YHWH
EXISTS

YHWH EXISTS

Volume I

JODELL ONSTOTT
YAH TZIDQENU

EMMANUEL PUBLISHING
BATON ROUGE, LOUSIANA

Printed in the United States of America.

www.emmanuelacademic.com
www.YHWHEXISTS.com

All Scripture references derived from The American King James Version
(Stone Engelbrite) unless otherwise specified.

All dictionary references are from Merriam Webster's Ninth New Collegiate
Dictionary unless otherwise specified.

Printed on acid-free paper.

LAYOUT BY EISENBRAUNS PREPRESS, WINONA LAKE, INDIANA.
www.eisenbrauns.com

Library of Congress Cataloging-in-Publication Data
Library of Congress Control Number: 2014958215

Dedication

*To my amazing family, who patiently endured
more than a dozen years of research.*

*May they discover an incredible double blessing from this
endeavor, which will last many generations to come.*

And for Bridget: a peg on the wall to finally hang your hat.

Table of Contents

PART 1

SCIENCE AND HISTORY:

A SURE FOUNDATION FOR GOD'S WORD

PART 2

LIFTING THE VEIL: THE TESTIMONIAL LAW

LIST OF FIGURES AND ILLUSTRATIONS

LIST OF TABLES

LIST OF MAPS

Preface

Having been raised a Seventh-Day Adventist, I have had a relationship with God for as long as I can remember. As an Adventist, I often felt the sting of being different from the more mainstream religions: we didn't go to football games on Friday night, we didn't dance, we didn't wear jewelry, and we went to church on Saturday instead of Sunday. I was taught that Adventism was the "true church." We were the "true Christians." Other denominations and believers either lacked a certain degree of sincerity or had somehow "missed the boat" in their belief system. We had a prophet, Ellen White, who cleared up a great deal of the fuzzy doctrine in the Old and New Testaments as she unveiled a religion that spoke to man's heart. Other churches didn't have *our* health message or *our* Sabbath. We were somehow set apart and more right than other denominations.

Funny thing: I grew older and came in contact with other people "in the world." I discovered they had been raised in the "true" church as well. My Baptist friends were more right than my Catholic friends, while my Church of God friends interpreted their doctrine more accurately than did my Church of Christ friends. In turn, my Messianic friends were sure they had it together better than any other religion out there.

This started to bother me. I wondered how each of us could have been taught so many different doctrines that were supposed to be right yet were considered wrong by other denominations. I knew that Seventh-Day Adventists didn't have all truth and neither did Baptists or Catholics; so I was left wondering what separates truth from error or good from evil. What made one belief right and another wrong? Was truth something man could decide for himself, or did it need to be God-given? I had been around long enough to know there were no simple answers. One Scripture passage could be interpreted five different ways, each meriting validity. These questions gnawed at my heart and soul. Why would God allow us to believe conflicting ideas about right and wrong?

About fifteen years ago, I read a couple of books that changed my life. Quite by accident, my spouse and I purchased a book that questioned Scripture's validity. The evidence was just as believable as the evidence that I knew existed for the varying interpretations of a particular Scripture passage. Compellingly, these books had science, history, and other academic research to back them up. I faced a dilemma. The relationship I had with my Creator was real; I had been through too much in my life to dismiss it lightly, but I also knew that my conscience could not rest until I found out for myself the truth to these difficult questions. I realized that questions relating to Scripture's validity were intricately entwined with doctrinal issues. What school of truth did the Creator actually sanction?

So, on the verge of becoming agnostic, I set out on a quest that lasted over a decade: to ascertain whether God existed. I needed to know if he was real or just a figment of my imagination. I threw away everything I had been taught, even cherished beliefs (that I had held so near and dear to my heart) in order to start from scratch. I could not dictate what God's word said; it had to speak for itself. Did God have any one particular truth? The following pages are the result of my study. I would not trade the knowledge I've gained from my research for anything in the world. I know God exists. I've seen his existence not only in my life but also through the very history and science that most scholars claim disprove him. He is real! His commands are there for our good—for our protection and blessing. What has satisfied my logical mind more than anything else is having found a nonconflicting set of doctrines that answer the many hard questions I had regarding Scripture's validity. Best of all, God's doctrine actually makes sense!

I thought others might wrestle with the same questions I had. I decided to prepare a case study from which I hope others will benefit. Before I present my evidence, I want to let you know how this book is organized. First, I based a significant portion of my research on the polemics of the very academics who claim that Scripture is nothing but folktales and reactionary political propaganda. My analysis defers to scholars who are foremost in their field of study. Second, wherever possible, I tried to use sources that are readily accessible on the internet or at local libraries. This way, if the reader wishes to verify a point or research a topic further, the resources are at his or her fingertips. Third, I tried to define Hebrew words using generally accepted, uncontroversial sources. The Hebrew meanings are usually based on the Brown, Driver, Briggs' *Lexicon* as well as *Strong's Exhaustive Concordance*. Fourth, letter points, such as (a) and (b) and emphasis, such as underlining, have been inserted into passages to aid further analysis. I hope these techniques will enable the reader to criticize issues without merely assuming that my points are valid. Rather, the reader can access specific elements to evaluate the evidence for him or herself.

I endeavored to keep my discussions conversational while maintaining integrity that merits the distinction of scholarship. My arguments are presented chronologically by building on the previous chapters' conclusions. Therefore, the reader will find that a sequential approach to reading this book is the most worthwhile approach. I hope this research will encourage further studies of this nature, fostering and rekindling interest in scholarship on authoritative Scripture.

Seek and You Shall Find

Once, America valiantly strove for biblical standards. Early American colonists risked the perils of new land in search of freedom and truth. Many of our forefathers laid down their lives for beliefs that they conceived important. They abandoned their European homes, hoping that a new land would provide liberty to walk in their faith. Our ancestors thirsted to know their Creator, to do what was right in his sight, and they were willing to uproot their lives for the sake of righteousness and truth.

Today, you and I have the religious freedom to pursue what they could only have dreamed. We have the freedom to believe as we choose, and there is presently little threat for expressing our beliefs. We do not need to hide our faith in the closet. Rather, we can freely promote our particular denomination. With the birth of the Internet and many recent archaeological discoveries, our generation possesses the tools and information for which our church fathers had longed. Yet, most of us are content that *our* church has *the truth*. We know logically that not every religion can be the "true" religion, but we are sure that our particular sect has it, or even more complacently, that truth is an elusive element that does not even exist.

Religious doctrine has become a matter that is in the eyes of the beholder. We each hold differing interpretations and beliefs, which is considered acceptable in our postmodern paradigm. Modern emergence of the doctrine of universal tolerance has obscured the lines between right and wrong. Religion has accepted the proposition that God has no absolute values and no absolute truth. Proposing that God may *not* tolerate certain interpretations, beliefs, or values has become politically incorrect and almost libelous. Dr. James Dobson, conservative author and founder of *Focus on the Family,* observes:

> This system of thought, also called moral relativism, teaches that truth is not only unknowable from God, whom postmodernism perceives as a myth, or from man, who has no right to speak for the rest of us. Rather, truth doesn't exist at all.

Nothing is right or wrong, *nothing* is good or evil, *nothing* is positive or negative. Everything is relative. All that matters is "what's right for me and what's right for you." Those ideas evolve from person to person as they go along. [1]

We have become complacent with the quest for knowledge in our churches, and many of us assume that finding an "absolute" interpretation of God's word is impossible.

Many earnest believers have pondered the various theologians who lived before our time. Every Protestant pioneer saw something slightly different in Scripture when they established the churches that our families have been brought up in today. If each of these pious theologians understood Scripture to support a slightly different doctrine, why should we be any different? We think that, if man has not found the truth by now, then truth is probably best left only to God to know or is a Pandora's Box better left unopened. Many believe that, if humanity has not found truth by now, he probably won't.

In many ways our churches have become quite polytheistic. Each church holds a particular view of who "God" is. Every church holds a different idea (doctrine) of what God teaches man to do or not to do. In essence, our churches have created many gods, all of whom we call the "one true God." We have become complacent in our quest for righteousness, as the church is often relegated to a social club status. Since we assume that truth is never attainable, doctrine becomes a matter of personal faith, while conflicting facts are all too often dismissed.

This modern complacency is far removed from Scripture's concepts of truth. The psalmist David prophesied, "For he comes, for he comes to judge the earth: he shall judge the world with righteousness, and the people *with his truth*" (Ps 96:13). The prophet Isaiah also encouraged his nation to seek the Creator in truth. "I have not spoken in secret, in a dark place of the earth: *I said not to the seed of Jacob, Seek you me in vain*: I Yahweh the Lord speak righteousness, I declare things that are right" (Isa 45:19). Jesus upheld this teaching by instructing, "Seek and you shall find, knock and the door shall be opened to you" (Matt 7:7–12; Luke 11:9–13). [2]

Jesus urged his followers to seek to know their God. He promised that if we follow this command we will find the one true God. Could it be that our many religious denominations exist today because our churches have allowed external influences to shape their idea of who God is? Could it be that if we look *only* to "the word of God" for truth we will find a path leading to one set of nonconflicting doctrines?

Scripture encourages people to question their ideas of God. The Creator desires that we prove him and his word rather than blindly tagging along. [3] The prophet Isaiah summoned ancient Israel to examine his word to see if it was righteous or not (Isa 1:18). The Apostle Paul indicates that by proving what is good and acceptable in the Creator's sight we change our preconceived ideas while renewing our minds (Rom 12:2). More importantly, Paul exhorts that we should examine ourselves and prove our beliefs (faiths) to see whether they stand on the word of God or not. [4]

Modern science, building on our ancestors' successes and failures, has discovered many truths about how the universe works. Academia has made great strides forward in astronomy, mathematics, chemistry, cosmology, technology, and medicine. Archaeology has equally excelled, as once-buried cities have been resurrected to divulge the background of biblical accounts. Scholars' studies have progressed substantially, enabling us to reconstruct ancient societies: their houses, temples, beliefs, and ways of life.

Over the past century, the field of comparative studies has equally excelled. Our understanding of the context of biblical accounts has enabled us to understand not merely the ancient's physical living conditions but the actual social context. The one endeavor, however, that I have yet to see scholars attempt is a thorough conceptual interpretation of the Hebrew Scriptures (i.e., Old Testament).

This quest is not without risk, which is probably why it has been avoided. Recent historians who have ventured down this path now view the Old Testament as a subjective work that was created during the reign of King Josiah, reducing most of its accounts to folktales written for political propaganda.[5] If this is *not* the case, there should be ample evidence demonstrating Scripture's historical validity to answer many of the disquieting questions posed by recent scholars.

History demonstrates that the scientific method works. Our lives have been blessed because Galileo Galilei, Sir Isaac Newton, Albert Einstein, and others followed this principle. Nevertheless, academics readily claim that religion is simply a matter of faith that can never be proven. Personal beliefs can never be validated or discredited. Yet which scientist has ever set out to prove this hypothetical claim right or wrong? If the scientific approach that scholars have applied to other fields of study were applied to Scripture, should not we expect to find that truth is attainable through a systematic collection and comparison of what God's word actually states?

If God is real, and he commands us to seek him, it stands to reason that he desires us to follow his brand of truth rather than our own.[6] If we were to search the Scriptures, could we find one true doctrine that preceeds modern religious interpretations? If we seek God, should not we be able to find him? If we find him, can we discover his truth rather than our version of it?

On God's Name

Ancient people worshiped a plethora of deities. The Greeks, for instance, identified over 400. Amidst the host of deities, all ancient nations acknowledged a single, usually supreme "Creator-god" in the pantheon. For the Greeks it was *Zeus*. For the Assyrians it was *An*, from whom all other deities descended. For the Babylonians it was *Anu*. For the Egyptians the sungod *Re*. And for the Canaanites *El*. In contrast to the polytheism of Greece, Assyria, and Canaan, the Old Testament's one Creator intended ancient Israel to stand alone as the one nation that preserved an accurate knowledge of him.[1]

Unlike deities of contemporary cultures, Israel's God required no pantheon to accompany him.[2] Israel's God, YHWH, was a single being whose name and theology distinguished him from gods of contemporary nations[3] (Isa 42:8; Ps 147:19). Surprisingly, modern Old Testament translations such as the King James Version have obscured this distinction by rendering God's name as "the Lord." The Hebrew Scriptures never attribute this title to God and, in fact, indicate that the Creator viewed this name quite disparagingly.[4] The word *lord* is actually an ancient name for a Phoenician-Canaanite deity called *Baal*.[5] Similarly, *Bel* was the Babylonian word for 'lord,' while the god *Marduk* was its Assyrian counterpart.[6]

The ancient Israelites developed a habit of associating the name of their God with pagan deities. One 8th century inscription excavated at Kuntillet 'Ajrud paraphrases Ps 97:5, Isa 55:12, Nah 1:5 and uses the name Baal to refer to YHWH.

> When God shines forth . . . [Y]HW[H]. . . The mountains will melt, the hills will crash . . . The Holy One over the gods . . . Prepare (yourself) [to] bless Baal on a day of war . . . to the name of El on a day of [w]ar.[7]

Throughout Israel's ancient history, her people conflated YHWH with other deities. John Day observes,

Prior to the discovery of the Ugaritic texts . . . it was sometimes supposed that 'the Baals' referred to quite distinct Canaanite deities, each Baal having its separate local identity. The Ugaritic texts revealed, however, that Baal, 'the lord,' was the epithet (though becoming a personal name) of one great cosmic deity, Hadad, so that the local Baals were, in fact, simply local manifestations of this particular deity.[8]

Israel's prophets wrote volumes against the *lies* found in the theology associated with the *lords* of Canaan's Baal or Babylon's Bel. The prophet Hosea foretold of a day when a righteous people would no longer call God after the names of Baal, saying,

> And it shall be at that day, says YHWH, that you shall call me Ishi; and shall *call ME no more Baali.* For I will take away the names of Baalim out of her mouth, and they shall no more be remembered by their name. (Hos 2:16–17)

Since *Baali* means *my lord,* God is saying that one day humanity will no longer call or look to him as an arbitrary lording master[9] but will instead see him as *Ishi,* a loving husband.[10]

The Creator intended for his name to distinguish his reputation from the "lords" of other nations. When God's messenger talked with Moses from the burning bush, Moses asked the name of the God who was sending him to Egypt.

> And Moses said to God, Behold, when I come to the Children of Israel, and shall say to them, The God of your fathers has sent me to you; and they shall say to me, What is his name? what shall I say to them? And God said to Moses, I AM THAT I AM: and he said, Thus shall you say to the Children of Israel, I AM has sent me to you. And God said moreover to Moses, Thus shall you say to the Children of Israel, YHWH God of your fathers, the God of Abraham, the God of Isaac, and the God of Jacob, has sent me to you: this is my name forever, and this is my memorial to all generations. (Exod 3:13–15)

The Creator tells us that his name is "I AM." This command to recognize his name as a memorial to all generations is so important that the Creator included it as the third commandment of the Ten Commandments, forbidding humanity to use it in vain (Exod 20:7).[11]

The Hebrew word for "I AM" is *Ehyeh,* from the root *hayah.*[12] It means 'to be' or 'to exist.'[13] This is the same word used in Gen 1:2, where Scripture states that the "earth *was* or existed without form." The concept found in this text embodies the ideology of a self-existent being: a God who simply "is" or simply "exists." The word YHWH derives from the root word *hyh* or *hayah.* Since ancient Hebrew did not employ vowels, it is written in consonants.[14]

The Creator's name may be more a scientific description of himself than a theological one. Renowned theoretical physicist Stephen Hawking in *A Brief History of Time* provides a description of an infinite universe that very closely parallels the Creator's description of himself. When describing the conditions of our universe, Hawking observes:

> The boundary condition of the universe is that it has no boundary. The universe would be completely self-contained and not affected by anything outside itself. It would neither be created nor destroyed. It would just BE.[15]

In other words, the universe simply *exists* or *is* in the same timeless manner that the Creator simply is: YHWH Exists.

The Creator told Moses his name should be a memorial for all generations. If we are to distinguish Israel's God from the customs and theology of other nations, we should begin by recognizing YHWH (alternatively, Yahweh or Yehovah) as the name of the God who gave ancient Israel her Scriptures. Hosea prophesied of a time when all other names for Israel's God would cease; perhaps this is the dawning of that day!

Abbreviations

AAAS	American Association for the Advancement of Science
ABD	Anchor Bible Dictionary (6 vols.; ed. D. N. Freedman; New York: Doubleday, 1992)
AKJV	The American King James Version
ANET	James B. Pritchard, ed., *Ancient Near Eastern Texts Relating to the Old Testament* (Princeton: Princeton University Press, 1969)
AEM	John F. Nunn, *Ancient Egyptian Medicine* (Norman: University of Oklahoma, 1996)
AnOr	*Analecta orientalia*
AOAI	Amnon Ben-Tor, ed., *The Archaeology of Ancient Israel* (trans. R. Greenberg; New Haven, CT: Yale University Press, 1992)
AUSS	Andrews University Seminary Studies
BDB	Francis Brown, *The Brown-Driver-Briggs Hebrew and English Lexicon* (Peabody, MA: Hendrickson Publishers, 2003)
BMJ	*British Medical Journal*
CAD	A. L. Oppenheim et al, eds., *The Assyrian Dictionary of the Oriental Institute of the University of Chicago* (21 vols.; Chicago: Oriental Institute, 1956–2011)
CDC	Centers for Disease Control
CGAE	Erik Hornung, *Conceptions of God in Ancient Egypt* (trans. John Baines; Ithaca, NY: Cornell University Press, 1982)
Diod	*Diodorus Siculus* (trans. Edwin Murphy; New Brunswick, NJ: Transaction Publishers, 1989)
EA	The El-Amarna Letters. William Moran, *The Amarna Letters* (Baltimore: Johns Hopkins University Press, 1987)
ESSP	James H. Breasted, ed., *The Edwin Smith Surgical Papyrus* (Chicago: University of Chicago, 1930)
Ebers	James Henry Breasted, *The Papyrus Ebers* (trans. Cyril P. Bryan; Letchworth, Herts: Garden City Press, 1930)
FTH	A. R. Millard, J. K. Hoffmeier, and D. W. Baker, eds., *Faith, Tradition, and History* (Winona Lake, IN: Eisenbrauns, 1994)
GDSAM	Jeremy Black and Anthony Green, *Gods, Demons and Symbols of Ancient Mesopotamia* (Austin: University of Texas, 1992)
GKC	Wilhelm Gesenius, *Gesenius' Hebrew Grammar* (ed. E. Kautzsch and trans. A. E. Cowley; Mineola, NY: Dover Publications, 2006)
HCJ	Victor Tcherikover, *Hellenistic Civilization and the Jews* (Philadelphia: Jewish Publication Society, 1959)
Herod	*Herodotus, The Histories* (trans. Aubrey de Sélincourt; New York: Penguin Books, 1972)
HP	Eliezer Oren, ed., *The Hyksos: New Historical and Archaeological Perspectives* (University Museum Monograph 96/8; Philadelphia: University of Pennsylvania Museum, 1997)
HPE	Gunther Hölbl, *A History of the Ptolemaic Empire* (trans. Tina Saavedra; London:

	Routledge, 2001)
HSM	Harvard Semitic Monographs
HTR	*Harvard Theological Review*
IHCANE	Hector Avalos, *Illness and Healthc Care in the Ancient Near East* (*HSM* 54; Atlanta, GA: Scholars Press, 1995)
ISBE	Geoffrey W. Bromiley, ed., *International Standard Bible Encyclopedia* (Grand Rapids, MI: Eerdmans, 1979)
JAMS	*Journal of the Ancient and Medieval Studies*
JANES	*Journal of Ancient Near Eastern Society*
JAOS	*Journal of the American Oriental Society*
JBL	*Journal of Biblical Literature*
JCS	*Journal* of Cuneiform Studies
JEA	*Journal of Egyptian Archaeology*
JETS	*Journal of the Evangelical Theological Society*
JFB	Robert Jamieson, A. R. Fausset, and David Brown, *Jamieson, Fausset, and Brown's Commentary* (Grand Rapids, MI: Zondervan, 1961)
JHRE	Aryeh Kasher, *The Jews in Hellenistic and Roman Egypt* (Tel Aviv: University of Tel Aviv, 1978)
JM	Timothy Freke and Peter Gandy, *The Jesus Mysteries* (New York: Three Rivers Press, 1999)
JNES	*Journal of Near Eastern Studies*
JSOT	*Journal for the Study of the Old Testament*
JSOTSup	Journal for the Study of the Old Testament, Supplement Series
JSS	*Journal of Semitic Studies*
JTS	*Journal of Theological Studies*
JSSEA	*Journal of the Society for the Study of Egyptian Antiquities*
KG	Henri Frankfort, *Kingship and the Gods* (Chicago: University of Chicago Press, 1948)
KK	László Török, *The Kingdom of Kush* (Leiden: Brill, 1997)
LXX	C. L. Brenton, *The Septuagint with Apocrypha: Greek and English* (London: Hendrickson Publishers, 1851)
MB	Mark W. Chavalas and K. Lawson Younger, Jr., eds., *Mesopotamia and the Bible* (Grand Rapids, MI: Baker, 2002)
MDAC	Aidan Cockburn, Eve Cockburn, and Theodore A. Reyman, eds., *Mummies, Disease, and Ancient Cultures* (Cambridge: Cambridge University Press, 1998)
Meg	John W. McCrindle, trans., *Ancient India as described by Megasthenes and Arrian* (New Delhi: Munshiram Manoharlal, 1926)
MW	Merriam Webster, *Webster's Ninth New Collegiate Dictionary* (Springfield, MA: Merriam-Webster, 1991)
NEJM	*New England Journal of Medicine*
NSE	Douglas W. Downey, ed., *New Standard Encyclopedia* (Chicago: Standard Educational Corp, 1995)
OHAE	Ian Shaw, ed., *The Oxford History of Ancient Egypt* (New York: Oxford University Press, 2000)
PB	Edwin M. Yamauchi, *Persia and the Bible* (Grand Rapids, MI: Baker, 1990)
PTMS	*Pittsburgh Theological Monograph Series*
SAAS	State Archives of Assyria Studies

SEC	James Strong, *Strong's Exhaustive Concordance* (Grand Rapids, MI: Baker Books, 1997) [denotes Strong's number only]
SIP	Second Intermediate Period
TMSJ	*The Master's Series Journal*
TWOT	R. Laird Harris, Gleason Archer, Jr., and Bruce Waltke, eds., *Theological Wordbook of the Old Testament* (2 vols.; Chicago: Moody Bible Institute, 1980)
UBD	Merrill F. Unger, *Unger's Bible Dictionary* (Chicago: Moody, 1957)
ULO	Michael Hudson and Baruch A. Levine, eds., *Urbanization and Land Ownership in the Ancient Near East* (vol. 2; Cambridge: Peabody Museum of Archaeology and Ethnology, Harvard University, 1999)
WWB	Richard E. Friedman, *Who Wrote the Bible?* (San Francisco, CA: Harper Collins, 1987)

Scripture Abbreviations

Tanakh/Old Testament

Gen	Genesis	Eccl	Ecclesiastes
Exod	Exodus	Song	Song of Solomon
Lev	Leviticus	Isa	Isaiah
Num	Numbers	Jer	Jeremiah
Deut	Deuteronomy	Lam	Lamentations
Josh	Joshua	Ezek	Ezekiel
Judg	Judges	Dan	Daniel
Ruth	Ruth	Hos	Hosea
1 Sam	1 Samuel	Joel	Joel
2 Sam	2 Samuel	Amos	Amos
1 Kgs	1 Kings	Obad	Obadiah
2 Kgs	2 Kings	Jonah	Jonah
1 Chr	1 Chronicles	Mic	Micah
2 Chr	2 Chronicles	Nah	Nahum
Ezra	Ezra	Hab	Habakkuk
Neh	Nehemiah	Zeph	Zephaniah
Esth	Esther	Hag	Haggai
Job	Job	Zech	Zechariah
Ps	Psalms	Mal	Malachi
Prov	Proverbs		

Apocrypha and Septuagint

1–2 Kgdms	1–3 Kingdoms	1–3 Macc	1–3 Maccabees

New Testament

Matt	Matthew	Titus	Titus
Mark	Mark	Phil	Philemon
Luke	Luke	Heb	Hebrew
John	John	Jas	James
Acts	Acts	1 Tim	1 Timothy
Rom	Romans	2 Tim	2 Timothy
1 Cor	1 Corinthians	1 Pet	1 Peter
2 Cor	2 Corinthians	2 Pet	2 Peter
Gal	Galatians	1 Jn	1 John
Eph	Ephesians	2 Jn	2 John
Phil	Philippians	3 Jn	3 John
Col	Colossians	Jude	Jude
1 Thess	1 Thessalonians	Rev	Revelation
2 Thess	2 Thessalonians		

Chronology

Archaeological Periods

Early Bronze Age (I–V)	3400–2000 BCE
Middle Bronze Age (I–III)	2000–1550/1500 BCE
Late Bronze Age (I–III)	1550/1500–1200 BCE
Iron Age (I–III)	1200/1150–539/500 BCE
Persian period	539/500–323 BCE

Part 1

Science and History: A Sure Foundation for God's Word

1

Concepts of Truth

I. ISRAEL'S CONTROVERSY

Today, twenty-first century theology tends to make religion a belief based upon faith rather than a belief of faith based upon fact. History, science, and conflicting Scriptures are all too often dismissed when they conflict with accepted creeds or dogma. Most Judeo-Christians are taught there are certain areas of their religion they should not question, causing the phrase "it is a matter of faith" to be well-worn and overused.

Scripture encourages individuals to question their idea of God. The prophet Isaiah indicates God's desire for man to seek truth, evidence, and facts when determining personal beliefs. He encouraged the ancient Israelites to see if their God was righteous and true, exhorting, "Come now, and let us reason together" (Isa 1:18). The act of "reasoning" involves discussions that analyze facts and consider various arguments before arriving at a conclusion of truth and validity or falsehood. The Psalmist David also placed value on a truth that conforms to facts, saying,

> **You desire truth in the inward parts**: and in the hidden part you shall make me to know wisdom. (Ps 51:6)

If a belief is based on facts, then the study of truth established by facts is paramount when a person is determining a belief founded in truth.

Many men in Scripture questioned God's judgments so that they could understand righteousness. After his calamity, Job questioned YHWH's judgment against him. He did not simply accept the Creator's judgment but reasoned and debated with his friends and with God to discover his punishment's cause. YHWH did not condemn Job's questions but desired that Job know the reason for his misfortune. Abraham likewise reasoned with God,

1

questioning the Creator's righteousness in destroying Sodom and Gomorrah. YHWH was not angry with Abraham's pleas for the salvation of the righteous who might live in the city (Gen 18:22–33) but desired Abraham to know and to understand his plans (Gen 18:17–18).

No prophet represents God's desire for man to question, analyze facts, and consider various arguments more than Micah. At the writing of his testimony (*c.* 800 BCE), ancient Israel had rebelled against her Creator's covenant, at the same time accusing YHWH, his way, and his Law of being unequal and unjust.[1]

The Creator challenged these allegations, desiring his people to exonerate him.

> (2) Hear you, O mountains, YHWH's controversy, and you strong foundations of the earth: for YHWH has a controversy with his people, and he will plead with Israel. (3) O my people, what have I done to you? and wherein have I wearied you? *testify against me.* (4) For I brought you up out of the land of Egypt, and redeemed you out of the house of servants; and I sent before you Moses, Aaron, and Miriam. (5) O my people, remember now what Balak king of Moab consulted, and what Balaam the son of Beor answered him from Shittim to Gilgal; that you may know the righteousness of YHWH (Mic 6:2–5; see also Numbers 23).

YHWH desires humanity to seek evidence in search of truth. To this end, he has put himself on trial, requesting his accusers to produce their witnesses. He solicits Israel to produce evidence proving he—his way, and his Law—has wearied her; or, to see if, in fact, he caused her to be free. In his own defense, YHWH offers his pleadings with the nation through his servants who prepared his way before the nation (v. 4) and revealed his truth. God's greatest rebuttal to Israel's charges is the reply that Balaam (son of Beor) gave to Balak (v. 5). YHWH indicates that Balaam's prophecy holds the key to his exoneration!

About three hundred years after Micah first introduced YHWH's controversy, we find the Israelites continuing their unrelenting accusations against YHWH's covenantal Law and his judgments. The Children of Israel criticized YHWH, telling the prophet Ezekiel that the Creator's Law, his way of life, and Yah's judgments of their rebellion were unfair. Ezekiel responded to the nation's complaint, referring to YHWH's age-old controversy.

> Yet you say, The way of the lord is not equal. Hear now, O House of Israel; Is not my way equal? Are not your ways unequal? . . . Yet said the House of Israel, The way of the Lord is not equal. O House of Israel, are not my ways equal? Are not your ways unequal? Therefore I will judge you, O House of Israel, every one according to his ways, said Adonai YHWH. *Repent, and turn yourselves from all your transgressions; so iniquity shall not be your ruin.* (Ezek 18:25, 29–30. See the entire context in Ezekiel 18 and 33)

The Children of Israel perpetually saw YHWH's way of life and his Law as unrighteous and unfair. In modern times, many if not most denominations inadvertently continue ancient Israel's polemic against Israel's God—the Father of the Old Testament—by viewing this Law and the way of life he prescribed for the ancient nation to be too difficult for humanity to observe or follow. In most Christian circles, the Father is seen as a harsh, judgmental, and exacting God from whose Law they desire to be delivered (Rom 7:1, 6). His Law and his requirements are seen as arbitrarily unfair, a way of life by which no one can be justified, be righteous, or be restored to a true relationship with God.[2] In many ways, YHWH's controversy with his people is still viable today.

If YHWH's case were tried, would we find his dealings with Israel righteous? Or, would we find him harsh, unmerciful, exacting, tyrannical, and unrighteous? Could we find that YHWH has been righteous in his dealings with humankind in general? Does it matter if the Creator has kept his word to Israel? Or, can he change his word at any time?

It is my purpose herein to reopen YHWH's controversy and try a case that has yet to be solved.[3] Does YHWH exist? If he does exist, is he righteous and true? Does it matter if the words of his prophets come true or if they fail to come to pass? The prophet Isaiah heralded a day wherein humanity would retry this case and finally judge their Creator righteous.

> Keep you judgment, and do justice: for my salvation is near to come, and *my righteousness to be revealed*. (Isa 56:1)

Can our investigation fulfill this ancient prophecy? Can we uncover the clue to Balaam's words,[4] which hold the key for revealing YHWH's righteousness today?

II. THE FOUNDATION

A. *Philosophy of Truth*

Modern philosophy holds many differing views of truth varying from Realism to Existentialism. The model against which we will try YHWH's case follows Bertrand Russell's correspondence theory of truth. The two basic elements of this view embrace that both truth and falsehood exist. A belief's truth or falsehood always depends on something that lies outside the belief itself.[5] In other words, truth consists in some form of correlation between belief and fact. Our goal for this investigation is to show whether or not YHWH's word provides enough facts in which people can base their beliefs so that falsehood can be eliminated, and the Creator can be exonerated from ancient Israel's allegations.

Since we will be conducting our investigation as a court trial, it is important to have clear, concise definitions on which to weigh this case. The Objectivist philosopher Ayn Rand points out modern philosophy's pitfall of "forgetting the existence of dictionaries and grammar primers" for defining basic ideas and concepts.[6] This aversion to concise definitions leads many modern philosophers to absurd vagueness and ambiguity regarding the most basic terms and ideas[7] (i.e., philosopher's quandary if a kitchen table really exists or if anything is real). Recent scholars have also validated the need for dictionaries to convey ideas accurately. Danish Egyptologist Kim Ryholt in his masterpiece on Egypt's Second

Intermediate Period has recently used a dictionary to convey and clarify the word *intermediate* in regard to Egyptian history.[8]

Our initial approach will establish a standard that YHWH's word must meet in order for it to be deemed both valid and good for humanity. Since definitions grant the ability to establish that standard, we will seek to define accurately the concepts governing this standard.[9] Although a dictionary may not be the preferable method in some researches, its ability to concisely define terms and its ease of accessibility for the reader serve the purpose of this discussion quite well.

B. *Does Science Exclude Theology?*

Mary Joan Leith (Stonehill College) has recently drawn attention to the difference between *Religious Studies* and *Theology*.

> The study of Religion has historically allied itself with science and reason and an interdisciplinary field using the methodologies of History, Linguistics, Anthropology—including Archaeology—and other university disciplines . . . as a neutral observer and reporter with no religious agenda (even if we know no one can be fully impartial). . . . By contrast, a Theologian studies her own religion as a believer . . . seeking to reconcile [discoveries] within an existing belief.[10]

While science and theology maintain a distinction, they naturally overlap. Scientific studies call for the scholar's assessment of the material at hand. This naturally leads to some judgment about God, the authority of his word, or the ideas that Scripture advances.

Leith challenges both disciplines to draw on each other in such a manner that critical biblical scholarship can respectfully engage the public by addressing theological perspectives. It is my hope that this present work successfully navigates both disciplines.

C. *What Is Truth?*

In the introduction, I mentioned my quandary when I realized that competing churches claimed that their set of beliefs or traditions embraced God's truth. This often occurs because one denomination discerns certain Scripture verses, texts, and passages as more important and others less important. Another denomination views these same subordinate passages as more important, basing their doctrine (i.e., divorce) on them while developing a dogma that totally contradicts that of the first group by reversing the importance of the same Scriptural texts.

Usually church denominations employ little rhyme or lucid reasoning in developing their doctrine because it is based on its own set of standards. Unfortunately, intellectual honesty and the standards of logic that we apply to all other areas of scientific learning and discipline all too often succumb to circular reasoning and arbitrary justifications where our beliefs are concerned. The very intellectual methods that have served humanity so well in regard to understanding physics, science, disease, medicine, history, and other academic disciplines are too often dismissed in order to support a denomination's particular set of beliefs of truth.

The circular reasoning that all too often pervades modern religious ideals is not at all what the prophet Isaiah intended when he pleaded for ancient Israel to "learn" (Isa 1:17) so that God and people could "reason together" (Isa 1:18). As many believers have experienced, little progress can be achieved in reasoning with a believer of a different denomination if the standard on which he or she bases his or her faith is different (which is of course why each of us can hold our differing beliefs). This is why it appears that Isaiah clarifies the ideals of reasoning together by stating that precept should be in line with precept and Scripture with Scripture (Isa 28:9–10).[11] Isaiah teaches us that it is not just the text that matters but also the philosophies or principles underlying the text.

In other words, the philosophies and ideals in one passage should be honestly and intellectually considered in light of other philosophies or doctrines conveyed in other texts of YHWH's written word. This is why Isaiah urges that integrity (which calls for adherence to a code of moral or artistic values) and honesty be applied to the basis of our Scriptural ideals. For modern humanity to find truth in YHWH's ancient Scriptures, our precepts or philosophies will need to be intellectually honest. We must ask tough questions in order to see if our modern *non*standard and arbitrary beliefs conflict with God's written word or if they measure up to the standards by which God judges truth. Further, we need to see if the standard by which God judges truth is righteous or unfair.

For these reasons, it is essential to define bedrock concepts on which this case will be tried. Without proper definitions, YHWH's case lacks credence and intellectual honesty and can be easily swayed or succumb to circular reasoning. To be intellectually honest, we must adhere to the standards of logic proven to work well in the real world of academic discipline. Scripture will also need to endorse and uphold these logical standards.[12] Only then can our discussion of doctrine progress out of the sphere of arbitrary personal interpretation into the light of truth (if such truth exists).

Concepts of truth must be the first foundation of this case. Without this standard, nothing can be proved or disproved. Today, most Judeo-Christians associate the word *truth* with vague ideals embodied in the terms "word of God" or "Scripture," often overlooking the practical definition of the word *truth*. What exactly does truth mean? Merriam-Webster defines truth as:

> Truth: FIDELITY, *CONSTANCY*; the state of being the case: FACT; the body of real things, events, and facts: ACTUALITY; the property (as of a statement) of being in accord with fact or reality.

YHWH's word must be founded on fidelity and constancy. This is our first conceptual standard on which this case will be tried. If this foundation is not solid, then there can be no exoneration of the nation's God. *YHWH's word must show evidence of being fact and a body of real things and real events.* Truth must be tried against the written word of the prophets in conjunction with archaeological and historical evidence. If YHWH's word is true, it must meet the test of "real things," "real events," and "real facts."

Noted scholar Joachim Rehork remarks:

> There is no lack of scholars—among them historians, theologians, philologists and archaeologists—who after conscientious examination of the biblical tradition have come to the conclusion that fundamentally it is of secondary importance whether the facts reported in the Bible are correct or not. According to them, the Bible is primarily 'prophecy.'[13]

Indeed, this is the trend of current theology and academic historiography, which place Scriptural accounts in the realm of Jewish tradition and folklore. But, if the accounts contained in Scripture are historically *invalid*, then how accurate can Scripture's prophecy be? Historicity is especially relevant considering that Israel's historical accounts are so intertwined with the prophets' testimonies that it could be questioned whether or not "prophecy" actually occurred, given Scripture's "redacted" accounts. In order for Scripture to be deemed true, it must meet the test of *real things* and *real events* as in Merriam Webster's definition of *truth*.

Rehork continues his observation:

> For the majority of Bible readers, on the other hand, as well as for a large number of biblical scholars, a great deal still depends on the question whether statements in the Bible can be proved. The Dominican father, Roland de Vaux, for example, one of the most prominent figures in the history of biblical antiquity, regarded the capacity to survive the Jewish and Christian faith as dependent upon the agreement between 'religious' and 'objective' history. He stated his opinion thus: 'if Israel's historical faith does not have its roots in history, then it is wrong and the same is true of our faith.' The no less distinguished American biblical archaeologist George Ernest Wright expressed the opinion that in biblical belief everything depends on whether the main events actually took place.[14]

Israel's history forms the basis of most Western theologies. If YHWH never physically spoke the "word of God" to Israel's patriarchs (Abraham, Isaac, and Jacob), the nation of Israel under Moses, or kings such as David, it would be senseless to believe in Israel's foundational history or theology. All stories would be man-made. Either the events recorded in the Old Testament actually occurred, or they did not. If YHWH is to be vindicated as a righteous God in this controversy, then establishing a faith based upon *real events* and *real facts* is imperative. Therefore, the *second step* of this investigation must seek to answer the question: Did Israel's history, as recorded in Scripture, actually occur?

D. Traits of Truth: Constancy, Fidelity, and Faithfulness

The second concept that will serve as a foundation in the case *Israel v. YHWH* is constancy—another concept of truth.[15] Merriam Webster defines *constancy* as:

Constancy: steadfastness of mind under duress: FORTITUDE; *FIDELITY*, LOYALTY; *freedom from change*.

To qualify as "truth," YHWH's word must exhibit attributes of steadfastness, even during times when Israel causes duress to YHWH by her idolatry and disobedience. Even during these times, YHWH must follow his covenantal word. Scripture must demonstrate fidelity and freedom from change. YHWH must not change his own word (recantation)! This last definition is paramount. Even if Israel has rebelled, God cannot change his word. *If YHWH can change his word and rescind agreements*[16] *that he has previously made, then he cannot meet the definition of truth.*

Fidelity: the quality of state of being *faithful;* accuracy in details: EXACTNESS.

The third foundation of truth on which Scripture must be built is detailed evidence and exactness. The word of YHWH must be faithful, witnessing exactness to the words written therein. If there are specific prophecies of events to occur, then their exact fulfillment should be demonstrated through history and/or Scripture.

Another bedrock of this case is *faithfulness,* a concept embodied in the definition of fidelity:

Faithful: steadfast in affection or allegiance: LOYAL; *firm in adherence to promises or in observance of duty*: CONSCIENTIOUS.

If YHWH is to be exonerated, he must show a "firm adherence to promises made." There can be no wavering. *Even if Israel is disobedient and walks in idolatry, YHWH's word cannot be revoked or rescinded.* The actions of Jacob's seed cannot annul the promises or covenants given to the nation or her patriarchs.[17] Even if it is to the Creator's own harm (Ps 15:4), he must uphold his promises to the ancient nation of Israel and keep his word!

E. Righteousness

One concept that has direct bearing on YHWH's trial is his *righteousness*. If we could establish that a particular truth did exist in the words of man's Creator, it would do little good if the Creator did not obey his own truth when he dealt with humanity. When Micah exhorted Israel to examine God, he indicated that the nation had charged her Creator with being unrighteous (Mic 6:3). In the prophet Ezekiel's days, Israel continued this accusation, saying that the way of YHWH was unfair (Ezek 18:25, 29; 33:17–20). So *if* Israel's God is to be exonerated from these allegations, then his word, his actions, and his judgments of humanity must meet the test of being righteous.

Webster defines *righteousness* as:

Righteous: *Acting in accord with divine or moral law*: free from guilt or sin.

For YHWH to be exonerated in this case, the Creator's words, actions, and judgments must demonstrate that he acts in accord with his own divine and moral law and that he is free from guilt or sin. This is the most pivotal point of our entire trial. Throughout the Old Testament, YHWH and his prophets claim that he is righteous.[18] God's perfection (2 Sam 22:31; Deut 32:4) and his freedom from sin and guilt are what separate "God" from mortals. If righteousness is an arbitrary idea that only God himself can understand or attain, how can we grow in his image to reflect his character in our lives? A standard must exist by which to define God's character as righteous.

The question of the Creator's righteousness has direct implications for humanity today. Each of us has a different belief of what truth is. Families, friends, and nations are often separated over doctrinal differences. If the Creator exists, he knows truth. Has he been righteous to withhold knowledge of truth from us? Or, is the Creator righteous to require man to seek out knowledge of truth for himself?

F. Righteousness Is Not Arbitrary

To ensure that the criterion on which we weigh evidence is both direct and specific, we must also define concepts that are contrary to our investigation. In other words, we need to know what concepts are excluded from the ideal of righteousness. The most helpful description of what is *not* righteous appears in the word *arbitrary*:

> Arbitrary: depending on individual discretion (as of judge) and *not fixed by law*; marked by or resulting from unrestrained and often tyrannical exercise of power; based on or determined by *individual preference or convenience rather than by necessity or the intrinsic nature of something*; existing or coming about seemingly at random or by chance or as the capricious and unreasonable act of will.

In order for the Creator to be righteous, he must obey his own divine Law. His judgments and words of truth given to Israel and her patriarchs must be constant, as opposed to being arbitrary. YHWH cannot use "individual discretion" or demonstrate an "unrestrained" or "tyrannical" exercise of power, *nor may he use favoritism* in his dealings with (or choice of) the nation of Israel. There must be clear-cut reasons for his judgments that manifest whether he has obeyed his own divine law.

Righteousness is not an arbitrary act. For YHWH to be righteous (and truthful), he cannot dismiss his own law and use random selection or chance to justify his actions with Israel or with humanity. For YHWH to be exonerated in this controversy, Scripture must evidence that the Creator acts in accord with his own divine law and written word. If YHWH's words are to meet the definitions of truth, they must corroborate scientific and historical evidence that they may be declared a word of faith based on facts rather than a faith that is based on subjective, personal criteria. Scripture must be objectively accurate rather than subjectively mystical.

These concepts of truth will serve as the structure for our examination of YHWH's controversy. However, before we can embark on our investigation, we need to see if Scripture supports the definitions of truth that we have profiled. This trial would be senseless if the premises on which this case is built were not upheld by Scripture. Does Scripture uphold Webster's concepts of truth and righteousness? Are there examples demonstrating that YHWH and his prophets upheld the same concepts of truth as outlined in the foundation of this case?

III. DOES SCRIPTURE UPHOLD THIS CASE'S CONCEPTS OF TRUTH?

A. *Constancy*

When the Moabites hired Balaam to prophesy against Israel's future, he said,

> God is not a man, that he should lie; neither the son of man, that he should repent: shall he say and not perform? Shall he speak and not keep to his word? And he said, "Blessed be YHWH God for behold, I have received command to bless: I will bless and not turn back." (Num 23:19, 20, rendered from the AKJV and the LXX)

Before Balaam's birth YHWH promised to bless Abraham and "his seed after him" (Gen 26:3). As a prophet, Balaam knew he could not change YHWH's word. Balaam understood YHWH's attribute of constancy, recognizing it as one of the Creator's greatest qualities. YHWH is *constant* and does not *turn back* on his word. If he does turn back on his word (i.e., recants), then both YHWH and his word are *not* true.

After Saul became Israel's first king, he rebelled against YHWH. The prophet Samuel upheld Balaam's parable when he prophesied against King Saul: "YHWH has rent the kingdom of Israel from you this day, and has given it to a neighbor of yours, that is better than you. And also *the Strength of Israel will not lie nor repent: for he is not a man, that he should repent*" (1 Sam 15:28–29). Samuel indicates that YHWH's command to strip Saul's kingdom could not be "rescinded." The Creator did not repent of what he had purposed to do. Rather, he followed through, keeping his own word as removing the kingdom from Saul's hand.

Scripture's constancy concept can be corroborated again with the account of a prophet who prophesied against Jeroboam's altar. YHWH commanded the Judean prophet to "eat no bread, nor drink water, nor turn again by the same way that he came" (1 Kgs 13:9). After the Judean prophet departed from Jeroboam, an older prophet *lied*, telling the younger prophet that YHWH had changed his word, so he could "turn again by the same way that he came." The younger Judean prophet disobeyed YHWH's instructions and returned to eat and drink in the older prophet's home. Consequently, YHWH sent a lion to kill the young rebellious prophet for failing this test.

The Judean prophet failed to understand the fundamental attribute of his Creator: YHWH does not change his word. Instead, the younger prophet disbelieved his God and listened to another person's lying words. Although the Judahite prophet was slain, the word that YHWH commanded him to speak against Jeroboam's altar *still came true* (2 Kgs 23:14–16). Why? Because according to the Hebrew Scriptures, YHWH does not waver or change his word (Ps 102:27). His previous statements stand firm, coming to pass regardless of man's rebellious and arbitrary actions.

The prophet Isaiah also upholds this ideal of constancy and firmness to YHWH's written and spoken word:

> And the glory of YHWH shall be revealed, and all flesh shall see it together: for the mouth of YHWH has spoken it. The voice said, Cry. And he said, What shall I cry? All flesh is grass, and all the goodliness of it is as the flower of the field: The grass withers, the flower fades: because the spirit of YHWH blows upon it: surely the people is grass. The grass withers, the flower fades: but *the word of our God shall stand forever*. (Isa 40:5–8)

Isaiah extols the ideal of truth; though seasons change like humanity's ideas of truth, YHWH's word is unchanging. Humanity's thoughts and beliefs—like grass (Isa 40:7)—come and go, but the word of YHWH is constant, unswerving, and unchanging. He is faithful to his written word. Notice too, Isaiah indicates that when YHWH's glory is revealed all flesh will see that YHWH's word *does* indeed unchangingly *stand* forever!

B. *Fidelity*

In the Book of Psalms, King David describes traits of righteousness, upholding the concept of fidelity, explaining: "In whose eyes a vile person is condemned; but he honors them that fear YHWH. *He that swears to his own hurt, and changes not*" (Ps 15:4). David champions the concepts of constancy and fidelity—the word of YHWH does not change. If the Creator is to be righteous, he cannot change what he has sworn to do. During a time of duress, *a righteous man* will keep his sworn word even if hurts him (Num 30:2). David's words support the fact that even the details of YHWH's word are unchanging.

This concept of constancy is witnessed once again when YHWH issues a covenant to David. "My covenant will I not break, nor alter the thing that is gone out of my lips" (Ps 89:34). YHWH indicates that once he has given his word he will not break his word or change what he has promised to do. Scripture must evidence this constancy and fidelity. It cannot deviate to the right or the left in what YHWH stated he will do (Deut 5:32). It must maintain exactness and detail, demonstrating fulfillment of prophecies in later Scripture and/or history. If YHWH has deviated, then Israel's Creator, the God of the Old Testament, cannot be exonerated in his controversy with Israel.

C. Faithfulness

Faithfulness is another concept of truth with which Scripture concurs. Moses certifies the definition of *faithfulness* as an attribute of YHWH: "Know therefore that YHWH your God, he is God, the faithful *God*, which keeps covenant and mercy with them that love him and keep his commandments to a thousand generations" (Deut 7:9). If Israel's God is faithful, then Scripture must demonstrate that he adheres to the promises he made to the descendants of Abraham, Isaac, and Jacob. He must fulfill the promises that he offered to the nation and her forefathers.

D. Righteousness Is Not Arbitrary

Our investigation into YHWH's controversy hinges on his righteousness. Israel's allegations condemned the Creator as an unjust and arbitrary God. She claimed his standards were too lofty to be observed (Ezek 18:25, 29). Only God himself was capable of observing his Law. Ancient Israel charged that not only was the Creator's Law harshly unrighteous, but he arbitrarily and erratically observed his own Law when judging humanity.

Scripture, however, does not support the charge of Israel's citizenry. Moses saw YHWH as a God of truth, whose judgments are full of justice, perfection, and without the stain of wickedness.

> He is the Rock, his work is perfect: for all his ways are judgment: a God of truth and *without iniquity*, just and right is he. (Deut 32:4)

The Hebrew word translated "just" is *tsaddiyq*, which means to be 'righteous, upright, correct, or just,' and is often translated "lawful" by the King James Version.[19] *Tsaddiyq* is derived from *tsadaq*, a root word that means 'to be right.'[20] Thus, to be righteous means to be just and equitable in accordance with divine Law. If YHWH is just and upright, if all his ways are perfect (2 Sam 22:31), and if he is a God without iniquity, then he does right and consistently obeys his own divine Law.

King Jehoshaphat's exhortation to Israel's judges confirms this interpretation. When Johoshaphat appointed judges over Israel's land, he explained that the judgments of humanity's ultimate judge were neither biased nor arbitrary: YHWH did not show favor to someone just because he or she brought gifts to him; rather, he judged according to his own Law.[21] Therefore there was no iniquity (perversity) in Israel's God. "Let the fear of YHWH be on you; take heed and do it: *for there is no iniquity with YHWH our God*, nor respect of persons, nor taking of gifts" (2 Chr 19:7).

King David also proclaims that YHWH's righteousness stems from obeying the truth found in the doctrine of his own Law:

> Your righteousness is an everlasting righteousness, and *your law is the truth*. (Ps 119:142)

The Hebrew Scriptures validate the precepts and philosophies that universally define and govern ideals of truth. This congruity allows our case to proceed. Now comes the test of seeing whose words will stand: Israel's or YHWH's. The prophet Micah has asked us to call our witnesses to see if Israel's charge is valid, or if YHWH can be vindicated as a righteous God. All of this matters little if Israel's God does not even exist. So our case must seek reasonable cause for Israel's allegations and discover if evidence can be uncovered for YHWH's existence. One key test this investigation must pass: Does external proof outside Israel's Scriptures exist to corroborate or lend credibility to Scriptural accounts?

IV. INNOCENT UNTIL PROVEN GUILTY?

Ancient Israel accused God of being unrighteous and unfair in his dealings with the nation: his way was "unequal." Today, most court cases follow the concept of presumed innocence until guilt is found (*Ei incumbit probatio qui dicit, non qui negat*). The trend of scholars over the last 30 years, however, is to blindly disregard this equitable principle.[22] More often than not, scholars require that the burden of proof should rest, *not* on the skeptical scholar, but on the scholar who accepts the statements in his source credible.[23]

Egyptologist James Hoffmeier has pointed out that

> many historians and biblical scholars now maintain that a text's claims must be corroborated before they can be considered historical. This expectation is the opposite of the Western legal tradition of "innocent until proven guilty." . . . In shifting the burden of proof to the ancient document and demanding that the maximalist historian "prove" the historicity of the text's claim, the minimalist historian commits a methodological fallacy. Historian David Hackett Fischer labels this practice the "fallacy of presumptive proof," which consists in advancing a proposition and shifting the burden of proof or disproof to others. Additionally, the minimalist approaches an ancient text as "guilty until proven innocent," whereas the maximalist accepts what appears to be a historical statement unless there is evidence to prove the contrary.[24]

Maximalists are those historians who *give the benefit of the doubt* to any ancient text, albeit Greek, Mesopotamian, Egyptian, or the Hebrew Scriptures. Minimalists are those historians who *reject an ancient text* unless it is corroborated by archaeological evidence. For instance, most minimalists rejected the historicity of the Davidic monarchy until discovery of a broken inscription from a Damascus king was excavated in an ancient city (Tel el-Qadi or Tel Dan). Now, most minimalists will accept that the Davidic monarchy actually existed.[25] Even the reknowned minimalist Israel Finkelstein has admitted that the David monarchy is historical.[26]

In his seminal work, *The First Historians*, Baruch Halpern justifies this method of investigation. "Historical knowledge is based upon evidence in just the way the deliberations of a jury are."[27] For this reason, this trial will avoid the error of presumptive proof. We will follow the procedure of presumptive innocence until guilt is found. This means that we will seek conclusive evidence to demonstrate YHWH's innocence in the face of Israel's charges against him.

To summarize, our purpose is to try ancient Israel's allegations against the concepts of truth and righteousness to see if the allegations can be substantiated or not. We will grant the standard legal rights that are afforded to most defendants: presumed innocence until guilt is found. We will assume that YHWH is righteous until evidence demonstrates Israel's God has either violated the objectives set forth in the *concepts of truth* or that he has indeed validated them. It may be remembered that according to the principles of presumed innocence, the burden of proof rests on the accuser. Therefore, the evidence recorded in the Hebrew Scriptures (presumably) by ancient scribes will be used as evidence to support Israel's allegations against her God. I will present considerable evidence so that our trial is complete. You, the reader, may draw your own conclusions about whether the extensive evidence brought forth is beyond reasonable doubt or still leaves YHWH's existence or righteousness imputed.[28]

For YHWH to be a God of truth without iniquity, he must obey his own divine Law: he cannot be above it. If YHWH is indeed a God without iniquity, his actions, his judgments of Israel, and of humankind in general should reveal his righteous adherence to his own divine Law so that he may be exonerated from Israel's allegations of unrighteousness.

V. SOURCES

Over the course of time, translations of ancient sources sometimes vary due to a translator's interpretations or biases. Geza Vermes, one leading authority on the Dead Sea Scrolls, terms this disparity "scribal creative freedom" when referring to a Qumran scroll's divergent translations.[29] If Scripture does uphold one particular set of doctrines, it stands to reason that the most ancient sources should better preserve the Creator's original words since subsequent manuscripts offer occasion for more creative freedom in translation.

Language itself is also affected by the passage of time. Languages lose idioms, as the meaning of words become lost within a language.[30] This requires a later scribe to interpret antiquated words into modern idiom that his audience will understand. One good example is 1 Sam 9:9, where the word *seer* had fallen out of use so Scripture's transcriber (or editor) needed to clarify that a seer was a prophet.

The Old Testament is preserved in two ancient sources. The first is the Hebrew Masoretic Text (MT). Modern scholars attribute the MT's formation to the time of Rabbi Aqiba, *c.* 100 CE.[31] The discovery of the "Dead Sea Scrolls has not only substantially confirmed this hypothesis, but is widely held to establish the existence of this text as ante-dating in essentials the Christian Era."[32] The King James Bible, JPS, and Artscroll Tanach rely on the MT.

The second ancient Old Testament source is the Greek Septuagint, usually designated "LXX," the Roman numeral for 70. The Septuagint was translated from the Hebrew Scriptures into Greek around 285 BCE.[33] While scholars once readily admitted that the Septuagint was a more corrupted version of the MT, they now find that many formerly assumed corruptions are in actuality preservations of an original text.[34]

Understanding events that transpired in Jerusalem following 220 BCE may also cause speculation regarding the traditionally held Masoretic Text.[35] The Essenes were a strict religious community that emerged around the third century BCE and appear to have used scribal creative freedom when it came to translating passages that supported their theologies.[36] It is unknown how greatly the Essene movement affected translations of prior manuscripts in Judea during this era. The Septuagint was translated before their movement and may preserve truth where the MT has failed.

It is reasonable to suppose that, if God has preserved the words of his prophets (so that humanity may seek and find truth), the Septuagint should demonstrate accuracy where the MT fails, and the MT should demonstrate accuracy where the Septuagint fails. If we compare one text against the other when a particular verse is in question, the truth should bear out. Our primary source for the Masoretic will be the King James Bible (Americanized).[37] When clarity is warranted, we will turn to the Septuagint.

VI. METHOD

Our forensics approach will examine what the word of YHWH actually states to ensure that we have an accurate context. We must put aside our emotions and preconceived ideas as we base concepts on YHWH's written word. We cannot add to or take away from the actual texts (Deut 12:32). If truth does exist in the Creator's words, then we should expect to find evidence of harmony in the Hebrew Scripture's doctrine (i.e., the Old Testament), demonstrating an underlying (normative) ethics-based system governing the ideas of right and wrong.

We have formulated the foundation of our case. Next emerges the task of collecting data through history and archaeology: testing the Word of YHWH to see if it demonstrates validity.[38] In his book *The Structure of Scientific Revolutions*, Thomas Kuhn argues that advances in a field are rarely the product of new data. Instead, Kuhn proposes that advances are the product of new questions and paradigms' being applied to data that already exist.[39] This case will examine evidence to see if Scriptural data already exists for the elusive element we call truth.

The exoneration of Israel's Creator must begin with Genesis, the beginning of YHWH's written word. As our journey of discovery progresses, we will uncover many hidden prophecies, seeing their fulfillment in history for the first time. We will try Israel's case to see if her God was unjust or if YHWH's righteousness can still be revealed!

VII. THE WAY

Our first procedure in this trial will use a sample to verify that the criteria allow us to work within the perimeters of this case. The words and actions of Israel's patriarchs and other persons whom Scripture deems godly should demonstrate affinity with YHWH's teachings and doctrines. This consistency would merit greater validity. If, however, the patriarchs' words and actions conflict with Torah's values,[40] we can conclude that all is subjective: no one body of doctrine exists. If, on the other hand, the patriarchs' actions, words, and lives do prove to harmonize with the Creator's teachings, they support the fact that God embraces a particular way of life or *doctrine*.

A. Love Your Neighbor

One of the basic commands found in Torah is for humanity "to love your neighbor as yourself" (Lev 19:18). YHWH established the Jubilee year on this precept.

> And if you sell anything to your neighbor, or buy anything of your neighbor's hand, ***you shall not oppress one another.*** . . . but you shall fear your God: for I am YHWH your God. You shall do my statutes, and keep my judgments, and do them; and you shall dwell in the land in safety. (Lev 25:14, 17–18; see also Exod 22:21; 23:9.)

The Creator's statutes and judgments teach individuals not to oppress their fellowman. Abraham's obedience to this command is evidenced in his interaction with his nephew Lot. When Abraham and Lot's servants quarreled over grazing land, Abraham did not attempt to control Lot's decision, nor did he try to manipulate the situation. He gave Lot freedom to choose the best, saying, "Is not the whole land before you? Separate yourself, I pray you, from me: if you will take the left hand, then I will go to the right; or if you depart to the right hand, then I will go to the left" (Gen 13:9). As an older man in authority, Abraham did not selfishly dictate to his nephew. Abraham pursued peace between himself and Lot, obeying the Law's command that he should not oppress another.

B. Bribes

Abraham's purchase of Machpelah is another instance of Abraham's knowledge of YHWH's way and his obedience to the Law in his personal life. Let us compare a law found in the Israelite Covenant with Abraham's transaction.

> And you shall take no *gift*: for the *gift* blinds the wise, and perverts the words of the righteous. (Exod 23:8)

Shacad is the Hebrew for "gift." It literally means 'a donation or bribe.'[41] A bribe involves giving in order to receive a biased or favorable judgment. Another text in Deuteronomy reiterates this command for justice: "You shall not decline judgment; you shall not respect persons, neither take a gift: for a gift does blind the eyes of the wise, and pervert the words of the righteous" (Deut 16:19).

When Sarah died, Abraham approached the Hittites for a family cemetery. He asked to buy the cave Machpelah at the end of Ephron's field. By this time, YHWH had made Abraham a mighty prince in Canaan (Gen 23:6), and Ephron had *regard* for Abraham's power and might, offering both the burial cave and field to Abraham as a donation. Abraham refused the "gift," insisting that he would pay a fair price for the field and its cave. He weighed 400 shekels of silver, and the field of Ephron was transferred to Abraham as a permanent possession.[42] Centuries later, King David conquered the Jebusites and faced the same situation; David reiterated this concept of rejecting gifts. "I will surely buy *it* of you at a price: neither will I offer burnt offerings to YHWH my God of *that which does cost me nothing*" (2 Sam 24:24). Abraham obeyed the law regarding bribes when he did not accept something for nothing.[43] His actions demonstrate that he observed the Creator's *way* as ordained in the later Israelite Law. Abraham's action qualifies as evidence supporting the constancy of Israel's God.[44]

C. *The Way of Life?*

Another Genesis account indicates that the *way of YHWH* has always naturally existed. Abraham knew YHWH's laws well before they were given to Israel at Mt. Sinai. The first time YHWH's angel appeared to Abraham he stated:

> Shall I hide from Abraham that thing which I do; Seeing that Abraham shall surely become a great and mighty nation, and all the nations of the earth shall be blessed in him? For I know him, that he will command his children and his household after him, *and they shall keep the way of YHWH, to do justice and judgment;* that YHWH may bring upon Abraham that which he has spoken of him. (Gen 18:17–19)

The King James Version translates *derek* as "the way." The Hebrew literally means 'the road or a course of life.'[45] YHWH knew Abraham would teach his children 'the way' of life, which is comprised of justice and judgment. In order for Abraham to instruct his children in YHWH's precepts, he first had to have knowledge of these judgments and statutes himself.

That Abraham indeed had knowledge of YHWH's laws, judgments, and statutes is evidenced in covenants confirmed with Abraham's son, Isaac:

> And YHWH appeared to him (Isaac), and said, Go not down into Egypt; dwell in the land which I shall tell you of: Sojourn in this land, and I will be with you, and will bless you; for to you, and to your seed, I will give all these countries, and I will perform the oath which I swore to Abraham your father; And I will make your seed to multiply as the stars of heaven, and will *give to your seed all these countries*; and in your seed shall all the nations of the earth be blessed; Because that Abraham *(a, see below) obeyed my voice, and kept my charge, (b) my commandments, (c) my statutes, and (d) my laws.* (Gen 26:2–5)

YHWH's selection of Abraham was not an arbitrary act. YHWH chose Abraham because he obeyed the Creator's instructions.[46] Isaac inherited his father's blessings due to (a, above) Abraham's obedience in keeping YHWH's charge, commandments, statues, and laws.[47]

These are the basic tenants of Israel's Law covenanted at Mt. Sinai. The Law's commandments (b) are defined in Exodus 20 and 34; the statutes (c) are defined in Exodus 21–24; and YHWH's (d) various laws are found scattered throughout the pages of Torah. This text strongly implies that Abraham kept all aspects of the later Israelite Law.

The Creator's philosophy taught that there was a particular way or course of life that benefited humanity. Genesis' record strongly implies that Israel's Law existed long before it was ratified at Mt. Sinai, and Abraham had observed it. Notice that Gen 18:17–19 augments this conclusion and clarifies the way YHWH would bring about his promises to Abraham.

> Shall I hide from Abraham that thing which I do; Seeing that Abraham shall surely become a great and mighty nation, and all the nations of the earth shall be blessed in him? For I know him, *that he will command his children and his household after him, and they shall keep the way of YHWH*, to do (a) justice and judgment; *(b) that YHWH may bring upon Abraham that which he has spoken of him*. (Gen 18:17–19)

YHWH indicates that his blessings did not occur just because YHWH was God or because YHWH chose Abraham. Rather, blessings were effected through a particular method. The Creator would fulfill his promises to Abraham through (b, see above) Abraham's obedience. "Keeping the way of YHWH to do justice and judgment" was the qualification for receiving YHWH's blessings. The Creator's philosophy on life was his truth; it would bring its own blessings for Abraham, his descendants, and all who obeyed. When YHWH called Israel out of Egypt (Hos 11:1; Exod 4:22), he established a Law that provided a written definition for the *way of YHWH*. This definition confirmed the (a) justice through judgments that had been alluded to in Gen 18:19. For ancient Israel, this verse implies that, as long as she observed his covenantal Law, she too would receive Abraham's blessings. However, when Israel rebelled, blessings could be withheld until she was again willing to obey.

YHWH's condition for receiving blessing qualifies as a nonarbitrary judgment. Just being the seed of Abraham did not entitle Israel to her forefather's blessings. Heirship had to couple obedience.[48] Samuel's words support this conclusion. "But if you will not obey the voice of YHWH, but rebel against the commandment of YHWH, then shall the hand of YHWH be against you, as it was against your fathers" (1 Sam 12:15). YHWH had chosen Abraham to bear his covenantal nation, based on Abraham's willingness to obey. Although Israel inherited Abraham's blessings, YHWH would judge the nation if she rebelled against YHWH's commandments. He would invoke contractual penalties, which regulated the methods at his disposal by which he could deal with a rebellious nation. Yet even then, YHWH could not rescind his promises to Abraham's children or disinherit them so as to forgo his promised blessings. Rather, YHWH would have to wait until Abraham's children were willing to choose their Creator's way of life at which point YHWH would again bless Abraham's descendants.

D. Abraham Alone Possessed YHWH's Truth

The Book of Genesis indicates that, early after the flood, humanity turned to vanity, compelling YHWH to choose someone to preserve his life-giving way (Gen 11:1–9). Abraham's obedience was one factor that prompted YHWH to choose him from all the people of the earth (Gen 26:5; In the next chapter, we will see that there was another factor in YHWH's choice of Abraham). He alone would preserve YHWH's truth and the knowledge of the right way to live.

Isaiah's theology echoes this theme:

> Listen to me, you that follow after righteousness, you that seek YHWH . . . Look to Abraham your father, and to Sarah that bore you: for *I called him alone*, and blessed him, and increased him. (Isa 51:1–2)

Isaiah implies that the knowledge of righteousness is found in Abraham's history. If we want to know righteousness, look to the story of Abram and Sarai. Why establish the knowledge of righteousness with Abraham? Why call Abraham alone?

Other nations had rebelled against *the way of YHWH,* or they had never known it. With the account of Noah and the Tower of Babel, only a few chapters before, Scripture demonstrates that, while the Amorites, Canaanites, Hittites, Babylonians, Egyptians, and other nations on earth had turned to idolatry and foolish practices, YHWH would establish truth with Abraham and his descendants through his written word. Abraham's seed—the nation of Israel—would be the only nation whose theology "alone" contained truth.

That YHWH indeed gave truth to Abraham's grandson, Jacob, is evidenced when Jacob states:

> I am not worthy of the least of all the mercies, *and of all the truth, which you have showed to your servant.* (Gen 32:10)

Jacob professed to possess YHWH's truth. If Jacob had truth, then YHWH must have confirmed Abraham's doctrine with Jacob. Since YHWH had "shown" his truth to Jacob, the younger patriarch understood the truth he had inherited from the teachings of his father, Isaac, and grandfather Abraham.

E. Evidence of Scripture's Adherence to Fidelity and Constancy

1. Fidelity: The Curse of the Ground vs. the Curse of the Fruit

For Scripture to meet the concepts of truth as outlined in the control for this case, Scripture needs to be accurate with the details regarding YHWH's actions. Does Genesis evidence fidelity in the Creator's words and actions?

Jeremiah's account of David's and Phinehas's covenants (with the monarchy and the priesthood) demonstrates accuracy and consistency between the minute details of YHWH's words.[49] The prophet uses the example of the Creator's covenant with the time allotted for day and night to demonstrate YHWH's faithfulness to David's and Phinehas's Houses.

> If you can break *my covenant of the day, and my covenant of the night, and that there should not be day and night in their season;* Then may also my covenant be broken with David my servant, that he should not have a son to reign on his throne; and with the Levites the priests, my ministers. (Jer 33:20–21)

When did YHWH establish his "covenant" with day and night that they should stay in their season? Though Jeremiah alludes to this event, Genesis records YHWH's promised covenant shortly after Noah departed from the ark.

> YHWH said in his heart, *I will not again curse the ground* any more for man's sake; for the imagination of man's heart is evil from his youth; neither will I again smite any more everything living, as I have done. While the earth remains, seedtime and harvest, and cold and heat, and *summer and winter, and day and night shall not cease.* (Gen 8:21–22)

YHWH did not establish his covenant with day and night until after the flood. It appears that prior to this covenant, YHWH used the ceasing of cold and heat, summer and winter, erratic daylight, and night's darkness to "curse the ground" and change seasons across the whole face of the earth. This inhibited the earth from producing fruit. The Israelite covenant is consistent with YHWH's seasonal/day covenant and does not again curse the "ground" of the entire earth. The exact wording of the curses found in the Law for Israel's breach of pact placed a curse on the "*fruit* of the ground" (Deut 28:4, 11, 23–24) and did not include a curse on the soil itself. When YHWH did withhold rain so that the "heaven that is over your head shall be brass, and the earth that is under you shall be iron" (Deut 28:23), he did not withhold rain over the entire face of the earth, but limited it to rebellious districts such as Israel and surrounding pagan nations. He never breached his promise of day, night, and the seasons' staying in their appointed times. As a result, YHWH's attention to detail in this particular action manifests fidelity.

2. Constancy: Evidence of the Curse of the Fruit of the Body

At Mt. Sinai, YHWH granted a Law to Israel within a constitutional covenant. This pact provided promises of prosperity (blessings) for keeping his Law and consequences of hardships (curses) for disregarding it. One consequence for breaking covenant resulted in a curse on offspring: "Cursed shall be the fruit of your body" (Deut 28:18). This terminology is broad. If applied, this curse could be evidenced by deformities, retardation, miscarriage, sterility, and a plethora of other congenital illnesses or diseases.[50] If YHWH constantly applied this penalty to disobedient societies, it would maintain the constancy and unarbitrary nature

Table 1.1. Cain's Seed Withheld

Genesis Text		Seth's Generations		Cain's Generations		Penalty Applied
Seth	Cain			Adam		
5:3–7	4:1	1	Seth	1	Cain	
5:7–10	4:17	2	Enos	2	Enoch	
5:10–13	4:18	3	Cainan	3	Irad	
5:15–16	4:18	4–5	Mahaleleel, Yared	4	Mehuyael	Seed withheld
5:18–21	4:18	6–7	Enoch, Methuselah	5	Methusael	Seed withheld
5:25–28	4:18	8–9	Lamech, Noah	6	Lamech	Seed withheld
5:30–32	4:19–22	10–12	Shem, Ham, Japeth	7–9	Yaabaal, Tubaal, Tubal-Cain	Children of Cain devise their own seed to get around curse
6:1–7, 11–13		Flood occurs as a result of Cain's corrupted blood line and evil nature				

of YHWH's Law. Can breach of this contractual law be evidenced in a disobedient society before the birth of the Israelite nation?

Cain had become the world's first murderer. His genealogy evidences a curse on offspring, which hampered his descendants' ability to procreate after the third generation (see Exod 20:5; 34:7; Num 14:18; Deut 5:9). Seth's offspring reproduced twice as quickly, probably securing the position as the dominant family culture. Table 1 demonstrates the "closing of the womb" that occurred to Cain's evil descendants (see Table 1.1).[51]

Seth's descendants evidence the blessing of progeny indicative of a strong society, which Abraham would later inherit. Cain's children procreated less frequently as they walked in their father's ungodly ways (a point we will examine in the next chapter). YHWH consistently rewards righteousness but places consequences on wickedness in order to thwart its tendency.

Thus far, Scripture's philosophies and precepts appear to agree.[52] YHWH consistently upholds the doctrine that people should love their neighbor as themselves (Lev 19:18). YHWH's instructions support this doctrine by commanding people to renounce oppression. The Creator also outlaws bribes, viewing them counterproductive to neighborly love. YHWH's word maintains fidelity by adhering to details since God did not violate his covenant with the day or night when he established Israel's curses, nor did he again curse the ground for the sake of humanity's sins. Interestingly, God never offers such a promise for offspring, a curse that can be witnessed in Cain's descendants and again later in Israel's descendants.

As I examined this evidence, I saw that a root of constancy and fidelity has been cultivated in the Creator's written word. But, I wondered: Did anything really important separate Abraham's theology from that of other nations? Was truth limited solely to Abraham's children? Remembering the verses where YHWH states that he sanctified Israel from "among the nations" (Exod 31:13; Lev 20:8), I was left contemplating if this excluded other nations from having known his truth. I was not satisfied with this paltry test of Israel's Scriptures, nor did I see that Israel's allegations had come close to being resolved. I needed more evidence and a better understanding of the "righteousness" YHWH had revealed to Abraham and why. I needed to know if anything was special or different about Abraham's religion.

2

The Genesis Connection: Survey in Ancient Religion

I. MYTHIC EGYPTIAN IMAGES

Before I could build a case for or against ancient Israel's allegations, I needed to see if these charges were credible history or folklore. There were several tests that Abraham's religion had to pass in order for it to merit credibility. First, it needed to be something that could be qualified and distinguished from other religious systems. This investigation required standards that could be measured in concrete ideas and systematically analyzed and compared.[1] The second test Scripture must pass for this investigation to be worthwhile is that Scripture must represent historiographic authenticity: in other words, the stories needed actually to have occurred. Why try a case based on allegations that never took place?

The problem I needed to investigate was whether Abraham's religion was special or different. I needed to see if Scripture promotes Abraham's and Jacob's truth as being unique when compared with other ancient religions. The first insight we glean arises in the *Law of Moses:*

> And you shall *not walk in the manners of the nations*, which I cast out before you: for they committed all these things, and therefore I abhorred them. (Lev 20:23)

God advised Abraham's children to refrain from following the customs of other Canaanite peoples. Although this does not distinguish Abraham's religion, YHWH does draw a distinction between the religious customs associated with his truth and those of contemporary nations.

23

Abraham's children eventually became the nation of Israel. King David distinguishes between the truth YHWH had given to ancient Israel and the lack of truth and equity that existed in other nations.

> He showed his word to Jacob, his statutes and his judgments *to Israel*. He has not dealt so with any nation: and as for his judgments, they have not known them. Praise you YHWH. (Ps 147:19–20)

The only nation YHWH singled out to bestow his word of truth was the ancient nation of Israel: YHWH did not deal so with any other nation! This means that neither Egypt, Assyria, nor Babylon had preserved YHWH's truth.

Deuteronomy reiterates this concept, further clarifying the differences between the righteousness revealed to Abraham and the values to which other nations adhered.

> Observe and hear (a) all these words which I command you, that it may go well with you, and with your children after you forever, when you do that which is (b) good and right in the sight of YHWH your God. When YHWH your God shall cut off the nations from before you, where you go to possess them, and you succeed them, and dwell in their land; Take heed to yourself that *you be not (c) snared* by following them, after they are destroyed from before you; and that you inquire not after their gods, saying, (d) How did these nations serve their gods? even so will I do likewise. (Deut 12:28–30)

YHWH commands Abraham's descendants to observe (a) all the commands in his constitutional Law, deeming them (b) righteous and good.[2] This is the first contrast we see between Israel's religion and other nations. Israel's God saw that his Law was good, thus implying that other law systems were deficient. YHWH instructs Israel to follow his commands yet warns them to not be (c) deceived into following contemporary religious customs. This implies that YHWH's covenanted commands were right and good,[3] while many beliefs, practices, and teachings advanced by other nations were dysfunctional and wicked. Further, foreign customs provided a deceptive, feel-good religion to which his people could succumb. YHWH clarifies that Abraham's children should not (d) serve him in the manner that other nations worshiped their gods. *This strongly implies that YHWH's requirements for salvation and his truth opposed contemporary customs and beliefs.*

In his constitutional Law,[4] YHWH warns Abraham's children that they would eventually rebel by worshiping imaginary gods, exasperating him with their dysfunctional theologies:

> They have moved me to jealousy with that which is not God; they have provoked me to anger with their *vanities*. (Deut 32:21; see also 2 Kgs 17:15)

Illustration 2.1. A tablet telling the legend of Ishtar's descent to the Underworld. From Nineveh, northern Iraq, Neo-Assyrian 7th century BCE.

Hebel, Hebrew for "vanities" means worthless.[5] Scripture often uses this expression to describe the customs, theology, and beliefs held by idolatrous nations. YHWH warns Israel regarding the danger in following a worthless and empty way of life, since the theology behind idol worship could bankrupt Abraham's nation.

Modern individuals often view idols and the people who worshiped them as primitive and quite naive. We think ancient man was just bowing down to wood and stone, nothing more. The reality is that the idol was just one part of this theology.[6] Every nation embraced particular doctrines or *truths* associated with the gods' physical manifestation (i.e., the idol).[7] George Mendenhall, a well–respected historian, observes "that deities—their symbols and rituals—were merely state-sanctioned expressions of entrenched social values."[8] What this means is that nations held philosophies underlying their beliefs about what God or society required man to do in order to be saved, cleansed from sin, and to enjoy an afterlife.[9] One German Egyptologist finds that the basic theology underlying idol-worship in Egypt's Isis and Osiris cult "from the very beginning . . . had to do with salvation and eternal life" (see Illustration 2.1).[10]

The Greeks, well known for paganism and idol worship, held many beliefs regarding sin and salvation as well. Idol worship pertained to the god's physical manifestation.[11] The first century pagan philosopher Celsus (175 CE) tells us that the "pagan representation of the gods are understood" by the believer "as having symbolic meaning and should not be taken literally, since they are 'symbols of invisible ideas and not objects of worship in themselves.'"[12]

The more important aspects of polytheism lay hidden in the initiation rites and the gods' various requirements.[13] "As long ago as the Homeric hymns (*c.* 800 BCE) we hear that ritual purity was the condition of salvation and that people were baptized to wash away all their previous sins."[14] Earlier than the Greeks, we learn that the Egyptians (during the very time that YHWH called Abraham and later spoke to Moses) held many of these same ideals regarding sin and salvation.[15]

During the very era when Greek and Egyptian theologies flourished, the prophet Jeremiah spoke volumes against these representative ideas and philosophies:

> Thus said YHWH, What iniquity have your fathers found in me, that they are gone far from me, and have *walked after vanity (hebel), and are become vain*? (Jer 2:5)
>
> Behold the voice of the cry of the daughter of my people because of them that dwell in a far country: Is not YHWH in Zion? Is not her king in her? Why have they *provoked me to anger with their graven images, and with strange vanities (hebel)*? (Jer 8:19)
>
> For *the customs of the people are vain (hebel)*: for one cuts a tree out of the forest, the work of the hands of the workman, with the axe. . . . But they are altogether *brutish and foolish: the stock is a doctrine of vanities (hebel)*. Silver spread into plates is brought from Tarshish, and gold from Uphaz, the work of the workman, and of the hands of the founder: blue and purple is their clothing: they are all the work of cunning men. (Jer 10:3, 8–9)

Jeremiah uses the Hebrew word *hebel* to describe false doctrines. Notice that Jeremiah associates false beliefs and distorted, empty doctrine with idol worship. The beliefs and doctrines surrounding pagan customs were as offensive to YHWH as the image itself. No text draws a clearer distinction between YHWH's ideals of truth and pagan ideas than Jeremiah's proclamation that YHWH's truth is nothing like pagan theology:

> They are *vanity, and the work of errors*: in the time of their visitation they shall perish. *The portion of Jacob is not like them: for he is the former of all things*; and Israel is the rod of his inheritance: YHWH of hosts is his name. (Jer 10:15–16; see also Jer 14:22; 16:19; 23:16; 51:17–19)

Jeremiah tells us that Jacob's God is not like the worthless and often destructive, self-gratifying doctrines found in the theologies of other nations. YHWH's way of life, his philosophy of life, and his religion precedes all others; it stood as truth both before and after the flood.

If YHWH's initial words in the Old Testament establish truth, then it follows that the theological core values of ancient societies who turned from their Creator should be at odds with the truth ordained in Scripture. Indeed, the prophet Ezekiel advocates that Israel's doctrine should not be confused with the basic tenet's of Egypt's religion. When YHWH commanded Ezekiel to reveal the sins of Israel's forefathers, the prophet obeyed by providing a short history lesson that referred to the nation's many rebellions after the exodus. Notice what he testifies regarding Israel's affiliation with Egypt's deities:

In the day that I lifted up my hand to them, to bring them out of the land of Egypt into a land that I had spied for them, flowing with milk and honey, which is the glory of all lands: Then said I to them, Cast you away every man the abominations of his eyes, and *defile not yourselves* with the idols of Egypt: I am YHWH your God. *But they rebelled against me*, and would not listen to me: they did not every man cast away the abominations of their eyes, *neither did they forsake the idols of Egypt*: then I said, I will pour out my fury upon them, to accomplish my anger against them in the middle of the land of Egypt. (Ezek 20:6–8)

The Egyptian idols to which Ezekiel refers may have been the Apis,[16] Osiris, Horus, or Hathor.[17] All four manifested as a calf and were associated with concepts of salvation (see Illustration 2.2).[18] The Apis bull was predominantly considered a manifestation of Osiris.[19] He became the most important of the sacred bulls in Egypt. This was probably the calf that Israel worshiped at Mt. Sinai (Exod 32:4–35) and that Jeroboam I instituted as the "gods that brought Israel out of Egypt" (1 Kgs 12:28–33).[20]

The Apis Osiris was Isis' son. He represented "an intermediary for mankind to communicate with the creator-god" through oracles.[21] The Israelites may have venerated the Apis as a surrogate Moses at Sinai since he had spoken to YHWH on Israel's behalf after Israel asked that YHWH no longer speak directly to the nation (Exod 20:19). This could very well explain both Moses' anger when he came down from the mount and saw the calf (Exod 32:19) and YHWH's disapproval of Moses' and Aaron's failure to sanctify him alone as Israel's God (Num 20:12). When Jeroboam I reinstated the Apis cult, he could have been trying to venerate Moses and Aaron as the two calves that

Illustration 2.2. The Apis, which was often associated with Osiris.

brought Israel out of Egypt (1 Kgs 12:28) and that spoke on their Creator's behalf. Jeroboam's cult thus merged Egyptian theology with Israel's history, an idolatrous practice archaeology attests Israel constantly employed.[22]

Illustration 2.3. A swimming merman from the detail of a monumental stone relief from the royal palace of the Assyrian king Sargon II (721–705 BCE) in modern Khorsbad.

Ezekiel alleges that Egypt's idols defiled Israel. This strongly implies that Egypt's theology debased Israel's pure creed. If this is indeed the case, Egypt's doctrine should be at odds when compared with Israel's original Abrahamic doctrine. After considering this evidence, I knew that the next step I needed to take was to retrace ancient theologies to see if I had inadvertently followed vanity in my own walk with God.

II. TRUTH OR MYTH?

In 1849, Henry Layard excavated Nineveh, uncovering a wealth of Assyrian texts. Many of these texts and reliefs depict doctrine paralleling modern beliefs and practices.[23] Early scholars and theologians who studied these texts, images, and reliefs readily recognized an intimate association between Catholicism and the "pagan" Babylonian and Assyrian mysteries.[24] Ralph Woodrow linked the papal miter to the same headdress worn by the Dogonish priests (and deities) depicted on Assyrian reliefs.[25] Other scholars perceived an association between religious symbols of crosses and fish icons in ancient Assyrian, Babylonian, and

Egyptian reliefs being mirrored by the Church today (see Illustration 2.3).[26] Still other theologians have seen a similarity between ancient pre-Christian religious rites and modern practices, such as: the communion sacrament, papal office, celibacy, Eucharist, and sainthood (see Illustration 2.4).[27] Much of this information led me to question, "How deep do these roots go"? Just how far has truth been enveloped by the shroud of paganism and folklore? Or, have tradition and folklore been disguised as "truth"?

Assyria is not the only ancient empire unearthed to reveal the secrets of her religious ideals. Ancient Babylon, Egypt, Ugarit, Nippur, Kish, Greece, Rome, and Persia have also been partially excavated to reveal stories with lasting images depicting theological

Illustration 2.4. A "fish-garbed figure," perhaps a priest.

beliefs.[28] The same ancient Sumerian and Babylonian texts that give reference to papal miters, sainthood, fish, and other "pagan" religious symbols also mention a beautiful garden, a serpent with a man and woman, and a flood—making the whole Scriptural account seem quite suspect and bringing me to question whether any truths or ideals really separated Abraham's religion (see Illustration 2.5).

Illustration 2.5. Epic of Creation dating to the 7th century BCE from Nineveh.

Faced with this evidence, I considered that there were at least two possibilites: 1). Scripture is just another myth; 2). Or, the flood accounts provide another witness to Scripture. I continued to question the possibilites. Did truth ever reside in Israel's Scriptures? Or did truth lie in the *pagan* Babylonian Mysteries? Or is truth an elusive concept? I even needed to consider whether Israel had borrowed her theology from other nations. Perhaps these ancient nations thought Israel important enough to assimilate a counterfeit religion paralleling the truth that the Creator had given to Abraham and Israel? Taking the issue to its very core, I had to ask: Did God Exist? I knew that I needed still more information and more evidence before I could draw any firm conclusions.

III. DID TRUTH EVER EXIST?

One strong consideration I saw for Scripture's authenticity is whether or not humanity had ever understood God. If biblical stories are accurate, then did those who lived before the flood (antediluvians) ever know truth? Did they know there was a Creator? If so, had Noah preserved that understanding through the flood? Israel's history demonstrates that the Creator bestowed a written law so that his words of truth could be preserved. Did the antediluvians or Noah have a law? Is there evidence of a system of equity and healthy living instituted for humankind before the flood? If evidence does exist, it buttresses the Creator's unchanging attribute. This evidence could demonstrate that a forum exists for truth to be preserved and sheltered from corruption. Does Genesis answer any of these questions?

I discovered that Genesis evidences a law bearing the basic framework of the later Israelite Law but without the greater detail of the Hebrew (or Israelite) Law. People before the flood knew about the ordinances for offerings (Gen 4:3–5).[29] Genesis 6–7 tells us that the antediluvians had grown violent. In contrast, YHWH calls Noah just, perfect (literally, 'entirely without blemish, complete'[30]), and righteous (Gen 6:8, 9; 7:1), indicating that humanity had a basic understanding of right and wrong.

Genesis may allude to some sort of law when YHWH states that early humanity had corrupted *his* way upon the earth.

> The earth also was corrupt before God, and the earth was filled with violence. And God looked on the earth, and, behold, it was corrupt; for all flesh had *corrupted his way upon the earth*. And God said to Noah, The end of all flesh is come before me; for the earth is filled with violence through them; and, behold, I will destroy them with the earth. (Gen 6:11–13)

The word translated "way" in v. 12 is *derek*. In the last chapter we saw that this term means the road or a course of life,[31] as referring to a pre-set philosophical course or value-precept-based way of living. When Abraham followed YHWH's *derek,* he adhered to the Creator's commandments, statutes, laws, and judgments, which effected justice (Gen 18:19; 26:2–5). This strongly suggests that Adam's descendants had a basic law quite similar to the instruction that YHWH later gave to Abraham. After the flood (Gen 6:18), Scripture tells us that YHWH promised to "*establish* his covenant with Noah" and his descendants because earth's inhabitants were evil and Noah was righteous. From the discourse in these first few chapters, Genesis makes it apparent that people had some sort of standard (i.e., law) by which to judge their lives. In spite of this standard, the antediluvians set themselves to do evil instead of good.

The word *establish* in Gen 6:18 literally means, 'to rise.'[32] It is often translated "confirm, rise up, establish, arise, or stand."[33] From the context of this verse, it appears that YHWH already had a covenant with the antediluvians, but they disregarded it. So YHWH *confirmed* his covenant with Noah, who obeyed his Creator and was righteous.[34] Genesis also records a prophecy spoken by Lamech, Noah's father, which implies YHWH had cursed cultivation during the antediluvian era, making farming an extraordinarily difficult endeavor. Lamech prophesied that Noah would

> comfort man concerning his work and toil of his hands, because of the ground which YHWH has cursed. (Gen 5:28–29)

If the Creator's "covenant with day and night" did not exist at this time,[35] then erratic seasons and lack of dew (Gen 2:5–6) were the most likely culprits for earth's difficult cultivation (Gen 4:12). The Creator fulfilled Lamech's prophecy for Noah in Genesis 8:21 by removing the Creator's curse on the soil, promising never again to curse the ground by this particular method.[36]

With the advent of the flood, we can discover numerous aspects of Israel's Law. YHWH told Noah to take animals inside the ark, commanding him to save two pairs of unclean animals and seven pairs of clean animals (Gen 7:2, 8). These descendants knew of the edible animal laws as prescribed in the later Israelite Covenant! Noah and his descendants also abstained from eating unclean animals, for if they had consumed unclean animals (Leviticus 11), species such as pigs would have quickly faced extinction.

Genesis 9:6 demonstrates the concept of an "eye for an eye and tooth for a tooth," as instructed in Abraham's and Israel's covenants by ordaining that a life would be given for life (Exod 21:24). Thus the Noahic Covenant established the judgment requiring lawful retribution for crime.[37] Genesis 9:4 continues the precepts of equity that are consistent with Israel's Law by commanding humanity to refrain from ingesting animal blood. The first penalties that YHWH ordains for murder and ingestion of animal blood establish precepts governing humankind and the animal kingdom. YHWH's commands and promises in Noah's Covenant apply to all Noah's descendants (i.e., the whole world).

At this point, I had to sit back and consider the evidence. Scripture indicates that the antediluvians had at one time known the Creator's way but had corrupted it (Gen 6:12). Surprisingly, Scripture states that antediluvians also knew the Creator's name—YHWH (Gen 4:26). In fact, Adam's grandson, Enos, is the first person, or at least the first generation, to have used YHWH's name. I had to consider the strong possibility that, after the flood, the whole world would have recognized this name, and it is probably why traces of YHWH's name have survived in various nonbiblical legends. Genesis 26:5 indicates that YHWH conferred true laws and statutes to Abraham and his children, while Genesis 32:10 states that Jacob knew truth. That Jacob indeed knew truth is evidenced when he served Laban for Rachel's hand in marriage (Gen 29:18) and followed the way of YHWH by observing the Seventh-year release statute (Deut 15:1). Jacob followed the judgments that YHWH gave Abraham's family. Jacob obeyed this statute *before* it had been given to the Israelites at Mt. Sinai, yet after the call of the nation's patriarch, Abraham, who kept the Creator's "commandments, statutes, and laws" (Gen 26:5). I had discovered strong evidence that the *way of YHWH* existed before he gave his Law at Mt. Sinai.

If Noah had preserved knowledge of YHWH through the flood, his first few generations would have used the Creator's name and observed animal offerings. They would have known about the flood and the Garden of Eden. Furthermore, they would have understood the law that predicated an "eye for an eye, and tooth for a tooth" concept of consequences that we later find both in the Torah (Old Testament Law) and generally in the ancient Near East (i.e., Hammurabi's Code). Scripture states that these patriarchs had truth and a law. Noah's Covenant broadly parallels the later Israelite Law. But I wondered if Scripture could make my quest clearer by indicating any possible errors to which Noah's descendants may have succumbed.

IV. FERMENTATION = COMMINGLED TRUTH AND ERROR

In the next step of this investigation, logic dictated that I focus on events after the flood. This led me to Babel, "the beginning of kingdoms on the earth" (Gen 10:10; 11:2). I needed to understand the elements influencing the postdiluvian era so I could trace the religious system that came out of Babel. Did Babel arise out of falsehood? Or did Babel arise out of truth that became corrupted and led to falsehood? If the early Babylonians did have truth, what truth did they possess?

Babel literally means 'confusion' and is derived from the word *balal*, which means 'to mix or mingle.'[38] The later name *Babylon* is derived from this city.[39] Thus, the Babylonian theology present at the Babel tower was a mixture of *truth* and *falsehood*, not simply falsehood. Therefore, we should find both truth and error in ancient Babylonian motifs. I was faced with the dilemma of how to separate what may have been a mythologized history from memories of a distant past. As we have seen, Scripture places responsibility on *the way* (*derek*) of YHWH to preserve truth. If we contrast this way of life to ancient societies' mythologies, then perhaps we can distinguish between myth and truth.[40] Scripture presents compelling evidence to support the theory that antediluvians possessed a law consonant with the later Israelite Law. But what hints, if any, does Scripture provide regarding false ideals embraced by humanity during this time?

The "Song of Moses" located at the end of Deuteronomy was written against a notoriously wicked generation who embraced Mesopotamian doctrines. A command in "Moses' Song" provides an excellent clue to the question of doctrinal falsehood.

> *Remember the DAYS OF OLD,* consider the years of many generations: ask your father, and he will show you; your elders, and they will tell you. *When the Most High divided to the nations their inheritance,* when he separated the sons of Adam, he set the bounds of the people according to the number of the Children of Israel. (Deut 32:7–8)

When did YHWH divide inheritances to the nations? When did he separate the sons of Adam?

And to Eber were born two sons: the name of one was Peleg; *for in his days was the earth divided.* (Gen 10:25, emphasis added)

The name *Peleg* means 'earthquake' or 'division'[41] and may have signaled the generation where Babel was destroyed and families of the earth divided.[42] Peleg was the fifth patriarch before Abram. The following list shows these generations in chronological order:

Noah	Reu
Shem	Serug
Arphaxad	Nahor
Eber	Terah
Peleg	Abram

As the children of Noah migrated from Mt. Ararat, they said, "Let us build us a city and a tower, whose top may reach to heaven; and let us make us a name, *lest we be scattered abroad on the face of the whole earth*" (Gen 11:4). At the building of Babel's tower, the nations had not yet been *divided* throughout the earth. After construction was well under way, YHWH confounded the builders' language, scattering them abroad (Gen 11:7–8). Languages were divided according to each of the families present, thus forming the nations of the earth (Gen 10:5, 18, 20, 31). Moses refers to this Babel epoch in his command for future generations to remember the days *when YHWH divided the languages and families of the earth.*[43]

Joshua obeys Moses' command to "remember the days of old at the dividing of nations at Babel" in Joshua 24:

And Joshua said to all the people, Thus said YHWH God of Israel, Your fathers dwelled on the other side of the flood *in old time*, even Terah, the father of Abraham, and the father of Nahor: and they served other gods. . . . Now therefore fear YHWH, and serve him in sincerity and in truth: and put away *the gods which your fathers served on the other side of the flood, and in Egypt*; and serve you YHWH. And if it seem evil to you to serve YHWH, choose you this day whom you will serve; *whether the gods which your fathers served that were on the other side of the flood,* or the gods of the Amorites, in whose land you dwell: but as for me and my house, we will serve YHWH. (Josh 24:2, 14–15, emphasis added)[44]

Moses had used the phrase "days of old" (Deut 32:7) to label the generation that lived during Babel's construction. Joshua uses "in old time" as an idiom to refer to this same generation. Joshua considers "in old time" to be before Jacob and his family migrated to Egypt, more in proximity with Terah's life. *Astoundingly, Joshua links the gods that people served in Terah's day with the same gods that people served in both Babel and Egypt.*[45] *If* both Terah and the

Egyptians were worshiping these "gods from the other side of the Euphrates River," then much of the early Egyptian and Babylonian theology should contain the same basic thematic elements in their theologies or doctrines.

In light of Moses' and Joshua's statements, Egypt's and Babylon's early theologies become increasingly important. It is paramount that we define the doctrines associated with these systems of worship, so error in Egypt and Babylon can be separated from the truth ordained in the words spoken to Abraham, Isaac, and Jacob. I knew that evidences for these "times of old" must stand on the facts of archaeology and history.

V. BABYLONIAN AND EGYPTIAN THEOLOGY

Scripture indicates that Israel lived in Egypt when Egyptian theology was quite primitive (*c.* 1900 BCE). Hinduism, one of the world's oldest religions, arises out of Egypt's theology and maintains many of the ancient philosophies and doctrines.[46] The Egyptian deity Osiris had been intricately woven into India's founder legends.[47] The ancient Greek historian Diodorus Siculus, who lived during the first century BCE, tells us that latter-day Indians were persuaded to claim the god as their own, asserting that he was born in India (*Lacus Curtius* I.19.7–8 and IV.6–7). Herodotus (II.123) grants credence to modern Hinduism's origins in Egyptian doctrine by citing Egypt's doctrine on immortality of the soul, "that after death it enters another creature at the moment of that creature's birth." This belief is still held by modern Hindus.[48]

Ancient Babylon, Egypt, and India were polytheistic in nature and devotion.[49] Along with the plethora of deities these nations worshiped, historical texts and archaeological evidence demonstrate that very specific ideals transcended national borders. From Babylon to Egypt, and throughout the Mediterranean lands, the following four ancient theologies are evidenced by ancient texts, archaeology, and ancient authors.

A. *Egyptians Worshiped Their Ancestors*

Egypt and Mesopotamia temple cults supported offerings for the dead.[50] Egyptians served the deceased by providing funerary offerings for their ancestors,[51] for which pharaohs were iconic deities.[52] Noted Egyptologist Erik Hornung observes that one of the hieroglyphs for the word 'god' was a cloth-wrapped staff (see Illustrations 2.6 and 2.7).[53]

Hornung associates this staff with the manifestation of power that was important for predynastic and early dynastic Egyptians.[54] He reasons that 'god' referred to all deceased[55] but was more narrowly applied to deceased pharaohs. "It is not surprising that terms for the deceased, such as *'hw* 'transfigured spirits' or *d'tjw* 'underworld dwellers' . . . for the dead are called 'gods' from an

Illustrations 2.6 and 2.7. The hieroglyph for "god" "staff bound with cloth."

early period on," Hornung tells us.[56] The deceased pharaoh's blessed "soul" took his place among the gods, where he was worshiped and often combined with another deity.[57] "The

Illustration 2.8. Isis and Osiris. The god Osiris holds the crook and flail, the sign of divine kingship.

deceased presented himself as a healer and avenger, and thus in the role of Horus."[58] Prayers, incense, and sacrifices were then directed to the deceased's soul, who could secure its patron's welfare.[59] With the patron's support, "The deceased had behind him the rites that have transformed him into a deified ancestral spirit" (see Illustration 2.8).[60]

> Offerings to the dead form a special feature of the Egyptian sacrifice. . . . The concern of the inscriptions appears to be to pray for their good reception in the land of the dead. The texts aim to promote the resurrection and ascension of the dead in order for them to join the company of immortal gods. The texts are also concerned with purification of the dead.[61]

Ancestor deification was no less prominent in Mesopotamia.[62] In one divination ritual, a sick man requests an intermediary to "speak to the ghost of my kin" to find the source of his illness.[63] Jeremy Black, an expert in Akkadian, Sumerian, and Babylonian literature and Fellow at Oxford University, is well known for his expertise in Mesopotamian deities. He has coauthored a book with accredited archaeologist Anthony Green, entitled *Gods, Demons and Symbols of Ancient Mesopotamia*. Regarding the practice of ancestor worship, the authors observe:

> The ancient Mesopotamians appear generally to have believed that after death most human beings survived in the form of a spirit or ghost which lived in the underworld. One of the duties of the living was to make funerary offerings (of food, drink and oil) to their deceased relatives. A special case is provided by extensive records from Girsu from the Early Dynastic Period of offerings made before the prayer statues of deceased rulers and members of the ruling family: these statutes were, it is assumed, originally dedicated by the living to stand in temples and pray constantly for them before the gods. After the death of their donors the statutes could not be moved and so came to be the recipients of offerings.[64]

The authors note that this practice did not necessarily imply ancestor *worship*, but failure to procure these offerings or sacrifices would cause the spirit to wander abroad.[65] Spirits could return to haunt the upper world, perhaps even the very family members who failed to procure their offerings.[66] "The dead, both of men and animals, occupy a prominent place among malignant beings who afflict the living."[67] Black and Green continue to observe, "The notion of an underworld populated by terrifying demonic beings, which fore-shadowed the medieval image of Hell, seems to have been a theological invention of the first millennium BC" (see Illustration 2.9).[68]

This ancient doctrine manifests one of the first dichotomies between pagan nations and Abraham's theology. YHWH's Law forbade bringing gifts for the dead into his sacred Temple precincts. YHWH commanded Israel's citizens to certify that they personally had *not*

given anything thereof for the dead: but I have listened to the voice of YHWH my God. (Deut 26:14)

YHWH disallowed votive offerings for the dead in his religious system.[69] This is one of the first doctrines ordained in Old Testament (Tanakh) theology that distinguished Abraham's beliefs from other ancient cultural values. Therefore, the theology of deification of the dead is one truth that separated Abraham's religion from the rest of the world.

B. Egypt Worshiped the Mother of a "Holy Child" Known as Isis, the "Queen of Heaven"

Worship of a deified child and his holy mother dominated many Eastern religions.[70] In Babylon, the Egyptian holy mother Isis was known as Ishtar and her holy son Tammuz.[71]

Illustration 2.9. The demon-god Pazuzu, "king of evil spirits," in a hell-like scene.

According to Greek Mycenaean tradition, the son's name was Adonis and the divine mother's name Aphrodite.[72] In India, the holy mother's name is Devaki and her divine son's name Krishna (Krsna).[73] In Hindu's ancient religion, the mother of the god-man was impregnated without seminal discharge.[74] During pregnancy, both the mother's and the child's lives were endangered by the ruler of the land.[75] The sovereign "patiently waited for the delivery of the child, expecting to kill him" as soon as he was delivered, yet the child miraculously escaped (see Illustration 2.10).[76]

When Herodotus wrote *Histories,* he easily identified Egypt's and Babylon's deities in his own Greek pantheon. He readily equated Babylon's Bel with his Greek counterpart, Zeus (I.181). He found Egypt's Horus god to be a duplicate of the Greek Apollo (II.156) and the Egyptian Osiris to counter the Grecian Dionysus (II.42).[77] Herodotus (II.4, 50, 51) tells us that the Egyptians accused the Greeks of plagiarizing their founding gods and that the Egyptian priests had sufficiently proved the validity of this claim. Diodorus (I.97, 19) also wrote of Grecian theology, venturing so far as to claim that Homer had borrowed his epic poems and their deities from Egypt.[78] Herodotus (II.4, 123) undoubtedly upheld this view, stating that certain Greek writers had borrowed Egypt's doctrines and "put them forward as their own." The Aegean's contact with Egypt (*c.* 1700 BCE) has recently been confirmed through pottery remains, which indicate a strong cross-influence on both cultures,[79] perhaps confirming Herodotus's account.

Another aspect of Egypt's theology associated deities with the heavenly kingdom.[80] Only the most important stars and constellations were conceived as gods.[81]

Illustration 2.10. Statute of Isis protecting Osiris, 6th *c.* BCE.

> *Sothis,* the brightest fixed star Sirius, acquired a cult as the herald of the inundation. From the early dynastic period on she was worshiped in cow form, *but was soon felt to be a manifestation of Isis,* just as Osiris was recognized in Orion.[82]

Throughout the Near East, cults associated holy mothers with heavenly bodies, which then acquired the appellation *Queen of Heaven* (see Illustration 2.11).[83] The prophet Jeremiah differentiates this doctrine from Israel's truth when addressing this cult.

> The children gather wood, and the fathers kindle the fire, and the women knead their dough, to make cakes to *the queen of heaven,* and to pour out drink offerings to other gods, that they may provoke me to anger. (Jer 7:18)

Illustration 2.11. Sacred
Babylonian mother and child.

Illustration 2.12. Bacchus (Dionysus),
a savior-god and the Greco-Roman
counterpart to Tammuz/Dumuzi.

If worshiping and providing offerings to a divine mother vexed YHWH's spirit and angered him, then this belief should not be associated with Israel's theology. YHWH commanded Israel not to worship him as other nations did (Deut 12:29–30). Jeremiah further emphasizes this point by stating that the core of YHWH's theology was wholly different from that of other nations ("They are altogether . . . a doctrine of vanities." Jer 10:8). It may be remembered that Isaiah—during the time these pagan beliefs were popular—tells us that YHWH sanctified a righteousness in Abraham and his descendants' theology that was unique, diverging from commonly held myths regarding righteousness, sin, salvation, and truth (Isa 51:1–2). If this is true, these contemporary religious beliefs should not be confused with Abraham's righteousness and truth.

C. Early Egyptians Worshiped a Savior-God Named Osiris

Osiris was the son of Isis, the Queen of Heaven,[84] who was resurrected from the dead. Egyptians believed Osiris to be the offspring of the supreme creator-god, Re.[85] In Egyptian theology, the half-human, half-divine Osiris died during the prime of his life. Followers of Osiris's cult participated in ritualistic weeping and mourning over the death of god's son, while other celebrations commemorated his resurrection.[86] A woman's sincere ritualistic grief (weeping) over Osiris/Tammuz played a special role which was seen in this mysterious religion to restore and make it possible for the slain god to come back to life (Ezek 8:14).[87] Both Osiris (Egypt) and Tammuz (Babylon) met with violent deaths and were resurrected (see Illustration 2.12).[88]

Egyptologist Erik Hornung observes, "The gods are rejuvenated in death and regenerate themselves at the wellsprings of their existence [i.e., youth]."[89] Plutarch tells us that people believed that Osiris descended into hell and then rose from the dead on the third day.[90] "One ancient Egyptian inscription promises the initiate that he will also be resurrected with his Lord: 'As truly as Osiris lives shall he live; as truly as Osiris is not dead shall he not die.'"[91] After resurrection, Osiris inherited the position of "judge of the dead."[92]

When Herodotus visited Egypt *c.* 450 BCE, he was so taken by the mysterious religious ceremony known as the "Passion,"[93] he could not even bring himself to describe it.[94] The Passion's rites and ceremonies[95] so closely paralleled those of his own Grecian theology that all he could bring himself to say was: "all the details of these performances are known to me, but—I will say no more" (II.171).[96] He felt it permissible to relate that the daughters of Danaus had imported this ceremony from Egypt and instructed the Pelasgian women in it (II.170–171; see Illustration 2.13).[97]

Illustration 2.13. A pre-Christian crucifixion from Ireland.

From ancient Egyptian texts we know that women wept yearly during Osiris's Passion Play, which was reenacted in the southern city of Abydos.[98] Regarding Osiris's Passion Play, Egyptologist Jan Assmann observes that in order to keep a person alive and be resurrected in the afterlife "it was above all important for one 'to turn his heart to him.'"[99] The text stresses the importance of the son of god (Osiris's) reconciling the social order on behalf of his father as the son proclaims, "I have acted on your behalf" in order to restore access to the father-god.[100] Perhaps most astoundingly, both these texts and the *Book of the Dead* indicate that in Egypt's polytheistic doctrine, salvation did not occur through works but through "divine grace" because "no one could hope to survive" the judgment of the dead "without divine grace" (see Illustration 2.14).[101]

Illustration 2.14. Osiris as the judge of the dead from a page of the *Book of the Dead* (Thebes, Egypt), 19th Dynasty, *c.* 1275 BCE.

Illustration 2.15. The goddess Indrani
and sacred child.

Illustration 2.16. Indian holy mother
Devaki and Krishna.

Alexander Hislop traced these four *foundation doctrines* to all ancient nations.[102] In Babylon, the mother and child duo were known as Ishtar and Tammuz (Dumuzi).[103] In India, this doctrine's foundation lay in the Isa and Iswara cult, where, like Egypt, Iswara is seen as a babe in his holy mother's arms.[104] In Asia the duo were known as Cybele and Dionysus, in Rome as Fortuna and Jupiter, in Greece as Apollo and Coronis, in Canaan as Baal and Anat, and in China and Japan the Madonna (holy mother) was known as Shing Moo (see Illustrations 2.15 and 2.16).[105] Alberto Green, of Rutgers University, observes,

> Culturally, the heterogeneity of (Syria) resulted in a series of borrowings, blending, and interchanges of populations. . . . Deities with similar attributes were identified, their personalities were fused, and even their ritual and regalia were commingled. To a certain degree, this may be considered characteristic of all of the cultures in the ancient Near East.[106]

Scripture and archaeology attest to Israel's trying to follow this practice of commingling YHWH with worship of other gods (most often with Ashteroth, Baal's consort).[107] In their thought-provoking research, Freke and Gandy observe:

> In the same way that Osiris was synthesized by the Greeks with their indigenous god Dionysus to create the Greek Mysteries, other Mediterranean cultures that adopted the Mystery religion also transformed one of their indigenous deities into the dying and resurrecting Mystery godman. So the deity who was known as Osiris in Egypt and became Dionysus in Greece was called Attis in Asia Minor, Adonis in Syria, Bacchus in Italy, Mithras in Persia, and so on. His forms were

many, but essentially he was the same perennial figure, whose collective identity was referred to as Osiris-Dionysus.[108]

Another scholar, James Frazer, also found these four doctrines to pervade ancient nations in his controversial book *The Golden Bough*. Henri Frankfort, another scholar, attempted to refute Frazer's thesis but was compelled to agree that basic ancient doctrines were universal.[109] Frankfort stressed, however, that the individual cult made them "specifically different."[110] Fascinatingly, *Frankfort recognized that Israel's religion did not conform to the universality of other national theologies.*[111] In his view, however, Israel's theological differences with other nations were a mitigating factor in the overall doctrinal dilemma. While Frankfort mitigates the conflict between ancient doctrine held by most nations and the Tanakh, our present study must recognize this distinction. Remember, our purpose in surveying ancient religions that existed "in times of old" is to distinguish them from the values and theology YHWH gave to Abraham's family, even if it is unpleasant to our sensibilities. As our study continues, we will discover a surprising reason for this apparent conflict in theology.

D. Egypt and Babylon Worshiped a Trinity (Three Beings United in One)

Triad unification of the gods formed another bedrock formula universal to Near Eastern theology.[112] One story of Isis and Re preserved on Ramesside papyri tells of the sun god's three chief manifestations: "Khepry in the morning, Re at midday, Atum in the evening."[113] Each manifestation is a separate deity or entity, that comprised Egypt's godhead, yet they are unified in one god: Re.

The stele of Ramesses IV, speaking directly of Osiris's unification with his father (Re) depicts Osiris's and Re's unity or oneness by stating that these unified gods "spoke with one mouth."[114] The Leiden hymn to Amun (the Egyptian "lord of all") states that "all gods are three" and continues to qualify the three attributes of the hidden deity's oneness (see Illustration 2.17).[115]

Illustration 2.17. Triad winged disc deity from Assyria, 8th century BCE.

Syncretism in the godhead[116] does not imply that the unified beings lose their personal identity.[117] Rather, the unification of two or three gods means that one is not lost in another but can once again be manifested separately.[118] Hence, although Osiris is "one" with his father, he is still an individual deity in the pantheon.[119] Alexander Hislop observes:

> While this was the theory, the first person in the Godhead was practically overlooked. As the Great Invisible, taking no immediate concern in human affairs, he was "to be worshiped through silence alone," that is, in point of fact, he was not worshiped by the multitude at all. The same thing is strikingly illustrated in India at this day. Though Brahma, according to the sacred books, is the first person of the Hindu Triad, and the relation of the Hindustan is called by his name, yet he is never worshiped, and there is scarcely a single temple in all India now in existence of those that were formerly erected to his honor.[120]

Illustration 2.18. Siva Trimurti: the triad of Brahma, Vishnu, and Siva. One god, three forms. Excavated at Mumbai, India.

Local deities (or patrons) were often incorporated into the national godhead, while deceased pharaohs were combined with two other national deities (i.e., Re, Osiris, Atum, etc. See Illustration 2.18).[121] The Greeks also believed in the unification of three-gods-in-one, for which Apollo-Helios-Hermes is a good example.[122]

It appears that monarchies propagandized the *son of god* doctrine for their own agenda.[123] The king's role was predicated on royal legitimacy, which prompted personified Osiris ideologies. As far south as Kush (Nubia), pharaohs practiced unification with Amun-Re, providing another example of triad unification (see Illustration 2.19).

Nubian scholar László Török observes that in Nubian theology, the divine ruler's birth was predestined before the creation of the universe.

The concept of the king's birth from the mystic intercourse between his earthly mother and the god Amun-Re, who took

Illustration 2.19. Slate statue of Ramsesnakht. On the naos is the sacred triad of Thebes: Amun, Mut, and Khons. From Karnak, 20th Dynasty, *c.* 1200 BCE.

Illustration 2.20. Stone panel from the North-West Palace of Ahsurnasirpal II, Nimrud, northern Iraq, Neo-Assyrian, *c.* 883–859. Winged figures show their divinity and carry buckets to sprinkle water on the Sacred Tree or Tree of Life.

on the form of the royal predecessor. . . . He received a part of his father's divinity and was legitimated and enabled to perform those duties in the world which his father performs in his cosmic realm. . . . The assimilation of the king with Amun-Re, the syncretistic deity uniting the creator Amun with the sun god (Re), was adopted under the influence of the Theban cult of Amun-Re.[124]

The ideals that legitimized kingship and authority through divinity were not exclusive to Africa.

Simo Parpola, an Assyriologist at the University of Helsinki, observed a similar phenomenon in ancient Mesopotamia. Assyria and Babylon expressed these ideals allegorically with the image of a tree planted on earth. "The sacred tree, usually represented in the form of a stylized palm tree, is the most common decorative motif in Assyrian royal iconography" (see Illustration 2.20).[125] In the throne room, the king is seen merging with the tree, thus becoming, as it were, its human incarnation.[126] Parpola opines in a controversial article,

Kingship was a sacred institution rooted in heaven, and the king was a model of human perfection seen as a prerequisite for man's personal salvation. By representing the king as the personification of the cosmic tree not only emphasized the unique position and power of the king, it also served to underline the divine origin of kingship. . . . Ashur was thus, by implication, the 'heavenly father' of the king, while the latter was his "son" in human form. The Father-Mother-Son triad constituted by Ashur, Ishtar and the king reminds one of the Holy Trinity of Christianity, where the Son, according to Athanasius, is 'the selfsame Godhead as the Father, but that Godhead manifested rather than immanent.' The notion of the king as the son of god held true only insofar as it referred to the divine spirit that resided within his human body. In Mesopotamian mythology, this divine spirit takes the form of a celestial savior figure. . . . symbolized by the cosmic tree. In short, he was god in human form, the 'perfect man,' the only person possibly fit to rule the world as god's earthly representative.[127]

Today when we think of government, we usually think of a person (or political party) who will either uphold rights of the individual or oppress these rights. Government is separated from religious life. This ideology, however, is far removed from concepts of rulership linked to kings in the ancient world. In the ancient Near East, kingship was always part of the national state religion, and monarchies were legitimized by their unification with the creator-god.[128] The king's power and legitimacy were manifested as he assimilated the attributes of *god's son*, Osiris (or Tammuz). Thus, the king always had a divine birth, he was god's dearly beloved son, a judge who sought to execute righteous judgments; he was beautiful, he was divine.[129]

The concept of *god's son* virtually became synonymous with the term *king*. If one was king, then one was considered a manifestation of the godhead—a son of god—usually the son of the nation's "great god" and likened to Osiris (or Tammuz), the earthly ruling agent or viceroy.[130] "The king appears in the concepts of predestination, 'election,' and divine sonship as if he were possessor of divine features since his conception (or even since the creation of the universe)," reflects Török.[131] The idea of god's son's being reborn in human form pervaded nations in the ancient Near East.

Confronted with these facts, I wondered if everything I had been taught was a lie. Did God exist? Was God a man-made fairy-tale? Or had I misapplied the data? I remembered what I had been taught as a child. My church taught that when Satan was cast out of heaven, he set up a counterfeit religion, paralleling the truth that he knew God would bestow to Israel. He did this to deceive the nations and, eventually, the Israelites. He set up polytheistic cults to mimic the very truth and plan of salvation that God was giving to Israel so that, later on, Israel and the world would not believe the truth when YHWH performed it with his own son.[132]

However, there was a contradiction in my church's doctrine that made me uneasy. In the very era when these counterfeit religions prospered in pagan nations, YHWH warned Israel to not "walk" in the same way as the nations who held these universal beliefs (Lev 20:23) or be snared into following them (Deut 12:29–31). When Israel rejected YHWH as ruler, the Creator told Samuel that Israel had rejected him only to substitute a king *like* the other nations. "For they have not rejected you, but they have rejected me, that I should not reign over them" (1 Sam 8:7). In the context of ancient ideals of kingship, coupled with Israel's continual desire for imaginary gods demonstrates that Israel rejected YHWH by exchanging him for older, fermented theology with views of the king as god-incarnate.

King David further distinguishes YHWH's religion from that of other dying-and-resurrection-savior cults by stating that YHWH "neither slumbers nor sleeps" (Ps 121:4) as other savior-deities did when they died, went to an underworld (hell), and were resurrected.[133] Ezekiel continues this subject by criticizing cults in which women wept for the death of God's son (Ezek 8:14–15). YHWH told the prophet that this aspect was an "abomination" to him (Ezek 8:15). If YHWH found this doctrine abominable, would he use it in his own theology? Could YHWH sanctify the very doctrine he condemned and yet be righteous?[134]

Jeremiah tells us that the utter core ("stock") of the theology on which these cults were based was a "doctrine of vanities" (Jer 10:8). Later on, Jeremiah wrote that Israel's God, "the portion of Jacob, is not like" the gods of other nations (Jer 10:15–16). If YHWH's truth is not similar to Osiris's or Tammuz's ideals (doctrines) of salvation, how can they represent a counterfeit religion? If Satan counterfeited YHWH's truth, would not YHWH have extolled these cult's virtues when he gave his truth to Abraham and Jacob? If YHWH were separating his truth from the beliefs of other nations, would he not have clarified the aspects of these cults that embraced true ideologies?

Instead, we find Moses telling Israel that the gods of other nations are unlike YHWH, "for their rock is not as our Rock" (Deut 32:31), consistently separating YHWH's theology from the ideals commonly held by other countries. Joshua continued in Moses' steps, encouraging Israel to forsake the gods she had worshiped in Egypt (Josh 24:2, 14–15), which was, as we have seen, a land that was entrenched in these four universal theologies, whose "doctrine was worthless" (Jer 10:8).

History and archaeology provide evidence for the "days of old" at the time when YHWH had divided the nations on the earth. But I wondered, *if* God considers these theologies false, from where did the source of their idolatry arise? Could I find evidence that these doctrines actually had a point of origin? If so, would it demonstrate a truth that had been counterfeited, or had history been regenerated into myth? Did any of the events transpiring *before* the flood generate later doctrine? The next step in this case was to focus on antediluvian accounts to help clear up this enigma.

VI. THE ANTEDILUVIAN CLUE

A. *Where Did the Perversion of Truth Gain Its Foothold?*

Most of us who read the Bible understand that YHWH destroyed Noah's generation for depravities such as violence. But what if a theological corruption also tainted this society's actions? Genesis 6:9 states that the generations of Noah were *tamiym*, which means 'entirely, wholly, and completely pure.'[135] If Noah and his ancestry were unadulterated, it is unlikely that idolatry and violence would have been perpetuated through Noah or his forefathers.

Cain, however, had selfishly divided his offering;[136] he was a murderer, and a much likelier candidate for harboring idolatrous intentions. By singling out Noah's generations as being "perfect" (Gen 6:9), Scripture implies that other lineages were impure and imperfect.

The only other lineage that Scripture mentions is Cain's descendants. Does Scripture afford any clues to the sins that were embedded in Cain's progeny? To identify any corruption that may have been perpetrated with Cain's line, we need to contrast the evidence that Scripture provides for Noah's ancestry with the evidence provided for Cain's descendants.

The pureness of Noah's ancestry is evidenced in his forefather, Enos, who had "faith to call on the name of YHWH."[137] The later Israelite Law had another command regarding the Creator's name. The Levites were instructed to bless Israel by using YHWH's name in the following manner.

> And they shall put *my name* on the Children of Israel; and I will bless them. (Num 6:27; see also Deut 28:10)

For most of Israel's history, the people followed this command. Although the English translation does not retain this evidence, the Hebrew spellings do. Names such as Chanan**yah** (Hananiah), Yirme**yah** (Jeremiah), Daniy'**el** (Daniel)**,** Shemuw'**el** (Samuel), Yesha'**yah** (Isaiah): all follow YHWH's command.[138] The evidence demonstrates that Israel followed the covenant's command in that their children were called by the name *YHWH Elohiym*. Could it be that YHWH had commanded the antediluvians to follow this practice, or at the very least they voluntarily called their children by YHWH's name?

(The letters J and V did not appear in these names until medieval times. Biblical Hebrew as we know it in the Old Testament used "Y," (*yod*) and "W" (*waw*). The J and V phonetic sounds did not enter the Hebrew language until Israel was in the Diaspora and had lost her national identity. Translating Scripture from Hebrew *to Latin* to English resulted in the letters J and V being used for *y* and *w*. So when Hebrew words are rendered in English, they are often spelled with a "J," rather than Hebraic "Y." For example, names pronounced Yared or Yosiah in Hebrew are spelled as Jared and Josiah in English.[139])

Did the antediluvians follow the Law's ordinance for blessing their children in the name of YHWH, as Israel would later do? Scripture attests the Creator's name throughout Noah's ancestry: Mahalale**el**, Mehu**yael**, and Methusel**ah**—yes, these antediluvian patriarchs contain the sacred name. A word study on the names of the Children of Israel is quite revealing. When Israel followed YHWH and was righteous, her descendants' names incorporated part of the Creator's name by using: "yh", "ah", or "el." However, when Israel lived in idolatry she called her children after the names of other gods by using the "bal'" or "bel" root in them. The *New Unger's Bible Dictionary* relates:

In times of lapse Hebrews compounded the names of their children with Baal—for example, Jerubbaal (Judg 7:1); Eshbaal (1 Chr 8:33; 9:39). Merib-baal (1 Chr 8:34; 9:40), which in times of revival and return to Jehovistic worship were altered, the baal element being replaced by 'bosheth,' meaning 'shame.' Thus pious Israelites expressed their horror of Baal worship; examples are Jerubbesheth (for Jerubbaal, 2 Sam 11:21), Ish-bosheth (for Ishbaal, 2 Sam 2:8), Mephibosheth (for Merib-baal; 2 Sam 4:4; 9:6, 10).[140]

This formula for giving a child a theophoric name was common throughout the ancient world, especially when kings were concerned. The name *Nebuchadnezzar,* for instance, translates: 'may the god Nebu protect the crown.'[141] Thus, in ancient times, names often revealed religious philosophies and associations.

The first glimpse into the cultural philosophies that Cain's descendants held is seen in three brothers (Gen 4:20–22) born in the same generation as Noah. Another man by the name of Lamech (not Noah's father) has three sons. His firstborn son's name, Yabal,[142] literally means 'he leads.' This name may reflect a firstborn child's tendency toward leadership within a family. Yubal means 'he is led,'[143] while Tubal-Cain means 'led by Cain.'[144] This latter name, though circumstantial, presents a strong possibility that Tubal-Cain walked in the ways of Cain, who was a murderer and whom YHWH had banished from his presence. Scripture also tells us that these brothers were not only the world's first inventors, but they also had very specific occupations.[145] Yabal's descendants lived in tents and raised cattle. Yubal played musical instruments, while Yubal-Cain forged metals.[146] They also had a sister named *Naamah* who was very beautiful (the word *Naamah* means 'beauty').[147]

We may miss the intent by assuming that this text refers only to Yabal's housing conditions. This reference more likely describes a place where he began to lead his family in worship. If Yubal followed his older brother, he may have initiated music in religious customs, while Yubal-Cain fashioned the images that this religion venerated. As sons of one of the first polygamous families, they may have used religion to legitimize their new role in society.

The second glimpse we see into Cain's lineage arises in a remark that Yabal's father made. Genesis records that Lamech spoke angrily to his two wives, saying,

> I have slain a man to my wounding, and a young man to my hurt. If Cain shall be avenged sevenfold, truly Lamech seventy and sevenfold. (Gen 4:23–24)

That Lamech had killed "to his own hurt" may mean he murdered one of his sons (perhaps Tubal-Cain); hence, he boasted of a greater, seventyfold, protection than YHWH had formerly afforded Cain. I have often wondered why Scripture records the history of Cain's descendants if they were simply destroyed in the flood. As I considered the evidence presented this far, I was left wondering if Scripture had provided this information for naught, or was there a reason for Cain's genealogy?

Probably the first clue to indiscretions that Cain's offspring may have perpetrated is found in the account shortly before the flood in Genesis 6.

> And it came to pass, when men began to multiply on the face of the earth, and daughters were born to them, that the *sons of God* saw the daughters of men that they were fair; and *they took them wives of all which they chose.* (Gen 6:1–2)

When YHWH created humanity, we became God's sons and daughters. Moses refers to YHWH as being our father in the sense that he has created us, asking, "Do you thus requite YHWH, O foolish people and unwise? *Is not he your father* that has bought you? Has he not made you, and established you?" (Deut 32:6). The prophet Isaiah also describes YHWH as humanity's father: "Doubtless *you are our father*, though Abraham be ignorant of us, and Israel acknowledge us not: you, *O YHWH, are our father*, our redeemer; your name is from everlasting" (Isa 63:16; see also Ps 68:5; 89:26). If YHWH is a Father to humanity simply because he has created us, then we are God's sons and daughters.

This concept is evidenced later in history when YHWH sought to redeem Abraham's children from captivity. He told Pharaoh that Israel was his son and commanded Pharaoh: "Let *my son* go that he may serve me" (Exod 4:23). The Creator further told Israel that they were his children: "You are the children of YHWH your God" (Deut 14:1). Therefore, it is possible that when Gen 6:2 states that the *sons of God* looked on the *daughters of men*, the text is building on the creation account by reflecting that mankind was created by YHWH (in his likeness and image) while womankind was created from man's rib, hence a by-product of man and, by extension, a "daughter of men."[148] But notice the clue found in this text.[149]

The sons of men, or more simply put, *men* found women so beautifully enticing, they began taking wives "of all which they chose."[150] This is the first Scriptural reference to polygyny (marriage to more than one wife). It appears that man was not content with the righteous paradigm established in Eden but greedily lusted after as much beauty as he could obtain. In response to this degradation, YHWH declared that his spirit would no longer exert a serious effort or energy where humanity was concerned since fleshly desires were consuming the goodness he created in man, therefore, he shortened the days in which humanity could do evil.

> And YHWH said, My spirit shall not always strive with man, for that he *also is flesh*: yet his days shall be an hundred and twenty years. (Gen 6:3)

Shagam,[151] translated also, draws attention to humanity's fleshly desires.[152] YHWH is condemning the fleshly desires that led to polygyny (the subject of the previous verse), as erring from his precepts. The text in Gen 6:3 has not yet introduced the idea of humanity's other depravities (6:5, 11). The context of the first four verses (6:1–4) deals strictly with humanity's perverse copulation that created "giants" (6:4). It is in this context that YHWH states he will remove his spirit. Thus, YHWH's judgment is against humanity's fleshly desires. He removes his spirit from contending with men's sinfulness, which ultimately shortened the number of years that men lived. Instead of living hundreds of years, mankind would live a mere 120 years without YHWH's spirit standing as an adversary to humanity's lusts.

Whereas the removal of YHWH's spirit was a judgment against polygyny, the flood was a separate judgment against the "the wickedness of man" and the "imagination of the thoughts of his heart," (v. 5), such as violence and destruction (v. 11–13). That the verse regarding withdrawal of YHWH's spirit is sandwiched in the context of unnatural marital unions indicates that it is a separate judgment from the judgment of the flood. The removal of YHWH's spirit, which strove against humanity's evil desire, was YHWH's judgment against humanity's fleshly desires that had led him to marry "all of which he chose," while the flood was a cleansing judgment against humanity's many other degradations.

One of the first distinctions we find between Noah's generations and that of his contemporaries is polygamy.[153] Lamech, one of Cain's descendants, was the first man renowned for entering into a polygamous marriage (Gen 4:19). Noah and his family, on the other hand, did not participate in polygamy. When Noah and his sons entered the ark, each had only one wife (Gen 7:13).

Polygyny is not the only practice that Genesis recognizes. Humanity corrupted the earth through violence (Gen 6:11) to such a horrific extent that YHWH's entire creation needed to be cleansed. It is hard to imagine what humanity did to corrupt the earth. However, if people were able to live for hundreds of years, imagine the scientific understanding they could gain of YHWH's handiwork, then apply to their own dysfunctional advantage.

Consider our modern era. Since the industrial and scientific revolutions, every year has marked significantly greater knowledge and understanding of our world and the laws by which it is governed.[154] We have progressed far beyond the primitive hand tools and manual labor that defined our daily life a mere 150 years ago. Very recent technological understanding has empowered us to see the weather by means of satellites; create communications that reach around the world; and genetically engineer and clone YHWH's creation—all in the last 70 years.

Our modern world has made these significant strides despite the fact that great scientific minds have lived an average of less than 80 years during this modern era. (Einstein only lived to be 76, while Isaac Newton lived to be 84.) Imagine the progress that the antediluvians could have achieved during an 800 or 900-hundred year life-span. Modern manipulation with genetic engineering began in the 1960's. Less than 50 years later, scientists learned to change the DNA structure of crops and clone animals such as sheep and horses,[155] and today scientists are looking at engineering trees with rabbit DNA in an effort to clean up our polluted environment. If the antediluvians lived for hundreds of years, there are boundless achievements that these people could have accomplished in understanding the organic world that YHWH had created.

Genesis may bear witness to humanity's endeavors to manipulate YHWH's creation, indicating the engineering of an unusual species of humankind before the institution of polygyny.

> There were giants (Heb. *nephiyliym*) in the earth in those days; and also after that, when the sons of God came in to the daughters of men, and they bore children to them, the same became mighty men (*giboriym*) which were of old, men of renown (lit., men of 'the name'). (Gen 6:4, parentheses added)

Scripture uses *nephiyliym*,[156] translated "giants," to denote a new race of people with increased stature. Not only were these giants (*nephiyliym*) tall, Scripture states they were *giboriym*, meaning 'mighty or powerful.'[157] Genesis 6:4 associates the *nephiyliym* with the "wickedness of man" and his "evil imagination" (Gen 6:5). Given the context of this chapter, the *nephiyliym* were one way that humanity had corrupted the earth (Gen 6:11). This species' staggering might enabled them to inflict violence (Gen 6:11) on the smaller, weaker individuals, and this violence only increased with the *nephiyliym*'s proliferation. This situation left YHWH with one solution: destroy his creation and humanity's manipulation of it (Gen 6:7).

(If Genesis 6:1–3 were referring to some type of divine beings [angels, Heb. *mal'ak*] that copulated with humanity, YHWH would have issued a judgment against the *mal'ak*, not mankind. Since YHWH's judgments [the flood and a shortened life] were directed solely at mankind, we are pretty safe in interpreting these texts as dealing solely with humanity.)

Genesis' texts may also imply that corruption had originated in Cain's progeny.[158] Scripture recognizes the violence and corruption after the *nephiyliym* entered history. YHWH had retarded Cain's reproductivity, while Seth's generations multiplied twice as quickly as Cain's (see pp. 19–21). His children needed to increase their reproductivity to survive. Lamech is the first recorded polygamist, and by his own admission he was a murderer (Gen 4:23). Could Lamech's forefathers have been *nephiyliym*? Had they attained greater strength and stature to prey on Seth's progeny? What about the fact that the name of Lamech's son connoted following after Cain?

The nexus tying all these questions together is Scripture's statement that Noah's generations were *tamiym*, 'perfect or pure.'

> Noah was a just man and **perfect in his generations**, and Noah walked with God. (Gen 6:9)

Tamiym, translated perfect means 'entirely, wholly, and completely pure.'[159] If Noah and his generations were pure, other lineages were not. YHWH had warned Cain that sin lay at the door of his heart if he did not learn to rule his thoughts, desires, and emotional impulses (Gen 4:7). Cain allowed jealousy and anger to control him to the point of murdering his own brother. When YHWH corrected him, Cain was more concerned about his own pride than rectifying the iniquity wrought by his deed (Gen 4:13–14). If Cain did not train himself to do right, then it is quite *un*likely that he possessed the self-discipline needed to train his children to rule their desires and impulses as well. Thus, Cain's progeny may have introduced self-gratifying iniquities into the world.

How does all of this tie in with pre-flood theology? The traits that would best characterize the cults perpetrated by Cain's descendants would emphasize self-gratification, fulfillment of fleshly desires, and maligning of traditional monogamy. Worship practices initiated by Lamech's children may have continued well after the flood in rituals such as fertility cults. This is where one possible theory develops. If Lamech's children were mighty powerful giants, it is likely that later stories of them transcended the divine. In later history, these stories of mere mortals morphed into mythological stories that eventually became part of cultic and anti-YHWH systems of religious expression. Although hypothetical, the Yabal brothers might have been the deified deceased ancestors that the Egyptians worshiped from the "days of old."[160] Could their epic tales have embodied the original Trinity? I wanted to examine all possible theories in my quest to understand the world thousands of years ago. As incredible as this premise was, it was actually supported by credible circumstantial evidence.

It is amazing how similar pagan cults were. After the flood, Ham's children settled in Egypt and Canaan (Gen 9:18; Ham's oldest son was *Mizraim*, which is the Hebrew word for "Egypt" Gen 10:6). Both Baal[161] and Osiris were associated with dying and renewal of the year in the fertility rites. As we have seen, the general premise of these cults was based on the suffering god's descent into the underworld, only to be resurrected a short time later.

Dumuzi was a popular Mesopotamian "suffering" god.[162] He was Mesopotamia's version of Egypt's Osiris or Babylon's Tammuz.[163] His name just happens to appear on a king's list from Sumeria that, according to Sumerian records, pre-dates the flood.[164] Could Dumuzi be the Sumerian equivalent of Lamech's son, killed at his father's hands? Some scholars have indeed posited that Dumuzi was an "historical figure who has been mythologized into religious tradition."[165] He may have been a king who began the entire process of participating in rites to ensure fertility, a core tradition associated with Dumuzi.[166] This theory fits quite appropriately with the Scriptural evidence, which demonstrates that Cain's progeny experienced handicapped birth rates when compared with Seth's line (see Table 1.1, p. 20). One scholar notes that, "once Dumuzi was deified, the pattern spread by identification to other localities and deities."[167]

Other names in ancient Sumerian lists are also tantalizing. Eridu, a city in the *Epic of Gilgamesh*, is listed in a Sumerian "antediluvian" city list.[168] Some scholars equate this town with Genesis' Irad (Gen 4:18), which was built by one of Cain's sons.[169] It is not easy to dismiss the association of another antediluvian Sumerian king, Enmeduranki, with the epic's hero Enkidu.[170] How do we account for this similarity unless these cults had a common epic from which their theological mythologies stemmed?

The factor most likely to have contributed to the Yabals' deification would have been the survival of Yabal's theology after the flood. What if Ham had married Naamah thereby continuing Cain's line through the flood? Ham's family could facilitate the belief system perpetrated by the imagery of Naamah's brothers, and she could have further nourished the memory of her brother, slain at her father's hand. I knew that scholars have demonstrated that ancient societies worshiped their ancestors. Add to this the fact that *all* of Cain's other children were destroyed in the flood, and there might have been a need to deify the memory of this lost line to epic proportions. While I knew all these theories and questions sounded like fanciful speculation, I came across genealogical evidence that could not be accounted for in any other way, if Noah's generations were indeed *tamiym*.

B. Nephiyl: Truth or Mythology?

During my examination of Israel's Scripture, I found evidence to support Ham's marriage to Cain's descendant, Naamah. When Joshua and Caleb spied in Canaan (a land formerly allotted to Ham's son, Gen 10:15–20), they saw a people called *Anakim*, whom Scripture

Illustration 2.21. Tenth century (BCE) shard excavated from Gath bearing the name, "Goliath."

identifies as *nephiyl* descendants. This is the only other place where the Hebrew Scriptures again use the word *nephiyl*, which the King James Version renders "giants":

> And there we saw the giants (*nephiyliym*), the sons of Anak, which come of the giants (*nephiyliym*): and we were in our own sight as grasshoppers, and so we were in their sight. (Num 13:33, parentheses added)

During Canaan's conquest, Joshua destroyed *all the Anakim* except for those in Gaza, **Gath**, and **Ashdod** (Josh 11:21–22). The *nephiyliym* were on the verge of extinction long before a young man killed one of their last remaining and best-known champions, Goliath.[171] It is not surprising then to find that Goliath's family resided in Gath (1 Sam 17:4), and his house bore the genetic malady that increased stature.[172] Second Samuel 21:20 acknowledges that Goliath's brothers also bore the genetic *nephiyl* mutation. King David and his men abolished the remaining Goliath household,[173] around 1050 BCE, driving the race to extinction (see Illustration 2.21).

Another *nephiyl* race called Emim, kin of the Anakims, is recorded in Deuteronomy (2:10–12). According to Deut 2:11, the Moabites called this giant tribe Emims while the Ammonites called them Zamzummims (Deut 2:20). Esau's and Lot's families destroyed these giant tribes, appropriating the land for themselves (Deut 2:19–22).[174]

> That also was accounted a land of giants (Heb. *Rephaim*): giants dwelt therein in old time; and the Ammonites call them Zamzummim; a people great, and many, and tall, as the Anakims; but YHWH destroyed them before them; and they succeeded them, and dwelt in their stead. (Deut 2:20–21)

Before the exodus, Scripture records that, in Abraham's days, King Chedorlaomer killed many giant nations including the Rephaims.

And in the fourteenth year came Chedorlaomer, and the kings that were with him, and smote the *Rephaims in* Ashteroth Karnaim, and the *Zuzim in Ham*, and the *Emim in Shaveh Kiriathaim.* (Gen 14:5)

The Rephaim were a Canaanite people, whose land YHWH had ceded to Abraham (Gen 15:20). As time progressed, it appears that the term *Rephaim* replaced the antiquated term *nephiyliym* to designate many of the giant tribes, or it may be that one dominant giant tribe of the *Rephaim* came to represent all other giant tribes (as the term German today designates many different ethnic tribes). Whatever the case may be, Scripture indicates that the giant *nephiyliym* existed as *Rephaim* well after this genetic corruption was supposed to have been destroyed in the flood.

Scripture and ancient Ugaritic texts consistently associate the Rephaim with the city of Ashteroth (see above, Gen 14:5). In Ugarit, a country not too far from Israel, the *nephiyliym* tribes were also called *Rephaim*. Ancient Ugaritic texts hale legendary *Rephaim* epic heroes, calling champions of Baal (like Goliath) "Rephaites."[175] This indicates that ancient Scriptural histories are supported by epigraphic accounts from other nations yet without the mythological theology that other nations appended to these legendary tales.[176]

This is not the only evidence that Scripture presents regarding the giant (*nephiyl*) tribes. When Israel's ten spies scouted the land of Canaan shortly after the exodus, their main fear was the giant Anakims, the sons of Anak (Num 13:22, 28, 33). In Deut 9:2–3, YHWH promised that Israel would very quickly conquer the feared Anakims. During the Conquest, Caleb defeated many of them, including three Anakim princes, driving them back to their stronghold in Arba (Josh 15:13–14), which under Israelite occupation became known as Hebron (Josh 15:13; 21:11). When Joshua divided the land, the city of Hebron was given to Caleb as an inheritance, since he had driven out the giant Anakim from the territory (Judg 1:20). It was also designated a Refuge City, the suburbs of which were to be shared with the Levites (Josh 21:10–13). Thus, Scripture consistently supports the idea that the *nephiyliym* reappeared *after* the flood.[177]

The account of the *nephiyliym* in 2 Sam 21:15–22 is quite telling. After Saul's death, it seems that the Anakim planned to assassinate King David (15–16). Even Goliath's brother Lahmi[178] led an expedition (v. 19) against the Israelites. Samuel's account identifies these giants with the Rephaim (the English reads "giants," 2 Sam 21:16, 18, 20, 22).[179] David waged at least four separate campaigns before exterminating the Anakims from the land of Canaan (chaps. 15–22). David's nephew even felled another Rephaim Baal-champion during one of Israel's last campaigns against the Anakims. The parallel account of David's four campaigns against Canaan's *nephiyl* is recorded in 1 Chr 20:4–8.[180] The prophet Isaiah recognized the Rephaim's former territory as the "Valley of Rephaim" (Isa 17:5) as late as the eighth century BCE.[181]

What are the implications that the *nephiyliym* have for Ham's genealogy? The antediluvian *nephiyliym* existed *after* the flood! Genesis 10 records that *Ham's descendants* settled south and east of the Mediterranean. These cities are the very places where accounts in the Books of Exodus and Joshua later record these powerfully large people as still living. If Noah's generations were pure and unadulterated (Gen 6:9), then how did giants genetically recur unless through the polluted genes of Cain's descendants? It was only through the marriage of Ham to Naamah that this species could have continued to exist.

Remember that *nephiyl* is not the only word that Genesis uses to distinguish Lamech's offspring. Scripture also states:

> There were giants in the earth in those days; and also after that, when the sons of God came in to the daughters of men, and they bare children to them, the same became *mighty men* (*gibboriym*) which were of old, men of renown. (Gen 6:4)

The word *gibboriym* means 'mighty or powerful people.'[182] This term would logically be applied to a giant race of people. The next text to employ the term *gibbor* is Genesis 10. This text again implicates Ham's descendants (through marriage to Naamah) as carriers of the *nephiyl/gibbor* genetic trait.

> Cush (Ham's son) begat Nimrod: he began to be a *mighty one* (*gibbor*) in the earth. He was a *mighty hunter* (*gibbor*-hunter) before YHWH: why it is said, Even as Nimrod the *mighty* (*gibbor*) hunter before YHWH. (Gen 10:8–9, parentheses added)

This text has *at least* two possible interpretations. The first interprets Nimrod as a mighty, powerful, tyrannical man who killed other mighty men. The second possibility is that, as Ham's descendant, Nimrod bore the genetic trait that caused the *nephiyl* to be powerful giants. He then sought to secure his kingdom by destroying other members of his clan whose genetic capabilities enabled them to be as mighty and as powerful as he (War of the Titans?). Nimrod may have even feared another flood should the *gibboriym* continue to procreate, and he may have sought to exterminate his own race. Scripture first defined the word *gibboriym* in context with the mutated *nephiyl*. Since this text (Gen 10:8–9) is the second time that Scripture employs *gibbor*, emphasizing that Nimrod was a 'gibbor-hunter,' the latter seems a more likely conclusion.[183]

In ancient times, the father was the head of the family[184] and served as a priest-king, much like Melchizedek did in Abraham's time. As head of his family, Ham would have been a priest and king in the doctrines that he and his clan embraced. Ham was the founding patriarch for his clan and served as a high priest and king in the Cainite-Yabalish religion. This conclusion is corroborated by the fact that Ham's son Mizraim founded Egypt, providing a framework for the evolution of Egyptian mythology which mirrored the Canaantie-Yabalish religion.[185]

This theory is further strengthened by another ancient Ugaritic text, which demonstrates that the *Rephaim* were considered underworld deities (deified upon death).[186] One text extols the *Repha* (singular form of the plural *Rephaim*) in an account quite similar to Genesis' account of Yubal's musical abilities (Gen 4:21).

> May Rp'u drink, the king of eternity. . . . the god who dwells in **Ashteroth**, the god who judges at **Edrei**, who sings and makes music with the harp and flute, with the tambourine and cymbals, with the castanets of ivory, among the good companions of Kothar.[187]

This text associates a deified Repha with musical talents similar to Yubal in Genesis, a person on whose origins Gen 6:1–4 casts in dubious light. The Ugaritic texts also associate the Rephaim as dwelling in Ashteroth-Karnaim. We learn from Scripture that Ashteroth and Edrei had been actual Rephaim occupied territory (Gen 14:5; Josh 12:4; 13:12). In his magnum opus, Oxford University's John Day points out

> The reference to "the god who dwells in Ashteroth, the god who judges in Edrei" strikingly resembles one of the ethnic Rephaim, "Og, king of Bashan, one of the remnant of the Rephaim, who dwelt at Ashteroth and at Erei." (Josh 12:4; cf 13:12)[188]

Scripture presents Og as controlling one of the last Rephaim strongholds (Josh 12:4; 13:12; Gen 14:5). Day continues to chart Ugaritic texts that *deify* the Rephaim as early as the second millennium BCE.[189] Day sees a strong association between the procreation account in Gen 6:1–4 and the Ugaritic Rephaim.[190] While Day supposes that the deified Rephaim gave rise to an ethnic Rephaim,[191] Scripture actually supports the opposite: the ethnic (antediluvian) Rephaim gave rise to deified giant Rephaim of whom Nimrod, the Yabal brothers, and Naamah (as Isis/Ishtar?) are early examples. Tales of their mighty, godlike exploits and histories were enshrined in many epic stories, such as Hercules, which called for reverence in the eyes of mere and normal mankind.

Adding to this evidence is Genesis' (6:4) statement that these *nephiyliym* and *gibboriym* were "men of renown." The Hebrew in this text literally reads "men of the name."[192] The "name" is normally a reference to God. Its usage here indicates a recognition, monument, or memorial that equaled (!) YHWH's own fame and recognition *by humanity*. Early humanity enshrined the *gibboriym*'s strength and memory in epic poems and mythological tales. Many Greek stories regarding the Titans may preserve fragmented remains of real history—a history like so many others throughout the Near East—tainted with aggrandizement and deification in the appending of mythic details. Humanity's worship of these early giants is what the Creator may have intended to destroy when he commanded Israel to "destroy their name from under heaven" (Deut 7:24–25). Thus, ample evidence from ancient Israel's Scriptures as well as texts from other nations support the theory that the antediluvian giants were worshiped in an earlier epic that corrupted truth. YHWH later reestablished truth with Abraham.

As I considered this evidence, it seemed possible that Scripture could contain historical facts that other nations had mingled with folklore and legendary tales. If records from ancient cultures bore witness to creation, the fall from the garden, the flood, and the Rephaim, perhaps ancient cultures had preserved a little truth in their vast mythical repertoire. Although I saw a contrast between Abraham's truth and the fables advanced by contemporary nations, I needed to know where the dividing line lay. What part of Israel's theology was truth, and what part of it was myth?

VII. MODERN EGYPTIAN THEOLOGY

The first concept I needed to establish for my own understanding of Abraham's God was whether Scripture upheld the contemporary Trinitarian views of Abraham's day. Was the Trinity fact or myth? For a moment, I placed myself in God's shoes and asked: If I were God and wanted to let my people know who I am, what would I tell them? If I gave a nation my truth and wanted them to know that other deities did exist—united with me in heart and mind—how would I communicate this idea to humanity? How would I tell Jacob that I was a Trinitarian God (see Illustration 2.22)?

Illustration 2.22. Ancient Siberian triad on medal from the Imperial Cabinet of St. Petersburg.

If, on the other hand, I were a God who wanted to distinguish myself from Trinitarian ideologies, what would I tell mankind? How would I tell my people that I am not united with any other deity?

Now came the test: Which message did YHWH convey? When he gave Israel his truth (Gen 32:10; Jer 10:15–16), did he communicate that he was a Trinitarian god or the *only* God?

Hear, O Israel: YHWH our God *YHWH is one*. (Deut 6:4)

Understand that I (singular) am He: before me there was no God formed, *neither shall there be after me*. (Isa 43:10)

I am YHWH, your Holy *One*, *the Creator* of Israel, your King. (Isa 43:15)

See now that I, even I, am he, and *there is no god (elohiym) with me*: I kill, and I make alive; I wound, and I heal: neither is there any that can deliver out of my hand. (Deut 32:39)

Thus said YHWH, your redeemer, and he that formed you from the womb, I am YHWH that *makes all things*; that stretches forth the heavens *alone*; that spreads abroad the *earth by myself*. (Isa 44:24)

To whom will you compare Me and make Me equal, or compare Me, that we may be alike? (Isa 46:5)[193]

As I meditated on these verses, I could find no expression of YHWH as a Trinitarian Godhead. In fact, Deuteronomy (32:39) tells us there are no other gods or pantheon that exists with YHWH. Isaiah asks to which of the pagan pantheon (all of whom had Trinitarian manifestations) we would assimilate YHWH or liken him.

Formulas for other religious systems described Re, Amun, or Osiris as one personality or manifestation of a godhead. If YHWH wanted us to know who he was so we could know him and worship him in sincerity and truth (Josh 24:14), then would he not have communicated this concept in terms readily understood by the ancient Hebrews? If God wanted Abraham's children to understand that he was a Trinitarian God, would he not have told them something to the effect that "I and my Son are Three?" This had been the common formula used to convey unity in a godhead's hidden Trinitarian oneness. If YHWH wanted Abraham's children to inherit his truth, to know, to understand, and to obey him so that they could completely love him, believe in him, and walk in all his ways, would he not have let them know he was a Trinitarian God? Yet YHWH repeatedly tells us that he is humanity's only Creator and that he created the earth himself (Isa 43:15; 44:24) without the aid of any other god.

I remembered my pastor teaching that the word *elohiym* in Genesis' creation account (Gen 1:26) was a plural term[194] that referred to a Trinitarian Godhead. *Elohiym* implied that there was more than one entity creating the world. Yet both Isaiah (44:6) and Deuteronomy (32:39) seem to contradict this modern belief by telling us there are no *elohiym* besides YHWH. Looking at the context of all these verses, I wondered if we had misplaced our understanding of Genesis' use of *elohiym*. I needed to see if the term had ever been used to depict a single deity.

Since I had been taught that the suffix *-iym* changed a Hebrew noun from singular to plural, I desired to know how this term fit in the above Scriptures.[195] Knowing numerous contradictions existed in modern theological interpretation (and among religious denominations), I thought it best to base my understanding directly on Scripture's actual Hebrew usage. What I found was eye-opening. There are Hebrew words that have the plural *-iym* suffix or other plural suffixes that are not actually plural nouns.[196] For a plural noun to be considered plural in Hebrew, both the verb and adjective surrounding the noun must maintain a plural form; if not, the noun is singular.[197] The prophet Isaiah, for example, uses the word lord (*adoniym*) in its plural form yet employs a singular verb and adjective:

> And the Egyptians will I give (singular) over into the hand of a (singular) cruel lord (*adoniym*—plural suffix); and a fierce king shall rule over them, said the Lord, YHWH of hosts. (Isa 19:4, parentheses added)

The context is that YHWH will give the Egyptians into the hand of a cruel king. Although the word *adoniym* has the plural *-iym* suffix, Isaiah uses a singular verb and adjective to define its usage, so the word "lord" is still singular. Thus, this verse denotes one absolute, powerful, cruel king who will reign over Egypt. This text does not denote two or even three kings, but one mighty, majestic and all-powerful lord (the term 'lord' in the phrase "the Lord, YHWH of hosts" is '*adown*, the singular form of "lord" in the above verse).

We find this same convention in Malachi:

A son honors his father, and a servant his master (*adonayw* —plural posses-
sive): if then I be a father, where is my honor? and if I be a master (*adoniym*
—plural), where is my fear? said YHWH of hosts to you, O priests, that despise
my name. And you say, Wherein have we despised your name? (Mal 1:6)

This text is not saying that YHWH is many masters but that, if YHWH is to be honored,
then he is one father and one master, not many fathers or many masters. Although Malachi
uses a plural suffix, *iym*, he joins it with a singular adjective, thus indicating that YHWH is
only one master. The next example brings this home.

When YHWH sent Moses to Egypt, he told him:

See, I have made you (singular) a god (*elohiym*–plural suffix) to Pharaoh: and
Aaron your brother shall be your prophet. (Exod 7:1)

The word *'el* or *elohiym* can also mean 'mighty or powerful ruler or judge' (see Exod 21:6;
22:8–9; Deut 28:32; 1 Sam 2:25; Ps 80:10; 82:1; 89:6; Mic 2:1).[198] YHWH uses the term *elohiym*
to say that he would make Moses mighty and powerful above Pharaoh. He is not saying that
he will make Moses into many gods but one powerful person. This does not imply that there
is a collective singular (i.e., many lords, many masters, or many gods) unless it is combined
with plural verbs, plural pronouns, and/or plural adjectives. In this case, the singular pronoun "you" goes with "Elohiym," thus rendering *Elohiym* singular.

The same type of construction is also found in the account of the patriarch Jacob. We
are told that the person who wrestled with Jacob was a "man" (*singular*, Gen 32:24). After
God's messenger blessed Jacob, the patriarch named the place Peniel (*lit.* 'face of God')
stating that he had seen "Elohiym face to face" (Gen 32:30). *Paniym*, the word "face" is
always rendered in the plural form even though it describes only one face (perhaps because
the face is comprised of many features).[199] Both *paniym* (plural form) and *Elohiym* (plural
form) are used to refer to a singular, mighty man, which is why both terms are singular in
meaning in this text.

In the account of Samson's birth, his parents also talked with YHWH's messenger or
angel (*mal'ak*—Judg 13:3). This angel is always referred to in the singular, "I" (Judg 13:4, 11,
13, 15–16), "you" (13:21), and "man" (13:3, 6, 8). Yet, when Manoah refers to this "angel of
YHWH" (13:16) he states that he had seen "Elohiym" (13:22). Manoah is not saying that he
saw many gods. Rather, he is stating that he saw one mighty or powerful person or angel.

Adding to this evidence is the fact that Scripture tells us,

So God (*Elohiym*—plural) created man in *his* image, in the image of God (*elohiym*) created *he* him" (Gen 1:27).

Scripture does not tell us that *Elohiym* created us in "their" image as would be indicative of a plural godhead, rather, humanity was created by a single being. Interestingly, when the Hebrew refers to YHWH as *elohiym*, it never refers to him as "they," but in the singular "he" or "him."[200] These texts use a singular verb and a singular adjective in conjunction with the plural elohiym. Scholars term this linguistic technique a "majestic plural" since it conveys a 'great, absolute or majestic' attribute of a Supreme Deity or Supreme Master who is "God of gods" and "Lord of lords."[201]

Joel Hoffman, a noted Hebrew linguist, provides another interesting perspective on Scripture's use of *elohiym*:

> The Hebrews' one God was seen as the equivalent of other cultures' many gods. In other words, the Hebrews were not (only?) trying to express the concept of "God" but also "gods." Every culture had their "gods," and so did the Hebrews. An obvious question, then, was how many gods were in the group "gods." For some cultures, the answer may have been a vague "many," or a particular number. For the Hebrews, the answer was "one."[202]

The ancient Hebrew term *elohiym* seems to have functioned in the same fashion as our modern term "God." The English word *god* traces back to polytheistic worship in Anglo-Saxon, German, Persian, and Hindu cultures.[203] Historically, this divine being could be fulfilled by any number of gods in the Hindu or German pantheon. Even today, if one speaks with a Hindu individual about "God," he or she can attach the idea of *god* to any member of the Hindu pantheon. For some individuals god will be Brahma, for others Shiva or Vishnu, while for other Hindu it could be Krishna or Buddha. But for the Hebrews, "God" meant *one and only one* Divine Being: YHWH.

> If elohiym means not only "God" but also the Hebrew equivalent of other cultures' "set of gods," then the statement makes sense. It claims first that Adonai is "the Hebrew set of gods," and then, recognizing that a set of gods generally contains more than one member, adds that this particular set contains but one member.[204]

That Hoffman's assessment is correct is validated by the Hebrew Scripture's constant clarification that YHWH Elohiym is but one God (see verses cited above), instead of the several gods that normally unified in a single godhead, as commonly accepted among other cultures.

This conclusion is further buttressed by the fact that Scripture readily accepts that the term *elohiym* could depict a Re, Zeus, or Anu type of godhead—a single deity that is chief over a pantheon. When Israel rebelled at Mt. Sinai by worshiping the Golden Calf, Aaron stated that "these" were Israel's gods, even though only one calf was constructed (Exod 32:8).[205] In this case, the word *elohiym* was joined with a plural pronoun and indeed refers to a plural god because Egypt's pantheon had a collective manifestation with the Apis at Sinai.[206]

This seems to be the reason that the Torah (Old Testament Pentateuch) continually emphasizes YHWH's absolute lack of partners.

Know therefore this day, and consider it in your heart, that YHWH *he is God in heaven above*, and on the earth beneath: *there is none else* (Deut 4:39). So *YHWH alone* did lead him, and there was no strange god with him (Deut 32:12). See now that I, even I, am he, and *there is no god with me*: I kill, and I make alive; I wound, and I heal: neither is there any that can deliver out of my hand . (Deut 32:39).

Who is God (*eloha*—singular)[207] besides YHWH? Or who is a rock save our God (*elohiym*)? (Ps 18:31, parentheses added)

You, even you, are YHWH alone; you have made heaven, the heaven of heavens, with all their host, the earth, and all things that are therein, the seas, and all that is therein, and you preserve them all; and *the host of heaven worships you.* (Neh 9:6)

The other purported evidence of the Trinity in the Old Testament, is the term "us" in YHWH's statement: "Let *us* make man in *our* image." If Abraham's religion embraced pure monotheism, to whom did the "us" in Gen 1:26 refer? Once again, I turned to the Hebrew Scriptures in search of evidence.

What I discovered is that YHWH has a heavenly council that helps him carry out his decrees. The prophet Micaiah describes a vision in which he sees YHWH sitting on his throne surrounded by his royal council, which consists of the "entire host of heaven."

I saw YHWH sitting on his throne, and *all the host of heaven standing by him on his right hand and on his left*. And YHWH said, Who shall persuade Ahab, that he may go up and fall at Ramothgilead? *And one said on this manner, and another said on that manner.* And there came forth a spirit, and stood before YHWH, and said, I will persuade him. And *YHWH said to him*, Where with? And he said, I will go forth, and I will be a lying spirit in the mouth of all his prophets. *And he said, You shall persuade him, and prevail also: go forth, and do so.* (1 Kgs 22:19–22; see also 2 Chr 18:18–21)

In this account, YHWH consults with his angels in the same way a flesh-and-blood king might consult the members of his *royal council*. YHWH is faced with a dilemma: How to cause Ahab's death. One spirit or angel comes to offer advice while another angel offers a different suggestion, until finally one angel offers an idea, which YHWH endorses. This angel then goes forth to effect YHWH's decree: to cause Ahab to die in battle (see also Isa 6:1).

Job also tells us about the sons of God attending two different meetings of his heavenly council:

> Now there was a day when the *sons of God* came to stand before YHWH. . . .
> Again there was a day when the sons of God came to present themselves before
> YHWH. (Job 1:6; 2:1)

The idioms *host of heaven* and *sons of God* in these contexts refer to the angels (*mal'ak*)
created by YHWH. The Book of Nehemiah tells us that "the host of heaven worships"
YHWH (Neh 9:6; see previous discussion and Ps 148:2). If the whole host of heaven worships
YHWH, where is there room for the other two members of the Trinity to be worshiped as
well? When God says, "Let 'us' make man in our image," YHWH is not referring to other
individuals or deities in the godhead but is referring to angels who form his holy council
and carry out his decrees.

Zechariah prophesies that when YHWH's people have learned to follow Abraham's
righteousness,

> YHWH shall be king over all the earth: in that day shall there be *one YHWH*,
> and *his name one*. (Zech 14:9)

Since ancient times, people have multiplied YHWH's name by believing him to be more
than one God. Whether Israel combined his worship with other pagan deities or believed
him to be only one member of the godhead, they still believed there was more than one
individual involved in being "God." When, however, YHWH establishes his kingdom on
earth, his people will finally comprehend monotheism: there will be only one YHWH, and
people will understand that YHWH is a single deity with one single name.

Thus far, Scripture supports Israel's religion as being unique. Moses and Joshua had
linked idolatries that were pervading at Babel "in old times" with the same doctrine and
philosophies that were taught in Egypt. We have seen that YHWH's Law and the books of
Ezekiel, Jeremiah, and Isaiah[208] tell us that, under no circumstances should YHWH's doctrine be confused with the "vanities" held by nations that were contemporary with Israel. Israel's Creator repeatedly tells the people not to not walk in pagan custom or to believe pagan
doctrines whose core is "altogether brutish and foolish: the stock is a *doctrine of vanities*" (Jer
10:2–3, 8). While other nations believed lies and vanity—a mixture of truth and error, the
Hebrew Scriptures support that only Abraham's religion solely established YHWH's truth.

> Look to Abraham your father, and to Sarah that bare you: for *I called him*
> *alone*, and blessed him, and increased him. (Isa 51:2)
>
> O YHWH, my strength, and my fortress, and my refuge in the day of affliction,
> *the Gentiles shall come* to you from the ends of the earth, and shall say, *Surely*
> *our fathers have inherited lies, vanity, and things wherein there is no profit.*
> (Jer 16:19)[209]

Jeremiah tells us that other nations will see that their cultures have inherited nothing but lies and vain doctrine in the latter days, while Israel has inherited YHWH's truth. This text strongly implies that many people today who seek righteousness and truth will come out of Babel's theologies, which pervade traditional Judeo-Christian doctrine.

So far, this evidence seemed to make sense, even if limited at this point. If modern Trinitarian beliefs were indeed false, I questioned whether the Creator had been righteous to allow this corruption. Ancient Israel accused YHWH of being unfair. I wondered if YHWH had been unfair to let us believe a lie. If YHWH is to be vindicated as righteous by unwavering in his word, it followed that the next foundation of this case (and in essence an understanding of truth) should be founded in the origins of the original promises that he made with humanity. Did YHWH uphold his covenants? Were his ways *equal,* i.e., fair and just? Or was YHWH's theology, the way of life embedded in his Law, an oppression from which humanity needed to be delivered?

3

Jacob's Ladder:
Songs of Ascent in the
Etymology of Israel's Covenants

My study of ancient religious concepts had produced some interesting results. Perplexingly, it raised more questions than it answered. Israel's religion appeared to have a concept of God that differed from other nations' concepts. YHWH was not unified with any other god, and his Law actually forbade the practice (Exod 20:3). However, this qualitative test was not capable of yielding comprehensive results. I still needed to study other areas of Scripture to see if they merited validity. Did they substantiate ancient Israel's accusations charging God with unrighteousness, or were the allegations false?

Israel's entire religion was based on YHWH's call of Abraham and blessings that YHWH established in several covenants. First, I needed to know if YHWH's supposed covenants with Abraham were historically valid. Second, I needed to understand what ideas, principles, or theology these covenants established.

I. HISTORICAL CONTEXT

A. Ancient Covenants

In order to understand Abraham's covenants, I had to place these covenants (also termed compacts and treaties) with God in their ancient Near Eastern context. George Mendenhall's landmark work on ancient treaties has transformed our entire understanding of ancient "covenants."[1] Although covenants as treaties existed throughout the ancient world, Israel's covenants most closely paralleled Hittite treaties of the fourteenth to thirteenth centuries BCE.[2] There were basically three types of treaties: *suzerainty* treaties, which bound only the inferior or weaker vassal by an oath to obey the king's commands (peasant to the king); the *parity* treaty that bound both parties to obey identical stipulations (treaties between kings);[3] and the third type of treaty is the *royal grant,* one of the most common formulas that Scripture records, used especially in regard to land (1 Sam 8:14).[4]

> The grant covenant constituted an obligation of the master to his servant. In the grant, a curse (a primary component of all ancient treaties, as we will see) is directed toward any entity who violates the rights of the king's vassal, while in the suzerainty treaty the curse is directed toward the vassal who violates the rights of his king. In other words, the grant served mainly to protect the rights of the *servant,* while the suzerainty treaty protected the rights of the *king.* What is more, while the grant is a reward for loyalty and good deeds already performed, the suzerainty treaty is an inducement for future loyalty.[5]

Although debates have developed over the type of treaty (suzerainty vs. grant) on which Israel's covenants were based, we will see that all three types of treaties are found in Israel's foundational covenants.[6]

Ancient covenants of the fourteenth century BCE followed a basic yet formal pattern.[7] (1) The document began with a preamble or title that identified the author of the covenant.[8] (2) The preamble was followed by a historical prologue or retrospect, citing previous relations and affinity between the covenantor and the covenantee.[9] (3) The third part outlined the stipulations or obligations laid on the vassal by the sovereign.[10] (4) The ancient treaty called for its deposit in the national sanctuary and (5) a periodic public reading.[11] (6) In the sixth division of a covenant, witnesses were listed.[12] One prominent feature of ancient covenants recorded (7) *curses for breach of pact* and (8) *blessings for compliance* with the covenant's stipulations.[13] (9) The ninth act of compliance was a self-imprecating oath taken to obey the treaty's stipulations, which was usually sealed by a sacrifice.[14] (10) The tenth feature and the only aspect that distinguished Israel's religious treaties from Hittite treaties was the sign of compliance that accompanied the covenant (Gen 15:17; Exod 31:13, 17; Deut 6:8; 11:18).

Israel's covenants were by very nature *parity* treaties (contra Mendenhall). If YHWH did not obey his own treaty of disallowing other gods, he could erect competing deities equal or superior to himself. Or, when he judged Israel, he could discipline her—not for breaching the stipulations of his covenant—but for any other miscellaneous infraction that perturbed him, in an arbitrary fashion that was similar to the gods throughout the ancient Near East. Our whole investigation hinges on YHWH's covenants with Israel functioning as parity treaties. If YHWH did not bind himself to the same Law that he required Israel to obey, the nation's charges of unfairness and arbitrary judgments would be substantiated.[15] Therefore, we will continue to consider the evidence to see whether YHWH is righteous by adhering to his own Law (parity) or is arbitrary by requiring man's obedience to the covenantal Law without acting consistently with the Law himself (suzerainty).

B. *Features of Ancient Covenants in Scripture*

I have discovered that it is important to have a thorough understanding of how each of these covenant features work. I found that there was no set order for how these 10 covenant features appeared in ancient covenants in Scripture. However, the preamble and historical prologue usually preceeded all other elements. Additionally, some covenants would drop one or two of these 10 features. For instance, the requirement for deposit and periodic public reading is not mentioned in the patriarchal covenants until these covenants are formally ratified again with the nation of Israel at Mt. Sinai.

Preamble or Title. Covenants were binding agreements. Scriptural covenants always begin with God's addressing the one with whom he is covenanting.[16] In modern times, the most famous preamble is that of the U.S. Constitution, which begins, "We the people." This statement signifies that the people are granting to themselves their own Constitutional Covenant based on their God-given divine right (a right, which historically had only been granted to kings). In Scripture, preambles or titles are usually identified by a form of direct address, such as "God spoke to—." Sometimes God speaks directly to someone as he did with Noah (Gen 8:15), or he may appear in a vision as he did to King Solomon (1 Kgs 3:5; see also Gen 15:1; 28:12). In some instances, he uses an angel or messenger to speak his words as he did with Abram and Jacob (Gen 22:11; 18:1; 32:24) or through a burning bush (Exod 3:2). In each case, the text specifies that God or God's agent is addressing someone. Within the words that follow God's appearance to a patriarch, we usually find the basic features of ancient covenants (i.e., stipulations, promises, blessing, curses, etc.).

Historical Prologue. The historical prologue mentions previous interactions or relationship between God and the person or family with whom he is covenanting.[17] We often find this formula in the statement referring to the covenant "which he swore to Abraham, to Isaac, and to Jacob" (Gen 50:24; Exod 13:5; Deut 4:21), which is mentioned over 70 times in the Tanakh (or Old Testament). In the covenant that Israel made with YHWH at Mt. Sinai, the prologue states:

> I am YHWH your God, which brought you out of the land of Egypt, from the house of bondage. (Exod 20:2)

Since the covenant made at Mt. Sinai and the covenant made on the plains of Moab (Deuteronomy) 40 years later basically incorporated the same stipulations, many features, such as the historical prologue and stipulations remained the same (Deut 5:6). The most significant differences between these two covenants, as we will see, were the means by which they were ratified and the sign for compliance.

Stipulations. Every covenant has something specific it requires.[18] The stipulations are binding both on YHWH and the patriarchs, and on YHWH and the nation of Israel. By their very nature, these are parity stipulations. God cannot change these stipulations or dismiss their relevance (see the foundation of this case in chap. 1). In Hittite covenants, we find that the stipulations defined a term of service that was required in exchange for some sort of compensation, whether money or provisions such as food and clothing.[19] Israel's covenants work the same way. God never requires something for nothing. He always pays for the benefit received. This means that these covenants are parity covenants and are mutually beneficial. The stipulations require such things as: not ingesting an animal's blood (Gen 9:4), refraining from murder (Gen 9:6), being circumcised (Gen 17:11), and the most famous stipulation is the 10 Commandments (Exodus 20). These are 10 categories or precepts that define the Torah doctrine since the entire Torah Law can be broken down into one of these 10 categories that define how humanity should interact with God and how people should interact with each other.

Safeguarding and deposit. Almost every ancient covenant required that it be deposited and safeguarded in the local temple.[20] Temples were not only responsible for ideals about God; they were the legal administrators of their district.[21] Although the early patriarchal covenants do not record this feature, the national Sinai covenant was the first biblical covenant that does (Exod 25:16).

> You shall put into the ark the testimony which I shall give you. (Exod 25:16).

The *Testimony* was YHWH's formal covenant with Israel (Exod 32:15–16; 34:28). It was separate from the *Law of Moses*, which included the more practical matters of applying the constitution's philosophy or precepts in legal proceedings. Once the Testimony was placed in the ark, the ark became known as the *Ark of the Testimony* (Exod 25:16, 21; 31:7; Deut 10:1–5; 31:24–8; Josh 4:16) or the *Ark of the Covenant* (Num 10:33; 14:44; Deut 10:8; 31:9, 25–26). Once the ark that bore the Testimony was installed in the Tabernacle, the Tabernacle became known as the *Tabernacle of Testimony* (Exod 38:21; Num 1:50; 10:10). The significance in this is stated in Exodus 25.

> Put the mercy seat above upon the ark; and in the ark you shall put the *testimony*. . . . *There I will meet with you, and I will commune with you* from above the mercy seat, from between the two cherubim which are on the ark of *the testimony, of all things which I will give you in commandment unto the children of Israel.* (Exod 25:21–22)

The importance of this statement is that all discussions God would have with Moses or anyone else for that matter would be based on the Testimony, which resided under the Mercy Seat. The Testimony would define the morals, ethics, rights, and responsibilities between individuals, and between individuals and the state, in the same manner as the United States Constitution is designed to do today. But more than the U.S. Constitution, Israel's constitutional covenant, as we will see, defined truth and doctrine for Israel and her descendants (Ps 119:142). Any conversation that God would have with humanity would be based on Israel's constitutional Testimony.

Periodic Public Reading. While other ancient Near Eastern nations may have had varying years in which the treaty was to be read,[22] in Israel it was read every seven years.

And Moses commanded them, saying, *At the end of every seven years, in the solemnity of the year of release, in the feast of tabernacles*, when all Israel is come to appear before YHWH your God in the place which he shall choose, you shall read this law before all Israel in their hearing. Gather the people together, men, and women, and children, and your stranger that is within your gates, that they may hear, and that they may learn, and fear YHWH your God, and observe to do all the words of this law. (Deut 31:10–12)

Of this provision, George Mendenhall opines,

This stipulation is almost self-explanatory. Since it was not only the vassal king, but his entire state which was bound by the treaty, periodic public reading served a double purpose: first, to familiarize the entire populace with the obligations to the great king; and second, to increase the respect for the vassal king by describing the close and warm relationship with the mighty and majestic Emperor which he enjoyed. Since the treaty itself was under the protection of the deity, it was deposited as a sacred thing in the sanctuary of the vassal state—perhaps also, to indicate that the local deity or deities would not and could not aid in breach of covenant.[23]

Although this feature may be self-explanatory, Mendenhall and other scholars miss a very important point in regard to Israel's covenant. Every time this covenant was read publicly, the people renewed or "pledged again" to uphold the stipulations set forth within the covenant. Probably the best example of covenant renewal is found during King Josiah's reign, when the Testimony (i.e., the Deuteronomy Covenant) had been rediscovered in the Temple. After the priests had asked the prophetess Huldah about the validity of the Testimony's curses (2 Kgs 22:14; 2 Chr 34:22), Josiah gathered the people together to renew the covenant:

And all the people, both small and great: and he (Josiah) read in their ears all the words of the book of the covenant which was found in the house of YHWH. And the king stood by a pillar and *made a covenant before YHWH*, to walk after YHWH, and to keep his commandments and his testimonies and his statutes with all their heart and all their soul, to perform the words of this covenant that were written in this book. And *all the people stood to the covenant*. (2 Kgs 23:2–3)

When the people "stood to the covenant," they were assenting to obey its stipulations. Israel's people pledged to follow this covenant wholeheartedly for another seven years.

Witnesses. Most ancient covenants contained a long list of gods as witnesses to uphold and enforce the penalties. In Israel's covenants, the witnesses include God and the person with whom he is covenanting. In the Circumcision Covenant, God stated that he was covenanting "between me and you" (Gen 17:2). The covenants made at Mt. Sinai and Shechem are contracted with the children of Israel (Exod 20:2; Deut 29:1–2).

One interesting example of a covenant's witnesses is a covenant that was not between God and a patriarch but was initiated by Jacob's father-in-law, Laban. In this covenant, Laban invokes several gods as witnesses to his covenant with Jacob:

> The God of Abraham, and the God of Nahor, the God of their father, judge between us. And Jacob swore by the fear of his father, Isaac. (Gen 31:53)

Laban appears to be invoking three different gods as witnesses to his and Jacob's pact. Rather than swear by a false deity, Jacob cleverly sidesteps the issue and simply swears by the fear of his father, Isaac. This may imply that Isaac ultimately feared YHWH; therefore, Jacob is swearing by Isaac's God. Whatever the case may be, Jacob does not assent swearing by another god or acknowledging other deities as witnesses.

Oath, seal, ratification. The oath and seal compare to signing one's name to a contract in modern times. The oath to obey the covenant was usually part of a ceremony and most often included self-imprecating sacrifices (see the patriarchal covenants below).[24] Not all covenants were ratified by blood. The Moab-Shechem covenant was ratified in the ceremony that placed the curses on Mt. Ebal and the blessings on Mt. Gerizim (Deut 11:29). The Circumcision Covenant was ratified by the literal act of circumcision. **The importance of this feature is that the covenantee gave verbal assent to live by the covenant's stipulations and to accept its consequences, if breached.** When this ceremonial oath accompanied sacrifice, the person consenting to the covenant would often slit an animal's throat and say something to the effect of "may what happens to this animal occur to me and my descendants if we do not uphold all the words of this covenant to do them" (see below). Thus this ceremony sealed the person and his descendants to uphold the covenant and to reap both its blessings and consequences.

One interesting record of covenant-making occurred after Athaliah (King Ahab's daughter) had oppressed the Kingdom of Judah for seven years.

> And the seventh year Jehoiada sent and fetched the rulers over hundreds, with the captains and the guard, and brought them to him into the house of YHWH, and *made a covenant with them, and took an oath* of them in the house of YHWH, and showed them the king's son. (2 Kgs 11:4)

The recorded oath in this text signified that Judah's aristocracy had assented to Jehoiada's covenant to install the rightful Davidic heir and to defend him. Fascinatingly, when Jehoiada and the rulers made Joash king, they installed him with the Testimony in his hand.

> Then they brought out the king's son, and put on him the crown, and *gave him the testimony*, and made him king. And Jehoiada and his sons anointed him, and said, God save the king. (2 Chr 23:11)

Jehoiada deliberately invested Joash with the Testimony. In English history, this compares to giving King John the *Magna Carta*. The Testimony, as we will see, defined: the limits on the king's power; his responsibility to God and the people; the laws by which he should rule and uphold; and the consequences that he and his people would face for breaching the covenant. Thus, reading the Testimony every seven years and making sure the people were aware of its stipulations were two of the king's primary responsibilities.

Blessings. There is a philosophy in Torah that the blessings enumerated in the covenants were not effected simply because an individual (or a community) was the seed of Abraham or had inherited the covenants. Keeping the covenant's stipulations naturally effected the promised blessings. This was mentioned, for example, shortly before God destroyed Sodom, when his messenger said,

> For I know (Abraham), that he will command his children and his household after him, and they shall keep the way of YHWH, to do justice and judgment; *that YHWH may bring upon Abraham that which he has spoken of him.* (Gen 18:19)

Notice the conditional nature of this statement. Blessings were not given simply because Abraham had covenanted with YHWH or simply because Abraham was a Hebrew (Gen 14:13). Blessings came from Abraham's observing and walking in *the way of YHWH*. This idea or philosophy is reiterated again in Deuteronomy's Moab-Shechem Covenant (Deut 28–30:14).

> Keep therefore his statutes, and his commandments, *that it may go well with you*, and with your children after you, and that you may prolong your days on the earth, which YHWH your God gives you, *forever.* (Deut 4:40)
>
> *Observe and hear all these words which I command you, that it may go well with you*, and with your children after you *forever*, when you do that which is good and right in the sight of YHWH your God. (Deut 12:28; see also Exod 19:5–6; Lev 26:2–4; Deut 5:16; 11:13)

The idea conveyed in these statements is that, not only does obeying YHWH's stipulations cause life to "go well" with humanity, but the Law he gave to Moses embraces *natural law*. Therefore, this covenant feature enumerated specific benefits from adhering to YHWH's philosophical life-style, including that a society could live "forever" (Deut 4:40; 12:28).

Curses. Just as obeying the Covenantal Law effects its own blessings, so disobeying it results in curses. Disobedience is a violation of natural Law. The "curses of the covenant" enumerated the specific consequences for breach of covenant. It is this feature, as we will see, that became known as Israel's formal *Testimony* (Exod 34:28; 32:15–16; Isa 8:16, 20). King David stated that "The secret of YHWH is with them that fear him; and he will show them his covenant" (Ps 25:14). In part two of this book, we will examine the covenant's Testimony to see if it is one of YHWH's greatest secrets.

Sign of compliance. This feature appears to have been unique to Israel's covenants. It was a special feature that acknowledged both acceptance and compliance. It was also a means by which either party could "look on" and determine very quickly whether the other party was in compliance with the covenant. When Noah offered YHWH a sacrifice, for instance, YHWH gave Noah a promise and sealed that promise with the sign of the rainbow: never again to destroy the entire earth by flood (Gen 9:16). In the Circumcision Covenant, YHWH provided a sign by changing Abraham's (Gen 17:5) and Sarah's names (Gen 17:15); the act of circumcision itself became a sign of Abraham's and Sarah's compliance with the pact. In the later Sinai Covenant, the observance of the Sabbaths was the sign by which Israel is recognized to be in compliance.

> Surely my sabbaths you shall keep: for *it is a sign between me and you* throughout your generations; that you may know that I am YHWH that does sanctify you. You shall keep the sabbath therefore; for it is holy to you: every one that defiles it shall surely be put to death: for whosoever does any work therein, that soul shall be cut off from among his people. (Exod 31:12–14)

Because many of YHWH's promises were made with the early patriarchs, these covenants were prophetic in nature and were fulfilled in the course of history. A covenant's "sign" is especially important in the context of Scripture, because it can contain a "window" into another prophecy.[25] Often Israel's covenants had the added feature (beyond Mendenhall's list) of an actual prophecy—i.e., something that would occur in the covenantee's (or his or her descendant's) future.[26]

Finally, every patriarchal and national covenant upheld and reissued the previous covenant. In other words, covenants build on each other by simply incorporating new stipulations and promises. There exists not one single instance in all of the Old Testament (Tanakh) where a covenant, stipulation, promise, blessing or curse was ever revoked, changed, or rescinded (as we will see throughout this chapter). Instead, one covenant often fulfilled an earlier covenant or prophecy. Tracing these covenants as they originated greatly aids our understanding of the various statutes ordained in the later national Israelite covenants. At this point, we will focus on the precepts that Israel's Scriptures establish for her God. Then, we will turn to more scientific data (see Table 3.1).

II. COVENANTS

In the process of time, YHWH enacted covenants with Noah, Abraham, Isaac, Jacob, Moses, the nation of Israel, Phinehas, David, and Solomon. Although the entire nation of Israel inherited her patriarch's covenants and blessings, the entire nation did not have a claim to covenants that YHWH made between individuals or families in Israel. For instance,

Table 3.1. Covenants of the Late Second Millennium BCE

1	*Preamble or title*	Identifies the author/grantor of the covenant
2	*Historical Prologue*	Mentions previous relationships with kindred
3	*Stipulations*	States what is required of the party accepting the treaty
4	*Storage or Deposition*	To be safeguarded in cultic sanctuary
5	*Periodic public reading*	Remembering and renewing of covenant
6	*Witnesses*	Long list of gods invoked to witness the covenant
7	*Oath*	Sealed or ratified by self-imprecation through sacrifice
8	*Promises for compliance*	Blessings
9	*Penalty for breach*	Curses
10	*Sign (Israel)*	An act, feature, or sign that demonstrates compliance

YHWH offered Aaron's son Phinehas a *covenant of peace* (Num 25:12). This covenant applied only to Phinehas and his descendants. Other Levites or Aaronic descendants were ineligible for the promises of Phinehas's covenant. It was a separate covenant within the Sinai compact.

Covenants defined the parameters of YHWH's truth. As we will see, the later Israelite Law predicated and incorporated all of YHWH's previous covenants with humanity. I discovered that understanding the history of these covenants allows us to chart clearly the words of promise and requirements of responsibility that YHWH spoke to humanity. In studying these covenants, we should be able to reconstruct a clear picture of Abraham's religious system so that we can see how or whether it differed from those of the rest of the ancient world.

III. NOAHIC COVENANT

After the flood, YHWH contracted a covenant with Noah and his descendants. This covenant originated with Noah's offering a sacrifice, once he was safely delivered from the ark (Gen 8:20–22). God responded to Noah's offering by extending a contractual relationship to Noah and his children in a *royal grant* treaty. Scholars recognize that the patriarchal covenants did not follow the suzerain form typical of the later national covenants, although they did share some common points.[27]

One of the first benefits that the Creator promised to Noah was that he would never "cut off all flesh any more by the waters of a flood; neither shall there anymore be a flood to destroy the earth" (Gen 9:11). The rainbow was YHWH's "sign" or seal of the Noahic Covenant. I have found that retracing the stipulations of this covenant and evidencing its various provisions sheds abundant light on the foundation of YHWH's truth.

The following text is the Noahic Covenant as recorded in Genesis 8 beginning with v. 15. Parentheses inserted into the Scriptural text indicate the aspects that we will examine afterward. (All covenants will be featured with a grey background.)

Preamble

And God spake to Noah, saying, Go forth of the ark, you, and your wife, and your sons, and your sons' wives with you. Bring forth with you every living thing that is with you of all flesh, both of fowl, and of cattle, and of every creeping thing that creeps on the earth; that they may breed abundantly in the earth, and be fruitful, and multiply upon the earth. (Gen 8:15–17)

Historical Prologue

And Noah went forth, and his sons, and his wife, and his sons' wives with him: Every beast, every creeping thing, and every fowl, and whatsoever creeps on the earth, after their kinds, went forth out of the ark. (Gen 8:8:18–19)

Noah's Oath or seal

And Noah built an altar to YHWH; and took of every clean beast, and of every clean fowl, and offered burnt offerings on the altar. And YHWH smelled a sweet savor. (Gen 8:20)

YHWH's Oath or seal: Stipulation binding on YHWH

And YHWH said in his heart, I will not again curse the ground any more for man's sake; for the imagination of man's heart is evil from his youth; *neither will I again smite any more every thing living,* as I have done. While the earth remains, seedtime and harvest, and cold and heat, and summer and winter, and day and night shall not cease. (Gen 8:21–22)

Promises

And God blessed Noah and his sons, and said to them, (a) Be fruitful, and multiply, and replenish the earth.

(b) And the fear of you and the dread of you shall be on every beast of the earth, and on every fowl of the air, on all that moves on the earth, and on all the fishes of the sea; into your hand are they delivered. Every moving thing that lives shall be meat for you; even as the green herb have I given you all things. (Gen 9:1–3)

Stipulations

But (c) flesh with the life thereof, which is the blood thereof, shall you not eat. And surely your blood of your lives will I require; at the *hand of every beast* will I require it, and at the *hand of man;* at the *hand of every man's brother will I require the life of man.*

(d) Whoever sheds man's blood, by man shall his blood be shed: for in the image of God made he man.

(e) And you, be you fruitful, and multiply; bring forth abundantly in the earth, and multiply therein. (Gen 9:4–7)

The Covenant's Sign

And God spoke to Noah, and to his sons with him, saying, And I, behold, I establish my covenant with you, and (f) with your seed after you; (g) And with every living creature that is with you, of the fowl, of the cattle, and of every beast of the earth with you; from all that go out of the ark, to every beast of the earth.

(h) And I will establish my covenant with you; neither shall all flesh be cut off any more by the waters of a flood; neither shall there any more be a flood to destroy the earth. (i) And God said, This is the *token* of the covenant which I make between me and you and every living creature that is with you, for *perpetual generations*: I do set my bow in the cloud, and it shall be for a token of a covenant between me and the earth. And it shall come to pass, when I bring a cloud over the earth, that the bow shall be seen in the cloud: And I will remember my covenant, which is between me and you and (g, above) every living creature of all flesh; and the waters shall no more become a flood to destroy all flesh. And the bow shall be in the cloud; and I will look on it, that I may remember the everlasting covenant between God and every living creature of all flesh that is on the earth. And God said to Noah, This is the token of the covenant, which I have established between me and all flesh that is on the earth. (Gen 9:8–17)

As the first recorded compact, Noah's Covenant establishes a pattern of promises of blessings and consequences of penalties to which all subsequent covenants will adhere. The preamble and prologue tell us that Noah, his family, and the animals have recently come out of the ark. Noah initiates a covenant with God through an oath of sacrifice. YHWH accepts this oath stating that he will never again "destroy every living thing" and that seasons should remain in place. The first blessing YHWH garnishes on Noah's family is the ability to have (a, above) a multitude of children. YHWH commands Noah and his family to actively pursue large families. As we will later see when we examine Abraham's covenants, humanity's need to repopulate the flooded earth was not YHWH's only reason for this blessing.

Striking distinctions can be observed between man's harsh state before the flood and his prosperity after the Noahic compact was contracted. The first marked distinction between Adam (b, above) and Noah's descendants was a "fear" that had been put on the animals for the sake of Noah's children.

Gen 9:4 (c) is the second place where Scripture records consequences for a breach of pact.[28] YHWH's covenant with Noah commanded: "Do not eat the blood of flesh." The *hidden judgment* for breaching this command warned that YHWH would require the offender's life at the hand of *each man's brother,* other men, and beasts.[29] If humanity consumed animals' blood while eating meat, the Creator would use these *three* venues to render judgment. He also enacted a penalty for manslaughter and bloodguilt by establishing that (d) "life would be given for life." This penalty formed the foundation of the bloodguilt doctrine that was reiterated in the later Israelite Law.

> And your eye shall not pity; but life shall go for life, eye for eye, tooth for tooth, hand for hand, foot for foot. (Deut 19:21; see also Exod 21:23)

YHWH removes humanity's pre-flood curses in Gen 9:7. Lamech's prophecy for Noah is fulfilled, and the curse on the soil is lifted, because the earth will now yield its bounty (Gen 5:28–29). YHWH restores man's ability to have children, as the curse (e) on Ham's seed is repealed. Although Cain's lineage survived the flood through Ham's marriage to Naamah, Cain's seed will no longer be withheld, as YHWH blesses Noah's children so that humanity can be fruitful and replenish the earth.

The (f) "recipient party" of Noah's Covenant included Noah, his sons, and their future offspring; thus, all humanity is a legal party to this binding agreement. Remarkably, humans were not the only covenantee. Animals (g) were also recipients of YHWH's covenant[30] and were ensured certain rights of justice when man "ate their flesh with the blood."[31]

Noah's Covenant appears to have set a precedent for formal treaties that ancient and modern nations continued to follow. In ancient times, both parties were required to offer a sign or seal to the agreement. While today we use a personal signature to "seal" compliance, sacrifices were the most common means of ratifying covenants and treaties throughout the ancient world. Thankfully, many ancient documents exist to clarify the exact role that the sacrifice played in the ratifying process.

One great example is an eighth century treaty that reads, "As this calf is cut to pieces so may Mati'el be cut to pieces," thus sealing Mati'el to the same fate as the sacrificial calf should he violate the treaty's stipulations.[32] In another ancient Near Eastern treaty, the donor king vows: "(May I be cursed) if I take back what I gave you,"[33] again sealing the consequential fate of the covenantor. Another eighth century (BCE) Assyrian document likewise attests:

> This ram was not taken from its flock for sacrifice. . . . If Mati'ilu (shall violate) the covenant and oath to the gods, then, as this ram, which was taken from its flock and to its flock will not return, and at the head of its flock shall not stand, so Mati'ilu with his sons . . . shall violate this covenant . . . as the head of this ram shall be struck off so shall his head be struck off.[34]

This text vividly outlines the consequences for breaching a treaty. *The sacrifice accompanying the sealing of a covenant depicted the fate of the one who benefited from the covenant if he should breach the stipulations to which he had agreed.*[35] In parity treaties, both parties would bear the "curse of death" symbolized by the sacrifice if they failed to uphold the ratified treaty.[36]

> The significance of this act may have varied from country to country and from century to century, although there seems to be a fairly *consistent interpretation of the act as a kind of self-imprecation, as though the participants in the treaty would say, 'If I break the treaty may this happen to me'*. In the Old Testament the practice is clearly described in several passages, and may be inferred in others. In the ancient Near East it was certainly in use in the eighteenth century BC at Mari and Alalaḫ while in the first millennium BC it is attested among the Aramaeans in the eighth century and among the Assyrians in the eighth and seventh centuries.[37]

Hence, Noah's sacrifice (Gen 8:20–21) quite literally "sealed" his fate and his children's fate should any of them fail to uphold the terms that YHWH set forth in his covenant for their benefit. YHWH's sign or seal of Noah's Covenant promised (h) that a flood would

Table 3.2. Noah's Covenant

Promise	Gen 8:21	Never again kill every living thing (unconditional)
	8:22	Seasons will remain constant (unconditional)
	9:11–15	Never will there be a worldwide flood again (unconditional)
Recipients/Prologue	9:9, 17	Humankind and animals and their posterity
Stipulation	9:4	Do not eat the blood of animals
	9:6	Do not murder mankind
	9:5–6	Precept for judgment: life for life
Oath	8:20–21	Noah's burnt offering
	8:21	YHWH's oath to never again "destroy every living thing"
Blessing	9:1, 7	Fruitfulness of humanity
	9:22–9:1	Fruitful land
	9:2–3	Animals become fearful of humans
Curse or Consequence	9:5	Death by animals (national war)
	9:5	Death by fellow man (civil war)
Sign	9:12–17	Rainbow

never again destroy all flesh, nor would a flood ever again destroy the earth. The sign that YHWH provided for the Noahic Covenant (i) as proof of YHWH's promise was a rainbow to *"perpetual"* or all future "generations," who were also recipients of Noah's Covenant.

In this grant treaty, YHWH bound himself to uphold the value judgments expressed in the covenant. This negated his right to offer any other treaty or covenant that violated these foundational principles. Equally, YHWH limited himself to never again sending a worldwide flood and to never again "smite every thing living" (Gen 8:21). This covenant indeed benefited both parties. YHWH benefited from the treaty by never having to destroy the earth again by a flood. He also profited from having a people who could follow a basic value system that enabled them to govern themselves. Noah and his progeny benefited from a defined value system on which to base their societies. Noah's descendants also profited from YHWH's self-imposed ban on the use of a global flood as a means of judgment (see Table 3.2).

At this point in my study, I wondered if any society had adhered to the ideals of justice as defined in Noah's Covenant. If so, it may further evidence that these values were history and not folklore. Interestingly, I found that ancient societies indeed embraced the same basic values in regard to justice. In the Hammurabi Code (196–97), King Hammurabi (*c.* 1728 BCE) reiterates the concept of a life given for a life as an "eye for an eye and tooth for a tooth," just as expressed in Noah's treaty (Gen 9:6).[38] Thus, at least in very ancient times, there is evidence that some ancient nations indeed embraced the ideals associated with the Noahic Covenant granting historical credence to its validity. Next, I needed to see other values or history that the Hebrew Scriptures defined as truth.

IV. NOAH DEFINES PROPHECY

After the flood, an event occurred that forever altered the prosperity of Ham's descendants. After waking from his wine,

> Noah . . . knew what his younger son had done to him. And he said, *Cursed* be Canaan; a servant of servants shall he be to his brothers. And he said, *Blessed* be YHWH God of Shem; *and Canaan shall be his servant.* God shall enlarge Japheth, and he shall dwell in the tents of Shem; and *Canaan shall be his servant.* (Gen 9:24–28)

Although this text treats Ham's offense evasively,[39] we know his malfeasance was severe enough for Noah to disinherit his younger son. With the entire earth's resources before him, the greatest assets that Noah possessed were: (1) the covenants that YHWH had granted to him, (2) land, and (3) his children's future. Knowing that his family hallmarked a new epoch in the earth's history, he used these resources to curse Ham's youngest son, Canaan.

There are two parts to Noah's prophecy. First, Noah removes a "birthright" from Ham, ceding it to Shem. Thus, *Shem and his children inherit a double birthright (or double portion),* while Canaan and his descendants inherit their father's curse. As we will see, Noah's blessing of Shem set the stage for YHWH to pass Shem's blessing to Abraham.

Second, Noah prophesies that Japheth will possess a spacious land and live within Shem's double birthright. The nature and context of Noah's words indicate that Shem's double blessing will be a land with double the area of Japheth's. The second part of this prophecy consigns Ham's children, Canaan, to be servants to *both* Shem and Japheth's descendants.[40] If Canaan's descendants become a landless people, they will naturally have to sell their labor since their society will not posess natural resources to sell or trade. Throughout history, people who do not own land tend to live in poverty, servitude, and serfdom. Noah's prophecy still functioned by one basic premise: during times of righteousness, his cursed offspring would not always bear the consequences of the curse. When, however, his children rebelled against the Noahic Covenant and YHWH's laws, the penalty of this curse would be applied.

If Scripture is true, it is from the Noahic Covenant and Noah's prophecy that *all* subsequent Scriptural covenants and prophecies will follow with constancy. Does Scripture or history reveal that Noah's prophecy has come to pass? Did Canaan's descendants become servants to Shem and Japheth?

A. Ham Serves Shem

In the opening chapter I discussed the importance of Scripture's truth supporting real facts and historical events. Unlike the *Iliad, Odyssey, Gilgamesh,* or Aesop's fables, which teach a moral lesson yet lack historical validity, Israel's Scripture needs to distinguish itself as comprising historical truths. Otherwise, this quest for reliability is as vain as searching for traces of the Cyclops on Crete. Scripture's promises, blessings, consequences, and prophecies must demonstrate historical validity for this case to be credible. In my quest for truth,

I needed to see if history confirms Noah's prophecies. This test should allow us to see if this portion of Scripture is a word of truth or mere folklore.

Noah's prophecy was initiated before Israel became a nation. Elam was Shem's first-born son (Gen 10:22) and would have been eligible to inherit Shem's double portion. When Abraham settled in Hebron, Ham's Canaanite descendants had served the Elamite king Chedorlaomer for 12 years (Gen 14:4).[41] Some 400 years later, Shem's descendants through Abraham occasionally dominated the Canaanites.[42] The strongest subjugations occurred during the days of Joshua, Judges, and later under David, Solomon, and Hezekiah. However, Israel's domination over Canaan was often thwarted by her own idolatry. So the question is: were Noah's words still binding during the times when Israel apostatized or when her military strength waned?

External evidence is found in Assyrian archives. Asshur, Shem's second eldest son, founded Nineveh. It is from Assur's name that the word *Assyria* is derived.[43] When Israel's power over Canaan waned, Shem's progeny, Assyria, still maintained lordship over Canaan. The first inscription regarding Assyria's domination over the Palestine region was written shortly before David's ascension. Tiglath-pileser I (1130–1090 BCE) tells us that he subjugated Lebanon, Sidon, and the entire country of Hatti.[44] Gen 15:20 lists the Hittites (Hatti) as Ham's descendants; thus, Assyria had mastery over the land belonging to Ham's offspring. In another inscription, Ashurnasirpal II (883–859 BCE) describes campaigns against the Hittites' remaining city-states, recording impressive tributes received from various Palestinian cities.[45] Following Ashurnasirpal II's ascension, almost every surviving Assyrian annal describes an invasion, subjugation, or deportation of Canaanite and Egyptian regions. Assyria's lordship over this territory reached its peak in the Third Intermediate and Late Period, when Esarhaddon conquered Egypt and established Necho I as his vassal.[46]

About 75 years later, King Nebuchadnezzar inherited Palestine's territories by conquering Assyria. Scripture does not record Nebuchadnezzar's lineage; however, scholars reconstruct Babylonia's origins based on its language and culture, which reflect a West Semitic origin similar to Israel's.[47] Scholars find that many Babylonian tribes (including the Chaldeans) were distant relatives of Abraham's clan.[48] Hence, Nebuchadnezzar inherited his right to subdue Canaan's tribal territories. Nebuchadnezzar's "Shemite" lineage allowed him to subjugate the Promised Land. Assyria and Babylon fulfilled Noah's prophecy when Israel's prowess declined. However, Noah's words stipulated that Ham's descendants would serve not only Shem's descendants but Japheth's as well. Does history evidence the fulfillment of this aspect of Noah's prophecy as well?

B. Ham Serves Japheth

Although Egypt was usually unaffected by Noah's prophecy, during times of *un*righteousness this curse also appears to have occurred in Egypt's history since Ham is implicated in what happened to Noah (Gen 9:22, 24). While this curse in no way ceded Ham's territory in Egypt to another people, it often affected the freedom Ham's children enjoyed. The first time we clearly see Egypt oppressed by foreigners was during the Second Intermediate Period (1800–1500).[49] During this era, Egypt was split in two and her kings driven out of the wealthy northern Delta region leaving all but a small petty Egyptian kingdom.[50] Although scholars recognize these invaders as Asiatics,[51] the prophet Isaiah recognizes an "Assyrian" (Isa 52:4) origin. Isaiah's assertion may be supported by the numerous Assyrian personal names attested during this era.[52] Although this information is not conclusive regarding the Shemite-Assyrian identity of Egypt's conqueror, it is a possibility during the Second Intermediate Period.

Assyria did not long outlast her kings who deported the Canaanites from their native homes under Ashurnasirpal and Esarhaddon. Assyria fell to Nabopolassar of Babylon, and Babylon soon fell to Persia. When a monarch lacks a son to perpetuate his heritage (name and lineage), according to Scripture (Num 27:8), a surviving daughter was to be substituted for a firstborn son and rightful heir.[53]

The ancient historian Herodotus tells us that Persia's King Cyrus II was the grandson of the Median king Astyages, who was survived by an only daughter (Herod 1.75, 91).[54] If Cyrus was Astyages' sole heir, Cyrus (through his mother—Astyages' only surviving offspring) carried not only the lineage of his Median grandfather but also the crown of his Persian father, Cambyses, although Herodutus' account is not without question.[55] According to the table of nations (Genesis 10), the Medes (Madai) were Japheth's descendants. When Cyrus inherited Canaan's territory from Babylon, he fulfilled Noah's words that Ham's children would become Persia's servants. Cyrus's Madain-Persian lineage gave him the divine "right" to conquer lands formerly inhabited by Canaan's seed. Cyrus's line ended with his son's death, and Darius (also a Mede) inherited Cyrus's lordship over Egypt and the land of Canaan.

Darius's sons exercised control over Canaan until Persia's fall to Alexander, whose lineage can be traced to another Japheth clan, Javan, Japheth's fourth son. His descendants are known as the *Ionians* or Greeks.[56] The Macedonians are a branch of the Greek family.[57] This is remarkable in light of the fact that Ham's seed became servants to the Macedonian sons of Japheth when Alexander conquered Egypt and Canaan in 332 BCE. When Alexander died, one of his generals, Ptolemy, of the Lagid Dynasty (a Macedonian family) ruled over the land of Egypt until its fall to Rome.[58] For almost 300 years, the sons of Japheth, the Ptolemies, were the lords of Egypt and Canaan.

> The whole burden of taxation was a heavy yoke upon the natives of the country (i.e., Egypt). The Greeks and Macedonians were not affected by it in the same measure as the Egyptians, for they were the conquerors and the Egyptians were the conquered. . . . Heavy compulsory labor such as the repair of canals, the paving of roads, and the construction of dykes, fell upon them alone. The natives were thus degraded to the level of people without rights, while the aliens ruled their country with a high hand.[59]

Egypt bore the heavy Ptolemaic yoke, and although Javan's lordship via the Ptolemies ended, it resurfaced with the Roman and later, Byzantine empires (Gomer, Tubal, Magog, Meshech—nations that also descended from Japheth—Gen 10:2). For well over 2,000 years, the children of Ham served Shem and Japheth's offspring. Noah's curse on Ham's children came to pass in these nations' early history, so their later history can be blessed (Gen 12:3).

The Noahic Covenant establishes the Creator's initial "words of truth." If YHWH is to be declared righteous and faithful, then all subsequent covenants, prophecies, and statutes must be consistent with the words that YHWH spoke to Noah. Though YHWH had not given Noah a prophecy against Canaan, Noah's prophecy had been based on his son's actions (Gen 9:22, 24). YHWH upheld and honored Noah's prophetic curse because Noah was righteous (Gen 6:8–9). The Noahic Covenant and Noah's prophecy form the basis of all subsequent "words of YHWH" and Old Testament prophecies. I had identified the foundation of any truth God had given to humanity. Next, came the task of seeing if subsequent covenants upheld these ideals.

V. ABRAHAMIC COVENANTS

A. *Migration Covenant*

I discovered that the three Abrahamic Covenants, like the Noahic Compact, resemble royal grants since they do not display the common features of later Near Eastern suzerainty covenants, as the later Sinai Compact does.[60] As more of a prototype of later covenants, the Abrahamic covenants include the following three main aspects: (1) stipulations or requirements; (2) blessings for obedience (no curses are listed for non-compliance); and (3) a sign or seal.[61] A sign or symbolic act that seals the patriarchal covenants is especially important, as we will see in our discussion below.

Table 3.3. The Four Abrahamic Covenants

Migration	*Promised-Land*	*Circumcision*	*Burnt-Offering*
Genesis 12:1–4	Genesis 15	Genesis 17	Genesis 22

Over the course of Abraham's life, YHWH covenanted four pacts: the Migration Covenant, the Promised-Land Covenant, the Circumcision Covenant, and the Burnt-Offering Covenant (see Table 3.3).[62] Each covenant was prophetic in nature with binding agreements placed on both parties (YHWH and Abraham). YHWH agreed to provide certain blessings for Abraham and his offspring, while Abraham and his children agreed to obey one particular request. Before Abram left Chaldea (Gen 12:31), YHWH extended the promise of his covenants, saying,

> Get you out of your country, and from your kindred, and from your father's house, *to a land that I will show you*: And I (1) will make of you a great nation, and (2) I will bless you, and (3) make your name great; and (4) you shall be a blessing: And (5) I will bless them that bless you, and curse him that curses you: and (6) in you shall all families of the earth be blessed. (Gen 12:1–3)

The stipulations of the Migration Covenant placed the greater burden on YHWH. The Creator asked Abram to migrate to a new country (stipulation), which meant leaving his native land and family ties. YHWH did not compel Abram or threaten him with misfortune should he choose to forgo this covenant. Rather, YHWH offered to reward Abram if he chose to enter into his covenant.[63]

If Abram complied with YHWH's request to migrate, YHWH promised to: (1) make Abram's progeny a great nation; (2) bless Abram and (3) make his name famous to future generations; (4) cause Abram's life to bless others; and (5) protect Abram and his offspring. YHWH would act favorably toward those who sought Abram and his descendants' welfare while afflicting those who sought their hurt; and (6) he would guarantee that Abram's migration would allow all the families of the earth to be blessed by Abraham's compliance in relocating to another land. Thus, the six obligations of this treaty were YHWH's to fulfill.

The responsibility of accepting this covenant rested on Abram. If he migrated (the sign of acceptance), YHWH knew that Abram had entered a covenant with him. When Abram entered the land, he sealed his covenant with YHWH through sacrifice (Gen 12:7). Although custom usually bound both parties to offer sacrifice, Abram was the only party to oblige at this point. YHWH did not yet offer any sign on his part to seal this treaty but the promises to Abram and his descendants of inheriting the land of Canaan.

> Abram passed through the land to the place of Sichem (Shechem), to the plain of Moreh. And the Canaanite was then in the land. And YHWH appeared to Abram, and said, To your seed will I give this land: and there built he an altar to YHWH, who appeared to him. (Gen 12:6–7, parenthesis added)

According to the genealogies listed in the Masoretic Text, at the time this promise was extended to Abram, Shem was still alive and saw both his blessing and his double-portioned birthright pass into Abram's hands (Gen 9:29; 11:10–31).[64] YHWH specifically bestowed the land of Canaan to Abram and his progeny. Notice that Scripture maintains the constancy of Noah's prophecy of dispossessing Canaan. YHWH's promise to Abram (in Genesis 12) served both to fulfill Noah's prophecy[65] by disinheriting Canaan and to define the parameters of future covenants that the Creator would grant to Abram and his offspring as the heirs of Shem's birthright and blessing (See Table 3.4).

Table 3.4. The Migration Covenant (Genesis 12)

Preamble	12:1, 7	YHWH reveals himself to Abram
Stipulation	12:1	Immigrate
Promises	12:1	*Shem's Birthright:* great nation; "land that I will show you."
	12:2–3	*Shem's Blessing:* material blessings; leadership of the nations
	12:2	Abram's name will become great
	12:3	He and his children's leadership will be a blessing to others
	12:2–3	YHWH empowers Abram's many children to inherit the blessing
	12:3	YHWH protects by bringing disaster on those who are against Abram and his descendants
	12:3	All of the earth will be blessed through Abram's offspring
Penalties		None. The grant covenant could be rejected without recourse
Sign	12:5–6	Abram immigrates to Canaan

B. Promised-Land Covenant

Abram was 75 years old when he accepted YHWH's covenant offer and migrated to Canaan (Gen 12:4). A short time later, harsh famines caused Abram to move to Egypt (Gen 12:10). When he returned to Canaan, YHWH gave Abram a vision that fulfilled the promise of land and offspring set forth in the Migration Covenant. Abram had been contemplating how YHWH would fulfill his promise of seed (offspring) when he and his wife were childless. This is the vision of the second Abramaic Covenant. (Parentheses inserted into the text indicate topics that will be examined below.)

C. Historical Background of the Promised-Land Covenant

Abram's petition seeks satisfaction since YHWH has failed to deliver on his promise that Abram will have offspring. Without children, Abram's high steward would inherit his estate along with his covenants. YHWH acknowledges Abram's request, but gently reaffirms his promise to give Abram his own child.

Preamble

After these things the word of YHWH came to Abram in a vision, saying, Fear not, Abram: I am your shield, and your exceeding great reward. And Abram said, Lord YHWH, *what will you give me, seeing I go childless,* and the steward of my house is this Eliezer of Damascus? And Abram said, Behold, to me you have given no seed: and lo, one born in my house is mine heir. (Gen 15:1–3)

Stipulation and Promise of a Son

And, behold, the word of YHWH came to him, saying, (1) *This shall not be your heir;* but he that shall come forth (2) *out of your own bowels* (*me'ah*) shall be your heir. And he brought him forth abroad, and said, (3) Look now toward heaven, and tell the stars, if you be able to number them: and he said to him, *So shall your seed be.* And (4) he believed in YHWH; and he *counted it to him for righteousness.* (Gen 15:4–6, parentheses added)

Historical Prologue

And he said to him, (a) *I am YHWH* that brought you out of Ur of the Chaldees, to give you this land to inherit it. (Gen 15:7)

Covenant's Sign

And he said, YHWH Adonai, whereby shall I know that I shall inherit it? And he said to him, (b) Take me an heifer of three years old, and a she goat of three years old, and a ram of three years old, and a turtledove, and a young pigeon. And he took to him all these, and divided them in the middle, and laid each piece one against another: but the birds divided he not. And when the fowls came down on the carcasses, Abram drove them away. (c) And when the sun was going down, a deep sleep fell on Abram; and see, an horror of great darkness fell on him. (Gen 15:8–11)

Prophecy

And he said to Abram, Know of a surety that (d) your seed shall be a stranger in a land that is not theirs, and shall serve them; and they *shall afflict* them four hundred years; (e) And also that nation, whom they shall serve, *will I judge*: and (f) afterward shall they come out with great substance. And you shall go to your fathers in peace; you shall be buried in a good old age. But in the (g) fourth generation they shall come here again: (h) for the iniquity of the Amorites is not yet full. And it came to pass, that, when the (i) sun went down, and it was dark, behold a smoking furnace, and a burning lamp that passed between those pieces. (Gen 15:13–17)

Promise of Land

In the (j) same day YHWH made a covenant with Abram, saying, To your seed have I given this land, from the river of Egypt to the great river, the river Euphrates: The Kenites, and the Kenizzites, and the Kadmonites, and the Hittites, and the Perizzites, and the Rephaims, and the Amorites, and the Canaanites, and the Girgashites, and the Jebusites. (Gen 15:18–21)

1. Part I: Stipulation and Promises

The Promised-Land Covenant fulfills the earlier promises in the Migration Covenant. YHWH offers this covenant as a grant since Abram has already obeyed YHWH's request and immigrated to Canaan.[66] YHWH is fulfilling the obligation that he previously assumed by means of the Migration Covenant. Abram had asked YHWH if his servant Eliezer would inherit his covenant (Gen 15:2). A contemporary Hurrian record reveals the context of Abram's question. The Nuzi documents show that it was customary during this era for servants of childless masters to inherit the former's estate.[67] The master "adopted" "an heir, called *ewuru* (CAD, IV, 415) in distinction to the direct heir, *aplu* (CAD, A/II, 173–77), who was a physical descendant. . . . The adopted son became the legally recognized heir to the estate."[68] Thus, Abram designates Eliezer as his *ewuru*[69] and questions YHWH if this legal maneuver is the means by which God will fulfill his promises to him.

The only stipulation that YHWH makes in the Promised-Land Covenant is (1, above) both to forbid Eliezer to inherit Abram's covenants (or his estate) as an *ewuru* and to define the terms for inheriting YHWH's covenants. *Binding on both Abram and YHWH* is the stipulation that determines the means by which Abram's children (2, above) can inherit his covenants: only Abram's *me'ah* (*lit.*, sperm)[70] qualify to inherit YHWH's covenants.[71] Even loyal, "adopted" servants may not substitute for Abram's physical offspring. *Abram had inherited Noah's and Shem's blessings because he was their physical descendant.* Likewise, only Abram's children were eligible for inheriting Canaan's land. Although Shem had other descendants who benefited from his blessings, only Abraham's descendants would benefit from YHWH's covenants with him, such as inheriting the Promised Land. The next blessing, however, was not exclusive.

YHWH, knowing the eternal value and worth of the family, (3, above) gave Abram the most powerful blessing on earth: children. (YHWH had first given this blessing to Noah in Gen 9:1, 7.) Not only would Abram's numerous children fill his heart with love and joy, but through them YHWH would fulfill his promise to make Abram's seed a mighty and powerful nation, to whom kings would listen and bow down. YHWH planned to use Abram's children to ensure a Torah-based culture and value system. Through the family, YHWH would build a mighty and righteous people who had the faith to live by his way of life and preserve its philosophical heritage for future generations.

Modern progressive societies often doubt the importance of large families. The sociopolitical attitude of America and many Western nations toward children is that they are simply another carbon footprint that depletes limited resources that society already has: children simply add to the earth's pollution, taxing limited resources. This philosophy, however, causes societies to collapse and fail because children are the strength and backbone of any nation's future.[72]

In order for any country, culture, or society to survive, families must produce an average of 2.11 children per family.[73] At this rate, society simply replenishes the parents' generation (not accounting for large-scale disasters). If births fall to an average of 1.9 children per family, then the overall population of nations such as Russia, Canada, and the U. K. will be cut by 1/4 within a generation, or about 30 years. Societies that only produce 1.3 children per family eventually shrink and collapse. Eventually, other more prolific cultures will replace the nations that have dwindling populations (see Table 3.5). [74]

Table 3.5. Population Sustainability

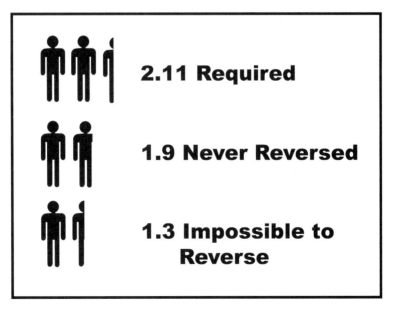

Modern-day Russia has become a victim of this crisis. Over the last 20 years, Russia's population has fallen exponentially. During a 16-year period beginning in 1976 (1976–1991), Russia had 36 million births.[75] Sixteen years later (1992–2007), however, the country experienced a 40% drop in the birth rate to only 22.3 million births. In 2005, Russia had a population of 143 million. This is expected to drop by about 20 million within 15 years to fall between 121 and 136 million by 2025.[76] The drop in birth rates has occurred due in large measure to the collapse of moral values. Marriage, in which 60% of women had participated in 1990, has dropped to less than 34% in 1996, because women opt for cohabitation relationships. With the decline of marriage, the popularity of abortion increased. Russian women had almost 13 abortions for every 10 live births in 2003.[77] Likewise, their depraved morals have led to the world's worst rates of death, induced by alcoholism and suicide.[78]

What does all of this mean in practical terms? Well, first, Russia will have a significantly smaller labor force. This means less government revenue from taxable income and a smaller gross national product (GNP). This ultimately translates into a lower standard of living for Russian families and less dominance in the global market. Consequently, neither Russia nor its policies will have as much influence with other nations in future years.[79]

Over the last few decades, the prevailing Western economic thinking is that a

> decline in fertility should mean a better material environment for newborns and children because a shift to smaller desired family size (all else being equal) should signify an increase in parents' expected commitments to each child's education, nutrition, health care, and the like. Yet in post–Communist Russia, there are unambiguous indications of a worsening of social well-being for a significant proportion of the country's children—in effect, a disinvestment in children in the face of a pronounced downward shift in national fertility patterns.[80]

Russia is only one country that demonstrates the ludicrousness of Western views on family fertility. Decrease in size of the family unit does not equal a better life-style for overall society but a worse overall socioeconomic status. The effect of Communism in post–Soviet Russia is not the abolition of capitalistic investments but an abolition of capitalism's most valuable resource—the family—as Marx himself had foreseen when writing the *Communist Manifesto*.[81]

Not only will Russia's standard of living and GNP decrease, her military prowess will be threatened as the population from which it can draw for its armed forces and with which it holds onto land diminishes. Ultimately, Russia's Communistic ideals have fulfilled Marxist prophecy of the "abolition of the family" because post-Communistic families possess no desire or incentive to reproduce. In realistic terms, abolition of the family is suicide for the nation. In the end, this means that other more prolific societies will dominate and eventually replace Russian society and its culture.

Why is a country or a culture's repopulation so important? Other nations, with better moral values will eventually replace deprived nations. Muslims, who uphold the value of proliferation, are overrunning most nations today. If, for instance, current population trends continue, Muslims will outnumber ethnic Russians in 30 years. There are now 25 million

Muslims in Russia, and they are projected to become 1/5 of the country's overall population by 2020. The *Washington Post's* foreign policy journal reports that

> many ethnic Russians are terrified at the prospect of becoming a minority in their own country. Alexander Belov, from the Movement Against Illegal Immigration, said: "History is a fight between races and religions." It's the law of nature . . . people are used to being with people like themselves, speaking the language their mothers taught them.[82]

Eventually, Russia faces the daunting reality of Muslim values' replacing traditional Russian values and the possibility that Sharia Law will replace the constitution of the Russian Federation. Since most Muslims have large families, their voice, power, and influence increase exponentially. This is especially true of nations, such as the U.S., in which "the fundamental principle is that the will of the majority is to prevail" (Thomas Jefferson).[83] In the end, the majority has the most power and will prevail over smaller cultures and populations. This is why YHWH granted Abram the gift of children, to ensure that his most powerful asset would not be dominated by societies that had grown corrupt.

When Abram heard YHWH's promises and understood his covenants, he believed the Creator's words and obediently acted on them. Because Abram (4) believed YHWH's promises and took YHWH at his word, the Creator credited Abram with righteousness. Thus, YHWH promised Abram that, if he and his children would believe his words and abide by them, they too would be righteous. Belief became the sign of Abram's compliance. These three promises became the underpinnings of the Promised-Land Covenant and all future covenants.

2. Part II: Foundation of the Covenant

The next section of the Promised-Land Covenant verifies who YHWH is and defines the consequence for breaching this pact. The Creator draws Abram's attention to who he is by (a) reestablishing the knowledge and importance of his name—YHWH. This is the same name Genesis' account tells us Eve had used when stating that "YHWH" had created her son (Gen 4:1). Enos, too, had used this name for God (Gen 4:26). Thus, according to Scripture, YHWH has been the name consistently attributed to the Creator since creation.

Once again YHWH seals his covenant with a sacrifice. The Creator asks Abram to prepare a five-part offering (b) consisting of a heifer, she-goat, and ram, each three years of age, and two undivided birds. In the evening time, (c) a "horror of great darkness" fell on Abram. The sacrifice that YHWH ordained for Abram to perform "depicts the self-destruction of the one making the contract in an analogous way: that the fate of the animal should befall him in the event that he does not keep the bᵉrît (covenant)."[84] Once again we see that sacrifice signaled the fate of the covenantee should he fail to uphold his pledge according to the covenant.[85]

This interpretation is consistent with Jer 34:18, where the Israelites again used a divided sacrifice to seal their covenant with YHWH. Jeremiah does not leave the symbolism of sacrifice to mystical ideals but plainly states the covenantee's fate should he fail to uphold his or her end of the covenanted pledge.

> I will give the men that have transgressed my covenant, which have *not performed the words of the covenant which they had made before me, when they cut the calf in two, and passed between the parts of it,* The princes of Judah, and the princes of Jerusalem, the eunuchs, and the priests, and all the people of the land, *which passed between the parts of the calf.* (Jer 34:18–19)

Jeremiah's prophecy demonstrates that this ceremony depicted the fate of those who failed to uphold their side of the covenant, or in more modern terms, "their end of the deal." Through this offering, Abram knew he would inherit the land promised to him if he complied. However, Abram had only prepared this sacrifice. It was YHWH—not Abram—who passed between the parts of a divided sacrifice *to seal his own compliance and his own fate* should he fail to deliver on his promises to Abram.[86]

3. Part III: Fulfillment of Noah's Prophecy

YHWH promised Abram (j) Canaan's land as an eternal possession for his children. The land and its nations (vv. 18–21) effectively covered all of Ham's descendants except for Mizraim's offspring in Egypt. The "hidden" prophecy in the Promised-Land Covenant judged Mizraim and established Abram and his children as the heir of Shem's double portion of the birthright.[87] YHWH specifically promised Canaan's land to Abram, a land that Noah removed from Canaan and promised to Shem's progeny.

4. Hidden Judgment Prophecy

The Promised-Land Covenant patterns the Noahic Covenant's model of penalty and judgment. YHWH foretells that Egypt will (d) afflict Israel. This situation will provoke YHWH to render (e) a Day of Judgment against the people that oppress them. Scholars observe that as early as the Old Kingdom (*c.* 2686–2181 BCE), Egypt dealt with national labor shortages through "forcible appropriation of people arbitrarily taken from the lands of one institution and forced to work on behalf of a different organization," usually temple-state organizations.[88] At the time that YHWH spoke this prophecy to Abram, Egypt had already established a tradition for oppressing and enslaving innocent people, especially those tied to agrarian careers.[89] Since Abram and his family were shepherds (Gen 46:32–34), YHWH knew that they would be an easy prey for Egypt's temple organizations.

When the time arose for YHWH to judge Egypt, the Creator would compensate Abram's children (f) by granting them their oppressor's wealth (gained by Israel's labor). According to Exod 9:16, the reason YHWH hardened Pharaoh's heart during the exodus plagues was "to show in you my power; and that my *name* may be declared throughout all the earth." Indeed, the exodus is one of the most-told Old Testament stories. If Israel had not migrated to Egypt, there would have been little cause for YHWH to show his power. The exodus not only delivered Israel; it also memorialized YHWH's fame for future generations, thus enabling us to talk and write about it today.

Gen 15:13 states that Abraham's seed (d) would serve Egypt 400 years. Most scholars define a generation as 20–30 years;[90] however, YHWH does not use the term *generation* in the modern sense. Rather, the term is used to describe the life-span of a generation. According to the genealogy of Exodus 6, four generations spanned Israel's migration to Egypt through her exodus from Egypt. Levi, immigrated to Egypt and lived to 137 years of age (Exod 6:16). His son Kohath lived to be 133 years old (Exod 6:18), and his grandson Amram lived to be 137 years of age (Exod 6:20). These *three* generations spanned 407 years. Moses was in the fourth generation and delivered Israel out of Egypt when he was 80 years old (Exod 7:7). Gen 15:16 adds the fourth generation (g), Moses' generation, to the 400 years (comprising the first three generations). Thus, the total time elapsed from migration to exodus should be approximately 420–30 years.

Interestingly, YHWH did not hand over Canaan to Abram at the time he contracted the Promised-Land Covenant because the Amorites' sins (h) had not yet "come to their fullness." Canaan had not become totally steeped in idolatry. The Creator could not render judgment against the Amorites by confiscating their land and fulfilling Noah's prophecy until their sins were completely degenerate.[91] *If he had, it would have been an arbitrary act.*[92] Evidence that the Amorites had not yet fully embraced idolatry during Abram's days is attested by the Amorite king Melchizedek, whom Scripture describes as "priest to the most high God" (see p. 353). As a priest who still upheld YHWH's values, Melchizedek had the ability to pronounce a blessing on Abram (Gen 14:18–20). YHWH knew that at the end of 430 years (400 years + the fourth generation) the Amorites, as a nation, would be steeped in idolatry, immorality, and other oppressive "ways of life" that called for national judgment.

To what extent had the sins of the Amorites "come to the full" when Israel inherited the land 430 years later? In Leviticus 18, YHWH commanded that Israel should not commit incest (vv.6–18) or adultery (v. 20). In v. 19 he commanded the Israelites to refrain from intercourse during menstruation and stipulated that their children should not be sacrificed to Molech (v. 21). YHWH also forbade homosexuality (v. 22) and bestiality (v. 23). Notice what the Creator states regarding the morality of the Amorites and other nations that Israel was to displace:

> Defile not you yourselves in any of these things: *for in all these the nations are defiled which I cast out before you: And the land is defiled: therefore I do visit the iniquity thereof on it,* and the land itself vomits out her inhabitants. (Lev 18:24–25)

When YHWH "visits iniquity" on a land, it indicates that the sins of that land have "come to a full." If the Amorites and other Canaanite peoples had committed the above trespasses mentioned in Leviticus 18, then they were ripe for judgment 430 years later, when Israel inherited their land.

5. Part IV: The Sign

The Promised-Land Covenant designated Abram's offspring to fulfill YHWH's judgment against Amorite sins by solidifying Israel's inheritance of Shem's double portion of the birthright (i.e., Canaan). This birthright granted Israel the privilege of fulfilling Noah's prophecy against Ham's offspring. Noah's prophecy was part of the reason that YHWH commanded Israel: "When you have passed over Jordan into the land of Canaan; Then you shall *drive out* all the inhabitants of the land from before you" (Num 33:51–52).

Abram had originally asked how he could be assured that YHWH's promises would indeed come true (Gen 15:8). He wanted a tangible sign to seal his covenant with YHWH. The (i) oath that YHWH offered to Abram for the Promised-Land Covenant was "a smoking furnace, and a burning lamp that passed between those pieces" of the divided burnt offering (Gen 15:17). When Judah's elders later made a similar covenant with YHWH (Jer 34:18), the Creator recognized those who "passed between the parts" of the divided sacrifice as being responsible for upholding the stipulations in the covenant, as was customary throughout the ancient world. The Promised-Land Covenant is unique in the fact that YHWH bound himself in this self-imprecating oath to the same fate as the divided sacrifice should he fail to deliver on his promises to Abraham.[93] Because YHWH obligated himself to the promises he made to Abraham, he (using a smoking furnace) passed between the pieces of the divided sacrifice, signifying both his commitment to the promises he made with Abram and his acceptance of Abram's previous covenant-offering (when he immigrated to Canaan).[94] Since YHWH committed himself to uphold his own promises or suffer the fate of the divided sacrifice (if he failed), Abram knew that his God would indeed cause his children to inherit Canaan's land.[95]

What was YHWH's (j) promise to Abram in this covenant?

> In the same day YHWH made a covenant with Abram, saying, *To your seed have I given this land, from the river of Egypt to the great river, the river Euphrates*: The Kenites, and the Kenizzites, and the Kadmonites, And the Hittites, and the Perizzites, and the Rephaims, and the Amorites, and the Canaanites, and the Girgashites, and the Jebusites. (Gen 15:18–21)

YHWH promised the land of Palestine to Abraham's progeny. Thus Israel's Promised Land spanned from modern Syria to the now-defunct Pelusiac branch of the Nile in Egypt (which included the Sinai Peninsula), granting the nation one of the most favorable trading positions in the ancient world.

Within this covenant's hidden prophecy, YHWH also provided an exact time for Canaan's judgment. How long does a generation exist before another generation begins? Currently, historiographers accept 20–30 years as the average span of a generation.[96] Does Scripture support its own covenants by demonstrating the fulfillment of this prophecy?

> Now the sojourning of the Children of Israel, who dwelled in Egypt, *was four hundred and thirty years.* And it came to pass at the end of the four hundred and thirty years, *even the selfsame day it came to pass,* that all the hosts of YHWH went out from the land of Egypt. It is a night to be much observed to YHWH for bringing them out from the land of Egypt . . . this is that night of YHWH to be observed of all the Children of Israel in their generations. (Exod 12:40–42)

Israel had entered Egypt on the 15th of Abib during Joseph's days and departed on the 15th of Abib 430 years later! The time frame that YHWH stipulated for Israel to dwell in Egypt, in this case, meets the test of fidelity.[97] Israel's deliverance accomplished YHWH's judgment on the apostacizing nations stipulated in the Promised-Land compact. (We will see more evidence when we look at Israel's exodus in chap. 10.) Through Abram, YHWH would drive out Ham's offspring and supplant them with Shem's progeny as the Amorites and other Canaanite nations' sins reached utter degradation. Thus far, I had seen that Scripture has maintained constancy in written prophecy and doctrine.

After studying these first few covenants, I saw that the Promised-Land Covenant fulfilled YHWH's obligation to bless Abram as promised in the earlier Migration Covenant. Although YHWH established stipulations for inheriting his covenants, he also promised Abram the means to fulfill the inheritance clause in his covenants (i.e., genetic offspring). Abram had accepted the stipulation of waiting on YHWH for a child. I also came to understand that YHWH wanted Abram to understand what would take place while his children waited for the Amorites' sins to degenerate, before he judged Egypt and delivered Israel. Abram needed to understand that his offspring would be afflicted in Egypt for over 400 years. This investigation had not uncovered much of anything that Abram needed to do to fulfill this treaty because he had already complied with YHWH's initial request for migration. The only stipulations that were binding for Abram were the terms of inheritance (i.e., genetic offspring) and the duration of time that Abram's children would have to wait until YHWH fulfilled his covenant to deliver Canaan to them.

Incredibly, I saw that YHWH's part of the covenant bore the greater responsibility. YHWH promised to give Abram his own children and to bless them with fertility. YHWH bore the added responsibilities of bringing Abram's children out of Egypt at the end of 430 years with "great substance," thus enabling them to inherit the Promised Land. YHWH delegated two responsibilities to Abram (stipulation for inheritance and waiting for the land) while placing the greater burden on himself. In contrast to Abram's two stipulations, YHWH bound himself to four stipulations: (1) disallowing adoption as a valid means of inheritance and acknowledging only Abram's physical offspring as rightful heirs of his covenants; (2) granting fertility; (3) bringing Abram's children out of Egypt with great wealth; and (4) causing them to inherit the Promised Land. Even more importantly, YHWH signaled his own fate (self-imprecation) by passing through the sacrifice should he fail to uphold or deliver on his promises to Abram and his descendants (see Table 3.6).[98]

Table 3.6. Promised Land Covenant of Grant (Genesis 15)

Preamble	15:1	YHWH appears to Abram in a vision
	15:1	YHWH is Abram's shield and his great reward
Historical Prologue	15:7	YHWH brought Abram out of Ur
(Issue/Petition)	15:2–3	Abram has no children—YHWH has not fulfilled the Migration Covenant
Stipulation (on Abram)	15:4	Eliezer disqualified to be Abram's son
	15:4	Disallows adoption as legal means of inheriting covenants
	15:4–5	Only Abram's *Me'ah* (lit., sperm) qualify to inherit Abram's covenants
	15:4–5, 18	Abraham's own offspring will inherit his promises
	15:4–5, 18	Inheritance of covenants based on biological seed
	15:5	Multitude of children
(Prophecy)	15:13	Children will migrate to another land and will be afflicted
	15:16	Wait for Amorites sins to become wholly reprobate
	15:13, 16	Children will return to Canaan 430 yrs. later
Hidden Judgment	15:14	YHWH will judge land to which Abram's children have immigrated
(Blessing for service)	15:14	Israel will leave the oppressor's land with great wealth
	15:16	Fourth generation will still be alive to inherit land
Promise/Blessing	15:5	Offspring as the sand of the seashore
Oath	15:18–21	*Shem's birthright*: to give Abram's descendants the Promised Land—Euphrates to the eastern (Pelusaic) branch of the Nile
Sign/ratified—YHWH	15:9–11, 17	YHWH's self-imprecating sacrifice
Sign—Abram	15:6	Abram believes

Thus far, the investigation has not revealed any contradictions in the words YHWH spoke to the patriarchs. The doctrine that the birthright (Promised Land) and the blessing (family leadership) would be inherited by Abram and his descendants has been consistent as each covenant has upheld and re-issued the previous promises. With the divergent stances that modern religions take on the inheritance of the Promised Land, I wondered: Would subsequent covenants rescind any of these promises or would YHWH continue upholding the pattern we have seen thus far?

D. Circumcision Covenant

Twenty-four years after YHWH had offered the Promised-Land Covenant to Abram (Gen 17:1, 24) he offered Abram another treaty. This covenant is significantly more specific and more detailed than the three previous covenants. In Noah's Covenant, YHWH had provided the rainbow as a sign. In the Migration Covenant, Abram signaled his willingness to enter into covenants with YHWH by moving to Canaan. With the Promised-Land Covenant, YHWH had sent a devouring lamp as a sign to seal his compliance to his own promises. He signaled his own fate if he failed to deliver on the promises he had contracted with Abram, thus offering the sincerest of pledges.

Similar to the Migration Covenant, the Circumcision Covenant does not involve sacrifice as part of its seal. In this treaty, both parties contribute signs to signal compliance.

Historical Prologue
YHWH appeared to Abram, and said to him, I am the Almighty God. (Gen 17:1)

Preamble
(a) *Walk before me, and be you perfect.* (Gen 17:1)

Promises
And I will make my covenant between me and you, and (b) *will multiply you exceedingly.* And Abram fell on his face: and God talked with him, saying, As for me, behold, my covenant is with you, and you shall be a (c) *father of many nations.* Neither shall your name any more be called Abram, but your name shall be Abraham; for a father of many nations have I made you. And I will make you (b) exceedingly fruitful, and I will make (c) nations of you, and (d) kings shall come out of you. *And I will establish my covenant between me and you and (e) your seed after you in their generations for an everlasting covenant, to be a God to you, and to your seed after you.* And I will give to you, and to your seed after you, the (f) land wherein you are a stranger, all the land of Canaan, for an everlasting possession; and *I will be their God.* And God said to Abraham, You shall keep my covenant therefore, you and your seed after you in their generations. (Gen 17:1–9)

The Seal and Requirement
This is my covenant, which you shall keep, between me and you and your seed after you; Every man child among you shall be circumcised. And you shall circumcise the flesh of your foreskin; and it shall be a *token* of the covenant between me and you. And he that is eight days old shall be circumcised among you, every man child in your generations, he that is born in the house, or bought with money of any stranger, which is not of your seed. . . . must be circumcised: and my covenant shall be in your flesh for an everlasting covenant. And the uncircumcised man child (g) whose flesh of his foreskin is not circumcised, that soul shall be cut off from his people; he has broken my covenant. (Gen 17:10–14)

YHWH's (a) only stipulation for the Circumcision Covenant requires Abram to walk with YHWH *tamiym*.[99] This is the word that, as we saw above (p. 46), means 'entire, complete, and whole-hearted.' The Hebrew word for "walk," *halak*,[100] means a value or principle-based course of life. The term is quite similar to *derek*, which we have already seen (pp. 16–17) means a 'way' or course of life. This is the same walk (*halak*) or value-based system to which Scripture records Enoch (Gen 5:24) and Noah (Gen 6:9) as having adhered. Hence, YHWH asks Abram and his children to be whole-hearted and to adhere completely to his principle-based way of life in their relationship with him. Later in the nation's history, King David is said to have walked (*halak*) before YHWH in truth (1 Kgs 3:6), completeness, and integrity of heart (1 Kgs 9:4; Ps 26:1). *Halak* is also used of King Amon (2 Kgs 21:21–22) to describe his adherence to value-based systems *contrary* to the way of YHWH.

As a reward for walking before YHWH wholeheartedly, Abram would gain certain blessings. YHWH reiterates and upholds the promise of (b) fertility.[101] As we discussed above, Scripture readily attests to the importance that children play in securing YHWH's blessings. This is emphasized during King David's reign.

> And Joab gave the sum of the number of the people to David. And all they of Israel were a thousand thousand and an hundred thousand men that drew sword: and Judah was four hundred threescore[102] and ten thousand men that drew sword. (1 Chr 21:5)

In addition to the joy of family, the blessings of seed indicates military prowess. Abram's descendants would possess military strength that would enable them to defend their country, secure their borders, and establish liberty in the Promised Land.

YHWH augments an additional blessing to his covenant with the promise that Abram's children (c) will become *many nations*. Kings (d) and monarchies will arise in Abram's progeny. YHWH specifically (e) promises to establish his covenant with Abram and his seed in subsequent generations for an everlasting covenant. Thus, YHWH maintains his position and authority as Israel's *only* God. **The wording of this covenant negates any possibility that YHWH could reject the seed of Abraham as inheritors of his covenants and yet be called a God of Truth.** It should be remembered that the definition of truth is:

> constancy and freedom from change even during a time of duress as embedded in the concepts of loyalty, fidelity, and faithfulness.[103]

If YHWH is to be a God of truth, then according to the concepts of truth discussed in chap. 1, he cannot recant or rescind his promises and reject Abram's descendants as inheritors of his covenants.[104] That the Creator is consistent and does not rescind his word is evidenced in the next aspect of the Circumcision Covenant wherein YHWH reaffirms (f) the Promised-Land Covenant's pledge, thus maintaining the faithfulness and constancy of his previous word.

The Hebrew word for token, *'owth* in verse eleven, means 'a sign.'[105] YHWH provided a sign in his part of this covenant by changing Abram's name from *Abram*, meaning 'high or first father,' to *Abraham*, meaning 'a father of multitudes.'[106] This significant sign reflected the prophetic promise of the Circumcision Covenant itself. Abraham's name became a "seal" or prophecy that ratified the blessing that would arise for his seed. In order for Abram and his seed to enter this pact, they contributed the "sign" of circumcision to ratify their agreement with the contract's terms.

This is the first time that YHWH includes explicit instructions for a covenantee's sign or seal of compliance. Circumcision, not sacrifice, signaled that Abram and his children were complying with the terms of this treaty. YHWH's only stipulation for Abram was to (a) walk before him wholeheartedly. Circumcision integrated this principle of cutting away the fleshy foreskin with cutting away other obstacles that prevented a whole-hearted walk with YHWH.[107] The Law later incorporated this idea, commanding Israel to "circumcise the foreskin of the heart to be no more stiffnecked" (Deut 10:16; see also Jer 4:4). In the later Moabite-Shechem Covenant (Deuteronomy, see below in this chap.), Moses cited the (e) ultimate fulfillment of this covenant, when "YHWH your God will circumcise your heart, and the heart of your seed, to love YHWH your God with all your heart, with all your soul, *that you may live*" (Deut 30:6; see Table 3.7).

Table 3.7. Circumcision Parity Covenant with Abram (Genesis 17)

Preamble or Title		17:1	I am YHWH your God
Historical Prologue		17:2	Walk before me and be perfect (reiterates requirement)
		17:2, 4	Recognizes previous covenants
(Recognizes Previous Promises)		17:2, 4–6	Multiply exceedingly; fruitfulness
		17:8	*Abram's birthright*: Promised Land
New Promises		17:6	Abram will be a father of many nations
		17:6	Added blessing of being "exceedingly" fruitful
		17:6	Nations and kings will come from Abram's seed
		17:7	Covenant given to Abram's perpetual generations (forever)
		17:7	YHWH will be the only God of Abram's children (Gen 15:1)
Stipulations	(YHWH)	17:7	Injunction: YHWH can never reject Abram's seed
	(Abram)	17:1	Injunction: Observe covenants, walk in the way of YHWH
		17:10, 12–14	Male circumcised on 8th day after birth
Witnesses		17:3	God and Abraham
Oath		15:9–11, 17	YHWH's promises—No sacrifice; YHWH had already given a self-imprecating oath. Nothing could be added to that surety.
Blessing for Compliance		17:2, 4, 7	All blessings of the promises in his covenants
Penalty/Curse for Breach		17:14	The offspring that are not circumcised will not be recognized as Abraham's legitimate heirs or seed. They lose access to covenants/blessings and are severed from Abram's children
Sign	(YHWH)	17:5	YHWH changes Abram's name to Abraham
	(Abram)	17:11	Circumcision

YHWH's ultimate objective in giving the Circumcision Covenant was to procure a people who would love and follow him wholeheartedly. We will delve into the prophetic implications of this covenant in part 2 of this book after we have resolved some questions of validity.

E. Sarahic Covenant

Within the Circumcision Covenant, YHWH covenanted promises to Abraham's wife, Sarai. YHWH acknowledged Sarai's authority and her voice in the upbringing of her children. If Sarai and her seed (i.e., females) would agree to circumcise their sons on the eighth day, YHWH would grant her certain blessings.

> And he that is (a) eight days old shall be circumcised among you. . . . And the uncircumcised man child whose flesh of his foreskin is (b) not circumcised, that soul shall be cut off from his people; he has broken my covenant. And God said to Abraham, As for (c) Sarai your wife, you shall not call her name Sarai, but Sarah shall her name be. And I will bless her, and give you a son also of her: yes, I will bless her, and (d) *she shall be a mother of nations*; kings of people shall be of her. Then Abraham fell on his face, and (e) laughed, and said in his heart, Shall a child be born to him that is an (f) hundred years old? and shall Sarah, that is (g) ninety years old, bear? And Abraham said to God, O that Ishmael might live before you! And God said, Sarah your wife shall bear you a son indeed; and (h) *you shall call his name Isaac*: and I will establish my covenant with him for an (i) everlasting covenant, and with his seed after him. And as for (j) Ishmael, I have heard you: Behold, I have blessed him, and will make him fruitful, and will multiply him exceedingly; twelve princes shall he beget, and I will make him a great nation. (k) *But my covenant will I establish with Isaac,* which (l) *Sarah shall bear to you at this set time in the next year.* And he left off talking with him, and God went up from Abraham. (Gen 17:12; 14–22)

In many ways, the Sarahic Covenant overlaps naturally with the Abrahamic covenant since the issue is Abram's and Sarai's unborn son. YHWH's (a) only stipulation in the Sarahic Covenant is for Sarai and her daughters to comply with male circumcision on the eighth day of life (Gen 17:12). Failure to comply with this request would (b) nullify Sarai's son's recognition as a legitimate heir of her husband's covenants with YHWH. As a reward for consenting to this one request, the Creator offers blessings to Sarai. He promises that Sarai will become the (d) "mother of nations." This equaled the promise that YHWH had given Abram (Gen 17:4–5), thus placing Abram and Sarai on equal footing. This blessing effectively cut off Hagar's son as a legitimate heir.

Fifteen years earlier when YHWH told Abraham that he would have a son, he readily believed God's word (Gen 15:6). Now (e) Abraham's faith wavered, and he laughed at YHWH's promise. Abraham was (f) 99 years old and by the time gestation would end, he would be at least 100 years of age. This seemed impossible! Furthermore, Sarah was now (g) 89 years of age. YHWH acknowledged the disbelief in Abram's heart, instructing him to name his future son (h) Isaac, meaning 'laughter.'[108] No doubt YHWH wanted to remind Abraham that nothing was impossible for him. Not even a child in Sarah's old age.

Table 3.8. Sarah's Circumcision Parity Covenant

Preamble or Title		17:1	I am YHWH your God
Historical Prologue		17:16–17	Sarah is old and has no biological children
		17:17; 18:11–12	Abram and Sarai have jested about having children because they are old
New Promises		17:16	Counterpart to Abraham: Mother of many nations
		17:16	Sarah will have a son
		17:16	Nations and kings will come from Sarah's womb
		17:19–21	Ishmael will not be Abraham's heir
		17:21	Isaac will be born within a year
Stipulations	(YHWH) (Sarah)	17:19	Injunction: YHWH can never reject Sarah's seed as Abraham's lawful heir
		17:19	Sarai will call her son Isaac
		17:10, 12–14	Males circumcised on 8th day after birth
Witnesses		17:3, 22	God and Abraham
Oath		15:9–11, 17	YHWH's promises–No sacrifice; YHWH had already given a self-imprecating oath: nothing could be added to that surety
Blessings for Compliance		17:16, 19, 21	Blessings of the promises of his covenants
Penalty/Curse for Breach		17:14	The offspring that are not circumcised are: not recognized as Abraham's and Sarah's legitimate heirs or seed and lose access to the covenants, birthright, and blessings; severed from Abram's descendants
Sign	(YHWH) (Sarah)	17:15	YHWH changes Sarai's name to Sarah
		17:10, 12	Allow her sons to be circumcised on the 8th day

In many ways YHWH's covenant with Sarai was political.[109] YHWH established her as the only legitimate mother of Abraham's (not-yet conceived) heir.[110] That this covenant recognized (h) Isaac as Abraham's only legitimate offspring is seen by YHWH's declaration that Abraham should make his "only son" a burnt offering in Gen 22:2, 12, and 16. The Sarahic Covenant continues to outline blessings for circumcision. Sarai's children will (i) also inherit YHWH's covenanted blessings as an "everlasting covenant." YHWH never promised this blessing to Sarah's servant, Hagar. Thus, YHWH esteems Sarah's position—as Abraham's first and only legitimate wife[111]—and his blessing of her seed alongside Abraham's, once again negating any possibility that Ishmael could lay claim to YHWH's covenanted birthright or blessing.

In accordance with cultural tradition,[112] Sarai had encouraged her husband to take her handmaid as a wife.[113] The deed had been done. At this point, Sarai needed to accept that YHWH would (j) bless her husband's child, Ishmael. YHWH acknowledges that he will cause Hagar's seed to burgeon into a great, yet wild and tumultuous multitude (a blessing previously bestowed on Hagar, Gen 16:7–15) even though Hagar's line would have (k) no claim to Isaac's birthright or blessing.[114]

YHWH offers two signs to seal his treaty with Sarai. The (c) first sign changes her name to Sarah. As sole heir of the Abrahamic covenants, Isaac's seed will become "many nations" (Gen 17:6–7). The Circumcision Covenant transforms both Abraham and Sarah's names as prophetic signs denoting blessings for their offspring. Thus YHWH offers the same stipulations, signs, and blessings to both Abraham and Sarah. The second sign that YHWH offers to Sarah reassures her that her long wait for a son is over. Her child will be (1) born one year later. Isaac's birth becomes the final sign to ratify and activate the blessings in the Circumcision Covenant. The only sign (a–c) that Sarai provides to seal her covenant with YHWH is to allow her son to be circumcised on the eighth day. In many ways the Abrahamic Covenants are not "male" covenants, but are family covenants since the promises in all covenants are for the Abraham-Sarah-Isaac family and their descendants (see Table 3.8).

F. Burnt-Offering Covenant

Within a few months of securing the Circumcision Covenant, YHWH sent messengers to tell Abraham about the fiery judgment he was soon to render on Sodom and Gomorrah (Gen 18:17–21). During the visit, YHWH's messengers reiterated YHWH's promise that Sarah would bear a son within a year. Sarah, much like Abraham, expressed her disbelief in YHWH's promised sign by laughing at the messenger's affirmation (Gen 18:10–14). Neither Abraham nor Sarah believed that YHWH would or could give Sarah a child in her old age.

Quite a bit of history had occurred between the Promised-Land and Burnt-Offering Covenants. Abraham had previously demonstrated his waning trust in YHWH. He had laughed at YHWH's promise that Sarah would have a son. Twice he had feared another nation (Gen 20:11; 12:12) instead of trusting in YHWH's covenanted protection. Nevertheless, YHWH had finally granted Abraham and Sarah their promised son (Gen 21:1–7). Sarah upheld her end of YHWH's covenant by allowing Isaac to be circumcised on the eighth day (Gen 21:4). Abraham had liberty to travel throughout the Promised Land. And YHWH had blessed him tremendously (Gen 13:5–6). YHWH had upheld his side of the treaty.

Now God needed to know if Abraham's heart was still trusting him. Did Abraham follow YHWH simply because of the miracle wrought in Isaac, or did he love YHWH above all else?[115] In order to know Abraham's heart, YHWH tested Abraham with the first covenant that involved sacrifice on Abraham's part.

Preamble and Historical Prologue

And it came to pass after these things that God did *tempt* Abraham, and said to him, Abraham: and he said, Behold, here I am. (Gen 22:1)

Stipulation

And he said, Take now your son, your only son Isaac, whom you **love,** and get you to the land of *Moriah;* and offer him there for a burnt offering on one of the mountains which I will tell you of. (Gen 22:2)

Nacah, Hebrew for "tempt," means to 'prove or put to the test.'[116] Unlike the English word *tempt,* the Hebrew does not include the connotation of 'enticing to do wrong.'[117]

Rather, YHWH is testing Abraham to see whether he will follow his instructions. YHWH will use this same method with Abraham's children, the nation of Israel, when they rebel against him in the wilderness.

> Then said YHWH to Moses, Behold, I will rain bread from heaven for you; and the people shall go out and gather a certain rate every day, that *I may prove them, whether they will walk in my law, or no.* (Exod 16:4)
>
> And you shall remember all the way which YHWH your God led you these forty years in the wilderness, to humble you, and **to prove you,** *to know what was in your heart, whether you would keep his commandments, or not.* (Deut 8:2)

YHWH's purpose for testing and trying Israel in the wilderness was to see whether the heart of the people was willing and compliant to follow his Law and walk in his way of life or if it would rebel to walk after its own desires.[118] Likewise, YHWH sought to know Abraham's heart: to know if he would sacrifice the one person his heart loved most and on whom all of YHWH's covenants had depended.[119]

Remember that the *Circumcision Covenant* had been pledged *specifically to Isaac* before his birth (Gen 17:19, 21), yet now YHWH was asking Abraham to destroy the very person to whom all his blessings were bequeathed. Previously, YHWH had provided a sign in the *Promised-Land Covenant* by passing through the divided sacrifice and signaling his own fate should he renege on his treaty with Abram.[120] With the *Circumcision Covenant* YHWH had provided a sign by changing Abraham and Sarah's names while Abraham and Sarah provided a sign of compliance by circumcising their son. Now YHWH asks that Abraham enter into a self-imprecating treaty as YHWH had done in the *Promised-Land Covenant.*

> And Abraham rose up early in the morning, and saddled his ass, and took two of his young men with him, and Isaac his son, and split the wood for the burnt offering, and rose up, and went to the place of which God had told him. . . . And Isaac spoke to Abraham his father, and said, My father: and he said, Here am I, my son. And he said, Behold the fire and the wood: but where is the lamb for a burnt offering? And Abraham said, *My son, God will provide himself a lamb for a burnt offering*: so they went both of them together. (Gen 22:3, 7–8)

Abraham did not hesitate to obey YHWH's request. As a prophet (Gen 20:7) who understood YHWH's way of life, he knew YHWH did not sanction human sacrifice.[121] But even more importantly, *Abraham knew that YHWH could not violate the previous treaties.* If he did, then God would also face the death penalty for his sin. Abraham was quite confident that YHWH would not change or rescind his previously contracted blessings. Therefore, Abraham could confidently tell Isaac that YHWH would provide an animal for this covenantal sacrifice.

> And they came to the place which God had told him of; and Abraham built an altar there, and laid the wood in order, and bound Isaac his son, and laid him on the altar on the wood. And *Abraham stretched forth his hand, and took the knife to slay his son.* And the angel of YHWH called to him out of heaven, and said, Abraham, Abraham: and he said, Here am I. And he said, Lay not your hand on the lad, neither do you any thing to him: *for now I know that you fear God, seeing you have not withheld your son, your only son from me.* And Abraham lifted up his eyes, and looked, and behold behind him a ram caught in a thicket by his horns: and Abraham went and took the ram, and offered him up for a burnt offering in the stead of his son. And Abraham called the name of that place Jehovahjireh: as it is said to this day, In the mount of YHWH it shall be seen. (Gen 22:9–14)

Abraham understood that YHWH was testing both his faith and his obedience.[122] Although he knew YHWH would not allow Isaac to be killed, he still had to prove himself obedient to YHWH's request. After Abraham offered the ram, YHWH's angel spoke to Abraham, offering the prophet the most generous covenant of all.

Blessings

And the angel of YHWH called to Abraham out of heaven the second time, And said, By myself have I sworn, said YHWH, because you have done this thing, and have not withheld your son, your only son: (a) *That in blessing I will bless you, and (b) in multiplying I will multiply your seed as the stars of the heaven, and as the sand which is on the sea shore; and (c) your seed shall possess the gate of his enemies;* (d) And in your seed shall all the nations of the earth be blessed; because you have obeyed my voice. (Gen 22:15–18)

Abraham lived in a world where treaties were usually sealed by sacrifice.[123] As we saw above, standard Hittite and Assyrian treaties were sealed or ratified by a religious ceremony that usually involved self-imprecating sacrifices.[124] When YHWH asked Abraham to sacrifice Isaac, Abraham understood the prophetic implications of this act—not for himself, but for his son, Isaac and his descendants. If YHWH had intended Abraham to be surety for his own covenant, then he would have asked Abraham to pass between the sacrifice. But he did not. YHWH asked Abraham to sacrifice Isaac, thus sealing a covenant with Abraham's offspring. **Abraham provided the sign for the burnt offering in his firstborn son.**[125] It may be remembered that covenant sacrifices always depicted the fate of the covenantee who violated the terms of contract. As long as his children remained faithful and obedient to Abraham's covenants, then God would bless them and "it would go well with them" (Gen 18:19; 26:5; Deut 4:40; 5:16; 12:25, 28; 19:13). **If they rebelled against his covenants however, their lives would be consumed in YHWH's sacrificial holocaust.**[126] Further, YHWH commanded Abraham and Isaac to travel to Mt. Moriah to perform this symbolic holocaust. *This tied the holocaust of the Burnt-Offering Covenant to Jerusalem (Mt. Moriah, 2 Chr 3:1) if Isaac's children rebelled and breached YHWH's covenants.*

YHWH rewarded Abraham's willingness to offer a prophetic holocaust from among his future progeny and his obedience to comply with YHWH's test by extending a covenant

Table 3.9. Burnt-Offering Parity Covenant (Genesis 22)

Preamble or Title	22:1	God has previously talked to Abraham
Historical Prologue	22:1	After these things, God tempts Abraham
Stipulations	22:2	Take your "only" son and sacrifice him
	22:2 (2 Chr 3:1)	Sacrifice at Mt. Moriah (later known as Jerusalem)
Witnesses	22:9–11	God, Abraham, Isaac
Oath	22:2, 6–10	Sealed by Abraham's self-imprecating sacrifice of his "only" son
Blessings	22:17–18	Blessings upon blessings
	22:17	More Blessings of children
	22:17	Will possess or own enemies' strategic "gates"
	22:18	*The blessing:* Isaac's children will be world leaders/ rulers
Penalty for breach	22:2, 6–10, 16	Self-imprecating: Sacrifice of Abraham's children for breach
Sign (Israel)	22:3, 16	Abraham's obedience to God's voice

more generous than any before. In YHWH's previous covenants, YHWH had given Shem's birthright to Abram (see Table 3.6, p. 92). With the Burnt-Offering Covenant, YHWH gives the (d) blessing of world leadership. The Creator continues to reaffirm his (b) blessing of prolific offspring. His promise magnified (a) all of Abraham's previous blessings so that they would compound and "increase exceedingly." Fulfillment of this prophecy is partly evidenced in Balaam's refusal to curse Israel (Numbers 24) because Balaam knew that YHWH had already blessed the nation. Therefore, Balaam blessed Israel on *every* side! The Circumcision Covenant guaranteed the multitude of children, numerous nations, and great kings who would arise out of Abraham's lineage. The Burnt-Offering Covenant added to this promise (c) by giving Abraham's children the power to possess or "own" the strategic, commercial, and maritime entrances to their enemy's lands. Israel's ability to own her enemy's strategic and economic "gates" further indicated that Abraham's children would exhibit military strength and enjoy great economic prosperity.

YHWH also promised Abraham that (d) through his many offspring *all* the nations of the earth would be blessed. This implies that there is a special blessing associated with the Burnt-Offering Covenant (see Table 3.9). Before his death, Jacob described how this covenant would be divided among the twelve tribes of Israel in *later days* (Gen 49:1). We will examine this prophecy when we analyze Jacob's divided blessings in the next chapter.

VI. THE ISAAIC COVENANT

And God heard their groaning, and God remembered *his covenant* with Abraham, *with Isaac, and with Jacob.* (Exod 2:24)

I found the above text interesting since it states that YHWH secured covenants with both Isaac and Jacob. In order to trace these covenants through time, I recognized that this investigation must continue by discovering the pledges that were spoken to these two patriarchs so that the contractual basis for these compacts can be understood or quantified.

I discovered evidence of the Isaaic Covenant in Genesis 26 with the initial time that YHWH's angel appeared to Isaac.

> And YHWH appeared to him, and said, Go not down into (a) Egypt; dwell in the land which I shall tell you of: Sojourn in this land, and I will be with you, and will bless you; for to you, and to your seed, (b) I will give all these countries, and I will (c) perform the oath which I swore to Abraham your father; And (d) I will make your seed to multiply as the stars of heaven, and will give to your seed (b) all these countries; and in your seed shall all the nations of the earth be blessed; (e) *Because that Abraham obeyed my voice, and kept my charge, my commandments, my statutes, and my laws.* And Isaac dwelled in Gerar. (Gen 26:2–6)

Isaac inherited blessings that stemmed from his father's (e) obedience.[127] Isaac's nonarbitrary inheritance of Abraham's blessings demonstrates God's faithfulness to which Moses spoke of: "the faithful God, which keeps covenant and mercy with them that love him and keep his commandments to a thousand generations" (Deut 7:9).[128] YHWH's faithfulness to Abraham is demonstrated by his reaffirmation of his covenant with Isaac, who also loved YHWH and kept his commandments.

YHWH again reaffirms the (d) *Circumcision Covenant*, promising many children, as well as the blessings for providing the prophesied burnt offering in his offspring. YHWH would exceedingly bless Isaac's children. Through Isaac's many descendants and their leadership, the patriarchal blessings would flow to the rest of the world. During Abraham's life, YHWH had blessed his friend in all things (Gen 24:1). Scripture reveals that Isaac inherited this blessing when he had "sowed in the land, and *received in the same year a hundredfold*: and YHWH blessed him" (Gen 26:12).[129] YHWH's blessings made Isaac very wealthy and powerful—so powerful that King Abimelech and his allies sought to solidify a peace treaty with Isaac (Gen 26:28–31). For Isaac's mere presence to have necessitated such an alliance, YHWH must have granted him a powerful and wealthy household.[130]

So far, I found that YHWH's words continue to be constant and unchanging. He reiterates the (c) Abrahamic promises that Isaac has inherited while reaffirming (b) the Promised-Land Covenant. He also specifies a requirement for Isaac's covenant. YHWH stipulates that Isaac must (a) not go down to Egypt but must stay in the land of Canaan, since the Creator saw that it was not yet time to fulfill the Promised-Land Covenant's 430-year prophecy. This is the only added stipulation to the patriarchal covenants. This stipulation would not be inherited by Isaac's children but would be totally fulfilled by Isaac's compliance with YHWH's request to stay in Canaan. The only sign that Isaac could offer for compliance with this treaty was his obedience, so he stayed in Gerar. But where was the customary and rightful sign that YHWH should have offered to secure this treaty?

VII. IN THE NAME OF ISAAC

Before I could investigate the Isaaic covenant any further, I needed to better understand two ordinances within Israel's Law that dictated how covenants were inherited: the birthright and the blessing.

Birthright: A Hebrew birthright is *"a right, privilege, or possession to which a person is entitled by birth."*[131] More specifically, the birthright entitled the eldest son to a "double portion" of the family estate (Deut 21:15–17). This was usually inherited by the firstborn.[132] When a prince inherited his father's kingdom, for instance, he was customarily the firstborn son (2 Chr 21:3). If he did not want the responsibilities associated with the role, or if circumstances necessitate a sellout, as in the case of Esau (Gen 25:32–34),[133] he was free to sell his birthright to another brother, *whose eligible offspring* would then fulfill this family office.[134]

A birthright also indicated the order in which sons inherit. When Joseph's brothers went to buy food in Egypt, he seated them in order of their birthright (Gen 43:33). If, however, a son proved himself unworthy, the father could revoke the son's birthright (Gen 48:13–20; 48:22; 49:3; 1 Chr 26:10). A Scriptural birthright specifically referred to the double portion of the family estate that was normally bequeathed to the firstborn.

The Hebrew custom of inheritance, called primogeniture, differed from other inheritance laws of their day. Hammurabi's Code (§§168–70, *ANET*, 173), Middle Assyrian Law (*ANET*, 185) and the Hurrian Nuzi texts (*ANET*, 220) all attest laws of primogeniture. Both the Code of Hammurabi and the Hurrian texts supported the firstborn heir's receiving a preferential portion. This is in contrast to the Lipit-Ishtar Code (*c.* 1934–1924 BCE) in which all sons inherited equally (§24; *ANET*, 160). The Israelite Law, however, differed from Hammurabi and the Middle Assyrian laws in three respects. First, it disallowed preferential treatment (Deut 21:15) based on a mother's or son's closer relationship to the father in polygamous households. Although the father could choose another son to have the birthright, his choice was to be dictated by his son's righteousness or lack of it (Gen 48:13–20; 49:3; 1 Chr 26:10). Second, the Israelite Law upheld the first wife's position as the lawful wife. *Thus the rights of the first wife and her son's right to inherit superseded the rights of a concubine or slave* (Gen 21:10). Third, unlike Mesopotamian law codes, Scripture allowed daughters to inherit their father's estate when no legitimate sons existed (Numbers 36).

Although some Scripture reference works[135] imply that the birthright and blessing were synonymous, I discovered that this was not the case. Both the birthright and blessing were the firstborn's "right or privilege," but they were not the same institution. If both had been the same, Isaac would not have planned to bestow the family blessing on Esau after Esau had already sold the birthright to Jacob.

Blessing: A Scriptural blessing "conferred prosperity or happiness upon: it protected, and preserved."[136] *A Scriptural blessing prophesied prosperity for a son or daughter's descendants.*[137] *In addition to physical blessings,* it bestowed family leadership or kingship.[138] This can be seen in Isaac's blessing, in which he conferred the blessing of leadership on Jacob: "Let people serve you, and nations bow down to you: be lord over your brothers, and let your mother's sons bow down to you" (Gen 27:29).[139] The physical blessings of economic prosperity and of a fertile land filled with natural resources provided the ability to lead and shepherd the nation effectively.

While blessings indicated prosperity and leadership, curses indicated poverty, hardship, distress, and oppression. In some cases, I discovered that the words or actions of a son or daughter dishonored the parents, and a blessing was withheld. If the dishonor was grave, as in Ham's case, a curse was issued instead of a blessing (Gen 9:25; 12:27; 27:37–40; 49:7).[140] *A curse was a negative prophecy against a person and his or her posterity.*[141] An example of this was Joshua's statement, "Cursed be the man before YHWH that rises up and builds this city Jericho: he shall lay the foundation of it in his firstborn, and in his youngest son shall he set up the gates of it" (Josh 6:26). This curse was fulfilled during the Divided Kingdom Era under Ahab: "In his days did Hiel the Bethelite build Jericho: he laid the foundation of it in Abiram his firstborn, and set up the gates of it in his youngest son Segub, according to the word of YHWH, which he spoke by Joshua the son of Nun" (1 Kgs 16:34). With an understanding of the birthright and blessing, we can grasp Isaac's promised blessing accurately.

YHWH had established many specific promises for Isaac before he was conceived. One of these prebirth blessings ordained his name:

> And God said, Sarah your wife shall bear you a son indeed; and *you shall call his name Isaac*: and I will establish my covenant with him for an everlasting covenant and with his seed after him (Gen 17:19).

Both Sarah and Abraham had laughed when YHWH told them Sarah would have a son; hence the irony of Isaac's name's meaning laughter (Gen 17:17; 18:12).[142] Isaac's name was a *memorial* to the belief that something impossible can be possible with YHWH. It would be a few years later, however, on the day of his weaning that Isaac's prophesied blessing would be given.

At Isaac's weaning celebration, Ishmael mocked his father's new heir. Sarah asked her husband to cast out the "son of the bondwoman." This request, though righteous, seemed quite harsh to Abraham. YHWH confirmed Sarah's judgment and offered comforting words, promising Abraham: "*in Isaac shall your seed be called*" (Gen 21:12). Qara', Hebrew for "called,"[143] is the same term used in Gen 1:5–10 to indicate the names that YHWH gave to parts of his creation. Adam used *qara'* when he called his wife "Eve." And the term is used throughout Scripture in the naming of the patriarch's sons (Gen 25:25–26), the naming of towns (Gen 19:22), or the naming of wells (Gen 26:18). Thus, YHWH promised Abraham that Isaac's children, the nation-heir to his covenants, would be named after Isaac.

When YHWH ratified Isaac's covenants, he stipulated that Isaac should not go down to Egypt, promising that: "in Isaac's seed shall all the nations of the earth be blessed" (Gen 26:4). Remember that a covenant requires a sign or seal. YHWH did not offer a sign when his angel appeared to Isaac, either at Gerar or at Beersheba (Gen 26:2–6, 23, 24). Why not? Can a covenant be valid without a sign? Did scribes simply forget to include this information? Or is possible that YHWH's promise to Abraham failed? Furthermore, the changing

Table 3.10. Isaaic Parity Covenants (Genesis 26)

Preamble or Title		26:2	YHWH appears to Isaac
Historical Prologue		26:5	Abraham had obeyed and walked perfectly with YHWH. Abraham had obeyed YHWH's voice, kept his charge, commandments, statutes, and laws.
Stipulations		26:2	Do not migrate to Egypt, stay in Promised Land
Witnesses		26:2	God, Isaac
Oath		22:2, 6–10	Isaac had already sealed by self-imprecating sacrifice at Mt. Moriah
Promises for Compliance		26:3	*Confirms birthright:* Gives Canaanite nations to Isaac's offspring
		26:3	YHWH will be with Isaac
		26:3–4	YHWH will bless Isaac
		26:4	Blesses offspring with numerous populations for a fourth time
		26:4	*Confirms blessing:* nations blessed by the leadership of Isaac's descendants
Penalty for Breach		26:3–4	Loses added blessings, which render a double fold blessing
Sign	(Isaac)	26:6	Isaac obeys
	(YHWH)	21:12	Isaac's children will be called by Isaac's name

of Abram's and Sarai's names had been paramount as "signs" in their covenants, so what about a sign for Isaac?

When YHWH confirmed the *Jacobic Covenant* with Isaac's son, YHWH's messenger changed Jacob's name, which meant supplanter (Gen 27:36),[144] to Israel (**Yisra'el**) meaning, 'he will rule as Elohiym' or 'prevailing with Elohiym' (Hos 12:3–5).[145] *Jacob's new name derived from his father's name—Isaac.* Abraham's seed was called by the name of **Is**aac by being named "**Is**rael." The later Jacobic Covenant fulfilled the promise to Abraham that "in Isaac shall your seed be named" (Gen 21:12). At the time that YHWH confirmed his covenant with Jacob, Isaac was still alive[146] and received the sign of this covenant through the changing of his son's name. Thus, Isaac's covenant continues to follow the concepts of constancy by fulfilling the words previously stated by YHWH with a future generation.

The second time the angel appeared to Isaac, he reestablished all subsequent covenants and promises.

> And he went up from there to Beersheba. And YHWH appeared to him the same night, and said, I am the God of Abraham your father: fear not, for I am with you, and will bless you, and multiply your seed *for my servant Abraham's sake*. And he built an altar there, and called on the name of YHWH and pitched his tent there. (Gen 26:23–25)

The second time YHWH's angel appeared to Isaac, he did not require anything additional from Isaac. Rather, YHWH simply reaffirmed his covenants with Isaac for "Abraham's sake." Thus, Abraham's covenants were granted to Isaac as gift or grant. Remember that, when we first examined Noah's and Abraham's covenants, we saw that they were sealed with sacrifices. Isaac's covenant consistently employs this practice, once again signaling his commitment to keep YHWH's covenants through self-imprecation: Isaac signals his and his offspring's fate should they breach their contract with YHWH (see Table 3.10).

VIII. JACOBIC COVENANTS

A. *Jacob's Struggle for Righteousness*

As we have seen so far, YHWH consistently maintained the concepts and stipulations of one covenant by reaffirming it in subsequent covenants. For instance, YHWH stated that the penalty for murder would be a life for a life in Noah's Covenant. "Whoever sheds man's blood, by man shall his blood be shed" (Gen 9:6). The Israelite Law built on this concept by stipulating penalties for injuries caused to others. "And if any mischief follow, then you shall give *life for life*, eye for eye, tooth for tooth, hand for hand, foot for foot, burning for burning, wound for wound, stripe for stripe" (Exod 21:23–25). The Law is consistent by upholding the philosophy that underlies the penalty of Noah's Covenant: "As you do to others so shall it be done to you, so treat others as you would have them treat you" (Lev 19:18, paraphrased).

King David continues to certify this precept, stating,

> With the merciful you will show yourself merciful; with an upright man you will show yourself upright; with the pure you will show yourself pure; and with the fraudulent you will show yourself devious. (Ps 18:25–26; see also 2 Sam 22:25–33)

As humanity's judge, YHWH requites a person's way back onto his own head, and Jacob's life is a prime example.

It took Jacob time to learn how to walk in *the way* of Isaac and Abraham. At Jacob's birth, YHWH had told Rebekah that Jacob would supplant his brother (Gen 25:23). He grew up knowing he would receive his brother's legitimate blessing and inheritance. His pride swelled, and he set about establishing these blessings himself, rather than waiting for God to establish them for him. Jacob insisted on buying Esau's birthright when his brother was at the point of starvation (Gen 25:30). This was hardly an act of mercy. He later deceived his father (Gen 27:11–29), so he could obtain his brother's blessing; this was not an act of honor or respect. Jacob's struggle to learn how to live in *the way* of YHWH marked his life. Although he received the blessings of prosperity (wealth) and offspring, unlike his fathers who lived righteously, his life met with crises and conflict. The way that Jacob lived in his younger years was reciprocated onto his own head throughout his life. As he had deceived his father, so was he deceived into marrying another woman, Rachel's older sister Leah.[147] During the two terms he served under Laban, his wages were constantly altered. Yet, it was during this trying time that Jacob finally began to understand *how* to walk in the way of his righteous fathers. When he returned to his promised inheritance, he met his brother with humility and graciousness,[148] subsequently restoring peace to their family. These aspects of Jacob's life as well as the fundamental precept of equity found in Noah's Covenant are reflected throughout Jacob's covenants (see Table 3.11).

Table 3.11. Jacobic Covenants

Diaspora Covenant	Prevailing Covenant	Covenant of Hope
Genesis 28:10–16	Genesis 34	Genesis 46:1–4

B. *Diaspora Covenant*

As Jacob was fleeing from Esau, YHWH offered his first covenant with Abraham's younger supplanter-heir. The promises made to Jacob on his journey to Padanaram occurred before he departed from his birthright possession.

> And Jacob went out from Beersheba, and went toward Haran. And he lighted on a certain place, and tarried there all night, because the sun was set; and he took of the stones of that place, and put them for his pillows, and lay down in that place to sleep. (a) And he dreamed, and behold a ladder set up on the earth, and the top of it reached to heaven: and behold the angels of God ascending and descending on it. And, behold, YHWH stood above it, and said, I am YHWH God of Abraham your father, and the God of Isaac: (b) the land where you lie, to you will I give it, and to your seed; (c) And your seed shall be as the dust of the earth, and (d) *you shall spread abroad to the west, and to the east, and to the north, and to the south: (e) and in you and in your seed shall all the families of the earth be blessed.* (f) And, behold, I am with you, and will keep you in all places where you go, and will bring you again into this land; for I will not leave you, until I have done that which I have spoken to you of. And Jacob awaked out of his sleep, and he said, Surely YHWH is in this place; and I knew it not. And he was afraid, and said, How dreadful is this place! This is none other but the House of God, and this is the gate of heaven. And Jacob rose up early in the morning, and took the stone that he had put for his pillows, and (g) set it up for a pillar, and poured oil upon the top of it. (Gen 28:10–18)

Much as in Isaac's covenants, YHWH does not request any additional requirements from Jacob other than obeying the conditions of Abraham's previous covenants (such as circumcision). YHWH simply and faithfully reissues Abraham's covenants. He does, however, augment the blessing with additional features for later fulfillment which reflect the history of Jacob's life. Previously, Isaac had sent Jacob to Laban in search of a wife (Gen 28:1–10). Since Jacob obeyed his father's instruction (Gen 28:7), YHWH may have viewed Isaac's command as representing his own. Thus, he extended the Abrahamic covenants to Jacob not only because of Isaac's blessing, but also because of Jacob's obedience to his father.

What sign did YHWH provide for Jacob's Covenant? It was the dream (a) of a ladder ascending to YHWH. The Creator reaffirmed the (b) Promised-Land Covenant and (c) the Circumcision Covenant's blessings. However, YHWH adds another factor to Jacob's covenant, which *precedes* ALL nations of the earth being blessed by Jacob's seed (in other words, before the blessings of the Burnt-Offering Covenant are fulfilled). **Before this blessing reaches its acme, Jacob's seed (d) will be scattered abroad to the four corners of the earth.** After this scattering has occurred, *all* nations (including Ham's descendants) will become (e) blessed through his offspring. YHWH grants an additional promise stating that he will not leave (f) Jacob (or his seed) until he has performed *all* he has promised. This statement indicates YHWH's constancy and fidelity regarding the word he has given to Jacob's progeny. As our examination turns to prophecy when we examine the Prophetic Law, it will be shown that all Israel's prophecies adhere to the basic structure outlined in Jacob's Diaspora Covenant.

As we have seen, covenants are often sealed with sacrifices. Jacob did not offer a sacrifice (because he was traveling and probably had none to offer). Rather, Jacob anointed a pillar. This was (g) symbolic of his children's anointing YHWH as their God and walking in his way *alone*. As a covenant's prophetic sign, Jacob's action indicated that YHWH would pour his anointing spirit on Jacob's children when they learned to walk in the way of YHWH. The fulfillment of the Diaspora Covenant would coincide with the outpouring of YHWH's spirit on Jacob's heirs and their subsequent reestablishment in the Promised Land.[149] These two events will be hallmarks of the pledge of the Burnt-Offering Covenant as Israel finally learns how to become a blessing to all nations (see Table 3.12).

The prophet Ezekiel built on the chronology set forth in the Diaspora Covenant when he prophecied that YHWH's spirit will be poured out on the House of Israel when the Diaspora is brought to an end:

> When I have brought them again from the people, and gathered them out of their enemies' lands, and am sanctified in them in the sight of many nations; Then shall they know that I am YHWH their God, which caused them to be led into captivity among the heathen: but I have gathered them unto their own land, and have left none of them any more there. Neither will I hide my face any more from them: for I have poured out my spirit on the house of Israel, says adonai YHWH. (Ezek 39:27–29)

C. Diaspora Covenant Engaged

Jacob's Diaspora Covenant had been a story that I had read my entire life; yet I had never really *read* it for what it meant. Seeing this covenant in the light of ancient Near Eastern treaties brought it to life. I also came to realize that YHWH understood that Israel needed to prove to herself whether or not his way of life worked. He therefore established penalties

Table 3.12. Diaspora Covenant (Genesis 28)

Preamble or Title	28:13	I am the God of Abraham your father and the God of Isaac
Historical Prologue	28:13	Mentions previous relationships with kindred
	28:13	*Confirms Birthright:* Jacob's seed will inherit Promised Land
	28:14	Blesses Jacob with many children
	28:15	Will be with Jacob; protect him until he has fulfilled all his covenants
Stipulations *(Jacob)*	28:14	*Injunction on the Blessing:* children/descendants will be scattered to the east, north, and south—across the face of the earth
	(Gen 18:19, implied)	Obey previous covenants' stipulations
(YHWH)	28:15	Stay with Jacob's offspring until he has fulfilled all covenants
Witnesses	28:12–13	God and Jacob
Oath	15:9–11, 17	Sealed by God's promise and his previous self-imprecating oath
Promises for Compliance	15:13–15	Confirms the blessings
Penalty for Breach		None—only penalties of previous covenants apply
Sign *(YHWH)*	28:12	Dream of ladder reaching heaven
(Jacob)	28:18	Anoints pillar with oil

if Abraham's children breached his covenants so that they would learn from their mistakes. YHWH's method for dealing with rebellion was (consistently) to exile individuals from their homeland. When Adam and Eve sinned, they were cast out of the land of Eden. Likewise, when the Amorites or Israelites sinned, they too were cast out of their homelands (Gen 15:16; Num 33:53–54).

In the opening section of chap. 3 (3.I), we discovered that Israel's ability to receive her forefathers' blessings was predicated on her obedience to *the way* of YHWH. After Jacob's children inherited the Promised Land, they violated every covenant YHWH had bestowed on their forefathers, including the covenant contracted at Mt. Sinai. Therefore, YHWH banished them just as he had Adam and Eve. The Book of 2 Kings states that YHWH caused Nebuchadnezzar to deport the people who remained in the country.

And he carried away all Jerusalem, and all the princes, and all the mighty men of valor, even ten thousand captives, and all the craftsmen and smiths: *none remained, save the poorest sort of the people of the land.* (2 Kgs 24:14)

Those not deported to eastern territories migrated to Egypt. (Jer 42:1–22)

During Cyrus's reign and Persia's glory years, only a small percentage of the nation returned to the Promised Land at Cyrus's decree (Ezra 2:1–70; Neh 7:6–73). Throughout the Second Temple Era, many families who had returned migrated to ethnic strongholds in Alexandria (Egypt) or Argos and Corinth (Greece).[150] In 70 CE, Titus obliterated Jerusalem. He destroyed Herod's Temple and razed Jerusalem's walls. In 132 CE, Julius Severus again raised the city, excommunicating individuals of Judean descent. He ordered Roman soldiers as well as Syrian and Greek civilians to be brought to live in the desolate city.[151] For over 500 years, the seed of Jacob was cast out of Judea and Jerusalem time and time again, so that only a minuscule number of Jews remained, while the House of Israel was left in complete Diaspora.[152] If the test of truth is "the state of being fact," then truly Israel has been sent into Diaspora and exiled from the Promised Land, as YHWH foretold in Jacob's Diaspora Covenant.

Is it possible to demonstrate that the Jacobic prophecy issued well over 4,500 years ago should be nearing fulfillment in these latter days? At present, the descendants of the Northern Kingdom of Israel and the Southern Kingdom of Judah are scattered to the west, east, north, and south—across the whole face of the earth. If the test of truth is consistency, then the Diaspora prophecy has been partially fulfilled, and its later blessing is a waiting completion. I wondered: Did Israel's prophets uphold the *Jacobic Covenant* by prophesying that the 12 tribes will return to the Promised Land in the latter days? Is their word consistent with the Diaspora Covenant? Do the prophets continue to uphold YHWH's truth? This is the evidence that I discovered from the *Law of Moses* and from the prophets.

Thus said YHWH, your redeemer, the Holy One of Israel; For your sake I have sent to Babylon, and have brought down all their nobles, and the Chaldeans, whose cry is in the ships. . . . Since you were precious in my sight, you have been honorable, and I have loved you: therefore will I give men for you, and people for your life. Fear not: for I am with you: *I will bring your seed from the east, and gather you from the west; I will say to the north, Give up; and to the south, Keep not back: bring my sons from far, and my daughters from the ends of the earth; Even every one that is called by my name*: for I have created him for my glory, I have formed him; yes, I have made him. Bring forth the blind people that have eyes, and the deaf that have ears. Let all the nations be gathered together, and let the people be assembled: who among them can declare this, and show us former things? Let them bring forth their witnesses, that they may be justified: or let them hear, and say, *It is truth.* You are my witnesses, said YHWH, and my servant whom I have chosen: that you may know and believe me, and understand that I am he: before me there was no God formed, neither shall there be after me. I, even I, am YHWH; and beside me there is no savior. I have declared, and have saved, and I have showed, when there was no strange god among you: therefore you are my witnesses, said YHWH, that I am God. Yes, before the day was I am he; and there is none that can deliver out of my hand: I will work, and who shall stop it? (Isa 43:14, 4–13)

For thus said YHWH: Sing with gladness for Jacob, and shout among the chief of the nations: publish you, praise you, and say, O YHWH, save your people, the remnant of Israel. Behold, I will *bring them from the north country*, and *gather them from the coasts of the earth*, and with them the blind and the lame, the woman with child and her that travails with child together: *a great company shall return there*. They shall come with weeping, and with supplications will I lead them: I will cause them to walk by the rivers of waters in a straight way, wherein they shall not stumble: for I am a father to Israel, and Ephraim is my firstborn. Hear the word of YHWH, O you nations, and declare it in the isles afar off, and say, *He that scattered Israel will gather him*, and keep him, as a shepherd does his flock. For YHWH has redeemed Jacob, and ransomed him from the hand of him that was stronger than he. Therefore *they shall come* and sing in the height of Zion, and shall flow together to the goodness of YHWH, for wheat, and for wine, and for oil, and for the young of the flock and of the herd: and their soul shall be as a watered garden; and they shall not sorrow any more at all. (Jer 31:7–12)

And I will *scatter you among the heathen*, and will draw out a sword after you: and your land shall be desolate, and your cities waste. . . . And **yet for all that, when they be in the land of their enemies, I will not cast them away,** neither will I abhor them, to destroy them utterly, and *to break my covenant with them: for I am YHWH their God.* But I will *for their sakes remember the covenant of their ancestors*, whom I brought forth out of the land of Egypt in the sight of the heathen, that I might be their God: I am YHWH. (Lev 26:33, 44–45; see also Gen 17:7 and Hos 9:17)

And [you] shall return to YHWH your God, and *shall obey* his voice according to all that I command you this day, you and your children, with all your heart, and with all your soul; That then YHWH your God will *turn your captivity*, and have compassion upon you, and will return and *gather you from all the nations, where YHWH your God has scattered you.* If any of yours be driven out to the outmost parts of heaven, from there will YHWH God gather you, and from there will he fetch you: And YHWH your God will *bring you into the land which your fathers possessed*, and you shall possess it; and he will do you good, and multiply you above your fathers. And YHWH your God will circumcise your heart, and the heart of your seed, to love YHWH your God with all your heart, and with all your soul, that you may live. (Deut 30:2–6, brackets added)

And *he remembered for them his covenant*, and repented according to the multitude of his mercies. He made them also to be pitied of all those that carried them captives. Save us, O YHWH our God, and *gather us from among the heathen*, to give thanks to your holy name, and to triumph in your praise. Blessed be YHWH God of Israel from everlasting to everlasting: and let all the people say, Amen. Praise you YHWH. (Ps 106:45–48)

For, see, I will command, and I will *sift the House of Israel among all nations*, like as corn is sifted in a sieve, yet shall not the least grain fall on the earth. All the sinners of my people shall die by the sword, which say, The evil shall not overtake nor prevent us. In that day will I raise up the tabernacle of David that is fallen, and close up the breaches of it; and I will raise up his ruins, and I will build it as in the days of old: That they may possess the remnant of Edom, and of all the heathen, which are called by my name, said YHWH that does this. Behold, the days come, said YHWH, that the plowman shall overtake the reaper, and the treader of grapes him that sows seed; and the mountains shall drop sweet wine, and all the hills shall melt. *And I will bring again the captivity of my people of Israel*, and they shall build the waste cities, and inhabit them; and they shall plant vineyards, and drink the wine of it; they shall also make gardens, and eat the fruit of them. *And I will plant them on their land, and they shall NO MORE be pulled up out of their land which I have given them, said YHWH your God.* (Amos 9:9–15, emphasis added.)

This prophecy could not have been fulfilled during the Second Temple Era. Amos says that the setting for this prophecy results in Israel's never again being cast out of the land. After a small remnant returned to Jerusalem during Nehemiah's days, however, Judea was again invaded and cast off the land. After Rome's invasion, Judea lost her independence. Both Titus and Rome again cast the few remaining Israelites out of Jerusalem and Judea when Rome destroyed Herod's Temple. Subsequent conquests excommunicated those of Judean lineage, banishing them from the residue of the land promised to Jacob's seed (see discussion on pp. 110).

Therefore say, Thus said the Lord YHWH; *I will even gather you from the people, and assemble you out of the countries where you have been scattered*, and I will give you the land of Israel. And they shall come here, and they shall take away all the detestable things of it and all the abominations of it from here. And I will give them one heart, and *I will put a new spirit within you*; and I will take the stony heart out of their flesh, and will give them an heart of flesh: (Ezek 11:17–19)

Notice the correlation between Israel's being brought back to the land—the end of the Diaspora—and YHWH's anointing the remnant with his spirit. When Jacob anointed the pillar with oil to seal his end of the Diaspora Covenant, his actions prophesied of the day when the Diaspora will be completed and YHWH will anoint his people with his spirit. Ezekiel's prophecy is consistent with the Diaspora Covenant.

For I will take you from among the heathen, and *gather you out of all countries*, and will bring you into your own land. Then will I sprinkle clean water on you, and you shall be clean: from all your filthiness, and from all your idols, will I cleanse you. *A new heart also will I give you, and a new spirit will I put within you*: and I will take away the stony heart out of your flesh, and I will give you an heart of flesh. *And I will put my spirit within you*, and cause you to walk in my statutes, and you shall keep my judgments, and do them. And you shall dwell in the land that I gave to your fathers; and you shall be my people, and I will be your God. (Ezek 36:24–28)

When I have brought them again from the people, and gathered them out of their enemies' lands, and am sanctified in them in the sight of many nations; Then shall they know that I am YHWH their God, which caused them to be led into captivity among the heathen: *but I have gathered them to their own land, and have left none of them any more there. Neither will I hide my face any more from them: for I have poured out my spirit upon the House of Israel,* says the Lord YHWH. (Ezek 39:27–29)

As a shepherd seeks out his flock in the day that he is among his *sheep that are scattered*; so will I seek out my sheep, and will deliver them out of all PLACES where they have been scattered in the cloudy and dark day. And I will bring them out from the people, and *gather them from the countries*, and *will bring them to their own LAND*, and feed them on the *mountains of Israel* by the rivers, and in all the inhabited places of the *country*. I will feed them in a good pasture, and on the high mountains of Israel shall their fold be: there shall they lie in a good fold, and in a fat pasture shall they feed on the mountains of Israel. I will feed my flock, and I will cause them to lie down, says YHWH Elohiym. I will seek that which was lost, and bring again that which was driven away, and will bind up that which was broken, and will strengthen that which was sick: but I will destroy the fat and the strong; I will feed them with judgment. (Ezek 34:12–16)

Therefore say to the House of Israel, Thus said YHWH Elohiym; I do not this for your sakes, O House of Israel, but for my holy name's sake, which you have profaned among the heathen, where you went. And I will sanctify my great name, which was profaned among the heathen, which you have profaned in the middle of them; and the heathen shall know that I am YHWH, says YHWH Elohiym, when I shall be sanctified in you *before their eyes*. For I will take you from among the heathen, *and gather you out of all countries, and will bring you into your own land*. (Ezek 36:22–24)

Arise, shine; for your light is come, and the glory of YHWH is risen on you. . . . Lift up your eyes round about, and see: all they gather themselves together, *they come to you: your sons shall come from far, . . . to bring your sons from far*, their silver and their gold with them, to the name of YHWH your God, and to the Holy One of Israel, because he has glorified you. For *the nation and kingdom that will not serve you shall perish*; yes, those nations shall be utterly wasted. . . . The sons also *of them that afflicted you* shall come bending to you; and all they that despised you shall bow themselves down at the soles of your feet; and they shall call you; The city of YHWH, the Zion of the Holy One of Israel. . . . You shall also suck the milk of the Gentiles, and shall suck the breast of kings: and you shall know that *I YHWH am your Savior and your Redeemer, the mighty One of Jacob. Violence shall no more be heard in your LAND, wasting nor destruction within your borders*; but you shall call your walls Salvation, and your gates Praise. The sun shall be no more your light by day; neither for brightness shall the moon give light to you: but YHWH shall be to you an everlasting light, and your God your glory. Your sun shall no more go down; neither shall your moon withdraw itself: for YHWH shall be your everlasting light, and the days of your mourning shall be ended. *Your people also shall be all righteous: they shall inherit the LAND forever*,[153] the branch of my planting, the work of my hands, that I may be glorified.[154] A little one shall become a thousand, and a small one a strong nation: I YHWH will hasten it in his time. (Isa 60:1, 4, 9, 12, 14, 16, 18–22)

You shall be named the Priests of YHWH: men shall call you the Ministers of our God: you shall eat the riches of the Gentiles, and in their glory shall you boast yourselves. For your shame you shall have double; and for confusion they shall rejoice in their portion: therefore *in their LAND they shall possess the double: everlasting joy shall be to them*. (Isa 61:6–7)

And I will gather the remnant of my flock *out of all countries where I have driven them*, and will bring them again to their folds; and they shall be fruitful and increase. And I will set up shepherds over them which shall feed them: and they shall fear no more, nor be dismayed, neither shall they be lacking, said YHWH. Behold, the days come, said YHWH, that I will raise to David a righteous branch, and a king shall reign and prosper, and shall execute judgment and justice in the earth. In his days Judah shall be saved, and Israel shall dwell safely: and this is his name whereby he shall be called, YHWH OUR RIGHTEOUSNESS. Therefore, behold, the days come, said YHWH, that they shall no more say, YHWH lives, which brought up the Children of Israel out of the land of Egypt; *But, YHWH lives, which brought up and which led the seed*

*of the House of Israel out of the north country, and from all countries where I
had driven them; and they shall dwell in their own land.* (Jer 23:3–8)

And he shall set up an ensign for the nations, and *shall assemble the outcasts
of Israel, and gather together the dispersed of Judah from the four corners of
the earth.* (Isa 11:12)

And YHWH shall *scatter you among the nations*, and you shall be left few in
number among the heathen, where YHWH shall lead you. And there you shall
serve gods, the work of men's hands, wood and stone, which neither see, nor
hear, nor eat, nor smell. *But if from there you shall seek YHWH your God,
you shall find him,* if you seek him with all your heart and with all your soul.
When you are in tribulation, and all these things are come on you, even in the
latter days, if you turn to YHWH your God, and shall be obedient to his voice;
(For YHWH your God is a merciful God;) *he will not forsake you*, neither
destroy you, *nor forget the covenant of your fathers which he swore to them.*
(Deut 4:27–31)

Deut 4:31 certifies the concepts of truth and constancy. If YHWH is to be vindicated as
righteous in these latter days, then according to the concepts of truth, the evidence must
show that God is faithful and does "not forget the covenant of Israel's forefathers which he
swore to them" (last quotation above). If YHWH were to forget, fail to uphold, or rescind his
enduring promises to Abraham's progeny then he could not be vindicated as a God of truth
in this trial. Therefore, YHWH must have a valid reason for not yet fulfilling the Diaspora
Covenant; otherwise his word has failed.

Granted, Israel's rebellion is no doubt one reason that YHWH has not fulfilled the
Diaspora Covenant. YHWH's promises were contingent on the nation's obedience to his
way of life (see chap. 3.I). If Israel followed YHWH's way of life, the nation would have effected her own blessings and fulfilled YHWH's promises. Likewise, rebellion against his way
resulted in failure to procure the Creator's promises. However, Israel's rebellion against the
way of YHWH in no way implies that the Creator's promises were made void or rescinded
(Lev 26:45–46; Deut 4:31). Rather, *if* the Creator is to be deemed righteous and true, he must
wait until the nation or her descendants become willing to walk in his way, then offer his
covenants to them.[155] Many believers today desire to do what is right in God's sight, so the
question remains: Why has this salvation languished?

For now, I will leave this question open-ended as we to continue to define the truth
established in the Creator's initial covenants. We will see whether the Hebrew Scriptures
exhibit internal consistency so they can be identified as truth, or whether they display internal contradictions that rescind (or nullify) God's words and thus should be classified as
the most incredible work of fiction. Then we will return to the question of why YHWH's
redemption has seemingly languished for 2,600 years.

D. Jacob's Ladder

The sign that YHWH gives to solidify his covenant with Jacob is a vision of angels ascending and descending a ladder leading to heaven. This vision was a prophetic promise, with each rung representing a covenant that YHWH has contracted with humanity. These covenants ascend the ladder until all the patriarchal covenants are fulfilled, causing YHWH to be known and sanctified in Israel and throughout the earth. It is with the completion of these covenants that Israel will fulfill the meaning of his name and "prevail with God."

E. Prevailing Covenant

The Prevailing Covenant departs from the standard pattern of "obedience effects blessing" that we have seen thus far. Rather, this covenant reflects a struggle to obey the stipulations ordained in previous covenants so that previously promised blessings can be inherited. The name *Jacob* means 'supplanter' (Gen 27:36). Jacob fulfilled his name by receiving Esau's birthright and his blessing and by supplanting his older brother as the firstborn and rightful heir. Jacob purchased Esau's birthright. Then he deceived Isaac into giving him Esau's blessing. Though Isaac's blessing rightfully belonged to Esau, Jacob was the person who actually received Isaac's words of blessing which, once spoken, could not be rescinded.[156] Notice, Scripture is faithful regarding not only YHWH's words but also a patriarch's words. Once the word has been spoken, it cannot return or be changed (Isa 45:23). That YHWH recognized Jacob, not Esau, as Isaac's rightful heir is reflected by the act of YHWH's messenger in changing Jacob's name to *Israel* to fulfill Isaac's blessing, rather than changing Esau's name. Although Jacob was younger, he supplanted his older brother's blessing, which could not be changed or rescinded regardless of Isaac's wishes.

1. Kingship and Priesthood

In Abraham's covenants, YHWH himself had established Isaac's patriarchal blessing. He did not do this, however, with Jacob. Isaac played the patriarchal role and established his own son's blessing, much as Noah had done for his sons. Isaac no doubt understood YHWH's plan for his family and based his son's blessing upon it. The blessing that Isaac gave Jacob further affected the parameters of YHWH's future covenants with Israel.

> Therefore God give (a) you of the dew of heaven, and the fatness of the earth, and plenty of corn and wine: Let (b) people serve you, and nations bow down to you: be lord over your brothers, and let your mother's sons bow down to you: (c) cursed be every one that curses you, and blessed be he that blesses you. (Gen 27:28–29)

Isaac's method of blessing Jacob follows the formula set forth in the Abrahamic covenants by establishing (a) material and physical blessings from the start. After these are in place, he bestows the family blessing, which allots other nations to serve Jacob's descendants. The concept of lordship (b) emphasizes the hereditary rights of government associated with the birthright and the blessing. Noah had followed a similar pattern in blessing his two sons, establishing their lordship over Ham's seed and a double portion for Shem. Isaac confers Shem's blessing and birthright upon Jacob's lineage. That non-Israelite nations would "bow down" to Jacob and his descendants (even his "mother's sons") indicates that Jacob's progeny would be powerful enough to dominate Esau's clan. That the Abrahamic-sovereignty birthright was intended for both Jacob (supplanting the firstborn) and his descendants is attested by YHWH's request for Pharaoh to let "Israel, his firstborn son," go free (Exod 4:22). Thus, the nation inherited *all* their father's blessings and covenants. Changing Jacob's name to Israel epitomized the fullest extent of Isaac's blessing, since it prophesied, "He shall prevail and rule with Elohiym."

The ability to rule as Elohiym was a basic right granted to YHWH's priests and prophets. It bestowed the authority to (c) bless or curse (Num 6:23, 27) peoples and nations. As a priest (Gen 14:18), Melchizedek was qualified to bless Abram. As a prophet (Num 23:26; 24:1–4), Balaam could bless or curse Israel. This is the reason that the Law provided a blessing for Israel's high priests to confer on the nation (Num 6:23). Noah, Abraham, Isaac, and Jacob were prophets because their words established their offspring's future. Moses, yet another prophet, issued both YHWH's blessings for Israel's future if they obeyed the covenant (Deuteronomy 33; 28:1–14; 30:1–14) and curses (Deuteronomy 32; 28:15–68; 29:18–28) should they choose to disobey. Isaac's blessing bequeathed both *YHWH's princehood and his priesthood* to Jacob's descendants (Exod 19:6).

The irony in this unusual blessing is that even if Jacob's enemies were to curse his descendants, they would effectually be cursing themselves. Their prosperity hinged upon Jacob's clan prevailing in the *way of YHWH* since YHWH had given the right of leadership to Jacob's descendants.

2. The Prevailing Covenant

The first time YHWH appears to Jacob occurs before Jacob left Canaan on his journey to Padanaram when YHWH established Jacob's Diaspora Covenant. The second time YHWH appears to Jacob occurs when he reenters his inherited land as he is about to confront his brother. Notice how this covenant seemed to epitomize Jacob's life.

> And Jacob was left alone; and there (a) wrestled a man with him until the breaking of the day. And when he saw that he prevailed not against him, (b) he touched the hollow of his thigh; and the hollow of Jacob's thigh was out of joint, as he wrestled with him. And he said, Let me go, for the day breaks. (c) And he said, I will not let you go, except you bless me. And he said to him, What is your name? And he said, Jacob. And he said, (d) *Your name shall be called no more Jacob, but Israel: for as a prince have you (e) power with God and with men, and have prevailed.* (Gen 32:24–28)

Jacob's second covenant is laden with signs. Jacob prevails with God by (a) wrestling and righteously contending with his Maker in order to receive his promised blessing. Once he prevails, (d) YHWH fulfills the Abrahamic blessing by sealing Isaac's covenant and calling Jacob by Isaac's name: *Israel*.[157]

Table 3.13. Prevailing Covenant (Genesis 32)

Preamble	32:1–2	Jacob saw an army of Elohiym
	32:9–12	Jacob calls out to God
Historical Prologue	32:3–5	Jacob had sent a peaceful delegation with gifts to his brother
	32:6	Esau was coming to meet Jacob with 400 men
	32:7–8	Jacob was afraid of his brother and divided his family
	32:9–12	Jacob prays for deliverance
	32:24	Jacob was alone
Witnesses	32:24	God's messenger and Jacob
Oath	32:26	"I will not let you go until you bless me"
Blessing	32:28	*Fulfills Isaac's Blessing:* changes Jacob's name to Yisrael
	32:28	*Jacob's Blessing:* A prince prevailing with God and man
	(48:22)	Jacob receives an "extra" blessing that is added to the birthright
Sign (YHWH)	32:24–30	Wrestles with Jacob
	32:25	Hollow of thigh—out of place (consequence of wrestling)
(Jacob)	32:28	Wrestling with God, prevails
	32:26	Will not let go until YHWH blesses him

One consequence of this match was that the (b) hollow of Jacob's thigh was put out of joint. A reminder of the consequences of living a life contrary to the way of God. This sign was later incorporated into Israel's offerings, thus signaling the prophetic implications of Israel's sacrifices.

> Therefore the Children of Israel eat not of the sinew which shrank, which is on the hollow of the thigh, to this day: because he touched the hollow of Jacob's thigh in the sinew that shrank. (Gen 32:32)

Jacob held onto the man of God, not willing to (c) release him until YHWH blessed him. Jacob prevailed in receiving YHWH's blessings because he behaved as a righteous prince who had power with Elohiym and with man.[158] The name Israel means (e) "he shall rule as El" or "having power with El."[159] That this is indeed a correct definition is explained in the Book of Hosea:

> He took his brother by the heel in the womb, and *by his strength he had power with Elohiym: Yes, he had power over the angel, and prevailed*: he wept, and made supplication to him: he found him in Bethel, and there he spoke with us; Even YHWH Elohiym of hosts; YHWH is his memorial. (Hos 12:3–5; see also Isa 60:12)

As this study continued, I wondered if I would see further aspects of Jacob's Prevailing Covenant within the nation's future treaties with God. It seemed to me that Jacob's Prevailing Covenant was perhaps the most symbolic for Israel today. As people begin to "prevail" in the way of YHWH, it should mark the end of Israel's Diaspora (see Table 3.13). If YHWH is righteous, he will fulfill the promises he ordained in Genesis, and Israel will completely inherit her ancestor's blessings. If the Creator is an unchanging God of truth who does not rescind his words, then *when* Israel becomes obedient, he must keep his promises, even if it is 1,000 generations later.[160] The Creator's eternal nature and the existence of Abraham's seed would cause these covenants to be valid still today.

F. A Covenant of Hope

The Prevailing Covenant prophesied that Jacob would master the ability to walk in the way of YHWH in order to receive his forefathers' blessings. The third time that YHWH spoke to Jacob occurred as he left the land of his his birthright to be reunited with Joseph in Egypt.

> And Israel took his journey with all that he had, and came to Beersheba, and (a) offered sacrifices to the God of his father Isaac. And God spoke to Israel in the visions of the night, and said, Jacob, Jacob. And he said, Here am I. And he said, I am God, the God of your father: (b) fear not to go down to Egypt; for (c) I will there make of you a great nation: I will go down with you into Egypt; and I will also (d) surely bring you up again: and (e) Joseph shall put his hand upon your eyes. (Gen 46:1–4)

Notice that Jacob seals his covenants with YHWH by (a) offering sacrifices, which symbolize his demise, should he or his progeny rebel against their agreement with YHWH. The Creator affirms that Israel's migration (b) to Egypt accords with his desire, as YHWH begins to fulfill the prophecy that he spoke to Abram in the Promised-Land Covenant (Gen 15:13–16). The Creator recertifies his promise of (c) numerous offspring while promising to (d) fulfill

Table 3.14. Covenant of Hope (Genesis 46)

Preamble	46:1	Jacob offers sacrifices to Isaac's God
	46:1–2	YHWH appears to Jacob as Isaac's God
Historical Prologue	45:25–28	Jacob has just learned that Joseph is alive in Egypt and wants the family to immigrate
Stipulation	46:3	Immigrate to Egypt
Blessing	46:3	Will make a great nation of Jacob while in Egypt
	46:3	YHWH will go with Jacob and his children to Egypt
	46:4	YHWH will deliver Jacob's children and bring them back to Canaan
Oath	46:4	Jacob will see his lost son, whom he believed to be dead
Sign (YHWH)	46:4, 29	Jacob sees and physically touches Joseph
(Jacob)	46:5–7	Jacob immigrates

Table 3.15. Patriarchal Covenants

Patriarch/ Matriarch	1st *Appearance*	2nd *Appearance*	3rd *Appearance*	4th *Appearance*
Noah	Before the flood, Gen 6:13	When Noah came out of the ark, Genesis 9	–	–
Abraham	Migration Covenant Gen 12:1–4	Promised-Land Covenant Genesis 5	Circumcision Covenant Genesis 7	Burnt-Offering Covenant Genesis 2
Sarah	–	–	Sarahic Covenant Gen 17:12, 14–22	–
Isaac	At Gerar, Gen 6:1–6	At Beersheba, Gen 26:23–24	–	–
Jacob	Diaspora Covenant Gen 28:10–16	Prevailing Covenant Genesis 34	Covenant of Hope Gen 46:1–4	–

the Promised-Land Covenant by bringing the Children of Israel out of Egypt again. Lastly, YHWH provides Jacob with a (e) promise of immediate hope—hope that he could believe and trust that he would see his long-lost son before his death. Prophetically, this promise should be applied to the generation that learns to walk in the way of YHWH. If they prevail, they too will receive their forefathers' blessings and live to be reestablished in the Promised Land (see Table 3.14).

I had seen that the Creator's covenants consistently established his words of truth with humanity. I had learned that patriarchs such as Noah or Isaac possessed authority to bless or to curse aspects of their descendants' lives. Patriarchal blessings or curses worked within the framework of the Creator's covenants. Abraham inherited Shem's double portion, a blessing that Noah had revoked for Canaan's progeny. I learned that YHWH had appeared to each patriarch at least twice, although YHWH offered Abraham four covenants and Jacob three, which are summarized in Tables 3.15 and 3.16. YHWH promised that Abraham's offspring would become many kingdoms and many nations (Gen 17:6, 16) who would possess the gates of their enemies. Jacob's patriarchal blessings built on these models. It established the identifying characteristics that the nations comprising Jacob's offspring will portray in the latter days of Diaspora when the Diaspora Covenant will be fulfilled as Israel's obedience qualifies her to be restored to the Abrahamic inheritance.

Thus far, I had seen that YHWH's initial covenants with humanity in Genesis consistently provided the foundation for all truth contained in the entire Old Testament. Now I needed to see how Jacob's divided blessing affected the patriarchal covenants so I could see how God's words should be applied in Israel's subsequent history. I had to continue testing the truth and consistency of Israel's doctrine before I could make any judgment regarding its validity or righteousness.

Table 3.16. Covenant Signs and Angel's Appearance

Covenant	Promises	Covenantee's Seal	YHWH's Sign
Noahic	Earth never again destroyed by flood	Burnt Offering	Rainbow
Migration	Abram will: (1) be a great nation; (2) be blessed; (3) receive a great name; (4) be a blessing to the world; (5) be protected	Migrate to Canaan	–
Promised Land	Promised Land; reaffirms Migration Covenant	Divided Burnt Offering	Devouring lamp passing between the sacrifice/ YHWH's self-imprecation
Circumcision	Abram is to be a father of many nations and is granted a fruitful seed that will bear kings; a covenant is promised to his seed after him in "their generations"	Circumcision	Gives Abram and Sarai new names to reflect promise fulfilled/Sarai will bear a son a year later
Sarah	Mother of nations; promise that she will have a son the following year; promise that Isaac alone will inherit Abraham's covenants	Circumcision	
Burnt Offering	Blessings upon blessings; seed multiplied further; descendants are given the gates of their enemies; all nations of the earth will be blessed through Abraham's seed	Firstborn Son as a Burnt Offering	Swore by himself to bless (self-imprecation)
Isaaic	Abraham's descendants will be called by Isaac's name; Isaac's offspring will inherit the Abrahamic covenants	Burnt Offering	Jacob's name changed to Israel
Diaspora	Abraham's seed will be scattered to the east, west, north, and south; YHWH will not leave Jacob or his seed until he has performed all that he has spoken	Anointed Pillar with Oil	Dream of ladder ascending to YHWH
Prevailing	"He shall prevail with El": receiving the blessings promised to Jacob's forefathers	Wrestling with the Man of God and Prevailing	Changes name to Yisrael to fulfill father's covenant
Hope	Jacob receives the promise before his death	Multiple Sacrifices	Joseph's hands touching Jacob's eyes so he may see

4

Blessings as Ensigns: Genesis 49 and Israel's National Covenants

I. DIVIDING JACOB AND SCATTERING ISRAEL

Before I could investigate Genesis 49's prophecies, I discovered that I needed to become familiar with a distinction made among Israel's descendants. When Jacob issues prophecies for Levi and Simeon in Genesis 49, he distinguishes between the terms *Jacob* and *Israel*, prophesying,

> I will *divide them in Jacob*, and scatter them in Israel. (Gen 49:7)

When Israel inherited the Promised Land, the tribe of Simeon was divided into Judah (Josh 19:1), and Levi's tribe was scattered throughout all the tribes of Israel (Num 18:23).[1] The prophet Isaiah also maintains this distinction.[2] What I learned from this study is that the birthright is always tied to a land territory. The birthright can be taken from Canaan and be given to Abraham and pass through Isaac and Jacob. When Jacob divides the land of Canaan among his sons (for their tribal inheritances), he can revoke or place stipulations on their land heritage, such as where that landed territory would fall. In the case of Simeon, his land fell within the tribe of Judah. (In modern terms, it would be similar to placing the state of New Jersey in the middle of the state of Texas.)

Reuben was Jacob's firstborn and rightful heir, but he greatly dishonored his father by sleeping with Jacob's concubine. For this sin, Reuben forfeited the firstborn's birthright or the leadership blessing of the family (Israelites). As we will see below, Jacob also disqualified his next two eligible heirs, Levi and Simeon, due to their crime against Shechem. This made Judah, Jacob's 4th heir, the first son eligible for the blessing. As a firstborn heir, *Judah inherited Jacob's name*. Hence, the prophecy of Simeon's division into *Jacob* (Gen 49:7) was fulfilled when Simeon's inheritance was divided into the midst of *Judah's* territory (Josh 19:1, 9).

Events transpiring over the next few centuries caused Judah's distinction to be broadened. Solomon turned from YHWH after covenanting with him twice. For his sin, YHWH rent the kingdom out of the hand of Solomon's son and gave it to Jeroboam. The ten tribes apportioned to Jeroboam I constituted the Northern Kingdom of Israel, often called *Ephraim* or *Samaria* after its capital city, although they were more formally distinguished as "Israel." YHWH allotted Solomon's son Rehoboam two tribes: Benjamin and Judah-Simeon.[3] These tribes composed the Southern Kingdom of Israel and were often called Jacob in accordance with the birthright apportioned to Judah.

After Jeroboam secured his throne, he feared that his ten tribes would revert in their loyalty to Jacob's monarchy when they journeyed to Jerusalem for the nation's three annual pilgrimage feasts (1 Kgs 12:27). To prevent this, Jeroboam cast the Levites out of Samaria's borders and installed the lowest people in the office of the priesthood. Jeroboam replaced YHWH with calves, which he reestablished as the "gods that brought Israel out of Egypt" (1 Kgs 12:28; 2 Chr 11:15). Being unlanded and dependent on government provisions, the Levites in the Northern Kingdom were left without income or resources to feed their families.[4] This forced them to emigrate from Ephraim's Northern Kingdom to the Southern Kingdom of Judah (2 Chr 11:12–15). For the rest of Israel's ancient history, Judah's Southern Kingdom comprised four tribes: Benjamin, Judah-Simeon, and Levi.

II.   JACOB DURING THE DIASPORA

The people living in Judah's Southern Kingdom eventually became known as the "Jews."[5] The word *Jew* was coined from the word *Judah* about a century before Nebuchadnezzar deported the Southern Kingdom.[6] Although Scripture describes the Southern Kingdom of Judah (Benjamin, Judah-Simeon, and Levi) as "Jews," the Hebrew Scripture *never* calls the Northern Kingdom "Jews."[7] The only time Scripture used this term was late in the nation's history, when the Northern Kingdom was almost completely deported from the Promised Land, leaving the Southern Kingdom as the lonely remnant of the former twelve tribes of Israel.[8]

That the term *Jew* only referred to the southern tribes is confirmed in many sources. Scripture and inscriptions from Assyrian kings such as Tiglath-pileser III and Sargon II attest to the late coining of the term "Jew" as a name for the citizens of the Southern Kingdom of Judah. The word *Jew* first appears in Israel's Scriptures during Ahaz's reign when Rezin, king of Syria, drove the Jews from Elah—a Judahite city (2 Kgs 16:6). At this time, Tiglath-pileser had severely weakened and deported most of Israel's Northern Kingdom, leaving only the capital city of Samaria to be conquered and deported at the time of Rezin's attacks.[9]

From their first contact, Assyria's kings designated the Southern Kingdom as "Judah" (*Ia-u-da-a-a* in Akkadian, Assyria's royal language). Both Tiglath-pileser III and Sargon II called the Southern Kingdom "Judah."[10] The first time Assyrian inscriptions used the term

Jew (*Ia-u-da-ai*) was when Sennacherib's scribes referred to King Hezekiah after Sennacherib's army had approached Jerusalem. This would have been about 20 years after Rezin's attack on Elah.[11] Before this, Tiglath-pileser had ample opportunity to designate Jehoahaz a "Jew" when the Judahite king brought his tribute to Assyria, but Tiglath-pileser did not. Instead, Assyria recognized Jehoahaz as a man of 'Judah' (*Ia-u-da-a-a*), demonstrating that the term "Jew" was coined after Samaria had fallen, and the Southern Kingdom of Judah was all that was left of the former United Israelite Kingdom.

Understanding how Scripture uses the word *Jew* helps us to understand YHWH's word. The strict technical definition of the word *Jew* is specifically "a descendant of the tribe of Judah."[12] Historically, this term was applied to the whole *Southern Kingdom* of Jacob. Esther and Mordecai were called Jews, although they were of Benjaminite lineage (Esth 2:5–7).[13] When the remnant returned to Israel at Cyrus's decree, the term *Jew* virtually replaced the name *Israel* and became synonymous with the people and the religion embraced during the Second Temple period.[14] Today, the word *Jew* does not denote a descendant of Judah, Jacob, or even Israel. It designates individuals who belong to a religion called *Judaism*. This term should not be confused with the historical definition of Jew, which indeed denotes a physical lineage, in contrast to the modern definition, which denotes the culture and religion evolving from the Second Temple Jews that bears no relation to *patrilineal* lineage. With this understanding, I could better grasp the patriarchal blessings that Jacob divided among his sons.

III. ENSIGNS AS STANDARDS

Toward the end of his life, Jacob called his sons together for an official blessing ceremony. His blessing of all 12 of his sons was quite similar to the blessings and curses that Noah gave his sons at the beginning of a new era in earth's history. YHWH had specified that the Abrahamic covenants could only be inherited by one of Abram's sons—Isaac. Likewise, Isaac chose only one son to inherit Abraham's covenants, even though Jacob subtlety subverted his choice. Jacob never faced the decision of which child would inherit the Abrahamic covenants—all of them would inherit the overall birthright and blessing, although the particular function of these rights would be distributed among the 12 tribes.

Jacob began by instructed his sons, saying,

> Gather yourselves together, that **I may tell you that which shall befall you in the last days**. Gather yourselves together, and hear, you sons of Jacob; and listen to Israel your father. (Gen 49:1–2)

Jacob prophesied that his words would be fulfilled in the *last days*. Scripture uses the word *'achariyth*[15] translated "last days," to designate events or epochs that were to occur in Israel's future. More generally, the term refers to any *later time* or even an 'end time,' shortly before the time allotted for the Diaspora has been completed, when *all* Israel's blessings and curses (negative prophecies) have been fulfilled.[16] Therefore, Jacob's prophecy encompasses an exceedingly broad time with implications for the world today.

YHWH's covenants with Abraham promised that his populous offspring would be not one nation,[17] but numerous nations (Gen 17:6, 16). Jacob's blessings add to the promise of numerous nations by prophesying individual attributes or *ensigns* these nations (full of his children) would display during the Diaspora's latter days.[18] *'Owth* is the word for 'sign,' which we saw earlier, accompanies a covenant (see pp. 94–95).[19] Hence, Jacob establishes signs, attributes, or *symbolic ensigns* that his children would display in the latter days. When *'owth* is used as a *standard* or *ensign*, the term conveys the idea of a sign or an emblem as a device, symbol, or figure adopted and used as an identifying mark (Num 2:2).[20] The first time that YHWH employed ensigns, he used them to identify the tribes during their wilderness encampments. The Book of Numbers (1:52–2:25) describes these standards. Both Moses' (Deuteronomy 33) and Deborah's Songs (Judges 5) add to Jacob's "identifying marks;" however, our investigation will focus solely on Jacob's words. Perhaps future studies will examine in greater detail these identifying marks in conjunction with Jacob's divided blessing.

IV. BLESSINGS DIVIDED

Noah had established a pattern of dividing blessings and curses among his sons. Jacob follows this custom[21] by dividing the Abrahamic birthright and blessing among his 12 sons. He based each son's blessing on the righteousness or unrighteousness exhibited in that son's life. As previously evidenced, patriarchs could extend a blessing to their children and grandchildren or use a curse if their child's life has proved decisively unrighteous. The Jacobic blessings further exemplify this method of inheritance and how the patriarchs established prophecy.[22]

Jacob blessed 10 sons, including Joseph's sons as half-tribes (Manasseh and Ephraim). He did not, however, bless Reuben, who sinned by sleeping with Jacob's concubine (Gen 35:22; Lev 18:8), or Simeon and Levi, who dealt unjustly with the men of Shechem.[23] Instead, Jacob issued a curse for their descendants.[24] Since Jacob disallowed the birthright to his first three sons, who would normally be the legitimate heirs of the birthright, the next child in line to receive the birthright was Judah (see Genesis 30 and 46). Jacob did not give Judah the full birthright but halved it with the Joseph tribes, bestowing the double portion of land (Gen 48:22) to Joseph, yet allowing Judah to retain the right of family leadership (monarchy) normally associated with the blessing. Jacob blesses all of his remaining sons, granting them very specific inheritances, yet the double portion of land associated with an extra birthright and blessings of prosperity are given to Joseph.

We saw above that YHWH upheld the rights of a first wife and her children's rights over the rights of concubines (see pp. 96–97). Jacob's blessings reflect this custom by blessing both Leah's first eligible offspring and Rachel's' first offspring over the handmaids' children.[25] Thus, the legal wives were again afforded greater privileges than the servants.[26] Although Rachel's handmaid had borne a child before Rachel bore Joseph, the child's birth did not negate Rachel's legal right to have her sons receive the first-born's greater portion of the inheritance.

Jacob's blessings fulfilled at least three obligations. First, he designated his legal heirs. These were the sons (tribes) that would inherit the greater portion of the birthright and blessing and bear the patriarch's name of "Jacob". Second, he divided the Promised-Land Covenant among his 12 sons, stipulating geographical features to mark the territory that each tribe will inherit. For instance, Zebulun was told that his inheritance would be coastal, while Issachar's lands would lie between two other tribes (see below). Jacob *removed a specific blessing* of the Promised-Land Covenant from his two cursed sons—Levi and Simeon. Levi and his children would be dispersed among all the tribes. Simeon would be subdivided into Judah's territory. This severely curtailed Simeon's autonomy as many of their policies would necessitate approval from Judah's leaders and any tribal "culture" would always be influenced by Judah's. Because their communities always fell in another tribe's inheritance, this left little self-governing tribal territory for the Levi and Simeon tribes.

Often, Jacob went beyond the simple designations of land (Judah, Issachar, Joseph)[27] to prophesy a particular type of political or geographical feature, cultural characteristics, or industry that would identify that particular tribe, both after the exodus and at the end of the Diaspora. For example, Reuben would display an unstable sociopolitical history, while Asher would have an abundance of food, enabling him to produce royal delicacies. Third, the attributes pronounced on each son/tribe predicted the cultural as well as the historical political and geographical features the tribes should display during the Diaspora when Jacob's children had become "many nations" (Gen 17:4–5). We will examine these prophecies in birthright order as listed in Gen 35:23–26 to see what truth Jacob's words established for Israel's current "latter-days."

A. Leah's Sons

1. Reuben

> Reuben, you are my firstborn, my strength, and the child of my vigorous youth. You are first in rank and first in power. But you are as unruly as a flood,[28] and *you will be first no longer.* For you went to bed with my wife; and you defiled my marriage couch. (Gen 49:3–4,[29] New Living translation)

Throughout the ancient world, firstborn sons were viewed as embodying their father's strength.[30] Reuben had trouble with self-control, seeking his own gratification over moral integrity. Thus, Reuben was morally weak. "Reuben is described as a very untrustworthy person, who like water in the Near East which can appear and disappear at any moment. Reuben is someone on whom one cannot build."[31] Though Reuben was Jacob's rightful heir, he had transgressed the Law (Lev 18:8) and disrespected his father when he slept with his father's concubine, Bilhah (Gen 35:22). For this sin, Jacob revokes Reuben's customary privilege of the birthright and blessing.[32] Unlike Noah with Ham, Jacob does *not* curse Reuben but leaves him and his descendants to their own instability. Applied as an ensign, Reuben's sociopolitical history will seek self-gratification over the logic of any natural law[33] and will remain unstable well into the latter days.

2. Simeon and Levi

> Simeon and Levi, brothers, (a) accomplished the injustice of their cutting off.[34] O my soul, come not you into their secret; to their assembly, my honor, be not you united, for in their wrath they slew men, and in their passion they houghed a bull (LXX). (b) **Cursed** be their wrath, for it was fierce, and their anger for it was cruel: (c) I will divide them in Jacob, and (d) scatter them in Israel. (Gen 49:5–7, LXX and AKJV)[35]

Jacob draws from Levi and Simeon's heinous crime at Shechem for this curse. Many scholars translate "houghed a bull" as "hamstringing a bull." One of the foremost scholars on this text, Raymond de Hoop points out that the "hamstringing of animals was nothing more than a postponed execution: the animal could not move any more to gather its water and food and thus had to die."[36] This analogy is quite applicable to Levi and Simeon's deception of Shechem by dishonestly offering his city a peaceful covenant.[37] The city of Shechem had acted on good faith and became circumcised so that they could enter into family relations with the Jacobic clan. Simeon and Levi slaughtered the town's citizens three days after the town's circumcision when the men were extremely sore (Genesis 34). Following typical analogy, the bull itself was a metaphor for the prince of Shechem.[38]

Both Simeon and Levi (b) inherit specific curses for (a) their acts of injustice. When Noah had cursed Canaan, he appropriated his tribal lands, giving his land instead to Shem's progeny. Likewise, Jacob's curse denies land inheritances to Simeon's and Levi's offspring. Their land inheritances would be scattered among other tribes, which is why *Simeon's* inheritance (c) was divided within Judah's inheritance. The Book of Joshua records:

> And the second lot came forth to Simeon, even for the tribe of the children of Simeon according to their families: and *their inheritance was within* the inheritance of the children of Judah. (Josh 19:1)

Jacob's curse of Levi (d) scattered his descendants among the entire 12 tribes as YHWH upheld Jacob's prophecy, disallowing Levi's children an inheritance of tribal land. Instead, each tribe (including Manasseh) allotted cities in which the Levites would dwell.[39] These cities served as the Levites' homes, since they received no arable lands to produce wealth like the rest of the Israelites were given. Thus, Simeon's and Levi's descendants would have little functional autonomy among the regions in which they lived. The tribe of Levi was virtually stripped of its ability to gain wealth through the highly lucrative grain industry. Although YHWH did not alter this curse in any way, he later added a blessing to this curse by giving the tribe of Levi the priesthood, thus providing for a highly diversified government, a subject to which we will return in chap. 7.

Thus far, this study had totally revolutionized the way I saw the ancient Israelite nation. I had always wondered why Simeon or Levi had not received the monarchy or double portion of land associated with the rights of the firstborn. Now I knew. I was curious to know if

Judah's blessing would change my understanding of the tribe's role in Israel's ancient history. How would Jacob's divided blessing affect Judah's future?

3. Judah

Judah, you are he whom (b) *your brothers shall praise*: (a) your hand shall be in the neck of your enemies; (b) your father's children shall bow down before you. (c) Judah is a lion's whelp: from the prey, my son, you are gone up: he stooped down, he couched as a lion, and as an old lion; who shall rouse him up? The (d) scepter shall not depart from Judah, *nor a lawgiver* from between his feet, until (e) Shiloh come; and to him shall the (f) gathering of the people be. Binding his foal to the vine, and his ass's colt to the choice vine; he washed his garments in wine, and his clothes in the blood of grapes: His eyes shall be red with wine, and his teeth white with milk. (Gen 49:8–12)

Jacob has just revoked his first three sons' rights to the birthright and the blessing due to their unrighteousness. Therefore, Judah is Jacob's first eligible heir. Jacob does not grant Judah the full birthright, but divides it between Judah and Joseph, giving Judah the rights of family leadership associated with the blessing and Joseph the double portion of land associated with the birthright. Jacob infuses Judah's birthright blessing with many prophecies. He bequeaths (a) military strength to Judah to dominate enemies and bestows on him (b, d) the right to rule his father's children. Judah is now reckoned the firstborn since (b, d) Reuben's birthright has passed to him.

The King James Version renders 1 Chr 5:1–2:

Now the sons of Reuben the firstborn of Israel, (for he was the firstborn; but, forasmuch as he defiled his father's bed, *his birthright was given to the sons of Joseph* the son of Israel: and the genealogy is not to be reckoned after the **birthright**. For Judah prevailed above his brothers, and of him *came the chief ruler*; but the **birthright** was Joseph's).

While Judah inherited Reuben's blessing of family rulership[40] and genealogical reckoning, which included the leadership of the family-nation, Joseph obtained Reuben's forfeited birthright of prosperity associated with the double portion of land, populous children, and possessions—a point that Moses reaffirms in Deut 33:13–16. When we look at Jacob's blessing of Joseph, we will see that Jacob divided the birthright and blessing between Judah and Joseph, allotting specific aspects of each to the two tribes.

Several facts demonstrate that Joseph did not receive the full blessing. First, Jacob bequeathed the (d) right to rule, to be the nation's "lawgiver" to Judah, not Joseph. Second, the northern tribes under Jeroboam (Manasseh and Ephraim) did not retain Jerusalem, the capital seat of government. It would have been very difficult for Ephraim or Manasseh to administer the blessing without retaining the "place where YHWH had placed his name out of all the tribes of Israel" (1 Kgs 14:21). Third, the prophets cite continual jealousy over

Ephraim's economic prosperity (Isa 11:13; Hos 12:8). Economic prosperity is associated with the blessing, not necessarily the birthright, although a double portion of land and labor force would surely contribute (Gen 27:29). Thus Jacob divided the birthright and blessing between Judah and Joseph. The Masoretic Text correctly asserts that Judah as Jacob's first eligible heir should be listed in place of Reuben as Jacob's firstborn son, not Joseph; however, Jacob places the name *Israel* on the Joseph tribes.[41]

The reason Judah retained the leadership portion of the blessing ahead of Joseph was quite simple: he was older than Joseph, and a birthright was based on the birth order of the legal wives' sons.[42] According to the chronology of Genesis 29–30, Leah had borne six sons (Gen 30:17, 19) before Rachel conceived Joseph (Gen 30:22–24). Had Judah disqualified himself by some heinous act as had Reuben, Simeon, and Levi, the birthright still would have fallen to Issachar then Zebulun before Joseph. In fact, the Law that Abraham and the patriarchs followed prevented Joseph from fully inheriting the birthright and blessing ahead of his elder brothers.

> If a man have two wives, one beloved, and another hated, and they have borne him children, both the beloved and the hated; and if the firstborn son be an heir that was hated: Then it shall be, when he makes his sons to inherit that which he has, that *he (a) may not make the son of the beloved firstborn before the son of the hated, which is indeed the firstborn: But he shall (b) acknowledge the son of the hated for the firstborn,* by giving *him a double portion* of all that he has: for he is the beginning of his strength; the right of the firstborn is his. (Deut 21:15–17)

The Book of Genesis also tells us that "Abraham obeyed my voice, and kept my charge, my commandments, my statutes, and my laws" (Gen 26:5). If Abraham and Isaac walked in the way of YHWH, then it is very likely that Jacob also followed YHWH's law regarding the inheritance the birthright and blessing of his sons. Judah (a) retained his rightful inheritance portion and the blessing of family leadership. Joseph received an extra portion of land outside the Promised Land of Canaan on the other side of Jordan since Joseph had been (b) "hated of his brothers." However, this extra portion does not appear to have infringed on Judah's lawful birthright inheritance because it lay outside the borders of Canaan.

First Chronicles also acknowledges that "Judah prevailed above his brothers" (1 Chr 5:1–2). Judah prevailed in at least two ways. First, his life was more righteous than Leah's older three sons' lives. Second, when Jacob's sons pleaded to let Benjamin travel with them to Egypt, Jacob refused. Reuben had initially pledged surety for Benjamin's safe return with his own two sons (Gen 42:37), but Jacob refused, not trusting Reuben for his beloved son's safe return. A few months later, Judah made the same plea and prevailed when Jacob allowed Benjamin to go to Egypt in Judah's care (Gen 43:8–11). Jacob did not trust Reuben's request until Judah echoed Joseph's demands. It was at this point that Jacob believed what his older sons had told him was true; thus Judah's integrity indeed prevailed above that of his brothers in securing the family's welfare because Jacob believed Judah's counsel to be credible.

Illustration 4.1. Ancient Egyptian "crouching lion" game piece.

Jacob's prophecy of (c) a lion's whelp conveys the idea of military strength.[43] "In literature, the lion is a favorite metaphor for warlike kings and fierce deities."[44] During the Monarchy, YHWH had used David of Judah to break the yoke of Israel's enemies. Applied as an ensign, Jacob's words indicate that Judah's dwindling latter-day military strength would need to be "roused up" (see Illustration 4.1). When Israel's enemies sought to destroy the nation after the Israelites left Egypt, they called a prophet to curse or reverse the nation's future. YHWH thwarted their intentions by ordering their prophet Balaam to uphold and reaffirm Jacob's latter-day prophecy for Judah some 400 years after Jacob had established YHWH's blessing:

> For there is no divination against Jacob, nor enchantment against Israel; in season it shall be told[45] to Jacob and Israel what God shall perform. Behold, the people shall rise up as a *lion's whelp*, and shall exalt himself as a lion; he shall not lie down till he have eaten the prey, and he shall drink the blood of the slain. (Num 23:23–24; rendered LXX)[46]

Balaam did not "turn back" or revoke Jacob's words. Rather, understanding YHWH's unchanging word, he confirmed Jacob's patriarchal blessing.

Micah continues the prophetic thread begun by Jacob (and augmented by Balaam) by defining the day Israel would "rise as a lion" and cause the heathen to perish out of the earth.

> And the remnant of Jacob shall be in the middle of *many people* as a dew from YHWH, as the showers on the grass, that tarries not for man, nor waits for the sons of men. And the *remnant of Jacob shall be among the Gentiles in the middle of many people as a lion among the beasts* of the forest, as *a young lion* among the flocks of sheep: who, if he go through, both treads down, and tears in pieces, and none can deliver. Your hand shall be lifted up on your adversaries, and all your enemies shall be cut off. (Mic 5:7–9)

Micah's words herald the completion of the Prevailing Covenant. Micah foretells the day when all Israel with Judah at the helm will have her strength restored.[47] Though the heirs of the patriarchal covenants are scattered among many nations, YHWH will strengthen and furnish them with power in the midst of foreign lands.[48] He will enable them to prevail against all their enemies so that none can deliver out of his people's hand.

Within Jacob's prophecy regarding Judah, Jacob recognizes a particular ruler who will be renowned for Judah's strength and peace that flourishes during his reign.

> The (d) scepter shall not depart from Judah, nor a lawgiver from between his feet, until Shiloh come; and to him shall the gathering of the people be. (Gen 49:10)

The Hebrew word for (d) scepter is *shebet*.[49] Like many Hebrew words, *shebet* has several meanings. The first definition means "to branch off" the tribe of a family clan, as translated in Exod 24:4; 28:21; Deut 1:15; 16:18; Josh 21:16; and 2 Sam 5:1. *Shebet's* second definition is "a rod" or "a staff," as translated in Exod 21:20 and Lev 27:32. The most common translation of *shebet* is "tribe," which the King James Version uses over 130 times.

Although translators preferred to use "scepter" for *shebet* rather than "tribe," this verse could also be accurately rendered:

> The *tribes*[50] shall not depart from Judah, nor a lawgiver from between his feet, until Shiloh come and to him shall the gathering of the people be. (Gen 49:10)

If this definition is correct, Jacob is recognizing an era during which his children would divide into two separate nations: the tribes would divide into Jacob and Israel when 10 tribes departed from Judah *after* Shiloh came.

The word (e) *Shiloh*[51] is derived from the root word *shalah*,[52] which means 'to be tranquil, to rest, or be secure and successful.' To be tranquil is to be "free from disturbance or turmoil." This prophecy could *not* refer to David since David's life was far from tranquil. Scripture testifies that his life was filled "with wars on every side" (1 Kgs 5:3–4). When David subjugated his enemies, Absalom rebelled, and once again peace was thwarted. In the Book of 2 Samuel, YHWH promised David a "sure house" (2 Sam 7:11–29) and passed Judah's Abrahamic blessing into the hands of David and his posterity. Hidden in YHWH's covenant of David's sure house is the prophecy of Shiloh:

> Also YHWH tells you that he will make you an house. And when your days be fulfilled, and you shall sleep with your fathers, I will set up your seed after you, *which shall proceed out of your bowels*, and I will establish his kingdom. *He shall build (a) an house for my name, and I will establish the throne of his kingdom forever.* I will be his father, and he shall be my son. If he commit iniquity, (b) I will chasten him with the rod of men, and with the stripes of the children of men: But my mercy shall not depart away from him, as I took it from Saul, whom I put away before you. And your house and your kingdom shall be established forever before you: your throne shall be established forever. According to all these words, and according to all this vision, so did Nathan speak to David. (2 Sam 7:11–17; see also 2 Sam 12:24–25)

When King David bestowed his blessing to his son Solomon on his deathbed, he acknowledged that Solomon would fulfill the Shiloh prophecy.

> David said to Solomon, My son, as for me, it was in my mind to build an house
> to the name of YHWH my God: But the word of YHWH came to me, saying.
> . . . Behold, a son shall be born to you, *who shall be a man of rest*; and I will give
> him rest from all his enemies round about: for *his name shall be Solomon, and I
> will give peace and quietness to Israel in his days. He shall (a) build an house for
> my name*; and he shall be my son, and I will be his father; and I will establish
> the throne of his kingdom over Israel forever. (1 Chr 22:7–10)

Solomon was the peaceable heir of whom Jacob had prophesied. He was the son who proceeded out of "David's bowels." Solomon affirms this political situation, testifying of his own peaceful life. "But now YHWH my God has given me rest on every side, so that there is *neither adversary nor evil occurrent*" (1 Kgs 5:4). Life without an adversary or evil occurrent meets the definition of tranquil found in the word Shiloh. King Solomon built David's (a) Temple, and YHWH blessed him with incredible military and maritime successes (1 Kgs 9:26–28). During his days (f, Gen 49:10, above), the people were gathered together. "There came of all people to hear the wisdom of Solomon, from all kings of the earth, which had heard of his wisdom" (1 Kgs 4:34). When Solomon committed iniquity, (b) YHWH did not take his mercy from him as he did with the many kings of Ephraim or like he had King Saul. Rather, he sent Ahijah who foretold that the tribes would depart from Judah when Shiloh's reign ended (1 Kings 11). YHWH waited until after Solomon's reign to cause the ten tribes to depart from Judah, thus fulfilling Jacob's words in Gen 49:10 that the "tribes would not depart from Judah until Shiloh came." Applied as an ensign, Judah's children should demonstrate strength, leadership, and prosperity amidst their enemies.

4. Issachar

> "Issachar is a strong ass couching down between two burdens: And he saw that rest was good, and the land that it was pleasant; and bowed his shoulder to bear, and became a servant to tribute" (Gen 49:14–15). The Septuagint renders v. 14: "Issachar has desired that which is good; resting between the inheritances."

When Joshua divided Canaan's territories, Issachar's land fell between two other tribes (Josh 19:17). Canaan's land distribution was proportional to tribal population (Num 26:25, 54; 33:54). Issachar had a large population (Num 1:29), so the tribe received a large portion of land located between two other tribes. Issachar's land was pleasant and easy to cultivate. However, he also bore heavy taxation and became a corvée laborer.[53] Since Jacob's prophecy encompasses the latter days, a key ensign of scattered Issachar today is the taxes that the people of this country pay. Of all the tribes blessed by Jacob or Moses, Issachar is the only nation associated with excessive taxation and some type of servitude (corvée labor).

5. Zebulun

> Zebulun shall dwell at the haven of the sea; and he shall be for an haven of *ships; and his border shall be unto Zidon.* (Gen 49:13)

Jacob uses geographical features to denote both Zebulun's (sea/harbor) and Isaachar's (arable land) ensigns. The word *haven* connotes safe seaports, and the word *Zidon* means 'fishery.'[54] When Moses apportioned Zebulun's inheritance, his territory laid at the seaside. Ancient Zebulun possessed calm seashores, natural harbors, and shelter for fishing fleets. That ships found refuge in his harbors, indicates prosperity from sea and international trade (see Map 4.1). A prosperous sea port would be the most distinguishable ensign for the nation of Zebulun today.

B. *Rachel's Sons*

1. Joseph

Before Jacob blessed his twelve sons, Joseph brought his two sons to visit their grandfather. During this visit, Jacob bestowed a special "extra" blessing on Manasseh and Ephraim. Since the words of later patriarchal blessings depended on previously spoken prophecies (patriarchs followed the precept of constancy by upholding their own previously binding words), Jacob's first blessing of Manasseh and Ephraim (Genesis 48) affected their blessings (Genesis 49) when the 12 sons were called together.

Noah had given Shem a double portion: one portion that already belonged to Shem and another portion, which Noah had taken from Ham's son Canaan. YHWH designated Abram to receive this inheritance, which later passed to Isaac, then to Jacob. When Jacob divided the inheritance among his sons, he separated one portion of the birthright, granting a double portion to Joseph's sons.

> And Jacob said to Joseph, God Almighty appeared to me at Luz in the land of Canaan, and blessed me, (a) And said to me, Behold, I will make you fruitful, and multiply you, and I will make of you a multitude of people; and will give this land to your seed after you for an everlasting possession. (b) And now your two sons, Ephraim and Manasseh, which were born to you in the land of Egypt before I came to you in Egypt, are mine; (c) as Reuben and Simeon, they shall be mine. And your issue, which you beget after them, shall be yours, and shall be called after the name of their brothers in their inheritance. (d) And as for me, when I came from Padan, Rachel died by me in the land of Canaan in the way, when yet there was but a little way to come to Ephrath: and I buried her there in the way of Ephrath; the same is Bethlehem. (Gen 48:3–7)

The first part of Jacob's blessing confers (a) the previous patriarchal covenants on Ephraim and Manasseh. Bequeathing the Promised Land and Circumcision Covenants to Manasseh and Ephraim allows Jacob to allot a separate portion of the Promised Land to both of Joseph's sons. Jacob passes the blessings given to (b) him onto his children and assimilates

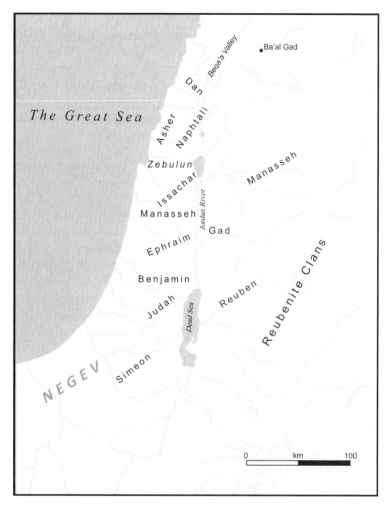

Map 4.1. Land Distribution Based on Genesis 49 with Zebulun's Safe Port.

Ephraim and Manasseh as his own sons, perhaps in place of Reuben and Simeon, his first two heirs who had been disqualified.[55] Jacob bequeaths (c) Reuben's forfeited birthright (double portion) to Manasseh and Ephraim (Ezek 47:13). Thus, Manasseh and Ephraim each receive part of the firstborn's double portion of land beyond Canaan's borders. Jacob's assimilation of Ephraim and Manasseh technically made Israel a thirteen tribe nation; however, Scripture makes it clear that Joseph's sons were still reckoned as a single tribe (Exod 24:4; 28:21; 39:14; Ezek 47:13) even though Joseph's sons were not called by Joseph's name, as was traditional. They were called after their own names, Manasseh and Ephraim. This birthright is why the two tribes received separate inheritances when the Promised Land was divided at the Conquest.

When Israel inherited Canaan, tribes were often allotted cities within another tribe's territory (Josh 16:9, 17:11; 19:50). This appears to have been the case with Bethlehem. Jacob (d) bequeathed Rachel's burial place near Ephrath (called Bethlehem) to her offspring. Although this city lay in Judah's borders, it was designated to belong to Joseph. Ephraim's and Manasseh's heritage would not belong to Judah since it was Joseph's mother that was buried there, not Judah's.

The following continues to chart Joseph's blessing, which was given before the blessing of the 11 other brothers gathered together.

And Joseph took them both, Ephraim in his right hand toward Israel's left hand, and Manasseh in his left hand toward Israel's right hand, and brought them near to him. And Israel stretched out his right hand, and laid it on Ephraim's head, who was the younger, and his left hand on Manasseh's head, guiding his hands wittingly; for Manasseh was the firstborn. And he blessed Joseph, and said, God, before whom my fathers Abraham and Isaac did walk, the God which fed me all my life long unto this day,

The Angel which redeemed me from all evil, bless the lads; and (a) let my name be named on them, and the name of my fathers Abraham and Isaac; and let them grow into a (b) multitude in the midst of the earth. And when Joseph saw that his father laid his right hand on the head of Ephraim, it displeased him: and he held up his father's hand, to remove it from Ephraim's head unto Manasseh's head. And Joseph said to his father, Not so, my father: for this is the firstborn; put your right hand on his head. And his father refused, and said, I know it, my son, I know it: he also shall become (c) a people, and he also shall be great: but truly his younger brother shall be greater than he, and his seed shall become a (d) multitude of nations. And he blessed them that day, saying, (e) In you shall Israel bless, saying, God make you as Ephraim and as Manasseh: and (e) he set Ephraim before Manasseh. And Israel said to Joseph, Behold, I die: but God shall be with you, and bring you again to the land of your fathers. Moreover I have given to you (f) *one portion above your brothers, which I took out of the hand of the Amorite with my sword and with my bow.* (Gen 48:13–22)

Today, children usually inherit their father's last name, but in ancient Israel, families did not use a last name. Rather, the firstborn son was called by his father's name and perpetuated the name of his father's house (e.g., Isaac ben Abraham). Jacob had substituted Ephraim-Manasseh for Reuben (his firstborn). This is (a) why Jacob states that his name should be placed "on them," claiming them as one of his sons and dividing the firstborn's birthright and blessing between Judah and Joseph. While the southern tribes were called by Judah's (and Jacob's) name, the northern tribes were called after Israel's name because Jacob had bequeathed that blessing to the Joseph tribes.

Jacob blesses Manasseh and Ephraim with populations (b) greater than the other tribes. When Manasseh entered Canaan (Num 26:34) his children were a great multitude. Although Jacob prophesied that (c) Manasseh would have a great population, he ordained Ephraim's seed to overpopulate Manasseh's. While it is true the tribe did become a great populace in the days of Joshua, nowhere does Scripture record Ephraim's population as surpassing that of Manasseh or the other tribes. After Jeroboam's reign YHWH began to diminish the population of the Northern Kingdom through wars, famine, and pestilence. During Israel's time in the Promised Land, this prophecy was unfulfilled and destined to be an ensign for Ephraim's latter days. Both economic prosperity and large populations are hallmarks of Ephraim's latter-day country.

Jacob ordained Manasseh to become one great nation with many people, and (d) Ephraim would become a greater people who would become *many* nations. If this prophecy has come to pass, it must have occurred after the Northern Kingdom's deportation (they did not become many nations during the Monarchy), during the Diaspora, or after the Diaspora's completion when the whole nation is gathered from the "four corners of the earth" (Isa 11:12) and restored to the Promised Land at the *second exodus* (Jer 16:14–21).

The blessings that Jacob bestows on the Joseph tribes will cause (e) other tribes (and nations) to desire their blessings. Although Ephraim was the youngest, his blessing will far surpass the blessings of Manasseh or any other tribe. As an ensign, this may be Ephraim's most distinguishing feature. Next, Jacob passes (f) Shem's double portion to the sons of Joseph. As discussed above, the double portion designated land; therefore, Joseph would have one "Amorite" portion of land greater than his brothers' portion.

That this was indeed the case is evidenced by Moses' division of the Promised Land.

> And Moses said to them, If the children of Gad and the children of Reuben will pass with you over Jordan, every man armed to battle, before YHWH, and the land shall be subdued before you; then you shall give them the land of Gilead for a possession: But if they will not pass over with you armed, they shall have possessions among you in the land of Canaan. And the children of Gad and the children of Reuben answered, saying, As YHWH has said to your servants, so will we do. We will pass over armed before YHWH to the land of Canaan, that *the possession of our inheritance on this side Jordan may be ours.* And Moses gave to them, even to the children of Gad, and to the children of Reuben, and *to half the tribe of Manasseh the son of Joseph, the kingdom of Sihon king of the Amorites*, and the kingdom of Og king of Bashan, the land, with the cities thereof in the coasts, even the cities of the country round about. (Num 32:29–33).

Manasseh's inheritance represented "one portion above your brothers, which I took out of the hand of the *Amorite* with my sword and with my bow." Thus Jacob's prophecy (Gen 48:22) was fulfilled after the nation came out of the Wilderness of Sin and inherited the Promised Land. Remember that YHWH did not bequeath this land to Abraham's descendants until the Amorites' sins had "come to the full" (Gen 15:16). This is why Manasseh's vast heritage fell on the other side of the Jordan River (Num 32:19).

Jacob's third blessing of Joseph occurred when the 12 brothers were called together for the patriarch's last will:

> Joseph is a fruitful bough, even a fruitful bough by a well; whose branches run over the wall: (a) The archers have sorely grieved him, and shot at him, and *hated him*: (b) But *his bow stayed in strength*, and the arms of his hands were made strong by the hands of the mighty God of Jacob; (from there (c) is the shepherd, the stone of Israel:) Even by the God of your father, who shall help you; and by the Almighty, (d) who *shall bless you with blessings* of heaven above, *blessings* of the deep that lies under, *blessings* of the breasts, and of the womb: *The blessings* of your father have prevailed above the *blessings* of (e) my progenitors to the utmost bound of the everlasting hills: they shall be on the head of Joseph, and on the crown of the head of him that was (f) separate from his brothers. (Gen 49:22–26)[56]

Jacob passes overflowing blessings to Joseph's sons. Joseph had been envied and harmed by his brothers, cast into a pit, sold into slavery—all but forgotten. Through it all, Joseph remained faithful. Therefore, Joseph's blessings far outweigh any prosperity that his brothers receive. When Jacob states that Joseph's children will live beside a "well," he indicates that their portion of land will be bountiful, arable, and self-sustaining. This portion is added to the Abrahamic blessings of children, monarchies, economic prosperity, and freedom. Unfortunately, prosperity (a) often results in envy by those who lack the prosperity (just as Joseph's brothers had envied him). In turn, this causes hatred and jealousy of the wealthy or intellectually prosperous. This seems to have been the case with Ephraim and Manasseh, who would be hated and envied for their prosperity, wealth, and natural resources. Although Joseph would be envied for his blessings, (b) he would possess military prowess to fight and defend himself against oppression and aggression.

Throughout Israel's history, YHWH established shepherds, such as Moses, Joshua, King David, or King Hezekiah to lead the flock of his people (Ps 77:20; Jer 23:4; Ezek 34:23). Hosea foretold that, during Israel's Diaspora, the nation would dwell without any king or priest to lead the people in the Creator's ways (Hos 3:4–5). However, at the end of the Diaspora, YHWH would again reestablish his covenants with the nation and set up his shepherds to lead the flock of his pasture (Jer 23:4; Ezek 34:23). Jacob's reference to a shepherd (c) established Joseph as the *latter-day* country, tribe, or territory in which one of Israel's foremost shepherds will be found in latter days. Jacob's prophecy, in particular, refers to Ephraim's possession of Bethlehem, which lay inside Judah's territory and bore Israel's most respected shepherd: King David.

Joseph is given the broadest and most encompassing blessing ever bestowed on a son. From the (d) heights above to the depths of the deep, even blessings of nourishment and healthy offspring, the blessings on the sons of Joseph are so great that they surpass (e) the blessings of Jacob, Isaac, Abraham, and Shem. Joseph's ensigns can be summarized in three ways. Jacob blesses Manasseh and Ephraim with wealth and population *before* the other 11 tribes. That is to say, before the Diaspora Covenant is fulfilled, Manasseh and Ephraim begin to receive the blessings of wealth and population. While being envied by other nations, they will have the armed forces to maintain their autonomy. Manasseh receives one portion of land more than his brothers. And perhaps Joseph's (Manasseh's and Ephraim's) most distinguishing ensign is that (f) his land *in the latter days* will be separated from his brothers' heritages (just as Manasseh's land had been separated by the Jordan River).

2. Benjamin

> Benjamin shall shred as a wolf: in the morning he shall devour the prey, and at night he shall divide the spoil. All these are the twelve tribes of Israel: and this is it that their father spoke to them, and blessed them; every one according to his blessing he blessed them. (Gen 49:27)[57]

Benjamin's most distinguishing feature is military strength: like a wolf, he pillages his enemies. This describes a fierce and aggressive people that accumulate wealth through conquest. At one time (morning) he devours his prey; at another time frame (evening) he divides the spoils taken from his enemies. It seems that this quest for prey and military conquest would also distinguish latter-day Benjamin.[58]

C. Sons of Concubines

1. Dan (Bilhah)

> Dan shall judge his people, as one of the tribes of Israel. Dan shall be a serpent by the way, an adder in the path, that bites the horse heels, so that his rider shall fall backward. I have waited for your salvation, O YHWH. (Gen 49:16–18)

Rachel had given her handmaid Bilhah to Jacob to bear her children. When Bilhah bore Rachel's first son, Rachel named him Dan because "God had judged her" (Gen 30:6) and given her a son through Bilhah. Jacob incorporates the meaning of Dan's name into his son's blessing.[59] Jacob's description of Dan is not so much about the land apportioned to him as it is a characterization of his descendants' tenacious and clever *modus operandi*. Jacob's blessing is an attribute that distinguishes Dan's progeny throughout the Diaspora until YHWH's salvation is granted. The nation who fulfills this prophecy will manifest a sound system of justice. His people will be militarily deceptive and historically a nuisance to those who desire their territory. Dan will be a people who wait and are ready for YHWH's latter-day salvation.

2. Naphtali (Bilhah)

> Naphtali is a hind let loose: he gives goodly words. (Gen 49:21)[60]

Jacob's words indicate that the tribe of Naphtali will have territory large enough to roam and the freedom to enjoy it. Additionally, Naphtali's people will either be known for good counsel or rich literary heritage. According to the Septuagint's translation, Naphtali's people would not be known for their words but for their children's beauty.

3. Gad and Asher (Zilpah)

> Gad, a troop shall overcome him: but he shall overcome at the last. Out of Asher his bread shall be fat, and he shall yield royal dainties. (Gen 49:19)[61]

Gad's and Asher's blessings will be an ensign clearly distinguishable in the latter days. At one point in Gad's history, an army overwhelms him, but he triumphs over his oppressors and establishes his independence before the Diaspora Covenant is completed. In Moses' blessing of the nation (Deuteronomy 33), Moses augments Jacob's prophetic blessings by saying that Gad will be found in the "portion of the lawgiver" (Deut 33:21); hence, in the latter days Gad will be found in Judah's territories. Jacob gives Asher land that produces much grain and supplies the rich dainties of the world's monarchies. Moses adds to this by saying that Asher will have many offspring and will be accepted among the other tribes (Deut 33:24–25).

The prophet Isaiah prophesies that ensigns will herald Israel's return to the Promised Land and fulfillment of his prophetic covenants.

> It shall come to pass in that day, that YHWH shall set his hand again the *second time* to recover the remnant of his people, which shall be left, from Assyria, and from Egypt, and from Pathros, and from Cush, and from Elam, and from Shinar, and from Hamath, and from the islands of the sea. And *he shall set up an ensign for the nations*, and shall assemble the outcasts of Israel, and gather together the dispersed of Judah from the four corners of the earth. The envy also of Ephraim shall depart, and the adversaries of Judah shall be cut off: Ephraim shall not envy Judah, and Judah shall not vex Ephraim. (Isa 11:11–13)

Isaiah prophesies that knowledge of Israel's defining geo-political characteristics (ensigns) will signal the day that YHWH restores unity to Abraham's children and fulfills the Promise-Land Covenant (see Table 4.1). I had discovered that Jacob's blessing provided prosperity, power, and freedom for his children. His blessings along with those added by Moses, Deborah, Jeremiah, and Hosea reveal the nation's defining, latter-day ensigns. There was only a couple more covenants that YHWH made with humanity before he covenanted with the nation of Israel at Mt. Sinai. I knew these would be the last stops before I examined the fairness or arbitrary and unrighteousness of the Law that YHWH gave to the ancient nation of Israel.

V. COVENANTS AFFECT HISTORY: THE MOSAIC COVENANT

The Mosaic Covenant was one of the last compacts contracted with man before Mt. Sinai. It affected Israel in at least two ways. It provided the place where YHWH would appear to Israel, and it designated Moses as the national deliverer, savior, or messiah. These are the verses that initiate Israel's deliverance.

Table 4.1. Political Blessings as Ensigns

Birthright Order	Tribe	Mother	Blessing	Political Feature	Geographical Feature
1	Reuben	Leah	—	Instablity	Unruly land?/ unstable governments
2	Levi	Leah	Curse	—	No tribal lands—divided among Israel
3	Simeon	Leah	Curse	—	No autonomy of tribal lands—divided within Judah
4	Judah	Leah	*Blessing*: Family/ World leadership	Strong army/warrior	Retains nation's capital
			No enchantments can stand against him	Latter days—Strength needs to be roused	
5	Issachar	Leah	Good, pleasant land	Excessive taxation	Between two other tribes
6	Zebulun	Leah	Coastal lands	Prosperous, safe sea ports	Border reaches to Zidon
7	Joseph	Rachel	*Birthright*: double portion of land/ double tribes/ double prosperity	Incredible economic prosperity	One portion of land more than the other tribes
			Additional blessings for being hated and cheated by his brothers	World is jealous of Joseph's prosperity	Incredibly fruitful and arable lands/ rich natural resources
			The latter-day "stone of Israel" comes from Joseph's land	Large population	Retains the city of Ephrath (Rachel's burial place) within Judah's inheritance
8	Benjamin	Rachel	Gains wealth through warfare	Warrior/ strong army	Border lands
9	Gad	Zilpah (Leah)	Fortune/ clever military	Warrior/ he will be raided/ but will attack the rear	Border lands
10	Asher	Zilpah (Leah)	Bountiful land/ prosperity	Manufactures royal danties/ plentiful harvests	Rich, arable lands
11	Dan	Bilah (Rachel)	Sense of judgment/ military trickery	Self-autonomy, sence of justice, judgment	Northern territory
			Waits for YHWH's salvation	Militarily deceptive/ difficult to subjugate	
12	Naphtali	Bilah (Rachel)	Peace/ good land	Rich literary heritage	Wide open territory

> Now Moses kept the flock of Jethro his father in law, (a) the priest of Midian: and he led the flock to the backside of the desert, (b) and came to the mountain of God, even to Horeb. (c) And the angel of YHWH appeared to him in a flame of fire out of the middle of a bush: and he looked, and, behold, the bush burned with fire, and the bush was not consumed. (Exod 3:1–2)

After Sarah died, Abraham married Keturah, who bore Midian (Gen 25:1). Although Midian had no stake in Isaac's birthright or blessing, Abraham gave him a portion and sent him away to the east (Gen 25:1–6). This text holds three clues. One, the "land of Midian" will lie to the east of Canaan. Two, (b) Mt. Horeb (also called Mt. Sinai) will lie in the land of Midian at the far part of the desert, or at least be close enough for Moses to pasture Jethro's flocks there. Third, Jethro (a) may have walked in the way of Abraham; he may have been schooled in the ways of justice and judgment, enabling him to serve as an honorable priest in the same manner that Melchizedek (Gen 14:18) did several centuries before. It appears that Jethro's knowledge of the *way of YHWH* (i.e., the Law) later enabled him to advise Moses so that Moses could ease his burden by establishing elders to judge in the nation's legal matters (Exod 18:14–26).[62]

In Exod 3:2 YHWH's angel made his first (c) appearance to Moses at Mt. Sinai. Although v. 2 states that the "flame of fire" was an angel, from there on the text treats this angel *as though it were YHWH himself.* Why does Scripture recognize the angel as YHWH? Because YHWH's name was in his messenger (Exod 23:21), and he was ordained to speak on his Creator's behalf. This method is consistently followed throughout the Hebrew Scriptures (Old Testament).[63]

> And Moses said, (d) I will now turn aside, and see this great sight, why the bush is not burnt. And when YHWH saw that he turned aside to see, God (Heb. *Elohiym*) called to him out of the middle of the bush, and said, Moses, Moses. And he said, Here am I. And he said, Do not draw closer: put off your shoes from off your feet, for the place where on you stand is holy ground. Moreover he said, (e) I am the God (Heb. *Eloha*) of your father, the God (Heb. *Eloha*) of Abraham, the God of Isaac, and the God of Jacob. And Moses hid his face; for he was afraid to look on God. And YHWH said, I have surely seen the affliction of my people which are in Egypt, and have heard their cry by reason of their taskmasters; for I know their sorrows; (f) And I am come down to deliver them out of the hand of the Egyptians, and to bring them up out of that land to a good land and a large, to a land flowing with milk and honey; to the place of the Canaanites, and the Hittites, and the Amorites, and the Perizzites, and the Hivites, and the Jebusites. Now therefore, behold, the cry of the Children of Israel is come unto me: and I have also *seen* the oppression with which the Egyptians oppress them. Come now therefore, and (g) I will send you to Pharaoh, that you may bring forth my people the Children of Israel out of Egypt. (Exod 3:3–10)

The sign (d) of Moses' Covenant was a burning bush that did not burn. YHWH established who (e) he was by stating that he was the God (Heb. *Elohiym*) who had covenanted with

Abraham, Isaac, and Jacob. YHWH called Moses, proposing (f) to fulfill the hidden judgment in the Promised-Land Covenant, using Moses to lead his people out of Egypt. YHWH commanded Moses to (g) "Bring my people out of Egypt."

> And Moses said to God, Who am I, that I should go to Pharaoh, and that I should bring forth the Children of Israel out of Egypt? (h) And he said, Certainly I will be with you; and this shall be a token to you, that I have sent you: **When you have brought forth the people out of Egypt, you shall serve God on this mountain.** (Exod 3:11–12)

YHWH offers a second sign (or token)[64] of his covenant with Moses. The sign is the actual fulfillment (h) of the Mosaic Covenant, which would bring YHWH's people out of Egypt and back to Mt. Sinai, thus fulfilling the prophecy of serving "God on this mountain."[65]

> And Moses said to God, Behold, when I come to the Children of Israel, and shall say to them, The God of your fathers has sent me to you; and they shall say to me, What is his name? (i) what shall I say to them? And God said to Moses, (j) I AM THAT I AM: and he said, Thus shall you say to the Children of Israel, I AM has sent me to you. And God said moreover to Moses, Thus shall you say to the Children of Israel, YHWH God of your fathers, the God of Abraham, the God of Isaac, and the God of Jacob, has sent me to you: **this is my name forever, and this is my memorial to all generations.** (Exod 3:13–15)

Moses' question (i) implies that the Children of Israel at this time did not know the God of Abraham, Isaac, and Jacob. Moses implies that Israel was serving Egyptian deities and would not know who Abraham's God was. David grants further credence to Israel's Egyptian idolatry, saying,

> What one nation in the earth is like your people, even like Israel, whom God went to redeem for a people to himself, and to make him a name, and to do for you great things and terrible, for your land, before your people, which you *redeemed to you from Egypt, from the nations and their gods?* (2 Sam 7:23)

That Israel needed to be "redeemed from Egypt's gods" indicates that Jacob's children worshiped them during their oppression. Although Israel may have cried out to false deities for deliverance, YHWH, who states "there is none else beside me," still heard their cry and purposed to fulfill his covenants with Abraham, Isaac, and Jacob.

The composition (j) of YHWH's name is *YH*, meaning 'I am' and *WH* meaning 'that I am.' Hence, 'I exist.'[66] Much like Isaac's name, this name established by the Creator is a memorial to humanity so that there should be no doubt about his existence. The Mosaic covenant establishes the name *YHWH* as the Creator's memorial, the name by which he wishes us to call him for "all generations."[67]

Go, and gather the elders of Israel together, and say to them, YHWH God of your fathers, the God of Abraham, of Isaac, and of Jacob, appeared to me, saying, I have surely visited you, and seen that which is done to you in Egypt: And I have said, I will bring you up out of the affliction of Egypt to the land of the Canaanites, and the Hittites, and the Amorites, and the Perizzites, and the Hivites, and the Jebusites, to a (k) *land flowing with milk and honey*. And they shall listen to your voice: and you shall come, you and the elders of Israel, to the king of Egypt, and you shall say to him, YHWH God of the Hebrews has met with us: and now let us go, we beseech you, three days' journey into the wilderness, that we may sacrifice to YHWH our God (Elohiym.) *And I am sure that the king of Egypt will not let you go, no, not by a mighty hand*. And I will stretch out my hand, and smite Egypt with all my wonders which I will do in the middle of it: and after that he will let you go. And I will give this people favor in the sight of the Egyptians: and it shall come to pass, that, *when you go, you shall not go empty:* But *every woman (l) shall borrow of her neighbor, and of her that sojournes in her house, jewels of silver, and jewels of gold, and raiment*: and you shall put them on your sons, and on your daughters; and *you shall spoil the Egyptians*. (Exod 3:16–22)

A land that flows with milk and honey possesses (k) vast natural resources. Rich, arable land, favorable precipitation, and mild climate all cause a land to flow with milk and honey. Thus, Canaan is marked by its abundance. An ancient text, dating to Egypt's Middle Kingdom (*c.* 2000–1780) allows us to glimpse the plenty that Canaan provided at the dawn of Israel's exodus.

> It was a good land, named Yaa. Figs were in it, and grapes. It had more wine than water. Plentiful was its honey, abundant its olives. Every (kind of) fruit was on its trees. Barley was there, and emmer. There was no limit to any (kind of) cattle.[68]

YHWH's angel instructed Israel's women (l) to borrow or demand gold and silver from their Egyptian neighbors and mistresses. This command initiated the fulfillment of the hidden judgment prophecy in the Promised-Land Covenant (Gen 15:14) by plundering the wealth owned by Israel's Egyptian lords (see pp. 88–89).

And Moses said to YHWH, O my lord, I am not eloquent, neither up until now, nor since you have spoken to your servant: but I am slow of speech, and of a slow tongue. And YHWH said to him, Who has made man's mouth? or who makes the dumb, or deaf, or the seeing, or the blind? Have not I YHWH? Now therefore go, and I will be with your mouth, and teach you what you shall say. And he said, O my lord, send, I pray you, by the hand of him whom you will send. (m) And *the anger* of YHWH was kindled against Moses, and he said, Is not Aaron the Levite your brother? I know that he can speak well. And also, behold, he comes forth to meet you: and when he sees you, he will be glad in his heart. And you shall speak to him, and put words in his mouth: and I will be with your mouth, and with his mouth, and will teach you what you shall do. *And he shall be your (n) spokesman to the people: and he shall be, even he shall be to you instead of a mouth, and you shall be to him instead of God.* (Exod 4:10–16)

Why did YHWH become angry (m) at Moses' unpretentious assessment of himself? YHWH had given Moses the sign of his power in the burning bush. He had shown that he could turn Moses' rod into a serpent (Exod 4:2–3) and make his hand leprous (Exod 4:4), yet Moses did not believe that YHWH could make him an effective deliverer. Moses asked for an intermediary to speak on his behalf. YHWH fulfilled this (n) request, telling Moses that he (Moses) would be as a God himself to the people and Aaron as Moses' spokesman. Exod 7:1 further defined this relationship by portraying Moses as God and Aaron as Moses' prophet.[69] "See, I have made you a god to Pharaoh: and Aaron your brother shall be your prophet."

YHWH further ordains that all of the signs that he will bring upon Egypt in order to deliver the nation, will be performed with Moses' rod:

> And you shall take this rod in your hand, with which you shall do signs. (Exod 4:17)

Moses' rod was the sign used to demonstrate to the people and to Pharaoh that Moses was YHWH's messenger, who spoke with YHWH's authority. This "rod of Elohiym" (Exod 4:20) was employed in every sign and wonder in which YHWH made Moses like himself (God).

YHWH consistently administers to nations their own oppression. The Israelite Law exhorts, "Love your neighbor as yourself" (Lev 19:18, 34; Deut 10:19). The Law specified that, if a person seeks to defraud, then the attempted fraud should be rendered on that person.[70] This precept was further evidenced in Solomon's prayer, which entreated YHWH to "hear from heaven, and do, and judge your servants, *by requiting the wicked, by recompensing his way on his own head;* and by justifying the righteous, by giving him according to his righteousness" (2 Chr 6:23). This precept is consistently evidenced in Moses' Covenant.

At Moses' birth, Pharaoh killed the Hebrew children. As judgment for this cold-blooded crime, YHWH would harden Pharaoh's heart so that he would not let Israel go. This would cause Pharaoh to withhold YHWH's firstborn son (Israel, Exod 4:22) from him. As judgment for not relinquishing YHWH's firstborn son, Pharaoh's firstborn son would be required as Pharaoh's way was recompensed on his own head.[71] Although many other signs and wonders were rendered on Egypt, the death of the firstborn was the final act of judgment. That Egypt was in need of correction is evidenced by Pharaoh's statement: "I have sinned this time: YHWH is righteous, and I and my people are wicked" (Exod 9:27).

And Moses took the rod of God in his hand. And YHWH said to Moses, When you go to return to Egypt, see that you do all those wonders before Pharaoh, which I have put in your hand: (o) but I will harden his heart, that he shall not let the people go. And you shall say to Pharaoh, (p) Thus said YHWH, *Israel is my son, even my firstborn*: And I say to you, Let my son go, that he may serve me: and if you refuse to let him go, behold, *I will slay your son, even your firstborn.* (Exod 4:20–23)

YHWH hardened Pharaoh's heart as a judgment on or (o) consequence of his own self-hardening. Pharaoh had already hardened his heart against Moses' appeal to free the Israelites. By hardening himself, he became always more confirmed in his obstinacy until he brought the final doom on himself, and his sin became its own punishment.[72]

The Mosaic Covenant recognized all of Jacob's children (p) as Abraham's firstborn son and heir (see also Exod 4:22). Thus, all the Israelites were heir to their father's covenants (the birthright and blessing) *and were viewed as the firstborn of all nations* of the earth.

Armed with this understanding, I was ready to investigate whether or not Israel's national covenants also upheld the initial words of truth given to her patriarchs. I had seen that covenants consistently upheld and incorporated all aspects of YHWH's previously spoken words (i.e., doctrine) to humanity. Would Israel's national covenants uphold this truth or would YHWH fail this test and arbitrarily rescind his promises?

VI. ISRAEL'S COVENANTS

A. *Sinai Covenant: The Ten Precepts*

As I began to look at the first covenant YHWH made with the Children of Israel at Mt. Sinai, I discovered something rather unique: the Creator himself spoke to the people. This is quite distinguishable from previous covenants made with Abraham, Isaac, and Jacob, in which a messenger or angel related YHWH's instructions and promises.[73] In YHWH's first covenant with Moses through the burning bush, a messenger had been sent to do YHWH's bidding (Exod 3:2), but when Moses returned to Mt. Horeb, YHWH himself "called aloud" to Moses.

> And Moses went up to God, and YHWH *called* to him out of the mountain, saying, Thus shall you say to the House of Jacob, and tell the Children of Israel; You have seen what I did to the Egyptians, and how I bore you on eagles' wings, and brought you to myself. Now therefore, if you will obey *my voice* indeed, and *keep my covenant*, then you shall be a peculiar treasure to me above all people: for all the earth is mine. (Exod 19:3–5)

The word "voice," *qowl* in Hebrew means 'to call aloud'; it denotes something actually spoken with a person's voice.[74] This same word is used to describe God walking in Eden and calling to Adam in Gen 3:8. At Mt. Sinai, YHWH audibly spoke to the Children of Israel, exhorting them to obey his Law.

> And *God spoke all these words*, saying, I am YHWH your God, which have brought you out of the land of Egypt, out of the house of bondage. (Exod 20:1–2; see also Exod 19:19)

The words that YHWH spoke in Exodus 20 are the Ten Commandments. After Israel heard YHWH speak these commands, the people cried out to Moses. "You speak with us, and we will hear: but do not let God (*Elohiym*) speak with us, lest we die" (Exod 20:18–19). Evidently, the sound of YHWH's voice accompanied by smoke and thunder was so frightening that the people feared hearing their Creator speak any longer. Deuteronomy certifies this event,

Table 4.2. The Sinai Constitutional Covenant

Preamble		Exod 20:1	"God spoke these words"
Historical Prologue		Exod 20:2	"I am YHWH your God, which have brought you out of the land of Egypt, out of the house of bondage."
Stipulation	YHWH	Exod 20:3–17	The Ten Commandments or Precepts
	Israel	Exod 20:18–20	*Self-imposed injunction*: People of Israel do not want God to talk directly to them
	Resolution	Exod 20:21–22	God gives his constitutional Law to Israel through Moses
Blessing		Lev 26:2-13, 44–46	Blessings for observing covenant "if, then"
		Exod 19:5–6	If Israel obeys, the nation will ultimately become a peculiar treasure, a kingdom of priests
Curse		Lev 26:14–46	Curses are chronologically and incrementally applied, eventually curses affect blessing
Oath/ Ratification	YHWH	Exod 3:8	YHWH is "come down" to deliver Israel "out of Egypt" and to fulfill the Promised Land Covenant
		Exod 3:20	YHWH will smite Egypt and Israel will not come out empty-handed (fulfill, Gen 15:14)
		Exod 13:3–4	Passover - The Passover sacrifice saves/delivers YHWH's first-born son Israel (Exod 4:22)
	Israel	Exod 12:11	Passover
Sign	YHWH	Exod 20:18	Descended on the mount with fire, thunder, and a great noise; all people heard YHWH's voice
	Israel	Exod 31:12–18	Sabbaths

reciting: "Did ever people hear the *voice of God* speaking out of the middle of the fire, as you *have heard*, and live?" (Deut 4:33). This evidences another point at which Scripture meets the test of fidelity: both Exodus and Deuteronomy are consistent in witnessing YHWH's speech at Mt. Sinai. YHWH accepted Israel's request as an injunction on his covenants and did not again speak directly to his people but used prophets to speak on his behalf.

Shortly after YHWH spoke his covenant, Moses ascended the mount, again talking with YHWH. Moses received the two stones of testimony (Exod 31:18), which defined YHWH's covenant with the nation. When he descended the mountain and saw Israel's rebellion, he shattered the tablets on which YHWH had written. A short time later, YHWH again provided a *written contract* of his Law. The second time Moses received the stone tablets, the Book of Exodus is clearer in regard to what was written on them.

And he was there with YHWH forty days and forty nights; he did neither eat bread, nor drink water. And he wrote on the tables the *words of the covenant, the Ten Commandments*. (Exod 34:28)

The Ten Commandments were the stipulations of Israel's Covenant. Remember that every covenant requires a sign or seal. At Moses' first ascent, YHWH had audibly spoken the sign that ratified Israel's covenant:

> Speak you also to the Children of Israel, saying, *Verily my sabbaths you shall keep: for it is a sign between me and you throughout your generations*; (a) that you may know that I am YHWH that does sanctify you. You shall keep the sabbath therefore; for it is holy to you: every one that defiles it shall surely be put to death: for whosoever does any work therein, that soul shall be cut off from among his people. Six days may work be done; but in the seventh is the sabbath of rest, holy to YHWH: whosoever does any work in the sabbath day, he shall surely be put to death. Why the Children of Israel shall keep the sabbath, to observe the sabbath throughout their generations, for a perpetual covenant. *It is a sign between me and the Children of Israel forever*: for in six days YHWH made heaven and earth, and on the seventh day he rested, and was refreshed. (Exod 31:13–17)

The Sabbaths are the sign of YHWH's covenant: written on the two tables of stone.[75] Israel's covenant continues to follow the Circumcision Covenant's formula by requiring the people to provide the sign that they are in agreement with the pact's terms by resting on the seventh day of the week and observing the sabbatical years. The Creator (a) indicates that by keeping his Sabbaths Israel will know who he is and understand that he has sanctified them. YHWH had given his covenant as a "deliverance from the house of bondage."[76] Both the stipulations regarding the Sabbath day and the requirements for the sabbatical year sought to relieve the oppression or bondage placed on the worker or laborer (whether slave or free). *By observing these Sabbaths, Israel would learn that to be in covenant with YHWH meant she should not oppress her countrymen.* Remember that in the last chapter, we saw that covenants consist of three primary parts: stipulation, penalty, and the sign. Israel's Sinai Compact continues to follow this formula as Leviticus 26 lists consequences or penalties should Israel breach her pact with YHWH. Leviticus 26 enumerates the consequences that would be applied in series of "seven times" if Israel rebelled. We will examine these penalties below, in chaps. 15–16.

Remember that covenants were sealed with self-imprecating sacrifices during biblical times. The sacrifice that Israel partook in to seal her covenant with YHWH was the Passover Sacrifice (Exodus 12 and Numbers 9). This sacrifice signaled the nation's fate should her citizens fail to uphold YHWH's covenant. Thus the Sinai Compact shifts from the patriarchal covenant of grant to that of parity or suzerainty type of covenant.[77] *YHWH established the Passover meal as the means by which Israel and her converts demonstrated that they were faithful to their covenantal agreement with YHWH* (Exod 12:43–49; Num 9:1–14). Observing the Passover ceremony was a sign of conversion that demonstrated that a foreigner would follow Israel's God and be held to the covenant's stipulations (Exod 12:43–50). The Passover ceremony signaled the convert's willingness to obey YHWH's Covenant while acknowledging its penalties for rebellion (see Table 4.2).

So far, I had not uncovered any aspect to the national covenant that rescinded or tried to annul YHWH's previously spoken promises. What I had discovered was a consistent message of truth that had been given to Abraham, Isaac, and Jacob, which appears to have been passed down to the nation of Israel. Quite unexpectedly, I learned that the Israelites were able to issue their own injunction on the covenant, which affected future generations (i.e., to not have God speak directly to them) and YHWH accepted it. I wondered if the next covenant would also reveal something new.

B. *The Moab-Shechem Covenant: Deuteronomy*

After YHWH brought Israel out of Egypt, the nation rebelled. She revolted persistently against YHWH and his covenant no less than ten times.[78] Due to the nation's barbaric and uncivilized defiance, YHWH forsook this generation (Num 14:35), choosing to establish his covenant with her children.[79] YHWH banned this belligerent generation from the Promised Land for 40 years (Num 14:34), condemning her to nomadism while her warriors died in the desert (Deut 2:14).

After Israel fulfilled her exile, the nation migrated to the plains of Moab,[80] a month before entering the Promised Land.[81] Moses outlined the covenant's parameters, in the plain of Moab in the 11th month of the 40th year of coming out of Egypt (Deut 1:3). Moses had instructed Joshua, the Levites, and the people to reconfirm and ratify this covenant inside the Promised Land on top of the two hills that overlooked Shechem.

> And it shall be *on the day when you shall pass over Jordan* to the land which YHWH your God gives you, that you *shall set you up great stones, and plaster them with plaster:* **And you shall write on them all the words of this law** (the Moab-Shechem Covenant), when you are passed over, that you may go in to the land which YHWH your God gives you. . . . Therefore it shall be *when you be gone over Jordan,* that you shall set up these stones, which I command you this day, in mount Ebal, and you shall plaster them with plaster. And *there shall you build an altar to YHWH your God, an altar of stones:* you shall not lift up any iron tool on them (see Exod 20:24). You shall build the altar of YHWH your God of whole stones: and *you shall offer burnt offerings thereon to YHWH your God.* (Deut 27:2–6, parentheses added)

Although Moses had confirmed this covenant in Moab, it was not actually ratified until about a month or two after Joshua had led Israel over the Jordan (Joshua 3) and conquered both Jericho and Ai (Joshua 5–8). This initial campaign carved out a peaceful region from which Israel could begin base operations to inherit the Promised Land.

Moses instructed the nation to administer her own blessings and curses.

> Behold, I set before you this day a blessing and a curse; A blessing, *if you obey* the commandments of YHWH your God, which I command you this day: And a curse, *if you will not obey* the commandments of YHWH your God, but turn aside out of the way which I command you this day, to go after other gods, which you have not known. And it shall come to pass, when YHWH your God has brought you in to the land where you go to possess it, that you shall put the blessing on mount Gerizim, and the curse on mount Ebal. (Deut 11:26–29)

Table 4.3. The Constitutional Moab-Shechem Covenant

Preamble	Deut 5:1/Exod 20:1, 18-20	Since Israel had requested that God not talk to her, Moses was calling Israel together to hear the words of the covenant: to learn, to observe, and to obey them. Israel was recovenanting with God.
	Deut 5:2	YHWH had previously made a covenant with Israel at Mt. Horeb.
	Deut 5:3	The Sinai Covenant was not just for Israel's forefathers but was for Israel "today."
Historical Prologue	Deut 5:4/ Exod 20:1, 18-20	"YHWH talked with you face to face in the mount out of the midst of the fire."
	Deut 5:5/ Exod 20:21-22	"I stood between YHWH and you at that time, to show you the work of YHWH: for you were afraid by reason of the fire."
(Re-issues Sinai Covenant)	Deut 5:6/ Exod 20:2	"I am YHWH your God, which have brought you out of the land of Egypt, out of the house of bondage."
Stipulation YHWH	Deut 5:7-21/ Exod 20:3-17	The Ten Commandments or Precepts
	Deut 5:22, 4:2, 12:32	*Injunction*: Do not add or take away from the words, precepts, stipulations of this covenant
Israel	Deut 5:23-29/ Exod 20:18-20	*Self-imposed injunction*: People of Israel do not want God to talk to them directly
	Deut 5:29	Clarification to Israel's self-imposed injunction: God desires Israel to have a heart to obey his law "that it may go well with the people." This implies a relationship with God.
	Deut 5:30-31/ Exod 20:21-22	God gives his Constitutional Law to Israel through Moses
	Deut 32-33	Moses encourages Israel to observe the Covenant that the nation may have a long life and inherit the promised land.
Blessings	Deut 28:1-14, 30-14/Lev 26:2-13, 44-46	Blessings for observing covenant "if, then." Disobedience leads to curses. Curses eventually affect blessings.
Curses	Deut 28:15-29:29/ Lev 26:14-46	Curses are chronologically and incrementally applied. Eventually curses affect blessing once the curses teach Israel to obey the covenant and Israel learns from her mistakes.

(Table continued next page)

Table 4.3. The Constitutional Moab-Shechem Covenant (continued)

Oath/ Ratification	YHWH	Exod 3:8	YHWH is come down to deliver Israel out of Egypt and to fulfill the Promised Land Covenant.
		Deut 5:24	God shows his glory (Heb., *kabod*) and greatness. God talks with man and he lives.
		Deut 9:3	YHWH will be a consuming fire to destroy Israel's enemies quickly.
		Deut 11:22-23	"If you obey . . . then YHWH will drive the natives out of the Promised Land, even nations that are stronger and mightier; no people can stand before Israel, that Israel may inherit the land" and fulfill all covenants.
		Deut 31:3	God will go before Israel to prepare her way so that she may inherit the Promised Land and fulfill the covenants. God names Joshua as Moses' successor.
	Israel	Deut 11:26-31, 27:1-30:14	Ceremony of placing the blessings on Mt. Gerizim and the curse on Mt. Ebal
		Deut 27:3, 8/ Josh 8:31-35	"Write all the words of this Law very plainly on the day that you pass over Jordan."
		Deut 27:6/ Josh 8:30-31	Build an unhewn stone altar to offer peace offerings and rejoice before YHWH.
Sign	YHWH	Deut 28:46	The history of the curses of the covenant (Deut 29:22-29)
	Israel	Deut 6:1-9, 11:18	Thinking and doing according to the Law: having the heart to obey the Law.
		Deut 11:19-20	Evidence that Israel's society is thinking and acting according to the Law: her people teach the covenants to their children, they talk of the laws and ways of YHWH often, they display the constitutional covenant in their homes and at their cities' entrances.

And Moses charged the people the same day, saying, These shall stand on mount Gerizim to bless the people, when you are come over Jordan; Simeon, and Levi, and Judah, and Issachar, and Joseph, and Benjamin: And these shall stand on mount Ebal to curse; Reuben, Gad, and Asher, and Zebulun, Dan, and Naphtali. And the Levites shall speak, and say to all the men of Israel with a loud voice. (Deut 27:11–14)

YHWH's division of Israel's tribes is quite striking. Those on Mt. Gerizim, the mount of blessing, are children of Jacob's lawful wives, Leah and Rachel (Gen 35:23–24): Simeon, Levi, Judah, Issachar, Joseph, and Benjamin. The tribes on Mt. Ebal, the mount of cursing, are Reuben, Gad, Asher, Zebulun, Dan, and Naphtali, sons of Bilhah and Zilpah—slave women belonging to Jacob's two wives (Gen 29:24, 29). Reuben and Zebulun are the exception.

The word *Ebal* means 'baldness,' signaling the mount's barren landscape, while the meaning of *Gerizim* is uncertain.[82] From the context of Moses' instructions, it appears that one mountain heralded the blessings of the nation while the other mountain signaled the national curses.

Joshua fulfilled Moses's instruction shortly after entering Canaan and blazing a trail from Jericho to Shechem.

> Then Joshua built an altar to YHWH God of Israel in mount Ebal, as Moses the servant of YHWH commanded the Children of Israel, as it is written in the book of the Law of Moses, an altar of whole stones, over which no man has lifted up any iron: and they offered there on burnt offerings to YHWH, and sacrificed peace offerings. And he wrote there on the stones a copy of the Law of Moses, which he wrote in the presence of the Children of Israel. And all Israel, and their elders, and officers, and their judges, stood on this side the ark and on that side before the priests the Levites, which bare the ark of the covenant of YHWH, as well the stranger, as he that was born among them; half of them over against mount Gerizim, and half of them over against mount Ebal; as Moses the servant of YHWH had commanded before, that they should bless the people of Israel. And afterward he read all the words of the law, the blessings and cursings, *according to all that is written in the book of the law. There was not a word of all that Moses commanded, which Joshua read not before all the congregation of Israel,* with the women, and the little ones, and the strangers that were conversant among them. (Josh 8:30–35)

Joshua's recovenanting at Shechem signaled the beginning of the nation's epochs. So many of YHWH's laws and his procedures dealt with issues that Israel could only obey once she entered the freedom afforded within the Promised Land.[83] Once she conquered the land to obtain this freedom, she could also be held accountable for upholding the covenant's stipulations. When Israel completed the blessing and cursing ceremony, her official "time" on the land began and was marked with the national Jubilees. Each Jubilee would mark the recovenanting of YHWH's constitution with a new generation (Leviticus 25, 27), who would pledge to walk in the way of Yah.[84] This not only kept YHWH's constitutional Law[85] the focal point of national patriotic values, it also served to inspire a new generation to affirm and recommit to walking in the way of Yah.

YHWH's requirements for the Moab-Shechem covenant were the same as they had been for the Sinai covenant: obedience to the Ten Commandments (Deuteronomy 5). YHWH did, however, broaden *the sign* of the Shechem covenant to include *all* the commandments, not just the Sabbath sign (Deut 6:8; 11:18).

> Hear, O Israel: YHWH our God is one YHWH. And you shall love YHWH your God with all your heart, and with all your soul, and with all your might. And these words, which I command you this day, shall be in your heart: And you shall teach them diligently to your children, and shall talk of them when you sit in your house, and when you walk by the

way, and when you lie down, and when you rise up. *And you shall bind them for a sign on your hand, and they shall be as frontlets between your eyes.* (Deut 6:5–8; see also Deut 11:18)

For Israel to show that she was in compliance with this covenant, her people had to train both their thoughts (the frontlet between their eyes) and their actions (hands) to be in accord with YHWH's ten stipulations (see Table 4.3). Thus, her willing obedience granted the sign of Israel's compliance in the Moabic covenant. The greatest difference between the Sinai Covenant and the Moab-Shechem Covenant were the consequences for breaching the Creator's pact, which are sited in Table 4.4. Leviticus 26 had outlined very general consequences that would be applied in series of "seven times." While the curses from the Sinai Covenant were incorporated into the Moab-Shechem Covenant, the latter covenant (Deuteronomy 29–30) outlined more specific and detailed judgments against the nation that included recognition of each national deportation.

Table 4.4. Sinai and Moab-Shechem Covenants

Israel's Covenants	Ratified or Sealed by:	Promise	Requirement	Penalty	Sign
Sinai	Passover	Israel will receive the blessings of the patriarchal covenants (Exod 12:25)	Ten Command-ments (Exodus 20)	"Seven Times" (Leviticus 26)	Sabbaths (Exod 31:12–17)
Moab-Shechem	Ceremonially placing blessings and curses at Shechem, writing a copy of the Law, peace offerings. (Josh 8:30–35)	The patriarchal covenants (Deut 1:11; 6:3; 12:20; 15:6; 8:18; 19:8; 26:18). YHWH's special blessing (Deut 30:1–14)	Ten Com-mandments/ do not add or delete from the constitution (Deuteronomy 5; 4:2; 5:22; 12:32)	Curses of the Law (Deuter-onomy 27–29)	Having a heart for Torah: Thinking and acting in accord with the Ten Commandments (Deut 6:8; 11:18)

Once again, Israel's national covenants had incorporated all aspects of the previously spoken words of YHWH to the patriarchs. (I have included further detail of the harmony between these covenants in chaps. 13–14.) Since I did not want to overlook any covenants that could have affected Israel's history, I turned to examine covenants that YHWH had made with individuals in Israel's society.

VII. COVENANTS OF PEACE FOR A LIGHT

There are two final covenants that greatly affected Israel's history and further defined YHWH's truth. The first covenant was contracted with Phinehas, the grandson of Israel's first high priest. God offered the second covenant to King David. Both of these covenants were *peace treaties* between YHWH and David and Phinehas and their offspring. Phinehas and David were responsible for ruling the people and ensuring that righteousness and justice prevailed in the land. YHWH's peace covenant granted extraordinary mercy to these two Houses when the nation rebelled. YHWH had previously awarded covenants to Abraham due to his obedience (Gen 22:18; 26:5). Both of these covenants followed this precedent when the men displayed outstanding loyalty to YHWH. They differed from the Abrahamic covenants only in the fact that Phinehas's and David's zealous actions had already provided the sign for their covenants. Therefore YHWH's covenants were offered as grants to these two men as recompense for their righteousness, and no additional signs were needed.

A. *Phinehas's Covenant*

Israel stayed in Shittim, and the people began to commit prostitution with the daughters of Moab. And they called the people to the sacrifices of their gods: and the people did eat, and bowed down to their gods. And Israel joined himself to Baal-peor: and the anger of YHWH was kindled against Israel. And YHWH said to Moses, Take all the heads of the people, and hang them up before YHWH against the sun, that the fierce anger of YHWH may be turned away from Israel. And Moses said to the judges of Israel, Slay you every one his men that were joined to Baal-peor. And behold, one of the Children of Israel came and brought to his brothers a Midianite woman in the sight of Moses, and in the sight of all the congregation of the Children of Israel, who were weeping before the door of the tabernacle of the congregation.

And when Phinehas, the son of Eleazar, the son of Aaron the priest, saw it, he rose up from among the congregation, and took a javelin in his hand; And he went after the man of Israel into the tent, and thrust both of them through, the man of Israel, and the woman through her belly. So the plague was stayed from the Children of Israel. And those that died in the plague were twenty and four thousand.

And YHWH spoke to Moses, saying, Phinehas, the son of Eleazar, the son of Aaron the priest, has turned my wrath away from the Children of Israel, while he was zealous for my sake among them, that I consumed not the Children of Israel in my jealousy. Therefore say, Behold, I give to him ***my covenant of peace***: And he shall have it, and his (a) seed after him, even the covenant of an (b) everlasting priesthood; because he was zealous for his God, and made an atonement for the Children of Israel. (Num 25:1–13)

Law enforcement was one of the Levites' governmental responsibilities. During the wilderness journey, Israel rebelled against the Law, and Phinehas fulfilled his role as judge by rendering retribution. Phinehas showed zeal for YHWH's sake, and his actions furnished the sign of this pact. YHWH's covenant of peace was made not only with Phinehas but with his descendants as well. What did the Creator promise? He promised establish Phinehas's House as the Aaronic line from which Israel's high priesthood would descend. At this point in Israel's history, the tribe of Levi had redeemed itself by the people's own righteousness. Moses, Aaron, and Miriam had led Israel out of Egypt and encouraged the nation to lean on YHWH (Exodus 15). Aaron's son, Phinehas, acted with zeal when no one else would stand up for Israel's God or for the covenant the nation had recently contracted. YHWH further divided the birthright, separating the priesthood from the family rulership (i.e., monarchy). Originally, the priesthood had been a right associated with the monarchy as we saw with Melchizedek (see pp. 55, 117). From this point forward in Israel's society, this birthright would be divided between Judah and Levi, providing a balance of power in the nation's governmental institutions.

B. Covenants with Women and Immigrants

There were at least two women in Israel's history who were also promised "sure houses." One was Shiphrah and the other Puah (Exod 1:15). Both of these women protected the lives of Israel's children when Pharaoh commanded them to kill Israel's newborns:

> And it came to pass, because the midwives feared God, that he made them houses. (Exod 1:21)

> Therefore thus says YHWH of hosts, the God of Israel; Jonadab the son of Rechab shall not want a man to stand before me forever. (Jer 35:19)

This same covenant was also given to the House of the Rechabites (Jer 35:1–19), who were not native Israelites but were resident-alien converts. The word translated "strangers" in v., 7 is the Hebrew *gerim*,[86] which designates individuals of non-Israelite extraction who had converted to walk in the way of YHWH. Although their ancestry did not trace to Jacob, YHWH still recognized the honor and obedience of the Rechabite descendants, promising that they would never "want for a male child" (Jer 35:19) to continue their heritage in the same way that Shiphrah and Puah would never want for offspring to continue their Houses (see Table 4.5).

Table 4.5. Covenants with Women and Immigrants

Shiphrah	Exod 1:15, 21	Covenant of Light—Sure house
Puah	Exod 1:15, 21	Covenant of Light—Sure house
Jonadab ben Rechab	Jer 35:19	Covenant of Light—Sure house

C. Davidic Covenant

After YHWH gave David peace from all his enemies, David rejoiced and desired to build a permanent house for YHWH. Although the Creator refused this offer because of David's war-torn past, YHWH did to David as David had tried to do for his Creator; YHWH promised David a sure house and a permanent lineage, even when his offspring rebelled.

> Now therefore so shall you say to my servant David, Thus said YHWH of hosts, I took you from the sheepcote, from following the sheep, to be ruler over my people, over Israel: And I was with you where ever you went, and have cut off all your enemies out of your sight, and have made you a great name, like to the name of the great men that are in the earth.

Moreover I will appoint a place for my people Israel, and will plant them, that they may dwell in a place of their own, and move no more; neither shall the children of wickedness afflict them anymore, as beforetime, And as since the time that I commanded judges to be over my people Israel, and have caused you to rest from all your enemies. Also YHWH tells you that *he will make you an house*. And when your days be fulfilled, and you shall sleep with your fathers, I will set up your seed after you, which shall proceed *out of your bowels*, and I will establish his kingdom.

He shall build an house for my name, and I will establish the throne of his kingdom forever. I will be his father, and he shall be my son. If he commit iniquity, I will chasten him with the rod of men, and with the stripes of the children of men: *But my mercy shall not depart away from him, as I took it from Saul, whom I put away before you. And your house and your kingdom shall be established forever before you: your throne shall be established forever*. According to all these words, and according to all this vision, so did Nathan speak to David.

Then went king David in, and sat before YHWH, and he said, Who am I, O YHWH God (Elohiym)? And what is my house, that you (singular) have brought me till now? And this was yet a small thing in your sight, O YHWH GOD; but you have spoken also of your servant's house *for a great while to come*. And is this the manner of man, O YHWH God? And what can David say more to you? for you, YHWH God, know your servant. For your word's sake, and according to your own heart, have you done all these great things, to make your servant know them. Why you are great, O YHWH God (Elohiym): for there is none like you, neither is there any God beside you, according to all that we have heard with our ears. And what one nation in the earth is like your people, even like Israel, whom God went to redeem for a people to himself, and to make him a name, and to do for you great things and terrible, for your land, before your people, which you redeemed to you from Egypt, *from the nations and their gods?* For you have **confirmed to yourself to your people Israel to be a people to you forever**: and you, YHWH, are become their God. And now, O YHWH God, the word that you have spoken concerning your servant, and concerning his house, establish it forever, and do as you have said.

And let your name be magnified forever, saying, YHWH of hosts is the God over Israel: and let the House of your servant David be established before you. For you, O YHWH of hosts, God of Israel, has revealed to your servant, saying, I will *build you an house*: therefore has your servant found in his heart to pray this prayer to you. And now, O YHWH GOD, you are that God, and your words be true, and you have promised this goodness to your servant: Therefore now let it please you to *bless the house* of your servant, that it may continue forever before you: for you, O YHWH GOD, have spoken it: and with *your blessing* let the house of your servant be blessed forever. (2 Sam 7:8–29)

Although YHWH established Phinehas's descendants as the Levitical high priesthood's rightful heirs, David's covenant established his line as the family from which Judah's leadership of Israel would descend. *David's House inherited Judah's birthright.*

From the outset of this investigation, I had formed my study on the concepts of truth: constancy and freedom from change (see Chap.1). I had also seen that internal constancy was an important consideration for Scripture's validity. As far as Israel's past was concerned, I had seen incredible consistency even in the small details. Now I needed to know if Scripture supported David's and Phinehas' promises as being permanent and unchanging. Are the Creator's promises to David and Phinehas still valid today? Or is it possible that YHWH could change or alter these covenants?

My covenant will I not break, nor alter the thing that is gone out of my lips. Once have I sworn by my holiness that I will not lie to David. (Ps 89:34–35)

My mercy will I keep for him for evermore, and *my covenant shall stand fast with him*. (Ps 89:28)

For thus said YHWH; (v. 17) *David shall never want a man to sit on the throne* of the House of Israel; *Neither shall the priests, the Levites, want a man before me* to offer burnt offerings, and to kindle meat offerings, and to do sacrifice *continually*. And the word of YHWH came to Jeremiah, saying, Thus said YHWH; If you can break my covenant of the day, and my covenant of the night, and that there should not be day and night in their season; Then may also my covenant be broken with David my servant, that he should not have a son to reign upon his throne; and with the Levites the priests, my ministers. As the host of heaven cannot be numbered, neither the sand of the sea measured: *so will I multiply the seed of David my servant*, and *the Levites* that minister to me.

Moreover the word of YHWH came to Jeremiah, saying, Consider you not what this people have spoken, saying, The two families which YHWH has chosen, he has even cast them off? Thus, they have despised my people, that they should be no more a nation before them. Thus said YHWH; If my covenant be not with day and night, and if I have not appointed the ordinances of heaven and earth; Then will I cast away the seed of Jacob, and David my servant, *so that I will not take any of his seed to be rulers over the seed of Abraham, Isaac, and Jacob: for I will cause their captivity to return, and have mercy on them.* (Jer 33:17–26)

Notice that v. 17 does *not* state that David will always have a son sitting on the throne, nor will Phinehas always have a son who will be performing priestly service. Rather, both David's and Phinehas's Houses will not lack children who could qualify and perform these services. In other words, they will never lack male progeny.

The value that YHWH places on his covenant with David was evidenced during Jehoram's reign (who was Ahab's grandson) when David's House continued all of Ahab's wickedness, "yet YHWH would not destroy Judah for David his servant's sake, as he promised *to give him always a light*, and to his children" (2 Kgs 8:19). YHWH established paralleled "covenants of light" to Phinehas and David—"sure houses" in both of their pedigrees, even during times of duress (see Table 4.6).

Table 4.6. Covenants with Israel's Houses of Leadership

Levi	Phinehas	Lev 25:12–13	Covenant of Light/Peace—Everlasting priesthood
Judah	David	2 Sam 7:8–29; Jer 33:17–26	Covenant of Light/Peace—Everlasting monarchy

If the word of YHWH is true, then Phinehas has descendants today who can perform the rights of the priesthood, and David has seed who can fulfill YHWH's word of sitting on the throne of David—for the day and night are *still* in their season. Notice also that Jeremiah 33 states that, *if* YHWH were able to cast away his covenant with the seed of David, then day and night would *not* be in their season. Only then would he be able to cast away Jacob's descendants and the promise of turning Israel's captivity today. Jeremiah's words are consistent with the Diaspora Covenant. If YHWH's word establishes truth and he is faithful to his promises, then this covenant is valid yet today, for day and night are still in their season. As our discussion turns to prophecy and history, the importance of these covenants will be manifest.

I had defined the ideas or doctrine that Scripture terms "truth." I knew that the next step in this investigation had to focus on the scientific validity of the Law that YHWH gave to Israel. Now it was time to see if Israel's charges were valid. Was YHWH's Law arbitrary or did it embrace natural laws that benefited all humanity? I also had to consider the possibility that Israel's Scriptures could demonstrate internal consistency but advocate a way of life that is unreasonable, irresponsible, or oppressive. Does the *way of YHWH* make his followers slaves to goals that we can never attain? Did God give us a Law simply to show us to be incapable of fulfilling it? The Book of Micah records Israel's view, that held YHWH's way of life and his Law were unrighteously unfair: a Law that could never be obeyed. I wanted to see for myself whether ancient Israel's allegations were yet to be substantiated. Was Israel's covenantal Law *a law of works* or a *law of equity*?

5

Laws of Reality, Part 1:
Vanquishing Modern Myths

In chap. 1, we heard Israel's accusation that YHWH had wearied and burdened the nation (Mic 6:3). The prophet Ezekiel sites a similar allegation during the Diaspora, when Israel complained that "the way of YHWH is not equal." Ezekiel rebutted the nation's claims, defending YHWH, saying, "Hear now, O House of Israel; Is not my way equal? Are not your ways unequal?" (Ezek 18:25). Since Israel's covenantal Law defines what YHWH requires of humanity, Israel's allegations are directed against the Law given at Mt. Sinai. The Israelites accused their Creator's ways (laws) of being harsh, unfair, unequal, and downright arbitrary. In his defense, the Creator maintained that it is man's ways that are unrighteous, but his ways that are just.

The Law was pivotal to my investigation of YHWH's righteousness. If the Creator was unrighteous or arbitrary in the Laws by which he ordained for the nation to live, then there can be no exoneration of Israel's God. Was the way outlined in his Law a way of death? Or did his Law ordain a way of life? Did the Creator establish righteous, fair, nonarbitrary, and equitable judgments? Or was the Law harsh and demanding: a Law whose demands could never be met? Truly, my entire investigation hinged on these questions. What good would it do if I found truth but found that truth to be unrighteous? For instance, would I really want to follow a Law that allowed a husband to beat his wife for not obeying his word? Or live in a world where free thought or a voiced opinion was prohibited?

Thus, Israel's allegations cannot be dismissed lightly. Establishing a firm understanding of Israel's Law and its intended use is imperative. Our investigation will search for evidence supporting the righteousness embodied in YHWH's way as described in his Law. We will weigh the righteousness of God's Law based on the following concepts:

Equity: justice according to natural law or right: freedom from bias or favoritism

159

Natural Law: a body of law or a specific principle held to be derived from nature and binding on human society in the absence of or in addition to positive law

Just: having a basis in or conforming to fact or reason: REASONABLE

Justice: The quality of being just or impartial, or fair: the principle or ideal of just dealing or right action: RIGHTEOUSNESS

—Merriam Webster's Ninth Collegiate Dictionary

I. FOUNDATION FOR THE LAW'S SCIENTIFIC INVESTIGATION

We have seen that YHWH ordained covenants for establishing and preserving truth found in "the way of YHWH." All patriarchal covenants were integrated into the nation's first Covenant, the Sinai Compact. This covenant was unique in that it actually defined the way of YHWH, having his constitutional Law attached to it.[1] Therefore, the Israelites' allegations challenged the fairness of their obligation to both the patriarchal covenants and the nation's divinely-ordained constitution.

In the introduction, I mentioned modern academia's view that religion can never be absolute. A person's firm belief in God can never be proven right or wrong. For most individuals, faith is simply choosing what he or she desires to believe (i.e., what feels good). But what if we applied the scientific method to Scripture? If we ask critical questions, research, construct hypothesis, test, and analyze the data, should we not be able to find solid evidence for or against YHWH's constitutional Law?

I have already defined the concepts governing my method of investigation (see chap. 1). Now it is imperative to ask critical questions to test Scripture's validity. Israel's Law must meet several tests to qualify as valid truth that is good for humanity. In addition to the concepts of truth defined in chap. 1 and the concepts of justice listed above, this case must ask the following questions:

Investigation question #1: Is the Law in harmony with the natural laws of nature?

Investigation question #2: Is the Law good for man?

Investigation question #3: Is the Law morally sound?

Investigation question #4: Does the Law contain freedom from "the house of servants," as Micah stated, or is it death, bondage, hard labor, and impossible to observe, as ancient Israel asserted?

II. INFALLIBILITY OF THE CHURCH

In the introduction of this book, I proposed that the Church has allowed spurious doctrines to be attached to God's word. The Church has often accepted popular opinion or one man's interpretation of God as the actual word of YHWH himself. Support for this view is probably no more evident than in the history of humanity's quest for knowledge and understanding in science, astronomy, and cosmology. For centuries, the Church maintained that the earth was the center of the universe.

The Church had endorsed Aristotle's view that the earth was at rest. The planets could move but in a flawed multiplicity of motions; only the "first heaven" attained the full perfection of the circle.[2] Noted scientific journalist Corey Powell observes:

> The Catholic Church, under the philosophical guidance of Aquinas in the thirteenth century, fused this cosmological model with Christian theology, so that the celestial spheres became the literal abode of the angels. This vivid picture is still a staple of popular culture, but it has cost the church dearly—once when Copernicus and Galileo argued powerfully that the Earth is not at the center of the universe, and again when Einstein developed the first comprehensive cosmological model rooted in physics.[3]

When Nicolaus Copernicus (1510 CE) presented evidence for the earth's rotation around the sun, the Church did not hesitate to dismiss his evidence as being absurd. Both Pope Paul V and Martin Luther argued against Copernicus's theories. Galileo Galilei charted the earth's orbit around the sun in *De Revolutionibus*, which the Church banned in 1616. In 1632, *The Inquisition* forced Galileo to renounce his views, and he lived the last nine years of his life under house arrest. Then Sir Isaac Newton, one of the foremost scientists in history appeared. His research could have advanced further had it not been for his prejudice fostered by the Church's medieval view of what God and his natural laws *ought* to be. Newton thought of God as "existing always and everywhere."[4] If God was everywhere, then it would be unthinkable that God's universe was not completely orderly with everything in its proper place: perfect circles, perfect distance, perfect distribution, perfect symmetry—perfectly static. He soon found that his conceptions were in error. Planets moved in elliptical motion, not circles. There were no uniform spaces or distances between planets. There was no perfect space, and the greatest finding of them all was—like weather patterns—the universe is constantly changing. Albert Einstein's research further revealed that the Church's view of the universe and the God who created it were quite flawed. One must ask whether the Church ever understood *who* God was in the first place. For if it had, should not its doctrine have reflected God's attributes as well as the reality of God's creation?

I have structured this case in such a way that Scripture's truth must be in accordance with facts and reality. *Webster's Dictionary* defines *truth* as:

> **Truth**: FIDELITY, CONSTANCY; the state of being the case: FACT; the body of real things, events, and facts: ACTUALITY; the property (as of a statement) of being in accord with fact or reality

If Scripture is truth, then its account of creation should be in accord with the realities that astronomers, mathematicians, and cosmologists have established through scientific experiment, observation, and verification. The Church has often let interpretations of Scripture be dictated by prominent Church leaders and Church politics. If the Old Testament is a word of truth, it should need no interpretation. Rather, we should find that it is in accord with the body of evidence presented by verified scientific discoveries today.

III. THE WORD OF YHWH: NATURAL LAW

It was imperative that I examine the Creator's Law to see whether it harmonizes with the laws of reality or is in fact contrary to natural law. The best *scientific* definition of *equity* is found in Sir Isaac Newton's Third Law of Motion. Newton's *Third Law,* also called the "action-reaction law," states:

> The actions of two bodies on each other are *always equal in magnitude and opposite in direction.*[5]

In other words, for every action, there is an opposite and equal reaction.

Scripture indeed embraces this natural law, but the terminology that Scripture uses for the action-reaction law is an *eye for an eye, and a tooth for a tooth*—opposite and equal reactions. While Scripture's terminology may seem archaic to us today, the concept embodied in this precept is timeless. YHWH employs this scientifically tried and true law as the basis for all his laws and covenants.[6] The ideology governing this precept is that, by learning from one's actions and their resulting consequence, humanity will not repeat adverse actions and choices.

A. The Word of YHWH: Tried and Made True

Scripture records many scientific descriptions of YHWH's universe. Jeremiah states:

> He (YHWH) has made the earth by his power, he has *established the world by his (a) wisdom*, and has stretched out the heavens by his (b) discretion. (Jer 10:12; see also Prov 3:19, 20)

The word *wisdom* denotes (a) an accumulated philosophic or scientific learning, knowledge and good sense, or judgment.[7] In other words, Jeremiah indicates that the Creator has gained knowledge and understanding. *Tavunah*, the word the King James translators render as "discretion," is a poor translation that may reflect the Church's medieval theology. The Hebrew (b) *tavunah*[8] means 'intelligence' or 'understanding,' and in most cases the King James Version does translate *tavunah* as "understanding." The word *understanding* conveys the concept of thorough skill or expertise.[9] Hence, Jeremiah asserts that the Creator stretched out the heavens (Ps 136:5) by understanding how the universe works. Israel's Law delineates the character and knowledge of the Creator. As the Creator has learned, so has he shared the foundation of that knowledge with the nation of Israel and through their Scriptures, to all humanity.

1. Earth's Crucible

King David often meditated on YHWH's word, gaining an understanding of the creation process. He adds to Scripture's description of creation, stating:

> For the oppression of the poor, for the sighing of the needy, now will I arise, said YHWH; I will set him in safety from him that puffs at him. *The words of YHWH are pure words: as silver tried in a furnace of earth, purified seven times.* You shall keep them, O YHWH, you shall preserve them from this generation forever. (Ps 12:5–8).

The word translated "purified" in v. 6 is the Hebrew *m'zuqqaq*.[10] It means 'to strain, exact, clarify, or refine.' Scripture uses this word to denote a refined or purified metal.[11] The word translated "tried," *tsaruf*, means 'to smelt, refine, or to test and prove as true.'[12] David indicates that YHWH has tried his own word in the earth and tested it so that it is true.[13] This, however, still fails to answer the fundamental question: How were the Creator's words tried or tested and refined in earth's furnace? Verse 6 is the only place in which Scripture uses the phrase "furnace of earth," and the word translated "furnace" specifically denotes heating that occurs during the purification process.[14] So, how do these verses bear on the Church's medieval view of creation?

It is very possible that King David is referring to earth's creation *processes* as the time when YHWH tried and proved his own word. Gen 2:4 states that the chronology recorded in the previous chapter (Genesis 1) is the history of earth's generations of creation. The word *toleidoth*, translated "generations," literally means 'descent' or 'history.'[15] Hence, Genesis 1 provides earth's long collective creation account, while Genesis 2 provides the history of the creation for earth's current "generation," which was initiated with the planting of Eden. After earth's six creations and YHWH's day of rest, YHWH planted the garden and put the man and woman that he had created in it.

2. The Beginning: A Dark Void

The opening verse of Genesis uses what we today call a *topic sentence* to tell the reader what the rest of the chapter will discuss. Gen 1:1 makes an introductory statement that YHWH (God) created the universe (i.e., heavens and the earth). Verse 2 begins by describing the actual creation process, before the earth actually existed. Notice how Scripture describes the planet earth.

> And the earth was *without form, and void*; and *darkness* was on the face of the deep. (Gen 1:2)

Why would the earth lack shape and structure? How could it be vacant and without light? Perhaps the writer is describing the conditions under which the earth was being created. Notice how closely Scripture's account parallels Stephen Hawking's description of a black hole:

a star that was sufficiently massive and compact would have such a strong gravitational field that light could not escape: any light emitted from the surface of the star would be dragged back by the star's gravitational attraction before it could get very far. . . . Although we would not be able to see them because the light from them would not reach us, we would still feel their gravitational attraction. Such objects are what we now call black holes, because that is what they are: *black voids* in space (see Illustration 5.1).[16]

Illustration 5.1. A black hole or black void in space.

Genesis' description of a void that was enshrouded with darkness accurately describes what one would see from a distance as a star's gravitational pull, sucked in all mass and energy (heat/light). If truth is to be found in Genesis' creation account, it will undoubtedly be from YHWH's perspective as he watched his creation unfold.

3. Creation from Nothing?

Far too many years have passed with scientists seeing Intelligent Design or Creation as conflicting with the Big Bang theory. Far too many years have passed with believers seeing the Big Bang as conflicting with Creation or Intelligent Design models. Einstein was one of the first to see that a field existed in which energy gained mass.[17] This field eventually became known as the Higgs field.[18] Amazingly, it was theorized that not every particle that passes through this field gains mass. Only the particles that can accept a Higgs boson can gain mass; all others pass through this field unaffected. Although this theory had been simply a theory, it was confirmed in July 2012, by two independent science teams due to the appearance of a "Higgslike" particle.[19] What this means for Intelligent Design or Creation models is that YHWH indeed took the particles in the universe and manipulated them in such a way as to give them mass. He thus created the universe from what appeared to be nothing (no visible particles). This observation is in line with cosmologists' theories regarding the Big Bang, demonstrating the harmony of both models, which was first described for humanity in the Tanakh (Old Testament).

4. 'Aliyl

The words of YHWH are pure words: as silver *tried in a furnace ('aliyl) of earth*, purified seven times. (Ps 12:6)

Over the past few decades, sciences such as mathematics, physics, cosmology, and astron-omy have discovered a great deal of evidence that supports creation via a Big Bang. What the laws of physics authenticate is that our universe was born at an instant when temperatures were extremely hot. As the creation process continued, gravity fused together two basic elements of hydrogen and helium forming the remaining 92 elements.[20] Fascinatingly, King David's use of 'aliyl (above), which the King James translates "furnace," more accurately de-notes a crucible.[21] At the time that King David had written of his understanding of YHWH's word, humanity had learned the importance of crucibles and applied the concept of this technology to pottery and metalworking. But what, exactly, is a crucible?

> 1: a vessel of a very refractory material (as porcelain) used for melting and calcin-ing a substance that requires a high degree of heat 2: a severe test 3: *a place or situation in which concentrated forces interact to cause or influence change or development.*

A crucible very accurately describes the forces at work when matter and energy converge under concentrated forces at unfathomably hot temperatures, as YHWH refined his own word seven times, during the seven days of creation. King David describes a Big Bang cre-ation in which YHWH's universe exploded into existence from complete nothingness, or more accurately, from an infinite density or point of singularity. Not only can Scripture and science coexist, science can help us understand and interpret the glimpses Scripture affords of that finite moment in eternity when YHWH created the world. In the chapters below, we will see that the Creator continues to use this crucible method of concentrated forces in order to try, understand, and refine humanity.

5. Day or Age?

Today, we define a year as the time it takes earth to complete its circuit around the sun. One day is also defined as the time it takes for the earth's axis to complete a full rotation into the sun's light, through darkness, and back to the point where it reenters the sun's light again 24 hours later. The Book of Genesis records that the sun, which defines both the year and the day, was not created until the fourth day. Thus, creation's early events could in no way be equated with a literal seven-day creation as we define a 24-hour *day* today.[22]

Scripture uses the word "day" to encompass many concepts. The Book of Psalms uses 1,000 years to define a *prophetic day*, stating,

> For a thousand years in your sight are but as *yesterday when it is past*, and as a watch in the night. (Ps 90:4)

Gen 5:4–5:31 uses the word "day" (Heb. *yowm*) to denote a period of time. Gen 6:4 uses the word *yowm* or day to refer *not* to a literal 24-hour day but to an undefined period or age in time, while Gen 7:4 uses *yowm* to define a literal/physical 24-hour day. Both the English and Hebrew words for "day" (*yowm*) convey the concept of an undefined period of time (an age) marked by one particular event that concludes with another change or event, marking the beginning of a new age or epoch.[23] I propose this latter concept is what is intended in Genesis' creation account since the sun that defines a literal 24-hour day had not yet been created. The prophet Jeremiah stated that there was a particular point in time when the Creator made a covenant with the day and the night (Jer 33:20) so that they would remain in their "appointed times."[24] This implies that, at one point in earth's history, the earth's rotation around the sun was rather erratic. In chap. 1, I proposed that YHWH's covenant with Noah brought stability and consistency to daily and seasonal cycles after the flood.[25] If this interpretation is correct, it further supports the theory that Genesis' account did not intend a literal 24-hour day as defined by the sun but an epoch or age.

6. Inflation: The Cosmological Constant

In his landmark book *Genesis and the Big Bang*, MIT graduate Dr. Gerald Schroeder charts harmony between science and Genesis' creation account. One event unexplained by academic theories at the time that Schroeder wrote his book was an antigravitational force that caused the universe to expand. After the Big Bang, the universe should have expanded and then retracted back into another black hole, based on the way that science currently understands the laws of gravity. But this was not the case.[26] MIT graduate Alan Guth and Soviet scientist Andrei Linde suggested that the universe may have gone through a brief period of very rapid expansion, then returned to normal conditions that put the universe back on the conventional Big Bang track. Schroeder builds on Guth's model, theorizing that, a few seconds

> after the beginning, the universe had a diameter of 10^{-24} centimeters. At that instant a unique, one-time force—a sort of antigravity—developed. This force, acting for a minuscule fraction of a second, caused an expansion of the universe at a rate far in excess of any rate prior to, or after, this episode. . . . The biblical allusion to this one-time inflation is found in Genesis 1:2 . . . and a wind of God [a one-time force, mentioned only here in all of Genesis] moved on the face of the water.[27]. . . A force, this wind of God, was required to start motion, the expansion of the black hole, which was the entire universe.[28]

This inflation caused creation out of almost complete nothingness! Fascinatingly, science has only very recently found that this expansion continues today (see below).

Six years after Schroeder wrote his book, scientists confirmed Guth's and Linde's thesis. At the time, scientists had been working on the theory that gravitation was slowing the universe's expansion, holding its own at a rate termed "critical" density. In 1998, two research teams headed by Saul Perlmutter and Brian Schmidt discovered that the exact opposite was true. The universe is accelerating under a mysterious repulsive influence that scientists have termed "dark matter." Cory Powell notes, "The true stunner was that Perlmutter and Schmidt also agreed that we live in a runaway universe where Lambda, not matter, controls our destiny."[29] Genesis had recorded this inflationary force that overwhelmed gravity's inward pull as a "wind of God moving over the face of the waters" (Gen 1:2) long before scientific evidence verified Genesis's or the prophet's creation accounts.

In another revelation, Guth noticed that inflation would have given the universe a stretching effect that would cause it to look flat. Scripture acknowledges this so-called stretching effect caused by "the wind of God" in Genesis, while Isaiah instills further insight into the creation processes.

> My hand also has laid the foundation of the earth, and my right hand has *spanned the heavens.* (Isa 48:13)

Tipach, the Hebrew word translated "spanned," means to 'to flatten out, extend, or unroll.'[30] The Creator takes credit for the effect that causes earth's universe to appear flat. Thus, there appears to be a great correlation between Scripture's accounts of creation and modern scientific verification.

Isaiah grants further insight into YHWH's creation of the heavens and the laws by which space is governed.

> Thus said YHWH, your redeemer, and he that formed you from the womb, I am YHWH that makes all things; *that stretches forth the heavens alone*; that spreads abroad the earth by myself. (Isa 44:24)

The word *noteh*, translated "stretches forth," actually conveys the idea of bending away,[31] while the word *roqa'*, translated "spreads abroad," is much closer in meaning to the English word 'stretch.'[32] Thus, in a more accurate translation from Hebrew, this verse reads: "I am YHWH who makes all things; *that bends away the heavens alone*; that *stretches forth the earth* by myself."

Isaiah indicates an understanding of the gravitational forces that "bent" space and time. This is the reason, of course, that the theory of relativity works so well in reality. Albert Einstein built his theory of general relativity on the ideas of the geometry of space-time curved by the forces of gravity (for which tidal waves are a prime example).[33] While Einstein expressed this concept relative to humans' perspective of the earth, Isaiah's statement is relative to the Creator's perspective as he bent or curved spacetime. In many ways, it seems that science has only recently returned to the knowledge that was once common among the ancients but then was obscured by the Church's prolonged medieval ideas. The Jewish sage Nahmanides, *c.* 1200 C.E. (Rabbi Moses ben Naḥman Girondi), proposed ideas that were consonant with the Big Bang long before modern scientific discoveries.[34]

7. Division of Light on the First Day

One of the greatest detractions from Genesis' account arises from the *creation* of "light" (Gen 1:3–5) before the *creation*[35] of the sun (Gen 1:14–19). How can light appear on the first day if the sun was not fashioned until the fourth day? The answer may rest in the fact that the first chapter of Genesis was written scientifically—perhaps not with the same jargon that we use today, but the events described are scientifically correct *according to the laws of nature.*

Science has demonstrated that, in the first age of the universe's existence, when temperatures were so unimaginably hot, light was compressed with matter, as the mix of photons and free electrons (light and matter) were in a turmoil of continual collision.[36]

> These photon-electron collisions had been so frequent that the photons (light itself) had been literally held within the mass of the universe. . . . When the temperature fell below 3,000° Kelvin, *a critical event occurred: Light separated from matter and emerged from the darkness of the universe.*[37]

Genesis records this event:

> And God said, Let there be light: and there was light. And God saw the light, that it was good: and God *divided* the light from the darkness. (Gen 1:3–4)

As the universe stabilized, the chaotic collisions were suddenly cleared of free electrons that, by being bound in stable atomic orbits, allowed the photons to travel freely. At that moment, they were able to separate or "divide" from the matter of the universe, as Genesis account accurately records. This process continued until our universe had expanded enough for the world to be created.[38] Once again, Genesis' account is consistent with scientific observations.

Today, science forms its theories and philosophies based on observations and the logic of cause and effect. Ideas of God rarely, if ever, have any bearing on formation or investigation. However, science affords independent evidence, a second witness to Genesis' creation account. That science has verified its facts and theories independent of Scripture only strengthens the validity of the long-before written word of YHWH.

B. *The Word of YHWH: Tahowr*

In the Book of Proverbs, Solomon states that laws governing wisdom and understanding existed before earth's creation. He poetically personifies Wisdom and Understanding as a woman, saying that "she" existed before earth's creation, and it was by "her" that YHWH created the earth. Had the Church read Solomon's words plainly, it no doubt would have denounced Solomon a heretic. Solomon states that the beginning of YHWH's way comprised the laws of wisdom and understanding (Prov 8:22). This strongly implies that YHWH himself follows or binds himself to natural law, regardless of whether he created it or not.

> Does not wisdom cry? and understanding put forth her voice? . . . For my mouth shall speak truth; and wickedness is an abomination to my lips. All the words of my mouth are in righteousness; there is nothing fraudulent or perverse in them. They are all plain to him that understands, and right to them that find knowledge. Receive my instruction, and not silver; and knowledge rather than choice gold. . . . I wisdom dwell with prudence, and find out knowledge of witty inventions.

The fear of YHWH is to hate evil: pride, arrogance, and the evil way, and the fraudulent mouth, do I hate. *Counsel is mine, and sound wisdom: I am understanding; I have strength. By me kings reign, and princes decree justice. By me princes rule, and nobles, even all the judges of the earth.*

I love them that love me; and those that seek me early shall find me. Riches and honor are with me; yes, durable riches and righteousness. My fruit is better than gold, yes, than fine gold; and my revenue than choice silver. I lead in the way of righteousness, in the middle of the paths of judgment: That I may cause those that love me to inherit substance; and I will fill their treasures.

YHWH possessed me in the beginning of his way, before his works of old. I was set up from everlasting, from the beginning, or before the earth was. When there were no depths, I was brought forth; when there were no fountains abounding with water. Before the mountains were settled, before the hills was *I brought forth*: While as yet he had not made the earth, nor the fields, nor the highest part of the dust of the world. *When he prepared the heavens, I was there*: when he set a compass on the face of the deep: When he established the clouds above: when he strengthened the fountains of the deep: When he gave to the sea his decree, that the waters should not pass his commandment: when he appointed the foundations of the earth: *Then I was by him, as one brought up with him: and I was daily his delight*, rejoicing always before him; Rejoicing in the habitable part of his earth; and my delights were with the sons of men. Now therefore listen to me, O you children: for blessed are they that keep *my ways*. Hear instruction, and be wise, and refuse it not. Blessed is the man that hears me, watching daily at my gates, waiting at the posts of my doors. For who finds me finds life, and shall obtain favor of YHWH. But he that sins against me wrongs *his own soul:* all they that hate me love death. (Proverbs 8)

The covenants that YHWH made with Abraham, Isaac, and Jacob support the idea that the way of YHWH embraces natural laws that govern how the universe works. His blessings were contingent on Abraham's following "The way of *Wisdom* and *Understanding*." If Abraham's children hated this way and failed to walk in it, they would naturally become weak and vulnerable, failing to prosper. Likewise, YHWH used *his way* to cause Abraham's people to become a strong and wise nation that was to be in harmony with the laws of his universe (Deut 4:6–10). So far, scripture's account of creation could not be discounted based on the scientific evidence.

David testified that YHWH's words were pure: "The words of YHWH are pure words: as silver tried in a furnace of earth, purified seven times" (Ps 12:6). The word translated "pure" is the Hebrew *tahowr*. It means pure in a 'physically, chemically, ceremonial or moral sense.'[39] If the words of Scripture are truth, then we should find that YHWH's words are pure and true because they accord with the laws of physics, science, chemistry, health, equity, and morality. Although science is often able to declare what the laws of nature are, the Torah should grant understanding on *the natural laws* of health, morality, and liberty that lead to a long life.

IV. A HOLY NATION (EXODUS 19:6)

A. *What Is a Holy Nation?*

Before we examine the various commands in Israel's Law, we must define the Law's purpose, scope, and intent along with its limitations according to Scripture. This ensures that we are not taking the Law out of context or trying to stretch its design more than intended. This is especially important as we establish whether or not the Law is unequal and incapable of being observed, as ancient Israel and modern religious denominations often maintain.

YHWH's irrevocable covenants with Israel's patriarchs designated the nation as inheritors of her forefather's birthright and blessings. In Exodus, the Creator told Israel that she was to be a *holy* or *set apart* nation, instructing, "You shall be to me a kingdom of priests, and an holy nation" (Exod 19:6).[40] This designated Jacob's seed as YHWH's chosen, representative people. As evidenced in chap. 3, YHWH's blessings depended on the people's adherence to YHWH's statutes, judgments, commandments, and laws.

After the Law had been given to Israel at Mt. Sinai, Moses continued to clarify that the nation's classification as a holy nation or set apart people would also depend on her citizens' obedience:

> This day YHWH your God has commanded you to do these statutes and judgments: you shall therefore keep and do them with all your heart, and with all your soul. You have avouched YHWH this day to be your God, and to walk in his ways, and to keep his statutes, and his commandments, and his judgments, and to listen to his voice: And YHWH has (a) avouched you this day to be his peculiar people, as he has promised you, and that you (b) should keep all his commandments; And to make you (c) high above all nations which he has made, in praise, and in name, and in honor; and (d) *that you may* be an holy people to YHWH your God, as he has spoken. (Deut 26:16–19)

Although the Creator chose Israel to be his (a) "peculiar people," their ability to be a (c) strong and mighty nation is realized through their obedience to (b) YHWH's commands. This grants the ability to be (d) a holy people to God. Another text indicates that the Creator intended for his natural law to be the mechanism that preserved the wisdom found in the *way of YHWH* (i.e., his precepts, philosophy, or doctrine).

His Law would teach Israel *how* to become a strong and mighty people.

> Now therefore listen, O Israel, *to the statutes and to the judgments*, which I teach you, for to do them, *that you may live*, and go in and possess the land which YHWH God of your fathers gives you. You shall not add to the word which I command you, neither shall you diminish anything from it, that you may keep the commandments of YHWH your God which I command you. . . . Behold, I have taught you statutes and judgments, even as YHWH my God commanded me, that you should do so in the land where you go to possess it. *Keep therefore*

> *and do them; for this is your (a) wisdom and your understanding in the sight of the nations, which shall hear all these statutes, and say, Surely this great nation is a wise and understanding people.* For what nation is there so great, who (b) has God so near to them, as YHWH our God is in all things that we (c) call upon him for? And what nation is there so great, that has statutes and judgments so righteous as all this law, which I set before you this day? (Deut 4:1–2, 5–8)

These words indicate that the nation's obedience is what (a) will enlighten national and domestic policies to effect a strong, mighty, and unique nation. *Segullah,* translated "peculiar," in Exod 19:5 and Deut 26:18, denotes a special type of treasure.[41] These verses imply that, by following the Law, Israel would attain the status of a righteous people who had wisdom and understood how their world worked. In short, they would be in touch with the *laws of reality*. YHWH required obedience in order to (b) be "near to them" and hear them (c) when they called. In order for the nation to have a relationship with her Creator, her people would need to walk in the way of YHWH and be responsible for their words, actions, and choices. This qualifies as another nonarbitrary attribute. YHWH had commanded human beings to love their neighbors (Lev 19:18). YHWH requires people to show this same respect for him that he commanded them to show to each other. Simply being a descendant of Israel did not obligate YHWH to bestow blessings on the wicked in their community. Blessings were for those with hearts willing to love and obey his commands.

B. Myths of Ancient Israel

There is an underlying and often unspoken argument among modern biblical scholars that, in order for the Israelites to be a set-apart nation embodying God's truth, they could not resemble or use contemporary customs or practices of the day.[42] Many scholars and theologians attribute modern ideologies of "coming out of Babylon" (Rev 18:2–4) to the concept of a holy nation and expect ancient Israel to have been isolated and to have withdrawn from cultural norms. The Amish and the Mennonites would be good examples of religious sects today that accept an antisocial interpretation of the concept of a holiness or set-apart people as they reject many modern technologies and customs.

Scripture indicates that YHWH intended his Law to establish righteousness and truth in an already existent social structure or social system. Unless duly warranted, YHWH's Law did not upheave an already functioning society. All evidence points to the fact that YHWH purposed his Law to establish righteousness, justice, and theological truth in the customs of the day. It did not nullify cultural custom or law just because they were common for other nations. Israel was, in fact, very contemporary with other nations.[43] For instance, all ancient Near Eastern nations invoked solemn oaths by their god(s)

> as means of creating contractual promises and of affirming testimony in court.
> . . . The same applies to the basic system of male inheritance: joint inheritance, followed by equal division of the initiative of the heirs, with an extra portion of the eldest son.[44]

Both of these customs, as we have seen, were foundational to Noah's blessing and later to Israel's tribal society. In another example, both Israel and Egypt employed proverbs in their literature on wisdom, such as Solomon's book on Proverbs.[45]

Solomon wrote the Song of Solomon as a love song for his Egyptian bride;[46] this type of poetry was a common literary style in Egypt and throughout the ancient Near East.[47] Israel, like other ancient nations, employed psalms for their temple liturgy.[48] The high priest's breastplate was intended for God's oracle pronouncements;[49] this was not wholly unlike the oracular practices surrounding the temples of other nations. Also, YHWH's basic structure for the Temple was similar to temple structures for other Near Eastern nations.[50] Although there were great similarities, as we discuss both the specific provisions of the Law and the prophecy that it established in part 2 of this book (chaps. 14–20), I will demonstrate that the exact structure of Israel's Temple and its *dissimilarity* from other ancient nations was significant for ancient Israel. However, these dissimilarities were rather subtle in comparison with modern concepts of Israel having been different from the pagan nations that surrounded her (see Illustrations 5.2 and 5.3).

Once a monarchy arose, Israel's government assumed administrative and archival functions similar to those of other nations, such as Assyria. In another

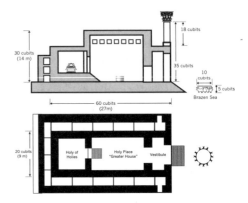

Illustration 5.2. The First Temple, commonly known as Solomon's Temple.

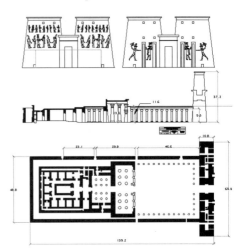

Illustration 5.3. The temple at Edfu dedicated to the Egyptian god Horus, Ptolemaic Era (c. 230 BCE). Notice the similarity between the inner vestibures of the First Temple and the Egyptian Temple. Both have a large pillar, an outer court, inner court, and most holy place.

similarity, Egyptian mummies attest circumcision throughout the dynasties until the practice was abandoned in the early Christian period.[51] Although YHWH required circumcision (Gen 17:10–14; Lev 12:3), contemporary nations observed this practice as well,[52] thus evidencing a once commonly held Noahic truth. In another parallel, scholars even assert that ancient Israel's cultic calendar functioned similar to the rules or standards underlying Babylon's lunar calendar, *c.* 600 BCE.[53]

In chap. 3, we charted evidence supporting Noah and his offspring's knowledge of basic laws for right and wrong.[54] Although many customs and traditions developed out of these basic ideas, nations such as Babylon or Assyria perverted many once-commonly-held truths. It appears that YHWH sought to reestablish and distinguish truth in Israel through his Law with Abraham and the nation of Israel. This conclusion is supported by the fact that, while the Law did not seek to make Israel *countercultural,* there were a number of ancient customs that the Law indeed forbade.

One of these stated:

> After the doings of the land of Egypt, wherein you dwelled, shall you not do: and after the doings of the land of Canaan, where I bring you, shall you not do: neither shall you walk in their ordinances. . . . Defile not you yourselves in any of these things: for in all these the nations are defiled which I cast out before you: *And the land is defiled*: therefore I do visit the iniquity thereof on it, and the land itself vomits out her inhabitants. You shall therefore keep my statutes and my judgments, and *shall not commit any of these abominations*; neither any of your own nation, nor any stranger that sojournes among you: (For all these abominations have the men of the land done, which were before you, and the land is defiled;). . . . Therefore shall you keep my ordinance, that *you commit not any one of these abominable customs, which were committed before you*, and that you defile not yourselves therein: I am YHWH your God. (Lev 18:3, 24–27, 30)

YHWH's Law is not so much concerned with what people believe as it is with what people do. Leviticus 18 outlawed practices such as incest (v.6–18), homosexuality (v. 22), and bestiality (v. 23). In ancient times, these practices were often associated with the temple cults or the official state religion.[55] One particular custom that YHWH deemed destructive to his peculiar treasure was the death and bereavement rituals. This is why Leviticus forbids the bereaved individual to cut his or her skin (Lev 19:27–28). In ancient times the bereaved practiced self-laceration or self-mutilation to demonstrate grief, or humility, or to seek a deity's favor.[56] Israel's Law did not forbid certain social customs, such as polygyny or slavery, but instead issued injunctions so that these practices would be tempered with justice (see Exod 21:2–10).[57]

Another avenue that modern scholarship takes is to presume that Israel's Law should have encompassed "all knowledge."[58] Polemicists often confuse the concept of truth with that of omniscience and suppose that the Law should have been almost as scientifically and technologically advanced as Western nations are today.[59] This is quite an assumption. YHWH never states that he intended to disclose or bestow "all knowledge" through his Law (Deut 29:29). What he did bestow was the framework—fundamental precepts and philosophy—a structure on which knowledge, truth, and understanding are based, by providing a political law that mirrored the natural laws governing the universe (Proverbs 8). Throughout this book we will see that, when man seeks truth, additional knowledge is readily available. Nevertheless, when humanity seeks superstition, falsehood, and error, the Creator may send a warning against humanity's unprofitable ways, but ultimately he allows us to learn from our own actions and the consequences of our own ways without interference (Jer 2:19).

Israel's Law simply formed a foundation for understanding how a righteous free society should operate by defining how a man should interact with his countrymen and his God. If truth is to be found in Israel's Law, we should find that its stipulations are in accord with scientific laws and observations, not that YHWH's Law explained diseases or bestowed *all* knowledge. Rather, Israel's Law should provide a constitutional paradigm or framework for any society, whether primitive or modern, that is in accord with the body of scientific evidence (realities) that often has only been discovered in recent times.

V. IS THE LAW GOOD FOR HUMANITY?

Our investigation to test whether YHWH's Law is good for humanity will be explored in five areas: YHWH's view of government, Israel's healthcare system, YHWH's definition of equity and justice, Israel's court system, and tribal-land heritages endowed to every citizen. We will discuss each of these by comparing textual and archaeological evidence for customs, traditions, and practices prevalent among ancient nations, including Israel. Next, we will examine the Law's judgments, statutes, and commands, comparing them with modern medical and other scientific findings. Given the extensive nature of this discussion, we will survey the evidence for each of the five topics outlined above. Hopefully, this discussion will stimulate further research on these topics.

The most progressive study on ancient healthcare has been Hector Avalos's *Illness and Health Care in the Ancient Near East*. We will rely on his comparative research regarding contemporary healthcare practices of the Near East. By comparing Israel with other nations, we should be able to see how Israel's theological ideals were similar to or different from other nation's practices.

A. *Function of Temple and Priesthood*

Today, when we speak of a church we are talking about a place where a group of believers gather to worship, praise, and fellowship. It is a place with auditorium-like seating and usually has a public dining hall. Separation of church and state is mandatory, and any governmental supervision is considered intrusive and oppressive. Priests, rabbis, and pastors are thought of as spiritual guides, leaders, teachers, or motivators. Their expertise is expected to be limited to the pulpit, congregation, knowledge of what is stated in Scripture, and its interpretation.

This is very far removed from the role played by a temple and its priesthood in ancient societies, where the temple was *always* part of the state and set public policies. Ancient temples in both Israel and Mesopotamia were far too small to accommodate even small crowds, so there was little room for large public gatherings except in the courtyards; certainly no permanent seating was provided,[60] although it was common to eat a meal in the temple precincts (Deut 12:5–7, 18) with the priests. The city-state, or in Israel's case, the nation-state was the high priest's "congregation." The high priesthood could be viewed as a hereditary presidential office that established a wide range of national policies. Branches in the priesthood specialized in a particular type of public service, usually passed down to subsequent generations.

Concepts of sin and its relationship to government differed greatly from modern religious ideas. Out of necessity, modern religious standards distinguish between Scriptural Law and governmental law (i.e., the law of a land). This distinction, however, was alien to ancient societies. *In Israel, the Temple was the state, and sin was a breach of government Law.*[61] YHWH's Law was the law of the land, and he expected it to be embraced by both the government and its citizenry. No separation existed between priesthood and state. Instead, the priesthood was an extension of the state and was given the divine right to teach the nation's judgments, statutes, commandments, and laws to the people in the same way American schools are supposed to teach the U.S. Constitution to its citizens today. Moreover, the priesthood was to judge the nation when the people rebelled. Priests were legal advisers, theologians,[62] judges,[63] scribes,[64] and public servants. As Marty Stevens observes:

> Worship is not disconnected from politics, economics, or sociology. If one central institution served multiple functions in ancient Israelite society, then society understood

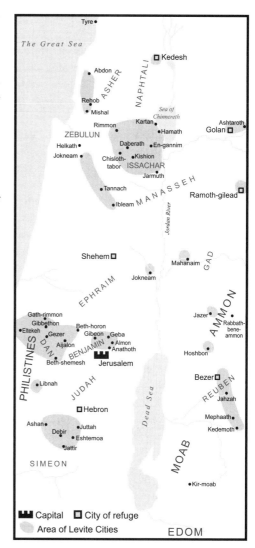

Map 5.1. Distribution of Levitical Territories

those functions to be integrated in life. Western democratic separation of church and state has artificially divided life into arenas of sacred and secular, divorcing economics from religion. . . I do suggest that the life of discipleship is not to be divided into sacred and secular, as our modern tendency. The biblical prophets precede me in this regard, announcing that worship without economic justice and societal righteousness is an abomination to the One we worship. I hope that understanding the economic role of the Jerusalem Temple may help us recapture something of the integrative, holistic character of life that our ancestors in the faith experienced.[65]

One public service that ancient temples performed was to maintain a public archive.[66] Their chief responsibility was storing records of land ownership and transfers.[67] At least in Israel, these were tied to a family's genealogical records,[68] so this function was vital to a nation whose land ownership (and citizenship) was based on tribal lineages. In chap. 8, I will demonstrate that during Israel's kingdom years the Temple and its priesthood became a royal archive center quite similar to Assyria's. Levitical priests became national historians, filling these government offices.

In addition to their archival function, temples served as a Federal Reserve System by establishing standard weights and measures for gold and silver currencies.[69] In most city-states, temples established rates of interest[70] and supported lending, investments, or ventures. This point reveals a significant dichotomy between Israel and other nations. YHWH outlawed interest on personal debt among Israel's citizens,[71] yet allowed Israel to collect interest on foreign investments or on personal loans to non-Israelites and foreign nations (Deut 23:20; 15:3). This is no doubt why YHWH stated that his *way* would make Israel economically powerful as a nation, by strengthening her own economy without the risk of debt.[72]

Centralization, another feature of Israel's Temple-state was another pivotal point of contrast with other nations.[73] When Israel first entered the Promised Land, Shiloh became the nation's administrative and judicial headquarters. Moses had instructed: "The place which YHWH your God shall choose out of all your tribes to put his name there, even to his habitation shall you seek, and there you shall come" (Deut 12:5). The Creator made sacrifices and offerings illegal in places other than the Temple city (Deut 12:6, 11–14). This structure was further strengthened by dividing the Levites (their homes and administrative centers) among the 48 satellite cities apportioned among the 12 tribes of Israel (see Map 5.1).

This provided a very cohesive government, not often seen in the ancient world. In Greek temple-states, for instance, power conflicts among competing temple factions existed from earliest times.[74] Mesopotamian temple theology was as divergent as its plethora of deities and so were the lands' internal conflicts. In contrast, Israel had one God, YHWH. Israel possessed one place where YHWH resided, one constitution that he sanctioned, and Israel's theology reflected the unity of the nation's doctrine. It appears that YHWH intended centralization to be a means for preserving the harmony, truth, and unity of the nation's brotherhood.

When the Philistines captured the Ark of the Covenant, YHWH removed his presence from Shiloh (Ps 78:60) and shortly thereafter he promised David that Jerusalem would be the only place where he would again place his name.[75] The Temple would be YHWH's dwelling place, and Jerusalem would naturally become the capital seat of government. Jerusalem's Temple served as a permanent headquarters for YHWH's government, replacing the original mobile Tabernacle. The Book of 1 Samuel indicates that, while YHWH supported a centralized government, he also ordained a very limited government. This appears to be one of the reasons he advised against the Monarchy, stating that the added bureaucracy would only serve to oppress citizens (1 Sam 8:8–22).

Astronomy was another branch of Temple service. Throughout the ancient Near East, where ancient calendars followed a lunar cyle, priests served as scientific keepers of time.

The week, its Sabbaths, holy days, and the months were often tied to lunar phases.[76] At creation (the beginning of time for earth), YHWH established the lights in the sky to "divide the day from the night; and to *let them be for signs, and for seasons, and for days, and years*" (Gen 1:14). *Moed* is the word that the King James Version translates "seasons."[77] This word is used again in Leviticus 23 (Lev 23:2–4, 37, 44), but the translators render it "feasts and seasons". Leviticus 23 highlighted the Creator's times of celebration by defining national holidays as times when the nation rested from work. A public assembly[78] and a ceremonial blow of the trumpet (Num 10:10; Lev 23:24) usually heralded these national holidays. These customs not only preserved knowledge of when the nation's Sabbaths occurred but provided a tradition rich in joyous, purposeful celebrations.

B. Taxation

Israel was one of many ancient nations that practiced taxation through tithing.[79] A tithe was a 10% flat tax. Throughout the ancient world, tithes were based on agricultural goods or other income producing goods and the money earned from selling them.[80] In most federations, monies from these taxes were used to support temples, their lands, and the priesthood. This granted considerable power to most temple federations. Temple-states were empowered to form corporate monopolies for business purposes. The temples dictated rates of interest and decided whose commerce the state would fund.[81] Their power and control was so great that they became "house and home" for a barrage of state laborers who became wards of the state.[82] As we shall see in chap. 7, YHWH's land distribution for Israel's priesthood—or, more accurately, lack of land—made this type of monopoly almost impossible in Israel's Temple system.

Israel's Tithe Code differed significantly from those of other nations' in that taxation was based on a citizen's economic income ability. YHWH ordained:

> Every man shall give as he is able, *according to the blessing* of YHWH your God which he has given you. (Deut 16:17)

The Hebrew word for blessing is *berakah*;[83] it means 'prosperity.' The Law established that, when the poor lacked prosperity, he did not pay a tithe. A Scriptural tithe was partially allocated for the widows' and orphans' benefit. YHWH commanded:

> When you have made an end of tithing all the tithes of your increase the (a) third year, which is the year of tithing, and have given it to (b) the Levite, (c) the stranger, the (d) fatherless, and the widow, that they may eat within your gates, and be filled. . . . (Deut 26:12)

Israel's economy and her festivals ran in cycles determined by national Jubilees. During the 49th and 50th years, *no* crops were planted, and the land observed a Sabbath year(s) of rest.

The first year after the 50th Jubilee (51st year), crops were planted but not harvested until the year's end, so the first two years (51st and 52nd years) replenished the supplies depleted during the national Jubilee years, when the land lay fallow.[84] During the (a) third year (53rd year), the nation would have enough increase to set aside and store provisions for the poor as part of the national tithe. YHWH viewed the nation's first year on the Promised Land (Josh 5:10–12) as though it were the first year of a new Jubilee cycle.

YHWH allocated Israel's flat tax for both (a) government support and indigent welfare. Since tax was only based on one's increase (net profit), YHWH's system (d) naturally exempted the poor (those without incomes) from paying tithes, which further decreased their need for welfare. YHWH's welfare system also allotted tax monies to help working, (c) poverty-stricken resident aliens (Heb. *ger*), who had no ownership of tribal heritages that naturally endowed Israel with incredible wealth.

Israel's land-based economic system made it very difficult for a person to be in poverty when the nation followed the Law. Land gave families the ability to farm, manufacture, raise livestock, rent their property, or simply a free place to live off the land. Historians observe that the countryside provided wealth for ancient societies in both domestic and foreign trade.[85] The blessing of arable land was the basis for tribal inheritances. This blessing granted the Israelites immense wealth from agricultural products such as grain, fruits, vegetables, and livestock.[86] Furthermore, owning land greatly impeded poverty. If this system did not provide enough economic prosperity for a family, YHWH commanded farmers and vineyard owners to reap their fields and vines only once (Lev 19:9–10), so the impoverished could glean the leftover produce for sustenance or income. This system also endowed descendants of Jacob tribal land for usage or leasing (Lev 25:13–16, 23–28). Israel's government did not burden the righteous with the indiscretions of individuals who lacked good judgment, nor was it unmerciful to the impoverished or unfortunate citizen. Rather, this system encouraged both mercy and personal responsibility concurrently.

There were two *specific* value-added taxes (VAT) that YHWH ordained, which were added to the flat income tax system. The first was the childbirth tax. Giving birth to a child incurred a period of uncleanliness when the mother was unable to approach the Temple precincts (Lev 12:4–5). The birth of a male child incurred 40 days of reserve (Lev 12:4–5), whereas the birth of a daughter subjected the mother to a significantly longer, 80-day period. This loss of cleanliness was compensated for or reflected in the Temple tax, for which the family paid a two-shekel-higher tax for a male child than it did for a female (Lev 27:6). As we saw on pp. 84–87, children add value to both a family and a nation by increasing the population that can produce, increase wealth, and defend itself. YHWH considered the child tax an honor for Israel's citizens since it acknowledged his blessing and compensated the Levites for the added responsibility of serving another citizen.

The census tax (Exod 30:11–16; Num 1:1–3; 3:39–51), the second VAT tax, functioned in much the same way as the childbirth tax. If the nation's leader required a census, every person counted in the census would pay a flat census tax, regardless of his or her income. "The rich would not give more, nor the poor less" (Exod 30:15). The government reaped the benefit of knowing how many people contributed to the nation's economy and how

Table 5.1. Constitutionally-Defined Federal Taxation

Tax	Tax based on	Allocated
Flat Income Tax	10% of all combined sources of yearly net income or increase	Government Support
Applied to:	Any person or entity earning an income or realizing a profit	
Exempted:	Indigent: poverty, slaves, terminal or disabled, those w/out income or produce	(small amount allocated for welfare)
VAT: Childbirth Tax	Son—5 shekels, flat—no graduation	Priesthood income
	Daughter— 3 Shekels, flat—no graduation	
VAT: Census Tax	Constitutionally pre-set, flat—no graduation	
Penalties for Misdemeanor Crimes or Sins (Lev 4:22–35, 5:7–13)	Graduated, based on personal income	Support government function/ Temple expenses
	Leaders paid a higher amount than the average citizen	
	High income earners pay less than leaders, but more than middle class	
	Middle class pay less than leaders, high income earners, but more than the poor	
	Those in poverty paid the least	
	Banned taxes	
Any Property Tax	Property or property-improvement taxes	Banned
Usury	Government lending in *Israel* to its own citizenry was banned (although Israel was *allowed* to lend/ apply usury to foreign nations)	

many males could be mustered for battle. However, this value-added tax naturally induced censuses to be highly unpopular with the majority of the citizens (hence, King David's census is the only recorded census outside the exodus, 2 Sam 24:1. David's census was taken in response to Israel's rebellion). While childbirth and census taxes were a predetermined value-added tax, sin offerings were not.

Sin offerings were not taxes or tithes. Rather, they were penalties on personal wealth for breaching national law. Livestock or other sources of wealth were lost in payment for trespass. YHWH intended for sin offerings to discourage disobedient words or actions that resulted in loss of income, in the same way that traffic tickets are used to discourage speeding violations today.[87] In these cases, the Law upheld a graduated system based on personal prosperity. The Leviticus Penalty Code (Lev 5:7) based reparations on ability, so the poor were not overly burdened. This system further benefited the indigent who lacked a father or other breadwinner to support the family. Notice the pattern set forth in the Law: tithes are a percentage of net income; VAT taxes are flat, predetermined amounts; and misdemeanor crimes and penalties are graduated based on economic ability.[88]

In addition to the poor and the resident alien, YHWH exempted two classes of citizenry from taxes altogether. Slaves constituted a poverty class of citizen. During their years of service, slaves were not viewed independently of their master's household and, as such, were not held liable for tithes. Another class exempted from taxation comprised individuals who had been diagnosed as being permanently unclean. "Leprosy" or other communicable diseases prohibited them from interacting with Israel's communities (Lev 13:46). Due to contagion, they also could not approach the Temple precincts (Num 19:19–22) and thus were excluded from the tithing system.

Another instruction in Deuteronomy provided for the poor by ordaining Israel to lend to her poor citizens without interest and "open her hand wide" to her countrymen.[89] If a poor individual was unable to repay his loan by the Jubilee year, the debt was forgiven altogether (Deut 15:9). YHWH states that the *only* reason the Moabic Covenant added this injunction to the Sinai Compact's previous welfare provisions was due to the nation's continual rebellion against the statutes and judgments that would have eliminated poverty altogether had they been followed.[90] Exemption from taxation, welfare, graduated penalties for breaching YHWH's Law, and debt forgiveness combined with tribal lands and gleanings from the farmer and vineyard owners' fields insured against Hebrew poverty or slavery with a high rate of certainty. I discovered that the Law supported a form of personal responsibility that did not burden an obedient society with the job of care-taking those whose lack of discretion or unfortunate circumstances led to poverty.

Remember that slavery itself provided a welfare system for the impoverished.[91] The last three resorts a person had for satisfying debt was to lease tribal lands (Lev 25:13–16, 23–28), hire himself for wages, or sell himself (and his family) into slavery. If he chose the latter option, he would come under the care and protection of his master's household. This was not always a negative situation.

> Memories of the African slave trade color our view of slavery, so that we cannot understand [gratitude in slavery]. But in ancient society slavery was the accepted way of bailing out the destitute, and under a benevolent master could be quite a comfortable status (cf. Joseph with Potiphar). Indeed the [Israelite] law envisages some temporary slaves electing to become permanent slaves rather than take the freedom to which they were entitled after six years of service. Ancient slavery at its best was like tenured employment, whereas the free man was more like someone who is self-employed. The latter may be freer, but he faces more risks.[92]

In exchange for the slaves' service, the master provided food, clothing, and shelter. YHWH commanded the nation to treat citizens entering the slave system with the honor and dignity of a hired worker (Lev 25:39–43).[93] I also disovered that Israel was the only nation in the ancient world that granted individual rights to slaves.[94] So when the nation followed the Law, a slave was well treated. Indigent families could come under the shelter and protection of another's house, while the master benefited from the slave's labor.[95] YHWH's Law consistently maintains the precept of personal responsibility, insisting that each person should bear the blessings or consequences of his or her own actions (Lev 5:1, 17; 24:15; see Table 5.1).

C. Israel's Healthcare System: Comparative Study

1. The Temple's Relationship to Illness

Israel's distinctiveness among contemporary nations was perhaps no more evident than in the nation's philosophy on health-care "doctrine." Throughout the Near Eastern world, temples served as a locus for the sick to find healthcare consultants. Greece provided what may be termed the first modern hospital. The *Asclepieia* encouraged the sick to come to its sacred site to live and be treated until they were healed. Hector Avalos, professor at Iowa State University, notes the problem with this temple function:

> Asclepieia, which were meant to cure the sick, may have unintentionally caused the spread of illness in the larger community by concentrating large numbers of sick people in small places. Thus visitors who came to be cured of Illness A at the Asclepieion may have contracted Illness B from other patients at the temple. Illness B may have then been transported back to their home.[96]

He continues by observing that ancient hospitals may have contributed to the spread of diseases that might otherwise have been halted by isolating the patients. "From a modern epidemiological standpoint, the Asclepieion may not have been the best type of healthcare to offer."[97] Egyptologists John Nunn and James Breasted state that Greek medical practices and perhaps even the original hospital may have originated in Egypt.[98]

Mesopotamia did not provide the "hospital" function as the Greek Asclepieia did, but its constituents still sought advisers from the temple's precincts (see Illustration 5.4). Once the ill secured a consultant, they proceeded to the ritual stage, where images were used to invoke deities. The patient stayed at the temple long enough for incantation images to be manufactured or purchased and all necessary documents transcribed.[99] In this manner, disease and contamination were spread throughout the community during the drawn-out ritual processes. When one ritual failed to procure healing, another had to be sought, keeping the ill patient in contact with a temple and its thriving community, readily spreading bacteria.

Illustration 5.4. Colossal marble head of Asclepius, Greek, found on Milos, Southern Aegean, c. 325 BCE.

YHWH states that the reason for establishing protocols for communicable diseases, such as leprosy, were to "teach when it is unclean, and when it is clean: this is the law of leprosy" (Lev 14:57). This implies that the scientific observation procedures established in Leviticus ch. 13 should be applied to diseases in general. Scholars note that leprosy in Scripture did not necessarily denote Hansen's disease, the modern equivalent.[100] The Hebrew term *tsara'ath*[101] denotes a plethora of skin disorders, which included Hansen's disease but were not limited to it.[102] Smallpox, psoriasis, skin cancer, vitiligo, abscesses, and lupus erythematosus are just a few diseases that could be denoted by the Hebrew term *tsara`ath*.[103] That Leviticus is indeed describing different forms of *tsara`ath,* rather than one disease is demonstrated by differing times allotted for quarantine periods and ch. 14's concluding statement that includes "leprosy" among scall, rising, scab, and bright spot (Lev 14:54–57). Another example of *tsara`ath's* broad meaning can be seen in the protocols dealing with household mold and blight that refer to a "plague being spread in the house" as a "fretting leprosy" (Lev 14:44).

Unlike other cults, YHWH did not permit his Temple to be part of the healing process. Once a person exhibited symptoms, a Levite from one of the nation's 48 satellite cities could be dispatched to the patient's home (Lev 13:2–3; Num 35:6–8) to determine contagion. If diagnosed in good health, the patient could come in contact with the Temple precincts and be considered part of the *tithable* Temple congregation (Lev 14:1–32). If he was diagnosed as having a disease, he was instructed to observe quarantine at home for 7–14 days (Lev 13:4–7). If he was pronounced healthy after this time, no other action was needed than an official "cleansing ceremony" (Lev 14:1–32). If, he was diagnosed with a persistent contagious ailment, the patient lived in isolation until healing or death, if YHWH did not grant healing (Lev 13:46). Only after healing occurred did YHWH allow citizens to come in contact with the Temple once again. For a society that lacked the understanding of how disease works, these primitive methods were the best means available to prevent contagious diseases from plaguing society.

Preventive medicine formed the core doctrine for YHWH's healthcare. He held the patient/citizens personally responsible for abstaining from certain meats and activities that caused ill health.[104] As our examination of the Law proceeds into modern medical discoveries, it will become clear that modern scientific studies lend support to YHWH's ancient standard for healthy living.

2. Illness and Sin

Throughout Israel and Mesopotamia, various people held that illness was a consequence of sin.[105] This contrasts with Greek theology, in which illness was separated from sin or immoral transgression.[106] Greek philosophy viewed illness and good health alike as an attribute of chance.[107] Rarely did Greek prescriptions enjoin a change in moral life to rectify illness.[108] Mesopotamia, in contrast, always viewed illness as an act of divine punishment that could be arbitrarily used by the gods.[109] Although illness was usually tied to sin, a god could send illness even if the patient did not do anything wrong, provided that the illness served the gods' best interests (see Illustrations 5.5).

This contradictory theology tied illness to the patient's "sins" and to the "sins" of other family members. If one family member angered the gods, then punishment could be inflicted on another family member.[110] Avalos states: "Even iniquities committed by family members might have been responsible for the supplicant's illness."[111] Once a person realized his infirmity, the patient and his (or her) priest/healthcare consultant embarked on the cumbersome task of determining which god was responsible for sending that particular illness. Usually these rituals involved enumerating any and all possible "sins," since sin in Mesopotamia was not defined absolutely (see Illustration 5.6).[112]

Illustration 5.5. Ivory figure of a griffin-headed de-mon, Utartian, from Toprakkale in eastern Anatolia, 8–7th BCE. Not all demons were evil. Many, such as the griffin were protective deities (similar to modern ideas of guardian angels).

Illustration 5.6. Pazuzu, an evil spirit, Neo-Assyrian bronze. While griffins protected the devotee, evil spirits such as Pazuzu inflicted misfortune.

Israel's health doctrine differed considerably in comparison with other ancient cultures' views of health. Israel's Law clearly defined the steps or precautions that a person needed to take in order to maintain good health. If YHWH rendered judgment on a person, it was for his sins and his sins alone and was not caused by other family members' sins.[113] YHWH always directed his judgment in response to specific infractions of his Law.

Hector Avalos, observing how Israel's theology contrasted with Mesopotamia's, states:

> Deuteronomy denies that illness is an arbitrary instrument of Yahweh. Since the conditions for a healthy life are so clear, a patient need only recall what the trans-gression was in order to find the cause of his/her illness. In contrast, Mesopota-mian medical theology assumes that illness is an instrument of divine policy for any and all matters which the gods may decide is in their interest, and such matters need not always be disclosed to the patient.[114]

Scripture indeed supports the idea that illness can be used as YHWH's instrument (Lev 14:34). The Book of 1 Samuel (16:14) states that YHWH sent an evil spirit to trouble King Saul and describes how this spirit was able to alter Saul's mental health. Uzza is another case in point. Since it was illegal for any person except the high priest or the Koathites to approach the Ark of the Covenant,[115] when Uzza put his hand on the ark, he was immediately struck dead (2 Sam 6:6). In another instance, YHWH used disease to judge Israel's rebellion. Af-ter Israel rebelled against David by following Absalom, YHWH provoked David to punish the people by numbering Israel. When a census was taken without procuring a Census

Tax, the Law stated that plague would be sent on the nation (Exod 30:12). 2 Samuel (24:17) records that the plague sent by the Creator for breaching this law as a destroying angel. When cause exists for judgment (such as in Egypt's case), the Creator waits until there is absolute certainty before rendering judgment (see Genesis 18).

The Law also supports the view that no man is an island. One man's negligence (such as driving drunk) can affect innocent bystanders. Any person who failed to abide by YHWH's quarantine standards could expose innocent people to his or her disease. *YHWH is responsible for these diseases only in the sense that he established the natural law that set the conditions*

Illustration 5.7. String of amulets in gold and semi-precious stones, Egyptian, Middle Kingdom, *c.* 1991–1750 BCE. In the center is a gold lotus pendant attached to a gold heh amulet (a seated god with arms raised holding year signs; a hieroglyph meaning 'millions of years').

for disease in motion. If a person consumed foods deemed unhealthy, he could also contract disease from or transmit disease to other people in his community. This is why the Law ordained equity in situations where one man's error or indiscretion affected or hurt his fellow man (see "Mediation" section below). Communicability, however, was not viewed as "judgment" from YHWH.

> The view that health is related to righteousness (and sickness to unrighteousness) is present in the Mesopotamian model of illness etiology. However, scholars have overlooked the fact that the Deuteronomistic view of the relationship between righteousness and health bears a significant difference. Whereas in Mesopotamia the gods may use illness for a variety of reasons, which may be entirely arbitrary from a human standpoint, Deuteronomy 28 limits the use of illness to the enforcement of the covenants. Deuteronomy 28 affirms that illness is not caused by any arbitrary reason that the deity may hide from the patient. Yahweh restricts his use of illness to the enforcement of stipulations that have been fully disclosed to the patient.[116]

YHWH's patient disclosure had been outlined in the curses listed in Deuteronomy 27–28, and his requirements for good health had been defined in his covenantal constitution with Israel.

The prophet Ezekiel represents Scripture best summary with regard to righteousness achieving good health, and its inverse, unrighteousness, procuring ill health:

As I live, said the lord YHWH, I have no pleasure in the death of the wicked; but that the wicked turn from his way and live: turn you, turn you from your evil ways; for why will you die, O House of Israel? Therefore, you son of man, say to the children of your people, The righteousness of the righteous shall not deliver him *in the day of his transgression*: as for the wickedness of the wicked, *he shall not fall by it in the day that he turns from his wickedness*; neither shall the righteous be able to live for his righteousness in the day that he sins. When I shall say to the righteous, *that he shall surely live*; if he trust to his own righteousness, *and commit iniquity*, all his righteousness shall not be remembered; but for his iniquity that he has committed, *he shall die for it*. Again, when I say to the wicked, You shall surely die; if he turn from his sin, and do that which is lawful and right; If the wicked restore the pledge, give again what he had robbed, *walk in the statutes of life*, without committing iniquity; he shall surely live, *he shall not die*. None of his sins that he has committed shall be mentioned to him: he has done that which is lawful and right; *he shall surely live*. (Ezek 33:11–16)

If a wicked person turned from a life of sin and death to YHWH's *statutes of life*, he and his society would enjoy the life-sustaining good health that comes from living in a righteously healthy way (Prov 3:8; 4:2, 22). He would eat from YHWH's tree of life as prescribed in his Law.[117] Likewise, when a righteous person turns from walking in the path that procures life, he will die because he will open himself up to "all the diseases of Egypt" (Exod 15:26). The penalties (curses) enumerated for breaching YHWH's covenantal agreement (Deut 28:22, 59) will take effect in the person's life. In chap. 6 we will see how YHWH's healthcare doctrine established good health for any nation that followed its instructions.

3. State Responsibility

Most ancient healthcare systems regarded the burden for the individuals' care to be a temple-state responsibility. The Greek Asclepieia followed a maximalist ideology, viewing the state as fully responsible for the infirmed people's healthcare.[118] Avalos theorizes that the Asclepius's cult not only supported the hospital, its land, and its consultant, but also provided economic support for the sick during the patient's hospital stay.[119] Mesopotamian idea of the state's responsibility differed only slightly: Mesopotamia did not use treatment centers that could be considered ancient hospitals. The king was still responsible for temple support as well as any salaries owed to the priests or healthcare consultants. Realistically, this expense was passed on to the citizens in the form of increased taxation.[120]

Mesopotamia's government played a particular role in supplying medical "ingredients." Avalos cites W. Farber's 1977 survey of medicine distribution which concludes that distribution of medical ingredients was a monopoly, subject to the policies of the state or temple bureaucracy.[121] He concludes that the Mesopotamian healthcare system also tended toward the maximalist view of state responsibility but not to the extent that the Greek did.[122]

YHWH's view of national healthcare resulted in a sharp dichotomy between Israel and other nations. Israel's system did not increase taxation of the healthy/wealthy populace for the indigent's support. Rather, Israel's welfare system exempted the ill from their tithe (tax) responsibilities altogether, entrusting the ill person's care to his or her family. Monies usually allotted for the tithe tax owed to the state could then be spent on the afflicted's healthcare as the family saw fit. That YHWH did exempt the ill from their tithe responsibility is evidenced in their exclusion from the Temple's precincts, which made their ability to bring tithes into the Temple impossible.[123]

4. Mediation

One final theology separated YHWH's people to be a holy nation. YHWH's exclusion of an intermediary deity is one of the most distinguishing factors in Israel's healthcare doctrine. Throughout Mesopotamia, temples recognized the power of an intermediary (usually female) healing deity called Gula or Ninisina, whom Avalos generically titles "G/N."[124]

> The intermediary role of G/N in healing is directly related to the Mesopotamian medical theology. . . . An illness could be caused by a host of gods, ancestors, hidden sins, as well as obvious physical causes. This use of G/N as an intermediary may be an attempt to simplify the search for a cure. . . . G/N was never able to replace totally other healing gods such as Marduk, and many healing rituals mention other gods alongside of her in incantations dealing with illness.[125]

In Egypt, G/N's counterpart was Isis, whose rituals were no less complex. Egyptologist James Breasted observes that the charms enumerated in the Edwin Smith Papyrus "operate not merely to banish the hostile powers, but also to call in beneficent divinities and spirits to aid in the protection of the patient"[126] (see Illustration 5.8).

Egypt and Mesopotamia needed to simplify their incantations and other "curing" prescriptions. One inscription tells King Esarhaddon to listen carefully to his healing ritual, since the ritual was "cumbersome."[127] The intermediary god's role served to simplify this process. Rather than appealing to every god in the heavenly pantheon individually, the patient's healthcare provider could simply seek *the god of mediation* to find the offended deity and intervene for the patient's cure.

Ancient priests continued this intermediary function, serving as liaisons in the healing process.[128] Hector Avalos sufficiently demonstrates that Mesopotamian or Grecian healthcare consultants

Illustration 5.8. Amulet with a figure of Lamashtu, designed to ward off evil (from Mesopotamia).

were not "physicians" because a magical element always surrounded their approach to curing illness.[129] What the various temples offered was a "remedy" or "therapy" for their ailment. Consultants indulged in "voodoo" healings, processes in which images were created to depict body parts or other places in need of healing.[130] Ancient temple excavations have unearthed hundreds of images used for these rituals in both Mesopotamia and Egypt.[131] One labor-intensive Mesopotamian ritual against disease (and) malaria prescribes the following ingredients:

> Illustrations of the following gods: the daughter of Anu, Namtar, Latarak
> A figurine of Death
> A substitute figurine made of clay (see Illustration 5.9)
> A substitute figurine made of wax
> . . . 15 drinking tubes of silver [. . . for?] Galua (and) Belet-weri
> . . . . 7 twigs] of tamarisk
> twigs of date palm
> [7 bot]tles of wine
> 7 bottles of beer
> [7 bottles] of milk
> 7 bottles of honey[132]

Another Mesopotamian text reflects how the complexity of its theology resulted in a labor-intensive systems of rituals. A Mesopotamian priest/healthcare consultant complains about the prescribed ritual, saying:

> We cannot execute it (the ritual);
> The tablets are (too) many.
> How will they copy them (in time)?
> Even the preparation of the figurines which
> The king saw (yesterday) took us 5–6 days.[133]

Avalos believes there is "a relationship between the complexity of rituals and the number of divine beings that must be contacted, expelled, or entreated."[134] Thus, the approach of Mesopotamia's healthcare reflected the complexity of the theology and multiplicity of gods.

Egyptian incantations were no less complex. The Edwin Smith Surgical Papyrus preserves examples of incantations that were to be spoken over deity images, "written with frankincense on a band of fine linen and attached to a man at his throat."[135] Likewise, The Ebers Papyrus (Ebers 465) preserves a cure for baldness, prescribing six animal fats from: a lion, hippopotamus, crocodile, cat, snake, and ibex (wild goat). The text continues to instruct that the bald person "make as one

Illustration 5.9. Terracotta figure, Elamite, from Susa, south-west Iran *c.* 1400–1200 BCE.

thing, smear (or anoint) the head . . . with it."[136] Bile, another favorite ingredient of Egypt's healthcare patricians, was usually placed on the eye or breast, but seldom taken internally.

The *intermediary* healthcare consultant continues to be one of the sharpest contrasts between the theology of other cultures and Israel's sanctification. Unlike Greek, Egyptian or Mesopotamian literature, Scripture contains no superstitious healing incantations.[137] Health and healing were viewed independently of YHWH's priesthood, and the Temple played no therapeutic role in the healing process.[138] No intermediary was required for access to YHWH or for his forgiveness.[139]

Hannah sought healing for her infertility at the Tabernacle without the aid of an intermediary. If rituals had been used by ancient Israel, someone would have divulged Hannah's condition to a priest. The fact that Priest Eli needed to question Hannah's intentions *after* she made her petition to YHWH supports the priesthood's limited healthcare role.[140] YHWH heard Manasseh's prayer in Assyria (2 Chr 33:18–19) and Israel's cries from Egypt. YHWH answered both petitions for deliverance without the presence of a Temple or intermediary (Exod 2:23–25 and Ps 106:41–45). Hezekiah was likewise able to request healing without an intermediary and without entering the Temple precinct. This is a sharp contrast to Asclepius's doctrine, which viewed the temple as the only place to contact the deity, or the only place where a deity could "hear" the petitions of his adherents.[141] YHWH could hear all those who called on his name, regardless of their location, and without mediation.[142]

The Law also upheld the patients' rights to self-medication. One of the few medications recorded in Israel's history was the astringent application of figs to Hezekiah's boil (2 Kgs 20:7), representing an herbal approach to medicine.[143] Ezekiel also refers to a restored Israel as using the leaves of the trees for medicine in the future (Ezek 47:12).

One theme continually seen throughout Israel's Law is the idea of personal responsibility, whether harm was intentional or not. YHWH commanded those responsible for another's injury to seek the best possible healthcare for the individual's recovery.[144] He instructed the culpable person to "cause" the victim "to be thoroughly healed" (Exod 21:19). If the injury resulted in lost wages, the culpable party compensated his victim's income, in addition to financing or supporting the victim's recovery.[145] Whereas Mesopotamia held the state responsible for the injured's cure, the Hebrew text holds the offender culpable for injury. No other person or collective group was held responsible.[146] Again, we see consistancy in Israel's doctrine, yet it contrasts with many philosophies and ritual practices prevalent among the nations during the Exodus Era.

One *spiritual* yet therapeutic healing ritual that the Old Testament did recommend was direct prayer to YHWH. Israel was the sole nation on earth holding YHWH's special glory. Regarding this presence, Exodus records,

> Then a cloud covered the tent of the congregation, and the glory of YHWH filled the tabernacle. And Moses was not able to enter into the tent of the congregation, because the cloud stayed thereon, and the glory of YHWH filled the tabernacle. (Exod 40:34–35)[147]

YHWH resided with the people of Israel, and he was ready to hear their petitions. No other invocation was necessary for YHWH to hear a humbled, repentant, contrite heart that was ready to walk in his way of life.[148]

Solomon requested that YHWH grant the petitions of all who prayed toward the Temple (1 Kgs 8:29–56). This *added* blessing was one of the very few "therapy" rituals ordained in Scripture. The Temple thus became

> a 'long distance' therapeutic device in itself without being a therapeutic locus. . . .
> The most significant aspect of the Prayer of Solomon is that it does not encourage
> the use of the temple as a direct petitionary or therapeutic locus for the ill . . .
> instead patients are to extend their hands toward the temple to receive healing. . . .
> The Prayer assumes that such instructions would be used by all patients whether
> in exile or in Israel.[149]

In comparison to other cultures, the Law's view of healthcare is significantly more practical. There were no complicated superstitious rituals, and healing was quite simple: prevention, direct prayer to YHWH, quarantine, and sanitation or purification. If a person had violated YHWH's preventive covenant, he or she would pay the penalty and be forgiven (this did not necessarily mean that the consequence was avoided).[150] Avalos sees that Israel's Scripture "does not provide any therapeutic advice because realistically there was not much anyone could do in certain cases."[151] He concludes that in many ways Israel was "more realistic about the incurability of some illnesses than the theologians of Gula or Asclepius."[152] Indeed, Scripture does acknowledge that there is often no recourse for disease other than abstinence, prevention, letting illness take its natural course, or occasionally, YHWH's divine intervention. Israel's Temple establishment followed a more realistic approach to the etiology and prognosis of illness.[153] Unfortunately, this realistic view did not bode well for the fairytale theology idolatrous ancient Israel desired.

5. The Placebo Religion

Although pagan rituals had no scientific validity, scholars observe that they did provide a particular level of comfort. John Nunn compares these rituals to the placebo effect in which belief is its own cure.[154] The patient's belief in the intermediary deity's healing power caused him to believe that he was getting well. Take the Asclepieion, for instance: it gave the patient access to someone he or she believed was personally acting on his or her behalf.[155] This service must not have been available at other temples, where the priests were not as indulging with regard to personal care and attention as they were attentive to other issues, such as rituals.[156]

Asclepius's theology provided another emotional attraction. According to the ancient historian Aelianus (*De Natura Animalium*, 8:12), Asclepius was the most human-loving of all gods.[157] The individual was all-important, as the god personally oversaw the patient's healing, regardless of the actions that may have caused the patient's illness. "Healing, and not political or other social differences (i.e., sins or crimes) was the focus" of the Greek cult.[158] This outlook relieved the patient of personal responsibility or culpability. He never had to face himself or turn from his ways. Healing was in a very real sense *easy*. Asclepius was so devoted to healing that the etiology of an illness only mattered if it enhanced Ascle-pius' miracles.[159] No doubt, an Israelite felt that his own nation's lack of complicated rituals left a theological emptiness or emotional void. Israel's priests lacked incantation rituals, did not offer a place to receive attention for ailments, and the patient was not absolved of personal accountability. This may be one reason that Canaan's more complex cults provided greater levels of self-indulgent comfort and "compassion" for the idolatrous nation. Ancient Israelites desired the placebo effect rather than following the way of their Creator.

The Law's ordinances for healthcare preserved YHWH's doctrine of personal respon-sibility while restraining the healthcare role that Israel's priesthood could assume. As I considered this evidence, it evoked several questions that I needed to understand: Is the Law's concept of personal responsibility too harsh? Are YHWH's laws too confining for a modern progressive society? Are YHWH's Laws good for all humanity, or are they unfair, as ancient Israel alleged? The next evidence this investigation needed to address was Scripture's relationship to disease.

6

Laws of Reality, Part 2: None of These Diseases

I. IS THE LAW HEALTHY FOR HUMANITY?

A. *None of These Diseases*

A nation's theology has historically determined how its citizens organize their political systems. Government functions according to doctrine. Philosophies that are attributed to popular deities determine what a government's doctrine will be. Greek theology separated action from consequence, while Egyptian dogma attributed the consequences of man's actions to the gods. Seth became an "evil god,"[1] while Bes and Isis either caused or aided the good[2] that happens in life. Again, there was little *cause and effect* directly tied to humanity's actions. When a consequence was directly tied to a person's actions (sin) in the ancient world, the cause was arbitrary and poorly defined. This sharply contrasted with YHWH's doctrine, which clearly defined sin and its consequences in the Torah.

Since YHWH was Israel's only God, he was responsible for both good and evil; there was no separation (Isa 45:7). He ordained human beings to reap the blessing or consequence of their actions.[3] If people walked in his way, they would be healthy, wealthy, and wise.[4] Likewise, if Israel failed to walk in his way, her actions would naturally correct her.[5] If her actions became deplorable, he would judge her by sending foreign oppression or disease (Deut 28:36–37, 59–61, 64). YHWH promised that, if Israel would obey his Law and walk in his way, he would not send any diseases on his people as he had on Egypt.

> If you will diligently listen to the voice of YHWH your God, and will do that which is right in his sight, and will give ear to his commandments, and keep all his statutes, *I will put none of these diseases on you, which I have brought on the Egyptians: for I am YHWH that heals you.* (Exod 15:26)

YHWH indicates that he was responsible for bringing disease on Egypt. While this statement probably refers to the exodus's ten plagues, YHWH may be denoting Egyptian disease in general.[6] I knew that the next logical question that I had to ask was: What diseases did YHWH bring on ancient Egypt?

Recent technological advances grant us the answer to this question via analysis of mummification samples. Mummies provide scientists the ability to study DNA and cadaver specimens so that disorders can be identified and classified. Pathology, MRIs, X-rays, and other modern diagnostic tools have greatly aided our understanding of ancient illnesses. These studies may be able to pinpoint some of the diseases that YHWH sent on Egypt as judgment for their oppressive sins. What diseases have scientists found in Egypt's mummies?

By far the most readily distinguished illnesses are vascular diseases:[7] aortic calcification, degenerative disease of the aorta and coronary arteries. Arteriosclerosis of the kidneys and myocardial fibrosis were also prevalent,[8] while bone diseases presented another set of problems. Scientists diagnosed osteoarthritis, osteomyelitis, spina bifida, and arthritis from a host of Egyptian cadavers.[9] Infectious diseases, such as tuberculosis (spinal), poliomyelitis, small pox, and malaria are also evidenced in Egyptian mummies.[10]

Leprosy was another fatal disease. An entry in the Ebers papyrus may reveal that leprosy (Hansen's disease) or bubonic plague was one of the exodus's plagues; although the term used was "the slaughter of Khonsu."[11] The Egyptian Ebers scroll states:

> Instructions for an anut-tumour of the slaughter of Khonsu. If you examine an anut-tumour of the slaughter of Khonsu in any part of a man and you find its head pointed and its base is straight; his two eyes are green and burning; his flesh is hot under it.... If you find them on his two arms, his pelvis and his thighs, pus [being] in them, you should not do anything against it. (Ebers 877)[12]

John Nunn, a retired member of the British Medical Research Counsel and member of the Egypt Exploration Society concludes that a diagnosis of leprosy would be difficult to refute, although he notes that inadequate translation could also miss a diagnosis of cancer, bubonic plague, or even neurofibromatosis.[13] Archaeologists recently discovered traces of black plague bacteria in fossilized fleas from the Workman's Village in Amarna, a city dating to 1350 BCE. Scientists cite this as "the first evidence of a non-Asian origin for the deadly plague."[14] Archaeologists consider the laborers' squalid living conditions to have made the village a likely place for this plague to populate. Thus, there is evidence that the Ebers papyrus could be referring to leprosy or bubonic plague.

One persistent problem for Egyptians, past and present, has been the overwhelming threat of parasites. Scientists have identified many parasites in Egyptian mummies. Most of these entered the host when a person came in contact with the Nile or drank water from it. One parasite known as *Schistosoma* causes a bleeding urinary infection and has been linked to bladder cancer.[15] The degree to which these parasites may have contributed to autoimmune diseases such as cancer and other ailments in ancient Egypt is relatively unknown. Cancer is usually harbored in body tissues, and these were usually discarded during the mummification process.[16] Given the extensive coverage that Egypt's many papyruses give to tumor treatments, tumors seem to have been a significant threat to the Egyptian population.[17] However, the technologies currently available to scientists indicate that, while tumors in mummies did occur, the incident is relatively low, and some former malignant diagnoses are now being reviewed.[18]

One parasite found in many cadaver samples was *Trichinella*, most commonly acquired from eating undercooked pork.[19] Herodotus (2.47) claims the Egyptians considered the pig unclean; however, archaeologists have discovered evidence of pig consumption throughout every dynasty.[20] Herodotus may have come in contact with one of Egypt's Jewish communities and assumed that their views reflected that of the entire Egyptian state, which archaeological evidence shows was not the case.

The Creator commanded humanity to abstain from pork, determining this animal to be unhealthy for human consumption (Lev 11:7). If YHWH judged Egypt for breaking his Law, then it is very possible that Trichinella *was* that judgment. The parasite resulted in disease, just as the Creator stated in Exod 15:26. YHWH did not stop the Egyptians from sinning. Rather, he allowed the Egyptians to experience the consequences of their ways.

In chap. 1, we defined two concepts of truth as constancy and freedom from change. If YHWH is to be considered truthful and constant, then obeying YHWH's commandments and statutes should procure good health for humanity today, even as it did in ancient times. Likewise, when a society dismisses YHWH's commandments and statues, we should expect to find vascular and cardiovascular diseases, arthritis, cancer, parasites, and other "Egyptian diseases" prevalent throughout society. Does YHWH's judgment of Egypt's diseases shed any light on humanity's health today?

B. *Modern Egyptian Diseases*

The United States of America is a society that dismisses many of the Creator's laws. The United States Department of Agriculture reports that *pork* accounts for about one-fourth of all U.S. meat consumed.[21] Shellfish and catfish, also unclean animals (Lev 11:12), are another American favorite. The National Marine Fisheries Service estimates that individual Americans consume approximately five pounds of shellfish and an additional 1.1 pounds of farm-raised catfish every year.[22] In 1980, the annual per-capita consumption of shrimp was 1.4 pounds, increasing to a record-breaking consumption of 3.7 pounds per consumer in 2002.[23] The total amount of unclean fish Americans eat is a little less than half of the total seafood industry.[24] If Americans (and other countries) have dismissed the Creator's prescription for health, we should expect to see a direct correlation between "Egyptian Diseases" and those nations that have forsaken YHWH's preventive health Law. Do modern societies that dismiss Israel's Law reflect YHWH's judgment by bearing Egypt's diseases?

Scientists observe ancient Egyptians "suffered many of the ailments that plague us now."[25] Vascular diseases affect well over 20 million Americans, and those with vascular disease are six times more likely to die of heart disease.[26] The Centers for Disease Control (CDC, U.S.) reports that heart diseases and other vascular disorders have been the leading cause of death for the past five years.[27] Cancers were the United States' second leading cause of death from 1999 to 2001.[28] As in ancient Egypt, bone disease is prevalent today. Arthritis afflicts well over 46 million Americans and is the leading arthritic cause of disability worldwide.[29] Researchers find that parasites that affected Egyptians over 5,000 years ago are still responsible for many diseases today, posing an enduring problem for people all over the world.[30] Moreover, pork and shellfish continue to be notorious for transmitting parasites to humans.[31]

The most recent outbreaks of Trichinella have occurred in such unclean animals as horse meat and cougar jerky.[32] That *non*-Torah-observant individuals[33] today bear the same diseases as the ancient Egyptian predecessors could be viewed as coincidental: *disease has always existed and has no direct relation to YHWH's statutes and commands; it is simply a fact of life, and a coincidence.* If this were the case, then similar to most Egyptian and Mesopotamian medical prescriptions of lion fat for baldness or bile for breast abscesses, there should be little or no scientific validity to Israel's Law. In other words, if YHWH's Law was just for ancient Israel, then its prescription for health should be just as outrageous as the healthcare prescriptions of other ancient nations. If, on the other hand, YHWH's statues and commands accord with the laws of nature and reflect the laws of reality, we should find that his law is validated by scientific evidence. This would greatly aid YHWH's case and rebut Israel's charges that his way was unequal, unfair, and too hard to obey. Thus, the remaining investigation into the question of whether the Law is good for humanity hinges on the results of scientific investigation.

C. *The Reality of Scientific Discoveries*

I have proposed that the Israelite Law not only defines the *way of YHWH* but also follows the laws of nature, or at least, the laws of nature are in harmony with Israel's Law. As demonstrated in the previous chapter on healthcare (chap. 5), YHWH viewed disease as a natural consequence for violating his Law: illness resulted from sin. There was no cure for disease unless the patient changed his life-style and/or YHWH divinely intervened and healed the patient. YHWH advocated what modern doctors call *preventive medicine*. His statutes and commands outlined foods, customs, or activities that he considered harmful for his children. He either outlawed these altogether or defined how they could be used without harming his people. For YHWH to be exonerated, these statutes and commands need evidence of scientific validity yet today. If they fail to be legitimate, the way of YHWH may be as arbitrary as ancient Egypt's and Mesopotamia's mystical and superstitious incantations. Does YHWH's Law prescribe a healthy way of life or vain superstition?

1. Circumcision

YHWH ordained the foreskin's removal in his covenant with Abraham. Later, he incorporated the Circumcision Covenant's sign in Israel's Law.

And in the eighth day the flesh of his foreskin shall be circumcised. (Lev 12:3)

Modern scientists have researched this topic more extensively than any other Scriptural Law. What the scientific evidence demonstrates is that if the tight, unretractable foreskin is not removed properly, cleansing cannot be readily performed.

> As a result many virulent bacteria, including the cancer-producing Smegma bacillus, can grow profusely. During sexual intercourse these bacteria are deposited on the cervix of the uterus, but if the mucous membrane of the cervix is intact, little harm results. However, if lacerations exist, as they frequently do after childbirth, these bacteria can cause considerable irritation. Since any part of the body, which is subjected to irritation, is susceptible to cancer, it is perfectly understandable why cervical cancer is likely to develop in women whose mates are not circumcised.[34]

A recent study published in the *New England Journal of Medicine* found that women who have sex with circumcised men have lower rates of cervical cancer and that circumcised men are less likely to develop genital warts.[35] In their analysis of seven studies across five countries and on three continents, a team led by Dr. Xavier Castellsague of Llobregat Hospital in Barcelona, Spain, found human papillomavirus (HPV) in nearly 20% of uncircumcised men, but fewer than 6% of all circumcised men. For women, the chance of developing cervical cancer was at least 58% lower if their partner was circumcised. Men with intact foreskins were three times more likely than circumcised men to be infected with human papillomavirus (HPV), which is believed responsible for up to 99% (percent) of cervical cancer cases, the second leading cancer among women worldwide.

Even more recently, at the 41st annual meeting of the Infectious Diseases Society of America (IDSA) in July of 2003, physicians associated with Johns Hopkins presented the results of a study observing the incidence of HIV among circumcised and uncircumcised men.[36] The study of 2,298 Indian men suggests that circumcised men have a *"profound 8-fold reduction in HIV-1 risk."* Steven J. Reynolds, M.D., M.P.H., a postdoctoral fellow in infectious diseases at Johns Hopkins University School of Medicine in Baltimore, Maryland, stated that the study results "not only add to the developing body of knowledge on circumcision and HIV transmission, but they also lend great support to studies now underway in Uganda, Kenya, and South Africa."[37] Compared with uncircumcised men, circumcised men had an adjusted risk of HIV-1 infection of 0.12, which was significant ($P = .003$).[38] This means that uncircumcised men had a significantly higher occurrence of HIV-1. The incidence of HIV-1 infection in uncircumcised men was 5.5% (percent) but it was just 0.7% (percent) among circumcised men.

These findings are nothing new. In the early 1900s Dr. Hiram N. Wineberg, while studying records of patients in New York's Mt. Sinai Hospital, observed that Jewish mothers (presumably following cultural norms, which dictated that their partners were circumcised) were almost free of cervical cancers.[39] Dr. Ira I. Kaplan and his associates studied the records at New York's Bellevue Hospital and also found the rate of cervical cancers among Jewish woman to be scarce.[40]

> In 1954 in a vast study of 86,214 woman in Boston, it was observed that cancer of the cervix in non-Jewish women was eight and one half times more frequent than in Jewish women.[41]

Dr. S. I. McMillen cites older studies in India in which race, food, and environment did not differ significantly for most citizens. However, among those who practice Islam (a religion that also observes circumcision), the rates of cervical cancer were significantly lower.[42] This has been the consistent result of circumcision studies performed in India for over a fifty-year period.

YHWH's law governing circumcision instructs that the procedure be performed on the eighth day of life. Physician and author Rex Russell remarks,

> It is routine procedure to circumcise babies during the first three days of their lives. The body's natural supply of the blood-clotting vitamin K, however, is not yet present. Research has now shown that this clotting factor in infants is at its lowest level on days two through five. Vitamin K begins to develop in the intestine as the infant nurses. After five to seven days of breast-feeding, infants have built up enough vitamin K to allow blood clotting to withstand circumcision.[43]

Another factor affecting the blood's clotting ability is the prothrombin protein. When injured, a blood vessel produces a signal triggering the conversion of prothrombin to thrombin. The thrombin protein plays a central role in provoking the assembly of other proteins to form the blood clot.[44] On the third day of a baby's life the available prothrombin is only 30% of the normal level. "Any surgical operation performed on a baby during that time would predispose to serious hemorrhage."[45] On the eighth day, however, prothrombin increases to a level even better than normal—110%; it then levels off to 100%.

> It appears that an eight-day-old baby has more available prothrombin than on any other day in its entire life. Thus one observes that from a consideration of vitamin K and prothrombin determines the perfect day to perform a circumcision is the eighth day. . . . It was the day picked by the Creator of vitamin K.[46]

But what are the consequences of not circumcising children? A study released in August of 2012 by Johns Hopkins University concluded that the 20-year decline of circumcision in the United States is costing America $2 billion in healthcare costs that could have been avoided.[47] The study found an exponential increase in cancers and sexually transmitted diseases among uncircumcised males as compared with their circumcised male counterparts.

> "Our economic evidence is backing up what our medical evidence has already shown to be perfectly clear," says Tobian, an assistant professor at the Johns Hopkins University School of Medicine. "There are health benefits to infant male circumcision in guarding against illness and disease, and declining male circumcision rates come at a severe price, not just in human suffering, but in billions of health care dollars as well."[48]

Scientific data support the value of circumcision as prescribed by the *way of YHWH*. Unlike Egypt's or Mesopotamia's mystical and superstitious rituals, the Creator's prescription for preventive medicine actually thwarts cancer, HIV, genital warts, and a host of other bacteria and infectious diseases. Not only is there evidence for the *preventive* effects, of circumcision but also for the safety ensured on day the Creator specifies that the procedure should be performed. Thirty-five hundred years after Mt. Sinai, studies show that one of YHWH's ways of life work.

2. Kashrut

a. *Seafood and Swine*

Circumcision was only one of the Creator's prescriptions for preventive medicine. He also deemed certain animals unfit for human consumption. The Book of Leviticus (ch. 11 and Deuteronomy 14) designates edible animals. The overall concept behind this Law is that food taken into the body should lead to health and long life. The Creator specifies the meats that are healthy for human consumption, distinguishing them from unhealthy meats.

There are two kinds of meat: clean and unclean. Clean meats include beef, chicken, goat, venison, and lamb. Only mammals that both chew the cud and have cleft hooves are clean (Lev 11:3). Unclean meats include pork (ham), camel, ostrich, dog, cat, reptiles, rabbit, squirrel, and other rodents. Fish must have both fins and scales to be healthy. A few examples of kosher seafood are salmon, flounder, red fish, and cod. Scavengers are classified as unclean seafood. For instance, shrimp, crawfish, catfish, lobsters, oysters, and all mullasks are considered unclean. Why does the Law exclude these for a healthy diet?

YHWH's forbidden foods are predominantly scavengers. These animals are the vacuums of their breed that help ensure a clean environment. They were created to be the "garbage collectors" (feces eaters) of their ecosystems; they were not intended for human sustenance. Pigs, for instance, are scavenger animals that will eat just about anything. Their appetite for less-than-wholesome foods makes them a breeding ground for potentially dangerous infections that can be passed to humans. Even cooking unclean foods for long periods is not enough preparation to kill many of the retroviruses and other parasites that they harbor.[49] Over the past few decades, scientists have found many toxins, parasites, and diseases that are especially associated with shellfish and pork.

The U.S. Food and Drug Administration (FDA) publishes more literature on shellfish (filter-feeding molluscs) toxins than any other food group. Their official toxins handbook states:

> Shellfish poisoning is caused by a group of toxins elaborated by planktonic algae (dinoflagellates, in most cases) upon which the shellfish feed. The toxins are accumulated and sometimes metabolized by the shellfish. *The 20 toxins* responsible for paralytic shellfish poisonings (PSP) are all derivatives of saxitoxin.[50]

The FDA attributes 20 different toxins to "paralytic poisonings" alone. This does not include other toxins that cause diarrhea, neurological disorders, or amnesia. The most famous poisons are those ingested by shellfish, which are then passed to humans through consumption.[51] Cooking cannot always eliminate the toxic effect caused by the substances that these creatures have ingested.[52] It appears that YHWH excluded seafood, such as shellfish, based on the poisonous or otherwise unhealthy substances initially consumed by the sea creature. Can this be evidenced in other meats that the Creator excludes?

Pigs, like shellfish, also serve as disease-transmitting vehicles. One organism-causing disease associated with pork is Necrotic enteritis (pig-bel), which is often fatal.[53] This bacterium frequently occurs in the animal's intestines and has two primary sources: the substances ingested by the animal and the "soil sediments" of their environment.[54] In other words, the unsanitary conditions in which pigs eat and wallow contain many virulent bacteria and parasitic diseases that harbor inside the pig. This is then transferred to humans via consumption or handling.[55] *Yersinia enterocolitica* is another bacterium associated with pork. Ingestion of this bacterium can cause gastroenteritis while attacking the appendix.[56] Researchers cite parasites in humans as one factor that reduces immune-system function and may even contribute to the body's inability to ward off cancer.[57] One recent study showed evidence of a parasite's ability to hide in body organs and resurface to reinfect the patient or be transferred to others.[58] While safe handling can eliminate some of the toxins and parasites present in many foods; pork, shellfish, and other unclean foods are especially loaded with parasites and bacteria toxins that may be ineradicable.

Dr. Rex Russell concludes,

> One reason for God's rule forbidding pork is that the digestive system of a pig is completely different from that of a cow. It is similar to ours, in that the stomach is very acidic. Pigs are gluttonous, never knowing when to stop eating. Their stomach acids become diluted because of the volume of food, allowing all kinds of vermin to pass through this protective barrier. Parasites, bacteria, viruses and toxins can pass in the pig's flesh because of overeating. These toxins and infectious agents can be passed on to humans when they eat a pig's flesh.[59]

YHWH saw that these many disease-causing agents made swine incredibly dangerous for humans. Of all his prohibitions against unclean animals, none was as explicit as YHWH's prohibition against eating swine or touching its carcass.

> And the swine, though he divide the hoof, and be cloven footed, yet he chews not the cud; he is unclean to you. Of their flesh shall you not eat, and their carcass shall you not touch; they are unclean to you. (Lev 11:7–8)

History abounds with stories of diseases. Many epidemics arise from swine and their corpses, thus verifying the wisdom of YHWH's doctrine. Well known is the fairly recent Swine flu pandemic. The First swine influenza outbreak occurred during the great 1918 pandemic, when pigs became sick at the same time as humans.[60] Swine influenza is a highly contagious, acute respiratory disease in pigs, caused by one of several swine influenza A viruses.[61] The H1N1 viral strain is often called "swine flu" because initial testing demonstrated that many of the genes in the virus were similar to influenza viruses normally occurring in North American swine.[62] Pigs are an unusual species in that they can be infected with influenza strains that normally infect other species. Swine can contract influenza strains, which infect three different species: pigs, birds, and humans.[63] This makes pigs a host where influenza viruses might exchange genes, producing new and dangerous strains.[64] Pigs are able to retain influenza strains long after these strains have disappeared from the human population, but they can later emerge to reinfect humans, once the human immunity to these strains has waned.[65]

Researchers have documented the dangers of handling swine. Over the last few years, 24 workers at pork-processing plants experienced symptoms that eventually lead to paralysis. In some cases, the syndrome rapidly disabled the patient. In every case, the infected workers had come into contact with pig brains and muscle tissue when the brains were forced out with a burst of compressed air. In the process, brain particles were exploded into a fine mist. Even though workers wore protective clothing such as gloves, glasses, and bellyguards, particles still permeated the air and were breathed in by the patients.[66] "When you're breathing in pig brain tissue, your body develops an antibody against it," said Mayo Clinic neurologist James Dyck, who helped treat the workers. Antibodies are chemicals used by the immune system to tag foreign bacteria and substances. "There's enough overlap between pig brains and human brains that it was a problem."[67] In other words, the similarity between the genetic makeup of swine and humans presents dangers for the human handling of pigs.

The most overlooked disease transmitted from pigs to humans is *Streptococcus suis* (S. *suis*), a form of meningitis that often leads to pneumonia, arthritis, and Toxic Shock Syndrome.[68] Although other unclean animals harbor this disease, pigs are the most prolific and dangerous of meningitis carriers. In 2005, S. *suis* rapidly infected 214 people in southwest China. In *less than two months*, 39 people died (a mortality rate of nearly 20%). Most victims caught this disease when slaughtering or preparing the pig's carcass or its by-products.[69]

Asian countries bear the highest incident of S. *suis*. However, several recent studies have concluded that the lack of Western (European and American) diagnosis of *Streptococcus suis* is due to a frequent misdiagnosis rather than a "true absence of disease."[70] In one study sponsored by the CDC, researchers discovered that people with more exposure to pigs had a higher number of antibodies to S. *suis* than non-swine-exposed persons had. More antibodies indicate exposure to disease, thus suggesting that human infection with S. *suis* is more common in the United States than previously thought.[71] Supporting this hypothesis are reports showing that S. *suis* has been mistaken for other types of meningitis or Streptococcus strains,[72] instead of being diagnosed accurately.[73]

Research in regional outbreaks has indicated that the annual incidence of S. *suis* meningitis is about 1,500 times higher in swine-handling people than the unexposed population,[74] while investigators in another study found the sero-positive incidence to be even higher, especially among meat handlers.[75] This has led the World Health Organization (WHO) to encourage extra precautionary measures for those who prepare or cook pork in their homes.[76]

So how do government agencies effectively deal with outbreaks of contagious diseases that occur from eating unclean animals? Once again, they return to the protocols outlined in Leviticus (Lev 14:21; 22:8; Deut 14:21). China "prohibited domestic slaughter of sick pigs or pigs that died of any illness," holding village leaders accountable during the last outbreak.[77] Then China began aggressive public-education campaigns to prevent and control human *S. suis* infections.[78] By eliminating the eating and cleaning of diseased swine carcasses, China quickly controlled the outbreak. However, if the Chinese people had followed the Tanakh's protocols in the first place, they could have saved many lives.

You shall not eat of any thing that dies of itself. (Deut 14:21)

That which dies of itself, or is torn with beasts, he shall not eat to defile himself with it: I am YHWH. (Lev 22:8)

The Creator may have known that many virulent diseases lurked in unclean animals, or he may have created those diseases himself as a test to see if we would violate his Law. Whatever the case may be, he states that, if we will follow his Law, he will put "none of these diseases" on us.

b. Other Unclean Species

Swine are only one unclean species that evidences the rightness of YHWH's prohibitions. Even more compelling are other species that harbor disease. In 2003, SARS (Severe Acute Respiratory Syndrome), similar to swine flu, became a sweeping epidemic that rapidly spread through China and around the globe. Hong Kong researchers initially traced the cause of this disease to ingestion of the unclean civet cat.[79] Since the SARS outbreak, the WHO has cited seven species that harbor this disease: palm civets, raccoon dogs, Chinese ferret badgers, cynomolgus macaques, fruit bats, snakes, and wild pigs,[80] all of which are unclean according to Scripture. People who handled these animals or the meat from them were tested sero-positive for the disease, although they displayed no symptoms. Contamination occurred through handling contaminated SARS flesh (meat). This is fascinating in light of Israel's Scriptures, since the Law prohibited touching an *unclean* animal's corpse.[81]

Ebola is another disease that scientists have recently traced to handling contaminated (usually unclean) meat after death. An article in *Science Magazine* shows that most secondary Ebola cases occur among family members in Africa.[82] The family hunter initially catches the virus when he kills an infected animal or handles an infected animal's carcass discovered in the forest. When the hunter becomes ill, his family cares for him, coming in contact with bodily fluids (vomit, sweat, saliva, or blood), all of which can contain the virus. Eventually, other family members become infected. The death rate from Ebola is 80%.[83] This whole process begins by handling or ingesting one infected corpse.

In another very recent study, an international team of researchers from Cameroon and the United States documented, for the first time, the transmission of a retrovirus from primates to people in natural settings. Dr. Wolfe from Johns Hopkins Bloomberg School of Public Health and his colleagues examined blood samples from 1,099 individuals from

Cameroon who were taking part in an HIV prevention program. All of the study partici-
pants reported exposure to primate blood (i.g., monkeys, gorillas) that occurred primarily
during hunting and butchering. The blood samples were screened for SFV (simian foamy
virus) antibodies, which were detected in 10 of the samples. These individuals were identified as being infected with viruses from three different primate species, which included De
Brazza's guenon, mandrill, and gorilla.[84]

SFV, like HIV, which causes AIDS, is a retrovirus that can integrate its genetic material
into the genome of its human host. Dr. Wolfe reported that these retroviruses are regularly
crossing into humans. In a very strongly worded statement to the press in March 2004,
Dr. Wolfe testified: "It is in all our interests to put into place economic alternatives to help
people move away from hunting and eating these animals."[85] Primates are unclean according to Scriptural Law, and the bacteria associated with eating their meat or handling their
flesh naturally transmits disease. YHWH's preventive formula forbids eating unclean meats,
the carriers of many diseases, and his Law designated that anyone touching their carcasses
would be unclean. His preventive prescription thwarts the spread of Ebola, SARS, small pox,
leprosy, Black Death, and a host of other infections and diseases. By following the Creator's
prescription for public health, diseases are contained and eradicated from society.

c. Blood and Fat

Unclean animals were only one source of disease. YHWH also deemed both blood and fat to
be unhealthy for human consumption. Recent research has uncovered the truth of this prohibition as well. David Macht's (Johns Hopkins University) profound study demonstrated
the toxic effects of meats on a controlled growth culture.[86] He found that animal flesh had
varying rates of toxicity. Fascinatingly, Macht found that toxicity in animal meat correlates
with Scripture's laws. The *most* toxic animals were swine, rabbit, bear, camels, eagles, bats,
and ravens, while the *least* toxic were sheep, goats, deer, cows, ducks, turkeys, chicken, and
quail. *In every case, he found that the animal's blood was more toxic than its flesh.*[87]

Israel's Law embraced the Noahic Covenant by forbidding the consumption of blood:
"for life is in the blood" (Lev 17:14). Blood carries any disease prevalent in the DNA of an
animal breed or species.[88] As charted in the case of pork or shellfish, animal illnesses can be
passed to humans through consumption or handling an animal corpse. So yet again, there
is evidence supporting the Creator's clean laws.

Equally important as abstaining from unclean meat is YHWH's prescription that the
fat covering the organs be removed and discarded. Dr. Russell observes,

> Animal fat is also a storage place for toxins and parasites. These toxins are found
> in the fat of all the animals we eat. Examples include DDT, insecticides, herbi-
> cides, antibiotics, hormones and various other chemicals the animals have in-
> gested, breathed or touched. In 1979, a hormone called DES (diethylstilbestrol)
> was removed from the market because researchers learned that this substance
> caused cancer in the vagina and cervix in daughters of women who had received
> the drug to prevent miscarriage. They found that the stockyards throughout the

United States injected beef cattle with large amounts of DES because it enabled the animals to gain weight rapidly. And sure enough, the hormone was stored in the animals' fat tissue.[89]

Fat poses a threat to overall human health since toxins are stored in an animal's fat. By avoiding fat in a one's diet, the risk of those toxins being transmitted from animals to humans is significantly reduced.

Another aspect of YHWH's preventive medicine with which modern science readily agrees is the command to avoid eating an animal that "died of itself or that which was torn with beasts" (Lev 17:15).[90] An animal that dies of "itself," usually does so due to disease.[91] As we have seen above, most Asian viruses arise from handling carcasses of unclean animals. Today, unless we were raised in the back hills of Mississippi or Tennessee or a third-world country, most of us would not contemplate eating an animal found as "road kill." Once again modern medicine agrees with the prescription for health ordained in YHWH's Law.

d. What about Mad Cow?

Like SARS, Ebola, or SFV, Mad Cow Disease (BSE) can be traced to humanity's defiance of natural law. Bovine are clean according to YHWH's Law. And they are natural vegetarians. Modern industrial methods have changed this natural practice by feeding cattle their own or other species, such as pig, in products such as meat and bone meal. On this practice, the WHO's official Web site states,

> The nature of the BSE agent is still being debated. Strong evidence currently available supports the theory that the agent is composed largely, if not entirely, of a self-replicating protein, referred to as a prion. *It is transmitted through the consumption of BSE-contaminated meat and bone meal supplements in cattle feed.*[92]

In other words, cattle are being exposed to disease by eating their own kind. Cannibalism and carnivorism cause mutation because herds are subjected to diseases common to other species if their feed contains lamb, pork, or other animal products or by-products.[93] Diseases native to unclean species, such as swine, can cross the species barrier, causing contamination.[94] This is then transmitted to humans through consumption. Humans can then contract diseases that originated in hogs or other unclean animals, or through genetic mutations passed on through species cannibalism. Thus, mad cow disease can also be traced to a violation of natural law.

Evidence shows that unclean animals carry more parasites and are more toxic to humans than are clean species. Blood is more toxic than meat. Toxins and parasites are stored in fat tissues, regardless of whether an animal is clean or unclean. It appears that the Creator desired to spare humanity from illness, infection, disease, and mutations that would evolve from the eating of these forbidden animals. In light of scientific data, it appears that YHWH did not forbid certain animals arbitrarily. In the future, scientific research is likely to find that heart disease, cancer, arthritis, and a host of other diseases are directly linked to consuming foods that the Creator forbade. In the case of YHWH's clean animal laws, there does not appear to be anything unequal or unfair. YHWH established protocols in his Law that would preserve Israel's health, so in this regard, Israel's charges against YHWH are unfounded.

3. Dealing with Disease

Quarantine was one form of prevention for community health. Since YHWH commanded his priests to educate their citizens about disease prevention, public education was one of the priesthood's chief concerns (Lev 10:11). YHWH viewed bodily fluids as vehicles of contamination: he deemed saliva,[95] blood,[96] menstrual blood,[97] semen,[98] and other body emissions as capable of spreading viruses or bacteria. If a person came in contact with one of these fluids, YHWH's basic formula was infection control (washing) and time provided for contaminants to die ("until the evening").[99]

During the Dark Ages, Europeans dismissed this preventive formula. This enabled diseases to spread through lack of basic Scriptural hygiene. The best-known diseases were two of Egypt's worst: leprosy and Black Death.

> Leprosy cast the greatest blight that threw its shadow over the daily life of the medieval humanity. Fear of all other diseases taken together can hardly be compared to the terror spread by leprosy. Not even the Black Death in the fourteenth century or the appearance of syphilis toward the end of the fifteenth century produced a similar state of fright. . . . Early in the Middle Ages, during the sixth and seventh centuries, it began to spread more widely in Europe and became a serious social and health problem. It was endemic particularly among the poor and reached a terrifying peak in the thirteenth and fourteenth centuries.[100]

Black Death was one of the greatest disasters ever to be recorded in European history, killing well over 40 million people, yet leprosy was dreaded even more.[101] Both these diseases raged out of control until governments (such as Venice) stepped in and instituted quarantine laws that were already laid down in Leviticus 13.[102] Only then were these diseases brought under control. When Norwegian physician Gerhard Armauer Hansen discovered that leprosy was a bacterial infection easily transmitted from person to person, Norway began separating its infected patients, instituting the Norwegian Leprosy Act, "requiring strict enforcement of the biblical precautions. In less than sixty years, Norway's leper count dropped from 2,858 to 69."[103] What is more astounding is that Hansen's disease is considered one of the least communicable of all infectious diseases, yet it plagued an entire civilization until societies implemented Scripture's precepts for preventing contagion.[104]

Even today, physicians find Leviticus's quarantine precept to be valid.[105] When SARS hit Asia and spread around the world, science encountered a very peculiar dilemma. SARS did not respond well to drug therapy,[106] and the patient remained contagious for a significant period after drug therapy had been initiated.[107] Government officials found quarantining to be the most effective treatment to deal with the disease. At one point, Hong Kong's police even quarantined an entire city block![108] Quarantine allowed the eradication of an extremely contagious disease in a very short time.[109]

The Creator's Law built upon scientific principles by teaching public servants to identify, classify, and diagnose heterogeneous symptoms. Leviticus 13 elucidates many overlapping characteristics of "leprosy," thereby teaching how to identify various skin disorders (Lev 13:2–44). The Law names at least five different categories into which "leprosy" symptoms might fall (Lev 14:54–56). Scripture states that the entire purpose for the law of leprosy was: "To teach when it is unclean, and when it is clean: this is the law of leprosy" (Lev 14:57). Leprosy's law followed a basic evaluation formula: identify the patient's symptoms (Lev 13:1–4); isolate patient if conditions warrant (Lev 13:4); reevaluate (Lev 13:5) and requarantine if need be; and rediagnose with a bill of good health or with chronic symptoms (Lev 13:6–8). This basic protocol for public health is still effectively employed today.

Observe how closely the WHO's official protocol for containing SARS parallels the Creator's law for disease:

> The evidence presented at the Global Meeting on the Epidemiology of SARS and published data have confirmed the efficacy of traditional public health measures, which include early case detection and isolation, vigorous contact tracing, voluntary home quarantine of close contacts for the duration of the incubation period, and public information and education to encourage prompt reporting of symptoms.[110]

The Creator's law for disease still works today, more than 3,500 years after it was given to Israel at Mt. Sinai. When a society observes the Law, diseases such as SARS and small pox are exterminated. Modern public health thrives by implementing YHWH's prescription for prevention and containment. Diseases, such as leprosy, Black Death, polio, meningitis, and others have either been eradicated or are very well controlled in nations that follow quarantine and infection control protocols. Quarantining restrains contamination, saving a community's health from compromise. In the case of YHWH's unclean Laws, Israel's charge of unfairness seems to be unsubstantiated.

II. IS THE LAW MORALLY SOUND?

A. *Family Function*

Society's health depends on family relationships. Relationships determine disease patterns, genetics and morality and can affect a family's emotional and psychological stability. The Law defines moral and healthy relationships by differentiating them from unhealthy relationships that constitute incest (Lev 18:6). Incestual relationships include marital-type unions between children and their father, mother, aunt, uncle, or sibling—even if the marriage is only to a half-relation (Lev 18:9, 11–14). YHWH deems it immoral for a son to marry his father's former wife, even if she is not his biological mother (Lev 18:7–8; 20:11; 27:20), or for a man or woman to be sexually involved with their grandchildren (Lev 18:10). The Creator's overall precept is protection and preservation of the family unit, making a special point to exclude half-sibling relations from marital unions:

The nakedness of your father's wife's daughter, begotten of your father, she is your sister, you shall not uncover her nakedness. You shall not uncover the nakedness of your father's sister: she is your father's near kinswoman. (Lev 18:11–12. See also Lev 20:17)

The pattern established by the Creator's Morality Code protects the function of family positions. Any step-children brought into a marriage are afforded the same office as any biological offspring. Thus, a man marrying a woman with children could never marry his wife's daughter, even if she were divorced (Lev 18:17; 20:14).

YHWH had promised Israel that he would send "none of these diseases" on her citizens if they obeyed his Law. Recent scientific discoveries have conclusively demonstrated that diseases often pass from parent to child.[111] So widely is this fact accepted that standard life insurance forms ask if there is a *family history* of heart disease, cancer, thyroid disorders, or other well-known *family diseases*. When close relations marry, the child is more prone to inherit diseases such as Down Syndrome that naturally become dominant in that particular family's genes. When a disease does enter a family, YHWH's Morality Code eliminates further risk by forbidding close relations to marry. Once again, YHWH's prescription for health is directly tied to "none of these diseases."

YHWH also deemed homosexuality and bestiality (Lev 18:22–23) to be void of any respectable attribute. Evidently these practices had played a role in Canaan's official cults, for YHWH stated that they were "ordinances" or "statutes" (Lev 18:30) practiced by nations that he intended to dispossess. Throughout the ancient near East, homosexuality was an accepted practice.[112] Psychiatrist and sexual historian Norman Sussman points out that

male and female prostitutes, serving temporarily or permanently and performing heterosexual, homosexual, oral-genital, bestial, and other forms of sexual activities, dispensed their [sexual] favors on behalf of the temple. The prostitute and the client acted as surrogates for the deities.[113]

Deuteronomy refers to these temple prostitutes as a *qadesh* or *qadeshah* (Deut 18:30). Scholars observe that no ancient records discovered thus far address lesbianism;[114] however, there is no reason to suppose that female prostitutes did not also participate in homosexual acts, because homosexuality was revered in most cults.[115] Based on the fact that YHWH (Leviticus 18) attacks the "statutes" associated with pagan cults and "perverse" family relations, YHWH's Morality Code would also prohibit lesbianism or other relationships that did not strengthen and unify the traditional family unit.

One question that arises is if the Morality code does not explicitly prohibit female homosexuality, is it permitted? Scriptural evidence demonstrates that the perversity is in the homosexual act, not the gender. For instance, the Law prohibits a man to sleep with both a woman and her daughter (Lev 18:17). There is no instruction in the Law that explicitly prohibits a woman from sleeping with a man and his son, as long as the woman is *not* married to: the man, his son, or another man (the latter would be classified as sins under other laws in Leviticus 18). Amos, however, cites as one of Israel's iniquities a situation where a father and son have slept with the same woman, regardless of whether the woman was married to one of them or not. "*A man and his father will go in to the same maid, to profane my holy name*" (Amos 2:7). The perversity or iniquity that occurred in this act was that both father and son entered the same woman, not that she was married to one of them. Although the Law does not *explicitly* forbid a woman to sleep with a father and his son, it does forbid a man to sleep with a woman and her daughter (Lev 18:17). Amos's castigation demonstrates that *a parent/child relation with the same partner was prohibited, regardless of gender.* The same precept would hold true for homosexuality. Scripture prohibits all homosexuality, regardless of gender.[116]

Another case demonstrating that the precepts of the Torah are concerned with how a person lives and are gender-neutral unless otherwise stated is the Sabbath regulations. YHWH established rest for all family members, yet the wife is not specifically mentioned (Exod 20:10–11; Deut 5:12–15). If we follow the logic that the homosexuality ban only applies to males, then wives could work on the Sabbath, since they are not explicitly mentioned (Exod 31:13; Deut 5:14). This is not the case. It was crucial that women also sanctify YHWH's Sabbath (Exod 31:14; Lev 23:3; Deut 5:12; 31:11–12). YHWH intended both his rest day and his ban on homosexuality to benefit women (and wives) as well as men.

Remember that the Amorites, Kenites, and other nations specified in the Promised-Land Covenant had provoked YHWH through dysfunctions that defiled their family lineages, corrupted the function of the family unit, thwarted procreation, and no doubt spread disease throughout the community thus corrupting their land (Lev 18:27).[117] YHWH had instructed,

> Defile not you yourselves in any of these things: *for in all these the nations are defiled* which I cast out before you. (Lev 18:24; see also Lev 20:23)

YHWH's Morality Code sought to protect the very family unit he had created in Eden. To this end, he sought to protect heterosexual relationships from having to compete with homosexual relationships (see below). The Morality Code protected the nation from disease, guilt, and shame while protecting the heart, soul, and psychological well-being of the family he had created (see below). These regulations then strengthened the nation militarily, economically, psychologically, and spiritually in the people's relationships with society and God.

B. Protecting Women

YHWH sought protection and longevity for women. Equal in the morality categories that we have touched on so far is prohibition of intercourse during menstruation. YHWH viewed a woman as susceptible to infection anytime she had in *utero* blood discharge: menstruation, postpartum, miscarriage, or other times outside menstruation when an issuing of blood occurred (Lev 12:2–5; 15:19–26). In the first study ever published on this topic, doctors Tanfer and Aral discovered that "the data demonstrate a distinct association between sexual inter-course during menses and STD experience."[118] They found that women were three times more likely to have a sexually transmitted disease if they had sex during menstruation.[119] The study focused on 1,669 women from various backgrounds and races. Referring to STDs, the authors conclude:

> The risk of upper tract infection in women appears to be influenced by the men-strual cycle. Evidence from clinical studies suggests that symptomatic gonococcal or chlamydial pelvic inflammatory disease occurs most frequently during the first week of the menstrual cycle. One reason for the increased risk for infection ap-pears to be the *relative penetrability of the cervical mucous during menses*; another reason is the reflux of potentially contaminated blood into the fallopian tubes during menstrual uterine contractions. For gonococcal infection, two other fac-tors may be responsible: iron, which is abundant in menstrual blood, may promote gonococcal growth, and the type of gonococcus that causes tubal infection may proliferate at the cervix during menstruation. . . . The menstrual cycle also has been shown to effect phenotypic changes in gonococci that may alter gonococ-cal virulence; *therefore, intercourse during the menstrual period may expedite the spread of gonococci from the cervix to the endometrium and fallopian tubes.* Further, associations with the menstrual period have been suggested for gonococcal and trichomonal infections of the lower genital tract. (emphasis added)[120]

In another analysis, the authors found that:

> More recently, the *presence of blood during vaginal intercourse* has emerged as a risk factor for heterosexual transmission of human immunodeficiency virus (HIV) in some studies. Because HIV has been found in menstrual fluids, inter-course during menses places male partners at increased risk for acquiring HIV through heterosexual intercourse. (emphasis added)[121]

The cervix provides a wall of protection against disease. A woman's ability to ward off disease is decreased when the cervix is open, such as during menstruation or the postpartum period. During these times, the cervix opens and provides a "housekeeping" function by shedding the nutrients in the endometrium and hormones needed to support a fetus.[122] A second line of defense is provided by the cervix's mucous membrane. If lacerations exist as they fre-quently do after childbirth, intercourse can cause considerable irritation, making the woman susceptible to infection and disease. The new mother has increased exposure to infection, and any lacerations that have occurred during the birthing process only increase this risk.

If these processes are not enough to put a woman at risk, a new mother often suffers from sleep deprivation because the demands of her infant interrupts her rest. Recent re-search strongly suggests that immunity is directly related to the amount and consistency of sleep.[123] By forbidding intercourse during menstruation or the postpartum period, YHWH's preventive prescription decreased stress and protected a woman and her partner when her risk of infection was most vulnerable. The mother's good health, in turn, protected the com-munity from contagion as well.[124]

C. Premarital Relations

YHWH observed that premarital relations were counterproductive to a family-based polit-ical society.[125] To protect both the family and individuals in Israel's society, YHWH prohib-ited all sexual relations that did not result in marriage. If a couple had intercourse outside marriage (being neither married nor engaged to another), they were encouraged to marry quickly (Exod 22:16–17). Although a father could refuse to give his daughter in marriage, it could have dire consequences for any illegitimate grandchildren conceived by the affair.

Israel's congregation formed the heart and soul of the nation's community,[126] and ille-gitimate sons were banned from this elite society for 10 generations (Deut 23:2). Therefore, it could take well over 300 years for his grandchildren to enter Israel's sanctified congregation. This tied the daughter's actions to her family's name and reputation. Her illegitimate sons would face difficulties in securing a spouse from a reputable family who would desire its grandchildren to participate in Israel's voting congregation (see pp. 267–74). The only option for obtaining a spouse for an illegitimate child may have been to purchase a wife from the nation's welfare system (i.e., slavery). So, YHWH discouraged the woman and her father from declining a marriage proposal. Thus, YHWH sought to preserve the integrity of the family unit. It was in the daughter's best interest to preserve her purity and integrity solely for her husband on her wedding day.

Unlike modern Sharia law, Israel's Law did not embrace or encourage honor killings. YHWH did not desire Israel's culture to be harsh or repressive. Rather, he desired to deliver Israel from the house of bondage[127] by establishing the best values for the nation's welfare. If a single woman had sexual relations with a man who did not wish to secure her as his bride, YHWH allowed her to experience the natural consequences of her actions. He did not add a death sentence to an already painful affair. If, however, the bride or her family represented her as a virgin to another man when she was not, the consequences were severe (Deut 22:20–21). This impeded promiscuity and sexually transmitted diseases, while preventing the woman and her family from hiding an unwed pregnancy by marrying a man more desir-able than the child's father. Since a male child or an only daughter was born with the right to inherit the husband's property, it was important that the husband not be deceived into allowing his inheritance to be given to a child who was not his true heir.

A father's refusal of marriage for his pregnant daughter had additional consequences for his illegitimate grandchild's future well-being. If the child were a son, he would have no claim to his biological father's land inheritance. For the child to be registered in the nation's genealogical archives or obtain an inheritance of land for his future household, the patrimony would come at the expense of the maternal grandfather who had refused marriage for his pregnant daughter (see pp. 267–68, 272–74). Her son would then be listed as his grandfather's heir in lieu of his biological father. Thus, the grandfather could have another claimant for lands rightly bequeathed to his own sons. Without the grandfather's gift, the child would need either to live in the city or become a servant in another household as he lacked the basic economic unit of land that ensured both his economic prosperity and freedom for his family.

Ancient nations viewed offspring in striking contrast to many modern societies. Biological fathers viewed children as preservers that strengthened the family clan. Children were an investment in the nation's future prosperity. A child was so highly desired by a father and his family that few men would shirk their fatherly obligations. YHWH placed the greatest value on the family unit by ordaining judgments, statutes, and protocols whereby the family could function at its greatest potential while protecting the family unit from dysfunctional practices that threatened society's moral values. These values in turn protected unsuspecting young people from marrying a person with a sexually transmitted disease.

The Tanakh (Old Testament) also discouraged sexual promiscuity, often terming it *whoredom* (*zanah, zenuth*).[128] Even though there is no regulation in the Law that treats promiscuity itself as a capital offense, the Morality Code certainly discouraged it. As we discussed, a couple who did have sexual relations were encouraged to marry quickly (Exod 22:16–17), while YHWH considered a woman's pretense of virginity to be a capital offense (Deut 22:20–21). Although this statute protected the husband from an illegitimate heir if his new bride falsely represented herself as a virgin,[129] YHWH's primary purpose was to limit sexual relations outside marriage, which "brought folly in Israel." This regulation served to prevent a woman from "playing the whore in her father's house" (Deut 22:23). Hosea (4:13–14) builds on this, stating that, while *adultery* (*na'aph*) harmed the husband and his lawful wife, *whoredom* or promiscuity (*zanah*) harmed both the father and his daughter's reputation.

Men also faced penalties for seducing an unmarried (and unengaged) woman.[130] If the woman's father refused to give his daughter to an undeserving lover, the man still had to pay the standard betrothal payment yet received no bride.[131] This penalty served to discourage men from taking advantage of women or sleeping around.

Sexual relations were sacred in YHWH's sight. So greatly did he see the importance of maintaining and protecting the function of the family unit in society that he sought to destroy perversions that threatened the family unit's well-being. This granted children a firm and stable upbringing—allowing children to trust adults without fear of harm, thus protecting a child's innocence and vulnerability. A younger or more vulnerable person did not need to feel guilty for a crime perpetrated by an aggressor. To this end, YHWH identified five instances when sexual perversions merited death: (1) adultery (Lev 20:10); (2) homosexual or (3) bestiality (Lev 20:13, 15); (4) incest (Lev 20:11–12, 14, 17, 19, 21); and (5) intercourse during menstruation (Lev 20:18). These were part of the statutes that would make Israel a wise, understanding, and economically powerful nation (Deut 4:6–8).

D. Divorce

YHWH's Morality Code also allowed divorce where harm had been found in the spouse (Deut 24:1–4). Although the family protections afforded in the Law encouraged the family unit to stay together, YHWH did not hold either partner in bondage. If a couple chose to divorce, the woman was free to remarry with no further obligation.

The only regulation governing divorce stipulated that once a couple divorced and the woman had sexual relations with another man (Deut 24:4), she could not remarry the first husband. It also prevented situations in which a woman divorced the first husband to marry an elderly man with no heirs. She could then claim his property and remarry her first husband, thus creating a nightmare among tribal possessions when her first husband laid claim to the second husband's tribal heritage.

Another reason for this statute may have been curbing hasty divorces or preventing a jealous or resentful ex-spouse from intervening in a new marriage. It also served to prevent the transmission of sexual diseases by introducing new partners to the original relationship (i.e., the wife's intercourse with other men).

One purpose of this injunction may have been economic, protecting the wife's interest from a cruel husband.[132] When a woman married, she usually brought wealth to the marriage in the form of a dowry (Gen 30:20; Exod 22:17). If the marriage ended in divorce and the woman remarried, this injunction protected the woman in the event of the second husband's death. The first husband could not take advantage of his ex-wife's vulnerable situation to lay claim to her heart and claim the deceased's wealth for himself by remarrying her.

Westbrook and Wells observe that this statute

> distinguishes between the termination of the two marriages: the first, ending in divorce for fault, leaves the husband with the wife's property (dowry), while the second, ending in death or divorce, leaves a wealthy widow or divorcée. The first husband cannot profit from his former wife's newfound wealth by remarrying her, when he profited from divorcing her by claiming she was unfit to be his wife.[133]

While Scripture does not tell us how dowry worked in Israel, it is unlikely that a woman's dowry would be forfeited to her husband since, in Israel's society; the husband always retained the family land heritage. A more likely scenario in Israel was the woman retained her dowry but left the family home, which was built on the family land belonging to her husband's family.

In the ancient Near East, divorce could legally be sought by either the husband or the wife.[134] While the Torah only mentions the husband's prerogative, no injunction existed to prohibit a woman from seeking divorce, in which case she would retain her dowry and perhaps a settlement from her husband's estate if he were found at fault. If she accused her husband of infidelity in court and he was put to death, she would retain the entire estate, and no divorce was necessary. This incredible legal right that the wife possessed further discouraged adultery and the heartache it brings. It additionally protected both partners from disease or economic duress while protecting the children from the heartache of a broken and divided home. The cost of infidelity, however, goes far beyond the immediate family to affect the health and prosperity of an entire nation.

E. A Nation's Departure from Morality Results in "All of These Diseases"

1. The Consequences of Immorality

Wisdom of YHWH's premarital standard is readily evident in nations that dismiss the Creator's Morality Code. Nations that adhere to the Morality Code enjoy very low rates of illegitimacy, offering children a much better beginning in life. But in nations that dismiss this code, standards for family relationships erode as less-moral values become mainstream. Take the United States, for instance. Less than a century ago, America adhered to YHWH's Morality Code, but today the United States has departed from the Creator's high moral standard and permitted promiscuity to flourish. America's low moral standards have resulted in a situation in which unwed mothers and their children constitute *more than one-fourth* of all families in America.[135]

Europe and the Russia Federation evidence similar statistics. Half of all children in France are born to unwed mothers, while one-third of all Russia-born children are illegitimate.[136] Fifty-six percent of all children in Sweden are born to unwed mothers, and in Britain 42% of all children are born to unwed mothers, according to the EU's official statistics branch, Eurostat.[137] "De facto unions are not as stable as those bound by a legal contract, and that in their wake they leave more children living with only one parent, with all the social, economic, and educational disadvantages that is widely acknowledged to bring."[138] The Western revolt against the traditional family and marriage has resulted in huge population decreases, leaving these nations economically, militarily, and culturally vulnerable to more prolific cultures such as Islam.[139]

Modern statistics reveal that premarital sex is one of the greatest threats to the family unit.[140] One government study observes:

> Increases in births to unmarried women are among the many changes in American society that have affected family structure and the economic security of children. Children of unmarried mothers are at higher risk of having adverse birth outcomes, such as low birth weight and infant mortality, and are more likely to live in poverty than children of married mothers.[141]

Uncommitted partners pose the greatest threat to a family system. Since the sex revolution of the 1960s, the number of unwed mothers has grown steadily in the United States. In 1980, about 18% of all births were to unwed mothers.[142] But, as the 60's philosophy burgeoned, the rate of unwed mothers grew to more than 33% forty years later (in 2000),[143] threatening the very fabric of family values and the idea of "family" itself. If this trend continues, within another decade or two, the family unit will be on the verge of extinction. When society accepts or even sanctions unwed relations, children are put at risk, and many of the child's natural needs go unmet.[144] Family values erode as a people's integrity of right and wrong become skewed in the wash of generalities.[145] Not only do children suffer, the single parent endures the stress of providing both parental roles (see Illustration 6.1).

The aim of this section is to determine whether the Creator's Law is valid. Do his laws lead to death, bondage, and hard labor, as ancient Israel asserted? Or, is the *way of YHWH* good for man? Is it morally sound? YHWH stated that he would protect Israel from disease (Deut 7:15) and ensure her prosperity (Deut 28:10–13) if she obeyed. Likewise, if Israel rebelled against his Law, disease (Deut 28:58–63) and hardship (Deut 28:38–45) would follow. So it is not surprising that the consequences for breaking the Creator's laws are easiest to identify in promiscuous individuals. Diseases carried by immoral persons outweigh the toxins carried by civet cat, shellfish, and swine put together.[146] A relation with one non-monogamous person can represent sexual contact with over 40 people. A person engaging in promiscuous sexual activity can be exposed to diseases that a partner contracted during or carried from previous relationships. It is little wonder that sexually transmitted diseases (STDs) pose one of the greatest threats to human health in the twenty-first century.

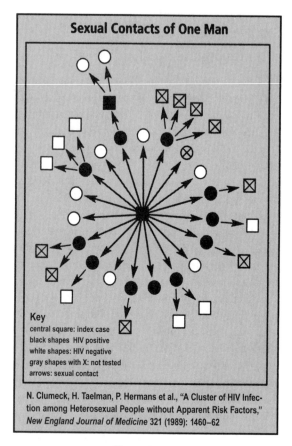

Sexual Contacts of One Man

Key
central square: index case ⊠
black shapes HIV positive
white shapes: HIV negative
gray shapes with X: not tested
arrows: sexual contact

N. Clumeck, H. Taelman, P. Hermans et al., "A Cluster of HIV Infection among Heterosexual People without Apparent Risk Factors," *New England Journal of Medicine* 321 (1989): 1460–62

Illustration 6.1.

2. STDs: All of These Diseases

There are many diseases that fall under the STD umbrella. Although the names and symptoms of each may differ, one thing is constant: the way STDs are contracted. STDs are contracted through intercourse with an individual infected with a an STD, who then transfers it to his or her subsequent partner. Statistics for STDs are one indicator of a society's moral values. Does the United States' departure from YHWH's Morality Code reflect disease?

The United States has the highest rate of STDs among the industrialized nations in the world.[147] Over 15 million cases alone were reported in 1996.[148] In 1997, CDC recorded 526,653 chlamydia cases.[149] After 1987, chlamydia cases rose from 47.8 per 100,000 persons to 207 per 100,000 persons by 1997.[150] This represents a 159.2% increase in the incident of this disease in just one decade! As of 2008, chlamydia cases had grown to more than 1.2 million (1,210,523).[151] And this is just one disease.

Gonorrhea, another STD, causes infertility, ectopic pregnancy, and cervical cancer.[152] America's faded social values have contributed to all sorts of STDs. In 1997, the CDC recorded 324,901 cases of gonorrhea and 8,550 cases of syphilis.[153] In 2004, the Richmond, Virginia metro area alone reported over 1,700 new cases of gonorrhea in one year.[154] Government agencies cite that there are well over 700,000 new cases of gonorrhea each year in the U.S.[155] Many of these STDs result in cancer. HPV (Human papovilla virus, an STD) especially causes cervical cancer in approximately 11,000 women each year.[156] As of 2010, there are over 70 million STDs in the United States with 19 million new cases being reported every year.[157] This again is evidence of a non-monogamous society in which rates of disease increase as moral standards of monogamous relationships decrease.

Not only do STDs incur life-long effects,[158] they also facilitate AIDS transmission.[159] In 2006, there were over one million people suffering with AIDS in the United States.[160] The WHO found that practicing homosexual men were twice as likely to contract HIV than heterosexual men.[161] Another study found that HPV was much more common among practicing homosexual men.

> Anal HPV prevalence is more common in HIV-positive men, at more than 60%, versus 17% in HIV-negative men. Another risk factor for HPV infection is the number of sexual partners. Up to two thirds of sexual partners of patients with condylomata acquire HPV infection. Among HIV-negative homosexual men, the prevalence of anal HPV infection has been reported to be as high as 78% by PCR. . . . Additionally, infection by multiple HPV types is common and carries an increased risk for anal squamous intraepithelial lesions (SIL, also known as anal intraepithelial neoplasia or AIN) and progression to HSIL over time. Multiple HPV types were found in 73% of HIV-positive and 23% of HIV-negative homosexual men.[162]

Globally, STDs are more devastating, claiming the lives of an astounding 40 million people.[163] The WHO estimates that more than 333 million people live with HIV, with new sexually transmitted infections occurring at a rate of 2.6 million every year.[164] Every year, over one-third of STD cases appear in young people under 25 years of age around the world.[165] These statistics hold true regardless of a person's religious affiliation: Christian, Islamist, Buddhist, Hindu, atheist, or Jew, if a person engages in promiscuity, he or she risks infection and risks infecting his or her partner.

All these diseases proliferate due to neglect of the Creator's precept for monogamous relationships. Modern technology is often ineffective in thwarting sexual contagion. Recent research has shown that latex condoms are often *in*effective at curbing STDs.[166] Realistically, there is no other method of avoiding contracting STDs than following YHWH's Morality Code. When the Law is followed, however, STDs, similar to Black Death, leprosy,[167] small pox, or other communicable diseases, can be eradicated from society so that disease is no longer transferred from one sexual partner to another.

3. Financial and Emotional Stress

Disease places an enormous burden on society. Disease severely weakens nations ridden with illness. Families endure the pain and grief associated with a loved one's illness or, worse, his or her loss. Nations battling disease lose strength and position among competing nations as resources are diverted to finance healthcare. The national CDC observes: "All Americans have an interest in STD prevention because all communities are impacted by STDs and *all individuals directly or indirectly pay for the costs of these diseases.*"[168] Africa provides a case in point for diseases' economic and emotional impact on society.

In just one year, Zambia lost 1,300 teachers to HIV. This was 70% of its new teachers, who had graduated and begun to teach. This resulted in larger class size and decreased public education. One WHO report explains that demographers in Africa used to speak of population pyramids but "now talk about population chimneys because of the lack of adults in the most productive years between 35 and 60," due to HIV infection and death. The authors of the study conclude: "This loss will weaken institutions such as governments and inhibit the growth of private-sector enterprises. As a result poverty will become more widespread."[169] Loss of a country's citizens weakens the nation. The loss of life decreases the ability of a nation to produce goods. This affects the economy for the entire nation, spreading poverty among the healthy.

Another report observes that in countries battling AIDS—like Tanzania—there is a direct correlation between the Gross Domestic Product (GDP) and disease. In many cases the GDP fell 1% per year in nations that battled the epidemic.[170] Desmond Cohen, Director of the UN's HIV and Development Programme (UNDP), is an economist and former Governor and Associate Fellow at the Institute of Development Studies. He cites one economic impact study in Thailand that generally excluded STDs and focused primarily on HIV.

> It confirms other studies which stress the virtual impossibility of families meeting from their own resources the health care costs of infected persons. Even at levels of treatment that exclude the most expensive therapies, the costs of health care would absorb some 30–50% of average household income in Thailand. Inevitably this will pose a major budgetary burden for the Thai Government, if it chose to try and meet it, and if it did so through traditional institutional mechanisms. Much more significant are the indirect costs, which are in the aggregate over the whole period 1991–2000 put at between US$ 7.3 billion and US$ 8.7 billion. The loss per AIDS death represented by these indirect costs is estimated at US $22,000, i.e., some 17.6 times the per capita GDP in 1991. Not only are the estimated direct and indirect costs very substantial, together they amount to an annual cost of some 16–18 times per capita GDP, but the study confirms that indirect costs to the economy due to foregone output far exceeds the direct costs due to health expenditures.[171]

What this study means is that HIV costs Thailand more money to care for its patients than the country generates in revenue. *The country simply does not generate enough income from its economy to care for the infected individuals.*

Direct medical costs of STDs in the United States are estimated to be $8.4 billion.[172] These estimates do not include indirect, nonmedical costs such as lost wages and productivity due to STD-related illness, out-of-pocket costs, or the costs incurred when STDs are transmitted to infants, which can result in lifelong expenses.[173]

More important than economic impact is the STD's attack on a nation's greatest national resource: human life. Lack of monogamy as a philosophical heritage has hit many African countries extremely hard. Sue Parry of the Farm Orphan Support Trust estimates that Zimbabwe alone will rear an entire generation without parents, an overwhelming 1.1 million orphans in 2005, whose parents have succumbed to AIDS.[174] Desmond Cohen sees:

> The economic and social costs of HIV are truly colossal. The epidemic, if unchecked, could transform the developmental performance of many countries. Not simply in terms of national economic growth rates, but also in terms of those broader social indicators that more accurately reflect improvements in the standard of living. No sectors of the economy are immune to the impacts of the epidemic, and all social strata will be affected.[175]

National costs of immorality are phenomenal. Economic resources normally spent on scientific discoveries, national defense, public education, or other advancements that strengthen nations are suspended as family and government divert resources to finance and care for those who suffer from disease. This causes a disease-ridden nation to lose its power and influence among rival nations. Rival nations that do not bear the economic burden of disease care can invest more resources into stronger armies and developing a greater GDP. This ultimately allows international political agendas and policies to favor stronger, wealthier nations.

Back in the 1930s, British social anthropologist J. D. Unwin studied 80 civilizations and concluded that every known culture in the world's history has followed the same sexual pattern. During a nation's early existence, premarital and extramarital relations were strictly prohibited, during which time the culture and scientific advancement prospered. Gradually, and much later in the cycle of society, standards and prohibitions against promiscuity slackened until society decayed and self-destructed. He predicted that a society could not sustain broad immorality beyond one generation.[176] His prophecy is currently being fulfilled in many African nations today, whose children will grow up parent-less. Given current statistics, it is unsettling to think how many of America's generations can survive before Unwin's cycle will be repeated in U.S. history as well.

4. Sins of the Fathers (Exodus 34:6–7)

As we continue to try YHWH's case, it is necessary to delve into a very sensitive and politically *in*correct topic for the purpose of demonstrating the consistency of the Creator's words. I have shown that if humanity keeps YHWH's law he "sends none of these diseases" on us. I have also deomonstrated that sexual diseases are more likely to occur when YHWH's statutes are breached. There is, however, another precept that determines how this statute works.

When YHWH passed before Moses at Mt. Sinai, he proclaimed the attributes of his character and the parameters by which mercy was governed.

> And YHWH passed by before him, and proclaimed, YHWH, YHWH God, merciful and gracious, longsuffering, and abundant in goodness and truth, Keeping mercy for thousands, forgiving iniquity and transgression and sin, and that will by no means clear the guilty; *visiting the iniquity of the fathers on the children, and on the children's children, to the third and to the fourth generation.* (Exod 34:6–7)

What does it mean for the father's iniquity to be passed to the third and fourth generations? The reality is that children often inherit their forefather's sins. Many children today are born with STDs.[177] In 1997 alone, 1,200 children were born with syphilis in the United States.[178] The WHO estimates that *over 3,600,000 children have been born with HIV*, many of whom have died.[179] Though the child does not deserve diseases inherited from his parent's actions, it is the way that genes and disease work. It is the legacy that the parent leaves for his or her unborn child. While we may complain about how unfair genetics are to the unborn, heredity is not arbitrary. The only way that society is to prevent genetic, congenital, or contagious diseases is by a return to YHWH's high standards, which define human relationships and eliminate "all of these diseases."

There is a pattern innate to Torah. The laws we have studied thus far contain preventive formulas that can be condensed into one word: RISK. A person may be able to consume pork, shellfish, civet cat, or other unclean animals and never see consequences in his lifetime. An individual may be able to consume animal blood and fat and never experience vascular or heart disease, although risk for it increases. Science has demonstrated that heart disease is passed down to children generation after generation,[180] so the parent may never see the consequences of his unrighteousness but passes on greater risk, an increased vulnerability to a particular disease as a heritage for his or her child as many studies are now discovering.[181] A parent may not have the protection of circumcision for himself and his wife, yet again he (or she) has an increased risk. A couple may engage in intercourse during menstruation, or the parties may move on to other partners. They may never receive any consequences in their lifetime, yet their risk for disease increases. And when they succumb to a risk, it is quickly passed on to other, often-uninfected individuals. All too often, the children do inherit their parents' sins. There appears to be one simple way to alleviate a child's un-deserved potential for congenital malformations: eliminate risk by following the *laws of reality*.

7

Laws of Reality, Part 3: The Blessing—Freedom or Bondage?

I. JUSTICE

Although healthcare formed a cornerstone of YHWH's constitution, it was only one aspect of his overall philosophy for a righteous or unique people (Exod 19:5). No nation can exist without law and order, so the Creator established a national constitution that defined how justice would prevail. Both YHWH's healthcare doctrine and his judicial doctrine were founded on precepts of equity.

The best definition for *equity* is found in the words of Sir Isaac Newton, known as Newton's Third Law of Motion, paraphrased: *For every action, there is an opposite and equal reaction.* The terminology used by Scripture for Newton's Law is "an eye for an eye, and a tooth for a tooth"—opposite and equal reactions. The ideology underlying this precept is that man will learn from the consequences of his actions and not repeat negative actions. The *entire* Law hinges on this precept. The following definitions will serve as the standard by which YHWH's Law must measure in order to qualify as fair and just.

Fair: marked by impartiality and honesty: free from self-interest, prejudice, or favoritism; b: conforming to the established rules

Impartial: not partial or biased: treating or affecting all equally.

Equity: justice according to natural law or right: freedom from bias or favoritism

Just: having a basis in or conforming to fact or reason: REASONABLE

Reasonable: not extreme or excessive; MODERATE, FAIR

Justice: The quality of being just or impartial, or fair: the principle or ideal of just dealing or right action: RIGHTEOUSNESS

Webster defines *equity* as being free from bias or favoritism. Does Israel's Law meet this definition of equity? A judgment in Exodus states,

> One law shall be to him that is home born, and to the stranger that sojourns among you. (Exod 12:49)[1]

Yes, this command encompasses the meaning of the word "equity." The Law did *not* show preference for a person just because he (or she) was the seed of Abraham.[2] Similar to Einstein's "metaprinciple," that all the laws of physics must be the same in every inertial reference frame, YHWH's Law worked the same for all people of the world. His laws are universally valid. Whether an individual was the offspring of Israel or the offspring of Egypt, one Law applied to all, and the rewards for keeping the Law (freedom from disease, justice, prosperity, relationship with God) blessed all who obeyed.

If YHWH had established two separate law codes in Israel's land—one for Abram's offspring and a separate code for immigrants from other nations—then social strife would have abounded. Israel would have faced the same type of unrest we see in European nations today, whose traditional law codes vie for social acceptance with Islamic Sharia law. Knowing that the key to national stability rested in national law, YHWH established a single code for harmony in the nation's borders.

The consistency of YHWH's Law is demonstrated in another judgment, in which YHWH commands the nation's judges to be impartial. The balance between mercy and justice were to be established through his Law (Exod 20:6; 25:17–22; 26:34; Deut 5:10). To this end, he barred judges from receiving contributions, donations, or more obviously, bribes.

> Keep you far from a false matter; and the innocent and righteous slay you not: for I will not justify the wicked. And you shall take no gift: for the gift blinds the wise, and perverts the words of the righteous. (Exod 23:7–8)

YHWH saw that contributions or other gifts would pervert a judge's sense of justice because his decision could be swayed by his own self-interests. Both YHWH's command that his Law is for *all* people and his command that forbids bribery uphold the concepts of fairness, impartiality, and equity. Thus, YHWH's ideals for fairness and impartiality are a bedrock principle for his entire Law. I wondered that, if the Law is fair, equitable, and impartial, is there evidence that his Law is also reasonable? Can it meet the requirement of being just?

A. Larceny

> If someone steals an ox or sheep and then kills or sells it, the thief must pay back five oxen for each ox stolen, and four sheep for each sheep stolen. If a thief is caught in the act of breaking into a house and is struck and killed in the process, the person who killed the thief is not guilty of murder. But if it happens in daylight, the one who killed the thief is guilty of murder. A thief who is caught must pay in full for everything he stole. If he cannot pay, he must be sold as a slave to pay for his theft. If someone steals an ox or a donkey or a sheep and it is found in the thief's possession, then the thief must pay double the value of the stolen animal. (Exod 22:1–4, *New Living Translation*)

When a thief failed to restore stolen property, he repaid four to five times the value of the stolen item. If the thief restored an article in the condition that he had taken it, he restored double that article's worth as a penalty for his crime. YHWH's restoration statutes both compensated the victim through fines and deterred thievery through penalized restitutions that had greater value than the stolen item(s). Unlike some contemporary law codes, Israel's Law did not place exorbitant penalties on crimes committed against the state (palace or the gods). The Laws of Hammurabi, for instance, called for a *thirtyfold* repayment when the crime had been perpetrated against "a god or the palace."[3] In Israel, God (his Temple and his priests) were compensated at the same pre-determined rates as the rest of Israel's society. Another distinction between Israel's Law and the Hammurabi Code was the term of repayment. The Hammurabi Code called for a *tenfold* repayment for theft committed against common citizens.[4] If the thief was unable to pay, he was put to death.[5] Israel's Law was significantly more lenient than Mesopotamian law, yet still held the theif accountable for his offense. If the thief could not make restitution, he was sold (through the court system) as an indebted servant until the theft had been repaid. He was not put to death for thievery. YHWH placed responsibility for the victim's loss on the culpable thief. He did not hold a slave's owner or anyone else responsible for an individual's actions. This formula is followed throughout the Law. YHWH's thievery judgments were not excessive or extreme, but appear to have been reasonable.

B. Noncriminal Negligence

> If a man shall cause a field or vineyard to be eaten, and shall put in his beast, and shall feed in another man's field; of the best of his own field, and of the best of his own vineyard, shall he make restitution. If fire break out, and catch in thorns, so that the stacks of corn, or the standing corn, or the field, be consumed by it; he that kindled the fire shall surely make restitution. (Exod 22:5–6)

If a man let his livestock feed in his neighbor's field, he was responsible for restitution, although he paid no further penalty. If a person started a fire and it accidentally grew out of hand, he was liable solely for restitution. Again, this judgment was not excessive or extreme. YHWH did not require the guilty person to pay four or five times the amount for an accidental circumstance; he simply compelled the guilty person to restore the owner's losses. Because the Creator set reasonable limits, I deemed that his laws (thus far) qualified as being just.

A nation's court system often determines the freedom of its citizenry. Governments that base policy on the best interest of its leaders end up oppressing the people, while governments that provide fair, unbiased, and reasonable verdicts maintain liberty for its citizenry. Historically, the United States of America has been the freest nation on earth, but now how do America's court verdicts compare with those established in YHWH's Law?

In the United States, many criminals earn a living through auto-theft. When the felon is apprehended and convicted, he is sentenced to do "time" in a local penitentiary. Rarely is the thief sentenced to work and repay his victim for the car he has stolen. The car owner almost never recovers his loss, or a third-party insurance pays the bill to cover the thief's actions.[6] When the car owner files his insurance claim, he is often penalized by increased premiums that offset the insurance company's loss. So, in effect, the victim actually pays for the thief's crime. This would hardly qualify as reasonable or just. While it may seem comfortable to assign restitution to a third party who had no part in the crime, indemnity (when it abrogates personal accountability) is an arbitrary institution.

The precept in Exod 22:1–4 (quoted above) holds only the thief who committed the crime liable for damages. This keeps the cost of living at a minimum. If the thief lacked the resources to pay his debt, he could sell his time in order to restore the car owner's loss. This in itself could deter a thief's criminal activities because labor would await crimes, not plush jail cells.

C. Culpability

Another verse that we examined in chap. 5 (p. 188) defines personal responsibility even further. Notice how closely the following judgment resembles "modern civil remedies".[7]

> If men strive together, and one smite another with a stone, or with his fist, and he die not, but keeps his bed: If he rise again, and walk abroad on his staff, then shall he that smote him be quit: only he shall pay for the loss of his time, and shall cause him to be thoroughly healed. (Exod 21:18–19)

This judgment compels the negligent to seek the injured party's full recovery. He pays the victim's lost wages and seeks the best medical treatment possible. If the victim can work again, there is no further vindication or compensation.

Compare this judgment with frivolous compensations awarded in America's courts. Catherine Crier, a former lawyer, judge, and well-respected legal commentator cites a case in Maine in which a woman hit an errant golf shot that landed near a set of railroad tracks. Her second shot hit the tracks, and the ball ricocheted back into her face. She sued the country club despite the fact there was a warning sign posted on the tee box and the obstacle was clearly visible from there. Her initial award of $250,000 was later reduced to $40,000 in recognition of her 'partial' fault in the accident. While these cases may sound absurd to the intelligent reader, law books are increasingly filled with such nonsense.[8]

Society as a whole is affected by these unjust and erroneous verdicts. We, the citizens, pay the court costs associated with these cases through higher taxes. The "victim's" compensation is either paid by an insurance company or is passed onto the consumer in the form of higher rates and fees.

According to Exod 21:18-19, this woman would not have received compensation if she were hit by her own wayward ball. If her shot had hit her golfing partner, she would be held responsible, and the country club owner would have had *zero* liability. The only way the country club owner could be held responsible would be if he (or someone from his institution) drove the ball. Even in this scenario, the only compensation that the injured would be awarded would be lost wages and medical treatment. In Israel's government there was justice, reasonable judgments, and freedom from absurdity, in comparison with current tort trends in America, where justice and "assumptive risk" are rapidly disappearing.

D. Involuntary Manslaughter vs. Premeditated Murder

Manslaughter greatly concerned YHWH's righteous government. His Law demonstrates an increased responsibility for prior knowledge and premeditated motives.[9] If a murder was premeditated, the killer was put to death.[10] If the act was involuntary manslaughter, the slayer escaped to a Refuge City (Num 35:6, 11-32; Josh 20:1-8).[11] These Refuge Cities were located throughout Israel, so one was never too far away (e.g., if a man had to flee, his family and his tribal land were not far away).[12] Refugees retained all personal rights and freedoms except one: they could not leave the city until the high priest's death. The refugee was free to enter into business, and his (or her) family could live with him. At the time of the high priest's death, he was free to leave the Refuge City and return to his family's heritage without fearing vindication from the victim's family. Society did not need to collect taxes to support jails, inmates, guards, or other facilities associated with incarcerating convicted felons. Man was not caged like a wild beast. He was treated with honor and respect throughout a tragic incident. A person was free to live and learn from the consequences of his actions—making restitution and treating his fellow man equitably. Thus far, Israel's Law would appear wholly in accord with the Laws of reality (natural law).

E. Ignorance Was Immaterial: Personal Responsibility Triumphed

Perhaps the Law's harmony with reality is nowhere more apparent than in an injunction in Leviticus, which states:

> And if a soul sin, and commit any of these things which are forbidden to be
> done by the commandments of YHWH; though he know it not, yet is he guilty,
> and shall bear his iniquity. (Lev 5:17)

An offender's awareness that his (or her) actions had breached the Law did not matter in
YHWH's eyes. *The trespasser's knowledge was irrelevant with regard to his guilt.* This placed
responsibility on individuals to be certain they were aware of YHWH's requirements and
adherence to them. A case could never be dismissed on the basis that the defendant was
"unaware" that his or her action was unlawful.[13] In this way, YHWH ensured that only
the guilty person would be responsible for restitution. This in turn granted great peace to
a society who knew there would be prompt consequences for an individual's actions and
speedy restitution when someone was wronged.

  Israel's Law was a "living" constitution. It was "living" in the sense that its original
principles would apply to new facts, not that the constitution changed to adapt to Israel's
new standards or culture. YHWH did not address every single scenario that might occur,
but he did provide enough judgments that the principles governing them could be applied
to new cases. In this way, YHWH's Law functioned as Israel's constitution in much the same
manner as the U.S. Constitution does the United States of America.

II. DOES THE ISRAELITE LAW ESTABLISH FREEDOM?

A. Family Value

Old Testament religion did not function independently of government. Rather, *the government prescribed in YHWH's Law defined Israel's religion.* YHWH's Law established a
righteous government that maintained equity between citizens (brethren) and between
humanity and God. While government law naturally does *not* delve into philosophical matters by explaining the fears, desires, or other factors that influence personal choice, by its
very nature national law does define the standards (precepts, philosophy) on which a society places value.[14] In other words, Israel's national constitutional Law established society's
cultural values. For instance, very few nations today institute laws bearing on morality.
Renowned conservative psychologist, Dr. James Dobson, in his book *Bringing up Boys*, cites
the consequences for Western society's departure from a morality code this way:

> Chief among the threats to this generation of boys is the breakdown of the family.
> Every other difficulty we will consider has been caused by or is related to that
> fundamental tragedy. It can hardly be overstated. We have been emphasizing for
> years that stable, *lifelong marriages provide the foundation for social order.* Every-
> thing of value rests on those underpinnings. Historically, when the family begins
> to unravel in a given culture, everything from the effectiveness of government to
> the general welfare of the people is adversely impacted. This is precisely what is
> happening to us today. The family is being buffeted and undermined by the forces

operating around it. . . In cultures where divorce becomes commonplace or large numbers of men and women choose to live together or copulate without bothering to marry, untold millions of kids are caught in the chaos.

If I may be permitted to offer what will sound like a hyperbole, I believe the future of Western civilization depends on how we handle this present crisis. Why? Because we as parents are raising the next generation of men who will either lead with honor and integrity or abandon every good thing they have inherited. They are the bridges to the future. Nations that are populated largely by immature, immoral, weak-willed, cowardly, and self-indulgent men cannot and will not long endure.[15]

American society in particular does not discourage childbearing out of wedlock, homosexuality, or adultery. There are no judicial laws or economic barriers to these actions, and current tort and welfare policies actually promote these behaviors.[16] This fact reveals that a society's philosophy places greater value on *personal preference* (which it may be remembered is a definition of *arbitrary*), which often undervalues standards rather than preservation of the family unit.[17] In contrast, YHWH's Law was quite concerned with the family's health and overall well-being. His Law prescribed the foundation for a healthy family. He realized that families are the core of any society and granted individual families the greatest power or voice in Israel's government. By their very nature, these laws not only display the value that YHWH places on family but also demonstrate the philosophy or precepts that the Creator holds for defining righteous behavior (such as the precept of personal responsibility), which in turn define his truth (Prov 4:2).

The *way of YHWH* sought to relieve stresses that pressure and contribute to dissolution of the family unit. This is why he apportioned permanent nontaxable (nontithable) property to every family. When Israel entered the Promised Land, Joshua divided Canaan among the 12 tribes of Israel.[18] We could call these "tribal territories."[19] Tribal territories were further divided into "clan territories," which designated the tribe's predominant hierarchy: probably the first three to five generations. Clan territories were further divided into family inheritances. Fathers apportioned the family inheritance when sons married or shortly before their death.[20] This ensured that every family owned a permanent piece of rural land (heritage), see Map 7.1.[21]

Heritages were directly tied to family self-government, and fathers were the governors of their land.[22] A father was responsible for seeing that righteousness and justice prevailed on his inheritance.[23] Individual families fell under the jurisdiction of their ruling clan, who in turn answered to the tribe's prince. Although families were autonomous, YHWH empowered the Levites to hold families accountable for their obedience to the Law. When the nation failed to obey, one of the Levites' functions was to render judgment on individuals who grossly rebelled against the Law.[24] Thus, YHWH balanced family autonomy with the power of his Levitical law-enforcement officers (see below).

YHWH's endowment of land shows the value that he places on the individual family unit. In ancient economies, agriculture provided great wealth. Columbia University Professor M. Van de Mieroop mentions one Babylonian family in Dilbat who owned considerable fields in the countryside (the equivalent to Israel's tribal lands), Mieroop observes that much

Map 7.1 Distribution of the Land among the 12 Tribes

of the family's wealth derived from its agricultural land.[25] Agricultural income allowed them to purchase substantial city real estate, which empowered them to increase their wealth. De Mieroop cites another man from Larsa who obtained substantial countryside holdings. His "primary income seems to have derived from his agricultural estates, including cereal fields and orchards. . . . With his wealth he was able to acquire a substantial amount of real estate in the city."[26]

Israel's economy was very similar to Mesopotamia's (Lev 25:15–16).[27] The value that Israel placed on its tribal lands is no better evidenced than in the story of Naboth's field.

> And it came to pass after these things, that Naboth the Jezreelite had a vineyard, which was in Jezreel, nearby the palace of Ahab king of Samaria. And Ahab spoke to Naboth, saying, Give me your vineyard, that I may have it for a garden of herbs, because it is near to my house: and I will give you for it a better vineyard than it; or, if it seem good to you, I will give you the worth of it in money. And Naboth said to Ahab, YHWH forbid it me, that I should give the inheritance of my fathers to you. And Ahab came into his house heavy and displeased because of the word which Naboth the Jezreelite had spoken to him: for he had said, I will not give you the inheritance of my fathers. And he laid him down on his bed, and turned away his face, and would eat no bread. (1 Kgs 21:1–4)

Naboth testifies that he inherited his forefather's land. Tribal heritages united a man and his family with their "roots." Close connection with ancestry gave families a sense of who they were, providing a rich heritage and a sense of self-worth. YHWH granted permanent heritages, and it appears that Naboth also inherited the family's vineyard business. Naboth rightly stated that YHWH had forbidden him to "sell" his family's property. The Law commanded:

> The land shall not be sold forever: for *the land is mine*; for you are strangers and sojourners with me. (Lev 25:23, emphasis added)

This statute granted families the ability to obtain and maintain their freedom. Family land could never be sold to pay debts.[28] Should a father make poor choices, which led to poverty or slavery, his "free" land would always be available for his children to begin again with a clean slate.

Tribal lands also allowed families to own two residences.[29] When Israel inherited Canaan's land, YHWH gave each tribe Canaan's former cities. Tribal lands provided permanent ownership while the city home functioned similarly to modern real estate.[30] This allowed families space to manufacture or produce goods in their own tribal lands, and the ability to easily sell them in a city home. Should a family decide to make the city its primary residence, the members were free to supplement their income by leasing their family heritage until the Jubilee (Lev 25:24–31). Thus, a family's land heritage provided a natural buffer against poverty. If the family made poor financial decisions or fell into a time of national duress, such as famine, a man could lease his tribal lands and live in the city, where he could hire his services out to further supplement his family's needs.[31] This gave him options other than slavery for dealing with debt.

Mesopotamia's earliest civilizations were based on tribal land systems very similar to Israel's.[32] Michael Hudson, a research professor of economics at the University of Missouri in Kansas City, writes that in early history temple-states did not have power to collect tax (even though they charged user fees, sharecropping rent, and interest).[33] Temples needed to be self-sufficient, so the temple personnel became entrepreneurs, forming enormous corporations.

> Temples housed the workshops where most export textiles were woven (in contrast to the homespun for subsistence use). They were endowed with resources to support their community's dependent labor to weave textiles and undertake other export production. Toward this end, much of the community's land was set aside for use by the temple to support their nonagricultural labor force and official staff.[34]

With the passage of time, the temple began to function as a business "corporation." Hudson observes the "'corporation's' labor originally consisted of 'unfortunates' such as the blind, orphan, widow, who were given an opportunity to earn wages."[35] These "unfortunates" eventually became wards of the temple, and their welfare was maintained by Mesopotamia's citizenry. The rise of temple-corporations coincided with a shift in land ownership. Tribal heritages evolved into real estate as "corporate groupings replaced their biological families"[36] and threatened the function of a family-based government system. Temples began to amass more and more land in order to support its priesthoods and labor forces,[37] which in turn displaced more families. Families were forced either to seek work inside a city or to become migratory (due to Mesopotamia's desert conditions). Without land, families often wandered around in search of food and home (Isocrates, *Panegyrikos*, 167–170).[38]

Scholars theorize that monarchies evolved as a way to balance the temple-state's newfound power. Monarchies were a divine office, and the nation's land officially belonged to the king.[39] If the king possessed the land, he could distribute it as he saw fit. In reality, monarchies only strengthened the temple's oppression by granting priesthoods additional allotments of land (in exchange for political support) and displacing still more citizens.[40] This further weakened the family unit, forcing migration to cities, where life and home focused around the family's ability to earn wages.

These factors no doubt factored heavily in YHWH's decision to exclude tribal lands from Israel's priesthood (Num 35:2–8) and to clearly define the borders of the Levite's suburbs (Num 35:4). YHWH was so adamant that the priests should not obtain tribal lands that he reiterates this point five separate times.[41] Thus, the power of Israel's priests and the responsibilities they could assume were severely limited by their lack of land resources.

In lieu of land, Levi received the treasured gift of public service. This position was a much less labor-intensive profession than farming, animal husbandry (shepherding), or manufacturing (industries such as basket weaving or pottery). After the nation's rebellion at Mt. Sinai, YHWH stated that he would take the Levites for public (temple) service in place of the average citizen.[42] This was a nontransferable, inherited membership in a caste supported by a 10% flat tax (tithe). Personal wealth was not tied to a particular branch of public service; rather, the priesthood's wealth correlated with the righteousness of the nation. When the nation obeyed, the Levites prospered, as tithes soared. Likewise, when the nation rebelled, tithes decreased, and the Levites' economic status declined. In extreme conditions, the Levites were compelled to seek work outside the Levitical governmental office.

Shortages of land resources in Israel or Mesopotamia naturally limited the responsibilities that a government could assume. Many nations offset and supplemented land income with interest income obtained from the temple's role as a nation's primary monetary reserve system.[43] This, of course, allowed a nation's government to gain even more power and control by assuming more responsibility. In YHWH's federal reserve system, the government could not charge interest from Israel's citizens (Exod 22:4; Lev 25:35–7; Deut 23:19–20). Not only did this serve to limit the priesthood's power and keep its prosperity directly tied to the nation's righteousness, it also ensured that the Levites did not embrace policies that benefited their own prosperity at the expense of YHWH's Law. Thus, promoting Torah obedience became the Levitical priesthood's only avenue to wealth.

YHWH's federal reserve policy, which banned interest, not only benefited the common citizen by restricting government power, it also fostered the entire nation's economic prosperity by restraining the cost of living. Since the Creator's primary concern was the individual family unit, he sought to shelter families from undue constraints. Families governed themselves yet were accountable to the Levites. This formed a natural balance of power. The family was held accountable to the Levites, and the Levites answered to YHWH, the nation's judge. The Creator intended for Israel's Law to be a paragon for a society based on personal freedom and righteousness. His Law achieved freedom by defining personal responsibility, ordaining family government, limiting Levitical government, and relieving family stress.

B. Social Stratification

1. Redistributed Land-based Capitalism

A society's economic prosperity is generally tied to land ownership. Inequities in land ownership cause economic stratification.[44] Most nations, both ancient and modern, ease this stratification through taxation and welfare systems that redistribute wealth.[45] The United States tries to ease the inequality in society through graduated income taxes and government-sponsored programs such as welfare, Medicaid, college tuition grant or loan programs, and small business grants and loans, among many other government-funded social programs. YHWH's system differs in that he granted every family tax-free land, thus giving the poor a means to procure their own sustenance (producing crops or other industry, gleaning fields, vineyards, or business and trade). The fact that Israel's flat-tax rate was only 10%, kept the redistribution of earnings at a minimum, while land granted every family the ability to produce, manufacture, or lease, as well as own a residence. Since land was a limited resource that had been equally distributed among the entire Children of Israel, this system kept one family from amassing large amounts of land. This kept social stratification limited to the amount of effort the individual wanted to invest in his income or to the number of estates that could be leased until the Jubilee.

One of the last recourses a man could take to avoid indebted slavery, or to gain wealth, was to lease his land, or a portion of his land, to the Levites until the Jubilee (Lev 27:16–19). The land's produce was valued at 50 silver shekels per homer (Lev 27:16). To put this into perspective, the flat census tax was only half a shekel per person (Exod 30:11–15), which was intended to establish Israel's entire Levitical government (Exod 30:16) while the first-born son's redemption (VAT) tax was only 5 shekels (Num 18:16). During Elisha's days, normal market values for a shekel could buy one measure of fine flour or two measures of barley (2 Kgs 7:1). Scholars theorize that a "measure," or *seah*, was about 1/30 of a homer, although the context in 2 Kgs 7:1 indicates an amount much smaller than 1/30 of a homer.[46] A homer of barley is equivalent modernly to about 9.5 bushels.[47] Conservative estimates allow for 20 bushels per acre with a profit of about 100 shekels. If a man leased 10 acres of land, this could net at least 1,000 shekels per year. Thus, this type of landed system provided immense wealth for Israel's citizens where, as long as the Levitical government realized tithe revenues, a buyer for commodities was guaranteed. If a man inherited land from a childless relative, that land could be sold to another near relation or the land leased to the Levites and yet more profits realized (Lev 27:20).

Up to this point we have focused on modern government practices that conflict with Torah Law. There are at least two areas in which United States policies are in accord with YHWH's philosophy. They are the freedom to compete and the freedom to choose one's occupation. This sharply contrasts to most ancient societies, in which caste systems resulted in rigid roles for the family. Caste systems divided society into classes of professional occupations. Each profession was assessed an *unchanging* percentage of wealth (income), privileges, and prestige.[48] Megasthenes (frag. 1.53) attests that ancient India had seven castes. Protocol forbade children to work or marry outside their caste.[49] In the first century BCE, the Greek historian Diodorus Siculus (1.74, 81) stated that Egyptian law forbade craftsmen to follow any other occupation than the occupation handed down to them from their parents.[50] Egyptologist John Nunn has found evidence of hereditary succession in Egypt's physician castes.[51] This meant that a child was never able to change his financial situation or occupation, even he disliked it or the family lived in poverty.

Israel's social system did not support this oppressive ideology. Citizens were free to vary both their financial situation and their occupation. While hereditary succession was customary, it was not mandated. Naturally, a son's land inheritance often dictated his profession. For instance, Naboth (1 Kgs 21:2–3) inherited his ancestor's vineyard. Although he was free to enter another profession, it would be costly, and the returns would not be as profitable. The Law, however, allowed Naboth the option to lease his vineyard and live in the city, where he could pursue another avenue of employment (Lev 25:15), if he did not enjoy his inherited career. This left a person *un*bound to a pre-set social position, thus enabling boundless upward economic mobility.

The Levites constituted the nation's only caste. This caste also functioned differently than in other nations. First, their profession did not solely determine the Levites' wealth. Rather, the priestly livelihood depended on the priests' role as teacher and instructor of YHWH's Law. If they correctly educated Israel's citizens to follow YHWH's Law, the nation became righteous and flourished economically. Likewise, during times of rebellion, when YHWH placed economic sanctions on the land, their wealth diminished. Second, most ancient castes constituted of lifelong professions. One was apprenticed in a trade during adolescence and practiced his or her trade until death. In contrast, the Levites were obliged to serve only 20 years in public service.[52] Levites retired at 50 years of age and retained the government's tithe pension until death (allocated from the nation's flat tax). Since the nation also lived on non-taxable land, their cost of living was minimal. Only the high priest's post was a lifetime profession (Num 20:23–28; 35:25–28). Third, a Levite's marriage was not confined in his tribe or profession. The Levites were free to marry women of other tribes as they saw fit. Only the high priest's office bore stipulations: he had to marry a virgin in Israel's lineage. He could not marry a divorced woman, widow, foreigner, or a promiscuous woman (Lev 21:1, 7, 13–15).

2. Elders and Youth

The only status or class distinctions existing among Israel's *righteous* citizens were the youth and the elderly. YHWH granted the aged distinction by instructing the young: "You shall rise up before the hoary head, and honor the face of the old man, and fear your God: I am YHWH" (Lev 19:32). The *International Bible Encyclopedia* observes that this class distinction placed greater value on the elders' experience and understanding.

> The value of young men to society was, indeed, found mainly in their physical strength, that of older men in their experience and ability to give counsel and guide the affairs of the community (Prov 20:29). Youth was thought to be characterized by inexperience (Judg 8:20; 1 Sam 17:33; 1 Chr 22:5; 2 Chr 13:7; Jer 1:6) and lack of wisdom (Prov 1:4; 7:7; 22:15) in contrast to old age. This conception of youth is the basis for hyperbolic use of *na'ar* in Solomon's prayer (1 Kgs 3:7) and stands behind the account of the beginning of Rehoboam's reign—not only did the young king reject the natural wisdom of age, he also adopted the reckless forcefulness of youth (1 Kgs 12:6–14; compare Isa 3:4–5).[53]

Youth was seen as a time of apprenticeship, when a child transitioned from the immaturity of adolescence to the maturity that comes with the experience of family responsibility. The distinction between the youth and the aged was so important to YHWH that he placed a curse on any who would set their esteem equal to their parents, saying, "Cursed be he that sets light by his father or his mother. And all the people shall say, Amen" (Deut 27:16). Israel's society always upheld its elders' honor and prestige, and no doubt, wages were also divided along these lines, with older generations receiving greater wages than the younger.

YHWH considered placing youthful power or youthful authority above the elders' authority offensive. He told Israel that, when she rebelled against his Law, immature and unqualified people would lead the nation.

> For, behold, the Lord, YHWH of hosts, does take away from Jerusalem and from Judah. . . . The mighty man, and the man of war, the judge, and the prophet, and the prudent, *and the ancient*, The captain of fifty, and the honorable man, and the counselor, and the cunning artificer, and the eloquent orator. And I will give children to be their princes, and babes shall rule over them. And the people shall be oppressed, every one by another, and every one by his neighbor: the child shall behave himself proudly against the ancient, and the base against the honorable. (Isa 3:1–5; see also Isa 3:12)

Immature and unqualified people are characterized by an inability to make tough decisions that are not always pleasant, but ultimately produce the best possible outcome (i.g., eliminating national debt). The ultimate consequence of immature policies brings society into severe oppression as people lack the self-control and self-discipline to make hard decisions that are ultimately in their best interest.

Much of the economic stratification caused by the elders' prestige would have been mitigated by the land ownership that YHWH granted to every citizen. Upon marriage, each son (and sometimes daughters) was apportioned part of the family's land. This inheritance was often a fully developed, income-producing estate, where an ancestor's home, furnishings, vineyard, farm, or other forms of wealth were already established. Sons either continued in the family business or began another line of work. Thus, the only defining stratification caused by YHWH's age distinction was prestige, not necessarily wealth.

The Abrahamic Covenants granted every citizen enormous prosperity. Because YHWH's Law is in harmony with the laws of equity, he placed every family on equal ground, granting them the ability to choose and determine their future.[54] At the same time, his natural law did not arbitrarily grant aid to the *un*righteous or those who had not rightly earned prosperity.

3. Natural Selection: The Righteous and the Unrighteous

Many of the principles in YHWH's Law embrace natural selection. Natural selection is the reason that YHWH permitted Israelites to sell animals that had died on their own[55] to other nations (Deut 14:21) yet forbade them to Israel's citizens. Natural selection is the reason that YHWH permitted Abraham's children to charge interest on loans issued to foreigners (Deut 15:3; 23:19–20) yet forbade usury within his nation.[56] By following the principles of natural selection, Israel would become the healthiest, wealthiest, and fittest nation (Deut 4:5–8). Since every nation bears the responsibility for prohibiting unclean foods to be sold in its own lands and to halt the practice of earning interest on its citizenry, YHWH allowed Israel to profit from another nation's *un*righteousness. If these nations embraced YHWH's Law, then they too would gain the strength that comes from walking in the way of YHWH, thereby growing successful as Israel had righteously done.

YHWH established natural selection to bless or prosper the most righteous people. For this reason, the Creator's Law established a difference between law-abiding citizens and the lawless. The righteous prospered while the wicked naturally became lower-class citizens. Sin offerings penalized wealth in much the same way that speeding tickets deter traffic violations today. Those who frequently violated the Law lost more wealth than the more obedient citizens. Israel's social stratification occurred simply as a consequence of personal or national breach of the covenant-constitution. So we see that one of the few dichotomies in Israel's socioeconomic system resulted from neglect of personal responsibility. By following the law of *natural selection*, those who obeyed YHWH's Law became the fittest of the nation, while those who disregarded his Law were the weakest on the land. Correspondingly, those who followed the Law were blessed with health, wealth, freedom, and success. This paradigm resulted in four naturally occurring, nonarbitrary stratifications in Israel's society as demonstrated by Table 7.1.

Table 7.1. Righteous-Aged Social Stratification

Righteous	Prosperity	↑	Aged
			Youth
Unrighteous	Poverty	↓	Aged
			Youth

Righteousness provided the dividing line between rich and poor, the honorable and the base. Older, righteous individuals (and their family) would obtain the highest wealth and prestige in Israel's God-fearing society, while the youthful unrighteous person was viewed with the most disdain and was more likely to be the weakest and poorest citizen. Even the poorest (and unrighteous) citizen, however, was afforded many liberties that deterred personal poverty.

C. Jubilees: Abolition of Slavery

1. Social Peace and Harmony

YHWH's national Jubilees united the land and further strengthened the family unit. In the Book of Leviticus, the Creator instructs people to love each other, teaching:

> You shall not hate your brother in your heart: you shall in any wise rebuke your neighbor, and *not suffer* sin on him. You shall not avenge, nor bear any grudge against the children of your people, but you shall love your neighbor as yourself: I am YHWH. (Lev 19:17–18)

The Jubilee statute built on this precept of love and liberty. The philosophy governing the Jubilee is so important that it is stated twice in Leviticus 25.

> And if you sell anything to your neighbor, or buy anything of your neighbor's hand, you shall not oppress one another . . . but you shall fear your God: for I am YHWH your God. Wherefore you shall do my statutes, and keep my judgments, and do them; and *you shall dwell in the land in safety.* (Lev 25:14, 17–18)

Love, justice, harmony, lack of oppression, and love of freedom in Israel's society were the basic elements that enabled her to develop the strongest and fittest culture. Israel's ability to dwell safely in her land (Lev 25:17–18) was predicated on obedience to YHWH's statutes, which taught her not to oppress her brothers. YHWH saw oppression as being especially counterproductive to the ability to love one's neighbor as oneself, so he established statutes that addressed oppression at its most basic level. His judgment stipulated that, if Israel's citizens rebelled against his instruction by oppressing fellow-citizens, he would turn their unjust ways on their heads, and Israelites would lose the freedom they had so carelessly exacted from their countrymen. Thus if Israel hypocritically misused the very freedom that YHWH's covenant ordained, the society would weaken, decay, and naturally lead to tyranny.

2. Release Years

The Law's national Jubilee ordained "freedom from oppression" by establishing national times of rest. Rest is so important to the Creator that he includes it in the Ten Commandments (Exod 20:10–11; 23:12) as the sign of observing his covenant (Exod 31:13). Isaiah saw rest as such a critical issue that he built on this precept by saying that Israel would be saved through "returning and rest" (Isa 30:15). The Creator considered repose from occupational labor to be vital to health, general welfare, and success of any nation. He observed that some of the greatest threats to personal and family freedoms were linked to occupation; therefore he established occupational limits[57] and year-long holidays for the labor-intensive agricultural industry which was called a *Release Year* (Deut 15:1–9).

This year was a national celebration which culminated in the reading of the entire Law during the Feast of Tabernacles and the citizens' recommitment to adhere to YHWH's way of life (Deut 31:10–11; 2 Kgs 23:2–3).[58] Farmers, vineyard owners, and other land-based occupations observed a year of rest every seven years.[59] During this time, no crops were planted or fully harvested.[60] Animals were allowed to glean fields and vineyards, which provided natural fertilizer while replenishing soil nutrients.[61] Since landowners did not reap fields or prune vineyards, the poor had access to an entire crop, not just the gleanings normally harvested during non-Release Years.[62] These foods greatly sustained the impoverished for future use. While farmers and society were allowed to eat and benefit from all that grew of its own accord, no crops or vineyards were tilled or planted (Lev 25:4–6).

YHWH promised to bless the land so that it sustained the people during this fallow time.

And if you shall say, What shall we eat the seventh year? Behold, we shall not sow, nor gather in our increase: Then I will command my blessing on you in the sixth year, and it shall bring forth fruit for three years. And you shall sow the eighth year, and eat yet of old fruit until the ninth year; until her fruits come in you shall eat of the old store. (Lev 25:20–22)

YHWH's Release Year statute taught Israel's citizens to plan for the future. Profits from productive years were stored and allocated for sustenance during the Release (and Jubilee) Years. Release sabbatical years provided an agricultural family with a year-long vacation. Fallow land freed families from labor-intensive farming responsibilities so they could turn their attention to other industries or simply retire for a year. Thus, this practice taught the people to diversify their income so that, during the Release Year, other pursuits could be realized or a much-needed rest enjoyed. Since farming was usually one of the wealthiest professions, the Release Years also served as a barrier to economic stratification, since the farmer would receive no income from his land during the Release Year.[63]

The precept governing both the Release Year, which occurred every 7th year, and the Jubilee which occurred every 50th year was the release from oppression (Lev 25:17). Farmers and their laborers were relieved from the hard labor of farming.[64] Likewise, the indigent were relieved when the nation's citizens forgave personal debts associated with indebted slavery (Deut 15:1–2, 9). Not only did this statute prevent an indebted nation, it prevented indebtedness from becoming an accepted cultural value (Prov 22:7). This helped those who had fallen on hard times to recover.[65] Thus, YHWH's attitude toward the poor did not penalize the wealthy for receiving the fruits of their labor and enjoying them, yet neither did he allow the prosperous to profit from oppressing the indigent.

3. The Jubilee: Abolition of Slavery

In the previous section (7.II.B), I demonstrated that YHWH's Law naturally caused those who followed it to prosper, while individuals who disregarded it drifted into poverty. Nevertheless, YHWH's Law was merciful to the impoverished by fixing occupational limits for Israel's welfare/slavery system by tying these limits to both the Release and the Jubilee years. Slavery in the Torah can be divided into three categories: impoverished Hebrews who were sold to pay debts (Lev 25:39–42); felons who were sold as satisfaction for their crime (Exod 22:3); and bondslaves, foreigners who were sold into the nation (Lev 25:44) or captured as a spoil of war (Deut 21:10).[66]

YHWH placed an injunction on Israel's debt slavery by commanding that Hebrew indebted slaves should not be treated as bondservants but as hired employees (Lev 25:39–40). Entering Israel's slave welfare system did not deprive individuals of personal rights or freedoms. During their term of service, slaves retained the income from leasing their tribal lands (Lev 25:15–16), money that enabled them to purchase their emancipation at any time the debt had been satisfied. Scripture calls the act of purchasing one's emancipation from the slavery system "redemption."[67] YHWH encouraged a slave's family to redeem their relatives if resources permitted (Lev 25:47–55).[68] A family's refusal to redeem a near relative could indicate the family's lack of resources (caused perhaps by national disparities, such as foreign tribute or famine) or the family's intolerance of the belligerent choices that had led to slavery.

Release Years designated times when Hebrew slaves were freed or "released" from their master's house (Exod 21:2). The maximum time an impoverished family could spend in Israel's slave system was six years (Exod 21:2–6).[69] At the beginning of the seventh year, the slave was always freed.[70] There were two special situations when a family remained in service to its master *even though its debt was satisfied.* The first occurred when a man married a woman slave from his master's house (Exod 21:5–6). The second occurred when a slave desired to continue service in the master's home rather than be freed. In these situations, a man and his family became slaves in the master's house "forever." However, Deut 15:17–18 indicates that even this period of "forever" continued to be defined as the six years allotted in Exod 21:2.[71] The only situations in which the Law allowed Israelites (Hebrews) to serve longer than six years occurred when: slavery had resulted from a crime (Exod 22:3)[72] or when a daughter had been sold as a concubine. If the slave did not redeem himself or his family did not redeem him before the national Jubilee, then the Israelite slave could always be released at the Jubilee. So the maximum time that he and his family could serve in another person's household was 49 years (Lev 25:54).[73]

The only exception to this rule was a woman who had been sold as a concubine, a practice that secured both a better life-style and better treatment for the debt-holder's daughter.[74] The Law ordained that she should not be treated as a slave but as any normal daughter-in-law marrying into a family (Exod 21:9).[75] The fact that children would be involved made this situation permanent because YHWH continually sought to protect and preserve the stability of the family unit. Even in this situation, a woman was protected under the Torah. If the husband took another wife, the concubine's rights and her standard of living could not decrease due to the added expense (Exod 21:10).[76] This meant that only the wealthiest men could afford an extra wife. If a man purchased an indebted man's daughter but did not marry her, she could be redeemed and freed from obligation.[77]

There were two main differences between a wife and a concubine. The first difference was with regard to the inheritance. Children from the purchased *second wife* would normally have no legal claim to their father's tribal heritage.[78] Second, whereas a legal wife had wealth (i.e., dowry, bride price, property, or other wealth) she brought to the marriage,[79] a concubine did not. If divorce occurred, a legal wife was issued a "bill of divorce" and property divided along lines of fault;[80] a concubine was simply manumitted (set free).[81]

Originally, YHWH had commanded masters to release their Hebrew slaves without any gifts or payments when the slave's term of service ended (Exod 21:2). Forty years after the Sinai compact, YHWH saw that Israel still did not desire to obey his laws or to walk in his ways.[82] Deliberately, YHWH added another economic deterrent to reentry into the slavery system by commanding masters to release their Hebrew slaves with gifts of wealth (Deut 15:12–15). Presumably, this would aid in re-establishing the impoverished family, helping them avoid reentry into the slavery system after they returned to their tribal lands.

Families were greatly strengthened by the nation's Jubilees. YHWH realized that finances were directly related to a family's freedom. Lack of prosperity resulted in oppression or, even worse, slavery. Therefore, he restored family lands that were leased during times of duress. Every *seventh* Release Year (49th year) initiated a two-year Jubilee period (Lev 25:8). All statutes that applied to the 7th Release Year applied to the 50th year Jubilee. What distinguished the Jubilee from other Release Years was the reverting of tribal lands back to the families who had leased them (Lev 25:13). This restoration provided a time of national restructuring during which the Levites archived tribal land ownership, tying it to the genealogical record, a custom that we will discuss below.

Bondservants, those bound to serve without wage compensation for their entire lifetime, were slaves obtained from other nations (Lev 25:39, 44–46). YHWH prohibited his free people, whom he had redeemed from the "house of bondage," and who had pledged to uphold his constitutional covenant from serving in this capacity (Lev 25:39). Yet YHWH granted even foreign bondservants certain rights and responsibilities. Foremost, YHWH commanded bondservants to observe national constitutional law.[83] The Creator indicated that Israel's weekly Sabbaths were for the rest and health of the nation and for the slave in particular. "Six days you shall do your work, and on the seventh day you shall rest: that your ox and your ass may rest, and the son of your handmaid, and the stranger, may be refreshed" (Exod 23:12; see also Deut 5:14). Failure to obey this command could result in the loss of the slave's life (Exod 35:2). At the least, the owner would be held responsible for his slave's violation of the Sabbath. So this command negated any possibility that slaves could be used as surrogate labor on the Sabbath Day; nor could it be argued the Law was intended just for Abraham's descendants.

Likewise, Jubilee years were designed for the bondservant's benefit.

> And the *sabbath of the land* shall be meat for you; for you, and for your servant, and for your maid, and for your hired servant, and for your stranger that sojourns with you. (Lev 25:6)

Although bondservants were not released during the Jubilee or Release Years, YHWH's Law ensured that they rested from their work during this time. This in turned caused the bonded servant to love YHWH's Law because it relieved their oppression.

YHWH allowed slaves purchased with money to join Israel's festivities. Males could be circumcised and enjoy all ceremonial aspects of Israel's congregation (Exod 12:43–49). A bondservant's children were considered their master's property and usually remained in their master's house for successive generations (Lev 25:45). But in some cases, trusted servants gained citizenship by marrying into their master's family (1 Chr 2:34–35). Children from these unions were considered free citizens.

YHWH commanded farmers to reap fields and vineyards only once so that the impoverished could obtain produce for sustenance (Lev 19:9–10). This further deterred poverty. Loans associated with slavery were forgiven every six years.[84] Clansmen were instructed to grant financial aid to disadvantaged relatives, which again deterred poverty (Lev 25:47–49; Deut 15:7–8). When an Israelite sold himself into the slave system, YHWH commanded Israelites (even the stranger living among them)[85] to treat him or her as an employee (hired servant), not to rule over him with harshness (Lev 25:39, 43). And very importantly, YHWH forbade Israel to sell her citizens as slaves to other nations, knowing that Israelites and their children would become bondmen and women in other societies (Exod 21:8; Lev 25:42). Had these provisions been followed, Hebrew slavery would have been weeded out of Israel's society.[86] Citizens from less righteous nations would have been Israel's only available slave resource (Lev 25:44–46). If other nations followed the Law, they too could have become economically fit by obeying the judgment that prohibited selling their countrymen to other nations.[87] Thus, YHWH's economic prescription would have abolished slavery and poverty altogether (see Table 7.2).

D. The Wealth of Israel

One modern myth about ancient Israel is that Israel was an isolated agrarian society. In this view, the family clans stayed on their tribal lands, grew their own food, used their own merchants, made their own clothes, and were very self-sufficient, needing little interaction or trade with other nations, especially the "cities" or the outside world. The reality of Israel's history is quite different.

Tribal lands formed the backbone of Israel's strength; land ensured freedom so a family could escape poverty and obtain shelter. It also provided a distribution of natural resources. YHWH bestowed many cities to the Children of Israel. Judah, for instance, procured well over 113 cities (Josh 15:20–63). With the exception of Hamath (Josh 13:5; 2 Kgs 14:28), all of Judah's cities lay within its tribal borders. Manasseh and Ephraim were an entirely different story. Six cities given to Manasseh lay in Asher and Issachar's tribal regions (Josh 17:11). Ephraim also held separate cities within Manasseh's inheritance (Josh 16:9). In order for Manasseh and Ephraim to colonize these cities, many families sought to live in cities outside their father's tribal lands.[88] This provided for a highly integrated and connected community, thus fostering both intertribal and international trade, which led to YHWH fulfilling the blessings promised to the Joseph tribes (Genesis 48; 49:22–26). The three major Levite clans further contributed to this national integration (Lev 25:31–34). Israel's non-aversion to city life is witnessed again in their metropolitan populations.

Beth-Shemesh accommodated well over 50,070 men (1 Sam 6:19). Assyria's King Sennacherib recorded similar numbers in Judah's outlying suburbs, listing 200,150 captives.[89] Scripture and history attest to the abundant number of cities and amount of commerce in the Promised Land. Many families lived in cities and used their inheritance or the city as a second home while others leased their property until the Jubilee.[90] While agriculture provided a backbone for society's food stores, sustenance, and commerce, the nation also had a diversified labor force of skilled craftsman. For instance, the Ashbeans produced fine linen (1 Chr 4:21), and Josiah sought for "carpenters, and builders, and masons" to build the Temple (2 Kgs 22:6).

Pottery, jewelry, carved cartouches, ivories, colorful garments, elephant hides, gold and silver vessels were all products that Assyrian kings say they received from Israel.[91] The

Table 7.2. Israel's Holidays

	Name of Holiday	Hebrew	Recur	Assemblies	Statute	Dates	Modern	Length
1	Weekly Sabbath	Shabbat	All year	Local communities	Don't work or conduct business: rest	Every 7th day	Saturday	1 day
2	(New Moons)	?	Monthly	Local communities	?Don't work: rest	1st of ea. month	Varies	?
3	Passover/Feast of Unleaven Bread	Pesach/ Chag Ha'Matzot	Yearly	Jerusalem	Celebrate Passover and constitutional Covenant; refrain from eating fermented/leavened bread; 1st and 8th days are Sabbaths—no work	1 mo./14-21st	March–May	8 days
4	Feast of Weeks	Shavuot	Yearly	Jerusalem	Grain offering; don't work: rest	7 Sabbaths —50 days after harvest begins	June/July	1 day
5	Day of Shouting	Yom Teruah	Yearly	Local communities	Don't work, rejoice	7th mo./1st day	Oct/Nov	1 day
6	Day of Atonement	Yom Kippur	Yearly	Local communities	Don't work; fast or afflict soul	7th mo./10th day	Oct/Nov	1 day
7	Feast of Tabernacles	Sukkot	Yearly	Jerusalem	Dwell in booths at Jerusalem 1st and 8th days are sabbaths—no work	7th mo./15-22nd	Oct/Nov	8 days
8	Release Year	Hasheba' Shemittah	All year— every 7th yr.	Covenant Renewal/ Jerusalem	Forgive debts, release slaves	1 year		
	Jubilee	Yovel	All year — every 50 yrs.		Return to heritage; realign tribal lands; Release Year statutes apply	1 year		

sizable tribute, to which Assyrian records attest indicates that Israel had a highly diversified and specialized market economy. Perhaps the best evidence supporting Israel's prosperity from its specialization of labor is recorded in the account of Judah's Diaspora:

> And he (Nebuchadnezzar) carried away all Jerusalem, and all the princes, and all the mighty men of valor, even ten thousand captives, and all the craftsmen and smiths: none remained, save the poorest sort of the people of the land. (2 Kgs 24:14, parenthesis added)

Unskilled labor today is still performed by the "poorest sort of people of the land." Individuals who are educated and skilled in a particular field (or trade) or business are the nation's most valuable resources and would be the first deported. These basic economic principles regarding skilled labor hold true in free market economies today.

Israel's economy not only followed sound economic principles, the nation also sought knowledge, technological advancement, and progress. The Creator instructed Joshua to build bulwarks for the deployment of what was at the time a modern appliance for siege and assault. He commanded Israel to build towers from trees so that men could scale fortress walls, and archers could attain better positioning. The nation's propensity for technological advancement is witnessed again during the time that YHWH was with Uzziah, and the king's men "made in Jerusalem engines, *invented* by cunning men, to be on the towers and on the bulwarks, to shoot arrows and great stones withal. And his name spread far abroad; for he was marvelously helped, till he was strong" (2 Chr 26:15). Hezekiah also used technology to improve Jerusalem's water access and sanitation: "The acts of Hezekiah, and all his might, and how he made a pool, and a conduit, and brought water into the city, are they not written in the Book of the chronicles of the kings of Judah?" (2 Kgs 20:20). YHWH's Law embraced natural economic laws, enabling Israel's citizens to prosper and become a strong power among the nations (Deut 4:5–8).

E. Genealogies

Shortly before his death, Jacob spoke to Joseph regarding his sons Manasseh and Ephraim: "And your issue, which you beget after them, shall be yours, and *shall be called after the name of their brothers in their inheritance*" (Gen 48:6). Jacob reckoned Joseph's sons equal to his other sons by placing any future children born to Joseph under the Manasseh and Ephraim tribes. Notice that Jacob's command is the first time we see that the division of Israel's land would be called in the name of Joseph's sons. This directly linked land ownership and its inheritance to the genealogical record.

This practice is no more revealing than in the request of Zelophehad's daughters:

> Then came the daughters of Zelophehad. . . . And they stood before Moses, and before Eleazar the priest, and before the princes and all the congregation, by the door of the tabernacle of the congregation, saying, Our father died in the

wilderness, and he was not in the company of them that gathered themselves together against YHWH in the company of Korah; but died in his own sin, and had no sons. Why should the (a) name of our father be done away from among his family, because he has (b) no son? Give to us therefore a (c) possession among the brothers of our father. And Moses brought their cause before YHWH. And YHWH spoke to Moses, saying, (d) The daughters of Zelophehad speak right: you shall surely give them a possession of an inheritance among their father's brothers; and you shall cause the inheritance of their father to pass to them. And you shall speak to the Children of Israel, saying, If a man die, and have no son, then you shall cause his inheritance to pass to his daughter. And if he have no daughter, then you shall give his inheritance to his brothers. And if he have no brothers, then you shall give his inheritance to his father's brothers. And if his father have no brothers, then you shall give his inheritance to his kinsman that is next to him of his family, and he shall possess it: and it shall be to the Children of Israel a (e) statute of judgment, as YHWH commanded Moses. (Num 27:1–11)

Zelophehad lacked any (b) sons to retain the family heritage. His daughters were concerned that their father's name (a) would cease to exist. Their land request directly related to preserving their father's name. This strongly implies a link between land ownership and the genealogical record. The daughters asked to be (c) substituted as their father's heir. YHWH granted their request, upholding the (d) rights of a daughter, equating her heirship with a firstborn son's. *Notice, however, that this (e) statute in no way permanently transferred the family's genealogical record to the woman's lineage.* In a similar case, 1 Chr 2:34–41 demonstrates a situation similar to Zelophehad, in which daughters were the only heirs in a Judahite family. Geneaology is again reckoned by the father through the firstborn daughter to the husband then through the male heirs again.[92] This demonstrates that as soon as the daughter obtained a son, he continued the genealogical record for his maternal grandfather's house.[93] Thus the woman's role in the genealogical process was only temporary until a male heir could be secured.[94] This account demonstrates that a woman's temporary role in genealogical records was *not* limited to the priesthood, as modern Judaism believes, but applied to the whole nation of Israel. Zelophehad was from Manasseh, yet his daughters were concerned with preserving his "name" and his land. So it appears that a daughter's function as a lineage liaison was temporary for the whole nation, not just the Levites.

Another account makes this distinction even clearer:

And the chief fathers of the families of the children of Gilead, the son of Machir, the son of Manasseh, of the families of the sons of Joseph, came near, and spoke before Moses, and before the princes, the chief fathers of the Children of Israel: And they said, YHWH commanded my lord to give the land for an inheritance by lot to the Children of Israel: and my lord was commanded by YHWH to give the inheritance of Zelophehad our brother to his daughters. And (a) if they be married to any of the sons of the other tribes of the Children of Israel, then shall their inheritance be taken from the inheritance of our fathers, and shall be put to the inheritance of the tribe where they are received: so shall it be taken from the lot of our inheritance. *And when the (b) jubilee of the Children of Israel shall be, then shall their inheritance be put to the inheritance of the tribe where they are received: so shall their inheritance be taken away from the inheritance of the tribe of our fathers.* And Moses commanded the Children of Israel according to the word of YHWH, saying, The tribe of the sons of Joseph have said well. This is the thing which YHWH does command concerning the daughters of Zelophehad, saying, Let them marry (c) to whom they think best; only to the (d) family of the tribe of their father shall they marry. *So shall not the inheritance of the Children of Israel remove from tribe to tribe*: for every one of the Children of Israel shall keep himself to the inheritance of the tribe of his fathers. And every daughter, that possesses an inheritance in any tribe of the Children of Israel, shall be wife to one of the family of the tribe of her father, that the Children of Israel may enjoy every man the inheritance of his fathers. Neither shall the inheritance remove from one tribe to another tribe; but every one of the tribes of the Children of Israel shall keep himself to his own inheritance. Even as YHWH commanded Moses, so did the daughters of Zelophehad. (Num 36:1–10)

The rights that YHWH had afforded an only daughter could cause her family's heritage to fall under the jurisdiction of another tribe if she (a) married outside her father's tribe.[95] Manasseh's citizens alleged that a woman's right to tribal inheritance would cause lands to (b) be assigned to the husband's tribe at the 50th Jubilee (Lev 25:28–31). This would cause a loss of purely tribal lands, and it could fracture the unity in that particular clan or tribe.

From a record keeping standpoint, genealogical accounting would be sheer mayhem! YHWH (d) therefore placed an injunction on a woman's right to tribal inheritance by stipulating that her possession would always stay in her father's tribe. This negated any possibility that a woman could be a long-term determinant in any genealogical recording process, since her heritage would always be reckoned to her husband's house at the 50th Jubilee, if a male heir had not been procured to perpetuate her father's line before the Jubilee. YHWH still allowed a daughter-heiress to marry whom she chose (c) as long as she chose from among her father's tribe.

Deut 25:5–10 built on this injunction, stipulating that near kinsmen should marry their tribe's childless widows.[96] This statute sought both to obtain heirs for deceased countrymen so the *name* of the deceased husband "be not put out of Israel,"[97] and to protect the wife from other kinsmen who might inherit the deceased husband's land and evict her. It was assumed that if the daughter-heiress married outside the tribe she would forfeit her right to her father's or her deceased husband's inheritance. Her heritage would then be assigned to her father's nearest kinsmen.

The above account also reveals scribal protocols. Notice that tribal inheritances were not (b) reckoned until the Jubilee year. This indicates that the Levites updated the nation's genealogical records every 50 years and probably deposited them in the Temple's archives.[98] We know from contemporary nations (Hitite, Mari) that depositing legal treaties in a temple's sacred precincts was a common legal practice (1 Kgs 8:9).[99] Leviticus 25 is consistent with this conclusion by indicating that only family estates were counted in the Jubilee, while cities were excluded (Lev 25:28–34). These estate records were then maintained by the local tribal Levites, who reported them to the Levites in Jerusalem.

F. National Citizenship Classifications

1. Ezrach

After centuries of religious persecution, the founders of the United States conceived a nation in which the powers of state and religion were separate. The U.S. Constitution granted religious freedom while prohibiting the church's power to use government to meet its own agenda. Likewise, the government was not supposed to interfere with its citizens' religious beliefs. For Americans, religion became a personal matter that varied from family to family and even region to region (hence "the Baptist belt"). American citizenship carried no ties to the philosophies or beliefs that her citizens or aliens held. Whether native born or an immigrant, there is no requirement for allegiance to God or to a specific moral code in order to be a citizen. Thus, there is no law or doctrine that encourages the immigrant to assimilate into the traditional American culture. While many of these ideals for separation of church and state have served a republic (with varied ideas of religious truths and to whose citizens God has never spoken) quite well, the separation of religion would have been quite damaging for Israel's ancient society, to whom God had actually spoken and given one unifying *doctrine of freedom*.

Israel was a theocratic constitutional republic. The Torah and the Levites were YHWH's guides for righteous governance. And citizenship was tied to the patriarchal covenants. Though many aspects of ancient Israel's national citizenship worked quite similar to modern ideals, it always included the added concept of religious and moral affinity. Based on this ethical precedent, five basic types of citizens and noncitizens were recognized in YHWH's government.

The first and most common citizen in ancient Israel was the *ezrach:* native-born Israelites whose biological genealogies traced through Abraham, Isaac, and Jacob.[100] The Hebrew Scriptures continually distinguish between native-born *ezrach* citizens and those whose lineage traces to other nations.

> And every soul that eats that which dies of itself, or that which was torn with beasts, whether it be one of your own country (*ezrach*), or a stranger (*ger*), he shall both wash his clothes, and bathe himself in water, and be unclean until the even: then shall he be clean. (Lev 17:15)

A person "of Israel's own country" was a physical descendant of Abraham, Isaac, and Jacob. The descendants' citizenship was recognized separately from that of the ger (the immigrant who chose to join Israel's covenant with YHWH), who joined Israel's native-born, *ezrach* citizens.

2. Nechar/Nokri

The second classification of citizen in Israel was the *nechar or nokri,* literally, the children of the uncircumcised Gentile who did not share religious affinity with the nation of Israel.[101] When YHWH offered the Circumcision Covenant, he stipulated that both Abram's offspring and the children of foreigners (*nechars*) who lived in Abram's house should be circumcised.

> And he that is eight days old shall be circumcised among you, every man child in your generations, he that is born in the house, or bought with money of any stranger (*nechar*), which is not of your seed. (Gen 17:12)

A nechar's lineage did not trace to Abraham or Jacob. *Nechars* were the children of the Canaanite, Assyrian, Egyptian, and other nations. YHWH placed certain limitations on the *nokri.* In chap. 3 (pp. 65–72), we saw that covenants were usually sealed with sacrifices.[102] When YHWH delivered Israel out of Egypt and offered his covenant to them, Israel sealed her covenant with YHWH *by partaking of the Passover sacrifice.* Her citizens agreed to live by YHWH's covenantal constitutional Law. Should her citizens fail to uphold YHWH's covenant, they would suffer the same holocaust fate as the lamb or goat used in the Passover ceremony. If the *nechar* had *not* joined himself to Israel to keep YHWH's covenant, he did not need to participate in the ritual that reminded him of the consequences for failing to uphold YHWH's covenant. Likewise, the *nechar* was not afforded the covenant's promises, and blessings either, since nechars were not citizens of Israel.

Since a nechar had not joined himself to YHWH's covenants, he was forbidden to

> eat the Passover (Exod 12:43); none of his animals was suitable for sacrifices (Lev 22:25); interest *could* be collected from those who had borrowed money from an Israelite (Deut 23:20); animals which had died a natural death could be sold to him for consumption (Deut 14:21).[103]

The *nechar* was a non-Israelite citizen. Yet *when* the stranger (*nechar*) became circumcised and pledged to uphold Israel's constitutional covenant and sought to follow YHWH and his Law, he was no longer considered a *nechar*, but a *ger,* a type of Israelite citizen that we will investigate shortly.

3. Zar

The third classification for citizenship was the *zar.*[104] This term designated uncircumcised and unconverted foreigners; however, the term more forcefully conveyed the idea of being strange or different from Israel's lineage, her customs, her laws, and her heritage. *Zarim* were often Israel's enemies.[105] This is evidenced when King David uses *zur* (variant, infinitive form) to designate the unconverted people of other nations who do did not know YHWH's Torah and were estranged from righteousness.

> The wicked are estranged *(zur)* from the womb: they go astray as soon as they be born, speaking lies. (Ps 58:3)

Naturally, a person born into a foreign nation who served pagan gods and lacked the knowledge of YHWH's Law would follow his or her parents, going astray as soon as he was born since he lacked any instruction in righteousness. The pagan *zur* was the antithesis of the *ezrach,* who did possess knowledge of YHWH's *written instruction for righteousness* from previous generations who had walked in the way of YHWH.

A *zur* could also designate an unconverted or non-Torah-observant Israelite even if he was an *ezrach.* Thus a *zur* could also designate Israelites who had made themselves "strange" to YHWH and his constitutional Law. Job uses this term to describe himself becoming strange or foreign to his own household:

> He has put my brothers far from me, and my acquaintance are verily estranged *(zur)* from me. . . . They that dwell in mine house, and my maids, count me for a stranger *(zar):* I am an alien in their sight. (Job 19:13, 15)

Job indicates that his calamities have caused him to become estranged from his household. His affliction separated him from them. The prophet Hosea also uses *zur* to designate Israel's unconverted children.

> They have dealt treacherously against YHWH: for they have begotten strange *(zurim)* children: now shall a month devour them with their portions. (Hos 5:7)

Hosea's use of *zur* has two possible interpretations: Israel had intermarried with uncircumcised and unconverted foreigners, so her children were *nechar;* or Israel's children had estranged themselves from YHWH's covenant, just as the pagan *zur* was naturally estranged from righteousness. The idea of being estranged or contrary to YHWH's Law is witnessed again when Aaron's sons used *zur* or "strange" fire in their censers.[106] Aaron's sons offered fire that did not meet the Torah's specifications. Basically, anything that departed, "turned aside," or declined from YHWH's Law could be classified as *zur.*[107] Although this did *not* in any way revoke inherited citizenship, it did change a person's social status under the covenant.[108] When a person committed heinous crimes or wantonly rebelled against YHWH's covenant, his social status equaled that of a *zur* who was "cut off from among the congregation" (Exod 12:19; 30:33, 38; Num 19:20). People with this status lost the voting rights associated with Israel's elite congregation, thus alienating criminals from Israel's commonwealth.[109] This compelled the wicked individual to become "strange" to Israel's righteous governing society. We will examine the voting function of Israel's congregation below.

4. Toshab

Toshab[110] is another term used to designate foreign resident aliens. However, the term is always used in conjunction with another term, such as hireling, which is often used to indicate situations involving debt repayment.[111] Today we might equate a *toshab* with one who possesses a working visa allowing prolonged albeit temporary alien residency, although even Israelites (*ezrach* and *gers*) could be hired help. Like the *nechar*, the *toshab* had not joined himself to YHWH's covenant; therefore, he could not partake of the Passover.

> A foreigner (*toshab*) and an hired servant shall not eat of it. (Exod 12:45)

But even with this status, the equality of YHWH's Law can be seen since YHWH protects the *toshab* from having to work on the national Sabbath holidays:

> And the sabbath of the land shall be meat for you; for you, and for your servant, and for your maid, and for your hired servant, and for your stranger (*toshab*) that sojourns with you. (Lev 25:6)

The Sabbath was the sign of YHWH's covenant. Even though the foreign *toshab* had not joined himself to Israel, he still benefitted from resting on the Sabbath. Unlike the *nechar/nokri* or the *zur*, the *toshab* was viewed with compassion as YHWH encouraged the nation to help out workers who paid taxes and made a valuable contribution to the nation's economy.

> And if *your brother* be waxen poor, and fallen in decay with you; then you shall *relieve him*: yes, though he be a *stranger* (*ger*), or a sojourner (*toshab*); that he may live with you. Take you no usury of him, or increase: but fear your God; that your brother may live with you. You shall not give him your money on usury, nor lend him your victuals for increase. (Lev 25:35–37)

Those who worked either as hired help or to repay debt were dealt with in compassion (both ezrach, gers, and foreigners). Although the *toshab* was not eligible for the benefits associated with Israel's welfare system, YHWH did command Israel's citizens to refrain from taking advantage of the *toshab*'s vulnerable economic status. If the foreign *toshab* fell into poverty, he could be sold into the nation's welfare system (Lev 25:45–47).

5. The Beloved Ger

The fourth and final class of citizen in Israel was the *ger*, or a *nechar* who became circumcised and joined himself to walk with YHWH in his covenants.[112] *Gers* were usually *nakori*, bondservants who had entered Israel's permanent slave system (Lev 25:47–54).[113] Once a convert, or *ger*, joined himself to YHWH, he became as one who was born in the land of Israel (*ezrach*)—there was no difference as far as ceremonial rights were concerned.

When a stranger shall sojourn with you, and will keep the passover to YHWH, let all his males be circumcised, and then let him come near and keep it; *and he shall be as one that is born in the land*: for no uncircumcised person shall eat of it. One law shall be to him that is homeborn, and to the stranger (*ger*) that sojourns among you. (Exod 12:48–49)

And if a stranger (*ger*) sojourn with you in your land, you shall not vex him. But the stranger (*ger*) that dwells with you shall be to you *as one born among you (ezrach) and you shall love him as yourself*; for you were strangers (*gers*) in the land of Egypt: I am YHWH your God. (Lev 19:33–34)

YHWH viewed the convert as an *ezrach* or homeborn citizen: *gers* were grafted into the body of Israel. *Gers* were entitled to the rights and privileges associated with Israelite citizenship,[114] complete with the blessings and promises found in YHWH's covenants.

Thus said YHWH, Keep you judgment, and do justice: for my salvation is near to come, and my righteousness to be revealed. Blessed is the man that does this, and the son of man that lays hold on it; that keeps the sabbath from polluting it, and keeps his hand from doing any evil. Neither let the son of the stranger (*nechar*), that has joined himself to YHWH, speak, saying, YHWH has utterly separated me from his people. . . . Also the sons of the stranger (*nechar*), that join themselves to YHWH, to serve him, and to love the name of YHWH, to be his servants, every one that keeps the sabbath from polluting it, and takes hold of my covenant; Even them will I bring to my holy mountain, and make them joyful in my house of prayer: their burnt offerings and their sacrifices shall be accepted on my altar; for my house shall be called an house of prayer for all people. YHWH God which gathers the outcasts of Israel said, Yet will I gather others to him, beside those that are gathered to him. (Isa 56:1–3, 6–8)

Throughout Scripture YHWH displays his love and desire for the foreigner (*nechar*) to convert and join his unique nation. The Promised Land was open to all who joined themselves to YHWH, to serve him, to love his name, to keep the Sabbath, the constitutional covenant, and to be numbered among his people. Once a foreign *nechar* joined himself to YHWH's people and took hold of YHWH's covenantal Law as his own (became circumcised), he was no longer a *nechar* but a *ger*. As we will see shortly, an individual's *ger* status lasted for only a few generations, at which time his or her family would be reckoned as native-born *ezrach* citizens with full voting rights in the nation's elite assembly.

YHWH's unbiased and open immigration policy toward converts was unprecedented in ancient times, when most foreigners were basically considered slaves. Though *gers* (similar to the Levites) were *not* entitled to arable tribal lands that ensured their prosperity and freedom, YHWH loved the convert so much that his Law ordained a small portion of the nation's crops to be allocated to alleviate the convert's (*ger*) financial disadvantage in Israel's economic system.

> At the end of three years you shall bring forth all the tithe of your increase the same year, and shall lay it up within your gates: And the Levite, (because he has no part nor inheritance with you,) and the stranger (*ger*), and the fatherless, and the widow, which are within your gates, shall come, and shall eat and be satisfied; that YHWH your God may bless you in all the work of your hand which you do. (Deut 14:28–29).
>
> YHWH preserves the strangers (*gers*); he relieves the fatherless and widow: but the way of the wicked he turns upside down. (Ps 146:9)

When YHWH divided the Promised Land among Israel's families after they entered Canaan, there were many *gers* who obtained tribal heritages alongside Israel. Caleb, the Kenezite, the scout who withstood Israel's unbelievers is one good example (Num 32:12; Josh 14:14).[115] Since Caleb did not belong to any tribe within Israel, YHWH instructed Joshua to give Caleb an inheritance in the tribe of Judah (Josh 15:13). After Joshua divided the land, however, no other arable land existed for converts in Israel's borders (unless the nation conquered new territories),[116] so when a person from another nation converted (i.e., became a *ger*), he could either live in the city or work in the household of an Israelite who held arable lands.

Since ancient economies were mostly based on agriculture, many *gers* who moved into Israel did not have land for a productive livelihood. This is why YHWH ordained that Israel's homeborn citizens allocate a small portion of their crops to help sustain and offset the *ger*'s disadvantage.

> And you shall not glean your vineyard, neither shall you gather every grape of your vineyard; you shall leave them for the poor and stranger (*ger*): I am YHWH your God. (Lev 19:10)
>
> And when you reap the harvest of your land, you shall not make clean riddance of the corners of your field when you reap, neither shall you gather any gleaning of your harvest: you shall leave them to the poor, and to the stranger (*ger*): I am YHWH your God. (Lev 23:22)
>
> But you shall remember that you were a bondman in Egypt, and YHWH your God redeemed you there: therefore I command you to do this thing. When you cut down your harvest in your field, and have forgot a sheaf in the field, you shall not go again to fetch it: it shall be for the stranger (*ger*), for the fatherless, and for the widow: that YHWH your God may bless you in all the work of your hands. When you beat your olive tree, you shall not go over the boughs again: it shall be for the stranger (*ger*), for the fatherless, and for the widow. When you gather the grapes of your vineyard, you shall not glean it afterward: it shall be for the stranger (*ger*), for the fatherless, and for the widow. And you shall remember that you were a bondman in the land of Egypt: therefore I command you to do this thing. (Deut 24:18–22)

YHWH's Law considered the *ger*'s disadvantaged position and lack of tribal lands equal to the orphan's and widow's lack of a provider. Therefore, YHWH provided a means for him to find sustenance and supplementary income. Beyond this, YHWH allotted a portion of the nation's 10% tithe to the convert's sustenance:

> And you shall rejoice in every good thing which YHWH your God has given to you, and to your house, you, and the Levite, and the stranger that is among you. When you have made an end of tithing all the tithes of your increase the third year, which is the year of tithing, and have given it to the Levite, the stranger (*ger*), the fatherless, and the widow, that they may eat within your gates, and be filled; Then you shall say before YHWH your God, I have brought away the hallowed things out of my house, and also have given them to the Levite, and to the stranger (*ger*), to the fatherless, and to the widow, according to all your commandments which you have commanded me: I have not transgressed your commandments, neither have I forgotten them. (Deut 26:11–13)

The statutes and commands in YHWH's Law provided sustenance for the convert while relieving his financial distress. He became a citizen with all the rights and privileges (i.e., access to the *ger*'s portion of tithe welfare, access to the Temple, participation in Passover and other ceremonies, and gained the ability to bring tithes and offerings, etc.).

YHWH also clarified that his Law applied *equally* to the seed of Abraham and the foreigner. His covenant nation embraced only one God and one constitution, which had been defined by the precepts established in his laws.

> One law shall be to him that is homeborn (*ezrach*), and to the stranger (*ger*) that sojourns among you. (Exod 12:49)

YHWH intended only one Law for his nation.[117] In fact he stressed this fact in the previous verses, which clarify that the regulations regarding the Feast of Unleavened Bread are the same for the convert (*ger*) as for the native-born (*ezrach*) citizen.

> Seven days shall there be no leaven found in your houses: for whosoever eats that which is leavened, even that soul shall be cut off from the congregation of Israel, whether he be a stranger (*ger*), or born in the land (*ezrach*). (Exod 12:19)

YHWH ordained only one constitution for all inhabitants to obey. YHWH again stressed the equality of the convert in his eyes in the Book of Numbers by outlining the same statutes and consequences for breaching the Law by the *ezrach* as for the *ger*.

> If a stranger (*ger*) sojourn with you, or whosoever be among you in your generations, and will offer an offering made by fire, of a sweet savor to YHWH; *as*

you do, so he shall do. One ordinance shall be both for you of the congregation, and also for the stranger (*ger*) that sojourns with you, an ordinance forever in your generations: *as you are, so shall the stranger (ger) be before YHWH*. One law and one manner shall be for you, and for the stranger that sojourns with you. (Num 15:14–16)

There is no separate "law of the *ger*" in Torah (Num 15:30–31). Rather, Torah teaches only one constitutional Law: the *way of YHWH*. Judaism, however, has traditionally interpreted this text as implying that there are two separate laws or two separate standards: one for the *ezrach* and another one for the *ger*. It was, however, for this very type of reasoning that YHWH condemned the ancient nation:

In the midst of you have they dealt by oppression with the stranger (*ger*)... yes, they have oppressed the stranger (*ger*) wrongfully. And I sought for a man among them, that should make up the hedge, and stand in the gap before me for the land, that I should not destroy it: but I found none. (Ezek 22:7, 29–30)

The interpretation that YHWH intended his Law *for only the nation of Israel* is an exclusivist and elitist doctrine that promotes contention and discord. Imagine if the United States had one set of laws for its native citizens and another for immigrants (i.e., the U.S. Constitution for Americans but Sharia law for Arab immigrants). Not only is this type of legal system untenable, it would produce a convoluted legal mess, stirring up immense controversy and righteous indignation by the underprivileged classes. Yet Judaism justifies its distinguishing between the status of the *ezrach* and the *ger* (convert) by two laws that allowed the Israelites to sell an animal that had "died of itself" and to charge interest from the *nechar*s, not the *ger*s.

You shall not eat of any thing that dies of itself: you shall give it to the stranger (*ger*) that is in your gates, that he may eat it; or you may sell it to an alien (*nokri*). (Deut 14:21)

For health reasons readily accepted today, YHWH forbade Israelites to eat animals that died prematurely. This is the only law in all of the Torah that at first glance appears to distinguish between the natural-born citizen and the convert-immigrant. The text appears to imply that Israel could not eat animals that died on their own while the *ger* (the immigrant-convert) and the *nokri* (non-convert) could. However, on further examination this traditional interpretation fails.

And *every soul* that eats that which died of itself, or that which was torn with beasts, *whether it be one of your own country, or a stranger (ger)*, he shall both wash his clothes, and bathe himself in water, and be unclean until the even: then shall he be clean. (Lev 17:15)

YHWH's Law had the exact same standard for the *ger* as it did for the native-born citizen. If either citizen (*ger* or *ezrach*) ate an animal "which died of itself," that person was to do laundry, take a bath, and wait until evening to be clean. Because both laundry and bathing were rather labor-intensive endeavors (fetch water many times to "draw a bath"; fetch water again to scrub clothes; and air dry), the cleanliness injunction would give the family pause to consider whether the work justified the cheap meal. It is assumed that poverty precipitated a family's temptation to eat sick or road-killed animals. Thus, Deuteronomy is not biased with regard to citizenship class. Otherwise, *two separate laws* would have addressed how citizens should be handled when they ate an animal that had not been slaughtered intentionally. *Instead, the Law has one way or one rule for dealing with this issue for both the* ezrach *as well as the* ger.

That YHWH intended his Law to be applied equally to the native citizen and the convert is demonstrated again when both are enjoined to refrain from eating blood, and the same rule and consequence are applied to both groups.

> And whatsoever man there be of the House of Israel, or of the strangers (*gers*) that sojourn among you, that eats any manner of blood; I will even set my face against that soul that eats blood, and will cut him off from among his people. (Lev 17:10)

Again, we see the law applied equally to the converted immigrant and to the seed of Abraham.

The second text that is traditionally used to infer a lower class for the stranger (*ger*) deals with what Judaism believes is Israel's right to lend money to them, which, in fact, YHWH prohibited the nation from doing to its own citizens (Lev 25:35–37).

> You shall not lend on usury to your brother; usury of money, usury of victuals, usury of any thing that is lent on usury: To a stranger (*nokri*) you may lend on usury; but to your brother you shall not lend on usury: that YHWH your God may bless you in all that you set your hand to in the land where you go to possess it. (Deut 23:19–20)

This text does allow Israel to earn interest—without a Release Year— from the *nokri*, a citizenship classification that we saw above designated someone who had not converted (become circumcised) to join YHWH's people or to uphold Israel's covenantal Law. This text did *not* allow Israel to earn interest from a converted *ger* who had indeed joined himself to Israel to obey YHWH's covenant.

> And if your (a) brother be waxen poor, and fallen in decay with you; then you shall relieve him: yes, though he be a (b) *stranger* (*ger*), or a sojourner (*toshab*);

> that he may live with you. Take you no usury of him, or increase: but fear your God; that your brother may live with you. You shall not give him your money on usury, nor lend him your victuals for increase. (Lev 25:35–37)

Common citizenship and equality under the Law are often referred to as "brotherhood" or "comradery." YHWH defines Israel's (a) brotherhood as including both the (b) *ger* and the *toshab*. In contrast to the *nokri* (Deut 23:20), Israel could not lend with interest to the *ger* or the working resident (*toshab*): both had protection from usury under YHWH's Law. Therefore, separating the *ger* as a "lower class" citizen in Israel is wholly unjustified.

Scripture consistently demonstrates YHWH's love and watchful care over the convert, promising that many converts will be among his people when he restores Israel in the latter days.

> For YHWH will have mercy on Jacob, and will yet choose Israel, and set them in their own land: and the strangers (*gers*) shall be joined with them, and they shall cleave to the House of Jacob. (Isa 14:1)

When YHWH restores Israel in the latter days, many converts will be among his dispersed people. According to Ezekiel, *gers* will be allotted an equal heritage in the Promised Land at the restoration, just as was done with Caleb at the Canaan conquest.

> So shall you divide this land to you according to the tribes of Israel. And it shall come to pass, that you shall divide it by lot for an inheritance to you, and to the strangers (*gers*) that sojourn among you, which shall beget children among you: and they shall be to you as born in the country among the Children of Israel; they shall have inheritance with you among the tribes of Israel. And it shall come to pass, that in what tribe the stranger (*ger*) sojourns, there shall you give him his inheritance, said the Lord YHWH. (Ezek 47:21–3)[118]

Throughout Israel's history, her people have tried to make themselves an exclusive society (Isa 65:5). Israel's native citizens have employed many tactics for segregating and oppressing the *ger*, such as adding stipulations and customs for culture, conversion, or citizenship to YHWH's Law that do not exist (e.g., shaving the head or requiring a drop of blood, kippas, prayer shawls, prayer liturgy, or man-made "cultural" ideals, etc.). Scripture is full of YHWH's chastisement of the nation for treating the convert different from a native-born Israelite[119] or for adding qualifications for citizenship and conversion to his Law (Deut 4:2; 12:32). Yet YHWH stresses the equality of the *ger* with Israel's native citizens that will happen at the latter-day restoration, when the nation will finally prevail to do what is right in his sight (see Table 7.3).

Table 7.3. Citizenship in Israel

Nationality	Citizenship	Type of Citizenship	Eligible for Welfare
Citizen of Israel	*Ezrach*	Natural-born citizen	(only orphans and widows)[120]
	Ezrach-zar	Citizens that forsook covenant/ Lost voting privileges	
	Ger	Converted *Nechar/nokri* from other nations	Entire family
Foreigners	*Toshab*	Work visa/Law-abiding, resident alien living and actively working in Israel	noneligible/could be bondservants
	Nechar/nokri *Nechar-zar*	Foreigners Israel's enemies	N/A

6. Genealogical Reckoning of Arable Land Heritages and Citizenship

Legal transactions and national archives were primarily a priestly-government function. The Levites maintained records regarding family heritages that were probably deposited in the Temple's archives.[121] Citizenship in Israel was based on male lineages.[122] The state's recognition of a family as an *ezrach* (native-born) citizen tied directly to land ownership since only native-born citizens inherited tribal estates.[123] For Israel's *ezrach* citizens, these lineages involved inheritance of land in the countryside.[124] As previously discussed, the Law forbade this land to be sold, although it could be leased (Lev 25:23–28). Marrying an Israelite woman was the only means for a foreign (*ger*) male to obtain a tribal-land possession for his offspring.[125] Under these circumstances, the foreigner's children would not be listed in the nation's genealogical archives unless the *ezrach* father-in-law granted his daughter (the *ger*'s wife) an inheritance from his tribal heritage.[126] If the father *did* give his daughter and son-in-law a land heritage, their offspring would be recorded according to the genealogical records of her father's house.[127] (This was the major reason for YHWH's command that Zelophehad's daughters marry in their own tribe, Num 36:6–9.) Foreign women who married into Israel automatically acquired the citizenship status of their husband because inheritance and citizenship were based on the male's status, *not* the woman's.

Citizenship in Israel was male-determinative.[128] In most ancient cultures women were not offered "citizenship" in the real sense of the word—that is, enjoying the same rights and status that the men enjoyed.[129] Women were usually considered their husband's or father's property.[130] A woman's social class was determined either by her mother's status as a wife, concubine, slave, or bondwoman, or by her own role as a wife, concubine, slave, or bondwoman.[131]

As we will see throughout this study, unless warranted, YHWH's Law did not alter an already-functioning society. YHWH's Law established righteousness, justice, and theological truth within the customs of the day. He did *not* nullify these customs just because certain customs were common in other nations. (The exception to this assent would be binding cultural customs, such as many rabbinic *takanot,* or required cultural customs that added to YHWH's Law, Deut 12:32). Regarding the fact that women were considered property, YHWH had pointed out the consequence of Eve's action, stating that her children would bear the curse of being dominated by men (Gen 3:16). YHWH's covenantal Law did not change this popular social structure, although he did establish justice for women within it. He allowed the curse to run its course until it would, in the latter days, die-off as women *finally* regained the equal status with which they had been created in the garden (Jer 31:22).[132]

YHWH afforded Israel's women many protections not equaled in other nations. One of the most important of these was her status. A woman virtually held the same citizenship as her father or husband.[133] If a woman was single (a virgin), she would hold whatever citizenship status her father possessed. When she married, she gained the same status as her husband. This is why the law allowed Israel's warriors to marry female war captives (Deut 21:10–14) whose families and gods the army had destroyed, yet forbade marriages to unconverted women in peaceful times when their gods were still available to worship (Deut 7:3–6). When an Israelite man married a foreign (*nechar*) woman, she automatically acquired the husband's citizenship status via marriage, thus being recognized as an *ezrach*.[134] If her husband died without an heir, she inherited all of his land, as in the case of Ruth, a foreign (*nechar*, Ruth 2:10) Moabitess who retained possession of her late husband's heritage (Ruth 4:5).[135]

The Law had ordained that, if a man leased his land and was unable to redeem it before the Jubilee, his next of kin could redeem it for him (Lev 25:25; Jer 32:6–14), a practice commonly called Levirate marriage.[136] Boaz's redemption of Chilion's land—and Ruth with it—demonstrates that women were a very temporary liaison in the genealogical process (Ruth 3:12; 4:4–10). As soon as an heir was born, he was recognized under the late husband's name (Deut 25:5–6), and the two lineages (the first and second husband's lineages) were joined together, even if separated by distance (in the same tribe). The heir was never recognized by his mother's house unless his father was a foreigner (*nechar*). Even in these circumstances, an Israelite son was not recognized by the mother's name but by her father's household name (Lev 24:11).

Had Ruth refused marriage, she would have retained Chilion's land until her death, at which time the field would be inherited by the next of kin. This practice in Israel's society protected a woman from being cast off her husband's land by claims of near kinsmen.[137] Thus, YHWH was concerned for a woman's safety and well-being by protecting her when her circumstances changed.

The fact that ancient societies considered a woman to be her husband's property combined with the fact that she had no real citizenship status outside the marriage is the reason that King David's lineage was not considered illegitimate. The Law excludes Moabite descendants for 10 generations (Deut 23:3). David was only the third generation from Ruth and Boaz (1 Chr 2:12–15). However, David was not reckoned by his great-grandmother's genealogy. He was reckoned by Boaz's lineage. Once married, Ruth shared her husband's citizenship status. Thus, YHWH's ban on the Moabite was *not racial* but political, a point that I will address in the next section.

Although women were barred from *permanently* owning arable lands, they could lease these lands. It is no doubt this type of property to which King Solomon refers when he states that a Godly woman "buys a field and plants a vineyard" with her own financial investment (Prov 31:16). A woman could either lease arable land or permanently purchase city real estate. The inheritance rules that governed male ownership of tribal lands did not apply to city property (Lev 25:29–30). After a year had passed, city property could be sold as modern real estate and women were free to purchase the land in cities. Thus, Israel's society granted women freedom to conduct business affairs.

G. The Blessing: Constitutionally-Defined Government

1. YHWH's Gift: Freedom from Oppression

When YHWH gave his covenants to Abraham and his children, he invested the birthright and blessing in Abraham's seed. His children would enjoy the birthright of a double portion of land. The family blessing indicates leadership. When Isaac blessed Jacob, he ordained that "his mother's sons would bow down to him" and that he would be "lord over his brothers" and that "nations would serve him" (Gen 27:29). It was through Abraham's blessing that his children would bless the entire earth (Gen 12:2; 22:18). This blessing was revolutionary.

Abraham's blessing not only established righteousness, truth, and justice; it also defined and limited the future nation's forms of government. YHWH's blessing established freedom from oppression. YHWH established this freedom foremost by his constitutional Law. YHWH's constitution established freedom in Israel by balancing power among the ruling families and her citizens at the national or federal level. His constitution only loosely addressed government at the tribal-state level, allowing tribal regions to work out their own policies. But even these policies needed to adhere to the precepts in YHWH's constitutional Law and, as we will see, if the family tribal-states over-stepped their authority, showed bias, or pursued oppressive policies, these issues could always be addressed by the nation's Levitical court, which bore the responsibility of correctly interpreting and applying YHWH's constitutional Law.

YHWH's political economy was based on Israel's land heritage. Land-ownership for every *ezrach* citizen formed the strength and backbone of that economy. The weekly, monthly and yearly Release and Jubilee years further strengthened the nation's economy and relieved the economic hardship that citizens could face.

Citizenship affected national unity and preserved the rights, freedoms, and economy of Israel's citizens. Landed heritages naturally discouraged large waves of immigration since the only place an immigrant could live was in the city, if he could not find employment with a landed citizen. Albeit, only the wealthiest immigrants could afford to live in Israel's cities. YHWH established constitutional boundaries for ancient Israel's "city limits" and suburbs (Num 35:1–8). This placed incredible demand on all available city real estate, keeping prices quite high because home and business values continually appreciated as the population expanded. This not only blessed Israel's economy, it also protected her from waves of immigrants who could transfer wealth out of the nation back to families in their homeland.

These constitutional precepts had formed the backbone of Israel's Abrahamic birthright and blessing. The birthright gave Abraham a free land for his children to establish a righteous government. The blessing that YHWH gave to Abraham and his seed restricted taxation so that the government could not impinge on the national economy and freedom of her citizens. Abraham's blessing limited, defined, and established accountability in Israel's government. It is this form of government embedded in the *way of YHWH* that is Abraham's greatest blessing.

2. Constitutional Monarchy

a. Limits of Power

When Israel came out of Egypt, YHWH ordained the Levites to serve in his government. One function that the Levites filled was that of a national or federal court, with the high priest being the nation's chief justice (see discussion in next section). During the Judges' Era, YHWH had been Israel's only king. The Judges had functioned as elected generals. This truly was an autonomous society with the most limited form of government.

YHWH foresaw that Israel, like other nations of the earth, would desire a more formal yet more oppressive form of government. His constitutional Law allowed for his authority over the nation to be transferred to a ruling house, or monarchy. YHWH placed several injunctions on the nation's ruling house to ensure that the office maintained the nation's freedom.

The first rule governing Israel's Monarchy was that only a descendant of the nation's forefathers (*those who initially entered Canaan under Joshua*) were eligible for leading YHWH's people (Deut 17:14–15). This restriction, similar to restrictions placed on the American presidency, intended to limit leadership to those who had the nation's best interests at heart—those who had a hereditary stake in the nation's prosperity. Thus, the child of an immigrant could never be eligible for the monarchy (as reckoned through the father). Not only did this stipulation maintain national unity, it served as another mechanism for ensuring that Israel's leaders understood their own theocratic constitutional heritage.

The Torah detailed the most stringent regulations for the Monarchy, theoretically limiting the institution's power.

> When you come to the land which YHWH your God gives you, and shall possess it . . . and shall say, I will set a king over me, like as all the nations that are about me. . . . (the king) shall not multiply (a) horses to himself, nor (b) cause the people to return to Egypt, to the end that he should multiply horses: forasmuch as YHWH has said to you, You shall henceforth return no more that way. Neither shall he (c) multiply wives to himself, that his heart turn not away: neither shall he (d) greatly multiply to himself silver and gold. And it shall be, when he sits on the throne of his kingdom, that (e) he shall write him a copy of

this law in a book out of that which is before the priests the Levites: And it shall be with him, and (e) he shall read in it all the days of his life: that he may learn to fear YHWH his God, to keep all the words of this law and these statutes, to do them. (Deut 17:14, 16–19, parenthesis added)

"Horses" often implied standing armies, especially in prophetic or poetic passages.[138] Funding large standing armies caused the people (b) to return to Egypt's "house of bondage." Originally, the Law provided no distribution of taxes to cover military expenditures, nor did it ordain a standing army (although it did provide for militias), so a monarchy would assess new taxes above and beyond the reasonable 10% tax ordained in the Law.

Another system that ancient monarchs maintained was an active corvée work force. It was this corvée labor about which YHWH protested through Samuel, saying that a monarchy would return Israel's citizens to the bondage from which they had been delivered (1 Sam 8:12–18; 1 Kgs 5:13–17; 9:17–23). Once a monarchy was installed, more tithe-tax was added to support the standing military, corvée laborers, and the administrative offices that the monarchy required (1 Sam 8:15), although tribute from other non-Israelite dependencies lessened some of this demand. This increased the people's oppression by raising taxes to a total of 15–20% per citizen, thus the reason for Samuel's adamant protests against this institution (1 Samuel 8).

YHWH's injunction in (b) Deut 17:16 prevented the king from instituting corvée labor from Israel's citizens. The king was also discouraged from maintaining a (c) large, costly harem by which his heart could be turned away from matters of state to personal indulgences and distractions. Additionally, YHWH encouraged the king (d) to not use his office to gain personal wealth. Rather, the monarch was to be a shepherd-servant who justly and righteously administered the Law on YHWH's behalf. To this end, the king (e) was commanded to write his own personal copy of the nation's constitutional Law to read and use when governing the nation. This would teach the king that, if he or his policies departed from YHWH's Law, YHWH would hold him and his House personally accountable (Exod 34:7).[139]

b. God's Son

The entire ancient world viewed kingship as a divine right. The king was God's son, reigning on earth in his father's stead. YHWH upheld this view of kingship with King David by covenanting with his House and establishing Judah's Monarchy in his lineage.

I will declare the decree: YHWH has said to me, You are my Son; this day have I begotten you. Ask of me, and I shall give you the heathen for your inheritance, and the uttermost parts of the earth for your possession. You shall break them with a rod of iron; you shall dash them in pieces like a potter's vessel. (Ps 2:7–9)

Reigning as God's son did not give the king indiscriminate authority or power. Instead, the office required fidelity to the God who had installed and sanctioned the king's office. YHWH had delegated much of his power and authority over the nation to the king. In return, the king was required to acknowledge the One who authorized his office by upholding YHWH's covenant with the nation. Pivotal to Israel's Monarchy was the stipulation that the king "fear YHWH his God, to keep all the words of this law and these statutes, to do them" (Deut 17:19). This aspect of YHWH's Law formed an integral part of his covenant with the king. By recognizing YHWH alone as Israel's God, the king demonstrated his submission to YHWH as the nation's ultimate authority.

Throughout the *Book of the Kings of Judah and Israel* (see chap. 6), Levitical scribes characterized each reign by the king's willingness to sanction YHWH alone as Israel's God and uphold his statutes. The scribe also characterized each king's reign based on the prevalence of idolatry. *Without fail, every single king of Judah and Israel that reigned over the nation was characterized by his adherence to the First and Second Commandments.* These statements were written in a fixed formula that stated righteous King X "did what was right" in YHWH's sight (1 Kgs 15:14; 22:43; 2 Kgs 12:2–3; 14:3–4; 15:3–4, 35; 18:3–4; 23:4–7) or "did what was evil" in YHWH's sight (1 Kgs 11:16; 14:22; 15:26, 34; 16:7, 19, 30; 21:20; 21:25; 22:25, 52; 2 Kgs 3:2, 18; 8:18, 27; 12:2; 13:2; 13:11). The Levites' goal was to recognize how well the king honored YHWH as Israel's ultimate authority. Judah's righteous kings were formally characterized by how well they sanctified YHWH alone as Israel's God. Thus, kings—even righteous kings such as Asa (1 Kgs 15:14), Jehoshaphat (1 Kgs 22:43), Joash (2 Kgs 12:2–3), Amaziah (2 Kgs 14:4), Uzziah (2 Kgs 15:3–4), and Jotham (2 Kgs 15:35), who may have walked before God with a perfect heart—were recognized for failing to remove rival gods or shrines from the Promised Land. Hezekiah (2 Kgs 18:3–4) and Josiah (2 Kgs 15:35) were the only two kings in Judah's history that followed the covenant, as King David had, by removing all YHWH's cultic rivals and sanctifying YHWH alone as the nation's God.

Ancient law historian Raymond Westbrook observes,

> By ordaining 'justice' for the land, particularly at the opening of his reign, a king demonstrated his quality as a ruler according to law. . . . It is worth comparing the activity of these same kings . . . whose primary purpose was to lay before the public, posterity, future kings, and above all the gods, evidence of the king's execution of his divinely ordained mandate: to have been a good shepherd-king.[140]

Westbrook also draws attention to the parallel between this ancient concept and the view of the responsibility of Hebrew kings when the priest recorded whether a king had "done justice in the eyes of Yahweh."[141] This view demonstrates that YHWH firmly delegated the power and authority to the Monarchy to ensure that the nation adhered to the constitutional covenant by observing the First and Second Commandments. Thus the kings who used their office to eliminate idolatry were acknowledged for their righteousness in sanctifying YHWH as the nation's only God. This demonstrates that one of the priestly functions was to hold the king personally accountable for his fidelity to God.

3. Balance of Power: Priesthood and Congregation

When our discussion turns to chronology in chap. 9, we will see that, *when* Judah's monarchs violated these constitutional ideals regarding the nation's freedom, the citizens (the *edah*) united with the priesthood to overthrow the king, installing another eligible heir in the place of the oppressive king. The reigns of Joash, Amaziah, Azariah, Ahaz, and Amon all demonstrate the role that the priesthood played in holding the Monarchy accountable to the covenant.

In the beginning of Joash's reign, the high priest Jehoiada and his wife Jehoshabeath aided the Monarchy by reinstalling Joash, David's legitimate heir. The limits placed on the nation's Monarchy are no more evident than when Joash was crowned king at the tender age of seven; he was installed based on Israel's constitutional covenant, which was formally called the *Testimony* (2 Kgs 11:12, 17; 2 Chr 23:11). This formal act served to remind Joash of the limits and responsibilities of his office. After Jehoiada's death, Joash turned from the covenant, and the priesthood began to prophecy against the king (2 Chr 24:17–27). When Joash killed Jehoiada's son for admonishing him for violating the covenant, YHWH sent a foreign army to chastise the nation (2 Chr 24:23–24). When this discipline proved ineffective, the people revolted, conspiring against Joash and hiring mercenaries to kill the wayward king (2 Chr 24:26). Thus, the priesthood and the congregation served as YHWH's right hand of judgment, balancing the Monarchy's power, and holding the king accountable to the constitution.

When Amaziah turned from YHWH, the congregation revolted against both the king's apostasy and his oppressive warfare against the nation's Northern brothers (2 Kgs 14:21–22; 2 Chr 25:27) by installing his son Uzziah in his stead. When Uzziah tried to usurp the constitutional authority delegated to the priesthood in Israel's covenant, "Azariah the priest went in after him, and with him 80 priests of YHWH, that were valiant men: And they withstood Uzziah the king" (2 Chr 26:17–18). YHWH himself judged Uzziah's gross usurping of authority and smote the king with leprosy (2 Kgs 15:5).

As soon as Ahaz inherited Judah's throne, Isaiah confronted the king to see if he would return to the covenant and refrain from oppressing Judah's citizens (Isa 7:1–13). Isaiah warned Ahaz (Isa 7:9) that *if* his actions did not demonstrate that he believed God's word, his kingdom would not be established. This strongly implied that the priesthood would not support Ahaz's regency. Ahaz is later recorded as "not doing right" in God's sight (2 Kgs 16:2–4) and a synchronized chronology of Judah's kings demonstrates that Ahaz's reign was cut short, as Judah's congregation, working with the priests, established Ahaz's righteous young son, Hezekiah, on the throne only six years later.

Probably the only reason that the priests and the congregation did not overthrow Manasseh's heinous rule was that the king eliminated all political dissent (2 Kgs 16:21); hence the reason that YHWH would no longer forgive the sins of the Monarchy (2 Kgs 24:4): the king had committed treason by eliminating the balance of power that YHWH had established. One of the last times the congregation conspired against the king was during Amon's reign, when the king tried to reinstitute his father's treasonous policies (2 Kgs 19:21–24). *Not once during Judah's Monarchic Era did anyone conspire against a Godly, constitution-abiding king.* However, the kings who violated the constitutional precepts established by YHWH's constitutional covenant were held accountable by both the priesthood and the congregation in the same way that Phinehas (with the congregation at his side) held the Northern tribes accountable in the case of the Altar of Ed (Josh 22:34).[142]

H. The Legislative Assembly: Role and Function

1. The 'Edah Senate

Israel's legislative assembly played a vital role in the nation's governmental affairs. It served several functions. One of the congregation's primary functions involved international policy. The assembly voted on national policies regarding contracts, covenants, and treaties. One of the first times that we see Israel's assembly participating in international affairs occurs when the congregation's (*'edah*) princes created a covenant with the Gibeonites.

> And Joshua made peace with them, and made a league with them, to let them live: and the princes of the congregation (*'edah*) swore to them. . . . And the Children of Israel smote them not, because the princes of the congregation had sworn to them by YHWH God of Israel. And all the congregation (*'edah*) murmured against the princes. (Josh 9:15, 18)

At the time Israel covenanted with the Gibeonites, she had two leaders: the high priest Eleazar and Joshua, who served as the nation's chieftain. YHWH had established a balance of power in Israel's government[143] similar to the balance of power found in Western nations today.[144] The high priest, king (judge or chieftain), and the assembly worked together to decide issues concerning the nation. In the case of the Gibeonites, both Joshua (the nation's leader) and the princely representatives for Israel's assembly made a treaty on behalf of the entire nation of Israel.

Though the congregation, or at least their princely representatives, voted on international affairs, the congregation's primary concern focused on domestic matters.[145] First, the assembly served as a jury in court cases, especially those involving manslaughter:

> Then the congregation (*'edah*) shall judge between the slayer and the revenger of blood according to these judgments: And the congregation (*'edah*) shall deliver the slayer out of the hand of the revenger of blood, and the congregation (*'edah*) shall restore him to the city of his refuge, where he was fled: and he shall abide in it unto the death of the high priest, which was anointed with the holy oil. (Num 35:24–25)
>
> When he that does flee to one of those cities shall stand at the entering of the gate of the city, and shall declare his cause in the ears of the elders of that city, they shall take him into the city to them, and give him a place, that he may dwell among them. And if the avenger of blood pursue after him, then they

shall not deliver the slayer up into his hand; because he smote his neighbor un-wittingly, and hated him not beforetime. And he shall dwell in that city, until he stand before the congregation (*'edah*) for judgment, and until the death of the high priest that shall be in those days: then shall the slayer return, and come to his own city, and to his own house, to the city from where he fled. (Josh 20:4–6)

'Edah is the Hebrew word for Israel's righteous congregation.[146] The term is derived from the root *ya'ad*[147] meaning, "to meet by appointment," indicating that Israel's legislative assembly convened in Jerusalem during YHWH's three set appointments (*mo'ed*[148]). "The *'edah* was expected to come where God promised to meet them,"[149] hence the word's relationship to YHWH's set appointed times. While the Hebrew Scriptures generally used *'edah* (and *qahal*, which we will discuss below) to denote any general multitude or assembly,[150] the term specified a legislative body of citizens who *merited* voting rights in the nation's affairs. Today we might say the *'edah* indicated a general body or classification of people, while the *'Edah* designated YHWH's voting assembly. Our discussion will address the *'Edah* as Israel's voting legislative assembly.

The *'Edah* formed the righteous body of people in Israel whose lives exemplified Torah. YHWH expected the *'Edah* to possess the wisdom and understanding of Torah (Deut 4:6) to judge accurately between a murderer and his victim's family.[151] Since the individuals in the *'Edah* actually lived by Torah, they would see how the precepts in YHWH's constitutional Law should apply to any given case. Notice that the account in Joshua (20:4–6) indicates that the congregation would not necessarily have been on hand to judge civil cases when they occurred. Though the city elders had heard the murderer's plea, it was not in their hands to render judgment. Rather, the reluctant murderer had to wait until the assembly convened for his case to be tried. We may assume that these cases were brought before Israel's voting assembly during one of the three annual pilgrimage feasts when all the Israelites came to-gether in Jerusalem.

2. The 'Edah Military

Israel's voting assembly *also* served as an active militia, ready to enforce either the judge's verdict, the congregation's judgment, or the high priest's word, should the need arise (Num 35:25 and *Deut 17:9–13*).

Bring forth him that has cursed without the camp; and let all that heard him lay their hands on his head, and let all the congregation (*'edah*) stone him. (Lev 24:14)

The congregation (*'edah*) sent there twelve thousand men of the most valiant,[152] and commanded them, saying, Go and smite the inhabitants of Jabesh-gilead with the edge of the sword, with the women and the children. (Judg 21:10)

Israel's *'Edah* had a direct interest in military matters.[154] This kept the congregation from voting for policies that would adversely affect military funding during times of duress.[155] The *'Edah's* personal interest in military operations would no doubt restrict the people's willingness to engage their forces in tactics that were not beneficial for the *'Edah* or that had not been sanctioned by the word of YHWH through his priests or prophets (2 Chr 14:11–15:1–8).

The *'Edah* did not function independently of Levi's or Judah-Ephraim's leadership,[156] the tribes that YHWH established to govern the nation. Rather, the *'Edah* was subject to both offices.

> And Moses spoke to YHWH, saying, Let YHWH, the God of the spirits of all flesh, set a man over the congregation (*'edah*), which may go out before them, and which may go in before them, and which may lead them out, and which may bring them in; that the congregation (*'edah*) of YHWH be not as sheep which have no shepherd (Num 27:16). And YHWH said to Moses, Take you Joshua the son of Nun, *a man in whom is the spirit,* and lay your hand on him; and set him before Eleazar the priest, and before all the congregation (*'edah*); and give him a charge in their sight. And you shall put some of your honor on him, that all the congregation (*'edah*) of the Children of Israel may be obedient. (Num 27:15–20; see also Deut 17:12)

The phrases "go out" and "come in" depicted military operations (Josh 14:11).[157] YHWH installed Joshua as a military leader since Israel's primary goal was conquering the Promised Land and driving out the native inhabitants (Num 33:51–54). Joshua inherited Moses' role as leader of the people, while Eleazar stood at his right hand to advise and seek counsel from YHWH.

Israel's constitution allowed verdicts and contractual agreements by any two of the nation's three branches of government: (1) the nation's leader (judge or king), (2) the high priest, or (3) the voting lay assembly.[158] We may theorize that each of these divisions could render judgment in criminal cases (such as adultery, murder, or blasphemy).[159] If there were differences of opinion between the king (judge)[160] and priest regarding judgment or policy issues, the high priest would take the case before the Holy Place for YHWH to decide (Exod 25:22; 30:6; Deut 1:17; 17:8), or he would allow the congregation to cast the deciding voice. Lots were also used where there was no clear-cut evidence regarding which way to judge.[161]

We have pretty good evidence that the *'Edah* was actively involved in state affairs.[162] In Judges 21, the formal *'Edah* came from all their tribes for deliberation. The *'Edah* gave advice with one unified voice in a domestic matter concerning one of Israel's rebellious tribes (Judg 20:7–8). The *'Edah* judged how the rebellious Benjamites should be engaged. In Lev 24:14, the *'Edah* executed judgment once Moses (under YHWH's guidance, Lev 24:12) judged that an Egyptian's crime merited death since the men in the *'Edah* formed the right hand of YHWH's Law and upheld his verdicts (Deut 17:11).

When Joshua, Phinehas, and the congregation believed that the Reubenites, Gaddites, and children of Manasseh had rebelled against YHWH (Josh 22:10–39), the *'Edah* moved to execute righteous judgment (Josh 22:16). When they confronted the northern tribes regarding what they believed was a pagan altar, the congregation sent their princes as representatives to hear the northern tribes' defense.

> And when Phinehas the priest, and the princes of the congregation (*'edah*) and heads of the thousands of Israel which were with him, heard the words that the children of Reuben and the children of Gad and the children of Manasseh spoke, it pleased them. (Josh 22:30)

The matter regarding the Altar of Ed did not concern foreign affairs but was both a theological and political question: Had the northern tribes rebelled against YHWH? This is why Phinehas—the man with the Urim and Thummim—led the nation's representatives while Joshua took a "back seat" to the high priest's authority as Israel's assembly stood ready to enforce Phinehas's verdict.

Once the Monarchy was instituted, it did not function independently of the priesthood. Rather, YHWH established the priesthood to offset the Monarchy's power and ability to depart from his constitutional Law. When King Saul rebelled against YHWH's word through Samuel, the prophet-priest,[163] held Saul accountable, relating that YHWH had rejected him and his House from governing his people (2 Samuel 13). When David sinned, the prophet Nathan denounced his sin by describing the long-lasting animosity that his actions had produced (2 Sam 12:7–12). When Athaliah usurped Judah's throne, the high priest Jehoiada (2 Kgs 11:4) exercised his authority to enthrone Joash as David's rightful heir. Likewise, when Uzziah tried to usurp the authority of the high priesthood, the high priest Azariah resisted the king with a force of 80 military guards (2 Chr 26:17). Thus the priesthood served to hold the Monarchy accountable for its actions.

It is interesting to note that the *'Edah* did not cease to function once the Monarchy was instituted (1 Kgs 8:5).[164] It was the *'Edah* that voted to revolt against Rehoboam's oppressive policies and installed Jeroboam as king (1 Kgs 1:12). When Amon followed Manasseh's wickedness, his servants assassinated him. The "people of the land" (2 Kgs 21:24), no doubt a reference to the *'Edah*, held the conspirators accountable by executing them for treason, installing Josiah (under the direction of the high priest Hilkiah) as David's legitimate heir, once again indicating the incredibly powerful alliance that the priesthood and the *'Edah* enjoyed.

Jeremiah tells us that, in the latter days, YHWH will restore both the priesthood and the monarchy.

> Thus said YHWH; If you can break my covenant of the day, and my covenant of the night, and that there should not be day and night in their season; *Then* may also my covenant be broken with David my servant, that he should *not have a son to reign* on his throne; and with the Levites the priests, my ministers. . . . Consider you not what this people have spoken, saying, The two families which YHWH has chosen, he has even cast them off? thus they have despised my

> people, that they should be no more a nation before them. Thus said YHWH;
> *If my covenant* be not with day and night, and if I have not appointed the ordi-
> nances of heaven and earth; *Then* will I cast away the seed of Jacob, and David
> my servant, so that I will not take any of his seed to be rulers over the seed of
> Abraham, Isaac, and Jacob: for *I will cause their captivity to return, and have
> mercy on them.* (Jer 33:20–21, 24–26)

Jeremiah prophesies that when the Diaspora Covenant has been fulfilled YHWH will again install David's and Phinehas's seed to govern Israel (at least as long as we have a 24-hr. day). Interestingly, Jeremiah also prophesies that, when YHWH reestablishes the nation in the latter days (Jer 30:24) after fulfilling the Diaspora Covenant (Jer 30:18–19), he will reestablish the *'Edah* (Jer 30:20) as well.

> Their children also shall be *as beforetime*, and their congregation (*'edah*) shall
> be established before me, and I will punish all that oppress them. (Jer 30:20)

This text indicates that the *'Edah* existed as another branch of power to withstand oppressive policies that any government (either domestic or foreign) might pursue against the general population. YHWH will reestablish this righteous balance of power in his latter-day government, when the Diaspora Covenant has been fulfilled.

3. Pre-arranged Congressional Assemblies

> Three times in the year shall all *your men* children appear before the Lord
> YHWH, the God of Israel. For I will (a) cast out the nations before you, and
> (b) enlarge your borders: neither shall (c) any man desire your land, when you
> shall go up to appear before YHWH your God three times in the year. (Exod
> 34:23–24)

YHWH promised both (c) peace and (b, a) the acquisition of new territory as being the direct result of obeying this command to attend the nation's three national conventions. When Israel's allies and enemies witnessed Israel's military forces' pilgrimage to Jerusalem, they would approach political relations cautiously: not wanting to attack or invade such a strong nation, capable of avenging insidious actions (Deut 4:5–8). The three annual feasts kept Israel ever-prepared in a manner unprecedented in the ancient world as her Congress addressed military, domestic, judiciary, and international policies during her holy days, when the *'Edah* convened in "the place where YHWH set his name."[165]

The annual feasts kept Israel connected to her God and his Law. At the beginning of every year, Israel's *'Edah* congress began its assembly in YHWH's holy city by renewing the nation's covenant with the Passover sacrifice (pp. 148, 153, 237, 766) This occurred before any legal matters were handled. The Wave Sheaf Offering (*Shavuot*) allowed a quick convening for any pressing issues (Leviticus 23), while the Feast of Tabernacles (*Sukkot*) was a time of festivity and national celebration. During the Release Year Sukkot debts were forgiven and freedom was given to slaves. This provided national solidarity. In addition, entire local communities rested and fellowshipped every Sabbath (Exod 12:16; Lev 23:3). This unity was further strengthened by priests' instruction of Torah, which ensured unity in righteousness.

Throughout YHWH's Law, he encourages his people to "put evil out of the land."[166] As a military force, *the lay congregation and voting assembly were* his right-hand men.[167] They were the power of his arm that stood ready to fulfill his word. Righteousness and justice were not left to the king or priest to enforce; rather, YHWH called on his righteous people to enforce his judgments so that his land did not fall into iniquity. Thus, the 'Edah citizen was the backbone of his government, ensuring that honesty, integrity, and adherence to his Law were passed down to future generations.

4. Qahal vs. the 'Edah

So far, we have seen that Israel's congregation, the *'Edah*, played an important role in the nation's legislative processes. There is another word that describes Israel's assembly whose meaning linguists consider to be almost synonymous with *'Edah*, since the two terms provide textual variety when used in proximity with each other.[168] The term *qahal* also means 'congregation' or 'assembly.'[169] The distinction between *qahal* and *'edah* appears when the text refers to Israel's voting assembly: then *qahal* designates 'a general multitude or gathering' and the *'Edah* applies to Israel's voting congregation. This distinction is readily seen in conjunction with the *'Edah*'s princely rulers and official representatives.

> And Moses called to them; and Aaron and all the rulers (*nasi'*) of the congregation (*'edah*) returned to him: and Moses talked with them. (Exod 34:31)

The word *nasi'* designates a ruler or one who has judicial authority among the people.[170] The term could designate a 'sheikh, chieftain, prince, or judge.' This position was usually a birthright office held by the firstborn families of Israel's tribes.[171] The *nasi'* were the leaders who represented the families in their tribe.

Scripture makes it quite clear that the princes represented only one division of power, authority, in Israel's government.

> That the princes (*nasi'*) of Israel, heads of the house of their fathers, who were the princes (*nasi'*) of the tribes, and were over them that were numbered. (Num 7:2)
>
> These were the renown of the congregation (*'edah*), princes (*nasi'*) of the tribes of their fathers, heads of thousands in Israel. (Num 1:16)

YHWH's command for summoning Israel further delineates the *nasi'* as territorial representatives for their respective clans. When Abiram and Dathan tried to usurp Moses' authority, 250 *nasi'* followed them (Num 16:2). This was only a fraction of the princes found in the nation's congregation or *'Edah*. Thus Israel's voting congregation (the *'Edah*) was very well represented in the nation's legislative processes.

When Zelophehad's daughters sought equal tribal rights, they presented their case to YHWH before Moses, Eleazar the high priest, and the princes of the *'Edah*.

> Then came the daughters of Zelophehad. . . And they stood before Moses, and before Eleazar the priest, and before the princes (*nasi'*) and all the congregation (*'edah*), by the door of the tabernacle of the congregation. (Num 27:1–2)

The *'Edah* were YHWH's right hand, ready to uphold and abide by the verdict that YHWH had spoken through Moses (see Deut 17:9–13). Scripture consistently uses the phrase "princes of the *'Edah*" (*nasi' ha'edah*) to designate Israel's voting assembly.[172] Scripture never uses *qahal* to refer to the rulers of Israel's legislative assembly since *qahal* more often denotes a general gathering.[173] In essence, the *qahal* can be part of the *'Edah,* however; the *qahal* is not always part of the *'Edah*. This is further demonstrated by the elders' association with *'Edah* in the Law of Moses.

> And the elders of the congregation (*'edah*) shall lay their hands on the head of the bullock before YHWH: and the bullock shall be killed before YHWH. (Lev 4:15; see also Judg 21:16)

The elders, like the princes, had a position of authority among the people. Their leadership is again associated with the *'Edah*. YHWH's heraldry statute further clarifies the distinction between the legislative *'Edah* and the lay *qahal*.

YHWH ordained that two trumpets should be blown when the entire *'Edah* was being called together for holy convocations, feasts, and other national affairs (see Illustration 7.1). When only the *'Edah*'s princely representatives (*nasi'*) were needed, only one trumpet was blown. When both trumpets were blown, both the *'Edah* and the princes (*nasi'*) met at the Tabernacle's door (later Temple courtyard).

> Make you two trumpets of silver; of a whole piece shall you make them: that you may use them for the calling of the assembly (*'edah*), and for the journeying of the camps. And when they shall *blow with them*, all the assembly (*'edah*) shall assemble themselves to you at the door of the tabernacle of the congregation. And if they blow but with *one trumpet*, then the princes (*nasi'*), which are heads of the thousands of Israel, shall gather themselves to you. (Num 10:2–4. See also Num 25:6–7 where the *'edah* convened at the door of the Tabernacle when part of the nation joined Baal-peor.)

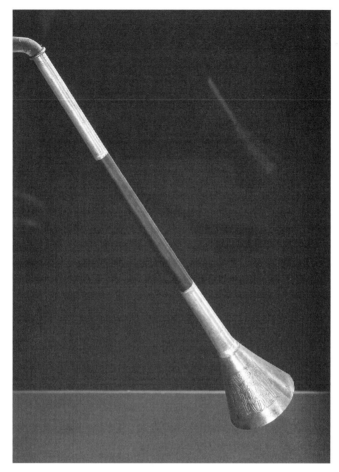

Illustration 7.1. Trumpet from the tomb of Pharaoh Tutankhamen, similar in design to Israel's silver trumpets.

Notice that Israel's legislature did not convene for long periods of time. Rather, the men assembled when matters of state arose or when there was an appointed assembly time.[174] YHWH's protocol for the blowing of trumpets consisted of at least four sorts of heraldry. In the first instance, two horns were used for calling together the general assembly (*'Edah*) or giving the camp marching orders (Num 4:10). Second, when the bugler blast one blow of the trumpet, only the princes of the *'Edah* took counsel (Num 4:10) in deciding policy regarding both domestic and international affairs. The third instance employed trumpets to herald a call to arms or signal troops in battle.[175] And fourth, the trumpets signaled the nation's holy days (Num 10:10; Lev 25:9).

Interestingly, a different type of trumpet heraldry was used for calling together the *'Edah* than for calling together the general *qahal*.

> And when they shall blow with them, all the assembly (*'edah*) shall assemble themselves to you at the door of the tabernacle of the congregation. And if they blow but with *one trumpet,* then the princes (*nasi'*), which are heads of the thousands of Israel, shall gather themselves to you (Num 10:2–4). . . . But when the congregation (*qahal*) is to be gathered together (*qahal*), you shall blow, but you shall not sound an alarm. (Num 10:7)

Notice that the *qahal* is separate from the *'Edah* and the elders. This text strongly indicates that the *'Edah* was a representative division of the larger *qahal*. Another subtle difference between the *'Edah* and the *qahal* was that the *'Edah* seems to have comprised only adult men, eligible to volunteer for war, while the *qahal* included men, women, and children.

For instance, it is the *'Edah* that was commanded to implement the death penalty (Lev 24:14–16; Num 35:15–36). *The qahal is never employed to implement judgment.* When the *'Edah* was numbered (Num 26:1–51), only males eligible for warfare were registered. "Take the sum of all the congregation [*'edah*] of the Children of Israel, from twenty years old and upward, throughout their father's house, *all that are able to go to war in Israel*" (Num 26:2). When the entire *'Edah* was registered, Scripture lists the names and numbers of Israel's families eligible for warfare. Women, children, servants, and *gers* are excluded from this record (with the exception of Asher's daughter, Num 26:46). Further evidence demonstrating that the *'Edah* consisted solely of adult men while the *qahal* included women and children is found in the Book of Joshua:

> There was not a word of all that Moses commanded, which Joshua read not before all the **congregation** (qahal*) of Israel, with the women, and the little ones, and the strangers** that were conversant among them. (Josh 8:35)

Joshua states that the *qahal* consisted of women, children, and *gers*. This was the general congregation, whereas the *'Edah* comprised men, of military age which formed Israel's lay governing body. This conclusion is further supported by the fact that only Israel's males are required to attend the nation's three annual feasts every year.

> Three times in the year *all your males* shall appear before YHWH GOD. (Exod 23:14–17)
>
> Thrice in the year shall all *your men* children appear before the Lord YHWH, the God of Israel. For I will cast out the nations before you, and enlarge your borders: neither shall any man desire your land, when you shall go up to appear before YHWH your God thrice in the year. (Exod 34:23–24)
>
> Three times in a year shall *all your males* appear before YHWH your God in the place which he shall choose; in the feast of unleavened bread, and in the feast of weeks, and in the feast of tabernacles: and they shall not appear before

> YHWH empty: Every man shall give as he is able, according to the blessing of
> YHWH your God which he has given you. (Deut 16:16–17)

YHWH did *not* forbid women and children to come with the *'Edah*. In fact, every seventh year, in the Release Year, YHWH commanded the entire nation, including women, children, and converts, to meet during the Feast of Tabernacles (*Sukkot*) before him in Jerusalem.

> And Moses commanded them, saying, At the end of every seven years, in the solemnity of the year of release, in the feast of tabernacles, When *all Israel* is come to appear before YHWH your God in the place which he shall choose, you shall read this law before all Israel in their hearing. Gather the people together, men, and women, and children, and your stranger that is within your gates, that they may hear, and that they may learn, and fear YHWH your God, and observe to do all the words of this law: And that their children, which have not known anything, may hear, and learn to fear YHWH your God, as long as you live in the land where you go over Jordan to possess it. (Deut 31:10–13)

YHWH did not command women to come up with the men throughout the year because he knew that pregnancy, child-rearing, and feminine hygiene issues (being in a state of *tahor* or uncleanliness) could be a burden or preclude them from travel. (Observe also that YHWH's command for the *ger* to attend the Release Year Feast of Tabernacles demonstrates that YHWH intended his Law for all people.) Later in Israel's history, Ezra and Nehemiah continued to associate the *qahal* with the entire nation, including women, children, and *gers* (Ezra 10:1; Neh 8:2).

The word *qahal* is never used in conjunction with Israel's princes, who had jurisdiction over the people, while the word *'Edah* is consistently used in regard to Israel's princes and elders, who had legislative authority over the nation's tribal territories. When the entire *qahal* met before YHWH every seven years, the priests read the Law to the entire nation (see Nehemiah 8; cf. 8:18), when the nation reconfirmed her commitment to YHWH's constitutional covenant (Deut 31:10–13). *Observance of the feasts, circumcision, and righteousness were only the first qualifications for membership in the congressional* 'Edah. YHWH wisely introduced additional stipulations for membership in his assembly so it could not be led astray by foreign or conflicting political interests.

5. Membership

a. Land Ownership

Membership in the elite "Edah assembly was tied to ownership of arable lands. This meant that only Israel's *ezrach* citizens could vote.[176] *Gers* could join the ezrach membership after 3 or 10 generations (see below) lived in Israel and had been upstanding citizens. The fact that tribal lands qualified voting rights appears to have naturally barred the nation's Levitical government from voting in the assembly. Their role was to teach, instruct, and perhaps even "lobby" for righteous causes; however, as recipients of the nation's tithes and members of a separate judiciary body, it is theorized that they were not allowed to vote for policies because of the potential for conflicts of interest. The Levites were not left without representation, however. The chief of their clan, the high priest, possessed final authority. It was his role to seek YHWH's final judgment in all matters (Exod 28:30; Deut 17:12; Num 27:15–20).

b. Righteousness

Israel's legislative assembly constituted a proven righteous body of people who voted on national matters. Though many families in Israel were native citizens or had converted, citizenship did *not necessarily* guarantee membership in YHWH's elite, *'Edah* congregation. YHWH based admittance into his righteous assembly on an individual's standing as a law-abiding citizen, which for Israel meant an individual's obedience to Torah.[177] This policy created a righteously wise body of people (Deut 4:6) who possessed the understanding to participate in and help direct the nation's policies.

The Law distinguished between common citizens and membership in Israel's elite congressional assembly. Although all *gers* readily obtained citizenship in Israel, not all *gers* could participate in the nation's voting assembly (*'Edah* or *qahal*). YHWH even placed restrictions on lawless native-born (*ezrach*) citizens, barring their participation in the nation's legislative and judicial affairs.

The first and primary qualification for membership or voice in the *'Edah* was that the citizen walk in the way of YHWH. "Therefore the ungodly shall not stand in the judgment, nor sinners in the congregation (*'edah*) of the righteous" (Ps 1:5). Righteousness was the second requirement for participation in YHWH's voting assembly (land ownership was the first, see above). YHWH promised his blessings to the nation through her compliance and love for his covenantal Law. Through the people's faithfulness, he could guarantee the nation's health, economic strength, security, and knowledge of him. He knew that achieving a righteous society did not simply occur by having a king or priest that sought counsel from him. The people also needed to live righteously in order to desire to follow their leadership.

When a person departed from YHWH's Law, the Creator banned him from participating in the voting assembly:

> Seven days shall there be no leaven found in your houses: for whosoever eats that which is leavened, even that soul shall be cut off (*karath*) from the congregation (*'edah*) of Israel, whether he be a stranger (*ger*), or born in the land (*ezrach*). (Exod 12:19)

> But the man that shall be unclean, and shall not purify himself, that soul shall be cut off (*karath*) from among the congregation (*qahal*), because he has defiled the sanctuary of YHWH: the water of separation has not been sprinkled on him; he is unclean. (Num 19:20)

The exact meaning of *karath,* translated "cut off," is uncertain.[178] In some contexts, it seems mean 'excommunication,'[179] yet in other instances it implies 'death,' perhaps depending on the crime committed.[180] What is certain is that, either way, a person could not participate in Israel's sanctified assemblies if he failed to: observe Passover and the prohibition on unleavened bread (Exod 12:19; Num 9:13–3); if he remained unclean (Num 19:20; Lev 7:20–21, 25–27; 19:8; 22:3); if he neglected to be circumcised (Gen 17:14); if he participated in immoral acts such as homosexuality or incest (Lev 18:29; 20:17–18); if he compounded the holy anointing oil (Exod 30:33, 38); if he sacrificed his child to Molech (Lev 20:3–6); if he failed to afflict himself on the Day of Atonement (Lev 23:29–30); or if he worked on the Sabbath day (Exod 31:14). *In every instance, a person banned or "cut off" from YHWH's congregation had rebelled against YHWH's covenant;* thus there is a word-play between "cutting a sacrifice" as the symbolic act of covenanting with God, and YHWH's "cutting off," which referred to the penalty for breach of pact. In every instance, "cutting off" played on this idea by removing the rebellious individual from the covenant's direct legislative benefit. In every instance, a person's righteousness and adherence to YHWH's covenantal Law were the qualifying factors for eligibility to participate in the 'Edah.

c. Eunuchs

A majority of the stipulations for membership in the congregation (*qahal*) of Israel are found in Deuteronomy 23. These stipulations not only dealt with membership in the 'Edah but also stipulated qualifications for the general congregation. The first stipulation forbade eunuchs to enter the nation's voting assembly or the general congregation:

> He that is wounded in the stones, or has his privy member cut off, shall not enter into the congregation (*qahal*) of YHWH. (Deut 23:1)

Although Deuteronomy appears to exclude eunuchs from the general assembly, the author probably intended the term to denote the congressional 'Edah.[181] Isaiah (56:3–8) clarifies that YHWH accepted a eunuch who took hold of his covenant and allowed him in the sacred Temple precincts. "Their burnt offerings and their sacrifices shall be accepted on my altar; for my house shall be called an house of prayer for all people" (Isa 56:7).

Throughout the ancient world, powerful rulers practiced male mutilation. Rulers discovered that, without properly functioning male genitalia, a man became more docile and submissive.[182] Even in our modern world, equestrians will render a stud a gelding so that the horse is more manageable. The lords and leaders of the ancient world discovered that, when a man lost both his ability to procreate and the strength of his testes, he lost the desire to seek his own well-being, which caused him to become loyal to the state.

YHWH's prohibition on eunuchs in his congregation primarily discouraged the practice.[183] He also saw that eunuchs lacked the strength to make tough decisions. Their condition naturally caused them to become softer and overly empathetic of others placed in situations beyond their control. For the eunuch, tough issues could become clouded, and they might pity an evil-doer (Deut 7:16; 13:8; 19:13, 21; 25:12).

Ancient cultures viewed children differently than most modern Westerners. Children were not only a joy and a delight, but they perpetuated their father's name, honor, and remembrance for future generations. A man's name and memory did not die with him, as customary today. Rather, future generations remembered a father's legacy and enjoyed the fruit of the labor invested in the family's land heritage. Because most eunuchs lacked offspring, they might lack the interest in seeking the welfare of the nation's future generations.

d. Converts from Hostile Nations

After YHWH delivered Israel out of Egypt, his people roamed the desert for 40 years. They were weary refugees migrating to a new land. When they sought to pass through Ammon's and Moab's territories, not only were they denied, but these hostile nations hired a prophet to curse and attempt to destroy Israel (Num 21:21–29). YHWH saw these actions and the hatred that accompanied them so heinous that they merited eternal consequences in relation to international and domestic affairs between the two nations.

> An Ammonite or Moabite shall not enter into the congregation of YHWH; even (a) *to their tenth generation* shall they not enter into the congregation of YHWH forever: Because they met you not with bread and with water in the way, when you came forth out of Egypt; and because they hired against you Balaam the son of Beor of Pethor of Mesopotamia, to curse you. Nevertheless YHWH your God would not listen to Balaam; but YHWH your God turned the curse into a blessing to you, because YHWH your God loved you. (b) You shall not seek their peace nor their prosperity all your days forever. (Deut 23:3–6)

Ammon and Moab's hatred of and utter contempt for Israel was a threat to the nation's security (as Iran is to the modern state). So YHWH barred even converts (*gers*) from hostile nations from participating in Israel's voting assembly. Though converts (*gers*) from these nations could be accepted in Israel and were granted equal citizenship, they could not lobby or vote in international or domestic affairs. This ban protected Israel from spies and political agendas that could be fronted under the auspices of conversion. This policy protected the country's security and overall well-being.

The wisdom of YHWH's exclusion of Ammonites and Moabites became evident in postexilic Judea. When the Second Temple Remnant failed to observe this prohibition, both the priests (Neh 13:28) and the congregation were willing to consider the best interests of Tobiah the Ammonite (Neh 4:3), who despised anyone who sought Israel's well-being (Neh 2:10). Tobiah and his comrades manipulated Israel's assembly (the *Knesset Gedolah* or Great Assembly) to serve their treacherous interests rather than YHWH's or his people's interests. The Remnant's voting assembly (not the *'Edah* but the *Knesset Gedolah*) foolishly supported their enemies' agendas and opinions to their own detriment (a situation that tends to plague many Western nations today).

When an Ammonite or Moabite did convert to serving YHWH (these were converts from hostile nations), God allotted (a) 10 generations to pass before these converts' children could join Israel's voting assembly. This prohibition prevented sedition and conspiracy against YHWH's people by foreigners who hated YHWH's people (perhaps an ancient form of anti-Semitism). While one, two, or even three generations might plot against YHWH's people to incite the congregation to policies that benefited the convert's former homeland or their own personal agendas, by the 10th generation (about 250–300 years), the *ger*'s family would have become fully grafted into Israel (by intermarrying with *ezrach*s for several generations). The foreigner's philosophy would change and grow as his family observed YHWH's Law, which would have caused him to love YHWH and his people. He and his children would begin to think of themselves as Israelites, not a foreigners.

The second stipulation that YHWH ordained regarding the nation's enemies (b) prohibited Israel's assembly from ever seeking policies that benefited their hostile Ammonite or Moabite neighbors. Today, we might equate this with a constitutional sanction or embargo. YHWH knew that Israel would become a powerful and wealthy nation by observing his Law (Deut 28:13; 4:6). YHWH wisely understood that if Israel ever allowed economic, military, or domestic policies to favor her enemies that Israel's blessings might spill over to strengthen her enemies and be used to fund her enemies' agendas against her.

e. Converts from Allied Nations

Converts from Israel's allies, such as Egypt or Edom, were welcomed into Israel's elite congregation (Deut 23:7–8). After three Torah-observant generations had lived on Israel's soil (Deut 23:8), converted Egyptians and Edomites (*gers*) were granted membership in the national *'Edah* congregation.

> You shall not abhor an Edomite; for he is your brother: you shall not abhor an Egyptian; because you were a stranger in his land. The children that are begotten of them shall enter into the congregation of YHWH *in their third generation*. (Deut 23:7–8)

YHWH did not consider converts from peaceable nations to be a threat to Israel's welfare as converts from hostile nations might be. Three generations were sufficient to deter sedition against his holy people. The Egyptian especially could relate to Israelites' leaving the house of bondage[184] when they migrated to Israel. From historical and archaeological sources, we know that not only did Egypt oppress foreigners, the pharaohs oppressed their own people, because Egyptians spent half the year working for the kingdom through corvée labor.[185] This sharply contrasts with the incredible freedom that YHWH gave to Israel within his Law—freedom most other nations could not even fathom. When an Egyptian left his former house of bondage to unite himself with Israel and her God, he came to understand Israel's history and relate to her past because he too had left Egypt's "house of bondage."[186]

f. Exclusion from Voting in the 'Edah *Did Not Negate the Convert's Importance*

Although YHWH forbade eunuchs and the first few generations of foreign converts to participate in legislative voting, Scripture makes it clear that this regulation did not preclude YHWH from loving the convert or eunuch less.

> Neither let the son of the *stranger* (*nechar*), that has joined himself to YHWH, speak, saying, YHWH has utterly separated me from his people: neither let the *eunuch* say, Behold, I am a dry tree. For thus said YHWH to the eunuchs that keep my sabbaths, and choose the things that please me, and take hold of my covenant; Even to them will I give in my house and within my walls a place and a name better than of sons and of daughters: I will give them an everlasting name, that shall not be cut off. (Isa 56:3–5)

Isaiah makes it clear that, even though YHWH had deferred the converted *nechar*'s participation and forbidden the eunuch's participation in the 'Edah, his intention was not to separate them from his chosen people. He loved converts and eunuchs and desired that they worship and obey him the same as any child of Israel. In many ways, his prohibition against *nechar*s and eunuchs in the voting assembly protected them as much as it did the *ezrach*. Immigrants and eunuchs were just as vulnerable as the *ezrach* should the *qahal* or 'Edah stray from YHWH and his constitutional Law. YHWH's prohibition on their voice in his assembly protected their interests as well as the native citizen's.

The exclusion of the convert from the 'Edah did not prevent him from keeping YHWH's covenant or coming into his holy Temple.

> Also the sons of the stranger (*nechar*), that join themselves to YHWH, to serve him, and to love the name of YHWH, to be his servants, every one that keeps the sabbath from polluting it, and takes hold of my covenant; Even them will I bring to my holy mountain, and make them joyful in my house of prayer: their burnt offerings and their sacrifices shall be accepted on my altar; for my house shall be called an house of prayer for all people. (Isa 56:6–7)

YHWH accepted the prayers, offerings, and sacrifices of the convert as he did those of the native citizen. YHWH freely accepted and loved the foreign convert, desiring that he come before him to submit petitions and offer his sacrifices and offerings.

g. Mamzers *and the Terminally Contagious*

Converts and eunuchs were not the only citizens whose membership in Israel's congregation was deferred for a few generations. YHWH also barred the *mamzer*, or illegitimate child, from entering the *qahal* for 10 generations (about 250–300 years):

> A bastard (*mamzer*) shall not enter into the congregation (*qahal*) of YHWH;
> even to his tenth generation shall he not enter into the congregation of YHWH.
> (Deut 23:2)

YHWH's ban on the *mamzer* served at least two functions. First, YHWH sought to discourage bearing children out of wedlock. He knew how damaging illegitimacy was for the child who lacked fatherly affection. Many recent studies have shown that a father's role in a child's life is essential to his emotional, psychological, and overall well-being.[187] This was especially true in Israel's patriarchal system, where men formed the backbone of society. YHWH saw that illegitimacy degraded the nation's moral values, placing children at risk of poverty since their livelihood and economic stability depended on tribal lands inherited from the father. If a child did not know who his father was, or if the father rejected the claim, the child would have no land heritage. Not only would the child be deprived of the rich legacy from his father's relations, but he would also face hardships and be at risk of slavery and poverty because he lacked land and sustenance to support his own family. This stipulation strengthened the nation's Morality Code by placing longlasting consequences on immorality while preserving the nation's moral standards.

Second, YHWH saw that corrupt moral standards under which illegitimate children had been raised could warp and degrade the judgment of his righteous law-abiding congregation. Their voice in Israel's affairs would no doubt tend toward leniency and pity (Deut 7:16; 13:8; 19:13, 21; 25:12) when circumstances had not merited mercy. An illegitimate, non-land-holding child did not have a vested interest in the land to support policies that benefited the long-term tribal inheritances. Their voice in Israel's assembly could be just as devastating as the insincere *nechar* who converted for seditious purposes because their opinions could lead Israel away from following YHWH's Law.

The only group excluded from membership in Israel's national assembly altogether was the contagious or permanently "unclean" group of people, who could be seen as a threat to the congregation's health.[188]

> And the leper in whom the plague is, his clothes shall be rent, and his head bare, and he shall put a covering on his upper lip, and shall cry, Unclean, unclean. All the days wherein the plague shall be in him he shall be defiled; he is unclean: he shall dwell alone; without the camp shall his habitation be. (Lev 13:46)

YHWH intended for his sacred Temple precincts to be a place of life and health. To this end, he only allowed persons who were clean (*tahor*) to could come into YHWH's sanctuary (Lev 7:20–21, 25–27; Num 19:13). If a person was in an unclean state, either by his/her own actions or by coming in contact with someone (or something) who was unclean, then she also became unclean and could not enter the Temple until he/she became clean again. This injunction also limited the power that the priests could assume in matters of healthcare and its delivery (see pp. 181–89). In this way, YHWH preserved the overall health, integrity, and sound judgment of his strongly wise people (Deut 4:6).

I. The Court

Courts in the ancient Near East functioned a little differently from courts today. First, no distinction was made between criminal and civil cases.[189] YHWH's Law was a living constitution—the law of the land—and its precepts could be applied to all cases. Second, Israel's court system, similar to its government, was family based.

At the time of Israel's exodus, Jethro, who may have been a descendant of Abraham and a Midianite priest, counseled Moses to establish judges throughout the nation to execute justice and judgment (Exod 18:14–23). When Moses met with YHWH on Mt. Sinai, the Creator confirmed this counsel, ordaining standards by which the nation should establish her judgments. When the nation recovenanted with YHWH in Moab, Moses recounted these events, reiterating the command for righteous judgments in Israel's courts.

> Take you wise men, and understanding, and known among your tribes, and I will make them rulers over you. And you answered me, and said, The thing which you have spoken is good for us to do. So I (a) took the chief of your tribes, wise men, and known, and made them heads over you, (b) captains over thousands, and captains over hundreds, and captains over fifties, and captains over tens, and officers among your tribes. And I charged your judges at that time, saying, Hear the causes between your brothers, and *judge righteously* between every man and his brother, *and the stranger that is with him.* You shall not respect persons in judgment; but you shall hear the small as well as the great; you shall not be afraid of the face of man; (c) for the judgment is God's: and (d) the cause that is too hard for you, bring it to me, and I will hear it. And I commanded you at that time all the things which you should do. (Deut 1:13–18)

Moses established Israel's judicial system through tribal judicial hierarchies. Wise leaders (chiefs) among Israel's (a) clans became tribal judges in the 'Edah. Clans were further divided, with (b) officers over them who carried out the judges' verdicts.[190] Moses stated (c) that, when a judge followed YHWH's judgments, he was acting as the Creator's agent. Consequently, the only thing a citizen needed to fear was failing to uphold YHWH's Law.

Notice that YHWH was not involved in every decision, nor did his theocratic government dictate every choice that Israel's 'Edah or the judges made. Rather, YHWH placed judgment in the hands of the people, ordaining self-government based on his constitutional Law.[191] Only when difficult (d) judicial matters or other questions of national policy arose did the people appeal directly to YHWH at his Tabernacle (e.g., Zelophehad's daughters, Exod 30:6; Num 7:89). It may very well be that cases could be appealed to the Levites, who may have served as an appellate court, especially for cases that involved inter-clan issues on which the judges' impartiality might be questioned.[192] The priest or king had the final jurisdiction as he sought counsel between the cherubim (Exod 25:22; Ps 99:1, 4, 6).

Israel's judges had two responsibilities: to uphold the Law and to grant mercy when it was warranted.[193] Never could a judge change the constitutional Law (Deut 4:2; 12:32), but he could defer penalty when there was lack of intent or other mitigating circumstances. This established a nonarbitrary judiciary, whose standards were never lowered due to trends or popular opinions.

Israel's court judged each case independently, based on its own merits. Witnesses were summoned to provide evidence, and the death penalty only applied if there were at least two or three witnesses (Deut 17:6–7).[194] Never could the testimony of one witness result in the defendant's death (Num 35:30).

People were *not* the only "witnesses" to crime or to the exoneration of it.

> Objects could also serve as physical evidence in court. According to Exodus 22:12, a herdsman who loses an animal to the predations of wild beasts is not liable to the owner for its replacement. The law, requires, however, that the herdsman bring as evidence the remains of the carcass, which the text actually calls a "witness" (*'ed*).[195]

Today, we call this type of witness "evidence." In the modern sense the Torah would consider forensic and DNA "witnesses" to be as compelling testimony in a court case, just as a dead carcass or a bride's last menstrual rags were in ancient times (Deut 22:13–19).

The judge's verdict was usually final although "there is some evidence that an appeal could be made to the king if one of the parties was not satisfied with the decision of the clan or judge (2 Sam 14:5). Cases were tried at the city gate, sometimes in the presence of the whole community; and these occasions called for great oratorical skill. Difficult cases were heard by the king himself (1 Kgs 3:16)."[196] Although similar cases may have provided good case studies in difficult situations, they did not necessarily constitute a rigid precedent for other cases to follow. Rather, the values, precepts, and principles governing the constitutional laws that YHWH gave at Mt. Sinai were applied to all cases when new situations arose. Thus, Israel's judges based their verdicts on the nation's constitutional Law and were not swayed by circumstances that were not relevant to new trials: the constitution was always the standard.

A little later, Moses again issued a command for Israel's elders to execute judgment as defined by YHWH's Law:

> Judges and officers shall you make you in all your gates, which YHWH your God gives you, throughout your tribes: and they shall judge the people with just judgment (Deut 16:18). . . . And you shall come to the priests the (a) Levites, and to the (b) judge that shall be in those days, and inquire; and they shall (c) show you the sentence of judgment: and (d) you shall do according to the sentence, which they of that (e) place which YHWH shall choose shall show you; and you shall observe to do according to all that they inform you:

> According to the sentence of *the law which they shall teach you,* and according
> to the judgment which they shall tell you, you shall do: you shall not decline
> from the sentence which they shall show you, to the right hand, nor to the left.
> And the man that will do presumptuously, and will not listen to the priest that
> stands to minister there before YHWH your God, or to the judge, (f) even that
> man shall die: and you shall put away the evil from Israel. And all the people
> shall hear, and fear, and do no more presumptuously. (Deut 17:9–13)

As the nation's instructors of justice, legal counsel was one of the Levites' (c) primary functions. The Levites may have (a) served as an appellate court.[197] They bore responsibility for correctly advising judges and their families on YHWH's Law. Family elders and chiefs of the 'Edah answered directly to (b) the high priest, the nation's supreme judge, who resided (e) at the capital seat of government.[198] The Tabernacle was at the capital, so YHWH's counsel was never far off. When the Levites (d) gave counsel, it was the people's responsibility to obey their judgment. If a person rebelled against their decree, he or she was put to death so that (f) "evil could be put away from Israel" (Deut 13:5; 17:7, 12; 19:19; 21:21; 22:22–24; 24:7).

During the Monarchy, local communities became corrupt and faced threats from biased judgments. Jehoshaphat reinstalled Levitical judges to hold the local community accountable (2 Chr 17:2, 7–9). These new court officers were "responsible to the king for the administration of justice in the districts under their control, and could rely on the support of the troops under their command to enforce their authority."[199] While local elders still played an important role in justice and policies established for their tribes, their authority was held in check by the Levites who acted as an impartial appellate court.[200]

Another advancement that Israel acquired under the Monarchy was the possibility of pardon, which was a totally separate function from an appeal process.[201] Today in America, both state governors and the president hold the power to pardon criminals without the consent of a court or other governing body. In Israel, this right was held solely by the king himself. We have a good example of how this process worked from a case presented before King David. One son had murdered his brother. The mother came to the king to ask for her son's pardon so that their family line was not extinguished in Israel (2 Sam 14:4). King David granted the one-time pardon, but under one condition: that the mother who sought the pardon take a self-imprecating oath should the son or his descendants continue to rebel against the covenant. David established this requirement so that he did not bear any future guilt should the woman's son again commit murder; David and his House would be free from the guilt incurred.

YHWH ordained the 'Edah to uphold Israel's Law (see pp. 253–58). Its standing militia was ready to enforce the court's decision. If a case was appealed to the high priest, who sought YHWH's counsel between the cherubim (Exod 25:22), the 'Edah stood ready to enforce his verdict. This ensured that people knew right away that there were consequences for evil actions, while granting relief to those who had been injured by another. In this manner YHWH's court system ensured that his land would increase in unity and brotherly love (see Table 7.4).

Table 7.4. Israel's Court System

YHWH
(Consitutional Covenant)

Priest

King

Appeal

Court System

Tribal/family
(State/municipal)

Levitical
(Federal)

J. Constitutionally Defined: Freedom of Speech

As we have seen thus far, YHWH ordained a free and limited system of self-government. This system is relatively similar to modern Western nations' governing systems except that its organization was tribe-based, both with regard to the land and within the family. YHWH's Law was ancient Israel's constitution. Not wholly dissimilar from modern constitutions, it was the apparatus that both ordained and preserved the freedom of God's people, protecting them from the "house of bondage."[202] Whereas modern constitutions are based on ideological statements that direct national policies and sanction the nation's functions, YHWH's constitution went beyond this archetype. Not only did YHWH's constitutional Law define and sanction the role that Israel's citizens and the Levites would play, but he provided practical laws that defined how his constitution should function in the real world.

For instance, the constitutional Ten Commandments prohibited stealing. While most constitutions simply define a concept, YHWH's law then established how the crime should be dealt with by listing possible situations (Exod 22:1–14). This helped both to limit spurious interpretations of his constitution and provide a model for applying fair and equitable consequences for violation. In another area, his constitutional Law ordained taxes but limited both the Levites' and the indigents' claim to taxes at 10%. This would be in contrast to apparatuses, such as the U.S. Constitution, that give power to the government to collect taxes and borrow on debt but do not establish its limits.[203]

The lack of these stipulations is what has allowed the U.S. government to assume debts well beyond its means and tax its citizenry excessively. Not only does this Constitutional ambiguity weaken the nation, it results in vast internal strife, conflict, and "class warfare." The end result is oppression and an ever-decreasing standard of living for the entire nation as the U.S. "becomes the tail," and stronger, less-debt-laden nations become the "head" (Deut 28:13, 44).

YHWH's constitutional Law discouraged national debt, pointing out that it would cause the nation to become the poorest and weakest of all nations (Deut 28:13). If Israel observed YHWH's constitution, she would become wealthy, allowing her to lend to many nations. But if she failed to follow his constitutional Law, she would only be able to borrow, thus becoming a vassal to all the nations around her (Deut 28:44).

Unlike the U.S. Constitution, which has demonstrated inadequacies, YHWH considered his Law perfect. The genius in YHWH's Law was that it provided specific and examples (precedents) about how it should be applied. Thus, YHWH considered his constitution full and complete: perfect (Ps 19:7). For this reason, he forbade any king, priest, member of the 'Edah or, qahal, or prophet from amending his constitution.

> You shall not add to the word which I command you, neither shall you diminish anything from it, that you may keep the commandments of YHWH your God which I command you. (Deut 4:2)
>
> What thing soever I command you, observe to do it: *you shall not add it it, nor diminish from it.* (Deut 12:32)

This injunction against amendment in the Deuteronomic law code thwarted attempts to change the covenantal Law's philosophical precepts (ethics). It also thwarted attempts to change *how* the Law should be applied. Thus it allowed Israel's constitutional Law to remain an archetype for society. Ultimately, it preserved the intent of YHWH's Law, his truth, thereby protecting it from the hand any later redactors.

Amendments to the constitution were not the only threat YHWH saw that Israel's society faced. The nation could not reach the harmony, unity, or blessing he had in mind for them if they did not uphold the constitution that ordained their freedom from oppression. To this end, he placed very *specific* limitations on free speech.

> Cursed be he that *confirms not* all the words of this law to do them. And all the people shall say, Amen. (Deut 27:26)

YHWH placed a curse in his Law against anyone who spoke against the validity of his constitutional and covenantal Law. This did *not* mean that valid debate could not transpire about how the Law should be applied or its intent. **But what it** did condemn **were those who sought to expunge the Law from society or proposed that his covenantal Law was no longer valid for their generation.** It would be similar to enacting a Law that prohibits U.S. citizens from discrediting the U.S. Constitution—to undermine the Constitution would be national suicide that would deliver America, like Israel, over to tyranny.[204] Notice also that this text did *not* curse people for failing to obey the Law (i.e., "to do the Law") but cursed them for speaking against the validity of the Law.

Table 7.5. Israel's Theocratic Government

YHWH to Be Sought at the Mercy Seat

Constitutional Covenant

	King	Priest	Edah Senate	Edah Congress	Qahal
Membership	Son of David through Solomon	Son of Phinehas through Zadok	Tribal Leader	Every Law-Abiding, Tribal land-holding citizen Mamzers after 10 generations Ger from friendly nations after 3 generations Ger from hostile nations after 10 generation	Men, Women, Children, Converts
Funtion	National & Military Leader	Ensure nation is compliant w/covenant (Supreme Court)	Foreign and Domestic	Judge in capital punishment cases; Militia; Domestic policy	Physically assemble in Jerusalem to participate in covenant renewal every 7 yrs
Court Function	Higher court: Judge in civil & criminal matters	Supreme court: Judge in civil & criminal matters	Lower court: Civil policies	Lower court: Criminal	N/A

Personal Relationship with God

Similar to protecting and strengthening the family unit, YHWH sought to protect Israel as a cultural society. YHWH's injunction on this particular aspect of free speech both preserved the honor and integrity of his covenantal constitution while unifying the citizens along common ethical, philosophical, political, and theological ideologies. He forbade progressive movements that sought to expand or restrict responsibilities under his Law.

Along these lines, YHWH placed one other limit on free speech.

> You shall not revile the gods, nor curse the ruler of your people. (Exod 22:28; see also Exod 20:12)

The use of "gods" (*elohiym*) in this text probably refers to YHWH as the nation's supreme deity.[205] This injunction prohibited cursing YHWH or those bearing jurisdiction in the government as his representatives. YHWH defined Israel's government. To curse the king or officials who represent "powers ordained of God, are in his stead, and represent him" was seen as a curse against YHWH's will.[206]

It may be remembered that cursing in Scripture meant issuing a negative prophecy against someone. When Shimei came to curse David, he issued a negative prophecy against YHWH's anointed.

> And thus said Shimei when he cursed, Come out, come out, you bloody man, and you man of Belial: YHWH has returned on you all the blood of the House of Saul, in whose stead you have reigned; and YHWH has delivered the kingdom into the hand of Absalom your son: and, behold, you are taken in your mischief, because you are a bloody man. (2 Sam 16:7–8)

The Benjaminite's curse negatively prophesied against David and his kingship. Shimei spoke in YHWH's name without YHWH's direction (Deut 19:20–22). This act stirred up greater strife between Benjamin (Saul) and Judah (David), thus fracturing a nation already on the brink of civil war (Absalom). YHWH's injunction against cursing God or the king sought to preserve national unity and harmonize ethical values. YHWH did not prohibit discussing political issues, but he did prohibit the public act of cursing. It may be remembered that YHWH had already ordained a balance of power in Israel's government system. Should there be an issue with a local judge, Levite, or the king himself, the matter could be appealed all the way to the nation's supreme counsel—the high priest to YHWH. But to issue a negative prophecy (curse) against the king did not benefit the nation in any way. YHWH sought to save his people from oppression, instilling in them the value of harmony and brotherly love, so they could enjoy the peace that observing his covenant afforded (see Table 7.5).

What did YHWH see as the end result of following his constitutionally defined government?

> Behold, I have taught you statutes and judgments, even as YHWH my God commanded me, that you should do so in the land where you go to possess it. Keep therefore and do them; for this is your wisdom and your understanding in the sight of the nations, which shall hear all these statutes, and say, Surely this great nation is a wise and understanding people. For what nation is there so great, who has God so nigh to them, as YHWH our God is in all things that we call upon him for? And what nation is there so great, that has statutes and judgments so righteous as all this law, which I set before you this day? (Deut 4:5–8)

III. THE MOABIC COVENANT: HARMONY OF DOCTRINE

One of YHWH's chief roles as God is to judge the earth by rewarding the righteous, condemning the wicked, and saving the disadvantaged from oppression.[207] "He does execute the judgment of the fatherless and widow, and loves the stranger, in giving him food and raiment" (Deut 10:18). YHWH desired to save the disadvantaged from bondage. After the exodus, however, YHWH saw that Israel did not delight to walk in his ways or to worship him alone, so he judged Israel and strengthened his Law in order that "man may no more oppress" (Ps 10:18) his brethren.[208]

As we have seen in this chapter, the statutes and judgments that YHWH gave to Israel at Mt. Sinai—had Israel followed them—would have abolished both poverty and the slavery system altogether (Deut 15:4). Since Israel despised YHWH's judgments, he added further stipulations in order to protect Hebrew slaves from oppression. YHWH's original judgment had commanded Israel to release her Hebrew servants at the Release Year, providing no compensation for the slave's service.

> If you buy an Hebrew servant, six years he shall serve: and in the seventh he shall go out free for nothing. (Exod 21:2)

When YHWH saw that Israel despised his judgments, such as those forbidding usury (Exod 22:25), he foresaw that her usury and oppression would continually afflict her poor brethren, never allowing them to achieve financial independence. So he added another stipulation to his Law commanding Israelites to pay their slaves upon their release from service.

> And if your brother, a Hebrew man, or a Hebrew woman, be sold to you, and serve you six years; then in the seventh year you shall let him go free from you. And when you send him out free from you, you shall not let him go away empty: You shall furnish him liberally out of your flock, and out of your floor, and out of your winepress: of that which YHWH your God has blessed you you shall give to him. (Deut 15:12–14)

The Moabic Covenant added an injunction to the release of Hebrew slaves stipulating that slave owners release their brethren with gifts at the end their service. This judgment served as an injunction against Israel's disdain of YHWH's former statutes and judgments, which protected the poor and the disadvantaged from the stronger citizen preying on them. But notice that this injunction had no long-term effect for Israel's citizens. If Israel followed YHWH's statutes and his judgments regarding the Release Year, the Jubilee, and his judgment on usury (lending with interest on consumer debt, Exod 22:25), Hebrew slavery would have been abolished altogether, and there would be no need for Israel to give compensation. YHWH did not increase the wealthy citizens' taxation; he simply had those who had benefited from indentured service offer compensation to enable the poor to "get back on their feet." YHWH's *compensation injunction* did not contradict his former judgment: the Creator still sought to free the disadvantaged from oppression. The doctrine and ethics of his Law remained constant.

Shortly before entering Canaan to claim the nation's inheritance, Israel recovenanted with God. YHWH ordained that the Moabic Covenant contracted "this day" in Moab should override or supersede the covenant made at Mt. Sinai.

> You shall keep therefore his statutes, and his commandments, which I command you this day, that it may go well with you, and with your children after you, and that you may prolong your days on the earth, which YHWH your God gives you, forever. (Deut 4:40; see also Deut 32:46)

> YHWH our God made a covenant with us in Horeb. YHWH made not this covenant with our fathers, but with us, even us, who are all of us here alive this day. (Deut 5:2–3)

> And now, Israel, what does YHWH your God require of you, but to fear YHWH your God, to walk in all his ways, and to love him, and to serve YHWH your God with all your heart and with all your soul, To keep the commandments of YHWH, and his statutes, which I command you *this day* for your good? (Deut 10:12–13)

> And what nation is there so great, that has statutes and judgments so righteous as all this law, which I set before you *this day*? Only take heed to yourself, and keep your soul diligently, lest you forget the things which your eyes have seen, and lest they depart from your heart all the days of your life: but teach them your sons, and your sons' sons. (Deut 4:8–9; see also Deut 6:16–17; 7:11–15; 8:1; 11:32; 27:9–10; 30:2, 8)

When Moses says, "Obey the statutes, judgments, and commands that I command unto you *this day*," he is referring to the Moabic-Shechem Covenant that YHWH made with Israel during the time she lived on the plains of Moab shortly before the nation entered Canaan (Deut 5:3; 29:1). Most scholars refer to this as the Deuteronomic Law or Deuteronomic Covenant.[209] YHWH wanted Israel to follow the Moabic Covenant's injunctions against oppression and rebellion instead of the less-stringent Sinai Covenant. To this end, he added a constitutional amendment forbidding anyone— priest, prophet, king, or citizen—to add to Deuteronomy's constitutional Law or take away from it.

> You shall not add to the word which I command you, neither shall you diminish ought from it, that you may keep the commandments of YHWH your God which I command you. (Deut 4:2)

> What thing soever I command you, observe to do it: you shall not add to it, nor diminish from it. (Deut 12:32)

> Behold, I set before you this day a blessing and a curse; A blessing, if you obey the commandments of YHWH your God, which I command you *this day:*[210] And a curse, if you will not obey the commandments of YHWH your God, but turn aside out of the way which I command you this day, to go after other gods, which you have not known. (Deut 11:26–28; see also Deut 30:15–20)

> Cursed be he that confirms not all the words of this law to do them. And all the people shall say, Amen. (Deut 27:26)

> Beware that you forget not YHWH your God, in not keeping his commandments, and his judgments, and his statutes, which I command you this day: (Deut 8:11)

> If you will not observe to do all the words of this law that are written in this book, that you may fear this glorious and fearful name, YHWH YOUR GOD; Then YHWH will make your plagues wonderful, and the plagues of your seed, even great plagues, and of long continuance, and sore sicknesses, and of long continuance. Moreover he will bring on you all the diseases of Egypt, which you were afraid of; and they shall cleave to you. Also every sickness, and every plague, which is not written in the book of this law, them will YHWH bring on you, until you be destroyed. (Deut 28:58–61)

After YHWH saw that Israel had hardened her heart against his statutes and judgments, he set a special blessing in the Moabic Covenant if she obeyed the Moabic constitution and a curse if she rebelled against it. Deuteronomy's law code not only *upheld and strengthened the Sinai compact* but superseded the Sinai Covenant with its added injunctions against oppression, limits on free speech, and prohibition against further amendments. *The Moabic Covenant strengthened YHWH's overall doctrine.* If Israel did not follow YHWH's statutes, judgments, and commandments as outlined in Deuteronomy, then "all of these diseases" would still afflict Israel's citizens (See Deut 28:58–61, above).

As humanity's judge, YHWH sought to protect the poor and the disadvantage citizen so they could share in the nation's blessings. The Creator sought to instill and preserve national solidarity. Though these judgments were added because of the nation's iniquity, *his Law continued to be a way of life that was good for the people.* It prolonged the days of their life (Deut 10:12–13; 4:40; 32:46). This is why he forbade anyone to add or take away from the Deuteronomic Law.

IV. DOES THE LAW LEAD TO DEATH AND BONDAGE?

Today, many societies place little value on a person's lineage. For the most part, Americans are ignorant of their ancestors' character or the country from which they originated. Likewise, most individuals barely consider the life of their offspring beyond their great-grandchildren. This contrasts sharply with the rich heritage of the ancient Near Eastern family. Much of a man's historical honor was bound up in the continuance of his offspring many generations later. Children perpetuated the name of their forefathers and provided a remembrance for their fathers' house. When people died, they were not simply forgotten; their memory and their name were preserved in future generations through the families' tribal land heritages. At Israel's Diaspora, over 22 generations had lived on their fathers' Promised Land, in their houses, and had remembered their forefathers' lives.[211]

The asset of seed or lineage is so important that it was not only promised to Abraham, Isaac, and Jacob but also to David and Phinehas (see pp. 153–58). In contrast to the previously mentioned righteous men, evil men like Ahab, Jeroboam, and Baasha died without children. The lack of seed extinguished a man's house, inheritance, and his remembrance upon the land. Any land that had once been in his *name* was then placed under the name of a near relative (Num 27:11). *So, the existence of a man's seed often indicated his righteousness.*

One great example of the depth of the Law's concept of freedom is evidenced by its tolerance of polygyny. As Israel broke her covenant with YHWH, penalties were enforced. One curse affected the ability to produce offspring: "Cursed shall be the fruit of your body" (Deut 28:18). When these penalties were enforced in idolatrous Israel, one wife could not bear children, so another was needed to carry on the family name, inheritance, and remembrance.

In *idolatrous* Israel, polygyny was quite practical. As Israel's sins increased, YHWH gave the nation into the hands of the enemy. If Israel had greatly departed from the Law, great casualties ensued that could deprive a particular tribe of many sons. Daughters too were lost when the victorious army sought its spoils. When the nation revolted against David and followed Absalom, 70,000 men died as a result of David's action in numbering Israel and provoking YHWH (2 Sam 24:15). More wives could produce more children than one wife, thereby strengthening the nation's armies and culture so they could better defend their land and their freedom.

YHWH had given one wife to Adam and established that a man should "leave his father and his mother, and shall cleave to his wife: and they shall be *one* flesh" (Gen 2:24). This command established the precept that a man should cleave to his "wife," not "wives."[212] The word used for "wife" is *ishshah*, the feminine of *'iysh*, which means an individual male person.[213] YHWH had instructed a man to cleave to one wife, not many (Gen 2:24). As we have seen, the first time that Scripture mentioned polygyny was with Lamech, Cain's proud-hearted son in Gen 4:19. Yet after this we find (in Gens 6:3) that, when men took many wives, YHWH removed his spirit from contending with humanity's lustful desires to please their own flesh. Therefore, the only time that YHWH sanctioned polygyny was in the command for men to marry a near relative's childless widow.[214]

Scripture demonstrates that ensuring seed through polygyny was not without great cost. Abraham's marriage to Hagar (Genesis 16), the account of Rachael and Leah (Gen 29:30–30:24), the story of Hannah and Peninnah (1 Samuel 1), and the rivalry among Gideon's sons (Judg 8:35–9:5) reveal the heartache and strife that this practice caused. Additionally, many children were born into households with no tribal inheritance and with a lower social status than children of the lawful wife, which no doubt strongly contributed to this strife (see pp. 49–50, 97, 103–4, 126).

The Law did not abolish this social institution, which helped ensure the nation's military strength during duress. Instead, YHWH included judgments so that a woman could be financially protected from this custom (Exod 21:10). The Law is consistent, however, by allowing people to experience the consequences, joy or sorrow, of their own ways. What YHWH accomplished was to establish the wife's basic rights and to ultimately preserve the family unit.[215]

What I discovered to be the greatest evidence for YHWH's love of freedom is witnessed in Abraham's Promised-Land Covenant. Land resources ensured personal freedom, which enabled families to walk in the Creator's natural law in order to become the fittest nation on earth. YHWH strengthened the nation by forbidding property taxes, while the Release and Jubilee years abolished Hebrew slavery. Although the House of Judah led Israel's people, individual families formed their own governments, which maintained the precepts of freedom found in the Law. YHWH ordained sons to ensure equity and justice in their house just as their father had ensured justice so that their land was in a good state to be inherited by their offspring (Num 35:34). In this manner the land promised to Abraham's descendants was at their personal discretion. They were free to live the way they wanted, do as they desired, and work as they saw fit under Torah's liberty.

V. SPIRITUAL VS. PHYSICAL LAW

A. Ancient Allegations-Modernized

The last aspect of Israel's Law that I needed to test was the Law's spiritual attributes. At the beginning of our investigation into YHWH's Law, I stated that YHWH's righteousness hinges on the righteous or arbitrary nature of his Law. When ancient Israel accused YHWH and his Law of being unequal, she alleged that she could never merit or fulfill the standards set forth in her Creator's Law. In short, the Israelites charged that the way of YHWH was insufficient and inadequate for their daily lives; thus, they could never be righteous (Mic 6:3; Ezek 18:25).

Many modern theologians unwittingly maintain Israel's ancient allegations by stating that YHWH's Law insufficiently provided for humanity's spiritual needs.[216] In effect, they believe that YHWH gave humanity his Law—a way of life that does indeed work—but he knew it was beyond humanity's ability to observe it.[217] This belief continues to maintain that the Creator gave his Law to humanity to show that humanity is incapable of keeping it—to demonstrate their need of him—while still punishing the Israelites when they failed to obey it.

As one popular Web site states,

> I am not trying to wander back into the legalistic rules of the Old Covenant—God knew we could never keep those to begin with. We needed the "Law" so that we could see our sin.[218]

Compare this doctrine to a parent giving a mentally delayed or mentally retarded child a course in science or math well beyond his ability or years. The parent knows the child is *in*capable of completing the coursework yet requires the child to reach perfection and punishes when the child fails to achieve—just to prove that the child needed the parent to take the science or math course for him. This doctrine implies that YHWH is harsh, unmerciful, demanding, arbitrary, tyrannical, and downright unrighteous by requiring people to obey a Law they were incapable of achieving in the first place. Since those who hold this view see the Law as only setting requirements for humanity's physical actions, they also believe YHWH's Law to have been spiritually lacking. In other words, his Law did not fulfill humanity's deep spiritual needs *to enable* people to develop qualities that are exemplary of YHWH's spirit so that his people could indeed keep the Law. Rather, YHWH simply gave the Law to show humanity's need of him.[219]

Another modern belief that inadvertently continues ancient Israel's accusation, associates righteousness with perfection. This belief is that humanity was unable to merit the standards of YHWH's Law since God required people to keep his Law perfectly (even though he knew humanity is incapable of observing his Law).[220] In other words, if an individual broke one law, he broke his whole entire Law. Thus if one sins at any point in his life, he is no longer deemed righteous. Thankfully, the Israelite Scriptures do *not* support this exactingly rigid and unmerciful definition of righteousness or completeness.

In fact, this theology could not be further from what YHWH's covenants teach. In no place does the Torah state or imply that the Creator intended Israel's citizens to observe his Law without ever sinning. To understand the incongruity of this line of thought, we must look at YHWH's paradigm. First, he ordained graduated penalties. Stealing, negligence, and unintentional manslaughter had *lesser* penalties than did adultery, intentional negligence, or premeditated murder. If YHWH had considered all sin to bear the same weight, he would have had one penalty for all sin, but he did not. Because YHWH viewed the citizenship status of the *ezrach* and *ger* equally, he ordained the same penalties for both when they violated his law. Thus, graduated penalties for sin demonstrate that YHWH did not view all sin under one giant umbrella or as having the same consequence.

Second, there are many people in Scripture who sinned, yet YHWH deemed them righteous. YHWH called Noah righteous (Gen 7:1). Abraham, although he deceived Pharaoh and Abimelech (Gen 12:11–20; Genesis 20),[221] is judged to be righteous (Gen 15:6). Moses, though he killed an Egyptian and disobeyed YHWH's instruction (Exod 2:11–12; Num 20:1–13), is counted righteous and is even called "the man of God" (Deut 33:1). King David, although he committed adultery and murder, but repented—is remembered for his righteousness (1 Kgs 3:6; 9:4; 14:8; 15:5). King Asa walked before YHWH with a perfect heart (1 Kgs 15:14; 2 Chr 15:17) until the end of his life, when he slid from YHWH's precepts (2 Chr 15:9–12). And, YHWH also considered Job to be perfect and upright (Job 1:1).

When YHWH afflicted Job, his three friends came to comfort him. Each offered his own reasons for Job's misery. After much debate, YHWH answered Job and his companions, stating that Job's three friends did *not* speak that which was right in his sight. Eliphaz's corrupted theology was stained with lies and untruths. Only *Job and Elihu* had maintained YHWH's truth:

> And it was so, that after YHWH had spoken these words to Job, YHWH said to *Eliphaz* the Temanite, My wrath is kindled against you, and against your two friends: *for you have* not *spoken of me the thing that is right,* as my servant Job has. (Job 42:7, emphasis added)

Eliphaz was not only a Temanite (Job 2:11, a city in Edom);[222] he was Esau's son (Gen 36:10).[223] Eliphaz, Bildad, and Zophar spoke lies and false doctrine in the Creator's name. Their doctrine did not maintain truth. One fundamental doctrine underlying Edomite theology was that humanity could never be righteous or "clean" in YHWH's sight.

> Eliphaz states: "Behold, he puts no trust in his saints; yes, the heavens *are not clean* in his sight." (Job 15:15)
>
> Bildad: "How then can man be justified with God? or how can he be clean that is born of a woman? Behold even to the moon, and it shines not; yes, the stars are not pure in his sight. How much less man, that is a worm? and the son of man, which is a worm?" (Job 25:4–6)

Both Eliphaz and Bildad believed that humanity could never be pure or clean in God's sight. For Eliphaz, God would never put his trust in his most elected saints. For Bildad, those born of a woman would always be as unclean worms. YHWH condemned these unrighteous doctrines, which precluded humanity's ability to be sanctified, justified, or "pure" in his sight.

In contrast, Job *correctly* maintained his righteousness before God and his friends, asserting that he could be righteous and clean in YHWH's sight:

> Job: "My righteousness I hold fast, and will not let it go: my heart shall not reproach me so long as I live." (Job 27:6)

Eliphaz and Job stood at two opposing spectrums regarding humanity's ability to be righteous or justified under the Law. YHWH applauded Job's doctrine while condemning Eliphaz and Bildad's doctrine. Humanity can be clean, righteous, and good in YHWH's sight.

> And YHWH said to Noah, Come you and all your house into the ark; for you have I seen righteous before me in this generation. (Gen 7:1)
>
> Speaking of Abraham: "And he believed in YHWH; and he counted it to him for righteousness." (Gen 15:6)
>
> Peradventure there be fifty righteous within the city: will you also destroy and not spare the place for the fifty righteous that are in it? (Gen 18:24)

Abraham's belief in YHWH led to obedience (Gen 22:18; 26:5). YHWH judged Abraham to be righteous because his heart desired God and led him to obediently seek to walk in the way of his God (Gen 18:19; 26:5). Later, Abraham asked if God would be willing to spare Sodom and Gomorrah for the sake of 50 *righteous* people who lived there. **Abraham's question shows that he not only understood that humanity could be righteous but indicated that there might be 50 righteous people existing in the heinously wicked city at this time!**

Isaiah also testified that Jerusalem was at one time a city filled with righteous people.

> How is the faithful city become an harlot! it was full of judgment; righteousness lodged in it; but now murderers. (Isa 1:21)

In order for Jerusalem to have been righteous prior to Isaiah's day, the men and women who lived there would have had to be righteous. Humanity can be good and righteous in the Creator's sight. Thus, I cannot find evidence of God's ideals (doctrine) supporting or upholding either ancient Israel's allegations or modern beliefs regarding man's *in*ability to keep the Law (Deut 30:11–14) or be righteous in his sight.

B. The Bread of Life

Modern theology views the spiritual realm separately from the physical world. The adherents of the "Law's insufficient spiritual nature" see the Law as works or deeds that humanity performs on the physical level only, having no bearing on a person's spiritual well-being. This concept was completely alien to YHWH's teaching because the Law provided both spiritual guidance and the understanding to apply it to the physical world. The natural laws that provided justice and righteousness, and procured health were the same natural laws that provided spiritual enlightenment and relationship with God. Physical laws illuminated spiritual truths. Spiritual precepts (ethics) granted insight on how to apply the Torah's physical laws. This way of life led to a purpose-filled day-to-day life.

YHWH granted Israel real, useful, eternal knowledge of himself in Israel's Law. This is why YHWH told Israel that his Law—his only word to Israel at this point in time—was her bread of life:

> And he humbled you, and suffered you to hunger, and fed you with manna, which you knew not, neither did your fathers know; that he might make you know that man does not live by bread only, but by every word that proceeds out of the mouth of YHWH does man live. (Deut 8:3)

The only words that had "proceeded" out of YHWH's mouth when God stated this in the Deuteronomic Covenant were his commands, statutes, judgments, laws, and covenants. These were the words that were capable of forever sustaining humanity's life. These were YHWH's words—his way—that breathed life into all who followed them, feeding his children with a spiritual food capable of lasting throughout eternity.[224]

This is especially true of the sign of the Sabbath. At Sinai, YHWH told the nation that he had "*delivered* Israel from the house of bondage," and the Sabbaths were *the sign* that the nation was complying with this covenant of deliverance (Exod 31:13–17). The weekly Sabbath afforded rest and rejuvenation, providing a national holiday for all laborers.[225] The sabbatical years afforded rest and deliverance for individuals sold into debt slavery. The overall precept governing the Sabbath institution was freedom from oppression: "freedom from the house of bondage." By physically observing this statute in the covenant, YHWH would know that Israel was adhering to his covenant, and likewise Israel would know that she would enjoy freedom from all oppression. Even more importantly, the Sabbaths taught Israel the spiritual precept and the philosophy that people should not oppress their fellow countrymen. Israel's ability to fully understand what it meant to be free from oppression and not oppress others rested on her physical obedience of the Sabbath command.

Solomon also understood that the way (*derek*)[226] of YHWH produced life everlasting for all who followed it:

> In the way of righteousness is life; and in the pathway (*derek*) of it there is no death. (Prov 12:28)

YHWH's perfect Law (Ps 19:7) defined righteousness and described how his people could walk in life everlasting. This is no doubt the reason that Ezekiel dubbed YHWH's Law the "statutes of life" (Ezek 33:15). The only question that remains pertaining to the life contained in YHWH's Law is whether human beings were ever capable of being righteous so that they could inherit this life (a point we will examine later in this chapter).

C. The Golden Rule

YHWH's Law taught that there was a particular way or path to everlasting life. YHWH shared his knowledge of that path with Israel. One primary spiritual/physical precept taught that stress, strife, and oppression shortened life while peace lengthened one's days.[227] This was one of the many reasons that he commanded his nation to love her brother as herself:

> You shall not (a) hate your brother in your heart: you (b) shall in any wise rebuke your neighbor, and not suffer sin on him. You shall not avenge, nor bear any grudge against the children of your people, but you shall (c) love your neighbor as yourself: I am YHWH. (Lev 19:17–18)

There are two parts to YHWH's command. The first forbade Israel to (a) hate her brother, while the second commanded her to (c) love her brother as herself. Both of these commands dealt with thoughts, emotions, and attitudes that take place in the heart and mind. YHWH further clarifies that the proper physical manifestation of brotherly love culminates in (b) rebuking a brother when he sinned. If a person sins and his brother rebukes him, it gives the sinner an opportunity to turn and repent from his ways so that he can be spared the consequences of his actions (Prov 9:8; 13:3; 19:25; 25:12; 28:23). YHWH did not command a person to love his brother above himself or below himself but as equal to himself. The Law's founding precept of equity is maintained in this command.

Notice YHWH's command for Israel to love her neighbor and to refrain from hatred were not "physical" commands. Compliance with the Golden Rule primarily involved the thoughts, feelings, desires, intentions, and spirit of the heart. The Creator desired his people to train and discipline themselves to refrain from hatred and other negative desires that were counterproductive to his eternal way of life.[228] YHWH grounded this spiritual truth in physical commands, telling his people, whom he dearly loved, that the way to love their brother was to reprove him when he sinned. Thus Israel clearly understood how to spiritually love her brothers because YHWH established the method by which his spiritual precepts *should manifest* themselves in the physical world.

D. Service of the Heart

YHWH had made humanity in his likeness and in his image (Gen 1:26–27). As a loving Creator, he thoroughly understood his creation's inner spiritual needs. This is why he addressed so much of his Law to his people, exhorting them to bring their whole heart and mind into order with his way of life. He knew that their hearts and minds were key to their spirits being fully grounded in his life-sustaining Law. If they fully immersed themselves in the precepts, principles, and ethics underlying his Laws, they could never be drawn away from their light.[229] YHWH deeply imbued his Law with matters of the heart and mind.

The Creator loved his people. He desired them to order their heart and their thoughts aright in his sight:

> This day YHWH your God has commanded you to do these statutes and judg-
> ments: you shall therefore keep and do them with all your heart, and with all
> your soul. (Deut 26:16)
>
> And now, Israel, what does YHWH your God require of you, but to fear YHWH
> your God, to walk in all his ways, and to love him, and to serve YHWH your
> God with all your heart and with all your soul, To keep the commandments of
> YHWH, and his statutes, which I command you this day for your good? Behold,
> the heaven and the heaven of heavens is YHWH's your God, the earth also,
> with all that therein is. Only YHWH had a delight in your fathers to love them,
> and he chose their seed after them, even you above all people, as it is this day.
> Circumcise therefore the foreskin of your heart, and be no more stiffnecked.
> (Deut 10:12–16; see also Deut 10:12–21; 1 Sam 12:24–25; and Josh 22:5)

YHWH's command for Israel to circumcise the foreskin of her heart was a spiritual command. However, the physical manifestation of performing spiritual circumcision was a
person's obedience to YHWH's physical Law. YHWH did not desire feigned obedience but
a servant's willing and joyful heart (Deut 28:47–48; Ps 100:2). Again, we see that spiritual
and physical precepts walk hand in hand in the Law. YHWH did *not* consider Israel to have
spiritual faith until her trust, like Abraham's (Gen 22:18; 26:5), manifested itself through
physical obedience, naturally displaying her confidence in the Creator's *bread of life*.

One of the commands that YHWH gave for Israel's heartfelt circumcision was to fear
him and his judgments:

> You shall not therefore oppress one another; but you shall fear your God: for I
> am YHWH your God. (Lev 25:17; see above, Deut 10:12)
>
> Only fear YHWH, and serve him in truth with all your heart: for consider how
> great things he has done for you. But if you shall still do wickedly, you shall be
> consumed, both you and your king. (1 Sam 12:24–25)

Walking in the fear of YHWH meant that a person believed that YHWH would hold him accountable for his actions (Exod 34:7). This precept taught humanity to be intellectually honest
and to apply that honesty to daily life. If a person sinned, there would be consequences (Ps
99:8). By believing that YHWH requires restoration or retribution from the guilty party, the
Law dissuaded people from sinning in much the same way that a hot stove naturally discour-
ages a person from touching it or a traffic ticket deters speeding. This call for complete and
whole-hearted honesty is found throughout YHWH's Law. If a person feared YHWH and
loved him with all his heart, he would naturally observe YHWH's life-giving instructions.

Notice how the eternal and unchanging spiritual truths in YHWH's Law are consistently applied to the physical world. His physical commands hinged on spiritual beliefs that
would naturally manifest themselves in physical actions when his people wholeheartedly

feared their God. The precepts of his Law taught people how to attain physical and spiritual peace (Ps 119:165), while granting them the education and philosophy needed to understand how to practically apply their Creator's physical truths to their daily life.

This is why King David attests that the fear of YHWH will endure throughout all eternity as it endows humans with the ability to obey YHWH's commandments in order to prevail spiritually.

> The fear of YHWH is (a) clean, (b) enduring forever (Ps 19:9). The fear of YHWH is the (c) beginning of wisdom: a (d) good understanding have all they that (e) do his commandments: (f) his praise endures forever (Ps 111:10).

David proclaims that fearing YHWH is (a) clean, *tahor,* meaning spiritually pure and undefiled.[230] The pureness and wholesomeness in fearing YHWH (b) endures forever; its importance will never fade, but will always be the (c) basis of wisdom, understanding, and (f) correctly worshiping and having a relationship with God (Deut 4:7–9). Fearing YHWH is what leads humanity to (e) obedience. Obedience then endows us with (d) understanding to judge what is true (Isa 42:1, 4). Fear, obedience, and trust are what enable mankind to correctly discern YHWH's spirit from competing emotions, agendas, and popular opinion (Deut 13:3–4; Isa 29:24).

> YHWH is my light and my salvation; whom shall I fear? YHWH is the strength of my life; of whom shall I be afraid? (Ps 27:1)

The spiritual truth found in fearing YHWH gave David confidence and strength. Fearing YHWH caused him to trust and believe that YHWH's Law was good for him (Ps 19:7; 119:39, 66, 68, 77, 97), and the *fear of YHWH* enabled David to receive YHWH's spirit[231] so that he could accurately discern YHWH's spiritual, physical, and prophetic Law.[232]

Jeremiah prophesied that YHWH will give Israel an everlasting covenant in the latter days. The trait that Jeremiah states will finally sanctify the nation is the fear that YHWH will place in a people's heart, which will cause them to fear him and his righteous judgments.

> Behold, I will gather them out of all countries, where I have driven them in my anger, and in my fury, and in great wrath; and I will bring them again to this place, and I will cause them to dwell safely: And they shall be my people, and I will be their God: And I will give them one heart, and one way, that they may fear me forever, for the good of them, and of their children after them: *And I will make an everlasting covenant with them,* that I will not turn away from them, to do them good; but I will put my fear in their hearts, that they shall not depart from me. (Jer 32:37–40)

The result of YHWH's everlasting covenant is his fear in our hearts. The *fear of YHWH* is the quality that sanctifies latter-day Israel. Walking in his fear—alone—will cause his people never again to depart from YHWH or his way of life. Once again we see that YHWH desires people to serve and worship him with their whole heart, not feigned physical compliance but genuine belief that YHWH will hold them accountable for their sins. They must fear the righteousness of their God, knowing that consequences always lie ahead. Thus, once again I find that modern allegations of the Law's spiritual inadequacy are unfounded because great spiritual depth can be evidenced in a constitutional Law given to an ancient Israelite nation.

E. Sin Begins in the Imaginations of the Heart

Many Torah commands were not concerned with "do's" and "dont's." Matters of the heart and mind were spiritual in nature and dominated YHWH's covenantal Law. YHWH desired his people to circumcise their hearts to love him. He desired that his people enter into a relationship with him.[233] YHWH readily saw that righteousness as well as sin began in the heart. A person's lack of fear, faith, or trust in him would eventually manifest itself in actions that violated the stipulations of his law. Sin began with thinking that YHWH's mercy would override justice and that he would not impute sin or hold the guilty responsible for their actions (Exod 34:7).

The first time we see YHWH condemning the imaginations of the human heart occurred shortly before the flood. YHWH saw that people's fatal flaw was in their thoughts and desires, which ultimately manifested in sinful actions. Humanity's lusts led to polygamy, violence, and other perversions devised by the human heart (Gen 6:5). YHWH condemned the "thoughts of the heart," since these thoughts brought negative consequences that led to death. This implies that YHWH considers evil thoughts to be erring from the precepts in his Law.

King Solomon upheld this interpretation when he declared that people who abstain from exercising good judgment and discipline in their thoughts have sinned in their minds.

> The thought of foolishness is sin: and the scorner is an abomination to men. (Prov 24:9)

Machashabah,[234] translated "thought" in Prov 24:9 is the same word used to denote the "thoughts of the imagination of the heart" in Gen 6:5, when YHWH sought to destroy mankind at the flood. Solomon tells us that, when a person's thoughts depart from YHWH's law, it is sin. The word for "sin," *chataa't,*[235] literally means 'sin' and is the name word associated with the offering (*hachataa't*) for sin.[236] Solomon termed the thoughts that occur in our innermost being—in our heart and mind—sin *when* our thoughts become folly by departing from YHWH's Law.

The fatal flaw with the thoughts of the heart is that they separate us from a relationship with YHWH because thoughts can become sinful actions. *Our desires determine our actions.* Isaiah readily acknowledges that desires in the heart eventually manifest into physical actions, whether by deed or by spoken word: "Out of the abundance of the heart the mouth speaks."

> In transgressing and lying against YHWH, and departing away from our God, speaking oppression and revolt, conceiving and uttering from the heart words of falsehood. (Isa 59:13)

Throughout the Hebrew Scriptures, YHWH's prophets readily recognize that sin originates in the thoughts and desires of the heart:

> And YHWH saw that the wickedness of man was great in the earth, and that every imagination of the thoughts of his heart was only evil continually. (Gen 6:5)
>
> But they listened not, nor inclined their ear, but walked in the counsels and in the imagination of their evil heart, and went backward, and not forward. (Jer 7:24)
>
> And you have done worse than your fathers; for, behold, you walk every one after the imagination of his evil heart, that they may not listen to me: (Jer 16:12; see also Jer 13:10; 14:14; Isa 55:7)

YHWH saw that the thoughts and desires (imagination) in the heart were crucial to humanity's salvation. This is why he exhorted Israel to place his Law in her heart so that she could set her heart on the spiritual truths that would endow her with his eternal bread of life.

> And these words, which I command you this day, shall be in your heart: (Deut 6:6)

> Your word have I hid in my heart, that I might not sin against you. (Ps 119:11)

> I delight to do your will, O my God: yes, your law is within my heart. (Ps 40:8)

> Give me understanding, and I shall keep your law; yes, I shall observe it with my whole heart. . . . My hands also will I lift up to your commandments, which I have loved; and I will meditate in your statutes . . . Let my heart be sound in your statutes; that I be not ashamed. (Ps 119:34, 48, 80)

> Listen to me, you that *know righteousness*, the people *in whose heart is my law*; fear you not the reproach of men, neither be you afraid of their revilings. (Isa 51:7)

YHWH's Law taught Israel that sin began with her heart's desires. She could easily avoid sin and sorrow if she loved the spiritual precepts (ethics) embedded in his Law, meditated on them (Ps 1:2; 63:6; 119:15, 23, 48, 78, 148), and lived by them. By loving YHWH's Law and choosing to walk in his way, Israel grew strong through YHWH so that she could easily obey his Law (Deut 30:11–14).

F. Covetousness: The Root of all Wickedness

YHWH saw sin as a process that began with an evil desire in the heart that eventually manifested itself into a physical action. This is why his covenantal Law forbade Israel *to desire* what did not rightfully belong to her. "You shall not covet your neighbor's house, you shall not covet your neighbor's wife, nor his manservant, nor his maidservant, nor his ox, nor his ass, nor any thing that is your neighbor's" (Exod 20:17). YHWH knew that the first step to sin involved desiring something that went contrary to his Law.[237] If an Israelite set his heart on his neighbor's wife, he could follow his desire and sin by committing adultery. If Israel desired another person's ox, the desire or lust for that object could lead people to steal. Likewise, if her people desired the gold and silver from graven images claimed during the nation's conquest of Canaan, her lust for the beautiful image could lead her to worship another god (Deut 7:25).

This is why the Creator warned Israel to

> remember all the commandments of YHWH, and do them; and that you seek not after your *own heart* and your own eyes, after which you used to go a whoring. (Num 15:39)

YHWH desired Israel to follow his commandments over the desires of her heart. He desired that she exhibit self-restraint and self-discipline so that she could walk in his way of life over her own deadly paths. The Creator warned the nation that, if her heart turned away from him to love and serve other gods, or if her heart turned from the good doctrine established in his Law (Prov 4:2), she would be drawn to worship fairy tale myths that departed from his sound doctrine (Ps 119:142). If she turned her heart to rebel against YHWH, her Creator would discipline the nation by allowing her iniquitous ways to naturally drive her from the land that had formerly guaranteed the blessings in his covenants.

> But *if your heart turn away*, so that you will not hear, but shall be drawn away, and worship other gods, and serve them; I will tell you this day that you shall surely perish, and that you shall not prolong your days on the land, where you pass over Jordan to go to possess it. (Deut 30:17–18)

YHWH bestowed his spiritual truth and doctrine in his physical Law. His spiritual truth encompassed the physical Law. So strongly did he ground Israel in the physical Law, which embodied his spiritual truth, that she could never be led astray *if* she obeyed. If another god or another religion taught her to dismiss any part of her Creator's Law, she could instantly know that god was false, since it contradicted the truth of the Law (Ps 119:142; Isa 8:20). Remember that one of the concepts of truth is constancy and freedom from change. If any god or prophet spoke *in YHWH's name* claiming that Israel no longer had to "remember all the commandments of YHWH *to do them*" (Num 15:39), then Israel could immediately be assured that the deity or prophet who spoke had *no* authority from YHWH.

> And you shall not go aside from any of the words which I command you this day, to the right hand, or to the left, to go after other gods to serve them. (Deut 28:14)

If a god's doctrine or theology contradicted YHWH's Law or taught Israel to forsake any part of his Law, she knew truth did not exist in that god. This point was driven home by YHWH's exhortation that *he would test Israel* with false prophets to see if she would depart from his Law to follow them.

YHWH desired to test his people to see if they truly loved him or if they simply desired superficial emotions, miracles, or blessings. Would Israel trust, worship, and obey the truth that her Creator bestowed in his Law? Would she follow the God that delivered her from all oppression? Or would she follow the miraculous deceptions that false prophets performed in the physical world? (For example, the miracles performed by Pharaoh's magicians—Exod 7:11–12, 22; 8:7, 18.)

> If there arise among you a prophet, or a dreamer of dreams, and gives you a sign or a wonder, *and the sign or the wonder come to pass*, whereof he spoke to you, saying, Let us go after other gods, *which you have not known*, and let us serve them; You shall not listen to the words of that prophet, or that dreamer of dreams: *for YHWH your God proves you, to know whether you love YHWH your God with all your heart and with all your soul.* You shall walk after YHWH your God, and fear him, and keep his commandments, and obey his voice, and you shall serve him, and cleave to him. And that prophet, or that dreamer of dreams, shall be put to death; because he has spoken to turn you away from YHWH your God, which brought you out of the land of Egypt, and redeemed you out of the house of bondage, to thrust you out of the way which YHWH your God commanded you to walk in. So shall you put the evil away from the midst of you. And all Israel shall hear, and fear, and shall do no more any such wickedness as this is among you. (Deut 13:1–5, 11)

Remember that YHWH had given humanity his truth within Israel's Law: "Your righteousness is an everlasting righteousness, and your law is the truth" (Ps 119:142). YHWH saw that as long as Israel delighted to love his constitutional Law and obey it, she would freely walk in righteousness and joyous truth, be free from oppression, and her cup would overflow with its blessings.

Yet, he warned her that if she turned from obeying his constitutional and covenantal Law that she could easily be *spiritually deceived* into worshiping false gods:

> And it shall come to pass, if you shall listen diligently to my commandments which I command you this day, to love YHWH your God, and to serve him with all your heart and with all your soul, (16) Take heed to yourselves, that your *heart* be not deceived, and you turn aside, and serve other gods, and worship them; (18) Therefore shall you lay up these my words *in your heart and in your soul*, and bind them for a sign on your hand, that they may be as frontlets between your eyes. And you shall teach them to your children, speaking of them when you sit in your house, and when you walk by the way, when you lie down, and when you rise up. And you shall write them on the door posts of your house, and on your gates: That your days may be multiplied, and the days of your children, in the land which YHWH swore to your fathers to give them, as the days of heaven on the earth. (Deut 11:13, 16, 18–21)

As it may be remembered, the sign of the Moabic Covenant was Israel living by YHWH's words, placing them in her heart and her very soul so that she could *think* and *act* according the spiritual precepts found within her Creator's Law (see pp. 149–53). If she obeyed, she could never be deceived or turned aside from the will of her God. Yet, if she rebelled against physically performing YHWH's spiritual truths, false gods and their ministers could easily deceive her heart and soul, robbing her of YHWH's spirit.

G. A God Who Tries, Proves, and Refines the Heart of Man

In the section entitled Earth's Crucible (see p. 163), we saw that YHWH uses the crucible method to try, prove, and understand his human creations. The crucible method is most evident in the way that YHWH deals with sin. Although YHWH sees that sin begins in the heart, he refrains from placing any judgment on a person *until* the sin in humanity's heart manifests itself in a physical action.

> And you shall remember all the way which YHWH your God led you these forty years in the wilderness, to humble you, and *to prove you, to know what was in your heart*, whether you would keep his commandments, or no. (Deut 8:2)
>
> And you, Solomon my son, know you the God of your father, and serve him with a *perfect heart and with a willing mind*: for YHWH *searches* all hearts, and understands all the imaginations of the thoughts: if you seek him, he will be found of you; but if you forsake him, he will cast you off forever. (1 Chr 28:9)

> The heart is deceitful above all things, and desperately wicked: who can know it? I YHWH search the heart, *I try the reins*, even to give every man according to his ways, and according to the fruit of his doings. (Jer 17:9–10; see also 1 Kgs 8:39; Ps 11:2–7; 26:2; 44:20–21; 2 Chr 6:30; 32:31)

When Adam and Eve sinned, YHWH sent a serpent to test them to see if the sin in their heart and words would manifest itself in a physical action. YHWH had told Adam not to eat the forbidden fruit (Gen 2:16–17). When Adam relayed YHWH's message to Eve, he added to YHWH's word by forbidding her to touch the fruit (Gen 3:3). Thus Adam revealed the *dis*trust that lay in his heart (Job 31:33) by adding to YHWH's word, an act YHWH's Law forbid (Deut 4:2; 12:32; Prov 30:6).

In another example, YHWH saw that the generation that exited Egypt was full of iniquity, distrust, and unfaithfulness, so he tried them with hunger and thirst to see if they would seek him and obey, or if they would rebel.

> And you shall remember all the way which YHWH your God led you these forty years in the wilderness, to humble you, and to prove you, to know what was in your heart, whether you would keep his commandments, or no. (Deut 8:2)

Although sin originated in the heart, YHWH did not punish human beings for the sins in their hearts and minds. Rather, he set those whose hearts had turned away from him in slippery places to see if the sin in their hearts would manifest itself in a physical action.

> For I was envious at the foolish, when I saw the prosperity of the wicked. . . . Until I went into the sanctuary of God; then understood I their end. Surely you did set them in slippery places: you cast them down into destruction. (Ps 73:3, 17–18)

After YHWH saw that a person's heart had turned from him to desiring (coveting) something such as a relationship with a married individual, stealing, bribery, or other crimes that went contrary to his way of life, YHWH put that individual in an unstable situation where the individual could either forsake his sin and get out of trouble or continue in his sin to reap destruction.[238] YHWH's application of this crucible method is again witnessed in the trial of Job and the many times that Israel rebelled against him during the Judges' Era. The Creator placed individuals and nations under oppression to see if they would return to him and obey or be crushed by their enemies.

Throughout this investigation, I have discovered that there was great wisdom in YHWH's method of judging sin. YHWH had committed the administration of his government and his Law to the Levites. The Levites were his earthly representatives, entrusted with overseeing the interpretation of his Law (Exod 18:20). If YHWH had set a precedent for punishing every sin in humanity's heart and mind, the Levites would have functioned as the Gestapo, searching for each citizen's secret sin and trying to convict him. If this had been the case, Israel would have been delivered into worse bondage then what she had ever seen in Egypt. Thankfully, YHWH did not ordain a police state but entrusted the individual to a great extent. YHWH trusted individuals with their own heart's obedience in the same way that a parent trusts his child to obey his instructions. YHWH knew that, when a person had indeed turned away from him, her actions would eventually betray her heart, at which point the matter could be taken up with Israel's God-appointed judges.

Once YHWH saw that sin and treachery overtook an individual or a nation, he used the "furnace of affliction" to prove and refine his creation into one that would not pollute his name or give his glory to any other god.

> I knew that you would deal very treacherously, and was called a transgressor from the womb. For my name's sake will I defer my anger, and for my praise will I refrain for you, that I cut you not off. Behold, I have refined you, but not with silver; I have chosen you in the furnace of affliction. For my own sake, even for mine own sake, will I do it: for how should my name be polluted? And I will not give my glory to another. (Isa 48:8–11)

Isaiah prophesies that YHWH will use the crucible method to refine a man and fashion him into a new creation—a creation that will walk humbly before him and finally obey his Law.

> I will punish the world for their evil, and the wicked for their iniquity; and I will cause the arrogancy of the proud to cease, and will lay low the haughtiness of the terrible. I will make a man more precious than fine gold; even a man than the golden wedge of Ophir. (Isa 13:11–12)

Moses provides what is probably the best metaphor for the way that YHWH tries humanity:

> You shall also consider in your heart, that, as a man chastens his son, so YHWH your God chastens you. (Deut 8:5)

As a parent who desires the best for his children, YHWH desired to teach his children to walk in the only way of life that would bring happiness, peace, prosperity, and a close relationship with him. When people erred from his way he would try, instruct, teach, and discipline them so they could learn to correctly walk in his way and discern when their hearts and souls were spiritually lacking in his sight. As Job's friend Elihu adeptly phrased it: "Yes, He renders to a man accordingly as each of them does, and in a man's path he will find him" (Job 34:11, LXX).

H. Sin, Iniquity, and Transgression

Many modern believers see sin as constituting a wide variety of thoughts and actions. These "sins" may or may not be tied to YHWH's Law.[239] This was not the case for the ancient Hebrew, who understood that there were three categories or types of sin.

Chata' or *chata'ah,* most often translated "sin," means to 'miss the mark' or to offend.[240] This type of sin specifically designated actions that violated a specific command in the Law, such as adultery, cleanliness injunctions, or eating of specific unclean foods.[241] *'Avon,* the second type of sin, which the King James Version fairly reliably translates "iniquity," means *perversity.*[242] This classification of sin designated the actions that violate the precepts in the Law, although the Law may not address the actual act.[243] *'Avon* depicts 'bending, twisting, or distorting' the Laws and commands in the Pentateuch.[244] Lesbianism and male prostitution would be actions that fall into this category since the Law does ban male homosexuality and female prostitution (Lev 20:13; 19:29). Even though it does not specifically address homosexuality among females or male prostitution, the perversity of these actions can be derived from the prohibition of the other gender; thus lesbianism and male prostitution would be classified as perversities or iniquities according to Scripture since both actions twist or distort the principle underlying the original command. The final type of sin, *Pesha' or ma'al* designates an open rebellion or wantonly perverse and sinful action.[245] This would include both of the previous types of sin mentioned, *chata'* and *'avon,* but is usually much stronger because it implies an *open rebellion* against YHWH and a defiant departure from his way of life: a change of allegiance away from YHWH and his covenantal Torah.[246]

Although YHWH wrote his Law based on precepts, we need to be careful what we construe as iniquity (perversity) and sin (breach of his Law). Although lesbianism or child molestation can definitely be considered "perversities" under the Law, the act of lying cannot. YHWH only forbids lying or deception when it is used *with the intent to defraud* or harm another. He did not forbid lying or deception when it was used for life-saving measures, such as the midwives' deception of Pharaoh (Exod 1:18–21), Rahab's lie to Jericho's guard that saved Israel's spies (Joshua 2; *6:17*), Jael's deception of Sisera, or Ehud's lie that lead to Israel's triumph over her enemies (Judg 3:15–30; 5:24–27). When YHWH desired to judge Ahab's wickedness, he caused the prophet Micaiah to lie to Ahab so that the oppressive king would be lulled into a false sense of security (1 Kgs 22:13–23). Ahab's false hope and false belief would then easily deliver him into YHWH's hands. YHWH's Law did not forbid lying or deception (*when done for righteous causes*), but it did forbid lying with the intent of defrauding one's neighbor (Lev 6:2–7; we will examine this in greater detail in volume 2). Thus, the actions that constituted sin were intimately tied to the statutes, commands, and judgments in YHWH's Law. *An action was not sin unless it actually breached the constitutional precept on which YHWH's Laws were based.*

When YHWH saw that Israel had openly rebelled (transgressed) against his covenantal Law, he still mercifully forgave if she repented and turned to him:

> Keeping mercy for thousands, forgiving iniquity and transgression and sin,[247] and that will *by no means clear the guilty;* visiting the iniquity of the fathers on the children, and on the children's children, unto the third and to the fourth generation. (Exod 34:7)

YHWH willingly and fully forgave people who treacherously rebelled against him, such as the many times that Israel rebelled in the wilderness (Ps 78:32–38). Although YHWH forgave perversity, rebellion, and the trespass of his Law for those who repented, he still allowed people to reap the consequences of their choices, often allowing children to learn from their parents' mistakes. When King David rebelled through adultery and murder, YHWH stated that his offspring would live in the strife that his actions had created (2 Sam 12:10). David left the consequences of his actions, the strife his disobedience had caused, as a legacy for his offspring, who had to "unlearn" their father's *un*righteous example. However, if YHWH's people offered the true sacrifices of the heart, mind, and spirit—giving them into their Creator's redemptive hands—then she could be freed from the sins that cowered at the doorstep of their heart (Gen 4:7).

I. True Sacrifice

We have seen that God wanted the best for Israel. He saw that guilt hindered the freedom he had ordained for her citizens. YHWH saw that feelings of culpability, inadequacy, and low self-esteem could destroy the confidence and strength that Israel could have by walking in his way of life. When he commanded Israel to love her neighbor and rebuke him when he sinned, YHWH intended to relieve his children from bearing the burden of guilt. If a person rebuked his brother's sin, then the brother could turn from his sin before the consequences (and the guilt) became too great. But even more than this, a brother's rebuke kept Israel's society firmly grounded in the Law so that people did not bear unnecessary guilt for actions that did not violate the Law. If, for instance, a husband committed adultery, the wife did not need to feel unnecessary guilt for not meeting her husband's needs or for provoking him to sin. Rather, she knew that her husband was solely responsible for his actions, and she was free from all guilt associated with her husband's crime. This not only maintained the honesty and integrity of Israel's society but kept the people from needlessly bearing iniquity and guilt—a way YHWH saw led to death (Exod 28:43; Lev 22:9; Num 18:22).

YHWH specifically tied the expiation of guilt to sacrifices.[248] If a person sinned against YHWH, he could bring his penalty to the Temple and leave the burden of his guilt at the altar, knowing that YHWH had accepted his offering, forgiven his sin, and restored the relationship. The individual did not need to continually wrestle with the question of whether or not he had been forgiven. Since he had provided an acceptable offering, he had obeyed YHWH's requirements for atonement and could enjoy the freedom of God's forgiveness.[249] YHWH grounded the spiritual and emotional aspects of sacrifice in the physical world so that an individual could know he had attained forgiveness and favor with his God.

This is why YHWH instructed that true sacrifice should cost some form of wealth (2 Sam 24:24). Penalties deterred people from committing the same offense twice. Although sacrifices for different sins had graduated economic values, they penalized the sinner, providing a consequence for his crime. Nevertheless, YHWH took into consideration the motive with which a person brought his sacrifice. If a person brought a sacrifice simply to fulfill the Law, without intending to change his ways, YHWH considered it abominable. "The sacrifice of the wicked is abomination: how much more, when he brings it *with a wicked mind?*" (Prov 21:27; see also Ezekiel 18). YHWH saw that true sacrifice would naturally lead to obedience when a person sacrificed the desire of the heart that led to trespassing the Law.

> The sacrifices of God are a broken spirit: a broken and a contrite heart, O God, you will not despise. (Ps 51:17)

True sacrifice is an attitude that is willing to obey even though it is not convenient. A willing, broken, and contrite heart will naturally seek to please its Maker. YHWH saw that if a person obeyed this doctrine *from the desire within her heart,* she could become a servant of righteousness, being made free from the burden of guilt and sin. Thus, Israel's ability to inherit the fruits of his spirit hung upon her willingness to circumcise her heart—to serve, obey, and worship him alone.

The physical nature of YHWH's spiritual Law did not leave Israel wondering if she had found favor, grace, and friendship with her God. Rather her physical compliance to his spiritual Law caused all who obeyed to know they merited his favor:

> But let all those that put their trust in you rejoice: let them ever shout for joy, because you defended them: let them also that love your name be joyful in you. For you, YHWH, will bless the righteous; *with favor* will you compass him as with a shield. (Ps 5:11–12)
>
> A good man obtains favor of YHWH: but a man of wicked devices will he condemn. (Prov 12:2)

Israelites' heartfelt obedience blessed them not only with physical blessings but with spiritual favor. They could find a friendly relationship (2 Chr 20:7; Isa 41:8) with God and he would reward them with all their hearts' desires (Ps 37:4) once they circumcised their heart to love YHWH and his law.

J. YHWH's Willing Spirit

Another accusation made by proponents of the Law's non-spiritual nature asserts that YHWH never endowed Israel with his spirit so that she could obey his Law.[250] In other words, God had never made his spirit available to empower humanity to choose to do right or to develop a Godly character or nature. This doctrine is untrue, however, according to Nehemiah who states that YHWH *had* given Israel his spirit at the exodus:

> You gave also your good spirit to instruct them, and withheld not your manna from their mouth, and gave them water for their thirst. Yet many years did you forbear them, and testified against them by your spirit in your prophets: yet would they not give ear: therefore gave you them into the hand of the people of the lands. (Neh 9:20, 30; see also Num 11:29)

King David credits YHWH's spirit with the ability to lead him into the land of the righteous:

> Teach me to do your will; for you are my God: your spirit is good; lead me into the land of uprightness. (Ps 143:10)

> Restore to me the joy of your salvation; and uphold me with your free spirit. (Ps 51:12)

> The Spirit of YHWH spoke by me, and his word was in my tongue. (2 Sam 23:2)

> Create in me a clean heart, O God; and renew a right spirit within me. (Ps 51:10)

> I said, YHWH, be merciful to me: heal my soul; for I have sinned against you. (Ps 41:4)

> Not by might, nor by power, but by my spirit, said YHWH of hosts. (Zech 4:6)

David stated YHWH freely granted his spirit to all who sought him (Ps 51:12) and that it was through YHWH's spirit that he wrote his psalms (2 Sam 23:2). When he sinned, David realized that YHWH's spirit needed to be renewed within him (Ps 51:10), and his soul healed (Ps 41:4) from the wound that his sinned had caused. Zechariah proclaimed that victory for the ancient nation, had not occurred through Israel's might but through the power of YHWH's spirit (Zech 4:6).

YHWH had freely given his spirit to Israel. She was capable of obeying his Law (Deut 30:11–14). His Law established parameters for her to walk with him so that she could have a close relationship with him. And his spirit was willingly available if his people would simply humble themselves to call on him and obey:

> For what nation is there so great, who has God so nigh to them, as YHWH our God is in all things that we call on him for? (Deut 4:7)
>
> YHWH is nigh to them that are of a broken heart; and saves such as be of a contrite spirit. (Ps 34:18)
>
> If my people, which are called by my name, shall humble themselves, and pray, and seek my face, and turn from their wicked ways; then will I hear from heaven, and will forgive their sin, and will heal their land. (2 Chr 7:14)

YHWH was willing to have a close relationship with any who were willing to humble himself to observe his Law (Deut 4:6). YHWH could willingly forgive humanity's sins and restore his righteous nature within them if only they humbled their own spirits to be submissive to his. YHWH was ever ready to develop and cultivate his spiritual character in his people so they could become a righteous example to all nations and a blessing to all people (Isa 60:1–3; 58:8–10; 49:6; Exod 19:6).

These examples demonstrate that ancient Israel indeed had the tools necessary to obey YHWH's Law. The Creator provided her with his willing spirit (Ps 51:12), endowed her with a spiritual Law that spoke to the needs of her heart, and willingly forgave her when she turned from her sins. His Law provided Israel with healthy precepts that could cure all her diseases (Exod 15:26) and provided a moral code to strengthen the relations in her society to effect perfect peace (Isa 26:3; Ps 37:37; 119:165) without death (Prov 12:28).

In the opening chapter of this book, I reopened YHWH's controversy to determine whether he was righteous. I established that truth would be the foundation for our investigation. YHWH's doctrine, his way, and his Law had to be in accord with reality, "the body of real things and real events," in order to meet the definition of being "true." I further refined my quest to see whether YHWH's truth was righteous or was arbitrary and inequitable. This had been ancient Israel's allegation (Mic 6:2–3; Ezek 18:25, 29). The nation accused her Creator and his Law of being harsh, demanding, inequitable, and too difficult to observe. My investigation over the last three chapters has uncovered enormous scientific validity for YHWH's Law. The way of YHWH is not just a matter of blind faith; the way of YHWH is based on scientific facts and realities that result in natural blessings for all who follow it, whether Jew, Gentile, Christian, Muslim, or atheist.

Therefore, Israel's accusation that YHWH's way is wearisome and burdensome so far lacks validity. The only time that the Creator forbids certain practices or customs is when they are harmful to humanity's physical and psychological well-being. YHWH's precepts reveal a father's earnest love for his children in patiently teaching and turning them to follow a productive way of life that works!

VI. SCRIPTURE'S PERSPECTIVE ON THE LAW

Thus far, evidence exists that the Law is physically, scientifically, spiritually sound and equitable. We have seen scientific validity for the practices of circumcision, clean foods, quarantine, and morality. Mercy was established for the poor and the ill by exempting them from taxation. YHWH introduced more than ten obstacles to the slavery system. Old Testament theology as outlined in YHWH's Law ordained freedom while advocating personal responsibility. It harmonized natural law with social justice by defining the Laws of reality by which man should live. However, as we have seen, modern theology (similar to ancient Israel's accusations) often teaches that the Law is difficult, if not impossible for man to keep.

Some modern scholars go so far as to assert that YHWH himself did not think man capable of observing his Law. Does Scripture uphold this viewpoint? Did YHWH think humanity incapable of obeying his Law? Did YHWH indicate that the Law was difficult for ancient Israel to obey, or that it is difficult for humanity in general to obey today?

This is what the Creator testifies:

> For this commandment which I command you this Day, it is not hidden from you, neither is it far off. It is not in heaven, that you should say, Who shall go up for us to heaven, and bring it to us, that we may hear it, and do it? Neither is it beyond the sea, that you should say, *Who* shall go over the sea for us, and bring it to us, that we may hear it, and do it? *But the word is very nigh to you, in your mouth, and in your heart, that you may do it.* (Deut 30:11–14)

> [Moses] said to them, Set your hearts to all the words which I testify among you this day, which you shall command your children to observe to do, all the words of this law. For it is not a vain thing for you; because it is your life: and *through this thing you shall prolong your days* in the land, where you go over Jordan to possess it. (Deut 32:46–47)

YHWH's Law is easy for humanity to obey. Observing YHWH's constitutional Law produces perfect righteousness in one's heart, mind, action, and spirit and leads to life. Humanity's very nature can be changed through meditating on and observing YHWH's Law (see Ps 119:34, 40, 69–70, 80, 92, 104, 128). The Book of Psalms upholds the Deuteronomic view, proclaiming:

> Oh that my people had listened to me, and Israel had walked in my ways! I should soon have subdued their enemies, and turned my hand against their adversaries. The haters of YHWH should have submitted themselves to him: but their time should have endured forever. He should have fed them also with the finest of the wheat: and with honey out of the rock should I have satisfied you. (Ps 81:13–16; see also Ps 119:142, 174)

> The prophet Isaiah echoes this sentiment, saying, "Thus said YHWH, your Redeemer, the Holy One of Israel; I am YHWH your God which teaches you to profit, which leads you by the way that you should go. O that you had listened to my commandments! then had your peace been as a river, and your righteousness as the waves of the sea. (Isa 48:17–18)[251]

There are four categories of the Law: all fall under the heading of "equity." The first category is the Ten Commandments. They divide the whole Law into (1) establishing equity between humanity and his Creator (Exod 20:1–4) and (2) establishing equity among people (Exod 20:5–10). The Ten Commandments are further divided into statutes, judgments, commandments, and laws that provide immeasurable freedom and individuality for citizens.

Of these categories, King David tells us:

> The *Law* of YHWH is perfect, restoring the soul: the *testimony* of YHWH is sure, making wise the simple. The *statutes* of YHWH are right, *rejoicing the heart*: the *commandment* of YHWH is pure, enlightening the eyes. The fear of YHWH is clean, enduring forever: the *judgments* of YHWH are true and righteous altogether. More to be desired are they than gold, yes, than much fine gold: sweeter also than honey and the honeycomb. Moreover by them is your servant warned: and in keeping of them there is great reward. (Ps 19:7–11)

The Law is perfect; it is able to restore (heal) the soul (Isa 30:15). YHWH's statutes are correct and equitable—a trait of justice for which we should rejoice! The Testimony in YHWH's Law reveals prophetic consequences for breaching his pact. The Testimonies' consequences are bound to occur and can enlighten those who lack understanding, thus educating the ignorant about YHWH's Law. The Creator's commandments open the eyes to understanding. His judgments are true, harmonizing with Isaac Newton's Third Law. And there are natural rewards for keeping Torah.

What are the rewards for keeping the Torah? They are freedom, health, long life, peace, prosperity, wealth, justice, and a relationship with one's Creator. These are all blessings resulting from living by the way of life that works, contained in the *Book of Life*.

I had found YHWH's Law to pass the tests of impartiality and reasonableness. The Torah formed a natural law that established equity, justice, health, and a balance of power for Israel's government where the citizens' voices could be heard. This, however, was only the tip of the iceberg. There were so many other issues that prevented me from stopping here. Many validity issues still remained. I wanted to know if Israel's Scriptures were historically valid. Or, where the Hebrew Scriptures simply written as political propaganda by Israel's priests?

8

Who Wrote the Hebrew Bible?

Although the scientific evidence for the reality of YHWH's Law may seem to invalidate Israel's charge of unrighteousness, many compelling arguments remain. Scripture's origins pose difficulty with consequences relating to Scripture's overall validity. Modern scholars view the Tanakh (Old Testament) as having been redacted for political reasons during the reign of Josiah (*c.* 630 BCE).[1]

The first writing phase of the Torah writing, according to some scholars, lasted from the tenth to the eighth centuries (BCE). Scholars identify four primary writers. Two writers have become known as "J" and "E" based on their prevalent usage of two names used for God. The former preferred to use "Yahweh" and the latter "Elohiym," as the name for Israel's God.[2] The second wave of invention occurred, according to currently accepted views, during the 7th century and is attributed to the Deuteronomistic ("D") and Priestly ("P") sources: the first redactor or group of redactors favored the Torah, and the latter showed bias toward the priesthood.[3] According to this theory, redactors or editors worked from the earlier J and E texts to compile a comprehensive narrative of the first four books of Torah. The Book of Deuteronomy was created during Josiah's reign and was incorporated into the J work. Recently, a newly developed computer algorithm program confirmed this general distinction of the predominate use of names of God based on variations of language and style, points of view, and duplications and repetitions in the text.[4]

Scholars are discovering that the Documentary Hypothesis, as it has come to be known, is not without problems.[5] Rolf Rendtorff, Professor of Old Testament at the University of Heidelberg, has identified formidable obstacles to identifying the J, E, P, and D sources as have Egyptologist James Hoffmeier and Assyriologist William Hallo.[6] Thankfully, Scripture preserves a record of its own authorship, so that we can know how to assign authorship to the various texts that developed during the course of the nation's history.

I. THE TORAH

A. *The Law of Moses*

The Book of Exodus records that Moses wrote the Law as it was given to him from the mouth of YHWH (Exod 24:4 and Deut 31:9). The Book of Numbers states that Moses recorded Israel's historical events (Num 33:2; Exod 17:14). The text then proceeds to list the places where Israel had journeyed and a description of which Moses had recorded.

> And *Moses wrote* **all the words of YHWH**, and rose up early in the morning, and built an altar under the hill, and twelve pillars, according to the twelve tribes of Israel. (Exod 24:4)

> And *Moses wrote* **their goings out according to their journeys by the commandment of YHWH**: and these are their journeys according to their goings out. (Num 33:2)

> And *Moses wrote this law*, **and delivered it to the priests the sons of Levi**, which bare the ark of the covenant of YHWH, and to all the elders of Israel. (Deut 31:9)

> And it came to pass, **when Moses had made an end of writing the words of this law in a book, until they were finished,** That Moses commanded the Levites, which bare the ark of the covenant of YHWH, saying, *Take this book of the law,* **and put it in the side of the ark of the covenant of YHWH your God,** that it may be there for a witness against you. (Deut 31:24–26)

One custom associated with ancient covenants was to store them inside a temple's sacred precincts (see pp. 66–68). The last text quoted above (Deut 31:24–26), states that Moses wrote all the words of "this law" in a book. This is a specific reference to the Book of Deuteronomy and its constitutional law code, which had been covenanted on the Moab plains. Moses gave this book to the Levites (Deut 31:9) to deposit in the Ark of the Covenant in the sacred precincts of Israel's Tabernacle. It was this Book of the Law that the Levites rediscovered (2 Kgs 22:8; 2 Chr 24:14) when making repairs to the First Temple during Josiah's reign.

According to texts listed above, in addition to recording Israel's covenantal Law and keeping a formal log of the nation's journeys, Moses recorded Israel's battles and other historical events. Some of these histories were written with prophecies, which were based on historical events.

> Joshua discomfited Amalek and his people with the edge of the sword. And YHWH said to Moses, **Write this for a memorial in a book,** and rehearse it in the ears of Joshua: for I will utterly put out the remembrance of Amalek[7] from under heaven. (Exod 17:13–14)

According to these texts, Moses wrote down: (1) the Law given to him at Sinai; (2) Israel's journeys in the wilderness; (3) Israel's history or chronicles; and the Moabic (Deuteronomy) covenant that was archived within the Ark of the Covenant. This would seemingly leave very little room for the Law to be originally recorded by another person other than Moses. However, scholars justifiably cite the account of Moses' death in Deut 34:5–7 as one of the most formidable challenges to Moses' authorship of the Torah.[8] If Moses wrote the Law, how did he record his own death?

Isaac de la Peyrère, a French Calvinist, added another criticism. He thought that the phrase "across the Jordan" (Deut 1:1) implied that Moses spoke to Israel on the other side of the Jordan, inside the Promised Land.[9] According to Scripture, YHWH banned Moses from entering the Promised Land (Num 20:12), and he died before entering Canaan. So how could Moses state that he was speaking to Israel "across the Jordan" if he never entered Canaan?

In yet another polemic about authorship, Spinoza, a sixteenth-century philosopher in Holland, observed that there were many third-person accounts of Moses, statements that Moses was unlikely to have made about himself.[10] In particular, Moses was unlikely to call himself "the humblest man on earth" as recorded in Num 12:3. The American Revolutionist Thomas Paine also noted that statements such as "unto this day" or "no man knows where the sepulcher is unto this day," (Deut 34:6) indicate that Deuteronomy was written well after Moses had lived.[11] If Moses did not write these portions of the Pentateuch, how can we be sure what Moses wrote?

Thankfully, Israel's scribes acknowledged the man who made editorial notations to Moses' work. Shortly before his death,

> Moses with the elders of Israel commanded the people, saying, keep all the commandments which I command you this day. And it shall be **on the day when you shall pass over Jordan** in to the land which YHWH your God gives you, that you shall set you up great stones, and plaster them with plaster: And you shall **write on them all the words of this law**, when you are passed over, that you may go in to the land which YHWH your God gives you, a land that flows with milk and honey; as YHWH God of your fathers has promised you. . . . and **you shall write on the stones all the words of this law very plainly.** (Deut 27:1–3, 8)

Israel passed over the Jordan River about one month later (chap. 9.III.C.2, p. 359). On the day Israel passed over the Jordan River, Joshua obeyed Moses' command to write a copy of the Law. Scripture records:

> And he [Joshua] wrote there on the stones **a copy of the Law of Moses**, which he wrote in the presence of the Children of Israel. (Josh 8:32, brackets added)

Joshua wrote a copy of the Law *after* Israel passed over the Jordan and obeyed Moses' command. Joshua's phrase "across the Jordan," refers to the Moab plains where Moses had indeed spoken to Israel. Joshua had worked side by side with Moses, knew his character, and saw the patience that Moses extended to a hardened and rebellious people. He was qualified to make character assessments regarding Moses' humility and to add more retrospective commentary to Moses' script.[12] The reason that YHWH commanded Moses to rehearse Israel's battle with Amalek in Joshua's ears (Joshua was not present on the hill with Moses, Exod 17:14, above) was so that Joshua could record this event in Israel's histories. YHWH had already chosen Joshua to succeed Moses as leader of his people and to chronicle the nation's history. As we will see, Joshua's role as chronicler was soon delegated to other scribes, who added yet more clarifying observations to Moses' original writing.

B. *The Testimony*

Scripture formally recognizes Israel's Law as the *Law of Moses*.[13] The *Law of Moses* comprised at least five parts: YHWH's charge, his statutes, his commandments, his judgments, and his testimony (1 Kgs 2:3; Ps 19:7–9). *'Eduwth*, Hebrew for "Testimony" means a 'warning' or a witness.[14] It is derived from the root *'ed*, meaning 'to bear witness.'[15] Though the Testimony was part of the Law, its division was far more distinct than the statutes or judgments (Isa 8:20). The Testimony was Israel's actual covenant, stating the terms of the Creator's pact with Israel.[16] It recorded the sign of YHWH's covenant, its blessing for compliance, and its penalties or consequences should Israel breach the covenant's regulations. These terms were given to Moses on two stone tablets formally known as the "Testimony."

> And YHWH spoke to Moses, saying, Speak you also to the Children of Israel, saying, Truly my sabbaths you shall keep: for it is a sign between me and you *throughout your generations*; that you may know that I am YHWH that does sanctify you. . . . Why the Children of Israel shall keep the sabbath, to observe the sabbath throughout their generations, for a perpetual covenant. It is a sign between me and the Children of Israel forever: for in six days YHWH made heaven and earth, and on the seventh day he rested, and was refreshed. And he gave to Moses, when he had made an end of communing with him on Mount Sinai, *two tables of testimony*, tables of stone, written with the finger of God. (Exod 31:12–18)

> YHWH said to Moses, Write you these words: for after the tenor of these words I have made a covenant with you and with Israel . . . And he wrote on the tables the words of the covenant, the ten commandments. (Exod 34:27–28; see also Exod 24:12; 31:18; 34:1; and Deut 4:13)

> Moses turned, and went down from the mount, and the two tables of the testimony were in his hand: the tables were written on both their sides; on the one side and on the other were they written. (Exod 32:15)

Although YHWH wrote the Ten Commandments on the two stone tables, these tablets were formally called the *Testimony*.[17] YHWH ordained the original Testimony to be housed in the ark;[18] hence the ark became known as the *Ark of the Covenant* or *Ark of Testimony* since it housed the original constitution, on which Israel was to base her theology, her government, and her way of life.

> You shall **put into the ark** *the testimony* **which I shall give you.** . . . And you shall put the mercy seat above upon the ark; and in the ark you shall put **the testimony** that I shall give you. And there I will meet with you, and I will commune with you from above the mercy seat, from between the two cherubim which are on **the ark of the testimony**, of all things which I will give you in commandment to the Children of Israel. (Exod 25:16, 21–22)

The rich, golden ark encased the originally engraved covenantal Testimony.[19] Scripture consistently interchanges the terms for the ark calling it both the *Ark of the Testimony*[20] and the *Ark of the Covenant*[21] since the Testimony was the formal written contract between YHWH and Israel (see chap. 3.I–II and chap. 14.I). Should any discrepancies arise among later documents, Israel's scribes could always ask the high priest to consult the original.[22] Since only the high priest had access to the original copy (written in stone and kept inside the Most Holy Place), YHWH limited the possibility that the authentic record could ever be altered (Exod 26:33; 28:29–35, 43).[23] The presence of YHWH communing with Israel above the mercy seat, which was atop the actual Testimony, implied that all discussions or negotiations would be based on the written constitution (Testimony) contained within the *Ark of Testimony.*

Moses or Joshua eventually merged the Sinai Testimony (inscribed on two stone tablets) into the collective written *Law of Moses*.[24] The practice of merging documents into a new canon is evidenced in ancient Egypt as early as the 18th Dynasty. Egyptologist K. Ryholt observes that five different sources were merged into the Turin King List. He theorizes that these sources were merged in the early 18th Dynasty,[25] directly from the kings' annals.[26] This date coincides with the very time that Israel had exited Egypt and Moses had written YHWH's Law.

As mentioned before, the Testimony comprised YHWH's written constitutional covenant with Israel at Mt. Sinai. The original Testimony consisted of three formal parts.[27] The first part instituted the 10 requirements. Today, this record is found in Exodus 20. The Sabbath sign constituted the second part of YHWH's Testimony and is today found in Exod 31:13–18. The third part of the Testimony listed blessings for compliance and penalties (or curses) should Israel breach her covenant with YHWH. This portion of the prophetic Testimony is today found in Leviticus 26.[28]

After those who rebelled after hearing the scouts' report had died in the wilderness (Num 14:23; 32:13; Deut 2:14), YHWH enacted the Moabic-Deuteronomy Covenant with their children, who had *not* entered into the earlier Sinai compact. Though Deuteronomy's

Covenant (Testimony) enumerated more-detailed stipulations for breach of pact (Deuter-onomy 27–30), these stipulations both clarified and expanded the stipulations of the original Sinai pact (Leviticus 26). The Moabic Covenant or Testimony was then added to the original constitutional covenant and housed in the Ark of Testimony.

> And it came to pass, **when Moses had made an end of writing the words of** *this law* **in a book, until they were finished,** That Moses commanded the Levites, which bare the ark of the covenant of YHWH, saying, **Take this book of the law, and put it in the side of the ark of the covenant of YHWH your God,** that it may be there for a witness against you. (Deut 31:24–26)

Both covenants were binding on Israel's people. The formal Testimony—the warning part of Israel's Law that described consequences for breach of pact—would encompass both the Sinai (Leviticus 26) and Moabic (Deuteronomy 28–30) contracts. The actual legal covenant was then edited into a story form with Moses' log of the nation's travels. YHWH com-manded that Moses rehearse Israel's battle with Amalek and include it in Israel's "memo-rial" (Exod 17:13–14). When Joshua obeyed this command, it added further detail to the "Law of Moses."

Thus, the entire Testimony has been divided in *The Law of Moses* and today is com-monly called the Pentateuch. Later, when we study the Testimonial Law, we will see that the consequences for Israel's breach of pact (Leviticus 26 and Deuteronomy 28–30) constitute the formal "Testimony." This division of the Law not only outlined consequences should the Israelites break their pact with their Creator, it *also provided a law for all prophecy.* Every one of Israel's righteous prophets based their prophecies on this chronologically prophetic law.

C. Colophons and Glosses

Colophons are "scribal notations" made at the end of a particular portion of text.[29] Colo-phons in ancient times were separated from the original text, thus allowing the scribe to append additional information that either helped to clarify the text he had just been work-ing with or supplemented it with more information not recorded in the original record.[30] Colophons are readily attested in Akkadian as well as Ugaritic documents.[31] Today, these colophons are not distinguished from the original copy but have been edited to appear as part of the original text. This is why we read that "Moses wrote" or "Joshua wrote" something in Scripture. A scribe appended a colophon to acknowledge the actual author but today this notation has become part of a particular chapter and verse in Scripture.

A gloss is a minor change or addition, such as the word Ramesses in Gen 47:11; Exod 12:37; and Num 33:3, 5. Glosses update obsolete terms or foreign words.[32] As we will see throughout this chapter, glosses and colophons consistently preserved knowledge about the original authorship. It is also the ancient practice of colophons that has unjustifiably given rise to criticism of anachronistic histories in Israel's Scriptures.

D. The Book of Wars

The Law of Moses, The Log of Israel's Wonderings, The Memorial of Israel's Battle with Amalek, and the *Testimony* were not the only books written before Israel's entry into Canaan. The Book of Numbers refers to a separate scroll that registered Israel's military campaigns:

> Wherefore it is said in the **book of the wars** of YHWH, (a) What he did in the Red Sea, and in the (b) brooks of Arnon, and at the stream of the brooks that goes down to the dwelling of Ar, and lies on the border of Moab. (Num 21:14–15)

The *Book of Wars*, which recorded Israel's battles, was originally a separate book from the *Law of Moses*. A later editor took the war book and interspersed it between the laws that YHWH had given to Moses. This is why the Torah retains a "story-like" feel rather than adhering to a formal law code (such as Hammurabi's Code), which would only have listed YHWH's laws. The merging of the *Book of Wars* into the Torah is what leads scholars to see different writing styles in the Torah and conclude that the Law had multiple authors.[34]

Today, the record of (a) "what YHWH did at the Red Sea" is Exodus 10–15, and Israel's victory at (b) Arnon is found in Numbers 21. YHWH's command for Moses to record Israel's battle with Amalek and the curse Moses issued against him may be another reference to the war chronicles. Portions of both Exodus and Numbers were excerpted from Israel's war chronicle, and it is likely that the books of Joshua and Judges, which primarily focus on military operations, were originally part of this scroll as well.

E. Archaeological Confirmation

Another piece of evidence supporting these conclusions is a text recently discovered by archaeologists working at modern Khirbet Qeiyafa.[35] Not only does this text date to King David and King Solomon's era, it bears implications for modern redactionary theories. Professor Gershon Galil of the University of Haifa, who deciphered the inscription, comments:

> It indicates that the Kingdom of Israel already existed in the 10th century BCE and that at least some of the biblical texts were written hundreds of years before the dates presented in current research.[36]

This text was written in a very ancient language that pre-dates Hebrew.[37] This demonstrates that the Law that Moses and Joshua had transcribed was also written in a language that foreshadowed scripts that eventually became known as Paleo-Hebrew or biblical Hebrew. What this ancient text confirms is that scribes existed at a very early time in ancient Israel's history. They were literate and capable of writing the nation's past. Additionally, the text confirms that the early Hebrew Law Code was indeed transmitted from one generation to another *via a written form*.

When Haifa University's Galil finally deciphered the text, he not only identified words unique to the Hebrew language but concepts in line with the Hebrew Law.

"It uses verbs that were characteristic of Hebrew, such as *asah* ('did') and *avad* ('worked'), which were rarely used in other regional languages," Galil said. "Particular words that appear in the text, such as *almanah* ('widow') are specific to Hebrew and are written differently in other local languages."[38]

Unlike most ancient texts, which are inscribed in clay (actually pressed into the stone), this ancient text is written in ink on a trapezoid-shaped piece of pottery about 6 inches by 6.5 inches (ostracon, an ancient kind of note paper). The text also appears to be a social statement, much in accord with the Hebrew Law, about how people should treat slaves, widows, and orphans (see Illustration 8.1). The ostracon may even have served as an order directly from King David or Solomon to direct local policies. In English, it reads (by numbered line):

Illustration 8.1. The ancient Hebrew inscription known as the "Galil-Ostracon."

1′ you shall not do [it], but worship the [Lord].
2′ Judge the sla[ve] and the wid[ow]/Judge the orph[an]
3′ [and] the stranger. [Pl]ead for the infant/plead for the po[or and]
4′ the widow. Rehabilitate [the poor] at the hands of the king.
5′ Protect the po[or and] the slave/[supp]ort the stranger.[39]

The content, which has some missing letters, is similar to some Scriptures, such as Isa 1:17, Ps 72:3, and Exod 23:3. Its form gives rise to the fact that it predated later authors. Similar to modern scholarly methods, David and Isaiah quoted directly from the Law in order to teach or draw parallels, in the same way that modern scholars quote from an article or other scholarly work they wish to study or advance.

II. JOSHUA

Titles for books of Scripture are often misleading. Titles that bear a person's name imply authorship. The Book of Joshua is a case in point. It is questionable whether Joshua made any entries into the chronicle that bears his name or whether the narratives were simply registered by several scribes who served under Joshua's administration. The Book of Joshua originally consisted of at least three books, though probably more.

The first few chapters of Joshua (through ch. 5) were, in their original state, part of the modern Book of Deuteronomy. This conclusion is drawn from the chronology presented in both books. The first chapter[40] of Deuteronomy states that Moses outlined the conditions and blessings for the nation's re-covenenting with YHWH in the *"fortieth year*, in the *eleventh month*, on the first day of the month"* (Deut 1:3). No other chronological information is presented until Moses' death, when the chronicle states that Israel mourned for him "thirty days" (Deut 34:8). The Book of Joshua continues this chronicle as though there is no break in text or chronology, and no clarification of dates is given. Rather, the opening of the book states that in three days (after the mourning period for Moses had ended) Israel needed to be ready to enter the Promised Land (Josh 1:11). This chronicle continues its account, stating that Israel crossed the Jordan on the tenth day of the first month, four days before Passover (Josh 5:10).

Clarification and a context for the "year" when these dates occurred are not provided until Josh 5:7, where the scribe clarifies that Israel crossed the Jordan in the 40th year after the exodus. This means that Moses had only died about 40 days prior to the account in Joshua 5. The fact that the first four chapters of Joshua continue the chronology established in Deut 1:3 indicates that the two records were originally one book. The scribe's reaffirmation that it was the 40th year when Israel actually entered Canaan in ch. 5 may signal the beginning of a new chronicle (or book) or the hand of a new scribe. What this evidence strongly supports is that Joshua or a scribe(s) under his administration originally edited the Book of Deuteronomy along with the first four or five chapters of Joshua. A later scribe, who organized various documents into the coherent history we read today, later divided the two records based on Moses' life. The scribe ended Deuteronomy with Moses' death and began the Book of Joshua with the beginning of Joshua's administration after Moses' death. If the chronology in these two books was quite well known at the time, the scribe may have missed the lack of clarity that this division brought to the date of the chronicle (see Table 9.4 on page 359).

The first significant break in the Joshua narrative[41] occurs in chaps. 14–17, which represent a summary of the "lots of inheritance" that Moses had established in the plains of Moab, about one month before Israel entered the Promised Land.[42] Well after Joshua had carved out a base area for Israel to launch her campaigns, Joshua charged scouts to record the unknown geographical features of Canaan's unexplored territories and to "write them in a book." Record of these territories is today found in Josh 18:10–19:51. *The Book of Distribution*, as some scholars call it, records the territories distributed to seven of Israel's tribes. The Book of Distribution was then entered into the "Joshua Chronicle" during the Shiloh (Release Year) assembly (Joshua 23–24) or at a later date.

Some of the confusion about the Joshua narrative may arise from the scribal practice of dual witnesses: two or more scribes provided an account of an event. Additionally, both Joshua and Judges manifest a relatively great number of editorial (colophons and glosses) remarks that served to clarify the context or update the nation's records (Josh 13:1–14; Judg 1–2). This is especially apparent in the section pertaining to the territories that Israel failed to conquer (Josh 15:63; 16:10; 17:12–13; Judges 1).

Recent scholarship has demonstrated genuine scribal practices in the Joshua narratives.[43] Egyptologist James Hoffmeier demonstrates contemporary scribal protocol in written

Egyptian records during the reign of Thutmoses III (*c.* 1458–1425).[44] What we learn from these records is that the Joshua narratives were drawn from other sources such as a Daybook and were written using a "history formula" that was common during the fifteenth century BCE. Hoffmeier cites six different components of the Joshua entries that demonstrate similarity with Egyptian formulas.[45] Not only are Egyptian scribal practices reflected in the Joshua account; many contemporary customs of warfare are included.[46] This lends credence to the possibility that, not only had Israel been in Canaan for several decades before Thutmoses III's campaigns in Canaan, but also that Israel was well-versed in Egyptian scribal practices during the fifteenth century. This indicates that Israel had entered Canaan long before the thirteenth-century date commonly accepted in modern academia, evidence that we will examine in chaps. 9–11.

III. JUDGES

The Book of Judges follows the same heavily edited pattern as Joshua. The first chapter of Judges through the Bochim (2:1–5) incident were probably originally part of the original Joshua narrative. In its original state, the Judges chronicle probably opened with Judg 3:1. A later scribe added the Conquest Summary that charted the military leave that Joshua gave to Israel's armies (2:6), which allowed the soldiers to establish their tribal heritages. This opening compendium repeated Joshua's death, giving an account of the Israelites' righteousness during the lives of those who outlived Joshua (2:10). Thus the scribe established both the terminus of the Joshua narrative and an overview of the entire Judges Era. Not only does Judg 2:6–23 begin a new record, it attests the hand of a scribe who lived long after the Judges Era and who could qualify and grant context to the events that the book recorded.

Levite scribes are the most likely candidates for authoring and editing other narratives found in the Book of Joshua. History writing was primarily a governmental function associated with the Temple.[47] In Israel's premonarchic history, chronicling was sporadic. The Song of Deborah, written about 200 years after Joshua's death, may attest to the chronicling and updating of the Book of Joshua and the beginning portions of the Book of Judges (Judg 1–5:31) during Deborah's administration.[48] Deborah tells us that, after Israel's battle with Jabin, scribes residing in Zebulun's territory (Judg 5:14) came to her. The tribe of Zebulun may have housed the Levite branch that registered the nation's chronicles during this era. The fact that Deborah used scribes (plural) indicates that more than one person edited and recorded parts of Joshua and Judges. Deborah and her scribes updated the nation's archives and they would have been contemporary with Ramesses II.[49] After Deborah's administration, the record of Israel's archives goes silent until Samuel's school of the prophets (1 Samuel 10). What role this school played in the nation's archives is uncertain. More certainly, Samuel (1 Chr 9:22) instructed David regarding the institutional aspects of the nation's archives in preparation for the time when he would inherit Saul's kingdom (1 Sam 19:18–22). We will return to the issues of editing in Israel's early history when we examine evidence for the Canaan Conquest in chap. 11, pp. 574–82. The entries in the books of Judges and Samuel indicate that the Levites inserted notations regarding events in the nation's history during the sabbatical years, when the nation had opportunity to renew the covenant (see chap. 9).

IV. PSALMS

In chap. 5.IV ("Vanquishing Modern Myths"), I mentioned that Israel's psalms were similar to psalms written for Temple services throughout the Near East. In Israel, psalms were official "state" prophecies that were hidden in praises to man's Creator. *Each psalm was an individual prophecy.* Some songs prophesied specific events. Psalm 137, for instance, foretold Israel's Diaspora in Babylon, while other songs prophesied of people who would play a role or function in Israel's history.

David wrote Psalm 72 as prophecy, ordaining events to occur during Solomon's reign. Psalm 72 is entitled "for Solomon": vv. 10 and 15 foretold Sheba's queenly visit, and v. 17 ordained that Solomon's name would endure forever!

> The kings of Tarshish and of the isles shall bring presents: the kings of **Sheba and Seba shall offer gifts.** Yes, all kings shall fall down before him: all nations shall serve him. And he shall live, and to him shall be given of the gold of Sheba: prayer also shall be made for him continually; and daily shall he be praised. . . **His name shall endure forever**: his name shall be continued as long as the sun: and men shall be blessed in him: all nations shall call him blessed. (Ps 72:10–11, 15, 17)

The fulfillment of this prophecy is found in 1 Kings 10 and 1 Chronicles 9. Even to this day, most people who attend church have heard of Israel's King Solomon; thus his name has endured "forever". One of the primary functions for the books of the Psalms was to ordain and prophesy about events and people that would play a role in Israel's history—whether it was for good or for evil.

In many ways, the prophecies in the Book of Psalms served as another witness to the prophets' testimony. The Psalms' "record of prophecies" not only ordained future commissions; it served as a mechanism to ensure the truthfulness of a later prophet's testimony. Should there be any question about the credibility of a prophet's claim, it could be compared with the Law of Moses (Josh 8:31), the Testimonial Law (Isa 8:20) and the Books of Psalms. We will further examine the Psalms' role in prophecy below, then pick up the topic again when we examine the Testimony, Israel's prophetic law, in part two of this book (chap. 14).

A. Authorship

The Hebrew title for Psalms is "Book of Praises." Although David was the Psalms' greatest contributor, he was *not* the book's only author. After Samuel anointed David to be king, he and David collaborated to establish Israel's various priestly offices for the Monarchy Era (1 Chr 9:22).[50] They instituted "the sons of Korath" as prophets and choir members to praise and prophesy in the Temple.[51] The sons of Korah were Levites who did not receive a commission to the priesthood (Num 4:2–4; 16:1–40) but usually served in the role of prophet (2 Chr 20:19–21). Samuel was a descendant of Korah (1 Chr 6:38–33) and the prophet whom YHWH had raised for Israel in Moses' stead (Deut 18:15–19).[52]

Israel's Temple choir consisted of singers (1 Chr 15:16; 16:4–7), harpists (1 Chr 25:3), trumpeters (1 Chr 25:5), and cymbalists (1 Chr 25:1). Asaph, the chief singer, served as a multifaceted conductor. He ministered before the ark, played cymbals (1 Chr 16:5), led the choir, prophesied, and contributed significantly to the Book of Psalms.

The Book of 1st Chronicles records:

> Moreover David and the captains of the host separated to the service of the sons of *Asaph, and of Heman, and of Jeduthun,* who should *prophesy* with harps, with psalteries, and with cymbals: and the number of the workmen according to their service was. (1 Chr 25:1)

Asaph, Heman, Jeduthun, and their sons were also prophets. 2 Chr 29:30 states that Asaph was a prophet whose prophetic songs were sung by the Levites. Jeduthun is listed both as a harp player and as David's prophet (1 Chr 25:52; 2 Chr 35:15), and Heman's sons are also listed as David's seers (prophets) in 1 Chr 25:5.[53] These three men wrote songs for the Temple, their sons inherited their role as choir members and prophets (2 Chr 20:14–19), and they greatly contributed to authoring the Book of Psalms.

Individual titles for each psalm usually provide the name of the person who authored it.[54] Asaph wrote 12 psalms (Psalm 50; 73–83). Heman authored Psalms 88 and 89. Moses authored Psalm 90, while Haggai and Zechariah wrote Psalms 146–148. And David probably authored many of the remaining praises.

B. Psalm Titles

Titles of psalms are crucial for understanding a particular prophecy's scope and intent. Many psalms ordained the epistle of Israel's prophets and are entitled "For instruction of the sons of Korah." David provided instruction for prophecy to Korah's sons in Psalms 42 and 44–49. Asaph instructed Korah's prophets in Psalms 85, 87, and 88. Asaph is himself listed as a Korite in 1 Chr 26:1 (and 6:39), and all three of the families that David established in the Temple choir were descendants of Korah (1 Chr 26:1; 6:33–37).

In some cases, a psalm's title contains a particular prophet's oracle instruction. David directed Jeduthun's prophecies (in Psalms 39; 62; 77; and 2 Chr 35:15), and he passes a "baton" or ordains a song for the singer (1 Chr 6:33) Hemen in Psalms 53. In other cases, a psalm may foretell or ordain prophets to receive YHWH's commission. For instance, Psalms 138 foretells of Haggai and Zechariah. Both of these prophets fulfilled David's prophetic instruction by prophesying during King Darius's second year. The Septuagint[55] titles this song: "A Psalm of David: For Haggai and Zechariah." David not only ordained their ministries, but provided their "prophetic" instructions.

Interestingly, Asaph often supplements a previous prophecy (psalm) by entitling it "*a song of a song.*" David also uses this "song of a song" method, opening a window on a prophetic song written in *earlier Scripture*[56] or on other prophecies in the Book of Praises itself. Thus, these additions further augmented David's, Deborah's, Asaph's, and Moses' many prophetic songs.

V. KINGS AND CHRONICLES

The books we know today as 1 and 2 Samuel, 1 and 2 Kings, and 1 and 2 Chronicles were, in their original format, voluminous manuscripts that were eventually edited into six simple books.[57] Israel's prophets wrote the Book of Kings. According to Scripture, the proper title for the Book of Kings is *The Book of the Kings of Israel and Judah*.[58] At the beginning of the Kingdom Era, these annals comprised the prophets' independent manuscripts.[59] During the reign of Asa, the prophets' record became a formal state document in a single archive: *The Book of the Kings of Israel and Judah* (2 Chr 16:11).

One special branch of the priesthood constituted the office of the scribe who narrated the Book of Chronicles.[60] Originally, there were two sets of Chronicle books: *The Book of the Chronicles of the Kings of Judah* and *The Book of the Chronicles of the Kings of Israel*.[61] Unhappily, the latter book has not survived and was probably destroyed during Samaria's siege.

A. Chronicles' Scribalship

Ancient Israel's scribal practices were contemporary with other nations'. By the twelfth to tenth centuries (BCE), royal Assyrian scribes were already using chronicles and other sources when composing their texts.[62] Ancient Israel similarly used chronicles, monuments, archives, and ancient sources to write history[63] that is not very different from the way we "remember the past" today. Assyriologist William Hallo observes:

> When biblical authors appropriated Bronze Age sources for the early Israelites history, they did so intelligently, purposefully, and selectively. . . . Their reflexes in biblical literature are neither free creations *de novo*, nor uncritical imitations of everything available. The case for the use of ancient Near Eastern materials is thus the same whether we are studying early Hebrew history or early Mesopotamian or Egyptian history.[64]

While the Scriptural record is virtually silent regarding how Israel recorded her history prior to the Monarchy, the evidence is quite substantial once the Kohite priest-prophet Samuel helped David to organize the nation's government institutions.

One of the first official posts that David established in the New Monarchy Era was the office of national historian. David

> appointed **certain of the Levites** to minister before the ark of YHWH, **and to record**, and to thank and praise YHWH God of Israel. (1 Chr 16:4)

The recorder marked or "remembered" events and registered them.[65] The second and more common designation was that of common scribe.[66] Basically, the scribe's duty was to count.[67] Isaiah gives some indication of this, inquiring: "Where is the scribe? Where is the receiver? **Where is he that counted the towers?**" (Isa 33:18). 2 Chr 26:11 also indicates that counting "fighting men" was the scribe's task.[68]

Uzziah had a host of fighting men, that went out to war by bands, according to the number of their account by the hand of **Jeiel the scribe**. (2 Chr 26:11)

In Hezekiah's days, Jeiel was reckoned among the sons of Levi (2 Chr 29:12–13). Early in Israel's kingdom years, the recorder wrote chronicles while the scribe provided numbers and was in charge of tallies, such as the composition of armies, or garrisons, the number of battle casualties, etc.; perhaps he was similar to a news reporter today.[69] The recorder no doubt used the scribe's data when he wrote the king's annals. In her study on Israel's administrative offices, Nili Fox argues that the recorder had a more oral role such as a heralder, rather than a scribal position. She sees the position as referring to an individual who makes announcements throughout the kingdom.[70] Perhaps a more accurate comparison of this post would be with the modern "press secretary" with expanded duties. The recorder's and the scribe's sons filled their offices when their service years were terminated (Num 4:47; 8:24–26).[71]

During the nation's righteous epochs, the Monarchy faithfully acknowledged Chronicles' authors. The first entry to record Israel's chroniclers appeared during David's reign:

Jehoshaphat the son of Ahilud was **recorder** . . . and Seraiah was the **scribe**. (2 Sam 8:16–17)[72]

Jehoshaphat wrote Israel's history during David's reign, a narrative preserved in 1 Chronicles 10–22. Seraiah provided the names of those who united with David during Saul's persecution as well as the Levites who ministered before the ark (1 Chronicles 11–12, 16), while Jehoshaphat compiled them into the actual Chronicle record. That the Levites authored the Book of Chronicles is confirmed by the following account:

And Shemaiah the son of Nethaneel the scribe, one of the Levites, *wrote* them before the king, and the princes, and Zadok the priest, and Ahimelech the son of Abiathar, and before the chief of the fathers of the priests and Levites: one principal household being taken for Eleazar, and one taken for Ithamar. (1 Chr 24:6)

Shemaiah's record of Eleazar's and Ithamar's House is today found in 1 Chronicles 23–27. During this time, the "Acts of Solomon," chronicles of Solomon's reign, were also written. Scripture registers the historian and scribe who held these offices during Solomon's days, indicating that Jehoshaphat chronicled both David's and Solomon's reigns: "Elihoreph and Ahiah, the sons of Shisha, scribes; **Jehoshaphat the son of Ahilud**, the recorder" (1 Kgs 4:3). Following Solomon's annals, however, the names of Israel's scribes and recorders rarely appear. Hezekiah's reign is the most notable exception, indicating that Hezekiah himself ordered the entry, following in the footsteps of his father David (2 Kgs 18:18; see also 2 Kgs 18:37; Isa 36:3).

B. *Transcribing and Updating the Archives*

Scripture evidences that one of the first tasks that the Levites undertook during King David's administration was copying, updating, and codifying the nation's loosely organized annals. Toponyms (names of geographical locations) are the primary evidence for the scribes' use of glosses for the purpose of clarifying context.

Scribes would update references to ancient cities or acknowledge that a certain feature (e.g., Rachel's pillar, Gen 35:20) still existed in their day.[73] The purpose of this practice was at least twofold: to update out of date material (1 Sam 9:9);[74] and to verify the historicity of the texts that the scribe was updating.[75] For instance, the scribe's eye witness account that the story of Achan was indeed factual was verified by the fact that the stones over Achan's body were still visible during the scribe's lifetime (Josh 7:26). This was in contrast to Moses' burial site, which the scribe could not verify (Deut 34:6).

The scribes' glosses primarily centered on ancient locations, such as cities or previously destroyed sites. For instance, a scribe used a gloss to state that Ai was still a "heap of stones" that had not been rebuilt "unto his day" (Josh 28:8–9). Another text states that the ancient city of Luz was the same place as "Bethel," since Jacob had renamed the former city, "Bethel" (Gen 28:19). Therefore, the scribe continually reminds the reader that Luz is Bethel (Gen 35:6; Josh 18:13; Judg 1:23). Why did the scribes consider all these editorial remarks so important?

Throughout the ancient world, cities were destroyed and rebuilt.[76] Sometimes they fell into decay, but more often they were conquered and destroyed by their rivals. Usually, parts of one city were used to build another city either on the same site or on another site some distance away (see the Tel Dan inscription, p. 605). In other instances, one city was destroyed only to be relocated at another site but using the same name. In the case of Luz, the scribe uses a colophon to explain the changes to the reader after the Joseph tribes had destroyed Bethel/Luz during the conquest. Later, a man went into Hittite territory to establish another city by the same name (i.e., Luz). Thus, the scribes' colophon preserved this information so that future generations would not confuse the two sites (i.e., *after the scribe's lifetime*, the older Bethel would not be confused with the modern Luz, which was separated from Bethel by a great distance. This would avert the readers from wondering how Jacob could rename the Hittite city of Luz).[77]

We also have evidence about the transcribing of Israel's records prior to David's administration. An earlier scribe used a gloss ("unto this day") to document the fact that during his days the Benjaminites still shared Jerusalem with the Jebusites (Judg 1:21). David purchased Jerusalem from Araunah, the Jebusite king (2 Sam 24:21–23), thus taking full possession of the mount. The scribe's notation may even have served as a record explaining when the text had been transcribed.

Some of the most controversial editing occurred with regard to the cities associated with Israel's exodus. As I have mentioned, cities did not always stand the test of time. They were often destroyed. This was especially true regarding the cities to which the scribe referred in Exodus: Pharaoh's store-city of Pithom and Pi-Ramses. By all *Scriptural accounts*,[78] Ramsses would postdate the exodus by some 150 years. So the reference to a city of Ramses would be anachronistic and suspect. However, this gloss (the practice of updating outdated terms) poses a number of questions in regard to scribal practices.

How would a scribe refer to ancient cities that no longer existed? What protocol would a scribe follow if a capital city had been abandoned by a later monarch? How should a scribe refer to a city that not only had been abandoned but whose monuments, temples, and other relics had been relocated to another site? In the Hebrew Scriptures, it appears that the scribe used a gloss to refer to the cities that Israel built during her time in Egypt.[79] The only conclusion that we can draw with certainty is that the reference in Exod 1:11 to Pithom refers to a store city,[80] while Pi-Ramses refers to Egypt's capital city. The scribe may have used Pi-Ramses so the reader would associate it with the Egyptian capital during his day, or the scribe could have been updating a reference to Avaris, an older city that lay buried underneath Pi-Ramses. I will return to the problems associated with this gloss when we look at the Exodus and Conquest.[81]

While the first official catalogue of Israel's history was organized under David's administration, the second or third commission for bringing the nation's archives up to date probably occurred during the righteous epochs of Hezekiah's and Josiah's reigns. As we will see below, each time a monarch commissioned this task, Scripture recognizes the Levites who held the official scribal office of national historian. These later modernizations and archiving of the nation's history provide evidence for the modern historian that the entire Pentateuch had been written by the sixth century (BCE).

C. *The Book of the Kings of Israel and Judah*

1. David

Before David ascended Israel's throne, Israel's histories were privatized, and had not yet become a function of the royal court. These annals were usually written by the Levitical prophet(s) who had direct interaction or direct contact with the king. The Hebrew Scriptures evidence that the books that the King James Version calls 1st and 2nd Samuel were, in their original state, three separate scrolls. Scripture uses a colophon[82] to acknowledge the original authors for this portion of its history.

> Now the acts of David the king, first and last, behold, they are **written in the book of Samuel the seer**, and in the **book of Nathan the prophet**, and in the **book of Gad the seer**. (1 Chr 29:29)

This verse attests three separate manuscripts written by three different prophets who recorded David's life. 1st Sam 10:25 states that Samuel wrote "in a book" the "manner of kingdom" Israel would have under a monarch. This indicates Samuel documented Israel's history before Saul and continued to record the first events of David's life before his (Samuel's) death.

The conclusion here is as follows: The prophet Samuel wrote 1 Samuel 1–21. Gad wrote about David's exile years, which constitute 1 Samuel 22–24–2 Samuel 6 and 2 Samuel

13–2 Samuel 23. The prophet Nathan wrote about David's last years, which constitute 2 Samuel 7–12 and 2 Samuel 24–1 Kings 1–4. Notice that each prophet/seer recorded one epoch of David's life with the exception of 2 Samuel 24. Although Gad might have recorded what is today 2 Samuel 24, the events in this text occurred toward the end of his life, when it is presumed that Nathan had assumed the recorder's role. At a much later date these manuscripts were edited into three books (1 and 2 Samuel [originally one book], and 1 Kings), which placed events in chronological order, ignoring actual authorship.[83]

2. Solomon

1 Kgs 11:41 records that Solomon's chronicles were originally written in a book entitled "The Acts of Solomon." Today, Scripture records these "acts" or "chronicles" in 2 Chronicles 1–9. As in the account of David's life, the scribe uses a colophon to acknowledge the persons who actually recorded "the acts of Solomon":

> Now the rest of the acts of Solomon, first and last, are they not written in the book of Nathan the prophet, and in the prophecy of Ahijah the Shilonite, and in the visions of Iddo the seer against Jeroboam the son of Nebat? (2 Chr 9:29)

This verse demonstrates that three prophets recorded both Solomon and Jeroboam's acts (annals or chronicles). Nathan began the writing of Solomon's life where he had ended the recording of David's. This constitutes 1 Kings 1–10. Ahijah wrote the prophecy regarding Jeroboam's claim to the ten tribes found in 1 Kings 11, having written this text during Solomon reign. Much later, Iddo wrote the words (vision) of Ahijah against Jeroboam I found in 1 Kings 12–14, because Ahijah was blind in his old age (1 Kgs 14:4) and could not write the prophecy for himself. Interestingly, although the prophet Ahijah was unable to write this vision for himself, a fellow prophet did record his words, thus maintaining the consistency of the Book of Kings' Levitical or prophetic authorship.

Other evidence for the prophet's authorship of *The Book of the Kings of Israel and Judah* (today 1 and 2 Kings) is found in a colophon appended to the record of Manasseh, king of Judah.

> Now the rest of the acts of Manasseh, and his prayer to his God, and the words of the seers that spoke to him in the name of YHWH of Israel, behold, they are written in the book of the kings of Israel. His prayer also,[84] and how God was intreated of him, and all his sin, and his trespass, and the places where he built high places, and set up groves and graven images, before he was humbled: behold, **they are written among the sayings of the** *seers*. (2 Chr 33:18–19)

There are no independent books written by Israel's prophets that record these "sayings of the seers." However, the words of Israel's seers against Manasseh are found in 2 Kings 21:10–15.

> And YHWH spoke by his servants the prophets, saying, Because Manasseh king of Judah has done these abominations, and has done wickedly above all that the Amorites did, which were before him, and has made Judah also to sin with his idols: Therefore thus said YHWH God of Israel, Behold, I am bringing such evil on Jerusalem and Judah, that whosoever hears of it, both his ears shall tingle. And I will stretch over Jerusalem the line of Samaria, and the plummet of the House of Ahab: and I will wipe Jerusalem as a man wipes a dish, wiping it, and turning it upside down. And I will forsake the remnant of my inheritance, and deliver them into the hand of their enemies; and they shall become a prey and a spoil to all their enemies; Because they have done that which was evil in my sight, and have provoked me to anger, since the day their fathers came forth out of Egypt, even unto this day. (2 Kgs 21:10–15)

The books of Kings serve as a testimony in the same manner as the works of Isaiah or Jeremiah. Israel's prophets wrote the Book of the Kings of Israel and Judah, ensuring the truth regarding Israel's history and YHWH's written word. And it appears that the "Sayings of the Seers" has been edited into the prophets' chronicles of the nation's history (see Table 8.1).

3. Rehoboam

Scripture provides evidence that two separate annals were begun at the dichotomy of Israel's kingdom (1 Kgs 14:19, 29). The proper titles of these two works were *Chronicles of the Kings of Judah* and *Chronicles of the Kings of Israel*. With respect to the authorship of Kings during Rehoboam's reign, the prophets' colophon states:

> Now the acts of Rehoboam, first and last, are they not **written in the book of Shemaiah the prophet**, and of **Iddo the seer** concerning genealogies? (2 Chr 12:15)

Table 8.1. Prophets and Kings

Date	Judah	Israel	Prophets	Reference
1023	David		Samuel	1 Sam 16
			Gad	2 Sam 24:11
			Nathan	2 Sam 7:2
			Asaph	2 Chr 29:30
			Jeduthun	1 Chr 16:41; 2 Chr 35:15
			Zadok	2 Sam 15:27; 1 Sam 9:9
			Heman and sons	1 Chr 25:5

Table 8.1. Prophets and Kings, *cont.*

Date	Judah	Israel	Prophets	Reference
983	Solomon		Nathan	1 Kgs 1:45
			Asaph, Jeduthun	2 Chr 5:12
			Heman and sons	2 Chr 5:12
			Ahijah	1 Kgs 11:29
			Iddo	2 Chr 9:29
944	Rehoboam	Jeroboam	Iddo (cont.)	2 Chr 12:15
927	Abijam		Ahijah	1 Kings 14:2
			Shemaiah	1 Chr 12:5; 1 Kgs 12–14
925	Asa	Nadab	Jehu ben Hanani	2 Chr 16:7; 1 Kgs 16
		Baasha	Azariah ben Oded	2 Chr 15:1, 8
		Omri		
885	Jehoshaphat	Ahab	Jehu ben Hanani	2 Chr 19:2
		Ahaziah	Micaiah ben Imla	2 Chr 18:18
			Eliezer ben Dodavah	2 Chr 20:37
			Elijah	1 Kgs 17–21
				2 Kgs 1:3; 2 Chr 21:12
864	Jehoram	Joram	Elisha[85]	2 Kgs 5:8
857	Ahaziah	Jehu		
	6 yrs. no king			
851	Joash	Jehu (cont.)	Elisha	2 Kgs 11–12; 2 Chr 22:10–24:27
		Jehoahaz	Jonah?	2 Kgs 14:25
814	Amaziah	Jehoash	Elisha	2 Kgs 13:14–25
			Hosea	Hosea 1:1
796	Amaziah/	Jeroboam II	Amos	Amos 1:1
	Uzziah	Menahem	Hosea	Hosea 1:1
		Pekahiah	Isaiah	2 Chr 26:22; Isa 1:1
744	Jotham	Pekah	Micah	Mic 1:1
			Oded	2 Chr 28:9
736	Ahaz	Hoshea	Hoshea	Hosea 1:1
722	Hezekiah		Isaiah	Isa 1:1
			Micah	Mic 1:1; Jer 26:18
694	Manasseh			
640	Amon			
639	Josiah		Jeremiah	Jer 1:1
			Zephaniah	Zeph 1:1
			Huldah	2 Chr 34:22
608	Jehoiakim		Uriyah	Jer 26:20
			Jeremiah	Jer 1:3
			Daniel	Dan 1:1
597	Zedekiah (Jehoiachin)		Ezekiel	Ezek 1:2

Iddo's genealogies are today scattered throughout 1 Chronicles 1–9.[86] The only "acts" of Rehoboam in Scripture are found in 1 Kings 12–14. This identifies Shemaiah as the author of this portion of the Kings' narrative (see above).

Notice the pattern set thus far? The Book of Chronicles witnesses an insertion in *The Book of Kings of the Kings of Israel and Judah,* while the Book of Kings, in turn, witnesses an entry into the Chronicles' archive.[87] These scribal colophons ensured the consistency and validity of any given entry. This practice of joint-recognition is consistently adhered to until the kingdom's twilight years, when the kings' annals were no longer the court's top priority due to political unrest. This same record-keeping pattern is often seen in Egypt, where periods of peace and prosperity are marked by abundant epigraphic material, while periods of unrest are manifest by the dearth of written materials[88] (i.e., Egypt's First and Second Intermediate Periods).

4. Jeroboam I (Ephraim)

> And the rest of the acts of Jeroboam, how he warred, and how he reigned, behold, they are written in the book of the **chronicles of the kings of *Israel.***
> (1 Kgs 14:19)

This is the first reference to a formal document called *The Chronicles of the Kings of Israel,* indicating that the king's annals have now become a formal state document rather than an individual record. The Israelite Chronicle of Jeroboam has been preserved in its entirety and was compiled with the Chronicles of Judah by a later editor. Jeroboam I's chronicle is found in 2 Chronicles 10–13. (A copy of this chronicle may have been taken to Jerusalem when Jeroboam cast the Levites out of his kingdom, which would explain its survival.)

The Levites' ability to record events in Israel's Northern Kingdom was severely thwarted when Jeroboam cast out the Levitical priesthood (1 Kgs 12:31; 13:33). The Northern Kingdom's only remaining chronicles state:

> And Rehoboam dwelled in Jerusalem, and built cities for defense in Judah. And the priests and the Levites that were in all Israel resorted to him out of all their coasts. **For the Levites left their suburbs and their possession, and came to Judah and Jerusalem:** for Jeroboam and his sons had cast them off from executing the priest's office unto YHWH. (2 Chr 11:5, 13–14)

Since Jeroboam expelled Levi's scribes, the Northern Kingdom's subsequent chronicles are severely lacking and northern kings are generally mentioned only when they came in contact with Judah's kings. Only once after Jeroboam I is a Samarian king written as an "Israelite entry" (see 2 Chr 25:17–25). This annal, too, has been edited into *The Book of the Chronicles of Judah.* The rest of Israel's chronicles were probably handled by royal scribes or priests installed by Jeroboam. The chronicles of Israel that did exist no doubt disappeared during the Northern Kingdom's deportations.

5. Abijah/Abijam (Judah)

> And the rest of the acts of Abijah, and his ways, and his sayings, are written in the story of the prophet Iddo. (2 Chr 13:22)

Since this text is an entry in the Chronicles' archive, it would normally imply that Iddo wrote an entry in the Book of Kings (1 Kgs 15:1–8), and he may have. However, the only record of Abijam's "ways and sayings" is 2 Chronicles 13. There are several possibilities: (1) Iddo's entry may be lost; (2) it is possible that a later editor switched the Chronicle with the testimony of Kings; or (3) most likely, as a prophet and Levitical scribe, Iddo wrote both entries.

6. Nadab–Baasha (Kings of Ephraim)
Asa–Jehoshaphat (Kings of Judah)

Nadab succeeded Jeroboam I and reigned for two years (1 Kgs 15:25). The only reference to his administration (1 Kgs 15:25–31) records Baasha's extermination of Jeroboam's House and conquering Samaria's throne during Asa's third year. 1 Kgs 15:31 mentions a correlating entry in Samaria's archives (*The Chronicles of the Kings of Israel*), this chronicle, however, is absent from Scripture. Scripture does refer to an entry for Asa in the King's record:

> The acts of Asa, first and last, see, they are written in the book of the kings of Judah and Israel. (2 Chr 16:11)

This is the first reference to a formal record of Judah's and Israel's kings as being the prophets' testimonies that were codified into a single state document. Following Asa's reign, recognition of the author-prophet who registered entries in the *Book of the Kings of Israel and Judah* is no longer cited, with the exception of Isaiah. The prophet Jehu *ben* ('son of') Hanani chronicled this portion of the *Book of the Kings of Judah and Israel* (today, 1 and 2 Kings). Jehu was the predominant prophet in the lives of both kings (2 Chr 16:7;[89] 1 Kings 16), and the events recorded in 1 Kings 15 and 16 are incidents that fulfilled prophecies issued by Jehu ben Hanani. This conclusion is further supported by an entry *in the Book of Chronicles* stating that the acts of Jehoshaphat were

> written in the book of Jehu the son of Hanani, who is mentioned in the book of the kings of Israel. (2 Chr 20:34)

If Jehu recorded the first and last events of Jehoshaphat, then it is conceivable that he recorded the previous lives of Asa and Baasha as well. Jehu's testimony is today found in 1 Kings 22.

7. Uzziah

A colophon in the *Chronicles of the Kings of Judah* tells us that Isaiah inserted an entry into the *Book of the Kings of Judah*. "Now the rest of the acts of Uzziah, first and last, did Isaiah the prophet, the son of Amoz, write" (2 Chr 26:22). Isaiah's record of Uzziah's acts begin in 2 Kgs 14:21 and continue through 2 Kgs 15:31. Thus the prophet Isaiah was one of the nation's final archivists (see Table 8.2).

D. *Genealogical Entries*

Israel's chronicles acknowledge four genealogical entries. Iddo[90] penned the first entry during Rehoboam's reign:

> Now the acts of Rehoboam, first and last, are they not *written in the book* of Shemaiah the prophet, and of Iddo the seer concerning genealogies? (2 Chr 12:15)

Identifying exactly which modern verses and chapters represent Iddo's genealogies is a difficult task for the simple reason that many of his lists have been interspersed throughout 1 Chronicles 1–9. While we have no reason to doubt his use of earlier sources,[91] the record's present state is rather fragmented. One of Iddo's sources appears today in Numbers 26, which seems originally to have been a military census.[92] That Iddo culled his data from older archives again supports Israel's use of records dated centuries earlier. Since, however, Iddo is mentioned in accounts dealing with Solomon, Jeroboam I, and Rehoboam (2 Chr 9:29; 12:15), the prophet-seer probably recorded the nation's genealogies through Rehoboam's lifetime or Asa's early reign at the latest. The chapters that contain most of Iddo's work are probably 1 Chronicles 1–2.

Scripture records a second genealogical entry penned during Jotham's reign:

> All these were reckoned by genealogies in the days of Jotham king of Judah, and in the days of Jeroboam king of Israel. (1 Chr 5:17)

This probably represents genealogies that begin where Iddo left off, covering lineages through Jotham's reign. The reference to Jeroboam in the above verse is to Jeroboam II. This text indicates at least two things. First, Jotham, who righteously followed YHWH (2 Kgs 15:32–34), ordered this genealogical entry and preserved the national records. Second, Jotham probably served quite a number of years as co-regent after YHWH struck his father with leprosy (2 Chr 26:19), since Jeroboam II had died at least 15 years prior to Scripture's recognition of Jotham's sole regency. These genealogies are again dispersed throughout the records, but can most readily be identified with 1 Chronicles 3–4.

The third genealogical entry occurred a short time later, in the days of Hezekiah. Shebna and Joah, Hezekiah's scribe and recorder, respectively (2 Kgs 18:18, 37), acknowledge this entry that was made during Hezekiah's reign.

Table 8.2. Record of Chronicles Authorship

| Kings of Judah | Acts Recorded | | Kings of Israel | Acts Recorded | |
	Kings	Chronicles		Kings	Chronicles
David	1 Sam 16–2 Sam– 1 Kgs 2:11	1 Chron 10–29			
Solomon	1 Kgs 1–11	2 Chron 1–9			
Rehoboam	1 Kgs 12–14	2 Chron 10–12	Jeroboam	1 Kgs 12–15	2 Chron 10–13
Abijam	1 Kgs 14:31–15:8	2 Chron 13			
Asa	1 Kgs 15:8–34	2 Chron 14–16	Nebat	1 Kgs 15:25–31	No Chron
			Baasa	1 Kgs 28–16:7	2 Chron 16:1–6[93]
			Elah		No Chron
			Omri		No Chron
Jehosephat/ Jehoash	1 Kgs 22–2 Kgs 3	2 Chron 17–20	Ahab	1 Kgs 16:28–22:40	2 Chron 18[94]
			Ahaziah	1 Kgs 22:51–1:18	2 Chron 20:35–37
Jehoram/ Ahaziah	2 Kgs 8:16–29	2 Chron 21–22	Jeroam		No Chron
Athaliah	2 Kgs 11:1–20	2 Chron 22:10–24:7	Jehu	2 Kgs 9–10	2 Chron 22
Joash	2 Kgs 11–12	2 Chron 22:10–24:7	Johoahaz	2 Kgs 13:1–9	No Chron
Amaziah	2 Kgs 14:1–22	2 Chron 25	Jehoash	2 Kgs 13:10–25	2 Chron 25:17–25[95]
Azariah (Uzziah)	2 Kgs 15:1–7	2 Chron 26	Jeroboam	2 Kgs 14:23–29	No Chron
			Zechariah	2 Kgs 15:8–12	No Chron
			Menahem	2 Kgs 15:14–22	No Chron
Jotham	2 Kgs 15:30–38	2 Chron 27	Pekahiah	2 Kgs 23–26	No Chron
Ahaz	2 Kgs 16	2 Chron 28	Pekah	2 Kgs 15:27–29	No Chron
Hezekiah	2 Kgs 17–20	2 Chron 29–32	Hoshea	2 Kgs 15:30; 17:1–4; 18:1–12	No Chron
Manasseh	2 Kgs 21:1–18	2 Chron 33:1–20			
Amon	2 Kgs 22:1–23:30	2 Chron 33:21–25			
Josiah	2 Kgs 22:1–23:30	2 Chron 34–35			
Jehoahaz		No formal entry, reigned for 3 months			
Jehoiakim	2 Kgs 23:34–24:7	2 Chron 26:4–8			
Jechoniah (Coniah)		No formal entry, reigned 3 months			
Zedekiah					
Nebuchad-nezzar					

> These mentioned by their names were princes in their families: and the house of their fathers increased greatly. . . . these **written by name came in the days** of Hezekiah king of Judah, and smote their tents, and the habitations that were found there, and destroyed them utterly unto this day, and dwelled in their rooms: because there was pasture there for their flocks. (1 Chr 4:38, 41)

The fourth and last genealogical entry was inserted after the Second Temple Remnant returned to the Promised Land under Cyrus, the king of Persia. Nehemiah mentions that Israel's "chief fathers" and Levite genealogies were recorded until the reign of "Darius the Persian" (Neh 12:22). These genealogies are recorded in the latter part of 1 Chronicles 8 and the beginning of ch. 9.

An entry made in 1 Chronicles indicates that the nation's genealogies were originally part of the *Book of the Kings of Israel and Judah*, although today Israel's genealogies have been added to the Book of Chronicles.

> So all Israel were reckoned by genealogies; and, behold, they were **written in the book of the kings of Israel and Judah**, who were carried away to Babylon for their transgression. (1 Chr 9:1)

Colophons, such as 1 Chronicles 9:1 that are anachronistic in the original text give rise to criticisms of the Hebrew source. How does a reference to Babylonian captivity (*c.* 590 BCE) appear in a text referring to the first few generations who entered the Promised Land?

In all fairness, the artificial chapter divisions have inadvertently separated the text from Benjamin's concluding genealogies, where this colophon would be relevant, placing the editorial remark at the beginning of Judah's genealogies. As we have seen throughout this chapter, Israel's scribes consistently used colophons and glosses to add context to the material they were transcribing and updating. Although the first major phase of archiving took place during the Samuel–David era, Scripture provides a great deal of evidence that a much later archiving and codifying process took place after the First Temple had been destroyed and Judah was deported from the Promised Land.

VI. EZRA

The validity of letters sent directly to a Persian king as recorded in Ezra has been a source of heated academic debate. Not until similar letters were unearthed in a Jewish community near Elephantine, Egypt, was any credibility given to Ezra's testimony. Acclaimed ancient Near Eastern historian, A. T. Olmstead wrote:

> The past few years have witnessed a dawning realization on the part of other Orientalists that the period has too long been neglected. Discovery of the archives from a Jewish mercenary colony near the first Egyptian cataract was truly

sensational. Here were the closest parallels in language and style to the Aramaic of Ezra. Prescripts from Persian kings were cited in Ezra; Old Testament critics had declared them unauthentic, but now there was ample proof that the critics themselves were in the wrong.[96]

Ezra's book grained further credibility when excavations unearthed a reference to the regional governor Tatnai (Ezra 5:3). The document calls him "Ta-at-tan-ni," the pahat or governor, subordinate to the satrap.[97] One archaeological discovery also confirms the name Gašmu, a local governor who opposed Nehemiah's efforts in Jerusalem (Neh 2:19). The artifact was a silver bowl from a temple at Tell al-Meskhûta in Lower Egypt. "The inscription written in the standard Aramaic of the Persian Period reads: 'Cain, son of Gašmu, king of Qedar.'"[98]

Illustration 8.2. Cyrus Cylinder, Babylon, 539–530 BCE. Cyrus describes measures of relief and restoration of various temples and the return of deportees to their homelands.

Another discovery, a Lycian cult charter, in 1973 added credibility to Ezra's testimony by providing striking parallels with Cyrus's decree for Temple restoration (see Illustration 8.2). Discovered in Xanthus, on the Lycian coast in southwest Turkey, the text was written in three languages: Greek, Lycian, and Aramaic. The most obvious parallels between Cyrus's decree and the Lycian are the facts that:

> It is a document issued in response to a local request, but one that would have received ratification from the Persian court; as in Ezra, amounts of sacrifices, names of priests, and the responsibility of the cult's upkeep are specified; the gods which are invoked to curse those who disregard the decree are local deities. Alan Millard concludes: Most obvious is the similarity of wording between Greek and Lycian requests and the satrap's Aramaic answer. Such resemblances in the Ezra passages, thought to show a forger's hand, are signs of normal practice. This practice explains how the Persian king or officer appears to know in detail about the cult in question; his information stems from its adherents. . . The further objection that the Persians would have paid no attention to such details falls away.[99]

The last 150 years of excavations have provided incredible archaeological support for Scripture. Assyrian inscriptions have corroborated the testimonies of Kings, Chronicles, Isaiah, Nehemiah, Zephaniah, and Jeremiah. As histories, the later testimonies of Ezra, Nehemiah, Esther, and Daniel have also gained credence from many recent archaeological discoveries. These external witnesses, however, are often outweighed by the numerous internal editorial remarks that demonstrate a scribe's hand late in the nation's history.

VII. EVIDENCE OF LATE-DATE ENTRY

Numerous textual clarifications (glosses and colophons) inserted into earlier written Scriptures indicate that the various books that today compose Joshua, Samuel, Kings, and Chronicles were edited into whole books at a date much later (*c.* 522 BCE) than when they were originally written.[100] One indication is a statement made in the genealogies of 1 Chronicles.

> So all Israel were reckoned by genealogies; and, behold, they were written in the book of the kings of Israel and Judah, who were carried away to Babylon for their transgression. (1 Chr 9:1)

That Israel's genealogies were written in the Book of Kings *after* Judah had been carried away to Babylon is evidence of late–date editing or compiling, which occurred after the government of Judah ceased to exist. The genealogies in 1 Chronicles 9 record the Remnant who were the "first inhabitants that dwelt in their possessions in their cities" (1 Chr 9:2) after Cyrus's emancipation decree. Many of these names appear in the books of Ezra and Nehemiah.

Nehemiah states:

> The sons of Levi, the *chief of the fathers*, were written in the book of the chronicles, even until the days of Johanan the son of Eliashib. (Neh 12:23)

The "last" chief fathers[101] are recorded in 1 Chronicles 9, indicating that the Levites made entries in the chronicle record after the Remnant returned to the Promised Land but ceased to record during Johanan's lifetime.

Another late-date account occurs in the penning of the high priest Jehozadak's captivity:

> And Jehozadak went into captivity, when YHWH carried away Judah and Jerusalem by the hand of Nebuchadnezzar. (1 Chr 6:15)

This entry was made in the chronicle after Jerusalem had been "carried away" and the state ceased to exist. In another example, 2 Kgs 25:27 states that Jehoiachin was seated above the other captive kings during the 37th year of his captivity (Jer 52:31), so this event was scribed at least 25 years *after* Solomon's Temple had been destroyed! Perhaps the strongest evidence of late-date entry can be found in the summary given in 2 Kgs 17:7–41. This entry exhibits characteristics of an editor who was knowledgeable in Israel's prophecies, grounded in the Law, and who understood the breach of the nation's covenantal constitution that caused Samaria's captivity.[102]

"Who" Scripture's late-date scribe or editor was is an important consideration for Scripture's credibility, validity, and overall constancy.[103] Yet again, Scripture furnishes evidence to solve this dilemma. Moses had ordained the Urim and Thummim be passed down through Levi's Aaronide line (Deut 33:8–11). When Cyrus permitted the Israelites to return to the Promised Land, Nehemiah forbade the priests to touch the tithes until a priest with Urim and Thummim returned to Jerusalem (Neh 7:65; Ezra 2:63). Ezra was the grandson of Seraiah, Israel's high priest at the time of the Diaspora (Jer 52:24). Ezra was a priest eligible for the high priesthood (Ezra 7:1–5), and Scripture acknowledges him to be the priest with whom the Urim and Thummim were found.

> This Ezra went up from Babylon; and he was a ready scribe in the Law of Moses, which YHWH God of Israel had given: and the king granted him all his request, according to **the hand of YHWH his God upon him.** (Ezra 7:6)

After Ezra arrived at Jerusalem, the priesthood began to function in an official capacity. That "YHWH's hand was on Ezra" is significant. Ezra worked with Nehemiah to reestablish Israel as a nation, much as Samuel worked with David to establish it in the beginning (Nehemiah 8).

Ezra was ordained to edit the nation's surviving archives. He understood YHWH, his prophecies, and the need for adding clarifications to texts that would seem ambiguous to later generations. Ezra's editing ensured that significant information remained accurate and truth was passed on to succeeding generations.[104] Of this conclusion, historian and author J. Llewellyn Thomas observes:

> It seems generally agreed that Ezra the great scribe and priest, who returned to Judea with the small portion of the captives of Judah from Babylon after the seventy years, was the editor who compiled these two separate histories into the one history as we have it in our Bible as the Second Book of Kings. The task of an inspired editor to make a single history out of the State Records of two separate nations would not be an easy one. He might have re-written the whole *de novo* in strict chronological order of events; but this would not have been exactly the work of an editor. The work rather consisted in piecing together the portions of the old records, without alteration, but with an opportunity of adding editorial remarks to elucidate the original texts, and of finishing off the story by the addition of much later events bearing on the subject, and of giving a review of the history.
>
> Thus a record of the entire reign of one king is given, and then the entire history of a contemporary or subsequent king of the other kingdom; and this even when the events of the two reigns took place at the same date. In this way the

events of a second section did not necessarily happen at the end of the previous section but at some earlier date. The ordinary reader might well think that the second section was a strict continuation (in point of time) of the previous one. In other words the events are not necessarily arranged in exact chronological order though the reigns are.[105]

Thomas' conclusion is quite accurate. The summary in 2 Kings 17 is one of the strongest indications of Ezra's late-date editing of the state's annals and chronicles. His is the hand that updated and provided political commentary for the cause of Israel's demise. He understood that Israel had broken her constitutional covenant with YHWH. Ezra's colophons recall that YHWH applied the penalties from Israel's Testimony, a point that we will return to in part two of this book.

Scholars who accept the JEPD theory may be correct to see at least four writing phases in Israel's history. We are not left in the dark to see how these phases occured. Scripture tells us when these collaborations took place and it has preserved who administered these writing phases: Moses-Joshua, Deborah, Samuel and the priests under the Monarchy, and Ezra.

VIII. SCRIBAL STANDARDS

A. *Lack of Codified Standards*

One area of Scripture that the minimalists eagerly attack is discrepancies in Israel's archives.[106] Critics point out that, if every word of the Old Testament was inspired by God himself, it should be flawless. As we have already seen, Israel's archives were a matter of state, not necessarily inspiration—with the exception of instances in which a prophet's testimony is recorded in the state's archives. Israel's state records were similar to the records of other ancient nations. Assyria's state archives also preserve variances and are an example of often-discrepant data.[107]

Assyria's records (like ancient Israel's chronicles) document factual events although numerical totals often conflict in the written annals. For instance, one of Sargon's inscriptions lists 27,290 Samarian deportees while another relief provides a figure of 27,280, which is 10 fewer than the first inscription.[108] Assyriologist John Russell considers that Assyria's records to have been based on the same primary source and offers several possibilities for these sorts of discrepancy. First, Assyrian reliefs were composed at different times than the written annals.[109] This would have allowed for recalculation of previous records and correction of previous errors. Second, Russell observes that differences between visual and verbal account for some variations as well as the fact that more than one person compiled the records. In this case, one engraver may have used the tallies of one scribe, while another engraver used a different scribe's calculations.[110] The third possibility lies in the purpose of state records may have been different from the purpose of visual displays.[111]

Another theory regarding Israel's seemingly conflicting standards is the simple fact that, throughout the ancient Near East, scribes did not codify spelling.[112] Scribes may simply have spelled words phonetically,[113] and different scribal schools (i.e., the priestly and the royal scribes) may have used divergent spelling methods.[114] Each school may have embraced different spelling, counting, and recording techniques or standards, although evidence also reveals an overall lack of codified standards.[115] Another suggestion pertains to the various Hebrew dialects. We know that the northern dialect was quite noticeable because the Ephraimites could not pronounce the שׁ ("sh") sound (Judg 12:6).[116] Different dialects may also account for different spellings of the same name (Jehoram vs. Joram) or place-name.

Regardless of the reasons, both Assyria's and Israel's archives demonstrate that there was an overall lack of scribal standards during this ancient era (at least by modern standards).[117] Non-standardization is why kings allowed conflicting tallies to be registered in the state record, and it would explain the variations in spelling of names of persons and cities. Whatever the case may be, both Assyria and Israel's scribes demonstrate congruent standards.

B. *Name and Honor*

In Scripture, some apparent discrepancies were intentional. In chap. 12, we will see that YHWH sought to memorialize the lives of the righteous while expunging the memory of the wicked (Ezek 33:13; Exod 17:14). Israel's scribes and prophets upheld YHWH's protocol for fame by employing shaming and defaming tactics to render ignominy to the nation's unrighteous kings. Probably the best example of this practice is the record of Jehoachin, whose name appears as Jehoachin, Jechoniah, and Coniah.[118] Though these names had the same meaning,[119] they were different spellings, which obscured Jechoniah's memory. Today, when we read about Jehoiachin, unless we are avid Bible readers, we rarely associate him with Coniah. This obscurity accomplishes both the scribe's and the prophet's intention of accurately recording Israel's history yet righteously denigrating Jehoiachin's memory. A similar method is evidenced in the scribe's interchange of Jehoash and Joash, which was intended once again to render ignominy to the memory of the unrighteous northern king by overshadowing him with Judah's righteous Joash (see 2 Kgs 13:25).

Another custom associated with honor and memorial is attested in Israel's choice of personal names. During Israel's kingdom years, Scripture does *not* record that any parent named his or her child after David, Moses, Abraham, Isaac, or Jacob. Notwithstanding, many incidents occurred in which two or more individuals shared the same name (Joash/Jehoash). The reasons for this variance are at least twofold. First, parents did not give their child the name of a renowned tribesman because it might diminish an honor that belonged to his predecessor.[120] If a mother called her son David and the child gained great fame, the child's achievements would always be eclipsed by the successes of his predecessor. Thus his "name and his renown" would not be his own. Second, giving a child his own name enabled him to establish a memorial all his own. Today, when we read the narratives of people such as Joash, Jehoash, or the Jeroboams, the person we are reading about seems obscure. However, when we read the memorial of Moses, David, or Solomon, there is no question about whom we are reading. YHWH's scribes have again succeeded in commemorating the righteous and obliterating the memory of the wicked.

IX. ISAIAH

Another trend in academic studies is to attribute the Book of Isaiah to at least two authors: *First Isaiah*, an eighth-century BCE author, wrote the first half of the book bearing his name, while *Second Isaiah*, who lived around the first century BCE, penned chaps. 40–66.[121] Most of this confusion arises from the fact that the prophet Isaiah wrote several books (scrolls) on very specific themes that were eventually compiled into a single manuscript.

Isaiah's first book dealt with YHWH's prophecies that Assyria would effect YHWH's judgment. YHWH himself specifically commanded Isaiah to write the prophecies about Assyria in *one* large book.

> Moreover YHWH said to me, Take you a great roll, and *write in it* with a man's pen concerning Maher-shalal-hash-baz. And I took to me faithful *witnesses to record*, Uriah the priest, and Zechariah the son of Jeberechiah. And I went to the prophetess; and she conceived, and bare a son. Then said YHWH to me, Call his name *Maher-shalal-hash-baz*. For before the child shall have knowledge to cry, My father, and my mother, the riches of Damascus and the spoil of Samaria shall be taken away before the king of Assyria. (Isa 8:1–4)

"Mahershalalhashbaz" marks the beginning of the first section of Isaiah's work. Today, this constitutes Isaiah 7–35. This portion of Isaiah deals directly with Israel and other nations in the Levant who opposed Assyria's might. *Although Isaiah narrated this section, the two Levitical scribes Uriah and Zechariah actually wrote this portion of the Book of Isaiah* (see Illustration 8.3).

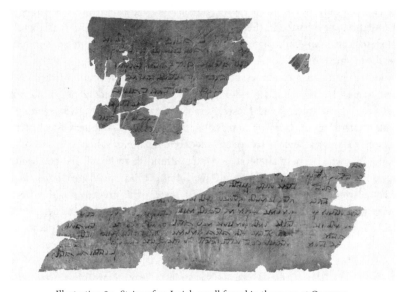

Illustration 8.3. Strips of an Isaiah scroll found in the caves at Qumran.

The second section of Isaiah's work records the fulfillment of the Mahershalalhash-baz prophecies, many of which occurred during Hezekiah's reign. Isaiah 36–39 chronicles Isaiah's interaction with Hezekiah and Assyria. The Book of Isaiah is unclear whether the prophet Isaiah actually wrote this book or whether other "faithful" scribes recorded these chronicles. Uriah and Zechariah probably penned this section of Isaiah's book, which is why modern scholars validly see it as having a different style from the latter third of his work.

The third section or third Book of Isaiah deals with issues regarding Israel's rebellion. YHWH commanded Isaiah:

> Now go, **write it before them in a table, and note it in a book,** *that it may be for the time to come* forever and ever: That this is a rebellious people, lying children, children that will not hear the law of YHWH. (Isa 30:8–9)

YHWH commanded Isaiah to write a book memorializing Israel's rebellion. Isaiah obeyed YHWH's command by writing,

> Who gave Jacob for a spoil, and Israel to the robbers? did not YHWH, he against whom we have sinned? **for they would not walk in his ways, neither were they obedient to his law.** (Isa 42:24)

This section primarily concerns Israel's hardness against YHWH's Law (Isa 42:4, 21, 24; 51:4, 7) and prophesies that YHWH will choose a future, righteous generation, that is willing to obey his Law in their stead. This third book follows the outline set forth in Jacob's Diaspora Covenant.[122] Isaiah prophesies against the rebellious and lying people of his day but overshadows them with a latter-day, righteous generation that will seek, find YHWH, and be restored to the Promised Land.[123] Although modern scholars attribute this portion of the Book of Isaiah (chs. 40–66) to a "Second Isaiah," this is the only section that can be identified as actually being penned by the prophet himself! This is why it is different in linguistic style from Uriah's or Zechariah's official priestly scribal office. Isaiah also wrote the opening 6 chapters of his book, which define his prophetic calling.

X. JEREMIAH

In recent years, the Book of Jeremiah has been thrown into the academic spotlight. Discovery of the "Lachish letters" in 1935 was one of the first helpful finds in this regard. These letters consist of correspondence between Hoshaiah, a subordinate in charge of a garrison located between Lachish and Jerusalem, and Yoash, Hoshaiah's commander at Lachish.[124] The Lachish letters were written shortly before Judah's fall to Babylon, and scholars observe that two letters in particular probably refer to Jeremiah. "Letter 6 refers to certain persons in Jerusalem discouraging (*lit.* 'weakening the hands of') the soldiers (presumably; see

Illustration 8.4).[125] A similar accusation in the same idiom was brought against Jeremiah (38:4; cf. 27:12–16)."[126] Two other letters (3 and 16) also mention a prophet (*nabi*), whom some scholars identify with Jeremiah or possibly Uriyah (Jer 26:20–23; see Illustrations 8.5 and 8.6).

Ilustration 8.4. Lachish Letter VI.

Illustration 8.5. Lachish Letter III, obverse.

Illustration 8.6. Lachish Letter III reverse.

A second discovery, published in 1980 by archaeologist Nachman Avigad, has caused even scholars critical of Scripture to acknowledge the legitimacy of Jeremiah's scribe Baruch. The artifact was a clay seal, impressed with the words:

lbrkyhw bn nryhw hspr
'belonging to Baruch son of Neriyah the scribe.'

"It was the first archaeological discovery ever of an object that was identifiable as having belonged to someone who is mentioned in the Bible. It is, in effect his [Baruch's] signature," notes Richard Friedman, author of *Who Wrote the Bible*.[127] Baruch wrote much of the work that bears Jeremiah's name (Jer 36:4, 18, 32; 45:1), especially issues dealing with Judah and Jerusalem (see Illustration 8.7)

Since Baruch wrote so much of the Book of Jeremiah, it is easier to distinguish portions written by Jeremiah than portions written by Baruch. The first passage that can be distinguished as having been written by Jeremiah is the book that Jeremiah told Seraiah (the high priest) to throw into Babylon's waters (Jer 51:61–64); it deals with prophecies against Babylon and other nations (Jer 51:60). This book has been preserved in Jer 50:1–51:64. Other notable books written by the prophet include the blessing of Baruch (Jeremiah 45) and Ebed-melech (Jer 39:13–18). When either Jeremiah or a later editor sought to compile all of Jeremiah's scrolls into one work, he placed one book after another book in chronological order as well as possible so as not to rewrite the original text. When I address Israel's Prophetic Law in chaps. 14–17, I will present evidence demonstrating that Isaiah and Jeremiah personally rearranged and edited much of their manuscripts into the versions that we have today.

For two millennia, many scholars have charged that Scripture's authorship is uncertain. This is not the case. During righteous epochs, scribes recorded the names of the authors of *Kings* and *Chronicles*; and during *un*righteous epochs, when monarchs were not careful to

Illustration 8.7. Bulla of "Baruch son of Neriyah the scribe."

order that entries be made in the chronicles, authorship can still be traced to the descendants who would have held the recorder's or scribe's office.

Through this research I discovered that Israel's archives recorded factual events, just as Assyria's inscriptions recorded actual wars, real kings (there really was a Sargon!), and real events. If we accept Assyria's history as valid, with all its divergent inscriptions and references to Assyria's gods, then we should admit the validity of Israel's history as well. This is especially true of the Book of Isaiah for which criticism is justified, but the scholarly consensus is awry by dating the "Second Isaiah" as a later work. Although Isaiah was indeed written by two different people (a "first" and "second" Isaiah), this in no way impinges on the factuality of Isaiah's testimony. The Book of Isaiah tells us that it originally consisted of several books and was written by three people: Uriyah, Zechariah, and Isaiah. Therefore I concluded that polemics against the authorship of the Hebrew texts fail to merit validity. Scripture names those who penned its ancient words.

From what I had learned, I came to understand that Israel's chronology helps us to place the Israelites in a historical context: from discerning who the Pharaoh of the exodus was to knowing how many years Saul reigned over Israel. Chronology allows us to place Israel in the real world that we call "history."

9

Chronology of the Book of the Kings of Israel and Judah

Unless one is a specialist with a passion for numbers, people would rather watch paint dry than discuss chronology. Chronology is, however, the most valuable tool for bringing real-world relevance to Scripture. Chronology is the vehicle that establishes Scripture's historical validity. Chronology allows us to "see" that Abraham lived until Jacob and Esau were 15 years of age or that Isaac died in the year that Joseph became vizier in Egypt. Chronology permits us to locate a specific prophecy in time (such as Isa 7:8) and trace its precise historical fulfillment.

Israel, in particular, provides the thread weaving together Assyrian and Egyptian dynasties. Both Egypt and Assyria campaigned extensively in Canaan, so Scripture's accounts often shed more light on the circumstances that necessitated invasion while chronology enables us to see when these events transpired.[1] In chap. 1, we learned that one definition of truth is factuality and historicity: the accounts in Scripture must be historically valid for the word of YHWH to be considered "truth." Consistently, chronology is one tool (or "control") that allows us to determine whether the stories that Scripture records meet the criteria that the archaeological data and written records of other nations provide. It is a study that, unlike paint, brings the Bible to life!

I. BACK TO THE BASICS

A. *Time*

Today, when we say that Jake was born in 1975, we mean that Jake was born one thousand nine hundred seventy-five years after the Christian or Common Era began. This system was implemented by the monk Dionysius Exiguus in AD 532.[2] Time for the Christian or

Common Era (CE) began with the birth of Christ in year 1 (there is no 0) and was called *Anno Domini* (AD). Jake was born 1,975 years after *Anno Domini,* or AD 1975. Time before *Anno Domini* is counted backwards and termed "before Christ" (BC) or "before the Common Era" (BCE).[3] When we say that King Cyrus issued his decree for the rebuilding of the Temple in Jerusalem in 538 BCE,[4] we mean five hundred thirty-eight years before Christ, or before the Common Era. Scholars determine Israel's chronology according to this system.

Chronologists usually pick an event in Scripture that is held in common with another nation, such as Babylon or Assyria, to reconstruct Israel's chronology. These events are usually referred to as "anchor dates" since the event anchors the relationship of one nation to the other. The best anchor date appears in two different Scripture accounts of Nebuchadnezzar's siege of Jerusalem in his 7th year and in Nebuchadnezzar's own inscription.[5] According to Nebuchadnezzar's 7th year annal, he sieged Jerusalem, captured Jehoiachin, and deported prisoners to Babylon.[6] Jeremiah confirms that Jerusalem's siege occurred during Nebuchadnezzar's 7th year (Jer 52:28), while 2 Kgs 24:12 informs us that it was Nebuchadnezzar's 8th year. The difference of one year in 2 Kings arises from the new year's dating. Nebuchadnezzar began to siege Jerusalem in Chislev (Nov/Dec), and the city fell in Adar (March), the last month of the year.[7] Jechoniah's deportation occurred during the following month, after the new year.[8] The scribe then reckoned the deportation in Nebuchadnezzar's 8th year. What these texts solidly affirm is that, between Nebuchadnezzar's 7th and 8th years, he deported Jechoniah and a large portion of Judah's citizenry. This event then serves as an anchor linking the chronologies of Babylon and Israel.

Since Nebuchadnezzar replaced Jechoniah with Zedekiah, who reigned for 11 years, we know that by Nebuchadnezzar's 19th year he had destroyed the Temple (Jer 52:12). The date that most scholars accept for Nebuchadnezzar's 7th year is 598 BCE, with the destruction of the Temple 11 years later, in 587 BCE.[9] As we examine Israel's chronology, we will see that there are a couple more anchor dates linking Israel's chronology with other nations.

Another device that scholars use to establish chronology is to determine the "benchmarks" internal to Israel's history.[10] Some mention contact with other kings or mark significant events. One significant benchmark in Israel's history is a scribe's notation in 1 Kgs 6:1 that Solomon's 4th year was 480 years after the exodus. This link to Solomon's 4th year provides a benchmark for reconstructing the nation's history both forward and backward.[11] What is needed to place Israel's chronology in "reality" is a point of contact with a king from another nation. The reign of Rehoboam, Solomon's son, provides just that. *The Book of the Kings of Israel and Judah* and *The Book of the Chronicles of the Kings of Judah* (1 Kgs 14:25; 2 Chr 12:2) tell us that Egypt's Shoshenq (biblical Shishak) invaded Judah during Rehoboam's 5th year. Shoshenq is known to have reigned over Egypt from *c.* 945 to 924 BCE, which is usually based, not on Egyptian chronologies, but on reconstructions of Israel's chronology.[12] This allows for about a 20-year window for this invasion to have occurred. Based on Scripture's internal synchronism with later Judahite and Samarian monarchs (which we will investigate below), Shoshenq's invasion occurred in 940 BCE, during the pharaoh's 6th or 7th year on the throne.

To discover the date of King Solomon's 4th year, we add Solomon's subsequent 35[13] years and Rehoboam's 5 years (35+5=40+940 BCE), landing at 980 BCE for King Solomon's 4th year (see Table 9.1). As we will see, this year had great significance since the construction of the original Temple coincided with the national sabbatical Release Year celebrations.

In past decades, chronologists have leaned heavily on ancient astronomical dates provided by Ptolemy's Canon (see below). The ancient world used astronomical events, such as eclipses, to date major events. These astronomical phenomena often conflict with monumental dating, however.[14] Thus, the direction of recent chronology methods has been to shy away from astronomical dating, allowing epigraphic and archaeological data to take precedence.[15]

B. Modern Dating Ideas

Scholars support a wide variety of dates for Solomon's 4th year. Egyptologist Donald Redford dates Solomon's 4th regnal year to 1016 BCE.[16] Silberman and Finkelstein cite 1005–930 BCE as the era in which both David and Solomon reigned,[17] thus placing Solomon's 4th year around 960 BCE, a date in line with John Bimson's.[18] Kenneth Kitchen places Solomon's 4th year at 967, a date that Andrew Steinmann, Rodger Young, and most biblical scholars also embrace.[19] Abraham Malamat places Solomon's independent rule at 967–66, which means that the king's 4th year was approximately 963/962.[20] Thus, the time frame that scholars generally accept for Solomon's 4th regnal year has a range from 1016 to 966, a span of about 50 years. The date 980 BCE used in this study is based on Israel's synchronistic chronology, a method most scholars only haphazardly employ. This date is 13 years higher than the Kitchen-Steinmann date but about midway between the ranges of generally accepted dating.

Many biblical scholars adamantly date Shoshenq's invasion (Rehoboam's 5th year) to 926/25 BCE.[21] While this date is certainly possible, nothing in Egyptian chronology rules out an earlier date. Shoshenq's inscriptions memorializing his victory over both Rehoboam and Jeroboam date to his 21st year.[22] Egyptian chronology simply does not allow for a precise date, thus allowing earlier possibilities.[23] As Egyptologist Karl Jansen-Winkeln has recently pointed out, it would be stretching the evidence to conclude that both the construction work on the temple at Thebes and the inscription occurred in the same year.[24] At most, the dating to Shoshenq's 21st year simply provides a lower limit for reconstructing Shoshenq's campaign against Israel's Divided Kingdom during this era.

If we apply 980 BCE to King Solomon's 4th year, then Jeroboam I probably fled to Shoshenq for refuge (1 Kgs 11:40) in Egypt during the year that the Libyan Shoshenq rose to power (946/945 BCE). Continuing Israel's chronology backward in time, David would have ascended Judah's throne 44 years earlier, in 1023 BCE. The scribe's notation in 1 Kgs 6:1 would mean that the Judges Era began in 1460 BCE (980 BCE + 480 yrs. = 1460 BCE). Thus the absolute latest (or lowest) possible date for the controversial exodus would be 1460 BCE.

C. Absolute Chronology

The trend in most studies dealing with biblical chronologies is toward reconstructing an "absolute" chronology, with little room for deviation.[25] The annoying fact when one tries to

Table 9.1. King Solomon's 4th year to Rehoboam's 5th year

BCE	Text	Judah	Samaria	Egypt
		Solomon		
980	1 Kgs 6:1, 37	**4**		
979		5		
978		6		
977		7		
976		8		
975		9		
974		10		
973	1 Kgs 6:38	**11**		
972		12		
971		13		
970		14		
969		15		
968		16		
967		17		
966		18		
965		19		
964		20		
963		21		
962		22		
961		23		
960		24		
959		25		
958		26		
957		27		
956		28		
955		29		
954		30		
953		31		
952		32		
951		33		
950		34		
949		35		
948		36		
947		37		Shoshenq I
946	1 Kgs 11:40—Jeroboam	38	Rehoboam	(945–924)
945	flees to Shoshenq	39	Jeroboam I	1
944		40	*1*	*1*	2
943			2	2	3
942			3	3	4
941			4	4	**5**
940	1 Kgs 14:25; 2 Chr 12:2	**5**	Shoshenq invades Judah	

synchronize the histories between Israel, Judah, Egypt, Crete, Assyria, Babylon, and Persia is that, while an absolute chronology may work well for one nation, it faces incredible contradiction when juxtaposed with another nation's internal chronology (or kings list). Rarely do national records afford the precise synchronism that we find in the case of Nebuchadnezzar's first siege of Jerusalem (his 7th year) during Jechoniah's reign. Thus, Assyrian chronology faces obstacles when synchronized with Egyptian chronologies. These differences have led to two different systems: one favoring an early (or high) date and another favoring a late (or low) date (about 60 years later).[26] Over the last decade, most scholarship has shifted toward a late (low) "absolute" chronology dating system.[27]

The frustration with chronologies arises because the ancient world had no continuing system by which to reckon "world chronology," as we do today. Instead, as Egyptologist Erik Hornung observes, "There was never an era with a constant continuous numbering of years: with each new Pharaoh, the count began anew."[28] This was true for all ancient nations. Although nations have left some wonderful chronologies embedded in kings lists, canons, and eponym lists, it is often difficult to match that chronology with a contemporary monarchy. While history for one nation can be reconstructed based on all the available chronological data that we have for, say Assyria, when it is then compared with all the available data that we have for, say Egypt, there may be a variation of 12 to 100 years. Since the Hebrew Scriptures teem with chronologies and synchronisms, some scholars (Kitchen, Wood, Hoffmeier, and Albright) see Israel as the link sowing these various nations together.[29]

Modern scholars have been able to distinguish between the formulas that Egypt and Assyria used to form a "continuing" chronology from one king to the next (see below). What is often missing in the various records of these ancient nations (including Israel) is the recognition of co-regency, when a father and son reigned at the same time, or a period of instability, when a usurper (even a rightful heir to the throne) reigned from another city in the empire.[30] Thankfully, Scripture provides many coinciding means by which to access the internal chronology before it is compared with other nations' contemporary histories.

II. OBSTACLE TO A TRADITIONAL EARLY/HIGH EXODUS DATE

Many biblical scholars date the exodus to 1446 BCE.[31] This would mean that Israel entered Canaan in 1406,[32] at the height of Egyptian power and control over Canaan. Both Thutmoses and his son Amenhotep II campaigned extensively in Canaan from about 1458 to as late as 1401.[33] Their inscriptions list thousands of captives and deportees, many who are described as *habiru*, a term which some scholars identify as the Hebrews.[34] Thutmoses installed a bureaucratic system with tight control over its Canaanite vassals,[35] leaving armed garrisons to enforce Egypt's policies. During the Amarna Period (1390–1332) Akhenaten also claimed to have captured and deported *habiru* from Canaan.[36] This situation opposes Scripture. The books of Joshua and Judges indicate that Israel faced no Egyptian threat at the *initial* Conquest, and the Israelites were safely out of Pharaoh's hand (Judg 2:1). In fact, the entire point of the exodus was to deliver Israel out of Pharaoh's hand and from the house of bondage (Exod 13:14; Josh 24:17) so the that people could enjoy the freedom and autonomy to establish YHWH's constitutional Law in the Promised Land. It is quite *un*likely, then, that YHWH would deliver Israel back into Egyptian bondage at the very time he had promised to establish the Promised-Land Covenant with Israel (Exod 6:4, 8; 12:25; 13:5, 11; 32:13; 33:1; Lev 20:24; Josh 11:23). The 1446 high/early date does not allow for a peaceful era during which foreign nations did not oppress Israel in Canaan.

In fact, Scripture not only indicates that Canaan was free of any Egyptian threat during this time but also that the region enjoyed tremendous military success. This situation would simply be impossible with Thutmoses's mighty forces standing by to protect his vassal states and secure its tribute between 1420 and 1390. Throughout the exodus account, Scripture states that Israel had come "out of Egypt" (Judg 2:1) and YHWH had fulfilled the promise of his covenant for Israel to inherit Canaan (Gen 15:18–20). This again indicates that Israel had initially faced no Egyptian obstacles in Canaan. This interpretation is bolstered by the fact that YHWH purposely led Israel out of Egypt by a route that avoided war with Egypt (Exod 13:7), implying that the people would *not* face war with Egypt inside Canaan at the initial Conquest. This evidence undermines the currently popular "biblical" exodus date.

Another obstacle to the traditional high/early date comes from the Book of Judges, which states that Israel's first oppression came from Aram-Naharim ("Mesopotamia" in Judg 3:8),[37] not Egypt. No Egyptian sources record any threat from Mesopotamia/Arameans during this period, and it is quite unlikely that Thutmoses or Amenhotep would have allowed another king to infringe on its borderlands. We know from the Amarna Tablets that Egypt enjoyed diplomatic relations with the east, even exchanging gifts. None of these demonstrates tension with Mesopotamia or invasion.

The trend in recent biblical scholarship to counter the obstacles (both evidence of Thutmoses's tight control over Canaan and the fact that the 1446 reconstruction does not allow for an initial Conquest) is simply to deny that a large-scale Conquest ever occurred.[38] In other words, to justify the lack of evidence for a Conquest, scholars recognize the Israelites as destroying only a very limited number of cities when they first entered the land. Biblical chronologist Andrew Steinmann limits these cities to Jericho, Ai, and Hazor.[39] The obstacle to this interpretation is that Scripture lists many of other cities, which should show at least some signs of destruction. Battles were waged against Libnah (Josh 10:29), Lachish (10:31), Eglon (10:34), Hebron (10:36), Debir (10:38), the hill country and southern Negev (10:40), Kadesh-barnea, Gaza, and Goshen (10:41). God would have to had provide divine protection to these *Canaanite* cities for them to escape signs of destruction from the aggressive war that Israel waged! The Scriptural view of the Canaanite Conquest extends far beyond the three cities cited by Steinmann. This evidence has led a second group of scholars to place the exodus in the thirteenth century, based on archaeological evidence of destruction throughout Canaan.[40] Lowering the Conquest to a later date, however, does not resolve all the conflicts with chronology or archaeology.

Joshua and Moses had destroyed cities on the east bank of the Jordan River, which should reveal decisive destruction archaeologically. The Book of Joshua attests that Hebron, Debir, Anab, and many other cities in the hill country had also been destroyed.

> At that time came Joshua, and cut off the Anakims from the mountains, from Hebron, from Debir, from Anab, and from all the mountains of Judah, and from all the mountains of Israel: *Joshua destroyed them utterly with their cities.* (Josh 11:21)

Further evidence of a large-scale conquest arises from Moses' account that he had destroyed Heshbon with fire (Num 21:28), a city that the Reubenites later rebuilt (Num 32:37). The obstacle that this evidence presents for both the high 1406 Conquest date and the low 1270 Conquest date is that no occupation is archaeologically attested in the thirteenth century, and certainly no sign of destruction,[41] thus bringing into question both of the traditional high/early and low/late exodus dates.

The initial Conquest had been quite substantial. Although Israel did not hold onto all the territory she conquered after she rebelled against the covenant (Judg 2:1), this fact does not negate the impact that the initial Conquest had. What the evidence suggests is that neither the High Conquest model dated to 1406, nor the Low date of 1270 is accurate, and the truth lies in another era. Can a detailed study of Israel's chronology help us reconstruct and reclaim this era?

III. THE EXODUS TO KING SOLOMON'S 4TH YEAR

A. *History of Ideas*

Through the years, the chronology of Israel and Judah has been one of the most debated topics in both academic and religious studies. Egyptian chronology unfortunately does not provide any firm anchor dates on which to base Israel's chronology.[42] Manfred Bietak, director of the excavations at Avaris (Tell el-Daba), Egypt, is, however, taking an interdisciplinary approach to this question that will likely narrow the possibilities in the near future.[43] Gaps in Assyria's and Babylon's annals allow deviations of a couple dozen years.[44] Israel's chronology is the nexus that unites and clarifies the chronologies of Egypt and Mesopotamia.[45]

In order for Israel's chronology to be relevant, it must be tied to a few compelling anchor dates of other nations. Biblical chronologists Andrew Steimann and Rodger Young provide a cogent study on Israel's chronology by reconstructing King Solomon's reign, taking into account 1 Kgs 6:1 (see discussion in the next section) and anchoring key events to accepted dates for Egyptian kings (Shishak's invasion in Rehoboam's 5th year) and tying them to other chronologies, such as the Tyrian King List, Josephus's reference to Hiram's reign (Tyre), and the Scriptural Jubilees.[46]

Overall, Steinmann's and Young's studies produce very appealing results for biblical chronologists with the Jubilees perfectly coinciding with both a talmudic source and the generally accepted high exodus date in 1446 BCE and 1 Kgs 6:1.[47] Their conclusions, however, are not without the inevitable (internal) Josephus chronology contradiction.

Josephus states that King Solomon completed the First Temple during the Tyrian King Hiram's 12th year on the throne (*Against Apion* 108, 126). This would have been Solomon's 11th regnal year. The problem with this synchronism is that Scripture places Hiram on the Tyrian throne long before Solomon's accession. David had conquered Jerusalem during the 7th year of his reign (2 Sam 5:5). When Hiram heard of David's success, he sent building materials for David's palace (2 Sam 5:7–12). Realistically, this would have been sometime between David's 8th and 14th years, before he brought the Ark of the Covenant up to Jerusalem (1 Chr 15:1–2) and long before David's affair with BathSheba (2 Sam 11:3). Hiram's 12th year would have occurred around David's 27th year at the very latest since David is recorded to have built palaces in the city of David (2 Sam 5:9–12; 1 Chr 14:1–2) before he brought the ark into Jerusalem (2 Samuel 6–7; 1 Chronicles 15–16; see Table 9.50 in Appendix A). Solomon's 11th year, when the Temple was completed, would probably have coincided with Hiram's 38th regnal year.

To resolve this contradiction, it is purposed that Solomon served as David's co-regent, based on Solomon's being anointed before David's death (1 Kgs 1:32–35, 46–47; 5:1; 1 Chr 23:1).[48] While Scripture does support Solomon's installation as a co-regent shortly before David's death (1 Kgs 1:1), 1 Kgs 2:12 strongly suggests that Solomon's reign was not reckoned as a co-regency. YHWH's injunction on building the Temple during David's reign further disallows a co-regency *reckoning* and contradicts Josephus's record of Hiram. According to 2 Sam 7:12–13, construction on the Temple could not begin until after David's death. This is in line with the chronology of 1 Kings 1–5, which presents Solomon's gathering of materials to build the Temple after David's death, then beginning construction during his 4th year. Once again, this would place Solomon's 4th year in approximately Hiram's 43rd regnal year. Scripture also disallows two separate Hirams (i.e., a son ruling in his father's name) since the Hiram who donated the Temple's building supplies is remembered as "ever being a lover of David" (1 Kgs 5:1), which references the prior friendly relations that Hiram had personally enjoyed with David. Josephus's record contradicts Scripture's chronology and undermines Steinmann's and Young's overall reconstruction of Solomonic chronology.

The second peg in the Steinmann-Young reconstruction is Israel's national Jubilee. Isa 37:30 is often considered to refer to Israel's national Jubilee in Hezekiah's 14th and 15th years.[49] The Steinmann-Young reconstruction dismisses the Hezekiah synchronization in favor of a talmudic source. The Talmud, similar to Josephus, contains many internal contradictions. In chap. 19, we will see that anyone dealing with the Talmud to reconstruct ancient Israel's history or theology should do so with the utmost caution.[50] When we discuss Israel's Jubilees (see chap. 9.V., pp. 366–75 below), we will see that the Release Year during Hezekiah's 14th regnal year should be preferred over the Talmud's chronology. The former method is central to our investigation, since our trial seeks to discover whether the Hebrew Scriptures constitute a credible source. We will see that both Israel's sabbatical Release Years (every 7 years) and the nation's Jubilee (50th year) are supported by Hezekiah's 15th-year Jubilee and that the reconstruction of these Jubilees both backward and forward in time helps to explain some of the Judges and early Monarchy chronology issues.

Perhaps Steimann's and Young's greatest contribution to the discussion of chronology has been advocating a system that distinguishes dual calendric systems. Young suggested that "n" be used for calendars that began in the spring and were based on the Hebrew month Nisan, and "t" be used for calendars that transitioned to the new year in the fall during the month of Tishri (7th month).[51] This method is quite useful in distinguishing between the calendric systems that the Divided Kingdoms of Judah and Israel employed, thus resolving many of the questions regarding internal synchronization. I will use this method throughout our chronology discussion.

Most chronologists consider the reference to Solomon's 4th year as being 480 years after the "exodus" as providing a central benchmark or peg for reconstructing chronologies. In the past, Kitchen, Dever, and other scholars have dismissed 1 Kgs 6:1 in favor of archaeological evidence that demonstrates destruction in Canaan during the 13th century. As we have seen, not even the 13th century can explain away the many contradictions that archaeology raises for this era, indicating that the truth of Israel's exodus must lie in a previous era. The question at this point is how the 480 years before Solomon's 4th year are pegged or linked to the exodus.

B. *The Judges Era—1 Kings 6:1: Five Witnesses*

1. Nineteen Generations

Chronology can be compared with engineering a building. Before one can construct the top floors, the foundation, structure, and lower levels need to be developed. For this discussion, the exodus and patriarchs are our upper floors, while the date of the destruction of Solomon's Temple in 587 BCE is our foundation. Solomon's 4th year in 980 BCE (discussed further below) provides our structure. In order to construct higher levels of Israel's history, we must build from 980 upward. The difficulty with this era is that controversies arise over the chronological methods that Israel used for recording history during this period. We will discuss the evidence for each period below.

Most scholars accept the patriarchal age as being pretty straightforward.[52] Patriarchal chronologies are linear, since they simply descend from father through son. This system changes in the intermediate period, following the exodus when there is no single patriarch with which to pin a linear genealogy. In order to reconstruct the time that elapsed during the exodus through early Conquest, the Judges Era, and the early Monarchy, we must establish several different controls in order to determine how this era can be reconstructed. These controls will be accessed by means of Scripture's internal chronological references that are directly stated or implied by the life-span of the early Conquest pioneers.

The Pentateuch presents 40 years as the time span of the nation's wilderness exile; however, this does not contribute to a continuing chronology. At this point, there is a definite break in the chronological record. Apparently, a scribe had access to material that was noted in a colophon. The notation asserts that Solomon's 4th regnal year was *480 years* after the nation's exodus.[53]

And it came to pass in the *four hundred and eightieth year after the Children of Israel were come out of the land of Egypt*, in the *fourth year of Solomon's reign over Israel*, in the month Ziv, which is the second month, that he began to build the house of YHWH. (1 Kgs 6:1)

This entry picks up where the patriarchal, exodus, and wilderness exile chronologies ended. The scribe's colophon (above) serves as the *first proof* for dating Israel's entry into Canaan at least 480 years prior to Solomon's 4th year. J. A. Thompson points out that this dating accords with the chronicler's genealogies.[54] Referring to Aaron's genealogies in 1 Chr 6:10–15 and 5:36–41, Thompson observes,

> With this reference we have twelve generations between Aaron and the building of the Temple. This would give twelve times forty, or four hundred and eighty years to agree with 1 Kgs 6:1. This is feasible reconstruction.[55]

According to some scholars, these twelve generations from Aaron to Solomon total approximately 480 years.[56] Although this reconstruction may be feasible, it fails to account for the generations listed in 1 Chr 6:33–37, which assigns 18 generations to the period from the exodus to King David.[57] Actually, the 18-generation genealogy covers Moses to Heman, a Temple musician in the time of David. If we add one more generation, we arrive at Solomon's 4th regnal year, thus totaling 19 generations from the exodus.[58] If we use the 30 years for a generation established in Genesis (Gen 15:16; Exod 12:40–41; see pp. 88–89), these geneologies allow roughly 570 years from Moses to Solomon. Alternatively, if we use the more accepted 25 years per generation, we arrive at 475 years, which is right in line with 1 Kgs 6:1.[59] Thus far, we have approached chronology from the exodus to Solomon by two different ways, examining both Aaron's 12 generations and the 19 generations mentioned in 1 Chr 6:33–37. These genealogies serve as a *second proof* supporting the scribe's colophon in 1 Kings 6:1, demonstrating that in no way could this era be collapsed into a shorter time frame.[60]

2. Jephthah's 300 Years

The scribe's chronology in 1 Kgs 6:1 also supports a statement made by Jephthah in the Book of Judges. Jephthah defends Israel's claim to the Amorites' former territories, claiming that, by the time of his (Jephthah's) days, Israel had already been in Canaan for 300 years.

> And the king of the children of Ammon answered to the messengers of Jephthah, Because Israel took away my land, *when they came up out of Egypt* (See Num 21:13–35), from Arnon even to Jabbok, and to Jordan: now therefore restore those lands again peaceably. And Jephthah sent messengers again to the king of the children of Ammon. . .*While Israel dwelled in Heshbon* and her towns, and in Aroer and her towns, and in all the cities that be along by the coasts of Arnon, *three hundred years*, why therefore did you not recover them within that time? (Judg 11:13–14, 26)

Israel had conquered the Amorite territory in Heshbon and Aroer shortly before entering the Promised Land (Numbers 21:13–35). This was the territory that the Patriarch Jacob had originally bequeathed to the Joseph tribes as the double portion or double blessing of his inheritance (Gen 48:20–22). During Jephthah's days, the Ammonites tried to reclaim this territory. Jephthah admonished Ammon's emissaries, reminding them that the Amorites' territory had long ago been inherited by Israel (Judg 11:24). To bolster his claim, Jephthah emphatically reminds the ambassadors that Israel had held this territory for well over 300 years. Since Jephthah lived about 140 years prior to Solomon's reign, his statement would be congruent with 1 Kgs 6:1. Jephthah's statement serves as the *third proof* in support of the scribe's colophon.

Jephthah's statement should not necessarily be taken as an exact figure but as an estimate that limits our range for reconstructing this era.[61] In modern times, we say that the U.S. has been a nation for 200 years when the exact figure is closer to 225 years. Jephthah's statement was used to prove the point that Ammon had no claim to the Amorites' lands, which Israel had held for *at least* 300 years. His statement was *not* a scribe's formal record of the nation's chronicle. Therefore, Jephthah's statement allows for Israel to have been in the Promised Land for *at least 300* but *less than 400* years. As we will see, Scripture indicates that the actual time that had passed since Israel had conquered the Amorites' territories was about 380 years at the time of Jephthah's remark.[62]

3. Judges' Linear Chronology

The Book of Judges forms a bridge between the way that the patriarchal chronologies are reckoned in Genesis–Exodus and the method by which they are reckoned under the later Monarchy. The scribe lists the reign of every judge in linear succession but intersperses the narrative with the time when Israel was oppressed;[63] thus, Israel was oppressed by x number of years, then saved by a leader who judged Israel for y number of years.[64] According to the chronology presented in the Book of Judges, the tumultuous Judges Era lasted about 340 years before Jephthah's statement (above).[65] Following Jephthah's statement, the Judges Era lasted another 91 years according to the Book of Judge's linear chronology.[66] This brings the *total of the Judges Era to 410 years.*[67]

Note that this 410 years *begins in Judg 3:8*, with Israel's full rebellion against YHWH's covenant. Like the scribe's colophon in 1 Kgs 6:1, this chronology *dismisses* the years for both Joshua and his immediate successor's administration(s), as well as the 40 years when Israel wandered in the wilderness (see below).[68] This evidence indicates that the scribe culled his information from the judges' records in the same manner that I have reconstructed it here.

Thus far, we have seen that there are three witnesses that fairly well agree on the amount of time that Israel lived in the Promised Land before instituting the Monarchy. What is not recorded is the length of time that Samuel judged Israel or the time amount of time Saul reigned over Israel. We know that David reigned over Israel for 40 years (2 Sam 5:5; 1 Kgs 2:11) and that the entry in 1 Kgs 6:1 referred to Solomon's 4th year. This leaves only about 26 years for Samuel–Saul.[69] If we add the 410 years of the Judges Era to David's 40-year reign and add Solomon's 4 years cited in the 1 Kings colophon, we arrive at 454 years, leaving only 26 years for both Samuel and Saul to have ruled over Israel. This places Saul's coronation at the very least 410 years after the Israelites first faced oppression, when the Book of Judges first began its formal chronology.[70] As we will see, Israel's sabbatical years aid in the reconstructions of this era as well.

At first, it appears that the omission of the length of Saul's reign is a scribal emendation made during David's administration. However, the entry in 1 Sam 13:1 follows the linear sort of chronological reckoning that we find in Judges.[71] Thus, Samuel or a student(s) under his administration archived both the information in Judges and the history in at least 1 Samuel 13–19 (see pp. 322–23). The Monarchy did not oversee the official historian's office until Samuel and David organized the kingdom (1 Chr 9:22; 16:4), probably while David was on the lam, a few years before Saul's death. Consequently, the only accounts that we have of Saul's reign are told from the priest's (Samuel's) perspective.[72] Meaningful to our discussion is that both the Judges' linear chronology and 1 Kgs 6:1 begin with Israel's oppression by Mesopotamia 8 years before Othniel judged the tribal federation. The time that 1 Kgs 6:1 accounts for that is not recorded in the Judges record is the 70 years that Israel's first three monarchs reigned over Israel (see below). All of these histories were registered by Levites in the scribe's office during David's and Solomon's reigns (1 Chr 9:22; 2 Sam 8:16–17; 1 Kgs 4:3; see chap. 8.V.). Thus, we see that the Levites had already established a linear (accession-year) chronology system well before the monarchy existed (see Table 9.2; see also Table 11.5, pp. 569–71).

4. Deborah and Hazor

A *fourth proof* of an early exodus date and for the long Judges Era comes from the account of Deborah. When Israel first entered the land, Joshua had thoroughly decimated Hazor. He killed Jabin, king of the Hazor kingdoms (Jer 49:28), burning the capital city to the ground (Josh 11:1–15), thoroughly routing Jabin's armies and annihilating Hazor's citizens (Josh 11:12). Deborah's account, however, attests that over 200 years later, the Jabin monarchy had re-established itself at Hazor (Judg 4:2–3) to oppress Judah.[73] According to the tribal distribution mentioned in Joshua, Judah had settled this area (Josh 15:21–25) but failed to drive out many of Canaan's natives (Josh 15:63; Judg 1:19).

Deborah could not have been contemporary with Joshua in any way for at least two reasons. First, Israel's armies faced obstacles in prevailing against Hazor's iron chariots at the initial Conquest but succeeded in utterly destroying them under Deborah (Josh 17:16–18; Judg 1:19). Deliberately, YHWH instructed Joshua to utterly destroy Hazor's chariots at the initial Conquest (Josh 11:6). The only way the Kingdom of Hazor (Jer 49:28) could replenish a 900-strong chariotry in Deborah's day (Judg 4:3) was for a significant time to pass during which the Jabins were able to reestablish and rebuilt their kingdom's chariot force.

Second, according to Deborah's account, Heber, a Kenite and a descendant of Reuel (Jethro), Moses' father-in-law,[74] had severed himself from Israel to ally with Hazor (Judg 4:11–12). He then betrayed Barak's (4:12) military plans to King Jabin. This act of treason is unlikely to have occurred under Joshua's or the elders' administrations, when Jethro had so firmly allied his family with his son-in-law Moses and Israel (Exodus 18). Obviously, Jael,

Table 9.2. Judges' Priestly Linear Chronology

Date	Text	Event	Years	Chronology
1460	Judg 3:8	Captivity: Mesopotamian King Chushan-rishathaim	8	8
1452	3:11	Saved: Othniel (Caleb's much younger brother leads Israel to a long era of peace)	40	48
1412	3:14	Captivity: Moab's King Eglon	18	66
1394	3:30	Saved: Ehud	80	146
1314	3:31; 5:6	Saved: Shamgar/Philistines	20	166
1294	4:3	Captivity: Hazor's King Jabin	20	186
1274	5:31	Saved: Deborah	40	226
1234	6:1	Captivity: Midian and Amalekites	7	233
1227	8:28	Saved: Gideon	40	273
1187	9:22	Coup: Abimelech	3	276
1184	10:2	Saved: Tola (of Issachar)	23	299
1161	10:3	Saved: Jair (Gileadite)	22	321
1139	10:7–8	Captivity: Philistines and Ammonites	18	339
1121	12:7	Saved: Jephthah	6	345
1115	12:8–9	Saved: Ibzan of Bethlehem	7	352
1108	12:11	Saved: Elon (Zebulunite)	10	362
1098	12:13–14	Saved: Abdon (Pirathonite)	8	370
1090	13:1	Captivity: Philistines (Samuel)	40	*410*
1051t	1 Sam 8:1	Israel asks for a king when Samuel is (80 yrs.?) old	(7)	436
	1 Sam 10:20–24	Saul	(19)	
1023t	1 Kgs 2:1	David enthroned over Judah	7	443
1016t	2 Sam 5:5	David enthroned over United Israel Kingdom	33	476
980	1 Kgs 6:1	Solomon's 4th year	4	*480*

Heber's wife, did not support her husband's alliance or his treachery against Israel's kindness to his tribe when she securely nailed her allegiance to Israel in the temple of Jabin's calculating general (Judg 4:17–21).

The strongest objection to 1 Kings' colophon and Judges' linear chronology (which places Deborah over 200 years after Joshua) arises in regard to claim that a King Jabin reigned from Hazor. Since both Deborah and Joshua cite a King Jabin, a number of scholars assume that these were the same king.[75] This assumption is unjustified.[76] History is laded with accounts of monarchs who ruled under a family name or in the name of a notable predecessor. Genesis lists Melchi-zedek (Gen 14:18) as king of Jerusalem. Another monarch is later listed as Adoni-zedek (Josh 10:1), Jerusalem's king during the Conquest. The same patronym custom is found with Syria's Ben-Hadad I and Ben-Hadad II and even with

Samaria's Jeroboam I or Jeroboam II. Egypt was no stranger to this custom either, because there exist in Egypt's royal kings' lists no less than ten *different* kings named Ramesses, four named Thutmoses, four different Amenhoteps, and two named Seti. Assyria also attests to monarchs who succeeded in the name of a notorious predecessor; hence, at least five *different* kings are named Shamshi-Adad and Shalmaneser, three are named Adad-nirari, three Shalmaneser, three Tiglath-pileser, and two Sargon. This custom spanned hundreds of years. In the case of Tiglath-pileser III (762 BCE), the royal name had been in use for about a 1,000 years. Thus, this objection to Scripture's chronology is naive and unfounded. This evidence has led some scholars to suggest that Jabin was a dynastic name rather than the name of an actual king.[77]

5. Israel's Ancient History Unbelievable?

One currently popular method of accounting for the Judges' chronology (Kitchen, Freedman, Albright, Wright) condenses the Judges Era by overlapping administrations.[78] Kenneth Kitchen, for instance, eclipses about 16 years of Israel's captivity under Moab's King Eglon into Ehud's 80-year administration. Thus, Ehud's 80 years is reduced to 64 years, and Judges' overall chronology shortened. Kitchen's assessment, however, ignores the fact that 1 Kgs 6:1 is itself based on the Book of Judges' linear chronology. Kitchen's theory does not account for Jephthah's statement[79] or for Hebron's renewed strength in Judges 4–5. Further, Kitchen refers to the early Conquest and Judges Era as an undetermined intermediate period,[80] when the rule of one judge overlapped that of another judge for an unspecified number of years. Although Kitchen is correct in stating that the early Conquest Era was an intermediate period the duration of which is not provided, we are not left without clues that allow us to reconstruct this period (see "Deutero-Joshua" below). Kitchen and scholars who thus telescope the entire Judges Era into 293 years are unjustified in discounting chronologies actually listed in Scripture.[81]

Egyptologist Donald Redford readily observes that the politically correct thirteenth century date for the exodus deconstructs and dismisses the validity of the text.

> The strength, however, of a confessional commitment to bolster a pre-judgment will not allow most conservative Jewish or Christian exegetes to discard the whole chronological arrangement. . . . The basic pattern of Patriarchal Age, Descent and Sojourn, Exodus and Conquest, and Judges *must* be essentially correct—Is it not inherently reasonable? Do you have a better one?—and consequently numerous ingenious solutions are devised. The most common trick has been to reduce time spans to generations: thus the 480 figure must really represent twelve generations: but 40 years per generation is too long, 20 being much closer to the average. Hence we can cut the figure in half and put the Exodus around 1255 BCE instead of 1486, and lo! it falls squarely in the reign of Ramesses II, and thus allusion to "Ra'amses" in Exodus 1:11 can be nicely accommodated! Similarly the 430 years of the Sojourn must simply be a curious equivalent of roughly four generations—does not Genesis 15:16 virtually prove it?—and so the Descent will come to rest about the

middle of the fourteenth century BCE, or at the close of the Amarna age. Although the Gargantuan ages of the patriarchs are not extraneous to the Genesis material as we now have it, but actually inform it, nevertheless these too are swept away or transmogrified into normal generation estimates; and thus the "Patriarchal Age" can occupy the fifteenth and early fourteenth centuries. . . . Such manhandling of the evidence smacks of prestidigitation and numerology; yet it has produced the shaky foundations on which a lamentable number of "histories" of Israel have been written.[82]

Redford is indeed justified in his criticism of this politically correct methodology of dismissing Scripture and trying to squeeze Israel's history in Egypt into a preconceived idea of what historical and archaeological evidence "should" demonstrate.

Not only does Kitchen's method undermine the validity of many details in Scripture, this telescoping method totally discounts the scribe's formal statement in Judges about "when" and how the Judges' chronology was reckoned.

> (Introductory Preamble) Nevertheless YHWH (a) raised up judges, which (b) delivered them out of the hand of those that spoiled them. And yet they would not listen to their judges, but they went a whoring after other gods, and bowed themselves to them: they turned quickly out of the way which their fathers walked in, obeying the commandments of YHWH; but they did not so.
>
> And (1) when YHWH raised them up judges, then YHWH was with the judge, and delivered them out of the hand of their enemies all the days of the judge: for it repented YHWH because of (3) their groanings by reason of them that (3) oppressed them and vexed them. And it came to pass, (2) when the judge was dead, that (3) they returned, and corrupted themselves more than their fathers, in following other gods to serve them, and to bow down to them; they ceased not from their own doings, nor from their stubborn way. (Judg 2:16–19, parenthesis added)

This text establishes the formula for the Judges' chronology. The introductory preamble introduces us to the Judges' subject matter as well as its basic theme: (b) Israel rebels so there is no protection from YHWH's covenant; subsequently the nation is delivered into oppression; YHWH (a) raises up judges to save the Israelites. The scribe then sets the formula for Judges' chronology. (1) YHWH raises up a judge and is with that judge (2) until his or her death. Thus, the life of the judge during his or her *judgeship* serves as x number of years for chronological purposes. Then Israel corrupts herself more (3) and is given over to oppression again. This is terminus y.[83] This interpretation of this text is supported further by the Judges' account listing a time for a judge to have ruled or for Israel to have been oppressed, followed by a scribal statement recognizing that, "after him," another judge ruled.[84] Naturally, this indicates a linear, descending chronology of judges, interrupted by a period of domination or vassal status, then returning to the leadership of another, perhaps elected judge.

Scribal commentary indicates that the Judges' material should indeed be dealt with in a linear fashion in lieu of the currently popular method of juxtaposing the rulership of one judge with another. The scribe's statement in Judg 2:16–19 serves as a *fifth proof* to 1 Kgs 6:1, demonstrating that according to all Scriptural accounts, the Judges Era lasted for at least 410 years,[85] not 293 years as scholars such as Kitchen posit.[86]

6. 430-Year Judgment Precedent

When we look at Israel's infiltration into the Promised Land, we see that Israel adhered to YHWH's covenant only during Joshua and his successors' lifetimes (Josh 24:31; Judg 2:7). After these pioneers passed away (30–45? years), the people began a downward-spiraling cycle.[87] Following Joshua's death, Israel's years in the land of Canaan were marked by continual disregard for the constitutional Law. In the Promised-Land Covenant that YHWH made with Abraham, the Creator established a 430-year precedent for a nation's sins to "come to the full" (Gen 15:13–16; Exod 12:41) before national judgment would be rendered.[88] Israel's request for a monarchy and Saul's accession to Israel's throne took place about 408 years after Israel had rebelled against the covenant at Bochim (Judg 2:1–5). By 1036, when the 430-year judgment was exhausted, YHWH had rejected Saul as king. The nation was on the brink of civil war as Saul chased David all over the countryside and the Philistines waged all-out war on Israel. The Tabernacle had been deserted, and the Ark of the Covenant resided in a layman's house. Unquestionably, chaos hallmarked Israel's state of affairs 430 years after Bochim.

David ascended Israel's throne 443 years after Bochim. David and his royal line ruled for exactly 430 years,[89] when the nation's sins again "came to the full," and YHWH rendered his Babylonian judgment on the nation. This 430-year judgment precedent is the *sixth (albeit tentative) proof* of the scribe's colophon. As we will see in upcoming chapters of this book, YHWH consistently withholds national judgment for 430 years and allows a nation to reach degradation (see Table 9.3).

From all accounts, the scribe based his notation in 1 Kgs 6:1 on Judges' *linear priestly chronology*. What neither chronology appears to account for is the 40 years that Israel roamed the wilderness before invading Canaan and the duration of Joshua (Judges 2:8) and his righteous successor's administration(s) after the nation first entered the land, which may have been another 30–60 years.[90]

Table 9.3. David's 430-Year Monarchy

David's House Rules over Judah	*Date*	
David ascends Judah's throne	1023	BCE
Zedekiah is killed	–587	BCE
Total	436	years
Athaliah's 6-year reign (857–851 BCE)	–6	
Total	430	years

C. Exodus to Judges: Deutero-Joshua

1. "Out of Egypt"

The scribe's entry in 1 Kgs 6:1 uses the phrase "after the children of Israel were come out of the land of Egypt" as a reference point or date. In the Book of Exodus, the phrase "out of Egypt" at first referred to Abib 14/15 when Israel left Egypt (Exod 12:17, 39, 41–42, 51; 13:3, 8, 14–17). After Israel crossed the Red Sea, the term *out of Egypt* included the crossing of the Red Sea (Exod 13:18), Miriam's sin (Deut 24:9), and Amalek's assault (Deut 25:17). Once Israel entered the wilderness the term "brought forth out of the land of Egypt" was no longer restricted to the exact "day" Israel left Egypt. Moses was careful to clarify when he meant the exact day that Israel came out of Egypt by identifying it with the month of Aviv (Exod 13:4; 23:15; 34:18; Deut 16:1) so that it was not confused with the ongoing journey out of Egypt, which came to include the covenanting at Sinai, and the wilderness sojourn.

By the end of the 40-year exile, Israel considered "coming forth out of the land of Egypt" to include the covenanting at Mt. Sinai (Deut 29:25). Israel did not make this covenant until three months (Exod 19:1) after departing Egypt. It is clear that the Wilderness Exile Period also came to be included in the tradition of Israel having "came out of Egypt."

> I made the children of Israel to dwell in booths, *when I brought them out of the land of Egypt.* (Lev 23:43; see also Deut 4:46)

Israel lived in booths or sukkahs throughout the entire wilderness exile. When Moses wanted to clarify the exact day Israel departed from Egypt, he used the phrase "day that you did depart out of the land of Egypt" (Deut 9:7). Shortly before Moses' death, he included the coming "forth out of Egypt" as bringing to "this place," in reference to the plains of Moab shortly before crossing the Jordan into the Promised Land (Deut 26:8–9). We see that this term was progressive and inclusive by including both the departure from Egypt and the entire Wilderness Exile Period until the recovenanting on the Moab plains, which *continued* the process of bringing Israel *out of Egypt.*

The Books of Joshua and Judges continue this reflective perception of "coming out of Egypt." Josh 2:10 includes the crossing of the Red Sea and battle with the Amorites in the time-period of "coming out of Egypt." The pattern that is displayed in all of these texts is that this term included the day on which Israel left Egypt until the day she crossed the Jordan into the Promised Land (see Judg 11:13, which took place several months after Israel left Egypt—Num 21:24).

The Book of Samuel continues a reflective view of the exodus. Whereas Moses had used the word *day* to refer to the exact day Israel walked out of Egypt, Samuel uses the term "day" as a general term to denote an era or period of time. "According to all the works which they have done *since the day that I brought them up out of Egypt* even unto this day, wherewith they have forsaken me, and served other gods, so do they also to you" (1 Sam 8:8). Israel did not rebel on the night she walked out of Egypt. She did not begin to complain until about

10 days later (Num 33:3–10) at the Red Sea (Exod 14:11) and continued complaining at the Waters of Marah (Exod 15:24). Therefore, Samuel's reference to Israel coming out of Egypt should not be taken as an exact *day* but a general era that includes the wilderness journeys. This conclusion is supported by another account in Scripture. King Saul used a broad and reflective perspective when using this phrase during his early campaigns. "And Saul said unto the Kenites . . . you showed kindness to all the children of Israel, *when they came up out of Egypt.*" (1 Sam 15:6). Moses's father-in-law, a Kenite (Judg 1:16), first showed kindness to Israel when the nation reached Mt. Sinai (Exodus 18) near his home settlement (Exod 3:1, 12; 4:18–19).

Under the Monarchy, this reflective perpsective continued as the exodus or "coming out of Egypt" is a generic epoch that included the time spent at Mt. Sinai/Horeb:

> There was nothing in the ark save the two tables of stone, which Moses put there at Horeb, *when YHWH made a covenant with the children of Israel, when they came out of the land of Egypt.* . . . . I have set there a place for the ark, wherein is the covenant of YHWH, *which he made with our fathers, when he brought them out of the land of Egypt.* (1 Kgs 8:9, 21; see also 2 Chr 5:10)

As we have seen, YHWH did not covenant with Israel on the day the people left Egypt. He did covenant with them 3 months later at Mt. Horeb/Sinai (Exod 19:1); however, the covenanting with Israel is included in the time frame *of bringing Israel out of the land of Egypt.* 1 Kgs 9:7 broadens this term to include the recovenanting on the plains of Moab 40 years later when YHWH appeared to Solomon in a dream.

> Israel shall be a proverb and a byword among all people. . . . And they shall answer, Because they forsook YHWH their God, *who brought forth their fathers out of the land of Egypt,* and have taken hold on other gods, and have worshipped them, and served them: therefore YHWH brought on them all this evil. (1 Kings 9:7, 9; see Deut 29:25)

YHWH's words to Solomon quote from the Testimonial Law in Deuteronomy (see, below and chap. 14). This covenant was contracted with Israel 40 years after the nation left Egypt. Notice how YHWH's admonition to Solomon is based on Deuteronomy 28. 1 Kgs 9:6 cites worshiping other gods and quotes from Deut 28:36, 64. 1 Kgs 9:8 refers to YHWH deporting Israel out of the land, which is a quote from Deut 28:25, 36, 41. 1 Kgs 9:7 refers to the people becoming a "proverb and a byword" is a quote from Deut 28:37. In 1 Kgs 9:9, YHWH quotes from Deut 29:25. YHWH is not referring to the Sinai Covenant as the covenant Israel made when she was "brought forth out of the land of Egypt" in 1 Kgs 9:8. He is referring to the Moab-Shechem covenant that was contracted 40 years later. When the scribe wanted to refer to the Passover "day" when Israel left Egypt, he referred to it as the "day" Israel came "out of Egypt" (1 Kgs 8:16; 2 Chr 6:5).

The term "out of Egypt" used in 1 Kgs 6:1 does not use any specific terminology to indicate that the scribe meant the Passover night on Abib 15. Instead, the scribe uses the generic "after Israel came out of Egypt," which included the 40 years in the wilderness. It is possible that the scribe dated the 480 years not from Abib 15 when Israel left Egypt but from Abib 15 when the Israelites had finally *finished their departure from Egypt* and had reached their goal: entering the Promised Land (Joshua 5; see below "40 Years"). What this means for our present study is that 1 Kgs 6:1 does not include the 40-year exile period in the phrase "after coming out of Egypt." The scribe dates his entry *after* the entire Wilderness Exile Period when Israel finally finished the journey out of Egypt and entered the Promised Land.

2. 40 Years

In chap. 8, we saw that the books of Deuteronomy and Joshua were updated by Joshua (Deut 27:3, 8; Josh 24:26) or one of his scribes once Israel entered the Promised Land. We also saw that Joshua 1, in its original form, had been part of the last chapter of Deuteronomy until a later scribe artificially divided the annal based on the lives of the nation's leaders instead of significant historical events. These later editorial practices have obscured much of the early Conquest and Judges Era.[91]

The chronology of the exodus picks up again in Deuteronomy, after the nation's 40 year exile.

> And it came to pass in the *fortieth year, in the eleventh month, on the first day of the month*, that Moses spoke to the Children of Israel, according unto all that YHWH had given him in commandment to them. (Deut 1:3)

This text places Israel on the plains of Moab to recovenant with YHWH (Deut 5:3; 29:1, 9, 12) at the tail end of the 40th year after coming out of Egypt. Israel is about to enter the Promised Land at the onset of the 41st year.[92] After Moses completed the recovenanting with Israel on the 1st of the 11th month of the 40th year, he died (Deut 34:5; see Table 9.4).

Table 9.4. Chronology of Deuteronomy–Joshua 5

Deut 1:3	40th year	11 month	Shebat 1	Moses gave instructions on renewing the covenant in the land
Deut 34:8		30 days	Adar 1	Israel grieves after Moses' death
Josh 1:11	41st year	3 days	Nisan 3	Leave the Moab plains to cross over Jordan
Josh 4:19		7 days later	Nisan 10	Crossed over Jordan
Josh 5:6, 7, 10		4 days later	Nisan 14	Observed Passover

Israel entered the Promised Land exactly 40 years after the exodus. She had departed Egypt on the 14th day of the 1st month (Exodus 12) and entered Canaan exactly 40 years later (at the onset of the 41st year) to establish her covenant with her God on the land he was laying bare before her (Exod 12:41).[93] This not only demonstrates the continuity of Israel's archives; it also demonstrates that Israel's scribes had access to very precise historical records. As far as the question of chronology is concerned, these texts firmly establish a 40 year epoch for which neither the scribe's colophon in 1 Kgs 6:1 nor the linear chronologies in Judges account.[94] Therefore, the wilderness epoch should be appended to the nation's 480-year chronology, totaling *at least* 520 years from the end of the exodus until Solomon's 4th regnal year.[95]

3. Israel's Intermediate Period

a. *From Leaving Egypt until Solomon's 4th Year*

Evidence demonstrates that we should proceed with caution when dating the exodus because there could be another 40–70 years (*including the 40-year exile*) appended to the nation's chronology that are not included in either the Judges' linear successions or the scribe's colophon in 1 Kgs 6:1.[96] Many scholars have carefully studied this era.[97] Kenneth Kitchen calculates that the chronology in Scripture for this unknown early Conquest Era could be 74 years, estimating the entire Monarchy and Judges Era to have lasted 554 years at the least and 596 years at its upper limit.[98] Josephus gives 112 years for this era in *Antiquities* (8.3.1); and 134 years in *Against Apion* (2.2), excluding the 480 years in 1 Kgs 6:1. John Bimson estimates that at least another 100–200 years could be added for this era, with 609 years being the upper limit for 1 Kgs 6:1, including the Joshua and the elders era and the 40 years in the wilderness.[99]

Egyptologist James Hoffmeier has also addressed the reconstruction of the 1 Kings colophon, wilderness exile, and Joshua's administration. He cites the work of previous scholars in this field:

> How then is the 480-year figure treated by scholars who reject it as a literal number? Petrie suggested that the number might have resulted from tallying up the duration of the Israelite judges from Saul back to Joshua. However, as Jack showed, if all the periods are added together, such as the 40 years in Sinai, the lengths of the judges, and periods of peace between judges, plus the length of leadership in Canaan and the length of Saul's kingship, which are not preserved, bring the total close to 600 years.[100]

Scholars allow up to about 600 years for the Joshua–Judges intermediate period. Although most scholars, including Hoffmeier, dismiss this high figure as absurd,[101] these scholars are usually equally critical of the current dates given for the exodus due to the lack of epigraphic and archaeological evidence of such a monumental event. Should we not find at least some evidence of this event if Scripture's accounts are indeed historical?

b. *Joshua and the Elders*

Since this study and the trial of YHWH are based *on the Scriptural text*, the question we must ask is: How long does Scripture allow for the Joshua–Judges intermediate period? Does Scripture give us enough information to reconstruct this undated era?

There are two entries that summarize this intermediate period. Two corresponding colophons in Joshua and Judges state that Israel followed YHWH's constitutional covenant during the lifetime of Israel's early pioneering settlers. These scribal notations focus on the nation's righteous time of blessing, when YHWH fought the Israelites' battles for them, which are reckoned according to the lives of the nation's founding fathers.

And Israel served YHWH (a) all the days of Joshua, and (b) all the days of the elders that outlived Joshua, and which (c) had known all the works of YHWH, that he had done for Israel. (Josh 24:31)

And the people served *YHWH all the days of Joshua, and all the days of the elders that outlived Joshua,* who had seen all the great works of YHWH, that he did for Israel. And Joshua the son of Nun, the servant of YHWH, died, being an *hundred and ten years old.* (Judg 2:7–8)

Both these texts confirm that during Israel's first intermediate period, Israel kept the Law (a) all of Joshua's days and all the (b) days of the young men who had: been in the wilderness, seen YHWH's miracles in (c) parting the Jordan (Joshua 3), eaten manna (Josh 5:12) and seen Jericho's destruction (Joshua 6). We learn at least two things from this text. First, Israel's Law played a very important role in the nation's early years in the land. This means that the nation's Release Years would naturally serve as times of renewal for the nation (i.e., Joshua 23–24). Second, "all the days of Joshua" and the "elders who outlived him" function as a timeline for calculating the nation's early, intermediate history. *Any valid Scriptural reconstruction of this era should take into account the lives of Joshua and the early elders as well as the role that Israel's Law played in early national policies.* The life-span of Caleb, Joshua, Othniel and the elders that "outlived" Joshua serve as the *seventh proof* of the Judges' linear chronology and coinciding 1 Kgs 6:1 account.

c. Caleb and Joshua

Caleb's and Joshua's lives serve as one terminus for the early Conquest Era. Caleb states that he was 40 years old (Josh 14:7) when he spied in Canaan, placing Caleb at 80 when the nation crossed the Jordan to set up a military post at Gilgal (Joshua 4–5). After warring for five years, Caleb petitioned Joshua at Gilgal, requesting that his tribal possession be distributed to him (Josh 14:10) when he was 85 years of age.[102] This is the only firm time frame we have for the Conquest Era. We do know that the Conquest continued well after Caleb's request, since Caleb and his family warred in the Hebron region after Joshua apportioned Caleb's inheritance.[103] Caleb's life serves as the *first terminus* for the early Conquest Era.

Joshua's age probably most closely mirrors Caleb's, placing both men at 40 years of age when Israel revolted after the scouts' report about the Promised Land.[104] After 40 years in the desert, Joshua would also have been around 80 years old when the nation invaded Canaan. This leaves about 30–40 years for Joshua to have led the people once the nation entered Canaan and before Joshua's death at 110 years of age.[105] (This also allows for Israel to have observed at least four Release Years and recovenanting periods with YHWH, Joshua 13–14, 18, 23–24). During Joshua's administration and his immediate predecessors', the nation adhered to righteousness and did not face oppression.[106] Thus, Joshua's life serves as the *second terminus* for the early Conquest Era, allowing 35–45 years for the early Conquest Era, before Joshua was succeeded by the "elders who outlived him."

d. Othniel

The third person whose age serves as a chronological terminus is Othniel, Caleb's much younger brother (Judg 1:13, 3:9). Othniel would have been somewhere between 20 and 59 years old when entering Canaan since YHWH banned any warrior aged 20 or more from entering Canaan (Num 14:29, 34). In other words, Othniel was included in the generation that saw YHWH's miracles when entering Canaan and "outlived" Joshua (Josh 24:31; Judg 2:7–8).

Based on the Judges' account, it appears that Othniel's life marked Israel's transitional or intermediate period between Joshua's administration and the later administrations by "judges." Othniel was at least 25 years old (Num 1:3) during the 5th year of the nation's initial Conquest campaign under Joshua's administration since he carried out Caleb's offensive at Kirjath-sepher (Judg 1:12). Othniel also was part of the first generation that faced oppression, living through eight years of Mesopotamian affliction before serving as an Israelite judge for 40 years after the nation broke free from Aram (Mesopotamia). While the text does not state how long Othniel lived, a safe estimate is between 105 and 115 years. Part of his life overlapped Joshua's administration (Josh 15:17). It is possible that Othniel lived long enough for there to be another 20 to 40 years not accounted by either the Judges chronicles or the 1 Kgs 6:1 colophon.

While Joshua's administration represented a righteous pioneering era, Scripture makes it clear that the nation did not rebel against YHWH's covenant until the *third generation* of those who entered the Promised Land. It was this generation that departed from YHWH and began the cycle of oppression and salvation; this may have occurred when Othniel was about 68 years old.

> And Joshua the son of Nun, the servant of YHWH, died, being an hundred and ten years old. . . . And also all that generation were gathered unto their fathers: and *there arose another generation after them, which knew not YHWH, nor yet the works which he had done for Israel.* And the Children of Israel did evil in the sight of YHWH, and served Baalim: And they forsook YHWH God of their fathers, which brought them out of the land of Egypt, and followed other gods, of the gods of the people that were round about them, and bowed themselves to them, and provoked YHWH to anger. And they forsook YHWH, and served Baal and Ashtaroth. (Judg 2:8, 10–13)

Othniel's life serves as the *third terminus* for the early Conquest Era, which transitioned into the Judges Era. If Joshua lived 30–40 years after entering Canaan, and Othniel lived another 40 years after Joshua's death, the upper limit for the early Conquest Era under Joshua's administration and the "elders that outlived him" was a *maximum* of 80 years. However, to Israel's scribes, Othniel's lifespan was not an independent administration like Joshua's or his successors' as much as it was a transitional time into the entire Judges Era. As far as any linear chronology is concerned, Othniel's life was eclipsed or coincided with the 8 years of Mesopotamian oppression before he became Israel's first judge. This evidence supports a 13-year intermediate period between Joshua's death and the Judges Era. Othniel's death still serves as a terminus for this era, but his age allows for only about 5–20 years of this transitional era to be in dispute.

The lives of Caleb, Joshua, and Othniel—our three "terminuses"—allow for the following chronological sequence. From the day that Israel entered the Promised Land until Joshua's death there were 35 to 45 years (perhaps longer, if Joshua was younger).[107] Subsequent to Joshua's death, Israel began another campaign to conquer the Promised Land (Judges 1). During this short era, Israel's power was at its zenith (Judg 1:28) yet, instead of driving out the land's natives as YHWH's covenant directed, the tribes offered suzerainty treaties, which obligated Canaan's tribute (Judg 1:31). Israel's greed, rebellion, and breach of YHWH's constitutional covenant prevented YHWH from fulfilling his covenantal promise (Judg 2:1–3) to drive out Canaan's natives or deliver the Promised Land into Israel's hand during this era (see Table 9.5; see also Table 11.5. on p. 569–71).

Table 9.5. Lifes-spans of Caleb, Joshua, and Othniel

Date	Text	Event	Chronology	Caleb	Joshua	Othniel
1548	Num 14:33	Age at desert exile		40	40	
1508	Joshua 23–24; 24:31	Israel enters Canaan	40	80	80	20
1503	Josh 14:6–14; Judg 1:13; 3:9–11	Joshua gives Caleb his inheritance/ Othniel champions Caleb's land	5	85	85	25
1478	Josh 24:29	Joshua dies[108]	25		110	50
1466	Josh 24:31; Judg 2:7–11	Elders that entered the land pass away	12	Intermediate period		
	Judg 2:1–5	Conquest terminates with Bochim/ 6th Release Year	6			68
1460	Judg 3:8	Captivity: Mesopotamian King Chushan-rishathaim	8			76
1452	Judg 3:11	Othniel—Caleb's much younger brother—leads Israel to a long era of peace	40			116

e. Third Generation and Bochim

Within Israel's covenantal Law, YHWH established limits for his mercy. He would extend mercy to those who rebelled against his covenant until the third or fourth generation (Deut 5:9). Caleb and Joshua had been part of the first generation that had exited Egypt. Othniel was part of the second generation, which was born in the wilderness and entered Canaan under Joshua's leadership. The children born in the Promised Land that had not seen the miracles associated with the Exodus (Judg 2:7–10) constituted the third generation. Since Israel had not been steadfast in her covenant with YHWH from the day he brought the nation out of Egypt (1 Sam 8:8), he terminated the mercy that the first three generations had enjoyed. At Israel's national covenant renewal assembly, YHWH addressed Israel's breach of his covenant. Israel had convened at Bochim, a word-play on Shechem, where YHWH refrained himself from fighting on Israel's behalf. The nation fell prey to Mesopotamia's Chushan-rishathaim (Judg 3:8) shortly thereafter.

This sequence of events allows for about 12 years in the Second Conquest Campaign during this transitional intermediate period before Israel was subjugated by Aram (Mesopotamia). Thus, the entire early Conquest Era lasted for about 42 years. If we add the 40-year wilderness exile, we conservatively arrive at about 88 years for both exile and early Conquest before the nation transitioned into the Judges Era with her subjection to Mesopotamia and the leadership of her first judge, Othniel.

Table 9.5 allows for 88 years for the combined wilderness exile, Joshua's administration, and the transitional intermediate period into the Judges Era, thus placing the Exodus about 1548 BCE This table estimates that there were 568 years from the day that Israel entered the Promised Land until King Solomon's 4th year (480+88 = 568). Thus, we see that Kitchen's estimate based on Scripture's chronology for this era closely harmonizes with the Scriptural account.

4. Perspective from the Eye of the Beholder

We have seen that there are at least five different Scripture "proofs" that support a time period of 480 years from the exodus until Solomon's 4th year (1 Kgs 6:1). The scribe began his chronology with the record of Mesopotamian captivity (Judg 3:8) and added the length of a particular judgeship to the time of captivity (refer to Table 9.2 on p. 353). This rendered 480 years from the year Mesopotamia first afflicted Israel until Solomon's 4th year. As we have seen, the phrase "after coming out of Egypt" (1 Kgs 6:1) did *not* include the 40-year exile period or Joshua and his successor's administrations (Josh 24:29–31; Judg 2:6–8). It is clear that the chronology from the point Israel entered the Promised Land (Josh 5:10) until the record of Israel's captivity to Mesopotamia (Judg 3:8) had either been lost, or had never been formally written. When the scribes compiled Israel's historical works they were not compelled to account for this "missing" intermediate period but used the lives of the nations founding patriarchs to bridge the gap.

Another factor affecting the continuity with which the Israelites viewed their ancient society during this era is that the generation that came out of Egypt was the same generation that inherited the Promised Land. Joshua was a young man when he left Egypt and scouted out Canaan.[109] After 40 years in the wilderness, Joshua and Caleb were remnants of a "normal" generation's lifespan.[110] From the scribes' point of view, there may have been no reason to arbitrarily demarcate a point in the middle of the nation's annals while Joshua, the nation's leader who came out of Egypt and shepherded the nation into the Promised Land was still alive. Therefore, when the scribe (1 Kgs 6:1) stated that it had been 480 years since the "coming out of Egypt," he may have seen the exodus as an epoch beginning with the plagues in Egypt and ending with the actual subjugation of Canaan. If this theory is correct, then there is a considerable span of time that neither the 1 Kgs 6:1 colophon nor the Judges record of the nation's early years on the land intended to include (Judges 1:1 to Judges 3:8).

IV. DATING THE EXODUS

So far, we have seen that Israel's history from Judges (3:8) through Solomon's 4th regnal year spans 480 years, placing the onset of the Judges Era at 1460 BCE. Neither of these sources accounts for the 40 year wilderness exile or for Joshua's and his successor's administrations.[111] As mentioned above, from the exodus to the beginning of the Judges Era are reconstructed to 88 years, which should be appended to 1 Kgs 6:1 to total 568 years from the time that Israel departed from Egypt until Solomon began to build the Temple his 4th year. Using the anchor date of 587 for the destruction of the First Temple, places Solomon's 4th year at 980, with Israel entering Canaan in 1508, and the exodus occurring 40 years earlier in 1548 (see Table 9.6 and Table 11.5).

Table 9.6. Exodus to Othniel

1548	Exod 12:41	Exodus		
	Num 14:33	Desert exile	40	40
1508	Josh 23–24; 24:31	Israel enters Canaan/First Conquest Campaign begins	5	45
1503	Josh 14:6–14	Joshua gives Caleb his inheritance		
1501	Joshua 13	1st Release Year—land distributed	2*	47
1494	Joshua 21	2nd Release Year—land distributed	7	54
1487	Joshua 23	3rd Release Year/Renewal of Covenant	7	61
1480	Joshua 24	4th Release Year/Renewal of Covenant	7	68
1478	Josh 24:29; Judges 24	Joshua dies at 110 yrs. of age	2	70
1478	Judges 1	Second Conquest Campaign begins under the elders	(12)	82
	Josh 24:31; Judg 2:7–11	Elders that entered the land pass away		
1466	Judg 2:1–5	6th Release Year/Conquest terminates with Bochim	(6)	88
		YHWH removes protection of his covenant, applies curses: delivers to bondage		
1460	Judg 3:8	Captivity: Mesopotamian king Chushan-rishathaim	8	96
1458	(Lev 25:10–11)	1st Jubilee		
1452	Judg 3:11	Third Conquest Campaign begins	40	136
		Saved: Othniel (Caleb's much younger brother leads Israel to a long era of peace)		

*Gray-shaded numbers are reconstructed, but not stated in the text.

V. NATIONAL JUBILEES

A. *Hezekiah's 14th Year*

Israel's national Jubilees provide another control or benchmark for dating the exodus.[112] Sabbatical years in Israel were universally fixed dates of national celebration (holidays).[113] If we know when one Jubilee occurred, we can work forward and backward to reconstruct chronology.[114] This allows us to reconstruct the national holidays when the nation would be most likely to convene and to renew the national constitution. These events are often alluded to in Scripture but are not given a datable context (see Joshua 13; 23; 24; Judg 2:1–5; 11:11; 1 Sam 7:2; ch. 8; 2 Samuel 6). Sabbatical years may be implied with qualifying statements throughout the Book of Judges, which states, "Israel forsook YHWH" (Judg 2:12–13), or Israel "again did evil" in YHWH's sight (Judg 3:7, 12; 4:1; 6:1; 10:6; 13:1). These statements may have been culled by Samuel from the Levitical scribe's record of Release/Jubilee years which Israel attended or failed to convene. The covenant had stipulated that Israel should meet during Sukkot (Feast of Tabernacles) every 7th year to read and renew the covenant.

> And Moses commanded them, saying, At the *end of every seven years*, in the solemnity of the year of release, *in the feast of tabernacles*, When *all Israel is come to appear before YHWH* your God in the place which he shall choose, you shall read this law before all Israel in their hearing. (Deut 31:10–11)

If the Israelites failed to show up at Shiloh to renew the covenant during the Feast of Tabernacles (Deut 31:10–13) every 7th year, as the constitution had legislated, then they had turned from YHWH to idolatry and oppression. It may be remembered that the sabbatical years and the Sabbath Day were the sign that the nation was in covenant with YHWH (Exod 31:13–17). Thus, it is not surprising to find many vague texts that appear to have coincided with these automatically occurring sabbatical years.

The best anchor that Scripture affords is Isaiah's reference to the Jubilee as the sign of Jerusalem's salvation (2 Kgs 19:29; Isa 37:30). Hezekiah's 14th year had been a national Release Year, and this was the reason Sennacherib chose to invade Jerusalem (2 Kgs 18:13), when food stores were low and the city was unable to endure a long siege. Jerusalem's deliverance could only be effected through divine intervention. Sennacherib had sent a letter to Hezekiah threatening Jerusalem and proclaiming Assyria's might. Laying Sennacherib's letter before YHWH, Hezekiah pleaded for deliverance. Encouragingly, Isaiah prophesied against Assyria's king, promising both Jerusalem's deliverance and Sennacherib's death. YHWH gave the following sign to Hezekiah as a token that his word would come to pass:

> And this shall be *a sign to you, You shall eat this year such as grows of itself; and the second year that which springs of the same: and in the third year sow you* and reap, and plant vineyards, and eat the fruit of it.[115] And the remnant that is escaped of the House of Judah shall again take root downward, and bear fruit

upward: For out of Jerusalem shall go forth a remnant, and they that escape out of Mount Zion: the zeal of YHWH of hosts shall do this. (Isa 37:30–32; compare with 2 Kgs 19:29–31)

Isaiah acknowledges that Judah's land will lie fallow for two years. If the nation's constitutional Law supports fallowing the land for two years, it supports the theory that this event was the 50th Jubilee. If, however, the land lay fallow the first year due to Sennacherib's siege, it simply demonstrates that Hezekiah's 15th year was the 49th Release Year (see below).[116]

Scripture outlined regulations for fallowing the land for two consecutive years, ordaining that during both the 49th and 50th years the land was to be left fallow.

But in the seventh year shall be a sabbath of rest to the land, a sabbath for YHWH: you shall neither sow your field, nor prune your vineyard. . . . And you shall number seven sabbaths of years to you, seven times seven years; and the space of the seven sabbaths of years shall be to you forty and nine years. (Lev 25:4, 9)

A Jubilee shall that fiftieth year be to you: you shall not sow, neither reap that which grows of itself in it, nor gather the grapes in it of your vine undressed. (Lev 25:11)

Scripture *does* indeed support a consecutive, two-year fallowing of the land.[117] In fact, the corollary account in 1 Kgs 19:29 and the original statute in Lev 25:5, 11 are the only texts that specifically refer to the fallowing of the land.[118] Thus, Isaiah's statement should not be taken to remark on Sennacherib's siege but on the 50th Jubilee.

Scripture is not the only source to support this conclusion. Sennacherib had campaigned in Israel as a junior king, under his father Sargon (see below). Sargon stated that he finally broke through the city of Azekah, which was a border city between Judah and Assyria during Hezekiah's "seventh time."[119] The exact meaning of this text is lost due to damage. However, the context indicates that Sargon had captured Azekah during this "seventh time."[120] William Shea interprets this text to refer to a Sabbath in Israel.[121] Similar to Young and Steimann, Shea discounts this reference based solely on rabbinic reckoning of the sabbatical years and concludes that the text refers to a weekly Sabbath.[122] This raises the question why one weekly Sabbath would be distinguished from another. The Release Year, however, would stand out to an enemy king since food stores and normal production would be suspended for the entire year (two years during the Jubilee), thus granting Sargon an opportune time to besiege Hezekiah's forces. Thus, both Scripture and an Assyrian inscription indicate that a Release Year and/or Jubilee took place during Hezekiah's 14th/15th years.

Steinmann's excellent treatment of this material demonstrates that an agricultural year began in the fall/winter and was harvested in the spring (April–June). During a normal sabbatical year, crops would be planted in the fall/winter of the 6th year and harvested in spring of the 7th year, although no spring/summer sowing would take place. Consequently, this meant that no fall harvest or sowing occurred in the fall/winter of the 7th year and no harvest during the spring of the 8th year.[123] Normal sowing would begin in the spring of the 8th year, with the first harvest occurring in the fall of the 8th year. During a Jubilee year, both the 7th and 8th years would be fallow years, with harvests beginning again in the fall of the 9th year (see Table 9.7).

Table 9.7. Seventh Release Year

	Season		Activity
Year 6	spring	harvest	sowing
	fall	harvest	sowing
Year 7	spring	harvest	*no sowing*
	fall	Fallow	*no sowing*
Year 8	spring		sowing
	fall	harvest	sowing
Year 9	spring	harvest	sowing

Note also that the only way Isaiah could use the Jubilee as a sign was *if* Israel was actually observing the Jubilee statute. For years, academics have debated whether Israel or her kings ever observed the sabbatical years. Scripture unequivocally states that David did.

> If you will listen to all that I command you, and will *walk in my ways, and do what is right in my sight, to keep my statutes and my commandments, as David my servant did*; that I will be with you. (1 Kgs 11:38)
>
> *David did* that which was right in the eyes of YHWH, and *turned not aside from any thing that he commanded him* all the days of his life, save only in the matter of Uriah the Hittite. (1 Kgs 15:5)

Similar to Abraham, who observed YHWH's statutes, commands, and laws (Gen 26:5), David also obeyed YHWH's covenantal Law. Remember that, unlike any other command, *all the Sabbaths*—both weekly and yearly were the sign (Exod 31:13–17) that the nation of Israel was in compliance with YHWH's covenant, especially since the covenant was renewed by the nation every Release Year (Deut 31:9–12; see chap. 4.VI, pp. 146–49). It is quite unlikely, then, that a Levitical scribe would characterize David's reign over Israel as "having done what is right" if he had not actually observed the sabbatical years and renewed the covenant. In fact, the scribe in 1 Kgs 15:5 states that the only parts of the Law that David failed to uphold were the precepts associated with the crime he committed against Uriah and Bathsheba. David was faithful in all else.

David's adherence to the Torah and commitment to run his administration by its precepts became a standard by which all future kings were measured. If a king did "what was right" in God's sight, his obedience was compared with David's. In all of Israel's and Judah's history, only Hezekiah (2 Kgs 18:2) and Josiah (2 Kgs 22:2) did what was right as David had. Thus, it is not surprising to find that Hezekiah's administration observed the Jubilee as required by the nation's constitutional covenant.

Since Scripture states that Hezekiah renewed Israel's covenant (2 Kgs 18:1–7), it is quite likely that he led the people to observe this statute and the release of Hebrew slaves that accompanied it. The last time we find a reference to the sabbatical year before the Diaspora occurred is when Jeremiah advocated for Zedekiah to return to the covenant and observe the Release Year, which the elders promised to do, even though they reneged a short time later (Jer 34:8–11). Jeremiah's push to reestablish the releasing of Hebrew slaves during the sabbatical year indicates that the nation had only recently abandoned this system. As we saw in chap. 7 (pp. 232–33, 262–63), Release Years allowed Israel's congregation to participate in local affairs and to uphold the nation's constitutional Law; when the people neglected this convention, the tribal and federal leaders had usurped their God-given constitutional authority by oppressing the people, just as Jeremiah's testimony indicates. Thus, trace evidence exists to indicate that the sabbatical years formed an integral backbone of Israel's cultural society, even during the Monarchy.

B. 49th Year vs. 50th Year Calculations

Another factor affecting the calculation of Jubilees is determining how to figure the 50th year. Jack Finegan, author of the *Handbook of Biblical Chronology*, favors a 50-year Jubilee count.[124] Steinmann and Young opt for counting the 50th year as the 1st year of the new Jubilee cycle, as advanced by several talmudic sources, leaving every Jubilee cycle to have 49 years.[125] Although the 49-year Jubilee count allows historians to reconstruct the exodus date (1446 BCE) conveniently by simply using multiples of 7, the method never allows for a 50th Jubilee because the last year of this system will always be the 49th year. In other words, there never is a 50th year in this system. In a 100-year time span, the second 50th Jubilee occurs in the 99th year instead of the 100th year. This complicates the natural archival functions for maintaining state records (see pp. 238–40). Over time, each Jubilee loses one year or shortens the chronology by one year. Over the span of 200 years, a system of calculation

Table 9.8. 49th and 50th Jubilee Fallowing Cycle

Jubilee Year	Consecutive	Fallowing	Season	Jubilee cycle	Activity
48th yr.	Year 6	(sustains for 3 yrs.)	spring	harvest	sowing
			fall	bountiful harvest	sowing
49th yr.	Year 7	1st fallow year	spring	bountiful harvest	no sowing
			fall	6th yr. sustains for	no sowing
50th yr.	Year 8	2nd fallow year	spring	3 yrs.	no sowing
			fall	(Lev 25:20–22)	no sowing
1st yr.	Year 9	3rd year harvest	spring		sowing
			fall	harvest	sowing
2nd yr.	Year 10		spring	harvest	sowing

that fails to include the 50th Jubilee will lose 3 years. The 49th-Jubilee method places more emphasis on talmudic sources[126] and less importance on Scripture. A similar ordinance for the Festival of Weeks (Shavuot) also adds the 50th year to the normal 7-year cycle (Lev 23:15–16). If one calculates these holidays by using a linear 50-year Jubilee, 50 years continually occur between each Jubilee cycle, and every two Jubilee cycles are equivalent to one century (see Table 9.8).

C. More Sabbatical Years

Although Hezekiah's reign provides a chronological benchmark for reconstructing Israel's Jubilees, it is not the only reference we have to the nation's sabbatical years. If we continue forward in time, Jeremiah's (34:8–10) plea for Zedekiah to observe the Release Year occurred during Zedekiah's 4th year. The nation's last sabbatical Release Year (not Jubilee) occurred during Zedekiah's final year, when Nebuchadnezzar burned the Temple to the ground and released the land to observe the sabbatical years that Israel had not observed during the Monarchy (2 Chr 36:21; Lev 26:34).

Going back in time from Hezekiah's Jubilee also allows us to reconstruct key ceremonial events in Israel's history. The construction of the First Temple began on a Release Year in Solomon's 4th year, in 980 BCE, and was completed 10 months before the next Release Year (1 Kgs 6:37–38), in 974. Solomon spent the remaining 10 months before the next Release Year fashioning the various Temple implements (1 Kgs 7:15–51), such as the candlesticks, censors, and the brazen sea (1 Kgs 7:43–50). On the subsequent Release Year, in 973, the Temple was dedicated during Sukkot (1 Kgs 6:1; 37–38; 8:2). Thus, Solomon's prayer for Israel at the Temple's dedication would have occurred during the Release Year festivities, when the nation customarily gathered in Jerusalem to renew the covenant. Solomon prayed according to the Testimonial Law, and YHWH agreed to add the blessings of prayer to the nation's covenant as part of this covenant renewal (2 Chr 6:19–22; 1 Kgs 8:22–62).

The command for Israel to hold national festivals during the Release Years provided natural occasions for the affairs of state to be handled. This recurring 7th Release-year interval is naturally best attested in the chronology that Scripture provides (based on 1 Kgs 6:1) which demonstrates that both Saul and David were installed during sabbatical Release Years.

King David was crowned king over *Judah* during a Release Year, in 1023n. He then became king over the *United Kingdom of Israel* when the nation naturally convened 7 years later, in 1016t (2 Sam 5:4–5). One of the most important Jubilees (50th year) occurred during the 16th year of David's reign. After seeing that YHWH had established his kingdom, David turned his attention to cultic endeavors (2 Sam 5:12, ch. 6, 7:16). Only 9 years had passed since David began to rule over a United Monarchy. This special event celebrated the nation's 10th Jubilee on the Promised Land and brought the Ark of the Covenant to Jerusalem (2 Samuel 6). Restoring the ark from the possession of the Philistines resonated with the idea of the freedom that the Jubilee statute ordained, prompting David to seek freedom for YHWH's constitutional Testimony. David understood the prophetic implications of bringing the ark—YHWH's mercy seat—to Jerusalem. This prophetic act was not only religious but political. By bringing the ark to Jerusalem, David sought to secure Jerusalem as his capital seat of government by installing the instrument that bore YHWH's sacred constitutional covenant and symbolically placed "YHWH's name" on the city (Deut 12:5–7). In the chronology Scripture provides, this event occurred in 1008 BCE. This would have been the nation's 10th Jubilee, marking the nation's first 500 years in the Promised Land, and culminated with David's merry celebration (2 Samuel 6). During the 37th year of David's reign, which would have been the last Release Year of David's life, he installed Solomon on the throne as co-regent (1 Kgs 1:32–35; 1 Chr 23:1; 28:11–13, 18–19), passing to him the pattern (blueprint) and commissioning him to build the First Temple. Solomon began to reign independently on David's death. He began to build the Temple in his 4th year, and it was dedicated during Sukkot in the 11th year of Solomon's reign (see Table 9.9).

Table 9.9. David's and Solomon's Sabbatical Years

Date	Text	Regnal Year	Release Year or Jubilee Event
1023n	2 Sam 2:5	1	David installed over Judah
1016t	2 Sam 2:5	7	David installed over a United Monarchy
1009	2 Sam 6:1–11; 1 Chr 13	14	Uzzah's breach
1008	2 Sam 6:12–17; 1 Chr 15–17	15	Jubilee/David brings Ark of the Testimony to Jerusalem
1001			
994			
987	1 Kgs 1:32–35; 1 Chr 23:1; 28:11–13, 18–19	37	David installs Solomon as co-regent/entrusts Solomon with building the Temple
980	1 Kgs 6:1, 37	4	Solomon begins building the Temple in his 4th year
973	1 Kgs 6:38	11	Temple is dedicated during Solomon's 11th year

The previous Jubilee, the 9th Jubilee transpired in 1058. During this national Jubilee convention, Israel petitioned Samuel for a king (1 Samuel 8). Saul was chosen and installed in the autumn of the subsequent Release Year in 1051t, when the nation reconvened during Sukkot. The Book of Samuel separates Israel's request for a king from Saul's coronation by inserting the story of the prophet's first encounter with Saul (1 Samuel 9). Later, Saul is formally chosen as king during another national convention. The Book of Samuel implies that 1 Samuel 8 occurred at the 9th Jubilee, in 1058, as the separate "Book of the Manner of the Kingdom" mentioned in 1 Sam 10:25, while 1 Sam 9:1–10:16 occurred during the intervening 7 years. The sabbatical year is implied again in 1 Sam 10:17–27, when Samuel again called Israel to the makeshift capital in Mizpeh in 1051t, both to renew the covenant and to install Saul as king. This chronology would allow 7 years for Samuel to judge Israel independently and 19 years for Saul to reign over the nation as king.[127]

The sabbatical year also explains why we find that the regnal reckoning of Judah's kings begins in the seventh month of Tishri. The Law had ordained that Israel convene every seven years during Sukkot to renew the covenant. This automatically recurring event provided the forum for Israel to formally petition Samuel for a king. Since Saul was installed during

Sukkot, his regnal years would naturally be reckoned from Tishri (the 7th month) instead of from the beginning of the normal cultic year, which was in Nisan. David's accession over Judah and Israel—seven years apart—would indicate that the Tishri calendar remained the formal Monarchic calendar, beginning with the transition of the kingdom to David's House, even though David had begun to rule over Judah in Nisan (1 Sam 5:5). As we will see, the Judah-Israel synchronisms conclusively demonstrate that Judah adhered to a Tishri system for reckoning regnal years throughout the entire era of the Monarchy.

The 10th Jubilee occurred in 1108, when Israel renewed the covenant and installed Elon as judge (Judg 12:11; 1 Sam 7:2–13). This era began to reverse the Philistines' domination over Israel, as Samuel faithfully upheld the covenant. The Book of Samuel contains an interesting chronology. At the convening in Mizpeh for the 10th Jubilee, Samuel states that the ark had been in Kirjath-jearim for 20 yrs. (1 Sam 7:2). This is significant in two respects. First, without the Ark of Testimony at the cultic site, Israel could not truly ratify or renew her covenant with God. Second, Samuel's remark allows us to reconstruct history, placing both Eli's death and the ark's capture in 1129/1128 BCE.

With the ark captured, YHWH withdrew his name from the nation's seat of government at Shiloh (Jer 7:12; Ps 78:60–64). Samuel and Israel's fighting forces retreated to Mizpeh's interior safety on the nation's northeastern border (1 Sam 7:5–7, 16; 10:17; see Map 11.5.). Prior to the sabbatical Release Year in 1123, the Ark of the Covenant had been captured, and the Philistine oppression raged strong. Samuel had been quite young when YHWH first called aloud to him in the Tabernacle. As a very young man, Samuel urgently pleaded for the Israelites to forsake idolatry and return to the constitutional covenant during the Release in 1123 (Judg 10:10–16). Evidently, the nation listened to the priest's counsel as Jephthah energetically delivered Israel from her enemies (Judg 12:7; see Table 9.10).

Table 9.10. Eli to David

1128	1 Samuel 4; 4:15	Ark Captured under Eli, who dies at 98 yrs. of age
1108	Judg 12:11; 1 Sam 7:3–13; 1 Sam 7:2	Saved: Elon the Zebulunite/*8th Jubilee* Samuel—priest/Israel puts away gods—Recovenanting/Ark in Kirjath-jearim for 20 yrs.
1058	1 Samuel 7–8	Israel asks for a king when Samuel is (80 yrs.?) old
1051t	1 Sam 10:20–24	Saul installed as king
1023n	1 Sam 5:5	David installed over Judah
1016t	1 Sam 5:5	David installed over United Kingdom of Israel

Working backward, the next preceding Jubilee that bears on Israel's history occurred in 1258. Deborah and Barak had successfully campaigned for 16 years in Canaan. For the first time since the initial Conquest, Israel had succeeded in conquering significant territory (see chap. 11.XII). By the 16th year of the campaign, when the 50th-year Jubilee rolled around, the nation again convened at Shiloh/Shechem. This holiday afforded the perfect opportunity for Deborah to work with the nation's scribes to update and compile the various scrolls that contained Israel's history and its covenantal Law (Judg 5:14). The Jubilee probably also occasioned *The Song of Deborah* in much the same way that the 10th national Jubilee was marked by David's celebrations, which had restored the ark. More will be said on this important chronological benchmark when we investigate Deborah's role in Israel's history in chap. 11 on the Conquest below.

No other sabbatical year stands out as significant until we go back to the Bochim incident during the early Conquest Era. Shiloh/Shechem had been Israel's capital, where YHWH had placed his name: the Tabernacle and mercy seat, his abode. Israel had faithfully convened at Shiloh every 7 years during Joshua's administration (Josh 18:1, 8–10; 21:2; 22:12; Judg 18:31; 21:19). The unfortunate Bochim event transpired during Israel's 6th Release Year (42nd actual year) in the land. This important sabbatical year hallmarked the epoch when Israel had thoroughly rebelled against YHWH and turned from the covenant (Judges 2). Since God's messenger pledged that YHWH would no longer fight Israel's battles, the most significant territorial Conquest had occurred during the previous 42 years, a point we will return to when we look at the archaeological evidence for the Conquest in chap. 11.

Several times the Book of Joshua records that Israel held a national convention at Shiloh/Shechem. Most of these meetings dealt with distributing the land among the tribes, although shortly before Joshua's death the meeting focused more on reestablishing the covenant (Joshua 24). At least four separate Release Years can be distinguished during this era, in 1480 (Joshua 24), 1487 (Joshua 23), 1494 (Joshua 21, 23), and 1501 (Joshua 13). Tracing back one additional Release Year brings us to the date Israel entered the Promised Land, in 1508/1509 BCE. Thus, the date when Israel's Jubilees indicate that Israel entered the Promised Land would be Nisan 1508, and the exodus would have occurred in 1548.

We have seen that both the 1 Kgs 6:1 colophon and the Book of Judges' linear chronology begin the Judges Era with Babylon's captivity of Israel in 1460 BCE. Notice that, when we reconstruct all the Jubilees backward, beginning with King Hezekiah's reign, the only date for Israel to have entered Canaan (after the exodus) would have been either 1508 or 1558 (when accounting for the Jubilee system). The problem with lowering this date is that by 1460 BCE Israel had been taken captive by Babylon (Judg 3:8). This allows no period of time for Israel to have conquered Canaan (Joshua 5–11) by vanquishing Jericho's territory (Josh 5–6), subjugating Shechem (Josh 8:30—Mt. Ebal was at Shechem) and the territory of Goshen in the Negev (Josh 11:16), or for several generations to have lived on the land before the people rebelled against the constitutional Covenant (Josh 24:31; Judg 2:7–11). Therefore, the date the Scriptural evidence supports for the exodus is 1548, with Israel entering the Promised Land in 1508. In chaps. 10–11 below, we will examine the surprising archaeologic and epigraphical evidence for a 1548 exodus and 1508 Conquest after we finish our investigation of Israel's chronology during the Monarchy and Second Temple Era.

My reconstruction of Solomon's 4th year is based on the anchor date for the destruction of the First Temple. The date 980 BCE is derived from the internal synchronizations and reign-lengths of Israel's kings during the period of the Divided Kingdom, a topic we will discuss in more detail below. Our reconstruction of the exodus and Solomon's 4th year is primarily based on the actual chronology of Israel's kings (as we will see), but this date just happens to coincide with Israel's national sabbatical years.

Table 9.11. Sabbatical Release and Jubilee Years Chronology

Date	Text	Event	Sabbatical year
1508	Josh 23–24; 24:31	Israel enters Canaan	
1501	Josh 13	Land distribution	1st Release Year
1494	Josh 21	Land distribution	2nd Release Year
1487	Josh 23	Covenant Renewal	3rd Release Year
1480	Joshua 24; Judges 1	Covenant Renewal	4th Release Year
1473	Josh 2:11?	Failed to convene and renew covenant?	5th Release Year
1466	Judg 2:1–5	Bochim	6th Release Year/YHWH removes protection—Israel not following covenant
1458			1st Jubilee
1408			2nd Jubilee
1358			3rd Jubilee
1308			4th Jubilee
1258	Judg 4–5	Song of Deborah, scribal activity	5th Jubilee
1208			6th Jubilee
1158			7th Jubilee
1108	Judg 12:11; 1 Sam 7:3–13; 1 Sam 7:2	Elon-Samuel/Israel puts away gods/ Recovenanting/ Ark in Kirjath-jearim 20 yrs.	8th Jubilee
1058	1 Samuel 7–8	Israel asks for a king	9th Jubilee
1051t	1 Sam 10:20–24	Saul installed as king	Release Year
1023n	1 Sam 5:5	David installed over Judah	Release Year
1016t	1 Sam 5:5	David installed over United Kingdom of Israel	Release Year
1008t	2 Samuel 6–7	David brings ark to Jerusalem	10th Jubilee/Covenant Renewal/David's Covenant of Light/ time of blessing
980	1 Kgs 6:1	Solomon begins Temple construction	Release Year
973	1 Kgs 8:1–2	Temple dedicated/Ark brought into Temple	Release Year/Sukkot mentioned in text
958			11th Jubilee/2nd Jubilee under the Monarchy
908	2 Chr 15:12–15	Asa re-covenants	12th Jubilee/3rd Jubilee under the Monarchy
858			13th Jubilee/4th Jubilee under the Monarchy
808			14th Jubilee/5th Jubilee under the Monarchy
758			15th Jubilee/6th Jubilee under the Monarchy

Table 9.11. Sabbatical Release and Jubilee Years Chronology, *cont.*

Date	Text	Event	Sabbatical year
708	2 Kgs 19:29; Isa 37:30	Hezekiah's Jubilee	16th Jubilee/7th Jubilee under the Monarchy
658			17th Jubilee/8th Jubilee under the Monarchy
608			18th Jubilee/9th Jubilee under the Monarchy
594	Jeremiah 34	Attempt to covenant	Release Year
587		Temple destroyed	Release Year

It is highly improbable that Israel's Release Years should perfectly coincide with so many national events: (1) the year that Solomon's Temple was completed and the year when construction began; (2) both David's accession year over both Judah and Israel; and (3) Saul's accession to the throne of Israel—unless these holidays had actually played an important role in the nation's administration throughout the Judges Era and the early Monarchy Era. Therefore, the Release and Jubilee years serve as the *eighth proof* supporting the chronology advanced by: (1) the 1 Kgs 6:1 colophon; (2) Judges' linear chronology; (3) the appended years of Caleb, Joshua, and Othniel's lives; (4) Israel's intermediate period; and the anchor date of King Hezekiah's Jubilee. There is one more chronological factor to consider when reconstructing the Judges and Monarchy Eras; a curse that was ordained in Israel's original covenant at Mt. Sinai (See Table 9.11).

VI. SEVEN TIMES

Sabbatical years aid in reconstructing Israel's chronology. These festival years, however, should *not* be over emphasized. No statute anywhere in the Law implies that the Jubilees had any chronological significance for Israel's history. Of course, national celebrations or state functions coincided with these naturally recurring events. *The same cannot be said for the Seven Times outlined in Leviticus that were based on the existence, location, and function of the Tabernacle or Temple.*

Although we will discuss the Testimonial Law in greater detail in part two of this book, the chronological implications of this system merit mentioning here. The Testimony was the part of the constitutional Law that contained Israel's actual covenant with YHWH.[128] Notably, (1) it comprised the 10 Commandments, (2) declared the required signs of compliance with the Sabbaths (Sinai Compact—Exod 31:12–18) in a formal treaty, (3) with consequences outlined for breaching the agreement. The consequence or penalty portions of both the Sinaitic Covenant in Leviticus 26 and the Moabic Covenant in Deuteronomy 27–30 set chronological limits or judgments on Israel's future apostasy (i.e., breach of covenant). Primarily, the consequence portion of the covenant is what is traditionally recognized as the formal division of the covenant's Testimony (Isa 8:20). In section two we will see how both systems (Leviticus and Deuteronomy) worked together. Important to our discussion on chronology is the cultic or religious demarcations that the Testimony of Leviticus 26 imposed on the nation's history. If Israel rebelled, YHWH would place adverse consequences (curses) on Israel in intervals of 7 Times (Lev 26:18, 21, 24, 28). This measuring line indicated 70 years of consequences (curses or penalties) associated with a particular 70-year epoch. Both Jeremiah's prophecy of Jerusalem's 70-year desolation (Jer 25:11; 29:10) and Isaiah's 65-year prophesy until "Ephraim would not be a people" (Isa 7:8) were based on the Testimonial Law's 7-Times judgment. Both of these prophecies and their relationship to Leviticus 26 will be discussed in greater detail in part 2 of this volume (see Table 9.12).

Table 9.12. Leviticus's 7 Times Cultic Judgment

Leviticus 16–17	1st	7 Times Judgment	years
18–20	2nd	7 Times Judgment	years
21–22	3rd	7 Times Judgment	years
23–26	4th	7 Times Judgment	years
27–33	5th	7 Times Judgment	years
		Total	350 years

A. The Tabernacle

The 7-Times judgments were in effect only when the nation's cultic shrines existed (Tabernacle or Temple). These curses or judgments were imposed when Israel had rebelled against the Law, and YHWH had formally acknowledged this breach of his covenant through the words of his prophets. The curse of the 7-Times judgment was applied to the nation for the first time at Bochim, where YHWH removed the protection his covenant afforded. Before the next Release Year, Israel fell into captivity to Mesopotamia. Lev 26:14–31 outlines five periods of 7 Times, equivalent to 350 years (5 x 70 = 350). Leviticus only allowed for five periods of 7 Times until the sanctuary (YHWH's dwelling place among the people) was destroyed.

At Bochim, the 70-year measuring line was stretched out over Israel in 1466 BCE. During the fifth and final 7th Time period for the Judges Era, the Ark of the Covenant was spoiled, and the Tabernacle at Shiloh was forsaken (1 Samuel 4, 4:15; Jer 7:12; Ps 78:60–64), perhaps destroyed in battle. In 1116, the final fifth 7 Times epoch ended. Since no tabernacle or temple existed at this time, the 7-Times judgment had already been fulfilled. The 7-Times judgment *would not be renewed until another national cultic shrine was constructed* under the Monarchy and the nation again rebelled against the covenant. Samuel's adept leadership returned Israel to a time of blessing under the covenant. What this demonstrates for a chronological perspective is that, from Bochim until the Monarchy, there had to have been *at least* 350 years. Since the Law had established provisions for a monarchy (Deut 17:14–20), there was no implication that the nation itself would end with the Judges Era, although her freedom would be severely curtailed by the bureaucratic functions that a formal government required (See Table 9.13).

Table 9.13. Tabernacle Era 7 Times

		The 7 Times Judgment Applied at Bochim
Date	*Text*	*Event*
1466	Judg 2:1–5	Sixth Release Year/YHWH removes protection of the covenant since Israel is not following the covenant
		1st 7 Times begins for Judges Era (Lev 26:14–17)
1393		1st 7 Times ends
1326		2nd 7 Times ends
1256		3rd 7 Times ends
1186		4th 7 Times ends
1116	Jer 7:12; Ps 78:60–64	5th 7 Times ends/YHWH has removed his name from Shiloh-Shechem/ No tabernacle/Covenant captured

B. *The First Temple*

David's and Solomon's reigns continued the righteous era initiated by Samuel. No national judgment or consequence was needed. Furthermore, no national shrine (temple or tabernacle) existed to validate the 7-Times curse if the nation again departed from the covenant until Solomon's 11th year on the throne. Although Solomon rebelled after the Temple was built, YHWH promised to withhold judgment for David's sake until Rehoboam's reign (1 Kgs 11:11–13). The fracturing of the kingdom into two nations marked the beginning of a new set of 7-Times that were applied to the nation because both kings (Rehoboam and Jeroboam I) revolted against YHWH's constitutional covenant (1 Kings 12). The fifth 7 Times ended with the destruction of the First Temple in Jerusalem in 587. This 70-year measuring line for both the Tabernacle and the First Temple (Judges and Monarchy) Era serves as the *ninth proof* for the synchronized chronology, demonstrating that Israel's chronology leaves very little room for being collapsed or shortened (see Table 9.14).

Table 9.14. First Temple Era 7 Times

		The 7 Times Judgment was applied when the tribes departed from Judah. Measuring line is first stretched over the Northern Kingdom, which never returns to the covenant
944	1 Kgs 11:29–40; 2 Chr 10:15	1st 7 Times begins
874		1st 7 Times ends
804		2nd 7 Times ends
734		3rd 7 Times ends
664	2 Chr 33:11	4th 7 Times ends/Samaria's sanctuary destroyed
657	(2 Chr 33:11)	(Omit 7 years for Manasseh in Assyria)
	2 Kgs 21:13	Samaria's measuring line stretched out over Judah
		5th 7 Time begins
587	Jer 52:12–27	5th 7 Time ends/Temple destroyed, people deported/
	2 Kgs 25:2	Land enjoys its Sabbaths

944–587–7 yrs. for Manasseh = 350 years for the 1st Temple Era

When the United Monarchy divided, YHWH initially placed the 70-year measuring line over Samaria (2 Kgs 21:13), since the Northern Kingdom never returned to YHWH's covenant. The prophet's writing, which had been inserted into *The Book of the Kings of Israel and Judah* during Manasseh's reign, explains that the Northern Kingdom's measuring line would be taken from Samaria and extended over Judah. At the end of this chronological measuring line, the Temple would be destroyed and Judah would cease to exist as a nation. The transfer of the measuring line from Samaria to Jerusalem occurred after Manasseh's exile when he reentered the city in 657 BCE.[129] This fifth and final 70-year epoch ended on a Release Year when the First Temple was destroyed, Zedekiah killed, and Judah deported to Babylon. Table 9.15 demonstrates how the 7 Times prophecy was applied first to Samaria and then transferred to Judah and its capital, Jerusalem.

Table 9.15. Samaria and Judah's 70-Year Chronicle

Date	Israel's Kings	Reign	Fulfills Levitical Law
1023	Samuel/David/Solomon		YHWH walks w/Israel—2 Chr 17:6
944	*The kingdom divides and epochs of 7 Times of consequences begin* *(Priestly/postdating method of calendric reckoning)*		
944	Jeroboam	21	Jeroboam's 18th yr. YHWH is not
	Nadab	0	with Israel, but he is with
	Baasha	23	Judah—2 Chr 13:12
	Elah	1	
	Omri	11	
	7 Times ends in Ahab's 14th regnal yr.	14	
874	1st 7 Times	70 yrs.	
	Ahab reigns 19 regnal yrs. (19–14 = 5)	5	
	Ahaziah	1	
	Joram	11	YHWH begins to cut
	Jehu	27	Israel—2 Kgs 10:32
	Jehoahaz	15	YHWH has not yet cast Israel
	7 Times ends Jehoash's 11th regnal yr.	11	off—2 Kgs 13:23
804	2nd 7 Times	70 yrs.	
	Jehoash reigned 15 yrs. (15–11 = 4)	4	YHWH not with Israel—2 Chr 25:7
	Jeroboam	41	
	Zechariah/Uzziah's 38th yr.	1	
	Menahem/Uzziah's 39th yr.	10	
	Pekahiah/Uzziah's 50th yr.	2	YHWH is angry with
	7 Times ends in Pekah's 12th yr.	12	Israel—Isa 9:11–12
734	3rd 7 Times	70 yrs.	

Table 9.15. Samaria and Judah's 70-Year Chronicle, *cont.*

Date	Israel's Kings	Reign	Fulfills Levitical Law
			Isaiah's 65-year prophecy (Isa 7:8)[a]
	Pekah reigns 20 yrs.	8	3
	Hoshea/Ahaz's 12th yr.	9	9
	Hezekiah reigns after Hoshea is taken[b]	23	23
	Manasseh captured/last	30	30	Ephraim deported by
664	4th 7 Times	70 yrs.		Ashurbanipal
	Isaiah's 65-yr. Prophecy of Ephraim fulfilled . . .		65 yrs.
	Samaria's (7 Times) measuring line stretched over Jerusalem when Manasseh returns from 7-yr. exile (2 Kgs 21:13)		
657	Manasseh returns 38th yr., reigns 55 yrs.	17	
	Amon	0	YHWH has cast Israel off
	Josiah	31	and will soon cast Judah off
	Jehoiakim	11	too—2 Kgs 23:27
	Zedekiah	11	
587	5th 7 Times	70 yrs.	
	Fulfills Lev 26:31's prophecy of the Temple's destruction		

[a]Pekah's 17th yr. is Ahaz's 1st official year after Jotham's death. Isaiah issued his prophecy for Ephraim's utter deportation at the end of Pekah's 16th year or at the beginning of his 17th year. Pekah reigned 20 years, so 4 years are subtracted to arrive at Pekah's 16th year, which is when Isaiah issued the Immanuel prophecy (Isa 7:8).

[b]Fulfills prophecy of Maher-shalal-hash-baz—Isa 8:1–8.

C. *The Second Temple*

After the First Temple had been reduced to ashes, *the land of Israel* enjoyed a 70-year Sabbath, during which no temple existed. The land rested (see Table 9.16). By implication, YHWH, who resided in the Temple (Num 14:10, 16:42; Ps 11:4; 18:6; 48:9) also rested. Exactly 70 years after the Temple had been destroyed, Zerubbabal and the high priest Jehoshua built the Second Temple in Darius's 6th year (Ezra 6:15). It was completed on Adar, the last month of the year. During this time the leadership of the nation reverted back to the priesthood, and David's descendants bore responsibility for the nation's policies (to be discussed in vol. 2).

Table 9.16. 70-Year Sabbath

587	Jer 52:12–27; 2 Kgs 25:2	5th 7th Time ends/Temple destroyed, people deported Land enjoys its Sabbaths
517	Jer 25:11; 29:10	Sabbath for land ends/Temple is being rebuilt
	587–517 = 70 years	

After Cyrus's emancipation decree and before the Second Temple was completed, the Second Temple Remnant had lived in the Promised Land for 25 years. Nehemiah's last memoir of the Remnant dates to 433 BCE. The Second Temple Remnant enjoyed well over 70 opportune years to confirm the covenant. Yet the Judeans during this era, like their forefathers, failed to establish YHWH's constitutional covenant. Therefore, the 7-Times judgment was stretched out over Judea with the completion of the Second Temple in Nisan 515 (see Table 9.17). We will return to this topic again when we discuss Israel's Testimonial or Prophetic Law in part 2.

Table 9.17. Second Temple Era 7 Times

520	Hag 2:10, 18	Temple begins to be rebuilt on Elul 24 in Darius's 2nd year.
516	Ezra 6:15	Temple is completed on Adar 3, in Darius's 6th year.
515		Since Adar 516 BCE was the last month of the year, the 7 Times Judgment begins again in Nisan the following year with dedication at Sukkot in 515 BCE (cf. Solomon's dedication).
445		1st 7 Times ends
375		2nd 7 Times ends
305		3rd 7 Times ends
235		4th 7 Times ends
165		5th 7 Times ends/Antichus Epiphanes has vandalized the Temple, rips the veil.
		Temple eventually falls into ruin and is forsaken.
		No legitimate Davidic or Aaronide heir refurbishes the Temple.

515 -165 = 350 years for the 2nd Temple Era

As our discussion continues, we will see how these 7 Times penalties affected Israel's history. Similar to the Jubilees, the 7 Times functions as another control in reconstructing a valid chronology during the Monarchic Era. With the date of the exodus established, we can now reconstruct the chronological history for the patriarchs before returning to the Monarchy Period.

VII. PATRIARCHAL NARRATIVES' LINEAR CHRONOLOGY

The Hebrew Scriptures do not provide a chronology for the patriarchs outside the number of years that they lived. Therefore, the best way to reconstruct a Scriptural chronology for this early period relies on genealogical accounts. The genealogies listed for the patriarchs are linear, which means they descend through only one child in successive progression.[130]

Since chronology issues are quite involved, I have placed the linear benchmarks in bold, with the more-detailed events following. To see an overview of the patriarchal era, you can just skim the bolded area.

A. Abraham

According to Scripture, Abraham (c. 2268 BCE) was 75 years old when he left Haran for the Promised Land (Gen 12:4). Twenty-five years later, Sarah bore Isaac when Abraham was 100 years of age (Gen 21:5).[131] During these 25 years several important events occurred. Ten years after entering Canaan, Abraham married Hagar (Gen 16:3), and Ishmael was born the following year when Abraham was 86 years old (Gen 16:16). Scripture's chronology is consistent, because Gen 17:1 states that Abraham was 99 years old in 2169 BCE when YHWH offered the Circumcision Covenant to Abraham, and Ishmael was 13 (Gen 17:25). At this time, Sarah was promised that she would have a son "next year" (Gen 17:16–17) as part of the Saraic Covenant. After YHWH offered the Circumcision Covenant, he sent messengers to Abraham stating that he was on his way to destroy Sodom and Gomorrah, thus placing the cities' demise in Abraham's 99th year (18:18–33). At this time the promise of a son "next year" was reiterated (Gen 18:10–14). Isaac was born when Abraham was 100 and Sarah 90 (Gen 17:1, 25), in 2168 BCE. This time frame is again confirmed by Abraham's assertion that he would be 100 and Sarah 90 at the time of Isaac's birth (Gen 17:17). Thus Scripture's internal chronology during Abraham's life is wholly consistent (see Table 9.18).

Table 9.18. Abraham-to-Isaac Chronology

Date	Text	Event	Years	Running Total
2268		Abraham is born		
2193	Gen 12:4	Abraham's age when departing Mesopotamia	75	
2183	Gen 16:3	Abraham marries Hagar 10 yrs. after entering Canaan	10	85
2182	Gen 16:16	Ishmael born following year	1	86
2169	Gen 17:24–25	Abraham 99 yrs. of age/Ishmael 13 yrs. of age	13	99
	Gen 17:1, 21	Sarah is 89, Abraham 99 when promise of son is given		
	Gen 18:16–19:29	Sodom and Gomorrah destroyed		
2168	Gen 17:1, 7, 21	Sarah is 90, Abraham 100 at Isaac's birth	1	100

B. Isaac

When Isaac was 60 years old, Rebekah gave birth to Jacob (Gen 25:26). This renders 160 years from Abram's birth until the birth of Jacob (100+60=160).[132] Several notable events are stabilized by the internal chronology and references that Scripture provides. The first event is Sarah's death, when the matriarch had lived to 127 (Gen 23:1). If Sarah bore Isaac at 90 years of age and died at 127, Isaac would have been 37 years old. Three years later, at age 40 (Gen 25:20), Isaac married Rebekah. The couple waited 20 years for the twins, Jacob and Esau to be born, when Isaac was 60 years old (Gen 25:26). Living be 175 (Gen 25:7), Abraham would have died when Jacob and Esau were 15 years old, in 2093 BCE (see Table 9.19).

Table 9.19. From Isaac to Ishmael's Death Chronology

2168	Gen 21:5	Isaac's birth when Abraham is 100 yrs. old		100
2131	Gen 23:1	Sarah dies at 127	37	137
2128	Gen 25:20	Isaac *m.* Rebekah at 40	3	140
2108	Gen 25:26	Jacob and Esau's birth	20	160
2093	Gen 25:7	Abraham dies at 175/Jacob and Esau are 15/Ishmael is 89	15	175
2045	Gen 25:17	Ishmael dies at 137	48	223

C. Jacob

At the age of 130, Jacob migrated to Egypt (Gen 47:9), where he lived for another 17 years (Gen 47:28). From Abraham's birth to the time when Jacob and his family migrated to Egypt was 290 years (160+130=290).[133] Scripture provides many dates for events that happened in Jacob's life. However, there is no point at which to anchor the date when Jacob left Canaan for Padan Aram, so the chronology must be worked backward from the point when Jacob and his family entered Egypt. From Gen 45:11 we know that Joseph revealed himself to his brothers when 5 years of famine remained. The original prophecy called for 7 years of plenty. This plenty was followed by 7 years of famine. Therefore, Joseph's brothers visited Egypt a second time during the second year of famine, implying that the first time his brothers had presented themselves to him occurred during the first year of famine, in 1979 BCE. Since Jacob was 130 years when he immigrated to Egypt, he would have emigrated the following year, in 1978.

If we add the 2 years of famine when Joseph revealed himself to his brothers to the previous 7 years of plenty, Joseph would have become vizier over Egypt 9 years before Jacob immigrated to Egypt. Scripture grants another tidbit. Joseph was 30 years old when he interpreted Pharaoh's dream (Gen 41:46) and became vizier in 1987. According to the way Egyptian chronology is currently understood, this would mean that either Amenemhat I or his son Senusret I, was the pharaoh under whom Joseph served. Joseph was appointed vizier when Jacob was 121 (130–9=121), placing Joseph at 39 years of age when his family immigrated to Egypt.

Considering that Joseph had been sold into slavery at the age of 17 (Gen 37:2), he would have spent 13 years as a slave in Egypt before Pharaoh elevated him to vizier. This makes Jacob 91 years old when Joseph was born and 108 years old when he believed Joseph to have been killed by a wild beast. Accordingly, Jacob spent 22 years believing Joseph to be dead.

Working backward still further, we discover that Joseph's life helps us connect Jacob's time in Haran (Gen 27:43). At the time of Joseph's birth, Jacob wanted to leave Haran (Gen 29:27; 30:25). Jacob had just completed his service to Laban (Gen 29:18, 27). However, Jacob stayed another 6 years near Haran working for wages and returned to Canaan after 20 years of service (Gen 31:38, 40). This means that Joseph lived the first six years of his life in Haran and eleven years in Canaan before being sold as a slave into Egypt at the age of 17.

If Jacob was 91 years of age at Joseph's birth (see above), he would have been 77 or 76 when he received Isaac's blessing and fled to Mesopotamia (91–14=77). This would place Isaac at 136 years of age when he passed on the patriarchal blessings to Jacob and 150 when

Joseph was born. Isaac died at 180 years of age (Gen 35:28), which would have been at least 44 years after blessing Jacob and 24 years after Jacob returned to Canaan (since Jacob had spent 20 years in Haran). Therefore, Isaac's death would have occurred during the year Joseph became vizier of Egypt, in 1987 (see Table 9.20).

Table 9.20. Joseph Chronology

2045	Gen 25:17	Ishmael dies at 137 yrs. of age		223
2031	Gen 28:2	Time that elapses between Ishmael's death and Jacob's receiving the patriarchal blessings/ Jacob is 76/77 when he leaves Canaan	14	237
2017	Gen 29:18, 27	Jacob serves Laban 14 yrs./Joseph is born at the end of the 14 yrs. of service when Jacob is 91 yrs. Old	14	251
	Gen 29:27; 30:25	Jacob wants to leave Laban soon after Joseph is born		
2011	Gen 31: 38, 40	Jacob serves Laban 20 yrs./Joseph 6 yrs. old/Returns to Canaan	6	257
2000	Gen 37:2	Joseph sold into slavery at age 17	11	268
1987	Gen 35:28	Isaac dies at 180	13	281
	Gen 41:53; 45:11; 41:46	Joseph becomes vizier in Egypt 9 yrs. before Jacob immigrates at age 30		
1980	Gen 41:29–30, 53–54	7 plentiful years end	7	288
1978	Gen 45:6, 11	In 2nd year of famine when Joseph's brothers come to Egypt 2nd time	2	290
	Gen 47:9; 41:1–36; 45:11	Jacob immigrates to Egypt in Nisan 1989 at age 130/5 yrs. of famine remain		
	Gen 15:13–16	Sojourn in Egypt begins for 430 years		
1973		Famine ends	5	295
1961	Gen 47:28	Jacob dies at 147 yrs. of age	12	307

D. 430 Years

Israel's 430-year (Exod 12:41)[134] period in Egypt began when Jacob was 130 years old (Gen 47:9). This renders 290 years between Abram's birth to Israel's residence in Egypt. Adding 290 years for the time that Abraham, Isaac, and Jacob lived to Israel's 430 years in Egypt, equals 720 years from Abraham's birth until Israel's exodus. Consequently, Abraham's life in terms of contemporary Egyptian chronology should be reckoned 720 years prior to Israel's exodus, roughly contemporary with Egypt's First Intermediate Period (c. 2180–2040).[135]

The patriarchal narrative ends with Jacob entering Egypt. The continuing chronology relies on the 430-year prophecy that YHWH had given to Abraham as part of the Promised-Land Covenant (Gen 15:13–16; see pp. 88–89). The Book of Exodus stresses the fact that Israel entered Egypt on the very same day that the people of Israel left Egypt: Nisan, 430 years later (Exod 12:17, 41, 51). This pragmatic association is quite realistic since Jacob and his family would have migrated to Egypt in the spring of what would normally (in non-drought years) be the beginning of Egypt's harvest season. What this means for our discussion is that Israel's patriarchal history, which began with the call of Abraham, began 720 years before the exodus. Thus the first era in Israel's history begins with Abraham leaving Mesopotamia in 2193 BCE and ends with the exodus in 1549/48 (see Table 9.21).

Table 9.21. Abraham to Exodus (Abridged)

Date	Scripture	Event	Years	Running Total
2268		Abraham is born		
2193	Gen 12:4	Abraham's age when departing Mesopotamia	75	
2168	Gen 21:5	Isaac's birth	25	100
2108	Gen 25:26	Jacob and Esau's birth	60	160
1987	Gen 41:53; 45:11	(Joseph becomes vizier in Egypt)		
1978	Gen 47:9	Jacob immigrates to Egypt	130	290
	Gen 15:13, 16	Sojourn in Egypt begins		
1628	Exod 7:7	(Moses is born/Pharaoh kills Hebrew boys)		
1548	Exod 12:41	Exodus	430	720
1508	Num 14:33	Desert exile ends/Enter Promised Land	40	760

As we have seen, 568 years passed during the pre-Solomon Monarchy and the Judges' Era. If we add this to Israel's 430 years in Egypt and the patriarchal era, the total time elapsed from Abraham's birth to Solomon's 4th regnal year was 1,288 years.[136] It is astounding that this information has been preserved over such a long period of time (see Table 9.22)

Table 9.22. Abraham to Exodus Unabridged Chronology

Date	Scripture	Event	Years	Running Total
2268		Abraham is born		0
2193	Gen 12:4	Abraham is 75 when he departed Mesopotamia	75	75
2183	Gen 16:3	Abraham marries Hagar 10 yrs. after entering Canaan	10	85
2182	Gen 16:16	Ishmael born following year	1	86
2169	Gen 17:24–25	Abraham is 99 yrs. of age/Ishmael 13 yrs. of age when Cir. Covenant is given	13	99
	Gen 17:1, 21	Sarah is 89, Abraham 99 when the promise of a son is given		
	Gen 18:16–19:29	Sodom and Gomorrah are destroyed		
2168	Gen 17:1, 7, 21; 21:5	Sarah is 90, Abraham 100 at Isaac's birth	1	100
2131	Gen 23:1	Sarah dies at the age of 127	37	137
2128	Gen 25:20	Isaac m. Rebekah at 40 yrs. of age	3	140
2108	Gen 25:26	Jacob and Esau's birth	20	160
2093	Gen 25:7	Abraham dies at 175/Jacob and Esau are 15 yrs. of age/Ishmael is 89	15	175

Table 9.22. Abraham to Exodus Unabridged Chronology, *cont.*

Date	Scripture	Event	Years	Running Total
2045	Gen 25:17	Ishmael dies at 137	48	223
2031		Time that lapses between Ishmael's death and Jacob receiving the patriarchal blessings/ Jacob is 76/77 when he leaves Canaan	14	237
2017	Gen 29:18, 27	Jacob serves Laban 14 yrs. /Joseph is born at the end of the 14 yrs. of service when Jacob was 91 yrs. Old	14	251
	Gen 29:27; 30:25	Jacob wants to leave Laban soon after Joseph is born		
2011	Gen 31:38, 40	Jacob serves Laban for 20 yrs. /Joseph was 6 yrs. old when they return to Canaan	6	257
2000	Gen 37:2	Joseph sold into slavery at 17 yrs. of age	11	268
1987	Gen 35:28	Isaac dies at 180	13	281
	Gen 41:53; 45:11; 41:46	Joseph becomes vizier in Egypt at age 30, 9 yrs. before Jacob migrates		
1980	Gen 21:49	7 plentiful years end	7	288
1978		2 yrs. of famine expired when Joseph's brother's come to Egypt	2	290
	Gen 47:9; 41:1–36; 45:11	Jacob immigrates to Egypt in Nisan 1978 at 130/5 yrs. of famine remain		
	Gen 15:13–16	Sojourn in Egypt begins and lasts for 430 yrs.		
1973		Famine ends	5	295
1961	Gen 47:28	Jacob dies at age of 147	12	307
c.1880		? Joseph dies		
c.1820		? Manasseh/Ephraim die		
1631		Aaron is born	(83 yrs. before exodus)	
1628	Exod 7:7	(Moses is born/Pharaoh kills Hebrew boys)	(80 yrs. before exodus)	
1548	Exod 12:41	Exodus (From Abraham to exodus)	413	720

(A brace spans from 1978 to c.1820 labeled "430 yrs.")

VIII. UNDER THE MONARCHY

A. Synchronism: Kings and Chronicles

Many formulas have been proposed for accurately interpreting ancient Israel's chronology.[137] The traditional approach to chronologies in the books of Kings and Chronicles is to add the number of years that a particular monarch reigned to the number of years of his predecessor in the same way that chronology was figured during the priestly account of the Judges' Era. Thus, for example, the eight years that Jehoram reigned (1 Kgs 22:50; 2 Chr 21:1–5; 2 Kgs

8:16, 17) are traditionally added to the 25 years that his father, Jehoshaphat, reigned, totaling 33 years from the beginning of Jehoshaphat's reign to the death of his son Jehoram. This method is quite hasty and fails to account for the overlapping year(s) when a father and son shared a co-regency.

Thiele's *magnum opus* has greatly contributed to chronology studies.[138] His methods, however, did not consistently recognize dual calendric systems or co-regencies, which smooth out many objections to the pattern of internal synchronization on which Scripture relied. Rodger Young sums up the situation nicely.

> Thiele realized that the data must be allowed to tell us if a co-regency was involved, and, if so, whether a given synchronism or length of reign was measured from the start of co-regency or from the start of the sole reign. It is of some interest that if this procedure is followed, there is enough information in the biblical texts to allow the construction of a coherent chronology for the kingdom period.[139]

Thiele was a pioneer from whom many scholars have benefited, and his acute observation of both the Scriptural data and contemporary practices allow this discussion today. He became disillusioned by what he considered conflicting internal synchronisms in the Book of Kings. This usually led him to opt for a successive, linear-type chronology.[140] This shift in his approach was unfortunate because the internal synchronisms are much more stable and reliable than normally realized. In fact, Scripture's internal synchronisms between Judahite and Israelite kings are what allow an accurate reconstruction of the Monarchic Era today.

B. *The Priestly and Civil Calendars*

1. Cultic Calendar

Throughout the ancient world, civilizations used two different calendar systems: a cultic calendar for religious festivities and a civil calendar for both the Crown's administration and the agricultural year. Both systems were luni-solar, which means they were based on calculable events common between both the moon and the sun.

At creation, YHWH had ordained the entire solar system to serve as humanity's time clock.

> And God said, Let there be lights in the firmament of the heaven to divide the day from the night; and let them be for *signs, and for seasons, and for days, and years.* (Gen 1:14)

Moed is the word the King James Version translates "seasons."[141] This word is used again in Leviticus 23 (Lev 23:2–4, 37, 44), only the translators rendered it "feasts and seasons." As we saw in chap. 5 (5.V.A), astronomy comprised one of the priestly functions. Israel, like other ancient nations, used the solar system to begin the year and to reckon time. Israel's *cultic or priestly* calendar closely mirrors the calendar in Mesopotamia but is less similar to the civil calendar in Egypt (as we will see in chap. 10). The year began with the spring equinox.[142]

The first day of the new year began on the first day of the first full month (or new moon) after the equinox, placing the new year between the end of March and the first part of May.[143] (We will look at this in greater detail in the next chapter.)

The Hebrew Scriptures only mention four of the months in Israel's original cultic calendar: Aviv, Ziv, Ethanim, and Bul.[144] Aviv was the first month of the year, Ziv the second, Ethanim the seventh, and Bul the eighth.[145] These names are quite similar to Canaanite names, from which we infer that Israel and Canaan may have shared the same yearly calendrical system since the seasons were the same for Canaanite territory.[146] By the time Ezra worked to update and codify Israel's various manuscripts, the names of Canaan's months had virtually been replaced by Babylonian names. As Andrew Steinmann observes, "During the Babylonian exile the Judeans apparently substituted the Babylonian names for the months into Hebrew. These names are occasionally used in the postexilic books of the Tanakh and are common in later Hebrew" (see Table 9.23).[147]

Table 9.23. Hebrew Calendar Months

	Monarchic	Postexilic	Modern Equivalent
1	Aviv	Nisan	March/April
2	Ziv	Iyyar	April/May
3		Sivan	May/June
4		Tammuz	June/July
5		Ab	July/August
6		Elul	August/September
7	Ethanim	Tishri	September/October
8	Bul	Marcheshvan	October/November
9		Kislev	November/December
10		Tebeth	December/January
11		Shebat	January/February
12		Adar	February/March

From Abraham to Paul: A Biblical Chronology © 2011 Andrew E. Steinmann. Used with permission of ConCordia Publishing House,. www.cph.org.

2. Civil Calendar

Before the Monarchy, Israel had relied solely on the cultic or priestly calendar established in the Torah. Since only one calendar was in play, it produced the straightforward linear chronology used during the Judges' Era. All this changed under the Monarchy, when Israel asked for a king, the people wanted a government similar to other nations (Deut 7:14; 1 Sam 8:20). One practice of ancient monarchies was to employ a second, "fiscal" or civil year.[148] Many synchronisms in Scripture indicate that after Samuel instituted the Monarchy, the nation transitioned to a civil calendar, similar to the civil calendars prevalent in Egypt and Mesopotamia.[149] While the priestly-cultic calendar began the new year in the spring with the vernal equinox,[150] the Monarchy's civil-agricultural calendar began with the autumnal equinox in the fall in the 7th month of Ethanim (1 Kgs 8:2), better known as Tishri.[151] The famed 10th century calendar excavated at Gezer is an example of the Tishri-based agricultural/civil calendar.[152] *This does not mean that the priestly calendar was abandoned but that a second, administrative system was in use by the end of King Solomon's reign.*

There were many reasons for a second calendar. The first had to do with administrative systems. Israel's priests served in many governmental capacities and were supported by part of the nation's 10% flat tax system. Using the same system may have confused the accounting of various government offices, especially since 1 Chr 9:22 indicates that the Levites also served administrative functions under the Monarchy (see chap. 8.V). A separate calendar clarified accounting for the king's administration and provided a second system for assessing taxes, similar to the way that corporations today use a "fiscal year."[153] Crops were also planted in the fall/winter and harvested in the spring between May and June.[154] The Gezer Calendar, perhaps coinciding with the latter end of Solomon's reign or the early part of Jehoshaphat's reign, demonstrates that the civil calendar began with two months of ingathering between September and November with the fall harvest and concluded at the beginning of the harvest in the following year.[155] While we do not know when tithes were assessed by the priests during the Judges Era, the Gezer Calendar demonstrates that taxes for the Monarchy were assessed during or shortly after the yearly spring harvest.

a. Civil Calendar: Solomon's Building of the Temple

Several Scripture passages demonstrate that the Monarchy followed a second, civil calendar-year. Israel's sabbatical years demonstrate that both Saul and David were installed during Release Years, implying that their "official" accession took place during the pilgrimage celebrations at Sukkot.[156] Since Sukkot falls in the 7th month, it would coincide with Ethanim or Tishri. Thus the Monarchic or civil calendar began with Saul and, later, David's accession over Israel in Tishri. This implies that chronological reckoning for the United Monarchy was counted from Tishri to Tishri, not Nisan to Nisan.

Several texts demonstrate this point. The most popular case used to demonstrate a two-calendar system is King Solomon's work on the Temple.[157] Solomon began construction on the second month of his 4th year (1 Kgs 6:1, 37). During his 11th year, Solomon completed the Temple (1 Kgs 6:38), with work having lasted almost 7 years (1 Kgs 6:38). Israel reckoned her chronology inclusively, which means that partial years were rounded up to the next whole year.[158] If the reckoning begins in the second month of the cultic calendar (Nisan) Solomon's 4th year, then 8 years are counted instead of seven (7 yrs. 6 months, which is rounded up to 8 yrs.) . If, the reckoning is according to Tishri years, there are closer to 7 years (6 yrs. 6 months, which is rounded up to 7 years).[159] Table 9.24 demonstrates that the Book of Kings reckons the building of the Temple and Solomon's reign according to a civil–Tishri New Year.

What this evidence demonstrates is that the scribes (perhaps Elihoreph and Ahiah, or Jehoshaphat—1 Kgs 4:3) used Tishri years to reckon 7 years from Solomon's 4th year to his 11th year. Understanding that the Monarchy used a civil calendar clarifies several chronological enigmas regarding Scripture's internal synchronizations.

Table 9.24. Solomon's 4th to 7th Years

		(Nisan counting is grey-shaded)					Temple Completed
	4th yr. 2nd mo.					11th yr. 2nd mo.	8th mo. Temple Dedicated
Nisan (spring)	4	5	6	7	8	9	10	11	12
Tishri (fall)	4	5	6	7	8	9	10	1 1	1 2
Tishri/ actual counting	Release Year 0	1	2	3	4	5	6	Release Year 7	
Nisan Couting	0	1	2	3	4	5	6	7	
BCE Dates	980	979	978	977	976	975	974	973	972

b. Dual Calendars: Asa and Ahab

After the Northern Kingdom split from Rehoboam, Jeroboam changed numerous policies in order to sever Samaria's confederacy with Judah. Well known is the fact that Jeroboam expelled the Levites, installing his own deities, priesthood, and cultic calendar (2 Chr 11:14); what is apparently less known is that he also changed the regnal (civil) reckoning to begin with Nisan. Numerous synchronisms reveal this fact and perhaps signal Jeroboam's revolt against Rehoboam and subsequent installment as king over Israel, which occurred the following Nisan (Passover) after Rehoboam's accession (the previous Tishri).

The first time that a two-calendar system appears is in the synchronization of Asa's and Ahab's reigns. According to 1 Kgs 16:29, Ahab began to reign over Israel (Northern Kingdom) the 38th year of Asa (1 Kgs 16:29, Southern Kingdom). Since Asa died in the 41st year of his reign, his son Jehoshaphat began to rule over Judah during the same year. From Asa's 38th year to his 41st year is only 3 years (41–38=3). Understanding that the Southern Kingdom of Judah used a different civil calendar from the calendar of the Northern Kingdom of Israel helps clarify this apparent discrepancy, manifesting that Asa's 41st year was certainly Ahab's 4th regnal year (see Table 9.25).

Table 9.25 Micro Judah-Israel Calendars for Asa-Ahab

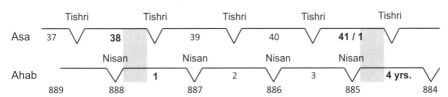

Scripture's internal synchronization implies that the two sister-nations used civil calendars, the accession-years of which began six months apart. Although our reconstruction in this case cannot tell us if the civil calendar that Judah used was a Tishri- or Nisan-based calendar, it can demonstrate the use of two different calendric systems. If Judah used a civil calendar that began in Tishri, then Ahab would have begun to rule over Israel somewhere between Nisan and Tishri (1st to 7th months) in 888 BCE. This would have been the beginning of Ahab's first official year, since the Northern Kingdom also used the Egyptian antedating/nonaccession-year-based system, in which the king's first year of rule was counted twice, first as the last year of his predecessor and second as the first year of his own reign (see VIII.C., "Accession," below). Therefore, the time period between Asa's 38th year and 41st year would be considered 4 regnal years of Ahab's reign. This places Asa's death after Nisan but before Tishri, since Ahab's 4th year began in Nisan (see Table 9.26).[160]

Table 9.26. Macro Asa-Ahab Synchronization w/Civil Calendar

Date	Judah		Israel		
		Asa	Omri		
892		34	8		
891		35	9	Ahab	
890		36	10	1	Co-regency
889		37	11	2	
888	1 Kgs 16:29	38	12	3	(1)
887		39	Jehoshaphat	4	(2)
886		40		5	(3)
885	1 Kgs 22:41	41	1	6	(4)
884			2	7	

There is one implication of this system that bears mentioning. The scribe who reckoned this synchronism omitted the 1 1/2–2 years that Ahab served as co-regent with his father. Although Jehoshaphat's 1st year over Judah was Ahab's 4th year as sole regent, the scribe intentionally omits the years when Ahab served as co-regent when it came to internal synchronisms, even though the entire reign length is included in the combined totals that formally register his reign (1 Kgs 16:29). As we will see, the Assyrian annals demonstrate incredible reliability with synchronizations in the Book of Kings, especially in the cases of Ahab and Jehu. We will come back to the implications of co-regencies below.

c. Dual Calendars: Amaziah and Jeroboam

Another synchronism demonstrates the same dual Judah-Israel calendric system. The beginning of Jeroboam's reign is tied to Amaziah's 15th year (2 Kgs 14:23). This would have been the year when Jehoash, Jeroboam's father, died, in 799 BCE. This annal places Jeroboam's

Table 9.27. Jeroboam II's Accession Synchronized with Amaziah's Reign

Amaziah 1 Kings 14:23

	Tishri 1	Tishri 2	Tishri 3	Tishri 4	Tishri 5	Tishri 6	Tishri 7	Tishri 8	Tishri 9	Tishri 10	Tishri 11	Tishri 12	Tishri 13	Tishri 14	Tishri 15[161]
	15	16	17	18	19	20	21	22	23	24	25	26	27	28	29[162]

Jeroboam II

	Nisan	Nisan	Nisan	Nisan	Nisan	Nisan	Nisan	Nisan	Nisan	Nisan	Nisan	Nisan	Nisan	Nisan	Nisan
	16 1	2	3	4	5	6	7	8	9	10	11	12	13	14	15

Jehoash[163]

BCE Dates 799 798 797 796 795 794 793 792 791 790 789 788 787 786 785 official accession after Nisan during Amaziah's 15th year. Scripture validates this synchronization with a continuing chronology. We are also told that Amaziah reigned for a total of 29 years and lived 15 years after Jehoash's death. As Table 9.27 demonstrates, the dual calendric system indeed accounts for all synchronisms.

The implication that a civil calendar has for our discussion on chronology is that the methods of reconstructing Scripture's chronology could deviate by only 6 months but appear as a one-year discrepancy. This is solid evidence that demonstrates two separate calendars were in play.

C. *Accession*

Another factor affecting ancient chronologies is the accession year. When a king died in the middle of a year, the problem was how to reckon the year: should the entire year be credited to his predecessor, or to the newly crowned monarch?[164] We know of two different systems of accounting. The first, called the **antedating system**, was popular in Egypt, where the "accession year was reckoned twice, as the last year of the deceased king and as the first year of the new king."[165] In Mesopotamian studies, this system is known as the **non-accession year**.[166]

The second system, in vogue with the Assyrians and Babylonians, the **postdating system**, worked just the opposite: "The accession year was reckoned only as the final year of the deceased king, and the new king's reign was regarded as formally beginning the following new year."[167] This system is also known as the **accession- year system** with the first partial year of the new monarch's reign being counted as 0 and credit for a full year given to the deceased predecessor.[168] It is this system, which produces a linear-type chronology in which the lengths of a king's reign can simply be added together, that appears to have been used by Levitical scribes during the Judges Era and the early Monarchy through King David's reign.

Regarding the effects that these systems had on Israel's chronology during the Monarchy, noted scholar David N. Freedman observes that Israel's early Monarchy may have followed the Egyptian-styled antedating system, while later chronologies, influenced by Assyrian practices, followed the postdating system. Thus, a shift may be discernible at some point in Israel's archives.

> The possible shift to a postdating pattern (under the influence of Assyrian domination and conquest) indicates that some of the figures may belong to a different pattern. We do not know whether the Deuteronomist compiled his own figures on the basis of a single scheme from the various sources or whether he simply incorporated the information from tables already prepared. *The net effect in any reconstruction is to leave a margin of adjustment of a least a year or two in reconciling the figures in the Israel-Judah dynastic chronology.*[169]

The importance of this information to our study is that the reign of one king may overlap with that of his son or successor. Andrew Steinmann observes that the net effect of this system is usually the overlap of the last year of one king's reign with the first year of his successor.[170] Indeed, this is the case. Many a king's reign was totally or partially eclipsed by this system of reckoning, as the synchronisms of Judah's and Israel's kings indicate.

D. Macro vs. Micro Chronology

One good example of the chronological eclipsing that occurred during the Monarchy is the synchronization provided in the Book of Kings for Nadab's and Baasha's reigns. Dual calendars and accession- year reckoning produce both micro and macro points of view. In the following example, the accession date for the heir or successor is tied directly to the years of Asa's regency, beginning with the year when he ascended the throne. What these synchronisms demonstrate when we look at the overall, continuing, macro view is that Nadab's reign was eclipsed by both his predecessor and his successor. Table 9.28 reconstructs these periods, when one monarch's death overlapped with the accession of the next. The *a* in the table demonstrates a monarch's accession year but does not represent a full year as it overlaps his predecessor's last year. The *n* or *t* on all chronology tables will indicate the calendar system used (Nisan or Tishri). Underlining is also used to demonstrate that the regnal year is specifically mentioned in Scripture and that it serves as an "anchor" for synchronization.

Table 9.28. Macro Chronology of Nadab's Regency

Date	Text	Judah			Israel		
		Rehoboam			Jeroboam I		
928			17	Abijam	17		
927	1 Kgs 15:1–2			<u>1</u>	<u>18</u>		
926		Asa	2		19		
925	1 Kgs 15:9–10	1a	3		<u>20</u>	Nadab	
924	1 Kgs 15:25	<u>2</u>			21	<u>1a,n</u>	Baasha
923	1 Kgs 15:28, 33	<u>3</u>			22n	2	<u>1a,n</u>
922		4					2

When a macro chronology is reconstructed, Nadab's reign is totally eclipsed. At first it appears that these synchronisms conflict with the actual number of years that the monarch is said to have reigned. However, when we look at the calendar at the micro level, taking the civil calendar into account in the succession list, we see that Nadab actually reigned for 1 year. Since Israel reckoned time inclusively (meaning all or part of a year was counted as a full year), Nadab's reign would then be registered as 2 years (see Table 9.29).

In this synchronization, Nadab succeeded Jeroboam after Nisan in Asa's 2nd year. He reigned for a full year and was killed after Nisan, one year later, during Asa's 3rd year. Because the Northern Kingdom used the antedating method, Nadab's first year correlates with Jeroboam's last (22nd) year. Nadab's succeeding year also corresponds with Baasha's accession year. So when we look at this chronology on the micro level, Nadab reigned for 2 years. When we "zoom out" to the macro chronology level, however, Nadab's entire reign is eclipsed by his predecessor and his successor, reducing the macro chronological effect to 0 (see Table 9.28, above).

Table 9.29. Micro Chronology of Nadab's Year

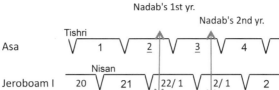

Nadab was not the only monarch to have his reign obscured on the macro chronology level. The regency of Judah's King Amon, Manasseh's heir, is reckoned the same way. Amon reigned for only 2 years. His first year is counted twice: first, as the last year of his father's reign as well as the 1st year of his own reign. Amon's 2nd and final year is eclipsed by his son Josiah because it is counted both as Amon's 2nd year and as Josiah's 1st year. Thus Amon's reign is eclipsed by both his father and his son, reducing the net chronological effect to 0. The macro view of Judah's chronology demonstrates that the reigns of Ahaziah and Amon are eclipsed. For Israel (Northern Kingdom), Nadab, Elah, and Ahaziah's reigns were

Table 9.30. Macro Chronology: Eclipsing Amon's Reign

Date	Text	King's Regnal Years		
		Manasseh		
641	2 Kgs 21:1		54	Amon
640	2 Kgs 21:19; 2 Chr 33:21	Josiah	55	*1*
639	2 Kgs 21:19	*1*	2	
638	2 Kgs 22:1	2		
637		3		

eclipsed before the nation shifted methods of regnal reckoning (see Table 9.30).

What the data imply is that, with one exception, the Southern Kingdom followed the antedating system through Josiah's reign.[171] Judah did not make the shift to the Babylonian or priestly postdating system until the end of Josiah's reign. Jehoiakim and Zedekiah are the only two monarchs whose reigns demonstrate the more eastern postdating tradition for the Southern Kingdom, although there was an exception, which we will discuss below.

The conclusion of regnal reckoning is as follows: the chronology of the Judges Era through the end of David's reign followed the linear, postdating system in which reign lengths were simply added together (a method currently popular in biblical scholarship). During this time, Israel's records and archives were handled by the priesthood (1 Chr 9:22; 18:16; 2 Sam 20:25). Under Solomon's administration, the linear-priestly system of reckoning chronology was abandoned in favor of the more sophisticated Egyptian antedating system, which depicted reigns more accurately. Solomon's strong ties with Egypt probably influenced this shift (1 Kings 9; see Table 9.31). This transfer probably occurred with the origin

Table 9.31. Shift from Priestly-Judges Era to Monarchy

Priestly Reckoning	Samuel	7
	Saul	19
	David	40
Monarchy Reckoning	Solomon/Rehoboam	40/1
	Rehoboam	17
	Abijam/Asa	3/1
	Asa/Jehoshaphat	41/1

of the new document called "The Acts of Solomon" (1 Kgs 11:41), which was later inserted into the *The Book of the Kings of Israel and Judah* (2 Chr 16:11; see chap. 8.V.).

This conclusion is supported by another fact. During David's reign, Jehoshaphat (ben Ahilud) and Seraiah were Levitical scribes who maintained Israel's historical annals (2 Sam 8:16–17). Although Jehoshaphat continued to be employed in the recorder's office during Solomon's reign, the scribe's responsibilities were transferred to two people, Elihoreph and Ahiah (1 Kgs 4:3), indicative perhaps of the increased bureaucratic stress that resulted from the institution of the Monarchy. The employment of new scribes in this official capacity would have provided the perfect opportunity for the change in regnal reckoning to occur, especially if the scribes were trained in an Egyptian school during Solomon's reign.

There is one shift during this era that "impersonates" a transition from the postdating to the antedating system during Jotham's and Ahab's reigns. What the text indicates is that both Jotham's and Ahaz's reigns (Judah) were reckoned by the linear-priestly postdating (or accession-year) system during the same period that the Northern Kingdom transitioned to the same postdating system. *Because Jeroboam had expelled the Levites, all synchronization is recorded from Judah's perspective.* That the regnal reckoning of both kingdoms reverted back to the priestly method at the same time strongly suggests that the Levitical scribe who recorded the Northern Kingdom's history at this time and provided the synchronization was the same scribe that recorded Judah's history.

The most likely candidate for this shift is Isaiah, who is known to have had contact with Jotham, Ahaz, and Hezekiah (Isa 1:1). As a Levite (see pp. 726–29), Isaiah naturally would have used the priestly-linear system of reckoning, which was equivalent to the postdating (accession-year) system. As we will see, the Jotham-Ahaz-Hezekiah era is obscured by overlapping co-regencies, which later scribes probably found confusing. After Hezekiah's reign, however, Judah had returned to Egypt's antedating (non-accession year) system. This shift was quite short-lived; the record reverts back to the Monarchy system of reckoning in the same generation, probably as soon as Isaiah or the scribes Uriah or Zechariah (Isa 8:2) transferred responsibility for the annals back to royal scribes.

The antedating system remained intact throughout Judah's Monarchy until the government came under direct Babylonian influence at Josiah's death. The reigns of Jehoiakim and Zedekiah, perhaps under the direction of Elishama, Elnathan, or Gemariah (Jer 36:12) or even Jeremiah shifted to the Levitical (Babylonian) method of regnal reckoning. This shift could indicate an administrative shift to reflect a more modern standard, or a political shift from the king's scribes back to the priesthood. The evidence demonstrates the continuity and consistency of the Southern Kingdom's regnal reckoning systems: changes were rare and deliberate. Thus we see the stability enjoyed by the Davidic Monarchy is reflected in the consistency of its chronicle systems (see Table 9.32).

Table 9.32. Judah's Shifts in Regnal Reckoning

1460–984	Priestly/postdating	Judges Era thru King David
983–745	Monarchy/antedating	Solomon thru Uzziah
744–722	(Priestly)	(Jotham thru Hezekiah's accession)
694–609	Monarchy/antedating	Manasseh thru Josiah
608–597	Priestly/postdating	Jehoiakim and Zedekiah

The Northern Kingdom (Samaria) made the switch from Egypt's antedating (*non-accession-year*) system to the priestly (postdating/*accession-year*) system late in its history. Jeroboam I, like Solomon, had strong ties with Egypt (1 Kgs 11:40). His administration followed Egypt's antedating system as demonstrated in Table 9.33. This system remained intact until Jeroboam II. Scripture indicates that Jeroboam II became highly involved in restoring the Northern Kingdom's grandeur (2 Kgs 14:23–29; 13:13–19), assuming personal responsibility for administrative systems (similar to the way that Thutmoses had revamped Canaan's administrative systems centuries prior). After Jeroboam II's coronation, the Northern Kingdom shifted to the postdating system. This remained the standard until the demise of the Northern Kingdom's Monarchy.

Table 9.33. Israel's Shifts in Regnal Reckoning

944–800	Monarchy/antedating	Jeroboam I thru Jehoash
799–725	Priestly/postdating	Jeroboam II thru Hoshea

These conclusions are supported by another fact. Uzziah (Azariah), king of Judah, enjoyed one of the longest and most stable reigns in the Southern Kingdom's history. The date that Scripture provides for Uzziah allows no other conclusion for Jeroboam II's reign but the use of the linear-priestly postdating (accession-year) method. From all indications, this method continued to be employed in the Northern Kingdom until the kingdom's annihilation under Sargon and Shalmaneser V.[172] Both of these systems are clarified by the scribe's synchronization of the regnal years of Judah's kings with the regnal dates of the kings of Israel (see Table 9.34).

Table 9.34. Azariah's Reign Synchronized with Jeroboam to Pekahiah

Azariah 2 Kgs 15:8   2 Kgs 15:13, 17

Winter Tishri Tishri Tishri Tishri Tishri Tishri Tishri Tishri Tishri Tishri Tishri Tishri Tishri Tishri Tishri Tishri Tishri

37 ∨ 38 ∨ 39 ∨ 40 ∨ 41 ∨ 42 ∨ 43 ∨ 44 ∨ 45 ∨ 46 ∨ 47 ∨ 48 ∨ 49 ∨ 50 ∨ 51 ∨ 52 ∨ 1 ∨

Jeroboam II

Spring Nisan Nisan Nisan Nisan Nisan Nisan Nisan Nisan Nisan Nisan Nisan Nisan Nisan Nisan Nisan

40 ∨ 41/6m ∨ 1 ∨ 2 ∨ 3 ∨ 4 ∨ 5 ∨ 6 ∨ 7 ∨ 8 ∨ 9 ∨ 10 ∨ 1 ∨ 2 ∨ 1 ∨ 2 ∨ 3

Jeroboam/Zechariah Shallum   Pekah   Pekahiah 2 Kgs 15:32
760 759 758 757 756 755 754 753 752 751 750 749 748 747 746 745 744

Notice that Jeroboam II's reign through Hezekiah's accession spanned the same years as Judah's only shift to the priestly postdating (accession-year) system. This means that both nations shifted to the linear-priestly method for regnal reckoning at the exact same time. Since this is not a very likely historical scenario and given the hostility between the two nations at this time, history-writing for this period of both nations must have reverted back to the priesthood, probably under Isaiah or a scribe who was working with the prophet. We have seen how both the accession year and the dual calendrical systems affect our understanding of chronology issues. The last three issues regarding chronology that we need to understand are (1) reckoned and (2) unreckoned co-regencies and (3) times of civil turmoil in which two monarchs (usually father and son) reigned from different cities in Judah.

E. *The Heir Apparent*

1. Sargon and Sennacherib

During the 12th Egyptian Dynasty, Pharaoh Amenemhet I instituted the first known practice of a father-son co-regency.[173] The son, a junior king or heir apparent, handled military matters, while the father ran the state. The son was a "king in training," a custom that became common throughout the Near East and was not exclusive to the 12th Dynasty.[174] As late as 700 BCE, this training was still practiced by many of Egypt's kings, and new evidence from the fairly recent translation of the Tang-i Var inscription indicates that the reign of Assyria's King Sennacherib converged with his father, Sargon's reign, with Sennacherib training in the role of heir apparent.[175]

Throughout the Near East, heirs apparent are attested as campaigning in foreign lands. As far south as the Kingdom of Kush, monarchies upheld the "Egyptian tradition of the appointment of the crown prince as commander-in-chief of an expeditionary force."[176] László Török notes that Kushite King Shebitqo, awaiting Assyrian attack, needed "an heir apparent to command his army, including the troops."[177] Sennacherib's third campaign occurred Hezekiah's 14th year (2 Kgs 18:13). Numerous kingdoms throughout the Levant had sought alliances with Egypt. Samaria's King Hoshea had participated in a similar alliance (2 Kgs 17:4; Isa 30:1–4). Sennacherib's general accused Hezekiah of collaborating in this defensive confederacy (2 Kgs 18:19–21).

Both Israel's and Assyria's records make it appear that Sennacherib's third campaign occurred well before his father's death, possibly placing Sennacherib as heir apparent with his "formal" accession occurring some five to seven years later. This theory is supported by at least three epigraphs.

The first, from one of *Sargon's* annals, asserts that Judah had allied with Egypt.

> The [kings] of Philistia, Judah, E[dom], Moab, who live by the sea, bearers of tri[bute and] gifts . . . sent words of falsehood (and) treacherous speech to incite enmity with me. To Pharaoh, king of Egypt, a prince who could not save them, they brought their good-will gifts and implored his alliance.[178]

It may very well be that Sargon sent his son against Jerusalem after he assumed that Judah had joined the Egyptian confederacy. Secondary evidence of a Sargon-Sennacherib co-regency comes from Sennacherib's many annals, which allege:

> Hezekiah had called upon the kings of Egypt (Mus(u)ri) (and) the bowmen, the
> chariot(-corps) and the cavalry of the king of Ethiopia (Meluhha). [179]

Sennacherib accuses Hezekiah of allying with Egypt. Israel's Scriptures record a parallel
version of Sennacherib's charges in the Book of Isaiah.[180] According to the Hebrew account,
Hezekiah had not conspired with Egypt (Isaiah 30, 31). What both of these Assyrian inscriptions
attest is that Sargon and Sennacherib carried out campaigns when Assyria believed
that Judah had sought alliance with Egypt.

One particular epigraph that bears directly on a Judahite-Assyrian synchronism is one
of Sargon's Nimrud inscriptions, which states:

> (*Property of Sargon,* etc.) the subduer of the country of Judah which is far away,
> the uprooter of Hamath, the ruler of which—Iau'bidi—*he captured personally.*[181]

If this inscription is actually Sargon's inscription (and not an epigraph attributed to Sargon
by his son), it further supports Sennacherib's invasion (2 Kgs 18:13–16; 2 Chr 32:1–8) as being
an heir apparent when he invaded Judah, since the only time that Scripture or Assyria's
annals indicate that Assyria subdued Judah was during Hezekiah's reign.

Another discovery that supports co-regency is the Tang-i Var Inscription, in which
Sargon recognizes Ethiopia's king as Shabataka/Shebitku. Respected author and scholar K.
Lawson Younger notes that the Tang-i Var Inscription indicates, "by naming Shabataka/
Shebitku as the king who extradited Yamani from Egypt, that Shebitku was already ruler by
706, *at least four years earlier than has generally been thought.*"[182] Thus, Sennacherib could
have served as a co-regent, with his third campaign against Hezekiah occurring before he
had officially ascended Assyria's throne.[183]

Whatever the case may be, both Sargon and Sennacherib attest that Hezekiah was king
during their reign. If Egypt, Kush, and Assyria employed heirs apparent as co-regents, it
would be quite plausible that Israel's Monarchy, which was fashioned after "the nations of
the earth" (Deut 17:14; 1 Sam 8:5, 20), employed heirs apparent as junior kings during this
era as well.

2. Scribes and the Heir Apparent

To compound these issues, it appears that scribes did not keep detailed records regarding
father-son co-regencies. This leaves the modern historian to reconstruct the overlapping
regnal years. Such is the case with Egypt's famed Turin King List. Although the king list is
thought to preserve a fairly accurate record of regnal years, co-regencies were not always
well documented.[184] These led later scribes to miss co-regencies all together. Regarding the
Turin's account of the 12th Dynasty, Egyptologist Kim Ryholt observes,

> Apparently the scribe did not realize that several of the reigns in question included
> a period of co-regency, and that the duration for the dynasty was therefore in
> reality much shorter.[185]

It appears that Israel's scribes, like Egypt's, were plagued by these same oversights, often failing
to recognize the co-regencies once the memory of the father's and son's lives had faded.
One tantalizing possibility for these oversights may have been an outdated regnal system.

In other words, a co-regent may have installed six months after the primary monarch yearly accession date (i.e., if the monarch had ascended the throne in the fall, the regent would be installed in the spring X years later). When later scribes edited the records or combined them, they missed an administrative tool for recording the co-regents' accession-year. It is hoped that future studies may explore this possible administrative devise.

The implications of co-regency for the Divided Kingdom's monarchies are: (1) part of the aggregate reign length of a king may have coincided with or been eclipsed by his father's reign, thus affecting the total number of years recorded for his reign; (2) there may be an unspecified co-regency, but the entire reign length of the heir was not reckoned until the father's death. (3) The accession date of a co-regency may be unknown, but it can be reconstructed with reference to internal synchronisms. As we will see, both reckoned and unreckoned co-regencies are attested in Scripture, although the latter unfortunately prevails throughout the Hebrew archives. Scripture's internal synchronizations do, however, allow us to reconstruct these unspecified co-regencies. The reign of Jehoshaphat (below) is one of the few exceptions to the normally garbled accounts of co-regencies in Israel's annals.

IX. SYNCHRONISMS WITH JUDAH'S HEIRS APPARENT

A. Jehoshaphat

The reigns of Israel's and Judah's kings for the most part are reasonably straightforward. What is confusing is the reign of an heir apparent. Our investigation will examine the kings whose synchronization indicates a co-regency. Table 9.35 on the opposite page demonstrates Israel and Judah's chronology. In the case of Jehoram, Scripture states:

> And in the fifth year of Joram the son of Ahab king of Israel, *Jehoshaphat being then king (melekh) of Judah*, Jehoram the son of Jehoshaphat king of Judah began to **reign** (malakh) . . . and he reigned eight years in Jerusalem. (2 Kgs 8:16–17)

Joram ben (son of) Ahab's 5th year would have been Jehoshaphat's 22nd year. Of Jehoram's 8 years, 4 years overlapped or eclipsed his father's 25-year reign (1 Kgs 22:42). Use of this detailed method renders 29 years for father and son in lieu of the chronological 33 years traditionally ascribed to them. Jehoram's 4-year sole regency cannot just be added to the 1st and only year that his brother Ahaziah reigned, because Ahaziah's only year overlaps with Jehoram's last year. Ahaziah began to rule at the tail end of Joram ben Ahab's 11th year and was killed by Jehu during Joram's 12th year (2 Kgs 8:25–26; 9:29). Thus, the time span from Jehoshaphat's 1st year until Ahaziah's death was *still* 29 years, as demonstrated by the macro chronology Table 9.35.

The internal synchronisms that Scripture provides help reconstruct this era. At first, 2 Kgs 9:29 and 8:25–26 appear to contradict each other regarding Ahaziah's accession year, one attributing it to Joram's 11th year (2 Kgs 9:29) and the other attributing it to Joram's 12th

Table 9.35. Jehoshaphat-Jehoram Co-regency

Date	Actual Yrs.		Judah		Israel		Assyria
			Jehoshaphat		Ahab		Shalmanassar
870	16			16		21 Ahaziah	5
869	17	1 Kgs 22:51		17	Joram 22	1	6
868	18	2 Kgs 3:1		18	1	2	7
867	19			19	2		8
866	20			20	3		9
865	21	2 Kgs 1:17- error	Jehoram 21		4		10
864	22	2 Kgs 8:16–17; 2 Chr 21:5	1 22		5		11
863	23		2 23		6		12
862	24		3 24		7		13
861	25		4 25		8		14
860	26		5		9		15
859	27		6		10		16
858	28	2 Kgs 9:29	Ahaziah 7 Athaliah		11 Jehu		17
857	29	2 Kgs 8:25–26; 10:36; 2 Chr 22:6	1t 8 1		12n 1		18

regnal year (2 Kgs 8:25–26). There is no contradiction in this synchronism; instead, it reveals the fact that one scribe wrote the account based on Samaria's Nisan, antedating system, while a Judahite scribe, using a Tishri year, reckoned Ahaziah's accession during Joram's 12th year. As the micro chronology in Table 9.36 demonstrates, Ahaziah began to reign during both Joram's 11th and 12th years.

Table 9.36. Ahaziah's Accession

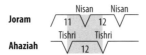

Throughout the entire Monarchic Period, there are a total of three errors in the synchronism of Judah's and Israel's monarchs. In every instance, the error occurs in glosses or editorial commentaries regarding the kings' reigns, thus betraying the hand of a later editor. The first error occurs in 2 Kgs 1:17, where the scribe states that Jehoram of Israel began to rule in the 2nd year of Jehoram of Judah. The previous synchronisms in 1 Kgs 22:51; 2 Kgs 3:1; 8:16; and 2 Chr 2:15 all agree that Joram began to rule in Jehoshaphat's 18th year, upon Ahaziah's death. In an effort to gloss over this error, biblical chronologist Dan Bruce has suggested that 2 Kgs 1:17 refers to a co-regency between a young Joram of Israel and Jehoram of Judah.[186] There are two obstacles to this suggestion.

First, the fracture of the Monarchy and the prophecy of taking the tribes out of Judah's hand (1 Kgs 11:11–13) make this scenario quite untenable. Second, 2 Kgs 1:17 is clear that in the narrative about Joram's (Israel) reigning in the stead of Ahazaiah. The statement that he reigned "because he had no son" refers to Ahaziah (2 Kgs 1:2). As Ahaziah's brother and Ahab's son, Joram (Israel) reigned in his brother (Ahaziah's) stead, which is consistent with other texts (2 Kgs 8:25). In no way can 2 Kgs 1:17 be construed to imply that a king in Judah ruled in Israel during the Divided Monarchy Period. Joram began to reign over Israel in Ahaziah's 2nd year, not Jehoram's (Judah) second year. It appears that a later editor confused the years Ahaziah' reigned over Israel with Jehoram's co-regency. This is an error made by a later editor.

B. Jehoshaphat, Ahaziah, and the House of Omri

1 Kgs 22:51 tells us that Ahaziah (Ahab's son) began to reign in *Jehoshaphat's seventeenth* year:

> Ahaziah the son of Ahab began to reign over Israel in Samaria the seventeenth year of Jehoshaphat king of Judah, and reigned two years over Israel. (1 Kgs 22:51)

Ahaziah reigned only 2 years. 2 Kings 3 states that Joram (Ahab's other son) began his reign in *Jehoshaphat's* 18th year (2 Kgs 3:1). These time frames overlap once again, because Ahaziah's 2 years should be reckoned chronologically as 1 year, since Ahaziah's 2nd year was also Joram's 1st year. This synchronism is confirmed by Assyria's

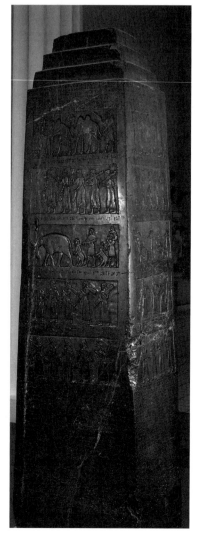

Illustration 9.1. Black Obelisk of Shalmaneser III, *c.* 850 BCE. One panel shows King Jehu paying tribute to Assyria his first regnal year.

annals. Shalmaneser's inscriptions tell us that he received tribute from the newly crowned Jehu in his 18th year (see Illustration 9.1).[187] Twelve years earlier, in the 6th year of his reign, "Shalmaneser claimed victory over a Syrian-led coalition of kings at Qarqar on the Orontes River as commemorated in the Monolith Inscription. Among the leaders of the forces opposed to Shalmaneser was King Ahab of Israel."[188] This exact correlation with

Assyria's archives demonstrates both the accuracy and the reliability of Scripture's Judah-Israel macro synchronizations (see Table 9.37).

Table 9.37. Judah-Israel-Assyria Synchronistic Chronology

Date	Judah			Israel			Assyria	
		Jehoshaphat		Ahab			Shalmaneser III	
874		12		_17_			1	
873		13		18			2	
872		14		19			3	
871		15		20			4	
870		16		21	Ahaziah		5	
869	1 Kgs 22:51	_17_	Joram	22	_1_		_6_	Shalmaneser
868	2 Kgs 3:1	_18_	_1_		2		7	confronts Ahab
867		19	2				8	in battle
866		20	3				9	
865	Jehoram	21	4				10	
864	2 Kgs 8:16–17; 2 Chr 21:5	_1_	22	_5_			11	
863		2	23	6			12	
862		3		7			13	
861		4		8			14	
860		5		9			15	
859		6		10			16	
858		7		11	Jehu		17	Receives tribute
857	2 Kgs 8:16–17; 2 Chr 21:5	8		12	_1_		_18_	from Jehu

Currently, the scholarly consensus is that Jehu's accession year was 841 BCE.[189] Scripture's synchronization presents this event as occurring 16 years earlier. This 16-year discrepancy is accounted for by an obscured era in Assyrian history that coincided with Hezekiah's reign. Scripture's synchronism, however, manifests precision when compared with Assyrian chronology, suggesting the reliability of the overall synchronistic method, which may in turn aid in accurately reconstructing the histories of contemporary nations.

C. Amaziah/Azariah (Uzziah)

In the second year of Joash son of Jehoahaz king of Israel reigned Amaziah the son of Joash king of Judah. He was twenty and five years old when he began to reign, and reigned twenty and nine years in Jerusalem. And his mother's name was Jehoaddan of Jerusalem. (2 Kgs 14:1–2)

Scripture evidences a co-regency again during Amaziah's reign.[190] According to the above text, Amaziah ascended Judah's throne during Jehoash's 2nd year and reigned for 29 years. The narrative of Amaziah's reign continues, citing the king's righteousness during his early years. Since the king sought to do right, YHWH blessed him with victory over Edom. When he returned from battle, however, he set up Edom's defeated gods as his own, then proudly challenged his brothers in Samaria (2 Chr 25:14–17; 2 Kgs 14:7–14). Samaria soundly defeated Amaziah. Soon after these debacles, the Southern Kingdom conspired against Amaziah by crowning his son Azariah (Uzziah) king.

This coup occurred *a few years* after Judah's humiliating confrontation with Israel, which was about 11 years before Amaziah's death.

> And Amaziah the son of Joash king of Judah lived after the death of Joash son of Jehoahaz king of Israel fifteen years. Now the rest of the acts of Amaziah, first and last, behold, are they not written in the book of the kings of Judah and Israel? *Now after the time that Amaziah did turn away from following YHWH they made a conspiracy against him in Jerusalem; and he fled to Lachish*: but they sent to Lachish after him, and slew him there. (2 Chr 25:25–27; see also 2 Kgs 14:19, 21–23)

This summary indicates that, shortly after Amaziah turned away from following YHWH, Judah's *'Edah* conspired against Amaziah, replacing him with his son Uzziah (Azariah).[191] Judah's sound defeat by the northern tribes no doubt brought about this coup:

> And Joash the king of *Israel* took Amaziah king of *Judah* . . . and brought him to Jerusalem, and broke down the wall of Jerusalem from the gate of Ephraim to the corner gate, four hundred cubits. And he took all the gold and the silver, and all the vessels that were found in the house of God with Obed-edom, and the treasures of the king's house, the hostages also, and returned to Samaria. And *Amaziah the son of Joash king of Judah lived after the death of Joash son of Jehoahaz king of Israel fifteen years.* (2 Chr 25:23–25; see also 2 Kgs 14:19–21)

At first glance, Chronicles and Kings appear to show Judah's sweeping revolt as occurring in one short movement. However, the evidence suggests that although Amaziah fled to Lachish, he lived another 15 years in exile after Judah's revolt. This conclusion is supported by a chronicler's subsequent entry. Although the English translation does not do this chronicle justice, the original Hebrew is clear.

> Then all the people of Judah took Uzziah, who was sixteen years old, and made him king [*malakh*, lit., **'to reign'**] *in the room of his father Amaziah.* He built

> Eloth, and restored it to Judah, after that the king [*melekh*, lit., '**the king**'] slept with his fathers. Sixteen years old was Uzziah when he began to reign, and he reigned fifty and two years in Jerusalem. His mother's name also was Jecoliah of Jerusalem. (2 Chr 26:1–3, brackets added)

At first this entry appears to record Uzziah's death after he had restored Eloth, but the context indicates otherwise. The Hebrew text states that Uzziah began to reign (*malakh*), not that he had actually become king (*melekh*). This is the same type of construction employed to describe the co-regency of Jehoshaphat and Jehoram (see p.398). The reference to the king's death in v. 2 probably refers to Amaziah's death, which occurred after Uzziah had restored Eloth to Judah. The usage of *malakh* (see above) to denote co-regency is consistent with 2 Kgs 8:16–17, where the text specifies that Jehoram began to reign (*malakh*) with his father, the king (*melekh*). The fact that subsequent portions of ch. 26 continue to highlight Uzziah's career before marking his death (2 Chr 26:21–23) demonstrates that v. 2 refers to Amaziah's death, while vv. 21–23 refer to Uzziah's death.

The archive in Kings also leads credence to this conclusion. While the chronicler's history separates the accounts of Amaziah's and Uzziah's reigns (2 Chronicles 25–26), the Book of Kings recognizes that Azariah (Uzziah) became king during his father's reign (2 Kgs 14:17–22) and that Jeroboam II became king before Azariah's (Uzziah's) sole regency (2 Kings 15).

The scribe's use of Uzziah's name is also telling. Throughout the ancient world, a king had a pre-throne name (or *nomen*), which was the king's personal name. The *prenomen* was the name given to the king when he officially ascended the throne. Kim Ryholt observes that scribes used the *nomen* and *prenomen* at random in Egyptian archives.[192] While the Book of Chronicles consistently recognizes Azariah by his *prenomen* (Azariah), the Kings' annals recognize him by his *nomen* (birth name), Uzziah, until the latter end of his reign, when perhaps Isaiah (see above) began to record the king's deeds (2 Kgs 15:13–34).

We know from the *Book of the Kings of Judah and Israel* that, during Joash's reign (Amaziah's father), Israel's King Jehoash ben Jehoahaz began to reign over Samaria:

> In the thirty and seventh year of Joash king of *Judah* began Jehoash the son of Jehoahaz to reign over *Israel* in Samaria, and reigned sixteen years. (2 Kgs 13:10)

Israel's Jehoash acceded to Samaria's throne when his father died. This entry bases Jehoash's (Israel) asccession on the 37th year of Joash's (Judah) reign. A later entry states that, in Jehoash's (Israel) 2nd year, Amaziah ascended to Judah's throne:

> *In the second year* of Joash son of Jehoahaz *king of Israel* reigned Amaziah the son of Joash king of Judah. He was twenty and five years old when he began to reign, and *reigned twenty and nine years in Jerusalem*. (2 Kgs 14:1–2)

If Amaziah ascended Judah's throne during Jehoash's 2nd year, this implies that he served as co-regent during the last three years of Joash's reign.

Remember, however, that Amaziah, "son of Joash king of Judah *lived after the death of Joash son of Jehoahaz king of Israel fifteen years.*" If Amaziah began to reign over Judah in Jehoash's 2nd year, reigned for 29 years, and lived only 15 years after Jehoash's death (2 Chr 25:25; 2 Kgs 14:17), then Jehoash's (Israel) death would have to have occurred in the 15th year of Amaziah's reign. This is consistent with 2 Kgs 14:23, which records that Jehoash's successor, Jeroboam II, ascended to Samaria's throne in Amaziah's 15th year (See Table 9.38).

Herein lies the dilemma with the Judean chronicles during this era. An entry in 2 Kings (2 Kgs 15:1), states that Uzziah's reign commenced in Jeroboam's 27th year.

> In the twenty and seventh year of Jeroboam king of *Israel* began Azariah son of Amaziah king of Judah to reign. Sixteen years old was he when he began to reign, and he reigned two and fifty years in Jerusalem. (2 Kgs 15:1–2).

This entry is impossible! Scripture states that Samaria's King Jeroboam II began to reign when his father died, during Amaziah's 15th year (2 Kgs 14:23). Amaziah reigned over Judah for a total of 29 years—including the 3 year co-regency with his father, Joash (2 Kgs 14:2). So, 15 years of Amaziah's rule occurred during Jeroboam II's reign. 2 Chr 25:25 and 2 Kgs 14:17 both testify that Amaziah lived only 15 years after Jehoash's death. This places Amaziah's death in the 15th year of Jeroboam II's reign, not his 27th year.[193]

According to 2 Kgs 15:1, Judah would have been without a king (interregnum) for well over 12 years. Whether or not this is the "errant pen" of the scribes to which Jer 8:8 refers or is a scribe's simple error is uncertain. What is certain is that Uzziah's rule began much earlier than Jeroboam II's 27th year. Given that Judah conspired against Amaziah from the time that he turned from following YHWH, probably shortly after Judah's defeat by their brothers in the north, and given the coup that forced Amaziah to flee to Lachish (2 Chr 25:25–27), supports that Uzziah's 52-year reign began much earlier in Jeroboam's reign than his 27th year. Since the Northern Kingdom does *not* evidence interregna (time without a monarch), it is quite likely that Uzziah's reign should correlate with the accession of Samaria's monarchs, as the later dates of Uzziah's reign indicate. Table 9.39 shows the synchronization of Israel's monarch's with the later years of Uzziah's (Judah) reign and demonstrates that interregna did not occur during this era. One interesting suggestion by Daniel Bruce is that 2 Kgs 15:1 does not refer to the 27th year of Jeroboam's reign but to the 27th year of his life.[194] Given, however, that all other synchronisms are worded in this manner refer to regnal years, this solution does not appear likely.

Synchronizing the Judah-Samarian annals supports the conclusion that 2 Kgs 15:1 is a second scribal error. Jeroboam reigned 41 years (2 Kgs 14:23), and his son (Zechariah) acceded to Israel's throne during Uzziah's 38th year (2 Kgs 15:8). If Jeroboam's ascension to Samaria's throne in Amaziah's 15th year (2 Kgs 14:23) is taken into account, then Uzziah's

Table 9.38. Coup against Amaziah

Date	Text	Judah			Israel	
					Jehoahaz	
			Joash			Jehoash
815	2 Kgs 13:10	Amaziah	<u>37</u>		17	1
814	2 Kgs 14:1–2, 20; 2 Chr 25:1	*1*	38			<u>2</u>
813	(co-regency or coup)	2	39			3
812		3	40			4
811		4				5
810		5				6
809		6				7
808		7				8
807		8				9
806		9				10
805		10				11
804		11				12
803		12				13
802		13				14
801		14				15
800	2 Kgs 14:17—15yrs.; 2 Kgs 14:23	<u>15t</u>			Jeroboam II	16
799	2 Chr 25:15–27	16			*1n*	
798		17			2	
797		18	Azariah (Uzziah)		3	
796		19	1	*Coup*	4	
795	2 Kgs 14:21–22; 2 Chr 25:27—coup	20	2	*d'état*	5	
794	Azariah crowned in Elah	21	3		6	
793	2 Kgs 15:2; 2 Chr 26:1–3	22	4		7	
792		23	5		8	
791		24	6		9	
790		25	7		10	
789		26	8		11	
788		27	9		12	
787		28	10		13	
786		29	11		14	

regency actually began in Jeroboam II's 4th or 5th year. Thus, Judah's coup occurred around the 19th year of Amaziah's reign. This chronology is consistent with the accession of Samaria's subsequent kings, which are reckoned according to Uzziah's reign: Zechariah began to rule in Uzziah's 38th year (2 Kgs 15:8), Shallum's and Menahem's reigns are based on Uzziah's 39th year (2 Kgs 15:13; 15:17), and Pekahiah began in Uzziah's 50th year (2 Kgs 15:23).

Table 9.39. Amaziah and Uzziah Chronology

Date	Text	Judah		Samaria	
			Joash	Jehoahaz	Jehoash
815	2 Kgs 13:10	Amaziah	37	17	1
814	2 Kgs 14:1–2; 2 Chr 25:1	1	38		2
813		2	39		3
812		3	40		4
811		4			5
810		5			6
809		6			7
808		7			8
807		8			9
806		9			10
805		10			11
804		11			12
803		12			16
802		13			14
801		14			15
800	2 Kgs 14:17—15yrs.; 2 Kgs 14:23	15t		Jeroboam II	16
799	2 Chr 25:5	16		1n	
798		17		2	
797		18	Azariah (Uzziah)	3	
796		19	1 coup	4	
795	2 Kgs 14:21–22; 2 Chr 25:27	20	2	5	
794	Azariah crowned in Elah	21	3	6	
793	2 Kgs 15:2; 2 Chr 26:1–3	22	4	7	
792		23	5	8	
791		24	6	9	
790		25	7	10	
789		26	8	11	
788		27	9	12	
787		28	10	13	
786		29	11	14	
785			12	15	
784			13	16	
783			14	17	
782			15	18	
781			16	19	

Table 9.39. Amaziah and Uzziah Chronology, *cont.*

Date	Text	Judah	Samaria	
780		17	20	
779		18	21	
778		19	22	
777		20	23	
776		21	24	
775		22	25	
774	2 Kgs 15:1—error	23	26	
773	If Jeroboam reigned 41 yrs. and	24	27	
772	Uzziah reigned 52 yrs., this would	25	28	
771	make Jeroboam's son Zechariah as-	26	29	
770	cending Samaria's throne in Uzziah's	27	30	
	14 yr., not his 38th yr.			
769		28	31	
768		29	32	
767		30	33	
766		31	34	
765		32	35	
764		33	36	
763		34	37	
762		35	38	
761		36	39	
760		37	40	
759	2 Kgs 15:8	<u>38</u>	41	Zechariah (6 mo.)
758	2 Kgs 15:13, 17	39t	*1n*	Menahem
757		40t		*1n*
756		41		2
755		42		3
754		43		4
753		44		5
752		45		6
751		46		7
750		47		8
749	2 Kgs 15:5—Jotham co-ruled because	48		9
748	Uzziah contracted leprosy	49	Pekahiah	10
747	2 Kgs 15:23	<u>50t</u>	*1n*	
746		51	2	Pekah
745	2 Kgs 15:27	<u>52t</u>	*1n*	

Thus, from Jeroboam's death until the disintegration of Samaria's monarchy, the Northern Kingdom was never without a king except for the 6 years when Omri and Tibni vied for Ephraim's throne. Although Judah's coup to usurp Amaziah's power by replacing him with Uzziah could hardly be seen as a co-regency, these texts do indicate a period of divided political alliances in Judah during which time Uzziah's and Amaziah's reigns overlapped (see Table 9.39).

D. Uzziah-Jotham-Hezekiah

The last co-regencies in Scripture involve four generations: Uzziah, Jotham, Ahaz, and Hezekiah.[195] Uzziah officially reigned over Judah for 52 years (2 Kgs 15:2, 27). Though he sought YHWH during most of his life, he failed to learn the lesson of obedience from his father's life. After YHWH had blessed him with incredible success, Uzziah revolted against YHWH by trying to usurp the high priest's responsibilities and burn incense in the Temple (2 Chr 26:16; Num 16:40). This move was not only religious but also political because Uzziah tried to usurp the high priest's authority and merge it with the monarchy, eliminating the constitutional balance of power. Scripture demonstrates that his son Jotham assumed his state responsibilities once YHWH struck him with leprosy.

> And Uzziah the king was a leper unto the day of his death, and dwelt in a several house, being a leper; for he was cut off from the house of YHWH: and *Jotham his son was over the king's house, judging the people of the land.* (2 Chr 26:21; see also 2 Kgs 15:5)

Although Jotham became co-regent[196] after his father was stricken with leprosy, his reign was not reckoned as a co-regency. Jotham officially ascended to Judah's throne upon his father's death, during King Pekah's (Israel) 2nd year on Samaria's throne: "In the second year of Pekah the son of Remaliah king of Israel began Jotham the son of Uzziah king of Judah to reign" (2 Kgs 15:32; see Table 9.40).

Judah's annals evidence that this period of co-regency was based on Uzziah's reign and not his son's (2 Kgs 15:17, 22–23, 27). One scribe does err, however, when he reckons that Hoshea's coup began in Jotham's 20th regnal year, a statement that is untenable.

> And Hoshea the son of Elah made a conspiracy against Pekah the son of Remaliah, and smote him, and slew him, and reigned in his stead, in the *twentieth year of Jotham the son of Uzziah.* (2 Kgs 15:30)

This entry contradicts another entry a few verses later (2 Kgs 15:33) as well as the chronicler's emphatic comment that Jotham reigned for *only* 16 years (2 Chr 27:1, 8).

Table 9.40. Uzziah-Pekah-Jotham Synchronization

Years	Text	Judah		Israel	
1	2 Kgs 15:5—Jotham co-regency/ Uzziah leper	Uzziah 49 Unreckoned	Pekahiah	Menahem 10	
2	2 Kgs 15:23	50 co-regency	1n		
3		51	2	Pekah	
4	2 Kgs 15:27	52 Jotham	1n		
5	2 Kgs 15:32–33; 2 Chr 27:1	1*	2		

*(Judah shifts to priestly-nonaccession-year system.)

Jotham was twenty and five years old when he began to reign, and *he reigned sixteen years in Jerusalem*. His mother's name also was Jerushah, the daughter of Zadok. . . . Now the rest of the acts of Jotham, and all his wars, and his ways, see, they are written in the book of the kings of Israel and Judah. He was five and twenty years old when he began to reign, *and reigned sixteen years in Jerusalem*. And Jotham slept with his fathers, and they buried him in the city of David: and Ahaz his son reigned in his stead. (2 Chr 27:1, 7–9; see also 2 Kgs 15:33)

The chronicler's record of the monarchy's regencies reveals no other inconsistencies. The only explanation for the incongruity between 2 Kgs 15:30 and this record is a scribe's error. The evidence shows that Jotham could not have been alive when Hoshea began to rule in Israel, and Jotham did not reign for 20 years since Scripture also tells us that Hoshea acceded to Samaria's throne in the 12th year of Ahaz's reign (2 Kgs 17:1). If Jotham only reigned in Judah independently for 16 years after becoming king in his 2nd year (2 Chr 28:1; 2 Kgs 16:1–2), he would have died in Pekah's 17th year. Hoshea's revolt did not occur until four years later! Table 9.41 exhibits the discrepancy in 2 Kgs 15:30 and reconstructs the corresponding co-regencies based on Israel's and Judah's synchronized annals and chronicles.

This evidence implies that a later editor was working with an original document but erred when copying it into the final compilation. Since both Kings and Chronicles agree that Jotham's reign lasted only 16 years and the synchronism with Israel's chronology demonstrates no periods without a king, 1 Kgs 15:30 must be a later addition. The error was actually a simple one to make if the scribe was working with the official annals and trying to provide internal synchronisms. Had Jotham lived another 4 years, Hoshea's 1st year would indeed have been Jotham's 20th year. There are well over 56 synchronisms and reign lengths listed in the Book of Kings. The fact that only 3 errors appear demonstrates the tediousness of the material and reveals that the same scribe or editor probably made all three errors.

This leads us to the next puzzle in Judah's chronology. When Jotham died in Pekah's 17th year, his son Ahaz ascended to Judah's throne.

Table 9.41. Synchronism Uzziah-Pekah-Hoshea Scribal Error

Date	Text	Judah		Israel	
		Uzziah		Pekah	
745	2 Kgs 15:27	52	Jotham	1n	
744	2 Kgs 15:32–33; 2 Chr 27:1	1t		2	
743		2		3	
742		3		4	
741		4		5	
740		5		6	
739		6		7	
738		7		8	
737		8		9	
736		9		10	
735		10		11	
734		11		12	
733		12		13	
732		13		14	
731		14		15	
730		15		16	
729	2 Kgs 16:1–2; 2 Kgs 15:32	Ahaz	16	17	
728	2 Chr 27:1	1t	17	18	
727		2	18	19	
726		3	19	20	Hoshea
725	2 Kgs 15:30—scribal error	4	20		1n

> In the seventeenth year of Pekah the son of Remaliah, Ahaz the son of Jotham king of Judah began to reign. Twenty years old was Ahaz when he began to reign, and reigned sixteen years in Jerusalem. (2 Kgs 16:1–2)

Ahaz assumed Judah's throne upon his father's death and, like his father, officially reigned over Judah for 16 years. The *Book of the Kings of Israel and Judah* records that Hoshea began to rule over Israel in the 12th year of Ahaz's reign:

> In the twelfth year of Ahaz king of Judah began Hoshea the son of Elah to reign in Samaria over Israel nine years. (2 Kgs 17:1)

What this means for our study is that the Northern Kingdom was never without a king during this era—a conclusion also supported by the annals of Assyria's Tiglath-pileser:

They [Israel] overthrew their king Pekah and I placed Hoshea as king over them.[197]

Hoshea's coup transpired during Ahaz's 12th year and gained Assyria's support when Tiglath-pileser legitimized Hoshea's revolt. Pekah had only reigned over Israel for 20 years (2 Kgs 15:27) before Hoshea's coup in Ahaz's 12th year (2 Kgs 17:1). This means that there were only 4 years from the point Ahaz officially ascended Judah's throne until Hoshea's successful revolution. Thus the span of Ahaz's reign from Pekah's 17th (2 Kgs 16:1–2) year until Hoshea's 1st year was only 4 years (see Table 9.42).

Table 9.42. Jotham-Ahaz-Hezekiah Co-regencies

Date	Scriptural Text	Judah		Israel	
			Jotham		Pekah
737		Ahaz	8		9
736		1	9		10
735	(co-regency)	2	10		11
734		3	11		12
733		4	12		13
732		5	13		14
731		6	14		15
730		7	15		16
729	2 Kgs 16:1–2; 2 Chr 28:1	8	16		17n
728	Isa 7:1; Mic 1:1	(1) 9/1t	17		18
727		(2) 10/2	18		19
726		(3) 11/3	19	Hoshea	20
725	2 Kgs 17:1 (2 Kgs 15:30—scribal error)	(4) 12/4	20	1n	
724	(Isa 7:1—Ahaz's kingdom is not established)	13/5		2	
723	2 Kgs 16—conspiracy against Ahaz?	14/6	Hezekiah	3n	
722	2 Kgs 18:1	15/7	1t	4	
721		16/8	2	5	
720		17/9	3	6	
719	2 Kgs 18:9		4	7	
718			5	8	
717	2 Kgs 18:10		6	9	

So far, Judah's chronology is fairly straightforward: Ahaz reigned for 16 years after Jotham's death. Four years passed from Pekah's 17th year to Hoshea's 1st regnal year. So Ahaz's son Hezekiah should have begun to reign 16–17 years after Pekah's 17th year, thus beginning at least 6 years after Assyria defeated Hoshea, and Israel's monarchy ceased to exist.[198] This conclusion is too eager, because Judah's annals make it very clear that Hezekiah was seated on Judah's throne 7 years after Jotham's death (2 Kgs 18:1). This leaves only 6 years for Ahaz (Hezekiah's father) to have reigned independently.

The scribe's account of Judah's King Hezekiah and Samaria's King Hoshea is one of the best synchronisms Scripture offers:

> And it came to pass in the *fourth year of king Hezekiah, which was the seventh year of Hoshea* son of Elah king of Israel, that Shalmaneser king of Assyria came up against Samaria, and besieged it. And at the end of three years they took it: even in the *sixth year of Hezekiah, that is the ninth year of Hoshea* king of Israel, Samaria was taken. (2 Kgs 18:9–10)

From Jotham's death to Hezekiah's ascension to the throne is a span of only 6 years, thus eclipsing 8 years of Ahaz's last 14 years of rule. This is consistent with 2 Kgs 16:1, which states that Ahaz began his rule in Pekah's 17th year, the year when his father (Jotham) died.[199] 2 Kings 17:1 also tells us that Hoshea acceded to Samaria's throne *Ahaz's 12th year*. This shows that Ahaz's co-regency commenced in Jotham's 9th year and that he reigned independently for only 6 years before Hezekiah became king. Continuing evidence is found in the prophet Isaiah's testimony (see Table 9.43).

Isaiah (7:1) notes that Pekah and Rezin began to harass Jerusalem during the "days of Ahaz." The prophet may be alluding to co-regency by writing that the Samarian-Syrian confederacy

Table 9.43. Hoshea-Hezekiah Synchronism

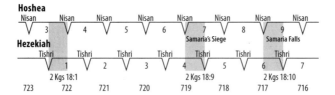

was disclosed "to the House of David" (Isa 7:2) and not specifically to King Ahaz. 2 Kgs 15:37 corroborates this supposition since the entry for Pekah's harassment of Judah was written *before* the entry for Jotham's death. In other words, when Isaiah (7:1) refers to the news of Pekah's revolt as being reported to the House of David, he is probably referring to Jotham's and Ahaz's co-regency.

The fact that the events of Isa 7:1 occurred soon after Jotham's death, early in Ahaz's independent reign, is evidenced by Isaiah's statement that, if Ahaz did not believe Isaiah's words, his kingdom would not be established (Isa 7:9). There would be no need for Isaiah to comment on establishing Ahaz's kingdom if he had already been reigning independently for a few years.

> And it came to pass in the days of Ahaz the son of Jotham, the son of Uzziah, king of Judah, that Rezin the king of Syria, and Pekah the son of Remaliah, king of Israel, went up toward Jerusalem to war against it, but could not prevail against it. And it was told the *House of David*, saying, Syria is confederate with

Ephraim. And his heart was moved, and the heart of his people, as the trees of the wood are moved with the wind. Then said YHWH to Isaiah, Go forth now to meet Ahaz, you, and Shear-jashub your son, at the end of the conduit of the upper pool in the highway of the fuller's field; And say to him, *Take heed, and be quiet; fear not,* neither be fainthearted for the two tails of these smoking firebrands, for the fierce anger of Rezin with Syria, and of the son of Remaliah. Because Syria, Ephraim, and the son of Remaliah, have taken evil counsel against you, saying, Let us go up against Judah, and vex it, and let us make a breach therein for us, and set a king in the middle of it, even the son of Tabeal: Thus said YHWH GOD, It shall not stand, neither shall it come to pass. For the head of Syria is Damascus, and the head of Damascus is Rezin; and *within threescore and five years shall Ephraim be broken, that it be not a people.* (9) And the head of Ephraim is Samaria, and the head of Samaria is Remaliah's son. *If you will not believe, surely you shall not be established.* (Isa 7:1–9)

Isaiah's reference to the "House of David" appears to refer to Jotham's and Ahaz's co-regency when Jotham sought after the Creator, and YHWH moved to help them (Isa 7:2, 4; 2 Chronicles 27). When Jotham died, YHWH then sought to establish Ahaz's kingdom, to which Isaiah refers to in v. 9.[200]

Isaiah's comment about establishing Ahaz's kingdom could also demonstrate the Levites' (allied with the *'Edah?*) resistance to the Monarchy. In other words, similar to Amaziah's administration, Isaiah implies that the priesthood would not support Ahaz's administration if he embraced wickedness (2 Kgs 16:2–4) but would supplant him with another legitimate heir, who would believe and abide by YHWH's constitutional word to the nation.

The *'Edah* had revolted against Amaziah to install his son Uzziah (2 Chr 25:25–27; 26:1–3) once the banished king rebelled against YHWH. There is no reason to doubt that the people would also have rebelled against Ahaz's wickedness by installing a godlier monarch. History indeed repeated itself. Both revolts took place after Israel (Northern Kingdom) had invaded Jerusalem, and YHWH had given Judah into their hand (2 Chr 25:2–5; 28:1–19). Ahaz's plea for Tiglath-pileser's support (28:16) may have been an attempt to preserve his throne from the people's revolt.

The opening words of the Book of Micah also support the theory of successive co-regencies during this era. Micah dates his testimony to the days of Jotham, Ahaz, and Hezekiah, thus indicating that these three kings reigned during a short time span (Mic 1:1). All of these observations accord with Table 9.50. Macro Synchronized Chronology of Israel and the Near East in Appendix A.

E. Synchronization with Egypt and Assyria

Israel's internal synchronization that I have presented here demonstrates about a 16-year difference between Judah-Israel's chronology and currently accepted Assyrian chronologies. The discrepancy arises during Tiglath-pileser's reign. The reigns of most kings, including Assyrian monarchs, are primarily reconstructed based on their annalistic inscriptions. Esarhaddon (similar to Ramesses II), who reigned about 80 years later, removed Tiglath-pileser's central palace slabs, on which his many inscriptions were written. He hacked them up and reused them in building his own palace.[201] This has left the reconstruction of Tiglath's reign somewhat ambiguous today.

1. Was Pul Tiglath-pileser?

In 1 Chr 5:26, the chronicler asserts that Pul and Tiglath-pileser were two separate monarchs. Scripture is not alone in recognizing an Assyrian king by the name of Pul. Berossus, a priest of the Akkadian god Bel in Babylon (*c.* 325 BCE) has preserved a Babylonian king-list (King List A) that reports a Pul reigning for 2 years over Babylon.[202] The first-century Jewish historian Josephus also mentions Pul when recounting Menahem's tribute (*Ant.* 9.11.1), and a Ptolemaic record (an Egyptian kings list) attests his name as well.[203]

Ptolemy's Canon, composed by the second-century (CE) astronomer Claudias Ptolemy, preserves a calendric list of kings that was used by ancient astronomers to date astronomical phenomena, such as eclipses. Its accuracy is generally acknowledged and has been confirmed by reference to other ancient king lists and has greatly aided our understanding of ancient chronology.[204] What is quite curious regarding Ptolemy's list is that, like the Hebrew chronicler, Ptolemy recognizes Pul and Tiglath-pileser as two separate people. Various theories have been advanced regarding these references to an Assyrian king by the name of Pul (2 Kgs 15:19) since he is not mentioned in any of Assyria's records. Two theories (Oppert) are that Assyria's records were flawed and (most widely held) that Pul and Tiglath–pileser were the same person. The latter theory is almost universally held by biblical scholars because both Ptolemy's Canon and Scripture list Pul's reign as being during the same period as the reign of Tiglath-pileser.[205]

According to the currently accepted Assyrian chronology, Tiglath-pileser only ruled for about 18 years.[206] However, a careful study of his inscriptions results in the same chronology as Scripture's synchronistic chronology. Tiglath-pileser records that, in his 3rd year, he received tribute from Azariah (Uzziah) "of the land of Judah."[207] It is likely that Tiglath received this tribute in Uzziah's 38th year. During this campaign, Judah lost Hamath and many of its northern tributary vassal territories to Assyria as Tiglath installed garrisons and erected administrative buildings to collect taxes.[208] A later undated inscription mentions Tiglath's receiving tribute from Judah's Jehoahaz, who is better known by his birth name, Ahaz. Scripture reports this same tribute (2 Kgs 16:7–10) to Tiglath-pileser when Judah sought to dissolve the Syria-Israel alliance that was aimed at overthrowing the Kingdom of Judah. What this means for chronological discussions is that Tiglath remained on the Assyrian throne for *at least* another 20 years than currently thought.

This theory is further supported by synchronizing monarchs with Israel's (Samaria's) monarchs. Both Scripture and Tiglath's inscriptions tell us that Menahem bought his throne by paying off Assyria (2 Kgs 15:19–20).[209]

One of Tiglath's fragmentary annals states that he installed Menahem in his "palace." Tiglath's inscriptions continue to chart his destruction of the Samaria-Syrian alliance against Judah. The ancient king tells us that, in a domestic coup, Israel overthrew Pekah, and Tiglath-pileser supported Hoshea's claim to Samaria's throne.[210] What this means for Assyrian chronology is that Tiglath-pileser reigned for 38 years (he died during Hoshea's 2nd year), a fact that is supported by both Shalmaneser's siege of Samaria in his 5th regnal year[211] (attested in Hoshea's 7th year) and Samaria's fall to Sargon 3 years later. What is clear from Scripture's internal synchronizations is that another 20 years must be accounted for in the Judah-Israel and Assyria synchronism for this era.

2. Sennacherib

The synchronization of Egypt's and Assyria's chronology for the period of Hezekiah's reign is also open to discussion. This period in Egyptian chronology is termed the Third Intermediate Period, due to rival dynasties competing for control over Egypt, leaving doubt regarding the precise chronology for this period.[212] Around 727 BCE, Egypt's northern territories were conquered by Nubia (a nation south of Egypt), which has today become known as the 25th Egyptian Dynasty. It is from this dynasty that both Scripture and Assyrian records demonstrate military conflict with Egypt.

As mentioned previously (pp. 396–97), the Tang-i-Var inscription indicates that Egypt's chronology during Sennacherib's reign began earlier than has previously been thought.[213] Egypt's Pharaoh Taharqa had campaigned in Canaan as a general under his brother Shebitku's reign.[214] The implication from Judah's record is that Sennacherib had also campaigned in Israel as heir apparent during the same campaign when his father (Sargon) was in Canaan dealing with Ashdod.

The famous Taylor Prism records Sennacherib's invasion of Judah and successful siege against Hezekiah during his third campaign. The prism chronicles through his eighth campaign and may have been written a few years afterward. Assyria had developed a unique method for reckoning "time" over the centuries so that dates, events, and kings (who often bore the same name) did not become confused for later scribes. Around 856 BCE, each year was named after a *different* Assyrian official, usually a governor.[215] Today, these years are termed an eponymy and the entire compilation is called an eponym list. Almost every year from *c.* 856–662 BCE is attested.[216] The issue with the Taylor Prism is that it is dated by the eponym "Gihilu of Hatarika," whose 'year' is listed two years before Sennacherib became king.[217] This may indicate that Sennacherib had campaigned as an heir apparent or co-regent for at least 9 years before Sargon's death.

It is quite likely that Tiglath-pileser's long reign meant that both Shalmaneser, who only reigned for 5 years, and his successor Sargon were old men. Sargon needed younger and more energetic leadership to marshal his campaigns. What this evidence suggests is that Sennacherib began commanding his father's forces during Sargon's 9th year, when Sargon campaigned against Ashdod, but he was not installed as co-regent until Sargon's 13th year. The Taylor Prism records Sennacherib's siege of Jerusalem during his third campaign. This would have been 2 years before the prince was actually installed as co-regent. It would also explain why Sargon could legitimately claim that he had subdued Jerusalem,[218] since Sennacherib simply acted as one of his generals.

These observations are in line with Kitchen's suggestion that Egypt's Shabaka and Shebitku may have been co-regents and that Taharqa's campaign may have occurred before he actually ascended to Kush's throne.[219] Thus, the evidence for this era accords with Scripture's chronology for this era.

In an effort to reconcile Israel's chronology with Assyria, Rodger Young has theorized that the Northern Kingdom split into two factions during Pekah's reign, as implied by Hos 5:5.[220] The fracture of the nation probably occurred during Menahem's horrific reign and continued to be an issue throughout the turbulent succession years until Hoshea's death. Scripture's synchronizations, however, demonstrate that the Northern Kingdom's chronology during this era was reckoned by the same linear method as it was after Jeroboam II's reign. This means, as Young has adeptly observed, that Ahaz and Hezekiah were coregent or Judah had revolted against Ahaz to install Hezekiah (see pp. 408–13).[221]

3. Samaria's Demise

Assyria had deported Samaria, placing her people in Assyria's Median territories (2 Kgs 18:11). Noted historian K. Lawson Younger observes that this deportation could not have occurred before 716 BCE.

> In the Assyrian sources, this would appear to be the area of Harhar (renamed Kār-Šarrukīn by Sargon) and its neighboring townships. *These Israelites could not have been deported before 716 BCE, simply because before that date Sargon had no 'cities of the Medes' within his provincial jurisdiction.*[222]

The synchronization in Scripture accords with Younger's assessment. It demonstrates that Samaria was destroyed in 717 BCE, and the people deported the following year after Sargon had secured the Medean territory where he planned to transplant Samaria's captives. Thus, the overall chronology that I have purposed accords with the Assyrian record.

4. Isaiah's 65 Years

When Isaiah exhorted Ahaz to believe in YHWH, he prophesied that within 65 years "Ephraim would be broken that it be not a people" (Isa 7:8). Assyria's method of deportation was bidirectional, meaning that, when Assyrian kings *deported* natives to Assyrian territories, they *imported* refugees from Mesopotamia into Israel's boundaries at the same

Table 9.44. Isaiah's 65 Years

728	Ahaz	6	yrs.
722	Hezekiah	29	yrs.
694	Manasseh	30	yrs.
664/663		65	years

time.[223] Isaiah's 65-year prophecy was fulfilled during Ashurbanipal's campaign, when Judah's King Manasseh was deported to Babylon (2 Chr 33:11–13), in 664 BCE.[224]

Isaiah issued the deportation prophecy against Ephraim during Ahaz's 1st official year, before his kingdom had a chance to be established (Isa 7:9; see pp. 412–13, Table 9.15 on p. 379). (Remember that Jacob's Diaspora Covenant had foretold this event.) Ahaz's 1st year as sole regent would also have been his 9th regnal year under co-regency (Pekah's 17th year—2 Kgs 16:1). Ahaz reigned independently for only 6 years before Judah revolted to install Hezekiah. After Hoshea's deportation, Hezekiah loosely governed the northern territory. Manasseh, Hezekiah's son, no doubt continued to pay his father's tribute to

Assyria until he decided to revolt and was deported by Assyria to Babylon along with the Ephraimite tribal confederacy. Table 9.44 demonstrates the fulfillment of Isaiah's prophecy in Manasseh's 30th year.

5. Manasseh's Deportation

Manasseh was temporarily deported, although Scripture does not document the duration of his exile, but we may evaluate circumstantial evidence regarding Nebuchadnezzar's exile to see if YHWH had set an "exile precedent." When Nebuchadnezzar attributed YHWH's deeds to himself, the Book of Daniel recorded that the Creator banished the haughty king.

> And they drove him from men, and his dwelling was with the beasts of the field: they made him to eat grass as oxen, and *seven times passed over him*, until he should know that the most High rules in the kingdom of men, and gives it to whomsoever he will. (Dan 4:32; see also vv. 16, 23, 25)

If YHWH used a period of 7 years to humble Nebuchadnezzar, then it is possible that 7 years were also employed to humble Manasseh. A 7-year exile would mean that Manasseh's release occurred during the 37th year of his reign. We will examine Manasseh's exile in light of the supporting Assyrian evidence in chap. 12 (see p. 623). We will investigate the implication of the covenant's curses of 7 Times and their relationship to Manasseh's reign when we look at the nation's Testimonial Law in part two of this book (chap. 14).

F. Josiah to Jehoiakim

After Pharaoh Necho killed Josiah, Manasseh's grandson, Judah's citizens (the 'Edah) installed Jehoahaz as their king. Only three months later, Necho deported Jehoahaz, placed Judah under Egyptian tribute, and crowned another one of Josiah's sons as regent. Four years later, during Nebuchadnezzar's 1st year, Babylon confronted Necho. Jeremiah provides a chronology from Josiah's reign until Jehoiakim's 4th year.

> The word that came to Jeremiah concerning all the people of Judah *in the fourth year of Jehoiakim* the son of Josiah king of Judah, that was the first year of Nebuchadrezzar king of Babylon. . . From the *thirteenth year* of Josiah the son of Amon king of Judah, even unto this day, that is the *three and twentieth year*, the word of YHWH has come to me, and I have spoken to you, rising early and speaking; but you have not listened. (Jer 25:3)

In order for there to be 23 years from Josiah's 13th year until Jehoiakim's 4th year, Jehoiakim's 1st year could *not* be reckoned to have overlapped with the last year of his father's reign (see Table 9.45), nor was any part of his reign reckoned as a co-regency.

Table 9.45. Jeremiah Prophecies from Josiah's 13th Yr.
to Jehoiakim's 4th Yr. = 23 Yrs. (Jer 25:3)

Date	Text	Judah		Total	Babylon
		Josiah			Nabopolassar
627		13		1	
626		14		2	1
625		15		3	2
624		16		4	3
623		17		5	4
622	(2 Kgs 22:3)	18		6	5
621		19		7	6
620		20		8	7
619		21		9	8
618		22		10	9
617		23		11	10
616		24		12	11
615		25		13	12
614		26		14	13
613		27		15	14
612		28		16	15
611		29		17	16
610		30	Jehoahaz/	18	17
609	2 Kgs 23:31	31	Jehoiakim	19	18
608	2 Kgs 23:34–36; Jer 52:1		1	20	19
607			2	21	20
606	Jer 25:1; 46:2—Nebuchadnezzar		3	22	21 Nebuchadnezzar
605	destroys Pharaoh Necho		4	23	1

G. Haran Inscription and Ptolemy's Canon

The proposed synchronized Judah-Samaria chronology is corroborated by two identical yet primitive autobiographical inscriptions of a priestess who lived a short distance east of Haran in Mesopotamia. Her long, 95-year career spanned the reigns of 7 kings.

> From the 20th year of Ashurbanipal, king of Assyria, when I was born, until the 42nd year of Ashurbanipal, the 3rd year of his son Ashur-etil-ili, the 21st year of Nabopolassar, the 43rd year of Nebuchadnezzar, the 2nd year of Awel-Merodach, the 4th year of Neriglissar, *during all these 95 years. . . .*[225]

The priestess's chronology perfectly coincides with the Scriptures' chronology for this era.

The canon created by the astronomer Ptolemy of Alexandria (mentioned above, pg. 414) *dis*agrees both with the Haran Inscription and Scripture's chronology *for the Assyrian era.* Ptolemy's Canon, however, perfectly coincides with both Scripture and the priestess's chronology during the Babylonian era, indicating that Ptolemy's source material for the Assyrian era was incomplete.

According to the chronology set forth in the Haran Inscription, Ashurbanipal's reign would have commenced during Manasseh's 24th year, shortly before Assyria completed Ephraim's deportations. Table 9.46 demonstrates that this 95-year chronology is in harmony with Scripture's chronology of Judah's kings and Jeremiah's 23-year prophetic mission.

Table 9.46. Haran Inscription and Scripture's Chronology

Date	Total	Text	Judah			Assyria and Babylon		Jeremiah's Chronology
652	0		Josiah			Ashurbanipal		
651	1		44			21		
650	2		45			22		
649	3		46			23		
648	4		47			24		
647	5		48			25		
646	6		49			26		
645	7		50			27		
644	8		51			28		
643	9		52			29		
642	10		53			30		
641	11		54	Amon		31		
640	12	2 Kgs 19:21/ 2 Chr 33:21	Josiah	55	1a	32		
639	13	2 Kgs 21:19	1a		2	33		
638	14	2 Kgs 22:1	2			34		
637	15		3			35		
636	16		4			36		
635	17		5			37		
634	18		6			38		
633	19		7			39		
632	20		8			40		
631	21		9			41		
630	22		10			42	Ashur-etil-ilani	
629	23		11				1	
628	24	Jer 25:3— Jeremiah prophecies	12				2	Jeremiah
627	25	from Josiah's 13th yr.	13				3	1
626	26		14			Nabopolassar	1	2
625	27		15				2	3

Date	Total	Text	Judah		Assyria and Babylon		Jeremiah's Chronology
624	28		16			3	4
623	29		17			4	5
622	30		18			5	6
621	31		19			6	7
620	32		20			7	8
619	33		21			8	9
618	34		22			9	10
617	35		23			10	11
616	36		24			11	12
615	37		25			12	13
614	38		26			13	14
613	39		27			*14*	15
612	40		28			15	16
611	41		29			16	17
610	42		30	Jehoahaz/		17	18
609	43	2 Kgs 23:31	31	Jehoiakim		18	19
608	44	2 Kgs 23:34–36; Jer 52:1	*1*			19	20
607	45		2			20	21
606	46		3		Nebuchad-nezzar	*21*	22
605	47	Jer 25:1; 46:2—	*4*			*1*	23
604	48	Nebuchadnezzar destroys Pharaoh Necho	5			2	
603	49		6			3	
602	50		7			4	
601	51		8			5	
600	52		9			6	
599	53	Jer 52:28	10	Jehoiachin /		7	Jer 52:31—Jechoniah's 37th yr.
598	54	2 Kgs 24:12	11	Zedekiah		8	1
597	55	2 Kgs 24:18	*1*			9	2
596	56		2			10	3
595	57		3			11	4
594	58	Jer 34:8–10	4			12	5
593	59	(Ezekiel 1–4)	5			13	6
592	60		6			14	7
591	61		7			15	8
590	62		8			16	9
589	63	Jer 52:4	Jerusalem sieged	9		17	10

Date	Total	Text	Judah	Assyria and Babylon		Jeremiah's Chronology
588	64	Jer 52:29; 2 Kgs 25:1	10	*18*		11
587	65	Jer 52:12–27; 2 Kgs 25:2	11	*19*		12
586	66	Jer 25:11; 29:10		20		13
585	67			21		14
584	68			22		15
583	69			*23*		16
582	70			24		17
581	71			25		18
580	72			26		19
579	73			27		20
578	74			28		21
577	75			29		22
576	76			30		23
575	77			31		24
574	78			32		25
573	79			33		26
572	80			34		27
571	81			35		28
570	82			36		29
569	83			*37*		30
568	84			38		31
567	85			39		32
566	86			40		33
565	87			41		34
564	88			42		35
563	89			43	Evil Merodach	36
562	90	2 Kgs 25:27–30; Jer 52:31–34			1	37
561	91	37th yr. of Jechoniah's captivity		(Neriglissar)	2	
560	92			*1*		
559	93			2	Nebuchadnezzar's 3rd generation	
558	94			3		
557	95	Priestess of Haran's 95 years		4		

X. DESTRUCTION OF THE FIRST TEMPLE

There are two dates that are generally accepted for the final destruction of Solomon's Temple. Rabbi Leibel Reznick and much of the Jewish community hold that Solomon's Temple was destroyed in 422 BCE.[226] This date, however, is not supported by epigraphic evidence from the nations that surrounded Israel and Judah and deported them (see chaps. 14–20). Most historians and other scientists date Nebuchadnezzar's first siege of the city, his 7th year, to 598 BCE and the city's final destruction in Nebuchadnezzar's 19th year to 587.[227] This date is based on converging chronologies of the nations that surrounded ancient Israel. Both of these sides hold the traditional chronological view that Solomon's Temple existed for about 410 years.[228] As evidenced in the method presented above, Israel's chronicles (Rehoboam through Zedekiah) actually spanned a much shorter time. The First Temple existed for 386 years. The Temple itself represented Israel's history (a point we will return to in part 2 of this book). The curses of 7 Times—cultic judgments against YHWH's sanctuary—began in 944 BCE, the year when the United Monarchy divided, and ended 357 years later with the First Temple's destruction, in 587 BCE.

As we have seen, only three errors exist in the entire Judah-Israel synchronization system. This indicates a deliberate attempt to preserve the Divided Monarchy's histories. Of the three errors, the latter was a simple mistake since the synchronism is correct, but the actual number of years reigned is incorrect. This leaves only two actual chronological errors out of 55 internal synchronisms. The scribe's error in 2 Kgs 15:1 might be seen as an attempt to correct the 15-year discrepancy. The problem with this theory is that it shifts the Judah chronology downward by another 15 to 24 years, causing both Judah and Israel to experience a 15-year period (at the same time) without a monarch on the throne when legitimate heirs were available. This is not a likely scenario. In every other case, the synchronisms between the Divided Kingdoms have been reliable. Our discussion has centered on the reliability and credibility of the Hebrew Scriptures. If we were to toss the synchronization that proved so accurate for the Ahab-Jehu-Shalmaneser era, then where would we limit this deconstruction?

We saw in the previous chapter that Scripture has indeed undergone many editing and transcribing processes. That only two errors are found in the entire chronological system is quite remarkable, demonstrating very tedious transcribing of the original texts. Throughout the last few centuries, Israel's chronology has come under attack. Many kings listed in Scripture were once thought to be fictional, but archaeology has now verified almost every single monarch mentioned in Scripture.

Chronology itself is a fluid study. It must be modified every time new epigraphic evidence comes to light. Over the years, Israel's chronology has been vindicated with almost every new inscription. The question is whether future discoveries will continue to clarify the eastern chronologies of this era as well.

XI. REMEMBERING JERUSALEM AFTER SEVENTY YEARS

A. *Seventy Years of Desolation Accomplished*

Many scholars attribute Persia's release of Israel to the fulfillment of Isaiah's prophecy. Isaiah had termed Cyrus "my shepherd" (Isa 44:28–45:7). Other scholars, critical of the Hebrew text, cite this as a contradiction to the Levite's record in 2 Chr 36:22, which states that Cyrus's release fulfilled Jeremiah's prophecy.[229]

> Now in the first year of Cyrus king of Persia, *that the word of YHWH spoken by the mouth of Jeremiah might be accomplished,* YHWH stirred up the spirit of Cyrus king of Persia, that he made a proclamation throughout all his kingdom. (2 Chr 36:22)

The truth is that Chronicles witnesses the fulfillment of both Isaiah's and Jeremiah's prophecies. Although Isaiah prophesied of Cyrus by name, Jeremiah prophesied of a specific time when Israel's banishment from the Promised Land would end.

> And this whole land shall be a desolation, and an astonishment; and *these nations shall serve the king of Babylon seventy years.* And it shall come to pass, when seventy years are accomplished, that I will punish the king of Babylon, and that nation, said YHWH, for their iniquity, and the land of the Chaldeans, and will make it perpetual desolations. And I will bring on that land all my words which I have pronounced against it, even all that is written in this book, which Jeremiah has prophesied against all the nations. (Jer 25:11–13)

Chronicles' scribe had Jeremiah's 70-year prophecy in mind when he wrote that Jeremiah's words had been fulfilled. Many scholars, however, refute Jeremiah's prophecy because only 47 years had elapsed from Nebuchadnezzar's destruction of Jerusalem to Cyrus's conquest of Babylon in 538 BCE. This, of course, in no way amounts to 70 years of desolation.[230] So the question must be asked: Did Cyrus's decree fulfill Jeremiah's prophecy?

Jeremiah's 70-year prophecy had not only built on Isaiah's prophecy about Cyrus (Isa 44:28–45:1–3, 13), it was also based on the consequences established in Israel's Testimonial Law. In the Book of Leviticus, the Creator established exile as the consequence for Israel's rebellion. He would allow the land to lie desolate and enjoy the Sabbaths that Israel failed to observe while she lived on his land.

> And I will make your cities waste, and *bring your sanctuaries to desolation,* and I will not smell the savor of your sweet odors. . . . Then shall the land enjoy her Sabbaths, as long as it lies desolate, and you be in your enemies' land; even

then shall the land rest, and enjoy her Sabbaths. As long as it lies desolate it shall rest; because it did not rest in your Sabbaths, when you dwelled upon it. (Lev 26:31, 34–35)

This was the prophecy on which Jeremiah had based his 70-year desolation (Jer 25:11–13; 29:10): the Promised Land would rest for one 7-Times (Lev 26:18–24).[231] Not only did both the Law and Jeremiah's prophecies account for the Temple's desolation, the Law also specified that the Temple and the Promised Land would rest for several "Sabbaths," which would have been at least 10 sabbatical Release Years. In chap. 14, we will see that Israel's Testimonial Law had defined the 70-year precedent on which Jeremiah based his prophecy. The sabbatical judgment against the sanctuary ended in 517 BCE (see Table 9.47).

Table 9.47. Jeremiah's 70-Year Sabbath

587	First Temple destroyed
538	Cyrus releases deportees/captives
537	7th month— foundation of Second Temple is laid during sabbatical Release Year
517	Jeremiah's 70 yrs. are completed (587–70 = 517)
516	Temple is completed in Adar (March), Darius' 6th yr. during a sabbatical Release Year
515	Second Temple is completed and dedicated at Sukkot/A new 7-Times begins

B. Laying the Second Temple's Foundation

Since Israel's annals end with Zedekiah's reign, it is tempting to consider Israel irrelevant once the nation had been deported from the Promised Land. It is during the Diaspora, however, that her history, the righteousness of her people, and their adherence to the nation's covenant matter the most.

Haggai's testimony reveals the short time frame that transpired between Cyrus's decree and the building of the Second Temple. In Darius's second year (Hag 1:1), the people commented that the 70-year desolation had not been fulfilled. "This people say, The time is not come, the time that YHWH's house should be built" (Hag 1:2). Despite this opposition, Haggai encouraged the Second Temple Remnant to begin the process of rebuilding the Temple.

Jeremiah's 70 years for the Temple's desolation (Jer 29:10) ended in 517 BCE, 4 years after Haggai called for Israel to rebuild the Temple. The Second Temple was completed the following year, in 516 (Ezra 6:15), during the sabbatical Release Year. This chronology perfectly harmonizes with Ptolemy's Canon for this era. YHWH had told Jeremiah that he would live long enough to see Israel's restoration to the land (Jer 16:1–4; 32:25; 43–44).

The books of Ezra, Nehemiah, Haggai, and Zechariah confirm this chronology. By the 7th month during the 1st year in which the Remnant had returned to the land, they built an altar on the Temple mount and observed Sukkot (Ezra 3:1–2). However, the foundation for the Second Temple had not yet been laid (Ezra 3:6). By the 2nd year, in the 2nd month (Ezra 3:8) the Remnant began to lay the Temple's foundation but did not finish it until Darius's 2nd year (Ezra 3:10; 5:16; Hag 2:18). This was a lapse of about 17 years.

At this time, there were many in Israel's congregation, especially priests and Levites, who had lived through the First Temple's destruction and witnessed this celebration.

> But many of the priests and Levites and chief of the fathers, who were ancient men, that had seen the first house, when the foundation of this house was laid before their eyes, wept with a loud voice; and many shouted aloud for joy: So that the people could not discern the noise of the shout of joy from the noise of the weeping of the people: for the people shouted with a loud shout, and the noise was heard afar off. (Ezra 3:12–13)

The laying of the Temple's foundation occurred before Cyrus's reign ended, somewhere between 537 and 530 BCE. According to Nehemiah's testimony, there were several notable people attending this ceremony: Jeremiah (Neh 10:2; 12:1, 12) and his royal scribe, Baruch (Neh 10:6), Daniel (10:6), Seraiah, who had been the high priest during Zedekiah's reign (2 Kgs 25:18–21), his son Ezra (Neh 12:1; Ezra 7:1–5) and grandson Yehoshua/Joshua (Neh 12:1), Mordecai (Ezra 2:1–2), along with Nehemiah. Ezra tells us specifically that many who had originally returned with him (Neh 12:1)—Zerubbabel, Yehoshua, Mordecai, and Nehemiah—were the very people whom Nebuchadnezzar had carried away to Babylon.

> Now these are the children of the province that went up out of the captivity, of those *which had been carried away*, whom Nebuchadnezzar the king of Babylon had carried away to Babylon, *and came again to Jerusalem and Judah, every one to his city. Which came with Zerubbabal*: Jeshua, *Nehemiah*, Seraiah, Reelaiah, *Mordecai*, Bilshan, Mispar, Bigvai, Rehum, Baanah. (Ezra 2:1–2)

Ezra and Nehemiah were both active during this initial return, and both are mentioned as returning with this Remnant under Zerubbabel and Yehoshua: "Now these are the priests and the Levites that went up with Zerubbabel the son of Shealtiel, and Jeshua: Seraiah, *Jeremiah, Ezra*" (Neh 12:1). Much like Othniel, Caleb, and Joshua, the lives of these older men can be used to reconstruct this murky era. It is highly unlikely that any of these events occurred later than 530 or 522 BCE. Jeremiah had prophesied as a young man during Josiah's 13 year, in 627 BCE, making the prophet at least 115 years old when the foundation was laid. Shortly thereafter, Jeremiah's sons are listed in his stead in the genealogical records (Neh 12:12) indicating that the prophet had died. This would also place Ezra and Nehemiah somewhere between 20 and 40 years of age in *c.* 530 BCE.

Ezra tells us that Judea's local enemies frustrated the building of the Second Temple all of Cyrus's days until the reign of Darius the Persian (Ezra 4:5), about 17 years if the Remnant had returned in 538 BCE. He also tells us that local chieftains thwarted attempts to construct the Temple during Cambyses's reign (Ezra 4:6–24), prior to Darius's accession (Ezra 4:24).

Under Haggai's and Zechariah's encouragement, the Remnant finally finished the Temple's foundation during Darius' 2nd year (Ezra 3:10; 5:16).

> Consider now from this day and upward, from the *four and twentieth day of the ninth month, even from the day that the foundation of YHWH's temple was laid*, consider it. (Hag 2:18)

The entire Second Temple was built 5 years later, in 516 BCE, being completed during the 11th month of the 6th year of Darius's reign.

> And this house was finished on the third day of the month Adar, which was in the sixth year of the reign of Darius the king. (Ezra 6:15)

Although many nobles were in Jerusalem for this dedication, it appears that Persia's kings recalled both Ezra and Nehemiah to Babylon and Susa. With the first Jubilee (50th year), Ezra returned to Jerusalem during Artaxerxes 7th year (Ezra 7:8) with another group from the Diaspora (Ezra 8). Nehemiah returned again during Artaxerxes's 20th year (Neh 2:1; 13:6). Each time they returned, both men found the Remnant trespassing and breaking the covenant worse than before (Nehemiah 5–6, 13; Ezra 9–10). As we will see, the Second Temple Remnant's rebellion against YHWH's covenant had dire consequences for their children when the 350 years of the Temple's 7-Times expired (see Table 9.48).

Table 9.48. Chronology of Second Temple Events

Chronology	Text	Events
Cyrus' decree for restoration	Nehemiah 7	The genealogy of those who returned with Zerubbabel. Nehemiah is listed among those who initially returned to Judah with Zerubbabel at Cyrus's order—Ezra 2:2; 2:63; Neh 7:65; 10:1
	Neh 7:7–ch. 10; Ezra 3	Remnant recovenant at laying of Second Temple's foundation
	Ezra 3:10–12; 5:15	Foundation work begun
Cambyses	Ezra 4	Foundation work suspended
Darius's 2nd yr.	Hag 2:18	Foundation work restarted
Darius's 6th yr.	Ezra 6:15	Temple construction completed
		Ezra and Nehemiah recalled to Babylon
Artaxerxes's 7th yr.	Ezra 8–11	Artaxerxes's 7th yr. = 1st Jubilee
		Ezra's arrival and the Remnant's recovenanting
	Nehemia 12	Genealogies of those who returned with Ezra
	Neh 13:1–4	Ezra and Nehemiah's cleansing. Nehemiah called back to Susa
Artaxerxes's 20th yr.	Neh 1–7	Nehemiah rebuilds Jerusalem's walls; installed as Jerusalem's governor
Artaxerxes's 32nd yr.	Neh 13:5–31	Nehemiah writes his memoirs

C. Aaron's Lineage

The high priests' lineage during this era also provides some chronological markers. Ye-hoshua worked with Zerubbabal to rebuild the Temple. Soon after this, his son Joiakim succeeded in his stead. Neh 12:1–25 clarifies that the Levitical genealogy of Joiakim was contemporary with both Ezra and Nehemiah.

These were in the days of Joiakim the son of Jeshua (Heb. *Yehoshua*), the son of Jozadak, and in the days of Nehemiah the governor, and of Ezra the priest, the scribe. (Neh 12:26)

Evidently, Yehoshua (Seraiah's grandson) did not live very long, and in a short time period his son Joiakim had succeeded him as high priest. However, Nehemiah attests that he and Ezra were still contemporaries at this time. Both men also draw attention to Eliashib, the most notorious and wicked high priest of this era, who collaborated with the enemy, Samarian governor Sanballat, while siding against his own people. Although Eliashib collected taxes and tithes from the people, he supplied Sanballat's coffers instead of the Temple's. Similar to Jeroboam I, centuries before, Eliashib left the priests without income or sustenance. Ezra and Nehemiah tried at least once or twice (if not more) to remedy this situation, but to no avail. Joiada had allowed Jonathan (Eliashib's grandson) to marry Sanballat's daughter, and the alliance was firm.

If this were not enough, the Jewish elders and leaders during this era ignored the Sabbath and oppressed the people by exacting usury, which led to the unlawful confiscation of tribal inheritances (Neh 5:11; Lev 25:23). The Second Temple's first 7 Times ended in 445 BCE (515−70=445), when Nehemiah returned to Jerusalem during Artaxerxes 20th year (see Table 9.49) Within this short time period, the Remnant had rebelled against every principle established in YHWH's constitutional covenant of freedom. When our discussion turns to prophecy, we will see that the implications of this era are more significant than previously conceived.

XII. IS 1548 TOO EARLY?

Thus far, our investigation of Israel's chronology has presented some interesting implications. The exodus occurred over one hundred years earlier than previously believed. The Conquest of Canaan is so early that no scholar has yet to seriously investigate the evidence for this era. The Judges Era likewise demonstrates that Israel's history in the Promised Land occurred at a very early date. I knew that chronology in itself is just a theory. I wondered if tangible archaeological or written evidence exists to support Scripture's internal chronologies? Could this evidence bring the 1548 BCE exodus date out of the realm of theories to demonstrate it really happened? The evidence is quite surprising.

Table 9.49. Second Temple Era Levitical Chronology

Estimated Dates	Text	High Priest Line	Chronology
		Seraiah	High priest under King Zedekiah
	Ezra 3:2, 8; 5:2; 12:26	Jehozadak	Born during captivity
c. 538–513	Ezra 3:2, 3:8; Neh 12:1, 7; 12:10; Hag 1:1, 14; 2:2–4	Yehoshua	High priest at Remnant's return and recovenanting with YHWH
c. 513–472	Neh 12:10, 12, 26	Joiakim	Contemporary with Ezra and Nehemiah
	Neh 12:22		Levites recorded until Darius's reign
			Ezra and Nehemiah recalled to Persia
c. 472–462	Neh 3:1, 20	Eliashib (High Priest)	Nehemiah rebuilds Jerusalem's walls/ Eliashib is high priest
	Neh 13:6–9		Eliashib confederates with Sanballat/ collects taxes for Sanballat
	Neh 13:10–13		Eliashib does not support Levites
	Ezra 7:7		Ezra arrives for the Jubilee in Artaxerxes 7th yr.
	Neh 13:23–27		Nehemiah learns that the Levites and people have again intermarried with pagan peoples
c. 462–450	Neh 12:11	Joiada	son marries Sanballat's daughter
c. 460–440	Neh 13:28	Jonathan (not high priest)	Marries Sanballat's daughter
	Ezra 10:6		Ezra learns of national and Levitical intermarriage
	Ezra 10:6		Collects Sanballat's taxes/does not support Levites
	Neh 13:28		Nehemiah casts Jonathan out of the Temple/Jonathan becomes ineligible for priesthood c. Artaxerxes 7th yr.
	Neh 13:30		Nehemiah cleanses priesthood
	Neh 13:15–22		Weekly Sabbath disregarded
	Neh 13:11–14		Nehemiah cleanses Temple, reinstates Levites, collects tithes to support them
	Neh 5:17–18		Nehemiah does without normal provisions for the sake of the people
c. 440		Jaddua	N/A

10

Critical Issues in Israel's History: Egypt to Conquest

Without a doubt, archaeology presents the most puzzling evidence for Israel's exodus and the early Conquest of Canaan. This topic has prompted many heated academic debates over the years that have done little to bring any scholarly consensus to the data.[1] For the most part, interpretation of archaeological finds remains strongly divided over questions of Scripture's historicity.[2]

Three dates are generally accepted for the exodus. A **low or late chronology** dates the exodus during Ramesses II's reign (*c.* 1294 or 1279 BCE).[3] A **high or early chronology** dates the exodus about 250 years earlier, between 1440 and 1470 BCE;[4] and the third, least-accepted date is based mainly on Josephus's (*Against Apion* I.73, 93, 227) equates Israel with the **Hyksos**, Asiatics who fled Egypt shortly before Egypt's New Kingdom Era (c. 1570–1530).[5] The problem with all three dates is that there is historical and archaeological evidence both supporting *and contradicting* them. The date embraced by most traditional biblical scholars (Albright, Courville, Wright, Kitchen, Dever) for the exodus is 1200–1300 BCE, during the reign of Ramesses II.[6]

We know Egyptian history today from four primary sources.[7] The first is Manetho, an Egyptian priest who, according to Plutarch (*De Osiride* 28), served as an adviser to Ptolemy I (300 BCE). Josephus (*c.* 50 CE) tells us that Manetho (*Against Apion* 1.73) committed Egypt's history to writing based on "sacred books" available in the priesthood's archives. Although none of Manetho's original works survives, other ancient historians' quotations from them are viable sources. The second group of sources is various inscriptions—some left by pharaohs and others by noblemen. The Palmero Stone, which records the last predynastic pharaohs before 3150 BCE and later kings through Neferirkare in the mid-5th Dynasty[8] along with various funerary biographies fall in this category.[9] A third group of sources is three king lists commissioned by various pharaohs. The *Royal King List of Karnak* lists Egypt's first kings down to Thutmoses III (1504–1450 BCE), and the *Royal List of Abydos* (still sitting on the walls of the Hall of Ancestors in the Temple of Seti I, 1291–1278 BCE) records Egypt's ancient kings.[10] The *Royal Canon of Turin* is another papyrus listing over 300 kings, compiled by Ramessid scribes.[11] It is the only record seen to rival Manetho's accounts, but unfortunately the papyrus is badly damaged and incomplete.[12] The fourth method for dating Egyptian history uses the Egyptian calendar, from which many inscriptions are dated. Scholars have been able to reconstruct this calendar and date events with a small margin of error.[13]

I. TRADITIONAL EXODUSES

A. *Evidence for a Low/Late Date*

Scripture. A low date for the exodus receives greater support from historical records and lesser support from Scripture and archaeological data. The Scriptural support that does exist for the low date comes from the exodus account, which documents that Israel departed from the city of Pi-Ramses (Exod 1:11; 12:37; Num 33:3, 5). Ramesses I ruled for two years around 1295 BCE and is not viewed as a very likely candidate for the pharaoh who was in power during the exodus.[14] Ramesses II, ruled in 1279 (or 1294) BCE and engaged in extensive building projects through slave labor; which is why he is seen as a more likely candidate for the exodus's pharaoh (see Illustration 10.1).[15]

History. Three sources support a low date. The first is a Hittite-Egyptian treaty inscribed on Egypt's Karnak temple walls and the Rameseum, which pledges Hittite support should Ramesses' "own subjects commit another crime against him."[16] The former "crime" could be viewed as the Israelite slaves' departure from Egypt during Ramesses' reign. Second, a stele

Illustration 10.1. Statute of Ramesses II *c.* 1250 BCE.

from Beth-shan records Ramesses' Transjordan campaign and another inscription from the Karnak temple mentions Ramesses' campaign in Moab.[17] According to Scripture, Edom confronted Israel with "much people and a strong hand" when Israel sought to pass through Edomite territories (Num 20:20). This would fit well in Ramesses II's campaigns into Edom and Moab, which date to about the same time and could be viewed as an Egyptian-Edomite coalition (of possibly conscripted) forces.

Third is an inscription commissioned by Merneptah (who succeeded Ramesses II) that mentions Israel by name, recounting Israel's sound defeat in battle. The method used to refer to Israel in the stele may also support a low date.[18] The Merneptah Stele distinguishes between a settled people and nomads by using a hieroglyphic determinative for a foreign country. Since Israel is not marked as a foreign country, many scholars interpret this evidence for Israel's entry into Canaan a short time earlier, before the nation had time to settle the land and become recognized as an official country by Egypt.[19] Another factor often considered in the low-date discussion is the Hyksos' takeover of northern Egypt. The word *Hyksos* comes from a Greek form of Egyptian and means 'rulers of foreign lands,' an epithet originally used to designate the heads of Canaanite families and tribes in Asia.[20] Scholars consider the Hyksos' incursion to be a likely time for Joseph to have risen to power.[21]

Archaeology—Egypt. Archaeological evidence for the low date comes from identifying Qantir, Ramesses II's Delta residence, as the Pi-Ramses of Exod 1:11.[22] This site was destroyed in earlier periods but rebuilt during the 19th Dynasty.[23] Other archaeological evidence comes from Ramesses II's wine-jar seals in the Ramesseum at Thebes. The workers are termed *Habiru* ('Hebrew'?) and a sharp reduction in seals occurs at this point in the archaeological record that has been connected to a significant loss in labor, which some scholars see as evidence for the exodus.[24]

B. Objections to a Low/Late Date

Scripture. The greatest obstacle to a low date for the exodus comes from Scripture. 1 Kgs 6:1 and Judg 11:26 attest that Israel had been in the Promised Land much longer than a 1200–1300 BCE Conquest allows (see chap. 9.I-IV., pp. 345–65).

Scholars who hang their shingle on the thirteenth century exodus do so because of a reference to Ramesses (Exod 1:11; 12:27; Num 33:3). They see the "new pharaoh" as a reference to the 19th Dynasty. This dating system, however, does not allow for the 80 years of Moses' life, since this transition from the 18th Dynasty to the reign of Ramssess II only lasted about 40 years.[25] This date dismisses not only 1 Kgs 6:1 but also Jephthah's statement that Israel had possessed Jordan for over 300 years.[26] Further compromised is the Scriptural account, leaving only a few years from Joshua's destruction of Hazor (Josh 11:11) to Deborah and Barak's final assault (Judg 4:2), thus collapsing the entire Judges Era to a mere 170 years.[27] The thirteenth-century date dismisses Scripture's statement that 18 or 19 generations had passed between Joshua and the later Judges Era.[28] The low dating only allows for 40–60 years between the time when Israel conquered the land and the time when the Philistines dominated Israel.[29] The problem with this is that, according to Scripture, Israel had totally decimated Hazor. The city revived to dominate Israel, then be destroyed by Israel again, well before a new wave of Sea People arrived on the scene, a point that we will investigate in chap. 11.

Scripture's use of "Ramesses" is another factor compromising the low dating. Gen 47:11 uses the place-name "the land of Ramses" to refer to the geographical location where Jacob and his family settled. In no way could Ramesses be construed to have reigned during or before Jacob's life. Therefore, either Scripture's account of Jacob is invalid, or another valid explanation exists.

One valid solution is to identify "Ramesses" with a city in Egypt that was named after the pharaoh instead of identifying a pharaoh named Ramesses as the pharaoh of the exodus. This solution can also be supported by the Levite's archival practices.[30] Manuscripts only lasted a few hundred years or less, if they were extensively used.[31] During the process of copying manuscripts onto new papyri, scribes often corrected or updated archaic or obsolete language.[32] This practice is probably best attested in Sam 9:9, where a later scribe felt compelled to clarify that in earlier times a *seer* was a prophet. Josh 15:15 and Judg 1:23 are other examples where the copier needed to update names of cities that had been abandoned since the Conquest Era.

For the scribe copying Israel's history onto new papyri around 1250 BCE, using the original place-names of the cities Israel had migrated from during the exodus posed one serious dilemma: the cities had been destroyed and lay buried underneath a new city—the city of Ramses.[33] If this theory is correct, then "the city of Ramses" and the "land of Ramses" denote the place where the Israelites worked and which they left. They did not depart during Ramesses' reign, since Ramesses built his city over Hyksos remains—a people that also employed slave labor (see below). Therefore, evidence for the exodus must be sought beneath the rubble of the more-recent city named Pi-Ramses.

History. It used to be thought that the historical data would be the most difficult to dispute for a low exodus date,[34] although parallels between Ramesses' campaigns and Israel's confrontation with Edom and Moab may be coincidental. Ramesses' Transjordan campaigns were an offensive move to pacify his eastern flank prior to concluding his treaty with the Hittites.[35] Ramesses may never have encountered Israel, since the Hittites were his primary objective. Scripture does not mention Egyptian forces in its accounts of Moab and Edom, while Egyptian reliefs in turn do not mention an Israel.[36] Similar objections to the low/more recent date arise when one assigns Joseph to the Hyksos dynasty—the strongest objection being the Hyksos' departure from ancient Egyptian customs and theology. Scripture's accounts of Joseph more accurately reflect a Middle Kingdom (12th Dynasty) culture than the culture of the Hyksos (Canaanite) occupation,[37] which again supports a much earlier date for Jacob's family's migration to Egypt and exodus from it.

Theology. An important argument against the low (more-recent) date is theological. When Israel entered Canaan, Joshua stated that Israel's God and his theology should not be confused with Egyptian theology (Joshua 24). As evidenced in chap. 2 (above), Egypt adhered to doctrines prevalent throughout the ancient Near East until a heretical pharaoh named Akhenaten assumed the throne, revolutionizing Egypt's religious world by introducing a Trinitarian monotheism into Egypt's religious culture around 1360 BCE (less than

100 years before Ramesses).[38] This poses a serious problem for the "originality" of Israel's religion. It could be argued that Israel's theology simply continued Akhenaten's monotheistic movement. The question remains: did anything separate Israel's religion from that of Egypt as Israel's prophets claim?[39]

C. Evidence for the Traditional High/Early Chronology

Scripture. Scholars who take Scripture as a valid historical record (Wood, Bimson, Kitchen, Younger) use 1 Kgs 6:1 to date the exodus. Many scholars assign Solomon's 4th regnal year to about 966 BCE, then add 480 years to bring the date of the exodus back to 1446 BCE (see chap. 9.I-III).[40] As we have seen, this period covers the Judges Era.

History. Historical support for the traditional, high date, 1446 BCE, is supported by the death of Thutmoses III, which would have occurred shortly after Israel's Passover[41]—an event that would parallel Scripture's account that Pharaoh died in the Red Sea (Exodus 14). X-rays of his mummy, however, reveal that he did not drown, so this scenario is not plausible.[42] Some scholars consider Thutmoses's store cities in Memphis to be Pithom and Pi-Ramses,[43] while other scholars consider Scripture's reference to Ramessid cities to be an editorial gloss that updated an earlier record.[44] The Syrian-Palestinian campaigns of Thutmoses III and his co-regent son, Amenhotep II, are considered to be a king's retribution for the evil that befell Egypt at the exodus.[45]

D. Objections to the Traditional High/Early Date

Scripture. In chap. 9, we saw that there were five different proofs for a 1548 BCE exodus date. However, the high chronology date evidenced by Scripture is not the high date that modern scholars traditionally have embraced. Modern scholars only account for 1 Kgs 6:1,[46] dating Solomon's 4th regnal year to about 966 BCE, then add 480 years to bring this date back to 1446 BCE.[47] In the previous chapter, we saw that the scribe's colophon was based solely on the Book of Judges' chronology, which spanned 410 years for the Judges Era and another 70 years for the Monarchy. Thus modern scholarship ignores the manner in which early Israel viewed her exodus by: (1) dismissing the 40 years in the wilderness, (2) the early years of Joshua's administration, and (3) the generation of the "elders who outlived him" (Josh 24:31; Judg 2:7) and were in authority during the early pioneering era. As we have seen, all three of these eras effect studies of Israel's early chronology.

Archaeology and Epigraphic Evidence. Most of the objections to the high chronology have been cited in the points previously listed. One formidable objection is the historical and archaeological evidence demonstrating Egypt's domination of Palestine throughout the post-Exodus Era from the reign of Thutmoses I to Ramesses II (1550–1150 BCE).[48] Many scholars see Egypt's strong control and its Palestinian campaigns as conflicting with Scripture's record, since Scripture does not attest to an Egyptian military presence during or after Israel's Canaan Conquest.[49]

A second compelling argument against a fifteenth century exodus is simply that there is no epigraphic evidence from Egypt to indicate that any plagues took place or that a large population fled Egypt.[50] Archaeology has not uncovered any mass graves to indicate that an epidemic involving the death of the firstborn ever took place. The third argument against dating the exodus to 1446 is the fact that the archaeological evidence does not reveal any of the destruction attested in Joshua's accounts of the early Conquest. Nor is there evidence that a population shift occurred in which a new people entered Canaan during this Era.

Scholars are quite justified in pointing out the lack of both historiographic and archaeological evidence for Israel's exodus during the traditional low or high dating systems (18th through 20th Egyptian dynasties).[51] As one Egyptologist adeptly puts it:

> The only question that *really* matters is whether any (non-biblical) textual or archaeological materials indicate a major outflow of Asiatics from Egypt to Canaan at any point in the 19th or even early 20th Dynasty. And so far the answer to that question is no.[52]

Noted archaeologist Israel Finkelstein likewise observes:

> The attempts to locate the events in the thirteenth century BCE, in the time of Pharaoh Ramesses II, have faced insurmountable difficulties. There is no mention of such an event in any New Kingdom Egyptian source, and there is no trace of the early Hebrews in Egypt. The northern coast of Sinai was protected by formidable Egyptian forts that could have easily prevented an escaping people from crossing the dessert.[53]

As we will see, there is plenty of evidence to support dating the exodus at the exact time when Scripture's chronology indicates that it occurred: in the sixteenth century.

II. THE HISTORICAL EXODUS

A. *The Revolution: Historical Context*

As we have seen, the greatest Scriptural support for both high dates is 1 Kgs 6:1, which documents that the 1st year of Solomon's reign was 480 years after the exodus event (see chap. 9.I-III). Since this text includes the month Ziv (the 2nd month) to date Solomon's 4th year, it seems that this entry for Solomon is accurately based on the original record. As we saw in the previous chapter, this 480-year date included the 410-year Judges Era. Another text that supports a high date is Judg 11:15–26, where Jephthah, one of Israel's later judges, states that Israel had controlled the Amorites' former territories for 300 years. If we place Solomon's 4th year in 991 BCE (chap. 9.III.) with the exodus occurring 568 years before, the exodus would date to *c.* 1548 BCE. In order to appreciate Scripture's account of the exodus, it is necessary to understand a little about Egypt's ancient history in general. To do this, we must step back in time to see how the Egyptians viewed their nation.

From the beginning of time, the Egyptians saw their country as two lands: Lower Egypt in the northern Delta region and Upper Egypt in the southern desert along the Nile, touching the borders of the ancient Kingdom of Kush (biblical Cush).[54] Early in the nation's history, these two lands were united in one kingdom for about 1,000 years.[55] Except for an interlude during the First Intermediate Period, this union lasted until about a century before Moses' birth (*c.* 1640 or 1670 BCE), when western immigrants fractured Egypt into two kingdoms.[56]

For two centuries, people from all over the world migrated to Egypt in search of the employment and the prosperity that Egypt had to offer.[57] Other people had been brought as captives during previous Egyptian campaigns into the Levant.[58] Many westerners, like Jacob's family (Gen 45:6–11), had migrated to avoid famines that had plagued western Asia.[59] The Egyptians called these people *Aamu*[60] or *western Asiatics*. Later Greek writers termed the rulers of these Asiatics *Hyksos*, equating the Aamu with rulers of foreign lands.[61] Archaeology as well as texts from earlier dynasties link the Asiatics with Canaanites.[62] Personal names also leave open the possibility of an Assyrian connection.[63] Scripture's chronology (see Table 9.22. on pg. 384–85) establishes that the Israelites were in Egypt by 1976 during what is known in Egyptian chronology as the Middle Kingdom (see Illustration 10.2).

Illustration 10.2.   Delegation of Aamu traveling to Egypt to sell eye paint.

During the Middle Kingdom (*c.* 1870 BCE), Senusret (alt. Senwosret) III revolutionized Egypt's entire system of government by annulling the power of Egypt's elite nobility. He replaced it with a centralized form of government.[64] Senusret divided the land into three administrative districts, each being administered by a counsel of senior staff who reported to a vizier.[65] Senusret's primary capital was Memphis in the north (Lower Egypt) and Thebes, a secondary capital, which governed six nomes (large counties) in the south (Upper Egypt).[66] A later king in the same dynasty eventually moved the southern Theban capital a few miles southwest of Memphis to the Faiyum region at Itjtawy, a site that has yet to be discovered.[67]

The Asiatics' migration into the Delta was widely accepted by the Egyptians,[68] probably in the same manner as Hispanic and Arab immigration into the United States is accepted today. These immigrants were able to live together with the native Egyptians without difficulty.[69] Gradually, the Asiatics (Canaanites) gained political positions in the empire.[70] Their rise to power was no doubt aided by the wealth from trading with their homelands.[71] The Asiatic's rise to power is further attested by the many foreign or Asiatic names of officials during this era.[72]

Egypt's government bureaucracy grew rapidly during this period as power was transferred from a strong centralized monarch to local rulers.[73] At some point, those living in the Delta began to question traditional Egyptian policies. "Officials" in the 13th Dynasty

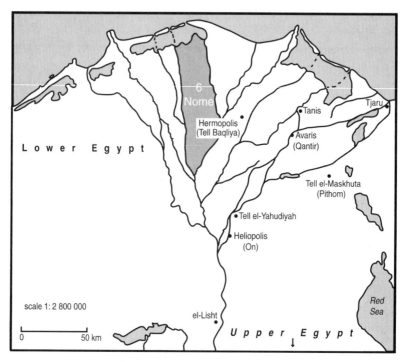

Map 10.1. Lower Egypt with 6th Nome

"with purely local authority abrogated to themselves royal epithets on their seals at a time and place where normally rigid protocols were no longer enforceable."[74] This apparently peaceful shift in authority led to a rival, immigrant (14th Dynasty) power ruling from the central western Delta (6th Egyptian nome, which had succeeded) sometime between 1800 and 1730 BCE.[75]

This left Egypt's legitimate, 13th Dynasty pharaohs controlling all of Egypt except the 6th nome (see Map 10.1).[76] Around 1720 BCE, however, the city of Avaris (which later became Pi-Ramses) likewise seceded.[77] Avaris was established in the 12th Dynasty as a defensive settlement to protect the eastern boundary, and archaeologists have discovered a 13th-Dynasty palace there.[78] During the Hyksos' occupation, the city covered an area of almost four square miles, which was twice as large as the later Ramessid city.[79] It is currently unknown to what extent the legitimate 13th Dynasty pharaohs retained control in the region at this time. Bubastis appears eventually to have become the 13th Dynasty's northern border.[80] We do know the Egyptians held onto Itjawy, slightly south of Memphis, before it finally fell into the hands of the Asiatic usurpers after 1674 BCE.[81]

Some northern regions that allied with the Hyksos in the northeastern Delta simply transferred allegiance from one authority (13th Dynasty) to another (15th Dynasty)[82]—perhaps similar to the recent U.S./UN transfer of authority in Iraq—in c.1630 or 1650 BCE, depending on one's system of dating.

After attaining a political majority in the northern Delta, the Hyksos formed an alliance with the Nubians (southern Kingdom of Kush)[83] and the dissident noble families whom Senusret had deposed a couple of centuries before.

> There was active cooperation between the Asiatics and the Egyptians within Egypt itself in the Amorite *coup d'état*. Disloyalty by important noble families may be understood in light of strong centralization of the administration by the pharaohs of the late Twelfth Dynasty. In the period of dynastic weakness, these families reasserted themselves. With the breakup of the land into the three departments of the previous Middle Kingdom administration, an Egyptian, Nehesy, had control of the North, probably with Asiatic cooperation. It was merely a step for Amorite princes themselves to take over the control of Lower Egypt and, in time, the whole of Egypt.[84]

The Hyksos (Asiatics) then extended their control over the entire Egyptian realm, placing all travelers along the Nile under tribute.[85] They established their capital at Memphis,[86] although Avaris remained their primary residence.

Egypt's weakened legitimate pharaohs retreated south to Thebes, and much of their history has been lost.[87] They appear to have been relegated to simple local authority.[88] Egypt's historians, such as Manetho, considered this to be the end of the 13th Dynasty. The Hyksos on the other hand enjoyed a century of economic prosperity from farming arable lands and from traditional Egyptian trade routes that brought wealth from Palestine, Nubia, and possibly Crete.[89] Unlike other invaders, the Hyksos assimilated with the Egyptian culture, intermarried with Egyptians, and took on Egyptian names for themselves.[90] Basically, the Asiatics became "Egyptians" culturally.[91] Then around 1685, the Hyksos appear to have pursued a more hostile and aggressive policy toward Egypt's legitimate (Theban) pharaohs, eventually becoming rulers over the land held by Egypt's traditional monarchs.

Meanwhile, the Theban kings, now considered the 17th Dynasty, grew tired of their diminished power and the provocation of an arrogant Hyksos king.[92] Although we do not know when the wars between the Theban and Hyksos dynasties took place, evidence points to these two powers vying for Egypt for several decades.[93] The mummy of Theban Pharaoh Seqenenre Tao II reveals that he died due to a war-time trauma (see Illustration 10.3).[94]

Seqenenre Tao II had ruled Upper Egypt (Thebes) since at least 1574,[95] and his goal, it appears, had been to rid the nation of the plague of Hyksos (foreign) rulers.

Seqenenre Tao was succeeded by his son, Kamose. According to one inscription, Kamose desired to chase all the "Asiatics" out of Egypt; but his counselors, at ease with their cattle pasturing in the Delta

Illustration 10.3. Badly damaged mummified skull of Seqenere (Tao II) *c.* 1580 BCE.

and tended by the Asiatics did not wish to upset the status quo.[96] Kamose felt sure the entire land would end up "weeping" if the Asiatics were allowed to stay, so he went against the wishes of his counselors and began a campaign to chase the Hyksos out of Egypt.[97] After his third year, he sacked the Hyksos capital at Avaris, plundering the city's vast wealth.[98] Unfortunately, Kamose did not live long enough to complete the expulsion, but his brother Ahmose completed the task of driving the Hyksos out of Egypt, back into Palestine.[99]

Although we know these accounts from inscriptions left by Kamose and one of his generals,[100] the much-respected second century (BCE) Egyptian priest Manetho also wrote on this period.

Note on My Approach to the Exodus and Conquest

In his assessment of the archaeological evidence for the Exodus and Conquest, archaeologist William Dever criticizes, not only the historicity of the exodus account, but also the approach taken by conservative scholars.[101] In particular, he singles out the objective approach taken by Egyptologist James Hoffmeier in his book *Israel in Egypt*. He criticizes Hoffmeier's analysis, pointing out that "Hoffmeier only makes a case that the exodus (or 'an exodus') *could* have happened, according the Egyptian evidence, not that it *did*."[102]

Most scholars decry less detached approaches that would lead scholars to personally endorse an exodus (while at the same time scorning anyone who did). However, this is exactly Dever's point of contention. Dever criticizes the detached approach, which simply assesses the evidence without actually endorsing that the exodus occurred. Therefore, if the evidence justifies Israel's historical exodus from Egypt, I will weigh the evidence objectively and critically. I will also draw clear, definitive conclusions when the evidence permits.

B. *Egyptian and Israelite perspectives*

1. Manetho's Testimony

Manetho was a second-century Egyptian priest who was fluent in the Greek language. He took it upon himself to preserve Egypt's history by bringing ancient records up to date. Although his original works are lost to us today, fragments of his work remain in quotation by other ancient authors. The Jewish historian Josephus (*Against Apion* 1.73) claims to quote directly from Manetho's ancient book *Aegyptiaca* when he writes:

> By main force they (i.e., the Hyksos) easily seized it (i.e., Egypt) without striking a blow; and having overpowered the rulers of the land, they then burned our cities ruthlessly, razed to the ground the temples of the gods. . . . Finally, they appointed as king one of their number whose name was Salitis. He had his seat at Memphis, levying tribute from Upper and Lower Egypt, and always leaving garrisons behind in the most advantageous positions.[103]

Although the Hyksos' capital was Memphis, their primary city was Avaris, modern Tell el-Dab'a.[104] As we will see, this site yields some very interesting artifacts. Manetho attested to the Hyksos' oppression of his ancestors, the local Egyptian population, once these immigrants had gained the upper hand.

Tutimaeus. In his reign, for what cause I know not, a blast of God smote us; and unexpectedly, from the regions of the East, invaders of obscure race marched in confidence of victory against our land. By main force they easily overpowered the rulers of the land, they then burned our cities ruthlessly, razed to the ground the temples of the gods, and *treated all the natives* with a cruel hostility, **massacring some and leading into slavery the wives and children of others.** Finally, they appointed as king one of their number whose name was *Salitis.* He had his seat at Memphis, levying tribute from Upper and Lower Egypt, and leaving garrisons behind in the most advantageous positions. Above all, he fortified the district to the east, foreseeing that the Assyrians, as they grew stronger, would one day covet and attack his kingdom.

In the Saite [Sethroite] nome he found a city very favorably situated on the east of the Bubastite branch of the Nile, and called Auaris (Avaris) after an ancient religious tradition. This place he rebuilt and fortified with massive walls, planting there a garrison of as many as 240,000 heavy-armed men to guard his frontier. Here he would come in summertime, partly to serve out rations and pay his troops, partly to train them carefully in maneuvers and so strike terror into foreign tribes. (*Aegyptiaca*, frag. 42, 1.75–79.2)[105]

Although Manetho has been maligned by scholars over the years,[106] much of his testimony has been vindicated by inscriptions discovered during archaeological excavations.[107] In the late nineteenth century, for instance, archaeologists discovered hieroglyphic steles mentioning a king Dudu-mose who is identified with Manetho's Greek Tutimaeus.[108] Egyptologist Donald Redford considers it unlikely that two Dude-moses (Tutimaeuses) were involved.[109] Manetho's assertion that the Hyksos employed slave labor may very well be confirmed by the extensive buildings and fortifications archeologists have uncovered in and surrounding Avaris.[110] Both archaeological and epigraphic evidence demonstrates that the Hyksos continued the pharaonic building tradition.[111] Tell el-Yahudiyah in particular raises questions. The site boasts a very large complex with sloping outer walls, yet very tall, impenetrable inside walls some 80 feet thick.[112] Some archaeologists identify this structure as a Hyksos "work camp."[113]

Another significant account is by Josephus, who again quotes Manetho. Josephus writes that Manetho had associated the Hyksos with the Israelites.

Our ancestors, tens of thousands of them, had come into Egypt and conquered the inhabitants. He (Manetho) then agreed that they had later gone into exile, occupied the land now called Judea, founded Jerusalem, and built the temple. (*Against Apion* 1. 228).[114]

From the Egyptian perspective,[115] Israel had come to Egypt from the east. Though they were Hebrews, the Egyptians would have considered them *Aamu* (Asiatics/Canaanites). Many Middle Kingdom texts use the Egyptian term *Hyksos* to designate a foreign ruling population from Syria–Palestine.[116] Though Israel should not be associated with the Hyksos who ruled over Egypt or the final Hyksos expulsion (see below), from the Theban perspective, the people of Israel were indeed Asiatics who entered the land of Egypt. Israel did leave Egypt and migrate to Canaan, a land that eventually became known as Judea. It is also true that Israel eventually conquered Jerusalem and erected a Temple there. Though Manetho appears to telescope these events and equate the Israelites with the Hyksos, which is not wholly accurate, his assertion that the Israelites were Asiatics who fled to Canaan is an accurate *Egyptian view* of Israel's history.[117]

2. Not Your Typical Egyptian Dynasty

Scripture opens the exodus account by recognizing a dynastic shift in Egypt.[118] In a land where pharaohs were not always succeeded by their children, dynastic transitions were quite common.[119] Unlike modern monarchies that are reckoned genealogically by a ruling "house" (e.g., England's Tudors or Windsors), Egypt recognized its dynasties based on the location of the dynasty's capital or by the rise of a competing dynasty.[120] This new dynasty that Scripture acknowledges, however, did not rise as other Egyptian monarchies.

> Now there arose up *a new king* over Egypt, *which knew not Joseph*. (Exod 1:8)

Joseph had served under the earlier, traditional *Egyptian* 12th Dynasty. The Hyksos' rise to power and a Hyksos pharaoh could very well explain the "king that knew not Joseph." This statement would have been unthinkable in traditional Egypt, which took pride in its own knowledge and understanding of the past.[121] Even during dynastic shifts, mortuary temples, steles, and other pieces of epigraphic evidence left by predecessors were rarely effaced.[122] In fact, most monarchs (even Ramesses) prided themselves on both maintaining and restoring their predecessor's memory.[123] Kings from the 18th and 19th Dynasties (in which scholars are apt to place a thirteenth or fifteenth-century exodus) were especially concerned with restoring ancient tombs and were thus very well acquainted with their historical past.

Well-respected commentator Albert Barnes remarks,

> The expressions in this verse are special and emphatic. "A new king" is a phrase not found elsewhere. It is understood by most commentators to imply that he did not succeed his predecessor in the natural order of descent and inheritance. He "arose up over Egypt," occupying the land, as it would seem, on different terms from the king whose place he took, either by usurpation or conquest. The fact that he knew not Joseph implies a complete separation from the traditions of Lower Egypt. At present the generality of Egyptian scholars identify this Pharaoh with Ramesses II, but all the conditions of the narrative are fulfilled in the person of Amosis I (Ahmose), the head of the 18th Dynasty. He was the descendant of the old Theban sovereigns, but his family was tributary to the Dynasty of the Shepherds, the Hyksos of Manetho, then ruling in the North of Egypt. Amosis married an Ethiopian princess, and in the third year of his reign captured Avaris. . . . the capital of the Hyksos, and completed the expulsion of that race.[124]

How could a king not know Joseph? The most likely reason is if he and his culture were generally unfamiliar with Egyptian history itself—a situation that would fit the Hyksos' situation quite well. The Hyksos' ignorance of Egypt is evidenced by their general lack of understanding of the written Egyptian language.[125] Hyksos royal seals reveal their clumsiness with Egyptian hieroglyphics since they often misinterpreted traditional pharaonic symbols for kingship.[126] If the Hyksos had this much trouble with the Egyptian language, it is highly improbable that they would have known anything about Joseph (a lesser vizier) or his family, who had migrated to Egypt several centuries before the Hyksos's rise to power.

Biblical commentator Spiros Zodhiates likewise observes,

> The expression "arose over Egypt" could better be translated "arose against Egypt." This probably refers to the invasion of the Hyksos, a people related to the Hebrews, who conquered Egypt. The Hyksos were never numerous, so the growing nation of Israel posed a threat to them (Exod 1:9). This threat ultimately led the Hyksos rulers to enslave the Jews.[127]

Not only did the Hyksos struggle with the Egyptian language (at least the written transmission of it), archaeological evidence strongly suggests that the Hyksos had no love for Egyptian history in general because their kings left very little evidence of monumental or epigraphic activity.[128] It is assumed that they desecrated the inscriptions of mortuary cults of earlier and contemporary dynasties.[129]

Scripture further endorses a non-Egyptian source of Israel's oppression. Though native Egyptians carried out the orders, the ultimate power that lay behind the orders was Asiatic. Citing Israel's sojourn in Egypt, the prophet Isaiah states that Israel was oppressed by the Assyrians, not the Egyptians.

> For thus says the Lord YHWH, My people *went down aforetime* into Egypt to sojourn there; *and the Assyrian oppressed them without cause.* (Isa 52:4)

Isaiah does not say that Israel went down to Egypt and the Egyptian or Libyan oppressed them (Egypt's pharaohs originated from both countries). "Assyrian" was perhaps the only cognate Hebrew term that Isaiah could use to denote Egypt's *Aamu* or Asiatic. If we understand the pharaoh of the exodus to have had ties with Assyria, the situation would match perfectly the scenario that we find during the Hyksos occupation.

Egypt's contact with Mesopotamia during the Hyksos era is bolstered by recent cuneiform discoveries at the palace of the Hyksos King Khayan (*c.* 1600). The first cuneiform script is in the Akkadian language and dates to the last decades of the Old Babylonian Kingdom. Manfred Bietak, lead excavator at the Hyksos capital of Avaris, concludes that the cuneiform found in the Hyksos context along with a lion sculpture bearing Khayan's name allows "far-reaching Hyksos connections (that) could be extrapolated right back to the Old Babylonian Kingdom."[130] In other words, Bietak sees strong ties between the Hyksos and Mesopotamia. Another inscription found at Khayan's palace "includes the name of a top governmental official who served during the Old Babylonian era under the reign of King Hammurabi (1792–1750 BC)."[131] This again links the Hyksos with Mesopotamia, leaving open the possibility of Assyrian origin.

Manetho asserts (cited in Josephus, *Against Apion* 1.74–92) that the Assyrians were a threat to the Delta kingdom. It is possible that Isaiah's text could be interpreted as though an Assyrian lineage had prevailed in the 15th Hyksos Dynasty. This possibility is strengthened by the Semitic origin of Khayan's name; Khyan is listed in an Assyrian king list among the ancestors of Assyria's Shamshi-Adad II (c. 1800).[132] While the Khayan listed in Assyrian archives should not be confused with the Hyksos king, the name Khayan itself reveals Assyrian affiliation during the time of the Hyksos' usurping of power in the Delta.

3. A Tyrannical Pharaoh

A few years before Moses' birth, the Asiatics who had migrated to Egypt during earlier dynasties asserted their independence. At first, it appears, they simply served as regional governors for Egypt over the immigrant populations. These local leaders succeeded in establishing their authority, and they seceded from Egypt's traditional authority.

> Egypt had suffered from civil war during the late Twelfth Dynasty, this may have provided the opportunity for the Canaanite population in the Delta to secede and eventually to proclaim its own ruler.[133]

Archaeology suggests this transition was far from peaceful.[134] The rival-(14th) Asiatic (Hyksos) Dynasty lasted for about 155 years.[135] Given the short reigns of these Asiatic kings (less than 2 years on average), it has often been proposed that these kings were elected to office.[136] In 1650 BCE, a Hyksos king named Khayan toppled the previous Asiatic (14th) and Egyptian (13th) Dynasties to begin his own "Hyksos" Dynasty.[137] At this point, both the 13th Dynasty (a continuation of the 12th Dynasty[138]) and the Asiatic (14th) Dynasty came to an end. Danish Egyptologist Kim Ryholt observes that the Hyksos were "more or less continuously at war with the Egyptian kings in Thebes."[139] The Hyksos would eventually subdue Egypt, extending their domain all the way to Thebes between 1649 and 1582 BCE.[140]

In the midst of this political climate, Moses was born. The chronology presented in chap. 9 demonstrates that Moses was born around 1639 BCE. Since Aaron's birth three years earlier (Exod 7:7) was not a population issue, it appears that a major political shift had occurred within this three-year span. Scripture does not specify whether the pharaoh at the time of Moses' birth was Egyptian or Hyksos. This leaves open two possible scenarios.

a. If Pharaoh Was Egyptian

Identifying the pharaoh associated with the Hebrew genocide is a problem of determining whether or not the 13th Dynasty still reigned from Avaris and controlled the Delta region.[141] Had the city itself been fractured in two (similar to East and West Berlin)? If so, the king during Moses' birth could have been one of the last kings of the 13th Dynasty, who might have slaughtered the Asiatic upstarts. Pharaohs during the latter end of this era only ruled for about 2–3 years each,[142] a situation that would allow for Aaron's birth to be unaffected by the pharaoh's decree. The damage done to the Turin Canon—our primary source for this period—destroyed the record of the last 19 kings of the dynasty, leaving Egypt's pharaoh unnamed.[143]

The fact that this pharaoh saw the Hebrews and more likely all Asiatics as a threat to his power supports a native Egyptian (13th-Dynasty) pharaoh. The Hyksos more than likely used conscripted forces in their armies. This helps to explain Pharaoh's decree, which solely targeted male progeny (Exod 1:9–10) in order to weaken Hyksos resistance. If this Egyptian pharaoh indeed massacred the Asiatic infants in the Delta, perhaps the massacre provoked the Hyksos' overall rebellion and subsequent campaign to occupy Egypt's southern territory as well.

b. If Pharaoh Was Hyksos

If Exodus's recognition of a dynastic shift (Exod 1:8) indeed refers to the Hyksos' usurpation, Moses' birth may be viewed under similar circumstances, but on the other side of the Nile. In this scenario, identifying Moses' pharaoh would be much easier. Evidence abounds for a power shift within the Hyksos Dynasty. Khayan, one of its most powerful kings dropped the association with the "Hyksos" and adopted traditional Egyptian royal titles.[144] The style of royal seals changed during Khayan's reign as well—again signaling a break with the past.[145] Unlike his predecessors, Khayan pursued a fiercely aggressive policy, subjugating Upper Egypt as far south as Thebes.[146] His rise to power also coincides with the time of Moses' birth.[147]

If Khayan was the pharaoh during Moses' birth, then the pharaoh's initial policy of genocide in all likelihood was an edict that applied to any group the Hyksos thought loyal to the Theban kings: hence, Manetho describing them as "massacring some," even of Egyptian nationality. If this slaughter was indeed historical, it is *un*likely that Egypt did not have a record of it. Thus, Egyptian texts may be able to clear up the question of whether the king during Moses' birth was Hyksos or Theban. We will return to this question when we examine the Egyptian historical evidence for Israelites and the exodus from Egypt below.

4. Moses: Truth or Legend?

The account of Yochebed's making a boat and placing Moses in the water is *not* without credibility. Egyptologist James Hoffmeier considers this type of abandonment to be similar to the modern practice of leaving a baby on the steps of a hospital or orphanage or at the door of a church.[148]

> The reason for the multitude of stories from across the Near East and Mediterranean of casting a children into the waters is that it may reflect the ancient practice of committing an unwanted child or one needing protection into the hands of providence.[149]

So widely is this type of abandonment accepted in modern times as a method to prevent harm to a child that most states in the U.S. have adopted "safe haven" or "baby Moses" laws that allow parents to abandon children without legal repercussions.[150] In a similar way,

Yochebed was trying to save her child by using the only method available to her: to cast her child into God's protection.

Another criticism often levied at Scripture's account of Moses' birth is that Pharaoh's daughter could not so easily have adopted Moses as her own, especially given that the Egyptians would have considered the Hebrews to be "vile Asiatics."[151] Egyptian kings, similar to later Greek monarchs, used children as hostages in order to forge alliances and to negotiate loyalty. In Egypt, these children were kept in a royal boarding school called the Kap.[152]

> The Kap was an institution at the royal court where children of both Egyptian and foreign nobility were brought to be raised in a manner that was meant to ensure future loyalty to the Egyptian King. However, not all children may have been sent voluntarily to the Kap, and by being present at the royal court away from their parents these children could by implication also be used as hostages if the necessity should arise. The children of the Kap were usually placed in positions of some standing once they reached adulthood, although these rarely included higher positions within the government.[153]

Moses may have fit right in with this crowd of children who were educated in the Kap. In this context, Moses would not have been considered a "prince" of Egypt, despite movies that popularize this notion.

If Moses was indeed born at Avaris, as the story would indicate (i.e., a palace lay nearby), Yochebed could easily have placed her son in the meandering pool, that (excavations have revealed) surrounded the palace at Avaris, without there being much danger from currents (see Map 10.2). Yochebed had confidence that women in Pharaoh's court would take compassion on Moses. This situation may evidence the polarity in Avaris itself, and Pharaoh's court was sympathetic to the plight of the Asiatic children.

Moses' name reveals an Egyptian origin.[154] In the Egyptian language, his name was *Msi* or *Msy*, meaning 'to give birth.'

> *Msi*, was a very common element in theophoric names. . . . Even Van Seters acknowledges that "few would dispute . . . it derives from the Egyptian verb *msy* ('to give birth') a very common element in Egyptian names." He cautions against allowing historicity to be assumed from this factor alone, maintaining it only shows "the name's appropriateness to the background of Israel's sojourn in Egypt."[155]

The name Moses indeed makes perfect sense in the Scriptural context. When Pharaoh's daughter named Moses, she associated his name with drawing him out of the water. "And she called his name Moses: and she said, Because I drew him out of the water" (Exod 2:10). It would have seemed to Pharaoh's daughter that the Nile had "given birth" to Moses, thus the correlation between his name and being drawn (birthed) from the Nile. Many kings of this era bore the theophoric *mose* name, which remained popular throughout the subsequent New Kingdom. Seqenenre Tao, who probably would have been contemporary with Moses' birth or ruled shortly thereafter, for some unknown reason, began the tradition of naming all his children with the *mose* ending but was particularly fond of the name Ahmose.[156]

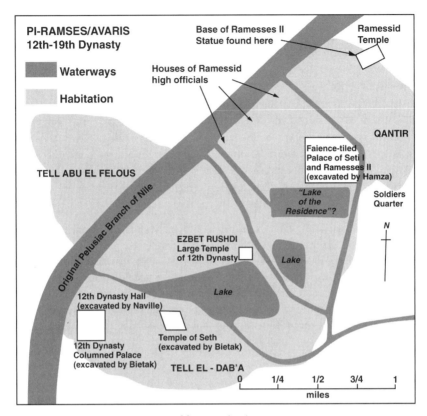

Map 10.2. Avaris

A tantalizing possibility that may explain Moses' strongly Theban Egyptian name yet account for his Hyksos upbringing appears in a treaty that Seqenenre Tao (with the Theban king being vassal) evidently made with Apophis, which was concluded with a diplomatic marriage. Evidence exists that a Theban princess, Tany, had been given to Apophis, or at least to one of his sons, as a wife.[157] If she were to have found a child whom she associated with her own people, her heart would no doubt have cried out in compassion to protect her people just as Moses' heart would years later when he stood up to protect the Hebrew slaves. She would have been the perfect surrogate to raise, nurture, and educate Moses, not only in leadership skills, but also in compassion for an oppressed people, with whom she could so readily identify.

5. A Crime Worthy of Exile

We probably do not appreciate just how horrific Moses' action of slaying an Egyptian was in Egypt's law-abiding society. Perhaps a similar circumstance would be the modern *pre*-civil rights era, when a crime by a black person against a white person was considered especially heinous.

Having been raised in the Kap, Moses would have qualified for a trusted position in the administration: either in the Crown's service or in one of the various temples. If Moses murdered an Egyptian of a superior social status, he would have been arrested and tried for murder: "When Pharaoh heard this thing, he sought to slay Moses. But Moses fled from the face of Pharaoh" (Exod 2:15).

The *Antef decree*, quite contemporary with Moses' upbringing in Egypt, grants a glimpse into the way in which individuals who committed crimes were treated. The decree outlines the crime of a particular servant in the temple of Min (an Egyptian deity) who was given the generalized theophoric name "Minhotpe." The prosecuting petitioner asked the king for "Minhotpe's" name to be expunged, which is why "Minhotpe" was simply recognized as "Tety's son" in the decree. The crime was so egregious that this servant was to be cut off from society.

> The temple staff of my father Min has petitioned My Majesty, saying, "A sorry affair has just (?) transpired in this temple: a hostile attitude (?) has been adopted by— damn his name!—Tety's son Minhotpe." Have him cast forth from the temple of my father Min, have him expelled from that temple office, sons and heirs (included), and excommunicated! His food rations and the contract of his meat salary are to be taken away so that his name be not mentioned in this temple, as is (normally) done to one of this sort who shows rebellion and hostility against his god. Destroy his documents in the temple of Min and in the treasury, and on any scroll of the temple likewise.[158]

The text continues to request that no king who pardoned this offender could rule in Upper or Lower Egypt. Any official who petitioned for a pardon for the offender would have his property confiscated and be relieved of his office, salary, and belongings, which would be given to another throughout their generations. If Moses faced a similar fate—his food, housing, and employment lost, and being cast out of society—he would have been willing to brave the hazards of the desert to find refuge in Midian. It would also explain why YHWH waited to call Moses out of Midian until the pharaoh who sought to arrest Moses had died (Exod 2:23).

6. The Arrogant Pharaoh of the Exodus

While identifying the pharaoh at Moses' birth presents some difficulties, the exodus's arrogant pharaoh stands out like a brandished sword. Royal inscriptions indicate that Khayan had intended his son to succeed him.[159] Instead, another king, Apophis, usurped the throne.[160] Fascinatingly, Apophis was known for his arrogance *not only* in Scripture, *but also* in Egyptian memory.

Apophis was still renowned for his egotism in New Kingdom, some 200 years later. A document dating to the Ramessid era (thirteenth century) tells the story of Apophis's inflammatory letter to Seqenenre Tao (the Theban king). The document, *Papyrus Sallier I*, states that "distress was in the town of the Asiatics."[161] Apophis was in Avaris, collecting taxes as well as the produce from the lucrative trade with other lands. The author claims that Apophis had forsaken the traditional Egyptian gods and worshiped only Seth, whom we know from archaeological remains was worshiped as an Egyptian form of the Canaanite god Baal.[162]

At this point, the document is damaged, but it indicates that Apophis had consulted with his counselors, who advised him to send an "an arrogant demand about the hippopotamus pool at Thebes." The text states that Apophis claimed these beasts (200 miles south of Avaris) were keeping him awake at night.[163] Seqenenre and his aides were dumbfounded with this ridiculous accusation. The Theban king consulted with his generals regarding the best course of action to take, but the conclusion of the story is, sadly, damaged. It appears that Apophis was intent on insulting the Theban king and provoking a conflict. If Seqenenre Tao's remains are any indication of this engagement, Apophis fared the better for it—at least temporarily.

Another point that is quite fascinating in this account is that apparently Apophis not only was challenging the Theban king to a duel, but was challenging his god(s) to a contest as well.

> [So we shall see the power of the god] is with him as protector. He relies upon god who is in the [entire land] except Amon-Re, King of the Gods.[164]

Noted near Eastern scholar James Pritchard understands this portion of the document to refer to the end of Apophis's and his counselors' challenge. "It pits their god Seth against the Theban god Amon-Re."[165] If Apophis won this contest, as it seems that Seqenenre's remains attest, then from the Asiatic viewpoint, Seth would have been victorious. However, this victory would have been short-lived because the Delta received the brunt of YHWH's plagues only a short time later, when he "executed judgment against all the gods of Egypt" (Exod 12:12). Thus, as far as a Scriptural background to the exodus account is concerned Apophis had already challenged the gods to a duel to see "whose god was with him as protector." Although Apophis trusted in Seth, not even Baal himself could save or deliver Apophis and his court out of YHWH's destructive hand a short time later.

Kamose's inscription at Buhen bolsters the accounts of Papyrus Sallier I by citing the enormous booty seized at Avaris.[166] Kamose (II) tells us that he captured hundreds of Hyksos trading ships filled with "bronze axes, gold, lapis, silver, and turquoise: 'all fine products of the *Retenu*,'" another Egyptian term for Canaan.[167] Kamose, whom most scholars identify as Seqenenre's older son also attests to Apophis's pride, which was so great that Apophis claimed he was without rival.[168] Kamose had such contempt for this arrogant king that he used the pejorative "Brave Ass" as a nickname for Apophis.[169] Thus far, the picture Egypt's history vividly paints is a scene of political unrest, which the first chapter of Exodus also attests. Other ideas, however, are not always as they seem.

7. "House of Bondage": Slavery Reconsidered

A recurrent theme found throughout the Tanakh is that YHWH "redeemed Israel from the house of bondage."[170] In fact, YHWH's salvation from the *House of Bondage* was the foundation of the Sinai Covenant.

> I am YHWH your God, which have brought you out of the land of Egypt, out of the house of bondage. (Exod 20:2)

In Disney's rendition of the *Prince of Egypt*, taskmasters were set over Israel as the pharaoh worked the Israelites to death, the way the cab drivers drove Ginger in the book *Black Beauty*. We might be surprised to find that, not only were the Hebrews not singled out for labor, they were not worked to such an extreme.

Surprisingly, the Tanakh (Old Testament) never actually calls the Hebrews in Egypt "slaves." While it does state that Israel worked under hard and difficult "service," *'abodah*[171] (Exod 1:14; 2:23), the text never refers to them as *bondservants*. In fact, the same type of work is later simply prohibited on the Sabbath (Lev 23:7). While it is clear that Israel's forced labor in Egypt was a type of slavery from which YHWH redeemed her, it was not the "plantation slavery" with which Americans often associate this institution.

Slaves (usually bondservants) rarely owned property or acquired wealth.[172] In contrast, Israel both owned her own property while in Egypt and she had possessions and forms of wealth.[173]

> And YHWH shall sever between *the cattle of Israel* and the cattle of Egypt: and there shall nothing die. . . . And YHWH did that thing on the morrow, and all the cattle of Egypt died: but of the *cattle of the Children of Israel* died not one. (Exod 9:4, 6)
>
> *Our cattle* also shall go with us; there shall not an hoof be left behind; for thereof must we take to serve YHWH our God. (Exod 10:26)

Israel was able to own wealth in Egypt. The pharaoh who appointed Joseph ruler in Egypt had given the Hebrews the best of the Delta in which to raise their cattle. Egypt's government allowed foreigners, such as Joseph's brothers, upward mobility.[174] This is evidenced when Pharaoh asked Joseph to place any qualified relatives in offices for supervising the Crown's cattle.

> The land of Egypt is before you; in the best of the land make your father and brothers to dwell; in the land of Goshen let them dwell: and if you know any men of activity among them, then *make them rulers over my cattle.* (Gen 47:6)

It is quite likely that the Hebrews' children inherited their fathers' offices, since that was the Egyptian custom.[175] It would therefore *not* be unlikely to have found Hebrews in charge of their own cattle as well as the Theban Crown's cattle at the time of the exodus (Kamose I).

If Israel owned wealth in the form of flocks and herds, how does Scripture view their oppression? From all indications, the type of bondage that YHWH condemned was compulsory civil service. Throughout the ancient world, kings compelled their own citizens to work for the government. Sometimes this was simply in the form of high taxes.[176] Those who could not afford steep taxes were obliged to give the sweat of their brow.[177] Egyptologists call this type of labor *corvée labor*, "meaning unpaid labor given to a feudal lord."[178] These policies were especially aimed at the lower classes.

> The enlistment of forced labor to carry out the building and agricultural programs of the state was common in the ancient Near East. Villagers, resident aliens, and the disenfranchised were the primary target groups for this sort of conscription.[179]

This was not "plantation slavery" but an obligation owed by every resident to the state. After Israel exchanged a portion of her freedom for a monarchy, King Solomon inflicted this system on Israel once more, although not nearly as oppressively as contemporary governments required. In Israel, this "form of servitude was of a limited nature. 1 Kgs 5:14 indicates three groups of workers (worked) on a three-month cycle. In Ugarit texts, corvée service ranged from two to sixty days per year to the Crown."[180] Surprisingly, Scripture also tells us that the oppression Israel faced in Egypt was indeed corvée labor.

> Therefore they did set over them taskmasters (*sarei misiym*) to afflict them with their burdens. (Exod 1:11)

The Hebrew word for "taskmasters" is *sarei misym*[181] and *mas* is most often translated "tribute" in the KJV. It was this same type of conscripted labor force King Solomon required of the people during the Monarchy (1 Kgs 5:13–14).

> The Hebrew terms for this type of corvée labor, *mas* and *sēḇel,* are cognates of the Akkadian terms *ma-as-sa* and *sa-ab-la-am*. In Israel the two were separately administered but the distinction between them is not entirely clear. . . . Under David and Solomon, Adoram was the administrator of the *mas* (1 Kgs 4:6; 5:13), and Jeroboam was over the *sēḇel* (1 Kgs 11:28). What is clear is that the northern tribes revolted, following Solomon's death, in no small part due to the burden of forced labor (1 Kgs 12:11); moreover they took that opportunity to stone Adoram to death (12:18).[182]

Solomon also employed a permanent corvée labor of non-Israelite peoples whom Israel had not driven out of the land during the Judges Era (1 Kgs 9:15; 2 Chr 8:8).

Israel's deliverance out of Egypt "from the house of bondage" was not necessarily a deliverance from slavery (the Israelite Law permitted slavery). Rather, it was a deliverance from an oppressive system of government, which required high taxes and compulsory civil service. It is this very system that YHWH condemned in 1 Samuel 8, when Israel asked for a monarch (1 Sam 8:11–20). While we may think that our modern economies are better advanced, many European nations still trade individual liberty and mortgaged prosperity for oppression, a political system into which America is quickly degenerating as well. There is every reason to discern that, when YHWH restores Israel again during the *second exodus*, these types of oppressive systems[183] (Ezek 34:2, 8; Zech 11:5) will cease to function in Israel.[184] Rather, taxation and obligation will be limited by the freedom established under YHWH's constitutional Law.

This brings us back to Manetho's account of the Hyksos oppression of Egypt, an account that echoes Scripture's. Manetho's statement should be considered from its Egyptian perspective. Today, for instance, citizens in many European countries do not mind paying high taxes or serving their own government as long as they and their families receive some benefit from civil labor and taxation: for example, libraries, highway systems, civil and criminal courts, law enforcement, schools, healthcare, and the list goes on. For ancient Egypt these benefits would have included food stored in preparation for times of famine, pottery wares, and clothing (manufactured by temples) at the very least. However, when these same systems are used to support foreign enterprises, and citizens receive little direct benefit, popular sentiment usually turns on them very quickly. This is the context in which Manetho's and Scripture's accounts of oppression should be understood: the Hyksos used Egyptian corvée labor to enrich the foreign elite, cutting out benefits for the citizens who actually provided the labor.

8. Israelite Armies in Egypt?

One anomaly I discovered in the Book of Exodus's account is the use of the word "armies" to refer to the Israelites when they left Egypt (Exod 6:26; 7:4; 12:17, 41, 51). The word *tsaba'* designates a standing army,[185] as, for example, in this verse:

> These are that Aaron and Moses, to whom YHWH said, Bring out the Children of Israel from the land of Egypt according to their *armies*. (Exod 6:26)

> But God led the people about, through the way of the wilderness of the Red sea: and the Children of Israel went up *harnessed* out of the land of Egypt. (Exod 13:18)

The word translated "harnessed" is *hamushiym* in Hebrew. It means an armed soldier, ready for combat (see Josh 1:14).[186] How did an enslaved and oppressed people have their own armed garrisons? While this account does not make sense in the 18th Dynasty under Thutmoses or 19th Dynasty under Ramesses II, it indeed makes perfect sense given the political situation at the end of the Hyksos Dynasty. According to the reverse side of the *Rhind Mathematical Papyrus*, by Kamose's 11th year he had surrounded Avaris from the south and cut the Hyksos off from Canaan on the northeast at Sile.[187]

At the beginning of the Hyksos Dynasty, Israel's population had been a liability. Almost a century later, the Hyksos had learned to dominate their rivals, and the Hebrews had learned to be dominated. Instead of Israel's male population being considered a liability, as it had been when Moses was born, it now became a conscripted force that aided Egypt's usurpers. Daggers discovered in burials are evidence of military armament during this era.[188] In fact, the Hyksos pharaoh desperately needed the Israelite forces in order to survive the threat from Egypt's legitimate 17th Dynasty.

Israel's labor force may have built several store cities. Exodus 1 mentions that the Israelites built store cities in Avaris (Pi-Ramses was later built over this Hyksos capital), Pithom, and according to the Septuagint, Heliopolis (Joseph's biblical city of On). This building program may have been part of a massive armament program that prepared for confronting the Theban threat and withstanding a protracted siege.[189]

Thus, much of Israel's slave labor probably supported a wartime program, and indeed Scripture supports this theory. The KJV erroneously translates "treasure" cities in this account.

> Therefore they did set over them taskmasters to afflict them with their burdens. And they built for Pharaoh *treasure* cities, Pithom and Ramses (KJV—Exod 1:11) and On, which is Heliopolis. (LXX)

The Hebrew, *mickenah*, means 'store' city and is translated as 'store' in every other context (1 Kgs 9:19; 2 Chr 6:14; 8:4, 6; 17:12; 32:28).[190] Scripture does not state that the Israelites lived in these cities, but that they built them (Exod 1:11). Thus, the Hebrews could have lived in the vicinity during the building season but had their own territory (which had been apportioned to them during the previous 11th or 12th Dynasty). Evidence of mud-brick grain-storage facilities is certainly not lacking at Avaris.[191] Recent archaeological discoveries demonstrate that the area did not always boast granary facilities.[192] However, as the city became a metropolis, large silos were built in the city adjoined to administrative complexes. Many of these storage facilities date to the 13th Dynasty (soon after the time of Joseph), but some were built shortly afterward as well.[193]

Manetho echoes this account of the Hyksos' employment of native conscripted forces to secure their foreign power.

> Toutimaios. . . . rebuilt this place (i.e., Avaris) and gave it impregnable walls and installed in it a *garrison of as many as 240,000 heavy-armed men* to guard his frontier. Here he would come in summertime, partly to serve out rations and pay his troops, *partly to train them carefully in maneuvers* and so strike terror into foreign tribes. (frag. 42, 1.75–79.2)[194]

Both Scripture and Manetho attest that Israel had a standing army while under the Egyptian corvée. Thus it was not out of place for Moses to write that the Israelites left Egypt in rank-and-file armed divisions:

> And it came to pass the selfsame day, that YHWH did bring the Children of Israel out of the land of Egypt by their armies. (Exod 12:51)

The Hyksos used conscripted garrisons, which Scripture also confirms. These forces were well trained to enter the Promised Land and claim their inheritance. Thus the history of Egypt and Scripture appear to agree. From the unrest that transpired at Moses' birth to the haughty pharaoh of the exodus, the political situation in Egypt mirrors the history in the Exodus account.

9. Stubborn King or Caged Bird?

> And I am sure that the king of Egypt will not let you go, no, not by a mighty hand. (Exod 3:19; 4:21)

Throughout the Exodus account, we find the recurrent theme that Pharaoh will not let Israel leave Egypt. How could YHWH be so sure that Pharaoh would not let Israel go? Exodus's abbreviated account makes it seem as though the plagues happened in rapid succession, one after another, so we wonder how Pharaoh could be as slow and inept as to hold onto Israel when every plague that Moses and Aaron predicted came true: why mess with Israel's God?

Learning about Egypt's political situation at this time again provides the answers to these questions. At the dawn of the exodus, the Delta was on the brink of war. The Theban Kamose had reclaimed almost all of the area south of Avaris and was about to conquer Sile, a fortress on the Hyksos' only escape route into Canaan.[195] The Asiatic pharaoh desperately needed Israel's garrisons to defend his territory. Pharaoh was not an ignoramus. He could not afford this loss of military support. From a practical position: could he tell whether Israel would defect to his enemy? YHWH, sending Moses and Aaron at the dawn of these final campaigns knew that pharaoh could not afford to let Israel go. Moses and Aaron's request defied basic military strategy for insuring the king's survival and for protecting his people residing in the Delta. To allow this able-bodied workforce to migrate during a wartime crisis would be national suicide.

To view this "Brave Ass" as helpless would be to underestimate Apophis entirely. He had sent a messenger to Kush, trying to urge the southern kingdom to revolt against Kamose, promising that Kush could have the southern half of Egypt, while Apophis would retain the Delta.[196] Apophis knew that Kamose's forces would be strapped and virtually incapable of fighting a war on two fronts. The Brave Ass's plans were thwarted, however, when Kamose captured Apophis's correspondent. Kamose took the messenger back to Apophis's territory so that he could describe to Apophis all that Kamose had destroyed of the Hyksos' former holdings in Upper Egypt. We can only speculate that perhaps Apophis was waiting for Kush to attack Kamose while the plagues were taking place. If he was, this might explain why he was reluctant to allow part of his armed forces leave: he believed that the tide was about to shift in his favor.

10. Goshen: A Separate Nome?

Scripture makes it clear that the "land of Goshen" where the Israelites lived just before the exodus was not the port city of Avaris. With the third plague, YHWH separated the "land" where the Israelites dwelt from their oppressor's land.

> And *I will sever in that day the land of Goshen, in which my people dwell*, that no swarms of flies shall be there; to the end you may know that I am YHWH

in the midst of the earth. And I will *put a division between my people and your people*: tomorrow shall this sign be. (Exod 8:22–23)

This text implies that Israel's land was divided by some geological feature, such as a distinct branch of the Nile. In the Egyptian context, the author probably intended the artificial territorial divisions called nomes (similar to counties or parishes today), which were often divided by the natural landscape that the Nile's path provided. Scripture associates Israel's corvée with three different nomes.

Israel's corvée force worked at Pi-Ramses, Pi-thom, and according to the Septuagint, On—more commonly known as Heliopolis (Exod 1:11; see Map 10.1 on p. 436). In Egypt, cities were recognized by the temples or gods who lived there.[197] We see this fact in the language of Canaan, where *Bethel* means 'House of El.' Similarly the Egyptian word "Pi" means 'house.'[198] Thus, the two cities in Exodus designate the 'House of Ramesses' and the 'House of Atum,' an Egyptian god.[199] Scholars have identified Avaris with the later Pi-Ramses, since the 13th-century pharaoh (Ramesses) built his capital city on top of the older Hyksos' metropolis. This city lay within the 20th Egyptian nome.[200] *On* is readily associated with *iwnw* in Egyptian but is called Heliopolis in Greek.[201] The city is located much farther south in the Delta. After an earlier pharaoh had promoted Joseph, he gave him a wife from On (Gen 41:45), and it is possible that some of Joseph's kin lived in this city.

The last city and most difficult to identify is Pithom. The word itself is a Hebraized version of the Egyptian *p(r) itim*, or 'House of Atum,' a prominent deity during the Ramessid era[202] at the time when Israel's archives were updated by Deborah's scribes. Two strong candidates for this site in the Wadi Timulat have emerged in recent years. The first, Tell el-Retabeh, and the second, Tell el Maskhuta, a short distance away.[203] The entire region where these sites lay was part of the 8th Egyptian nome. During the Hyksos period, this area was lush, fertile farmland.[204] Because its nearby arm of the Nile silted up hundreds of years ago, it is now a vast desert region (see Map 11.1.).

Another area often associated with Goshen is Tanis, which was in the 19th nome.[205] This site is supported by Asaph's song, which states that Israel saw YHWH's miracles "in the field of Zoan." Scripture does not say that Zoan was the place where Israel lived but identifies it as the area where most of YHWH's miraculous plagues took place:

Marvelous things did he in the sight of their fathers, in the land of Egypt, in the Field of Zoan. (Ps 78:12, 43)

The Field of Zoan in Scripture was called the Field of Dja'u in Egyptian due to its rich fishing marshes.[206] It lay directly to the east of the 16th nome; its Asiatic immigrants Manetho (see Josephus, *Against Apion* 1.78) tells us revolted prior to the Hyksos' takeover of Avaris. Unfortunately, this site has not been excavated enough for any connection to Israel to be found. In May 2011, scientists from the University of Alabama (Birmingham) used satellite and infrared imaging to reveal that it was a massive settlement, significantly larger than Avaris, complete with at least 17 pyramids.[207] These images were later confirmed by on-site excavations.[208] However, much of this site dates centuries later than the exodus. It will take archaeologists decades to excavate through the layers of this city to see if any Hyksos, Asiatic, or even Hebrew associations can be discovered in these ruins.

What this means for our study is that the three cities mentioned in Exod 1:11 may represent three different nomes.[209] This conclusion would *not* deny Israel's residence or corvée labor in other cities but would identify the three nomes (8th, 19th, and 20th) in which the Israelites were *most actively* employed. If Avaris was a major Hyksos trading port and metropolis,[210] then perhaps the Israelites were part of seasonal work crews there who had permanent residence in either the 8th or 19th nome. Thus, the land of Goshen would have been recognized as a separate district, not only by Israel but also by the Egyptians, in a territory on the farthest eastern Pelusic Nile branch near Sinai.

C. Circular Consensus

Understanding the politics underlying the current scholarly consensus, which embraces a 12th-century exodus helps us grasp some of the elements affecting research in this era. As mentioned above (see beginning of this chapter), in the early 1900s most scholars accepted the 1400s (18th Dynasty) as the date for the exodus, based exclusively on 1 Kgs 6:1. Archaeological digs in Israel–Palestine revealed a "wave of destruction" that spread across much of Canaan.[211] Pioneering scholars and archaeologists optimistically associated this destruction with Israel's Conquest of Canaan and dated this era to the thirteenth century.[212] Although this dating contradicted the Scriptural evidence, scholars considered the archaeological evidence for the thirteenth-century date to be irrefutable.

This situation did not last long. In the 1940s and 50s Kathleen Kenyon's thorough and detailed excavations at Jericho turned "Biblical Archaeology" on its heels, revealing that the massive wave of destruction did not occur in the thirteenth century, as enthusiastic scholars had maintained; rather, it occurred at least two centuries earlier, around 1550 BCE.[213] At this point scholars became divided: only the "fringe" considered it remotely possible that Israel's history should stretch back yet another 200 years (even though Scripture's chronology supported it).

Two camps emerged with this post-Kenyon evidence, aided by additional studies that supported various redactional theories regarding Scripture's original composition.[214] One conservative group of scholars still embraced a very limited and much-revised theory of a twelfth-century exodus (Kitchen, Albright, Wright). The second group of scholars (Finkelstein, Dever, Silberman, Redford) dismissed any notion of an actual or historical exodus, instead preferring to consider this account as a folktale mixed with various traditions spanning several centuries; it was redacted (and propagandized) during the sixth century under King Josiah (or later) as a biography of Israel's origins.

The problem that the first group of scholars has presented for biblical studies of this era is more or less a catch-22. First, they are the group that represents or accepts Scripture as a more or less valid testimony of Israel's history. Their stalwart resolve to retain their mentor's (professor's) dating system has prevented any real discussion of the evidence supporting a historical exodus. The second group is more or less hampered by the first group. Since the second group does not claim to accept Scripture as a valid historical source, it yields to the scholars who do. This does not mean, however, that the second group does not have some valid ideas. Quite the contrary, it is the second group that raises the most valid opposition to the current politically correct dating of a twelfth-century exodus. Many scholars in this second group have also hinted at the ample evidence that exists for a sixteenth-century exodus.

For instance, Egyptologist Donald Redford, who falls in the second group, observes:

> No one can deny that the tradition of Israel's coming out of Egypt was one of long standing. . . . There is only one chain of historical events that can accommodate this late tradition, that is the Hyksos descent and occupation of Egypt. . . . And in fact it is in the Exodus account that we are confronted with the Canaanite version of this event.[215]

Redford makes this observation while accepting a 1440 date for Israel's exodus.[216] He is apparently unwilling to engage the capacious Scriptural evidence, which places the exodus at least 100 years earlier between 1546 and 1576 (see chap. 9.III-IV.), during Kamose's reign.

Israel Finkelstein likewise sees Scripture's accounts of the exodus as folktales and oral traditions of generations past that were telescoped into a story at a much later date.[217] Given their demur against the current twelfth-century date and given the fact that these scholars see Israel's association with the Hyksos as at least a somewhat viable history, it is surprising that these scholars have not presented a valid alternative to the generally accepted date. What has probably thwarted their desire to re-date the exodus most is their reliance on various redactional schemes. The question, however, that remains for this present study is this: what evidence does Egypt exhibit for the historical validity of Scripture's account of the exodus?

D. *The Egyptian Evidence*

1. Archaeological

a. *Canaanite/Amorite Names*

One of the strongest associations between Israel and an Asiatic population in the Delta arises from the strong presence of Amorite (Syrian) names.[218] Some names such as Yakbim and Ya'qub-Har (Ya'qub-baal) frequently appear on royal seals from this era (*c.* 1800–1650) and bear a striking similarity to the name of the patriarch Yaakob ('Jacob' in Hebrew). While there is nothing to suggest that the biblical Yaakob (Jacob, *c.* 2100–1960) should be associated with these seals or with the Hyksos, their existence does reveal that there was an Amorite population in the Delta region at the same time when Scripture places Israel in Egypt (see Illustrations 10.4 and 10.5).[219]

Illustration 10.4. Yakbim, nomen/prenomen   Illustration 10.5. The Ya'qub-Har nomen/ prenomen

Some scholars theorize that the massive wave of Amorite migrations prior to the Hyksos resulted from famines abroad.[220] Egyptologist Kim Ryholt finds that the "seeds" of the Amorite presence in Egypt during this time (the Second Intermediate Period or SIP) were

> found in the Twelfth Dynasty, during which a migration of Semitic people from Canaan to the Egyptian Delta took place. . . . These migrations had begun already in the late 3rd millennium BCE and had led to the collapse of the 3rd Dynasty of Ur and to the establishment of several Amorite dynasties in Babylonia and Syria. The migration of people from Canaan into Egypt would similarly lead to the collapse of the Twelfth Dynasty and to the establishment of a West Semitic dynasty in the Delta.[221]

The Israelite/Hebrew presence in Egypt was symptomatic of Asiatic presence in Egypt as a whole. Nothing would overtly distinguish the Israelites (Hebrews) from any other Canaanite peoples. Yet, the presence of names—direct parallels of the names recorded in Scripture—would attest to the likelihood of Israel's presence in Egypt during this era.

b. Asiatic (Canaanite) Customs

Abraham and his children lived in Canaan for about 200 years before his grandson Jacob moved the clan to Egypt. From Egypt's perspective, the Hebrews were Canaanites or Asiatics. There are several customs that, we learn from archaeology, distinguished the Asiatics from the native Egyptian populations. Fascinatingly, *some* of these customs demonstrate an affinity with Hebrew practices. The first was the Hyksos' practice of intermixing burials with the living community,[222] a practice for which YHWH later chastised Israel (Ezek 34:7–9). Second was the Asitatics' practice of taking on Egyptian names.[223] In the story of Joseph, the new vizer retained his Hebrew name but was also given Zaphnath-paaneah (Gen 41:45) as an Egyptian name.[224]

The third trait shared between the Asiatics and the Israelites, which was unearthed at Avaris, was use of the four-room, Syrian-styled home that date to the Hyksos' occupation.[225] Scholars usually associate this style of home with Israelite building customs.[226] However, not all the data gleaned from archaeology present a straightforward picture, because many of these homes contained Minoan and Cretan pottery.[227] The fourth custom unique to the Asiatics and shared with the Israelites was (Canaanites) the practice of using family tombs.[228] Genesis tells of Abraham's purchase of the cave of Machpelah (Gen 23:9) as a family tomb in which to bury Sarah. Three generations later, we find that this tomb was still in use when Joseph buried Jacob (Gen 50:13). Thus, at least four customs are attested for both the Israelites and the Asiatics in Egypt during the Second Intermediate Period.

c. Slavery: Evidence of Concentration Work Camps

During the Middle Kingdom, Egypt's pharaohs raised taxes and conscripted corvée labor.[229] These policies were especially aimed at the lower classes. Gae Callender observes that during the Middle Kingdom,

> there was a system of enforced labor, whereby men and women of the middle and lower classes were enlisted to undertake specific physical tasks, including military service. This corvée system was organized through town officials, but there was central control under the office of the "organization of labor." Although it was possible to escape the burden of the work legitimately by paying another person to do it, those who avoided the corvée altogether were punished very severely, and their families, or anyone aiding their evasion, were also punished. [230]

As early as Amenemhet III (c. 1840), Senusret III's successor, Asiatics were part of the labor force of a religious institution under the "priest of the corps of Sopdu, Lord of the East." This corps may have reported directly to an administrative official, "the superintendent of works of the Northern department."[231] Like other administrative services that the Hyksos inherited, this system continued well into the 17th Dynasty.[232] Although this system had been instituted during previous dynasties, the Hyksos made use of it since contemporary texts refer to "camps of Asiatic workmen" (see Illustration 10.6).[233]

Illustration 10.6. Tell el-Yahudiyah ware.

As mentioned before, Tell el-Yahudiyah demonstrates a work-camp type structure, perhaps similar to a concentration camp. The outer walls are sloped while the inner walls rise vertically to a height of about 70 feet.[234] Flinders Petrie, who originally excavated this walled enclosure, estimated that the camp could house 40,000 workmen.[235] The site is also known for its iconic el-Yahudiyah pottery,[236] which may have been mass-produced under corvée conditions, perhaps similar to sweatshops in third-world nations today. "Trade was the

Illustration 10.7. Tell el-Yahudiyah, a work camp during the Hyksos Era.

King's monopoly."[237] Tell el-Yahudiyah came to an end shortly before the last Hyksos stratum (D/2) at Avaris (Tell el-Deb'a).[238] This may indicate a loss of territory and consolidation of labor resources with the threat of war looming on the horizon (see Illustration 10.7).

Manfred Bietak, lead excavator at Avaris has unearthed "reed huts erected in systematic fashion under and in the artificial deposits (which) probably served to accommodate laborers for what seems to be a palace project."²³⁹ These huts are perhaps further evidence of forced Asiatic labor. It seems evident that the Theban monarchs lost corvée labor to the usurpers. *Theban building projects* at the end of the 13th Dynasty and the beginning of the succeeding 17th Dynasty were quite modest, demonstrating a lack of labor, a lack of resources, and a lack of capital to effect the large-scale projects undertaken by their predecessors.²⁴⁰

Manetho tells us,

> By main force they easily overpowered the rulers of the land, they then *burned our cities ruthlessly*, razed to the ground the temples of the gods, and *treated all the natives* with a cruel hostility, *massacring some and leading into slavery the wives and children of others*.²⁴¹

Manetho's assertion that the Hyksos burned Egyptian cities may be bolstered by recent excavations at Avaris, which demonstrate that an earlier structure was burned and replaced by King Khayan's heavily fortified palace.²⁴²

The initial Hyksos conquest may have served to quash individuals loyal to the traditional Theban kings. It is apparent that the Hyksos-occupied Delta reached a comfortable equilibrium with native Egyptians, and it appears that Egypt's nobles probably profited from the Hyksos' prosperity. Kamose's stele indicates that his counselors' investments in the Delta region were unaffected by Hyksos' rise to power. Thus, their freely grazing livestock may still have been managed by loyal Hebrew descendants (Gen 47:6). This may explain why the nobles in Kamose's counsel did not fear the Hebrews' defection to Hyksos profiteers. Strewn pottery sherds from Tell el-Maskhuta, a site near the biblical Pi-tham, have been interpreted by archaeologists as being indicative of a pastoral community.²⁴³ This may bolster support for both Scripture's account of Hebrew herdsmen in Egypt and Kamose's claim. The Hebrews' loyalty to the Theban dynasty would therefore have been considered seditious by the Hyksos upstarts when the struggle for power ensued at the time of Moses' birth.

The Hyksos tried to become Egyptians and, in many ways, the Hyksos kingdom still resembled the Middle Kingdom it had usurped.

> The Hyksos introduced a method of government which was to prove equally successful for all the later invaders who applied it to Egypt: instead of attempting to impose their own governmental structures on the country, they immersed themselves in the existing Egyptian political system.²⁴⁴

Under the Hyksos, native Egyptians served as commanders in the Hyksos' garrisons²⁴⁵ and intermarried with Asiatics.²⁴⁶ The Hyksos' use of native Egyptians to control the local population would accord with Scripture's accounts of Egyptian taskmasters (*sarei misiym*, corvée officers—Exod 1:11; 3:7; 5:6–14) ruling over the Hebrews. According to Scripture, the Egyptians established officials among the Hebrew population to hold Israel accountable to their authority as well (Exod 5:14–15, 19). This type of control has been used by many governments throughout history. More recently, the United States' use of local tribesmen to implement American (or U.N.) policies and objectives in Iraq in return for large distributions of foreign aid (without a conscripted service) would probably be a similar parallel.

Scripture echoes Manetho's view of the Hyksos' policy, citing slavery as the Hyksos' tool for subduing Hebrew allegiances. One of the reasons Scripture gives for Pharaoh's enslaving of Israel is that the vast Hebrew populace could side with the king's enemies if war arose.

> Now there arose up a new king over Egypt, which knew not Joseph. And he said *to his people*, Behold, the people of the Children of Israel are more and mightier than we: Come on, let us deal wisely with them; lest they multiply, and it come to pass, that, when there falls out any war, they join also to our enemies, and fight against us, and so get them up out of the land. (Exod 1:8–10)

This account is curious because war seems to be a foregone conclusion. It is also intriguing that, in this account, the pharaoh consults with "his people." If this pharaoh's native people were Egyptians, why not just state that "Pharaoh said to the Egyptians"? A similar account is found 80 years later in Exod 8:21 when the pharaoh's "people" appear to be distinguished from the "houses of the Egyptians." The Septuagint also states that Pharaoh spoke to "his nation" and does not call them Egyptians (Exod 1:9, LXX). Although I am speculating with this text, these passages do at least give rise to suspicion.

In the chronology presented in chap. 9, Israel's migration into Egypt occurred shortly after the First Intermediate Period in 1976 BCE, possibly during the 11th or 12th Dynasty, about 200 years before the Hyksos exerted power over the Delta regions (see chap. 9.IV). The Hyksos may have deemed these Asiatic Hebrews to be "natives" of Egypt, and they may be part of the "natives" whom Manetho says a Hyksos king massacred and enslaved. By all accounts, the later Theban kings who chased the Hyksos out of Egypt warred with them off and on for about 70 years.[247] This is the background for Scripture's depiction of the pharaoh of the exodus, who sought to massacre an ever-burgeoning population (Exod 1:22) that might easily have sided with the legitimate Egyptian pharaohs.

Both Manetho's testimony and the archaeological data quite accurately parallel Scripture's description of Israel's sojourn in Egypt. Recent scholars, however, have questioned Manetho's accounts, opting instead to view the Hyksos' takeover as a peaceful invasion.[248] Both views are indeed accurate, based on one's perspective. While Manetho is recounting the effects of the Hyksos' occupation, scholars such as Ryholt observe that the Hyksos' initial transition into Egyptian pharaohs was peaceful process but later degenerated into conflict.[249]

Egypt's loss of the Delta region had been aided by the establishment of regional territories, which had eventually allowed Asiatics to hold positions of authority. While Egypt does not yet yield documents demonstrating how the Asiatics usurped Lower Egypt, we may be able to infer that their trading contacts[250] and business savvy allowed them upward mobility in Egypt's society. As their population increased, they naturally sought to establish an independent state. Once they achieved independence, they took advantage of the lower classes, enslaving them and using an already functioning corvée system to their own gain.

d. Evidence of Plundering

Egypt's archaeological record for the Hyksos period reveals the violence of the Hyksos era. From the end of the 12th Dynasty to the beginning of the 15th Dynasty, graves manifest a society with a large warrior class. Even though the graves had been extensively plundered, "50 percent of the male burials yielded weapons, which indicates that warriors played an important part in society."[251] This type of archaeological evidence matches the account of Moses' birth, in which a pharaoh is concerned that the male population could easily side with his enemies (Exod 1:10, 22). This is the reason that Pharaoh singles out the Hebrew males for slaughter. This evidence would also lend support to Scripture's account that the Israelites had their own, no doubt conscripted forces at the time of the exodus (Exod 6:26). This would most certainly support an association of Israel's armies with Avaris's "warrior class."

Fascinating parallels exist not only between Exodus 1–12 and the beginning of Egypt's Second Intermediate Period, but also between Exodus 1–12 and the end of Hyksos era. Not only were temples destroyed in the Delta during the SIP, but native tombs and graves were plundered. Danish Egyptologist Kim Ryholt observes,

> In addition to the destruction of temples, there are indications that the Fifteenth Dynasty was also responsible for the plundering of certain royal tombs of native Egyptian kings within the territory they conquered.[252]

Due to the fragmented state of the records of this era, there is much debate about whether Kamose had indeed plundered Avaris or had only plundered the territories he had captured on his campaign to Avaris.[253] The current consensus is that Kamose challenged Apophis to engage in battle at Avaris. Apophis refused, and Kamose retreated south to Karnak.[254] Both Apophis and Kamose died (unexplainably),[255] and Kamose's adolescent brother, Ahmose, who had been co-regent, became king.[256] Ahmose waited 11 years to mature before he engaged the new Hyksos king, Khamudi, in battle (a chronology that is questioned among scholars)[257] and chased the remnant Hyksos to Sharhuen (in Canaan), where he besieged the city for 3 years and captured it.[258]

While scholars correctly associate this devastation with Hyksos occupation[259] and Kamose's subsequent sack of Avaris,[260] it is quite possible that some plundering happened either by the Hebrews or by local residents who were eager to see the Hebrews leave.

> And I will give this people favor in the sight of the Egyptians; and when you go, *you shall not go empty*, but each woman shall ask of her neighbor, and any woman who lives in her house, for silver and gold jewelry, and for clothing. You shall put them on your sons and on your daughters. *So you shall plunder*[261] *the Egyptians*. (Exod 3:21–22, KJV 2000).

Remember that the hidden prophecy in the Promised-Land Covenant foretold of YHWH's judgment against Egypt's land. He promised that, when the Israelites left Egypt, they would leave with considerable wealth:

> And also that nation, whom they shall serve, will I judge: and afterward *shall they come out with great substance.* (Gen 15:14)

If tombs and graves were raided as a result of wanting to appease the Hebrews and their God, these actions—from an archaeological point of view—would be indistinguishable from Kamose's raid on Avaris, when he subjugated the area a short time later. The discovery of Tutankhamun's tomb in 1907 revealed for the first time the incredible treasures that such tombs could hold. Scripture's accounts of the gold and fine linen employed to adorn the Tabernacle (Exodus 25–30, 36–39), when Israel's only resources came from Egypt, indicate that in one way or another the Hebrews had indeed "plundered the Egyptians," as the archaeological record also attests.

e. Epidemic

Perhaps the most fascinating archaeological discovery was unearthed during the painstaking excavations of Manfred Bietak at the Hyksos' capital at Avaris. The last Hyksos occupation stratum of the city revealed that an epidemic took place at Avaris shortly before the city was abandoned:[262] "In several parts of the site, Bietak has found large communal graves in which many bodies were placed, without any discernible ceremony."[263] To the ancient individual, this type of burial was detrimental to helping the dead travel to a joyous afterlife, which was effected through burial rituals.[264] The graves lie in shallow pits 20–40 cm deep, and the "bodies in most of the pits burials were in a casual, extended position; it is apparent that the bodies were sometimes thrown into the pit."[265]

These mass burials may very well evidence Scripture's account of the death of the firstborn (Exodus 12), an epidemic that may have been caused by famine, pursuant to the previous plagues. As Ryholt observes, "longer famines often lead to plagues in ancient times."[266] This particular plague, however, only affected Egypt's firstborn.

Currently, archaeologists do not date the stratum to the latter half of the Hyksos period, but to the city's initial expansion around 1715 BCE. However, the current method of dating this epidemic and Avaris as a whole is a hot topic of scholarly debate. Regarding the excavation at Avaris in general, Egyptologist Janine Bourriau observes,

> The material is found in nine strata (H-D/2), the upper and lower ends of which have been linked by the Austrian excavator Manfred Bietak to the reigns of two Egyptian kings, respectively Amenemhat IV (1786–1777 BCE) and Ahmose (1550–1525 BCE). He divides the resulting period by nine, allotting roughly thirty years to each stratum and thus obtaining a framework of absolute dates for this relative sequence. However, when these dates have been imported to sites in Syria-Palestine where objects similar to those from Tell el-Dab'a have been found, there have sometimes been clashes with the existing chronology. The resulting fierce debates, when resolved, will eventually demand radical revisions not only in the dating of strata at Tell el-Dab'a but in the methods used for dating the Middle Bronze Age over the whole east Mediterranean region.[267]

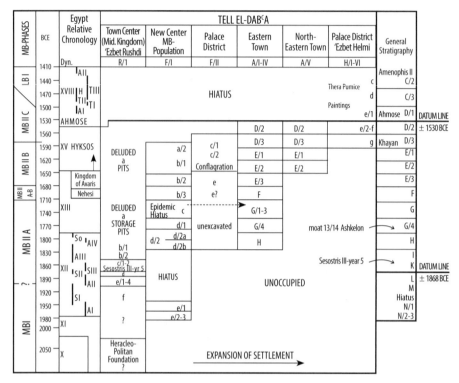

Table 10.1. Avaris Stratum[271]

The problem in determining the strata for this city is the moist and muddy region, which simply allows for no discernible layers at Avaris the way that distinct strata are found in Canaan or more arid regions.[268] This often causes a loss of context even when written inscriptions that bear a ruler's name are uncovered.[269] *What this means is that the last plague cannot be ruled out as the cause for this epidemic.* Adults and children were buried together, indicating that they had died at the same time, yet quite surprisingly, there is no evidence of illness as the cause of death (see Table 10.1).[270]

Both the Hearst Papyrus and the London Medical Papyrus written in the early 18th Dynasty (1570–1530 BCE, shortly after Israel's exodus,) mention an "Asiatic disease."[272] This has led scholars such as Manfred Bietak to question whether this epidemic and the "Asiatic disease" could be related.[273] Interestingly, these references to an "Asiatic" catalyst for disease were written shortly after the Theban kings chased the Hyksos out of the Delta.

According to Scripture, Israel left Egypt accompanied by a mixed Egyptian-Asiatic multitude (Exod 12:38) on the very night that the death plague took place (Exod 12:29–42). Thus, not only would this area face depopulation from an epidemic but also from a massive Egyptian and Asiatic/Hebrew migration. It is not known whether the Egyptian-Hyksos priests "cleansed" the city after the plague, before expanding again. If so, another period of destruction could have occurred shortly before the city expanded again.[274] Bietak has drawn similar conclusions in regard to the mass graves and hurried burials that occurred at the end of the Hyksos period.[275] If cleansing was a deliberate effort, it might have skewed the archaeological evidence, resulting in an apparent shorter span of time between stratum than normally expected.

This epidemic presents yet another curiosity. Most scholars agree that Kamose (see Illustration 10.8) began the conquest and pillage of Avaris or at least of its districts.[276] However, his final campaign appears to have been cut short not only by his own untimely death, but also the death of his opponent, Apophis (Apepi, below).

> It was at least eleven years before an army under Ahmose began to fight its way north again. The reason for the lull was that both Kamose and his opponent Aauserra Apepi had died.[277]

Interestingly, Kamose's coffin was unusually plain, indicating an accidental or unexpected death.[278] His remains also lacked the more sophisticated mummification processes because it had crumbled to dust by the time researchers opened his sarcophagus.[279] Equally enigmatic is the fact that Ahmose's firstborn son (Kamose's nephew), Ahmose-ankh, preceded his father in death sometime between

Illustration 10.8. Limestone shabti figure of King Ahmose, 18th Dynasty, c. 1520 BCE.

Ahmose's 17th and 22nd regnal years raising the issue of the death of the firstborn once more.[280] Ahmose's mummy reveals that he died at about 35 years of age.[281] The radiocarbon dating for the beginning of his reign is 1570–1544 BCE,[282] which is right in line with the date of 1548 purposed for the Exodus in chapter 9. Added to these points of interest is the fact that Ahmose suddenly found himself king outside the capital and had to rush home to secure his throne after a devastating flood (see discussion of the *Storm Stele* below). Linking all these deaths to the exodus's plague is probably too ambitious. It is hoped that future chronology studies in Egyptology will take the Scriptural evidence into consideration in this discussion.

f. Evidence of a Loss of Corvée Labor

> The initial expansion of Tell el-Dab'a was checked temporarily by an epidemic. . . . Thereafter . . . the patterns of both settlements and cemeteries suggest a less egalitarian society than before. Large houses with smaller ones fitted in around them, more elaborate buildings on the center than on the edge of the settlement, servants buried in front of the tombs of their masters: all suggest the social dominance of a wealthy élite group.[283]

Discoveries at Avaris show that Egypt's nobles reasserted their status in the Delta region (after the exodus). If Israel's exodus drew Asiatics (from the Egyptian perspective, this would include Hebrews) and Egyptians from the corvée system (Exod 12:38), then the change in settlement patterns could be considered an opportune time for Egypt's traditional nobility (whom Senusret had diminished) to reassert their status now that "the people" were gone. The fact that servants' quarters appear to have been so closely linked with large houses[284] may indicate that a lost workforce had been replaced by a more privatized and individualized labor system. Some Asiatics were

> captured in engagements or taken as part of the booty and dispersed as domestics among the Egyptian troop; but these were relatively few, and the *absence in Egypt during the next fifty years of a servile community of aliens* speaks against the postulate of a seizure of a large segment of the Hyksos population by the liberators.[285]

Had this been any normal campaign, Pharaoh would have availed himself of an already active and functioning workforce in Avaris and its environs, as Ramesses did two centuries later.[286] The fact that Egypt's pharaoh did not or could not avail himself of this workforce surely demonstrates that an exodus from the Delta had occurred prior to Ahmose's final attack on the city. The fact that Egypt did not recover its corvée system for 50 years fits perfectly in the scenario that Israel and her mixed multitudes were in the wilderness of Kadesh (Num 33:36) and effectively out of Egypt's periphery during this epoch.

As mentioned previously, there are conflicting chronologies proposed for this period. A majority of scholars estimate that Kamose died somewhere between 1570 and 1549.[287] If Kamose's death indeed marks Israel's exodus, there remains at least a twenty-year period unaccounted for by this chronology. The instability of this era would explain Scriptures' account of a large Egyptian population that exited Egypt with Moses (Exod 12:38). With war on the horizon, extensive obligations to Egypt's corvée system, and the power of Israel's God, many weary citizens were eager to escape this system to a new land and a "covenant of freedom" with the Hebrew's God. After the exodus, YHWH set out formal Passover stipulations, to include the substantial number of Egyptians and other races who left Egypt with Israel, freely allowing these refugees to join the host of YHWH's people, as Caleb the Kenezite (Num 32:12) is a prime example.

g. Evidence of Migration

Avaris (Tell el-Dab'a) is not the only city that appears to have a history similar to the history recorded in the Book of Exodus. Tell el-Makhuta, which some scholars associate with Pi-thom (Exod 1:11),[288] has also exposed some interesting and parallel artifacts. What may be of significance in regard to Tell el-Maskhuta is the large number of infant and adolescent burials that date to the Hyksos period that are seemingly disproportionate in relation to adult burials (see Illustration 10.9).[289] In fact, adult burials are virtually absent, but many infants as young as 2–4 months are buried there.[290] This could evidence the infanticide perpetrated by Pharaoh at the time of Moses' birth. The site maintained "store" granaries as well as industrialized pottery-manufacturing facilities.[291] These facilities would fit Scripture's

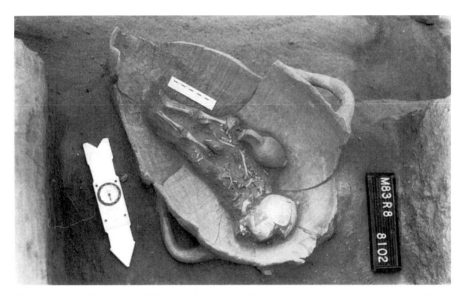

Illustration 10.9. Hyksos era child burial, 2–6 months old in Canaanite Storage-jar R8112 (misnumbered in photo).

account of "store cities" quite well. Even more fascinating is the fact that the people of this town appear to have had a pottery tradition similar to the Canaanite city of Shechem,[292] a place where Jacob and his family lived prior to migrating into Egypt (Gen 37:13). Excavators at the site concluded that the community that lived there leaned more toward hereditary interaction than the social-ranking system common in traditional Egyptian society,[293] another trait that would suit Jacob's tribal descendants quite well.

In another parallel, John Holladay, who excavated this site concluded that people peacefully emigrated from this city, taking everything of value with them.

> Everything portable was picked up, and the population quietly moved elsewhere, prior to the final occupational stage (Stratum D/2) at Tell el-Dab'a (Avaris).[294]

Similar to Avaris, Tell el-Maskhuta's graves were plundered before the people moved away from town.[295] Pottery sherds around this site may also be evidence of the Hebrews' pastoral society. Pi-thom (Etham), probably mentioned in Num 33:6 is listed as one of the first cities Israel journeyed to after departing from Avaris during the exodus. Numerous pottery sherds were strewn about this settlement, indicating the presence of cattle and shepherds,[296] but they could also be the remains of a large emigrating group of people (or both). Similar to Avaris, Tell el-Maskhuta was discontinued before the last period of Hyksos occupation.[297] What this implies is that Israel exited Egypt quite a few years before Ahmose chased the remnants of the international trading dynasty to Sharhuen and "expelled" the remaining Asiatics from Lower Egypt. Thus, Avaris is not the only Egyptian city to produce archaeological evidence that supports the historicity of the Hebrew Scriptures.

2. Epigraphic

a. Ahmose's Tempest Stele

Archaeological data are not the only evidence of Israel's exodus at the end of the Second Intermediate Period. Several recently discovered inscriptions also grant legitimacy to the Exodus accounts. The first inscription is the *Tempest Stele* of Ahmose (or *Unwetterstele* of Ahmose), which was *erected* shortly after the expulsion of the 15th Hyksos Dynasty.[298] The stele itself was found in the temple at Karnak in Thebes between 1947 and 1951 and pieced together as fragments were unearthed during excavation. In this stele, Ahmose refers to an "all-wreckening storm." While he does not date this event, the fact that he memorializes this "storm" shortly after expelling the Hyksos evokes concurrence with the plagues described in the Book of Exodus.

Ahmose, the Theban pharaoh who finally expelled the Hyksos refers to "storms," the like of which Egypt had never before seen (v. 18). While some scholars envisage this inscription as simply a poetic reaction to the Hyksos' occupation,[299] both the words and the timing of this stele, along with numerous other epigraphic data from this era demonstrate that the text should be taken literally as describing a weather-related storm.[300]

The Egyptian culture always interpreted events in terms of the king's ability to deal with them.[301] Thus, Ahmose's stele is based on an actual storm, and it contains the undertones that the Hyksos were responsible for the gods' anger and the storm that resulted from it.[302]

The inscription begins with Ahmose living in his older brother Kamose's town of Wése,[303] Thebes, shortly after he had become king: perhaps he was co-regent, keeping order at home while Kamose was campaigning and regaining territory in the north.[304] Two scholars, Malcom Weiner and James Allen have recently reexamined this text. Allen's careful work restores the opening lines to read "at the coming of His Incarnation," words that indicate that Ahmose had just ascended the throne during the year when this stele was written.[305] The stele also indicates that Ahmose had been *crowned prince outside the capital city*,[306] due to Kamose's recent and unexpected death. The authors see Ahmose's return to Karnak as confirmation that he was securing his throne.[307] The story of the storm is told in lines of the stele that deal with Ahmose's recent coronation. Let Ahmose tell what occurred:

> (7) The gods were vexed, (8) they were angry. . . . of (?) the gods. The sky came on with *a [rain]-storm, and [darkness]* was in the western heavens; (9) it *rained without [let-u.* . . . the cr]y of the people, powerful [. . . .] *[the thunder] upon the mountains,* louder than the noise of (10) the 'Cavern' which is in Abydos. Then every house and hut [where] they had repaired [collapsed and the detritus was] (11) in the *flood of water, like reed canoes, at the very gate by the palace; and for a period of [. . .] days (12) no lamp was ever lit in the Two Lands.*
>
> Then said His Majesty: 'This is much more serious than god's punishment, greater [than] the gods' [judge]ment!' [308]

Ahmose states that the storm came from the "western heavens" (v. 8) as storms in Egypt are prone to do.[309] Had he meant this metaphorically as a political reaction to the Hyksos'

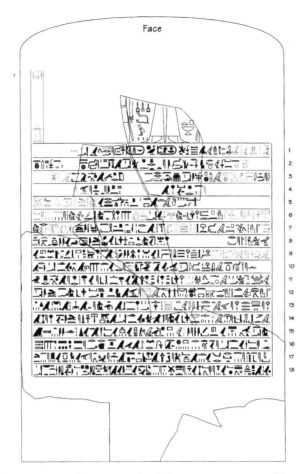

Illustration 10.10. The Tempest Stela of Ahmose. Reconstruction of the Face.

destruction instead of a literal storm, he would have claimed that the storm came out of the east, not the west. Ahmose compares this loud thunderstorm to the Cavern at Abydos (v. 10). This is a reference to the wailing for Osiris (Egypt's counterpart to Tammuz) in the passion play that was enacted yearly at Abydos.[310] He continues to relate that the (11) flooding made houses (huts)[311] float like reed canoes, which reached the very palace threshold. Given the variable levels of the Nile, the king's residence was located at the highest elevation. That flood debris would reach the very palace "gate" indicates that this was a tremendous and unusual flood.[312]

Theban kings often recorded the Nile's flooding. An *earlier* stele by one of Ahmose's 17th-Dynasty predecessors states that the king had walked through the "broad hall" of the temple to find it filled with water during the inundation.[313] That Ahmose's stele likewise attests a violent, "howling" storm would be in character with the type of "news" recorded on the temple walls at Karnak during this era (see Illustration 10.10).

Very recent archaeological evidence at Memphis reveals that flooding occurred shortly before Ahmose's sole regency. The stratum immediately preceding the early 18th Dynasty (Ahmose's Dynasty) evidences water-borne destruction.[314] While the upper layers demonstrate a strong association with the 18th Dynasty, lower levels were covered by sand and destroyed in such a way as to indicate that water had played a part. Beneath this stratum, the excavations revealed a continuum with the earlier 13th Dynasty and scattered ties to the Hyksos upstarts.[315] Another inscription describing Ahmose's support of a Karnak temple is also telling. He donated the most simple and basic furniture and equipment, indicating that perhaps better gifts had been water damaged or washed away.[316] Interestingly, none of his dedications involved precious metals, implying that Ahmose still did not have access to these after his brother's death.[317] This would indicate that the Hyksos had not yet been expelled from Lower Egypt (since the Hyksos had controlled the lucrative Sinai).

Ahmoses's stele states that not only were houses flooded and torn apart by the torrent, (10) but there was also a period of darkness (12) that lasted for an unspecified number of days.[318] Unfortunately, the text is damaged where the duration of the darkness would appear. Since the text does state "days" instead of "day," we know that the dark days lasted for at least two days. What is interesting about this account, as we will see when we compare it with the Scriptural version, is Ahmose's assertion that, not only was it dark for a period of time, but it was impossible to light a lamp in either Upper or Lower Egypt. What is beyond dispute is that the pharaonic regime interpreted these events as "god's punishment."[319] Other texts of this era considered the catalyst for this punishment to be the Hyksos' occupation of the Delta, which had divided the land along with the goading of an arrogant king.

The next section of the stele indicates that Ahmose then traveled north. Later, he states that his army had (v. 13–14) denuded themselves to propitiate the god for his punishment.[320] Ahmose then returned south (v. 14) to "Wése to create a divine golden image "to receive what he desired."[321] This refers to the concluding coronation ceremonies that culminated in the new king's gilding a divine image to show that he had united with the god Re to rule the land.[322] This again implies that Kamose had died unexpectedly around the time of the storm.

Ahmose's *Storm Stele* goes on to state,

> (17) Residence did His Majesty take up within the Great House. Then they reminded His Majesty of the *destruction of the townships, the collapse of buildings, the demolition of the temples and the devastation of the pyramid-tombs*—(18) '*What had never been done (before) is what has (now) been done!*'—Thereupon His Majesty commanded to restore the temples which had fallen into ruin throughout this entire land, to set up (19) the gods' monuments ... to re-introduce the images into their shrines, *which had been scattered about on the ground. . . .* The rations of the office-holders were to be doubled, and the land restored to what it was in the beginning.[323]

After Ahmose's throne had been solidified, when he had taken up residence at the capital (Thebes), his advisors formally reminded him of the destruction wrought by the storm: buildings had collapsed, temples had been "demolished," and the mortuary (pyramid) tombs had been compromised.[324] Every semblance of order had been overthrown, and "that which had never before been, was": chaos prevailed. Ahmose's claim in line 19 regarding the gods' images' being scattered on the ground has an interesting parallel in the later account of the Philistines' taking the *Ark of the Covenant* and placing it inside Dagon's Temple, only to find the god's image "scattered about the ground" (1 Sam 5:4) when morning came. This could indicate YHWH's judgment against Egypt's gods. That Ahmose was able to reestablish the cults throughout Egypt as before the storm may very well indicate that the legitimate Theban Dynasty was on its way to triumph over the Hyksos after a large portion of their population had left by the time the Storm Stela was erected.

Scripture's report of the plagues provides a fascinating parallel to Ahmose's stele: rainfall was enough to flood pyramids, houses, and mortuary temples (line 17), causing incredible damage. It is quite compelling that Scripture also cites a downpour that "had never before been seen in all Egypt since Egypt was a nation."

> Behold, tomorrow about this time I will cause it *to rain* a very grievous hail, *such as has not been in Egypt since the foundation thereof even until now.* (Exod 9:18) And Moses stretched forth his rod toward heaven: and YHWH sent thunder and hail, and the fire ran along on the ground; and YHWH *rained hail on the land of Egypt.* So there was hail, and fire mingled with the hail, very grievous, such *as there was none like it in all the land of Egypt since it became a nation.* (Exod 9:23–24) And Moses went out of the city from Pharaoh, and spread abroad his hands to YHWH: and the thunders and hail ceased, and the rain was not poured on the earth. And when Pharaoh saw that *the rain and the hail* and *the thunders* were ceased, he sinned yet more, and hardened his heart, he and his servants. (Exod 9:33–34)

It appears that we have two accounts of the same event. One from the Egyptian perspective, and the other from the Hebrew. From Ahmose's Theban perspective, it would have appeared that the Hyksos were causing destruction in Egypt: Moses and Aaron had visited the Delta pharaoh, who refused to let Israel go. Scripture's statements that rain and hail of this sort had never fallen in Egypt "since the foundation of it until now" and that "there was none like it in all the land of Egypt since it became a nation" read like the common Egyptian motif of order versus chaos.[325] Ahmose's stele describes the same scene but is couched in traditional Egyptian language:

(18) *What had never been done (before) is what has (now) been done!*

Both Scripture and Ahmose's stele support the idea that this storm was a new form of chaos, a punishment of the god(s) that had never occurred before in all of Egyptian history.[326] Both accounts cite thunder and rain. This western storm stretched from the Delta region where Israel labored all the way to Thebes, indicating the enormity of this system.

Ahmose's stele and the Scriptural account mirror each other with incredible fidelity. Both accounts tell of a miraculous storm filled with rain and thunder, for which there was no parallel. And, both accounts attest a period of darkness. Regarding the plague of darkness, the Hebrew Scriptures tells us:

> And Moses stretched forth his hand toward heaven; and there was a *thick darkness* in all the land of Egypt three days: *They saw not one another, neither rose any from his place* for three days: but all the Children of Israel had light in their dwellings. (Exod 10:22–23)

Traditional interpretations of this text conclude that a prolonged but normal sandstorm engulfed Egypt.[327] While this is certainly a possibility, it is quite implausible for sandstorms in Egypt to include catastrophic flooding. Scripture described this as a plague of darkness "that can be felt" (Exod 10:21), indicating that there was something "in" this darkness. Ahmose's account likewise attests that the Egyptians were "unable to light a torch anywhere," which parallels Scripture. Weiner and Allen interpret Ahmose's stele to indicate that "the darkness was so intense that not even a torch could relieve it."[328]

A very unusual storm, possibly the result of a volcanic eruption, such as an ash plume could also match this description. This type of storm would explain why the Egyptians could not leave their residences (i.g., ash with so much moisture that was it was impossible to ignite a torch). Archaeologists have discovered at least some evidence of volcanic activity during the Hyksos period.[329]

> Of particular interest is the find at several sites within the citadel of numerous nodules of pumice, all of which appear in stratification of the early Eighteenth Dynasty. According to scientific analysis, the pumice derives from the eruption of the Santorini volcano (Thera). [330]

Based on the currently accepted dating system, the early 18th Dynasty falls anywhere between 1570 and 1530 BCE.[331] Radiocarbon dating on Ahmose's mummy also fell in this same range: 1570–1544 BCE (see p. 463). This firmly allows for the debris to be associated with the beginning of Ahmose's reign as well as Israel's exodus. John Holladay, observes that Tell el-Maskhuta (Pi-thom?) demonstrates evidence of an earthquake,[332] which normally precedes volcanic activity. Bietek recognizes that pumice has been discovered (and documented) on top of Hyksos-period occupation layers in northern Sinai at Tell el-Hebwa I.[333] Scientific analysis likewise traces these volcanic deposits to Thera.[334] Bietak plans to attempt to recover volcanic ash at Avaris in the near future. However, he is unsure if a firm context can be provided due to the reconstruction of this area by later pharaohs (i.e., Ramesses) and the disruption of soil by modern farmers.[335]

Based on this archaeological evidence, both Ahmose's stele and the Book of Exodus appear to refer to the same rare and miraculous event. While not every plague in the Exodus account should be associated with volcanic activity, a few may very well be related. Ahmose telescoped the events of the last couple of plagues into one almighty storm of "the great god" against all the "other gods." This context allows for a violent rainstorm to preceded volcanic eruption a month later.[336] Ian Wilson's excellent treatment of this subject has demonstrated that an ash cloud would not necessarily have to cover Egypt for darkness to prevail. If the force of the blast went high enough into the atmosphere, the ash plume could darken the sky for a few days.[337] Malcolm Wiener has also pointed out that radiocarbon data reveals the likelihood of a peak in volcanic activity in 1565 BCE.[338] This once again closely coincides with the date of Scripture's chronology for a 1548 exodus.

Archaeologists likewise question whether the increase in Aegean pottery, specifically Minoan and Cretan, with frescoes in the strata at Avaris may evidence a displaced Aegean population.[339] Manfred Bietak notes Avaris' direct contact with Thera artists in the subsequent early 18th Dynasty (1570–1530). Not only does late Minoan pottery bear ties to the Knossos palace on Crete, but some frescoes (Minoan IA) appear to have the same details as those on Thera, thus demonstrating a chronological link with a Thera, Kea, Cretan and overall Minoan society shortly before[340] Thera's eruption and strong ties afterward. The most telling evidence, however is the White Slip I ware from Thera, which does not appear in Egypt prior to the 18th Dynasty;[341] what this means is that Thera's eruption did not occur during the Hyksos period but at the end of it. The data once again coincide with Scripture's account of the plagues.

Another fascinating parallel to Ahmose's stele and the exodus is the Pharaoh's account that "Egyptian temples and funerary chapels were destroyed."[342] When YHWH threatened to kill Egypt's firstborn, he stated that he would execute judgment not only on the Egyptians but also on their gods.

> For I will pass through the land of Egypt this night, and will smite all the firstborn in the land of Egypt, both man and beast; *and against all the gods of Egypt I will execute judgment*: I am YHWH. (Exod 12:12)

According to the Egyptian account, "As the catalyst of all the events, it is said that the gods were angry, and the resulting torment is described as being 'greater than the wrath of the great god' (lines 7–8, 12)."[343] In particular, Wiener sees this as a clash between "the great god" and "the (other) gods."

> . . . the "great god" on one hand, and "the gods," on the other. (Wiener quotes from line 10 of the *Amose Stele*:) "How much greater is this than the impressive manifestation of the great god, than the plans of the gods!"—indicates that both "the great god" and "the gods" were considered agents of its (the storm's) occurrence.[344]

This is the exact scenario that Scripture presents. According to Scripture, the reason YHWH exercised his power and his wrath on Egypt was to "to show in you my power; and that my name may be declared throughout all the earth" (Exod 9:16). Scripture states that he planned to judge Egypt's gods to demonstrate their impotence as well as to make his fame known as the only viable deity. Uncharacteristically, Egyptian texts admit the powerlessness of the nation's pantheon.

There are at least at least nine parallels between Ahmose's Tempest Stele and the Exodus account. First, Ahmose ascended the throne shortly after his brother's untimely death, which occurred shortly after a destructive storm. Second, this violent storm came out of the west (not the east), supporting the theory that Ahmose was indeed referring to a literal weather-related storm and was not referring to the invading, vile Asiatics who hailed from the east. Third, thunder (Exod 9:23–29) was a characteristic of the seventh plague, which destroyed Egypt's early cereal grains (flax and barley) in the Scriptural account. Thunder was likewise mentioned in Ahmose's description of the unprecedented storm. Fourth, if this epic storm lasted for a couple days, it is quite likely that flooding could ensue, at least to levels common during the yearly flooding of the Nile. The only difference between this flood and the annual inundation was that normal precautions were not taken (since Egypt was not expecting floods at this time of year). Fifth, darkness was the curse of the eighth plague. While Ahmose's stele does divulge the duration of the darkness, it does indicate that it lasted for more than one day. Sixth, both Scripture and Ahmose's stele manifest the idea that these plagues originated from "the great God." Ahmose's view is in line with Gen 15:14, where YHWH prophecies of the nation's future judgment. Seventh, and related to point six is Ahmose's juxtaposing of "the great god" with the "other gods": the same motif is used in Scripture, where YHWH intends to show just how helpless Egypt's deities are and how not even they can deliver the people out of his hand (Exod 12:12). Eighth, we find evidence supporting the destruction of tombs and temples—either due to the storm or due to plundering that occurred a few days before the exodus. Ninth, both Ahmose and Scripture describe this as an unprecedented storm, the likes of which Egypt had never before seen: "What had never been done (before) is what has (now) been done" or that "there was none like it in all the land of Egypt since it became a nation." Thus we see that all the key elements of the exodus were present at the onset of the 18th Dynasty.

b. Bitter Memories of Destruction: Hatshepsut

About 70 years after the Hyksos' expulsion, Queen Hatshepsut commissioned an inscription that once again describes the "ruin" that the Hyksos had brought to the northern lands. The theme of her inscription describes her role in restoring the ancient monuments (mortuary temples and pyramids) that were lost during Hyksos occupation. Her inscription at Speos Artemidos testifies that Hatshepsut restored the following:

> . . .(14) The roads that were (formerly) blocked on all sides, are (now) trodden; my troops which (formerly) had nothing, are (now) equipped with the finest things since my accession as king. . . . Great Pakhet who courses through the valleys in the eastern desert, who opens the (20) rain-swept road. . . . (36) I have restored what was destroyed, I raised up what had formerly been shattered, (37) since Asiatics were in the midst of the Delta (at) Avaris, when the nomads in their midst (38) were destroying what had been made. They ruled without Re, nor did he act by divine decree right down to my majesty('s time)![345]

Similar to Ahmose's claim, Hatshepsut's account associates the destruction of Egypt's cults with the Hyksos who did not even rule by the traditional Egyptian god Re but had chosen his enemy, Seth (see below). She echoes Ahmose's claim of destruction by stating the Pakhet (a local protective lion-goddess) had cleared "rain-swept" roads. While it is likely Hatshepsut is simply referring to the annual flooding of the Nile, it is also possible that she is referring to Ahmose's epic volcanic storm, which devastated the land less than a century before. As we saw earlier, there is evidence that Memphis had been flooded shortly before Ahmose's reign. This interpretation is bolstered by the fact that Hatshepsut still identifies the Asiatics as the cause of Egypt's devastation. Weiner also sees allusions to Ahmose's Tempest in this text, categorizing it as "genre of permanent records describing the restoration of order."[346] Thus it is possible that both these texts retain the memory of the devastating and unprecedented spring storm that YHWH sent on Egypt shortly before he delivered the Israelites.

c. Celebrating the Delta's Destructive God

One of the last inscriptions to mention the Hyksos dates to the last king of the 18th Dynasty, Horemheb (1321–1293), who succeeded the famous Tutankhamun. Horemheb sent his vizier, Seti I (Ramesses' father), to Tanis to celebrate the 400th anniversary of the Egyptian god Seth by erecting a stele. What is particularly ironic is that Seth is not represented in traditional Egyptian style but as an Asiatic deity in "distinctively Asiatic dress."[347] During the Hyksos period, the Asiatics had associated Seth with the Canaanite deity Baal.[348] And the stele seems to indicate that the king's association with a Seth-Baal god was intentional. Scholars speculate that this stele commemorated the founding of Seth as "king" over the Hyksos.

That Horemheb needed to recognize an Asiatic Seth 400 years later may indicate that the Asiatics whom the Egyptians had been deported from Canaan to the Delta during previous administrations (i.e., Thutmoses III) were again becoming a burgeoning population. In theory, no Egyptian king ruled without being granted that right by god (usually Re). Thus, by recognizing Seth, Horemheb was legitimizing his rule[349] over the 19th nome in a preemptive move to counter the possibility that this territory would secede as it had during the SIP.

d. Admonitions of Ipuwer

i. ADMONITIONS AS HISTORY

In the past, scholars have been hesitant to view literature such as *The Admonitions of Ipuwer*[350] as a historical narrative, instead viewing it as a political commentary. Recent studies have demonstrated that, quite the contrary, every nation writes history according to "the framework of their own beliefs" in much the same way that the Israelite writers recorded history in Scripture or even as we do today.[351] That a theological philosophy governs ancient literature does not devalue its historical content; if anything, it helps us to see how the ancient nations interpreted their past.[352]

The validity of this approach is no more apparent than in *The Admonitions of Ipuwer*. This particular text gains validity from at least five sources: archaeology, Ahmose's *Storm Stele*, Queen Hatshepsut's inscription from Speos Artemidos, Manetho, and Scripture.

The Admonitions of Ipuwer is a single document (Papyrus Leiden 344). The papyrus dates to the 19th Dynasty (c. 1290–1185), but the text is a copy of an older document.[353]

Admonitions is the work of an adviser (Ipuwer), who laments the calamities of the Second Intermediate Period and uses a history lesson to instruct the king.[354] When scholars first began discussing this document, they were apt to associate it with Egypt's First Intermediate Period;[355] however, scholars now realize that it bears a striking resemblance to the Second Intermediate Period (i.e., Hyksos) instead.[356] The dilemma that scholars face when attributing it to the First or Second Intermediate Period of Egyptian history is that the events it describes are typical of Egypt's trouble with Asiatics during both epochs.

Ipuwer presents his advice to the king as an indictment of a past Asiatic uprising in the Delta (see Illustration 10.11). He draws attention to the legitimate pharaoh's inability to retain law and order during anarchy. The text appears to provide an accurate description of the SIP civil war while re-assuring the people of the legitimate Egyptian pharaoh's ability to handle the Asiatics. The occasion of this work, may indicate that the 18th Dynasty king whom Ipuwer addresses was facing pressure from his nobles and citizens for trans-Jordan campaigns, which brought large booty of Asiatic captives back into Egypt just as Senusret III had done in the Middle Kingdom. It was the offspring of these captives that, from all accounts, rose to overthrow

Illustration 10.11. An Egyptian scribe.

the 13th Dynasty during the SIP and Ipuwer uses this history to teach the king to avoid similar policies. *Admonitions of Ipuwer* is too long to be given justice here, but a few points beg observation.

ii. CORVÉE SLAVERY

Scripture is not the only text, which indicates a fierce political shift had occurred about the time of Moses' birth. As we saw earlier, Manetho (in Josephus, *Against Apion* 1.76) states this shift coincided with the Hyksos king "slaughtering some and enslaving the wives and children of others." Manetho may have been quoting directly from the history of Ipuwer, which recounts:

> Lo, citizens are put to the grindstones, Wearers of fine linen are beaten with [sticks]. . . . Lo, [ᵣtombᵣ]-builders have become field-laborers, Those who were in the god's bard are yoked [to it].[357]

Ipuwer recounts the reversal of fortune. The same nature of which Scripture tells us occurred when the Hebrews suddenly found themselves under corvée labor (Exod 1:11). As we saw earlier (pp. 449–54, 457–59, 463–64), archaeology for this era demonstrates strong corvée ties, ties that appear severed for at least 50 years after Israel and her mixed company left Avaris. Thus, Manetho, Ahmose, Ipuwer, Scripture, and archaeology may all appear to evidence the same event; at the very least, these sources allow for it.

iii. DESTRUCTION OF TEMPLES AND GODS

In the *Storm Stele,* Ahmose claimed great damage had occurred to the mortuary temples, tombs, and gods during his reign. About 70 years later, Hatshepsut made the same claim as the theme of her inscription at Speos Artemidos (cited above) focused on recommissioning the various cults that had fallen into disuse after the plunder by the "Asiatics in the midst of the Delta."[358]

Archaeological data demonstrate that tombs were indeed plundered during the Hyksos' southern advance, which attempted to overtake the nation's traditional Egyptian monarchs as far south as Abydos.[359] Bietak observes that "all the graves (at Avaris) were plundered."[360] The same appears true of the tombs at Tell el-Maskhuta[361] prior to the final Hyksos occupation.

Manetho also describes great destruction to Egypt's "temples and their gods," associating it with the Asiatic rebellion in the Delta. Scripture states that YHWH intended the final Egyptian plague to "execute judgment: against all the gods of Egypt" (Exod 12:12), which we saw earlier could have indicated a physical destruction or plundering of Egyptian mortuary temples. Ipuwer appears to be citing first-hand accounts of this destruction:

> Lo, those who were entombed are cast on high ground. . . . What the pyramid hid is empty. See now, the land is deprived of kingship. . . . By a few people who ignore custom. . . . He who could not make a coffin owns a tomb.[362]

About 30 years after the exodus, Amenhotep I made the "radical decision to site his mortuary temple away from his burial place."[363] This could be seen as a reaction to the Hyksos' recent plundering of mortuary temples and tombs, and Amenhotep's attempt to secure his soul's successful journey into the afterlife. This would be in line with Hatshepsut's remarks a few years later that she had continued Ahmose I's policy (*Tempest Stele,* line 17) of restoring the temples and tombs (*Speos Artemidos,* lines 36–38) the Asiatics had "ruined." Thus, Manetho, Ahmose, Hatshepsut, archaeology, Ipuwer, and Scripture all seem to refer to a judgment of Egypt's gods (Exod 12:12) resulting in the plundering and usurping of sacred burial sites.

iv. THE PEOPLE'S REVOLUTION

Religious thought defines societies and empires. Beliefs precede action. This is perhaps no more evident than in the SIP (Second Intermediate Period). The most important religious development of this era concerned the cult of Osiris,[364] who had in Middle Kingdom times become the "Great God of all necropolises."[365] Previous to this era, Senusret III lavished Osiris's cult at Abydos with wealth.

> The growing influence of Osiris must have derived to some extent from active promotion of the site of Abydos and the so-called mysteries of Osiris. . . . The growth

of the Osirian cult was accompanied by a cultural phenomenon sometimes described as the 'democratization of the afterlife': the extension of once-royal funerary privileges to ordinary people. Large numbers of stelae at Abydos in particular show that it was becoming increasingly common for private individuals to take part in the rites of Osiris, thus receiving blessings that had once been restricted to kings. As a result of this development, the funerary beliefs and rites of the entire population began to change. [366]

For the first time, individuals had direct access to "god" and were able to participate directly in the mysterious passion play, a rite previously held only for the very elite.[367] With this new sense of independence and self-worth, the people saw themselves as individuals who were important to the state for the first time. The individual mattered. He had access to god himself. He was important enough in the god Osiris's eyes to be allowed into the afterlife and receive his blessings.

This new-found importance of the individual is no more evident than in the titles that upper government officials took for themselves. So many of these officials usurped royal titles normally reserved solely for Pharaoh himself that it is almost impossible to sort out who was a legitimate ruler during the SIP.[368] The later, 13th-century scribe obviously had problems with these as well and simply lumped them all together in one dynasty (14th Dynasty).[369] Ipuwer's history lesson for the king may help us piece together the fragments left of this fragmented era.

Ipuwer tells us that, at the beginning of his history, uprisings were rampant in the Delta region as brother raised hand against brother to shed blood.

> The Delta [-dwellers] carry shield. . . . A man regards his son as his enemy . . . Hostility[———] another. . . . Foreigners have become people everywhere. . . . There is blood everywhere, no shortage of dead. . . . Lo, many dead are buried in the river. The stream is the grave, the tomb became a stream. Lo, the river is blood.[370]

Social order had broken down. Bloodshed was pandemic: civil war had overturned the realm. Had it not been for obvious Egyptian cultural references, this history could very well be the French Revolution under Napoleon or the Bolshevik revolution in Russia. The tenor of this history could very well be written in modern times as a "people's revolution," in which the over-taxed, oppressed, and ignoble lower classes form alliances with generations of immigrants, disenfranchised nobles, and international trade connections to oppose and to overthrow their oppressive lords.

> Lo, poor men have become men of wealth, He who could not afford sandals owns riches. . . . Lo, men's slaves, their hearts are greed. . . . Lo, nobles lament, the poor rejoice, Every town says, "let us expel our rulers. . . . The robber owns riches, [the noble] is a thief. . . . Lo, —-noblewomen, Their bodies suffer in rags, Their hearts ⌈shrink⌉ from greeting [⌈each other⌉]. Lo, every have-not is one who has, Those who were people are strangers whom one shows the way. . . . One can't distinguish the son of man from the pauper. . . . The serf becomes an owner of serf. . . . beggars come and go in the great mansion. . . . Lo, there is much hatred in the street. . . .

Men stir up strife unopposed. . . . The coward is emboldened to seize his goods. . . . The king has been robbed by beggars. . . . See, the poor of the land have become rich, The man of property is a pauper.[371]

Like many revolutions, this popular uprising lacked any direction or thought about the future beyond humbling the upper classes. Uneducated and unskilled commoners occupied vast estates and "private"[372] properties in the *coup*. Not even rare and precious possessions were spared. The vilest of prisoners were freed: "Those who never saw daylight go out unhindered."[373] Thus, in effect, the lower classes stripped the very reserves and resources that ensured their welfare. Had this account not been removed by 3,000 years, it could almost describe Egypt's modern-day revolt, in which the Egyptian Library in Cairo was burned and tens of thousands of ancient documents relating to the people's own heritage were destroyed in December 2011.

> Lo, trees are felled, branches stripped. . . . Food is lacking. . . . Lo, the great hunger and suffer. . . . *Lo, chests of ebony are smashed, Precious ssndm-wood is chopped*[374][—]He who did not weave for himself owns fine linen. See, he who did not build a boat for himself owns ship. . . . Their owner looks at them: they are not his. . . . See, the poor of the land have become rich, The man of property is a pauper. See he who had no loaf owns a barn, His storeroom is filled with another's goods. . . . He who could not find plow-oxen owns cattle. . . . The output of craftsmen is lacking. . . . He who lacked grain owns granaries, He who fetched grain on loan issues it. Lower Egypt weeps. . . . The King's storehouse is "I go-get-it," for everyone, and the whole palace is without its revenues. . . . Towns are ravaged, Upper Egypt became wasteland. . . . Lo, grain is lacking on all sides, Lo, people are diminished. . . . Lo, the desert claims the land, The nomes are destroyed, Gold is lacking; ⌐materials⌐ for every kind of craft. What belongs to the palace has been stripped. Everyone says, "There's nothing." The storehouse is bare, Its keeper stretched on the ground[375.] . . . See now, the transformations of (foreign) people. See the judges of the land are driven from the land, The nobles are expelled from the royal mansions. . . . Princes in the workhouse. . . . See, those who owned robes are in rags. . . . See, the mighty of the land are not reported to, the affairs of the people have gone to ruin.[376]
>
> [The King answers Ipuwer:] "For every man slays his (own) brother, and the troops we recruited for ourselves have become foreigners, and have turned to pillaging. The outcome of that will be to let the Asiatics realize the condition of the land. . . . But (this will be) said of you in later years: [. . .] destroyed itself."[377]

Archaeological excavations demonstrate that the "inhabitants of Avaris suffered to an extremely high degree from deficiency diseases and anaemic states caused by periodic scarcity of food."[378] This is especially attested when private inscriptions state that upper government officials took on royal titles for themselves; the inscriptions memorialize their ability to sustain themselves during famine. Donald Redford sees these epitaphs reflecting "a southland victimized by natural disaster, famine, and the depredations of foreigners."[379] This is the exact situation that Ipuwer relates: "Food is lacking, there is great hunger," every man helped himself to Egypt's food stores—a situation that would have led to food shortages for several years. All these circumstances could easily have been exacerbated if the Nile had failed to flood and contributed to the instability of the overall revolution.

V. TRAFFIC BLOCKADE

One passage reveals Ipuwer's Theban origin. Similar to Kamose's lament that Apophis had placed all travelers along the Nile under tribute; Ipuwer laments the loss of trade routes with Byblos and access to cedar wood for the deceased.

> No one sails north to Byblos today. How shall we replace for our mummies the cedar wood, the importation of which makes possible the making of coffins of the priests.[380]

Van Seters ties Ipuwer's statement to the Hyksos era by using the archaeological evidence that coffins from Upper Egypt (Thebes) were no longer made from cedar, a product of Syria, but hollowed-out logs of local sycamore trees.[381] Thus trade between Upper Egypt and the Levant had been effectively usurped by the Hyksos tariffs on the Delta's trade routes.[382] This places Ipuwer's lament squarely in the Hyksos era of Egyptian history.

Interestingly, Hatshepsut had stated that she had to clear and reopen roads and perhaps even the trade routes that the Asiatics had blocked. "The roads that were (formerly) blocked on all sides, are (now) trodden" (Speos Artemidos, v. 14). Ipuwer provides a third witness to the fact that the Asiatics had blockaded traffic and trade during the Hyksos era:

> Lo, the whole Delta cannot be seen. . . . Lower Egypt puts trust in trodden roads (trade blockade). Lo, the ways are [blocked], the roads watched. Lo, gone is what was yesterday was seen, The land is left to its weakness like a cutting of flax.[383]

During the height of Hyksos power, Apophis subjected all travel and trade along the Nile to tribute (see Kamose I). It is very possible that Hyksos garrisons kept a close watch over the land routes, missing no opportunity to tax trade or travel along Egypt's highways.

vi. INFANTICIDE

What may be the strongest ties between Ipuwer's history, the Hyksos' occupation of the Delta, and Moses' birth is the claim that the trouble-makers of this rebellion slaughtered children and infants.

> Lo, children of nobles are dashed against walls, Infants are put out on high ground. . . . Lo, children of nobles are dashed against walls, Infants are put out on high ground. Lo, terror kills. . . . Lo, women are barren, none conceive.[384]

Manetho had asserted that the first Hyksos king had "treated the inhabitants with the utmost hostility, slaughtering some and enslaving the wives and children of others." This is the exact setting in which Scripture places Moses' birth as the Hebrew Asiatics' children were slaughtered shortly after birth (Exod 1:16, 22). As we saw above, Tell el-Maskhuta demonstrates a substantial number of infant and adolescent burials, disproportionate with adult graves, perhaps indicating a situation where both native Egyptians and Hebrews (any loyal to the traditional Egyptian Dynasty) faced execution by the usurping Hyksos. In the Scriptural account, midwives were directed to kill the new-borns. This situation would have caused many women to avoid pregnancy so that their infants did not face death, thus the "women would be barren and none conceive."

Ipuwer's *Admonitions* appear to relate the history of the SIP from the beginning of a revolution and its hostile takeover until the land was once again restored to peace—an epoch covering 100–200 years. The similarities among Manetho, Scripture, and archaeology are extensive. Those at ease and with some social status and property were suddenly thrust into low-status jobs, probably associated with corvée labor. Mortuary temples and graves were plundered by foreigners and the lower classes. Egypt's gods were helpless to protect their own shrines. Traffic and trade from Upper Egypt endured such stiff tariffs that they all but ceased to exist. Some of these routes may later have been blockaded by the storm (seventh plague)—the focus of Ahmose's stele. The murder of small children is quite accurately depicted by both the Scriptural account of this era and the archaeological remains, thus demonstrating that Ipuwer's history must fall squarely within the SIP.

e. No "Destruction of Mankind"

> The interest of the tale lies, of course, in the theme of human wickedness arousing the divine wrath and resulting in a partial destruction of mankind.[385]
> ~ Miriam Lichtheim, *Ancient Egyptian Literature of the New Kingdom*

No discussion of the exodus would be complete without addressing one piece of Egyptian literature that, at first glance, appears to grant historical validity to the exodus's plagues. The "Destruction of Mankind" appears on the walls of the thirteenth-century tomb of several kings at Thebes: Seti I, Ramesses II, and Ramesses III. While this story dates to the New Kingdom, "the language used and the corrupted state of the text show that it followed an older original,"[386] prompting most scholars to place this story in the Middle Kingdom (2040–1720 BCE).[387] Most literature of the New Kingdom (1570–1070 BCE) Era was written in Late Egyptian, whereas the "Destruction of Mankind" is written in Middle Egyptian.[388] In other words, the tale is much older than the reign of Ramesses, where biblical scholars (Kitchen) are often prone to place the exodus.

During the earlier Middle Kingdom, the relationship between the gods was poorly defined. All this appears to have changed in the New Kingdom (after Ahmose), when "a well-articulated set of relationships between these gods emerged."[389] The redefining, interconnection, and merging of the gods are nowhere more apparent than in the Ramessid Pyramid Texts.

The "Destruction of Mankind" is a tale of rebellion against the very aged god Re.[390] According to the text, the rebels had escaped to the desert.[391] Hathor, who was usually worshiped for her kind and protective nature, suddenly changes into another god, Sekhmet in order to avenge mankind's transgressions (see Illustration 10.12). Re sends Hathor, now

Sekhmet, to destroy the transgressors. Hathor-Sekhmet becomes so delighted in destroying mankind that she does not stop. In an effort to quell her thirst for blood, Re sends to the south to obtain "red ochre," a dye found near Elephantine.[392] The red ochre is ground and mixed with 7,000 jars of beer-mash, "and it became like human blood."[393] Re floods the Delta then uses a "Nile that has turned to blood" to trick Sekhmet into drinking it. She becomes drunk and her thirst for blood is satisfied. She then reverts to the kind, protective deity Hathor.[394]

The text continues by referring to a period of darkness that gives way to light[395] and human sacrifice, which is translated as the "slaughter of sacrifice."[396] Hathor's vengeance is said to have begun at Herakleopolis (Suten-henen in Egyptian) *during the night* when Hathor "waded in the blood of men."[397] Her slaughter is said to have occurred when mankind "travels south,"[398] perhaps alluding to the harvest season, when

Illustration 10.12. Sekhmet, from the temple at Kom Ombo in Upper Egypt.

Nile levels were low and torrents manageable—the only time southern travel was possible (i.e. February-July). Later in the legend, the very aged Re creates Thoth, who has power "to turn back northern people."[399] Hathor is conveniently retired to the sparsely populated far western part of Lower Egypt.[400] Sekhmet continues to be associated with plagues, pestilence, and healing from plagues throughout the New Kingdom.[401]

James Allen sees this pyramid text as a "literary parallel" to the Ahmose Stele[402] because the events it describes appear to be related. Attempts to associate this tale with Scripture's exodus, however, appear unjustified. Egypt's ancient kings refer to Sekhmet's plagues and destructive nature. As early as the 16th Dynasty (*c*. 1649–1570 BCE), King Senakhenre Montuhopti refers to "Sekhmet's year of pestilence" as though it is a standing conceptual motif.[403] It is true that the story appears to redact and redefine the relationship of the gods based on past history. While the story could be an Egyptian parallel to the exodus, there is currently not enough evidence to judge whether the particular plagues enumerated in the "Destruction of Man" were a common literary formula before the Hyksos period. While the tale indeed satisfies all the historical facts regarding the Asiatic invasion and the exodus, the tale may apply equally to many eras in Egyptian history, describing and justifying the causes of chaos and couching it in terms of being caused by Asiatic immigrations. Until future research proves otherwise, the original story appears to predate the exodus.

Egyptologist Janine Bourriau has recently argued that in reality the Middle Kingdom continued through the Hyksos era (SIP) until the rise of the 18th Dynasty.[404] In other words, there may be no significant break with tradition until Ahmose and his successors installed new literary styles and perhaps even revamped and realigned Egypt's gods. Although the original story of the "Destruction of Man" was indeed written toward the end of the Middle Kingdom, perhaps even during the SIP, its importance and popularity grew during the New Kingdom. Its popularity during Seti's and Ramesses' reigns (it appears in three different king's tombs) could be interpreted as a political reaction to justify the events that took place during the Hyksos period and the exodus. Ramesses and his New Kingdom predecessors had captured and deported many Asiatics as prisoners of war or as hostages, settling them in the Delta once more. Thus, this tale may have been a response to justify the causes for events that were still fresh in society's collective memory.

The "Destruction of Man" does pose some curious questions. Four events parallel Scripture's account of the exodus: water turning to blood, a period of darkness, a great loss of life during the night (which occurred in the spring), and a people who have escaped into the desert. As we saw when we looked at Ahmose's Tempest Stele, there was a volcanic eruption that "darkened" the land of Egypt for a couple of days, and evidence exists for a flood—events that coincide perfectly with Scripture's chronology for the Exodus Era. The likelihood that these stories portray separate events or even that both are valid is slim. So how do we account for the similarities?

Egyptian theology contained no concept of monotheism.[405] Even when one deals with a particular deity, "there is never the exclusivity" that occurs in monotheism. Thus, the only way the Egyptians could understand Israel's God was to associate him with one of their own, or for YHWH to deal with Egypt as though he were one of its gods. If the Egyptians associated YHWH with Sekhmet, this would explain why she was elevated to the "mightiest one" and her popularity increased in the subsequent New Kingdom Era.[406] However, more research is needed on this topic to resolve these issues in light of an earlier exodus.

Strong evidence exists for dating Israel's exodus in the Hyksos era. First, Israel's chronology firmly places the exodus in 1548, contemporary with Thera's eruption. Second, early Asiatic names associated with the 14th Dynasty attest an Amorite presence with names such as Yakbim and Ya'qub. While these names do not refer to the Hebrew patriarch, they do attest its contemporary popularity. Third, archaeology reveals customs that are also recorded in Scripture: family tombs, placing burial sites in the community, taking on Egyptian names, and four-room Syrian-style homes are all typically associated with Israel. Fourth, the Hyksos era evidences the garrison forces referred to in Scripture, an account that does not make much sense in the latter Ramessid era. Fifth, corvée labor (a type of slavery) is attested by Scripture, archaeology, Egyptian state documents, and Manetho. There is evidence that an Asiatic servile community left Egypt around 1550, and the next 50 years demonstrate (archaeologically) a loss of labor. This period conspicuously coincides with the time when Israel would have been in the wilderness. Sixth, tombs, graves, and mortuary temples exhibit plundering, either by natives, Asiatics, Hebrews or all three. YHWH had told Abraham and Moses that when the Israelites left Egypt, they would "plunder" Egypt's wealth. Seventh, mass burials evidence an epidemic and may attest to the cleansing of the city afterward. Strangely, it appears both that Kamose, Apophis, and Ahmose's firstborn son died sometime during this short period.

Eighth, Tell el-Maskhuta also presents some interesting parallels. Strewn pottery shards probably demonstrate a pastoral society. Yet, they could also evidence Israel's final exodus, as the people journeyed from Avaris to Pi-thom. Maskhuta's early society evidences numerous infant burials indicative of infanticide, which also occurred at the time of Moses' birth. The city further satisfies Scripture's description by revealing store facilities and ties to Shechem. Fascinatingly, the final inhabitants quietly took everything portable with them when they left in peace.

Ninth, the epigraphic evidence is even more convincing. Ahmose commissioned a stele to record a mighty storm, the like of which Egypt had never seen before. The stele strongly suggests that the storm occurred shortly before Ahmose acceded to the throne, perhaps shortly after his brother's death. Thunder, flooding, and a period of darkness were part of this tempest. Tenth, Archaeological evidence as well as scientific tests reveal that Thera indeed erupted during the last phases of Hyksos occupation, shortly before Ahmose began to rebuild the empire. Eleventh, seismic data places this event sometime around 1565 BCE (a date that fits well with Scripture's chronology). Additionally, Memphis may evidence flooding at the end of the Hyksos period, shortly before Ahmose expelled the remaining Hyksos and reclaimed the Delta. All these data are supported by the archaeological evidence for an increasing Aegean population shortly before Thera's eruption, with ties to the Theran population, who it appears decorated the palace with their frescoes shortly after Thera's final blow. Ahmose understood this storm to be the product of "the great God," rendering his judgment on all the "other gods" of Egypt— a view that Scripture likewise shares.

Twelfth, 70 years after Ahmose chased the remaining Asiatics from the Delta, Hatshepsut was still reciting Egypt's disdain toward the Asiatics and the chaos wrought by their occupation. Roads were blockaded, perhaps "rainswept," and temples destroyed: all because Asiatics had overtaken the Delta and fractured the land. Thirteenth, Ipuwer's *Admonissions* likewise witnessed social unrest during the entire Second Intermediate Period. The upper classes became corvée laborers, temples were plundered, civil war raged, trade was hindered by tariffs and was blockaded and, most of all, "children of nobles are dashed against walls, infants are put out on high ground" during the horrors perpetrated during the civil war and women ceased to become pregnant for fear of their children's future.

And Fourteenth, in the subsequent New Kingdom Era, Sekhmet and Seth—both gods of destruction—excelled in popularity; much of the folklore about Sekhmet echoes the plagues that took place when YHWH sent plagues on Egypt when Thera erupted. In this case, it appears that significant evidence exists for Israel's historical exodus.

III. THEOLOGICAL PERSPECTIVE OF THE EXODUS AND THE PLAGUES

A. *The Pejorative God: Religion, Politics, or Both?*

The Asiatics' ties to Canaan are most discernible in the religion that they embraced after emigrating to Egypt. Scholars mostly agree that the Hyksos worshiped the Canaanite Baal.[407]

Baal was the Canaanite version of the Egyptian Osiris[408] or the Babylonian Tammuz. There is some debate as to whether Asiatics residing in the Delta founded Seth's cult or if it was founded by native Egyptians in prior centuries.[409] What is ironic with Baal's association with Seth is that he treacherously assassinated his brother and rightful heir,[410] a scenario that seems to echo the Hyksos usurpation quite well.

To the Egyptians, Seth was Osiris's antagonist. He was associated with chaos and destruction.[411] But it does not appear that the Asiatics identified him as such. For the Asiatics in the Delta, Seth was Baal. This may very well explain Israel's later comfort with and apostasy to Baal throughout her history. It is also in this light that Joshua's statement that Israel should put away the gods she had worshiped in Egypt should be understood (Josh 24:14). Israel would be facing the exact same doctrine from similar gods once she arrived in Canaan.

Above, we saw that Apophis had sent a challenging and insulting letter to Kamose's father, Seqenenre Tao. Not only did the arrogant king challenge the southern Theban king to a duel but also his god to a duel. We saw that this challenge "pits their god Seth against the Theban god Amon-Re."[412] Although Seth would have seemed victorious in Apophis's defeat over the Theban king Seqenenre Tao, this victory would be short-lived. Apophis had challenged the gods to a duel to see which god would "be with him as protector."[413] The Delta was about to see that neither Apophis's god Seth nor any of the other of the gods of Egypt could protect the people from Israel's God. YHWH would answer Apophis's challenge. The Delta would receive the brunt of YHWH's plagues when YHWH "executed judgment against all the gods of Egypt" (Exod 12:12). Thus, as far as a Scriptural background to the Exodus account is concerned, it was the perfect setup. While Apophis trusted in Seth, not even Baal himself could save or deliver Apophis and his court out of YHWH's destructive hand.

It is in this context that YHWH states that he raised Apophis to the monarchy, so that he could reveal his own power and glory.

> And in very deed for this cause have I raised you up, for to show in you my power; and that my name may be declared throughout all the earth. As yet exalt you yourself against my people that you will not let them go? (Exod 9:16–17)

It appears that Apophis's usurpation of Egypt's throne was no accident. Rather, YHWH chose the most base and arrogant man to rule over Egypt.

After Apophis's death, it appears that Egypt's traditional priests were at a loss with how to treat this particularly offensive king. All Egyptian pharaohs, including foreign usurpers, were customarily deified upon death (though not worshiped).[414] Yet, how were they to deal with a king who had defied all the gods? It may be that the priesthood used the only tools it had at its disposal: defame Apophis's memory.

The god Apophis is *unattested before* the Hyksos' occupation of Egypt.[415] Unlike traditional pharaohs, Apophis was considered a malevolent, destructive god. He was associated with unexplained darkness, earthquakes, thunderstorms, and chaos.[416] If Apophis was indeed the pharaoh at the exodus, this fact would explain his later deified attributes, memorializing the events that transpired during his reign. Chaos prevailed when YHWH sent destructive thunderstorms to destroy crops, and three dark days ensued, while an earthquake was preceded by Thera's eruption—all causing chaos in Egypt's orderly society.

In the New Kingdom (19th Dynasty),[417] Apophis was represented as a snake like the Greek Hydra: no matter how many times he was killed, or his head was chopped off or eaten, he always came back.[418] This association could stem from his contact with Moses: though Egyptian magicians could produce snakes, it was Moses and Aaron's snake that devoured and destroyed the snakes belonging to Apophis's magicians. Fascinatingly, Apophis was often associated with the Hyksos deity Seth.[419] Like Sekhmet or Apophis, the Egyptian Seth was associated with destructive forces. Eventually, Seth united with Egypt's creator-god Re to destroy Apophis at last. At a much later date in Egyptian literature, Apophis became "the sun god's arch enemy," from whose chaos the world needs to be saved.[420] Thus, Apophis may be one origin of modern ideas regarding "the devil" (see Illustration 10.13).

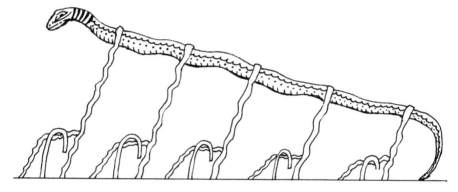

Illustration 10.13. The evil god Apophis bound to the earth. Apophis "existed at the creation of the world and must be defeated for the first time by the creator god and driven out of the ordered world of existence" (*CGAE*, 159).

B. Note on Miracles

Credible studies regarding the science behind the plagues are severely lacking. Two observations bear mentioning. All miracles occur by some scientific method, whether we understand it or not. While not every plague should be associated with volcanic activity, credible evidence exists to support that the theory that the plagues associated with a horrific storm and darkness were indeed caused by Thera's volcanic eruption. These plagues were caused by a real phenomenon. However, their catalyst or cause was directed by YHWH. The same would be true of other phenomena from the parting of the Red Sea and the Jordan River to the sun's standing still (Josh 10:13). These were effected by manipulation of the laws of physics, not mysticism. It appears that the God who created the laws of the universe knew how to work within these laws—perhaps by quantum mechanics—to effect "supernatural" phenomena at the very moment that he chose them to occur.

One last observation regarding the plagues of gnats and locusts and the appearance of Israel's quail in the wilderness. We do not know whether the Egyptians struggled with these pests prior to the exodus. These infestations do continue to recur every few years, although to a lesser degree as recorded in Scripture. Swarms of locust occur in northern Egypt every 40 to 70 years (see below).[421] And, the coriander-like manna substance that Israel ate in the wilderness still appears overnight in the desert in very small quantities.[422] Even if these miracles had not occurred prior to the exodus, the remnants of the mechanisms that YHWH put in place to effect his miracles still function today but on a much smaller scale.

C. The Egyptian Calendar: A Theological Perspective

1. The Lunar-Solar Civil Calendar

The story of Egypt's plagues in the Book of Exodus gives the impression that all of these outbreaks recurred in rapid succession, lasting a few weeks to possibly a month. This perspective is influenced by the telescoped nature of the Exodus account, which condensed the major points of conflict and Moses' interaction with Pharaoh into a short narrative easy for readers to follow. Taking a critical look at this account, an entirely different picture emerges.

Using a forensics approach, we can find many clues to the duration of the Egyptian plagues. In order to understand the context in which the plagues occurred, it is necessary to understand the Egyptian calendric system. Unlike our modern, Julian-Gregorian calendar, which is based on the solar seasons, the Egyptian civil calendar was astronomically based.[423] Instead of four seasons, it had three seasons. The first was Akhet (meaning 'inundation') when the Nile flooded the Delta, this season lasted from July to early November. The second was Peret, meaning 'seed.' This season coincided with the time when crops were planted: from early November through early March. And the last season was Shomu, meaning 'harvest,' in which crops were harvested. This season lasted from early March through the end of June.[424] These three seasons were further divided into 12 months with 30 equal days.[425] At the end of each year, 5–6 days were inserted to keep the civil calendar in line with the solar year and the seasons in the correct months.[426]

The Egyptian new year began when the star Sirius (Sopdet in Egyptian) "was observed to rise just before dawn; this was its heliacal rising."[427] Although the civil year began with the heliacal rising, the agricultural year began with the inundation. This could be a few days to 25 days after Sirius's appearance; hence, the Egyptian times for planting and harvest could vary by this same amount of time (7–25 days).[428]

2. Moses Elohiym and Aaron Mal'ak: Scripture's Plagues in Their Egyptian Context

When YHWH sent Moses to Egypt, he stated that he would make Moses a god to Pharaoh and Aaron would be his prophet.

And YHWH said to Moses, See, *I have made you a god (elohiym) to Pharaoh*: and Aaron your brother shall be your prophet. You shall speak all that I

> command you: and Aaron your brother shall speak to Pharaoh, that he send
> the Children of Israel out of his land. And I will harden Pharaoh's heart, and
> multiply my signs and my wonders in the land of Egypt. (Exod 7:1–3)

The extent to which YHWH would make Moses a god to Pharaoh is missed without understanding the Egyptian calendar. The plagues appear to follow the Egyptian civil calendric
cycle, with the genesis of each plague challenging the power of that the season's gods. Initial
investigation indicates that one plague occurred every month.[429] This means that Moses,
Aaron, and the elders first appeared before Pharaoh before the beginning of the Egyptian
new year (which began with the rising of Sirius), shortly before the Nile flooded the Delta
region (modernly around mid- July).[430]

a. Season: Akhet. Month: Tekhi—Mid-July to Mid-August

1st Plague: Water to Blood

Egyptian harvests occurred earlier than harvest time in Israel.[431] The entire harvest was
completed by June, a couple of weeks before the inundation[432]—the time of year when
the snows melted in the mountains, and the Nile overflowed its banks. Using a scientific
forensics approach allows us to see the details: the first plague occurred after the harvest yet
before the inundation, which means that Moses first came to Pharaoh between mid-June
and mid-July.[433]

Scripture records that at this time Israel was employed in brick-making (Exodus 5).
Brick-making would not have been an option during the harvest season, when all hands
were busy harvesting the land.[434] The inundation was traditionally the "season when the
work-force, essentially consisting of peasants, was available for the corvée work that they
were obliged to undertake for the king."[435]

The second clue to the time of year when the first plague occurred is Scripture's statement that the Israelites used straw to make their bricks:

> You shall no more give the people straw to make brick, as before: let them
> go and gather straw for themselves. . . . So the people were *scattered abroad
> throughout all the land of Egypt to gather stubble* instead of straw. (Exod 5:7, 12)

This text reveals at least two things: first that straw as
harvest "leftovers" was available for Israel to gather.
The second is that Israel was able to go throughout the
land of Egypt to gather straw. This places Moses and
Aaron's first encounters with Pharaoh after the harvest,
when stalks littered the fields and threshing floors. This
again indicates that Moses first spoke with Pharaoh after the harvest, shortly before the Nile's inundation.

Illustration 10.14. Akhet: The
Egyptian horizon. The Akhet season
ran from mid-July to mid-November.

This would have been during the month of Tekhi in the first season of Akhet (see Illustration 10.14).

Egypt's various religious cults were tied to the nation's civil calendar. Each Egyptian month marked the veneration of a different Egyptian god. Within the first Egyptian month of Tekhi, the god Djehuty (Gk. Thoth) was worshiped.[436] The center of his cult was Hermopolis in southern Egypt. The mythological tradition with Thoth was that the deity invented writing and was a recorder of time. Also important to his cult was his ability to command magic.[437] Pharaoh Apophis had challenged the gods to a duel, claiming that Seth (and probably his Delta pantheon) was the most powerful god of the land. YHWH seized this opportunity to demonstrate that these deities were nothing more than folklore and tricks of the magicians. Hence, Moses and Aaron's "magic" was stronger than Djehuty's when Moses' serpent ate the magicians' snakes (Exod 7:9–12). Thus, YHWH's power was greater than that of Egypt's gods.

Illustration 10.15   Hapy, the god of the Nile.

YHWH would demonstrate that his power superseded that of any god in Egypt: he would prove they were fake by demonstrating that no god could deliver Egypt out of his hand. The next deity that Moses and Aaron challenged targeted the Nile. Since Egypt did not receive significant rainfall to sustain agriculture, the Nile's inundation or lack thereof led to either feast or famine. That the very first plague targeted the Nile supports the correlation between the plagues and Egypt's calendric-agricultural cycle, indicating that the plague occurred in the first Egyptian month. When the Nile turned to "blood," it was severe enough to make the water undrinkable (Exod 7:24), yet when channels were dug to allow seepage, the soil purified the water enough so it could be drunk. This suggests the presence of a microorganism that caused this plague, which lasted for seven days (Exod 7:25; see Illustration 10.15).

The Egyptians called the inundation "the arrival of Hapy," since Hapy was the Nile god.[438] Hapy may naturally have been associated with the entire inundation season since the first three plagues challenged the almighty Nile thereby challenging Hapy's powers. While Moses' "magic" had challenged Djehuty's power (Thoth), the first plague demonstrated that Hapy, the god of the Nile was unable to protect Egypt from the power of the God of the Hebrews' ability to turn the water to blood.[439] Thus, Hapy could not protect Egypt any more than Djehuty could.

b. Menkhet: Mid-August to mid-September

2nd Plague: Frogs

> I will smite all your borders with frogs: And the river (*Hapy*) shall bring forth frogs abundantly, which shall go up and come into your house, and into your bedchamber, and on your bed, and into the house of your servants, and on your people, and in your ovens, and in your kneading troughs. (Exod 8:1–7, parenthesis added)

The second Egyptian month, Menkhet (Gk. Phaophi), celebrated the god Ptah (see Illustration 10.16).[440] His cult was centered in Memphis to the south. Ptah was venerated both as the creator-god and was the patron deity of skilled craftsmen who was known for hearing prayers. Specifically, Ptah was extolled for his ability to create by his spoken word.[441] YHWH had put Moses in his stead as a god to Pharaoh. Moses' and Aaron's actions in "creating" frogs challenged both Ptah's and his priests' authority and power. From the Egyptian perspective, the second plague demonstrated that Ptah was not the only god with power to create (see Illustration 10.17).

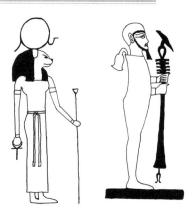

Illustration 10.16. Illustration 10.17.
Menkhet   Ptah

The plague of frogs also continued to challenge Hapy, the Nile god, who was known as the "lord of fishes and birds." Numerous crocodile and frog goddesses were in his retinue.[442] From the Egyptian perspective or even from Israel's perspective, it would have appeared that YHWH had control over Hapy. YHWH was causing chaos for Hapy and his fellow deities by throwing them out of control and showing that they were unable to protect the Nile or the Delta region it nourished. By the end of the second plague, at least four deities (Seth, Thoth, Hapy, and Ptah) were unable to protect or aid Apophis in his challenge to the gods.

c. Khenet Het-Hert: Mid-September to mid-October

3rd Plague: Gnats (KJV–lice)

> YHWH said to Moses, Say to Aaron, Stretch out your rod, and smite the dust of the land, that it may become lice throughout all the land of Egypt. . . . And the magicians did so with their enchantments to bring forth lice, but they could not: Then the magicians said to Pharaoh, This is the finger of God. (Exod 8:16–19)

The Jewish commentator Philo (*On Moses* 1.19) tells us that 2,000 years after the exodus these gnats still persisted during the inundation, although probably to a much lesser degree. Two important things occurred with the third plague. First, Egypt's magicians were no longer able to "create": Djehuty and Ptah had been defeated. Second, Egypt's priests began to recognize YHWH's power, even though the arrogant Pharaoh did not.

The third plague probably occurred in the month of Khenet Het-Hert ('Voyage of Het-Hert'). Het-Hert is better known as the female goddess Hathor, meaning 'House of Horus' (see Illustration 10.18).[443] The Greeks associated her with Aphrodite, although in the Delta region she was associated with the Egyptian goddess Bast.[444] According to Egyptologist Erik Hornung, she was "probably the most universal Egyptian goddess"[445] and was associated with the cow. As a protective deity, she was the god of choice for women. Hathor was extolled for both her motherly protectiveness and her female traits of love and sexuality.[446] In later times, she was identified with Isis. From the Egyptian point of view, this month and the next month were intricately entwined. While Hathor was a loving, protective god of "goodness," she would suddenly morph into Sekhmet, the destructive god of plagues during the subsequent month in the tale of the *Destruction of Mankind*, which was probably circulated as propaganda in the New Kingdom Era to justify the exodus events.

The gnats associated with this plague were still associated with the Nile thousands of years later:

Illustration 10.18. Hathor, the cow goddess who was at times the mother, wife, and daughter of the sun god Re. She later became associated with Isis.

> The Gnats, or the third plague, were not "lice," but σκνῖφες, *sciniphes*, a species of gnats, so small as to be hardly visible to the eye, but with a sting which, according to Philo and Origen, causes a most painful irritation of the skin. They even creep into the eyes and nose, and after the harvest they rise in great swarms from the inundated rice-fields.[447]

Gnats swarmed during the height of the inundation, around October.[448] This reveals that the third plague occurred in the third Egyptian civil month of Khenet Het-Hert, around October. Gnats or even mosquitoes swarm around swamps. This phenomenon could even have led to the infection associated with the next plague (perhaps malaria or anthrax?) a couple months later. That these pesky creatures would come out of the Nile shows that YHWH was demonstrating that Hapy still had no power to protect Egypt during the normal joyous time of inundation.

The third month recognized Hathor as a protective deity. In the New Kingdom, Hathor was reinvented as the destructive Sekhmet.[449] The overwhelming effect that these plagues had on the Egyptian collective memory was probably rationalized by reinventing and recasting Egypt's gods to account for the ongoing misfortune Egypt had faced during the exodus.

The New Kingdom priesthood simply updated the calendar and modernized its cults to reflect the nation's history. The Hebrews' flight from Egypt was followed by the Hyksos' expulsion, which crippled the nation's workforce, which probably only continued the misery that Egypt felt during the Exodus epoch.

d. Nekheb-Kau: Mid-October to mid-November

4th Plague: Flies or Mosquitoes

> Thus said YHWH, Let my people go, that they may serve me. Else, if you will not let my people go. . . . I will send swarms of flies on you, and on your servants, and on your people, and in your houses: and the houses of the Egyptians shall be full of swarms of flies, and also the ground where they are. And I will sever in that day the land of Goshen, in which my people dwell, that no swarms of flies shall be there; to the end you may know that I am YHWH in the midst of the earth. And I will put a division between my people and your people: tomorrow shall this sign be. (Exod 8:20–24)

The cult associated with the fourth Egyptian month of Nekheb-Kau recognized Sekhmet, the destructive deity into whom Hathor had degenerated.[450] The plague of flies seemed to reiterate the fact that Egypt's gods could not offer any protection, while the Hebrew deity YHWH was perfectly capable of protecting the Hebrews. It may be remembered that this was Apophis's original challenge: was the Hyksos or the Theban god stronger? By demonstrating that neither the Theban nor the Delta gods were able to stand against him, YHWH was demonstrating that he was the strongest God (even though Egypt had no concept of monotheism).[451]

Sekhmet's association with plagues is another bit of evidence showing that several plagues had already occurred: hence the need to justify their cause during the New Kingdom. Hathor/Sekhmet now becomes the Egyptian god responsible for all of Egypt's woes. And the priests had a very vulnerable group of people on which to hang all their troubles. In *The Destruction of Mankind*, Re sent Sekhmet to render his judgment on the land for their "blasphemy" against him.[452] Thus, from the Egyptians' perspective, all these plagues were caused by the Asiatics (including the Hebrews). This myth then provided a motif by which Egyptians could interpret and understand their misfortunes.

The fourth plague was the last to be associated with the Nile, as the inundation came to an end. The Nile (Hapy) had crested and begun to recede. During the season that celebrated Hapy's inundation, the Egyptian deity could not protect himself or his devotees from the power of Israel's God. Significantly, the plague of flies is the first plague that the Hebrews did not receive. They had seen that YHWH was the only God. While Egypt's gods offered no hope or protection, the Hebrews' God did. That YHWH could separate Israel's land at this time may indicate that the land of Goshen or its Nile tributaries had receded more quickly than the primary arteries that ran through the Delta region.

e. Season: Peret (Growing). Month: Shef-bedet—Mid-November to mid-December

5th Plague: Murrain of Cattle and Herds

Thus said YHWH God of the Hebrews, Let my people go, that they may serve me. For if you refuse to let them go, and will hold them still, Behold, the hand of YHWH is on your cattle which is in the field, on the horses, on the asses, on the camels, on the oxen, and on the sheep: there shall be a very grievous murrain. And YHWH shall sever between the cattle of Israel and the cattle of Egypt: and there shall nothing die of all that is the children's of Israel. And YHWH appointed a set time, saying, Tomorrow YHWH shall do this thing in the land. (Exod 9:1–5)

Peret marked a new season.[453] This was the time of year when seeds were planted and crops began to grow. Shef-bedet ('swelling of emmer-wheat') was the first month of the peret season, and YHWH's plagues now focused on livestock and agriculture, since the season of the inundation of the Nile had ended. Two gods were associated with the month of Shef-bedet, the male deity Min and the female deity Mut (see Illustration 10.19).[454] Min was a fertility god associated with agriculture. Egyptians brought their first ears of corn from the new harvest to him.[455] Mut was located in Thebes. She was the great mother and queen of the gods. Interestingly, she was the southern counterpart of the goddess Sekhmet who resided in the northern Delta.[456] Mut is unattested in any textual sources or representations before the New Kingdom,[457] when the gods were probably "reinvented."[458] A continual trend can be seen with the various priests redacting or explaining away the exodus's plagues within the various cults by aligning Mut with Sekhmet in southern Egypt during the subsequent New Kingdom Era.

Illustration 10.19. The female goddess Mut.

The fifth plague aimed at the next agricultural phase: flocks and herds. The inundation had provided the perfect environment for the next plague to foment. The fact that the fifth plague targeted cattle reflects the fact that winter had just begun when the nation's attention indeed focused on livestock and sowing. Neither the fertility-god Min nor the "mightier than the gods"[459] mother Mut could protect his/her devotees from the chaos and death with which Israel's God plagued the livestock.

Once the inundation ended, the next agricultural phase was livestock. Peret marked the beginning of a new lambing season, which lasted from November to January.[460] Egypt's administrators would be busy counting the Crown's herds, which had swelled during the calving season.

With the fifth plague, YHWH shifted from menacing and annoying plagues to more drastic diseases that weakened and undermined Egypt's economy. YHWH again challenged the power of Egypt's gods to protect the nation while demonstrating that he was perfectly capable of protecting his people in Goshen. The livestock disease served to weaken the Delta's (Lower Egypt's) economy. The fact that Israel's territory was unaffected by this plague means that this domain (nome) remained economically viable.

When Pharaoh heard that Israel's cattle had not died in the previous plague, he hardened his heart once more, refusing to let YHWH's firstborn son (Israel, Exod 4:22) leave Egypt. While we may think that Apophis was dense, remember that it would have appeared to him that he had just proved the power of Seth-Baal in his previous confrontation with the Theban dynasty, so he had cause for (false) hope. Added to this, he probably viewed the Hebrews' livestock as a viable resource to sustain his people to withstand the siege that was being threatened by Egypt's legitimate, Theban kings.

Illustration 10.20. The sister and wife of Osiris and mother of Horus. Isis became one of the most popular Egyptian dieties.

f. Rekeh-Aa: Mid-December to Mid-January

6th Plague: Boils

> YHWH said to Moses and to Aaron, Take to you handfuls of ashes of the furnace, and let Moses sprinkle it toward the heaven in the sight of Pharaoh. And it shall become small dust in all the land of Egypt, and shall be a boil breaking forth with blains on man, and on beast, throughout all the land of Egypt. . . . And the magicians could not stand before Moses because of the boils; for the boil was on the magicians, and on all the Egyptians. (Exod 9:8–11)

The previous series of plagues had attacked the natural agricultural cycle. There was no distinctive "agricultural" event during the winter. Therefore, the sixth plague in the month of Rekeh-Aa ('big burning') targeted the people themselves, once again demonstrating that Egypt's gods were powerless to protect the people from YHWH. This month specifically challenged the power and authority of the priests themselves (Exod 9:11). Not even they or their cattle were immune to the plagues of Israel's God.

The sixth month was the month of Aset (Isis; see Illustration 10.20).[461] She was the deity who tricked Re (Amun) into revealing his "secret name."[462] She was viewed as a protective, motherly deity for the kings of Egypt. Once again, in the month that honored her, she could offer no protection to Egypt. Rekeh-Aa was the second month after the land was sown. Notice, once again the theory of monthly plagues is supported by the fact that the fifth and sixth plagues were not aimed at the Nile or any crops, since there were no crops yet available to plague.

g. Rekeh-nedjes: Mid-January to Mid-February

7th Plague: Storms, Thunder, Hail, Frost

> And Moses stretched forth his rod toward heaven: and YHWH sent thunder and hail, and the fire ran along on the ground; and YHWH rained hail on the land of Egypt. So there was hail, and fire mingled with the hail, very grievous, such as there was none like it in all the land of Egypt since it became a nation. And the hail smote throughout all the land of Egypt all that was in the field, both man and beast; and the hail smote every herb of the field, and break every tree of the field. Only in the land of Goshen, where the Children of Israel were, was there no hail. (Exod 9:23–26)

Amun was the god venerated in the seventh month of Rekeh-nedjes.[463] He was known as the invisible creator-god. He is often called "The Hidden One" and was associated with invisibility.[464] The ancients regarded him as being behind and in all things, a deity too complex to describe in one name or even to depict in his true form.[465] Therefore, another name was "He who abides in all things."[466] "Hidden of aspect, mysterious of form" and "the *ba* of all things" are other epithets. They also called him "asha renu" which meant 'rich in names.'[467] In modern times, his month would coincide with mid-January through mid-February.[468] The seventh plague targeted agriculture as well as livestock. This indicates that early crops had matured to a state where they could be struck down. This again demonstrates a synchronism between the cycle of plagues and the Egyptian civil calendar.

The storm plague preceded Thera's eruption. Storms and erratic weather often foreshadow volcanic activity.[469] They are caused by gases that the volcano releases into the atmosphere.[470] What this plague may demonstrate is that Thera's eruption was imminent. It would not be surprising to find that the first waves of diaspora from Thera into Egypt and the Levant occurred about this time. Ahmose's *Storm Stele* probably telescopes the seventh through tenth plagues into one grand national catastrophe—Catastrophe that was caused by Thera's eruption, and Thera's eruption that was effected by the Creator—YHWH. It is Scripture's account that provides the greatest information for synchronizing the seventh plague with the seventh month of the Egyptian civil calendar and its coinciding agricultural context.

Egyptian Agriculture: Flax and Barley

> For I will at this time send all my plagues *on your heart*, and on your servants, and on your people; that you may know that there is none like me in all the earth. For now I will stretch out my hand, that I may smite you and your people with pestilence; and you shall be cut off from the earth. (Exod 9:14–15)

From all accounts—Scriptural and Egyptian sources—the seventh plague was the most devastating for Egypt. It was this storm that it appears Ahmose had called an "all wreckening storm": the result of a duel between the gods (lines 7–8, 12), perhaps, in part, a reference to Apophis's challenge.[471] In order to appreciate the economic impact of this plague, we need to step back in time to see how essential flax was to Egypt's viability, culture, and economic prosperity.

Flax was Egypt's primary export: by trading with it she was able to obtain wares from all over the world.[472] The ancient world prized Egypt's fine linen, which derived from a highly technical industrial process.[473] This trade provided Lower Egypt with considerable wealth.[474]

Since Egypt's entire society depended on flax, the Egyptians may have considered this plague the most devastating, which was why YHWH told Pharaoh that the seventh plague would touch Egypt's very heart (Exod 9:14, above; see Illustration 10.21).

Illustration 10.21. Painting in the Tomb of Sennedjem (workmen's tomb) depicting the tomb owner and his wife ploughing and reaping flax and wheat.

> Behold, tomorrow about this time I will cause it to rain a very grievous hail, *such as has not been in Egypt since the foundation of it even until now.* Send therefore now, and gather your cattle, and all that you have in the field; for on every man and beast which shall be found in the field, and shall not be brought home, the hail shall come down on them, and they shall die. (Exod 9:18–19)

Scripture provides the most specific agricultural information for determining the time of year in which the seventh plague occurred.

And the flax and the barley was smitten: for the *barley was in the ear, and the flax was bolled*. But the wheat and the rye were not smitten: for they were not grown up. (Exod 9:31–32)

This statement is key for dating the seventh plague. A flax boll, or seed pod, appears after flowering toward the end of maturity, shortly before harvest.[475] The entire process from planting to harvest takes about 95–110 days, and the boll appears about a month before harvest.[476] Thus, if the Egyptians planted in mid-November,[477] flax would flower at the end of January,[478] and be bolled toward the end of February. That the flax had already entered the "bolled" state indicates that harvest was due in only a couple of weeks.

In his book *Natural History*, the ancient Greek author Pliny (*c.* 70 C.E.) writes about Egypt's agriculture. His accounts give a glimpse into Egypt's traditional agriculture before modern farming techniques entered the region. Pliny tells us that flax was the earliest Egyptian crop.

Flax is mostly sown in sandy soils, and after a single ploughing only. There is no plant that grows more rapidly than this; sown in spring, it is pulled up in summary.... There are four varieties of it, the Tanitic, the Pelusiac, the Butic, and the Tentyritic—so called from the various districts in which they are respectively grown. (Pliny, *Natural History*, Book 19) [479]

While four main varieties of flax existed, the one most often depicted on tombs and other scenes is the species *Linum usitatissimum*, from which fine linen is derived.[480]

The task of sowing flax seeds was carried out in the *middle of November* following the annual inundation of the Nile Valley. There are numerous representations of sowing scenes in Old and Middle Kingdom tombs, thus allowing the process to be followed and reconstructed. Often the sowing of cereal grain and flax is shown combined.... *Flax plants take about three months to mature*; once the flowers have died away and the seed heads appear, the plants are almost ready to be harvested. *The timing of the harvesting is important, because the age of the plant affects the uses to which the fibres can be put.* Thus, if the flax plants are harvested while *still young and green* then a fine textile can be produced, and if it is harvested when slightly older then the fibres are suitable for a general, good quality cloth. However, if the harvesting takes place when the plants are old, then the resulting flax is usable only for coarse cloth and ropes.[481]

That the flax had bolled but had not yet been harvested before the seventh plague demonstrates that the flax was still tender and green, thus indicating that the seventh plague occurred about the end of January to the middle of February.

Like flax, barley was another early crop. Barley was not only an important grain for bread but also for beer, a common staple of Egyptian diet.[482] However, the Egyptians did not sow barley independently. Ancient inscriptions depict barley as being sown in the same field as other cereal grains,[483] a depiction that is confirmed by archaeological evidence.

In traditional agriculture a mixture of two or more cereal or pulse species are sometimes sown together for a variety of reasons (e.g., as a way of reducing the risk of failure of any single species), and these crops are known as maslins. Archaeobotanical samples from Egypt and elsewhere in the Near East often contain a mixture of wheat and barley and based on ethnographic observation, it has been suggested that, in some cases, this mixing of cereals may have occurred at the sowing stage rather than as a later accident of storage or through the subsequent mixing of debris during disposal. [484]

The archaeological evidence confirms various ancient Egyptian reports that barley and other cereal grains were sown in the same field. When YHWH gave Israel his Law at Mt. Sinai, he outlawed this practice (Lev 19:19).[485] Whether this regulation aimed only at the mixing of specific types of grains (similar to the *sha'anez* garment[486]) or a more general combination is uncertain.

Pliny tells us that in ancient Egypt barley was reaped in the sixth month of the Egyptian calendar and wheat in the seventh during his day:

> In Egypt, we find barley cut at the end of six months, and wheat at the end of seven, from the time of sowing. (Pliny the Elder, *Natural History*, 18.10)

If crops were sown in mid-November, then barley would reach maturity in mid-March, depending on the timing of the Nile's inundation in that particular year.[487] This leaves open a time frame from mid-February to March.

Regarding this plague, Carl Friedrich Keil and Franz Delitzsch observe:

> The barley is ripe about the end of February or beginning of March; the wheat, at the end of March or beginning of April. . . . Consequently the plague of hail occurred at the end of January, or at the latest in the first half of February; so that there were *at least eight weeks* between the seventh and tenth plagues.[488]

Scripture also supports a January date for this plague:

> He gave also their increase to the caterpillar, and their labor to the locust. He destroyed their vines with hail, and their sycamore trees *with frost*. He gave up their cattle also to the hail, and their flocks to hot thunderbolts. (Ps 78:46–48)

Scripture mentions frost separately from hail. That Egypt's low-lying Delta should experience such extreme temperatures along with humidity is unusual, even for the moist Delta region.[489] In the southern United States, it is not uncommon for frost to follow a tumultuous storm. One day might have temperatures in the 80s and a few hours later it can be in the 30s, with frost or even freezing temperatures occurring before daybreak the next morning. If a similar situation had accompanied this plague, it could have caused massive destruction to already saturated and heavily damaged crops. Thus, from an Egyptian point of view, it would have reached to the very heart of Egypt's economy and probably also to Egypt's psyche. Not even the unseen Amun, a primary Egyptian deity, could save Egypt from the destruction wrought by Hebrews' God.

The timing alluded to in both Ahmose's *Storm Stele* and the redacted story of *The Destruction of Mankind* for this plague was spring. Both texts indicate a time when the Nile was manageable, and southern travel was possible—well after the inundation.[490] Thus, all indications are that the seventh plague occurred in late January to early February, during the seventh Egyptian month of Rekeh-nedjes, in the planting season of peret.

Once Moses had left "Pharaoh's city" (Exod 9:33), probably Avaris, he caused the storm to cease. Once again the Brave Ass pharaoh hardened his heart, refusing to let YHWH's firstborn son, Israel (Exod 4:22), go free.

h. Renen-wetet: Mid-February to Mid-March

8th Plague: Locusts

> Tomorrow will I bring the locusts into your coast: And they shall cover the face of the earth, that one cannot be able to see the earth: and they shall eat the residue of that which is escaped, which remains to you from the hail, and shall eat every tree which grows for you out of the field. And they shall fill your houses, and the houses of all your servants, and the houses of all the Egyptians; which neither your fathers, nor your fathers' fathers have seen, since the day that they were on the earth to this day. And he turned himself, and went out from Pharaoh. And Pharaoh's servants said to him, How long shall this man be a snare to us? Let the men go, that they may serve YHWH their God: know you not yet that Egypt is destroyed? (Exod 10:4–7)

The god associated with the eighth month was the female goddess Renenutet.[491] She was known as the

"Lady of the fertile land" and "lady of granaries." Not only was she a deity of fertility and harvest but she was also a protector of linen: especially bandages (for mummification), children and their nourishment. She was mother of the grain god Nepri. . . . People made offerings to her during harvest time and she was depicted either as a snake or a human with a snakeś head. Under Greek influence in much later times, she became associated with Isis. Her main cult was Faiyum in Lower Egypt.[492]

Renenutet's association with the protection of linen[493] indicates that the harvest and production of linen usually occurred during her month (see Illustration 10.22). Toward the end of this month, the first cereals, such as barley began to ripen, from which we infer that the locust plague occurred during the flax and early barley harvests.

Illustration 10.22. Renenutet: goddess of grainaries.

The harvest season in central Israel runs about three weeks later than Egypt's,[494] which the 10th century Gezer Calendar also confirms. The Gezer Calendar was excavated in 1908 and records the monthly agricultural activities at Gezer in Israel.[495] In his landmark work on Israel's festival calendar, Jan Wagaanar demonstrates that in the Gezer Calendar the flax and barley harvests "seem to concur with the simultaneous flowering of the flax and ripening of the barley" in Israel.[496] Even though Israel's agricultural season began later than Egypt's, the harvest season was similar with flax maturing shortly before the ripening of barley. The plague of locusts challenged Renenutet's ability to protect and ensure a fruitful harvest. Once again, YHWH prevailed over Egypt's gods (see Illustration 10.23).

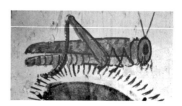

Illustration 10.23. Locust from a scene in the tomb of Pharaoh Horemheb *c.* 1300 BCE.

> And *YHWH turned a mighty strong west wind, which took away the locusts, and cast them into the Red sea*; there remained not one locust in all the coasts of Egypt. But YHWH hardened Pharaoh's heart, so that he would not let the Children of Israel go. (Exod 10:19–20)

This is one Egyptian plague that still occurs today. Abnormally wet conditions provide the perfect breeding ground for an enormous locust population explosion.[497] During the spring, grasshoppers are blown into Egypt from off the Mediterranean.[498] A strong westerly wind blows the grasshoppers into the Delta, where they can ravage crops. The last devastating swarms occurred in 2004 and in the 1950s.[499] The creatures are then blown from east to the west, where a northwest wind carries them into the Sudan (their breeding grounds on the coast of the Red Sea).[500] These pesky creatures can eat twice their body weight per day and over 50,000 tons of crops per swarming season.[501]

i. Season: Shomu (Harvest). Month: Khonsu—Mid-March to Mid-April

9th Plague: 3 Days of Darkness, Thera Erupts!

> And YHWH said to Moses, Stretch out your hand toward heaven, that there may be darkness over the land of Egypt, even darkness *which may be felt.* And Moses stretched forth his hand toward heaven; and there was a thick darkness in all the land of Egypt three days: They saw not one another, neither rose any from his place for three days: but all the Children of Israel had light in their dwellings. (Exod 10:21–23)

The first month of the harvest season celebrated the moon-god Khonsu (see Illustration 10.24). In his form *Khonsu heseb-ahau,* he was known as 'Keeper of the Books of the End of

Illustration 10.24. Khonsu as a falcon-headed god.

the Year',[502] possibly attesting an earlier Egyptian calendar system in which the new year coincided with the spring (vernal) equinox. Both Richard Parker and Leo Depuydt have demonstrated that Egypt's original calendar was indeed lunar based.[503] Depuydt successfully demonstrated that the last lunar month prior to the "astronomical" new year was a straddle month, in which the "New Year's Day" occurred in the last month of the year.[504] The first new moon after the "astronomical" or solar year marked the first month of the year.[505] If this observation is correct, Khonsu's form as Khonsu heseb-ahau *may* retain a distant memory of an earlier lunar-based calendar when the month of Khonsu (modern mid-March to mid-April) served as the last month of the year. As we will see, this theory is tentatively supported by the festival regulations that YHWH ordained during Egypt's last plague. It is hoped that future studies will take into account Egypt's calendrical system(s) when reconstructing Israel's festival calendar.

One of Khonsu's functions was to determine who would live and who would die during the upcoming year. The 10th plague, may have challenged Khonsu's ability to predict who would be written in his death book, since, during the very next month all of Egypt's firstborn were killed. In addition to handling the "Books of the End of the Year," Khonsu was also the god of the night.[506] It was his duty to see to it that night safely passed. YHWH's act in rendering three dark days in Egypt once again rendered another Egyptian deity powerless. Nine gods, nine months, and nine plagues: none of the gods could withstand the power of Israel's God.

Scripture may preserve a passing reference to Apophis's eminent death:

> But YHWH hardened Pharaoh's heart, and he would not let them go. And Pharaoh said to him, Get you from me, take heed to yourself, see my face no more; for in that day you see my face you shall die. And Moses said, You have spoken well, *I will see your face again no more.* (Exod 10:27–29)

If, in fact, Moses never again saw Apophis's face, Apophis may have died in the 10th plague. Thus, the pharaoh who finally allowed Israel's people to go free may have been Apophis's son. Another possibility is that Kamose's (or Ahmose's) forces may have sacked Avaris, slaughtering its Asiatic population and King Apophis. Since Israel's settlement lay outside the city, the blood on the doorpost may have marked Israel's opposition to the Hyksos king and her allegiance to YHWH. Thus Egypt's Theban kings would have spared the Hebrews, who may have remained faithful to the traditional Theban monarchy, whose cattle they had pastured in the Delta region, when Kamose attacked Avaris a month later.

j. Khenet-KhetyPerti: Mid-April to Mid-May

10th Plague: Death of Firstborn

> And Moses said, Thus said YHWH, About midnight will I go out into the midst of Egypt. And all the firstborn in the land of Egypt shall die, from the firstborn of Pharaoh *that sits on his throne*, even to the firstborn of the maidservant that is behind the mill; and all the firstborn of beasts. And there shall be a great cry throughout all the land of Egypt, such as there was none like it, nor shall be like it any more. But against any of the Children of Israel shall not a dog move his tongue, against man or beast: that you may know how that YHWH does put a difference between the Egyptians and Israel. (Exod 11:4–7)

The last month that Israel spent in Egypt was the month of Khenet-KhetyPerti. It was in this month that Horus, one of Egypt's most famous and universally worshiped deities was venerated.[507] He was often conceived as a sun deity and fused with the great Re.[508] Horus was also known as the *God of Kingship*, who was the son of Isis and Osiris, and struggled against the evil god Seth to retain the throne of Egypt.[509] In later times, Horus became virtually synonymous with Osiris.[510] Horus epitomized the pagan motif of a good god warring against an evil god who was bent on destroying the kingdom. In many ways, YHWH's vanquishing of this great Egyptian god was the vanquishing of all gods.

Egyptian-Hebrew Calendar Synchronism. This Egyptian month is the second time the Hebrew text provides a synchronism between Egypt's harvest season and the Hebrew cultic/festival calendar.

> And YHWH spoke to Moses and Aaron *in the land of Egypt*, saying, *This month shall be to you the beginning of months*: it shall be the first month of the year to you.(Exod 12:1–2)
>
> *Remember this day, in which you came out from Egypt*, out of the house of bondage; for by strength of hand YHWH brought you out from this place: there shall no leavened bread be eaten. This day came you out *in the month Abib*. (Exod 13:3–4)

Egypt's civil calendar recognized the first sighting of Sirius as the beginning of its new year since Sirius "rose" at the beginning of the inundation.[511] This made sense for the Egyptians, whose agricultural year began with the flooding of the Nile, but this system made no sense for Israel because the Nile did not affect Canaan. With Exodus 12–13's injunctions, YHWH distinguished the solar-lunar new year that Israel's calendrical system would use. YHWH made the above statement to Moses in the Egyptian month of Khenet-KhetyPerti. Modernly, this month coincides with mid-April to mid-May. Israel's cultic calendar would begin its new year *after* the vernal equinox (modernly, March 20th).[512]

The Hebrew term *teqūfat haššānā*, often translated "turn of the year," "end of the year," or "beginning of the year" (Exod 23:16; 34:22; 2 Sam 11:1; 2 Chr 24:23) refers to the spring and autumn equinoxes, *lit.*, 'when the year turns.'[513] In Exod 34:22, the count for the Feast of Weeks occurs after the spring equinox, while Sukkot begins after the autumnal equinox. The concept of a six-month equinox was conventional in most ancient cultic-festival calendars.[514] Scripture parallels this customary six-month equinox "year" in Exod 23:16 and Deut 11:12. It was not that the rest of the year did not exist, but no harvests or festivals took place between November and March; therefore this period was not as significant agriculturally, economically, or religiously. Most scholars are unanimous in reading equinox in these verses since almost every Semitic language uses a cognate of *haššānā* (turn of the year) to denote the New Year.[515] In Akkadian, ancient Assyria's language, *mūṣē šatti* meant 'the end of the year,' which most scholars see as a "direct parallel to the biblical Hebrew בְּצֵאת הַשָּׁנָה."[516]

Ugarit (the ruins of which are on the modern north Syrian coastline) attests a similar calendar as the famous 10th-century Gezer Calendar. Exod 23:16 uses the "going out" of the year, *yatsa haššānā*, and similar terminology as used in Ugaritic texts.[517] The interesting fact about Ugarit's calendar and some Mesopotamian calendars is that they celebrated a spring and a fall festival that coincided with the equinox.[518] In fact, the "Festival of Huts" (Deut 16:13, 16) finds parallels with the fall festival in early Ugaritic texts, since similar Sukkot and equinox terminology (i.e., "huts") is used.[519] Some of the first Mesopotamian calendars also appear to parallel ancient Israel's cultic calendar by observing a spring, early summer, and fall festival.[520] In Mesopotamia, the spring festival (similar to Israel) was called a Feast of Firstfruits and the fall festival was called a Feast of Ingathering.[521]

At creation, YHWH had ordained the entire solar system to serve as humanity's time clock.

> And God said, Let there be lights in the firmament of the heaven to divide the day from the night; and let them be for *signs, and for seasons, and for days, and years.* (Gen 1:14)

Moed is the word the King James Version translates "seasons."[522] This word is used again in Leviticus 23 (Lev 23:2–4, 37, 44), only the translators render it "feasts and seasons." Israel, like other ancient nations used the solar system to begin the year and to reckon time. Israel's *cultic* or *priestly* calendar closely mirrors the calendar in Mesopotamia but is less similar to the civil calendar in Egypt.

In his excellent treatment of Israel's festival calendar, Jan Wagenaar observes that the month or season of Abib occurs at the beginning of the barley harvest.[523] Fascinatingly, Wagenaar concludes that the Abib season begins in the *second* month after the vernal equinox, not the first.[524] This would place *Israel's* barley harvest in April or May. If there is a deficiency in Wagenaar's treatise, it is threefold. First, he does not address the general logic of calendars for lunar-solar based calendar systems (Gen 1:14).[525] Second, he does not distinguish between Israel's cultic calendar and the later civil calendar that was put into place during the Monarchy (the Gezer Calendar coincides with the Monarchy). And third, his reliance on popular redactional theories precludes a fully objective reconstruction of a legitimate ancient calendar system for Israel.

Wagenaar is correct that Israel's barley harvest likely occurred during the second month after the equinox, but he fails to account for the way that ancient Egyptians reckoned their lunar-solar calendar. Scripture, Egypt's calendar, and the monthly plague cycle all point to Israel's New Year beginning the first full lunar month after the "astronomical event," in this case, the vernal equinox.[526] *Therefore, the first full month (or new moon) after the equinox would be the second lunar month after the vernal equinox, yet the first month of the New Year.*[527] In modern terms, this would place Israel's New Year (in Abib) occurring between the end of March and the first part of May, depending on when the first new moon after the equinox occurs. What this means for our present discussion is that Wagenaar's independent conclusions regarding Israel's festival calendar, which place Abib in the second agricultural month after the equinox perfectly coincide with the synchronism of the Egyptian civil calendar and the exodus plague cycle which support that the 10th plague, the exodus, and the first month of Abib occurred between mid-April and early May. It is hoped that future studies will address these synchronisms more fully.

The Destroyer. When YHWH gave Moses instructions regarding the last plague, he counseled Israel to plunder the Egyptians (see pp. 460–61). Specifically, YHWH stated that he would give Israel favor in the eyes of the Egyptians so that the Egyptians would give Israel treasures of wealth. He stated that Pharaoh "shall surely *thrust you out*" (Exod 11:1–3). All the previous misfortune YHWH had brought on the land of Egypt had probably placed fear in the Egyptians' hearts: appease the Hebrews' God by giving a peace offering to his people. However, YHWH set the stage for greater generosity by bringing Kamose's forces ever closer to Avaris in the days that preceded Passover. Thus, the Egyptians may have wanted their treasures to be "safe" with the Hebrews instead of being plundered by the southern pharaoh.

It is interesting that the Book of Exodus states that an unnamed pharaoh would "thrust" Israel out of Egypt altogether. This act is generally attributed to Ahmose's expulsion of the Hyksos, who may be termed the "destroyer" in Scripture:

> For YHWH will pass through to smite the Egyptians; and when he sees the blood on the lintel, and on the two side posts, YHWH will pass over the door, and will *not suffer the destroyer* to come in to your houses to smite you. (Exod 12:23. See also Isa 54:16)

Throughout Israel's history, YHWH used kings to effect his judgments. King Cyrus, whom YHWH termed a "messiah" (Isa 45:1), allowed his subjects to return to their homelands. The Assyrian "bee" fulfilled YHWH's judgment by deporting the Northern Israelite Kingdom (Isa 7:18). And at the Conquest of Canaan, YHWH sent two Amorite "hornets" (see chap. 11) to drive out and destroy Canaan's natives (Deut 7:20; Josh 24:12), as he prepared for Israel to inherit the Promised Land. "The destroyer" whom YHWH had sent to effect his judgment on the Delta region was probably King Kamose.[258]

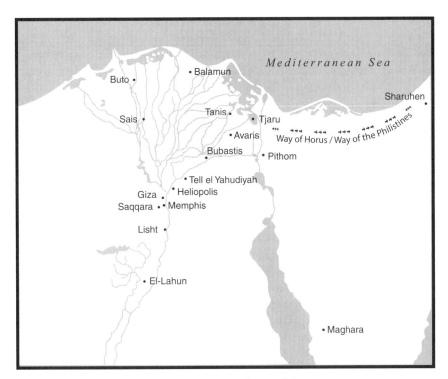

Map 10.3. Lower Egypt with Way of Horus

The reverse of the *Rhind Mathematical Papyrus* records a scribe's notes. During an unnamed king's 11th year, the fortress city of Sile had been taken.[529] Sile lay on the traditional highway to Canaan, often called *The Way of the Philistines* (Exod 13:17) or the *Way of Horus*.[530] Sile (Tjaru) had been taken at the end of the month of Akhet, the first month of the year, while Heliopolis (biblical On—Gen 41:45) had been taken in the end of the 10th month of Khenet-KhetyPerti.

Regarding the reverse of the *Rhind Mathematical Papyrus's* text, Egyptologist Kim Ryholt observes,

> While the jottings do not mention Avaris itself, the fact that Heliopolis and *Sile* and been taken would suggest that Avaris was now surrounded, and it therefore seems highly probably that it would have fallen soon after.[531]

The question that arises when one is interpreting the text is whether the scribe's jotting of events refer to Apophis or his successor Khamudi.

> 11th regnal-year, 2nd month of Shomu: Heliopolis was entered (i.e., taken).
> 1st month of Akhet, 23rd day: He of the South (i.e., Kahmose or Ahmose) strikes against Sile. . . . 25th or 26th day: It was heard that Sile had been entered (i.e., taken).[532]

According to this text, Kamose/Ahmose had captured Heliopolis (biblical, On) in the 10th month of Khentekhtai-perti (the 2nd month of the harvest season Shomu). The Theban forces continued their northward advance bypassing Avaris to capture Sile on the Mediterranean coast. This important strategic position not only allowed the Theban kings to cut off the Hyksos' livelihood and recognizance from Canaan, it also prevented the Asiatics at Avaris from retreating by the only land-route to Canaan, the Way of Horus. This indicates that Kamose did not intend to expel the Delta's Asiatics but to utterly vanquish and subjugate them. The first plague would have coincided with Kamose's forces taking Sile (Tjaru), hence Apophis' resolve in holding onto the Hebrew garrisoned forces. Sile had been captured by the end Tekhi, the first month of Akhet (when Moses turned the Nile into blood) with a strike on Avaris eminent.

If one or both Theban brothers converged on Avaris during a daring, stealthy attack at night, when Avaris was sleeping and least expecting battle, the Thebans could achieve huge success. Kamose's inscriptions tell us that he successfully plundered the riches of Avaris's harbors,[533] a feat not readily achieved during active warfare, when ships are set ablaze, looted, or sunk by their owners to prevent their falling into enemy hands. The second text that suggests that both brothers contributed to this campaign is Ahmose's *Storm Stele*. The text suggest that Ahmose was north of Thebes when Kamose died unexpectedly. Ahmose then needed to rush back to Thebes to secure his throne. If the Theban pharaohs and their officers had been on friendly relations with the Hebrews who tended their cattle (see pp. 448–50), the blood on the lintel of the door-post could signal not only their fidelity to the Hebrew God but also allegiance to the Theban kings' claim to the Delta region. When the Hebrews deserted the Delta, bypassing Sile, Kamose may have considered the act treason, and sought to capture his workforce. When Kamose died during the battle or by chasing the Israelites to the Red Sea (Exod 10:19), Ahmose had to withdraw to Thebes and secure his throne, thus postponing his campaign against the Asiatics by a few months to as long as eleven years later.

IV. THE EXODUS ROUTE

A. Sile

The reverse of the *Rhind Mathematical Papyrus* allows another piece of the puzzle to fall into place. Scripture tells us that, when YHWH delivered Egypt, he did not take them by "The Way of the Philistines," even though it was a direct route to Canaan, because war loomed along this highway. The Egyptians knew this highway as the *Way of Horus*.[534]

> And it came to pass, when Pharaoh had let the people go, that God led them not through the *way of the land of the Philistines, although that was (a) near*; for God said, Lest peradventure the people repent (b) *when they see war*, and they return to Egypt, (Exod 13:17)

We learn at least two details from this text. First, the *Way of Horus* was (a) near the place where Israel lived in Egypt. Second, if Israel used this traditional route to enter Canaan, (b) she would see war. This implies that the alternative Sinai route did not face the same risks. The question is why.

It is easy to consider the threat of war as arising from a confrontation with the Canaanites. But if so, why did a Sinai-Midian (Exod 2:15; 3:1, 12) route prove any less daunting, since it still led Israel into Canaan, where war was more likely and was even commanded (Num 33:51–4)? Understanding the political situation in Egypt at this particular time, however, allows us see that the Exodus's account makes perfect sence during the 16th century but not during any other century.

The reverse of the *Rhind Mathematical Papyrus* tells us that Pharaoh Kamose had surrounded Avaris and cut off any support from the land of Canaan months before the exodus. His base of operations was at Sile, which was a military fortification.[535] This city lies directly on the *Way of Horus,* which led to Canaan. Thus, the threat of war was not from Canaan but from Egypt. Had an army of Asiatics (Hebrews) tried to pass through this fortification, it is quite likely that Ahmose's army would have challenged these forces: first on military grounds, second on the grounds of not wanting to lose such a capable corvée work force, no matter how loyal it had been to Egypt's Theban Dynasty.

B. *The Sinai and Exodus Route*

One objection that critics of the exodus often draw attention to is the unlikelihood that a group of people could escape through the heavily patrolled and heavily garrisoned Sinai.

> The escape of more than a tiny group from Egyptian control at the time of Ramesses II seems highly unlikely, as is the crossing of the desert and entry into Canaan. In the thirteenth century, Egypt was at the peak of its authority—the dominant power in the world. The Egyptian grip over Canaan was firm; Egyptian strongholds were built in various places in the country, and Egyptian officials administered the affairs of the region.[536]

Silberman and Finkelstein adeptly point out the obstacles to a thirteenth-century exodus. Once Ahmose had seized the Delta, he reopened the Sinai mines, re-garrisoned the defensive *Wall of the Ruler,* and sent patrols throughout the Sinai Peninsula.[537] This system remained intact throughout the New Kingdom (*c.* 1500–1070), when scholars are apt to place Israel's flight through the Sinai.[538]

Scripture's account of the exodus makes it clear that Israel traveled through the edge of the Sinai Peninsula.

> In the third month, when the Children of Israel were gone forth out of the land of Egypt, the same day came they *into the wilderness of Sinai.* For they were departed from Rephidim, and were come to the *desert of Sinai,* and had pitched in the wilderness; and there Israel camped before the mount. (Exod 19:1–2)

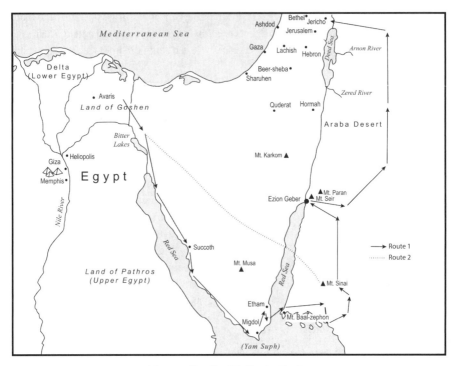

Map 10.4. Two Possible Exodus Routes

What becomes a topic for debate at this point is the route that the Israelites followed once they left Avaris (Pi-Ramses, according to the Deborah's scribes—Exod 1:11; 12:37; Num 33:3, 5; See chap. 11.XII.D., pp. 578–582 for discussion on Deborah's scribes). While various theories have been proposed, the route that is best supported by the Scriptural text traverses the edge of the tip of the Sinai Peninsula and crosses at the Gulf of Aqaba.[539]

Unfortunately, it is the least-discussed and least-pursued route by modern scholars.[540] Most treatments of the Exodus route accept the traditional location at St. Catherine's Monastery. However, this site lacks almost every geographical feature mentioned in Scripture: the bitter waters of Marah (Exod 15:23); the cleft rock at Horeb (Exod 17:6) that poured out water for thousands of people; the fissure in which Moses hid (Exod 33:22) and to which Elijah later fled (1 Kgs 19:1); and the boundary markers (Exod 19:12).

When we examined the Mosaic Covenant, we also saw that, when Moses stopped at the burning bush, he was in the land of Midian (not an Egyptian province). Additionally, we saw that Midian was one of Abraham's sons, whom the patriarch sent away to the east (Gen 25:6). Therefore, this places Mt. Horeb both to the east of Egypt and southeast of Canaan. Unfortunately, the only attention that this route has received has been from amateurs, treasure hunters, and documentaries presented by the Discovery Channel or religious organizations. As is well known, these investigations do not necessarily adhere to scientific methods. While the initial scholarly treatments of this route have been negative,[541] enough supporting evidence (such as the remains of chariot wheels in the Gulf of Aqaba) has been presented to justify more-rigorous attention.

The Scriptural text provides a "journal" to reconstruct the path Israel took when leaving Egypt. Israel departed from Succoth, probably modern Tell el-Maskhuta, and camped at Etham "on the edge of the Wilderness" (Exod 13:20; Num 33:5–6). From Etham they traveled (along the coastal plain?) to the foot of Pi-hahiroth, which is said to be "between Migdol and the sea, over against Baal-zephon . . . by the sea" (Exod 14:2–3; see Map 10.4). This would imply that the route Israel traveled was on the coastal regions of the Sinai Peninsula.

Our investigation began with ancient Israel's allegations, charging that YHWH's Law and his way of life were unfair. While this chapter optimistically demonstrates that Israel's history—as recorded in Scripture—is indeed valid, it does nothing to vindicate Israel's God. I have only provided a historical context in which Israel's allegations may be understood. Modern scholars have charged that Israel's history and Scriptures are nothing more than folktales and legends written 1,500 years after the nation's fictional exodus. Quite surprisingly, we will find that both Scripture and archaeology can debunk these naïve and contradictory redaction theories with the evidence for the subsequent Conquest and Judges Era.

11

Critical Issues:
The Canaan Conquest

Thomas Kuhn observed that scientific revolutions do not always occur because new discoveries are unearthed. Instead, scientific enlightenment often emerges when we ask new questions about the old information that lead us to draw new conclusions and result in a "paradigm shift."[1] The reality of Kuhn's observation is readily demonstrated by the new questions our investigation has asked and the new conclusions that we have drawn. Kuhn's theory remains true when we apply these new conclusions to Scripture's history of the Conquest Era.

In the past, popular scholars nonchalantly dismissed the internal Scriptural evidence supporting a sixteenth-century exodus.[2] We have seen, Scripture supports the exodus at *c.* 1548 BCE (see chap. 9). We have also seen that substantial archaeological, epigraphic (*Ahmose Stele*), and even scientific evidence (archaeology and the date of Thera's eruption) link Israel's exodus with this same period. Yet, perhaps even more-compelling evidence exists in the archaeological record of ancient Israel–Palestine alongside Scripture's description of Canaan's cities during the Conquest Era. As we will soon discover, Scripture's straightforward chronology turns the old thirteenth-century exodus and Conquest model into a relic of paradigms past.[3] The known history and archaeology of Canaan falls precisely in place with Scripture's sixteenth-century Conquest.

I. CANAAN C. 1550 BCE

A. Hazor

Many scholars have observed that the Conquest account describes a much earlier era than is popularly accepted. In particular, some scholars note that the Book of Joshua reflects a period that came to an abrupt end in the sixteenth-century, *c.* 1550/1530 BCE.[4] One clue that leads to this conclusion is Scripture's characterization of the city of Hazor as the powerhouse of the city-state federations that existed when Israel infiltrated Canaan:

> For Hazor formerly was the head of all those kingdoms. (Josh 11:10–11)

Scholars such as Egyptologist Donald Redford who accept a much later Conquest consider this reference to be a "dim memory" of Hazor's former "Middle Bronze Age importance."[5] Characterizing this account as a faint recollection is questionable. The context of Joshua's statement (Joshua 11) refers to Hazor as a powerful city that Joshua and Israel had very recently defeated. Scripture is not describing a bankrupt city that had ceased to exist some 300 years earlier, as Redford opines. Rather, the Book of Joshua reflects the fact that Hazor was suzerain of the city-states at the time when Israel defeated its king. This is the first indication in the historical record that the Canaan Conquest was at least three centuries earlier than is now generally accepted.

The second clue to a much earlier Conquest of Hazor, is Joshua's mention of a king "Jabin" (Josh 11:1). An Old Babylonian text recently excavated at Hazor that dates to between the eigthteenth and sixteenth centuries bears the name "Ibni."[6] Noted archaeologist William Dever observes that, not only was this a dynastic name; it was also the Hebrew equivalent of the name Jabin:

> Now it happens that Akkadian "Ibni" is the exact linguistic equivalent of Hebrew "Yabin," the name of the king of Hazor in Joshua 11:1.[7]

We have a situation in which not only was Hazor the head of all kingdoms during the sixteenth century but the ruling monarchy to which Joshua refers is attested by written evidence unearthed at Hazor: evidence, that appears to support a much earlier Exodus and Conquest.

The archaeology of Hazor also demonstrates a two-phase destruction (see Illustration 11.1). The first in the sixteenth century and the second in the thirteenth century (we will discuss this below). This basic chronology is also supported by Scripture, which cites one assault on Hazor by Joshua at the initial Conquest and another by Deborah and Barak several centuries later, during an era when Israel adhered to the Covenant.

B. Jericho

The Book of Joshua unequivocally cites Jericho as the first city that Israel assaulted after crossing the Jordan (Joshua 5–6). This again presents an "early" view of Canaan. Archaeology reveals that the city was obliterated in the sixteenth century (see Illustration 11.2). Jericho is one of many cities that demonstrate destruction between 1550 and 1500 BCE.[8] In fact, famed archaeologist Kathleen Kenyon wrote a painstakingly detailed report of the excavations at Jericho that is so convincing that very few academics challenge her conclusions.[9] Fascinatingly, Jericho was not rebuilt or inhabited during the traditional twelfth or thirteenth century Conquest dates.[10] There was no city of Jericho in the thirteenth century:

Illustration 11.1. Upper and Lower Hazor. Lower Hazor begins with the dark paving stones in the upper center of the photo.

Illustration 11.2. Ancient Jericho was built on the top of a large hill or tell.

no walls to come tumbling down. This destruction had already occurred 300 years prior. Hence, the picture presented by the Deutero-Joshua narratives reflects an earlier, sixteenth century era, which agrees both with the archaeological evidence and with recent carbon-14 dating in a disputed destruction layer at Jericho.[11]

C. *Knowing the Lay of the Land*

We have seen that Scripture presents a very early date for both Jericho and Hazor. This early era is also evidenced by the general topography (layout of the land) Scripture describes. What we know about the archaeology of Canaan during later eras (when scholars are apt to date the Conquest) is again quite at odds with the Scriptural account. Archaeologist William Dever, who specializes in the archaeology of this era observes: "Certainly the biblical writers and editors show little familiarity with the topography and settlement patterns of the early Iron Age."[12] Dever's statement is made in the context of cities that were on the eastern side of Jordan (i.g., Heshbon). And he is wholly correct in concluding that Scriptures' description of the topography does not reflect the early Iron Age. As we will see, however, the situation that Scripture describes perfectly reflects a Middle Bronze Age topography.

D. *Walled and Heavily Fortified*

Another anomaly found in the popular, thirteenth-century Conquest model arises from Scripture's accounts of vastly walled and fortified cities, such as Hazor. There is no doubt that the Pentateuch portrays Canaan as a network of heavily fortified federations. Shortly before Israel entered the Promised Land, the Children of Israel recognized these fortification systems as being obstacles to conquering the land.

> Nevertheless the people be strong that dwell in the land, and *the cities are walled, and very great.* (Num 13:27–28)
>
> Where shall we go up? our brothers have discouraged our heart, saying, The people is greater and taller than we; *the cities are great and walled up to heaven.* (Deut 1:28)

Israel's spies had scouted Canaan shortly after the exodus in 1548. The congregation rebelled when they heard the spies' report, doubting YHWH's ability to deliver these strong, impregnable cities into their hand. The rebellion cost Israel 40 years of wilderness exile, until all the seditionists of that generation had died. When the nation began the conquest of the land 39 years later, walls were still standing around the settlements in central Canaan and in the Amorite territory east of the Jordan River (Heshbon). This is the very territory that Jacob had bequeathed to the Joseph tribes shortly before his death (Genesis 48–49).

Remember that, when Jacob distributed the birthright and the blessing among his sons, he ordained that the Joseph tribes should have one portion of land more than the other tribes.

> I have given to you one portion above your brothers, which I took out of the hand of the *Amorite* with my sword and with my bow. (Gen 48:22)

Jacob's birthright to the Joseph tribes indicates that Israel would conquer a particular Amorite territory through warfare. Israel claimed this portion on the eastern side of the Jordan after the exile. Moses himself attests to the vast walled defenses that these cities maintained at the time of the Conquest.

> So YHWH our God delivered into our hands Og also, the king of Bashan, and all his people: and we smote him until none was left to him remaining. And we took all his cities at that time, there was not a city which we took not from them, threescore (60) cities, all the region of Argob, the kingdom of Og in Bashan. *All these cities were fenced with high walls, gates, and bars; beside unwalled towns a great many.* (Deut 3:3–5)

These heavily fortified cities remained in Canaan and its periphery 40 years after Israel exited Egypt (*c.* 1508 BCE).[13] A month after Moses made this speech, Jericho's heavily walled fortress fell flat before Israel's peaceful assault.

> The people heard the sound of the trumpet, and the people shouted with a great shout, that the *wall fell down flat,* so that the people went up into the city, every man straight before him, and they took the city. (Josh 6:5)

Every evening, the city of Jericho closed the city gate (Josh 2:5). Rahab had permitted the spies to escape over the city wall (Josh 2:15), probably part of the lower-level fortifications. Thus, there is no denying that Scripture supports the perception that Canaan's vast fortification systems "reached up to heaven."[14]

E. Lightning campaign

Many scholars interpret the biblical account as supporting a *blitzkrieg* campaign that destroyed the most impregnable cities, a situation quite unsupportable in any later era. Israeli archaeologists Israel Finkelstein and Neil Silberman observe, "The Book of Joshua tells the story of a lightning military campaign during which the powerful kings of Canaan were defeated in battle and the Israelite tribes inherited their land."[15] Donald Redford also observes that cities fell quickly in the Conquest accounts. Summarizing the Scriptural record, Redford opines, "Cities with massive fortifications fall easily to rustic nomads fresh off the desert (mighty Lachish in only two days according to Josh 10:31), a feat Pharaoh's armies had great difficulty in accomplishing."[16]

Indeed, Scripture does support a sudden demise of the cities that Israel assaulted.

> YHWH your God is he which goes over before you; as a consuming fire he
> shall destroy them, and he shall bring them down before your face: so shall you
> drive them out, and *destroy them quickly*, as YHWH has said to you. (Deut 9:3)

The archaeology of later periods demonstrates a gradual overthrow of Canaan's cities (see below). The only massive wave of destruction that quickly swept across Canaan occurred in the sixteenth century, once again causing one to question the credibility of the thirteenth-century Conquest model.

F. Destruction

Another text indicates that Joshua's army had a policy of razing the battlements and other fortifications of nearly every city that Israel conquered. After Joshua had razed Jericho, he cursed anyone who would rebuild or refortify the city.

> Cursed of YHWH be the man who shall *undertake to fortify* this city of Jericho:
> he shall lay its foundations at the cost of his firstborn, and set up its gates at the
> cost of his youngest. (Josh 6:26)[17]

At the least, this text indicates a policy of defortifying towns. Scripture provides a clear sixteenth-century account of the Conquest. This sweeping destruction is attested archaeologically only in the sixteenth century. Canaan consisted of a federation of well-fortified city-states, of which Hazor was a major capital. Jericho, another kingdom-state, also attests walls and destruction only in the sixteenth century. When Israel attacked these impregnable fortresses, they fell before her quickly. Cities such as Ai remained "ruinous heaps" throughout Israel's history. The critical issue at this juncture is whether or not these accounts are real. Did a conquest of Canaan take place in the manner described by Scripture?

II. THE THIRTEENTH-CENTURY MIRAGE

When archaeologists began digging up the Holy Land at the turn of twentieth century, they believed that they had found vast evidence supporting Joshua's conquest of Canaan. This euphoria did not last long. As the science of archaeology gained precision, these discoveries were dated so much earlier that no reasonable scholar would believe Israel's history could be so ancient. The debate over historicity has continued into the modern era, but now, the accounts themselves are deemed to be fuel for debate.

These polemics are strengthened by scholars who support a thirteenth-century Conquest. The archaeological evidence does not demonstrate a vastly fortified Canaan during either the fourteenth or thirteenth centuries.[18] Nor are large-scale settlements between the fifteenth and thirteenth centuries attested.[19] Thus many academics deduce that the Conquest never occurred (Finkelstein, Dever, Van Seters, Alt, and Noth).

In their best-selling book *The Bible Unearthed*, Israel Finkelstein and Neil Silberman cite archaeological anachronisms that challenge Scripture's accounts of walled cities and strong fortifications during the Canaan Conquest.

> The cities of Canaan were unfortified and there were no walls that could have come tumbling down. In the case of Jericho, there was no trace of a settlement of any kind in the 13th century BCE and the earlier Late Bronze settlement, dating to the 14th century BCE was small and poor, almost insignificant, and unfortified. There was also no sign of destruction. Thus the famous scene of the Israelite forces marching around the walled town with the Ark of the Covenant, causing Jericho's mighty walls to collapse by the blowing of their war trumpets was, to put it simply, a romantic mirage.[20]

This assessment is wholly *accurate* if one is looking for archaeological evidence of the Conquest in the thirteenth, fourteenth, and fifteenth centuries. Even the fourteenth century lacks evidence of "hordes of uprooted people leaving their villages."[21] This leads Silberman and Finkelstein to conclude that:

> It is also noteworthy—in contrast to the Bible's accounts of almost continual warfare between the Israelites and their neighbors—that the villages were not fortified. . . . No weapons, such as swords or lances, were uncovered—although such finds are typical of the cities in the lowlands. Nor were there signs of burning or sudden destruction that might indicate a violent attack.[22]

No archaeological evidence demonstrates that a *blitzkrieg* campaign decimated towns and cities across Canaan during the twelfth through fourteenth centuries.[23] However, an entirely different picture emerges in the previous, sixteenth century, when nearly every city was indeed walled and heavily fortified, only to be destroyed at the end of the Hyksos Era (1550–1500 BCE).[24]

III. ARCHAEOLOGY OF CANAAN AT THE SIXTEENTH CENTURY CONQUEST

A. First Conquest Campaign

While the late-twelfth to fifteenth-century dates for the Conquest are historically, archaeologically, and Scripturally untenable, a sixteenth-century Conquest is not. In fact, the period marked by the end of the Hyksos period in Egypt, *c.* 1530, coincides with every detail of Scripture's account of the Conquest in Canaan.

During the Hyksos' control over Lower Egypt, Hazor had indeed emerged as the head of the nations in the Jordan Valley, just as the Scripture records.

> Hazor in the north Jordan Valley had been a major power center, presumably exercising control over much of northern Palestine and the Golan. . . . Hazor would have maintained its powerful position through most, if not all, the Hyksos period.[25]

Illustration 11.3. City walls dating to the 12th century CE. Walls in Canaan, which were built on top of hills, or were fortified to greater hights would have been many times higher. For perspective, notice the Bedouin in the lower right of the photo.

Not only was Hazor a major power-player, but the last phase of this era demonstrates that Canaan's cities were walled and heavily fortified.[26] Many cities had not exhibited walls in the previous centuries prior to 1650 BCE.[27] As the Hyksos Era in Egypt ended, Canaanite fortifications rapidly increased. Archaeologist William Dever observes that at the end of the MB II phase (1650–1530 BCE) nearly every city in Canaan had become heavily fortified.

> First, the fact that now (and only now) nearly *every* site in Palestine is heavily fortified—even sites as small as Tel Mevorakh, less than four acres. The rest of the later sites that had not been previously fortified, like Shechem and Gezer, now boast multiphase, truly monumental fortifications exactly contemporary with the Fifteenth Dynasty/"Hyksos" interregnum in Egypt.[28]

These fortifications were massive, some 70 feet or more in height (see Illustration 11.3).

The impressive fortifications of the Middle Bronze Age were based largely on glacis systems and huge earthen embankments. In the course of the Middle Bronze Age, and even more so with the destruction of the cities, occupation levels within the fortified enclosures rose nearly to the height of the ramparts.[29]

Archaeological discoveries dating to the Middle Bronze Age (III) very accurately reflect the accounts of Israel's spies. Scholars date this era to 1550/1530 BCE.[30] This means that Israel's spies were scouting Canaan at the very zenith of Canaan's impregnable fortifications. Yet, at the height of the dominion by Canaan's ostensibly invincible fortresses, the cities were, at least from an archaeological account, "mysteriously" obliterated. Archaeology demonstrates that in a very short time these fortifications had either fallen out of use or provided little shelter to refugees inside the city because destruction claimed almost every city.[31] Once again, archaeological evidence reinforces the same scenario that is presented by the Hebrew Scriptures.

In fact, of 337 known Middle Bronze Age Canaanite cities, scholars estimate that 204 were still functioning as late as 1800–1530 BCE (MB III).[32] At the end of the era, however, almost every city was overthrown.[33] Most were left uninhabited for centuries (see Table 11.1).[34] William Dever observes,

> It is generally accepted that it (MB III) is closely related both chronologically and culturally to the Asiatic 15th Dynasty in Egypt, which is quite well dated to about 1650–1540/1530 BCE (parallel to the 17th Dynasty). The end of the period, in particular, can be dated closely *by the destructions at nearly every site in Palestine.*[35]

In order for almost every site to have been "mysteriously" decimated during this period, a very quick campaign that lasted perhaps as little as 5–7 years must have preceded this destruction. (The cities listed in bold in Table 11.1. are specifically listed in Scripture's account of the Canaan Conquest)

This evidence seems to be a remarkable confirmation of Manetho's Hyksos-Israel equation (at least from an Egyptian perspective). Many scholars, such as Dever attribute this massive wave of destruction to the retreating Hyksos or Egypt's pursuing armies.[36] Egyptologist Donald Redford draws attention to the *implausibility* of this scenario. He points out that Egypt's traditional Theban kings were incapable of effecting the destruction that swept across Canaan.

> The assumption (is) that . . . it was the Egyptian armies of Ahmose that effected this devastation in their pursuit of their fleeing enemy. Yet a moment's reflection will demonstrate the improbability of this view. The Egyptians of Ahmose's time were notoriously inept when it came to laying siege to, or assaulting, a fortified city: Avaris defied their attempts for more than one generation, and Sharuhen for more than three years.[37]

Redford's analysis adeptly describes the Theban forces' limited capabilities. If a small fortress such as Sharuhen took over three years to breach, how could Ahmose's forces sweep across Canaan, quickly penetrating and annihilating Canaan's 200 vastly fortified cities?

The dearth of written historiographical evidence for the end of this era has led Redford to conclude "that a most significant page is missing in the record."[38] Indeed, the thirteenth-century Conquest hypothesis misses the most significant testimony, which fills the gap of this intermediate era. Scripture's record not only fills in the missing record but is firmly buttressed by tangible archaeological and written evidence.

Table 11.1. Palestinian Middle Bronze Age Sites

	2000–1800/1750 BCE	MBII(=IIB)	1650 BCE MB III(=IIC)	1550/1500 BCE LB IA
City	*Occupied*	*Growth*	*Continued Growth*	*Destruction*
Dan	Tomb	Embankment, domestic levels	Fortified	Gap?
Hazor	Tomb	Wall, embankment	Fortified	partial gap
Ginnosar	Tombs	Tombs	Fortified	Gap
Megiddo	Tombs	Wall, gate, glacis	Fortified	(continues)
Ta'anach		Occupied	Walls, glacis	Gap?
Beth-shan	Tombs	Gap/Mound grows	Fortification- unknown, lost	Gap?
Rehov	Tomb	Continues previous occupation	Fortified	Gap?
Barqai	Tomb	Tomb	Continues previous occupation	?
Kabri	Palace	Occupied	Continues previous occupation	Gap
Naharivh	Early Sanctuary	Fortifications	Later phases of Sanctuary	Gap
Akko	Sherds	Embankment, Gate	Fortified	Gap
Achzib	Occupied	?	Embankment, Walls	Gap
Tel Nami	Occupied	Continues previous occupation	Embankment, Walls	Gap
Tell Far 'ah	Occupied	Continues previous occupation	Glacis, Embankment, Gate	Gap
Shechem	Occupied	Temenos/Occupied/Walls	Embankment, Walls, Growth	Gap
Tell el-Havvat	Occupied	Continues previous occupation	Continies previous occupation	Gap
Jericho	Occupied/ tombs	Wall, gate, glacis	Fortified, Growth	Gap
Gibeon	Occupied	Continies previous occupation	Tombs, ?Fortified	Gap
Jerusalem	Occupied	Walled	Fortified	Gap
Bethel	Sherds	gap?	Wall, Gate, Domestic levels	Gap
Beth-shemesh	Occupied	Tombs	Wall, Gate	Gap?
Gezer	Occupied	fortifications	Growth	Gap
Bas el-Ain/Aphek	Occupied	Walls	Fortified	Gap
Tel-Aviv/Jaffa area	Occupied/ tombs	Fortifications, domestic levels, tombs	Fortified	Gap
Lachish	sherds/ occupied	Tombs, Glacis, Revetment	Fortified	Gap?
Ashkelon	Gate/Glacis	Continues previous occupation	Fortified	?
Tell el-Hesy	city	gap?	City, defenses	Gap?
Tell el-Ajjul (Sharuhen)	cemetery	city II, Palace II	Fortified	City Palace III/Gap
Tel el-Hammam (Bashan?)	Occupied	Growth, fortifications	Fortified	Gap

B. *Israel's First Intermediate Period*

The overall dating of the Second Intermediate Period in Egypt is a topic of heated academic debate. Scholars' chronology systems often differ from 50 to 100 years for this era.[39] As we saw in chap. 9, the Tanakh provides at least five internal proofs supporting a 1548 date for the exodus. Thus, the internal chronology of Scripture falls squarely in the range of accepted synchronisms and deviations for this era. The transition from the Exodus through Wilderness Exile, to period of the Conquest and Joshua's later administration, was truly an "Intermediate Period" in Israel's history.[40] Our chronology allowed 42 years for this intermediate era (1508–1460 = 42 yrs.). Josephus, however, suggested 112 years (*Antiquities* 8.3.1) to 134 years (*Against Apion* 2.2) for this period. While the latter figure would seem quite far-fetched, we cannot disregard the fact that our proposed 568-year chronology, which begins with Israel's walking out of Egypt and ends with King Solomon's 4th year, could indeed include another 20–40 years, bringing us back to Kenneth Kitchen's 596 years for the Exodus, Exile, Joshua–Judges, and early Monarchy Era.[41] Thus, the high and low chronologies presented here are in line with standard deviations in chronology studies for this era. Having established the timing of the Exodus and Conquest, we can turn our attention to the plausibility of the patriarchal accounts.

IV. THE PATRIARCH ACCOUNTS IN THEIR ARCHAEOLOGICAL CONTEXT

Ur stood as a commanding empire in southern Babylonia and Canaan in its sphere of influence. Abraham left Ur about 200 years before Ur fell. The tribes that migrated out of Ur spoke a West Semitic language that is generally dubbed "Amorite."[42] Egypt later recognized these people as Aamu or Asiatics, a classification into which Abraham's language would have fallen.[43] Egypt had recognized the approximate territorial boundaries that YHWH established in the Promised Land (Gen 15:18) as a single geographical area called Canaan from very early times and associated it with West-Semitic-(Amorite)-speaking peoples such as Abraham.[44]

During Abraham's days, Canaan had been dotted by small, unfortified cities.[45] This period of time is known as Early Bronze Age IV (2300–2000 BCE), otherwise known as a "Dark Age" in Canaan's history.[46] Farming and husbandry characterized this city-state society.[47] Around 2000 BCE, these small settlements, rural villages, and the surrounding pastoral nomadic sites were abandoned, most of them permanently.[48] This collapse of Canaanite society probably coincided with the famine that Canaan faced[49] when Abraham migrated to Egypt (Genesis 12) during the early First Intermediate Period (2180–2040 BCE).

When the Asiatic society moved back to Canaan, they chose favorable sites with locations that were suitable for agriculture and where water was easily accessed.[50] Several hundred new cities popped up all over Palestine.[51] These early settlements eventually gave way to the large cities that Israel later destroyed.

Under Ur's influence, Canaan had been exposed to the Mesopotamian culture for a few hundred years.[52] Akkadian was the written language of early Mesopotamia. Toward the end of this era, the first truly *alphabetic* script emerged in Canaan, marking the "zenith" of Middle Bronze Age Palestine.[53] This development would have enabled Abraham to write and record the promises and responsibilities associated with the patriarchal covenants.

Archaeological discoveries of this era demonstrate the presence of "monumental palaces," while the presence of weapons in tombs suggests that Canaan's cities had standing armies.[54] This evidence accommodates Scripture's description of Abimelek and his standing army quite well (Gen 21:22, 32). Abimelek was king of Gezer, a city that dates to the early resettlement phase in Canaan.[55] Abimelek's treaty with Abraham may have been occasioned by the fact that Gezer had only very recently secured its position as a city-state in the region, and a treaty with a powerful sheik such as Abraham was the next logical step.

According to Scripture's chronology, Israel's tribes migrated to Egypt around 1978 BCE, during Egypt's 11th or 12th Dynasty. While Israel sojourned in Egypt, Canaan continued to experience urbanization. At least 199 cities are attested in archaeological surveys, which demonstrate increasingly larger populations.[56] Flight to cities for refuge may have been motivated in part by Egypt's policy of plundering Canaan for slaves to support its monumental work force. Senusret I had captured 1,500 Canaanite prisoners of war, confiscating their weapons, ships, vast amounts of silver, copper, and other valuable commodities and food stores.[57] Threats such as these led citizens to seek shelter in impregnable fortified mountain defense posts. Dever estimates that as much as 80% of the population was now living in the 400 cities attested in the Middle Bronze Age (1785–1530 BCE).[58]

Large waves of immigration threaten the stability of any society. The immigration to Egypt of Abraham and the rest of the Amorites from Canaan during the First Intermediate Period induced social upheaval.[59] In an effort to secure Egypt's borders, the pharaohs established a defensive border called "The Wall of the Ruler" to keep Canaanites from immigrating *en mass* and causing the same sort of chaos as they had during the First Intermediate Period.[60] This defensive system that stretched into the Sinai did not eliminate immigration, but controlled it. This left Egypt's trade relations with northern Canaan (Byblos, Ebla, Ugarit) intact, although these relations were later usurped by the Hyksos.

By the end of this era (*c.* 1650), Canaan had rapidly developed into the cities familiar to us in Scripture: Hazor, Gezer, Kedesh, Dor, Ashkelon, Lachish, and Akko, became fortresses "walled up to heaven." Hazor's fortifications expanded to a whopping 200 acres.[61] Heavy fortifications hallmark the Canaanite city-states with an

> increasing pace and complexity of the defensive constructions. Not only are many more sites fortified in MB II, but the defenses now begin to incorporate elaborate *glacis* systems that are more technologically advanced than the earlier earthen embankments or ramparts. In addition, multiphase masonry and mudbrick city walls and standardized triple-entry-way gates now proliferate—probably influenced by the spread of Syro-Anatolian and Hittite prototypes as Palestine became more internationalized.[62]

These *glacis* were quite similar to those at Tell el-Yahudiyah in Egypt and compare to earthen ramps and moats that surrounded later European castles. The only entrance into the city was guarded by a watch-tower gate.[63] These defenses were specifically designed to withstand siege engines, indicating that military aggression threatened the autonomy of Canaan's city-states.[64] These phenomenal defenses were "mysteriously" destroyed at the very same time when Scripture indicates Israel was entering Canaan. This dramatic destruction characterizes the end of this era, around 1530/1550 BCE (MB III).[65] Rounding out the evidence of a 16th-century Conquest is the fact that the "first well-documented, large-scale ethnic movements of foreign peoples into Canaan are attested archaeologically,"[66] because new populations displaced Canaan's native citizenry.

Toward the end of this phase, numerous Cypriot styles begin to appear in the archaeological record. Remember that this was the same situation presented in Avaris (Tell el Dab'a); trade and displacement of people occurred shortly before and subsequent to Thera's eruption (pp. 470–71, 481–84, 493, 498). Places such as Alalakh in southern Turkey suddenly boasted frescoes that demonstrate affinity with Santorini,[67] a similar development also seen at Avaris. Once again, sites along the Levant evidence the infiltration of people from the island of Thera. Many of these sites were destroyed 40 to 60 years later, during the period of the Israelite Conquest.

V. SCRIPTURAL ACCOUNT OF THE CANAAN CONQUEST

A. "One Extra Portion"

Central Canaan is not the only area that evidences destruction during the sixteenth century. Archaeology also attests a massive destruction on the eastern side of the Jordan. Quite uncoincidentally, Israel's first campaign targeted the corridor east of the Jordan River that belonged to the Amorites (Num 21:23–25). Israel conquered this land from "Dibon to Nophah, which reaches to Medeba" (Num 21:30) on the east side of Jordan. After these victories, Moses continued campaigning against the Amorites, turning his attention to the giant nephiyl Og, king of Bashan, whom Israel defeated in battle at Edrei (Num 21:31–33; see also pp. 52–56).

Like central Canaan, this region came to an abrupt and "mysterious" end according to archaeology, right at the very time when Scripture indicates that Israel was entering Canaan (1550/1530 BCE). One particularly interesting site is modern Tel el-Hammam, which sits opposite Jericho and rises above the Jordan plain. Not only does this summit allow a view of the Promised Land, but Tel el-Hammam like Tel Nimrin (another MBA city in east Jordan), was destroyed during this time. In fact the excavators of this site draw attention to the fact that many other "Jordan Disk" sites were destroyed about 1530 BCE, which was "followed by its own five-to seven-century occupational hiatus."[68] (An "Occupational hiatus" is an archaeological term used to describe the period a city lay vacant, thus no one lived in this area for 500–700 years.) There was no economic or military reason for Egypt, the Hurrians, or the Hittites to conquer the Jordan Disk area. It lay outside favorable trade routes. No explanation exists for this devastation other than the record preserved in the Hebrew Scriptures about Israel's Conquest.

B. Canaan Conquest

The Amorites had been suzerain over Moab's territory (Num 21:26) at the time of the Conquest. Moses pacified this territory during the 40-year exile, and Israel set up camp on the Moab Plains opposite Jericho (Num 26:63) where she re-covenanted with YHWH. After Moses had spoken the words to Israel found in the Book of Deuteronomy, he numbered the men of war, who were 601,730 men strong (Num 26:51). With this army, YHWH would conquer Canaan's thriving but lawless city-states.

The record of Israel's Conquest in Canaan's interior appears in Joshua 5 through the summary of Judges 1. What is fascinating about these accounts is that almost every city mentioned in Scripture evidences destruction in the sixteenth century: Lachish, Shechem, and Jerusalem all the way down to Sharuhen and the "land of Goshen" (see bolded cities in Table 11.1, above). Archaeology soundly attests the destruction and abandonment to which Canaan's cities succumbed during the sixteenth century.

Previously, YHWH had used Joseph to bring his brothers into Egypt until the iniquity of the Amorites had "come to the full" (Gen 15:16). At the Conquest, YHWH did not judge and destroy a God-fearing people but a wantonly perverse and immoral people, who had no love for his Law or his healthy way of life.

C. Land of Goshen

The Hyksos Kingdom in Egypt stretched from Avaris to Sharuhen in southern Canaan.[69] The Book of Joshua offers tantalizing clues to the fact that the Hyksos had either not yet been driven out of Egypt at the time of the Conquest or they had been so recently expelled that Israel still recognized this territory as a Hyksos dependency during the initial Conquest. The "land of Goshen" was within Israel's tribal inheritance (Josh 11:16). This was the territory that YHWH had "severed" from Egypt during the plagues (Exod 8:22; 9:26). As we saw in chap. 10, this land lay on the eastern side of a now-defunct branch of the Nile (Josh 13:3; Isa 23:3; Jer 2:18). When YHWH had established Israel's borders, he gave the nation access to the two most powerful economic trading routes that existed in the ancient world: The Euphrates in the north and the Pelusiac branch of the Nile in the south (Gen 15:18; Num 34:5; Josh 15:4, 47–51).

Scripture lists the "land of Goshen" as part of the Negev (Josh 10:41). Both archaeology and satellite images demonstrate that the Negev during this era (MBA II–III) was not the vast desert that it is today.[70] A canal penetrated the district, allowing ships to travel into its ports and waterways.[71] This internal water supply sustained cultivation and a strong trade network. While Scripture's recognition of a southern "land of Goshen" does not make sense during a Thutmoses or Ramessid era, it fits the situation at the close of the Hyksos Era perfectly and should probably be equated with the Kingdom of Sharuhen, the Hyksos settlement that stretched to Gaza.[72]

Sharuhen had been the military and political headquarters of southern Canaan. Its city and palace were built during the later Hyksos Era (MB II–III). The area grew rapidly under highly supervised and organized urban planning.[73] It was here that the Hyksos took refuge when Ahmose expelled them from Egypt, besieging the city for three years.[74]

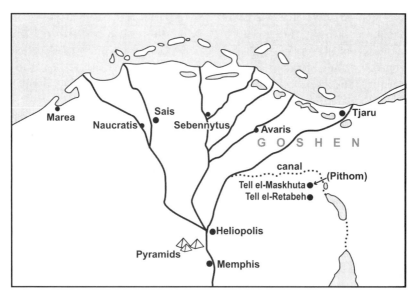

Map 11.1. Goshen

This political situation fits well with Scripture's account of Gaza and Ashkelon as being well equipped with chariots (Judg 1:18–19)—chariots that enabled the Hyksos colonies to withstand Israel's forces. Scripture also supports the scholarly consensus that the Hyksos' control over Canaan was limited: thwarted perhaps by Hazor's control of Canaan's interior.[75] These conclusions are supported by the fact that, after the Hyksos' expulsion, Egypt had placed garrisons in Sharuhen but shifted them to Gaza once Sharuhen ceased to be a region.[76]

Later in the Conquest, Goshen is listed along with 11 other cities (Josh 15:47–51) belonging to a southern city-state federation that Joshua and Israel subdued. Sharuhen is subsequently listed as the head of "thirteen cities and their villages" (Josh 19:6), a designation that probably replaced the earlier "land of Goshen" after the Hyksos had been expelled from Egypt. Israel's ability to conquer this region was no doubt aided by Ahmose's siege of Sharuhen. The scant evidence, however, does not permit specific dating of either Israel's conquest or Ahmose's siege, which may have occurred about 18 years apart from of each other.

Similar to Avaris and many cities across Palestine, Sharuhen evidences contact with Cyprus and the Aegean during its final period since Cypriot bichrome Ware begins to appear in the archaeological context.[77] This is again evidence of a massive Aegean Diaspora, probably prompted by the threat of Thera's volcanic activity just before Israel's exodus.[78]

VI. PARADIGM SHIFT

A. Equine

It is not surprising to find that many earlier Canaanite customs ended abruptly with the massive wave of destruction that swept across Canaan. Ceremonial donkey burials are one such custom. From Greece to Hyksos-occupied Egypt through Canaan and into Mesopotamia, equid (donkeys, asses, and horses) burials distinguished the Middle Bronze Age.[79] Scholars believe this ceremonial custom originated with the Mesopotamian cult of Shakkan and was later brought to the Aegean by the Amorites who migrated into Canaan.[80] Interestingly, it is evidence of this custom that most archaeologists use to identify "Hyksos" cities in both Egypt and Canaan.[81]

Equids played an important ceremonial role in Canaan's culture.[82] At Avaris, donkey burials were a hallmark of Hyksos society. Excavations have revealed the popularity of this custom throughout Canaan during the era (Late Bronze Age IIA thru LBA IA[83]). Places such as Jericho, Lachish, Azor, Tel Haror, and Tell el-Ajjul all exhibit the popularity of donkey burials.[84]

In Mari, a country on the Euphrates near northern Syria, covenants were ratified with the ritual slaying of a donkey's foal to make the ceremony binding (compare to p. 76).[85] Many equid burials were used in ceremonial foundation deposits.[86] In other instances donkeys were eaten as part of a sacrificial meal. More popular, however, were the donkey sacrifices associated with human funerary customs. The question that has perplexed archaeologists is: why did this practice suddenly come to an end?

> The survey of equid burials shows that the ritual inhumation of donkey. . . . was a region-wide phenomenon. While the incidences of the practice in Greece are the most distinctive, close attention to the specifics shows that there are no attributes that are regionally distinct. . . . An interesting question that remains is why, given its ubiquity in the late third and early second millennia, the phenomenon did not continue.[87]

The only explanation that reasonably satisfies the question why this custom suddenly ceased at the end of the Bronze Age (c. 1500 BCE) is Israel's Conquest of the region. Israel was the only entity whose religion forbade equid sacrifices altogether. There were at least three different laws in Israel's constitution that banned equid sacrifices, both as viable commodities for ratifying covenants and for funerary practices.

The first regulation that prevented equids' ritualistic use in Israel was YHWH's command that Israel consume only animals that chewed the cud or had a cleft foot (Leviticus 11 and Deuteronomy 14). Since equids do not meet these criteria, they could not be used in sacrificial meals. Second, YHWH had banned funerary cults and offerings for the dead (Deut 26:12–14; 14:1; Lev 19:28). Third, YHWH had specifically singled out the donkey as not even fit for the normal "firstborn redemption" offering.

> When YHWH brings you into the land of the Canaanite. . . . you shall set apart to YHWH all that open the matrix, and every firstling that comes of a beast which you have; the males shall be YHWH's. And *every firstling of an ass you shall redeem with a lamb; and if you will not redeem it, then you shall break his neck*: and all the firstborn of man among your children shall you redeem. (Exod 13:11–13)

As the primary means of transportation, donkeys held particular value in the ancient world, similar to the modern value of cars and trucks. Because donkeys were worth so much, the contribution of a donkey indicated the great piety of an owner. Although YHWH required firstborn male animals to be given to him, he allowed donkeys to be redeemed with the less costly and more plentiful lambs. This allowed donkeys to play a strong role in Israel's society without obtrusive religious or ritualistic demands. These regulations also made it clear that equids were not viable sacrifices for Israel's God. The donkey was the only animal YHWH specifically rejected; all others were set aside for him.[88] Interestingly, the donkey was the only unclean animal that is even mentioned in all of Torah that had to be redeemed. Even if a person chose not to redeem a donkey's firstborn male offspring, it could not be offered as a sacrifice. Rather, its neck was broken.

Israel's extraordinary Conquest of Canaan was a type of "shot heard around the world,"[89] sending out ripples that affected normal customs. While donkey rituals would have naturally ceased in Canaan under Israelite occupation, Israel's impressive victory may also have affected ritual equid trends around the entire region.

B. Appropriating a Previous Era

One challenge that archaeologists face when excavating Canaan's remains is the lack of artifacts, house types, and pottery that are distinctively "Israelite." As frustrating as this may be for an archaeologist or scholar studying this era, Scripture indicates that we should not expect to find anything distinctively "Israelite" from the time of the Conquest. YHWH granted the small tribal federations the very houses, fields, furniture, pottery, and possessions previously owned by the land's dispossessed inhabitants:

> When YHWH your God has cut off the nations . . . and you succeed them, and (shall) *dwell in their cities, and in their houses.* (Deut 19:1; parenthesis added.)

Joshua attests that YHWH had fulfilled this promise during his lifetime since many Israelites had overtaken Canaan's houses, cities, and fields.

> I have given you a land for which you did not labor, and cities which you built not, and *you dwell in them*; of the vineyards and olive yards which you planted not do you eat. (Josh 24:13)

Israel had driven out Canaan's natives (Num 33:52–54) and claimed their houses, fields, and possessions as the spoils of war.[90] While Egyptologist Donald Redford is critical of other aspects of Israel's history, he acknowledges the limitations of archaeology.

> While the cultural continuum between the Canaanite LB II and Iron I is a fact, the origin and identity of the Iron I peoples of the highlands cannot be sought among the fugitive Canaanite peasantry of the lowlands. Egyptian texts describe the highlanders clearly as transhumant pastoralists, and the fact that they borrowed

Canaanite house types cannot be used to disprove this. (I myself have sat in houses on the Medeba plains that, by the same kind of reasoning, might be used to prove the presence there of people from Jaffa or Haifa, so closely do they conform to a Palestinian style; yet their occupants, my hosts, were recently settled bedu.) If Egyptian texts do describe any movement of people it is always hills-to-plains, not the other way around.[91]

When an ethnic group of people enter a new land, one of two things happens. The people either assert their dominance and maintain their identity, or they become assimilated with the culture of the land's natives. This is comparable to many cultural groups immigrating to the United States who adapt America's holidays, America's dress, America's language, and other social customs, which often include conversion to Christianity. The simple fact is that, if one is to be successful in a particular country, a family must adopt the customs, practices, and especially the language of the adopted nation. As the old saying (of St. Ambrose) goes, "When in Rome, do as the Romans do".

Scripture shows that Israel struggled hard with these same issues. YHWH had commanded Israel to purge the land of all traces of idolatry and other negative social influences (Num 33:51–54). His command not only judged Canaan but established the Hebrews' independence in this region. Israel's religious and cultural "nationality" could only be established by replacing former perversions and governments with YHWH's righteous kingdom—something that the Israelites never achieved during their rebellious, post-Conquest Era. Although YHWH had given them all the tools to subjugate the land, many Israelites sought to integrate with the Canaanite culture instead. This affinity with local populations caused the entire Conquest to become a long, drawn-out process throughout the Judges Era.

VII. NOT BY HAND OR BOW

A. *The Hornet*

To attribute Canaan's destruction solely to Israel's invading armies is too eager an endeavor, which Scripture does not support. Although Joshua had conquered most of the cities in central and southern Canaan, YHWH sent foreign armies to devastate northern strongholds. At the exodus, 40 years before Israel entered Canaan, YHWH told Israel he would use other nations to drive the natives out of the Promised Land.

> Moreover *YHWH your God (a) will send the hornet among them*, until they that are left, and hide themselves from you, be destroyed. You shall not be frighted at them: for YHWH your God is among you, a mighty God and terrible. (b) *And YHWH your God will put out those nations before you by little and little*: you may not consume them at once, lest the beasts of the field increase on you. But YHWH your God shall deliver them to you, and shall destroy them with a mighty destruction, until they be destroyed. And he shall deliver their kings into your hand, and you shall destroy their name from under heaven: there shall no man be able to stand before you, until you have destroyed them. (Deut 7:20–24. See also Exod 23:28–30)

This text tells us at least two things. First, when Israel gathered on the Moab plains (before crossing the Jordan), YHWH had not yet sent the "hornet" to drive out Canaan's natives. Second, Israel would not destroy every city but inherit the land bit by bit, generation after righteous generation. This view is confirmed by the subsequent archaeological record.

> Many modern archaeologists point out that while Jericho and a few other towns were clearly sacked about this time, most other towns, although abandoned, do not show signs of violent destruction. Thus, many argue that this period is more complex than previously thought.[92]

Later in this chapter, we will see that the complexity of this era is easily explained by Israel's continuing Conquest surges, which coincided with Israel's cycles of obedience. The picture unearthed by archaeology illustrates that the Israelites indeed "drove out" many of the nations as YHWH had commanded (Num 33:50–54), appropriating houses and cities for themselves (Josh 24:13).

Scripture consistently uses the symbolism of hornets and bees to denote foreign armies. Seven hundred years later, Isaiah used the term "bee" to designate Assyria's armies that would sting and chase Israel from her heritage.

> YHWH shall bring upon you. . . . *the king of Assyria*. And it shall come to pass in that day, that YHWH shall hiss *for the fly* that is in the uttermost part of the rivers of Egypt, and *for the bee that is in the land of Assyria*. And they shall come, and shall rest all of them in the desolate valleys, and in the holes of the rocks, and on all thorns, and on all bushes. (Isa 7:17–19. See also Deut 1:44)

Isaiah uses "bees" as a metaphor for Assyria's invading armies. If Scripture is consistent (a concept of truth), then YHWH promised Israel that if she would obey his Law he would use other armies to drive out Canaan's inhabitants before her. Therefore, if we are to find historicity in Scripture's accounts, we should find "hornets" and "bees" invading, deporting, and weakening the Promised Land shortly after Israel's initial ingress into the Promised Land.

This view is bolstered by Joshua's claim that many victories over the nations mentioned in the Promised-Land Covenant (Gen 15:18–21) were won by the "hornet" that YHWH sent ahead of Israel. Joshua clarifies that neither Israel's sword nor her bow had gained the victory, but YHWH's forces had.[93]

> And you went over Jordan, and came to Jericho: and the men of Jericho fought against you, the Amorites, and the Perizzites, and the Canaanites, and the Hittites, and the Girgashites, the Hivites, and the Jebusites; and I delivered them into your hand. And I sent the *hornet before you*, which *drove them out from before you, even the two kings of the Amorites; but not with your sword, nor with your bow*. (Josh 24:11–12)

Joshua begins this discourse by reciting Israel's campaigns chronologically. After Israel had conquered Jericho, YHWH sent "two Amorite kings" as a "hornet" before Israel to weaken and drive out Canaan's residents. This raises the question: just who were these two Amorite kings?

The first king may be identified with the Hittite King Hattusilis I, who was roughly contemporary with the later years of Pharaoh Ahmose (1570–1546/1552–1527 BCE).[94] He launched an attack against Alalakh, a dependency of Aleppo, a mighty city-state in North Syria, comparable to Hazor. Not only did Hattusilis destroy Alalakh; he also annihilated cities along the Euphrates just north of Carchemish.[95] Hattusilis' grandson, Mursilis I, completed the Hittite campaign by utterly destroying Aleppo itself and obliterating Canaan's northern federations. Even more importantly, the Hittites annihilated Babylon shortly before 1530 BCE, alleviating the entire Canaan region from any threat from Mesopotamia for several decades (see Illustration 11.4).[96]

Illustration 11.4. The great King Hattuṣili III offering a libation to the weather god.

The significance of these campaigns for Israel cannot be overstated. The Hittites' home base lay in modern-day Turkey. Their decimation of Syria left a vacuum into which the Hurrians migrated, ultimately creating a protective buffer for Canaan.[97] The Hurrians claimed the territory around the Euphrates River, establishing the Mitannian Kingdom.[98] This buffer zone virtually isolated Canaan from outside threats by the Hittites or Mesopotamia (Babylon or Assyria). The northern hornets that YHWH promised to send against Canaan provided a protective covering, allowing the Israelites to fulfill the Promised-Land Covenant. However, when these invaders became too strong or began to infringe on Israel's inheritance,[99] YHWH sent Egyptian hornets from the south to prevent any further Hurrian ingress into the Promised Land until Israel grew strong enough to defend her own land. Thus, the only obstacle to stand in Israel's way was her rebellion against her covenant with God.

B. *Reality Check*

Archaeology and Scripture attest Israel's sweeping devastation of Canaan. It consisted mainly of "hit-and-run" campaigns that prevented threats from nearby towns but did not necessarily occupy them. At the end of Joshua's life, YHWH outlined the campaigns that still lay ahead.

> Now Joshua was old and stricken in years; and YHWH said to him, You are old and stricken in years, and *there remains yet very much land to be possessed.* This is the land that yet remains: *all the borders of the Philistines, and all Geshuri, From Sihor, which is before Egypt, even to the borders of Ekron northward, which is counted to the Canaanite*: five lords of the Philistines; the Gazathites, and the Ashdothites, the Eshkalonites, the Gittites, and the Ekronites; also the Avites: From the south, all the land of the Canaanites, and Mearah that is beside the Sidonians, to Aphek, to the borders of the Amorites: And the land of the *Giblites, and all Lebanon*, toward the sunrising, *from Baal-gad under mount Hermon to the entering into Hamath. All the inhabitants of the hill country from Lebanon to Misrephoth-maim*, and all the Sidonians, them will I drive out from before the Children of Israel: only divide you it by lot to the Israelites for an inheritance, as I have commanded you. (Josh 13:1–6)

YHWH had previously told Israel that he would not deliver Canaan into Israel's hand all at once but in increments, as Israel obeyed his Law, and her population subsequently increased (Exod 23:23–30). The archaeological record would supports this fact. Israel Finkelstein observes, "Transformation was not sudden in every place. The archaeological evidence indicates that the destruction of Canaanite society was a relatively long and gradual process."[100] The initial conquest had lasted 35–50 years. At the close of Joshua's life, Israel had secured the central and southern highlands, while the Hittites and Hurrians had weakened the north. The only task left for Israel was to fulfill YHWH's commands so they could inherit the Promised Land.

In particular, YHWH had commanded Israel to

> *Drive out* all the inhabitants of the land, and *Destroy all their pictures, and Destroy all their molten images, and quite pluck down all their high places: Dispossess* the inhabitants of the land, and *Dwell* there in: for I have given you the land to possess it. *Divide the land* by lot for an inheritance among your families. (Num 33:52–54)

> But if you will not drive out the inhabitants of the land from before you; then it shall come to pass, that *those which you let remain of them* shall be pricks in your eyes, and thorns in your sides, and shall vex you in the land wherein you dwell. Moreover it shall come to pass, that *I shall do to you, as I thought to do to them.* (Num 33:55–56)

YHWH specifically commanded Israel to drive out the Amorites, to dispossess them, and to expel them from their homeland. Yet, after Joshua's death, when the land had been prepared for the Israelites' victory, the nation greedily settled for suzerainty over Canaan's cities, which secured tribute revenue while allowing the Canaanites to remain in the Promised Land.

Judges 1 summarizes all of the cities and territories that Israel failed to destroy, drive out, and dispossess. The author characterizes Israel's policy, saying,

> And it came to pass, when Israel was strong, that they put the Canaanites to tribute, and *did not utterly drive them out*. (Judg 1:28)

YHWH's command for Israel to dispossess the native Canaanites was multifaceted. First, YHWH had waited 430 years for the Canaanites' sins to "come to the full." He judged their transgressions (Gen 15:14–16) and intended to cast them out of the land. Second, he had given Israel a constitutional Law to live by, which established her system of government. The Canaanites had no reason to abide by this Law. They had neither heard YHWH's voice at Mt. Sinai nor seen his miracles in Egypt. Yet as many modern European nations can presently attest, having a land with two competing law codes (e.g., European civil law versus *Sharia* law) breeds strife and civil unrest. So in order to establish a peaceful land and to fulfill Noah's prophecy (see chap. 3.III), YHWH commanded Israel to expel the Canaanites. Third, God knew how deceptive Canaan's cults were. He understood how easily his people could be led astray. In order to protect them from Canaan's deviant theologies, he sought to destroy and expel the heathen. This policy would have completely secured the land without any threat to Israel's constitutional liberty.

VIII. THE CONQUEST'S PROTECTED YEARS:
1508-1460

A. Israel: Joshua–Othniel/Egypt: Ahmose–Hatshepsut

YHWH actively protected Israel. During the nation's early years in Canaan, the Babylonian, Assyrian, and Hittite regions were plagued by intrigue and crises—situations that were hardly coincidental. Even Egypt's power over Canaan could be thwarted by Nubian threats, a female pharaoh's interest in international trade, or another pharaoh's cultish proclivity to serve a particular god to the detriment of state affairs. Later, the long, peaceful life of a mighty pharaoh allowed Israel to thrive while it led Egypt to coups and, later, civil wars.

While the Hittites and Hurrians had provided a protective buffer-zone in the north, Egypt had been pacified in the south. Any threat of Hittite resurgence had been thwarted by palace revolutions and Hurrian resurgence.[101] That the Hurrians in Mitanni had not yet infiltrated Canaan in *c.* 1500 is attested by the fact that, when Thutmoses I (1524–1518 BCE) led an exploratory expedition all the way to the Euphrates, no one fought against him.[102] It was not until at least 36 years later that Mitanni is listed as Egypt's "enemy."[103]

After Ahmose's death, Egypt was ruled by several kings who were primarily concerned with securing their southern, Nubian border.[104] For at least half a century after Israel's exodus, Egypt focused on reestablishing a united kingdom.[105] Around 1463, a complicated succession allowed Queen Hatshepsut to exert her power over Egypt. Her primary concerns were not conquest but international trade, maintaining a healthy economy, and restoring Egypt to its former cultural glory (see Illustration 11.5).[106] This again left Israel unmolested, allowing YHWH's covenanted people to establish a tribal federation in the Promised Land. For two generations (Josh 24:31; Judg 2:7), Israel followed YHWH's command to cleanse and possess the land.

After Joshua's death, Israel surged to claim new territory during the **Second Conquest Campaign**. Safe from foreign threats, she had the manpower and the strength to completely drive out the Canaanites (Judg 1:28). However, she relinquished her inheritance to Canaan's natives in exchange for tribute due to her greed for wealth and power. Within a decade of Joshua's death, Israel preferred suzerainty to war.

The security threats posed by the Canaanites were real. Within 60 years (3 generations), Israel had rebelled against YHWH's covenant. Israel congregated at Shiloh (Shechem, Josh 22:12; 24:1) to renew the covenant with

Illustration 11.5. Hetshepsut, the woman Pharaoh.

YHWH, an event that very likely coincided with the nation's first national Jubilee (Judg 2:1–5). This celebration collapsed into mourning when YHWH invoked his right under the covenant to withhold aid on Israel's behalf. Within a decade, Israel fell prey to Aram-Naharim's Chushan-rishathaim (Judg 3:8), who is perhaps to be identified with Kadashman-harbe I of Kassite Babylon (*c.* 1450) and who is known to have raided the Suteans, a people living in Canaan who are later attested in the el-Amarna Letters (see below).[107]

Aram-Naharim (Kassite Babylon?) humbled Israel for eight years, receiving the very tribute that Israel had so greedily required from Canaanites she was to displace. Israel soon learned her lesson and returned to obeying YHWH's covenant (Judg 3:9). Caleb's much younger brother, Othniel, became Israel's first savior-judge. Not only did his term mark an era of liberty, Israel also sought once more to obey the command in Numbers 33 to expel the indigenous Canaanites during Israel's **Third Conquest Campaign**.

Israel seemed to have faith in YHWH only as long as there was a national leader in whom she could trust. She apostacized after Caleb and Joshua died and repeated this mistake after Othniel's death. It is probably not coincidental that the 17 years that Israel served Moab (*c.* 1412 BCE) may have coincided with the 18 campaigns that Thutmoses III waged in Canaan (see below).[108] However, Scripture's silence regarding Egypt's vast campaigns in Canaan during the Judges Era poses the strongest polemic against a sixteenth-century Exodus and Conquest.

B. *Where's Egypt? The Scribe's Values and Standards*

One of the strongest arguments against a sixteenth-century exodus is Scripture's silence on the fact that Egypt engaged in vast and fierce campaigns across Canaan during the Judges' Era. In many cases, Pharaoh conquered the very cities that Scripture reports Israel had overthrown during the early Conquest. If Israel's Scriptures indeed provide valid records of this era, why are there no references to Egypt?

The answer to this perplexing question may simply be protocol. The Israelite scribe's primary concern was to record the nation's allegiance to the covenant with YHWH. Israel's peace depended on this covenant, a fact that we will see is made poignantly clear in the second part of this book. At Mt. Horeb and in the Moab plains, YHWH had promised certain blessings for obeying his covenant. Israel had agreed to abide by YHWH's statutes, judgments, and commands. Levitical scribes were commissioned to witness whether or not both parties had faithfully fulfilled their contractual obligations.[109]

Between c. 1580 and 1460, YHWH had created a political situation that allowed Israel to subjugate Canaan completely. To facilitate the full observance of his constitutional Law, YHWH specified the Canaanite tribes that Israel was to expel from the Promised Land. Her failure to obey this command meant that she would receive the very fate of the Canaanites she was to have dispossessed (Num 33:55–56; see p. 529–30).

Thus, the scribe's pen highlighted Israel's obedience to YHWH's command or her rebellion against it. This naturally dictated the scribe's fixation on the peoples whom YHWH had commanded Israel to expel from Canaan, to the exclusion of others, since Canaan's indigenous population would be the source of conflict—a political situation quite similar to modern Palestinian relations today. YHWH's covenantal Law had forewarned, "*Those which you let remain of them . . . shall vex you*" (Num 33:55). Egypt was not a land that was given to Israel, nor were the Egyptians a people that she was commanded to drive out. From the scribe's perspective, Egypt was irrelevant. If Israel obeyed the command to cleanse Canaan, YHWH would protect her from Egypt's forces, and "no one would desire her land" (Exod 34:24). If Egypt, Babylon, or Assyria subjugated her people, she had rebelled against YHWH's covenantal Law.

This in no way diminishes the fact that Egypt's armies often comprised local Canaanite forces. Israel's early scribal protocol dictated that her scribes ignore foreign coalitions or conscripted forces. Had Israel driven the Canaanites from the land as commanded, Egypt would have had no cities to leverage against Israel (see Egyptian campaigns below). When local states clashed with Israel's armies, her scribes acknowledged only the local henchmen who were now vexing her, despite the fact that many of these henchmen were aided by foreign garrisons or were vassals supported by Egyptian forces. A good example of this is Pharaoh Merneptah's campaign (c. 1230),[110] which coincided with Midian, as a vassal-lord, collecting the territory's tribute (Judg 6:1, see below). Egypt's inscriptions refer to Israel as one of the peoples whom Merneptah assaulted. Israel's archives are silent on Egypt's activity in Canaan, however, since her scribes recognized only the local "middle-men" federations that vexed Israel.[111]

A great example of this scribal practice in later years is the scribes' protocol that mentions the Northern Kingdom's wars and alliances with Syria but fails to mention that Ahab's last battle (1 Kgs 22:1–3; 31–39) with Syria (as an ally) was fought against Assyria's Shalmaneser III.[112] Assyria had invaded Syria–Palestine as a direct offensive *against Syria* (not Israel), and Israel's scribes only acknowledged local contact with Syria (since Israel was not the objective of Shalmaneser's campaign).

In contrast, Egypt's invasion of Judah under Shoshenq in Rehoboam's 5th year (*c.* 950 BCE) was a direct attack that did not arise from a local dispute that required reinforcements. Because this campaign was a direct Egyptian offensive (1 Kgs 14:25), Israel's scribes acknowledge Egypt as the aggressor. Later scribal entries also recognized both Shalmaneser V's and Sennacherib's Syro-Palestinian invasions. Both campaigns, like Shoshenq's, were direct Assyrian offensives, independent of any local disputes.

If the theory that Israel's scribal protocol was to recognize only local nations in their disputes with Israel is correct, then at least some of Egypt's Syro-Palestinian campaigns should correlate with the times when Israel rebelled against the *way of YHWH*, when the Creator placed the nation under the control of local Canaanite forces, perhaps garrisoned by Pharaoh's armies.

IX. CYCLE OF DISOBEDIENCE: 1412–1394

A. Israel: Captivity under Moab/Egypt: Thutmoses III and Amenhotep II

After the initial Conquest, Israel rebelled against the covenant (Judg 2:1–5). YHWH allowed a political situation to develop that threatened Israel's autonomy. Queen Hatshepsut had scarcely been laid to rest before her co-regent nephew began "Napoleonic" campaigns in North Syria since Mitanni was now a powerful force.[113] The Hyksos had enjoyed international trade with Byblos and the Aegean regions. Ahmose and his successors simply inherited these trading partners after expelling the Hyksos. Mitanni had perhaps sought to replace Egypt as the world's preeminent trading partner—something akin in modern times to Mexico or Venezuela supplanting America's trade relations with China. Thutmoses III (see Illustration 11.6) would not stand for this economic threat or the possibility of Asiatic invasion again; therefore, he enforced trade relations by military force in the Levant.[114]

In previous campaigns, the princes in Northern Syria had pledged their allegiance to Thutmoses's predecessors.[115] As suzerain, Egypt garnered tribute. By Thutmoses's first campaign, these local princes had switched allegiances from Egypt to Mitanni, rapidly fortifying themselves against any future incursions.[116] According to Thutmoses, Canaan's Kadesh and Megiddo had aligned with Naharin and Mitanni to war against Egypt.[117]

Thutmoses's initial campaign targeted Megiddo in north-central Canaan, which linked trade in the Levant with Mesopotamia. He besieged Megiddo for seven months. When the city fell, Thutmoses III captured its king, utterly despoiled the city, describing its value as being "worth a thousand towns"![118] Thutmoses and his son not only depopulated the land but also confiscated weapons of warfare. At Megiddo's fall, Thutmoses carried off 2,041 horses, 924 chariots, 502 bows, a couple coats of mail, and 329 Hittite warriors.[119] Thutmoses's son, Amenhotep II, claimed to have captured *1,092 chariots* and 13,050 weapons of war during his Canaanite campaigns. This policy weakened and depleted the munitions that Canaan would have on hand to face Israel a decade later, when Israel returned to YHWH's covenant. The question at this juncture is: how did Thutmoses's campaigns fit in Israel's history or affect it?

During the *initial Conquest surge*, Joshua had killed the king of Megiddo and allotted this territory to Manasseh (Josh 6–8; 12:21); however, Israel never expelled Megiddo's citizens (Josh 17:11). Megiddo is listed along with other cities and territories whose people Israel did not drive out or conquer.

Illustration 11.6. Thutmoses III.

And Manasseh had in Issachar and in Asher Beth-shan and her towns, and (a) **Ibleam** and her towns, and the inhabitants of **Dor** and her towns, and the inhabitants of Endor and her towns, and the inhabitants of (b) **Taanach** and her towns, and the inhabitants of (c) **Megiddo** and her towns, **even three countries** known to the Egyptians as the Djahi region.[120]

Yet the children of *Manasseh could not drive out the inhabitants of those cities; but the Canaanites would dwell in that land. Yet it came to pass, when the Children of Israel were waxen strong, that they put the Canaanites to tribute; but did not utterly drive them out.* (Josh 17:11–13)

Although Israel did not drive out the peoples or conquer these territories as YHWH had commanded, Thutmoses III did. Most of Thutmoses's campaigns served to conquer, drive out, and dispel the very peoples whom Israel failed to dispossess herself. Thutmoses deported

43 from (a) Ibleam, 42 people from (b) Tanaach, and (c) 340 prisoners from Megiddo while having killed 83 men.[121] The most prominent cities in Megiddo's federation were Yanoam, Nuges, and Herenkeru.[122] From these vassals, Thutmoses deported 38 warriors, 84 children of princes as hostages, and 1,796 slaves—totaling 2,503 prisoners in all.[123]

Thutmoses's inscriptions describe a political situation reminiscent of Joshua's earlier conquests. When Thutmoses faced Megiddo, he claimed that "330 princes, every one of them having his (own) army," came out against him.[124] This is the exact sort of federation that Joshua had faced about 50 or 60 years before.

> When Jabin king of Hazor had heard those things, that he sent to . . . *the kings that were on the north of the mountains, and of the plains south of Chinneroth,* and in the valley, and in the borders of Dor on the west, And to the Canaanite on the east and on the west, and to the Amorite, and the Hittite, and the Perizzite, and the Jebusite in the mountains, and to the Hivite under Hermon in the (a) land of Mizpeh. And they went out, they and all their hosts with them, much people, *even as (b) the sand that is on the sea shore in multitude,* with horses and chariots very many. And when all these kings were met together, they came and pitched together at the waters of Merom, to fight against Israel. (Josh 11:1–5)

Scripture previously recognized the (a) "land of Mizpeh" as the region of Gilead in Syria where Jacob and Laban had covenanted together (Gen 31:47–49). It was a seven-days' journey (Gen 31:23) from Padanaram (Gen 31:18). Joshua referred to Hazor's forces as (b) the "sand on the seashore." Thutmoses similarly described the Mitanni federations as being "millions and hundred-thousands of men, the individuals of every foreign country in their chariots."[125] Thus Joshua and Thutmoses gave roughly contemporary and similar accounts of the military prowess of Canaan's federations.

Thutmoses successfully defeated the federations in Northern Syria, extending the "frontiers of Egypt" all the way to Niya, south of Carchemish, and north of the Euphrates.[126] During subsequent campaigns, he secured northern Phoenician harbors, taking 492 political prisoners and 494 male captives from Tunip in far Northern Syria.[127] With these incursions, Thutmoses secured Egypt's supreme access to cedar or other precious goods in the Levant.[128] Egypt would not be denied access to this precious wood for her pharaohs' coffins or for her building programs, as she had been during the Hyksos' occupation (see pp. 477–78). Thutmoses's foreign objectives alleviated any pressure the Hurrians (Mitanni) or the Hittites might have intended to exert on Canaan's interior.[129] This situation once again allowed Israel to develop on the Promised Land without any external threats from the north.

Another territory that Israel had difficulty subduing was the district of Sharuhen ("land of Goshen") in the Negev, south of Gaza (Judg 1:19). Amenemheb, one of Thutmoses' warriors, tells us that he captured 3 prisoners from this district.[130] Thutmoses's military records at Karnak list 57 captives as being taken from the Negev, as Egypt once again weakened and depopulated the very areas that Israel had trouble securing herself.

With the Mitannian threat securely eliminated, Thutmoses's latter years were peaceful as his attention turned to building programs.[131] His son Amenhotep only attests three campaigns aimed specifically at Mitanni, which may have already occurred when he was co-regent with his father.[132] Egypt had become the world empire. Tribute flowed in from Babylon, Assyria, and the Aegean.[133] Hittite pressure on Mitanni finally forced an alliance between the two contending empires. Canaan's border along the Orontes River became firmly fixed by the marriage of Amenhotep's son Thutmoses IV to a Mitannian princess.[134] Although Thutmoses IV used a "show of force" upon succession, his reign initiated three generations of peace between Egypt and the East.[135] This peaceful alliance again provided the perfect environment for Israel once again to assert her right to inherit the Promised Land and to fulfill her covenant with God under the leadership of Ehud, an Israelite judge who would lead Israel's **Fourth Conquest Campaign**.

B. Contemporary Warfare Policies

One method that archaeologists often use to identify the chronology of a region or people they are examining is to identify contemporary pottery, customs, or other corresponding artifacts and practices. Not surprisingly, we find that Thutmoses and his son Amenhotep employed the same conquest policies as Israel. First, Thutmoses was friendly with towns

that opened up to him but plundered towns and killed those that resisted.[136] He burned and sacked towns he could not rehabilitate.[137] This policy very closely mirrors YHWH's instructions regarding Israel's campaigns in Deuteronomy's war-policy instructions (Deut 20:10–14). For Israel, this policy did not apply to the heartland of her inheritance, only to her outlying territories (Deut 20:15). No peaceful options were permitted in places where Israel was actually to live (Deut 20:16).

Second, Israel and Egypt shared the same policy in regard to Canaan's indigenous people: drive them off the land or deport them. Thutmoses dealt with Canaan's revolts by deporting the citizens—either conscripting them into corvée labor or selling them into slavery. During his 16 campaigns into Canaan, Thutmoses deported well over 7,300 people.[138] A few years later, his son, Amenhotep II (Illustration 11.7) claims to have deported 89,600 men (or 101,128 men may be more accurate), not counting women and children.[139] One hundred years later, Pharaoh praises Egypt's policy in "causing" Canaan's people to "[abandon] their towns."[140] Thus both Israel and Egypt sought

Illustration 11.7. Amenhotep II

to depopulate, drive out, and deport Canaan's residents, thus fulfilling YHWH's judgment against the Amorites' sins.

Donald Redford observes that Amenhotep's policies had severely depopulated the entire hill country.

> In consequence the hill country was virtual depopulated and the country severely weakened. . . . Never again could the Asiatics use Palestine as a base from which to attack Egypt . . . the territory was held as "insurance" against the hostility of Egypt's neighbors.[141]

This is significant (as we will see) because Israel's subsequent rebellion against YHWH's Law permitted her only to secure the depopulated hill country after the Third Conquest Campaign.

It is hardly coincidental that Amenhotep lists *Habiru* (Hebrews, see below) among the people he deported to Egypt.[142] For Israel's tribal federation, Amenhotep's campaigns had a silver lining, removing any possibility that the Hittites or other foreign entities could forge alliances with Canaanite federations against Israel or Egypt. In the subsequent peaceful era, Israel could once again assert her claim to Canaan's lands.

Third, both Joshua and Thutmoses held a disarmament policy. When Joshua conquered Hazor, he did not confiscate chariots or horses but utterly destroyed them (Josh 11:9). Thutmoses III similarly confiscated weapons of warfare, such as in the case of Megiddo cited above. This once again weakened the native population.

Fourth, both Joshua and Thutmoses had a policy of razing and burning cities that resisted them. Joshua set fire to cities such as Jericho (Josh 6:24), Ai (8:19), Hazor (11:11), and Jerusalem (Judg 1:8). When Egypt warred against Mitanni's vassals, Thutmoses III claimed to have set fire to "towns and tribes."[143] His son followed this same protocol. Inspired by a dream, Amenhotep III captured Migdol-yeneth (an unknown city in Canaan).[144] He took all the captives (numbering above 400), booty, and weapons of warfare, dug two ditches around them and set all on fire. The king watched over this dreadful scene until all was consumed: men, women, and children.[145] Thus, it appears that, where Israel had failed to fulfill Noah's prophecy or was timid to conquer the land, YHWH sent the hornet of Egypt to subjugate and tame the land for her.

Thutmoses's policy, which mirrored Deuteronomy's Conquest protocol, may be interpreted as Egypt rendering YHWH's judgment on Canaan in lieu of Israel. At no later time in Egypt's history do we find pharaohs following these directives. Despite Israel's rebellion, the archaeological and historiographical evidence suggest that YHWH indeed kept his promise to drive off Canaan's natives, providing another chance for Israel to believe his acts, fear him, and obey his Law.

C. A City and Its God

Thutmoses had inaugurated the custom of listing his conquest accomplishments on the temple walls at Karnak, and his predecessors followed in his footsteps.[146] Amenhotep II and his father often associated towns or people with their supreme deity. These inscriptions state the name of the city and its god. Amenhotep's inscriptions at Karnak and Memphis mention cities such as Shamash-Edom.[147] Shumash (Chemosh) was Edom's supreme deity (Num 21:29; Judg 11:24).[148] Two other cities—Joseph and Jacob—are also associated with the god El,[149] a supreme deity in Canaan that Egypt may very well have equated with YHWH.[150] A few centuries later, Ramesses III would similarly recognize another people in Canaan as Levi-El. Thutmoses's and Ramesses' recognition of cities in Canaan with names that are so strikingly Israelite in origin can hardly be dismissed as coincidental or "Egyptian folklore."

Sometime after Amenhotep's second campaign, he captured 3,600 *Habiru*, 15,200 *shasu* Bedouin, 36,300 Horites, and 15,070 Neges.[151] The term *Habiru* is phonetically equivalent to the word "Hebrew."[152] The king's victories are listed by geographical region, beginning with the *shasu* Bedouin in the south, the Horites of Syro–Palestine, and the Neges, a people of Northern Syria.[153] Not only did Egypt recognized the Habiru as a separate people during Amenhotep's campaign, these captives may represent Israelite tribes that had entered into alliances with the very cities that Thutmoses III and Amenhotep II conquered, a controversy we will soon address.

Earlier, we saw that recent scholars have observed similarities between Israel's scribal practices and those of Egypt and the rest of the ancient Near East.[154] This fact, alongside Scripture's chronology, attests Israel's well-established presence in Canaan at least two and a half centuries before the "politically-correct" twelfth-century Conquest date. Not only do Israel's scribal customs suggest contemporaneity with Egypt; her military policies toward Canaan reflect an earlier era. Thus, the evidence for a sixteenth-century Exodus and initial Conquest is supported by archaeological data, scribal practices, warfare protocol, and the protective buffer created by the Egyptian-Hurrian-Hittite stalemate.

D. *Evidence for an Earlier Exodus*

1. Names of Cities and Territories

In my study of cities that Thutmoses and Amenhotep conquered, I discovered that quite a few were indeed apostate Israelite cities or at least cities that had defied YHWH's command to not covenant with the Canaanites.[155] Several cities bear familiar Hebrew names. Two cities in particular stand out: Jacob-El, perhaps a reference to southern Israel (Judah); and Joseph-El, perhaps a reference to northern Israelite tribes.[156] In much the same way that Cyrus would be anointed years later, it would appear that YHWH sent Thutmoses III to accomplish his judgment. He disposed of and drove out any that stood in the way of Israel's fulfilling her covenant: both Canaanites and apostate Israelites. Thus, in some cases Thutmoses indeed "did to Israel as YHWH had thought to do to the Canaanites" (Num 33:56, paraphrased). Thutmoses deported 102 people from Jacob-El and 78 from Joseph-El (see Table 11.2).[157] Notice the implication: Israel's cities would have to have been firmly established in the Promised Land well before Thutmoses's rise to power for them to be deported back to Egypt.

These conclusions are bolstered by an inscription attributed to Amenhotep III. His temple south of Aswan records his victory over various nomadic tribes. One of the tribes mentioned is the "Shasu of Yhw."[158] The Egyptian word "Yhw" is phonetically equivalent to the Hebrew word "Yahweh."[159] This alludes to the fact that Israel had migrated into the land of Canaan and was at least partially seminomadic during the 18th Dynasty. Some scholars, however, reject associating Israel with a nomadic people during the New Kingdom period.[160] This view, however, contradicts the Hebrew account of its own history.

The characterization of Israel as *shasu* or nomads fits Scripture's accounts of the tribes' living in tents during the early Conquest (Josh 3:14; 22:6) and later during the Judges Era (Judg 4:11, 20–21; 8:11; Isa 38:12; 2 Kgs 13:5).[161] The tribes that secured their inheritances lived in houses (Deut 6:11; 19:1; Judg 18:22), while the tribes that had yet to subjugate their inheritances lived in tents inside other tribes' safe territories. While portions of Judah, Benjamin, Ephraim, and other tribes settled down to permanent residences or appropriated the residences of the natives they had driven out (Deut 6:11), a large portion of society still lived in tents until at least the time of Deborah (Judg 4:11, 20–21). The account of Jael using a tent stake to kill Sisera leaves little doubt about the type of dwelling the (*ger*) Kenites had lived in prior to Deborah's administration. The story of the Levite's murdered concubine (Judges 20) also demonstrates that Israel was a mixed-dwelling society (Judg 20:8). Those who had secured the tribal inheritances that Joshua had allotted to them lived in houses. But families who were living in the land temporarily or pursuing a shepherding life-style lived in tents, constantly moving to the outer periphery as the territory became secure.

According to the books of Isaiah (38:12) and Jeremiah (6:3; 4:20; 35:7; 49:29), families pursuing a career in shepherding often lived in tents and at least periodically lived a nomadic life-style as late as the sixth century (i.e., Jeremiah's days). This type of life-style is called *transhumance* and is often confused with *nomadism*.[162] Therefore, Israel's early life-style fits with the Egyptians' view of Israel as YHWH's nomads or "semi-nomads" at this early point in her nation's history, since YHWH was the only God the Hebrews served. Thus Egyptian records that attest to Israel's presence in Egypt during this early era should not be discounted.

2. The Berlin Canaanite Pedestal Relief

Despite the objection of so many scholars that "no Egyptian text ever found contains a single reference to 'Hebrews' or 'Israelites,'"[163] there is actually written evidence to the contrary. Egypt's records do mention both Israel and the Hebrews in general.

Recent translation of a warehoused inscription in the Berlin Museum has sparked lively scholarly debate.[164] Munich University's Manfred Görg studied the Berlin Canaan relief and found that it contained three nations written on a cartouche that an unnamed pharaoh had conquered and carted off as captives. The inscription itself is strikingly similar to the Merneptah Stele (*c.* 1208/1230), which most scholars consider the first inscription to mention the people of Israel.[165] The Merneptah Stele lists three city-states in geographical order: Ashkelon, Gezer, and Yanoam. A similar order and geographical orientation is implied in the earlier Berlin Canaan relief. The first cartouche mentions Ashkelon, followed by "Canaan" in a spelling that indicates the Canaanite lowlands.[166] The third cartouche is written in hieroglyphic as *Y3-šr-il* or *'I3-šr-Il*,[167] which at least five different scholars render as "Israel" (see Illustration 11.8).[168]

Table 11.2. Cities Thutmoses Captured that are Attested in Scripture during the Joshua–Judges Era

City	# of Prisoners	City Conquered During Joshua Era	Tribe's Territory	Early Israelite Possession	Vassal	Conquered During Judges Era
Aleppo						
Laish			Dan			Judges 18
Anaharath	52	Josh 19:19	Issachar		(Commingled)	
Ashteroth		Josh 9:10; 12:4; 13:12; 13:31	Manasseh (Josh 13:31)/Reuben (Josh 12:6)	X		Judg 2:13; 10:6
Beth-anath	111	Josh 19:38	Naphtali (Josh 19:32–38)		(Commingled)	Judg 1:33
Beths-shan	110	Josh 17:11, 16	Manasseh-Issachar (Josh 17:11)		X	Judg 1:27
Carchemish	270					
Chinneroth	34	Josh 11:2	Reuben/Gad/Manasseh (Josh12:6)			
Dibon	98	Num 21:30; 32:3, 34; Josh 13:9; 13:17	Gad/Reuben (Num 32:3–6, 31)			
Hamath	16	Num 13:21; 34:8; Josh 13:5	Dan?		X	Judg 3:3
Hazor	32	Joshua 11; 12:19; 15:25; 19:36	Naphtali (Josh 19:32–39)			Judg 4:2, 17
Edrei	91	Num 21:33; Deut 1:5; 3:1, 10; Josh 12:4; 13:12, 31; 19:37	Reuben/Gad/Manasseh (Josh 13:7–15)	X		
Gezer	104	Josh 10:33; 12:12; 16:3; 16:10; 21:21	Ephraim (Joshua 16)	X	(Commingled)	Judg 1:29
Ibleam	43	Josh 17:11	Manasseh (Josh 17:11)		X	Judg 1:27
Jacob-El	102		?Judah	X		
Joseph-El	78		?Ephraim	X		
Kadesh	1	Num 13:26, 20				Judg 11:16–17

Makkedah	30	Josh 10:10, 16–17, 21, 28–29; 12:16; 15:41	Judah (Josh 15:21–41)		X	
Megiddo	2	Josh 12:21; 17:11	Manasseh-Issachar or Manasseh-Asher (Josh 17:11)		X	Judg 1:27; 5:19
Merom	12	Josh 11:5, 7		?		
Mishal	39	Josh 21:30	A Levitical city in Asher (Josh 21:30)	X		
Negeb	57	Josh 10:40–41; 11:16; 15:51 (KJV "south country" or "country of Goshen"	Judah (Josh 15:21–51)	X		
Rabbah	105	Josh 13:25; 15:60	Judah (Josh 15:60) Rabbah was formerly an Ammonite city (Josh 13:25; 2 Samuel 11:1, 12)		X	
Rehob	87	Num 13:21; Josh 19:28–30; 21:31	Asher (Josh 19:24–30)		X	Judg 1:31
??Rosh-Kadesh	48	Num 13:26; 20:1, 14, 16, 22; 27:14; 33:36–37				Judg 11:17
Shamash–Edom	51	Num 20:14; Judg 11:17–18				
Shunem	38	Josh 19:18	Issachar (Josh 19:18)			
Sharuhen		Josh 19:6	Simeon (Josh 19:1–6)	X	X	
Taanach	42	Josh 12:21; 17:11	Manasseh-Issachar or Manasseh-Asher (Josh 17:11)		(Com-mingled)	Judg 1:27; 5:19

Unlike the Merneptah Stele, however, the Berlin Canaan relief uses language indicative of a much earlier Egyptian period.[169] Christoffer Theis and Peter van der Veen took a fresh look at the relief and found that both spelling and language usage coincide with other linguistic formulas common during the early 18th Dynasty (1548–1400 BCE). Those who have studied this relief broadly date it from the Second Intermediate Period (*c.* 1650) to as late as the reign of Ramesses III (*c.* 1152).[170] What this relief shows is that Israel was in the land of Canaan *at least* a century prior to the thirteenth-century.[171] Theis and Van der Veen's study of the stele allows for a more precise dating, however.

Both scholars cite at least four characteristics of language and spelling that demonstrate affinity with the inscriptions of Thutmoses III and Amenhotep II (traditionally, *c.* 1458–1401). The first of these is the use of a shorter spelling for "Canaan." During the later Ramessid period, this word took on a longer spelling.[172] Second, the names are written conso-

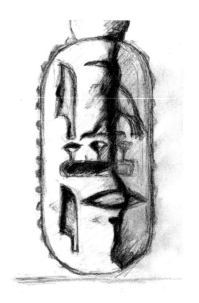

Illustration 11.8. Peter van der Veen's reconstruction of the third name ring on the Berlin Pedistal Relief.

nantally, which again parallels other inscriptions by Thutmoses and Amenhotep, but was modernized during the subsequent, 19th (Ramessid) Dynasty.[173] This means that the Berlin Canaan relief would have been written before the 19th Dynasty. Third, the name *Y3-šr-il* contains the theophoric element of the divine name El, similar to Hebrew names such as Samuel, Daniel, and Israel.[174] The rendering of a name with the divine element first became popular during Thutmoses's and Amenhotep's reigns.[175] As we have seen, the temple at Karnak records the territories or tribes of Jacob-El and Joseph-El during the reign of Thutmoses III, a custom that continued as late as Seti I, when his scribes recognized the tribe Levi-El.[176] The fourth element that links the pedestal relief to the Thutmoses-Amenhotep era is the use of the hieroglyph *r* to represent an *el*.

Lamed is the Hebrew letter *el* in the word *Israel*. Unfortunately, Egyptian hieroglyphic did not possess a separate sign to represent lamed with a vowel so the hieroglyph *r* took its place.[177] Again, Theis and Van der Veen demonstrate other uses for this character to represent an *el* in such words as *Jerusalem* and *Ashkelon* during Thutmoses and Amenhotep's reign and during the subsequent Amarna Period. The inscription on the pedestal does not allow enough space to allow another hieroglyph for the name to read anything but "Israel."[178]

The most controversial element of this translation, which Egyptologist James Hoffmeier contests, is the fact that "Israel" is written with a *śin* (שׂ) instead of with a *šin* (שׁ), which is basically the difference between an *s* and an *sh* sound. This renders the word *Ishrael* in lieu of *Israel*. This objection becomes moot if we consider that many ancient nations did not distinguish between these two sounds.[179] Even within Israel's dialects, this sound was not uniform. While the (southern) Judahites could pronounce the *sh* sound, the (northern) Ephraimites could not.

During a short period of civil war in Israel, which probably occurred within a century of this relief, the Gileadites blockaded the Jordan fords, using the password *Shibboleth* (Judg 12:5–6), which the Ephraimites could not pronounce. Since the Ephraimites could only pronounce the *s* sound, their origin was exposed. The author states the proper way to pronounce *Shibboleth* was with the *sh* sound, not with the *s* sound. What this demonstrates is that even in Hebrew there were regional dialects influencing these two sounds. For the Egyptians who came in contact with Israel, the two sounds may have been used interchangeably in the regional dialects that Thutmoses's forces encountered. Thus, Hoffmeier's objection in this case is unsubstantiated.

3. Synchronism

Egyptian chronology is a highly specialized field that normally resists discussion of new ideas or theories being applied to accepted divisions. It is necessary, however, to present a hypothetical scenario for the reigns of Thutmoses III and Amenhotep II that, if valid, would serve to partially resolve conflicts between Egyptian and Israelite chronology of the Judges Era.

The implication of this vast evidence is that most of Thutmoses III's reign was as co-regent, first with Hatshepsut and then with his son Amenhotep II. Thutmoses reigned for 33 years after Hatshepsut's death. It is quite possible that Amenhotep became co-regent long before the generally accepted two-year co-regency.[180] Redford observes that from year 20, Hatshepsut made "bellicose statements" in her inscriptions. He considers these statements to imply that Thutmoses III was either taking more liberties or assuming more authority under an ailing Hatshepsut.[181] Historical information from Thutmoses's and Amenhotep's reigns indicates that the real threat came from Thutmoses's strengthening his power by appointing Amenhotep as co-regent during the 32nd year of his reign, which would have been Hatshepsut's 20th year. Amenhotep's inscriptions appear to imply this very scenario. Inscriptions from Amenhotep's second and third campaigns claim that each one was his first campaign. Most scholars take this ambiguity to reflect his accession as being a 2-year co-regency before Thutmoses's death, with the second campaign being during his first official year after Thutmose's death. However, it is quite possible that it reflects the same scenario except that he was appointed co-regent during Hatshepsut's 20th year. His first campaign occurred in his 2nd year. This was Hatshepsut's 21st year. Since Hatshepsut died in her 22nd year, Amenhotep's 3rd campaign would have been his first campaign as sole co-regent with his father (see Table 11.3).

According to the above synchronization, Amenhotep's third campaign would have been Thutmoses's 8th campaign in Thutmoses's 33rd year, and the latter's second campaign against Mitanni. It also would have been Amenhotep's first campaign against Mitanni and the first campaign for father and son after Hatshepsut's death.

The possibility for this synchronization is further evidenced by the accession dates for all three monarchs. Thutmoses ascended the throne on April 24th, which means his regnal

Table 11.3. Thutmoses, Hatshepsut, Amenhotep Co-regencies

Dates[182]	Coincides w/ Israel	Thutmoses Regnal Year	Campaign	Amenhotep II Regnal Year	Campaign	Hatshepsut Regnal Year	campaign
1424		10					
1423		11					
1422		12				1	
1421		13				2	
1420		14				3	
1419		15				4	
1418		16				5	
1417		17				6	
1416		18				7	
1415	Israel's	19				8	
1414	18 yrs. of	20	Alone			9	Punt/Alone
1413	oppression	21				10	
1412	1	22	1st campaign			11	
1411	2	23	2nd Megiddo			12	
1410	3	24				13	
1409	4	25				14	
1408	5	26				15	
1407	6	27				16	Both/Thutmoses
1406	7	28				17	
1405	8	29	5th—Phoenicia/ Syria			18	
1404	9	30				19	
1403	10	31	7th—Phoenicia/ Syria			20	Both/Thutmoses
1402	11	32		1		21	
1401	12	33	8th—Mitanni	2	1st	22	Hatshepsut's death?
1400	13	34	9th	3	1st Mitanni		
1399	14	35	10th	4	Turah quarries		
1398	15	36		5			
1397	16	37		6			
1396	17	38	13th	7	Syria		
1395	18	39	39th	8			
1394		40	Tribute/	9	Sea of Galilee/		
1393		41	Peaceful	10	Peaceful		
1392		42		11			

1391	43	12	
1390	44	13	
1389	45	14	
1388	46	15	
1387	47	16	
1386	48	17	
1385	49	18	
1384	50	19	
1383	51	20	
1382	52	21	
1381	53	22	
1380	54	23	
1379		24	
1378		25	
1378		26	

years would be counted from the spring every year. Since Hatshepsut also reckoned her reign according to Thutmoses's regnal years, her reign should also be counted from the spring, as indicated by an inscription that (Urk. IV 367, 3–5) transitions from her 15th to 16th year during the month of April (Shemu I). Amenhotep did not become co-regent in the spring but during the fourth Egyptian month of Akhet (November), seven months later. Thus his regency was reckoned 6 months later, which can produce deviations up to a year (see civil calendars discussion, pp. 386–90). This makes Amenhotep's ascension year correspond to both Thutmoses's 31st year and Hatshepsut's 20th year. Amenhotep's first campaign as co-regent would have occurred in his 2nd year (Hatshepsut's 21st and Thutmoses's 32nd year) while his first campaign after Hatshepsut's death would have occurred during her 22nd year and Thutmoses's 33rd year. This synchronization shortens Thutmoses's reign by 23 years and dates Hatshepsut's co-regency as beginning in the 13th year of Thutmoses's reign, leaving only three years for Amenhotep to reign independently. Amenhotep's accession could also help explain why he desecrated and defaced Hatsehpsut's many monuments.[183]

This synchronism is also supported by what we know from Egypt's inscriptions. Thutmoses's last incursion into Canaan met with quite a bit of resistance, and he apparently avoided campaigning in the territory after his 42nd year in order to simply enjoy the tribute and the peace that his empire had accomplished. This would have been Amenhotep's 9th regnal year, which was also Amenhotep's last incursion into Canaan. Both monarchs mention a sizable tribute in the following year, which again supports synchronization.

Another indication that most of Amenhotep's reign converged with his father's is the similarity of the campaigns and the inscriptions that describe them. One inscription from Karnak tells us that Thutmoses commanded his victories from years 23 to 42; however the inscription lacks a summary. Interestingly, a summary appears in Amenhotep's 9th-year annal at Karnak, which appears to cull the total number of deportees from both Thutmoses's and Amenhotep's Canaanite campaigns—tallies that include the captives from Thutmoses's 23rd and 33rd-year campaigns, along with those who were deported during Amenhotep's co-regency. From Thutmoses's 23rd to 42nd year is a span of 19 years. From a Scriptural point of view, Thutmoses's and Amenhotep's combined 19 years of oppression of Canaan perfectly coincide with the 18 years that Egypt most actively campaigned in the region before Israel gained relief from the local tribes that had been exacting Egypt's tribute.

It should be noted that the purposed association between Moab's oppression of Israel and the campaigns of Thutmoses III is tenative. Based on currently accepted chronologies, Thutmoses's reign would be dated 35 to 40 years later than what is currently accepted. It would also resurrect the question of Hatshepsut's claim to have been co-regent with her father or for her to have reigned independently for a time.[184] This theory assumes that three generations of Thutmoses III's sons continued to practice long coregencies in order to strengthen their hold on Egypt's throne. If Amenhotep III (Amenhotep II's grandson) was 45 years old at death, and reigned for 39 years,[185] it is doubtful that he would have ascended Egypt's throne at 6 years of age. It is more likely that he served as co-regent with his father Thutmoses IV for a few years. It is hoped that future studies will take into account the strong association of Israel's captivity by Moab with Thutmoses and Amenhotep's campaigns.

X. CYCLE OF OBEDIENCE: 1394-1334

A. *Israel: Ehud/Egypt: Amenhotep III–Horemheb*

The Conquest began in 1508. At least three generations had lived on the Promised Land (Judg 2:7) when Israel rebelled and God gave them to serve Kadashman-harbe I of Kassite Babylon (Judg 3:8; see p. 363–64) around 1460 BCE. Scripture allows for a 40-year era of peace under Othniel, followed by 18 years of oppression by Eglon of Moab (Judg 3:12–14). It may not be coincidental that Thutmoses III also campaigned in Canaan for 18 years.[186] As we have seen there is evidence that Amenhotep II's Canaan campaigns occurred while he was co-regent with his father. Only during his 2nd and 9th years do we find incursion into Canaan around the Sea of Galilee,[187] which may have occurred while he was heir apparent, if we take into account the fact that his father had himself been co-regent with Hatshepsut for quite a while.

According to Scripture, Ehud delivered Israel from Moab and then enjoyed 80 years of peace.[188] It is not surprising then to learn that the next 74 years of Egyptian politics were focused on culture, trade, and a few Nubian campaigns.[189] Texts are remarkably silent about any significant Egyptian campaigns into Canaan's interior during Thutmoses IV's 34-year reign or Amenhotep III's 40-year reign, except for the latter's 5th year (during an apparent co-regency). During Amenhotep III's reign, Egypt finally entered into a treaty with Mitanni through the diplomatic marriage of a princess to Thutmoses IV.[190] Peace appears to have prevailed throughout Canaan. During this era, many of the Canaanite city-states that Joshua and Thutmoses III had vanquished regained power, providing the political backdrop attested by Ehud's acquisitions, once Egypt turned its attention homeward (see Map 11.2).

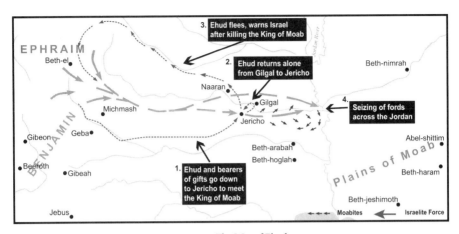

Map 11.2. The War of Ehud

During the latter part his reign, Amenhotep III was plagued by a disease to which he eventually succumbed.[191] Campaigning in Canaan was the least of his worries. His son Amenhotep IV, better known as the heretical Akhenaten, succeeded him. Both the latter half of Amenhotep's reign and the entire reign of Akhenaten are known as the Amarna Period, when Akhenaten moved his royal residence to Amarna. There are only a few hints of very limited Egyptian activity in Canaan. In stark contrast to Thutmoses's and Amenhotep II's aggressive policies, the Amarna Period marked an era when Egypt deliberately ignored the political issues in Canaan. This situation once again allowed Israel (and other Canaanite cities) to grow strong. Thus, part of Ehud's or even Shamgar's judgeship would have converged with Egypt's Amarna Period as Israel began her **Fourth Conquest Campaign** in Canaan. It is hoped that future scholars will give more consideration to these synchronisms with Egypt.

B. The Bubble Bursts

Mitanni had needed the treaty with Egypt more than Egypt had needed Mitanni. Two forces were trying to destroy the Hurrian state: the Assyrians in the east and the Hittites in the west. The Hittites quickly formed alliances, encroaching on Mitanni's sphere of influence. As the Canaanite cities began to reestablish their independence during Egypt's Amarna Period, some federations sought to throw off the Mitanni yoke by aligning with the Hittites.[192] By 1377, Mitanni had been fractured, finding herself a simple vassal state—her power forever stripped.[193]

Suppiluliumas I, the Hittite king who acquired Mitanni's territory, carefully avoided violating Mitanni's Egyptian boundary so that he did not incur Akhenaten's wrath.[194] While Egypt's diplomatic relations with the Hittites began under Amenhotep III, Akhenaten formally recognized the Hittite claim to the Mitannian frontier through a treaty.[195] Shortly thereafter, city after city began to defect from Egypt to the Hittites on the basis of more-reliable and favorable suzerainty terms.[196] This brought the Hittite border well in Northern Syria, which Egypt considered part of its realm. The Hittites justified this incursion by identifying these northern cities as Mitanni's territory before Egypt's treaty with the Hurrians, but in reality this ingress violated the current Hittite-Egyptian pact. Egypt did nothing during Akhenaten's reign, and Akhenaten's successor, Tutankhamun was too young and ineffective to change course. Since Tutankhamun was unable to produce children, with his death (*c.* 1325) the 18th Dynasty, which had begun with Ahmose, came to an end.

The Amarna Era allowed Israel and many other Canaanite federations to reassert their former independence. There is clear evidence during the Amarna Period that Israel allied with other Canaanite cities to topple Egypt's vassal states. The Israelites succeeded in this endeavor under Ehud and perhaps Shamgar, until her sins overcame her once more and there arose another pharaoh to subjugate her.

C. Israelite Influence

1. Treaties

By the end of the Amarna Period (*c.* 1334), Israel had lived in the Promised Land for many generations. Treaties are the first custom to demonstrate a strong affinity between Canaan and Israel. When Israel covenanted with YHWH at Mt. Sinai and in the Moab plains, she followed a formal, ten-part treaty formula (see chap. 3.I-II). After the initial Conquest surge, Israel illegally covenanted with the Canaanites (Exod 23:32; Deut 7:2; Judg 1:28). Her elders probably used this same formula when securing allegiances. Israel's activity in Syria is probably best attested by her influence on treaties in general. By the fourteenth and early thirteenth centuries, the Sinai covenant formula had become standard protocol.[197] Kenneth Kitchen observes:

> Nearly all the known treaties of the 14th/13th centuries BCE follow this pattern closely. Sometimes some elements are omitted, but the order of them is almost invariable, whenever the original texts are sufficiently well preserved to be analyzed. This is, therefore, a stable form in the period concerned. Earlier than this, the pattern was apparently somewhat different.[198]

Israel's treaty formula prevailed among the cities that covenanted with the Hittites (see Illustration 11.9). Almost every Hittite treaty follows Israel's covenant pattern.[199] In effect, Israel's treaties inadvertently introduced a new standard and a more-formalized written treaty protocol, which would last well into the first millennium.[200] This evidence implies that many of the northern Canaanite federations that cast off Egypt's yoke in favor of the Hittite were indeed led by Israelite tribes as they sought to carve out and secure a greater homeland.

Illustration 11.9. A 13th *c.* Hittite treaty.

2. Fashion

Another interesting custom found in Northern Syria may also attest Israel's influence on the local population. YHWH had established regulations for Israel's dress, ordaining blue fringes on the borders of her garments. "Tell them to . . . put on the fringe of the borders a ribbon of blue (Num 15:38–39). As the Late Bronze Age (1550–1400 BCE) dawned in Canaan,

a new stage in costume development had set in. Well-to-do Asiatics from North Syria and Mitanni now appear, from the reign of Thutmoses III onward, in a tight-fitting white gown *with blue or red hems*, reaching from neck to midcalf, with tight, wrist-length sleeves.[201]

This association may attest Israel's early compliance with YHWH's Law and Israel's ability to influence local fashion. As in the case of the covenant formula, it appears that Israel set many new trends in Canaan and influenced protocol due to her (at least) partial observance of YHWH's Law (see Illustrations 11.10 and 11.11).

Illustrations 11.10 and 11.11. Portrayal of Canaanites with blue or red hems in an Egyptian wall painting *c.* 14th century BCE.

D. Who Were the Israelites?

People are distinguished in many ways. Sometimes ethnicity is based on place of origin, sometimes on race, and other times on language. For instance, a Spanish-speaking person from Honduras is generically termed a "Mexican," even when his or her nationality bears no relation to Mexico. This type of situation is probably comparable with Egypt's broad classification of the *Aamu* or Asiatics, which Donald Reford recognizes as based on similar languages.[202] Linguistically, the Hebrews would have fallen into this broad classification, since their language was so similar to Canaanite, Ugaritic, and the language of the Aramaeans.[203]

Scripture calls Abraham and his descendants *Hebrews* (*ibri* in Hebrew, Gen 14:13; Exod 7:16). The term *Hebrew* is derived from Abraham's ancestor Eber (Gen 10:21),[204] Shem's fourth-generation grandson. Assyria's royal archives appear to list Eber's name as Ḥarḥaru, which according to custom, became "Hebrew."[205] Patriarchal names were used to designate children in ancient times. The late great Abraham Malamat of Hebrew University in Jerusalem observed, "each son, in turn, acts as an eponym of one of the twelve tribes of Israel; the tribes encompass broad lineages which are divided into maximal, major, minor and minimal lines."[206] Given the affinity that Israel's laws and customs had with other ancient Near Eastern nations',[207] there is no reason to doubt that eponyms did not originally define most ancient clans throughout the Near East.

Malamat observes that in the course of time some Hebrew terms "ultimately expanded their scope—that is, they underwent an 'anaemic' process so to speak, namely, a loosening of blood ties in the kinship system."[208] Eber/Ḥarḥaru, originally designated the Hebrews or someone who had married into the clan.[209] The term *Hebrew* or *Habiru* is attested throughout Mesopotamia and Egypt well before the Children of Israel existed.[210]

The general term *Hebrew*, like *Amorite*, could have designated a people who spoke a "Hebrew" tongue and whose lineage traced back to the patriarch Eber. According to Gen 10:5–20, the languages at Babel were divided along family lines, apparently during Eber's lifetime. Abraham was only one of Eber's descendants. Thus, from a Scriptural perspective, the term *Hebrew* not only designated the Abrahamic clan; it also designated Eber's other descendants through Joktan (Gen 10:25) and Peleg (Gen 10:25; 11:17–27), who are often identified as Greeks (see Appendix 9.51). After Babel, the term may have evolved to designate all people who spoke the Eber/Hebrew language, in lieu of an actual tribal association, thus supplanting bloodline with language.[211]

Scripture readily acknowledges that other Hebrews existed outside Abraham's lineage.[212] Terah, Abraham's father, for instance, and most of his clan settled in Ur (Gen 11:28). When Abraham sought a wife for Isaac, he sent his servant to his brother Nahor (Gen 24:47–48), who as an Eber descendant would also have been considered a Hebrew and evidently spoke the same tongue. Unsurprisingly, we find Eber's children scattered throughout Mesopotamia, Mari, and the Near East in general and referred to as *Apiru* or *Habiru*. These terms become the most prevalent in Egypt and Canaan during Ehud's leadership of Israel, when the Hebrews realized one of the most significant acquisitions in territory since the initial Conquest.

E. 'Apiru/Habiru/Sa.Gaz

1. El-Amarna Tablets

The term *Hebrew* is found in many ancient texts in different languages. In Akkadian, the standard diplomatic language of Mesopotamia, the term appears in a logogram (not phonetic) as *Sa.Gaz*.[213] In other languages, the term *Hebrew* appears as *Apiru* or *Habiru*.[214] Many ancient Sumerian, Akkadian, Hittite, Mitanni, and Ugaritic texts refer to the Habiru well before Israel became a nation.[215] Not coincidentally, the term died out as the people of Israel became a nation during the Monarchy.[216] Texts from Alalakh, in North Syria and roughly contemporary with the patriarch Jacob (*c.* 1975), mention a treaty between King Semuma and the Habiru warriors.[217] This event was a significant turning point in national relations, and an entire era is dated by the event.[218] Although most scholars dismiss the Habiru, as having no direct link to Israel,[219] some allow for the fact that the term may have referred to an ethnic group of people called Hebrews.[220]

Since their discovery a century ago, the el-Amarna Tablets have sparked controversy over whether they bear record to Israel's ongoing Conquest. The letters refer to groups of Habiru that made alliances with local Canaanite rulers. Guerilla warfare marked the tactics of Canaan's up and coming foe, who burned and destroyed towns while driving out Canaan's natives. These warriors are recognized by two names. In southern Canaan where Egyptian hieroglyphics were employed, the Amarna Tablets call the invaders *apiru* or *habiru*.[221] In the north, where Akkadian was the standard diplomatic language for correspondence, the invaders were designated with the Sumerian logogram Sa.Gaz.[222]

Over the years, I have studied quite a number of works dealing with the Habiru/Hebrew issues.[223] Most scholars timidly refrain from equating this group of people with the Hebrews in Scripture even though their names are phonetically similar.[224] Although scholars have raised arguments against associating the Habiru with the Scriptural *'ibri* ('Hebrews'), each study that I have read has been rather myopic, failing to consider the Scriptural perspective or the implications of an earlier exodus date.

The current scholarly consensus is that the Sa.Gaz/Habiru were a nomadic or semi-nomadic society composed of rebellious outlaws, raiders, and mercenaries—always on the fringe of society.[225] As we have seen, Scripture demonstrates that Israel's society was semi-nomadic, because many tribes lived in tents throughout the Judges Era (see pp. 525–26, 539). The fact that Israel continued her assault on Canaan's native population lends further support to an Hebrew-Habiru equation. Thus the Habiru's seminomadic trait fits with Scriptural evidence of Israel's partial seminomadic tent-dwelling society.

One scholarly view considers the 'Apiru to be strictly mercenaries.[226] The problem with this theory is that Habiru are listed with just about every occupation, from shepherds to skilled laborers, even kings and slaves.[227] Meredith Kline observes that the Habiru population was found "with its own property holdings and cattle, with its share of government officials, aristocracy, military officers, and cultic functionaries along with its contributions to the lower ranks of . . . shepherd."[228] Since kings did not offer treaties to dependent social classes,[229] the Habiru was a people strong enough that no king could ignore. This quite accurately reflects Abraham's ability to muster a powerful regiment to assail Lot's captors (Genesis 14) or the significance of King Semuma's treaty with the Habiru warriors. Thus, to classify the Habiru strictly as a mercenary class or to identify them as a marauding social class prejudices the interpretation.

Common to almost all people designated as *Habiru* is the fact that they were uprooted from their original political and social framework and forced to adapt to a new environment.[230] What scholars have yet to address is: what would cause an ethnic-linguistic group such as the clan of Abraham, Terah, and the Hebrews in general to become migratory or to develop a strong mercenary class?

We know that during early Mesopotamian history people had a tribal society of inalienable land ownership, similar to what YHWH later ordained in Israel.[231] As priests and kings amassed more and more power, they began to purchase or confiscate lands and displace families.[232] This practice and an unstable political environment no doubt compelled Terah's and Abraham's migration shortly before the great Ur kingdom collapsed. Notice the implication that this had for displaced Hebrews in general. Forced from their homeland, the Hebrews would look for sustenance from labor in lieu of land.[233] Thus, movement to safe-havens for employment would become their hallmark, in much the same way that Hispanics often immigrate to America and work for several generations before they can acquire valuable real estate.

Like other scholars, Meredith Kline sees a link between the Habiru and the Mesopotamian concept of migration.

> All the antinomies can be resolved by the supposition that the *Habiru* were refu-
> gees, men who had fled their native lands. This would explain why they appear as
> strangers, why they are found well-nigh everywhere, and why they have such a
> variety of names. It would account for the fact that some settled down in assigned
> places subject to the local authorities, while others organized into independent,
> outlaw bands. It would account, too, for the fact that while some may have been
> absorbed into the new culture, others preserved some of their native traditions
> and thus are found, for example, to have their own gods (Rachel and Laban). It
> would also explain why the term *Habiru* sometimes denotes a social class (i.e.,
> fugitives) and yet is used as the equivalent of an ethnic term. . . . What fortune,
> from kingship to slavery, might not befall the fugitive *ha-BI-ru*?[234]

It is quite possible that these displaced Hebrews gave rise to the concept "to ḫabāru" or 'to
migrate,'[235] as an ethnic tribe evidenced a trait that seemed to characterize the entire clan. A
similar phenomenon is observed with the ethnic Medjay tribe that aided Ahmose as "regular policemen" against the Hyksos.[236] The tribe performed the office so well that the term
"'Medjay' virtually became synonymous with 'policeman.'"[237] Although the Medjay were
law-enforcers, their occupation did not discount an ethnic tribal association.[238]

The first time we encounter the Habiru in Egyptian sources is during the campaigns
of Thutmoses III and Amenhotep II, when 3,600 Habiru were deported from Canaan into
Egypt.[239] Their number was much *less* than the 5,200 *shasu*, 36,300 *Horites* (Kharu), 15,070
Neges (Northern Syria) listed in the same inscription.[240] It is clear that Egypt recognized the
Habiru as a separate ethnic group.[241] They are distinguished from immigrants and foreign
Horites and *shasu*, yet they *are* listed among (and equal to) other ethnic peoples, such as
the Horites.

Later, Akhenaten deported the "Habiru of the pasture land" and settled them in the
land of Kush, although Egypt's records do not inform us of the number of captives.[242] That
Akhenaten needed to designate the place from which the Habiru derived indicates that they
were not domiciled in a particular region but scattered throughout Canaan. If the Habiru
were Hebrews who had exited Egypt under Apophis/Ahmose and had formerly conquered
Canaan with the intent of fulfilling the Promised-Land covenant, how do we explain the
Habirus' later subjugation and deportation by Egypt's kings during this early era?

2. Habiru in Ships

The covenant that Israel compacted with YHWH had stipulated consequences for breach of
pact. Ultimately, the penalty returned Israel to the very house of bondage from which she
had been delivered. A curse in the law prophesied:

> And *YHWH shall bring you into Egypt again with (a) ships*, by the way whereof
> I spoke to you, "You shall see it no more again" (see Exod 14:13); and there you

shall be sold to your enemies for bondmen and bondwomen, and (b) no man shall buy you. (Deut 28:68)

At Bochim (Judg 2:1–5), YHWH's messenger told Israel that he would no longer fight on Israel's behalf. YHWH invoked the covenant's penalties, citing Israel's capacious infraction of making suzerainty alliances with the Canaanites instead of driving them out of the Promised Land, as instructed:

> I made you to go up out of Egypt, and have brought you into the land which I swore to your fathers; and I said, I will never break my covenant with you. And *you shall make no league with the inhabitants of this land; you shall throw down their altars: but you have not obeyed my voice: why have you done this?* Wherefore I also said, I will not drive them out from before you; but they shall be as thorns in your sides (see Num 33:55), and their gods shall be a snare to you. (Judg 2:1–3)

Bochim occurred within 50 years of Israel's entering the Promised Land. Although Israel indeed returned to YHWH after serving Aram-Naharim (Mesopotamia or Kassite Babylon) for 8 years, 40 years later her tendency to treaty with the Canaanites stubbornly persisted. With Othniel's death, Thutmoses III and Amenhotep II executed YHWH's judgment until Israel again learned her lesson. Interestingly, Thutmoses indeed used ships to deport captives, many of whom were not sold to individuals but reentered Pharaoh's corvée, as "*boatloads* of Canaanite slaves were regular arrivals in Egyptian ports."[243] Redford points out that Thutmoses indeed sent Canaan's war captives back to Egypt in ships! Since, most of these became Egypt's corvée laborers, the captives were not sold to individuals (hence, "no man bought" them) but became assets of the state when they reentered Egypt's *house of bondage*. Thus, YHWH completely sold these rebellious tribes back into the house of bondage from which they had recently been redeemed.

F. *Thorns, Snares, and Vassal-Lords*

When YHWH's messenger told Israel that God would no longer fight for the nation (Judg 2:1–3; see above), he quoted from the judgment of Numbers 33 by stating that the Canaan's indigenous people would be "thorns" in Israel's side and their gods a snare. The messenger at Bochim quoted directly from Numbers 33:

> But if you will not drive out the inhabitants of the land from before you; then it shall come to pass, that those which you let remain of them shall be pricks in your eyes, and *thorns in your sides, and shall vex you* in the land wherein you dwell. (Num 33:55–56)

Israel's friendly policy toward the Canaanites resulted in continual warfare and civil strife. Canaan's federations could be easily manipulated against Israel and her interests by greater powers such as Egypt. Local kingdoms simply enacted Pharaoh's policies and collected his tribute.

After Thutmoses III's campaigns, Canaan lost considerable independence. Her monarchies were reduced to petty administrations or replaced with regional governors.[244] Each king and his cabinet members swore allegiance to Pharaoh as suzerain. His throne was now considered a courtesy appointment by Pharaoh.[245] Canaan's formerly strong federations had yielded considerable power over weaker districts, enjoying tribute as overlords. Now these same kings were themselves weaker vassals, obliged to oversee and collect Pharaoh's tribute. Thutmoses took advantage of well-established government structures, adapting them to the organizational structure used in Egypt's own government.[246] Thus, former powerful kingdoms now fell to the status of tax-collector. This proved to be a delicate balancing act. "If they appeared to be 'Egypt's man' to an excessive degree, they ran the risk of being assassinated; but if they failed to cooperate with the imperial administration, they ran the risk of being dragged off to Pharaoh's court to answer charges."[247]

YHWH had commanded Israel to drive out and dispossess Canaan's indigenous peoples (Num 33:52–53). Had Israel obeyed this command instead of making peace, Egypt's kings would have lacked established systems to leverage against vassals like Israel. Likewise, if Israel had obeyed Numbers 33's judgment to drive out and dispossess the Canaanites, the land would have been so depopulated that neither Thutmoses IV nor Amenhotep III would have had any desire to invade, deport, or subjugate Canaan's cities. Indeed this theory is confirmed by the political situation in Canaan after Amenhotep II had severely depopulated (over 89,000 captives) the region and Egypt all but lost interest in any further deportations or campaigns in Canaan for the rest of the dynasty.

Because Israel had treated with the Canaanites, these peoples became painful pricks in Israel's eyes and thorns in her side, vexing her on Pharaoh's behalf. Finally, "YHWH did to Israel as he had sought to do to the Canaanites by spewing them out of his land" (Num 33:55–56).

Before Thutmoses III's reign, the only land that Israel controlled and possessed had stretched from Jericho north to Shechem (Joshua 6–7; 17:7; 20:7; 21:21; 24:1, 25, 32) and south to Jerusalem (Josh 10:1–5; 15:63; Judg 1:7–8), with scattered enclaves around Mt. Ephraim and the surrounding countryside (Josh 17:8; 19:50) and around Gezer (Judg 1:29). This is in addition to the extra portion on the Jordan's eastern side. After YHWH refused to fight Israel's battles, her strength languished. Moab seized this opportunity, banding with the Ammonites and Amalekites to occupy Jericho's former dominion and subjugate Israel (Judg 3:13), Moab's much-hated foe (Numbers 21–24; Josh 24:9).

We really do not know if Moab succumbed to Thutmoses III or his successors during this era. The fact that Moab is absent from Thutmoses's list of conquered cities and peoples seems to indicate that both Jericho and Israel lay on the periphery of Thutmoses's vision. Although Egypt deported certain rebellious Hebrew towns, Moab still claimed suzerainty over Israel either independently or as Egypt's henchman.

After serving Moab for 18 years, Israel enjoyed a subsequent 80–100 year revival as Ehud led the nation to topple Moab's authority. At this time, Egypt only displayed a half-hearted interest in Canaan. Amenhotep III spent much of his time trying to find a cure for his life-threatening disease, while the interest of his son Akhenaten lay more in serving the god Aten than in tending to Egypt's Canaanite interests.[248] This era, commonly known as the Amarna Period, marked one of Israel's strongest attempts to possess Canaan's interior (see below), due to the Canaanites' cultic immorality that allowed the perfect opportunity for Israel's advance.

G. Amarna Period (1391–1334): An Era of Instability

1. None of These Diseases

After Thutmoses III died, Israel was again ready to return to YHWH's covenant. Ehud as-sassinated Moab's king in a revolt that swept across Canaan.[249] While alliances with Canaan still plagued Israel's policy, Israel had grown strong and populous enough to advance her own cause. While YHWH did not provide the divine intervention that he had during the initial two Conquest phases, neither Canaan nor Israel could escape the natural laws that govern any society.

In chap. 6, we saw how YHWH's Law accords with natural law. Following his Law natu-rally brings blessing, while departure from it causes sickness, disease, and poverty. When nations depart from the Law, disease and political unrest run rampant. Excavations dating to the twelfth and thirteenth centuries BCE "reveal a stunning story of upheaval, war, and widespread social breakdown."[250] Social breakdown is exactly the scene we should expect to find if Scripture's account of the ongoing Conquest Campaign is correct. Canaan's departure from the social order afforded by YHWH's natural law provoked his judgment and called for the people's expulsion (Lev 18:24–25, 27–28; Gen 15:16–21).

The Amarna Letters describe the diseases to which some of Canaan's cities had suc-cumbed. Pharaoh's appointee King Abdi-Aširta is "very sick" unto death (EA 95).[251] He recovered, only to be killed a short time later (EA 101). In another tablet, Rib-Addi, the king of Byblos writes to Pharaoh, stating that he is "old and his body is afflicted with a severe disease" (EA 137, 106).[252] In another letter, a chief writes to Rib-Addi, asking if the "plague in Sumura" is among the animals or the people. Biridija, the ruler of Megiddo, also fears that his city will succumb to plague (EA 244); and Milkili, ruler of another Canaanite province needs "myrrh for medicine" (EA 269).[253]

When nations grossly depart from YHWH's Law, the Creator seeks to drive them from their homeland and cleanse the land from their diseases (Lev 18:24–29). The Amorites sins had "come to the full" (Gen 15:16). YHWH proposed to fulfill his covenant of Promised Land with Abraham's descendants and use Israel to "spew out" Canaan's inhabitants for their callous violation of his Law (Lev 18:27–29), establishing in their stead a people circumcised to his natural Law. Although Egypt had deported a small portion of Israel's rebellious tribes under Thutmoses III and Amenhotep II, the Hebrews still possessed the ability to fulfill YHWH's covenant.

Egypt's stiff tribute no doubt contributed to disease, producing food shortages in lean years. This weakened, depopulated state of affairs gave Ehud the perfect advantage to throw off Egypt's yoke as he led an 80-year campaign to conquer Canaan. Egypt's power had been fractured in the north, and Canaan's city federations began to assert themselves once more, as Israel finally seized her opportunity.

2. Social Breakdown

> There is evidence elsewhere that the breakdown of familial and personal relationships almost always accompanies the destruction of political organizations and the consequent radical drop in population.[254]

The El-Amarna Tablets span 50 years of correspondence[255] between Egypt and Syria–Palestine, dating from Amenhotep III (variant Amenophis, *c.* 1391 BCE) to no later than the first year of Tutankhamun (*c.* 1334 BCE). Most correspondence dates to the reign of Akhetaten, Egypt's heretical pharaoh.[256] The early Amarna Letters portray very stable sociopolitical relations in Canaan. Disputes between cities are minor and infrequent. The major points discussed between Egypt and her Canaanite vassals are gift exchanges and marriage proposals.

As time passes into Akhenaten's reign, kings try to grab their neighbor's territories and accuse each other to Pharaoh, as Canaan's unrest mounts. Suwardata, king of a region near Hebron claims that Abdi-Hiba, king of Jerusalem, bribed one of his vassal cities to unite with Jerusalem against him (EA 280). In another letter, Biridija of Megiddo, accuses Labaja, another ruler, of harboring intentions to destroy Megiddo (EA 244), while Aiab, king of Bihisi, accuses the king of Hazor of capturing three of his cities (EA 256a).

To complicate matters, Canaan had been under the direction of a regional deputy who had recently been recalled to Egypt and whose post Pharaoh left unattended.[257] This was during an outbreak of widespread disease. But by far, the outcry of the later Amarna Tablets is the accusations against local governors who have defected to unite with the *Habiru/Sa.Gaz.* Each governor (or king) writes to Pharaoh, fearing that Egypt will lose control over his territory, and asks Pharaoh to send reinforcements to fight against the Habiru to "protect the land of the king."

H. *The Amarna Habiru*

Unlike the inscriptions that occasionally mention the Habiru during earlier periods in Mesopotamia, the Amarna Tablets repeatedly refer to specific Habiru activities. Throughout the Amarna Letters, Canaan's vassals decry the fact that city after city has colluded with the *'Abiru*-Israelites, becoming *Habiru*.

> The expression "to become Habiru," which is repeated in many letters from all areas of Canaan, implies desertion from the Pharaoh and his representatives, the various rulers of the city-states, and defection to the side of their opponents, who were regarded as outlaws.[258]

The Amarna Letters portray the craftiness of Israel's tribal federations by forging alliances to play one city against the other,[259] the ultimate intent being to provide enough intrigue to eliminate the "thorns" now plaguing the nation. After Thutmoses III's campaigns, Egypt considered Canaan part of its realm.[260] The Hebrews' rebellion against the vassal-lords that Egypt had established to govern and collect her taxes would indeed lead Egypt to view Israel as outlaws. From the Egyptian perspective, "the Hebrew" was the cause of lawless anarchy and chaos throughout Canaan.

Since Israel was assaulting Canaan's land, we should hardly expect the governors to refer to the Hebrews in a favorable light. The derogatory way in which Canaan's vassals refer to the Habiru attests renewed effort on Israel's part to occupy Canaan's strategic interior, granting credence to the threat that Israel's forces posed. The same can be seen today in the wake of 9/11, when Americans have developed derogatory expressions for Muslims, their culture, and their "terrorist proclivity." This was the same sort of response that we find in the correspondence of the Canaan vassal-states that Israel sought to dispel.

Israel's activity is best attested in Northern Syria. Shortly before the Amarna Period, an Amurru country emerged near modern-day Lebanon that had allied with the Habiru.[261] At the end of Joshua's life, this region had yet to be occupied (Josh 13:5). During the Amarna period, the Hebrews took advantage of Egypt's tranquility, forging alliances with the Amurru, who were led by the powerful sheik Abdi-ashirta. Donald Redford refers to the Amurru as an Habiru community that evolved into a Habiru state.

> The tactics of both Abdi-ashirta and Aziru (his son) were irregular for the times and confused their contemporaries, as they continue to confuse some modern investigators. . . . But Amurru was an 'Apiru (variant Habiru) community, but lately graduated from that type of stateless, lawless brigandage for which 'Apiru bands throughout the Levant were notorious. And it was the tactics of a brigand that Aziru used in all his diplomatic dealings with his equals. If a town could be taken and pillaged or a territory ransacked, Aziru did so without a second thought. If resistance was encountered, or was likely to be encountered, a more circuitous route was adopted: a conspiracy against the local mayor might be hatched, or a rebellion fomented among the peasantry . . . such peasant revolts arose endemically in the present instance where a quintessential 'Apiru state met and impinged upon settled, agricultural communities (see Illustration 11.12).[262]

Illustration 11.12. Letter of the ruler Aziru to Pharaoh, Tell el Amarna *c.* 1365.

The Amuru-Habiru alliance of northern tribes encompassed only one territory in which Israel actively campaigned. The cries and pleas of Canaan's governors sounded from Tyre,

Byblos, and Sidon on the Mediterranean coast, to Megiddo and Gezer in the central foot-hills, to Jerusalem—all faced the Habiru threat.

Joshua had allotted Tyre and Sidon to the tribe of Asher (Josh 19:28–29), but Israel had yet to drive out their citizens at the beginning of the Judges Era (Judg 1:31). Megiddo is listed as a Manasseh-Issachar town that had not been taken at the end of the initial Conquest (Judg 1:27–28). Gezer is listed as a city allotted to Ephraim (Judg 1:29) in which Canaanites still lived. Although Benjamin inherited Jerusalem, the tribe could not drive out the Jebusites but lived among them (Judg 1:21). Thus, Israel's campaigns during the Amarna Era sought to conquer and subjugate the territories into which the Hebrews had infiltrated but which they had not yet overthrown.

The campaigns of Thutmoses III and Amenhotep II, along with their drastic depopula-tion policies, provided the perfect opportunity for Israel. During the earlier Conquest under Joshua, kingdoms had banded together to withstand Israel's forces. Now, these kingdoms' alliances were fractured, thwarted by Egypt's presence in Canaan. As Israel returned to the covenant, YHWH caused disease and religious compulsion to distract Pharaoh's interests in Canaan, once again creating the perfect opportunity for Israel to seize the day.

The Amarna Letters are the best testament of Israel's ongoing Conquest. There are more than 80 Amarna Letters that ask for help against the Habiru, so we will just look at a few.[263] Remember that the term *Sa.Gaz* was the Akkadian word for the *Habiru*. The Habiru posed a threat to security, and their guerilla tactics instilled fear in the surrounding cities. Cities that are mentioned in the Books of Joshua and Judges will be in bold in the following Amarna Letters and the Scriptural reference will be inserted into the text. These campaigns occurred during Ehud's leadership (according to the Judges' chronology); however, these territories would have been assaulted during Joshua's administration with conflicts continuing well into the Amarna Period.

> Abimilki of Tyre to the King (3rd letter)—The king of **Zidon** (Josh 11:8; 19:28; Judg 1:31) takes daily my infantry, so let the king give attention to his servant and give orders to his deputy. . . . Since he has begun hostilities, he has not fulfilled the agreement. There is no infantry here. He who has desolated the land of the king is the king of *Zidon* (Josh 11:8; 19:28; Judg 1:31; 10:6). The king of **Hazura** (Hazor—Josh 11:1; 10–11, 13; 15:25; Judg 4:2) has left his city and has united with the Sa.Gaz-people. . . . The land of the king has fallen to the *Sa.Gaz*-people. Let the king ask his deputy, who knows Kinahna. (EA 148 II)[264]

> Zimriddi of Zidon to the King—May the king know that I have made preparations before the arrival of the archers of the king, my lord. . . . May the king, my lord, know that the war against me is very severe. All the cit[i]es that the king put in [m]y ch[ar]ge, have been joined to the 'Ap[ir]u. May the king put me in charge of a man that will lead the archers of the king to call to account the cities that have been joined to the 'Apiru, so you can restore them to my charge that I may be able to serve the king, my lord, as our anscestors (did) before. (EA 144)[265]

Majarzana of Ḥazi to the king—K[no]w the deed, which Amanḥatbi (a descendant of Dan?—Num 1:12), the man of Tušulti, has done against the c[i]ties of the king, my lord, a[f]ter the soldiers of the *Sa.Gaz*-people h[a]d commit[ted] an hostile act against me and taken the cities of the king, my lord, my god, my sun. The *Sa.Gaz*-people have conquered Maḥzi[b]ti, a city of the kin[g], my lord, and **they have plundered and have set it on fire**. And the *Sa.Gaz*-people have come to Ama[nḥatb]i. And the *Sa.Gaz*-people have conquered **Gil[uni]**, a city of the king, my lord, and they *have plundered it and have set it on fire, and scarcely a house has escaped in Giluni*. And to Amanḥatbi have come the *Sa.Gaz*-people. And the *Sa.Gaz*-people have conquered **[M]agd[a]li** (Migdal-el?—Josh 19:38), a city of the k[in]g, my lord, my god, m[y] sun, a[n]d they have plundered it and set fire to it, a[n]d sca[r]cely a h[ou]se has escaped in Mag[da]li. And to Ama[nh]atbi the S[a.G]az-people came. And Ušte, a [ci]ty of the king, my lord, the *Sa.G[az]*-people have conquered, and they ha[ve] plundered [i]t. . . . And, behold, the *Sa.Gaz*-people have oppressed Hazi, a [c]ity of the king, my lord, and we have delivered a stroke against the *Sa.Gaz* people and smitten them. So forty *Sa.Gaz*-people went to [Amanḥ]atbi, and he received those who had gone forth, a[nd]—Paḥmi and the *Sa.Gaz*-peopl[e Amanḥ]atbi. And we [h]ea[rd th]at there were *Sa.Ga[z]*-people[e wi]th Amanḥatbi, and then my brothers (and) my sons, your servants, mounted chariots and went to A[m]anḥatbi, and my b[r]oth[e]rs said to Amanḥatbi: "Give up the *Sa.Gaz*-people, enemies of the king, our lord. We want to ask them what the *Sa.Gaz*-people have [sa]id to you concerning the fact that they have c[on]quered the cities of the king, and set them on fi[r]e." And he accepted the gift of the *Sa.Gaz*-people; but he took them to---and fled to the *Sa.Gaz*-people. So, behold, Amanḥatbi is an enemy, so let the king, my lord, ask him (whether) he fled from him. Let the king, my lord, not hold back so that Amanḥatbi may not dishonor another man, and that he permit not to enter enemies into the faithful [l]and of the king, my lord. (EA 185;[266] compare with Josh 10:1–4 for a similar situation).

Sum---to the king—[Let] the king . . . [kn]ow [tha]t the regents, [who were] in the city . . . have come to an end, [and (that) the who]le land of the king, my [lor]d, has fallen away to the *Sa.Gaz*-people. And let the king, my lord, enquire of his deputy concerning that which [i]s d[on]e in the land of the k[ing. . . . a[n]d let the king, my lord, order his soldiers, his —- to m[e]. (EA 272)[267]

Biridija of *Megiddo* (Josh 12:21; 17:11; Judg 1:27) to the king (#2)—I have heard the words of the king, my lord and my sun, and, behold, I protect **Makida** (Josh 10:10, 16–17, 28–29; 12:16; 15:41) the city of the king, my lord, d[a]y and night (l[I-e]l. By day I guard [fr]om the fields. With chariots and s[oldiers] I protect the walls of the king, my lord. Any verily, power[ful I]s the enmity of the S[a].Gaz-people in the land. So let the king, my lord, care for his land. (EA 243)[268]

Later tablets from Megiddo tell us that another local ruler, Labaja, joined the *Sa.Gaz* (EA 246) and threatened to conquer Megiddo. They besieged the city, preventing those inside its walls from tending their crops on the outside. Thus, Labaja's siege increased the risk of plague in the city (EA 244).

> Abdi-Ḫiba of *Jerusalem* (Josh 10:1–5; 12:10; 15:8, 63; 18:28; Judg 1:7–8, 21)—Let the king care for his land. The land of the king will be lost. All of it will be taken from me; there is hostility to me. . . . Now the Ḫabiru are taking the cities of the king. No regent is (left) to the king, my lord; all are lost. Behold, Turbazu has been kill[ed] in the gate of Zilû (Ziddim?—Josh 19:35), yet the king holds himself back. Behold, Zimrida of Lakisi—servants, who have joined with the [Ḫ]a[b]i[r]u, have smitten him. . . . [Fo]r if there are no archers this year, all the lands of the king, my lord, will be lost (*abadat*). (EA 288)[269]

> Abdi-Ḫiba—The land of the king has fallen away to the Ḫabiru; and now in addition to that a city of the land of Jerusalem, whose name is Bit-Ninib a city of the king, has gone forth where the people of Kilti are. Let the king listen to Abdi-Ḫiba, your servant, and send archers that they may again restore the land of the king to the king. But if there are no archers the land of the king will desert to the Ḫabiru. This (will be) the fate of the la[nd]. (EA 290)[270]

Based on Scripture's chronology, Israel finally gained control of the central highlands—the area attributed to the Habiru in the Amarna Tablets.[271] Though many scholars reject equating the Habiru with Israel, it cannot be denied that the Habiru claimed the same territories as Israel in Canaan at the same time when Scripture attests that Ehud led a revival of the Conquest Campaigns (*c.* 1390–1313 BCE).[272]

I. *The Habiru Israelites*

The summary in the Book of Judges indicates that Judah maintained control of the highlands but failed to secure the coastal lands.

> And Judah went with Simeon his brother, and they slew the Canaanites that inhabited Zephath, and utterly destroyed it. And the name of the city was called Hormah. Also Judah took Gaza with the border, and Askelon with its border, and Ekron with it border. And YHWH was with Judah; *and he (a) drove out the inhabitants of the mountain; but could not drive out the inhabitants of the valley,* because they had chariots of iron. And they gave Hebron to Caleb, as Moses said: and he expelled there the three sons of Anak. And *the children of Benjamin did not drive out the Jebusites that inhabited Jerusalem; but (b) the Jebusites dwell with the children of Benjamin in Jerusalem unto this day.* (Judg 1:17–21)

One conspicuous parallel between the Amarna Tablets and Scripture is the allegations of Egypt's regents in Canaan. Judah drove out the inhabitants of the (a) mountains but not those of the valley and coastal regions during the initial Conquest. Benjamin also did not drive out the (b) inhabitants of Jerusalem but resided among them. This history is corroborated by the Amarna correspondence, which alleges that Abdi-Ḫiba, who ruled Jerusalem's extensive territory and the Judean highlands,[273] became allied with the Habiru, thus furnishing a parallel account with Scripture from the Canaanite perspective.

Canaan's governors allege that other regents had defected to the *Sa.Gaz/Habiru*. It may be remembered that Israel's proclivity to treaty and ally with native Canaanites was the factor preventing YHWH's divine intervention in securing Israel's possession of Canaan's vast territories. It appears that Israel continued to rely on these tactics well into the Amarna Period.

Hazor was one particular Egyptian vassal in the northern highlands with which Israel allied in order to secure her interests. In the early correspondence, Abdi-Tishri, the king of Hazor, communicated his fidelity to Pharaoh. He indicates that he is protecting Egyptian interests in the region, and specifically refers to Hazor as being "your [i.e., Pharaoh's] city" (EA 228).[274] Later, Abdi-Tishri apparently aligned himself with Israel because the king of Tyre accused him of defecting to the Habiru (EA 148).

In an interesting parallel, notice how closely a scholar's view of the Habiru (*'Apiru*) mirrors Scripture's Conquest accounts.

> The success enjoyed by the 'Apiru enclaves in the north Lebanon in carving out a kingdom for themselves is not paralleled elsewhere by the bands of 'Apiru operating in Amki, Bashan, and the *Palestinian highlands* at the close of the period covered by the Amarna Letters. . . . Ever since the great deportations of Thutmose III and Amenophis II, the northern empire and Palestine especially had suffered a weakening brought on by underpopulation. Not only did *the 'Apiru bandry now take advantage of the vacuum in the highlands*, but nomads from Transjordan also began to move north into Galilee and Syria and west across the Negev to Gaza, Ashkelon, and the highway linking Egypt with Palestine.[275]

Scholars such as Donald Redford readily admit that the Habiru established enclaves in the highlands.[276] It is quite conspicuous that even archaeologists who are critical of Israel's history attribute settlements in the Palestinian highlands to the Israelites.[277] Notice how closely archaeologist Timothy Harrison's observations of sites that have been deemed "Israelite" parallel the very areas attributed to the Habiru: "Surveys in the central hill country of Canaan reveal an explosion of small sedentary settlements—between 250–300 of them. . . . Descriptions in the Book of Judges (see Judg 1:19) indicate that this was precisely the territory settled by the early Israelites."[278] The archaeology of Canaan also evidences "population disruption" during the Amarna Period. What this means is that people moved out of the highlands and into the valleys and coastal plains, thus "leaving the highlands sparsely occupied."[279]

The Habiru connection with Shechem is especially telling. Scripture tells us that Shechem was one of the first city's that Israel had secured (Joshua 24). Over 100 years later, during the Amarna Period, Shechem was a secure territory in which the Habiru could "freely operate."[280] The city's sphere of influence stretched from Megiddo to the Jordan and south to Gezer, probably indicating that Israel had settled in Gezer and migrated toward the coasts during Ehud's administration (Judg 1:29). One Egyptian scribe during the Amarna Period complained that Ashkelon, Gezer, and Lachish had aided the Habiru (EA 287:14–16), perhaps under tribute obligation (Judg 1:28).[281] Thus, Scripture shows that Israel controlled the exact same city as the Habiru at the exact same time that the Habiru were active in the region. This establishes that the Israelites were the Habiru who controlled Shechem.

The Habiru were active in the highlands at the same time that Scripture's chronology places Israel's resurgence under Ehud. The Habiru name was linguistically similar to Hebrew (see p. 538). The Habiru targeted the very cities that Joshua had previously allotted to the 12 tribes of Israel. These assaults, especially in the northern hill country, continued into the reign of Seti I and Ramesses II as the pharaohs' campaigns focused on Habiru activity in Beth-shan and Mt. Yarmuta.[282] And, the Habiru's method of treaty and assault continues to mirror that of the early Judges Era, for which YHWH's messenger had condemned Israel at Bochim. Egypt's vassal cities viewed the Habiru as anarchists, intent on reversing Egypt's established order. This view is in line with the threat that Israel posed to Canaan's citizens as Israel sought to drive out and dispel the land's residents. Additionally, we find Israel's influence on treaties, especially in the northern regions, as her tribes sought to align with and garner support from the Hittites.[283] Thus, as Nicolas Grimal concludes, The 'Apiru "are synonymous with the Hebrews mentioned in the Amarna correspondence."[284] (See Appendix C, "The Hapiru Hebrews," for further discussion.)

J. Five Shall Chase a Hundred

Another question often raised against the biblical Conquest account is how so few Israelites could capture strong fortifications with such small forces. If Scripture's accounts are true, however, Israel's ability to topple large populations was the fulfillment of YHWH's promise:

> Five of you shall chase an hundred, and an hundred of you shall put ten thousand to flight: and your enemies shall fall before you by the sword. (Lev 26:8)

If Scripture is historically accurate, small contingencies were be able to devastate numerous Canaanite cities *during Israel's righteous epochs*. Notice, fascinatingly, that Redford's description of the Habirus' tiny but mighty forces parallels Scripture's promise.

> The 'Apiru and nomadic dissidents always had the upper hand: to the Canaanite headmen they were "mighty enemies" (EA 318:9), and *as few as forty were sufficient to capture and destroy 'cities'.* (EA 185:47; 186:50)[285]

Redford is referring to the Amarna account of 40 Habiru who had captured five cities, committed them to flame, and "hardly one family escaped" (EA 185:24–25). The Amarna Tablets demonstrate that a fighting force of 400 men was a sizable army during this chaotic period (EA 76).[286] Thus, it appears that Israel fits the description of the 'Apiru during the Amarna Period. Ehud's campaigns were so effective that, by the time of the great Ramesses II, Egypt had lost the greater part of her Asiatic Empire.[287]

K. After Amarna: 1334–1294

The next time that documents indicate Egyptian activity in North Syria was during Tutankhamun's short 9-year reign with Horemheb as a general and tax-collector. This small expedition tackled Hittite alliances with Egypt's former vassals.[288] Egypt did not recover this territory, which meant that Egypt's frontier receded back to the Lebanon region.[289] This was a far cry from Thutmoses's horizon, which had extended all the way to Carchemish on the Euphrates.

Tutankhamun's Restoration Stele tells us that the entire land was "topsy-turvy" *before* he ascended the throne. If the army was sent to Northern Syria "to extend the frontiers of Egypt, no success of theirs came at all."[290] One of Horemheb's inscriptions (as Tutankhamun's general) describes Israel's ongoing Conquest Campaign during the Amarna Period when he refers to the Asiatics during Akhenaten's reign.

> They mustered [every] foreign country [into a confederacy] unknown since Re. Their battle cry in their hearts was one."[291]

Another damaged relief tells of a group of Asiatics that came to Egypt seeking asylum from Canaan's chaos. The residents were being displaced, towns are laid waste and burned with fire, and crops were pillaged as the residents fled to the mountains for safety. Referring to the Asiatics, Horemheb's account shows that people had been expelled from their homes while other peoples claimed them (Deut 6:11). Towns were sieged and burned to the ground, leading to massive starvation among the general Canaanite populace.

> others have been placed in their abodes they have been destroyed, and their towns laid waste, and fire has been thrown . . . [they have come to entreat] the Great in Strength to send his mighty sword before. Their countries are starving, they live like goats of the mountain. [292]

Horemheb's description of Canaan at the end of the 18th Dynasty would be an accurate description of (Israel's) the Habiru campaigns that sought to drive out Canaan's natives and fulfill the Promised-Land Covenant under Ehud's administration.

Horemheb had served as Tutankhamun's general. When Tutankhamun died without an heir, the 18th Dynasty came to an end. Tutankhamun was succeeded by his father's aged vizier who reigned only 4 short years, and Canaan apparently held no interest for him. After his death, the military took control of Egypt as Horemheb took charge.[293]

Akhenaten's policies of restricting activity to Amarna had severely depressed Egypt's economy.[294] Horemheb planned to reverse Egypt's waning fortunes and restore its former glory. During his 28-year reign, Horemheb's attention focused solely on reestablishing law, order, and justice, which had degenerated during the Amarna Period.[295] Apparently, this effort consumed his attention, leaving him very little energy for Canaan's affairs, although his reforms,[296] especially with regard to taxation, probably benefited the entire realm, including Canaan.

The 19th Dynasty began when Horemheb, lacking an heir, appointed his vizier Ramesses I to succeed him. Ramesses came from a military caste[297] and was an old man when

Horemheb died. He reigned for 2 years, and there is no evidence of campaigns into Canaan until the reign of his son, Seti, who ruled Egypt for 12 years. This period comprised at least 50 years of peace in Canaan, as former federations continued to ignore Egypt's appointed administrators in hopes of regaining former glory.[298] At the beginning of the 19th Dynasty, Egypt lost Canaan; even Sinai resisted her might.[299] Including the Amarna Period, roughly 100 years passed during which Canaan enjoyed independence and autonomy, and Israel could claim her inheritance. Canaan's revival came to a halt when a military-minded Seti inherited the throne (or at least became co-regent) and began to punish the Habiru for falling away from YHWH's covenant once more.

By the beginning of the 19th Dynasty, Israel again rebelled against YHWH's covenant, and the Hebrews fell prey to Hazor's rekindled independence. It should not be surprising then, to find that Hazor's subjugation of Israel developed as vassal-lords who were implementing Egyptian policies. This cycle continued throughout the Judges Era until Egypt faced internal crises and the Philistines supplanted their authority in Canaan. When Israel returned to YHWH's covenant, she successfully threw off Egypt's yoke. But when she apostacized, Egypt had a system in place to discipline the nation, and Egypt employed "thorns," to vex Israel with Pharaoh's ever-increasing tribute.

XI. CYCLE OF DISOBEDIENCE: 1294-1274

A. *Israel: Captivity by Hazor/Egypt: Seti I and Ramesses II*

And the Children of Israel again did evil in the sight of YHWH, when Ehud was dead. And YHWH sold them into the hand of Jabin king of Canaan, that reigned in Hazor; the captain of whose host was Sisera, which dwelt in Harosheth of the Gentiles. (Judg 4:1–2)

Israel's 100-year expansion into Canaan came to an abrupt end soon after Ehud's death. Israel rebelled against YHWH's covenant, and YHWH gave the Hebrews over to Egypt's vassal-king in Hazor. For 20 years, Hazor ruled over the Hebrews. This era coincided with the reigns of Seti I and Ramesses II (*c.* 1292–1274).[300] Both pharaohs invaded the very territories that the Habiru had acquired during the Amarna Period. This oppression lasted until Deborah and Barak finally cast off Egypt's yoke around 1274 BCE. This suggests that Egyptian chronology as a whole should be pushed back another 15 years, with Ramesses being co-regent during Seti's reign, thus placing Ramesses II's accession to the throne in 1294 BCE. Seti's and Ramesses' campaigns were similar to Thutmoses's and Amenhotep's campaigns. The *uncanny similarity* between Seti and Ramesses' (as co-regent) campaigns into Transjordan with Scripture's account of Hazor's oppression over Israel is difficult to ignore. Both Egyptian and Israelite histories allow for similar time spans for Ramesses' activity in Canaan, and both attest a strong policy in Israel's hill country, suggesting that these campaigns occurred during a period of co-regency, although this suggestion has been dismissed by Kitchen.[301]

It appears that Israel's alliance with Hazor after the Amarna Period soured. With the rise of a new dynasty, Egypt renewed its interest in Canaan again.[302] Israel had turned from YHWH (Judg 4:1), and Hazor began to exact steep tribute from Israel, becoming Pharaoh's middleman once more.[303]

Seti retraced Thutmoses's trail in Canaan, swiftly moving up the Gaza Strip and the Palestinian coast.[304] Like Thutmoses, he secured Phoenician ports to supply his troops, carting off captives and war booty. Seti apparently recovered Kadesh from the Hittites. For the first time, Egypt directly challenged Hittite expansion that had been ignored by Akhenaten.[305] Seti listed the cities he conquered on the temple walls at Karnak, just as Thutmoses had before him. He recorded the number of captives he took from each city (see Table 11.4).

Table 11.4. Cities Seti I Assaulted and Number of Captives Taken

Beth-shan	51	Megiddo	assulted	Naharin	23	Tyre	57
Hazor	64	Raphia	65	Qatna	30	Kadesh	28
Yanoam	52	Lower Canaan	24	Upper Canaan	25	Beth-anath	59
Migdol	32						

Many familiar cities such as Megiddo and Hazor were once again assaulted by the Egyptians.[306] This indicates that Hazor's oppression of Israel was as a "thorny" vassal-lord. Seti concentrated on rebellious cities, campaigning in Beth-shan near the Jordan Valley—the very hill country in which Manasseh and Issachar lived according to Scripture (Josh 17:11; Judg 1:27–28). Prior to Ehud, Israel had not expelled the Canaanites but had placed its citizens under tribute (Judg 1:27). Thutmoses III had previously deported 110 people from this area, and Seti now extradited 51 captives. An inscription excavated at Beth-shan describes the rebellion of two local towns (Hamath and Pella) against Beth-shan fomented by the Habiru, an uprising that Ramesses apparently suppressed.[307] Similar to Thutmoses, Seti and Ramesses' focused their attention on many cities that proved to be "thorns in Israel's side." Although Seti did not depopulate the land to the extent that Thutmoses had, his control over the region weakened not only internal alliances but also the resources by which Canaan could fund her independence.

At least part of Seti's mission addressed Israel's aggression and lack of submission to Egyptian vassal-lords, a conclusion supported by another commemorative stele, in which Seti I and his son Ramesses state that the *Apiru of Mount Yarmuta* have attacked the "Asiatics of the Rehem."[308] Mt. Yarmuta is listed as "Jarmuth" in Josh 21:29, a refuge city belonging to Manasseh. This "news" refers to Israel's activity in this area during the previous, Fourth Conquest Campaign under Ehud (Judg 3:27–30).

Seti's initial campaign targeted the *shasu* in the hill country—the very territory again, Scripture says that Israel had settled and where the Amarna Tablets attest Habiru aggression. Egypt considered the *shasu* to be pastoral (shepherding) peoples.[309] Since many Israelites pursued this life-style, Egypt may have applied the "Habiru" and "shasu" terms terms to

Israel's unsettled and permanent populaces, respectively.[310] His reliefs reveal that rebellious *shasu* attacked the "Asiatic Horites,"[311] a people who was probably included among the Canaanite and Amorite groups (Gen 15:21) that YHWH commanded Israel to expel. Interestingly, Ramesses (II) identified these 'Apiru as "Asiatics."[312] As we have seen, the earlier Egyptians (Manetho) associated Israel with Asiatics in general at the time of the exodus, perhaps because they shared a similar language.[313] Thus, the *Egyptians viewed* Israel as Asiatics, whether as a subgroup of 'Apiru or as a separate people (nation).[314]

Seti's 2nd year focused on Kadesh and the Amurru country in the north, the very territory claimed by Dan and Asher (see Map 4.1 on pg. 135). In his 3rd year, he addressed Libyan aggression to the west of the Egyptian Delta.[315] If Canaan thought this a reprieve, she would have been disappointed the following year when Seti again confronted Hittite aggression in northern Canaan.[316] Egypt had secured allegiances in such cities as Megiddo and Beth-shan that were pivotal to her trade with Mesopotamia. The interior continued to be very loosely administered, with outposts stationed along the main highways that were being constantly attacked and raided by the locals.[317]

B. Highways Were Unoccupied and Villages Ceased

The prophetess Deborah, who lived during Seti's and Ramesses' days, recounted the hazards of the highways during this era. Villages and highways were deserted. If one traveled, it was by obscure routes, outside the strong arm of Pharaoh's administrators, outposts, and vassal-lords.

> In the days of Shamgar the son of Anath, in the days of Jael, *the highways were unoccupied, and the travelers walked through byways. The inhabitants of the villages ceased*, they ceased in Israel. (Judg 5:6–7)

Deborah's account indicates a general expulsion of people from their own lands as oppression, taxation, and violence threatened the Habirus' tribal inheritances. Not even the highways were safe from Pharaoh's roaming armies or his native henchmen.[318] It would not be surprising if many of the tribes that raided Pharaoh's outposts were Hebrews.

Indeed this is the same scenario that archaeologist Rivka Gonen discovered in the Late Bronze Age (1400–1180 BCE): highways were avoided and villages deserted.

> This state of affairs appears to be related to Canaan's location on the route of the Egyptian armies northward; at times it even served as the theater of battle. It may be assumed that for each military campaign that passed through the countryside, the local population was expected to supply auxiliary forces, labor, and provisions and to clear roadways. The supreme Egyptian interest was to keep the routes open and the Canaanite population submissive. The pressures on the Canaanite population may have been unendurable (witness the occasional uprisings against Egyptian rule), and many inhabitants likely left the towns to avoid the constant Egyptian demand for supplies and manpower. [319]

Gonen's observations regarding this era precisely reflect the description by Deborah in Judges 5:6–7, the highways and villages were deserted in order to avoid the demands that Pharaoh and his vassal-kings placed on local populations. This also mirrors the threat to Canaan's interior posed by Seti's and Ramesses' campaigns.

After Seti's fourth campaign, Egypt's aggression ended at Kadesh's southern border, and Canaan was left alone for the remainder of his reign. Thus, Seti's policy in Canaan did little to disrupt the revival enjoyed by Canaan's old city-states other than to reestablish the payment of tribute and to take a few captives for corvée labor.

C. Ramesses

Ramesses succeeded his father in 1294 and we do not know how many years he had been co-regent.[320] In his 5th year, he and his aged father, Seti, followed Thutmoses III's campaign strategy, securing Canaan's coast and directly confronting the Hittites.[321] Barely avoiding disaster from misinformation, Ramesses failed to achieve the success that Thutmoses III had enjoyed centuries earlier. Calamity avoided, the northern frontier remained in precarious limbo as Ramesses retreated to Avaris, which was now being rebuilt as Pi-Ramses. Canaan perceived that Egypt was not the powerhouse it had been under Thutmoses and revolted.[322] The Hittites likewise took advantage of this opportunity, infiltrating Canaan south of Beirut.[323] It is during this period that Kenneth Kitchen finds numerous treaties between the citizens of Syria (Habiru) and the Hittites that follow the same pattern as the Sinai compact.[324]

In his 7th year, Ramesses confronted revolts and assessed loyalties. This brought him directly in contact with the regions where Israel lived as he accosted the enemies that threatened Israel's future generations. Edom and Moab were Ramesses' first targets.[325] Although Ehud had thrown off Moab's yoke 100 years before, Ramesses now guaranteed that Moab would never again threaten YHWH's covenant people. Edom would not be allowed to harass YHWH's people either, because Ramesses' campaigns rendered them powerless *again* in the 18th year of his reign.[326]

Ramesses also attacked both Jerusalem and Jericho, where Israel had settled, and where the Amarna Letters tell us the Habiru had caused so much trouble.[327] While the Egyptian evidence does not tell us whether Ramesses killed or deported any Israelites, if Thutmoses's campaigns are any indication, we can safely assume that he did. An inscription on the temple at Karnak lists nine captives from Jacob-El (southern Canaan) but none from the northern tribes of Joseph-El,[328] probably near Hazor. It was during Ramesses' reign that 111 prisoners of war were taken captive from a region called Levi-El.[329] Given, Israel's resurgence a few years later, it is obvious that Ramesses took the weakest of the Hebrew population, since Israel achieved one of the greatest victories in the nation's history a few short years later under Deborah.

From Jericho, Ramesses crossed the Jordan before marching to Heshbon and Damascus via Ammon, east of the Jordan, to confront Hittite threats.[330] Ramesses' first 21 years, from 1294–1274 (or 1279–1258) BCE, checked Hittite aggression and annexation of Canaan. Thus the "bee" of Egypt served on YHWH's behalf to secure Israel's future while disciplining Israel's present transgression.

After playing a cat-and-mouse game for almost two decades, the Hittites and Egyptians were ready to call a truce in Ramesses' 21st year (1275 BCE).[331] The next 46 years of Ramesses' 67-year reign were peaceful for Canaan.[332] The Egyptian-Hittite alliance finally brokered permanent peace, relieving all threats on Canaan's northern border. For two centuries, Egypt had fought for a northern empire. Now Egypt became docile on Canaan's southern border as Ramesses turned his attention to Egyptian cultural endeavors, leaving Canaan unmolested for at least 45 years.[333] Neither Israel nor the native populations needed to worry about threats from north of the Euphrates until 500 years later, when YHWH delivered Canaan into Assyria's hand. YHWH had used Egypt's hornets to secure Israel's northern border while vanquishing Edom and Moab on Israel's eastern front. This set the stage for the most incredible surge of Israelite-Habiru Conquest, perhaps the greatest in Israel's history (see Table 11.5.).

XII. CYCLE OF OBEDIENCE: 1274-1234

A. *Israel: Deborah/Egypt: Ramesses II*

During the previous Amarna Period, as well as in Ramesses' later reign, Canaan's city-states had renewed old alliances and reasserted authority over weaker populations. The Amarna Letters refer to Hazor as Hasura.[334] Abdi-Tishri had been king of Hazor during Akhenaten's reign (*c.* 1360). Hazor's resurgence had been fueled by Pharaoh's endowments, which supported Hazor as a vassal that collected the Crown's tribute while enjoying a lion's share of the profits. The fact that Jabin could successfully acquire and maintain 900 chariots implies that Egypt did not question Hazor's dominion in this region (Judg 4:3) and may even have supplemented Hazor's supplies.

Hazor, along with other districts such as Kadesh in the north, Tunip in central Syria, and Ugarit on the Mediterranean coast constituted the status "Great Kingship," which meant suzerainty over surrounding territories.[335] Donald Redford observes that each of these states

> controlled a territory comprising farmland, towns, and occasionally subjugated cities, but was constantly in a state of expansion or contraction.[336]

This situation mirrors Scripture's description of the Canaanite states during the fifteenth through twelfth centuries. A "kingship" such as Moab expanded to dominate Israel during Thutmoses III's reign (Judg 3:12–15) but then contracted when Israel cast off the king's yoke by renewing YHWH's covenant (Judg 2:13–22; 3:16–30). The same scenario can be seen again with Hazor as the city expanded to subjugate the surrounding Habiru territory in order to satisfy Seti and Ramesses' tribute demands but was destroyed three decades later, when Deborah and Barak decimated its stronghold.

Papyrus Anastasi I is a literary controversy between two Egyptian scribes who argued over the geography of Syria–Palestine under Ramesses II.[337] The document demonstrates that the Egyptians and their Canaanite vassals only loosely controlled the hill country after Ehud's death, probably just enough to extract tribute. Egypt's primary goal was to guard access to strategic highways and trade routes in order to expand her economy.[338]

Table 11.5. The Book of Judges and Egyptian Chronology

Date	Scripture	Event	Years	Total	Accepted Egyptian and Mesopotamian Chronology w/ Thutmose II and Amenhotep II Co-regency
1548	Exod 12:41	Exodus			1548–1523: Ahmose I / Hittite: King Hattusilis I
	Num 14:33	Dessert Exile	40	40	1545/1530: Hyksos expelled/ Ahmose campaigns in Canaan
1508	Josh 23–24; 24:31	Israel Enters Canaan/First Conquest Campaign Begins			1523–1496: Amenohotep I
1503	Josh 14:6–14	Joshua gives Caleb his inheritance	5	45	c. 1530 (Hittite): Mursilis I
1501	Josh 13	1st Release Year—land distributed			
1494	Josh 21	2nd Relase Year—land distributed			1496–1483: Tuthmosis I (campaigns in Syria)
1487	Joshua 23	3rd Release Year (reconstructed)/Renewal of Covenant	16	61	
1480	Joshua 24; Judg 1	4th Release Year/Renewal of Covenant			1483–1469: Thutmoses II
1478	Josh 24:29	Joshua dies at 110 yrs. of age	9	70	
1478	Judges 1	Second Conquest Campaign begins under the elders			
	Josh 24:31; Judg 2:7–11	Elders that entered the land pass away	12	82	
1466	Judg 2:1–5	Conquest terminates with Bochim/6th Release Year	6	88	1469–1415: Thutmoses III
1463		1st 7 times begins (Lev 26:14-17)			1463–1441: Hatshepsut
1460	Judg 3:8	Captivity: Mesopotamian King Chushan-rishathaim	8	96	1450 (Babylon): Kadashman-harbe I
1458		1st Jubilee			
1452	Judg 3:11	Saved: Othniel/ Third Conquest Campaign Begins	40	136	1447–1428: Thutmoses III begins Syria-Palestine campaigns
1412	Judg 3:14	Captivity: Moab's King Eglon	18	154	1438–1412: Amenhotep II
1408		2nd Jubilee			1412–1402: Tuthmosis IV
1393		1st 7 times ends			

Date	Scripture	Event	Years	Total	Accepted Egyptian and Mesopotamian Chronology w/ Thutmoses II and Amenhotep II Co-regency
1394	3:30	Saved: Ehud / Fourth Conquest Campaign begins	80	234	1402–1365: Amenhoteop III
1358		3rd Jubilee			1369–1353: Amenhotep IV (Akhenaten)/1353–1351: Smenkhkare
1326		2nd 7 times ends			1351–1342: Tutankhamun/1342–1348: Ay
1314	3:31; 5:6	Saved: Shamgar/Philistines	20	254	1338–1310: Horemheb/1310–1308: Ramesses I
1308		4th Jubilee			1308–1295: Seti I
1294	4:3	Captivity: Hazor's king Jabin	20	274	1295–1228: Ramesses II, The Great
1274	5:31	Saved: Deborah/ Fifth Conquest Campaign begins	40	314	c. 1275: Ramesses makes a treaty with Mitanni
1258		5th Jubilee			
1256		3rd 7 times ends			
1234	6:1	Captivity: Midian and Amalekites (non-Egyptian)	7	321	
1227	8:28	Saved: Gideon	40	361	1228–1218: Merneptah/Sea people
1208		6th Jubilee/1223 or 1208 Merneptah Stele			1218–1215: Amenmesses/1215–1209: Seti II
1187	9:22	Coup: Abimelech	3	364	1209–1206: Setnakhte
1186		4th 7 times ends			1206–1204: Twosret/ 1204–1201: Setnakhte
1184	10:2	Saved: Tola (of Issachar)	23	387	1201–1170: Ramesses III /Sea people
1161	Judgs 10:3; 1 Sam 4:18	Saved: Jair (Gileadite)/ Eli -High Priest	22	409	1170–1166: Ramesses IV
1158		7th Jubilee			1166–1154: Ramesses V and VI—Unrest, "fear from enemy"
	10:6	Israel turns from Law again			1154–1147: Ramesses VII
1139	10:7–8	Captivity: Philistines and Ammonites	18	427	1154–1147: Ramesses VIII
1128	1 Samuel 4 (4:15)	Ark Captured under Eli/ Eli dies at 98 yrs. of age			1147–1129: Ramesses IX
1123	Judgs 10:10– 18; 10:13	Israel cries out to YHWH/ YHWH pledges not to deliver			1129–1119: Ramesses X: Egypt is weakend
		The Israelites have to deliver themselves			

Date	Scripture	Event	Years	Total	Accepted Egyptian and Mesopotamian Chronology w/ Thutmose II and Amenhotep II Co-regency
1121	Judg 12:7	Saved: Jephthah/Sixth Conquest Campaign	6	433	1124–1103 (Babylon): Nebuchadnezzar I
1116	Jer 7:12; Ps 78:60–64	Release Year/ 5th 7 Time ends/ YHWH removes name from Shiloh-Shechem/No tabernacle/ Ark of the Covenant has been captured			c. 1115–1077 (Assyria): Tiglathpileser I
1115	Judg 12:8–9	Saved: Ibzan of Bethlehem	7	440	1119–1091: Ramesses XI/civil war
1108	Judg 12:11; 1 Sam 7:2–13	Saved: Elon (Zebulonite)/8th Jubilee Samuel/ Israelites puts away their gods—Recovenanting/ Ark in Kirjathjearim for 20 yrs.	10	450	
1098	Judg 12:13–14	Saved: Abdon (Pirathonite)	8	458	
	13:1	Israel rebels			1091: Civil war intermittantly for next 120 years
1090	13:1	Captivity: Philistines/(Samuel)	40	498	
1058	21:24 21:24	9th Jubilee/ Curses of 7 times "reset" under the Monarchy/ Seventh Conquest Campaign (Samuel–Saul)			
	1 Sam 8:1	Israel asks for a king when Samuel is 80? yrs. old	(7)	505	
1051t	1 Sam 10:20–24	Saul/Release Year	(19)	524	c. 1074–1057 (Assyria): Asharid-apal-Ekur Ashur-bel-kala
1028?		Samuel dies at 102? yrs. of age			c. 1067–1046 (Babylon): Adad-apla-iddina
1023	1 Kgs 2:1	David/ Eighth and Final Conquest Campaign	40	564	
1016		David installed over United Israel			c. 1016 (Assyira): Ashur-nirairi IV/ Ashur-rabi II
1013?		"When David went forth against Mesopotamia and A'-ram-zo'-bah and Jo'-ab smote E'-dom" (Ps 60:1–title)			c. 1013: Assyria: Ashur-rabi II attacks the Ahlamu-Aramaeans
1008	2 Samuel 6–7	10th Jubilee/Covenant Renewal/Ark brought up/David's Covenant of light/ time of blessing			1003–987 (Babylon): Eulma Shakin-Shumi
980	1 Kgs 6:1	Solomon's 4th year	4	568	978–959 (Egypt): Siamun/946: Shoshenq I (1 Kgs 11:40)

Of particular interest are Hazor's *maryannu,* men who formed an elite chariot-driving class of citizenry.[339] The prophetess Deborah tells us that Hazor maintained over 900 chariots (Judg 3:4). Evidently these were manufactured locally because inscriptions speak of metalworkers throughout the region.[340] One hundred fifty years earlier, Thutmoses III stated that he had faced an army of 924 chariots in Canaan, thus Deborah's account is quite in line with the Egyptian record.[341] The Amarna Letters list bronze and teams of horses "for chariots" (EA 25, 37) as tribute sent to Egypt. Pharaoh may have redistributed these items throughout Canaan to help support its governors. It appears, however, that Hazor's army was greater than anything that Egypt would have provisioned, and thus the need for Egypt to subdue Hazor during Thutmoses' campaigns,[342] but for Hazor to dominate the central highlands on her own behalf.

During Ramesses' earlier years, Hazor served as the "thorn" to prick and oppress Israel due to Egypt's mounting and arbitrary tribute demands.[343] After a generation (approx. 30 years), Israel once again learned her lesson and came back to YHWH's covenant. Ramesses had signed the treaty with the Hittites in December 1275 (or 1259) BCE.[344] Barak immediately sought Deborah's counsel and began to campaign against Hazor the next spring (*c.* 1274). The Egyptian-Hittite truce led to 80 years of "unparalleled prosperity,"[345] roughly spanning the same period beginning with Deborah through the end of Gideon's leadership of the nation (1274–1234). This was Israel's Fifth and most significant Conquest Campaign. Israel gained the greatest extent of territory (before the Monarchy) and enjoyed the prosperity of a free homeland until she rebelled once more, and the Philistines had grown strong enough to subdue her.

B. *Thirteenth-Century Hazor*

The archaeology of Hazor is probably the best evidence for the purposed sixteenth-century Exodus and Conquest. Scripture specifically states that Israel sacked Hazor on two separate occasions, reducing the city to flames both times (Josh 11:11; Judg 4:24).[346] Joshua sacked Hazor in the sixteenth century, while Deborah and Barak devastated the city again 300 years later, in the thirteenth century (Judg 4:24).[347]

Archaeology attests that Hazor was partially decimated in the massive wave of destruction that swept across Canaan in the sixteenth century.[348] Archaeology also attests that Hazor regained strength after Joshua's assault and continued to be an impregnable fort well into the thirteenth century.[349] Had Joshua *thoroughly* razed Hazor, he would have destroyed the city's defensive rampart. However, the wall existed throughout the Middle Bronze Age until at least 1250 BCE.[350] This archaeological evidence reinforces the Scriptural account of a two-stage destruction (Joshua 11; Judges 4; see Map 11.3).

Map 11.3. Upper and Lower Hazor

Archaeologist William Dever observes that thirteenth-century Hazor

> was so thoroughly destroyed that its Bronze Age history of 1500 years came to an abrupt and permanent end. Now we also know that the smaller Late Bronze Age upper city, or acropolis, was also violently destroyed. Ben-Tor (Hazor's excavator) has discovered a monumental Canaanite royal palace complex of the 14th–13th century BCE, very similar to those well known from Syria, which was deliberately looted and then burned in a fire so intense that it left great blocks of dense basalt masonry blackened, cracked, and shattered.[351]

If Hazor had simply been plundered and its people carted off as spoils of war, this could be explained by any number of scenarios. However, this is not all that Hazor's destruction reveals! Her destroyers specifically targeted her idols, smashing and effacing these snares, just as YHWH had commanded in Num 33:51–54.[352] After examining some of these smashed and decapitated idols, Egyptologist James Hoffmeier reports,

> I have examined one of the now restored decapitated statutes . . . and a rectangular hole of a chisel that severed the head from the neck is evident. This demonstrates that the removal of the head from the neck was calculated. . . . Since 1991, Amnon Ben-Tor has renewed excavations at Hazor, and further examples of desecrated statutes have been uncovered. Of particular interest are those that are both de-capitated and have hands chopped off in destruction layers filled with ash. There is only one ancient source that alludes to this practice, and it is in the Bible.[353]

As a prophetess, Deborah cast Israel's victory in light of obedience and the fulfilling of YHWH's covenants (Judg 4:6–7). Both the Moabic Covenant and the Judgment of Numbers 33 had required Israel to smash Canaan's gods "that they be not a snare to you" (Deut 7:16).[354] Archaeology would indeed provide evidence that Barak and Deborah led Israel to obey these very commands.

Hazor's destruction occurred during the reign of Ramesses II. An object, which is often interpreted as an offering table was recovered during archaeological excavations. A "few preserved hieroglyphic signs are enough to tell us that the object was most probably dedicated by the high priest Rahotep, who served under Pharaoh Ramesses II, and should probably be dated "to as late as the third decade of Ramesses II's reign [1250 BCE]."[355] Bry-ant Wood accurately points out that Hazor's destruction did not occur at the beginning of Deborah's campaign.

> The battle described in Judges 4 took place at the Kishon River some 35 miles south-southwest of Hazor. The victory at the Kishon River resulted in Jabin being "subdued" (Judg 4:23). Following this, the "Israelites grew stronger and stronger against Jabin" until they "destroyed him" (Judg 4:24). The destruction of Jabin implies the destruction of his capital city Hazor.[356]

What this means for our discussion is that Hazor was not burned to the ground for probably another 10 years after Deborah and Barak's campaigns began, thus dating Hazor's destruction to c. 1265 at the earliest.

YHWH delivered such an impressive victory into Israel's hands that Hazor never again rose from the ashes. So what accounted for Deborah's impressive victory? According to the prophetess, Israel finally learned her lesson and did make alliances during this era. Deborah summarizes by saying:

> The kings came and fought, then fought the kings of Canaan in Taanach . . . they *took no gain of money*. (Jdgs 5:19)

Despite the fact that Israel did not own a spear or shield among 40,000 men (Judg 5:8), the nation's obedience to YHWH's covenant allowed the Creator to fight on Israel's behalf. Bochim was repealed during Deborah's days. The highlands were secure, and no other thorns remained to prick Israel. Now if she rebelled, her enemies would lie outside the area in which she lived and thrived. After Deborah and Barak's impressive victories, the nation was emboldened to finally claim the land that YHWH had promised her three centuries prior, when Joshua had allocated the tribal inheritances.

C. Fifth Conquest Campaign

Deborah and Barak's fidelity to YHWH's covenant led Israel to one of the greatest successes since the initial Conquest under Joshua and the elders back in the sixteenth century. Of this era, Finkelstein and Silberman observe:

> One by one the old Canaanite centers fell in sudden, dramatic conflagrations or went into gradual decline . . . On the coastal plain, Aphek was destroyed in a terrible fire; a cuneiform tablet dealing with a vital wheat transaction between Ugarit and Egypt was found in the think destruction debris. Farther south, the imposing Canaanite city of Lachish was torched and abandoned. And in the rich Jezreel valley, Megiddo was set aflame and its palace was buried under six feet of burnt brick debris.[357]

A few decades after Hazor's destruction, the Egyptian stronghold in Beth-shan was destroyed. Idols were again targeted but not taken as war booty. A thin gold plaque from the temple there was intentionally ripped from its base, wadded up and thrown down near a staircase.[358] Thus, Hazor is not the only city that exhibits this type of effacement and destruction that occurred during Deborah's campaigns.

Finkelstein points out that this transformation was not sudden in every place.[359] Scripture concurs (Exod 23:30). Some areas were destroyed years later during Gideon's administration or during the administration of other saviors. The last period of history to which the city of Lachish attests is revealed by a fitting for the main city gate that bears the name of Pharaoh Ramesses III (*c.* 1205).[360] Lachish's demise occurred sometime thereafter, probably under the leadership of Tola of Issachar (c 1172). Beth-shan, where the Hebrews (Habiru) had been active during Seti's and Ramesses' earlier campaigns finally fell to Israel around 1150,[361] probably under Samuel's leadership (1 Sam 7:13) with Jair the Gileadite commanding the troops. Megiddo's last testament to Canaanite civilization is a statue's metal base that bears the name of Ramesses VI (*c.* 1143),[362] which was destroyed under Jair's and Samuel's leadership (Judg 10:3), shortly before the nation turned from the Law again and faced another round of oppression from the Philistines. Thus, both Scripture and archaeology evidence continued Conquest cycles until Israel again completely rebelled against YHWH's covenants and this time were given into the hands of the Philistines and Ammonites (Judg 10:7–8) since Egypt was no longer capable of pacifying Canaan.

Under Deborah's leadership, Israel did not serve Egypt or her vassal henchmen for the first

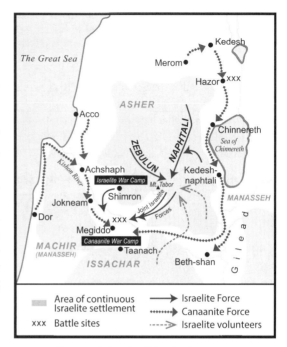

Map 11.4. Deborah and Barak's Campaigns.

time in 200 years (since Thutmoses III). Israel had learned her lesson as she drove out and dispelled Canaan's native citizens (see Map 11.4). It was at this point that the archaeological data indicate Israel was righteous in adhering to YHWH's covenantal Law. Even William Dever, who is usually critical of Israel's "history" in Canaan observes,

> All authorities today agree that the major break in the archaeological sequence in Palestine that would have to be correlated with a shift from "Canaanite to Israelite" culture occurred at the end of the Bronze Age *c.* 1250–1150 BCE.[363]

Except for the short period of Midian's subjugation of Israel, during which time Merneptah directly attacked Israel (see below), the Hebrews did not face any threats for the next 135 years (from Deborah to Jair). It is not surprising then that archaeology attests to Israel's strength (through obedience to YHWH's covenantal Law) during this same period.

We saw that Joshua's campaigns had obliterated the customs associated with equine burials (pp. 523–25). Now, under Deborah, Gideon, and subsequent leaders, Israel finally began to prevail to observe YHWH's Law as she obliterated Canaan's pagan culture. Archaeology demonstrates that by the twelfth century (Iron Age I)—the very time when Deborah had prevailed against King Jabin—the customs of the people living in the highlands no longer evidence pagan roots. This is especially true of the death and bereavement rituals. As Israel grew strong in the Law, she no longer participated in these foolish cults. Of this era, Israel Finkelstein observes,

> We know almost nothing about burial customs, apparently because graves were simple and the dead were interred without offerings. Likewise, there is almost no indication for cult. No shrines were found in the villages, so their specific religious beliefs are unknown.[364]

The absence of cultic shrines and death rituals would indeed witness to a righteous era in Israel's history. Yet, evidence of this righteous epoch does not end here. While archaeology demonstrates that other nations such as the Philistines, Ammonites, and Moabites ate pork in this era, Israel finally obeyed the cleanliness laws regarding animals, from about the twelfth century through the Monarchic Era.[365]

> Bones recovered from the excavations of the small early Israelite villages in the highlands differ from settlements in other parts of the country in one significant respect: there are no pigs. Bone assemblages from earlier highlands settlements did contain the remains of pigs and the same is true for later (post–Iron Age) settlements there. But throughout the Iron Age—the era of the Israelite monarchies—pigs were not cooked and eaten, or even raised in the highlands.[366]

Israel's obedience to YHWH's covenantal Law strengthened (Deut 4:6–8) her society to realize the greatest expansion of her borders since the Israelites entered Canaan 300 years earlier.

Following Deborah's and Gideon's campaigns, there was a wave of new settlements along the Mediterranean coast.[367] Israel began to spread out of the highlands[368] into the coastal cities originally parceled out by Joshua. At the initial Conquest, Joshua had allotted this territory to Judah (Josh 15:11–12), but it is clear that Israel did not claim it at this time (Josh 13:1–4). It is during Israel's Fifth Conquest Campaign that "Ekron all the way to Gath and their coasts" were built up by Israelite-Habiru occupation (1 Sam 7:14), which the Philistines would later subdue.[369] The colophon in Josh 16:9–10 mentions that Israel had settled in and around *Gezer* but paid tribute to the Canaanites "unto this day"—perhaps a notation made under Deborah's authority (see below).

It is interesting that after the initial Conquest there are very few references to the Philistines (the exception is Shamgar—Judg 3:31) until well after Gideon's administration. Even the coastal regions where the Philistines were active during Jair's and Eli's days lack Scripture references to the Philistines. These coastal towns are noted with the generic "Canaanite" peoples. This would support the theory that new waves of Sea Peoples (Philistines) had not yet migrated into Canaan (see also below). This point was not lost on Bimson. He observed that the lack of Scripture references to Philistines through the time of Deborah "implies that the greater part of the period of the judges should be placed before the time of the Philistine expansion."[370]

Archaeology also attests another biblical account of the Judges Era: there were no kings. Throughout Mesopotamia, Syria, and Canaan, small kingdoms were ruled by a monarch who lived in a royal palace.[371] Royal palaces are surprisingly few and far between in Canaan during the Judges Era (Late Bronze Age *c.* 1500–1180 BCE).[372] Scholars such as Rivka Gonen are usually inclined to interpret the lack of monumental edifices as a sign of the poverty of the local population,[373] which is hardly the case. Since judges led Israel until the Monarchy, the tribes had no need for these massive or centralized governmental structures. In fact, while many Middle Bronze Age (1800–1500) palaces are attested in Canaan, not one seems to have survived into the Late Bronze Age (c. 1200 BCE) except Hazor.[374] The only times when we should expect to find palaces in Israel's settlements are when leaders such as Gideon's son (Judges 9) exceeded the normal authority granted to a judge.

Another source for evidence of Israel's culture during Deborah's leadership is Canaan's pottery. Pottery of this era does not evidence a new culture or style as much as it attests poverty, consisting of a poorer quality of materials than during previous eras.[375] Some scholars see this as evidence of a new people in Canaan (i.e., 13th century, recently immigrated Hebrews).[376] Other scholars simply see this shift in pottery as reflecting changes in style, fashion, or economics during this era.[377] In fact it is the latter scenario that Scripture affirms. Poverty pervaded due to the steep tribute that Ramesses and Hazor had exacted from the region.[378] Once Israel's tribes fought for independence, they were focused on war, *not* the finer arts of earthenware. Hence, raw materials were probably hastily quarried, with emphasis being placed on the safety and security of quarrying and quality of material being a lesser concern. The same is true of the apparently rapid production,[379] because most of the society's energies were concentrated on supporting the war effort. This conclusion is quite in line with a Canaanite pottery style, which continued through the later Conquest cycles.[380]

The pottery of the coastal territories also evidences greater trade with the Mediterranean.[381] As Israel grew to be the prevailing population throughout Canaan, the society grew more homogeneous and stable, and more wealth-building venues could be pursued. This is evidenced by the increased trade that Israel and the Canaanites enjoyed with Cyprus and the Mediterranean in general during this era.[382]

In his Law, YHWH had instructed Israel to make no offerings for the dead (Deut 26:14). From the point that Israel began to keep the Law during Deborah's administration, the nation obeyed this instruction. Archaeology attests that from about 1200 BCE onward the dead "were buried in simple inhumations located outside settlements, in open fields with no grave goods."[383] Thus, archaeology attests the importance of the Fifth Conquest Campaign during Deborah's administration.

After the death of Joshua and the elders (Josh 24:1; Judg 2:7), Israel had struggled to walk in the way of YHWH (Judg 1:28, 30, 33, 35). Since she did not dispel Canaan's citizens, their gods became a snare to them because Israel had simply borrowed many of the cultural practices in the same way that many Hispanics or Europeans assimilate to American culture today. This epoch of disobedience is attested by Egypt's constant hand on Israel whenever her rebellion reached such a degenerate state that YHWH could no longer withhold the penalties of his covenant (Judg 2:15). Yet after almost 300 years, Deborah and Barak led the Hebrews to one of the nation's greatest expansions as Israel (at least, six tribes—Judg 5:14–18) expelled pagan nations from the territories in which she lived. The corresponding victories that Israel achieved only emboldened the Children of Israel in their resolve to keep the covenant. This righteous epoch (omitting the short lapse prior to Gideon) lasted until the nation became comfortable with peace and once again departed from the covenant, being snared by the gods of the heathen nations that still surrounded them. At the end of this righteous, 135-year era, when Israel turned from the covenant once more, YHWH delivered Israel into the hands of a new enemy: the Philistines.

D. Deborah and the Scribes

The Song of Deborah (Judges 5) is a poetic summary of Israel's victory over the Canaanites, expressly Hazor. Deborah lists the six tribes that aided Israel in this Conquest (Jdgs 5:14–15, 18): Ephraim, Benjamin, Issachar, Zebulun, Naphtali, and Manasseh (Machir and Gilead— Gen 50:23; Num 26:29). Deborah recognized not only the tribes that fought for the cause but also those that did not. Reuben appears to have been too afraid (Judg 5:15–16), while Dan and Asher remained in their northern territories along the Mediterranean coast (Judg 5:15–17), perhaps preparing to beseige Ugarit.

An interesting point about Deborah's account is that she not only recognizes the particular tribes that contributed to the war effort; she recognizes *what* they contributed. Ephraim fought against Amalek, while Zebulun and Naphtali engaged battle on the open field or on treacherous terrain, depending on interpretation (Judg 5:14–15, 18). The princes and leaders of Issachar all contributed to the war effort. Zebulun and Machir's contribution is the most interesting. Deborah tells us that Zebulun donated scribes to help advance the Conquest, and even more likely, to write and update the first "official" record of the nation's history. Deborah specifically states that Zebulun's scribes were with her during Israel's campaigns.

> Out of Ephraim was there a root of them against Amalek; after you, Benjamin, among your people; out of Machir came down (a) *governors*, and *out of Zebulun they that handle the (b) pen of the writer*. And the princes of Issachar (c) *were with Deborah*; even Issachar, and also Barak: he was sent on foot into the valley. (Judg 5:14–15)

The KJV states that Machir's (a) "governors" aided the effort. This is a poor translation. The Hebrew word for "governors" is *chaqaq*,[384] literally meaning 'to inscribe.' It is most often translated "lawgiver" (Gen 49:10; Deut 33:21; Ps 60:7; 108:8; Isa 33:22) or "to inscribe" (Job 19:23; Isa 49:16; Ezek 4:1; 23:14). This implies that scribes, perhaps Levitical, came from both Manasseh and (b) Zebulun during Deborah's judgeship.

That Israel employed scribes' during this era is not surprising since *contemporary* Egyptian records attest that Syrian scribes were also among Thutmoses's Canaanite captives.[385] Archaeology further indicates that a scribal school existed at Megiddo during this era.[386] Several decades later, Scripture lists several scribal clans descending from Caleb's family (the Kenite who warred with Joshua). His descendants are listed as housing "families" of scribes at Jabez (1 Chr 2:55), thus demonstrating a core literacy in Israel's tribal society.

The significance of scribes' attending Deborah and Barak's standing army is lost without an understanding of the relationship between scribes and the army during this era. Our study on chronology has revealed that Deborah's leadership converged with the reign of

Ramesses II. What we learn from documents dating to Ramesses' reign is that scribes were predominantly part of the military corps, just as Scripture depicts in Deborah's account.

One such Ramessid document, Papyrus Anastasi I, describes Egyptian qualifications for messengers who carried military orders or recorded battle casualties, directing:

> The king's messenger must be a 'choice scribe,' and able serviceman, leader of troops, head of the host, listed in every office, a good charioteer and archer.[387]

Scribes during this era served with the army and held military offices. Donald Redford observes, "Countryside military scribes were attached to each barracks, fort, and temple estate to keep local lists up to quota and to assist in the mustering. When the call-up came, every company was assigned its own scribe."[388] Scribes held the most important military ranks.[389] The "scribe of infantry" was almost equal in rank to a general.[390] Fascinatingly, scribes were usually military servicemen and less often civil officers.[391] This shows that Deborah's scribes were observing contemporary military protocol. Her scribes probably served as archers, charioteers, and messengers in addition to providing administrative and historical services, as they continued to do until Judah's demise (2 Kgs 25:19; Jer 52:25).

The implication that Israel's army had scribes informs more than the immediate war effort. It also explains a glaring anachronism. One of the main reasons that scholars support a thirteenth-century exodus (the very time when Deborah and Barak destroyed Hazor), is because Scripture states Israel built and escaped from Pi-Ramses (Exod 1:11; 12:37; Num 33:3, 5). As we have seen, neither the history nor the chronology that Scripture portrays can be collapsed into a short, 170-year period before the Monarchy (see pp. 347–65).

If Deborah's scribes updated and codified the scrolls bearing Israel's history, they would naturally have used contemporary language and customs. Scribes would have referred to locations by their modern names. They would not have referred to a city by using an ancient and archaic name that no one recognized.[392] Although Deborah's scribes often mentioned an archaic name, for cities in Canaan with which Israel was familiar, there was no reason for them to use Pi-Ramses' older name, since the Israelites during Deborah's days would never see Pi-Ramses or become familiar with its earlier history (or at least they hoped not! If an Habiru saw the new city, it was as a slave).

Israel had left the Hyksos city of Avaris at the end of the Second Intermediate Period (c. 1548). Some 300 years later, when Deborah called upon Israel's scribes to update and codify the nation's archives, Avaris had long since been abandoned and ceased to exist. Ramesses, however, built an impressive city over the former Hyksos capital. Thus, Israel's scribes accurately refer to the Delta area as the "land of Ramesses" (Gen 47:11) or the city as "Pi-Ramses," since Ramesses was indeed king at the time when the scribes updated the nation's archives.[393] Understanding that Israel's scribes added a gloss in order to add context to the territory that Israel had resided in 300 years earlier no doubt aided the readers' understanding of their nation's history during Deborah's era (see p. 312).

Scripture's chronology dates these scribal activities c. 1250 (see Table 11.5, pp. 569–71), right in line with Egyptologist James Hoffmeier's observations that these glosses would have occurred during the Egypt's New Kingdom period between c. 1270 and 1120 BCE: "Given the limited window when Pi-Ramses flourished, this would mean that the glossing occurred between *c.* 1270 and 1120 BC."[394] Scripture indeed places the Hebrews' scribal activities in the period Pi-Ramses flourished. Since Pi-Ramses had such a limited time of occupation, there would have been no reason for later authors, such as Asaph (Ps 78:43), to recognize a city that had long since been claimed by the desert.

We have seen that, under the prophetess's authority, the scribes updated the names of ancient cities in Canaan and inserted glosses stating that a particular landmark still existed at that point in time (see pp. 312, 316). Our reconstruction of Israel's Jubilees indicate that this codifying and updating of the Hebrew scrolls occurred *c.* 1258 in conjunction with the normal administrative functions associated with the Jubilee. It should not be surprising if future scholars discover that many literary features such as phrases or protocols about the written Pentateuch through the writing of the Book of Judges (*c.* 1548–1101) bear similarities to literary practices of Egypt during the time of Ramesses II.[395]

In fact, there are at least four such features. The first is the use of Pharaoh's name. In earlier eras, Egypt had recognized its pharaohs by their throne names.[396] During the Ramessid era (1300–1100), this protocol changed to simply recognizing a generic, no-name "pharaoh." Egyptologist James Hoffmeier observes that

> Throughout Genesis and Exodus, the well-known title "Pharaoh," derived from *pr*
> *3*, literally "great house," is used . . . but as an epithet for the monarch, it does not
> occur until the 18th Dynasty, sometime before the reign of Thutmoses III (1479–
> 1425 BCE). By the Ramesside period (1300–1100 BCE), "Pharaoh" is widely used
> and continued to be popular in the late period. From its inception until the 10th
> century, the term "Pharaoh" stood alone, without juxtaposed personal name. In
> subsequent periods, the name of the monarch was generally added on.[397]

Hoffmeier continues by noting that Scripture's use of the term "pharaoh" is in line with the Egyptian practice from the fifteenth through eleventh centuries.[398] Taken in context, this scribal practice obscured both the name of Joseph's pharaoh and the pharaoh of the exodus.[399] Fascinatingly, this custom once again attests the work of Deborah's scribes during the thirteenth century.

A second feature reveals influence of Egyptian literary style. This style is evidenced by the glowing editorial colophon summarizing Joshua's success in Canaan (Josh 21:43–45). Although it is true that YHWH had performed every word of his covenant and subdued the land before Israel (archaeology verifies, this massive wave of destruction in the sixteenth century), it is also clear that much of the land had yet to be occupied at the end of Joshua's life (Josh 13:1–6, 23–24). A similar statement is made in Josh 10:33, when the scribe writes that, after Joshua's campaign against Gezer, he "left none remaining." Yet we find later (probably as late as Deborah) that, Israel had settled in Gezer's suburbs next to the native residents (Judg 1:29), implying that Joshua had left quite a few Gezerites "remaining" in the land.

These literary styles are quite similar to Pharaoh Merneptah's (*c.* 1231) euphoric statement that he had "wiped out" Israel's seed or that he had made the Horites "widows." While such statements describe a real and literal destruction, the scribes' use of this exaggerated literary device to vastly over-state accomplishments is simply hyperbole that makes a particular battle or campaign more distinguished. Taken in context, the colophon in Joshua (probably appended by Deborah's scribes after subjugating Hazor) euphorically summarizes the progress achieved during Joshua's administration by using contemporary hyperbole to emphasize the point of success.

A third literary device was an "allegorical lament" used to depict a defeated foe. Deborah employed this device to depict the grief that Sisera's mother would feel when her son did not return and she discovered he had been slain in battle.

> The mother of Sisera looked out a window, and cried through the lattice, Why is his chariot so long in coming? Why tarry the wheels of his chariots? Her wise ladies answered her, yes, she returned answer to herself, Have they not sped? have they not divided the prey; to every man a damsel or two; to Sisera a prey of divers colors, a prey of divers colors of needlework . . . on both sides, meet for the necks of them that take the spoil? So let all your enemies perish, O YHWH: but let them that love him be as the sun when he goes forth in his might. (Judg 5:28–31)

Ramesses II was succeeded by his son Merneptah. His famous "Merneptah Stele," also known as the "Israelite Stela," uses a similar literary motif when describing Merneptah's victory over the Tjehenu (Libyans). He relates how he conquered their leader, Meriy. He burned the Libyans' tents and confiscated their provisions. The stele then uses the "allegorical lament" to paint a picture of the homecoming that the defeated and dishonored Meriy would face (see Illustration 11.13 on page 583).

> When he reached his country, he was in laments; every survivor in his land was loath to receive him. "The chief whom an evil fate has shorn of the feather!"[400] all those of his town were saying about him.[401]

Both Deborah's Song and the Merneptah Stele anticipate the mourning that will result from their foe's defeat. Both paint a picture of the grief and conflict that will arise from their enemy's death. This suggests that Israel's scribes had received formal training in Ramessid schools.

Another motif employed by both Deborah and Merneptah is a curse pronounced against their enemy. Deborah issued a curse against a particular city (?) that did not come to Israel's aid during the Fifth Conquest:

> Curse you Meroz, said the angel (messenger) of YHWH, curse you bitterly the inhabitants thereof; because they came not to the help of YHWH, to the help of YHWH against the mighty. (Judg 5:23)

Perhaps as few as 20 years later, Merneptah issued a similar curse:

The lord of the Black Land has cursed his name. Meriy is an abomination of the With-Walled City (i.e., Memphis).⁴⁰²

Merneptah curses his Libyan foe because he attacked Egypt. Although other curses are issued in both Egyptian literature and Scripture, the fact that both occur in a context of so many other similarities (hyperbole, allegorical lament, use of a nondescript "pharaoh," mention of Ramssess) indicates that Israel's scribes had an Egyptian education. We know that Megiddo and Beth-shan boasted scribal schools where Israel's writers could be educated.⁴⁰³ Israel's nobles could also be captured in battle, educated, and "Egyptianized" in the Crown's Kap in Egypt proper.⁴⁰⁴

There is one other element of Deborah's Song that links her to the reign of Ramesses II. When Egypt warred against Israel (the Habiru) and took captives, these slaves entered into an institution called "His Majesty's Captivity."⁴⁰⁵ These slaves were distributed throughout Egypt, often stocking the temple workhouses.⁴⁰⁶ When Israel had recovenanted on the Moab plains, YHWH had outlined the consequences (curses) for rebelling against his covenant. Thus, when YHWH's stated that he would bring Israel "to a nation which neither you nor your fathers have known; and *there shall you serve other gods, wood and stone*" (Deut 28:36), this curse can be taken literally! Pharaoh indeed consecrated Israel to serve the very falsehoods for which she had lusted. Deborah's Song had called for Barak to "lead his captivity captive." This veiled reference may indicate the threat that Barak faced as a warring Habiru who could be captured by Hazor and sold into His Majesty's captivity if he did not obey YHWH's command to lead Israel's forces.

XIII. CYCLE OF DISOBEDIENCE: 1234–1227, ISRAEL: OPPRESSION BY MIDIAN, AMALAK, AND EGYPT/ EGYPT: RAMSSESS II–MERNEPTAH

A. *Merneptah's Invasion: Israel's Perspective*

Canaan's traditional federations had been fractured and fragmented during Ramesses' reign. In earlier eras, these city-states had been bolstered by Egypt's administration.⁴⁰⁷ But now, no central power buttressed Canaan's puppet-men. After Ramesses' treaty with the Hittites, he turned to more peaceful endeavors; this allowed Israel to expand her borders in Canaan's interior. By the time of Ramesses' death, Israel had once again become complacent in regard to the consititional covenant and had rebelled once again.

During the latter half of Deborah and Barak's leadership, Israel began challenging the Canaanites' claim to the lowlands. **Gezer** had been a refuge city allotted to Ephraim (Josh 16:10) in the lower foothills. Up until this time, Ephraim had not yet driven out the natives but had settled among them (Josh 21:21; Judg 1:29). The summary in Judges 1 (probably written by Deborah's scribes) tells us that Judah and Simeon had seized Ashkelon's dependencies in the highlands but had not yet taken the capitol city itself (Judg 1:18–19). At some point during Deborah and Barak's leadership (Judg 3:31; 5:6), Shamgar (Samson) assaulted Ashkelon (Judg 14:16). Israel was pushing into the lowlands, placing pressure on both **Ashkelon and Gaza**. When Deborah died, however, Israel again forsook the covenant (Judg 5:31–6:4), and Egypt was once again ready to render YHWH's corrective judgment.

Both threats that Israel now faced came from territories that Ramesses II had formerly suppressed. The fact that two separate people now dominated Israel indicates that the Hebrews had grown large enough to populate more than one territory (i.e., the hill country). Israel's former campaigns under Deborah and Barak were effective in the sense that no one power would ever dominate Israel again. Israel had finally destroyed the old city-state federations that had plagued her peace since the initial Conquest.

This time when Israel rebelled, YHWH did not immediately send Egypt to punish her. Instead, he sent the nomadic Midianites and Amalekites from the eastern desert fringes. These assaults proved extremely harsh—so severe that Israel sought refuge in the "mountains, *caves,* and strongholds" (Judg 6:1–4). When Israel cried to YHWH for deliverance, he once again sent his Egyptian bee to chase the *shasu* Midianites from Israel's inheritance.

B. Merneptah's Invasion: Egypt's Perspective

When Merneptah ascended to Egypt's throne, he faced a new set of problems.[408] The Hittites were facing a horrible famine and invoked their treaty with Egypt by asking Pharaoh to send food supplies.[409] In Merneptah's 5th year, a coalition of Libyans and Sea People attempted to force their emigration into Egypt.[410] Merneptah's Stele at Thebes relates that Merneptah slew at least 6,200 "uncircumcised" refugees.[411] Nubia had offered support to the Libyans, so Merneptah then turned his campaign south to bring Nubia back into subjection. His famous stele appears to summarize the political situation during the previous four years and his response to it during the 5th year of his reign (see Illustration 11.13).[412]

Merneptah's famous "Israelite Stele" is the first Egyptian source that scholars agree is referring to Israel.[413] The cities that Merneptah assaulted appear in the same order as the cities in the Berlin Canaan Relief (from Thutmoses III): Ashkelon on the Mediterranean coast, Gezer in the central foothills, and Yanoam across the Jordan. These territories are followed by a reference to the people of Israel. As we have seen, Yanoam was the territory in which the Habiru had been active during Thutmoses's reign (see pp. 535, 564–66).

Illustration 11.13. The large Merneptah Stele is the first inscription scholars accept to mention a people called "Israel."

The parallels among what we know about the reign of Merneptah, his stele, and Judges 6 are astounding. First, both Judges 6 and history attest that a famine plagued most of the world.[414] This famine caused Merneptah to fulfill the Egypt's covenant with the Hittites and to supply them with grain. It also led the Midianites-Amalekites to raid Canaan's fertile coastal regions. This was probably the famine that led Elimelech and Naomi to seek refuge in Moab (Ruth 1:1).

Second, this epic famine caused the desert nomads to resort to violent attacks on settled territories. These terroist-like invasions caused Israel to seek refuge in caves.

> And the Children of Israel did evil in the sight of YHWH: and YHWH delivered them into the hand of Midian *seven years*. And the hand of Midian prevailed against Israel: and because of the Midianites the *Children of Israel made them dens which are in the mountains, and CAVES, and strong holds*. And so it was, when Israel had sown, that the *Midianites came up, and the Amalekites, and the children of the east*, even they came up against them; And they *encamped against them*, and destroyed the increase of the earth, till you come to *Gaza*, and left no sustenance for Israel, neither sheep, nor ox, nor ass. (Judg 6:1–4)

Merneptah's Stele presents a similar story. About these chaotic and unstable times, Merneptah wrote that it was

> advantageous to hide since one is safe in the cave.[415]

Both the Book of Judges and Merneptah attest that the hostile nomads caused the native populations to seek refuge in caves. No other Egyptian account before or after refers to a turbulent era wherein the population resorted to caves. This places Merneptah's account squarely in the same context as Judges 6.

The Midianites and Amalekites had an agenda to drive Israel off the land. Scripture tells us these lords pillaged Israel's crops (Judg 6:3–4), probably due to famine. The region of assault against Israel reached all the way down to Gaza (Judg 6:4), where the Midianites and Amalekites raided and terrorized Israel's cattle, sheep, and donkeys. The assault was so severe that Israel retreated to mountain strongholds and caves. Notice that, if the towns and countryside were not safe from the marauding Midianites-Amalekites, the normal highway routes would have been even less secure.

Third, an interesting parallel between Scripture and Merneptah's Stele is their the characterization of the Midianites and Amalekites as nomads, whom the Egyptians would have referred to as *shasu*.[416]

> For *they came up with their cattle and their tents*, and they came as grasshoppers for multitude; for both they and their camels were without number: and they entered into the land to destroy it. And Israel was greatly impoverished because of the Midianites; and the Children of Israel cried unto YHWH. (Judg 6:5–6)

The tribal Midian-Amalek alliance had infiltrated through the central region all the way south to Gaza. Gideon later confronted these nomads in the Jezreel Valley (Judg 6:33), which indicates that they had pillaged Gezer all the way to Ashkelon (see Map 11.5).

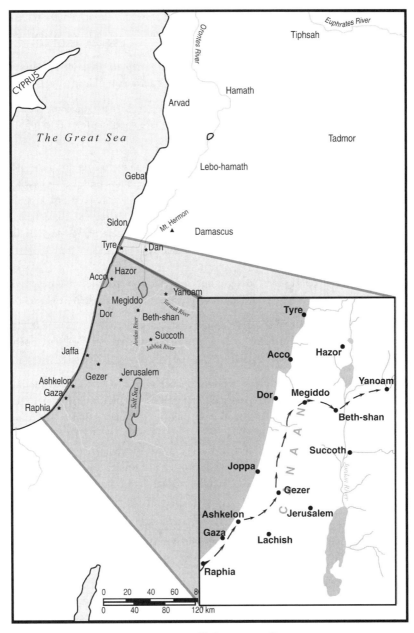

Map 11.5. Merneptah's Campaign in Canaan.

The *shasu's* assault on Yanoam, Ashkelon, and Gezer prompted Egypt to strike.[417] The bottom of Merneptah's Stele tells us that he targeted the marauding *shasu* nomads that were harassing the coastal regions. Merneptah indicates that he had vanquished the *shasu* Midianites and Amalekites, claiming that "all the restless peoples are now stilled."[418] Merneptah's deliverance did not come without a cost: while Pharaoh indeed relieved Canaan of the *shasu* threat, he also targeted Israel's rebellious tribes surrounding **Gezer, Gaza, Ashkelon,** and the coastal plain.

Fourth, Merneptah's Stele indicates that, *prior* to Merneptah's invasion of Canaan, the *shasu's* hostilities had led the Canaanites to seek shelter across the Nile in Egypt.

> Field and cattle are left as freely roaming herds (see Judg 6:4); no longer are herdsmen crossing the river's flood . . . No longer is there shouting for aid at night; "Help, help!" Has ceased from the mouths of strangers.[419]

Although Merneptah claims to have restored order so that shepherds no longer needed to take refuge in Egypt, the text is thus implying that shepherds *had* fled to Egypt prior to his campaigns in Canaan. Remember that during Horemheb's reign a similar situation existed when the Fourth Hebrew (Habiru) Conquest of the region had caused the *shasu* (nomads) to seek shelter in Egypt (see p. 563). The story of Elimelech and Naomi indicates that Israel was fleeing to caves or abroad as the Israelites sought shelter from both famine and invasion.

Fifth, Merneptah tells us that "foreign countries" had harassed the land, preventing his messengers from safely traveling on Canaan's highways. Merneptah claims to have

> defended the one who is distressed because of any foreign country. . . . One walks freely upon the road. Fortresses are left alone to themselves, and wells are open (accessible) to messengers.[420]

Remember that at the end of this inscription Merneptah stated that he had vanquished the *shasu.* Judges 6 tells us that the *shasu* had distressed Israel, indicating that not even the highways were safe. Merneptah claims to have relieved this oppression by restoring the former order to the coastal regions.[421]

The sixth parallel is found in Merneptah's claim that his campaigns caused people to return from the caves to resettle towns. While crops had formerly been pillaged, now the residents could eat their own produce, since Merneptah had restored the nobles to their native inheritances.

> Towns are resettled once again. The one who sows his crop will consume it. . . . (Merneptah) let nobles regain their possessions and let private persons frequent their towns.[422]

This account parallels the revival that Israel enjoyed under Gideon. The enemy was defeated, crops were sown, cattle freely roamed, roads were open, and the land was free of distress. It appears that once Israel returned to YHWH, he ended the famine in the land (e.g., Boaz had bountiful harvests—Ruth 2).

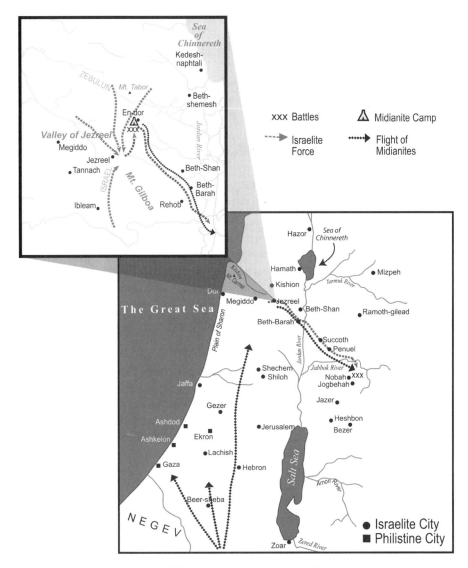

Map 11.6. Gideon's Campaign against the Midianites.

The seventh parallel between the Merneptah Stele and the Judges account is the activity in the Yanoam region. Once Gideon had slain 120,000 men of the Midianite-Amalekite federation (Judg 8:10), he pursued the enemy, crossing the Jordan near Beth-shan into a district Egypt that called Yanoam (see Map 11.6). Gideon pursued the Midianites all the way south to Succoth and Penuel.[423] Gideon asked these two cities to provision his troops since he was chasing a mutual enemy (Judg 8:4–9). This was a service Israel was accustomed to providing the Egyptians and local vassal-lords.[424] Yet, both Succoth and Penuel refused. Gideon pledged revenge on these cities for refusing to aid their own cause. After successfully warring against Midian, he returned to Succoth and Penuel to demonstrate that he had firmly an-nulled the cities' alliances with the Midianites (Judg 8:6, 15) and to punish their leaders for their lack of support. He tore down the *migdal* (a defensive temple-tower) at Penuel and slew its militia (Judg 8:17). At Succoth, he killed the elders of the city, perhaps even setting the city on fire (Judg 8:16). Merneptah's words in his inscription about Yanoam probably refer to both the threatening Midian *shasu* and Gideon's response to their marauding.

The eighth and probably most fascinating point linking Midian's oppression of Israel with Merneptah's campaigns comes not from the inscription itself, but from the temple walls at Karnak that depict the battles Merneptah fought and are recorded on the famous stele. The similarity of these battle scenes with Judges' history again provides another fascinating parallel.

C. Israel's Chariots

From an Egyptian perspective, there really was no transition in Canaan from Deborah's to Gideon's administrations. During the seven years when Israel faced oppression from the *shasu* Midianites-Amalakites, Canaan theoretically remained part of the Egyptian realm. Viewing this era as one continual 87-year era would be accurate. What this means for our present study is that Deborah's and Barak's policies spilled over and affected Gideon's campaigns.

Merneptah's reliefs at Karnak indicate that Deborah and Barak had adopted a new policy with regard to disarmament. Whereas Joshua had destroyed weapons of war, such as chariots, Deborah and Barak confiscated them.[425] King David followed a similar policy (2 Sam 8:4), also reserving for his men a portion of the chariots captured in battle. This may in part account for the success that the Israelites had across Canaan during Ramesses II's later years. How do we know that Deborah and Barak appropriated Hazor's chariots?

One custom that Egypt, Assyria, and Babylon followed was to "picture" significant conquests on the temple or palace walls. Battle "scenes" or victories were depicted and etched on the temple (or palace) wall in chronological order so that the first city mentioned in the inscription matched the first battle scene and the second scene described a victory over a second group people or battle. A stele, such as the Merneptah Stele, accompanied these scenes, providing a more complete record (see Illustration 11.14). Frank Yurco, who has intensively studied these scenes observes:

> These four battle scenes of Merneptah and their data correspond exactly to the retrospective text on Merneptah's "Israel Stela," where Ashkelon, Gezer, Yano'am, and Israel are all named specifically; and most significantly, the determinative used for the writing of the name of Israel in the stela suits exactly the *fourth battle scene*, depicting a people in open country without a fortified town.[426]

Intriguingly, in the coordinating fourth battle scene, Israel is depicted as battling Egypt from chariots. How could Israel have obtained chariots unless the nation had confiscated a por-tion of Hazor's 900 iron chariots? Israel had either used them during Deborah's campaigns

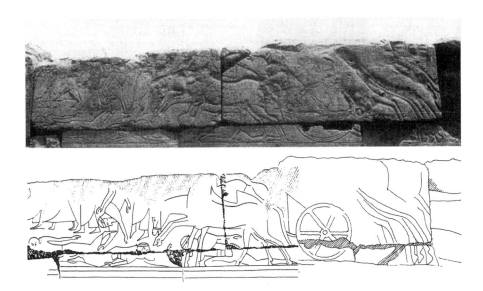

Illustration 11.14. The corresponding panel depicts the events described in the famous Merneptah Stele. Frank Yurco believed this scene to depict the people of "Israel" mentioned in the Stele.

or hidden them for later assaults (such as Gideon's campaign). No other war in Canaan is attested by Merneptah, and the remainder of his reign appears to have been peaceful.[427]

One point of contention regarding this battle scene is the Canaanite dress that Israel is depicted wearing.[428] As we saw above, the stipulations for the colored fringe along the border of Israel's garments indeed paralleled Canaanite fashion (see p. 549). The dress in which Israel is depicted is the same style as the garments of the warriors defending Ashkelon, Gezer, and Yanoam.[429] As we saw above, Israel (Habiru) had claimed the territory of Gezer and settled the coastal regions during Ehud's administration during the Amarna period (see pp. 550–64). Israel settled among the Canaanites and charged them tribute. All three cities depicted in Merneptah's reliefs are the same cities that were accused of aiding the Habiru during the Amarna Period. This implies these reliefs indeed depicted Merneptah's campaign against Israelite-dominated territories. Vanquishing Gezer was such a feat that Merneptah even took it as one of his epitaphs, referring to himself as the "Binder of Gezer."[430] This indicates that, in the vacuum left by Hazor's annihilation, Gezer had become the "lord" of the region during Deborah and Barak's campaigns.

The question that arises at this point is how Israel could have defended herself with chariots against Merneptah but failed against the *shasu*. The answer may lie in the fact that chariot battle usually took place in the open field. The *shasu* probably pitched their tents in areas that were inaccessible to chariots and employed guerilla tactics to lay claim to Israel's food sources.

The Merneptah Stele prompts one last observation regarding the Israelites. Within 100 years of the initial Conquest, Thutmoses III and his son had referred to Israel as the generic "*Shasu* of YHWH" (pp. 538–39). This term appears to have developed quickly into an ethnic distinction, and Israel began to be identified as an Asiatic group called the *Habiru*, perhaps based partly on their association with YHWH but more likely on having a kindred language. During the Amarna Period and early Ramassid times, the term *Habiru* (Hebrew) was the most common designation of Israel's tribes. Although Thutmoses did indeed refer to Israel and her connection with Ashkelon and the Canaanite low-lands on the Berlin Pedestal Relief, the name Israel does not appear again until Merneptah's reign. After Israel had campaignd another 40 years, the Hebrews became their own independent authority. Merneptah recognizes Israel as a people, citing the cities in which Israel lived (i.e., Ashkelon, Gezer, and Yanoam). As Israel's history passes from the Judges Era into the early days of the Monarchy, the term *Habiru* falls into complete disuse; the nation retains its tribal designation *Children of Israel* or just simply *Israel*.[431] Thus we see a progression from nomads to small states and tribal territories into finally a nation: a history that perfectly reflects the Scriptural account.

There are at least eight different parallels between the account of Midian's oppression in Judges 6–8 and the Merneptah Stele. History attests to famine in this era, which led the Midianites and Amalekites to raid the produce of Israel's more fertile lands and cattle. Both Merneptah's Stele and Scripture mention that crops and cattle had been plundered. This assault causes Israel to seek refuge in caves and on the hillsides or to flee to Egypt as the highways become dangerous again. Both the Merneptah Stele and the Book of Judges tell us that the Midianites were nomads (*shasu*). And both accounts attest to their pillaging during this era. Merneptah claims to have reversed these conditions, bringing peace to the land, and restoring tribal possessions. His campaigns targeted the very areas that Midian had assaulted, from Ashkelon, through Gezer, all the way up to Yanoam. It was probably in this district that Merneptah confronted Israel's chariot corps, which he claims to have brought into subjection. These eight parallels do not include the similar literary styles of employing the allegorical lament, "the curse against the foe" in Deborah's Song, the parallel usage in New-Kingdom protocol of referring to a generic "pharaoh" or Scripture's reference to Ramesses during an era Deborah's scribes codified the Hebrew history.

Scripture's account of this era accurately depicts what we know of Israel's interaction with Egypt. Israel was a subject people during the 20 years that Seti and Ramesses were active in Canaan. When Israel sought to follow YHWH's covenant, they enjoyed freedom as Ramesses pursued more-peaceful endeavors. Once Israel trusts in her own strength by rebelling against the covenant, YHWH delivers her over to marauding nomads. When she cries for deliverance, YHWH sends Egypt both to vanquish the *shasu* so they can no longer harass the coast and to render his own corrective judgment on the cities in which Israel resided: all of these cities and even the people involved in the conflict of this era are mentioned on Merneptah's Stele and depicted on the temple's walls at Karnak. Thus, evidence does exist for the reliability of the Scriptures during this period.

XIV. OBEDIENCE: FORTY YEARS OF STRENGTH, 1227-1187, ISRAEL: GIDEON/EGYPT: MERNEPTAH, SETI II, RAMSSESS III

The long reign of Ramesses II presented many internal succession problems for Egypt.[432] While his reign had allowed for about a half century of peace in Canaan, it eventually led to conflict and the end of his dynasty. Merneptah had been an old man when he inherited his father's throne and he ruled for less than a decade.[433] Since some of Ramesses' sons were still alive at Merneptah's death, a coup ensued. The remaining 25 years of the 19th Dynasty were weakened.[434] With all of Egypt's internal conflict, Canaan became the least of the Crown's concerns. This decline "led to its withdrawal from Canaan 60 years later."[435]

The 20th Dynasty began under Setnakhte who evidently dealt with Asiatics' migrating into the Delta the way the 18th Dynasty had 300 years earlier.[436] It was not until his son, Ramesses III, that Egypt was able to take a final aggressive approach to Canaan. Ramesses, however, did not direct his campaign toward the Canaanites but toward the hordes of invading Sea People who had left their western homelands to enjoy the bounty of Egypt.[437] Some tribes of Sea People had allied with the Libyans on the western Delta, while others invaded along the coastal regions from the north. Women and children migrated with ox carts that carried their possessions, as ships guarded their progress.[438] In year 8, Ramesses III raced up the Palestinian coast, violently contesting their ingress.[439] Ramesses' inscriptions tell us that he settled some of the invading tribes in Canaan.[440] The remaining 23 years of Ramesses' reign appear to have been relatively peaceful for Canaan, as Pharaoh once again turned his attention toward building programs and economic crises at home.[441]

This was Egypt's last stand. In the years following, Egypt was riveted with internal coups, succession issues, and, most of all, the power of rival temples, which had profited from the vast wealth that Ramesses III had appropriated from the Sea Peoples.[442] This led to a century of intermittent civil war. No longer would Egypt dominate Canaan. The role of dominating an apostate Canaan would now be inherited by the Sea Peoples.

Only with the Sea Peoples' invasion and Ramesses III's campaign was there any show of Egyptian power in Canaan during this period. In the north, the Sea Peoples brought an end to the Late Bronze Age (c. 1150).[443] The Hittite Empire was destroyed; Alalakh and Ugarit were razed to the ground, never to be rebuilt. The Sea Peoples destroyed Syria, as the Hurrian "bee" had done three centuries prior. Ramesses III, however, thwarted the Sea Peoples' attempt to infiltrate Canaan fully, accosting them on the old Hittite boundary.[444] This new wave of immigrants became firmly established in Israel's coastal inheritances. If Israel rebelled against YHWH's covenant, the consequences would be both immediate and severe.

XV. DISOBEDIENCE: CIVIL WAR, 1187-1161

After Gideon's death, Abimelech—who had no lawful claim to his father's inheritance—instigated the first recorded coup in Israel. He allied with his other relatives in Shechem and slaughtered his brothers; only Jotham escaped. The latter issued a curse against Abimelech and the conspirators, stating that his brother would destroy Shechem, but that refugees in a citadel would destroy Abimelech (Judg 9:7–20). According to Judges 9, the Israelites in Shechem worshiped the 'god of the covenant,' Berith (who was perhaps seen as one aspect of Israel's God YHWH). Three years after the coup, YHWH fulfilled Jotham's prophecy, and Shechem revolted against Abimelech's excessive and arbitrary taxes (Judg 9:28). The Shechemites found less affliction in serving the Canaanites than in serving Gideon's wayward son.

Gaal, the son of Ebed, led the revolt (Judg 9:28) against Abimelech. Warned by his confederate governor in Shechem (Judg 9:30–34), Abimelech prevailed in the battle. Abimelech razed Shechem and *salted its fields* (Judg 9:45). Gaal and the Shechemites fled to the Temple of Berith for protection (9:47), which Abimelech burned down to the ground. Shortly thereafter, Abimelech seized the city of Thebez (9:50). A woman in the citadel threw a stone at his head and killed the power-hungry Abimelech.

Fascinatingly, the archaeology of Shechem tells the same story as Judges 9. During the time of the judges (Late Bronze Age, c. 1500–1180), temples served as massive defensive fortifications.[445] The people of Shechem built the Temple of Berith using scraps from the previous city,[446] which was destroyed during the initial Conquest under Joshua. Not only have archaeologists unearthed this temple; they have also discovered that its defensive watchtower was indeed destroyed in about 1180 BCE[447]—right in line with when Scripture's linear chronology dates Abimelech's coup to have taken place. Even more convincing proof of the Scriptural account is the fact that archaeologists have discovered the large commemorative stele set up at Shechem (Josh 24:26), where the Shechemites crowned Gideon's son king (see Illustration 11.15).[448]

Illustration 11.15. A pillar at Shechem from the temple of Baal-Berith, 'Lord of the Covenant.' Bryant Wood dates this pillar to the time time of Abimelech. The fortress temple was destroyed c. 1125 BCE.

XVI. ISRAEL: 1161–1139

The early years of Gideon's leadership coincided with the final years of Merneptah's reign. The next 87 years were relatively peaceful years for Israel. Israel enjoyed 40 years of peace under Gideon and another 55 peaceful years under Tola and the Gileadite Jair, who had conquered 23 cities in the land of Gilead (1 Chr 2:22) and extended Israel's territory. When Jair died, Israel again wantonly departed from the covenant. YHWH placed the nation in a squeeze, with the Philistines on the west and the Ammonites on the east. This oppressing situation lasted for 18 years (Judgs 10:8). During this wave of Philistine assaults, the Ark of the Covenant was taken, and the capital city of Shiloh was abandoned (1 Sam 4:4; Ps 78:60; Jer 7:12). The high priest Eli had judged Israel perhaps as early as Gideon (1 Sam 4:18). His counsel no doubt aided the nation in walking righteously before her God.

XVII. ISRAEL: OPPRESSION BY THE PHILISTINES AND AMMONITES, 1139–1121

There is no denying Scripture's perspective regarding the Philistines. From the Hebrew point of view, the Philistines had lived in Canaan long before the invasions under Merneptah and Ramesses III.[449] We know that the "Sea People" had migrated into Canaan and the Egyptian Delta before Thera's eruption, back in the sixteenth century at the time of the exodus. In fact, both pottery and mosaics from the sixteenth century demonstrate strong Aegean contact.[450] Joshua battled five Philistine lords (Josh 13:2–3), who continued to be a problem at least 40 years later (Judgs 3:3). Abimelech, the king of Gerar with whom Abram made a treaty was

Illustration 11.16. Relief on a temple wall showing Ramesses III dismounted from his chariot, shooting at the Philistine ships in naval battle.

also called a Philistine. Several hundred years later, the prophet Jeremiah connected the Philistines with Caphtor, better known as Crete (Jer 47:4; Amos 9:7).[451] Despite the claims of scholars to the contrary,[452] there simply is not enough evidence to verify or dismiss these claims. All we can say for sure is that a *new wave* of Philistine immigrants entered Canaan at the close of the thirteenth century.[453]

Scripture identifies these Sea Peoples as Philistines based on ethnicity; they were the offspring of Ham (Gen 10:6–19). While various tribes may have sailed across the Aegean and back, Scripture appears to lump all Sea Peoples into one broad category as "Philistines." Scripture recognizes a resurgence of Philistine power and dominance after massive migrations occurred during the reigns of Merneptah (*c.* 1228/1213) and Ramesses III.[454] After Ramesses had settled these people on Canaan's seacoast,[455] they began a thrust inland to occupy more territories.

The first time Israel was oppressed by the Philistines was (*c.* 1139) about 80 years after the first massive migrations are recorded by Merneptah. This scenario is quite realistic, allowing about two to three generations for the new immigrants to strengthen in the Promised Land before asserting authority over Israel. The Philistines' power was probably strengthened by subsequent migrations, as families and tribes reunited on Canaan's shores.[456]

XVIII. CYCLE OF DISOBEDIENCE: JEPHTHAH–SAMUEL, 1121–1051

The rebellion after Jair's administration (*c.* 1150) was the first time the Philistines had grown strong enough to subjugate Israel (Judg 10:5–6). Israel had again rebelled to serve the gods of Ammon and Philistia (Judg 10:5–6). During this oppression by Ammon and Philistia, shortly after Jair's administration, Eli served as high priest. His life came to an end when the Philistines captured the Ark of the Covenant, *c.* 1128. Samuel may have been as young as 10 years old at this time. YHWH removed his own name (Jer 7:12) from Shiloh, and Israel remained without a capitol for well over 100 years. Once Samuel grew into young adulthood, he beckoned Israel to Jepheth's hometown of Mizpeh (1 Sam 7:5) in the north. Samuel called for a renewal of the covenant (7:1–9), during which time Jephthah committed to freeing Israel from Ammon's hold (Judg 10:17; 11:11). [457]

The Philistines were pressing Israel on the west while the Ammonites pushed from the east, thus subduing the entire nation. Jephthah led Israel to her last Conquest surge as the nation's sins weakened her to such an extent that she faced being driven out like the Canaanites before her. Although Jephthah's campaign successfully alleviated the threats from the Ammonites on Israel's eastern side, his efforts did nothing to confront the powerful Philistine federations, which may have backed down after Jephthah's show of force and success on Israel's eastern front.

The princes of Gilead, a clan in the Manasseh tribe (Josh 17:1; Judg 10:18) appointed Jephthah, since he had displayed valor in battle (Judg 11:1). YHWH blessed Jephthah's efforts to fulfill the Effacement Judgment (Judg 11:29), and he conquered 20 cities for Israel (Judg 11:33) during the nation's **Sixth Conquest Campaign**. Megiddo and Taanach may have been

Map 11.7. Israel's Retreat from Shiloh to Mizpeh during Samuel's and Jephthah's Leadership.

among them. Both cities evidence destruction that occurred in about 1125, and they lay unoccupied for a long time.[458]

Envy soon arose between Ephraim and the Gileadites, and a civil war ensued. Scripture does not say how long this dispute lasted, but possibly as long as two years (Judg 12:1–7), after which Jephthah was victor. During the previous wars with the Philistines, Shiloh had been abandoned, and Jephthah called Israel to his hometown of Mizpeh. This region was one of the territories that Israel had secured by driving out the Canaanites during the initial, six-teenth- century Conquest (Josh 11:8). Now that the coastal regions were vulnerable, Mizpeh was a safehaven. That Jephthah uttered "all his words before YHWH in Mizpeh" (Judg 11:11) indicates that Israel had met there to renew the covenant (see Map 11.7).

Israel's eighth Jubilee in 1108 occasioned the next significant covenant renewal of this era (1 Sam 7:3–13). Along with this event, Samuel provided chronological data that aid us in reconstructing this era. Samuel states that, after the ark had been captured, it was quickly returned to Israel seven months later (1 Sam 6:1). At the onset of the nation's eighth Jubilee, we learn that the ark had been at Kirjath-jearim for 20 years (1 Sam 7:2). This dates both Eli's death and the capturing of the ark to 1128, when Samuel was between eight and twelve years of age. During this Jubilee, Elon of Zebulun had been installed to marshal Israel's forces.

By about 1090, Israel had once again rebelled against YHWH and was again having to pay tribute to the Philistines (Judg 13:1). The priesthood increasingly began to play a leadership role, as Samuel sought to bring back his people to the constitutional covenant. Under Samuel's administration, Israel recovered the territories lost to the Philistines 40 years before. When Israel had lost the Ark of the Covenant (after Jair's administration), Israel had also lost the cities of Ekron and Gath (1 Sam 7:14). Samuel recovered these cities (probably as tributaries) and restored Israel's former borders. This move secured the best position for Israel to follow the covenant and once again assert her claim to the entire land. Samuel mentions both the Philistines and the Ammonites as a threat that YHWH had enabled him to subdue during his administration (1 Sam 7:14), and peace prevailed during his later years. Scripture states that YHWH's hand was against the Philistines all of Samuel's days, as he continue the Sixth Conquest Campaign.

This campaign, however, was not finalized by another judge like Jair, Samuel, or Ehud. Rather, Israel asked for a king at the nation's subsequent, ninth Jubilee, in 1058. Samuel anointed Saul during Sukkot that year, and he was installed as king over Israel during the next sabbatical-year festival at Sukkot, during Tishri of 1051. Saul continued the task of driving the Philistines and Ammonites out of Israel's homeland initiating the **Seventh Conquest Campaign** (1 Sam 11:11; 12:12; 14:47).

Shortly after Saul's coronation, the Ammonites assaulted Jabesh-gilead. The Ammonites offered the territory a traditional vassal alliance if its men would submit to having their right eyes gouged out (1 Sam 11:1–2)! When Saul heard these repulsive terms, he sprang into action and delivered the region (1 Samuel 11) from the Ammonites' barbarous intent. Two years later, Saul assaulted a Philistine garrison in Geba and began a long campaign against the Philistines, which David later inherited. Saul died in battle while warring against the Philistines on Mt. Gilboa (2 Samuel 31).

A recent reexamination of the Qeiyafa Ostracon determined that it may record the actual transition from the Judges Era to the Monarchy. As we saw above (pp. 313–14), the Qeiyafa Ostracon is one of the oldest writings yet discovered, dating to the early Monarchy (see Illustration 8.1, p. 314).[459] The inscription contains basic ideals that are comparable with Israel's Law: do not oppress the widow or the foreigner. But a new examination by Émile Puech, reading the text from left to write (Hebrew is normally read right to left) demonstrates that this may be a new directive written directly to Israel's judges. The Book of Samuel indicates that the judges had corrupted justice (1 Sam 8:3). The Qeiyafa Ostracon preserves a directive that, under the king's new administration, judges will serve God and judge righteously.

> Puech tells us that when he had completed deciphering the text of the Qeiyafa Ostracon, he was "surprised to find that [it] contained all of the essentials" that are in the biblical text: (1) the need for judges who will not oppress the foreigner and those less fortunate (e.g., the widow and the orphan) and a need for those who will protect them from annihilation, (2) the installation of a king, (3) the existence of servants who serve the king, (4) the injunction not to oppress, but to serve God and (5) most importantly the designation of a new monarch.[460]

This new interpretation may indeed evidence a transition to a monarchy. Unfortunately, the sherd is broken, and some of the context lost. It is hoped that future examinations may shed more light on this intriguing possibility.

Israel did not finally have rest from all her enemies until David slew the Philistines (2 Sam 8:1), Moabites (2 Sam 8:2), Syrians (8:3), and Edomites (8:14) between 1037 (as the anointed yet persecuted heir apparent) and 1008 BCE. Places as far as Hamath on the Euphrates became tributary regions (8:9–13), as David brought the entire Promised Land into subjection during the **Eighth** and final **Conquest Campaign**. David sought YHWH, who in turn blessed Israel's small but well–organized and well-trained army.

XIX. DAVID: 1023–984

A. Dating David

The last synchronism that Scripture offers during the early Monarchy appears in the title of Psalm 60. David states that his general, Joab, warred against Edom at the same time that Mesopotamia confronted the Arameans. David superscribed his song with a "date marker":

When he (David) strove with Mesopotamia and with A'-ram-zo'-bah and Jo'-ab smote E'-dom (Ps 60:1, superscription)

David's campaign coincides with the reign of Ashur-rabi II, who fought with the Arameans, and whose predecessor (Tiglath-pileser I) had garrisoned their cities about a century before.[461] David's superscription to Psalm 60 was probably written in the early years of his reign, when Joab placed garrisons in Edom (2 Sam 8:14).

Archaeology has recently unearthed cultic shrines that mirror the religion described in the Torah. During David's reign, cultic implements were simple architectural designs, lacking the more "pagan" elements of animal and image manifestation of the gods.[462] Preliminary analysis of the recent excavations at Khirbet Qeiyafa (a border city of Judah opposite the Philistine city of Gath) indicate that Samuel and David had renewed Israel in the covenant. The religious implements at Qeiyafa not only lack normal pagan iconography but the accompanying offerings are devoid of pig remains, thus indicating that the shrines were used by Israelite households.[463] Thus archaeology once again unearths a record of Israel that agrees with Scripture (see Illustrations 11.17).

B. David's Genealogy

David's genealogy provides another great example for the chronology presented in chap. 9. When Jacob had divided his blessing among his sons, Judah had inherited the Monarchy of the family nation because his three older brothers had been disqualified (see pp. 127–33). David's right to govern Israel was based on his lineage, which ascended through Boaz, Nahshon, Hezron, Pharez, to Judah (1 Chr 2:4–5, 9–14). The Pentateuch and 1 Chronicles mention Ram (1 Chr 2:9–10; Ruth 4:19; Job 32:2), Amminadab (Num 2:3; 1 Chr 2:10–11), and

Illustrations 11.17. Unpictured pottery arks discovered at Khirbet Qeiyafa.

Nahshon as David's ancestors who lived in Egypt. Nahshon lived during the 40 years of exile (Num 1:7; 3:2; 7:12, 17; 10:4; Ruth 4:20–22) and died in the wilderness. The record becomes "silent" once Israel enters the land until Ehud's administration when Salma (variant, Salmon, 1 Chr 2:11; Ruth 4:20) is mentioned. Remember, this is the same "silent" or "intermediate period" that is demonstrated in Israel's chronology and is simply noted as "Joshua and the elders that outlived him" (Judg 2:7; see pp. 354, 360–64). Thus, there are one to two generations that have been omitted from David's lineage simply because the Levites did not record during this early era when the nation was warring and simply trying to survive.

Once the genealogical record picks up again during Ehud's administration, geneaologies appear to have been faithfully noted. Salma, for instance, would perhaps have been born toward the beginning of Ehud's administration around 1394 BCE. Although the scribes under Ehud recorded genealogies, they probably did not make a formal genealogy record for another 140 years, simply because they did not have enough generations to record. Deborah's scribes may have been the first to organize more formal genealogy lists for Israel's families based on the families' tribal land ownership.

These conclusions are supported by the histories within the books of Ruth, 1 Chronicles, and Judges. When we reconstruct this era,[464] it allows for Salma to be born *c.* 1394. If Salma bore Boaz at age 55, then Boaz would have been born in *c.* 1238. From the book of Ruth, we learn that Elimelech, Naomi, Mahlon, and Chilion had emigrated to Moab *c.* 1233 due to the famine that began several years prior, which caused the Midianites and Amalekites to invade Israel (Ruth 1; Judg 6:1–7; see pp. 583-86). Naomi's sons were young enough to be single when the family moved to Moab and the family lived there long enough for Elimelech to die, for his sons to marry, and for both of his sons to die (Ruth 1:1–5). This is, perhaps, a period of 20–30 years. This means that the earliest Boaz could have married Ruth would have been between 1215–1205. It is unlikely that Obed was born right away, and could have been born 20 years later when Boaz was about 55 years of age in 1183. If Obed was 59 when Jesse was born, then Jesse would have been born in 1124, right about the time that the Ark of the Covenant had been captured by the Philistines (see pp. 571, 593–96). Jesse had six sons before he had David (1 Chr 2:12–15), and we know that David was 30 years old when he became king over Judah (2 Sam 5:4–5). This dates David's birth to 1053 and means that Jesse was about 70 years when David was born.

David's genealogy evidences that Deborah's scribes could only trace Israel's genealogies to Ehud's administration. This would indicate that Israel's early pioneers (c. 1508–1394) did not keep detailed records of the nation's genealogies until Ehud's administration. These genealogies parallel Israel's early historical record by demonstrating a time of silence during Joshua's administration and "the elders that outlived him" when the record of genealogies was not the nation's top concern and all efforts were probably focused on basic survival of day to day living, farming, and Conquest of the land. Thus, the evidence consistently demonstrates the chronology purposed in chap. 9.

In chap. 10, we saw extraordinary evidence for Israel's exodus toward the end of Egypt's Second Intermediate Period. Not only does the epigraphic evidence appear to support this association, the archaeological record supports it, as does Thera's eruption. Within 40 years of Thera's eruption and the Hyksos' retreat from Egypt, Canaan also exhibits a massive wave of destruction.

Scripture supports a sixteenth-century Canaan Conquest with its descriptions of the destruction at Hazor and Jericho. Hundreds of Canaanite towns demonstrate catastrophic ruin with a gap in occupation. YHWH promised that he would send his "bees" to drive out the Canaanites until Israel's armies increased enough to handle the job themselves. The Hurrians were the first to provide a protective buffer so that Israel could establish the covenant and increase on the land. However, Israel faced continual encroachment from Egypt every time she rebelled. Canaan had been severely weakened during Thutmoses III's and Amenhotep II's campaigns, which depopulated the land, eliminated food stores, and disarmed Canaan during the years when Egypt dominated Israel's inheritance. This not only rendered judgment on rebellious Israelites for allying with the Canaanites, but also weakened Canaanite federations so that future Hebrew generations could claim greater territorial conquests. YHWH indeed fulfilled his word to Israel, for which both historical and archaeological evidence exists.

Israel's two northern threats disappeared as the Hittites annexed many Hurrian strongholds, thus destroying the Mitanni Empire. Yet when Israel departed from YHWH and his Law, Egypt reappeared on the scene to punish Israel's covenant breach, simultaneously alleviating the Promised Land of Hittite and Hurranian threats by securing a firm border, thus protecting Canaan from northern hazards and enabling Israel's future covenant-abiding generations.

Many towns *that* do not reveal archaeological evidence for destruction during the initial sixteenth-century Conquest do show signs of gradual decline, with utter ruin occurring after Deborah and Barak took hold of the YHWH's covenant to obey it. During these eras of obedience, Egyptian documents attest the *Habiru* activity in Canaan and archaeology demonstrates utter ruin at sites such as Hazor, Lachish, and Gezer.

Scripture attests a new wave of Philistine power at the same time when Egyptian and Ugaritic records attest their peoples' migration and plundering activity in the Levant. The Sea People eliminated the remaining Hittite threats toward the end of the Judges Era, yet supplanted Egypt in rendering YHWH's judgment when Israel rebelled against his covenant. After a few generations, the Philistines grew strong enough to oppress Israel, capturing the Ark of the Covenant in Eli's days. Samuel encouraged Israel to observe YHWH's covenant, and the nation began to recover the territory she lost to the Philistines.

Despite this victory, the nation grew weary of fighting her enemies and even more impatient with corrupt judges who had no accountability. Both of these situations pressured Israel to ask for the more-controlled yet oppressive Monarchy system. Saul and David finally brought the Philistines under control and led the nation into a prosperous and peaceful era. So far, the evidence that my investigation had uncovered indicates that historicity exists in the Scriptural record and, not only does it exist, but it is accurate. I really had not expected this outcome. I still had to wonder: Does the same hold true for the Monarchy Era?

12

Critical Issues in Israelite History: The Effacement Judgment

I. NUMBERS 33

In chap. 3.IV, we examined Noah's covenant and his blessing of his sons, which defined prophecy and bequeathed Canaan's tribal inheritances to Shem's progeny. To fulfill Noah's words, YHWH covenanted with Abraham, promising Canaan's lands (Gen 15:18–21) to his offspring. YHWH waited 430 years from the time that he covenanted with Abraham so that the Amorites' perversity (iniquity) could "come to the full" (Gen 15:16). Four hundred thirty years later, Scripture shows that these nations had indeed reached maximum degradation by marrying close relatives and by participating in homosexuality and bestiality (Leviticus 18; 20:12–27, 24–30). YHWH sought to judge the Canaanites by driving them off their native land and ceding it to Israel.

A. Effacing Israel

YHWH gave Israel specific instructions for cleansing the Promised Land (Num 33:50–54) and securing the nation's military, economic, and environmental prowess. Israel was commanded to perform what herein will be called the five D's.

1. **D**rive out all the inhabitants of the land from before you (Num 33:52), and
2. **D**estroy all their pictures, and **d**estroy all their molten images, and quite pluck down all their high places (Num 33:52):
3. **D**ispossess the inhabitants of the land (Num 33:53), and
4. **D**well therein: for I have given you the land to possess it (Num 33:53).
5. **D**ivide the land by lot for an inheritance among your families: and to the more you shall give the more inheritance, and

to the fewer you shall give the less inheritance: every man's inheritance shall
be in the place where his lot falls; according to the tribes of your fathers you
shall inherit. (Num 33:54)

YHWH commanded Israel to drive out Canaan's natives, to destroy their memorabilia, to
dispossess them, to dwell in the Promised Land, and to divide the land among themselves.
Notice, that obeying the second command eliminated many archaeological artifacts! Pictured objects, such as reliefs, tombs, epigraphs, and other monuments would all qualify as
items for destruction. Epigraphic pottery without pictures was almost the only artifact that
this judgment did not include.

B. Fame and Righteousness

Why would YHWH command Israel to destroy and eliminate what we today consider
archaeological evidence? The purpose was to erase the memory of a particular people or
nation. It is quite probable that our ancient ancestors knew they were the first of many
generations to populate the earth and sought to carve a memory of their existence into
stones and other lasting objects. Ancient kings considered recognition of their accomplishments a divine right, so they committed their fame to stone monuments, the words of which
called down wrath on any who removed or damaged their memorial. For instance, a Sargon
inscription reads, "May Shamash destroy the potency and make perish every offspring of
whosoever damages this inscription. . . . May Anu destroy the name and . . . finish off the
offspring . . . to whosoever destroys this inscription."[1] The seal of an Assyrian general makes
similar threats against those "who blot out my inscribed name, may Assur and Adad destroy
his name and his land."[2]

For a man's fame and recognition to outlast his lifetime was considered a great honor;
in fact it amounted to immortality.[3] Offspring, who bore their father's name added to the
father's memory and fame. Likewise, extinguishing a man's offspring caused his memory to
be forgotten. This can be seen again in the decree of Seti I (1318–1301 BCE), who called for
revenge against thieves, stating that Osiris would "be after him (the thief), after his wife, and
after his children, *to wipe out his name.*"[4] Seti's curse sought to expunge the memory of the
thief and his house (offspring). Likewise Sennacherib's purpose for flooding Babylon was
(in his own words) "that in days to come the site of that city . . . may not be remembered."[5]

Monarchs such as Sennacherib or Seti sought to expunge the memory of individuals
considered evildoers, yet sought their own name to be remembered for "time immemorial."
Cyrus, the king of Persia, certainly considered himself to be famous and honorable. According to Arrian (6.29), his tomb bore the epitaph:

Mortal! I am Cyrus, son of Cambyses, who founded the Persian Empire, and was
Lord of Asia. Grudge me not, then, my monument.

Deuteronomy supports this concept of tying fame to a name, stating that, if a man died
without heirs, his nearest relative should father a child who would "succeed in the name of

his brother which is dead, *that his name be not put out of Israel*" (Deut 25:6). The prophet Isaiah also links fame among Israel's congregation to righteousness. He states that YHWH will give eunuchs who keep the covenant's Sabbath "a *name* better than of sons and of daughters . . . *that shall not be cut off*" (Isa 56:4–5, emphasis added). Daniel may be a good example of a righteous eunuch whose name YHWH caused "not to be cut off" (since his name is commemorated by the Book of Daniel). YHWH sought to honor the righteous and to *slight* or expunge the memory of the wicked.

Slighting was a great dishonor, and God used it as a tool for judgment. For instance, Deut 25:19 commanded that the name of Amalek, the Edomite king who raided Israel after the exodus, be expunged from Israel's national archives so that no remembrance of his existence or his wicked deed would remain (Exod 17:8–16; Num 24:20). *Machah*, translated 'blot out' in v. 19, means erasing or obliterating: expunging.[6] Moses also used this word when he sought to make atonement for Israel's idolatry, asking the Creator to "*blot* me, I pray you, out of your book which you have written" (Exod 32:32). Moses sought to expunge his own memory from Israel's "historical monument"—YHWH's written word in Scripture— if YHWH would not forgive Israel's idolatry. In light of ancient values, Moses made a very generous offer.

Not only was the Creator concerned with expunging the memory of the wicked, he also sought to expunge the memory of their deities. This was why he commanded Israel not to mention the names of other gods.

> Make no mention of the name of other gods, neither let it be heard out of your mouth. (Exod 23:13)

The prophet Zechariah prophesied of a time when this command would be fulfilled, and memory of all false gods would cease to exist.

> And it shall come to pass in that day, says YHWH of hosts, that I will cut off the names of the idols out of the land, and they shall *no more be remembered*: and also I will cause the prophets and the unclean spirit to pass out of the land. (Zech 13:2; see also Hos 2:16–17)

Throughout the ancient world, people considered it an honor for a name to outlive a person's lifetime or the lifetime of a person's descendants. YHWH's Effacement Judgment commemorated righteousness and expunged evil.

C. *The Effacement Judgment Initiated*

The Creator's Effacement Judgment in the Book of Numbers sought to remove the memory of wicked nations, their kings, and their offspring. This served at least two purposes. It removed the "evidence" or memorial of a people by wiping their very existence from the land. And it "blotted out" knowledge of their evil practices, so the customs could be brought to an end (Deut 13:12–17; 20:18).

Scripture reveals that Israel followed Numbers' Effacement Judgment during Joshua's days, which would have lasted as long as 35 to 45 years after Israel entered Canaan, and at intervals during the Judges Era. When Jericho fell to Joshua,

> The people went up into the city, every man straight before him, and they took the city. And they *utterly destroyed* all that was in the city, both man and woman, young and old, and ox, and sheep, and ass, with the edge of the sword. (Josh 6:20–21)

Similar accounts are given for Makkedah (Josh 10:28), Lachish (Josh 10:32), and Eglon (Josh 10:34–35). A short time later, YHWH again confirmed Numbers 33's Effacement Judgment against Canaan.

> All the inhabitants of the hill country from Lebanon to Misrephoth-maim, and all the Sidonians, them *will I drive out* from before the Children of Israel: only *divide you it by lot to the Israelites* for an inheritance, as I have commanded you. Now therefore *divide this land* for an inheritance unto the nine tribes, and the half tribe of Manasseh. (Josh 13:6–7)

Sennacherib's inscription demonstrates that Assyria had once executed an effacement judgment that was perhaps similar to YHWH's command to Israel. Notice how thoroughly Sennacherib sought to eliminate any evidence of the city of Babylon:

> The city and (its) houses, from its foundation to its top, I destroyed, I devastated, I burned with fire. The wall and outer wall, temples and gods, temple towers of brick and earth, as many as there were, I razed and dumped them into the Arahtu Canal. Through the midst of that city I dug canals, I flooded its side (*lit.*, ground) with water, and the very foundations thereof (*lit.*, the structure of its foundation) I destroyed. I made its destruction more complete than by a flood. *That in days to come the site of that city, and (its) temples and gods, might not be remembered*, I completely blotted it out with (floods) of water and *made it like a meadow.*[7]

We have seen that Israel obeyed Numbers' Effacement Judgment during Joshua's days (Josh 24:31), similar to the way that Sennacherib sought to efface Babylon. However, Israel vacillated in her obedience to Numbers' Effacement Judgment, at times obeying and at other times ignoring YHWH's commands. This half-hearted obedience led to Israel being driven off the Promised Land. What evidence has survived of Israel's life in Canaan is known to us today from records of other nations, such as Egypt and Assyria. Very little evidence has been found in Israel's tribal borders to confirm the existence of her monarchies. The evidence that does exist, bolsters the history that the Hebrew scriptures record.

II. DAVIDIC DYNASTY

A. *Historical Evidence*

David was one of Israel's most righteous kings, and YHWH rewarded him by giving fame and honor to David's name. The Book of 2 Samuel notes, "I was with you wherever you went, and have cut off all your enemies out of your sight, and have made you a *great name*, like unto the name of the great men that are in the earth" (2 Sam 7:9).

In the summer of 1993, a fragmentary text discovered at the ancient site of Tel Dan in northern Israel confirmed the existence and fame of David's House. Most scholars attribute this fragmented black basalt monument to Hazael, king of Damascus, who ruled around 835 BCE (see Illustration 12.1).[8] The Aramaic inscription reads:

> [I killed Jeho]ram son of [Ahab] king of Israel,
> and [I] killed [Ahaz]iahu son of [Jehoram kin]g
> of the House of David. And I set [their towns into
> ruins and turned] their land into [desolation].[9]

Illustration 12.1. The Tell Dan inscription.

Hazael's text had been broken, almost completely destroyed, and reused as a stone in a city wall. This shows that the Israelites had at one time observed Numbers' command to destroy epigraphic material (Num 33:52), thus atomizing King Hazael's monument and erasing memory of the land's former inhabitants. Thankfully for us, use of the fragments in other construction also preserved epigraphic evidence outside Israel's Scriptures to demonstrate that David and his sons were indeed legitimate.

The following year, in 1994, the excavator, Abraham Biran, discovered two more fragments of this stele.[10] The new pieces contain what appears to be the partially preserved names of Jehoram, king of Israel, and Ahaziah, king of Judah.[11] Scripture tells us that Jehoram had fought against Hazael of Damascus and was injured at Ramoth-Gilead (2 Chr 22:5). Scholars theorize that one of Hazael's generals had erected the original stele, commemorating Syria's victory over Israel.[12]

Another monument, the Moabite Mesha Inscription, discovered intact in 1868, also bears reference to David's House (see Illustration 12.2). In this stele, the Moabite King Mesha reports conquering

Illustration 12.2. Victory stele of Mesha, King of Moab, celebrating his victory over king Omri of Israel. The Israelites had established a fortress at Atharot, threatening Dhibon, Mesha's capital.

Israel's territory east of the Jordan and humiliating the tribe of Gad. Mesha even purports to have captured the vessels of "Yahweh." Since the intact Mesha Inscription's discovery, this stele has also been broken and the surviving fragmented and restored text now resides in France's historical museum, the Louvre. These two texts have caused scholars to acknowledge David as a viable king in Israel's history. Critical scholar Israel Finkelstein even concludes, "The House of David was known throughout the region"[13]

In 2005, archaeologists working in the ancient city of Gath (modern Tell es-Safi) unearthed an important artifact. The ostracon (an inscription on a broken pottery piece, used as ancient "note paper") bears the equivalent of the name *Goliath* in a very early Proto-Semitic script.[14] Dr. Aren Maeir, a professor at Bar-Ilan University and director of the excavation, points out that, while the discovery is not definitive evidence of Goliath's existence, it does support Scripture's depiction of life at the time that David battled Goliath.[15] "What this means is that at the time there were people there named Goliath," he said. "It shows us that David and Goliath's story reflects the cultural reality of the time." Maeir said that finding the scraps lends historical credence to the biblical story. The sherd dates back to around 950 BCE, making it the oldest Philistine inscription ever found and quite contemporary with the biblical account (see Illustration 2.21, pp. 53–54).[16]

In 2009, archaeologists Yosef Garfinkel and Saar Ganor were working at a tell in modern Khirbet Qeiyafa.[17] The site was an

> Israelite fort on the border with Philistia dating to the late 11th—early tenth century BCE, the time of David and Solomon. It was occupied during this period and was then abandoned (until the Hellenistic period), so there is no question about the dating and the implications are considerable.[18]

The archaeologists working at this site identify it with the biblical Sha'araim mentioned in 1 Sam 17:52.[19] The name Sha'araim means 'two-gates.'[20] "Khirbet Qeiyafa is the only site in the Kingdoms of Judah and Israel" that is archaeologically attested "with two gates."[21]

Garfinkel and Ganor found this ancient community to be quite impressive. The wall (casemate) surrounding the hilltop required more that 200,000 tons of boulders and the city's four-chambered gates weighed almost 5 tons. *Biblical Archaeology Review* editor Hershel Shanks points out that

> it took a well-organized, technologically proficient state society to construct something like this. This fort was not built by some tribal chiefdom. Qeiyafa is thus a powerful antidote to scholars like Tel Aviv University's Israel Finkelstein, who claims that Judah never existed as a state in the tenth century and that the "Kingdom" of David and Solomon was a tribal chiefdom at most.[22]

Although the city itself was impressive, the city is not what archaeologists consider to be their prize find. In one administrative office in this walled city, archaeologists also discovered a 6-inch ostracon that had been written on in ink. Though the ink has faded, this ancient text demonstrates that it was written using an ancient script referred to as Proto-Canaanite or Proto-Sinaitic, which means that this is one of the oldest pieces of writing ever discovered in this region. The text also demonstrates that Israel was a literate society, whose scribes were actually capable of writing and recording Israel's history. The fragment itself appears to be in line with ancient Israel's Law Code since it is either a layman's copy of the Law or the king's command to obey it. Thus, archaeology evidences a strong, Torah-observant Davidic Kingdom in its early years.[23]

How great was David's kingdom? Significant enough to be referred to in the Persian archives 500 years later. Ezra records that, when Artaxerxes searched for records of Israel's history, he found references to Israel's grandeur.

> There have been mighty kings also over Jerusalem, which have ruled over all countries beyond the river; and toll, tribute, and custom, were paid to them. (Ezra 4:20)

Ezra (6:2) tells us that these records were housed in the Median capital of Ectaba, which the King James Version renders as "Achmetha."[24] Recent excavations confirm this site as one of Persia's archive centers; however, modern urban development precludes adequate excavation. It is quite possible that the record Ezra refers to remains buried in Ectaba today.[25]

B. David's Borders

After the exodus, YHWH established Israel's borders from Hamath of Syria in the north to the "river of Egypt," probably the now defunct Pelusiac branch of the Nile, on Egypt's southeastern side.[26] Joshua once subjugated this region (Josh 10:41; 11:16), and Goshen is later mentioned as a territory belonging to Judah (Josh 15:51). Judah's control over this region was short-lived, however. As Israel's apostasy continued, the nation lost control over Goshen and many other territories. Under David's mighty arm, the southern boundaries were reestablished (1 Kgs 4:21; 2 Chr 9:26), and Goshen once again became an Israelite province.

When YHWH gave his covenants to Abraham, he intended to give Israel

> *power to get wealth,* that he may establish his covenant which he swore to your fathers. (Deut 8:18)

This statement alludes, in part, to the Burnt-Offering Covenant, wherein YHWH promised Abraham: "Your seed shall possess the gate of his enemies" (Gen 22:17). Under David's leadership Israel stood as a great power, owning many enemies' strategic or economic "gates." In the north, David subjugated the Syro-Palestinian region to the Euphrates River, possessing Tiphsah on the west bank of the Euphrates, above the confluence of the Blikh (1 Kgs 4:24).[27] The Tiphsah fort or "gate" contained great economic resources. It occupied the end of the great trade road that extended from Egypt, through Phoenicia, into Syria, Mesopotamia, and the kingdoms of inner Asia.[28]

David secured another key economic and militarily strategic location in the "entrance of Hamath" (Num 13:21; 1 Kgs 8:65). Of this entrance the *International Standard Bible Encyclopedia* states,

It seems that instead of translating, we should read here a place-name, 'Libo of Hamath.' The presence of the ancient site of Lebo (modern Lebweh) fourteen miles North-Northeast of Baalbek, at the head-waters of the Orontes and commanding the strategic point where the plain broadens out to the North and to the South, confirms us in this conjecture.[29]

This strategic location not only ensured defense against foreign attack, its location provided an indispensable economic trading center that ensured the nation's wealth as Israel imported and exported goods with other countries and collected toll, tribute, and customs from the nations that David regulated (see Map 12.1).

III. NUMBERS' HIDDEN JUDGMENT

A. *Hidden Judgments*

When YHWH made the Promised-Land Covenant with Abraham, he "hid" a judgment against Egypt delivering Egypt and much of her wealth into Israel's hands (see pp. 88–89). He allotted 430 years for the Amorites' sins to come "to the full" before delivering Canaan into Israel's hand. Numbers 33's Effacement Judgment was designed to eliminate evidence that the Canaanites ever lived on the Promised Land, intending that their memory should "perish forever" (Num 24:20; Deut 7:24). Scripture is constant in use of this hidden-judgment methodology, because each Book of the Torah contains a "hidden" or "obscured" judgment against Israel should she rebel against YHWH's covenant by hardening her heart against obeying YHWH's commands.

> But if you will not drive out the inhabitants of the land from before you; then it shall come to pass, that those which you *let remain of them shall be pricks in your eyes, and thorns in your sides, and shall vex you in the land where in you dwell.* (Num 33:55)

This last verse of Numbers 33's Judgment foretells the consequences for not driving out Canaan's natives. YHWH had intended to use Abraham's descendants to fulfill Noah's curse, which ceded Canaan's inheritance, his tribal lands to Shem's progeny (see pp. 78–81). YHWH could not fulfill this curse until Canaan's progeny became wholly degenerate (Gen 15:16). If Israel also rebelled against the way of YHWH, as Canaan had, the Creator would judge Israel by the same standard. Although the judgment prophecy against Israel begins in v. 55, YHWH's final act of judgment is found in v. 56:

> Moreover it shall come to pass, that *I shall do to you, as I thought to do to them.* (Num 33:56)

YHWH foresaw that Israel would become ensnared by Canaan's religious customs if she did not dispose the land's native inhabitants. Remember that the Law's founding precept was grounded in opposite and equal reactions. YHWH followed his own Law with this judgment against Israel: as YHWH sought to do to the Canaanites, so YHWH would do to the Israelites if they followed the same perversities. This further evidences YHWH's unbiased character. The

Map 12.1. David's and Solomon's Kingdom with Tribute.

judgment he ordained for the Amorites and other nations stipulated in the Promised-Land Covenant was the same judgment he pronounced on Israel for her rebellion against his Law.

The Effacement Judgment outlined in Numbers 33 would be applied to Israel for not "driving out" the current residents. So, if the tables were turned, we would find that there would be (2, p. 601) very little remembrance of Israel left in the Promised Land. YHWH's people would be captured, deported, or otherwise (1) driven off, and (3) dispossessed of Canaan. Israel's land (4, 5) would then *be divided among the Gentiles by lot for an inheritance*. The very few Israelites left in the Promised Land would be just enough to be (6) thorns in the sides of the heathen. That this judgment has been so completely fulfilled is attested by the "absence of evidence" and the fulfillment of Numbers 33's prophecy, which has led many archaeologists and historians to conclude that Israel's historical writings were created during Josiah's reign.

B. Israel's Effacement Judgment—Fulfilled

Israel never did fulfill Numbers' Effacement edict. Israel never fully dispossessed the Amorites, Perizzites, or any other nation stipulated in the Promised-Land Covenant (with the exception, perhaps, of the Rephaim). Before Israel entered Canaan, Moses prophesied that YHWH would apply Numbers' judgment to Israel when the nation rebelled against YHWH's commands. "I said, I would scatter them into corners, I would make the *remembrance* of them to cease from among men" (Deut 32:26).

The author of 2 Kings continues this prophetic thread:

> And I will *wipe* Jerusalem as a man wipes a dish . . . he does *wipe* and turn it upside down. (2 Kgs 21:13)[30]

YHWH would wipe Jerusalem so clean that there would be almost no trace of Israel's existence left in Jerusalem. *Maḥah,*[31] translated "wipe," is again the word we examined above that Scripture uses to say that YHWH would "wipe, blot out or otherwise obliterate Israel's existence in Jerusalem from humanity's memory."

To what extent has YHWH's Effacement Judgment been rendered against Israel's kingdom? Monarchs of most great Near Eastern nations such as Assyria, Babylon, Egypt, and Persia are known to us today by the inscriptions, tombs, graves, monuments, pottery, royal palaces, and other artifacts they left behind that have been excavated and restored to our knowledge. Israel's epigraphic grave is quite barren. Archaeologists have yet to find any tombs or inscriptions commissioned during David's or Solomon's reigns. Furthermore, the only two testimonies that archaeologists have discovered that witness David's House originated in other nations.[32]

One fairly recent Hebrew discovery that has survived to evidence Judah's Monarchy is an inscription etched into a tunnel far beneath Jerusalem. The Siloam Inscription, as it is now called, describes how two sets of engineers tunneled their way toward each other from opposite ends of a conduit in order to fortify Jerusalem (2 Kgs 20:20; see Illustration 12.3). Of this feat, Israel Finkelstein notes: "Such an extraordinary achievement did not escape

Illustration 12.3. The Siloam inscription, a Hebrew text commemorating the excavation of a tunnel between the Gihon spring and the pool of Siloam inside the walls of Jerusaelm. Built under King Hezekiah, the tunnel brought water to the city during the Assyrian siege by Sennacherib.

the attention of the biblical historians and represents one of the rare instances when a specific project of a Hebrew king can safely be identified archaeologically."[33] Another recent discovery is the highly contested Jehoash Inscription, which charts Jehoash's repairs to the Temple. It also lacks any pictured relief.

Archaeology's "new vision of ancient Israel" supports the fact that YHWH fulfilled his judgment against the nation by erasing her memory from his land. Absence of evidence attests the constancy of the Creator's word and fulfillment of his effacement prophecy. Thankfully, Assyria's archives have preserved much of what has been lost in Israel's Effacement Judgment.[34]

IV. ASSYRIA

A. Shalmaneser III

The first significant account of Assyrian prowess in Syria–Palestine (*c.* 900) is found in an inscription of Shalmaneser III. According to 1 Kgs 20:30–34, Israel's (Northern Kingdom) King Ahab entered into a covenant with Syria's King Ben-hadad. Evidently, Syria promised to restore all the possessions that Ben-hadad's father had formerly seized from Israel. This effected a three-year truce between Syria and Ephraim, which evidently included a military alliance (see Illustration 12.4).

Ahab supplied Syria with Israelite troops when Shalmaneser III, in the 6th year of his

Illustration 12.4. The Kurkh Monolith of Shalmaneser III mentioning King Ahab of Israel, Ben-hadad of Damascus, and the Battle of Qarqar.

reign, campaigned against Syrian territories. This was the year that Ahab died. Shalmaneser's inscription states that "Ahab, the Israelite," sent troops to help the provinces allied with Syria.[35] According to the inscription, this battle was so decisive in Shalmaneser's favor that bodies filled the plain, and the "vast field gave out when it came to bury them."[36] Shortly after this battle, Assyria claimed the territory of Hamath, which had previously been obtained by

David. Israel lost her strategic trade entrance "gate" to the north. The prophet Jonah, who prophesied shortly after Ahab's death, foretold that YHWH would send Israel a savior who would reclaim Hamath for Judah (2 Kgs 14:25). Jeroboam II fulfilled Jonah's prophecy when he conquered Damascus for Samaria and Hamath for Judah (2 Kgs 14:28) at what may have been a time of Assyrian unrest at the beginning of Ashur-dan III's reign (c. 789 BCE). During the 1903–4 expedition at Meggido, archaeologists unearthed a seal that reads, "Shema, servant of Jeroboam" (see Illustration 12.5) Most scholars attribute this to a court official of Jeroboam II.

Illustration 12.5. Found at Megiddo, a signet belonging to a servant of Jeroboam II.

Assyrian inscriptions exhibit many references to Israel following King Ahab. Shalmaneser III (c. 874 BCE) records receiving tribute from Jehu, son of Omri.

> Tribute from Jehu son of Omri; I received from him silver, gold, a golden saplu-bowl, a golden vase with pointed bottom, golden tumblers, golden buckets, tin, a staff for a king and a wooden puruhtu.[37]

Although King Jehu was not the "son of Omri," Assyria's first contact with Israel occurred during Omri or Ahab ben (son of) Omri's reign, so naturally all subsequent kings were recognized as Omri descendants. Assyria called the Northern Kingdom 'Omri Land' while they called the Southern Kingdom 'Judah' (*Ia-u'-da-a-a*; see Illustration 12.6).

Illustration 12.6. Jehu, King of Israel, prostrating himself before King Shalmaneser III of Assyria. Bas-relief on the black stele of Shalmaneser III (9th c. BCE).

B. *Tiglath-pileser III*

After Shalmaneser, many Assyrian inscriptions referring to Israel are corroborated by Judah's annals. Such is the case with Tiglath-pileser III's first incursion into the Northern Kingdom. This text cites Assyria's invasion during Israel's King Menahem's reign.

> Pul the king of Assyria came against the land: and Menahem gave Pul a *thousand talents of silver*, that his hand might be with him to confirm the kingdom in his hand. And Menahem exacted the money of Israel, even of all the mighty men of wealth, of each man fifty shekels of silver, to give to the king of Assyria. So the king of Assyria turned back, and stayed not there in the land. (2 Kgs 15:19–20)[38]

A fragmentary annalistic text from Tiglath-pileser corroborates the Hebrew testimony.

> [As for Menahem, I ov]erwhelmed him [like a snowstorm] and he . . . fled like a bird, alone, and bowed to my feet. I returned him to his place and imposed tribute upon him, to wit: gold, silver, linen garments with multicolored trimmings . . . great I received from him. Israel (lit., 'Omri-Land) . . . *all its inhabitants (and) their possessions I led to Assyria.* They overthrew their king Pekah and I placed Hoshea as king over them. I received from them 10 talents of gold, *1000 talents of silver* as their tribute and brought them to Assyria.[39]

Both Israel's and Assyria's texts attest Ephraim's 1,000 silver-talent tribute. What Tiglath-pileser's text reveals and what is *not* recorded in Scripture is that Israel's *first deportation* occurred during Menahem's reign.

Tiglath-pileser's inscriptions also record the tribute charges and invasion of Judah during Azariah's (Uzziah's) reign. After Assyria had deported much of Syria and northern Israel, Azariah (similar to Hezekiah and Josiah) sought to consolidate the northern regions under his control. During the early years of his regency, Azariah sought YHWH, and the Creator helped strengthen him.

> And he went forth and warred against the Philistines, and broke down the wall of Gath, and the wall of Jabneh, and the wall of Ashdod, and built cities about Ashdod, and among the Philistines. And God helped him against the Philistines, and against the Arabians that dwelled in Gur-baal, and the Mehunims. And the Ammonites gave gifts to Uzziah: and his name spread abroad even to the entering in of Egypt; for he strengthened himself exceedingly. Moreover Uzziah built towers in Jerusalem at the corner gate, and at the valley gate, and at the turning of the wall, and fortified them. (2 Chr 26:6–9)

With his great success, Azariah became proud, however, and sought to burn incense in the Temple, a right given only to the high priest (2 Ch 26:6–9, 16). After this sin, Judah rebelled, and YHWH began to shorten the extent of his kingdom.

An inscription from Tiglath's reign tells us Assyria had received tribute from "Azariah of Judah."[40] Evidently, he considered Azariah (Uzziah) a significant rival. Tiglath devotes a very fair amount of his inscriptions to his act in vanquishing Azariah and receiving a steep tribute from him.

> 19 districts of Hamath, together with the cities of their environs, which (lie) on the shore of the sea of the setting sun, which had gone over to Azariah, in revolt (*lit.*, sin) and contempt of Assyria, I brought within the border of Assyria. My officials I set over them as governors. 30,300 people [I carried off from] their cities and placed them in the province of the city of Ku–.[41]

Fascinatingly, this inscription quite precisely parallels Scripture's account of Azariah's reign. Scripture does not tell us the particulars of Tiglath's invasion into Samaria's former territories, but it does provide the background behind YHWH's weakening of Judah. For critics who claim the books of Kings and Chronicles were simply plagiarized from Assyrian annals, this record (which is not recorded in Scripture) demonstrates the disconnected nature of both Assyria's and Israel's archives, which actually recorded historical events, and as we will later see, fulfilled Israel's Testimonial (Prophetical) Law.

The reign of Assyria's Tiglath-pileser continued during King Ahaz's administration, when war again prevailed between Pekah (Northern Kingdom) and Judah. Pekah had aligned with Rezin, king of Syria, seeking to conquer Judah. In desperation, King Ahaz

> sent messengers to Tiglath-pileser king of Assyria, saying, I am your servant and your son: come up, and save me out of the hand of the king of Syria, and out of the hand of the king of Israel, which rise up against me. And Ahaz took the silver and gold that was found in the house of YHWH, and in the treasures of the king's house, and sent it for a present to the king of Assyria. And the king of Assyria listened to him: *for the king of Assyria went up against Damascus, and took it, and carried the people of it captive to Kir, and slew Rezin.* (2 Kgs 16:7–9)

Tiglath-pileser's inscription witnesses this tribute, stating that Tiglath received tribute from "Jehoahaz king of Judah."[42] Another building inscription corroborates Scripture's account of Damascus's deportation.

> I laid siege to and conquered the town Hadara, the inherited property of Rezon of Damascus, the place where he was born. I brought away as prisoners 800 of its inhabitants with their possessions . . . of the 16 districts of the country of Damascus I destroyed making them look like hills of ruined cities over which the flood had swept.[43]

This same building inscription, which dates to after Tiglath-pileser's 9th year, recounts that in "former campaigns" Assyria had deported Syria's cities.[44] Tiglath states, "The town of Samaria only did I leave."[45]

Another fragmented Akkadian text (Assyria's royal language) with an unknown year cites that Assyria deported Naphtali and other Ephraim territories:

> Byblos, Simirra, Arqa, Zimarra, Uznu, [Siannu], Ri'-raba, Ri'sisu. . . . the towns of the Upper Sea, I brought under my rule. Six officers of mine I installed as governors over them. . . . the town Rashpuna which is situated at the coast of the Upper Sea, [the towns . . .]nite, Gal'za, *Abilakka which are adjacent to Israel (Bît Ḫu-um-ri-a) and the wide land of Naphtali, in its entire extent, I united with Assyria*. Officers of mine I installed as governors upon them.[46]

Scripture corroborates Pul's conquest of this region as well as Israel's second deportation.

> In the days of Pekah king of Israel came Tiglath-pileser king of Assyria, and took Ijon, and Abel-Beth-Maachah, and Jonoah, and Kedesh, and Hazor, and Gilead, and Galilee, *all the land of Naphtali, and carried them captive to Assyria.* (2 Kgs 15:29)

The Book of Chronicles is a third witness to this invasion.

> And the God of Israel stirred up the spirit of *Pul king of Assyria, and the spirit of Tiglath-pileser king of Assyria*, and he carried them away, even the Reubenites, and the Gadites, and the half tribe of Manasseh, and brought them to Halah, and Habor, and Hara, and to the river Gozan, to this day. (1 Chr 5:26)

Scripture's record is in accord with Tiglath-pileser's inscriptions, supporting the claim that by the 9th year of his reign Samaria was about the only city left unseized. As we will see when we study the Testimonial Law, which outlined the consequences for breaching the covenantal pact, each of these deportations had been foretold before Israel entered the Promised Land to claim Abraham's inheritance.

C. Shalmaneser V and Sargon II

Scripture tells us about Samaria's final days.

> In the twelfth year of Ahaz king of Judah began Hoshea the son of Elah to reign in Samaria over Israel nine years. And he did that which was evil in the sight of YHWH, but not as the kings of Israel that were before him. Against him came up *Shalmaneser king of Assyria*; and Hoshea became his servant, and gave him presents. And the king of Assyria found conspiracy in Hoshea: for he had sent messengers to So king of Egypt, and brought no present to the king of Assyria, as he had done year by year: therefore the king of Assyria shut him up, and bound him in prison. Then the king of Assyria came up throughout all the land, and went up to Samaria, and besieged it three years. (2 Kgs 17:1–5)

The Babylonian Chronicle (i.28) agrees with this account, citing: "He [Shalmaneser] ruined Samaria" (see Illustration 12.7).[47] Although Scripture and the Babylonian chronicle agree, King Sargon's inscriptions tell quite a different story. In eight different inscriptions Sargon asserts that *he* was Samaria's conqueror. There is some question whether Sargon actually took Samaria or whether he just attributed the achievements of his predecessor (Shalmaneser) to himself to justify his throne. Adding to this dilemma, Assyrian texts indicate that Sargon II was not Shalmaneser's son or a member of the royal house. From all accounts his legitimacy as a royal heir is questionable. According to K. Lawson Younger, a scholar of Mesopotamian studies at Trinity University,

Illustration 12.7. Tablet with part of the Babylonian Chronicle from southern Iraq (Neo-Babylonian) *c.* 550–400 BCE. The tablet is one of a series that summarizes the principal events each year from 747 BCE to at least 280 BCE.

> Sargon II came to power with the death of Shalmaneser V, who apparently died of natural causes. . . . The ensuing internal difficulties indicated in the sources demonstrate that there was a significant struggle for the throne in Assyria at this time. The accumulative evidence seems to point to an illegitimate power seizure by Sargon (whose name means 'legitimate king'). It was in the midst of this less than smooth transition of power in Assyria in the last years of the 720's that Samaria, the capital of the northern kingdom of Israel, was captured.[48]

Younger concludes that Sargon's conquest of Samaria was part of a campaign that resulted in the capture of Ekron, Gaza, and Raphia on the Egyptian border, but was a separate military campaign from Shalmaneser V's initial siege against Samaria.[49] At any rate, vanquishing Samaria must have been a victory great enough to strengthen the legitimacy of Sargon's reign; Samaria was worth boasting over.

Assyria's siege of Samaria gave Hezekiah opportunity to expand Judah's interests. The Book of Kings records that Hezekiah

> smote the Philistines, even to Gaza, and the borders thereof, from the tower of the watchmen to the fenced city. (2 Kgs 18:8)

The Azekah Inscription confirms Scripture's account, recording Hezekiah's victories over the

> royal city of the Philistines, which [Hezek]iah had captured and strengthened for himself.[50]

It may very well be that Shalmaneser began besieging Samaria, which occupied most of his forces, giving Hezekiah the advantage over Philistia's cities after Shalmaneser's death until Sargon secured his throne and finally toppled Samaria, and deported her people.

1. Only in Isaiah

In the mid 1800s, most scholars doubted that any king by the name of Sargon ever existed. The Book of Isaiah was the only ancient source witnessing this Assyrian king. No other classical writer (not even Herodotus) had testified of Sargon's reign, so the validity of Isaiah's reference was highly contested by nineteenth-century scholars.[51] Not until the archaeologist M. Botta discovered Sargon's palace at modern Khorsabad in the late 1800s did Isaiah's account gain credibility.

Isaiah's once-contested account records,

> In the year that Tartan came to Ashdod (when Sargon the king of Assyria sent him,) and fought against Ashdod, and took it; At the same time spoke YHWH by Isaiah. (Isa 20:1–2)

Sargon's inscriptions not only attest Sargon's existence, they also confirm Isaiah's report.

> In the ninth regnal year I [marched] against [the cities of Ashdod, which is on the coast of the Great Sea.[. . .][the city] of Ashdod.[52]

That Sargon stayed in Assyria while sending his general to do his dirty work is attested by an Eponym Chronicle, which tells us that Sargon stayed "in the land."[53] Sargon's inscriptions also confirm that he captured both Gaza and Ashdod during this campaign, just as Isaiah reports.

2. Israel's Effacement Judgment Imposed

> At the beginning of my royal rule. . . . . the towns of the Samarians I besieged, conquered (2 lines destroyed) for the god who let me achieve this my triumph. . . . *I led away as prisoners 27,290 in habitants* of it and equipped from among them soldiers to man 50 chariots for my royal corps. . . . The town I rebuilt better than it was before *and settled therein people from countries which I myself had conquered.* I placed an officer of mine as governor over them and imposed upon them tribute as is customary for Assyrian citizens.[54]

Sargon's many inscriptions documenting the tribute that he received after his victory over Samaria also record Israel's third deportation. Numbers' Effacement Judgment had stipulated that Israel would be "dispossessed" and "driven out," of the Promised Land if she failed to uphold YHWH's command. The land would then be "divided by a lot among the heathen" (Num 33:54–55). Sargon's inscription witnesses the role that Assyria played in fulfilling this prophecy. Scripture provides a second witness to Sargon's transplanting of foreigners to Canaan's soil, who would be "thorns in the sides" of the few Israelites who remained in the Promised Land.

> And the *king of Assyria brought men* from Babylon, and from Cuthah, and from
> Ava, and from Hamath, and from Sepharvaim, *and placed them in the cities of
> Samaria instead of the Children of Israel*: and they possessed Samaria, and dwelt
> in the cities thereof. (2 Kgs 17:24)

Both Scripture and Sargon's inscription agree. Sargon deported Samaria (Northern Kingdom) while bringing pagan nations to live on Israel's soil. Thus, two sources witness YHWH's
division of the Promised Land, awarding it as an inheritance to the heathen as YHWH
continued to fulfill the Effacement Judgment.

D. Sennacherib

Throughout this era, Canaanite tribes
were forging alliances with Egypt, antic-
ipating deliverance from Assyria's devastating blows. King Hoshea (Samaria) had
joined this sedition, provoking Shalmaneser's invasion (Isa 30:1–4; 2 Kgs 17:4).
Momentum behind this insurgency had
been gaining speed when Sennacherib
directed his third campaign toward the
west, targeting Hezekiah's victories over
Philistia (2 Kgs 18:8). It became obvious to
Hezekiah that Assyria's invasion was in-

Illustration 12.8. Hezekiah's Tunnel.

evitable. In preparation for a prolonged siege, Hezekiah built a conduit to bring water inside
the city walls (2 Kgs 20:20; see Illustration 12.8). Of Sennacherib's siege against Jerusalem,
Scripture records:

> Now in the fourteenth year of king Hezekiah did Sennacherib king of Assyria
> come up against all the fenced cities of Judah, and took them. And Hezekiah
> king of Judah sent to the king of Assyria to Lachish, saying, I have offended;
> return from me: that which you put on me will I bear. And the king of Assyria
> appointed to Hezekiah king of Judah *three hundred talents of silver* and *thirty
> talents of gold*. And Hezekiah gave him all the silver that was found in the house
> of YHWH, and in the treasures of the king's house. (2 Kgs 18:13–15)

Assyrian records provide parallel and fascinating details about Sennacherib's campaign and
siege of Jerusalem as told from the Assyrian perspective. It seems that the territory of Ekron
had originally made peace with Assyria; probably at the cost of a considerable tribute by
Ekron's citizens. Evidently the Ekronites were not enthralled with their king's covenant with
Assyria and defected to Judah's Hezekiah, revolting against their king. Ekron was part of
Philistia's territory, and King Hezekiah had captured the Ekron king, incarcerating him in

Jerusalem. When Sennacherib attacked Jerusalem's suburbs, he took the cities that Hezekiah had conquered, restoring them to their independent tributary status. He also placed a stiff penalty on Hezekiah's aggression into territory that was quickly becoming income tribute for Assyria's coffers. Let Sennacherib share his story:

> The officials, the patricians and the common people of Ekron had thrown Padi, their king, into fetters because he was loyal to his solemn oath sworn by the god Ashur, and had handed him over to Hezekiah, the Jew and he (Hezekiah) held him in prison, unlawfully as if he (Padi) be an enemy. He (Hezekiah) had become afraid and had called for help upon the kings of Egypt and bowmen, the chariots and the cavalry of the king of Ethiopia, an army beyond counting—and they actually had come to their assistance. . . . I fought with them and inflicted a defeat upon them. In the melee of the battle, I personally captured alive the Egyptian charioteers with their princes and also the charioteers of the king of Ethiopia . . . I made Padi, their king, come from Jerusalem and set him as their lord on the throne, imposing upon him the tribute due to me as overlord.

> As to Hezekiah, the Jew, he did not submit to my yoke, I laid siege to 46 of his strong cities, walled forts and to the countless small villages in their vicinity, and conquered them by means of well-stamped earth-ramps, and battering-rams brought thus near to the walls combined with the attack by foot soldiers, using mines, breeches as well as sapper work. *I drove out*[55] of them 200,150 people, young and old, male and female, horses, mules, donkeys, camels, big and small cattle beyond counting, and considered them booty. Himself I made a prisoner in Jerusalem, his royal residence, like a bird in a cage. I surrounded him with earthwork in order to molest those who were leaving his city's gate. His towns which I had plundered, I took away from his country and gave them over to Mitinti, king of Ashdod, Padi, king of Ekron, and Sillibel, king of Gaza. Thus I reduced his country, *but I still increased the tribute and the presents due* to me as his overlord . . . did send me, later, to Nineveh, my lordly city together with *30 talents of gold* and *800 talents of silver*, precious stones.[56]

Illustration 12.9. The Taylor-Prism, from Niniveh, northern Iraq *c.* 691 BCE. This six-sided baked clay document is a foundation record, intended to perserve Sennacherib's achievements for posterity and the gods. The prism records Sennacherib's third campaign, the destruction of 46 cities in Judah and the deporation of 200,150 people. Hezekiah, king of Judah, is reported to have sent tribute to Sennacherib.

Remarkably, both Assyrian and Israelite annals mention the 30 gold talents that were required as Judean tribute (see Illustration 12.9). The 500-talent discrepancy (the difference between the reference to 300 talents of silver in Judah's record and the 800 talents in the Assyrian record) between these two accounts might be explained by Hezekiah's scribes' composing his annals before Sennacherib "increased the tribute and presents due." The recorder's statement in 2 Kgs 18:15, "And Hezekiah gave him all the silver that was found in the house of YHWH, and in the treasures of the king's house," may reflect a later insertion into the record to witness the increased silver tribute.

It has been argued by some scholars that during Judah's latter years ambassadors were sent to gather information from Assyria's royal archives so that Judah could redact or re-create its national history in the form of nationalistic propaganda. If this were true, we should expect to find complete harmony between Judah's and Assyria's annals, since Judahite scribes were just "copying" Assyria's texts.[57] Had there been uniformity between Assyrian and Hebrew (Israelite) texts, there would be just cause for concern. That there are minor deviations between records testifies to the authenticity of Israel's records, not plagiarism of Assyria's archives.

1. Lachish

During Sennacherib's Palestinian campaigns, he besieged Lachish. The prophet Micah witnessed this city's destruction and the deportation of its citizenry, prophesying against Lachish's sins.

> O you inhabitant of Lachish, bind the chariot to the swift beast: she is the beginning of the sin to the daughter of Zion: for the transgressions of Israel were found in you . . . make the bald, and poll you for your delicate children; enlarge your baldness as the eagle; for *they are gone into captivity from you.* (Mic 1:13, 16; see also Isa 36:2; 37:8)

Sennacherib considered Lachish's conquest to be such a feat that he ordered three different epigraphs to commemorate the city's final defeat (see Illustration 12.10).

2. Sennacherib's Death

During Sennacherib's campaign, he reviled Israel and her God. His general purposely spoke in Hebrew (2 Kgs 18:26-8) so that all Jerusalem could hear his polemic against Israel's God. He advised Hezekiah not to put any trust in YHWH: all the other Palestinian nations had trusted their gods, but they were no match for Assyrian might (2 Kgs 18:29-35). To top it off, Sennacherib's general arrogantly claimed to have YHWH on Assyria's side (2 Kgs 18:25). Isaiah prophesied against Assyria's king:

> Behold, I will send a blast on him, and he shall hear a rumor, and return to his own land; and I will cause him to fall by the sword in his own land. (Isa 37:7)

Scripture records the fulfillment of this prophecy.

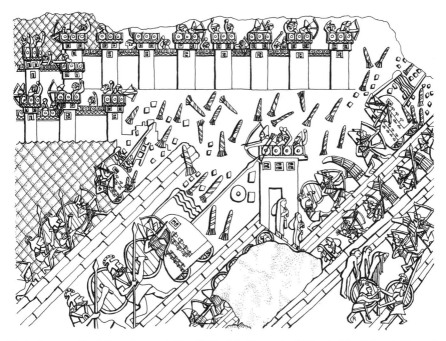

Illustration 12.10. Depiction of a carved 8th *c.* BCE relief at Sennacherib's South-West Palace in Nenevah. The bas-relief scene depicts the seige of the Judahite city of Lachish.

> Sennacherib king of Assyria departed, and went and returned, and dwelled at Nineveh. And it came to pass, as he was worshipping in the house of Nisroch his god, that Adrammelech and Sharezer his sons smote him with the sword; and they escaped into the land of Armenia: and Esar-haddon his son reigned in his stead. (2 Kgs 19:36–37; see also Isa 37:37–38)[58]

A Babylonian Chronicle (BM 84–211, 92) provides corroborating evidence of Scripture's account: "On the 20th day of Tebitu Sennacherib, king of Assyria, was slain by his son in a revolt."[59] Sennacherib's younger son and appointed heir apparent, Esarhaddon, tells the story in his own words:

> A firm [determination] "fell upon" my brothers. They forsook the gods and turned to their deeds of violence, plotting evil word(s) and deed(s), contrary to the will (lit., heart) of god, they perpetrated against me. Unholy hostility they planned behind my back. . . . To gain the kingship they slew Sennnacherib, their father. (Prism S)[60]

Evidently, Sennacherib had chosen his youngest son, Esarhaddon, as his successor. He took oaths from the Assyrian nation and his older sons to uphold this decision. When

Esarhaddon entered the former crowned prince's palace, it dawned on his brothers that their younger brother would be king over them. The older brothers proceeded to Nineveh, provoking a revolt that Esarhaddon easily squelched. The brothers then "fled to an unknown country."[61] The annals of Esarhaddon's son, Ashurbanipal, describe these rebels' fate:

> The others, I smashed alive with *the very same statues of protective deities with which they had smashed my own grandfather—Sennacherib*.[62]

That Ashurbanipal employed idols as the implements with which to kill Sennacherib supports Isaiah's testimony that Sennacherib's death occurred in an Assyrian temple. Thus once again there is harmony between Scripture and history.

E. Esarhaddon and Ashurbanipal

After Samaria's deportation, Assyria's "Omri-Land" no longer existed. During this era, Assyrian texts simply refer to Ephraim's former territories as "Hatti," in reference to the Hittites who had once dominated the Palestinian region before Israel's exodus. Esarhaddon's and Ashurbanipal's texts use the term *Hatti* as including Judah in its territory. The Book of Ezra records that Esarhaddon and Ashurbanipal twice imported foreign nations into the Promised Land as YHWH continued to enforce the Effacement Judgment and divide Israel's land for an inheritance among the heathen:

> Then they came to Zerubbabel, and to the chief of the fathers, and said to them, Let us build with you: for we seek your God, as you do; and we do sacrifice to him since the days of Esar-haddon king of Assur, which brought us up here. (Ezra 4:2)

Of this Syro-Palestinian Campaign, Esarhaddon's annals state:

> I settled therein people from the mountain regions and the sea(shore) of the East, those who belonged to me as my share of the booty. I set over them officers of mine as governors.[63]

Esarhaddon deported native Egyptians into eastern Assyrian lands, subduing the entire Levant. Unlike his father, however, Ashurbanipal spent more time quelling insurrections than conquering new territories. During one of the many "Hatti" rebellions, foreigners were again imported into the Promised Land as Israel's Effacement Judgment continued to be fulfilled. YHWH continued to fulfill the covenant's penalties for Israel's breach of contract.

In another account, Ezra describes Assyria's former campaigns on Israel's soil. Ezra recounts Assyria's resettlement of her captives, referring to Ashurbanipal as "Asnappar":

> Then wrote Rehum the chancellor, and Shimshai the scribe, and the rest of their companions; the Dinaites, the Apharsathchites, the Tarpelites, the Aphar-sites, the Archevites, the Babylonians, the *Susanchites,* the Dehavites, and the

Elamites, And the rest of the nations whom the great and noble Asnappar brought over, and set in the cities of Samaria, and the rest that are on this side of the river. (Ezra 4:9–10)

Ashurbanipal's inscription corroborates Ezra's account of Elam's deportation and his sack of Susa (Ezra's Susanchites, mentioned above).

I broke their gods, appeasing the heart of the lord of lords. His gods, his goddesses, his goods, his property, the people small and great I carried off to Assyria. Sixty double-hours within Elam (Susa's capital city) I laid waste, scattering salt and tares thereon.[64]

According to Ezra's account, Ashurbanipal later transplanted these vanquished people into Samaria's former territory. During this campaign, Ashurbanipal invaded Judah, capturing King Manasseh. The Book of Chronicles records:

Wherefore YHWH brought on them the captains of the host of the king of Assyria, which took Manasseh among the thorns, and bound him with fetters, and carried him to Babylon. And when he was in affliction, he sought YHWH his God, and humbled himself greatly before the God of his fathers, and prayed to him: and he was entreated of him, and heard his supplication, and brought him again to Jerusalem into his kingdom. Then Manasseh knew that YHWH he was God. (2 Chr 33:11–13)

Both Esarhaddon's and Ashurbanipal's inscriptions attest that Manasseh was king of Judah during their reigns.[65] Manasseh is listed along with 12 Kings from the "land of Hatti," which included Tyre, Gaza, Ashkelon, Ekron, and Ashdod; and he is further designated as a king by the "sea coast." Assyria's kings usually invaded after tribute was abjured, requests were not complied with, or an uprising occurred. Assyria's invasion evidences that Manasseh had thrown off Assyria's yoke, no doubt aligning himself with King Tarha-qa of Egypt.[66]

Ashurbanipal had a knack for subduing stubborn kings who refused to oblige tribute. One inscription relates how Ashurbanipal handled one obstinate Arab king.

I "put a dog's collar on him and made him watch the bar of the city's gate." A paralleled inscription records: "I put a pillory on his neck together with a bear and a dog and made him stand on guard (duty) at the gate in Nineveh."[67]

If Ashurbanipal imposed a punishment on Manasseh for his rebellion similar to this Arabic king's, we can see the humor in Manasseh's soon-found humility to "greatly humble himself before the God of his fathers" (2 Chr 33:12).

V. NINEVEH

Nineveh was a magnificent city. The ancient historian Diodorus Siculus (2.3) gives Nineveh's dimensions as 150 stadia on the two longest sides of the quadrangle and 90 on the opposite, the square being 480 stadia or about 60 square miles. Jonah states that the city took three days to cross (3:3). When Henry Layard uncovered the empire's remains in 1848, he discovered that the original city encompassed four building sites.

> If we take the four great mounds of Nimroud (Nineveh), Kouyunjik, Khorsabad, and Karamles, as the corners of a square, it will be found that its for sides correspond pretty accurately with the 480 stadia, or 60 miles of the geographer, which make the three days' journey of the prophet. [68]

Within its vast walls, Nineveh supported cattle and croplands, which enabled the city to endure sieges for several years. The Greek historian and mercenary Xenophon (*c.* 400 BCE) calculated Nineveh's circumference to be about 24 miles (*Anab.*3.4)

Judeo-Christians often focus on the God of the Old Testament as being concerned with justice and righteousness in Israel alone and having little or no concern for those who were not "the seed of Abraham." This is hardly the case. During Assyria's epoch as superpower, YHWH sent Jonah to warn Nineveh to turn from her iniquity. This call for repentance not only demonstrates that Assyria was to some degree familiar with YHWH's Law, it also demonstrates that at one time Assyria understood YHWH's righteous standard. It also underscores the Creator's desire to save Nineveh from her suicidal policies. Jonah's mission was effective. Even the king and nobles repented (Jonah 3). YHWH did not overthrow the city at the end of Jonah's 40-day period. History attests, however, that Nineveh's repentance was short-lived because the people quickly returned to their sins. YHWH caused Nabopolassar (Nebuchadnezzar's father) to destroy the city a short time later.

Zephaniah had poetically prophesied of Nineveh's destruction:

> He will stretch out his hand against the north, and destroy Assyria; and will make Nineveh a desolation, and dry like a wilderness, *And flocks shall lie down in the middle of her.* (Zeph 2:13–14)

Three hundred years after Nineveh's destruction, the city remained barely visible for the Greek historian Xenophon (*Anab.* 3, 4, 7) to describe its remains. Today, some 2,500 years later, Nineveh is a parched land—a wilderness covered with layers of sand and silt. Fascinatingly, archaeologists find that springs once flourished in this region,[69] which is ironic considering Zephaniah's prophecy. Before Layard's rediscovery of Nineveh's ruins in the 1800s, the natives of this region called one of the mounds covering the ancient city Tel Kouyunjik, 'Mound of Many Sheep.' See Illustrations 12.11 and 12.12 to see how completely desolate Nineveh is today.[70]

Illustration 12.11. Flocks of sheep pasture on top of modern-day Nineveh's once prominent gate.

Illustration 12.12. Sennacherib's once illustrious palace throne room (Room 1) at Sennacherib's Palace Site Museum, Nineveh.

VI. BY THE WATERS OF BABYLON

A. *Nahum Brings Comfort*

YHWH banished Israelites from the Promised Land, exiling them to lands far east of the Euphrates. Assyria deported Samaria four times, deporting the Southern Kingdom of Judah once during Hezekiah's reign, as YHWH divorced a rebellious generation (Isa 50:1; Jer 3:8). After Esarhaddon had vanquished the Northern Kingdom, Ephraim was "no more" a nation (Isa 7:8). Assyria's super-prowess, however, came to an end even before Israel ceased as a nation. Soon after Jonah's visit, Nineveh returned to its injustices and wicked ways. It was at this time that Nahum sent prophecy to comfort Jacob (Judah) by describing Assyria's fall and the end of her vexation of Judah.

> And it shall come to pass, that all they that look on you shall flee from you, and say, Nineveh is laid waste: who will bemoan her? From where shall I seek comforters for you? (Nah 3:7)

Nineveh's fall would be a public example of a once-impregnable city obliterated. It was the ancient "shot heard around the world."

In the closing years of Assyria's majesty, the Chaldeans organized under Nabopolassar, who labeled himself "the king of Akkad."[71] Nabopolassar began campaigning against Assyria during his 10th year. Two years later, the Medians attacked, plundered, and massacred Assyria's population. Nabopolassar allied with these plundering Medes, establishing a covenant with their king, Cyaxares, in Nabopolassar's 12th year.[72] Cyaxares retreated from his assaults, recognizing Nabopolassar's territorial rights to Assyria as Akkad's king. Two years later, Nabopolassar, in his 14th year, called on his covenant with Cyaxares to march against Nineveh and, in his own words, turned Nineveh into "ruin-hills."[73] Nineveh's history was finished.

B. *Nebuchadnezzar*

1. "My Servant Nebuchadnezzar"

YHWH termed Nebuchadnezzar "my servant" when he brought Babylon against Jerusalem, foretelling,[74]

> Behold, I will send and take all the families of the north, says YHWH, and Nebuchadnezzar the king of Babylon, *my servant*, and will bring them against this land, and against the inhabitants thereof, and against all these nations round about, and will *utterly destroy* them, and make them an astonishment, and an hissing, and perpetual desolations. (Jer 25:9)

YHWH recognized Babylon as the tool he would employ for fulfilling the Effacement Judgment because of Israel's breach of the Numbers 33 command. Nebuchadnezzar was YHWH's servant because he fulfilled the Creator's judgment by "destroying Israel's pictures, all their molten images; deporting them to Babylonian and former Assyrian territories; and plucking down (burning) all their high places," which included Solomon's Temple. Nebuchadnezzar left only the poorest of Israel's citizens to be "pricks and thorns" in the eyes and sides of the heathen whom Assyria had imported into the land (2 Kgs 24:14).

2. Babylon's Record

The harmony between Nebuchadnezzar's inscriptions and Scripture is extraordinary. Jeremiah reports that Nebuchadnezzar's reign commenced during Jehoiakim's 4th year (Jer 25:1). Seven years later, he besieged Jerusalem, replacing Jehoiakim's son, Jehoiachin (also known as Jechoniah or Coniah), with his younger brother Mattaniah, and changing his name to Zedekiah. Nebuchadnezzar's 7th-year annal records this event:

> Year 7, month Kislev: The king of Akkad mustered his army and marched against Hattu. He encamped against the city of Judah and on the second day of the month Adar he captured the city (and) seized (its) king. A king of his own choice he appointed in the city (and) taking the vast tribute he brought it into Babylon. (ABC 5)[75]

Scripture attests that 11 years later Nebuchadnezzar once again besieged Jerusalem.

> Now in the fifth month, in the tenth day of the month, which was the nineteenth year of Nebuchadnezzar king of Babylon, came Nebuzaradan, captain of the guard, which served the king of Babylon, into Jerusalem, and burned the house of YHWH, and the king's house; and all the houses of Jerusalem, and all the houses of the great men, burned he with fire: and all the army of the Chaldeans, that were with the captain of the guard, broke down all the walls of Jerusalem round about. (Jer 52:12–14)

Jeremiah's chronology of Nebuchadnezzar's reign coincides directly with Babylon's inscriptions. Jer 52:12 even preserves the name of Nebuchadnezzar's captain of the guard, calling him Nebuzaradan, whereas Nebuchadnezzar's prism inscription calls him "Nabuzeribni."[76] Another recently translated Babylonian temple receipt confirms another official whom Jeremiah mentions in Jerusalem's final siege. Jeremiah lists Nebo-Sarsekim (Jer 39:3) as one of Nebuchadnezzar's chief rulers. The recently translated receipt confirms Nebo-Sarskim (Nabu-sharrussu-ukin in Akkadian) served as chief eunuch.[77]

Cuneiform and classical sources agree that Nebuchadnezzar reigned 43 years.[78] This is consistent with Jeremiah's testimony that the 1st year of Evil-merodach (Akkadian, Amel-Merduk) occurred during the 37th year of Jehoiachin's captivity (Jer 52:31–34; 2 Kgs 25:27–30). From this point forward, the Babylonian chronicles become very confusing. Nebuchadnezzar's son Amel-Merduk (Evil-merodach) reigned at least 2 years, and the "prince" Nergal-sharezer mentioned in Jer 39:3 is known to have ascended to Babylon's throne.[79] After this, Babylon's annalistic texts and inscriptions become even more indecipherable, due perhaps in part to the fact that Cyrus effaced Nabonidus's inscriptions, his predecessor, and sought to defame his memory as part of Persia's propaganda policy.[80]

Nabonidus, Babylon's last reigning monarch, may very well be the "Nebuchadnezzar" to whom Daniel refers. Scholars observe striking parallels between the Babylonian accounts of Nabonidus's mental instability and Daniel 4.[81] According to Babylonian records, Belshazzar's 1st year corresponded with Nabonidus's 1st year away from Babylon.[82] Some scholars conclude that Nabonidus was Nebuchadnezzar's son-in-law.[83] This fits well into Daniel's chronology, which places Nabonidus's mental illness before the rise of his son Belshazzar. It also explains Daniel's elevation to the "third" position in the kingdom and not the second (Dan 5:7, 16, 29). Many Babylonian usurpers had tried to commandeer Nebuchadnezzar's fame and reputation by attributing his name to themselves, which may be why Daniel called Nabonidus "Nebuchadnezzar."

YHWH promised *his servant* Nebuchadnezzar that his lineage would retain Babylon's throne for three generations.

> Now I will hand all your countries over to my servant Nebuchadnezzar king of Babylon; I will make even the wild animals subject to him. All nations will *serve him and his son and his grandson* until the time for his land comes; then many nations and great kings will subjugate him. (Jer 27:6–7, NIV, 1984)

Nebuchadnezzar's line remained in power for two generations after his death. His line ended when Cyrus executed Nebuchadnezzar's grandson, Belshazzar. YHWH similarly used this method with King Jehu, who had rendered a service to YHWH by destroying Ahab's offspring. He, too, was promised a royal line until the fourth generation (2 Kgs 10:30). YHWH had established the limits of his mercy for righteous deeds in his Law.[84] Since Nebuchadnezzar served YHWH by fulfilling the Creator's judgment of Jerusalem, the Creator bulwarked Babylon's throne for three generations until, like Jehu, his sons became steeped in wickedness. Then YHWH judged Babylon by the same standard as he did Israel or Nineveh, using Persia's Cyrus to render his judgment against Babylon and Nebuchadnezzar's House.

C. Jeremiah's Desolation

1. Prophecy of Psalm 137

Throughout the ancient Near East, temple liturgists performed songs in the temple's sacred precincts.[85] Israel's Psalms were not intended just to praise the Creator; they were also meant to prophesy. Perhaps no psalm demonstrates this better than Psalm 137.

> By the rivers of Babylon, there we sat down, yes, we wept, when we remembered Zion.
>
> We hung our harps on the willows in the middle of it. For there they that carried us away (a) captive required of us a song; and they that wasted us required of us mirth, saying, Sing us one of the songs of Zion.

How shall we sing YHWH's song in a (b) strange land?

(e) If *I* forget you, O Jerusalem, let *my* right hand forget her cunning. If I do not remember you, let my tongue cleave to the roof of my mouth; if I prefer not Jerusalem above my chief joy. Remember, O YHWH, the children (c) of Edom in the day of Jerusalem; who said, Raze it, raze it, even to the foundation of it. O daughter of Babylon, (d) who is to be destroyed; happy shall he be, that rewards you as you have served us. Happy shall he be, that takes and dashes your little ones against the stones.

Jeremiah borrows much of Psalm 137 in his prophecies against Babylon by building on King David's former psalm. Jeremiah lived during the twilight of Israel's kingdom years, as Numbers' Effacement Judgment concluded and the Jerusalemites began to hang their harps on Babylon's willow trees. Knowing that (a) captivity and (b) exile were the Creator's determined decree, Jeremiah encouraged Jerusalem to submit to Babylon's yoke and avoid further bloodshed:

> Seek the peace of the city where I have caused you to be carried away captives, and pray to YHWH for it: for in the peace there of shall you have peace. (Jer 29:7; see also Jer 20:4).

Jeremiah's message for Israel to submit was not exclusive; he encouraged all Syro-Palestinian nations to yield to Nebuchadnezzar's yoke (Jeremiah 27).

Jeremiah continues to follow and fulfill David's prophecy in Psalm 137. Jeremiah (c) "remembers the children of Edom" in Jeremiah 49 and prophesies of a holocaust for Esau's wicked children that would compare with Sodom and Gomorrah's overthrow. Notice how closely Jeremiah's words parallel David's:

> Concerning Edom, thus said YHWH of hosts; Is wisdom no more in Teman? is counsel perished from the prudent? is their wisdom vanished? Flee you, turn back, dwell deep, O inhabitants of Dedan; for I will bring the calamity of Esau on him, the time that I will visit him. . . . But I have made Esau bare, I have uncovered his secret places, and he shall not be able to hide himself: his seed is spoiled, and his brethren, and his neighbors, and he is not. Leave your fatherless children, I will preserve them alive; and let your widows trust in me. . . . For I have sworn by myself, said YHWH, that Bozrah shall become a desolation, a reproach, a waste, and a curse; and all the cities of it shall be perpetual wastes. . . . For, lo, I will make you small among the heathen, and despised among men. . . . Also Edom shall be a desolation: every one that goes by it shall be astonished, and shall hiss at all the plagues of it. As in the overthrow of Sodom and Gomorrah and the neighbor cities thereof, said YHWH, no man shall abide there, neither shall a son of man dwell in it. . . . Therefore

hear the counsel of YHWH, that he has taken against Edom; and his purposes, that he has purposed against the inhabitants of Teman: Surely the least of the flock shall draw them out: surely he shall make their habitations desolate with them. (Jer 49:7–8, 10–13, 15, 17–18, 20)

David's decree in Psalm 137 prophesied against Babylon's offspring by calling them *the daughter of Babylon*: "O daughter of Babylon, (d) who is to be destroyed; happy shall he be, that rewards you as you have served us." Jeremiah reissues and continues David's prophecy in Psalm 137 by prophesying:

For thus said YHWH of hosts, the God of Israel; The *daughter of Babylon* is like a threshing floor, it is time to thresh her: yet a little while, and the time of her harvest shall come. Nebuchadnezzar the king of Babylon has devoured me, he has crushed me, he has made me an empty vessel, he has swallowed me up like a dragon, he has filled his belly with my delicates, he has cast me out. (Jer 51:33–34)

Another part of David's decree stated, "Happy shall he be, *that rewards you as you have served us*" (Ps 137:8). Compare David's decree with Jeremiah's carefully worded "reward" prophecy for Babylon:

The violence done to me and to my flesh be on Babylon, shall the inhabitant of Zion say; and my blood on the inhabitants of Chaldea, shall Jerusalem say. Therefore thus said YHWH; Behold, I will plead your cause, and take vengeance for you; and I will dry up her sea, and make her springs dry. And Babylon shall become heaps, a dwelling place for dragons, an astonishment, and an hissing, without an inhabitant. (Jer 51:35–37)

David's prophetic psalm commissioned Jeremiah's prophecy. *King David passed a "prophetical baton" to Jeremiah, commissioning his prophetic message.* Jeremiah fulfilled his role in Israel's history by continuing David's prophecy and adding more information to it. In every instance, Jeremiah used Psalm 137 as his guide when prophesying in regard to Babylon, Edom, and Jerusalem.

2. If I Do Not Remember

In the opening chapters of Jeremiah's testimony, he states that YHWH knew him before his birth.

Before I formed you in the belly I knew you; and before you came forth out of the womb I sanctified you, and I ordained you a prophet to the nations. (Jer 1:5)

No other prophet writes that YHWH knew him before conception. So why would Jeremiah acknowledge that YHWH knew him and ordained his work before his birth?

King David, through YHWH's spirit (2 Sam 23:2), ordained Jeremiah's prophetic mission to Israel and the nations of the world. Ps 137:5 ordained the "remembering of Jerusalem" after its citizens had been deported:

> If (e) *I* forget you, O Jerusalem, let my right hand forget her cunning. If **I** do not remember you, let **my** tongue cleave to the roof of **my** mouth; if **I** prefer not Jerusalem above my chief joy. (Ps 137:5–6)

Notice the usage of the personal pronoun "I." Psalm 137 is written as the prophecy of a specific person who would remember Jerusalem as YHWH's chief joy. Reassuringly, Jeremiah fulfills David's prophecy and obeys his commission when he "remembers" Jerusalem again. He prophesies:

> For thus said YHWH, That after seventy years be accomplished at Babylon I will visit you, and perform my good word toward you, in causing you to return to this place. For I know the thoughts that I think toward you, said YHWH, thoughts of peace, and not of evil, to give you an expected end. (Jer 29:10–11; see also Jer 3:17)

Jeremiah fulfills David's prophecy by ordaining the reestablishment of Jerusalem. But how does this demonstrate that YHWH knew Jeremiah before conception? The title of Psalm 137, which was written well over 200 years before Jeremiah's birth, prophesies: "A Psalm of Jeremiah."

VII. JEREMIAH 50-51

Modern doctrine often associates the Old Testament's prophecies against Babylon with modern political and religious systems that are perceived as retaining Babylon's ancient ideologies (Rev 18:4). Israel's prophets, however, specifically recognize "Babylon" as a distinct territory of land, despite any nation that obtained control over the region (Assyria, Chaldea, Persia, Greece, etc.). The words of Israel's prophets focus on the "land of Babylon" and not necessarily on the Chaldeans per se.

This is the case with events that transpired after Babylon's fall to Persia. Originally, Jeremiah wrote prophecies against Babylon during Jehoiakim's 4th year (Jer 46:2). Jeremiah commissioned these prophecies to be written in a separate book (Jer 51:59) from his prophecies about Egypt (Jer 51:59–64) or Israel. Today, his prophecies regarding Babylon comprise chaps. 46–51. This particular book contains prophecies against Canaan's many nations and describes world history by outlining events to befall each nation. Ch. 46 is written against Egypt; ch. 47 against Philistia; 48 against Moab; and ch. 49 against Ammon, Edom, Syria–Damascus, and Kedar of Hazor.

A. Jeremiah's Five-Step Judgment Plan

Jeremiah's prophecies begin with an era of judgment: Nebuchadnezzar will subjugate Syria–Palestine, judgment will continue until lands are nothing but dry deserts; then, at last, there will arise latter-day salvation, redemption, and restoration. Jeremiah's words against the nations maintain the constancy of prophecy found in the Diaspora Covenant by outlining each nation's judgment, Diaspora, captivity, and latter-day restoration.[86] Jeremiah's prophecy establishes five phases of world history:

1. The coming of Babylon, which commences an era of Judgment against the nations—Jer 46:13, 26; 49:28; Nah 2–3:7.

2. Judgment continues: the nations become drunk in Babylon's wine (doctrine)—Jer 48:26; 49:12; 51:7, 39, 57; Nah 3:11.

3. Nations join together—Jer 49:14; 50:9, 41; Joel 3:2–15.

4. The nations are made desolate and scattered while continuing in Babylonian doctrine and drunkenness from her wine—Jer 48:42, 44; 49:17–18, 33, 35–38; 50:12–13, 26, 39, 45; 51:43; Zeph 3:8; Nah 3:18; Isa 63:6.

5. In the latter days, each nation is restored to its inherited land and learns to live righteously—Jer 30:18–22; 48:47; 49:6; 50:17–20, 39; 51:9–10.

B. Babylon's Judgment Day

Although the "Day of Babylon" judgment commenced when the nation fell to Cyrus, king of Persia, it did not end there. YHWH would also judge the gods in whom she trusted and on whom she leaned for protection just as he had the Egyptians back in the sixteeth century. Many of these deities were associated with the ceremony that legitimized the Babylonia king's right to rule over Babylon. By destroying these protective deities, YHWH proved that they had no power to restore the Babylonian monarchy or its national fortunes.

Jeremiah continues his chronological testimony in ch. 50: "Declare you among the nations, and publish, and set up a standard; publish, and conceal not: say, Babylon is taken, Bel is confounded, Merodach is broken in pieces; her idols are confounded, her images are broken in pieces" (Jer 50:2; see also Isa 46:1; Jer 51:44). Scholars attribute Jeremiah's prophecy to what befell Babylon's deities when Xerxes "made Babylon an ordinary satrapy. He ordered the destruction of Marduk's great temple, E-sagila, which Alexander found in ruins, and removed from it the statute of Marduk, thus rendering meaningless the accession ceremony of taking the hands of Bel."[87]

After YHWH destroyed Babylon's images, Jeremiah describes the Second Temple Remnant's return to Zion under Ezra in v. 4–5, foretelling:

> They shall *ask the way to Zion* with their faces toward it. (Jer 50:5, KJ Bible 2000/2003)

This event was fulfilled when Ezra and his company sought the safest way to return to Jerusalem, also known as Mt. Zion.[88] Ezra states that he

> proclaimed a fast there, at the river of Ahava, that we might afflict ourselves before our God, to *seek of him a right way for us*, and for our little ones, and for all our substance. (Ezra 8:21)

Truly, Ezra fulfilled Jeremiah's words when his company sought the way to Zion.

King Solomon had requested of YHWH to listen to Israel when she prayed toward the Temple (1 Kgs 8:30). YHWH agreed to this request. When Israel lived too far away to visit the Temple or in a time of captivity (1 Kgs 8:46–54; 9:3). Daniel claimed this promise by praying toward the Temple (Dan 6:10), and certainly Ezra (Ezra 8:23, 31) and his party claimed YHWH's promise as well by asking the way "with their faces toward Jerusalem," fulfilling Jeremiah's prophecy.

Jer 50:5 continues the prophet's chronology of world events, predicting that the Second Temple Remnant would "join themselves to YHWH in a perpetual covenant that shall not be forgotten." This event transpired during the nation's first Jubilee back in the Promised Land, in Artaxerxes' 7th year, when the Remnant renewed Israel's ancient covenant with YHWH:

> Now therefore let *us make a covenant* with our God to put away all the wives, and such as are born of them, according to the counsel of my lord, and of those that tremble at the commandment of our God; and let it be done according to the law. (Ezra 10:3)

Nehemiah affirmed Ezra's account. After the priest Ezra's arrival, the elders "made a sure covenant, and wrote it; and their princes, Levites, and priests, sealed to it" (Neh 9:38; see Table 9.48, on p. 426).[89] Thus, the returned Remnant, the Daughter of Zion, agreed once again to all the covenants' blessings and curses (i.e., Deut 27–30).

Jer 50:6–7 continues the chronology of the Second Temple Remnant by stating that soon after Ezra's and Nehemiah's days this Remnant would follow many false shepherds:

> My people have been lost sheep: their shepherds have caused them to go astray, they have turned them away on the mountains: they have gone from mountain to hill, they have forgotten their resting place. (Jer 50:6)

Jeremiah's prophetic accusation is substantiated by the testimony of Ezra, Nehemiah, and Zechariah, who wrote that this wicked generation rebelled against every Law that YHWH had given (Nehemiah 5, 13; Ezra 9). As we shall see in the chapters below, the shepherds, the leaders of Israel were Judah's chief offenders.

Jer 50:8 continues Jeremiah's prophetic chronology by foretelling events to transpire on Babylon's land. Mass exodus out of Babylon would be a hallmark of this epic. Heeding Jeremiah's warning of Babylon's impending Day of Vengeance, many people would flee her territory. Jeremiah (50:9–14) continues to describe the nations that would continue to assault Babylon during the Second Temple Era, until she was finally rendered desolate.

> Remove out of the middle of Babylon, and go forth out of the land of the Chaldeans, and be as the he goats before the flocks. For, see, I will raise and cause to come up against Babylon an assembly of great nations from the north country: and they shall set themselves in array against her; from there she shall be taken: their arrows shall be as of a mighty expert man; none shall return in vain. And Chaldea shall be a spoil: all that spoil her shall be satisfied, said YHWH. Because you were glad, because you rejoiced, O you destroyers of my heritage, because you are grown fat as the heifer at grass,[90] and bellow as bulls; Your mother shall be sore confounded; she that bare you shall be ashamed: behold, the *last* of the nations shall be a wilderness, a dry land, and a desert. Because of the wrath of YHWH it shall not be inhabited, but it shall be wholly desolate: every one that goes by Babylon shall be astonished, and hiss at all her plagues. (Jer 50:8–13; see Illustration 12.13)

The Hebrew *'achariyth,* "last" in Jer 50:12 means 'a latter end.'[91] This is the same word that Jacob used in Gen 49:1 to express the events to occur in the 12 tribes' last days. Therefore, Jeremiah's prophecy could not denote Babylon's fall to Cyrus, when the city was subjugated and lost prominence but still existed. Rather, Jer 50:9–14 addresses her ultimate latter days, when she had wholly become a "wilderness, a dry land, and a desert that shall not be inhabited" (Jer 50:12–13). Jeremiah 50–51 continue to "laminate together" or synchronize this prophecy in several layers. This repetitive process in effect hides or veils the events in Babylon's near future.

The rest of Jeremiah's prophecies against the nations continue to delineate the veil cast over the nations through the drunkenness of Babylonian-based doctrines (Jer 51:7; 48:26; 49:12). And Jer 50:44 speaks of Alexander, the youthful Babylonian king (Alexander conquered Babylon) who will liken himself to YHWH and who will destroy many nations, including the land of Babylon.[92] Jeremiah 49:19 appends another layer to world history when his prophecy of Alexander falls in prophecies against Edom and coincides with those against Babylon. As we study Israel's Testimonial Law, we will see that Jeremiah 50–51 directly follows the chronology set forth in Israel's Prophetic Law, as Jeremiah once again bases his testimony on the covenantal Law bestowed at Mt. Sinai.

Illustration 2.13. Modern day ruins of the once bustling city of Babylon.

VIII. HADASSAH, MORDECAI, AND PSALM 45

The Book of Esther tells us that Nebuchadnezzar deported Mordecai along with Ezekiel and Jeconiah (Est 2:6 and Ezek 1:2) when he established Zedekiah on Judah's throne. Nabopolassar had wasted Nineveh only five years before, and it is likely that Cyaxares remained the Median king at the time of Mordecai's captivity. The Assyrians had established Israelite communities in the Median cities of Halah and Habor (2 Kgs 17:6, 1 Chr 5:26) during Samaria's exile, and Nebuchadnezzar probably deposited refugees into these already established Israelite communities.[93]

The Book of Esther tells us that Mordecai was Esther's cousin (she was his "uncle's daughter"—2:7). While Mordecai was old enough to raise Esther, there probably were no more than 50-60 years between them in age. What this implies is that Esther's husband and king should be identified with either Cyrus or another Persian monarch before him. If Esther was born after her parents' deportation in 597 BCE, then she was a young maiden no later than 540-530 BCE. Even allowing for her to be born 20 years later (although her father would probably have been a generation older than Mordecai), this still means that Esther was at a marriageable age no later than 510 BCE. Thus, Cyrus and other nobles in the Persian Empire probably should be identified as Esther's sons.

A. Susa

Elam, the patriarch of the Elamite nation, was a descendant of Shem (Gen 10:22). Elam's capital was located in "Shushan" or "Susa." The Assyrians once devastated this territory, and Ezra tells us that Ashurbanipal transplanted Elamite and Susaite refugees to Israel's Samaria–Palestine during Ephraim's last deportation.[94] When Nineveh fell to Nabopolassar, the Chaldeans firmly secured Susa as a Babylonian province.[95] Babylon had held Susa for quite some time before Daniel saw a vision while he resided at the palace in Susa. The Septuagint renders this text:

> In the third year of the reign of King Belshazzar, a vision appeared to me, even me Daniel, after that which appeared to me at the first. *And I was in Susa the Palace, which is in the land of Elam, and I was on the bank of the Ubal.* And I lifted up my eyes and saw . . . (Dan 8:1–3, LXX)

According to Daniel, Babylon held onto Susa as late as Belshazzar's 3rd year before Susa fell to Persia.

Susa boasted an impressive palace. Although the Persians erected many palaces, Susa became their favorite. Strabo (15.3.3) tells us that the Persians "adorned the palace at Susa more than any other." Darius I left an Old Persian inscription that described the building of his Susa palace:

> The gold was brought from Sardis and from Bactria, which here was wrought. The precious stone lapis lazuli and carnelian which was wrought here, this was brought from Sogdiana. The precious stone turquoise, this was brought from Chorasmia, which was wrought here. The silver and the ebony were brought from Egypt. The ornamentation with which the wall was adorned that from Ionia was brought.[96]

Darius's inscription parallels Esther's account, accurately describing Susa's Achaemenid home:

> Where were white, green, and blue, hangings, fastened with cords of fine linen and purple to silver rings and pillars of marble: the beds were of gold and silver, upon a pavement of red, and blue, and white, and black, marble. (Est 1:6)

Esther's reference to tapestry hangings is intriguing in light of texts excavated at Susa that manifest the city to be a center for textile production.[97] Fascinatingly, scholars observe that these tablets refer to garments of various styles and colors and to carpets and bed coverings.[98] Once again, Scripture is historically accurate and gains increasing reliability when compared with other historical and archaeological data.

B. Psalm 45

Many Christians, who are only slightly familiar with Scripture have heard the story of Esther. Most people, however, are unaware that David foretold of Esther's heroism long before she was born. How long before Esther's birth did he prophesy of her?

King David prophesied about Hadassah (Esther's Hebrew name) some 400 years prior! Psalm 45 speaks of Hadassah. Remember that the Psalms are prophecies hidden within praises to Israel's God (see chap. 8.IV). The prophecy in Book of Psalms foretells *not only* events to occur in Israel's future but also of people who will play an important role in the nation's story. (Evidence demonstrating the fulfillment of this prophecy will be inserted into parentheses in the text.) Let King David tell you what would happen to Hadassah in his own words:

My heart is inditing a good matter: I speak of the things which I have made touching the king: my tongue is the (a) pen of a ready writer. You are (b) fairer than the children of men *(Hadassah as a "maid was fair and beautiful"— Esth 2:7)*: grace is poured into your lips: therefore God has blessed you forever. Gird your sword on your thigh, O most mighty, with your glory and your majesty. And in your majesty ride prosperously because of truth and meekness and righteousness; and your right hand shall teach you terrible things. Your (c) arrows are sharp in the heart of the king's enemies; whereby the people fall under you. Your throne, O God, is forever and ever: the sceptre of your kingdom is a right sceptre. You love righteousness, and hate wickedness: therefore God, *your God, (d) has anointed you with the oil of gladness above your fellows (Esth 2:9).* All your garments smell of myrrh, and aloes, and cassia, out of the (e) ivory palaces *(Esth 2:12)*, whereby they have made you glad. Kings' daughters (f) were among your honorable women: on your right hand did stand the queen in gold of Ophir.

Listen, *O daughter*, and consider, and incline your ear; (g) forget also your own people *(fulfilled—Esth 2:10, 20)*, and your father's house; So shall *the king greatly (d) desire your beauty (Esth 2:17): for he is your lord*; and worship you him. And the daughter of Tyre shall be there with a gift; even the rich among the people shall intreat your favor. The king's daughter is all glorious within: her clothing is of wrought gold. She shall be brought to the king in raiment of needlework: the virgins her companions that follow her shall be brought to you *(indicates the maids in waiting of another would be given to Hadassah).* With gladness and rejoicing shall they be brought: they shall enter into the king's palace. Instead of your fathers shall be your children, *whom (h) you may make princes in all the earth. I will make (i) your name to be remembered in all generations*: therefore shall the people praise you forever and ever. (Psalm 45, parentheses added)

Hadassah fulfilled this psalm. She was (b) beautiful; chosen above all others; and lived in an (e) exquisite palace. Esther (g) forgot her own people before she was chosen to be queen, but remembered her people and her father's house when she used her womanly (c) arrows to save her people from the hatred of an evil governor. Since she was faithful and beautiful in every way, the king greatly (b, d) admired her and she found favor in his sight. Quite uncoincidentally, Hadassah was given another queen's (f) maids in waiting (i.e., Vashti).

And, Esther's hand (a) was ready both to write her own biography and to write orders protecting her people (Esth 8:1–13). Today, Hadassah's Babylonian (i) "name has been very well remembered unto all generations." From preschool to adulthood, Esther's heroic story is retold. Psalm 45 also provides a very interesting clue in Scripture's chronology of (h) Persian kings. "Instead of your fathers shall be your children, *whom you may make princes in all the earth*" (Ps 45:16). This verse clearly states that Esther will make her sons "princes in the earth." Does Scripture evidence that this indeed took place? Nehemiah's request for permission to go to Jerusalem presents a tantalizing possibility:

> Then the king said to me, For what do you make request? So I prayed to the God of heaven. And I said to the king, If it please the king, and if your servant has found favor in your sight, that you would send me to Judah, to the city of my fathers' sepulchers, that I may build it. And the king said to me, (*the queen also sitting by him*,) For how long shall your journey be? and when will you return? So it pleased the king to send me; and I set him a time. (Neh 2:4–6)

Why would Nehemiah mention a queen sitting beside the king? Could it be that the queen was Artaxerxes' mother (or grandmother), Hadassah? Nehemiah provides another clue by intentionally using *shegal*[99] as the word for queen in v. 5. The only other time this word is used is in Ps 45:9 when referring to the queen of Ophir.

The Book of Psalms prophesied that Jeremiah would remember Jerusalem and that the story of Hadassah's becoming queen would be remembered unto "all generations." YHWH both foresaw and foretold Israel's history. David knew what to prophesy for Israel's future when he wrote Psalms since he looked to the nation's Prophetic Law (Isa 8:20) and statutes (Ps 119:54), which defined all of Israel's prophecies. YHWH's spirit further led him to see how to apply his covenantal Testimony. Jeremiah also understood the 70-year period for Israel's exile by looking to the nation's Testimonial Law. As we shall see in the next section, the Testimony outlined, defined, and foretold Israel's future chronologically. The Testimonial Law, given as part of the nation's covenantal constitution, is where we can begin to test and see whether YHWH is righteous.

Part 2

Lifting the Veil: The Testimonial Law

13

Tabernacle of Testimony

I. THE NATURE OF PROPHECY

A. *The Constitutional Testimony*

Up till now, our study has focused on establishing the historical validity of the Hebrew Scriptures. Thus far, we have seen that Israel's Scriptures demonstrate fact, "the body of real things and real events" (see chap. 1.II.C). At this point, we will shift gears to focus on the theology that YHWH gave to Israel. We will develop our understanding of this theology directly from the written Hebrew Scriptures. When I had studied these issues, there were several questions that I needed to discover for myself. Is YHWH's word constant (chap. 1. II.C-D)? Does he rescind promises or contradict himself? Does he adhere to his own Law that he may be shown righteous? We will build on what we have learned in part 1 of this book in order to see how this understanding helps us to interpret Israel's theology, beginning with Israel's Testimonial Law (Isa 8:16, 20).

In chap. 3, we saw that one of the final aspects of ancient treaties consisted of penalties for breach of agreement. In ancient treaties, these consisted of blessings for complying with the treaty or curses for breaching the covenantal pact.[1] YHWH had given Israel two national covenants: the Sinai Covenant and the Moab-Shechem (Deuteronomy) Covenant. The covenant, its blessings and curses were customarily deposited in the national temple archives, to be read periodically to the people.[2] In Israel, this public reading occurred during the Release-year at Sukkot, every seven years (Deut 31:9–13; 1 Kgs 8:8:9), when the nation gathered to reaffirm the nation's treaty. Moses had deposited Israel's two national covenants (the Sinatic and Moabic) into the *Ark of Testimony* (Deut 10:1–5; 31:24–28).

Historically, ancient covenants consisted of nine formal parts. The most important parts were the Preamble, Prologue, Stipulations, and the blessings for obedience and curses for disobedience. Scriptural covenants had the added (tenth) feature of the sign of compliance. For the Sinai Compact, the sign was the Sabbath holidays (Exod 31:13–17). **Israel's Testimony—the formal document that YHWH had originally etched in stone—was the formal covenant document and was deposited in the Ark of the Testimony inside the Temple (Exod 25:16).** While the Ten Commandments were the stipulations of Israel's covenant (Exodus 20), the blessings and curses formed a chronological Law all prophecies followed based on Leviticus 26. It is this formal covenant-treaty that forms the nation's formal Testimony (see pp. 68–72, 310–312). Thus, the promises and penalties (blessings and curses) portion of Israel's covenant with God forms an entirely separate division of Israel's Law that formally became known as the "Testimony" (Isa 8:20; Ps 19:7).

Moses merged the two tablets containing YHWH's Testimony into the *Law of Moses* today known as the Pentateuch. YHWH specifically commanded Moses to place the Testimony inside the *Ark of the Testimony* or *Ark of the Covenant*. "You [Moses] shall put into the ark *the Testimony* which I shall give you" (Exod 25:16). This formal treaty declaration lay safely encapsulated in the protective ark, safe from any who would seek to alter or deface any facet of YHWH's treaty with the nation.

B. Veiling the Testimony

The second time that Moses received YHWH's covenant at Mt. Sinai, he fulfilled YHWH's request by placing the Ten-Commandment Testimony in the *Ark of the Covenant:*

> At that time YHWH said to me, Hew you two tables of stone like to the first, and come up to me into the mount, and make you an ark of wood. And I will write on the tables the words that were in the first tables which you brake, and *you shall put them in the ark.* . . . And he wrote on the tables, according to the first writing, the ten commandments, which YHWH spoke to you in the mount out of the middle of the fire in the day of the assembly: and YHWH gave them to me. And I turned myself and came down from the mount, and *put the tables in the ark which I had made*; and there they be, as YHWH commanded me. (Deut 10:1–5)

The Tabernacle housed the ark bearing YHWH's covenantal Testimony. The Testimony defined the ark's purpose and the Tabernacle's prophetic structure as the ark of the Covenant became known as "the Ark of Testimony" (Exod 25:22; 26:33–34) and the Tabernacle became the "Tabernacle of Testimony" (Num 1:50, 53; 9:15). Although Moses merged the book (or inscription) of Testimony into of the *Law of Moses* (the Pentateuch), **Israel's prophets consistently recognized the Testimony as a separate but parallel Book of the Law (Ps 78:5; 19:7; Isa 8:20).** By symbolically placing the Testimony inside the ark in the Holies of Holies and setting it behind the veil, YHWH symbolically *hid* the Testimony's consequences for Israel's breach of pact.[3]

Notice that it was not the *Law of Moses* (i.e., requirements—statutes, judgments, and laws) YHWH veiled, but the Testimony (consequences for breaching the covenant) that

YHWH had Moses symbolically hide, veil, and enshroud in the Tabernacle's most Holy Place. This is why a later Levitical scribe divided the written record of the Testimony's stipulations (the Ten Commandments—Exodus 20) from the Testimony's curses (Leviticus 26) in the Pentateuch by placing each in separate manuscripts. This division obscured the straightforward penalties for breaching the pact. YHWH hid the Testimony (prophecy) found in the covenant's penalties by dividing the Testimony in the Law of Moses, thus separating the covenant's penalties from the covenant's stipulation. In this way, YHWH hid the Testimony in his Law, leaving it to a latter-day generation to seek and find his truth.[4]

After Israel rebelled in the wilderness, YHWH cast off Israel's rebellious generation, choosing to reestablish his covenant with their children. He offered the next generation the same covenant (the Ten Commandments, Deuteronomy 5) in the plains of Moab, as he had at Mt. Sinai. The penalty portion of the Moab Covenant, however, granted more detail and greater specificity than Leviticus 26's penalties had by foretelling each national deportation. Today, the penalty for the breach of the Moab–Shechem Covenant is found in Deuteronomy 27–30.[5]

C. The Prophetic Testimony

YHWH's Testimony demonstrates his fidelity and faithfulness to Abraham's descendants as *the covenants that were contracted with Israel's patriarchs (Noah, Abraham, Isaac, and Jacob) form the bedrock of the entire Testimonial or Prophetic Law* (see Table 3.16 on p. 121). The Testimonial Law listed YHWH's judgments against Israel until the nation's latter-day restoration, when the Diaspora Covenant is fulfilled. The dividing of the Testimony both hid and obscured YHWH's judgments for Israel's breach of pact, and it is the reason that Israel's prophets write that YHWH will cause the judgments found in his Testimony to rest for a light to his people in the latter days (Isa 51:4; Zeph 3:5).[6]

Accurately foretelling Israel's future, the Testimony provided a chronological *Prophetic Law* that all Israel's prophets faithfully followed. Today the Testimony has been scattered throughout the Torah, with each Book of the Law containing a very distinct but *parallel* prophecy for Israel's future. The following table shows the abridged Prophetic Law:

Table 13.1. Abridged Testimonial Law

Genesis	Covenants form a chronological outline	All patriarchal covenants
Exodus	Tabernacle of Testimony	Exodus 25–31
Leviticus	Seven Times	Leviticus 26
Deuteronomy	Blessings and Curses	Deuteronomy 27–30
Numbers	Balaam's Blessing	Numbers 23–24

When YHWH offered the Promised-Land Covenant to Abraham (Genesis 15), he hid in it a prophecy against Egypt that called for a Day of Judgment. YHWH's method of hiding of a time of judgment is consistently employed. Intriguingly, he hides a "Day of Judgment" against Israel inside his covenantal Law.[7] Remember that Abraham's divided sacrifice (Gen

15:10) symbolized the fate of the one offering the covenant, if that person did not fulfill his promises. This self-imprecating sacrifice symbolized YHWH's fate should the Creator fail to uphold his part of the covenant (pp. 70–76, 90–92, 99–101, 106, 147–48). It was this act that had caused Abraham to believe his God (Gen 15:6). Later, Israel took a similar self-imprecating oath when she partook of the Passover sacrifice and entered into a covenant with God at Mt. Sinai. She had pledged to obey YHWH's constitutional Law and to walk in his ways or to bear the judgment penalties for breach of contract. Within the curses outlined in the Testimony, YHWH specifies several very specific days or eras of judgment when the penalties in his Law would rain down on the people in a horrific sacrificial holocaust.

Though YHWH had openly and fully disclosed these consequences, the manner in which the Hebrew Scriptures were later edited obscured and hid these blatantly-disclosed consequences. YHWH's Testimonial Law (Leviticus 26 and Deuteronomy 28–30) follows the precedent established in the Promised-Land Covenant by hiding YHWH's judgment of Israel's breaching her covenant with YHWH. Israel's prophets, who consistently adhered to the Testimonial Law, followed this precedent of a hidden judgment by obscuring YHWH's *Day of Vengeance* against Israel in their testimonies as well. The following prophecies in Israel's Law show specific Days of Eras or judgment.

Table 13.2. Specific Days (Times) of Judgment

Effacement Judgment	Num 33:50–56
The "Day of YHWH" (KJV: "Day of the Lord")	Deuteronomy 32; Gen 9:5
Burnt-Offering Covenant	Genesis 22
Jealousy Judgment: Drinking Cursed Waters	Numbers 5; Deut 29:18–21
Judgment against Israel's enemies	Deut 32:39–43; 30:7

Israel's prophets intentionally obscure, veil, or hide Israel's Judgment Day in their books. This is why Isaiah writes, "*To the law and to the testimony: if they speak not according to this word, it is because there is no light in them*" (Isa 8:20; see also Ps 19:7). While the Law demonstrates the precepts for a way of life that works, the Testimonial aspect of the Law provides a chronological prophetic timeline for Israel's future.

II. YHWH'S WITNESSES

When the Levites judged court cases, YHWH had commanded that truth could not be established by the word of only one witness.

One witness shall not rise up against a man for any iniquity, or for any sin, in any sin that he sins: at the mouth of two witnesses, or at the mouth of three witnesses, shall the matter be established. (Deut 19:15).[8]

There is a proverb within this verse: the testimony of two or three witnesses establishes a matter. YHWH has obeyed his own Law (he has not acted arbitrarily) with the prophets commissioned to warn Israel. When he ordained his prophets to witness against Israel's sins or to testify what would befall other nations, *there were at least two or more prophets witnessing the same account.* In other words, for every prophecy spoken by the mouth of one prophet, one or two other prophets speak the same word.

Contrast this to a false prophecy. The Book of Enoch (*c.* 200 BCE) is a testimony that did not make the Catholic canon but is quoted throughout the Gospels of the New Testament. The author of Enoch states that *only he* had knowledge of the secrets that the "lord of the spirits" gave him (1 Enoch 19:3). This statement is an example of one way to detect falsehood. Truth will be established in the mouth of two or three prophets, or in the case of the Law and its prophecies, the entire nation of Israel witnessed YHWH's Testimony (Josh 24:22; Exod 20:18–22; and Isa 43:10).

III. TESTIMONIAL LAW/PROPHETIC LAW

During Moses' conversation with YHWH on Sinai, YHWH established Israel's first prophecy in the Tabernacle's structure and statutes. The *Tabernacle of Testimony*'s prophetic structure coincided with the Testimonial Law, the latter defining the structure and statutes used in the Tabernacle. Both the Tabernacle in the wilderness and the First Temple (along with the Law's statutes and judgments) synchronize with the Testimonial Law of Leviticus 26 (Sinai) and Deuteronomy 28–31 (Moab-Shechem). The Book of Psalms continues to "laminate" the Testimonial Law by adhering more detailed layers to the Law's already-stated chronological prophecies.

David tells us that the Law's statutes had governed his many Psalms, as the statutes surrounding the Tabernacle had inspired his many prophetic praises.

Your statutes have been my songs in the house of my pilgrimage. (Ps 119:54)

David understood the purpose and symbolism of the statutes used in the Tabernacle. He based his prophetic praises on the Law's prophetic statutes. David's many "Psalms of Statute" continue to hide and preserve the Tabernacle's symbolism, structure, furniture, and purpose. We will examine many aspects of the Testimonial-Prophetic Law and its relationship to the books of Psalms and Proverbs in the chapters below.

IV. TABERNACLE OF TESTIMONY

The Prophetic Law in the Book of Exodus is found within the structure and statutes surrounding the Tabernacle. This structure prophesied Israel's future and ordained the testimony of her prophets. Both the Tabernacle in the wilderness and the later Temple designed by David represented the nation of Israel. When YHWH deported the Israelites, and they ceased to exist as a nation, the Temple was destroyed. Likewise, when the nation returned to the land after King Cyrus's decree, the Temple was rebuilt. It is on the Temple's statutes and structure that David and his chief musician, Asaph, based the Psalms, which provide wonderful definitions for understanding the Tabernacle's and Temple's implements.

A. Lamp of Seven with Pure Candlestick

When YHWH's glory descended upon Mt. Sinai, a cloud veiled the mount for six days. On the seventh day the Creator called Moses to the summit. They first discussed plans for a tabernacle. Central to the Tabernacle's service was a seven-branched pure golden candlestick (see Illustration 13.1). This was the instruction YHWH spoke to Moses:

> Their knops and their branches shall be of the same: all it shall be one beaten work of pure gold. And you shall make the *seven lamps* of it: and they shall light the lamps of it, that they may give light over against it. (Exod 25:36–37)

> You shall command the Children of Israel, that they bring you pure olive oil beaten for the light, *to cause the lamp to burn always.* (Exod 27:20; see also Lev 24:2, 4)

Illustration 13.1. A reconstruction of the First Temple menorah.

David used the Tabernacle's statutes to form the bedrock of his prophetic Psalms by using meaningful symbolic imagery and definitions within his songs. Such is the case with Ps 119:105, which defines the golden lamp as representing YHWH's word:

> *Your word* is *a lamp* to my feet, and a light to my path. (Ps 119:105)

There are many Hebrew words for "lamp." Gen 15:17, for instance, refers to a "smoking furnace, and a burning *lamp*" that "passed between the pieces." The Hebrew word for lamp here is *lappiyd*, which means 'to shine or flame' and is usually indicative of a torch.[9] This is not, however, the word used for the Tabernacle's pure golden lamp. *Niyr* is a primary root word meaning 'to glisten: as in a lamp or a light.'[10] The first time Scripture employs this word is in Exodus's description of the seven-branched candlestick. So when David refers to the *niyr* in Ps 119:105, he is referring to the seven-branched candlestick that represented YHWH's word of truth to his people. The lamp gave light to the *path of life* that YHWH had given Israel to follow by endowing her with the knowledge of his Law.

The prophet Samuel maintained David's definition of the *niyr* as YHWH's word.

> And the child Samuel ministered to YHWH before Eli. *And the word of YHWH was precious in those days; there was no open vision.* . . . And ere *the lamp (niyr) of God* went out in the temple of YHWH, where the ark of God was, and Samuel was laid down to sleep. (1 Sam 3:1, 3)

The Tabernacle's lamp symbolized the truth (word) and knowledge (light) that YHWH sends to his people. This is why 1 Sam 1:1 qualifies the extinguished lamp with the fact that there was no other source for truth. Although the lamp's light burned out due to Eli's blindness, this event symbolically represented knowledge ceasing in Israel and the nation's dwelling in darkness.[11] A short time later, the Philistines captured the Ark of the Covenant (1 Samuel 4), and the Tabernacle at Shiloh was abandoned as the people reaped the consequences for their idolatry. Similarly, the prophet Zechariah, saw a vision of a seven-lamped candle and was told that it represented *the word of YHWH*.

> And said to me, What see you? And I said, I have looked, and behold a candlestick all of gold, with a bowl on the top of it, and his *seven lamps on it,* and seven pipes to the seven lamps, which are on the top of it: And two olive trees by it, one on the right side of the bowl, and the other on the left side of it. So I answered and spoke to the angel that talked with me, saying, What are these, my lord? Then the angel that talked with me answered and said to me, Know you not what these be? And I said, No, my lord. Then he answered and spoke to me, saying, **This is the word of YHWH** to Zerubbabel, saying, Not by might, nor by power, but by my spirit, says YHWH of hosts. (Zech 4:2–6)

B. Showbread

The showbread, literally, the 'bread before your face,' also represented God's open word.[12] Being unfermented[13] it was pure and uncorrupted.

> And you shall set on the table shewbread before me always. (Exod 25:30)

God's unleavened bread represented his pure, un-fermented word of truth to Israel. It sat out in the open, fully disclosed to the entire nation of Israel. She had no need to wonder about or fret over what YHWH required of her. YHWH had fully disclosed his covenant's requirements at Mt. Sinai and ratified them again in Moab-Shechem. Israel's pure bread was made daily and was always present to Israel so she could live by the word of her God:

> Man does not live by bread only, but by every word that proceeds out of the mouth of YHWH does man live. (Deut 8:3; see Illustration 13.2)

C. Stones and the Altar of Earth

YHWH established a symbolic and prophetic definition for stones in the statutes surrounding the Tabernacle. Although Scripture uses the word "stones" in various instances, there is one meaning intended: stones represent the 12 tribes of Israel.

Illustration 13.2. The Table of Showbread was always visible to Israel's congregation.

> And you shall take two onyx stones, and grave on them *the names of the Children of Israel: Six of their names on one stone, and the other six names of the rest on the other stone, according to their birth.* . . . And you shall put the two stones on the shoulders of the ephod for stones of memorial to the Children of Israel: and Aaron shall bear their names before YHWH on his two shoulders for a memorial. (Exod 28:9–12)

> And you shall make the breastplate of judgment with cunning work. . . . *And the stones shall be with the names of the Children of Israel, twelve, according to their names, like the engravings of a signet; every one with his name shall they be according to the twelve tribes.* . . . And Aaron shall bear the names of the Children of Israel in the breastplate of judgment on his heart, when he goes in to the holy place, for a memorial before YHWH continually. And you shall put in the breastplate of judgment the Urim and the Thummim; and they shall be on Aaron's heart, when he goes in before YHWH: and Aaron shall bear the judgment of the Children of Israel on his heart before YHWH continually. (Exod 28:15–22, 29–30)

Both the stones in the shoulders of Aaron's ephod and those on the breastplate represented the 12 tribes of Israel. Scripture contains two notable references to stones in an *earthen altar* that consistently maintain the idea of stones as symbolically representing Israel's 12 tribes.

> And Elijah *took twelve stones, according to the number of the tribes of the sons of Jacob*, to whom the word of YHWH came, saying, Israel shall be your name: And with the stones he built an altar in the name of YHWH. (1 Kgs 18:31–32)

> An altar of earth you shall make to me, and shall sacrifice thereon your burnt offerings, and your peace offerings, your sheep, and your oxen: in all places where I record my name I will come to you, and I will bless you. *And if you will make me an altar of stone, you shall not build it of hewn stone: for if you lift up your tool on it, you have polluted it.* Neither shall you go up by steps to my altar, that your nakedness be not discovered thereon. (Exod 20:24–26; see also Deut 27:5)

Elijah's actions demonstrate that even stones in an earthen altar represent the 12 tribes of Israel: each stone depicting one tribe. Daniel also follows the Law's statute (Exod 20:24–26) in his prophecy of a "stone cut without hands" (Dan 2:34) that destroys the nations. *A stone that is not cut with hands is an unhewn stone.* Daniel's prophecy is consistent with the Diaspora Covenant, which prophesies that a righteous, latter-day nation will become a great mountain that will fill the whole earth.[14]

The Hebrew word for "stones" (in the above verses) is *'eben*, which means an ordinary stone that is used in the building process.[15] Scripture uses a different word, *tsuwr*, to refer to the Creator. *Tsuwr* means a large cliff or large boulder.[16] While Scripture uses ordinary (or even precious) stones to represent Israel, YHWH is symbolically represented as a "mighty cliff" or "rock" (*tsuwr*):

> Because I will publish the name of YHWH: ascribe you greatness to our God. He is the *Rock (tsuwr)*, his work is perfect: for all his ways are judgment: a God of truth and without iniquity, just and right is he. (Deut 32:3–4)

> And he said, *YHWH is my rock (tsuwr)*, and my fortress, and my deliverer; *The God of my rock*; in him will I trust: he is my shield, and the horn of my salvation, my high tower, and my refuge, my savior; you saved me from violence. I will call on YHWH, who is worthy to be praised: so shall I be saved from my enemies. (2 Sam 22:2–4)

> Truly my soul waits on God: from him comes my salvation. He only is my rock (*tsuwr*) and my salvation; he is my defense; I shall not be greatly moved. (Ps 62:1–2)

YHWH is the massive, mighty rock. Israel is a stone that is *not* cut out of the rock by human hands but by YHWH's divine calling. Israel will become the stone YHWH cut out of the *tsuwr*, which will supplant all nations.

D. Horns of the Altar

At each corner of the Tabernacle's altar were peaked points, thrusting upward, called horns (see Illustration 13.3). These horns symbolically represented strength. Israel's prophets often employ horns to depict strong nations. David, in particular, associates strength and salvation with his usage of horns:

Illustration 13.3. Reconstruction of an ancient Israelite horned altar (based on the remnants of the original one) as it was used to sacrifice animals at Beersheba.

> YHWH is my *rock*, and my fortress, and my deliverer; my God, *my strength*, in whom I will trust; my buckler, and the *horn of my salvation*, and my high tower. (Ps 18:2)
>
> For you are the *glory of their strength*: and in your favor our *horn* shall be exalted. (Ps 89:17)
>
> He also exalts the *horn of his people*, the praise of all his saints; even of the Children of Israel, a people near to him. Praise you YHWH. (Ps 148:14)
>
> Amos also associates horns with strength. "For you have turned judgment into gall, and the fruit of righteousness into hemlock: You which rejoice in a thing of nothing, which say, Have we not taken to us *horns by our own strength*?" (Amos 6:12–13).[17]

A horn's righteous strength is based on the constitutional precepts and judgments found in YHWH's Law. When a person takes unrighteous horns by his own strength, he dismisses the Law's sound precepts of equity to follow a way of life that is unjust. The prophets consistently use horns to depict strength, regardless of whether that strength that is righteous or not.

E. Veiling the Holy of Holies

> And you shall hang up the veil under the clasps, that you may bring inside *within the veil the ark of the testimony*: and the *veil shall divide to you between the holy place and the most holy*. And you shall put the *mercy seat* on the ark of the testimony in the most holy place. And you shall set the table without the veil, and the candlestick over against the table on the side of the tabernacle toward the south: and you shall put the table on the north side. (Exod 26:33–35)

And he took and put the testimony into the ark, and set the staves on the ark, and put the mercy seat above on the ark: And *he brought the ark into the tabernacle, and set up the veil of the covering, and covered the ark of the testimony;* as YHWH commanded Moses. (Exod 40:20–21)

YHWH's glory resided within the most Holy Place (Exod 40:34–38), yet it was veiled and hidden from the sight of both the common priest and the people. Both Israel's Testimony and the mercy seat rested behind this curtain. The high priest was the only person ever to see the seat of mercy or the ark bearing Israel's Testimony. Moses' act of veiling the *Ark of Testimony* portrayed YHWH's hiding the knowledge of who he is by *obscuring the evidence for his mercy*, the non-arbitrary nature of his righteousness, and the prophets' prophetic adherence to his Law. King Solomon indicated that the Creator's reasons for obscuring (or hiding) truth were so that, when humanity is finally ready to adhere to his Law, YHWH can be sought out and glorified by the knowledge of what had been hidden within Scripture. "It is the glory of God to conceal a thing: but the honor of kings is to search out a matter" (Prov 25:2). "The *secret of YHWH* is with them that fear him; and *he will show them his covenant*" (Ps 25:14). When humanity searches for his Creator in sincerity and truth (Josh 24:14), YHWH will be glorified through the covenants that he has contracted with Israel's patriarchs.[18]

1. Wine Symbolizes Doctrinal Error

One instruction that affected the *Tabernacle of Testimony's* role in Israel's history was YHWH's command that forbade the high priest to drink wine or other liquor when he entered the Tabernacle.

YHWH spoke to Aaron, saying, **Do not drink wine nor strong drink**, you, nor your sons with you, when you go into the tabernacle of the congregation, lest you die: it shall be a statute forever throughout your generations: And that you may put difference between holy and unholy, and between unclean and clean; And that you may teach the Children of Israel all the statutes which YHWH has spoken to them by the hand of Moses. (Lev 10:8–11)

YHWH introduced this injunction so that the high priest could accurately discern between truth and error and correctly teach God's precepts to Israel. Imagine what could happen if the priest entered the Tabernacle drunk and imagined that YHWH had spoken to him when he had not? Thus, the instruction was practical.

Second, Scripture consistently used this allegorically rich symbol of wine to represent doctrinal error, as demonstrated in the following texts.

But they also have **erred through wine**, and through strong drink are out of the way; the priest and the prophet have **erred through strong drink**, they are swallowed up of wine, they are out of the way through strong drink; they err in vision, they stumble in judgment. For all tables are full of vomit and filthiness, so that there is no place clean. (Isa 28:7–8)

The princes of Zoan are become fools, the princes of Noph are deceived; they have also seduced Egypt, even they that are the stay of the tribes thereof. *YHWH has mingled a perverse spirit in the middle thereof:* and they have caused Egypt **to err** in every work thereof, **as a drunken man staggers** in his vomit. (Isa 19:13–14; see also Isa 29:8–16)

For their rock is not as our Rock, even our enemies themselves being judges. For their vine is of the vine of Sodom, and of the fields of Gomorrah: their grapes are grapes of gall, their clusters are bitter: **Their wine** is the poison of dragons, and the cruel venom of asps. (Deut 32:31–33)

Wine is a mocker, **strong drink** is raging: and **whosoever is deceived** thereby is not wise. (Prov 20:1)

Babylon has been a golden cup in YHWH's hand, that made all the earth **drunk:** the nations have **drunk of her wine**; therefore the nations are mad. (Jer 51:7)

The priest's abstinence from wine symbolized the soundness of his doctrine, while drunkenness denoted doctrinal error. At Israel's exodus, YHWH instructed the nation to observe a feast of "unfermented" or "unleavened" bread for seven days (Exod 12:15). Ancient societies did not use the commercial granules of yeast we use to make bread today. In ancient times, flour and water were allowed to sit in the open air to collect yeast and become *fermented* as the dough rose.[19] A prior batch of fermented dough could be added to a new loaf of bread, but even this was allowed to sit and ferment until it soured and became ready to bake, usually 12–24 hours later. (This method is very similar to what we today call "Amish bread" or sourdough bread.)

Fermentation was the common method for making bread, very similar to the fermentation process used to procure wine. So YHWH's command for Israel to abstain from "fermented" things during the feast of unleavened bread indicated an era during which YHWH bestowed truth to Israel as the nation journeyed to Sinai to receive the covenantal Law. That YHWH had indeed given the nation "unfermented" doctrine is evidenced in the words of Deuteronomy.

You have *not eaten bread, neither have you drunk wine or strong drink*: that you might know that I am YHWH your God. (Deut 29:6)

The feast of "unfermented bread" celebrated this time in Israel's history, when the Creator established his uncorrupted truth with Abraham's descendants as promised in Gen 17:7 and symbolized it in the showbread.

Compare the statute that forbade wine (Lev 10:8–11) with the Law's instructions' calling for many of Israel's sacrifices (holocausts) and offerings to be accompanied with wine (drink) offerings. YHWH even ordained the daily sacrifice (Num 28:2–6) that was offered in the Holy Place to be sacrificed with "strong wine."[20] This symbolic ritual prophesied of false doctrines entering into Israel's most sanctified and set apart beliefs. This implied that doctrinal error or doctrinal drunkenness would be the issue that provoked YHWH's judgment, thus affecting Israel's many prophetic sacrifices or holocausts during the day of YHWH.[21]

> And I will *tread down the people in mine anger*, and make them **drunk** in my fury, and I will bring down their strength to the earth. (Isa 63:6)

Both David and Asaph built on the Law's statutes, which associated wine (doctrinal error) with YHWH's wrathful judgments in their prophetic songs.

2. Wine (False Doctrine) Brings YHWH's Judgment

Today, we see all sorts of negative effects from intoxication. Few of us have not been touched by someone who has a drinking problem—from the drunk who searches for the right key to his car to no avail to the drunk who finds it but then loses the road ahead, or worse, loses the road, only to run into another car or tree to injure himself, his passengers, or another car head on. False doctrine often works the same way. Sometimes our error only affects us as we lose our way: our ideas and philosophies of right and wrong, truth and error live in a shade of gray. Other times, we find a way but go down a wrong path. Sometimes we injure ourselves; other times we make it home fine. However, when we consistently follow a risky path, the chances are that we will end up injuring others through our error before we let go of the substance that appears to give us so much comfort. Yet, much like the "blue pill,"[22] it is the drug that blinds us to the truth of its own destructive nature.

YHWH saw that a persons' lust for comfort and his desire to evade personal responsibility were much like strong drink. In fact, the Israelites' charge against YHWH's way of life had alleged that their children's teeth were "set on edge" (Jer 31:29–30), not because of their own defective choices, but because YHWH had given his covenantal Law to them to prove them incapable of obeying it.[23] YHWH, knowing the drunken state to which these irresponsible beliefs led, gave his prophets an "owner's manual" for life to understand how this intoxicated belief system would corrupt truth and justice. The statutes in his Law demonstrated that Israel's drunken iniquity would require his judgment to set things straight (Hos 4:1–6).

Like David, Asaph built on the Tabernacle's instruction-manual statutes, which implied that truth would be veiled: hidden through inebriation.

> For in the hand of YHWH there is a **cup, and the wine is red; it is full of mixture**; and he pours out of the same: but the dregs of it, all the wicked of the earth shall wring them out, and drink them. (Ps 75:8)

In another Asaph psalm, the orchestra-conductor prophet clarified the question about "when" drunkenness would occur in Israel. He declared that the cup in YHWH's hand would be poured out when the "people returned to Israel," after the Babylonian Diaspora.

> They are corrupt, and speak wickedly concerning oppression:[24] they speak loftily.[25] They set their mouth against the heavens, and their tongue walks through the earth. **Therefore his people return here: and waters of a full cup are wrung out to them.** (Ps 73:8–10; see also Isa 1:22; 30:20; and Jer 8:14; 9:15)

Isaiah built on the words of Psalm 73 by prophesying of the Second Temple Remnant's apostasy.

> Therefore you have forsaken your people the House of Jacob, **because they be replenished from the east, and are soothsayers like the Philistines, and they please themselves in the children of strangers.** (Isa 2:6; fulfilled—Ezra 9)

The "east" refers to the Diaspora in Babylon and Assyria. When Israel returned to the Promised Land after the 70-year exile, she brought back doctrines similar to the Philistines' theology. And the Judean Remnant did not build up her own kingdom. Rather, the Second Temple Remnant "pleased themselves in the children of strangers" by marrying and building up the kingdoms of the nations around them that were Israel's enemies (fulfilled, Neh 13:23–30).

Much of Psalm 73 correlates with Ezra's and Nehemiah's testimonies, which testified to the pride, oppression, lawlessness, and rebellion exhibited by the newly returned exiles in the sixth century BCE. Asaph continued limning Israel's wicked generation by stating that he did not understand their end "until he went into the sanctuary of God." When Asaph went into the Temple, he saw the prophetic implements and considered the statutes that governed the Temple's services. From the Tabernacle's prophetic, structure he understood that YHWH would bring this wicked generation "into desolation, as in a moment!" and that they would be "utterly consumed with terrors" (Ps 73:17–19) as YHWH applied the crucible method of holocaust to try and refine his creation of man into a new creation that would wholeheartedly adhere to his constitutional covenant.[26]

As previously mentioned, one of the Psalms' primary objectives was to interpret the Law's statutes. Isaiah built on the Psalms' foundational prophecies by foretelling the *Judgment of Delusions* (Isa 66:4) that YHWH would render on this wicked people, prophesying:

> And I will tread down the people in mine anger, and **make them drunk in my fury,** and I will bring down their strength to the earth. (Isa 63:6)

Isaiah paints a vivid picture of a people whose iniquity has provoked the Creator to render a *Judgment of Delusions* that spawns doctrinal inebriation. Of all nations to fall into a drunken stupor, Judah and Jerusalem were to become the most outrageous:

> Woe to Ariel, to Ariel, the city where David dwelled. . . . And *the multitude of all the nations* that fight against Ariel, even (a) *all that fight against her and her fortification*, and that distress her, shall be as a dream of a night vision. It shall even be as when an (b) hungry man dreams, and, behold, he eats; but he wakes, and his soul is empty: or as when a thirsty man dreams, and, behold, he drinks; but he wakes, and, behold, he is faint, and his soul has appetite: so shall the multitude of (a) *all the nations* be, that fight against mount Zion. Stay yourselves, and wonder; cry you out, and cry: **they are drunken, but not with wine; they stagger, but not with strong drink.** *For YHWH has poured out on (c) you the spirit of deep sleep, and has closed your eyes:* **the prophets and your rulers, the seers has he covered.** (Isa 29:1, 7–10)

Isaiah's prophecy lists a (a) multitude of nations fighting in Jerusalem whose (b) blood thirst for the city would never be quenched.[27] Though they battle against Jerusalem, their desire to control her is never satisfied. That this prophecy of Zion and her inebriated state has not yet been *fully* accomplished can be witnessed in the current Muslim, Palestinian, Christian, and Jewish conflicts in the territory today. Isaiah continues this prophetic thread in ch. 51 when writing of a righteous latter-day generation who would awake from the red wine's deeply intoxicating sleep and be restored to the Promised Land:

> Awake, awake, stand up, O Jerusalem, which **has drunk** at the hand of YHWH the cup of his fury; you have drunken the dregs of the cup of trembling, and wrung them out. (Isa 51:17)

Notice that YHWH will cause (c, above) Judah and Israel to be both blind and drunk. Isaiah (51:17–23) and Jeremiah[28] further describe Israel's blindness by depicting YHWH as veiling himself from all nations through the delusion of strong wine. It is this veil cast over the eyes of *all Israel* and over the eyes of *all nations* that will be destroyed in the latter days, when Isaiah prophecies:

> And in this mountain shall YHWH of hosts make to all people a feast of fat things, a feast of wines on the lees, of fat things full of marrow, of wines on the lees well refined. And he will destroy in this mountain **the face of the covering cast over all people, and the veil that is spread over all nations.** He will swallow up death in victory; and YHWH Elohim will wipe away tears from off all faces; and the rebuke of his people shall he take away from off all the earth: for YHWH has spoken it. And it shall be said in that day, Yes, this is our God;

we have waited for him, and he will save us: **this is YHWH**; we have waited for him, we will be glad and rejoice in his salvation. (Isa 25:6–9)[29]

When the veil covering the most Holy Place is withdrawn, YHWH's mercy and his righteousness, which have been obscured by the veil of intoxicating illogical and contradictory doctrine (which departs from his constitutional Law) will be seen and understood by all nations and peoples of the earth.

F. *Ark of the Covenant*

You shall make a *mercy seat* of pure gold: two cubits[30] and a half shall be the length of it, and a cubit and a half the breadth of it. And you shall make two cherubim of gold, of beaten work shall you make them, in the two ends of the *mercy seat*. (Exod 25:17–18)

The Ark of the Covenant rested behind the curtain, concealed from the people's sight. The high priest was the only person ever to see this implement (see Illustration 13.4). The veiling of the mercy seat again symbolizes YHWH's hiding of who he is, so that humanity can seek him and discover his mercy. Because the Psalms interpreted the Tabernacle's statutes (Ps 119:54), they provide many wonderful definitions of the Temple's furniture.

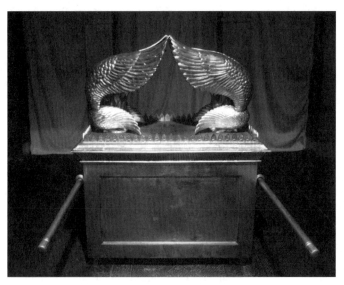

Illustration 13.4. The Ark of the Covenant.

One technique David often uses in a song is a "topic sentence." He opens a psalm with a topic sentence, then describes the subject matter in the rest of the song. Such is the case with the opening statement of Psalm 99, where David conceals a symbolic definition of the Ark of the Covenant and its cherubim.

> YHWH reigns; let the people tremble: he sits between the cherubim; let the earth be moved. (Ps 99:1)

David's opening statement defines four subjects that Psalm 99 will encompass: (1) the reigning of YHWH; (2) how the people will tremble; (3) a *description of the cherubim*; (4) and David's foretelling of YHWH's methodology for world judgment. The following demonstrates David's four discourses in Psalms 99:

1. YHWH reigns:

> YHWH is great in Zion; and he is high above all the people. (Ps 99:2)

2. Let the people tremble:

> Let them praise your great and terrible name; for it is holy. (Ps 99:3)

3. He sits between the cherubim:

> **The king's strength also loves judgment; you do establish equity, you execute judgment and righteousness in Jacob.** Exalt you YHWH our God, and worship at his footstool; for he is holy. (Ps 99:4–5)
>
> **Moses and Aaron among his priests, and Samuel among them that call on his name; they called on YHWH, and he answered them.** He spoke to them in the cloudy pillar: they kept his testimonies, and the ordinance that he gave them. (Ps 99:6–7)

4. Let the earth be moved:

> You answered them, O YHWH our God: you were a God that forgave them, though you took vengeance of their inventions. Exalt YHWH our God, and worship at his holy hill; for YHWH our God is holy. (Ps 99:8–9)

The first part of this Psalms 99 (v. 2) designates a time when YHWH was greatly exalted in Zion. The second division (99:3) declares a day when YHWH was magnified and the importance of his name understood. The third segment (99:4–5) identifies the cherubim facing the mercy seat as the king and the priest: Israel found justice and mercy in the counsel of the king and priest before YHWH, who sat or resided between the cherubim. *Mercy and judgment were always based on the constitutional Testimony that lay beneath the mercy seat.* In the fourth division (99:8–9), David declares that, when YHWH forgives, he still takes vengeance on the actions that pervert justice;[31] forgiveness does not necessarily erase consequences or judgment.

YHWH ordained the Levites as a very limited government for Israel, leaving families free to govern themselves. Later, when the people cried out for a ruler to govern them, Israel's Testimony became intricately entwined in the history of Judah and Levi—the two tribes who inherited the covenant leadership of the people.[32] For this reason, these two families are repeatedly portrayed in the structure of Solomon's Temple since their history is vital for understanding Israel's prophetic "Temple of Testimony."

V. SOLOMON'S TEMPLE

The First Temple is often identified with Solomon, the king who built it. However, it would be just as appropriate to call this David's Temple. David had written a copy of the Law for himself (Deut 17:18; 1 Chr 28:19), and YHWH's spirit caused him to understand every detail of the future that should be reflected in the Temple to be built by his son, Solomon. David bequeathed the Temple's pattern to Solomon in front of the whole congregation of Israel, an action that transitioned the kingdom from David into Solomon's care (i.e., co-regency).

> Then David gave to Solomon his son the pattern of the porch, and of the houses of it, and of the treasuries of it, and of the upper chambers of it, and of the inner parlors of it, and of the place of the mercy seat, **And the pattern of all that he had by the spirit**, of the courts of the house of YHWH, and of all the chambers round about, of the treasuries of the house of God, and of the treasuries of the dedicated things: Also for the courses of the priests and the Levites, and for all the work of the service of the house of YHWH, and for all the vessels of service in the house of YHWH. . . . And for the altar of incense refined gold by weight; and gold for the pattern of the **chariot of the cherubim**, that spread out their wings, and covered the ark of the covenant of YHWH. **All this, said David, YHWH made me understand in writing by his hand upon me**, even all the works of this pattern. (1 Chr 28:11–13, 18–19)

Deut 17:18 was a general instruction for all kings to write a copy of the Law for themselves. More specifically, the text also prophesied that the priests would witness a righteous king in Israel who would write a copy of the Israel's constitutional Law for himself. David attests that he performed this feat by "writing" the words of the various statutes, commands, judgments, and laws. From his transcription of the *Law of Moses*, David came to understand that the Temple should reflect the Torah's statutes, judgments, laws, and Testimony. YHWH's spirit caused David to understand every prophetic structure that would be represented by Israel's physical Testimony. YHWH opened David's eyes to the various purposes contained in the Tabernacle's stipulations, and this is the reason so many Psalms parallel the Law, Testimony, and Temple implements and structures.

A. *Molten Sea*

1. Tabernacle

> Every man of the Children of Israel shall pitch by his own standard, **with the ensign of their father's house:** far off about the tabernacle of the congregation shall they pitch. And on the east side toward the rising of the sun shall they of the standard of the camp of Judah pitch throughout their armies: and Nahshon the son of Amminadab shall be captain of the children of Judah. (Num 2:2–3)

Both the Tabernacle and the later Temple provided symbolic representations of the patriarchal covenants. After the exodus, Moses divided Israel's tribes into four divisions, placing them on the four sides of the Tabernacle (Num 2:3, 10, 18, 25). *This division symbolized the Diaspora Covenant* by prophesying the Day when Israel would be scattered to the north, south, east, and west: Issachar, Judah, and Zebulun were to the east; Naphtali, Dan, and Asher were to the north; Benjamin, Ephraim, and Manasseh were to the west; and Gad, Reuben, and Simeon were to the south (see Illustration 13.5).

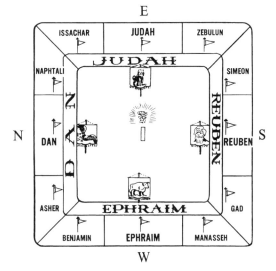

Illustration 13.5. The Israel encampment with standards[33]

2. Temple

Solomon's Temple also incorporated the Diaspora Covenant's prophecy. The Temple's inner precincts represented Israel in the Promised Land. David incorporated Jacob's Diaspora Covenant into the Temple's prophetic structure while the molten sea was placed outside the Temple. This was the plan that King David handed to the heir apparent (i.e., Solomon).

He made a molten sea of ten cubits from brim to brim, round in compass, and five cubits the height of it; and a line of thirty cubits did compass it round about. And under it was the similitude of oxen, which did compass it round about: ten in a cubit, compassing the sea round about. Two rows of oxen were cast, when it was cast. It stood upon **twelve oxen, three looking toward the north, and three looking toward the west, and three looking toward the south, and three looking toward the east: and the sea was set above upon them, and all their hind parts were inward.** And the thickness of it was a handbreadth, and the brim of it like the work of the brim of a cup, with flowers of lilies; and it received and held three thousand baths. (2 Chr 4:2–5)

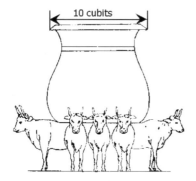

Illustrations 13.6. The oxen under the Molten Sea faced north, south, east, and west. The oxen represented the Diaspora Covenant (Gen 28:14) which prophesied of Israel's national Diaspora, while the Molten Sea prophesied of the refining and cleansing of Israel that would take place during the Diaspora.

The molten sea's 12 oxen paralleled the Tabernacles' ensigns or standards (see Illustrations 13.6). Both structures (the Tabernacle and the Temple) prophesied that three tribes would be scattered to the north, three tribes to the south, three tribes to the east, and three tribes to the west; hence, Israel and Judah were to be scattered to the four corners of the earth (Isa 11:12). According to 1 Chr 28:12, YHWH's spirit had shown King David that the Diaspora Covenant should be cast as a sacred implement that both displayed and reminded Israel of her future judgment should she rebel. This indicates that many of the political blessings that Jacob had bequeathed to Israel would occur "outside" the land of Israel. Similar to taking a daily bath, Diaspora would be the mechanism that would finally cleanse the nation of her idolatry and rebellion against YHWH's way of life.

B. *Chariot of Cherubim*

> And for the altar of incense refined gold by weight; and gold for **the pattern of the chariot of the cherubim,** that spread out their wings, and covered the ark of the covenant of YHWH. All this, said David, YHWH made me understand in writing by his hand upon me, even all the works of this pattern. (1 Chr 28:18–19)

Solomon's engineers constructed the chariot of the cherubim that David had ordained. The *Acts of Solomon* records this accomplishment:

> And in the most holy house he made two cherubim of image work, and overlaid them with gold. . . . The wings of these cherubim spread themselves forth *twenty cubits: and they stood on their feet, and their faces were inward.* (2 Chr 3:10, 13)

In order to understand the prophetic nature of these implements, we must digress for a moment. In Ps 99:6–7, David defined the cherubim covering the Ark of the Covenant: one depicted the priest and prophet, while the other depicted the king (Ps 99:1, 6–7). Samuel in particular fulfilled the role of "cherubim" by interceding for the nation. In the Moab-Shechem Covenant, YHWH foretold that he would raise a prophet up in Moses' stead.

> YHWH your God will raise up to you a prophet from the middle of you, of your brothers, like to me (Moses); to him you shall listen. . . . I will raise them up a prophet from among their brothers, like to you (Moses), and will (a) **put my words in his mouth;** and he shall speak to them all that I shall command him. And it shall come to pass, that (b) who so ever will not listen to my words which he shall speak in my name, **I will require it of him.** (Deut 18:15, 18–19; parenthesis added).

As a Levitical priest of the sons of Korah, Samuel was of Moses' "brothers" (1 Chr 6:33–8—Samuel's genealogy is listed in ascending order). He was also an Ephraimite (1 Sam 1:1). Joshua had divided Ephraim's cities, distributing 13 cities to the Korahites (Josh 21:20–22; 1 Chr 6:66–70).[34] This Levitical heritage was the reason that Elkanah (1 Chronicles 22–28), Samuel's father, served in the Tabernacle on a yearly basis: to offer sacrifices and to serve at the Tabernacle in his place in the service rotation, similar to the rotation that was later instituted under Samuel and David (1 Chr 28:13, 21).

Samuel acted as Moses toward Israel. Like Moses, Samuel spoke directly with YHWH (Samuel 3). When the people rebelled by asking for a king, Samuel stood as their advocate before YHWH (1 Sam 8:5–9), just as Moses had formerly protested against the nation's sins

(Exod 32:30–34) centuries earlier. Samuel (a) spoke on YHWH's behalf (1 Samuel 8), just as Moses had spoken on YHWH's behalf at Sinai and Moab. Samuel also worked with David to organize the government under the Monarchy, just as Moses had worked under YHWH's direction to order the priesthood and to define the limits of Israel's constitutional government.[35]

Samuel also held the people (b) accountable. When the people sinned, Samuel summoned YHWH to send rain and hail down from heaven to destroy Israel's harvest (1 Sam 12:16–18), even as Moses called for plagues in Egypt (Exodus 1–11). And again, when King Saul rebelled against Samuel's word, the prophet held the king accountable, renouncing the kingship to Saul's progeny (1 Samuel 13, 15). This act fulfilled Deuteronomy's prophecy of "requiring it" of Saul for "not listening to the words Samuel spoke in YHWH's name." Samuel continued to mirror Moses' role by petitioning for YHWH's mercy, even though the Israelites continued in their iniquity (1 Sam 12:20–23) with little or no repentance during the Tabernacle Era, as Moses had prayed for YHWH's mercy centuries earlier (Exod 32:9–14).

Samuel was one of Israel's great cherubim, but he was far from being the only special cherub. The structure that David ordained in the First Temple foretold of another prophet in particular who would again fulfill the cherubim role in Israel's future, holding the nation and her king accountable during the Kingdom Era.

The "Chariot of the Cherubim" symbolically foretold of another prophet in particular who would live during the First Temple Era—a prophet who would stand out above all others: a prophet who would be the *Chariot of the Cherubim* (see Illustration 13.7). Who was Israel's chariot of the Cherubim? A prophet who stood apart from all others?

It was Elijah. Like Moses, Elijah spoke directly with YHWH at Mt. Sinai (1 Kgs 19:12). Elijah served as a covering to Israel time and time again, seeking

Illustration 13.7. Tututankhamen's gold gilded chariot, perhaps similar to the chariot depicted in the First Temple.

YHWH's mercy for Israel by rebuking her, entreating her to turn from her iniquity, return to the Law, and to call on YHWH (1 Kings 18). When a chariot of fire separated Elijah from his younger apprentice, Elisha, the younger prophet coined the now-famous line "My father, my father, the chariot of Israel and the horsemen thereof."

> And it came to pass, as they still went on, and talked, that, behold, there appeared *a chariot of fire*, and horses of fire, and parted them both asunder; and Elijah went up by a whirlwind into heaven. And Elisha saw it, and he cried, **My father, my father, the chariot of Israel, and the horsemen thereof.** And he saw him no more: and he took hold of his own clothes, and rent them in two pieces. (2 Kgs 2:11–12)

A chariot of fire separated the two friends, and a double portion of Elijah's spirit rested on his apprentice Elisha (2 Kgs 2:9). Years later, when Elisha was much older and had fallen sick, Ephraim's King Joash proclaimed the same phrase to Elisha that had been previously attributed to Elijah, saying, "O my father, my father, the chariot of Israel, and the horsemen thereof" (2 Kgs 13:14). Elisha recognized this plea for special intervention. He used Joash's own enthusiasm to establish his ability to save the people out of his enemies' hand (2 Kgs 13:15–19).

Samuel and Elijah are the only two prophets in Israel's history who are recorded to have spoken directly with YHWH like Moses. Samuel and Elijah-Elisha (both prophets bore the same spirit—2 Kgs 2:9–12) are the only two Old Testament prophets to whom (like Moses) miracles are attributed.[36] Later, Elijah and Elisha prayed to YHWH, bringing a boy back to life (1 Kgs 17:17–24; 2 Kgs 4:8–37). Both Elijah and Elisha parted the waters and walked through on dry land (2 Kgs 2:8–9, 14). Elisha sought YHWH and healed a poisonous soup (2 Kgs 4:38–41), and he fed 100 men with only 20 loaves of bread (2 Kgs 4:42–44), while Elijah had called fire down from heaven (2 Kings 1). In short, Elijah and Elisha performed the exact same miracles that YHWH had performed through Moses: parting the Red Sea, calling fire from heaven to give the nation light, and feeding a hungry nation during the wilderness.[37] Other prophets, in comparison, only prayed for YHWH's mercy or foretold YHWH's judgments based on Israel's Testimonial Law. This is why David ordained the *Chariot of Cherubim* to stand out above all other cherubim (priests, prophets, or kings): he possessed a unique dispensation of YHWH's spirit to perform miracles and to speak in YHWH's name.

C. Boaz and Jachin: Pillars of the Temple's Porch

As we have seen, the Temple's structure prophesied Israel's future. David's and Phinehas's covenants were crucial in this era of Israel's history. The Temple's pillars represented the two tribes whom YHWH had charged to govern his people. Whereas the cherubs covering the mercy seat depicted the mercy and justice aspect of the nation's leadership, the pillars represented the actual history experienced by Judah's and Levi's descendants. Judah, the left pillar, was named for David's great-grandfather Boaz, while Levi, the right pillar, was called Jachin.

> And he set up the pillars in the porch of the temple: and he set up the right pillar, and called the name of it Jachin: and he set up the left pillar, and he called the name of it Boaz. (1 Kgs 7:21)

The Book of Chronicles provides further definition of these two pillars:

> Also he made before the house *two pillars of thirty and five cubits high*, and the *chapter that was on the top of each of them was five cubits*. And he made chains, as in the oracle, and put them on the heads of the pillars; and made an hundred pomegranates, and put them on the chains. And he reared up the

pillars before the temple, one on the right hand, and the other on the left; and called the name of that on the right hand Jachin, and the name of that on the left Boaz. (2 Chr 3:15–17)

The Boaz and Jachin pillars epitomized the Temple porch. Each cubit represented a generation of Boaz's and Jachin's children who lived in the Promised Land. Hence, 35 cubits prophesied of 35 generations that would live in the Promised Land before these particular genealogical lines became extinct in YHWH's great Judgment Day. YHWH's covenant with David officially began the generational count, with David representing the pillar's first cubit. Above the pillars rested a chapiter five-cubits high (Jer 52:22). This represented the five main princes of Judah, who had exited Egypt and *were recorded* to have lived before YHWH established his covenant with David: Nahshon, Salma (variant Salmon), Boaz, Obed, and Jesse. The *Acts of Solomon* as recorded in 2 Chr 4:13 relates that the first two chapters on the pillars were covered.

To wit, the two pillars, and the pommels, and the chapiters which were on the top of the two pillars, and the two wreaths to cover the two pommels of the chapiters which were on the top of the pillars; And four hundred pomegranates on the two wreaths; two rows of pomegranates on each wreath, *to cover the two pommels of the chapiters* which were on the pillars. (2 Chr 4:12–13; see also 1 Kgs 7:18–22)

The two covered chapiters delineated at least two generations in David's pedigree who were covered or hidden from view. Remember, one or two generations after Nahshon had been "silenced" or "hidden" due to the fact that they had never been written in the nation's archives (see pp. 597–99). These two covered generations represented the generations prior to Boaz: Nahshon through Salma (respectively). Nahshon had been Judah's prince when Israel came out of Egypt (Num 2:3) and had died in the wilderness. Salma (Salmon), Boaz's father, lived during Ehud's days, however, his life was otherwise unnotable. Boaz was quite prominent in the nation's history. His wife wrote her biography[38] and Boaz was a prominent leader in Judah's House. Obed and Jesse completed the chapiters' fourth and fifth generations of Judah's House before YHWH established his "sure house" covenant with David. Thus, David and his household officially began the pillar itself.

As mentioned above, David wrote his plan for the Temple based on the Law and Israel's history. Since the national archives were silent regarding the first one or two generations that lived during Israel's first "intermediate period" (Judg 2:7), David did not include these in his plans for the Temple. This firmly demonstrates that David used a written text to construct the blueprints for the Temple and that he did not rely on any oral tradition regarding Israel's histories.

D. Hollow Brazen Pillars

Scripture draws attention to a set of smaller hollow pillars manufactured of brass. These pillars continued to symbolize David's and Phinehas's lineages, as each cubit represented a generation (see front book cover).

> For he cast two pillars of brass, *of* **eighteen cubits high apiece: and a line of twelve cubits** did compass either of them about. And he made two chapters of molten brass, to set on the tops of the pillars: the height of the one chapter was *five cubits*, and the height of the other chapter was five cubits. (1 Kgs 7:15–16)

> Concerning the pillars, the height of one pillar was **eighteen cubits; and a fillet of twelve cubits did compass it**; and the thickness of it was four fingers: **it was hollow**. And a chapter of brass was on it; and the height of one chapter was **five cubits**, with network and pomegranates on the chapters round about, all of brass. The second pillar also and the pomegranates were like unto these. And there were ninety and six pomegranates on a side; and all the pomegranates on the network were an hundred round about. (Jer 52:21–23)

Pillars consistently represent the historical aspects of Levi's and Judah's Houses. The pillars' 18 cubits depict 18 generations of David's and Levi's Houses that would live in the Promised Land before the nation's final deportation by Babylon. These generations began with David and the Davidic Covenant and progressed to King Zedekiah's generation, which ended with the First Temple's destruction. The

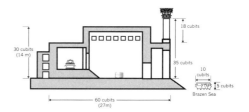

Illustration 13.8. The Pillars of Boaz and Jachin

chapters' 3 cubits (2 Kgs 25:16–17) represented the 3 generations preceding David (i.e., Jesse, Obed, and Boaz). Listed below in Table 13.3 are the 18 generations of David's sons who fulfilled the prophetic pillars of Solomon's Temple:

The editors of the Hebrew Scriptures *intentionally* recorded the names of each king's mother so that father-son relationships could be distinguished from brothers. Fascinatingly, the 18 generations of the Temple's pillar coincide exactly with Israel's record of the Davidic Monarchy.

Jeremiah draws attention to another interesting symbolic facet of these pillars by mentioning a fillet of gold that runs through only 12 cubits.

> The height of one pillar was eighteen cubits; and *a* **fillet of twelve cubits did compass it** . . . and; it was hollow. (Jer 52:21)

Table 13.3. The Symbolic, Hollow 18-Cubit Brazen Pillar

1. David
2. Solomon
3. Rehoboam
4. Abijam (mother—Maachah, dtr. of Absalom)
   Asa (mother—Maachah, dtr. of Absalom)
5. Jehoshaphat
6. Jehoram—marries Ahab's daughter, Athaliah
7. **Ahaziah—Ahab's grandson through Athaliah; David's offspring through Jehoram**
8. Joash
9. Amaziah
10. Azaraiah (Uzziah)
11. Jotham
12. Ahaz
13. Hezekiah
14. Manasseh
15. Amon
16. Josiah
17. Jehoahaz—mother, Hamutal (dtr. of Jeremiah of Labnah)—brother of Zedekiah
    Jehoiakim—mother, Zubudah (dtr. of Pediah of Rumah)—brother of Jehoahaz
    Zedekiah—mother, Hamutal (dtr. of Jeremiah of Labnah)—brother of Jehoahaz and Jehoiakim
18. Jehoiachin (aliases: Jeconiah, Coniah)

The golden fillet represented 12 generations of Ahab's seed in the Houses of both David and Levi. When a man dies without a male heir, the Law considers a surviving daughter to be like a firstborn son (Num 27:8). Jehoshaphat was one of Judah's righteous kings (2 Chr 17:3–12). He sought an alliance with Israel through the marriage of his son Jehoram to Ahab's daughter Athaliah. As Ahab's only surviving offspring, Athaliah carried the name and the lineage of her father's house. Her son Ahaziah was the legal heir to both Ahab's and David's thrones (after Jehu had slain all of Ahab's other male heirs). Ahab's seed entered into David's "sure house" in the 7th generation and continued for 12 generations, keeping Ahab's cursed line alive in the Children of Israel (2 Chr 21:6).

Ahab's seed also entered the priesthood in the same generation when the high priest Jehoiada took Jehoshabeath (Ahaziah's sister and the daughter of Athaliah) for his wife (2 Chr 22:11). As a priest who respected YHWH's Law, Jehoiada no doubt understood the implications that his marriage to Jehoshabeath would have for his children, which is why he took a second wife (2 Chr 24:3), so his seed could exist in the latter days. Scripture does not provide the genealogy for Jehoiada, but it does for David (see Table 13.4).

In order to understand the implications of the pillar's golden 12-cubit fillet, we should review the prophecies concerning Ahab's posterity. Israel's prophets had prophesied against

Table 13.4. The Sons of David and Seed of Ahab

The Brazen Pillars' Twelve-Cubit Fillet	
Judah	*Levi*
1. Ahaziah, son of Athaliah	Jehoiada the priest marries Jehoshabeath, dtr.
2. Joash	of Athaliah, and sister of Ahaziah
3. Amaziah	
4. Azariah (Uzziah)	Azariah
5. Jotham	
6. Ahaz	
7. Hezekiah	
8. Manasseh	
9. Amon	
10. Josiah	Hilkiah
11. Eliakim (alias Jehoiakim; Mattaniah-alias Zedekiah, and Jehoahaz)	Seraiah (taken captive by Nebuchadnezzar, 2 Kgs 25:18)
12. Jechoniah (alias: Coniah, Jehoachin)	

King Ahab and his lineage, stating that YHWH would utterly extinguish Ahab's House so that his lineage would never again see male offspring.

> Behold, I will bring evil on you, and will take away your posterity, and will cut off from *Ahab him that urinates against the wall*, and him that is shut up and left in Israel, And will make your house *like the House of Jeroboam the son of Nebat*, and like the *House of Baasha* the son of Ahijah, for the provocation with which you have provoked me to anger, and made Israel to sin. (1 Kgs 21:21–22; see also 2 Kgs 9:8–9)

Baasha's and Jeroboam's families were so wicked that they were left without *any* descendants.[39] As evidenced in previous chapters (pp. 335, 602–03), in ancient times the existence of a man's descendants generations later demonstrated the righteousness of his life. If a *righteous* man's children were *unrighteous*, YHWH would show them mercy for the sake of their progenitor's obedience. If a man lacked descendants three or four generations later, this condition indicated his own unrighteousness because YHWH would show no mercy to his children *when they rebelled*. Ahab's line entered David's sure house through Athaliah. Ahab's Davidic offspring were shown mercy for the sake of David's obedience. YHWH's mercy to David, however, could not annul or rescind the judgment passed on Ahab's wicked offspring.

2 Kgs 10:11 witnesses the judgment applied to Ahab's wicked House shortly before Ahab's daughter usurped David's throne.

> So Jehu slew all that remained of the House of Ahab in Jezreel, and all his great men, and his kinsfolks, and his priests, until he left him none remaining. (2 Kgs 10:11)

The Chronicles of Judah also refer to this event:

> And it came to pass, that, when Jehu was executing judgment on the House of Ahab, and *found the princes of Judah, and the sons of the brothers of Ahaziah,* that ministered to Ahaziah, he slew them. (2 Chr 22:8)

Before Jehu killed Ahaziah and his brothers, Ahaziah's father, Jehoram, had slaughtered his own brothers after Jehoshaphat's death (2 Chr 21:4). While Jehu was executing judgment on Ahaziah's brothers, Ahab's daughter Athaliah annihilated her husband's (Jehoram's) offspring after her son Ahaziah's death. Her children would have wholly perished had not Athaliah's daughter Jehoshabeath hidden her nephew Joash (Ahaziah's son and Athaliah's grandson) in the Temple for six years.

During the reigns of Joash, Uzziah, Hezekiah, Jehoiakim, and Jechoniah, the seed of Ahab still existed even though YHWH had foretold:

> The whole House of Ahab shall perish: and I will cut off from Ahab him that urinates against the wall. (2 Kgs 9:8).

Thus far, our study has shown that YHWH keeps his word; he does not rescind it. But what happens when a cursed line marries into a sure house? If YHWH promised to obliterate Ahab's House the way he had Jeroboam's and Baasha's, why did YHWH wait to wipe out Ahab's wicked lineage that existed in David's lineage?

> Yet YHWH would not destroy Judah for David his servant's sake, as he promised him to give him always a light, and to his children. (2 Kgs 8:19)

For the sake of YHWH's mercy and his covenanted promise to David, YHWH withheld judgment against Ahab's seed even though it was in David's House. YHWH's judgment, however, would not be deferred forever. He *would* execute judgment and extinguish Ahab's persistently wicked line in a later Judgment Day that had been hidden in Israel's Testimonial Law.

E. The Hidden Judgment Day

When Ahab was at the height of his reign, he surveyed his neighbor's field and coveted it. The field lay in proximity to Ahab's palace. The king thought the field would make an excellent herb garden, so he met the owner, requesting to buy the field. The vineyard/field belonged to Naboth, the Jezreelite. Naboth refused to forfeit his land to Ahab because it was his inheritance and his children's heritage, which would sustain the family for many generations to come. Returning home, Ahab sat down on his bed. He sulked and pouted, stubbornly refusing to eat. While he was still lying on his bed, Jezebel (his wife) devised a plan whereby he could obtain Naboth's vineyard. She would write letters in Ahab's name and seal them with the king's signet. They ordered Naboth to be put on trial for blaspheming YHWH and Ahab. She paid two accomplices to testify falsely against him. Naboth was erroneously convicted, and he and his sons were stoned to death (1 Kgs 21:1–16; 2 Kgs 9:26).

When Ahab heard that Naboth was dead, he rose off his bed from his depression and took possession of Naboth's bloody field. After this, the prophet Micah recorded one of the first judgment prophecies against the Temple pillar's symbolic *hollow* fillet:

> Woe to them that devise iniquity, and work evil upon their beds! When the morning is light, they practice it, because it is in the power of their hand. And *they covet fields, and take them by violence*; and houses, and take them away: so *they oppress a man and his house, even a man and his heritage*. Therefore thus said YHWH; **Behold, against this family do I devise an evil**, from which you shall not remove your necks; neither shall you go haughtily: for this time is evil. *In that day* shall one take up a parable against you, and lament with a doleful lamentation, and say, We be utterly spoiled: he has changed the portion of my people: how has he removed it from me! turning away he has divided our fields. **Therefore you shall have none that shall cast a cord by lot in the congregation of YHWH**. (Mic 2:1–5)

Micah prophesied of the great evil that YHWH planned to render on Ahab's wicked seed— so evil that Ahab would have not have a single heir left in YHWH's congregation in the latter days.

The next thread (or continuation) of the fillet prophecy is found in 2 Kings:

> I will stretch over Jerusalem the line of Samaria, and **the plummet of the House of Ahab**: and I will wipe Jerusalem as a man wipes a dish, wiping it, and turning it upside down. And I will **forsake the remnant** of mine inheritance, and deliver them into the hand of their enemies; and they shall become a prey and a spoil to all their enemies. (2 Kgs 21:13–14)

The word *mishqeleth*, "plummet," in the above verse literally means 'a plumb-line used for leveling.'[40] Micah had predicted a time when *YHWH would weigh Abab's censured lineage and render his judgment—not in Samaria, where Ahab had lived—but in Jerusalem.* Micah wrote his prophecy against Ahab's House during the days of Jotham and Hezekiah (Mic 1:1). This would have been about 150 years after Ahab's death. The prophecy from 2 Kgs 21:13–14 was written in the days of Manasseh, who reigned about 205 years after Ahab had lived. However, both of these prophecies designate a future *Day of Judgment* when Ahab's House would be "weighed" over Jerusalem, and the words of Mic 2:5 fulfilled.[41] Hidden in the structure of the Boaz and Jachin pillars was a *Judgment Day* prophecy that told of a specific time when David's and Phinehas's *hollow* 35-cubits or 35-generations would be extinguished.

VI. THE SECOND TEMPLE: THE FIRST TEMPLE REBUILT

Long before Cyrus became king of Persia, Isaiah had prophesied of Cyrus by name. Isaiah foretold that Cyrus would authorize freedom for Israel's dispersed exiles (Isa 44:24, 28). The Book of Ezra registers the specific instructions regarding Cyrus's edict.

> In the first year of Cyrus the king, the same Cyrus the king made a decree concerning the house of God at Jerusalem, Let the house be built, the place where they offered sacrifices, and let the foundations of it be strongly laid; the (a) *height of it threescore cubits, and the breadth of it threescore cubits;* (b) *With three rows of great stones, and a row of new timber:* and let the expenses be given out of the king's house. (Ezra 6:3–4)

The measurements for the Second Temple correspond to those of the First Temple. The height of (a) 30 cubits decreed by Cyrus matches the measurements of Solomon's Temple in 1 Kgs 6:2. The (b) three rows of stone also correspond to the record of Solomon's Temple (1 Kgs 6:36). The only noted structural difference between the First and Second Temple was its width. The First Temple measured 20 cubits, whereas the Second Temple was broader, at 30 cubits (1 Kgs 6:2; 1 Chr 3:3). The Second Temple was Solomon's Temple rebuilt. This is significant since the Temple's structure represented Israel while the nation lived in the Promised Land.[42]

The Boaz and Jachin pillars were reestablished after the Babylonia Diaspora, and their symbolism prophesied Israel's future once more. While the inner pillars of YHWH's house were only 18 cubits, the lineage of David, Ahab, and Jehoiada still existed in the outer court's pillars of "Boaz and Jachin," which represented not 18 generations *but 35 generations* of Judah's and Levi's descendants in the Promised Land. Eighteen of these 35 generations lived during the First Temple Era, with 12 generations fulfilling the prophecy embedded in the structure of the hollow brazen pillars. When the Remnant returned with Nehemiah, Zerubbabel, and Mordecai (Neh 7:7), Ahab's line still existed within the Houses of David and Phinehas. The Temple of Testimony demonstrates that Ahab's seed *would continue for yet 17 generations* until YHWH rendered the prophesied judgment, weighing Ahab's House against Jerusalem and bringing Ahab's seed to destruction.

Table 13.5. Davidic and Aaronide Descendants of Ahab

Generation	David		Aaron/Phinehas/Zadok	
18	Jechoiachin	Deported to Babylon 11 years before the First Temple was destroyed	Seraiah	Deported at Jerusalem's fall
19	Pedaiah		Jehozadak	
20	**Zerubbabel**	Returned with Remnant at the decree of Cyrus	**Yehoshua**	Returned with Remnant at Cyrus's decree
21	Hananiah		Joiakim	
22	Shechaniah		Eliashib	Collaborated w/enemy
23	Neariah		Joiada	
24	Elioenai		Jonathan	
25	Seven sons	Hodaiah, Eliashib, Pelaiah, Akkub, Johanan, Dalaiah, and Anani	Jaddua	
26–35	No genealogical record			

The genealogical records of 1 Chr 3:16–24 provide the last information regarding the David-Ahab line. Table 13.5 shows the continued line, beginning with the 18th generation.

The hollow brazen pillars had depicted 12 generations within David's and Phinehas's Houses. The judgment associated with this structure occurred when the 12 cubits or generations expired: Nebuchadnezzar deported Judah, and the Davidic Monarchy terminated. Similarly, the Boaz and Jachin pillars prophesied a more devastating holocaust that would occur when the 35 generations expired.

In chap. 3, we saw that Scripture defines a generation as 30 years (Gen 15:16; Exod 12:41).[43] If Nebuchadnezzar destroyed Solomon's Temple around 587 BCE, this date would serve both as the ending date of the 12th generation and the initial marker for Boaz and Jachin's remaining 17 generations. If we multiply the remaining 17 generations by 30 years (per generation), we arrive at 510 years later, when Israel's generations would again cease to exist in the Promised Land. Thus, Israel's judgment would occur *c.* 88–76 BCE, roughly the time when Rome, under Pompey, forever ended the Jewish nation's independence and autonomy.

Josephus seemingly confirms this hypothesis (*Ant* 20.10.1) by stating that the House of Zadok through the high priest Yehoshua ben Seraiah continued at least 15 generations until the reign of King Antiochus V Eupator (164–162 BCE), when the Seleucid king killed the high priest Onias III and replaced him with a Levite who was not of the House of Zadok.[44] Josephus's 15 generations are only 2 generations shy of the 17 symbolized by the Temple pillars. A short time later (35 BCE) Herod, a descendant of Esau, executed Levi's remaining Hasmonian House and, with them, Judea's sovereignty forever came to an end.

Israel's Temple of Testimony foretold an era or *Day of Judgment* for a generation that had rebelled against YHWH's covenant and his Law—a generation whom YHWH would forsake and leave to reap the consequences of their own intoxicating false doctrine, which both added to and diminished from YHWH's Law. The First Temple does not stand alone in this prophecy. The Prophetic Law of Leviticus 26 and Deuteronomy 27–30 provide greater definition and understanding for Israel's future Judgment Day, painting a clearer picture of the circumstances surrounding the extermination of the Boaz and Jachin pillars. The constitutional covenant at Mt. Sinai had prophesied of plagues to occur in series of Seven Times. These plagues were directly tied to the presence of a national Temple in Jerusalem. The First and Second Temples were based on the Testimonial Law, which incorporated all of the covenants YHWH had made with Israel's patriarchs. It is these collective covenants that, David claims, hold YHWH's greatest secret (Ps 25:14)—the Testimonial Law (Isa 8:16, 20).

14

The Testimonial Law

Fidelity: the quality of state of being faithful; *accuracy in details: EXACTNESS.*

In chap. 1, we established parameters for the trial *Israel v. YHWH*. Israel alleged that YHWH had wearied her, and the Creator sought to have this case investigated to see if the charges levied against him were merited. We have reopened this controversy to see if Israel's God was righteous (Mic 6:1–5). While we have seen evidence supporting both the accuracy and validity of the Hebrew Scriptures, this contributes little to the discussion of YHWH's righteousness, for which he is on trial. Ancient Israel was a real nation with an actual history. The Israelites had accused God and his way of life as being unfair. While we have seen many benefits from Israel's covenantal and constitutional Law, the Law was not all blessing. If Israel rebelled, YHWH promised to place curses of consequence on the nation both to discipline her and to limit her wickedness. But were these curses fair? Were these curses righteous? Or did YHWH's Law predestine the nation to failure, as ancient Israel had charged (Jer 31:29–30; Ezek 18:2)?

I. THE PROPHETIC LAW

The covenants that YHWH contracted with Noah, Abraham, Isaac, and Jacob were combined into a chronological Prophetic Law in the books of Leviticus and Deuteronomy. Israel's formal covenant had ten parts (chap. 3), which were etched on the tablets that YHWH gave to Moses at Sinai. The most important aspect of these were the Preamble, Prologue, Stipulations, and Consequences for breach of contract, which culminated in the blessings for obedience and curses for disobedience, and the sign of compliance. While the Ten Commandments constituted the Stipulation for Israel's covenant, the blessings and curses formed a chronological Law that all prophecies followed. It was the formal covenant treaty that

673

formed the nation's Testimony, and more specifically the Testimony referred to the blessing and cursing portions of the Law (Isa 8:20). For this reason I have also termed the Testimony the "Prophetic Law."

Both the Sinai and Moabic-Shechem covenants present parallel prophecies for Israel's future. The Moabic Covenant (Deuteronomy) granted a more thorough, simultaneous Testimony for both Judah and Israel until the day when the Diaspora Covenant will be fulfilled and Israel will be restored to the Promised Land. Below is Leviticus's prophetic outline for Israel's history. *The Sinai Covenant—Leviticus 26's Testimony—provides a more detailed picture of the Northern Kingdom's history than the Southern Kingdom, referring only to Judah after Samaria was exiled from the Promised Land.* In the following chapters we will examine the blessings and curses in detail beginning with Lev 26:1–13 to see when they were fulfilled.

A. *Time of Blessing: Leviticus 26:1–13*

> You shall make you no idols nor graven image, neither rear you up a standing image, neither shall you set up any image of stone in your land, to bow down to it: for I am YHWH your God. You shall keep my sabbaths, and reverence my sanctuary: I am YHWH.
>
> If you (a) walk in my statutes, and keep my commandments, and do them; Then I will give you rain in due season, and the land shall yield her increase, and the trees of the field shall yield its fruit. And (b) your threshing shall reach to the vintage, and the vintage shall reach to the sowing time: and you shall eat your bread to the full, and dwell in your land safely. And I will give **peace** in the land, and you shall lie down, and none shall make you afraid: and I will (c) rid evil beasts out of the land, neither shall the sword go through your land. And you shall chase your enemies, and they shall fall before you by the sword. And five of you shall chase an hundred, and an hundred of you shall put ten thousand to flight: and your enemies shall fall before you by the sword. For I will have respect to you, and make you fruitful, and multiply you, and establish my covenant with you. And you shall eat old store, and bring forth the old because of the new.
>
> **And I (d) will set my tabernacle among you**: and my soul shall not abhor you. And I will walk among you, and will be your God, and you shall be my people. I am YHWH your God, which brought you forth out of the land of Egypt, that you should not (e) be their bondmen; and I have broken the bands of your yoke, and made you go upright. (Lev 26:1–13)

Lev 26:1–13 begins with a time (or day) of blessing for Israel. The people are (a) walking in the Law of YHWH, keeping his statutes, honoring the Sabbaths, and observing his commandments. During this era, Israel has (c) subdued her enemies; she is (b) prosperous, being entirely free of (e) paying tribute to other nations. This prosperous epoch is epitomized when YHWH (d) places his name on Jerusalem[1] and sets his holy Tabernacle as a permanent dwelling place on earth in the Temple designed by David and built by Solomon. A permanent Temple signaled YHWH's fellowship with the nation. He was ready to hear the people's requests, to lead, and to heal the nation. During this epoch of blessing, Solomon

Table 14.1. Epoch of Blessings

1116–1051	Samuel's leadership during the Judges Era	65
1051–1023	Saul	19
1023–984	David	40
983–944	Solomon	40
	Epoch of blessing	164 years

secured even greater blessings for Israel as he prayed according to the Testimonial Law at the Temple's dedication and YHWH granted his request.[2]

One of the promises made in YHWH's covenants to Abraham affirmed that his off-spring would "possess his enemies' gates" (Gen 22:17). During David's and Solomon's reigns, YHWH began to fulfill this blessing as David subjugated many an enemy, and Solomon collected tribute as far away as Tyre (1 Kgs 9:14–15, 21–22). Over 500 years later, when Arta-xerxes made an inquiry regarding Persia's state records, he found that "there have been mighty kings also over Jerusalem, which have ruled over all countries beyond the river; and toll, tribute, and custom, was paid to them" (Ezra 4:19–20). The tribute payments allowed Solomon to establish great institutions, including a navy that embarked on two-year voyages in search of treasure and tribute. Though this era of blessing could have lasted forever; it was cut short once again by Israel's rebellion against YHWH's constitutional covenant, which defined how to walk in YHWH's way of life (see Table 14.1).[3]

B. Curses Outlined but Not Yet Applied: Leviticus 26:14–16

The epoch of blessings continued until Israel began to depart from the Law. Solomon's idolatry led to dire consequences for Israel's citizens. National blessings began to decline as YHWH imposed the consequences (curses) outlined in Leviticus's and Deuteronomy's Testimonies. YHWH twice appeared to Solomon and granted his heart's desire, awarding him a covenant of wisdom. After Solomon received his request, he turned from YHWH to sacrifice to other gods, thus violating the very foundation of YHWH's covenant with the Monarchy (see pp. 253–56 for discussion). For his disregard of the nation's covenant, YHWH divided Israel and Judah into two nations at the beginning of Rehoboam's (Solomon's son's) reign, and the tribes departed from Judah (Gen 49:10). Ten tribes were transferred to Jeroboam, but Judah and Benjamin remained under the rule of David's descendants.[4] *The separation of Samaria from Judah marked the beginning of Leviticus's plagues and curses on the Northern Kingdom.* Judah had not yet openly rebelled against YHWH's covenant, so Leviticus's curses did not yet apply to Judah. Even though the Testimony's curses began to fall on Ephraim, YHWH was still with both nations (2 Chr 11:16) at the time of the United Monarchy's dis-union (see Appendix A: 9.50/8–9, pp. 893–95).

Soon after the national fracture, Jeroboam feared that his people would rejoin the House of David when journeying to Jerusalem for the annual festivals.[5] So he instituted his own Samarian feasts and installed his own priests (1 Kgs 12:25–13:3). Israel was appalled the first time that Jeroboam celebrated his own pagan feasts, so the people adhered to the national constitution by observing the feasts and ordinances in Jerusalem (2 Chr 11:14–16). YHWH strengthened Rehoboam's hand (who sought to do good at the time—2 Chr 11:17), and other cities joined Judah due to the apostasy of Jeroboam's new-sprung religion. Although YHWH both withered and healed Jeroboam's hand (1 Kgs 13:4–6), Samaria's king still did not trust his Maker to secure his kingdom. Once again, he reinstated common people as priests in his commingled pagan-Israelitish religion.

Leviticus's Testimonial Law continues to outline this era of national decline as Ephraim disregarded YHWH's Law.

> But if you will not listen to me, and will not do all these commandments; And if you shall despise my statutes, or if your soul abhor my judgments, so that you will not do all my commandments, but that you break my covenant: I also will do this to you; I will even appoint over you terror, consumption, and the burning ague, that shall consume the eyes, and cause sorrow of heart: and you shall sow your seed in vain, for your enemies shall eat it. (Lev 26:14–16)

Lev 26:14–16 marks a transitional time in Israel's history. The Northern Kingdom rebelled, refrained from listening to YHWH, and then despised his statutes, judgments, and commandments. It had been early in Jeroboam's reign when he first replaced the Levites. In the 18th year of his reign, he set up non-Levites as priests for the second time. With this act of rebellion, YHWH departed from Ephraim (2 Chr 13:12; 15:2–4).

> Now for a long season Israel has been *without the true God*, and without a teaching priest, and without law. (2 Chr 15:3)

This era marks YHWH's departure from walking with the Northern Kingdom. Lev 26:16 outlines the curses of terror and disease that would prevail against Samaria as the nation continued to rebel against YHWH's Laws that had formerly ensured national prosperity.

The Levites' chronicle witnesses the fulfillment of this portion of Leviticus's Testimony, which stated that the people would "not listen to YHWH," by describing Ephraim's abhorrence of the way of YHWH and Jeroboam's rebellion against YHWH's covenant. *Every* king to rule over Ephraim from this point forward would "walk in the ways of Jeroboam the son of Nebat who made Israel to sin."[6] Not one Samarian king would ever turn from Jeroboam's apostasy. The following text is the penalty (Testimony) for breaching the Sinai Covenant.[7]

C. Time of Curses: The Penalty of Seven Times—Leviticus 26:16-33

(16) I also will do this to you; I will even appoint over you terror, consumption, and the burning ague, that shall consume the eyes, and cause sorrow of heart: and you shall sow your seed in vain, for your enemies shall eat it. (17) And I will set my face against you, and you shall be slain before your enemies: they that hate you shall reign over you; and you shall flee when none pursues you.

(18) And if you will not yet for all this listen to me, then I will punish you *seven times more* for your sins. And I will break the pride of your power; and I will make your heaven as iron, and your earth as brass: And your strength shall be spent in vain: for your land shall not yield her increase, neither shall the trees of the land yield their fruits.

(21) And if you walk contrary to me, and will not listen to me; I will bring *seven times more* plagues on you according to your sins. I will also send wild beasts among you, which shall rob you of your children, and destroy your cattle, and make you few in number; and your highways shall be desolate (see Illustration 14.1).

(23) And if you will not be reformed by me by these things, but will walk contrary to me; Then will I also walk contrary to you, and will punish you yet *seven times* for your sins. And I will bring *a sword on you, that shall avenge the quarrel of my covenant:* and when you are gathered together within your cities, I will send the pestilence among you; and you shall be delivered into the hand of the enemy. And when I have broken the staff of your bread, ten women shall bake your bread in one oven, and they shall deliver you your bread again by weight: and you shall eat, and not be satisfied.

Illustration 14.1. Scripture employs the symbolism of beasts, such as sphinxes, to describe invading foreign nations.

(27) And if you will not for all this listen to me, but walk contrary to me; Then I will walk contrary to you also in fury; and I, even I, will chastise you *seven times* for your sins. And you shall eat the flesh of your sons, and the flesh of your daughters shall you eat.

(30) And I will destroy your high places, and cut down your images, and cast your carcasses on the carcasses of your idols, and my soul shall abhor you. And I will make your cities waste, and bring your sanctuaries to desolation, and I will not smell the smell of your sweet odors.

(32) And I will bring the land into desolation: and your enemies which dwell therein shall be astonished at it. And I will scatter you among the heathen, and will draw out a sword after you: and your land shall be desolate, and your cities waste. (Lev 26:16–33)

The Creator acknowledged the penalty portion of his covenant by stating that he would "avenge the quarrel of his covenant" (v. 25). YHWH desired justice for Israel's breach of contract with him. The Sinai Covenant outlined *penalties of 7, or 7 Times* that the Creator would render against his beloved people if they breached his constitutional covenant through national apostasy. **The covenant's "7 Times" are penalties applied in 70-year increments:** 5 periods of 7 times during the First Temple Era; another 5 periods of 7 times during the Second Temple Era, for a total of 10 periods of sabbatical Release cycles.[8] For every 70 years that Israel rebels against YHWH's covenant, the plagues associated with that particular 7 Times occur.

Table 14.2. Leviticus's 7 Times Cultic Judgment

Leviticus 16–17	1st	7 Times Judgment	70 years
18–20	2nd	7 Times Judgment	70 years
21–22	3rd	7 Times Judgment	70 years
23–26	4th	7 Times Judgment	70 years
27–33	5th	7 Times Judgment	70 years
		Total	350 years

The first time the Law *states* 7 Times would be allotted for disobedience occurs in v. 18:

And if you will not yet for all this listen to me, then I will punish you *seven times more* for your sins. (Lev 26:18)

Yacaph, Hebrew for "more," indicates that these plagues were not the first set of 7 Times.[9] The 7 Times mentioned in v. 18 is the *second* 7 Times placed on the Northern Kingdom. The "plagues of 7" begin to occur in v. 16 after Ephraim (Northern Kingdom) despises YHWH's statutes, judgments, and commandments. Tables 14.2 and 14.3 demonstrate the chronological application of Leviticus 26's plagues of seven (see also chap. 9.VI., pp. 375–76).

Table 14.3. Samaria and Judah's 70-Year Chronicle

Date	Israel's Kings	Reign	Fulfills Levitical Law
1023	Samuel/David/Solomon		YHWH walks w/Israel—2 Chr 17:6
944	*The kingdom divides and epochs of 7 Times of consequences begin* (Priestly/postdating method of calendric reckoning)		
944	Jeroboam	21	Jeroboam's 18th yr. YHWH is not
	Nadab	0	with Israel, but he is with
	Baasha	23	Judah—2 Chr 13:12

Table 14.3. Samaria and Judah's 70-Year Chronicle, *cont.*

Date	Israel's Kings	Reign	Fulfills Levitical Law
	Elah	1	
	Omri	11	
	7 Times ends in Ahab's 14th regnal yr.	14	
874	1st 7 Times	70 yrs.	
	Ahab reigns 19 regnal yrs. (19–14 = 5)	5	
	Ahaziah	1	
	Joram	11	YHWH begins to cut
	Jehu	27	Israel—2 Kgs 10:32
	Jehoahaz	15	YHWH has not yet cast Israel
	7 Times ends Jehoash's 11th regnal yr.	11	off—2 Kgs 13:23
804	2nd 7 Times	70 yrs.	
	Jehoash reigned 15 yrs. (15–11 = 4)	4	YHWH not with Israel—2 Chr 25:7
	Jeroboam	41	
	Zechariah/Uzziah's 38th yr.	1	
	Menahem/Uzziah's 39th yr.	10	
	Pekahiah/Uzziah's 50th yr.	2	YHWH is angry with
	7 Times ends in Pekah's 12th yr.	12	Israel—Isa 9:11–12
734	3rd 7 Times	70 yrs.	

			Isaiah's 65-year prophecy (Isa 7:8)[a]	
	Pekah reigns 20 yrs.	8	3	
	Hoshea/Ahaz's 12th yr.	9	9	
	Hezekiah reigns after Hoshea is taken[b]	23	23	
	Manasseh captured/last	30	30	Ephraim deported by
664	4th 7 Times	70 yrs.		Ashurbanipal
	Isaiah's 65-yr. Prophecy of Ephraim fulfilled		65 yrs.	

Samaria's (7 Times) measuring line stretched over Jerusalem when
Manasseh returns from 7-yr. exile (2 Kgs 21:13)

Date	Israel's Kings	Reign	Fulfills Levitical Law
657	Manasseh returns 38th yr., reigns 55 yrs.	17	
	Amon	0	YHWH has cast Israel off
	Josiah	31	and will soon cast Judah off
	Jehoiakim	11	too—2 Kgs 23:27
	Zedekiah	11	
587	5th 7 Times	70 yrs.	

Fulfills Lev 26:31's prophecy of the Temple's destruction

[a]Pekah's 17th yr. is Ahaz's 1st official year after Jotham's death. Isaiah issued his prophecy for Ephraim's utter deportation at the end of Pekah's 16th year or at the beginning of his 17th year. Pekah reigned 20 years, so 4 years are subtracted to arrive at Pekah's 16th year, which is when Isaiah issued the Immanuel prophecy (Isa 7:8).

[b]Fulfills prophecy of Maher-shalal-hash-baz—Isa 8:1–8.

D. *Jeremiah's 70 years: Leviticus 26:34–35*

Psalm 137 had prophesied of Jeremiah, ordaining that if he did not remember Jerusalem, his right hand would forget its cunning and his tongue cleave to the roof of his mouth (Ps 137:5–6).[10] When Jeremiah *did* remember Jerusalem, he based his prophecy on Leviticus's plagues of 7, ordaining 70 years for Jerusalem's desolation. "After seventy years be accomplished at Babylon I will visit you, and perform my good word toward you, in causing you to return to this place" (Jer 29:10). Jeremiah knew that 70 years was the allotted time for the Promised Land's Sabbath because he looked to the Law's Testimony, which foretold seven times (70 years) of consequences (see Table 14.4).

Table 14.4. First Temple Era 7 Times

The 7 Times Judgment was applied when the tribes departed from Judah. Measuring line is first stretched over the Northern Kingdom, which never returns to the covenant		
944	1 Kgs 11:29–40; 2 Chr 10:15	1st 7 Times begins
874		1st 7 Times ends
804		2nd 7 Times ends
734		3rd 7 Times ends
664	2 Chr 33:11	4th 7 Times ends/Samaria's sanctuary destroyed
657	(2 Chr 33:11)	(Omit 7 years for Manasseh in Assyria)
	2 Kgs 21:13	Samaria's measuring line stretched out over Judah
		5th 7 Time begins
587	Jer 52:12–27	5th 7 Time ends/Temple destroyed, people deported/
	2 Kgs 25:2	Land enjoys its Sabbaths

944–587–7 yrs. for Manasseh = 350 years for the 1st Temple Era

Then shall the land enjoy her sabbaths, as long as it lies desolate, and you be in your enemies' land; even then shall the land rest, and enjoy her sabbaths. As long as it lies desolate it shall rest; because it did not rest in your sabbaths, when you dwelled on it. (Lev 26:34–35).

E. *During the Diaspora: Leviticus 26:36–39*

And on them that are left alive of you I will send a faintness into their hearts **in the lands of their enemies**; and the sound of a shaken leaf shall chase them; and they shall flee, as fleeing from a sword; and they shall fall when none pursues. And **they shall fall one on another**, as it were before a sword, when none pursues and you shall have no power to stand before your enemies. And you shall perish among the heathen, and **the land of your enemies shall eat you up**. And they that are left of you shall pine away in their iniquity **in your enemies' lands**; and also in the iniquities of their fathers shall they pine away with them. (Lev 26:36–39)

This phase of the Sinai Covenant's penalties included the Diaspora Covenant that YHWH had made with Jacob, which foretold that his children would be scattered to the four corners of the earth *before* becoming a blessing to all humanity.[11] As long as YHWH banishes the Israelites from the Promised Land, these curses will cleave to them, until they become an astonishment, proverb, and byword to all the nations to which YHWH has scattered them (Deut 28:37). Only in the latter days, when YHWH remembers his covenants with Israel will these curses finally be lifted from the Israelites' descendants (Lev 26:44–45) and the nation will become a blessing to the whole earth.

F. A Hidden Judgment: Leviticus 26:36–39

In Jacob's Prevailing Covenant, YHWH promised that Israel's ultimate blessing would begin when the nation fulfilled the meaning of Israel's name, to 'prevail with God,' by establishing a nation founded on God's constitutional precepts.[12] YHWH's righteous people would never again be fractured or overthrown. Amos testifies:

> And I will bring again the captivity of my people of Israel, and they shall build the waste cities, and inhabit them; and they shall plant vineyards, and drink the wine thereof; they shall also make gardens, and eat the fruit of them. And I will plant them on their land, *and they shall no more be pulled up out of their land which I have given them, said YHWH your God.* (Amos 9:14–15)

Micah also prophesies of this Day:

> But in *the last days* it shall come to pass, that the mountain of the house of YHWH shall be established in the top of the mountains, and it shall be exalted above the hills; and people shall flow to it. And *many nations* shall come, and say, Come, and let us go up to the mountain of YHWH, and to the house of the God of Jacob; and *he will teach us of his ways, and we will walk in his paths:* for the *law* shall go forth of Zion, and the word of YHWH from Jerusalem. And he shall judge among many people, and rebuke strong nations afar off; *and they shall beat their swords into plowshares, and their spears into pruninghooks: nation shall not lift up a sword against nation, neither shall they learn war any more.* But they shall sit every man under his vine and under his fig tree; and none shall make them afraid: for the mouth of YHWH of hosts has spoken it. (Mic 4:1–4)

Isaiah also prophecies of Israel's return to the Promised Land.

> And it shall come to pass in that day, that YHWH shall set his hand again the *second time to recover the remnant* of his people, which shall be left, from Assyria, and from Egypt, and from Pathros, and from Cush, and from Elam,

> and from Shinar, and from Hamath, and from the islands of the sea. And he shall set up an ensign for the nations, and shall assemble the outcasts of Israel, and gather together the dispersed of Judah *from the four corners of the earth.* The envy also of Ephraim shall depart, and the adversaries of Judah shall be cut off: Ephraim shall not envy Judah, and Judah shall not vex Ephraim. But they shall fly on the shoulders of the Philistines toward the west; they shall spoil them of the east together: they shall lay their hand on Edom and Moab; and the children of Ammon shall obey them. (Isa 11:11–14)[13]

Today, most theologians teach that Israel's everlasting return to the Promised Land was "supposed" to have occurred when Cyrus released Israel to rebuild Solomon's Temple.[14] Yet, for some mysterious reason, the return never effected eternal peace. This hasty assumption overlooks many prophecies in the Testimonial Law and the prophets that had yet to be fulfilled. Since nothing became of Israel (nationally) when she returned to Canaan after the decrees of Cyrus and Darius, the Testimony of YHWH's Law and his prophets is untrue, or traditional theology has overlooked an important fact. And it has: the hidden prophecies of Israel's Judgment Day.

Notice what the Prophetic Law foretold would occur during Israel's Diaspora.

> And on them that are left alive of you I will send a faintness into their hearts **in the lands of their enemies**; and the sound of a shaken leaf shall chase them; and they shall flee, as fleeing from a sword; and they shall fall when none pursues. And they shall **fall one on another**, as it were before a sword, when none pursues: and you shall have no power to stand before your enemies. And you shall perish among the heathen, and the land of your enemies shall eat you up. **And they that are left of you shall pine away in their iniquity in your enemies' lands**; and also in the iniquities of their fathers shall they pine away with them. (Lev 26:36–39)

These verses hide Israel's Judgment Day by foretelling *well in advance* the events to occur during the nation's exile. As long as the nation lived outside the Promised Land, she would live in fear, languishing in her iniquities. What YHWH's Law and his prophets forewarned would occur after Cyrus released the Remnant and the people returned to the Promised Land is "the rest of the story."

G. After the Land's 70-Year Sabbath: Leviticus 26:43

> If they shall (a) **confess their iniquity, and the iniquity of their fathers, with their (b)** trespass which they trespassed against me, and that also (c) they have walked contrary to me; And that (d) I also have walked contrary to them,[15] and (e) **have brought them into the land of their enemies**; if then their uncircumcised hearts be (f) **humbled, and they** then accept of the punishment of their iniquity: Then **will I (g) remember my covenant with Jacob**, and also my covenant with Isaac, and also my covenant with Abraham will I remember; and I will remember the land. (Lev 26:40–42)

Contemporaries Ezra and Daniel acknowledged that they lived during this phase of Leviticus's Prophetic Law. Both men made supplication to YHWH, praying according to the words of Lev 26:40. Both men humbled themselves before their Creator, acknowledging Israel's trespass, and confessing YHWH's righteousness in walking contrary to the nation.

The text below is Daniel's prayer, which will be followed by Ezra's prayer. The points inserted into Leviticus's text (above) will be linked to both Daniel's prayer and Ezra's prayer (below) to demonstrate that both Daniel and Ezra prayed according to Lev 26:40-42. The following is Daniel's prayer which parallels Lev 26:40-41. Notice how the inserted points correlate with the Testimony of Leviticus 26:

I set my face to YHWH God, to seek by prayer and supplication, (f, see Lev 26:40-42, above) with fasting, and sackcloth, and ashes: And I prayed to YHWH my God, and made my confession, and said, O YHWH, the great and dreadful God, keeping the covenant and mercy to them that love him, and to them that keep his commandments; We (a, above) have sinned, and have committed iniquity, and have done wickedly, and have rebelled, even by (b) departing from your precepts and from your judgments: Neither have we listened to your servants the prophets, which spoke in your name to our kings, our princes, and our fathers, and to all the people of the land. O YHWH, righteousness belongs to you, but to us confusion of faces, as at this day; to the men of Judah, and to the inhabitants of Jerusalem, and to all Israel, (e) that are near, and that are far off, through all the countries where you have driven them, because of their trespass that they have trespassed against you. O YHWH, to us belongs confusion of face, to our kings, to our princes, and to our fathers, because we have sinned against you. To YHWH our God belong mercies and forgivenesses, though we have rebelled against him; (c) Neither have we obeyed the voice of YHWH our God, to walk in his laws, which he set before us by his servants the prophets. Yes, all Israel have transgressed your law, even by departing, that they might not obey your voice; *therefore the curse is poured on us*, and *the oath that is written in the Law of Moses*[16] the servant of God, because we have sinned against him. And he (d) has *confirmed his words, which he spoke against us*, and against our judges that judged us, by bringing on us a great evil: for under the whole heaven has not been done as has been done on Jerusalem. (v. 13) *As it is written in the Law of Moses, all this evil is come on us*: yet made we not our prayer before YHWH our God, *that we might turn from our iniquities, and understand your truth*. Therefore has YHWH (d) watched on the evil, and brought it on us: *for YHWH our God is righteous in all his works which he does: for we obeyed not his voice*. And now, O YHWH our God, that has brought your people forth out of the land of Egypt with a mighty hand, and has gotten you renown, as at this day; we have sinned, we have done wickedly. O YHWH, according to all your righteousness, I beseech you, let your anger and your fury be turned away from your city Jerusalem, your holy mountain: *because for our sins, and* (a) *for the iniquities of our fathers, Jerusalem and your people are become a reproach* to all that are about us. Now therefore, O our God, hear the prayer of your servant, and his supplications, and cause your face to shine on your sanctuary that is desolate, for YHWH's sake.

O my God, (g) incline your ear, and hear; open your eyes, and behold our desolations, and the city which is called by your name: for we do not present our supplications before you *for our righteousnesses, but for your great mercies*. O YHWH, hear; O YHWH, forgive; O YHWH, listen and do; defer not, for your own sake, O my God: for your city and your people are called by your name. (Dan 9:3–19, emphasis added)

Notice that in v. 13, Daniel acknowledges that the Law of Moses foretold Israel's desolations. Daniel is specifically referring to the covenant's Testimony, today preserved in Leviticus 26. Daniel humbled himself through fasting (f) while seeking the Creator's mercy. He confessed his iniquity, the inquity of the nation, and (a) the sins of his fathers with their (b) trespasses by declaring that the nation had (c) walked contrary to God. Daniel acknowledges that YHWH righteously walked contrary to Israel (d) because she rebelled, and he recognizes that it was YHWH who had brought them into (e) their enemy's land. Daniel appeals for YHWH's mercy to remember Israel and Jerusalem. The Creator listened. Following Daniel's petition, the Creator did (g) remember his covenant with Jacob and restored Israel to the Promised Land. King Cyrus ordered freedom for Israel's captives and restoration of the First Temple. YHWH reestablished the Children of Israel, granting her opportunity to thrive and prosper once more.

Both Daniel and Ezra humbled themselves before YHWH: Daniel with fasting and sackcloth, Ezra by rending his garments. Ezra grants further insight into the epoch following the land's 70-year Sabbath. The following is Ezra's prayer when he heard of the Second Temple Remnant's rebellion. (The letters inserted into the text correlate with the points inserted in Lev 26:40–42 above).

And when I heard this thing, I rent my garment and my mantle, and (f) plucked off the hair of my head and of my beard, and sat down astonished. Then were assembled to me every one that trembled at the words of YHWH of Israel, because of the transgression of those that had been carried away; and I sat astonished until the evening sacrifice. And at the evening sacrifice I arose up from my heaviness; and having rent my garment and my mantle, I fell on my knees, and spread out my hands to YHWH my God. And said, O my God, I am ashamed and blush to lift up my face to you, my God: for (a) our iniquities are increased over our head, and our (b) trespass is grown up to the heavens. Since the days of our fathers have we been in a great trespass to this day; and for our iniquities have we, our kings, and our priests, been delivered to the hand of the kings of the lands, to the sword, to (e) captivity, and to a spoil, and to confusion of face, as it is this day. And *now for a little space* grace has been showed from YHWH our God, to leave us a remnant to escape, and to give us a nail in his holy place, that our God may lighten our eyes, and *give us a little reviving in our bondage*. For we were slaves; yet our God has not forsaken us in our bondage, but has extended mercy to us in the sight of the kings of Persia, to give us a reviving, *to set up the house of our God*, and to repair the desolations of it, and to give us *a wall in Judah and in Jerusalem*. And now, O our God, what shall we say after this? (c) *For we have forsaken your commandments*, which you have commanded by your servants the prophets, saying, The land, to which you go to possess it, is an unclean land with the filthiness of the people of the lands, with their abominations, which have filled it from one end to another with their uncleanness. Now therefore give not your daughters to their sons, neither take their daughters to your sons, nor seek their peace or their wealth forever (see Deut 7:1–4): *that you may be strong*, and eat the good of the land, and leave it for an inheritance to your children forever. And after all that is come on us for our evil deeds, and for our great trespass, seeing that you *our* (d) *God have punished us less than our iniquities deserve*, and have given us such deliverance as this; *Should we again break your commandments, and join in affinity with the people of these abominations? Would not you be angry with us till you had consumed us*, so that there should be no remnant nor escaping? O YHWH God of Israel, you are righteous: for we remain yet escaped, as it is this day: behold, *we are before you in our trespasses: for we cannot stand before you because of this*. (Ezra 9:3–15, emphasis added)

Notice Ezra's reference to a "little space of grace" and a "little reviving from bondage" (in bold above). Ezra acknowledges this phase of the Prophetic Law. He recognizes that the Second Temple period was *not* the final latter-day righteous kingdom of which the prophets had prophesied. He testifies that the newly returned Remnant "again broke YHWH's commandments, and joined in affinity with the people of abominations" (Ezra 9–10; Neh 5:1–13). Additionally, Ezra acknowledges the Creator's mercy in extending a space of peace and rest from the nation's enemies during this epoch of Israel's history.

If the Creator does not change but is committed to his word and his own methodology, then it stands to reason that YHWH will judge the Second Temple Remnant for rebelling against his covenant in the same manner that he had judged their forefathers. Ezra's era was a space of "a little grace," but the Remnant abused this grace by breaking YHWH's commandments and joining with the nations they were commanded to expel (Ezra 9:14; Gen 15:17–21). So if YHWH judged Israel for rebelling against his covenant during the Monarchy, would he not also judge the Second Temple Remnant for condoning the same offenses?

The continuing chronology of Leviticus 26 foretold the day when YHWH would once again expel Israel from the Promised Land:

The land also shall be left of them, and shall enjoy her sabbaths, while she lies desolate without them: and **they shall accept of the punishment of their iniquity**: because, even because they despised my judgments, and because their soul abhorred my statutes. (Lev 26:43)

YHWH would divorce the Second Temple Remnant and cast them out of his sight, so that the Promised Land could once again enjoy its Sabbaths from Israel's iniquities. Lev 26:33–35 had forewarned of Judah's deportation and the 70-year rest that the land would observe during the land's Sabbath, while vv. 36–39 outlined the Day of Judgment when YHWH would judge his wicked people, during their Diaspora. Lev 26:40–42 continued the chronology by recognizing the reestablishment of his people in the Promised Land and the renewal of the covenant (Ezra 10:3; Neh 9:38). Lev 26:43 prophesied that YHWH would once again judge his people for their rebellion. He would judge the Second Temple Remnant for rebelling against his Law, even as their fathers had done during the days of King Zedekiah. Verse 43 refers to the *Day of YHWH,* when Israel's judge would allow his people to receive the consequences of their ways by sending a violent Roman army to once again drive Israel out of YHWH's land (see Table 14.5; we will explore this further when we compare Leviticus's Testimony with the Testimony of Deuteronomy.)

Table 14.5. Second Temple Era 7 Times

520	Hag 2:10, 18	Temple begins to be rebuilt on Elul 24 in Darius's 2nd year.
516	Ezra 6:15	Temple is completed on Adar 3, in Darius's 6th year.
515		Since Adar 516 BCE was the last month of the year, the 7 Times Judgment begins again in Nisan the following year in 515 BCE (cf. Solomon's dedication).
445		1st 7 Times ends
375		2nd 7 Times ends
305		3rd 7 Times ends
235		4th 7 Times ends
165		5th 7 Times ends/Antichus Epiphanes has vandalized the Temple, rips the veil.
		Temple eventually falls into ruin and is forsaken.
		No legitimate Davidic or Aaronide heir refurbishes the Temple.

515 -165 = 350 years for the 2nd Temple Era

H. Numbers 33: The Second Temple Remnant Expelled from the Promised Land

The covenant's Testimony that foretold of the penalties for breaking YHWH's covenant testified that the Creator would cast Israel out of the Promised Land again after he had "remembered" his covenants with Abraham, Isaac, and Jacob (Lev 26:42) and reestablished Israel in the land after Jeremiah's 70-year desolation. The Creator's inaugural covenant with Abraham purposed to fulfill Noah's prophecy and transfer Canaan's lands to Abraham and his descendants. Numbers' Effacement Judgment upheld Noah's words intending to transfer Canaan's lands to Shem's offspring. As we discussed in chap. 12, YHWH commanded Israel to drive out Canaan's natives, destroy her pictures, images, and high places, and to "dispossess the inhabitants of the land, and dwell there" (Num 33:52–54).

During Israel's covenanting at Mt. Sinai, YHWH stated that he would prepare the land so that Canaan could be driven out easily.

> I will deliver the inhabitants of the land to your hand; and you shall drive them out before you. *You shall make no covenant with them,* nor with their gods. *They shall not dwell in your land,* lest they make you sin against me: for if you serve their gods, it will surely be a snare to you. (Exod 23:31–33)

As we have seen, during Joshua's days and the early days of the judges, Israel obeyed the command to drive out and dispossess Canaan's descendants. Soon after Joshua died, the Israelites adopted Canaan's traditions, so YHWH weakened them and placed them in captivity. After Joshua's death, every tribe rebelled against Numbers' Effacement Judgment and put the inhabitants to tribute and servitude rather than obeying the command to drive out Canaan's offspring, as YHWH had commanded (Judges 1). In David's and Solomon's days YHWH conferred blessings, and the nation once again began to "drive out" the Canaanites' descendants.[17] After the division of the kingdom, the nation's idolatries took hold again and "the heathen's snare turned her from YHWH."[18] At this epoch, YHWH began to place plagues of seven on her as other nations nearby began to drive her out of her own land.

> And YHWH sent against him bands of the Chaldees, and bands of the Syrians, and bands of the Moabites, and bands of the children of Ammon, and sent them against Judah to destroy it, according to the word of YHWH, which he spoke by his servants the prophets. (2 Kgs 24:2)

In chap. 1, we saw that one of the concepts of truth is constancy and freedom from change—loyalty even during a time of duress. At Bochim (Judg 2:1), YHWH's messenger stated that YHWH would "never break his covenant" with Israel. If YHWH is to be true and consistent, then his command in Numbers' Effacement Judgment (which Israel never fulfilled) was still binding on the Remnant-nation when its people returned to the Promised Land during Ezra's and Nehemiah's days. So the question must be raised: Did YHWH provide the Second Temple Remnant with the *opportunity* to fulfill Numbers' Effacement Judgment?

I. A Time of Blessings: The Second Temple Remnant Made Strong

1. Curses Are Removed

During Persia's reign of the civilized world, Judea enjoyed incredible blessings. During Darius's 2nd year (Hag 1:1), YHWH's spirit remained strong among the Remnant as YHWH reestablished the Sinai Covenant (Hag 2:5). Prior to Darius' 2nd year, the First Remnant struggled—not only with obedience but also with drought, disease-ridden crops, and a life worsened by heavy taxation (Hag 1:6, 9–11). These curses of the Law had adhered to the

Remnant through the destruction of the First Temple and continued after Cyrus's release (Hagai 1–9). In 520 BCE (Darius's 2nd year), YHWH promised the Remnant that he would remove the curses of the Law so that they had the power to rebuild the Temple and establish his covenant once more (see Table 9.48 on p.426 and Appendix A: 9.50/8-9 on pp. 893–95).

> Consider now from this day and onward, from the four and twentieth day of the ninth month, even from the day that the foundation of YHWH's temple was laid, consider it. Is the seed yet in the barn? Yes, as yet the vine, and the fig tree, and the pomegranate, and the olive tree, has not brought forth: *from this day will I bless you.* (Hag 2:18–19)

The laying of the Temple's foundation marked a time of blessing. YHWH removed the curses of his Law for the Israelites who resided in the Promised Land. They would enjoy a period of blessing that enabled them to establish YHWH's constitutional Covenant, which would in turn allow them to fulfill the judgment of Numbers 33. In spite of YHWH's spirit leading the nation, or the blessing that YHWH poured out on the Remnant, Ezra and Nehemiah witness that this wicked generation rebelled against every Torah precept and command, which prevented oppression and established the nation's freedom. If these sins were not enough, the leaders usurped the constitutional authority of the Levites to establish their own traditions, which they substituted for Israel's Law (see below).

2. Opportunity Knocks

The Persian Empire dominated the Levant until its fall to Alexander the Great. During this time, the Second Temple Remnant enjoyed peace and freedom in their borders.[19] Alexander the Great invaded Samaria. It appears that Judea enjoyed peace during his campaigns (*Ant.* 11.8.4–6).[20] After Alexander's death, the Didoches awarded Seleucus (king of Persia and Babylon—modern Iran and Iraq) Palestine, although he did not secure his possession since Ptolemy of Egypt had already appropriated the Judean province as his own. Seleucus did not press his claim, and Judea remained at peace under Ptolemaic Egyptian rule, enjoying "almost a century of prosperity despite conflicts between the successors of Ptolemy and Seleucus."[21] Throughout this century of prosperity (*c.* 320–220), the Remnant had opportunity to obey Numbers' Effacement but never sought to do so.

During the fourth Syrian War (219–217 BCE), Judea's peace dwindled as the Seleucids and Ptolemies fiercely battled for Judea's territory, which at the time was called "Coele-Syria and Phoenicia." In the subsequent war (the fifth Syrian War, 202–195 BCE) Syria finally established the Seleucid claim in Judea. Some 30 years later, when a humiliated Antiochus Epiphanes retreated from Egypt, he unleashed the wrath of his bruised pride on Jerusalem's inhabitants. With this Judean onslaught, the Aaronide (Levite) Mattathias stood up to lead the Judeans, and his sons, the Maccabees, ushered in an era of strong Judean independence.

When Mattathias died, his son Judas led the Second Temple Remnant to thier greatest independence during the Second Temple Era. Judas and his brothers not only expelled Syria from Judean territory, his forces were able to annex many Ptolemaic and Seleucid holdings. By the time of Jannaeus's death in 76 BCE, the Maccabees had "virtually restored the Kingdom of David and Solomon."[22] YHWH strengthened the Hasmoneans (another name for the Maccabees), empowering them to fulfill Numbers' Effacement Judgment, which stipulated that Abraham's heir-nation should "drive out and dispossess" the nations stipulated in the Promised-Land Covenant. But did the Hasmoneans—when YHWH had made them strong—obey YHWH's command to drive out the nativites?

Noted historian Michael Avi-Yonah observes Israel's policy during the acme of the Second Temple Era:

> The Jewish rulers therefore of necessity placed before the inhabitants of the *cities the choice of either adopting the Jewish religion or of emigrating.*[23]

The Jewish rulers did not drive out the Canaanite natives. Instead, the Second Temple Remnant followed the same rebellious and oppressive protocol as their forefathers, seeking to convert[24] Palestine's inhabitants rather than "driving them out" as YHWH had commanded. As in the days of the Judges, YHWH strengthened Judea, granting her independence and freedom from servitude. When the Jewish rulers had opportunity to obey YHWH's command, they sought to make a covenant—through conversion—with the nations that Noah had ordained should be cast out of Canaan's land (this conversion was often employed by force).[25] In previous times, when Israel first inherited the land, YHWH stated that Canaan's inhabitants would ensnare her (Exod 23:31–33). Canaan's religions were no less deceptive during the second century (BCE) than they had been during the sixteenth century (BCE). Less than a century later, Judea would become the bloody victim of the very nations and peoples whom she sought to convert.

Not only had Judea's rebellious Remnant revolted against YHWH's command to drive out and dispossess Canaan's inhabitants, the Judeans also intermarried with the Canaanites throughout the Second Temple Period. The Second Temple Remnant did not keep YHWH's statutes, judgment, commands, or laws. Rather, the sages and elders corrupted YHWH's word with their own teachings and oral traditions, which Israel came to believe should supersede YHWH's written Law (we will discuss this in chap. 19). Due to Judea's many rebellions against the constitutional covenant, the *Day of YHWH*, which is depicted by the priests' many ceremonial and prophetic holocausts (sacrifices), began to occur. YHWH would leave Judea-Israel, refusing to hear her cries until she had finally learned "to accept the punishment of her iniquity" (Lev 26:43) and returned to YHWH alone. The Testimonial Law leaves this Remnant in "slippery places" (Ps 73:18) until the day (or era) his people finally learn that departing from the constitutional way of YHWH only leads to oppression (Deut 28:29).

J. The Day of Salvation Begins: Leviticus 26:44–45

The chronology of the Prophetic Law of Leviticus 26 leaves Israel in Diaspora until the latter days, when the nation accepts the punishment of her iniquity and is ready to obey the constitution (Lev 26:43). Leviticus's Testimonial Law picks up again in Israel's final days of Diaspora shortly before the Creator again "remembers" the covenants of Abraham, Isaac, and Jacob.

And yet for all that, (a) **when they be in the land of their enemies**, I will not cast them away, neither will I abhor them, to (b) destroy them utterly, **and to (c) break my covenant with them**: for I am YHWH their God. But I will *for their sakes* **remember the covenant of their ancestors**, whom I brought forth out of the land of Egypt in the sight of the heathen, that I might be their God: I am YHWH. (Lev 26:44–45)

This epoch of the Prophetic Law occurs when Israel is (a) scattered "in the land of their enemies." YHWH will (b) not abhor her, utterly destroy her, or break his covenant with Abraham's descendants. Leviticus 26 maintains YHWH's character of faithfulness to Israel. Even though he scatters them among their enemies and destroys those who rebelled, he will not break the covenants contracted with Abraham, Isaac, Jacob, or the nation of Israel. Rather, YHWH will wait until the nation is ready to obey his Law and then choose her willing children again in the latter days.

Of all the evidence presented thus far, the above two verses best demonstrate YHWH's constancy, fidelity, and faithfulness to Abraham's descendants. Even when the nation rebelled after Cyrus's decree for restoration, YHWH still would not (c) break his covenant with Israel's ancestors! YHWH promised to remember his covenants, for Israel's sake and for his name's sake. His covenants benefited Israel by granting long life, liberty, and not only the pursuit of happiness but its realization as well.

Many prophets followed the Testimony's instruction, prophesying of the day when YHWH would restore his covenants with a righteous latter-day nation.

Seek YHWH, and his strength: seek his face evermore. Remember his marvelous works that he has done; his wonders, and the judgments of his mouth; O you seed of Abraham his servant, you children of Jacob his chosen. He is YHWH our God: his judgments are in all the earth. *He has remembered his covenant forever, the word which he commanded to a thousand generations.* Which covenant he made with Abraham, and his oath to Isaac and confirmed the same to Jacob for a law, and to Israel for an everlasting covenant, Saying, To you will I give the land of Canaan, the lot of your inheritance. (Ps 105:4–11)

The works of his hands are verity and judgment; all his commandments are sure. They stand fast forever and ever, and are done in truth and uprightness. He sent redemption to his people: *he has commanded his covenant forever:* holy and reverend is his name. The fear of YHWH is the beginning of wisdom: a good understanding have all they that do his commandments: his praise endures forever. (Ps 111:7–10)

Sing, O barren, you that did not bear; break forth into singing and cry aloud, you that did not travail with children for more are the children of the desolate than the children of the married wife. . . . Fear not; for you shall not be ashamed: neither be you confounded; for you shall not be put to shame: for you shall forget the shame of your youth, and shall not remember the reproach of your widowhood any more. For your Maker is your husband; YHWH of hosts is his name; and your Redeemer the Holy One of Israel, the God of the whole earth shall he be called. For YHWH has called you as a woman forsaken and grieved in spirit, and a wife of youth, when you were refused, said your God. For a small moment have I forsaken you; but with great mercies will I gather you. In a little wrath *I hid my face from you* for a moment; but with *everlasting kindness* will I have mercy on you, said YHWH your Redeemer. *For this is as the waters of Noah to me: for as I have sworn that the waters of Noah should no more go over the earth; so have I sworn that I would not be wroth with you, nor rebuke you.* For the mountains shall depart, and the hills be removed; but my kindness shall not depart from you, *neither shall the covenant of my peace be removed*, said YHWH that has mercy on you. . . . And all your children shall be taught of YHWH; and *great shall be the peace of your children*. (Isa 54:1, 4–10, 13; see also Hos 2:18–23)

For I YHWH love judgment, I hate robbery for burnt offering; and I will direct their work in truth, and *I will make an everlasting covenant with them*. And their *seed* shall be known among the Gentiles, and their offspring among the people: all that see them shall acknowledge them, that they are the *seed* which YHWH has blessed. (Isa 61:8–9)

Thus said YHWH, which gives the sun for a light by day, and the ordinances of the moon and the stars for a light by night, which divides the sea when the waves of it roar; YHWH of hosts is his name: *If those ordinances depart from before me*, said YHWH, *then* the *seed* of Israel also shall cease *from being a nation* before me forever. Thus said YHWH; If heaven above can be measured, and the foundations of the earth searched out beneath, I will also cast off all the *seed* of Israel for all that they have done, says YHWH. (Jer 31:35–37)

Behold, I will gather them *out of all countries*, where I have driven them in mine anger, and in my fury, and in great wrath; and *I will bring them again to this place*, and I will cause them to dwell safely: And they shall be my people, and I will be their God: and I will give them one heart, and one way, that they may fear me forever, for the good of them and of their children after them: *And I will make an everlasting covenant with them*, that I will not turn away from them, to do them good; but I will put my fear in their hearts, that they shall not depart from me. Yes, I will rejoice over them to do them good, and *I will plant them in this land* assuredly with my whole heart and with my whole soul. For thus said YHWH, like as I have brought all this great evil upon this people, *so will I bring on them all the good that I have promised them.* (Jer 32:37–42; see also Lev 26:45 and Ezek 16:59–63; 34:25–31)

During Israel's Judgment Day, YHWH had hid his face, but in the latter days he will return to Israel with everlasting kindness. This phase of the Law occurs while Israel's descendants are still in Diaspora. Once YHWH's people return to him, he will take a new remnant with the seed of Jacob, taking them from all nations to reestablish them in the land to fulfill the Promised-Land Covenant and to inherit all the blessings that come from obedience that their forefathers' had rejected.

K. Israel's Redemption

And (a) *he remembered for them his covenant*, and repented according to the multitude of his mercies. He made them also *to be* (b) *pitied* of all those that carried them captives. Save us, O YHWH our God, and (c) *gather us from among the heathen*, to give thanks to your holy name, and to triumph in your praise. Blessed be YHWH God of Israel from everlasting to everlasting: and let all the people say, Amen. Praise you YHWH. (Ps 106:45–48)

Scriptural redemption freed citizens sold into slavery (Lev 25:47–55). Redemption, closely associated with the Jubilee year, restored the family's land (Lev 25:23–31). When YHWH states that he will (a) remember the Promised-Land Covenant and (c) redeem Israel from the nations, he bases his promise/prophecy on the redemption ordinance in his Law. When Israel returns to her Creator and seeks him, YHWH will cause Israel to be (b) pitied in the sight of the nations, and he will fulfill the Diaspora Covenant.

Notice how the words of the Moab-Shechem Covenant and the prophets parallel the Prophetic Law of Leviticus 26:

And (you) shall return to YHWH your God, and *shall obey* his voice according to all that I command you this day, you and your children, with all your heart, and with all your soul; That then YHWH your God *will turn your captivity*, and have compassion on you, and will return and *gather you from all the nations, where YHWH your God has scattered you.* If any of yours be driven out to the outmost parts of heaven, from there will YHWH God gather you, and from there will he fetch you: And YHWH your God will *bring you into the land which your fathers possessed*, and you shall possess it; and he will do you good, and multiply you above your fathers. And YHWH your God will circumcise your heart, and the heart of your seed, to love YHWH your God with all your heart, and with all your soul, that you may live. (Deut 30:2–6)

And I will bring again the captivity of my people of Israel, and they shall build the waste cities, and inhabit them; and they shall plant vineyards, and drink the wine of it; they shall also make gardens, and eat the fruit of them. *And I will plant them on their land, and they shall no more be pulled up out of their land which I have given them, said YHWH your God.* (Amos 9:14–15)

———————

As a shepherd seeks out his flock *in the day that he is among his sheep that are scattered*; so will I seek out my sheep, and will deliver them out of all *places* where they have been scattered in the cloudy and dark day. And I will bring them out from the people, and *gather them from the countries*, and *will bring them to their own land*, and feed them on the *mountains of Israel* by the rivers, and in all the inhabited *places* of the country. I will feed them in a good pasture, and on the high mountains of Israel shall their fold be: there shall they lie in a good fold, and in a fat pasture shall they feed on the mountains of Israel. I will feed my flock, and I will cause them to lie down, said YHWH God. I will seek that which was lost, and bring again that which was driven away, and will bind up that which was broken, and will strengthen that which was sick: but I will destroy the fat and the strong; I will feed them with judgment. (Ezek 34:12–16)

———————

And I will gather the remnant of my flock *out of all countries where I have driven them*, and will bring them again to their folds; and they shall be fruitful and increase. And I will set up shepherds over them which shall feed them: and they shall fear no more, nor be dismayed, neither shall they be lacking, said YHWH. Behold, the days come, said YHWH, that I will raise to David a righteous Branch, and a King shall reign and prosper, and shall execute judgment and justice in the earth. In his days Judah shall be saved, and Israel shall dwell safely: and this is his name whereby he shall be called, YHWH OUR RIGHTEOUSNESS. Therefore, behold, the days come, said YHWH, that they shall no more say, YHWH lives, which brought up the Children of Israel out of the land of Egypt; *But, YHWH lives, which brought up and which led the seed of the House of Israel out of the north country, and from all countries where I had driven them; and they shall dwell in their own land.* (Jer 23:3–8)

———————

And YHWH shall *scatter you among the nations*, and you shall be left few in number among the heathen, where YHWH shall lead you. And there you shall serve gods, the work of men's hands, wood and stone, which neither see, nor hear, nor eat, nor smell. *But if from there you shall seek YHWH your God, you shall find him,* if you seek him with all your heart and with all your soul. When you are in tribulation, and all these things are come on you, even in the *latter days*, if you turn to YHWH your God, and shall be obedient to his voice; (For

YHWH your God is a merciful God;) he will not forsake you, neither destroy you, *nor forget the covenant of your fathers which he swore to them.* (Deut 4:27–31)

Come, and let us return to YHWH: for he has torn (Jer 15:3), and he will heal us; he has smitten, and he will bind us up. *After two days will he revive us: in the third day he will raise us up, and we shall live in his sight.* Then shall we know, *if we follow on to know YHWH:* his going forth is prepared as the morning; and he shall come to us as the rain, as the latter and former rain to the earth. (Hos 6:1–3)

Although YHWH had scattered Israel to the four corners of the earth, in the latter days he will not forget the covenants contracted with her ancestors. When Israel has humbled herself and is willing to obey and seek YHWH, she will be restored to her Creator. It is with a righteous latter-day generation who will be raised up in their forefathers' stead, that YHWH will reestablish his covenants and plant his people in the Promised Land. Thus, the Law demonstrates great fidelity by fulfilling the Seven Times outlined in the Prophetic Law of Leviticus 26. From the day when Israel and Jacob were separated until the day they were banished from their land of freedom, the Testimony ordained in the wilderness foretold Israel's future. This fidelity further supports that truth has been established and defined in Israel's Law. The following outline demonstrates the division of each 70 years of Leviticus 26's chronology, beginning with the era of blessings under Samuel, David, and Solomon.

II. OUTLINE OF THE PROPHETICAL
LAW OF LEVITICUS 26

The outline of Israel's Testimonial Law is based on Leviticus 26. After briefly examining each of its points, we will investigate each era in greater detail, providing historical support and comparing it with the Testimonial Law in Deuteronomy.

Lev 26:1–13	Blessings, including YHWH's setting his Tabernacle among the Children of Israel. Priest/Kings: Samuel, David, and Solomon
Lev 26:14–17	Curses, seed sown in vain, given as tribute to enemies. Freedom diminishes. Kings: Jeroboam–Ahab 1st 7 Times ends (70 yrs.)
Lev 26:18–20	Curses, famine, pride of power broken. Kings: Ahab–Jehoash 2nd 7 Times
Lev 26:21–22	Curses, increase of land spent in vain—given as tribute to foreign nations. Wild beasts multiplied, becoming few in number—Assyrian invasion. Diaspora Covenant goes into effect. Kings: Jehoash–Pekah 3rd 7 Times
Lev 26:23–26	Curses, YHWH walks contrary to Israel (he is not with Israel)—Ephraim is left few in number/no more a nation. "Staff of bread broken again"

(v. 26) indicates Samaria's siege. Isaiah's 65-year prophecy (Isa 7:8) fulfilled—Northern Kingdom is deported when Ashurbanipal (Assyria) takes Manasseh prisoner to Babylon (Ezra 4:10; 2 Chr 33:11–13). Kings: Pekah, Hoshea—No more a nation. 4th 7 Times

Lev 26:27–33 Samaria's measuring line of 7 Times is stretched over Jerusalem "for the sins of Manasseh which YHWH would not pardon" (Amos 7:7–9; 2 Kgs 21:13–14). This 7 Times commences at the end of Manasseh's years in exile. Siege of city—eat flesh of children for want of food; sanctuaries and high places destroyed. Scattered among heathen. Num 33:56 applied. Kings: Manasseh–Zedekiah. 5th 7 Times

Lev 26:34–35 Land lies desolate and enjoys Sabbaths—Jer 25:11; 29:10. 6th 7 Times—70 years of desolation

Lev 26:36–39 Foretells or prophecies of Israel's "Hidden Judgment Day."

Lev 26:40–42 YHWH remembers covenant with Israel—Cyrus's 1st year over Babylon—decrees for the Second Temple Remnant to return and rebuild Solomon's Temple. Prayers of Daniel (Daniel 9) and Ezra parallel this phase of the Prophetic Law (Ezra 9:8–9; Neh 9:2).

Lev 26:43–44 Second Temple Remnant cast off/land to enjoy Sabbaths. Judgment of Numbers 33 is put into action a second time. The nation is to accept punishment for her iniquities in the "Day of Judgment": Epiphanes–Rome.[26] Burnt-Offering Covenant is fulfilled. Israel is cast off for 2 days and left in captivity (Hos 6:2), Rome–Present (2,000 yrs.).

Lev 26:45 Latter Days when the Day of Salvation begins—Israel has been made willing to obey and seeks YHWH alone. YHWH remembers his covenants with Abraham, Isaac, Jacob, the nation of Israel, Phinehas, and David (Hos 6:3; Judg 5:2—see LXX translation). Dispersed Israel is made strong while scattered among the nations. Israel's curses begin to be placed on her enemies. Israel's exiles return to the Promised Land, and the Diaspora Covenant, Promised-Land Covenant, Circumcision Covenant, and Prevailing Covenant are fulfilled.[27]

III. THE PROPHETIC LAW OF DEUTERONOMY

A. *Freedom of Choice*

As we continue our discussion of Israel's Prophetic Law, I will cite evidence demonstrating YHWH's fidelity in applying the covenant's penalties against Israel. It could be argued that this evidence demonstrates that the Creator does not allow human beings to choose for themselves, that people are "predestined to do good or predestined to do evil": an individuals' choice to do right or wrong is never his or her own. (In fact, this had been part of Israel's original controversy!) It could then be argued that the Creator had actually influenced Israel to sin and then punished the nation for the sins he induced. If this were the case, the Creator could *not* be righteous, nor could he be exonerated in this trial. Does Scripture demonstrate that humanity is able to choose for himself? Does Scripture support the theory that humans have the power and the ability to do right and wrong outside of God's control?

One of the first examples demonstrating humanity's ability to choose for himself arises in Joshua's exhortation for Israel to choose which god she would serve:

> Now therefore fear YHWH, and serve him in sincerity and in truth: and put away the gods which your fathers served on the other side of the flood, and in Egypt; and serve you YHWH. And if it seem evil to you to serve YHWH, *choose you this day whom you will serve; whether the gods which your fathers served that were on the other side of the flood, or the gods of the Amorites,* in whose land you dwell: but as for me and my house, we will serve YHWH. (Josh 24:14–15)

The people of Israel had the ability to choose to serve YHWH or the ability to choose to serve other deities. In no way does Joshua imply that their choice was "predestined" for them. Moses' words to Israel also demonstrated a person's ability to choose:

> Behold, I set before you this day a blessing and a curse; A blessing, *if you obey* the commandments of YHWH your God, which I command you this day: And a curse, *if you will not obey* the commandments of YHWH your God, but turn aside out of the way which I command you this day, to go after other gods, which you have not known. (Deut 11:26–28)

Moses' prophecies depend on Israel's actions. "If" the people obey, the outcome is blessing. But "if" the people of Israel disobey, the consequences are curses. The power to obey YHWH's commandments or disobey them lay in the people's hand. Another text strongly indicates an individual's power to choose for himself or herself:

> **If** you shall listen to the voice of YHWH your God, to keep his commandments and his statutes *which are written in this book of the law*, and *if* you turn to YHWH your God with all your heart, and with all your soul. For this commandment which I command you this day, it is not hidden from you, neither is it far off. It is not in heaven, that you should say, Who shall go up for us to heaven, and bring it to us, that we may hear it, and do it? Neither is it beyond the sea, that you should say, Who shall go over the sea for us, and bring it to us, that we may hear it, and do it? *But the word is very near to you,* in your mouth, and in your heart, that you may do it. See, I have set before you this day life and good, and death and evil; In that I command you this day to love YHWH your God, to walk in his ways, and to keep his commandments and his

statutes and his judgments, that you may live and multiply: and YHWH your God shall bless you in the land where you go to possess it. *But if your heart turn away*, so that you will not hear, but shall be drawn away, and worship other gods, and serve them; I denounce to you this day, that you shall surely perish, and that you shall not prolong your days on the land, where you pass over Jordan to go to possess it. I call heaven and earth to record this day against you, that I have set before you life and death, blessing and cursing: *therefore choose life, that both you and your seed may live*: That you may love YHWH your God, and that you may obey his voice, and that you may cleave to him: for he is your life, and the length of your days: that you may dwell in the land which YHWH swore to your fathers, to Abraham, to Isaac, and to Jacob, to give them. (Deut 30:10–20)

Notice that the promises and curses depend on the people's own choices. Although the Law is "very close" or is easy for a person's heart to do and to live by, it is still up to the individual to choose to obey. The Prophetic Law demonstrates fidelity by foretelling well in advance the *exact consequences* for Israel's actions. **In essence the Testimony defines the judgments that YHWH will perform to limit the nation's wickedness.** Does this contradict an individual's ability to choose for himself?

The Prophetic Law demonstrates that YHWH's judgments are a consequence of the people's choice to disobey. YHWH simply placed time "limits" on the people's choices. If the people embraced actions or beliefs that violated his covenant, then the Creator would bring about certain consequences, thus limiting the time when humanity could do wickedness.[28]

The Creator knew his people. He understood their propensity to rebel against him by their actions during the wilderness exile. The Prophetic Law chronologically defined his judgments for the nation's breach of his covenant. **The Testimony did** not **"predestine" the nation's actions or choices,** but it did predestine the consequences for her choices. The fulfillment of the Creator's judgments in the Testimony demonstrates YHWH's fidelity to his own word and establishes "truth."[29]

Deuteronomy 27–30 provide the fullest detail regarding Israel's future. Remember, the Prophetic Law incorporated the covenants made with Noah, Abraham, Isaac, and Jacob into a very particularized Testimonial Law. Deuteronomy's Prophetic Law provides an event outline that coincides with and parallels Leviticus 26. While Leviticus provided 70-year increments for the Northern Kingdom's rebellion, Deuteronomy provided an overview for both the Northern and Southern Kingdoms, including the nation's history after the 70 years of desolation mentioned in Lev 26:34–35 (and Jer 25:12; 29:10). This continues throughout the long Diaspora as YHWH establishes judgments to limit Israel's ability to continue to do wickedly and specifies the judgments that YHWH would use to teach the nation to finally forsake wickedness.

B. A Symbolic Act

Shortly before Israel entered Canaan, Moses separated the Children of Israel into two groups. He ordained that the nation administer its own curses and blessings when she entered the Promised Land. This is the *test* that YHWH set before the nation of Israel:

> Behold, I set before you this day *a blessing and a curse*; A blessing, *if you obey* the commandments of YHWH your God, which I command you this day: And a curse, *if you will not obey* the commandments of YHWH your God, but turn aside out of the way which I command you this day, to go after other gods, which you have not known. And it shall come to pass, when YHWH your God has brought you in to the land where you go to possess it, that you shall put the blessing on mount Gerizim, and the curse on mount Ebal. (Deut 11:26–29)

The blessing and the curse that Moses presented to Israel represented epochs in the nation's future. Though Moses established these epochs before his death, they were not validated until Israel entered the Promised Land and established an altar of cursing on Mt. Ebal (Deut 27:2–10) to remind them of the consequences of breaching YHWH's contract. Moses charged that once Israel entered Canaan the people should ceremonially administer their own blessings and curses while the Levites supervised (see Illustrations 14.2 and 14.3).

> These shall stand on mount Gerizim *to bless* the people, when you are come over Jordan: Simeon, Levi, Judah, Issachar, Joseph, and Benjamin: And these shall stand on mount Ebal *to curse*: Reuben, Gad, Asher, Zebulun, Dan, and Naphtali. And the Levites shall speak, and say to all the men of Israel with a loud voice. (Deut 27:12–14)

Deuteronomy's Testimonial Law (the consequence or penalty portion of the covenant) begins with Israel administering her own blessings and curses in the ceremony quoted above and continues (through chaps. 28–30) until the curses near fulfillment in Deut 30:1 when Moses reports:

> And it shall come to pass, when **all these things** are come on you, the **blessing and the curse**, which I have set before you, and you shall call them to mind **among all the nations**, where YHWH your God has driven you, and shall return to YHWH your God, and **shall obey His voice according to all that I command you this day, you and your children, with all your heart, and with all your soul.** (Deut 30:1–2)

After *all* the Law's curses have befallen Israel, the Diaspora Covenant will be fulfilled. Israel will return to YHWH as her only God. YHWH will then return those who keep his covenant to the land of freedom promised to Abraham, Isaac, and Jacob—never again to be uprooted. Evidence that Deuteronomy's Testimony continued to be valid during Josiah's

Illustration 14.2. Mt. Ebal has a natural amphitheater built into the side of the mountain that would have echoed to Mt. Gerizim, opposite. Shechem lies between the base of Mt. Ebal and Mt. Gerizim.

Illustration 14.3. Shechem in the foreground with Mt. Gerizim on the left and Mt. Ebal on the right.

days is demonstrated by the Levites' discovering a copy of the Deuteronomic constitutional Testimony in the Temple, and reading it to Josiah (2 Kgs 22:8–20). After the Levites read the Testimonial Law to Josiah, he asked the prophetess Huldah if what he heard was yet to take place. She responded, "Thus said YHWH, Behold, I will bring evil on this place, and on the inhabitants of it, *even all the curses* that are written in the book which they have read before the king of Judah" (2 Chr 34:24). Huldah confirmed that Judah would receive the penalties listed in Deuteronomy for breaching YHWH's Covenant. As we shall see, the curses outlined in the Moab-Shechem (Deuteronomy) Covenant provided greater detail regarding consequences than the Sinai Covenant had. The outline below lists the chronological Testimonies contained in the Torah. Over the next few chapters we will show, in detail, the fulfillment of Leviticus's and Deuteronomy's simultaneous Testimonial Law.

IV. THE PROPHETIC LAW OF DEUTERONOMY WITH PARALLEL LEVITICUS LAW

Deut 27:14–26 Outlines general curses against those who break specific commands in the Law. No specific chronological designation—applies to all of Israel's lineage.

Deut 28:1–14 **Blessings**—YHWH sets his Tabernacle among the Israelites (1116–944
Lev 26:1–13 BCE). Israel's Shepherds: Samuel, David, and Solomon

Deut 28:15–21 **Curses**—outlined, defined, and divided into 5 parts, paralleling Leviticus 26. Curses begin to be applied when the nation splits into two nations: Samaria-Ephraim and Judah (Judah, Simeon, Benjamin, Levi).

Deut 28:22 **Curses** in field and fruit of body begin and increase (944–874 BCE).
Lev 26:14–17 Kings of Samaria: Jeroboam–Ahab/Judah: Rehaboam–Jehoshaphat. 1st 7 Times (70 yrs.) fulfilled.

Deut 28:23–24 **Curses**—Rebuke, pestilence, famine. See Lev 26:19 and Deut 28:23
Lev 26:18–20 (874–804 BCE). The Temple's 12-cubit fillet of the Boaz and Jachin pillars enter into the Monarchy and Priesthood.[30] Kings of Samaria: Ahab–Jehoash/Judah: Jehoshephat–Amaziah. 2nd 7 Times fulfilled.

Deut 28:25–27 **Curses**—Wild beasts multiplied: Assyrian invasion against Menahem. 1st
Lev 26:21–22 deportation (804 BCE–). Israel loses population; YHWH is angry at Israel
(Num 33:55–56) (Isa 9:11–12); Diaspora Covenant goes into effect. Judgment of Num 33:55–56 begins. Kings of Samaria: Jehoash–Pekah/Judah: Amaziah—Jotham. 3rd 7 Times *begins*.

Deut 28:27–29 **Noon Day Curse**—Judgment against knowledge. Noonday (Deut 28:29) occurs the first year (745 BCE) of Pekah's reign: First "Day of Darkness" and faintness of heart (Deut 28:28; continues previous 7 Times).

Deut 28:30-33 **Curses**—Israel is so evil, the land fails for justice. 2nd deportation (Deut
Lev 26:23-25   28:31; -734 BCE) The Northern Kingdom is given no more deliverers.
Kings of Samaria: Pekah/Judah: Ahaz–Hezekiah. 3rd 7 Times *ends.*

Deut 28:34-37 **Curses**—The Northern Kingdom is deported along with her king; 3rd
Lev 26:26   deportation; prophecy (734 BCE-) of Jezreel fulfilled (Hos 1:4); 1st depor-
tation of Judah. Kings of Samaria: Pekah–Hoshea/Judah: Hezekiah–
Manasseh. 4th 7 Times *begins.*

Deut 28:38-41 **Curses**—Deportation of Ephraim and fulfillment of Isa 7:8; Ephraim's 4th
deportation, which (-664 BCE) fulfilled prophecy of Lo-Ruhamah—"I
will utterly take them away" (Hos 1:6). Manasseh is deported (continues
previous 7 Times). Samaria has no more kings/Judah's kings: Hezekiah
and Manasseh. 4th 7 Times *ends.*

Deut 28:42-46 **Curses**—Measuring line of Samaria stretched over Jerusalem (2 Kgs
Lev 26:27-28   21:13): curses fall on Jacob (657 BCE-). Judah becomes tail—tribute to
Pharaoh Necho (2 Kgs 23:33). Judah's kings: Manasseh, Josiah, Jehoahaz,
Jehoiakim. 5th 7 Times *begins.*

Deut 28:47-51 **Curses**—Foreign tribute; 2nd deportations of Judah under Jehoiakim;
(Babylon's 1st deportation); Moabites, Syrians, Chaldees, and Ammo-
nites deport Judah (2 Kgs 24:2-3). Judah's kings: Jehoahaz, Jehoiakim,
Zedekiah (Continues previous 7 Times).

Deut 28:52-57 **Curses**—Fall of Jerusalem in 598 BCE; Judah's 3rd and 4th deportations;
Lev 26:29-31   18 cubits (representing 18 generations) of the outer porch end; Judgment
(Num 33:56)   of Numbers 33 is fulfilled against Israel (-587 BCE).
Temple is destroyed. No more kings of Judah. 5th 7 Times *ends.*

Deut 28:58-62 **Curses**—Plagues inherited by Israel's descendants. Prophecies of Israel's
Lev 26:32-33   afflictions during the Diaspora.

Deut 28:63-64 Prophecy (early warning) of the future Judgment Day during Diaspora.
Lev 26:33-35   (587-517 BCE). Land enjoys its Sabbaths. 6th 7 Times *begins.*

Deut 28:65-67 **Curses on the heart**. Israel is left to her own unrighteousness. She
Lev 26:36-39   continues to live in her fathers' iniquities. There is uncertainty of life;
prophecies of world judgment for breaking the Noahic Covenant.

Deut 28:68   **Curses**—Israel goes back to the "House of Bondage" (587-447 BCE).
6th 7 Times *ends.*

Deut 29:1-15   **Blessing—Renewal of Israel's Covenant.** The Remnant returns with
Lev 26:40-42   Zerubbabel (515-445 BCE). The Temple is rebuilt in 517-516 BCE. The
covenant is renewed with Ezra, Nehemiah, Yehoshua, and Zerubbabel.

Jeremiah's 70 years are completed. Temple's pillars reestablished and the golden fillet still exists. YHWH stretches Samaria's measuring-line over Jerusalem one last time (Zech 1:16; Dan 9:24). 7th 7 Times *begins*.

Deut 29:16–17   Curses—Recognizes the Diaspora. Diaspora Covenant reactivated. Israel has fulfilled the curse of worshiping "new gods" in their new homelands in other nations (Deut 28:36, 64). (Continues previous 7 Times.)

Deut 29:18–28   The Dreaded Curse: The Day of Judgment/Day of YHWH. Temple
Lev 26:43   violated, veil removed (165 BCE–??). Hellenistic and Roman eras. Civil
(Gen 9:5)   war, penalty of Noah's Covenant. Burnt-Offering Covenant. Israel is cast
(Genesis 22)   to the "molten sea" of 2,000 baths (Hos 6:2), which represent two
(Numbers 5)   prophetic days (Ps 90:4) or 2,000 years. Toward the end of the two and a
(Deuteronomy half days (2,500 years) of darkness, Israel's descendants will consider and
32)   understand the curses YHWH placed on the land (Deut 29:22–28).
                           The 7th 7 Times *ends* in 377 BCE.

Deut 29:29   Blessing—The third "Day of Darkness" is completed and the judgment of Noonday is lifted. The veil cast over the nations is removed (Isa 25:7). Covenant of Hope (Gen 46:1–4).

Deut 30:1–6   Blessing—Latter-Day remnant return to YHWH and obey. Remnant are
Lev 26:44–45 delivered (redeemed) to the Promised Land and all prior covenants
(Num 23:8–10) (Promised-Land, Circumcision, Diaspora, and Prevailing) are fulfilled. Israel's heart is circumcised to YHWH. Balaam's prophecy of Israel's latter end is fulfilled.

Deut 30:7–15   Blessing—Day of Judgment against Israel's enemies. Curses fall on Israel's enemies. Temple is rebuilt. Judgment against the nations who have sought to destroy Israel and Jerusalem (Deut 32:39–43; 30:7; Zech 12:9). Israel becomes the "head," other nations the "tail" (Lev 26:45); Israel lends but does not borrow. Israel is blessed and becomes a blessing to all other nations by establishing righteousness and justice. Other nations then learn to walk in the way of YHWH and to enjoy constitutionally defined righteousness and justice in their own lands.

Charting the fulfillment of the Law's curses allows us to confirm or refute the validity of Scripture's Testimony. In the next few chapters, we will investigate the events prophesied in Deuteronomy to see if their precise fulfillment can be synchronized with Leviticus's Prophetic Law to see if they have come to pass in either history or Scripture. In the subsequent segments of this chapter, we will begin to examine these national epochs (or prophetic days).

V. DETERONOMY'S CURSES OUTLINED

We have outlined the Testimonies of the Sinai (Leviticus 26) and Moab-Shechem (Deuteronomy 27–30) Covenants. Deuteronomy's covenant issues general curses against those who would break the following commands:

> And the Levites shall speak, and say to all the men of Israel with a loud voice,
>
> Cursed be the man that makes any graven or molten image, an abomination to YHWH, the work of the hands of the craftsman, and puts it in a secret place. And all the people shall answer and say, Amen.
>
> Cursed be he that sets light by his father or his mother. And all the people shall say, Amen.
>
> Cursed be he that removes his neighbor's landmark. And all the people shall say, Amen.
>
> Cursed be he that makes the blind to wander out of the way. And all the people shall say, Amen.
>
> Cursed be he that perverts the judgment of the stranger, fatherless, and widow. And all the people shall say, Amen.
>
> Cursed be he that lies with his father's wife; because he uncovers his father's skirt. And all the people shall say, Amen.
>
> Cursed be he that lies with any manner of beast. And all the people shall say, Amen.
>
> Cursed be he that lies with his sister, the daughter of his father, or the daughter of his mother. And all the people shall say, Amen.
>
> Cursed be he that lies with his mother in law. And all the people shall say, Amen.
>
> Cursed be he that smites his neighbor secretly. And all the people shall say, Amen.
>
> Cursed be he that takes reward to slay an innocent person. And all the people shall say, Amen.
>
> Cursed be he that confirms not all the words of this law to do them. And all the people shall say, Amen. (Deut 27:14–26)

The curses outlined at the beginning of Deuteronomy's Testimonial Law held no specific chronological designation. Each of these curses highlighted specific personal breaches of the Law. Succinctly, these served as prophecies against any individual who "did" the things listed in each curse. The nation of Israel administered these curses herself, indicating that these were self-imprecating curses. *Hence, these curses would apply to all those of Israelite lineage, regardless of whether the offspring knew they were Israel's descendants.* We will briefly examine each of these curses. (Each general curse will be noted with an asterisk.)

> *Cursed be the man that makes any graven or molten image, an abomination to YHWH, the work of the hands of the craftsman, and puts it in a secret place. And all the people shall answer and say, Amen. (Deut 27:15).

Israel's covenant, the Ten Commandments, forbade worshiping graven images (Exod 20:4–5). YHWH placed a curse on, or negative prophecy against any Israelite who would forge a graven image to worship it.

> *Cursed be he that *sets light* by his father or his mother. And all the people shall say, Amen. (Deut 27:16)

The Fifth Commandment ordained that children should honor their parents (Exod 20:12). The word *honor* connotes: "a good name or public esteem; reputation; a showing of usually merited respect: recognition; a person of superior standing . . . fame, credit."[31] Parents merit this respect through their experiences in life and the wisdom gained from the years they have lived. This is why YHWH articulates in the Ten Commandments that the blessing from honoring one's parents is long life (Exod 20:12).

Leviticus 19 built on the precept of honoring parents: "You shall rise up before the hoary head, and honor the face of the old man, and fear your God: I am YHWH" (Lev 19:32). The Israelite Law distinguished between a child and an elder. The honor due to an older adult was *not* to be shared with an immature child. When YHWH applied the curses of the Law and removed the hoary head from ruling over the nation, Isaiah prophesied

> And I will give *children* to be their princes, and babes shall rule over them. And the people shall be oppressed, every one by another, and every one by his neighbor: *the child shall behave himself proudly against the ancient*, and the base against the honorable. (Isa 3:4–5)

Israel's older generations attained greater maturity and wisdom than the younger generations had. They learned from their lives' experiences and could pass that knowledge to future generations.

Regarding the respect a child should show his parents, Dr. James Dobson explains:

> It is imperative that a child learns to respect his parents—not to satisfy their egos, but because his relationship with them provides the basis for his later attitude toward all other people. His early view of parental authority becomes the cornerstone of his future outlook on school authority, law enforcement officers, employers, and others with whom he will eventually live and work. The parent-child relationship is the first and most important social interaction a youngster will have, and the flaws and knots experienced there can often be seen later in life.[32]

Older generations created an honorable reputation for themselves and their families by the manner in which they instructed and interacted with society. Israel's culture considered it dishonorable for a person who had lived 40, 60, or more years and had earned respect and gained maturity to be ruled over by a less-mature, younger person. The devastating effects of immaturity and ego can be seen in many modern governments' officials today as they embrace impulsive and oppressive policies that reap economic and political benefits for the present with little or no thought about how their policies will affect future generations. The next concept in this curse is closely related.

The Hebrew word for "light" in Deut 27:16 is *qalah,* which specifically connotes 'contempt.' This same word was used in 1 Samuel 18, when David states that he had no social position to enable him to become Saul's son-in-law because he was "a poor man, and *lightly esteemed.*" Isaiah again used this term when he predicted, "The child shall behave himself proudly against the ancient, and the *base* against the honorable" (Isa 3:5). The low-class and ungodly citizen would scorn the righteous, viewing the upright as vile and worthless rather than looking to the righteous for the leadership and the self-discipline they needed. Thus, YHWH would apply the penalty (Deut 27:16) to Israelites who "set light" by lightly esteeming or acting proudly regarding parental instruction and authority.

*Cursed be he that removes his neighbor's landmark. And all the people shall say, Amen. (Deut 27:17)

Being one of the most valuable assets, arable land (farmland) provided landowners incredible wealth. When Israel inherited the Promised Land, Joshua and the elders divided the land, granting each family a permanently fixed portion of land that YHWH forbade anyone to alter.

> You shall not remove your neighbor's landmark, which they of old time have set in your inheritance, which you shall inherit in the land that YHWH your God gives you to possess it. (Deut 19:14)

YHWH's curse on removing an ancient landmark addressed at least two issues. The first was stealing adjacent lands through appropriation. Second, the landmark gave families a sense of identity by honoring or remembering the founding family who inherited the Promised Land and by continuing the family legacy. YHWH sought to establish justice and unity in Israel's land, so he made the boundaries between family inheritances permanent and cursed any who would pervert justice by stealing his neighbor's land.

*Cursed be he that makes the blind to wander out of the way. And all the people shall say, Amen. (Deut 27:18)

This curse stemmed from a command in the Law that stated: "You shall not curse the deaf, nor put a stumblingblock before the blind, but shall fear your God: I am YHWH" (Lev 19:14). When YHWH passed before Moses' sight, he proclaimed his own righteousness by clarifying that although he was merciful he would "*by no means clear the guilty*" (Exod 34:6–7; see also Exod 20:5–6). When a person curses someone who cannot hear the words of his curse or puts a stumblingblock before someone who cannot see, it is cruel and unjust. As humanity's judge (Isa 33:22), YHWH will hold people accountable for the way they treat others, so YHWH's curse in Deut 27:18 was an evil prophecy affecting inhumane persons who dealt cruelly with the physically disadvantaged, thus protecting the handicapped from being exploited.

> *Cursed be he that perverts the judgment of the stranger, fatherless, and widow. And all the people shall say, Amen. (Deut 27:19)

YHWH's mercy and tenderness toward the widow and the fatherless are woven throughout Scripture. Notice how the following penalty for afflicting the widow and the fatherless child demonstrates the Law's founding precept of opposite and equal reactions:

> You shall not afflict any widow, or fatherless child. If you afflict them in any wise, and they cry at all to me, I will surely hear their cry; and my wrath shall wax hot, and I will kill you with the sword; *and your wives shall be widows, and your children fatherless.* (Exod 22:22–24)

YHWH commanded Israel's citizens to abstain from placing any hardship or affliction on widows or children who had lost their home's financial provider. The covenant made in Moab built on this Law:

> Circumcise therefore the foreskin of your heart, and be no more stiffnecked. For YHWH your God is God of gods, and YHWH of lords, a great God, a mighty, and a terrible, which regards not persons, nor takes reward: *He does execute the judgment of the fatherless and widow, and loves the stranger*, in giving him food and raiment. Love you therefore the stranger: for you were strangers in the land of Egypt. (Deut 10:16–19)

As humanity's judge, YHWH sought to protect the disadvantaged and recompense the oppressor. Ultimately, he sought to protect and defend the individual family unit from oppression and injustice, thereby preserving the nation's ethical and moral fabric.

> *Cursed be he that lies with his father's wife; because he uncovers his father's skirt. And all the people shall say, Amen. Cursed be he that lies with any manner of beast. And all the people shall say, Amen. Cursed be he that lies with his sister, the daughter of his father, or the daughter of his mother. And all the people shall say, Amen. Cursed be he that lies with his mother in law. And all the people shall say, Amen. (Deut 27:20–23)

In the ancient world incest was common in royal familes. Marriage between brothers and sisters kept wealth and control in a powerful family while preserving strong family characteristics.[33] Incest also fueled family feuds and aided disease.[34] This curse was built into the Morality Code of Leviticus 18, which forbade marital relationships between close relatives (Lev 18:6–11, 23). As we have seen, YHWH aspired to drive the Canaanites' offspring out of the land since they had perverted their lineages and defiled the land through immoral behavior (Lev 18:27–28). The curses of Deuteronomy 27 fell on individual Israelites who committed the atrocities of the land's indigenous peoples to corrupt their families' and the nation of Israel's health and morality.

*Cursed be he that smites his neighbor secretly. And all the people shall say, Amen. (Deut 27:24)

This curse is again based upon violating a direct Law in Israel's Covenant: "You shall not murder" (Exod 20:13). This curse was issued against any individual Israelite who murdered and concealed it. When David secretly killed Uriah, YHWH applied this curse against David and his house:

> The sword shall never depart from your house; because you have despised me and have taken the wife of Uriah the Hittite to be your wife. Thus said YHWH, Behold, I will raise up evil against you out of your own house, and I will take your wives before your eyes and give them to your neighbor, and he shall lie with your wives in the sight of this sun. For *you did it secretly*: but I will do this thing before all Israel, and before the sun. (2 Sam 12:10–12)

YHWH did not show bias or favoritism toward David just because he had covenanted peace with him. Though David was one of Israel's most righteous kings, YHWH obeyed his own Law by placing a curse on David and his House if his sons rebelled against YHWH. Thus no person was exempt from Deuteronomy's curses.

*Cursed be he that takes reward to slay an innocent person. And all the people shall say, Amen. (Deut 27:25)

This curse built on the Law that commanded:

> You shall take no gift: for the gift blinds the wise, and perverts the words of the righteous. (Exod 23:8)
>
> You shall not wrest judgment; you shall not respect persons, neither take a gift: for a gift does blind the eyes of the wise, and pervert the words of the righteous. (Deut 16:19)

When Ahab's House sought to appropriate Naboth's vineyard, Ahab's wife bribed men to testify falsely against Naboth, so he could be executed. The above curse would apply to the men who accepted a reward for falsely testifying against Naboth. This was one of the reasons that YHWH cursed Ahab's House, obliterating it without any offspring (1 Kgs 21:16–26).[35]

> *Cursed be he that *confirms* **not all the words of this law to do them.** And all the people shall say, Amen. (Deut 27:26)

The word for "confirm" means 'to give new assurance for the validity of.' *This curse would apply to any person of Israelite lineage who failed to provide new assurance for the constitutional Law's validity.* Remember that YHWH had placed a constitutional injunction prohibiting any person or government from adding to or deleting from his constitutional Law (Deut 4:2; 12:32; see pp. 278–80). YHWH considered his constitution to be perfect (Ps 19:7), having no need for alteration. This curse placed an injunction on free speech, stipulating that future generations should confirm, uphold, and grant 'new assurance' to his covenanted constitution; it did *not* curse someone for breaking the Law.

Remember that the definition of truth is "fidelity, constancy; the state of being the case: fact; the body of real things, events, and facts; the body of true statements and propositions; fidelity to an original or to a standard."[36] This curse admonished Israel to support the "body of true statements, propositions and show fidelity to the standard of the Law." Any person in Israel's lineage who taught that Israel's Law was *in*valid or that it no longer needed to be obeyed or observed would be breaching the Law and would be considered "cursed." Israel's choice to obey YHWH or to turn from his Law determined whether she would receive YHWH's blessings or his curses. As we continue our study, we will see how these curses were fulfilled in Israel's history and still affect many societies today.

15

Epochs of Blessings and Curses

I. AN EPOCH OF BLESSING:
THE UNITED MONARCHY ERA

Deut 28:1–14	Blessings, including YHWH's setting his Tabernacle in Israel (1116–944
Lev 26:1–13	BCE). Shepherds: Samuel, David, and Solomon.

YHWH equipped Israel with two covenants. The first contracted with the people who rebelled in the wilderness (Sinai), and the second was made with their children (Moabic). The penalties of both covenants were the same. The second Testimony not only incorporated the Sinai Covenant and all previous patriarchal covenants; it also added a significant number of details.

The first phase of Deuteronomy's Law parallels the beginning of Leviticus 26 by designating a time of blessing. This prophetic era or "day" begins with the time of blessings under Samuel, David, and Solomon. (The inserted points reflect parallels between Leviticus and Deuteronomy that will be discussed after the text.)

> Lev 26:1–13: You shall make you no idols nor graven image, neither rear you up a standing image, neither shall you set up any image of stone in your land, to bow down to it: for I am YHWH your God. You shall keep my sabbaths, and reverence my sanctuary: I am YHWH. *If you walk in my statutes, and keep my commandments, and do them; Then* I will give you (a) rain in due season, and the (b) land shall yield her increase, and the trees of the field shall yield their fruit. And your (c) threshing shall reach to the vintage, and the vintage shall reach to the sowing time: and you shall eat your bread to the full, and (d) dwell in your land safely. And I will give peace in the land, and you shall lie down,

and none shall make you afraid: and I will rid evil beasts out of the land, neither shall the sword go through your land. And you shall chase your enemies, and they shall fall before you by the sword. And **five of you shall chase an hundred, and an hundred of you shall put ten thousand to flight**: and your enemies shall fall before you by the sword. For I will have respect to you, and make (e) you fruitful, and multiply you, and establish my covenant with you. And you shall eat (f) old store, and bring forth the old because of the new. And I will set my (g) tabernacle among you: and my soul shall not abhor you. And I will walk among you, and will be your God, and you shall be my people. I am YHWH your God, which brought you forth out of the land of Egypt, that you should not be their bondmen; and (h) I have broken the bands of your yoke, and made you go upright.

Deut 28:1–14: And it shall come to pass, if you shall listen diligently to the voice of YHWH your God, to observe and to do all his commandments which I command you this day, that YHWH your God will set you on high above all nations of the earth: And all these blessings shall come on you, and overtake you, *if you shall listen to the voice of YHWH your God.* Blessed shall you be in the city, and blessed shall you be (b) in the field. Blessed shall be the (e) fruit of your body, and the (b) fruit of your ground, and the fruit of your cattle, the increase of your cows, and the flocks of your sheep. Blessed shall be (f) your basket and your store. Blessed shall you be when you (d) come in, and blessed shall you be when you go out. YHWH shall cause your enemies that rise up against you to be smitten before your face: they shall come out against you one way, and **flee before you seven ways**. YHWH shall command the blessing on you in your (c, f) storehouses, and in all that you set your hand to; and he shall bless you in the land which YHWH your God gives you. YHWH shall establish you (g) an holy people to himself, as he has sworn to you, if you shall keep the commandments of YHWH your God, and walk in his ways. And all people of the (g) earth shall see that you are called by the name of YHWH; and they shall be afraid of you. And YHWH shall make (c, e) you plenteous in goods, in the fruit of your body, and in the fruit of your cattle, and in the fruit of your ground, in the land which YHWH swore to your fathers to give you.

YHWH shall open to you his good treasure, the heaven to give the (a) rain to your land in his season, and to bless all the work of your hand: and (h) you shall lend to many nations, and you shall not borrow. And YHWH shall **make you the head, and not the tail**; and you shall be above only, and you shall not be beneath; if that you listen to the commandments of YHWH your God, which I command you this day, to observe and to do them: And you shall not go aside (i) from any of the words which I command you this day, to the right hand, or to the left, to go after other gods to serve them.

This phase of the Testimonial Law blessed Israel's obedience. During ancient times, cattle, crops, clothing, jewelry, and pottery were assets of wealth.[1] In his promises, YHWH granted wealth, health, and prosperity while strengthening Israel's families. The blessings that Israel reaped from adhering to the Law included (a) rain for (b) fertile crops, cattle, and sheep: (c) prosperity that furnished food stores to excess. Her cup ran over (Ps 23:5) so that there was not room enough to receive it (Mal 3:10). Since Israel obeyed the Law, disease died out (Num 15:24) while (e) good health was established for her children. YHWH promised Israel (d) military success,[2] and everything else she set her hand to do while walking in the *way of YHWH* would prosper. All nations would (g) see that YHWH walked with Israel and would fear her. Her wealth would become so extensive that she could (h) lend to many nations with no need to borrow from any; she would enjoy perfect freedom. All these blessings were predicated in the first commandment, which forbade (j) "Israel to go after other gods to serve them."

Evidence that Israel's blessings occurred during this epoch arises from David's years in exile, when he befriended Abigail's husband, Nabal. The prophet Gad records that Nabal, an incredibly prosperous man, owned "possessions in Carmel. And the man was very great, and he had three thousand sheep, and a thousand goats" (1 Sam 25:2). Another account of Israel's blessings during David's exile years covers the period when David sought refuge with the Philistines.

During this time David and his militia conquered many Canaanite cities leaving neither man nor woman to reveal his exploits.[3] His band of men returned from these campaigns with numerous sheep, oxen, asses, camels, and apparel. David and his men received the financial blessings outlined in this phase of the Law. When David's Ziklag home had burned and his family and possessions were taken captive, David again recovered tremendous spoil (1 Sam 30:18–20) and sent this spoil to the elders of Judah (1 Sam 30:26–31); many Judahite households were blessed with the wealth from David's conquests.

After the kingdom was transferred to David (2 Sam 3:10), YHWH granted military success. On every side, "YHWH caused their enemies that rose up against them to be smitten before their face: they that came out against them one way, fled before them seven ways and YHWH blessed David and his people in all that they set their hand to because they followed the commandments of YHWH" (Deut 28:7, paraphrased; see 2 Sam 5:19–25). This verse accurately describes the epoch of Israel's blessing as her enemies fled before her in seven directions.

During this epoch of national blessing, Samuel and Saul began to subjugate the Canaanite region, while David established Israel's borders, united the tribes, and inaugurated a time of peace. Solomon's wealth increased abundantly as nations far and near brought their gifts and observed his wisdom. Israel became "an holy people who were called in the name of YHWH, who were feared" (Deut 28:10). This was the era when Israel became the head and lender to many nations, with no need to borrow (see another example of David's wealth in 1 Chr 27:25–31). Solomon's tripartite voyages through trade and exploration procured incredible wealth of gold and other precious metals (1 Kgs 9:26–28). Solomon's insatiable scientific curiosity generated zoological and botanical gardens, no doubt comparable with Babylon's hanging gardens or Cyrus's orchards (Eccl 2:4–5). Solomon's appreciation for culture is attested in Eccl 2:8 where he relates his delight in the humanities, including singing and instruments similar to modern choirs and orchestras.

The First Temple was the zenith of this era, as YHWH established a permanent dwelling place among his people. He was ready to hear petitions, render judgment, and direct the nation's steps. Israel enjoyed freedom in every way (exception given for the increased burden of supporting the Monarchy—1 Sam 8:9–18). But like most great nations, her prosperity and grandeur quickly slipped away as she ceased to use the philosophy of sound principles to guide her in wisdom and understanding (Deut 4:6). By the time Rehoboam inherited Israel's throne, her sins or at least her monarch's sins began to catch up with her, and the first curse, which fractured the brotherhood of the united nation, came into effect (see Appendix A: Table 9.50/2, p. 880–81)

II. AN EPOCH OF CURSES:
THE DIVIDED KINGDOM ERA

The second phase of Deuteronomy's Testimonial Law is a time of curses as the people turn from righteousness to do the evil listed in Deut 27:10–26. Deut 28:15–21 marks a transitional time in Israel's history because the curses are outlined but not yet fully applied.

> Lev 26:14–16: But if (a) you will not listen to me, and will not do all these commandments; And if you shall despise my statutes, or if your soul abhor my judgments, so that you will not do all my commandments, but that you break my covenant: I also will do this to you. . . .
>
> Deut 28:15–20: But it shall come to pass, if you will (a) not listen to the voice of YHWH your God, to observe to do all his commandments and his statutes which I command you this day; that all these curses shall come on you, and overtake you: Cursed shall you be in the city, and cursed (b) shall you be in the field. Cursed shall be your basket and (c) your store. Cursed shall be the (d) fruit of your body, and the fruit of your land, the (e) increase of your cows, and the flocks of your sheep. Cursed shall you be when you (f) come in, and cursed shall you be when you go out. YHWH shall send on you cursing, vexation, and rebuke, in all that you set your hand for to do, until you be destroyed, and until you perish quickly; because of the wickedness of your doings, whereby you have forsaken me.

The end result of the curses thus far: "YHWH shall (g) make the pestilence stick to you, until he have *consumed you from (h) off the land*, where you go to possess it." (Deut 28:15–21) The above verses outline all the curses that will be applied to the nation throughout the Kingdom Era. The blessings issued at the beginning of the Kingdom Era (Deut 28:1–14) are turned into curses at this phase of the Testimony. These curses were activated because Israel breached the covenant by doing the cursed things mentioned in Deut 27:15–26.

After YHWH granted Solomon his heart's desires, he (a) rebelled against "listening to YHWH . . . to do all the commandments and his statutes" (Deut 28:15). For Solomon's sin, YHWH divided the kingdom, and ten "tribes departed from Judah" (Gen 49:10).[4] Fracturing of the kingdom was the beginning of the first era of curses (see Appendix A: Table 9.50/2, pp. 880). YHWH's curses had consequences for the health and productivity of Israel's (b) fields, (c) food stores, (e) sheep, and cattle. This loss of wealth would weaken the nation and her resources so that she would no longer be a strong or feared nation (Deut 4:4–9). Instead, Israel would fear other nations, paying tribute to greater and more powerful nations.

Another curse during this era affected Israel's ability to procure healthy (d) offspring. As we saw in chap. 6, when parents are close family members, greater probability exists for the children to inherit diseases that are dominant in that particular family. Likewise, when humanity departs from YHWH's Morality Code, children often inherit sexual diseases contracted by a parent. This particular curse was a consequence for Israel's breaking natural laws. Israel's unhealthy life-styles brought disease on her children and her communities.

In the wilderness, YHWH had promised to send his messenger to drive out the lands' native inhabitants if Israel obeyed YHWH's voice and commandments (Exod 23:20–24). Israel rebelled against YHWH, and the angel of YHWH's presence stated that he would no longer fight Israel's battles for her. God left the heathen that Israel failed to drive out as "thorns in their sides and their gods a snare to them" (Judg 2:3). At the beginning of the Monarchy Era, this angel was fighting for Israel once again, empowering Israel's victories. As the nation began to turn from her Creator during Solomon's and Rehoboam's reigns, this angel ceased to be a source of strength, and frequent military (f) defeats ensued.[5] While Israel rebelled against walking in the way of YHWH, all that she would set her hand to do would eventually fail. Her actions betrayed the fact that the people had forsaken their Creator. Once again the Creator would cause the heathen around about the nation to become "thorns in their sides and their gods a snare to them."[6]

What was the end result of the curses during the Divided Kingdom epoch? Numbers 33's Effacement Judgment stipulated that the Israelites would be driven off the land and dispossessed if they did not expel the Canaanites. Deuteronomy 28's curses incorporated Numbers 33's Judgment, upholding the verdict that Israel would perish off the (h) Promised Land for refusing to obey YHWH's command in Num 33:55–56. Though (g) pestilences aided YHWH's cause in driving Israel off her land, we will see that later on Deuteronomy's curses stipulated that pestilence would continue to cling to Israel and her descendants during the Diaspora, until the day when YHWH will redeem her. This is the overview of all the curses that occur during the Divided Kingdom Era. The Prophetic Law had fortold exactly when these curses would occur.

III. CURSES APPLIED

A. The First 70-Year Epoch (944–874 BCE)

Deut 28:22	Curses in: field, fruit of body, increase.
Lev 26:14–17	Kings of: Samaria: Jeroboam I–Ahab/Judah: Rehoboam–Jehoshephat 1st 7 Times (70 years)

Deut 28:22: YHWH shall smite you with a (a) consumption, and with a (a) fever, and with an (a) inflammation, and with an (a) **extreme burning**, and with the (b) sword, and with (c) blasting, and with (c) mildew; and they shall pursue you until you perish. (The inserted letters mark parallel points that will be examined in the following discussion.)

> Lev 26:16: I also will do this to you; I will even appoint over you (b) terror, (a) consumption, and the (a) **burning ague**, that shall consume the eyes, and cause sorrow of heart: and (c) you shall sow your seed in vain, for your enemies shall eat it.

Deut 28:15–26 outlines the consequences for Israel's breach of contract with YHWH. The dividing of Israel into two nations launched these specific curses. Notice how the testimonies of Leviticus 26 and Deuteronomy 28 mirror each other precisely. Both prophecies acknowledge the specific curse (c) placed on the seeds of produce. While Leviticus forewarns that Israel's food will be sown in vain and given as tribute to her enemies, Deuteronomy states that mildew and blight will infect her crops.

Siddapon,[7] translated (c) "blasting," means 'blight' and denotes a plant's disease or injury that results in withering, cessation of growth, and dying. Blight is often caused by pathogenic organisms, such as bacteria and mildew that lead to infection.[8] Similarly, the Testimony noted that (c) *Yeraqon,*[9] translated "mildew" (parasites or fungi), would ravage the bountiful crops as YHWH reduced Israel's bounty.[10] Notice the similarity between Leviticus's and Deuteronomy's Testimonies as the two books describe the (c) hardships that YHWH would bring up on Israel's soil during this epoch.

> The terms *siddapon* and *yeraqon* constitute a stereotyped pair in the topos of the "catalogue of calamities." Some scholars define *yeraqon* as "the fading of the tips of the green grain resulting from 'worm growth' during a period of prolonged drought." The noun *yeraqon* is used five times in the OT to denote a disease infecting grain; it always follows *siddapon*. It appears in v. 22 of Deut 28:15–68 (a curse); in 1 Kings 8:37 (par. 2 Chr 6:28), in the prayer of dedication of the Temple as a plague that causes the people to resort to prayer; and in Amos 4:9, in the context of an invective against the cult pilgrims, as a plague that should cause them to repent and return to Yahweh.[11]

The word translated (a) "fever" in Deut 28:22 is *qaddahat.*[12] This same Hebrew word is used in Lev 26:16 but the translators render it "burning ague" in the KJV.[13] *Charchur,* translated "extreme burning," denotes an especially violent fever resulting from various infections and diseases.[14] Scripture demonstrates that the curse of fever indeed began to occur shortly after the kingdom divided, during Jeroboam I's days. "At that time Abijah the son of Jeroboam fell sick. . . . And Jeroboam's wife arose, and departed, and came to Tirzah: and when she came to the threshold of the door, the child died" (1 Kgs 14:1, 17).

While Scripture does not specifically state that Jeroboam's son died of a high fever, fever does generally accompany many viruses, diseases, and bacterial infections. So it is quite likely that "burning ague" accompanied the sickness of which Jeroboam's child died.

Deuteronomy also prophesied of an imminent (b) sword waiting to fall in retribution on an apostatizing people. Leviticus had established 70 years as the length of time for each epoch of Israel's curses, and the first phase of Israel's curses began during Jeroboam's reign and continued throughout Omri's and Ahab's reigns. In order to follow the Testimonial Law's fulfillment during this era, we need to see if these curses occurred during the first phase (70 years/7 Times). The verses quoted below show that the "sword" prophesied in Deut 28:22 and Lev 26:16 was fulfilled during the first epoch.

> So Ben-hadad listened to king Asa, and sent the captains of the hosts which he had against the cities of Israel, and **smote** Ijon, and Dan, and Abel-Beth-Maachah, and all Cinneroth, with all the land of Naphtali. (1 Kgs 15:20)

When Rehoboam's son Abijah acceded to the throne, he planned to regain the territories his father had lost to Jeroboam I and civil war broke out around 926 BCE (see Appendix A: Table 9.50/2, pp. 880–81.

> Jeroboam caused an ambushment to come about behind them: so they were before Judah, and the ambushment was behind them. . . . And the Children of Israel fled before Judah: and God delivered them into their hand. And Abijah and his people *slew them with a great slaughter: so there fell down slain of Israel five hundred thousand chosen men.* Thus the Children of Israel were brought under at that time, and the children of Judah prevailed, because they relied on YHWH God of their fathers. And Abijah pursued after Jeroboam, and took cities from him, Bethel with the towns of it, and Jeshnah with the towns of it, and Ephraim with the towns of it. (2 Chr 13:13, 16–19)
>
> Regarding the above civil war the prophet Azariah, son of Oded states: "And in those times there was no peace to him that went out, nor to him that came in, but great vexations were on all the inhabitants of the countries. And nation was destroyed of nation, and city of city: for God did vex them with all adversity" (2 Chr 15:5–6).

Azariah witnesses that YHWH was with Judah during this epoch but he had abandoned the Northern Kingdom of Samaria (2 Chr 15:2–4).

> And it came to pass, when he reigned, that he smote all the House of Jeroboam; he left not to Jeroboam any that breathed, until he had destroyed him, according to the saying of YHWH, which he spoke by his servant Ahijah the Shilonite. (1 Kgs 15:29)

All four texts tell us that the sword came against the Northern Kingdom due tor the nation's choice to disregard YHWH's constitutional Law. This curse had not occurred during David's or Solomon's days, when the nation lived in peace and unity. During the United Monarchy, Israel had wielded a sword rather than being wounded by the sword. But in the Testimony's first 70-year epoch of curses, the circumstance were drastically reversed. At the end of 70 years, while Ahab (Samaria) and Jehoshaphat (Judah) were still on the throne, a new 70-year epoch began, forcing the sister nations to face a whole new set of consequences (curses) that limited the nation's ability to do evil.

B. The Second 70-Year Epoch (874–804 BCE)

Deut 28:23–24	Curses: rebuke, pestilence, famine.
Lev 26:18–20	Kings of: Samaria: Ahab–Jehoash/Judah: Jehoshaphat–Amaziah.
	2nd 7 Times (70 yrs.)

> Deut 28:23–24: And your **heaven that is over your head shall be (a) brass**, and the **earth that is under you shall be (b) iron.** YHWH shall make the rain of your land powder and dust: from heaven shall it come down on you, until you be destroyed.
>
> Lev 26:19: And I will break the pride of your (c) power; and I will **make your heaven as (b) iron, and your earth as (a) brass.**

Israel's national power declined sharply during the reigns of Ahab and Jehoash. Moab revolted (2 Kgs 1:1; 3:5–7). Assyria captured Hamath, which had previously been subjugated by David. The "sons of Omri" became vassals to Assyria's kings.[15] While Samaria once controlled smaller, weaker local nations, she now fell prey to nations stronger than herself.

The phrase (a, b) "heavens as brass and earth as iron" refers to the lack of rainfall and to the hardness of soil. Lack of rainfall causes the earth to harden as brass due to the lack of evaporating water, which causes the heavens to fuse as a molten alloy over Israel's land (comparable to the Negeb in modern times).[16] This era marked the most notorious famines in the nation's history.

Siddapon ("blasting" or 'blight') resulted in "the fiery east winds which *still blow* irregularly across Palestine for days at a time, drying up vegetation, ruining the crops, and damaging property. The sky is hazy and there is a glare as if the sun were reflected from a huge *brass* tray."[17] Thus, evidence of this curse still persists today.

The following texts will evidence a few of the famines that occurred during the second 70-year epoch. Probably the most outstanding curse is the words Elijah the Tishbite spoke to Ahab. "As YHWH God of Israel lives, before whom I stand, there shall not be dew nor rain these years, but according to my word" (1 Kgs 17:1). This famine lasted for three years (1 Kgs 18:2). Later, the following events occurred during the reign of Joram ben Ahab:

> And there was a great famine in Samaria: and, behold, they besieged it, until an ass's head was sold for fourscore pieces of silver, and the fourth part of a cab of dove's dung for five pieces of silver. (2 Kgs 6:25)
>
> Then spoke Elisha to the woman, whose son he had restored to life, saying, Arise, and go you and your household, and sojourn wheresoever you can sojourn: for YHWH has called for a famine; and it shall also come on the land *seven years.* (2 Kgs 8:1)

Amos wrote his book shortly after Jehoash's days, during Jeroboam II's reign. This was the Testimony's *third* 70-year epoch of curses. Amos's testimony demonstrates that the curses of Deut 28:22–24 had already been applied to Israel in *previous* years epoch.

I have smitten you with *blasting and mildew*:[18] when your gardens and your vineyards and your fig trees and your olive trees increased, the palmerworm devoured them: yet have you not returned to me, said YHWH. I have sent among you the *pestilence after the manner of Egypt: your young men have I slain with the sword,* and have taken away your horses; and I have made the stink of your camps to come up to your nostrils: yet have you not returned to me, said YHWH. *I have overthrown* some of you, as God overthrew Sodom and Gomorrah, and you were as a firebrand plucked out of the burning: yet have you not returned to me, said YHWH. (Amos 4:9–11)

Amos's description accurately portrays the curses that befell Israel before his written testimony. Deuteronomy's former curse of blasting (blight) and mildew had already fallen on Israel's land (between 874–804 BCE).

Lev 26:19 prophesied that YHWH would break Israel's (c) pride of power. Amos describes the fulfillment of this prophesy during the second epoch of the Testimony's curses, when the enemy's sword overthrew Samaria's warriors as Israel's enemies began to prey on the vulnerable nation. Moab invaded, deported, and controlled swaths of Samaria's former holdings during the second 7 Times epoch as well. Mesha, the king of Moab, tells us:

As for Omri, king of Israel, he humbled Moab many years (lit., days). . . . And his son followed him and he also said, "I will humble Moab." In my time he spoke (thus), but I have triumphed over him and over his house, while Israel has perished forever! (Now) Omri had occupied the land of Medeba, and (Israel) had dwelt there in his time and half the time of his son (Ahab), forty years; but Chemosh [god of Moab] dwelt there in my time.[19]

The breaking of Samaria's power continued during Ahab's reign, when Assyria's Shalmaneser fought against the Syrian-Samarian alliance. According to Shalmaneser's inscriptions, Ahab had sent 10,000 foot soldiers but encountered mass casualties during the ensuing onslaught that finally killed Israel's wicked king (Ahab).[20]

Judah's power also waned during this epoch. Edom and Libnah revolted from Jehoram (2 Kgs 8:20–22). Boldly, Edom proclaimed its independence by installing its own king (2 Chr 21:8). YHWH also sent the Philistines and Arabians to break the Southern Kingdom's power. The "Philistines and the Arabians, that were near the Ethiopians, came up to Judah, broke into it, and carried away all the king's house, and his sons also, and his wives; so that there was never a son left him, save Jehoahaz, the youngest of his sons" (2 Chr 21:16–17. Evidently Jehoahaz was Ahaziah's birth name, 2 Chr 21:17; 22:1–2, while *Ahaziah* was his throne name.) Judah's rebellion against YHWH's Law was growing stronger, so Samaria's curses began to fall on the Southern Kingdom during the second phase of the Prophetic Law, even though the Creator was *still with* the Southern Kingdom of Judah (see Appendix A: Table 9.50/3–4, pp. 882–85.

C. *The Third 70-year Epoch Begins (804–734 BCE)*

Deut 28:25–27 Curses: Wild beasts multiplied—Assyrian invasion against Menahem.
Lev 26:21–22 Israel is left few in number; 1st deportation of Israel. Diaspora Covenant
initiated. YHWH is angry with Israel (Isa 9:11–12). Kings of: Samaria:
Jehoash–Pekah/Judah: Amaziah, Uzziah, Jotham, Ahaz
3rd 7 Times (70 years) begins

Deut 28:25–26: YHWH shall cause you to be smitten before your enemies: you shall go
out one way against them, and flee **seven ways** before them: and shall be (a) **removed to
all the kingdoms of the earth**. And your carcass shall be meat to all fowls of the air, and
to the (b) **beasts of the earth**, and no man shall fray them away.

Lev 26:22: I will also send (b) **wild beasts** among you, which (a) shall **rob you of your
children**, and destroy your cattle, and make you few in number; and your highways shall
be desolate.

Scripture employs the symbolism of (b)
wild beasts to describe conquering nations and their armies.[21] Hosea depicts
wild beasts as an analogy for foreign nations that robbed Israel of her children
and deported them off the Promised
Land. It may be remembered that in
Noah's Covenant, YHWH stipulated
that the consequence for eating animal
blood was being slain by "every beast"
(Gen 9:5). Israel's Testimonial Law incorporated this curse. YHWH would
become an adversarial beast to Israel: "I
will meet them as a bear that is bereaved
of her whelps, and will rend the lobe
of their heart, and there will I devour
them like a lion: the wild beast shall
tear them" (Hos 13:8). When YHWH
fulfilled Hosea's curse (negative prophecy), he used the wild Assyrian lion to
tear Israel away from the land promised
to her (Isa 10:5; see Illustration 15.1).

Illustration 15.1. Battlefield Palette (obverse) showing a
lion and vultures preying on bodies after battle.

Deut 28:25 reiterates Jacob's Diaspora Covenant (see pp. 107–15), acknowledging that
(a) Israel would be "removed into all kingdoms of the earth." This prophecy accurately
depicts the first nation-wide deportation, during Menahem's reign. While Scripture does
not mention this deportation, Tiglath-pileser's building inscription does.

As for Menaheim I overwhelmed him like a snowstorm and he . . . fled like a bird, alone and bowed to my feet. I returned him to his place and imposed tribute on him, to wit: gold, silver, linen garments with multicolored trimmings. Israel (lit. 'Omri-Land') *all its inhabitants and their possessions I led to Assyria.*[22]

Both Scripture and history attest the truth and fidelity of the covenant's Testimonial Law. When Israel had covenanted with YHWH in the Moab plains, he had openly warned of Samaria's deportation as occurring during the *third* epoch of Leviticus's plagues of 7. YHWH's constitutional Testimony recognized each national deportation.

Deut 28:27: YHWH will smite you with the botch of Egypt, and with tumors, and with the scab, and with the itch, **whereof you can not be healed**.

Why was the botch of Egypt so feared? Lev 13:20 illuminates the symptoms of leprosy (Hansen's Disease) or bubonic plague.[23] Both diseases manifested with a rash. When the rash was associated with a boil or abscess, with the whitening of the hair (Lev 13:19, 20), the diagnosis was positive.[24] "The sore botch of Egypt" may have been the plague that was previously employed to kill the firstborn and deliver Israel out of Egypt (Exod 11:1). The Testimony set a precedent of requiting with the very plagues that were once used to vanquish the Egyptians, if Israel violated YHWH's covenant (see Exod 15:24). YHWH's curses during this phase of the Prophetic Law continued to send "pestilence after the manner of Egypt" (Amos 4:10) to the nation of Israel. The third "7 Time" epoch was evidenced by Uzziah's battle with leprosy (see Appendix A: Table 9.50/4–5, pp. 884–87.

After YHWH granted Uzziah great military success and technological advancements (2 Chr 26:6–15), Uzziah exalted himself by seeking to burn incense on YHWH's altar (2 Chr 26:16–21). The Law stipulated

that no stranger, which is *not of the seed of Aaron*, come near to offer incense before YHWH; that he be not as Korah, and as his company. (Num 16:40)

Uzziah was not Aaron's descendant. The king usurped the constitutional limits of his authority. When the priests tried to correct the king, he hardened his heart to their repoofs, pushing through their protests. For this sin, YHWH struck Uzziah with leprosy until the day of his death. Though YHWH could have used various forms of chastisement, he chose leprosy. Thus, Deut 28:27's curse of the "botch of Egypt" was evidenced in Uzziah's life with no remission (i.e., no healing).

For YHWH to be exonerated in the case of *Israel vs. YHWH*, the Creator's actions with Israel must demonstrate the attributes of righteousness and truth. Thus far, our study of the Testimonial Law of Deuteronomy has met the test of fidelity, constancy, loyalty, and faithfulness—all concepts that are embedded in the definition of truth. The Prophetic Law has demonstrated (thus far) that the words YHWH used in the early patriarchal covenants were consistently incorporated into the Prophetic Law, which was incorporated into the structure of the Temple, the prophecies of the Psalms, and the words of the prophets. However, the prophecy that lies around the next corner is quite surprising!

IV. NOONDAY

A. *Full Disclosure*

At Mt. Sinai, YHWH had openly revealed his entire Law to Israel. YHWH taught her to walk in his paths without reserve, establishing his Law for truth and doctrine—a way of living that leads to everlasting life (Ezek 33:15).[25] The first time YHWH's angel appeared to Abraham, he stated:

> *Shall I hide* from Abraham that thing which I do; Seeing that Abraham shall surely become a great and mighty nation, and all the nations of the earth shall be blessed in him? For I know him, that he will command his children and his household after him, *and they shall keep the way of YHWH, to do justice and judgment;* that YHWH may bring on Abraham that which he has spoken of him. (Gen 18:17–19)

The King James Version translates *derek* as "the way." The Hebrew literally means 'the road or a course of life.'[26] YHWH knew that Abraham would teach his children the way of life, which comprises justice and judgment. Israel's constitutional Testimony incorporated this *derek* or way of life as one of the blessings arising from obeying YHWH's covenant.

> If you **walk in my statutes, and keep my commandments, and do them**; Then I will give you rain in due season, and the land shall yield her increase. . . . and you shall eat your bread to the full, and dwell in your land safely. (Lev 26:3–5)

YHWH's statutes, judgments, and commandments are codified in Israel's covenantal Law. At Mt. Sinai YHWH himself spoke to Israel from the cloud, clearly disclosing the stipulations of his constitutional Law (Exodus 20). This Law openly established YHWH's truth doctrine:

> Your righteousness is an everlasting righteousness, and *your law is the truth.* (Ps 119:142)
>
> I give you good doctrine, forsake you not my law. (Prov 4:2)
>
> All the paths of YHWH are mercy and truth to such as keep his covenant and his testimonies. (Ps 25:10)

Throughout Abraham's days, the days of Moses and the Judges Era, and through David's and Solomon's reigns, YHWH's Law stood as a light; easily understood to all who read it.

> For this commandment which I command you this day, **it is not hidden from you**, neither is it far off. It is not in heaven, that you should say, Who shall go up for us to heaven, and bring it to us, that we may hear it, and do it? Neither is it beyond the sea, that you should say, Who shall go over the sea for us, and bring it to us, that we may hear it, and do it? But **the word is very near to you, in your mouth, and in your heart, that you may do it**. (Deut 30:11–14)

YHWH did not desire to hide who he was. Nor did he desire to hide the path to life. Rather he desired all humanity to know and understand him (Jer 31:34). YHWH did not hide himself or his plan of salvation to Israel, but openly declared his way of life through his Law.

> *I have not spoken in secret*, in a dark place of the earth: I said not to the seed of Jacob, Seek you me in vain: I YHWH speak righteousness, I declare things that are right. (Isa 45:19)

If YHWH did not speak from a secret or dark place *then* he gave his truth openly, without reserve.

> Come near to me, hear you this; *I have not spoken in secret from the beginning*; from the time that it was, there am I: and now the Lord YHWH, and his Spirit, has sent me. Thus says YHWH, your Redeemer, the Holy One of Israel; I am YHWH your God which teaches you to profit, *which leads you by the way that you should go*. (Isa 48:16–17)

Throughout Israel's early history YHWH had endeavored to lead Israel in his paths of righteousness (Ps 23:3). He desired humanity to love him and to emulate his character. Despite YHWH's earnest pleas, proddings, promises, warnings, and disciplining of his people, his children continued down a destructively rebellious path.

YHWH's Testimony openly forewarned the day when YHWH would hide and obscure the clear knowledge and understanding of his path of life. He would take the constitutional Law—the way of life—that the Israelites so bitterly despised away from them. He would blind the nation so she could no longer discern YHWH's truth, understand his precepts, or see the consequences for breach of contract with God. With this understanding, we can appreciate the next judgment listed within the curses of the Moab-Shechem Covenant.

B. The Noonday Curse (745 BCE)

> YHWH shall smite you with madness, and blindness, and astonishment of heart: And **you shall grope at noonday, as the blind gropes in darkness**, and you shall not prosper in your ways: and you shall be only oppressed and spoiled evermore, and *no man shall save you*. (Deut 28:28–29)

When YHWH endeavored to deliver Israel at the exodus, one of the last plagues he used on Egypt was darkness (Exod 10:22). The Noonday curse requited this Egyptian plague over the whole nation of Israel (see Amos 4: 10). Israel's noonday darkness was not a literal dark day, as it was for Egypt, but a blindness that darkened or veiled Scripture, removing man's ability "to see" or discern truth.

Isaiah also refers to this darkened day.

> For YHWH has poured out on you *the spirit of deep sleep*, and has *closed your eyes*: the prophets and your rulers, the seers has he covered. (Isa 29:10)
>
> Let their eyes be darkened, that they see not; and make their loins continually to shake. (Ps 69:23)
>
> For, behold, the darkness shall cover the earth, and gross darkness the people. (Isa 60:2)

David also prophesied of the sleeping spirit that *YHWH would send forth* at the Noonday epoch, stating that the "evil spirit" would be sent at Noonday.

> You shall not be afraid of terror by night; nor of the arrow flying by day; nor of the evil thing (KJV—pestilence) that walks in *darkness*; nor of calamity and *the evil spirit at noon-day*. (Ps 91:5–6, LXX)[27]

When YHWH sent plagues to Egypt, he caused darkness to fall on the nation first, then sent pestilences, culminating in the death of their firstborn. YHWH ordained this spirit of slumber as a judgment to fulfill the Temple's prophetic veil to hide the knowledge of his unfailing and unchanging covenants with Israel—a judgment plainly disclosed in the Testimony, which Israel had publically accepted for herself (Josh 8:30–35) and which stipulated the consequences for Israel's disobedience to his constitutional Law. This curse obscured the true doctrine in YHWH's Law (Prov 4:2; Ps 119:142), as Israel began to turn to the precepts of men for understanding YHWH's truth (Isa 29:13) instead of the words and precepts in YHWH's *written* constitutional Law.

YHWH would judge Israel for her rebellion, covering the nation with blindness and madness, leaving his people to grope in the darkness (Deut 28:28) that would fall so unexpected. The aftermath of this curse was the vastly differing interpretations of Scripture. YHWH's judgment closed Scripture to the eyes of Israel; it became a vision

> as the words of a book that is sealed, which men deliver to one that is learned, saying, Read this, I pray you: and he said, I cannot; for it is sealed: And the book is delivered to him that is not learned, saying, Read this, I pray you: and he said, I am not learned. . . . Therefore, behold, I will proceed to do a marvelous work among this people, even a marvelous work and a wonder: for the wisdom of

their wise men shall perish, *and the understanding of their prudent men shall be hid.* (Isa 29:11–12, 14)

YHWH sent forth a spirit of blindness to darken and hide the prudent's understanding because Israel had "removed their heart far from him and their fear toward him was taught by the *precepts* of men" (Isa 29:13). Therefore YHWH covered the very truth they despised with a veil of sleep and slumber. He gave his people over to their own lusts and their own hearts' desires and the vanities of their oral traditions. "Their own way would correct them and their own backslidings reprove them, so that the nation might know that it is evil and bitter, that they had forsaken YHWH their God" (Jer 2:19).[28] Thus, YHWH's judgment concealed Scripture in darkness, causing every blind man to go his own way, *as though* Scripture was too high above to understand (Deut 30:11–14).

Isaiah again refers to the Noonday's darkness, reporting that YHWH would turn the world upside down (Isa 24:1). As humanity turned away from his Law by esteeming the counsel of the scribes and elders above the word of God, wrong would begin to seem right in humanity's eyes (Isa 5:20–25). Her leaders would pervert YHWH's pure constitution by adding to and deleting from it.

I will bring the blind by *a way that they knew not;* I will lead them in paths that they have not known: I will make darkness light before them, and crooked things straight. These things will I do to them, and *not* forsake them. *They shall be turned back, they shall be greatly ashamed.* (Isa 42:16–17)

Israel's idolatry continually blinded the nation and led her people down *unfamiliar paths.* So YHWH would apply the opposite and equal reaction of the Law by placing stumbling blocks before the nation. When a blind person is brought down a path unfamiliar to her, she will often stumble and fall. This verse symbolized Israel's seeking life outside the covenantal Law that both protected the nation from oppression and disease while preserving knowledge of truth. Previously, the only path that YHWH had led Israel along was the truth of his Law, and her sight was clear. The basis of Israel's doctrinal blindness, however, would be the *ideals and precepts of men*, which depart from the precepts of his Law, causing her to go down a different path, to her own shame.

But my people would not listen to my voice; and Israel would none of me. So I gave them up to their own hearts' lust: and they walked in their own counsels. (Ps 81:11–12)

Wherefore the Lord said, Forasmuch as this people draw near me with their mouth, and with their lips do honor me, but have removed their heart far from me, and their fear toward me is taught by the precept of men:[29] Therefore, look, I will proceed to do a marvellous work among this people, even a marvellous work and a wonder: for the wisdom of their wise men shall perish, and the understanding of their prudent men *shall be hid*. (Isa 29:13–14; see Isa 28:7–13)

The Tabernacle's prophetic structure had foretold the veiling of the most Holy Place, which represented hiding the knowledge and truth of the Creator's unchanging words in his unchanging constitutional covenants. Israel had sought the wine of false doctrine since her infancy, so YHWH's judgment at Noonday obscured and veiled the Creator's truth, established by his covenants, so that he could in a later epoch give the people the false doctrine they had lusted after for so long.[30]

C. One Nation under Darkness

Up to this point in the Testimonial Law and in the nation's history, Leviticus's and Deuteronomy's curses predominantly fell on the Northern Kingdom. Many of Judah's kings, such as Hezekiah and Josiah turned from their forefathers' sins, and the nation met with reprieve. In contrast, no Samarian king ever returned to walk in the way of YHWH. This is why many of the curses, such as Diaspora from the land (Deut 28:21; Num 33:50–56) and the final judgment in this phase of the Prophetic Law befell the Northern Kingdom first. The Noonday curse, however, fell on both nations, not just Ephraim. Understanding exactly when Noonday occurred greatly enlightens our interpretation of the prophets' written word. Seeing when each prophet lived and wrote his testimony is essential for comprehending the Noonday curse.[31] Amos and Micah lived before Noonday prevailed against the nation's prophets; their testimonies provide crucial understanding about what would happen at the Noonday Judgment.

D. Light of the Prophets

Amos' testimony ended a few years before his son Isaiah's testimony began. Amos began to prophesy (*c.* 800 BCE) during Jeroboam II's reign or about 130 years before Ephraim's last deportation. His "plumbline" prophecy began a thread of the Law's *Darkness at Noonday* on which other prophets would build; they would give greater definition to the pattern of YHWH's strange and marvelous work. Amos' prophecy (cited below) referred to the Prophetic Law's Noonday and ensuing Day of Judgment (Day of YHWH) ordained in the Song of Moses (Deuteronomy 32).

YHWH has sworn by the excellency of Jacob, Surely I will never forget any of their works. Shall not the land tremble for this, and every one mourn that dwells therein? and it shall rise up wholly as a flood; and it shall be cast out and drowned, as by the flood of Egypt. (9) And it shall come to pass in that day, said YHWH God, that I will cause the *SUN TO GO DOWN AT NOON, and I will darken the earth in the clear day*: And I will turn your feasts into mourning, and all your songs into lamentation; and I will bring up sackcloth on all loins, and baldness on every head; and I will make it as the mourning of an only son, and the end of it as a bitter day. (11) Behold, the days come, said YHWH God, that I will send a famine in the land, not a famine of bread, nor a thirst for water, but the hearing of the words of YHWH: And they shall wander from sea to sea, and from the north even to the east, they shall run to and fro to seek the word of YHWH and shall not find it. In that day shall the fair virgins and young men faint for thirst. They that swear by the sin of Samaria, and say, Your god, O Dan, lives; and, The manner of Beer-sheba lives; even they shall fall, and never rise up again. (9:1) I saw YHWH standing on the altar: and he said, Smite the lintel of the door, that the posts may shake: and cut them in the head, all of them; and I will slay the last of them with the sword: he that flees of them shall not flee away, and he that escapes of them shall not be delivered. Though they dig into hell, there shall my hand take them; though they climb up to heaven, there will I bring them down: And though they hide themselves in the top of Carmel, I will search and take them out there; and though they be hid from my sight in the bottom of the sea, there will I command the serpent, and he shall bite them: *(9:4)* **And though they go into captivity before their enemies, there will I command the sword, and it shall slay them**: *and I will set my eyes on them for evil, and not for good.* And YHWH God of hosts is he that touches the land, and it shall melt, and all that dwell therein shall mourn: and it shall rise up wholly like a flood; and shall be drowned, as by the flood of Egypt. It is he that builds his stories in the heaven, and has founded his troop in the earth; he that calls for the waters of the sea, and pours them out on the face of the earth: YHWH is his name. Are you not as children of the Ethiopians to me, O Children of Israel? Said YHWH. Have not I brought up Israel out of the land of Egypt? and the Philistines from Caphtor, and the Syrians from Kir?

Behold, the eyes of YHWH God are on the sinful kingdom, and I will destroy it from off the face of the earth; saving that I will not utterly destroy the House of Jacob, said YHWH. (9:9) For, see, I will command, and I will sift the House of Israel among all nations, like as corn is sifted in a sieve, yet shall not the least grain fall upon the earth. All the sinners of my people shall die by the sword, which say, "The evil shall not overtake nor prevent us." (Amos 8:7–9:10)

Notice how Amos's chronology follows the Testimonial Law. The sun goes down at noon (Amos 8:9); then there is no word from YHWH (8:11); this is followed by a dark Passover for the people of Israel (9:1). While still in captivity, the sword will begin to slay during YHWH's holocaust (Amos 9:4; see Lev 26:33); and finally, Israel is sifted into all nations (Amos 9:9). Notice also that only sinners among the people will be slain (Amos 9:10). Amos's testimony parallels the Prophetic Law of Deuteronomy and Leviticus precisely.

Micah also prophesied before the sun went down at noon. He was the second prophet to foretell of the day's darkening and subsequent judgment. Micah was a contemporary of Amos and began to write his testimony during Jotham's reign, shortly after Amos's testimonies had ended (see Table 8.1. on p. 324–25). He prophesied against the family of Ahab, whose descendants were still part of the House of David in Michah's days. This is what Micah testified regarding Noonday:

> Thus said YHWH concerning the prophets that make my people err, that bite with their teeth, and cry, Peace; and he that puts not into their mouths, they even prepare war against him. **Therefore night shall be to you**, that you shall not have a vision; and it shall be **dark** to you, that you shall not divine; and *the sun shall go down over the prophets, and the day shall be dark over them.* Then shall the seers be ashamed, and the diviners confounded: yes, they shall all cover their lips; **for there is** *no answer* of God. (Mic 3:5–7)

Micah foretold that YHWH would darken knowledge so that the false prophets who turned Israel away from him could no longer prophecy according to his Testimony. The sun would "set" on the prophets as YHWH refused to answer their questions or give word to his people. Micah's prophecy parallels Amos's testimony. YHWH sent his prophets to fully disclose and warn about his Noon Day Judgment. The question now to be asked is: when did Noonday occur?

E. Isaiah—A Son of Korah?

David's transcription of the Law opened his eyes to see the multifaceted purposes of the Law's statutes, the Tabernacle's ordinances, the statutes, and the Temple furniture. From this understanding, YHWH's spirit caused David to see many prophets and events that would occur in Israel's future.[32] In chap. 8.IV, we saw that many of David's and Asaph's psalms were prophecies hidden within praises to YHWH (see Illustration 15.2).

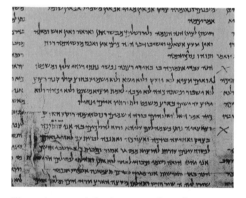

Illustration 15.2. A few lines in Hebrew from one of the two scrolls of Isaiah found in the cave at Qumron.

Many psalms were written as instruction for Israel's prophets and are entitled "for instruction of the sons of Korah."[33] The sons of Kohath were Levites who were separated to serve in the Tabernacle but were not given the priesthood (Num 16:8–10; 3:30–31). Korah was Kohath's grandson who rebelled in the wilderness, seeking the priesthood, and disappearing into the earth (Num 16:27–30). Korah's sons were not destroyed in this judgment (Num 26:11), and the descendants of Kohath traditionally held the role of prophet. This is why the Tabernacle's prophetic vessels were covered and hidden from their view (Num 4:4–15; 3:31). The independent testimony of Korah's sons added another witness to the Tabernacle's structure and its prophetic implements.

Scripture includes at least two direct references to the sons of Korah and Kohath as serving in the role of prophet (see 2 Chr 29:30; see also 1 Sam 9:9). The Book of 1st Chronicles tells us: "Moreover David and the captains of the host separated to the service of the sons of Asaph, and of Heman, and of Jeduthun, **who should prophesy** with harps, with psalteries, and with cymbals: and the number of the workmen according to their service" (1 Chr 25:1). Asaph is listed as a Kohathite and David's seer (1 Chr 26:1; 2 Chr 29:30); Heman is also listed as a Kohathite and David's seer (1 Chr 6:33; 25:5). Jeduthun's Kohathite lineage held the profession of harpist (1 Chr 25:3), and Jeduthun is listed among David's prophets (2 Chr 35:15). The best example of Korah's sons' serving in the role of prophet is found in a prophecy issued by two of Asaph's sons:

> Then on Jahaziel the son of Zechariah, the son of Benaiah, the son of Jeiel, the son of Mattaniah, **a Levite of the sons of Asaph**, came the Spirit of YHWH in the middle of the congregation; And he said, Listen you, all Judah, and you inhabitants of Jerusalem, and you king Jehoshaphat, Thus said YHWH to you, Be not afraid nor dismayed by reason of this great multitude; for the battle is not yours, but God's. Tomorrow go you down against them: behold, they come up by the cliff of Ziz; and you shall find them at the end of the brook, before the wilderness of Jeruel. You shall not need to fight in this battle: set yourselves, stand you still, and see the salvation of YHWH with you, O Judah and Jerusalem: fear not, nor be dismayed; tomorrow go out against them: for YHWH will be with you. . . And the Levites, of the children of the **Kohathites, and of the children of the Korhites**, stood up to praise YHWH God of Israel with a loud voice on high. (2 Chr 20:14–17, 19)

When David and Samuel established the various Levitical offices (1 Chr 9:22),[34] they made the Korahites (variant Korhite/Korahite) role as prophet a hereditary post.[35] This is why Asaph's son Jahaziel is listed among the Kohathites who praised YHWH. Another account describes the hereditary role of prophecy more clearly:

> The sons of Asaph: Zaccur, and Joseph, and Nethaniah, and Asarelah, the sons of Asaph under the hands of Asaph, **which prophesied according to the order of the king**. (1 Chr 25:2)

David ordered the Levites to prophesy in the Temple before YHWH, and their prophetic psalms foretold Israel's future.

A psalm's title explains its purpose. Psalm 72, for instance, prophesied of events to occur in Solomon's life, while Psalm 45 prophesied about Hadassah (Esther).[36] Psalm 137 ordained Jeremiah's role as prophet while prophesying of Judah's Babylonian Diaspora. David wrote Psalm 138 as instruction for Haggai and Zechariah.[37] David and the Korathites looked to the Law—its statutes (Ps 119:54), ordinances, and Testimony (Isa 8:16, 20)—when prophesying. They took the prophecies they had come to understand in the Law and based many of their Psalms on them. Such is the case with Psalm 87, which foretold a particular prophet whom YHWH would send to Israel. Psalm 87 is entitled "A Psalm of a Song for the sons of Korah."

The following text is David's instruction to a particular prophet—a son of Korah—whom YHWH would send to Israel.

His foundations are in the holy mountains. YHWH (a) loves the gates of Zion more than all the tabernacles of Jacob. Glorious things have been spoken of you, O city of God. Pause.

I will make mention of (b) Rahab and Babylon to them that know me: behold also the Philistines, and Tyre, and the people of the Ethiopians: these were born there. A man shall say Zion is my mother; and a man was born in her; and the Highest himself has founded her. YHWH shall recount it in the writing of the people, and of these princes that have been born in her. Pause. The dwelling of all within you is as the dwelling of those that rejoice.[38] (Psalm 87, LXX)

When the author of Psalm 137 prophesied and ordained Jeremiah's testimony, he used the personal pronoun "I" to distinguish what Jeremiah would do (see pp. 628–31). Psalm 87 continues to use this persona device. This psalm ordains the role of another prophet whom YHWH would send to Israel, who would fulfill all the points mentioned above. Of whom did Psalm 87 prophesy? Who was the prophet that would mention Rahab and Babylon? It was Isaiah. Both Isaiah and his father, Amos, were sons of Korah.[39] No other prophet (a) remembered the love YHWH had for Zion more than Isaiah. He proclaimed "YHWH's love for Zion's gates, more then all the dwellings of Jacob" in Isaiah 18, 33, and 52. He continued to fulfill this prophecy by establishing the righteous glory of Zion as the overwhelming hope of the latter-day remnant:

Zion shall be redeemed with judgment, and her converts with righteousness (Isa 1:27). I have put my words in your mouth, and I have covered you in the shadow of my hand, that I may plant the heavens, and lay the foundations of the earth, and say to **Zion, You are my people.** (Isa 51:16; see also Isa 51:2–4; 46:13; 35:10)

Isaiah obeyed David's instruction by (b) "making mention of Rahab" when he wrote his prophecy in a book: "Are you not it that has cut **Rahab**, and wounded the dragon?" (Isa 51:9). Isaiah fulfilled David's command to testify of Babylon in Isaiah ch. 13; and of Philistia in Isa 11:14 and 14:29–31; Tyre in ch. 23; and the people of Ethiopia in Isaiah 20. David passed a "prophetical baton"[40] to Isaiah, empowering him to speak in the name of YHWH. Isaiah lived during the Noonday epoch and was the key prophet who wrote during Pekah's and Hezekiah's reigns. *YHWH's specific mission to Isaiah fulfilled the Noonday Judgment against Israel.*

F. *Isaiah Obeys YHWH's Commission to Blind Israel*

Isaiah inherited a unique mission. During the last year of Uzziah's reign, YHWH appeared to Isaiah, commanding him to blind Israel. YHWH commissioned Isaiah to "shut Israel's eyes," so she could not see (Isa 6:10; 44:18), thus fulfilling the Testimony's Noonday curse. The Law had prophesied that YHWH would "smite you with madness, and blindness, and astonishment of heart: **And you shall grope at noonday, as the blind grope in darkness**, and you shall not prosper in your ways: and you shall be only oppressed and spoiled evermore, and no man shall save you" (Deut 28:28–29). Isaiah's prophetic role and his written testimony veiled Scripture, hiding knowledge of humanity's Creator.

This was YHWH's commission to Isaiah:

> In the year that king Uzziah died **I saw also YHWH sitting on a throne**, high and lifted up, and his train filled the temple. . . . Also I heard the voice of YHWH, saying, Whom shall I send, and who will go for us? Then said I, Here am I; send me. And he said, **Go, and tell this people, (a) Hear you indeed, but understand not; and see you indeed, but perceive not.** Make the heart of this people fat, and make their ears heavy, and **shut their eyes**; lest they see with their eyes, and hear with their ears, and understand with their heart, and (b) convert, and (c) be healed. (Isa 6:1, 8–10)

Isaiah's vision (a) established Scripture's darkness as the Noon Day Judgment. YHWH commissioned Isaiah in the last year of Uzziah's reign, in *c.* 745 BCE. This would also have been the first year of Pekah's reign over Samaria (Isa 6:1; see Table 9.39 or 9.40 on pp. 406–7, 409). **So Pekah's first year is the benchmark for the Noonday epoch.** Notice that Isaiah's commission to veil Scripture and to blind Israel would (b) prevent Israel from returning to YHWH and (c) being healed. The word of YHWH in Isaiah's book becomes the first "sealed" book in Israel's history (Isa 29:11).

Isaiah's testimony built on the words of the Law, the Psalms, and the Books of Amos and Micah by prophesying that YHWH would pour out "the spirit of deep sleep" (Isa 29:10). YHWH would "close" the "eyes of the nation, their prophets, their rulers, and their seers" so that they should walk in Scriptural darkness (Isa 30:27–28). How did YHWH cause a spirit of deep sleep to cover the people of Israel? Isaiah blinded Israel by mixing up the chronology of events to befall Israel. He shuffled the chronology established in the Testimonial Law, often using "in that day" to specify when an epoch or event is to occur rather than adhering to the Testimony's chronological timeline.[41] The words that Isaiah speaks are doctrinally true and wholly in accord with the precepts of the Law, but his chronology is not. Many of his prophecies are written obscurely so that the details contained in his prophecies find increasing importance. It is only by looking to the Prophetic Law (i.e., Testimony) that the Book of Isaiah can be accurately understood (Isa 8:16). This is why Isaiah writes: "To the Law and to the Testimony: if they speak not according to this word, it is because there is no light in them" (Isa 8:20).

G. Thrones of Judgment

David and the Levites established many symbolic definitions and concepts in their praises. When we sought to understand the symbolism of the Tabernacle's fixtures, we discovered that the Book of Psalms had preserved definitions for: the golden candle, the altar's horns, the stones of the earthen altar, the cherubim, the mercy seat, and even the purpose for veiling the Holy of Holies.[42] Another Psalm defines the symbol of *thrones*.

> But YHWH shall endure forever: he has prepared his **throne for judgment**. And he shall judge the world in righteousness, he shall minister judgment to the people in uprightness. (Ps 9:7–8)

David, the author of Psalm 9, understood a throne's purpose. As Israel's king, he issued judgments (verdicts) in the cases brought before him.[43] Isaiah understood that the "throne" was the place where judgment occurred: rewarding the righteous and condemning the wicked (Deut 25:1). Isaiah builds on David's symbolic use of "thrones" as the place where judgment occurs. "I saw also YHWH **sitting on a throne**, high and lifted up" (Isa 6:1). Isaiah indicates that the mission YHWH handed to him while sitting on his throne was to fulfill the Creator's judgment against a wicked nation. This further supports Isaiah's role of also fulfilling YHWH's Noonday judgment in Deut 28:28–29.

Before sunset prevailed in Israel, the Books of Amos and Micah had followed the chronology set forth in the covenant's Testimony. But now Israel's prophets would no longer speak to the people in a literal style. Isaiah's testimony signaled the epoch of Noonday, which commenced in Pekah's 1st year (see Appendix A: Table 9.50/5, pp. 885–87). As Israel entered her first darkened day, the word of YHWH would be written in a hidden and obscure manner. From this time forward, the only distinguishable light from the Testimonial Law (Isa 8:20, 16) would fade into obscurity as prophets, elders, and wisemen looked outside the covenant to define their precepts of truth.

> But the word of YHWH was to them precept on precept, precept on precept; line on line, line on line; here a little, and there a little; **that they might go, and fall backward, and be broken, and snared, and taken.** (Isa 28:13)

That Noonday had already been fulfilled in Josiah's day is evidenced by the name *Zephaniah*, meaning 'Yah has secreted.' Zephaniah, who prophesied about 100 years after the Noonday epoch, followed Isaiah's example by mixing up the sequence of events to befall Israel. Zephaniah fulfilled the meaning of his name by veiling the chronological order of YHWH's judgments and by mentioning Israel's hidden Judgment Day as though it occurred before Israel's deportation (Zeph 1:7–18); he prophesied of Noonday as though it would occur in the future, rather than having already occurred in the past (Zeph 2:4). Zephaniah and subsequent prophets followed Isaiah's example of mixing up Israel's chronological prophecy. It is only by looking to the Testimonial Law that we can understand the prophets who lived after Isaiah.

16

The Testimony Ordains Israel's Deportations

I. THE THIRD 70-YEAR EPOCH ENDS (804-734 BCE, CONTINUED)

Deut 28:30-33	Israel is so evil that the land fails for justice (v. 31). Saviors are no
Lev 26:23-25	longer sent to deliver Israel. Samaria's 2nd deportation occurs.
	Kings of Samaria: Pekah/Judah: Ahaz–Hezekiah
	3rd 7 Times ends/4th 7 Times begins

Deut 28:30-33: You shall betroth a wife, and another man shall lie with her: you shall build an house, and you shall not live in it: you shall plant a vineyard, and (a) shall not gather the grapes of it. Your ox (b) shall be slain before your eyes, and you shall not eat of it: your ass shall be (c) violently taken away from before your face, and shall not be restored to you: your sheep shall be (d) given **to your enemies**, and you shall have none to rescue them. (e) **Your sons and your daughters shall be given to another people**, and your eyes shall look, and fail with longing for them all the daylong: and there shall be no might in your hand. The fruit of your land, and all your labors, (f) **shall a nation which you know not** eat up; and you shall be only oppressed and crushed always.

Lev 26:23-35: And if you will not be reformed by me by these things, but will walk contrary to me; Then will I also walk contrary to you, and will punish you yet seven times for your sins. And I will **bring a sword on you**, that shall avenge the quarrel of my covenant.

During this epoch, Israel walked contrary to the way of YHWH. The Northern Kingdom's degradation escalated as idolatry, adultery, thieving, murder, and other injustices prevailed.

The national punishment outlined in the third phase foretold that Assyria's (c) sword would "violently take away" Samaria's (d) ass, sheep, and (b) cattle, while remaining livestock would be taken as (d) tribute paid to Israel's enemies. The nation that YHWH employed to punish Israel would be one that (f) "they knew not." Thus, the Testimony indicated that this enemy would not be native to Israel's borders but would come from a far-off land. This wording precluded any Canaanite or Egyptian nation from rendering justice to Israel at the end of the Testimony's third epoch (see Appendix A: Table 9.50/5, pp. 885–87).

The Law once again evidences that (e) Samaria's "sons and daughters would be given to another people." The Testimony acknowledges Israel's second deportation at the hand of Tiglath-pileser, which occurred during Pekah's reign.

> In the days of Pekah king of Israel came Tiglath-pileser king of Assyria, and took Ijon, and Abel-Beth-Maachah, and Jonoah, and Kedesh, and Hazor, and Gilead, and Galilee, all the land of Naphtali, and *carried them captive to Assyria*. (2 Kgs 15:29)

Although Ephraim had (a) planted vineyards, the people never had a chance to harvest them. Assyrian tablets also witnessed Israel's second deportation. A fragmentary annalistic text of Tiglath-pileser III testifies: "Gal'za, Abilakka which are adjacent to Israel and the wide land of Naphtali, in its entire extent, I united with Assyria. Officers of mine I installed as governors upon them."[1] Assyria's archives evidence Naphtali's deportation, confirming the Law's fidelity to its own standards by pre-ordaining Israel's deportations as judgments, which limited Israel's wickedness.

II. THE FOURTH EPOCH OF 7 TIMES (734–664 BCE)

Deut 28:34–37 **Lev 26:26**	The Northern Kingdom is deported along with her king. Prophecy of Jezreel (Hos 1:4); Ephraim's 3rd deportation; 1st recorded deportation of Judah. Kings of Samaria: Pekah–Hoshea/Judah: Hezekiah–Manasseh 4th 7th Time begins

Deut 28:34–37: So that you shall be (a) mad for the sight of your eyes which you shall see. YHWH shall smite you in the knees, and in the legs, with a (b) sore botch that cannot be healed, from the sole of your foot to the top of your head. YHWH shall (c) **bring you, and your (d) king which you shall set over you, to a nation** which neither you nor your fathers have known; and (e) **there shall you serve other gods, wood and stone.** And you shall become an (f) astonishment, a proverb, and a (g) byword, among all (h) nations where YHWH shall lead you.

Lev 26:25–26: And when you are gathered together within your cities, I will send the (b) pestilence among you; and (c, d) you shall be delivered into the hand of the enemy. And when I have (i) broken the staff of your bread, ten women shall bake your bread in one oven, and they shall deliver you your bread again by weight: and you shall eat, and not be satisfied.

A. *Sunset Has Prevailed against Truth*

The phrasing of Deuteronomy's text (a) indicates that the Noonday Judgment has fallen. Jeremiah upholds this conclusion. When he began receiving YHWH's word in Josiah's 13th year (Jer 25:3), Jeremiah indicated that the Noonday had already passed. "Hear now this, O foolish people, and without understanding; which *have eyes, and see not; which have ears, and hear not*" (Jer 5:21). Isaiah had blinded Israel by veiling Scripture with a darkened cloak. Isaiah's mission to cause the people to "hear indeed, but understand not; and see you indeed, but perceive not" (Isa 6:1, 8–10) has been accomplished. Judah and Samaria are blind to understanding truth or the constitutional precepts on which it was based. This fact is further evidenced in words spoken by Jerusalem's elders.

Jeremiah had prophesied against the capital city proclaiming that YHWH would uproot Jerusalem, just as he had Shiloh. His testimony angered the priests, false prophets, and other Jerusalem zealots into an uproar, provoking them to prosecute Jeremiah for blasphemy. The elders tried Jeremiah's case at the entry of the new gate of YHWH's house. Judah's leaders defended Jeremiah, arguing that he spoke in YHWH's name. The Judean elders spoke on Jeremiah's behalf, citing the prophet Micah, who had also foretold Jerusalem's destruction. The elders blindly cited Micah's prophecies to refute Jeremiah's testimony, claiming that Micah's prophecies had not occurred because YHWH had repented of the evil proposed against Jerusalem!

> Micah the Morasthite prophesied in the days of Hezekiah king of Judah, and spoke to all the people of Judah, saying, Thus said YHWH of hosts; Zion shall be plowed like a field, and Jerusalem shall become heaps, and the mountains of the house as the high places of a forest. Did Hezekiah king of Judah and all Judah put him at all to death? Did he not fear YHWH, and besought YHWH, and **YHWH repented him of the evil which he had pronounced against them?** Thus might we procure great evil against our souls. (Jer 26:18–19)

The polemic of Judah's elders demonstrates that the knowledge of truth had already been hidden from Judah's sight long before the Diaspora. The people had not repented from their rebellious ways; their eyes were closed to understand the Law and YHWH's prophets. In subsequent epochs, the teachings of Judah's blinded elders and sages would continue to confuse Israel and pervert truth. Many of Judah's elders who defended Jeremiah lived to see the evil that Micah had prophesied against Jerusalem be fulfilled.

B. *Pestilence*

Deuteronomy's Testimony, which aligns with the fourth 7 Times epoch, specifies that plagues would once more prevail against Israel: "And *when you are gathered together within your cities*, I will send the pestilence among you" (Lev 26:26). Cholera, dysentery, Bubonic

Plague, Black Death, and other diseases emerge from poor sanitation. These diseases are easily transmitted from one host carrying bacteria, infection, and other parasites to another host. Protracted sieges often lasted several years, providing the perfect breeding ground for many diseases.[2]

Deuteronomy witnessed that the (b) "sore botch that cannot be healed" would fall on Israel again in the fourth epoch (Deut 28:34–35). Scripture describes one such plague that occurred in Jerusalem during Hezekiah's reign:

> In those days was Hezekiah sick to death. And the prophet Isaiah the son of Amoz came to him, and said to him, Thus said YHWH, (a) Set your house in order; for you shall die, and not live. Then he turned his face to the wall, and prayed to YHWH, saying, I beseech you, O YHWH, remember now how I have walked before you in truth and with a perfect heart, and have done that which is good in your sight. And Hezekiah wept sore. And it came to pass, before Isaiah was gone out to the middle court, that the word of YHWH came into him, saying, Turn again, and tell Hezekiah the captain of my people, Thus said YHWH, the God of David your father, I have heard your prayer, I have seen your tears: behold, I will heal you: on the third day you shall go up to the house of YHWH. And I will add to your days fifteen years; and I will deliver you and this city out of the hand of the king of Assyria; and I will defend this city for my own sake, and for my servant David's sake. And Isaiah said, Take a lump of figs. And they took and laid it on (b) the *boil*, and he recovered. (2 Kgs 20:1–7)

The Testimony's "sore botch" occurred in Hezekiah's lifetime and it was the reason that Hezekiah was "sick to death." Isaiah was familiar with the covenant's Testimony. He knew that the Law withheld healing during this era, so he advised the king to prepare his house for his death. When Hezekiah pleaded for YHWH's mercy, the Creator agreed to heal Hezekiah due to the king's righteous desire to walk in his way wholeheartedly. Since Hezekiah obeyed, YHWH mercifully healed during an era when healing was otherwise withheld.

C. Samaria's Siege (717 BCE)

Ancient cities were walled and gated for protection. These defenses usually proved futile against the terrifying tactics tirelessly employed during siege. First, any water that could be diverted was redirected from the city. Food stores outside the wall were raided. Merchants were banned from the city. Trees were felled, and ramps were erected to scale the enemy's walls or batter through them while archers were positioned atop latters.[3] The city, on the other hand, was usually well prepared to withstand an attack, having secured a large quantity of food and military supplies. Some cities could withstand a siege for a few months; others a few years. One of the longest sieges ever recorded was Nebuchadnezzar's war on Tyre, which lasted a whopping 13 years! Sometimes sieges ended by the enemy's penetrating the wall, but more often they ended because the inhabitants were driven to starvation, malnutrition, and devastating diseases (plagues).[4] When disease erupted, it weakened the population, thus forcing the city's surrender (see Illustration 16.1).

Shalmaneser began to besiege Samaria in Hezekiah's 4th year. During the three-year siege, Samaria's (i) "staff of bread was broken and was given to her by weight, yet it was not enough to satisfy the pangs of hunger" (Lev 26:26, paraphrased). Israel's Testimony accurately predicted the final days of Ephraim's Kingdom as she faced utter destruction during this phase of the Testimony, which had foretold the consequences for breaching covenant.

> Deut 28:36: YHWH shall (c) bring you, and (d) your king which you shall set over you, to a nation which neither you nor your fathers have known.

Illustration 16.1. Warriors scaling walls with ladders: bas-relief from the palace in Nineveh, *c.* 7th century BCE.

The Prophetic Law consistently recognizes each national deportation. The Law not only foretold Ephraim's deportation, it accurately prophesied the (d) demise of the Northern Kingdom's Monarchy. Ephraim's (c) 3rd deportation occurred in Hezekiah's 6th year (2 Kgs 17:6; 18:10), when Sargon captured King Hoshea, and the strength of the people was "delivered into the hand of their enemy." Sargon's texts corroborate the Testimony's prophecy.

> At the beginning of my royal rule . . . the town of the Samarians I besieged, conquered. . . . I lead away as prisoners 27,290 inhabitants of it and equipped from among them soldiers to man 50 chariots for my royal corps. . . The town I rebuilt better than it was before and settled therein people from countries which I myself had conquered.[5]

Judah's 1st deportation also occurred during this phase. Sennacherib had besieged 46 "strong cities" belonging to Judah, including Lachish. His annals record Judah's first deportation. "I *drove out* of them 200,150 people, young and old, male and female, horses, mules, donkeys, camels, big and small cattle beyond counting, and considered them booty."[6] Ephraim's 3rd deportation and Judah's 1st deportation continue to fulfill the prophesied consequences of the nation's rebellion against YHWH's command to drive out Canaan's inhabitants as well. Although YHWH delivered Hezekiah and Jerusalem from Assyria's hand, Ephraim's and Judah's outlying cities were not protected.

D. YHWH Sends Israel to Serve Other Gods

> YHWH shall bring you, and your king which you shall set over you, to a nation which neither you nor your fathers have known; and (e) **there shall you serve other gods, wood and stone**. (Deut 28:36)

YHWH's founding precept based judgment on an "eye for an eye and a tooth for a tooth" principle: opposite and equal reactions. Israel had sought to worship false gods of wood and stone since her infancy. During her Egyptian enslavement she had worshiped Egypt's gods (Josh 24:14; 2 Sam 7:23; Ps 78:56–57). Once she entered the Promised Land, she turned to worship Canaan's deities. YHWH's judgment at this epoch gave Israel the very idolatry she had lusted after for so long: but her lust would be satisfied in foreign nations. She would not fulfill her desire within YHWH's covenanted land.

When YHWH delivered Israel out of Egypt she was the youngest of all nations of the earth (Deut 32:8). Older, well-established nations had already stopped walking in his way, so the Creator chose Israel to preserve his truth (see chap. 2.I). Moses warned Israel that if she made images of YHWH's creation, her lust would drive her to worship the work of her hands, leading her in the footsteps of former nations (Deut 4:14–19). Like other nations, YHWH would give his people over to serving false gods.

> Lest you lift up your eyes to heaven, and when you see the *sun, and the moon, and the stars, even all the host of heaven*, should be driven to worship them, and serve them, *which YHWH your God has divided to all nations under the whole heaven*. (Deut 4:19)

Halaq, the Hebrew word for "divided," means to 'to give, deal, distribute, apportion, or equip.'[7] Moses is saying that YHWH gave false gods to other nations as judgment for their rebellion. The Creator himself apportioned the "whole host of heaven" to rebellious nations to worship. This is why the ancient world associated its gods with stars and planets, and it is the reason that doctrine throughout the ancient world was so similar.[8] All nations worshiped the matriarch of the godhead, the "queen of heaven."[9] In Egypt, she was Isis and was identified with the star Sothis (Sirius). In Mesopotamia, the planet Venus was worshiped as Inana (Istar), who was known as the "lady of heaven." She was believed to be the daughter of the moon-god Nanna and sister of the sun-god Utu.[10] YHWH apportioned these false deities of the "heavenly host" among rebellious nations, allowing them to quench their sinful desires by receiving the consequences of their own choices (Ps 81:12; Jer 2:19).

When Assyria deported Samaria to Halah, Habor, Hara, and the Gozan River (1 Chr 5:26), Israel came in contact with Assyria's deities for the first time. The deities that Assyria worshiped were not the same gods that Israel's "father's had known." Mesopotamia's deities had different names, customs, rites, physical manifestations (images), temples, and cultures from the gods of Canaan. YHWH gave Israel to her sinful lusts just as he had former nations (see Illustration 16.2)

Illustration 16.2. Captives from Judah's city of Lachish carrying baggage on their way into exile. Part of a relief from the Palace of Sennacherib at Nineveh, 8th century BCE.

YHWH's method of judgment demonstrates fidelity and constancy because Deut 28:36 prophesied for Israel the very judgment YHWH had used on other nations (for their apostasy); thus, Israel was deported to foreign lands to worship false deities. YHWH freed Israel from his covenant so she (e) could seek the bondage of falsehood to her heart's content; however, her oppressive idolatry would no longer occur on YHWH's land (Lev 25:23). During the Diaspora, YHWH's land would enjoy the freedom of its Sabbaths (Lev 26:34–35), resting from Israel's iniquities, as YHWH let the bitter bondage, the consequence of Israel's lusts, correct her (Jer 2:19).

E. Israel Becomes a Taunting Proverb During the Diaspora

And you shall become an (f) astonishment, a proverb, and a (g) byword, among all (h) nations where YHWH shall lead you. (Deut 28:37)[11]

During the fourth 7 Times, a large portion of the nation was deported. YHWH informed these deportees that he would lead them through (h) many "nations." Assyria was only the first nation. Therefore, this curse evidenced a long Diaspora, when the whole House of Israel would be "sifted among" many nations (Amos 9:9). Each nation would bring Israel into contact with a new idea of God. Her doctrine would evolve as she served "new gods," and the wine procured from this strange mixture would render its own judgment, even though she was exiled from his land.[12]

During her long Diaspora, Israel would become a (g) byword, an adage for a desolate, God-forsaken nation.[13] Other nations would deride her people, taunting about whether YHWH had ever "chosen" Israel and questioning whether she had ever understood YHWH's truth. She would face continual persecution. Other nations would not believe that YHWH had established his eternal covenant with her. Other nations would not see that YHWH had given her a constitutional Law that was good for her, "wherein there is no death" (Prov 12:28), or that she possessed the Promised-Land birthright. Even fewer nations would believe that her national archives (Scripture) were historical. That this curse has been fulfilled is evident today in many academic publications. Scholars who do *not* believe the historicity of Scripture's accounts tauntingly dub scholars who do believe as "maximalists," implying that they distort evidence to support Scripture when little evidence exists. During Israel's long Diaspora and up to the present day, Israel has become a source of mockery and disbelief.

III. "NOT A PEOPLE" (~664 BCE)

Deut 28:38–41 Deportation of Ephraim fulfills Isa 7:8 and prophecy of Lo-Ruhamah—
"I will utterly take them away" (Hos 1:6); Ephraim's 4th deportation.
Manasseh is deported. Kings of Judah: Hezekiah–Manasseh
4th 7th Times ends

Deut 28:38–41: You shall carry much seed out to the field, and shall gather but little in; for the locust shall consume it. You shall plant vineyards, and dress them, but shall neither drink of the wine, nor gather the grapes; for the worms shall eat them. (a) You shall have **olive trees** throughout all your coasts, but you shall not anoint yourself with the oil; for your olive shall cast his fruit. (b) **You shall bear sons and daughters, but you shall not enjoy them; for they shall go into captivity.**

Verse 38 marks a transitional time, as Ephraim's plagues of seven begin to fall on Judah for her disobedience. This epoch was fulfilled during the prophet Hosea's life, when (a) the oil from Ephraim's olive trees was spent to satisfy Egyptian tribute. "Ephraim feeds on wind, and follows after the east wind: he daily increases lies and desolation; and they do make a covenant with the Assyrians, and *oil is carried into Egypt*" (Hos 12:1). Previous curses had included pestilences against Samaria's fruit (Deut 28:22–24, 30, 33). Egypt would claim as tribute payment the fruit that had survived the pestilence, during the 4th Testimonial epoch of Leviticus's Prophetic Law (see Appendix A: Table 9.50/5–6, pp. 885–89)

The Prophetic Law foretold that Ephraim's and Judah's taxation would increase. Evidence of Judah's tribute during Hezekiah's reign appears in Sennacherib's annals: "Thus I reduced his country, but *I still increased the tribute and the presents due to me* as his overlord."[14] Although Hezekiah sought YHWH and was one of Israel's most righteous kings, the people had not returned to follow their Maker. So, they bore the heavy burden by satisfying Sennacherib's ever-increasing tribute.

The accuracy and reality of the Testimony's prophecy is evidenced by Assyria's archives. Nineveh's texts support the Testimony, stating that there were no Samarian kings in the "land of Omri" following Hezekiah's reign (see Appendix A: Table 9.50/5, pp. 885–87). Assyria's archives demonstrate that Ephraim no longer maintained a Monarchy just as the Testimony had long before openly foretold (Deut 28:36). Deuteronomy's Prophetic Law is consistent with its own prophecy by mentioning each Assyrian deportation (b) of the Northern Kingdom. Ephraim's 4th and final deportation occurred during Ashurbanipal's reign.[15] The prophetic judgment was fulfilled (b) when "YHWH brought on them the captains of the host of the king of Assyria, which took Manasseh among the thorns, and bound him with fetters, and carried him to Babylon" (2 Chr 33:11). Israel bore sons and daughters but did not enjoy them, for they went into captivity or were sold into slavery.

Isaiah was a son of Korah who understood Leviticus's Prophetic Law. When he prophesied to Ahaz that Ephraim would be "not a people" (Isa 7:8), he knew that 5 years had already passed since the beginning of the 4th "7 Times" epoch. Isaiah understood that "7 Times" denoted 70 years, which left only 65 years remaining for that era: Ephraim would be wholly deported, never to be a nation again (see Table 14.3 on p. 678–79). By the time Jeremiah began to prophesy, Isaiah's 65 years had long since been accomplished. That Ephraim had been totally deported before Josiah's reign is evidenced by YHWH's instruction to Jeremiah to prophesy that he would "entirely" cast off Judah just as he had Samaria. "And I will cast you out of my sight, as I have cast out all your brothers, *even the whole seed of Ephraim*" (Jer 7:15).

IV. JERUSALEM INHERITS SAMARIA'S LINE (657-587 BCE)

Deut 28:42–46 Samaria's measuring line stretched over Jerusalem (Amos 7:7–9):
Lev 26:27–28 curses fall on Jacob (Judah). Judah becomes the tail—paying tribute
to Pharaoh Necho (2 Kgs 23:33). Kings of Judah: Manasseh, Josiah,
Jehoahaz, Jehoiakim.
5th 7 Times begins.

Deut 28:42–46: All your (a) trees and fruit of your land shall the locust consume. The stranger that is within you shall get up above you very high; and you shall come down very low. He shall lend to you, and you shall not lend to him: he shall be the head, and (b) you shall be the tail. (c) **Moreover all these curses** shall come on you, and shall pursue you, and overtake you, till you be destroyed; because you listened not to the voice of YHWH your God, to keep his commandments and his statutes which he commanded you: **And they shall be on you for a (d) sign and for a wonder, and on your seed forever.**

Lev 26:27–28: And if you will not for all this listen to me, but walk contrary to me; Then I will walk contrary to you also in fury; and I, even I, will chastise you seven times for your sins.

A. Tribute and King Manasseh's Return

Leviticus prophesies of a transitional epoch as Samaria's 70-year plumbline was stretched over Jerusalem. The plumbline began to measure Jerusalem when (c) Manasseh reentered the city after completing his 7-year exile in Assyria.[16] Remember that Manasseh was the fruit of Ahab's cursed lineage, and he had been Judah's most wicked king. Although YHWH mercifully redeemed him from exile, *he would not forgive Manasseh's sins (2 Kgs 24:4).* As a consequence for his heinous crimes (2 Kgs 21:11), YHWH would

> stretch over Jerusalem the line of Samaria, and the plummet of the House of Ahab: and wipe Jerusalem as a man wipes a dish, wiping it, and turning it upside down. (2 Kgs 21:13)

Only 70 years would pass from the day that Manasseh reentered the city until Jerusalem's final siege in Zedekiah's 12th year (see Appendix A: Table 9.50/6–7, pp. 888–91). YHWH had promised David that he would never take his mercy away from David's children as he had King Saul's (1 Chr 17:13; 2 Chr 21:7). But as David's seed grew increasingly evil, it became more merciful for YHWH to destroy this particular Davidic line than to let them continue in their self-destroying and oppressive iniquities (Jer 2:19). YHWH would allow them to finally experience the consequences of their choices.

During Manasseh's and Jehoiakim's reigns, the curse against the (a) fruit of the field intensified, and (b) foreign tribute was increased. While the blessings of YHWH's Law had ensured both health and economic prosperity,[17] the penalty for rebellion brought the *Curse of pestilence and indebtedness.*

The king's prophet-authored annal confirms the fulfillment of the curse of indebtedness, which led to poverty.

> And Pharaoh-nechoh put him (Jehoahaz) in bands at Riblah in the land of Hamath, that he might not reign in Jerusalem; and *put the land to a tribute of an hundred talents of silver, and a talent of gold.* And Pharaoh-nechoh made Eliakim the son of Josiah king in the room of Josiah his father, and turned his name to Jehoiakim, and took Jehoahaz away: and he came to Egypt, and died there. And Jehoiakim gave the silver and the gold to Pharaoh; but he taxed the land to give the money according to the commandment of Pharaoh: *he exacted the silver and the gold of the people of the land,* of every one according to his taxation, to give it to Pharaoh-nechoh. (2 Kgs 23:33–35, parenthesis added)

B. "All of These Diseases"

When YHWH had outlined the curses on Israel, he told the Israelites that he would cause pestilence to cling to them until it consumed the land (Deut 28:21). YHWH purposed to drive Israel off his land for breaching his covenant. Genetic, bacterial, and infectious diseases characterized the fifth epoch, which Israel brought on herself by departing from the natural Law that had preserved her health.

YHWH had promised,

> If you give careful attention to *the voice* of YHWH your God, do what is right in his sight, *give ear to his commandments, and keep all his statutes*, **I will put none of these diseases on you**, which I have brought on the Egyptians; for I am YHWH who heals you. (Exod 15:26)

This phase of the Prophetic Law was the final judgment—withholding YHWH's blessing of health.

> Because you listened *not to the voice* of YHWH your God, *to keep his commandments and his statutes* which he commanded you: Moreover all these curses shall come on you and pursue you, and overtake you, till you be destroyed. *And they shall be on you for a (d) sign and for a wonder, and on your seed forever.* (Deut 28:45–46, order of text reversed)

Notice that this text specifies that misfortune and disease would plague Israel's children throughout the Diaspora. The Israelites would bear the "sins of their fathers" well into their third and fourth generations and longer (Exod 20:5; 34:7) in the houses that disregarded the covenant's safeguards. Although this specific curse fell on the entire nation, the plagues of pestilence and indebtedness were especially aimed at the Northern Kingdom, who had been weakened at the end of the previous epoch. Throughout Israel's long Diaspora, she would continue to be a (d) sign and a wonder; she would battle disease and indebtedness as long as she disregarded YHWH's commandments and his statutes.

V. YOKE OF BONDAGE

Deut 28:47–51 Foreign tribute; prophecy of Babylon; 2nd deportations of Judah under Jehoiakim; Moabites, Syrians, Chaldees, and Ammonites deport Judah (2 Kgs 24:2–3); Jeremiah's Yoke. Kings of Judah: Josiah–Jehoiakim 5th 7 Times continues

Deut 28:47–51: Because you served not YHWH your God with joyfulness, and with gladness of heart, for the abundance of all things; Therefore shall you serve your (a) enemies

which *YHWH shall send against you*, in hunger, and in thirst, and in nakedness, and in want of all things: and he shall (b) **put a yoke of iron on your neck**, until he have destroyed you. YHWH shall bring a nation (c) against you from far, from the end of the earth, as swift as the eagle flies; a nation whose tongue you shall not understand; A nation of fierce countenance, which shall not regard the person of the old, nor show favor to the young. And he shall eat the fruit of your cattle, and the fruit of your land, (d) until you be destroyed: which also shall not leave you either corn, wine, or oil, or the increase of your cows, or flocks of your sheep, until (d) he have destroyed you.

Israel's national Testimony foretold each national deportation. YHWH sent many (a) enemies against Judah during the Testimony's fifth phase. Pharaoh Necho was the first to despoil Judah. He invaded Jerusalem and "carried away Jehoahaz" (2 Chr 36:4). After Egypt's deportation of Judah,

> Nebuchadnezzar king of Babylon came up, and Jehoiakim became his servant three years: then he turned and rebelled against him. And *YHWH sent against him bands of the Chaldees, and bands of the Syrians, and bands of the Moabites, and bands of the children of Ammon*, and sent them against Judah to destroy it, according to the word of YHWH, which he spake by his servants the prophets. . . to remove them out of his sight." (2 Kgs 24:1–3)

Babylon's 1st deportation of Judah (Judah's 2nd deportation) occurred in Nebuchadnezzar's 7th year (Jer 52:28), when he deported Jeconiah, Daniel, Mordecai, and Ezekiel. Once again the Testimony foretold the constitutional limits to which YHWH would hold Israel's citizens accountable as he applied the covenant's penalties (see Table 16.1).

A. Iron Yokes

Iron yokes (b) depict excessive oppression that diminishes all hope of freedom. The Prophetic Law foretold Necho's iron yoke (Deut 28:48), which had exacted gold and silver tribute (2 Kgs 23:35). It also prophesied of Nebuchadnezzar's iron yoke. Judah would serve Babylon and bear her yoke, just as oxen served their master. If Judah did not comply with the curse of tribute, there was always the threat of invasion and deportation into slavery.

When Jeremiah looked to the Law, YHWH's spirit caused him to see what should be written in his testimony. He understood the curses in the fifth epoch and he understood how the Creator would apply them. YHWH instructed Jeremiah to wear (b) a yoke about his neck to signify the fifth and final Monarchy epoch. He directed Jeremiah to send this implement of oppression to neighboring nations, advising all nations that submitted their necks to Nebuchadnezzar's yoke would prosper (Jer 27:8).

YHWH told Jeremiah to wear the yoke until instructed otherwise. He wore the yoke from the beginning of Jehoiakim's reign (Jer 27:1–2) until Zedekiah's 4th year (Jer 28:1, 10), when the false prophet Hannaniah snatched the yoke off his neck and broke it. In response, Jeremiah prophesied,

Table 16.1. Deportations of Israel and Judah

BCE Date	Deportation	Assyrian/Babylonian	Israel	Judah	References
c. 757	Israel's 1st	Tiglath-pileser (Pul)	Menahem	Azariah	2 Kgs 15:19–20
744	Israel's 2nd	Tiglath-pileser (Pul)	Pekah	Jotham/ Ahaz	2 Kgs 15:29; 1 Chr 5:26
717	Israel's 3rd	Shalmaneser V/ Sargon II	Hoshea	Hezekiah	2 Kgs 17:3–6; 18:9; Isa 8:1–8; Hos 1:4–5
709	Judah's 1st	Sargon II/ Sennacherib	No King	Hezekiah	2 Kgs 18:13; 2 Chr 32:1–9; Isa 36:1–2; Hos 1:7
664	Israel's 4th and Final	Esar-Haddon/ Ashurbanipal		Manasseh	2 Chr 33:11; Ezra 4:2; Isa 7:8; Hos 1:6
605	Judah: Invasion— no deportation	Nebuchadnezzar 4th yr.		Jehoiakim	No deportation, part of Egyptian campaign—2 Kgs 24:1
598	Judah's 2nd	Nebuchadnezzar 7th yr.		Jehoiakim/ Jechoniah	2 Kgs 24:10–14; 2 Chr 36:5–11; Jer 22:24–25; 52:28
587	Judah's 3rd	Nebuchadnezzar 18th/19th yr.		Zedekiah	2 Kgs 25:1–3, 8, 21; Jer 39:1–3; 52:4, 12, 29
583	Judah's 4th	Nebuchadnezzar 23rd yr.		No King	Jer 52:30

Go and tell Hananiah, saying, Thus said YHWH; You have broken the yokes of wood; but you shall make for them yokes of iron. For thus said YHWH of hosts, the God of Israel; I have put a *yoke of iron* on the neck of all these nations, that they may serve Nebuchadnezzar king of Babylon; and they shall serve him: and I have given him the beasts of the field also. (Jer 28:13–14)

Rebelling against Babylon's yoke was rebellion against YHWH, who had sent Nebuchadnezzar to judge an apostatizing and oppressively rebellious nation. The Testimony had foretold that yoke. The Testimony had not mentioned it in previous epochs, even when Samaria had been oppressed and then deported. Rather, Israel's righteous prophets who looked to the nation's Testimony (Isa 8:20) saw that iron yokes were not placed on YHWH's people until the fifth 7 Times epoch.

B. A Nation from Afar

One of the first prophecies to mention foreign inavasion was in Balaam's blessing. When the prophet Balaam blessed Jacob's children, he foretold Assyria's domination of the Canaanite region (Num 24:22–24). The Effacement Judgment had similarly predicted that many Canaanite nations that Israel had been commanded to drive out (such as the Ammonites) would in turn drive Israel out of the Promised Land (Num 33:56). Deuteronomy mentions another nation that would follow in Assyria's footsteps to subjugate the Promise Land during this phase of the Prophetic Law.

> YHWH shall bring a nation against you *from far*, from the end of the earth, as swift as the eagle flies; a nation whose tongue you shall not understand; A nation of fierce countenance, **which shall not regard the person of the old, nor show favor to the young.** (Deut 28:49–50)

Deuteronomy foretold (c, p. 742) Babylon's rise to supremacy. She would come from a far land and have an efficient military. She would speak a foreign tongue. This was not, however, what distinguished Babylon from Assyria. Rather, it was Babylon's lack of compassion for the life of the young and the old. Notice how closely Chronicles' account of Babylon parallels the nation's ancient Testimony:

> Moreover all the chief of the priests, and the people, transgressed very much after all the abominations of the heathen; and polluted the house of YHWH which he had hallowed in Jerusalem. Therefore he brought on them the king of the Chaldees, who slew their young men with the sword *in the house of their sanctuary*, and *had no compassion on young man or maiden, old man, or him that stooped for age*: he gave them all into his hand. (2 Chr 36:14, 17)

Babylon did not pity woman, child, or the elderly. Nebuchadnezzar slew some of the young men and took the rest as booty. Jeremiah saw that Jerusalem's people would not turn from their oppressions. He looked to this phase of the Prophetic Law to see what YHWH's judgment would be (d) if the people did not repent. Hence the reason he exhorted the Judahites to submit to Babylon's yoke and obtain mercy. The Testimony foretold that Babylon would prevail against Judah (d) until she was "destroyed" off the land, as YHWH fulfilled the Numbers 33 judgment and divorced Judah, just as he had Samaria.

VI. JUDAH IS NO LONGER A PEOPLE

Deut 28:52–57 Jerusalem's final siege
Lev 26:29–32

Deut 28:52–57: And he shall besiege you in all your gates, until your high and fenced walls come down, wherein you trust, throughout all your land: and he shall besiege you in all your gates throughout all your land, which YHWH your God has given you. And you shall (a) eat the fruit of your own body, the flesh of your sons and of your daughters, which

YHWH your God has given you, in the siege, and in the narrow place, with which your enemies shall distress you: So that the man that is tender among you, and very delicate, his eye shall be evil toward his brother, and toward the wife of his bosom, and toward the remnant of his children which he shall leave: So that he will not give (a) to any of them of the flesh of his children whom he shall eat: because he has nothing left him in the siege, and in the narrow place, with which your enemies shall distress you in all your gates. The tender and delicate woman among you, which would not adventure to set the sole of her foot on the ground for delicateness and tenderness, her eye shall be evil toward the husband of her bosom, and toward her son, and toward her daughter, and toward her young one that comes out from between her feet, and toward her children which she shall bear: for she shall eat them for want of all things secretly in the siege and straitness, wherewith your enemy shall distress you in your gates.

Lev 26:29–32: And you shall (a) eat the flesh of your sons, and the flesh of your daughters shall you eat. And I will destroy your high places, and cut down your images, and (b) **cast your carcasses on the carcasses of your idols**, and my soul shall abhor you. And I will make your cities waste, and bring your sanctuaries to desolation, and I will not smell the savor of your sweet odors. And I will bring the land into desolation: and your enemies which dwell therein (c) **shall be astonished at it.**

Jeremiah had chaperoned Judah's older priests and citizens to the Hinnom Valley, where idolatrous Israel had traditionally sacrificed her children. There, he prophesied destruction for those who had burned incense to idols, saying that YHWH would

> do to the inhabitants of it, and even make this city as Tophet: And the houses of Jerusalem, and the houses of the kings of Judah, *shall be defiled* as the place of Tophet, *because of all the houses on whose roofs* they have burned incense to all the host of heaven, and have poured out drink offerings to other gods. (Jer 19:12–13)

Jeremiah's words coincided with Leviticus's (b) prophecy of "carcasses being cast on their idols." Housetops often served as high places in the city.[18] There, Israel worshiped idols and burned incense. So when Jeremiah referred to "defiling" Jerusalem's houses, he was referring to Babylon killing Israel's people as they clung to her idols for protection. Jeremiah continued this prophecy by breaking a potter's jar, symbolically demonstrating that, like the potter's vessel, Judah and Jerusalem would soon be broken and destroyed (Jer 19:10–11). He continued to enumerate events to befall them when a "nation from afar" encroached on her borders. Judah would

> fall by the sword before her enemies, and by the hands of them that seek her life: and her carcasses would be given to be meat for the fowls of the heaven, and for the beasts of the earth. And [YHWH] would make this city (Jerusalem)

desolate, and an hissing; every one that passes by shall be astonished[19] and (c) hiss because of all the plagues of it. And *I will cause them to eat the flesh of their sons and the flesh of their daughters, and they shall eat every one the flesh of his friend* in the siege and narrow place, with which her enemies, and they that seek her life, shall straiten them. (Jer 19:7–9; pronoun tense modified)

This prophecy regarding Jerusalem was fulfilled during Nebuchadnezzar's two-year siege when "famine prevailed in the city, and there was no bread for the people of the land" (2 Kgs 25:1–4).[20] The famine was so devastating that Jerusalem (a) resorted to cannibalism. YHWH applied the Testimony's curses until the entire nation had been destroyed or removed from the land (see Map 16.1). Every epoch of the Testimony's prophecy had been fulfilled during the Monarchy Era. But, YHWH's Testimony for the nation did not end with the Monarchy's demise. The Testimony foretold Israel's future throughout the long Diaspora era.

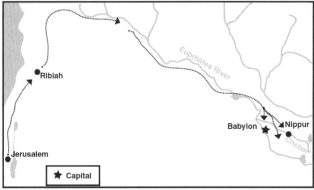

Villages of Exile on Chebar River near Nippur, Tel-abib, Tel-mela, Tel-harsha

Map 16.1. Judah's Deportation to Babylon

VII.   DURING THE DIASPORA

> **Deut 28:58–62**   Plagues on Israel and her seed during the Diaspora until she is re-deemed a "second time" (Isa 11:11).

Deut 28:58–62: If you will not observe to do all the words of this law that are written in (a) **this book**, that you may fear this glorious and fearful name, YHWH your God; Then YHWH will make **your plagues wonderful, and (b) the plagues of your seed, even great plagues, and of long continuance, and sore sicknesses, and of long continuance.** Moreover he will bring on you all the (c) **diseases of Egypt**, which you were afraid of; and they shall cleave to you. Also (d) **every sickness, and every plague, which is not written in the book of this law**, them will YHWH bring on you, until you are destroyed. And you shall be left few in number, whereas you were as the stars of heaven for multitude; because you would not obey the voice of YHWH your God.

When YHWH outlined the consequences for breaking his Law, he foretold Israel's future from the perspective of the Promised Land—that is, as the people were in contact with the Promised Land or severed from it. Earlier in the nation's history, the *Curse of pestilence and indebtedness* (Deut 28:42–46) had prophesied of plagues and judgments that Israel and her children would bear during her banishment from the land. Although these curses began to fall on Judah when Manasseh reentered Jerusalem, the earlier curse against the nation's health (Deut 28:42–46) was specifically aimed at the Northern Kingdom and its descendants during Diaspora (see pp. 739–41). The Testimony stipulated that all the Law's curses would continue to cling to the Northern Kingdom's offspring throughout their long captivity until Israel's latter-day redemption.

Deut 28:58–62 (above) issued this same curse once again as YHWH dispelled Judah from the land. Judah's offspring would also bear all the Law's curses—consequences that had originated from Israel's disregard for the Law while she lived in on the land. The curses on her health would cling to her descendants just as the curses against the Northern Kingdom had already commenced. Thus, the Law's curses were to adhere to *all* of the Israelites' descendants throughout their Diaspora until the latter-day redemption.

A. No Stone Unturned

In the opening chapter, I established that we would try the case of *Israel vs. YHWH* based on the concepts of truth. We accepted that YHWH's written word as contained in Israel's Scriptures would define truth within the *word of God* (chap. 1.II.B). It was further established that the Creator must perform what he stated he would do in order to be exonerated as a God who is righteous in keeping his own word and so that his word can be deemed an unchanging "truth." It is important that no stone is left unturned in our search for evidence of YHWH's righteousness in keeping his own word, or his unrighteousness in failing to keep it.

When YHWH covenanted his blessings to the patriarchs, he promised that multitudes and nations would be born from their descendants. Jacob later divided the patriarchal blessing and birthright among the tribes of Israel to serve as an ensign for identifying the tribes' geographical, economic, and sociopolitical features. The Testimony added another element to these defining features, stipulating that all the Law's penalties will adhere to disobedient Israel throughout the long Diaspora. At this point, it is necessary to digress for a moment to see if the curses found in the Law are evident in societies today. Ancient Israel's descendants are today scattered across the face of the earth. If YHWH's word is true, we should find evidence of the Testimony's curses still adhering to Israel's seed during her exile from the Promised Land. Thus, if Israel's descendants still exist, these curses should manifest in them today (if we are to accept that YHWH has neither rescinded his word nor annulled his covenant). Is it possible that the signs of Israel's disobedience are evident in modern societies today?

B. *Fever, Consumption, Blight, and Fungus*

> YHWH shall smite you with (a) consumption, and with (b) a fever, and with (c) an inflammation, and with an extreme burning, and with the sword, and with (d) blasting [blight] and with mildew; and they shall pursue you until you perish. (Deut 28:22)

The first part of this penalty concerns health. (b, c) Fever and inflammation are curses readily identified in almost every society today. Children rarely reach adulthood without having experienced a febrile illness of an unknown origin, and some of these are severe. Ireland's national disease control center reports that "at least ninety percent (90%) of enteroviral infections are either asymptomatic or result in non-specific febrile illness."[21] "Outbreaks of infections have been reported worldwide and may be very large, affecting entire countries. Nationwide outbreaks of viral meningitis have been reported from Romania (4,734 cases), Japan (4,061 cases) and other countries."[22] Viral meningitis is only one febrile illness. Influenza, bronchitis, encephalitis, neo-natal infections, and hundreds of other infections are also associated with the body's febrile immune response to illness.

(a) Consumption is an antiquated term denoting an illness that results in the patient's emaciation.[23] Many diseases cause a patient to waste away: cancer, multiple sclerosis, tuberculosis, and AIDS are only a few in a myriad of dehabilitating diseases. Crohn's, one degenerative disease, affects as many as one million Americans.[24] Inflammatory bowel diseases (IBD) such as Crohn's

> tend to run in families, so we know that genes definitely play a role in the IBD picture. . . . IBD also appears to affect certain ethnic groups more than others. For example, American Jews of European descent are four to five times more likely to develop IBD than the general population. IBD has long been thought of as a disease predominantly affecting whites; the prevalence rate (the number of people with a disease at a given time) among whites is 149 per 100,000. However, there has been a steady increase in reported cases of both Crohn's disease and ulcerative colitis among African Americans. . . For reasons that are not yet clearly understood, IBD is largely a disease of the developed world-principally, the U.S. and Europe.[25]

In his best-selling book *The Maker's Diet*, Jordan Rubin, a Christian with an American-Jewish heritage, describes his battle with Crohn's disease that almost killed him until he returned to the diet prescribed in Israel's Law. Within three months, Rubin totally recovered from the disease and its symptoms. Today—over ten years later—he is an advocate for the diet prescribed in Israel's Law.[26] Rubin is only one story. Many other people struggling with illness have returned to the Law and have been healed as well.[27]

Israel's ill health during her Diaspora would not only affect her children; disease would damage her crops. *Shedephah*, the Hebrew word (d) for '"blight," denotes a 'parasite, disease or condition that damages crops'.[28] Sometimes this was manifested in a blistering, blasting east wind that scorched and dried everything in its path.[29] Other effects of this curse were parasitic and fungal diseases. Crops that survived the curse of blight often succumbed to mildew, a fungus that feeds on food.[30] Are the curses of blight and mildew evident today?

One of the best countries in which to witness this curse is the United States of America, where agricultural statistics are carefully maintained. According to one government source, in 1996, 76% of all farm acres were treated with insecticides.[31] Farmers use insecticides to fight parasites and insects that feed on crops. If farmers choose to farm organically, the yields are much lower, and the risks of infection are higher. The latest statistics demonstrate that the virulent curses affect farmland today.

> World pesticide expenditures totaled more than $35.8 billion in 2006 and more than $39.4 billion in 2007. . . . U.S. pesticide expenditures totaled $11.8 billion in 2006 and $12.5 billion in 2007, in proportions similar to those of world expenditures, with a relatively larger proportion of total U.S. expenditures on herbicides. In 2007, U.S. expenditures accounted for 32% of total world on pesticides, 38% of world expenditures on herbicides, 39% of world expenditures on insecticides, 15% of world expenditures on fungicides, and 25% of world expenditures on other pesticides.[32]

The curse of disease and fungus is not limited to the industrialized agricultural market. These curses can also be found on the land of ordinary citizens.

> Pesticides are used by homeowners (and/or family members) in a majority of U.S. households, including lawns, gardens and any other outside areas. As of 1990, 69 million households used one or more types of pesticides, which equaled 81.6 percent of U.S. households that year. In other words, about one-fifth of households did not use any pesticides. Insecticides and fungicides are the most commonly used conventional pesticides in homes and gardens. About 60 percent used an insecticide and about 40 percent used a fungicide.[33]

Israel's curse of blight and mildew is today found worldwide but is especially evident in the United States. Commercial farmers and home gardeners spend thousands of dollars every year to treat fields so that disease and fungus will not destroy their crops. The cost of pesticides and fungicides is then passed on to the consumer, reflected in higher prices at the grocery store, not to mention the pesticides' many adverse health side effects from the farmer's effort to maintain viable crops.[34]

Mold, one type of fungus, is not only found in crops but also in the home. An article published by the insurance industry's *Claims Magazine* warned: "Mold and Mildew: A Creeping Catastrophe," charting the rising costs associated with mold and the importance of timely diagnosis.[35] The authors observe that the Book of Leviticus provides one of the first historical descriptions of household molds and how to deal with them:

> Mold, mildew and fungi are hardly new problems. In the book of Leviticus, chs. 13 and 14, there is reference to a plague, also called mildew in some translations. The description seems to fit that of a toxic mold. In Leviticus, the solution was to try cleaning: "Watch the plague and if the plague spreads, the unclean item or property must be removed and destroyed."[36]

In one insurance case in 1998, a mold expert was exposed to mold from a water-damaged home. "The expert found himself throwing up for hours after spending just 30 minutes in the house. He has a severe hearing loss in one ear from his exposure to the mold."[37] Today, the insurance industry usually follows Leviticus's prescription for dealing with mold: if damage cannot be effectively eradicated from a home, the house is condemned and rebuilt. Twenty-five hundred years after Israel ceased to exist, Israel's curses are still evident in the world today; yet these curses are still healed and cured by following Israel's constitution for health that stipulated razing mold-infested structures.

C. *"All of These Diseases"*

Then YHWH will make your plagues wonderful, and the plagues of your seed, even great plagues, and **of long continuance, and sore sicknesses, and of long continuance**. Moreover he will bring on you *all the diseases of Egypt*, which you were afraid of; and they shall cleave to you. Also every sickness, and every plague, which is *not* written in the book of this law, them will YHWH bring on you, until you be destroyed. (Deut 28:59–61)

Cancer, AIDS, heart disease, stroke, and diabetes are but a few diseases of "sore and long continuance." In chap. 6, we saw that it has only been within the last decade that science has connected these diseases to DNA, showing that many people's health is effected by their forefathers' genes. Physicians today have accepted the DNA link to diseases so widely that it has become a standard part of paperwork filled out by patients visiting the doctor's office. The first questions these forms often ask is whether there is a "family history" of heart disease, diabetes, or cancer.

Many of Egypt's diseases are evidenced in America today. In 1999 alone, 725,192 Americans died of the nation's deadliest killer, heart disease, while 549,838 Americans died of cancers—another disease of "sore sickness and long continuance."[38] Cerebrovascular diseases, a "great plague of Israel's seed" in 2004, killed 150,147 Americans, while diabetes claimed 72,815 American lives, and Alzheimer's killed 65,829 Americans in just one calendar year.[39] These statistics only reflect disease in the United States; however, the U.S. is not alone in battling these diseases. People all over the world battle these diseases, as new diseases for failing to abide by the Law continue to emerge.

One new disease in European nations (Belgium, France, Sweden, and the Netherlands) is Lymphogranuloma venereum (LGV) encountered by the gay and bisexual community. The infection is very easy to misdiagnose and is caused by specific strains of chlamydia, a sexually transmitted disease, and usually marked by genital ulcers, swollen lymph glands, and flu-like symptoms.[40] Although the disease is uncommon in industrialized nations, the American Centers for Disease Control expects the illness to spread to the United States in the near future.[41] After three millennium, the curses for breaking YHWH's Morality Code are still in force today. The signs and wonders of Israel's disobedience adhere to Israel's seed today, even though the people have been scattered among all nations.

D. Curse on Bearing Children

Cursed shall be the fruit of your body. (Deut 28:18)

The wording of this curse is broad. Hence, the casting out of early fruit through miscarriage or pre-term labor is one consequence of this curse. Retardation, birth defects, stillbirths and congenital diseases are also depicted in the open terminology of this consequence. Once again evidence for this curse is readily seen in the United States. In 1999, over one-fourth of all newborn births ended in death (ages 1–12 months). Almost 20% of these deaths were caused by congenital malformations, deformations, and chromosomal abnormalities.[42] Disorders relating to short gestation (the casting out of early fruit) and low birth weight represented about 15% of infant deaths, while about one-quarter of all infants die from respiratory and circulatory diseases, SIDS, newborn bacterial sepsis, and maternal and newborn complications in the first year of life.[43] In 2000, almost twelve 12% of all births were pre-term.[44] The U.S. vital statistic reports notes:

> The increased incidence in preterm births is of concern because of their heightened risk of morbidity and early mortality. Almost one-fifth of all very preterm infants do not survive the first year of life, compared with about 1 percent of infants born moderately preterm (32–36wks) and .3 percent of infants born at term (37–41 wks). Preterm newborns who do survive are more likely to be neurologically impaired.[45]

Pre-term births and low birth weights are another risk threatening children today. Around the globe, children are killed by sexually transmitted diseases contracted due to the parents' life-style. Children bear the curse of their father or mother's sexual conduct. Surely many of our children bear the signs of Israel's curse today. Yet, as we saw in chap. 6, if society returns to Israel's Law these curses will cease to exist.

The strongest evidence for this theory appears in Uganda, a country riveted with the highest incident of AIDS in the world during the 1980s. After Ugandan President Yoweri Museveni and his wife, Janet, initiated a behavioral-change-based abstinence program, the country's incidence of AIDS fell to 14th worldwide and continued to diminish.[46] If returning to morality was saving a country as small as Uganda from one of the curses of the Law, just think of the peace it could bring to the rest of the world!

E. Diaspora

YHWH shall **scatter you among all people, from the one end of the earth even to the other**; and there you shall serve other gods, which neither you nor your fathers have known, even wood and stone. (Deut 28:64)

Israel is scattered among all nations today. Through the prophecies in Genesis 49, Deuteronomy 33, and Judges 5, Israel's migrations can be traced to Britain, Ireland, Denmark,

France, the Netherlands, the United States, and many other countries.[47] During her long Diaspora, Israel has ignorantly served gods other than YHWH, and she has been unaware that the healthy ways of life prescribed in Israel's constitutional Law could have saved her from catastrophic outbreaks of Black Death, Bubonic plague, and leprosy and could have restored her to long life (Ps 19:7).

F. *Egypt's Three Days of Darkness*

> YHWH shall smite you with madness, and blindness, and astonishment of heart. (Deut 28:28)

One consequence of this curse is vastly differing interpretations of Scripture. Most Judeo-Christians base their beliefs on the Old Testament; however, there are well over 1,500 Christian denominations in the United States today.[48] Although the basic tenants of Christianity are universal, doctrine is not. For instance, the largest churches are divided between two primary denominations: Roman Catholic and Eastern Orthodox. Doctrines held by Protestant churches are even more diverse: Baptist, American Baptist, Southern Baptist; Methodist, Lutheran, Evangelical Lutheran; Presbyterian; Reformed Presbyterian; Seventh-Day Adventist; Jehovah's Witness; World-Wide Church of God; United Church of God; Church of God Latter-Day; Church of God; and Church of Christ, are only a few Protestant sects found all over the world. The chasms between Judaism's sects are no narrower or less confusing: Orthodox (whose branches include: Hasidic Judaism, Haredi—"Ultra-Orthodox"—Judaism, and Modern Orthodox), Reform, Conservative, and Reconstructionist. All of these religious sects believe that Israel's God is humanity's Creator, yet each religion teaches humanity a different view of who God is and what he expects of humanity.

Surely, YHWH has continued to smite Israel with madness, blindness, and astonishment of heart during the past 2,500-year Diaspora. Most of the world today, like Israel's fathers "in old time," still clings to doctrines originating from Babylonian and Egyptian theology. This would very well explain why there are so many different denominations, all of which have roots in the God of the Old Testament yet differ so broadly on the definition of "truth" and what God requires of us. Truly, Israel is still under every curse of the Law today!

Isaiah foretold our present darkened state over 2,000 years ago:

> For YHWH has poured out on you the spirit of deep sleep, and has closed your eyes: the prophets and your rulers, the seers has he covered. And the vision of all is become to you as the words of a book that is sealed, which men deliver to one that is learned, saying, Read this, I pray you: and he said, I cannot; for it is sealed. And the book is delivered to him that is not learned, saying, Read this, I pray you: and he said, I am not learned. Wherefore YHWH said, Forasmuch as this people draw near me with their mouth, and with their lips do honor me, but have removed their heart far from me, and their fear toward me is taught *by*

the precept of men: Therefore, behold, I will proceed to do a marvelous work among this people, even a marvelous work and a wonder: for the wisdom of their wise men shall perish, and the understanding of their prudent men shall be hid. (Isa 29:10–14)

Most laymen today still turn to a learned authority such as a pastor, rabbi, or scholar to interpret Scripture for them. Yet the world's doctrine remains divided. Jeremiah foretold the glorious *Day of Restoration* where humanity would no longer need to look to learned authorities to understand doctrine.

But this shall be the covenant that I will make with the House of Israel; After those days, said YHWH, I will put *my law in their inward parts, and write it in their hearts*; and will be their God, and they shall be my people. And they shall teach no more every man his neighbor, and every man his brother, saying, Know YHWH: for they shall all know me, from the least of them to the greatest of them, said YHWH; for I will forgive their iniquity, and I will remember their sin no more. (Jer 31:33–34)

YHWH's judgment on truth occurred in 745 BCE, when Isaiah began to write his testimony. For 2,500 years Israel has borne the curse of blindness as each descendant today gropes in darkness, searching for humanity's Creator, or giving up the quest all together. Will this curse continue forever? Will religion continue to oppress and divide humanity?

Both the Law and the prophets recognized the plagues of Egypt as falling on Israel's children. Egypt's plague of darkness lasted three days.[49] When will Israel's three days of darkness be lifted? When will YHWH remove the veil cast over all nations? The Tabernacle of Testimony provides the answer. The oxen under the molten sea faced the "four corners" of the earth and prophesied of Israel's Diaspora.[50] The sea above the oxen held 2,000 baths (1 Kgs 7:26). These 2,000 baths represent 2,000 years of dispersion and exile from Israel's Promised Land.

Hosea built on this structure, prophesying of a time that Israel would return to her Creator, and he would heal all her curses.

Come, and let us return to YHWH: for he has torn, and he will heal us; he has smitten, and he will bind us up. *After two days will he revive us: in the third day he will raise us up,* and we shall live in his sight. Then shall we know, if we follow on to know YHWH: his going forth is prepared as the morning; and he shall come to us as the rain, as the latter and the former rain to the earth. (Hos 6:1–3)

Hosea's two prophetic days paralleled the Temple's 2,000 baths, depicting a former time when YHWH had "torn and smitten" Israel (Nebuchadnezzar and the Diaspora). After

2,000 years are completed, in the third millennium, or "day," Israel will turn wholeheartedly to YHWH, and YHWH will return to Israel's descendants. He will heal them, bind them up, bring them back, and redeem them to the Promised Land to live in his sight.

Isaiah tells us that Israel's diverse Scriptural interpretations and divisions among believers will finally cease, and unity will be restored when YHWH redeems Israel to the Promised Land.

> Your watchmen shall lift up the voice; with the voice together shall they sing: *for they shall see eye to eye, when YHWH shall bring again Zion.* (Isa 52:8; see also Isa 60:19–22; Zech 14:6–7)

Isaiah's testimony follows the Prophetic Law of Deut 29:29–30:6 and Lev 26:45 by stating that unity and truth will be restored when latter-day Israel is redeemed to the land. By understanding Israel's beginning and end, as set forth in the foundational words of YHWH in the Covenants with Noah, Abraham, Isaac, and Jacob, humanity today has hope for coming out of the bondage of "blindness, madness, and astonishment of heart" that YHWH had convicted the nation's forefathers to but will today lift from the eyes of those who seek him.

> Thus said YHWH GOD; Behold, I will take the Children of Israel from among the heathen, where they be gone, and will gather them on every side, and bring them into their own land: and I will make them one nation in the land on the mountains of Israel; and one king shall be king to them all: and they shall be no more two nations, neither shall they be divided into two kingdoms any more at all: **Neither shall they defile themselves any more with their idols, nor with their detestable things, nor with any of their transgressions**: but *I will save them* out of all their dwelling places, wherein they have sinned, and will cleanse them: so shall they be my people, and I will be their God. And David my servant shall be king over them; and they all shall have one shepherd: **they shall also walk in my judgments, and observe my statutes, and do them. And they shall dwell in the land that I have given to Jacob my servant, wherein your fathers have dwelled; and they shall dwell therein, even they, and their children, and their children's children forever: and my servant David shall be their prince forever**. Moreover I will make a covenant of peace with them; it shall be an everlasting covenant with them: and I will place them, and multiply them, and will set **my sanctuary in the middle of them for evermore**. My tabernacle also shall be with them: yes, I will be their God, and they shall be my people. **And the heathen shall know that I YHWH do sanctify Israel, when my sanctuary shall be in the middle of them for evermore.** (Ezek 37:21–28)

VIII. THE DIVIDED KINGDOM ERA ENDS

(587-517 BCE)

Deut 28:63-64	Judah's 3rd and 4th deportations; Land enjoys its Sabbaths; Prophesy of
Lev 26:33-35	the Hidden Day of Judgment.
(Num 33:56)	Num 33:56 fulfilled; No more kings of Judah.
	The 5th 7 Times ends

Deut 28:63–64: And it shall come to pass, that as YHWH rejoiced over you to do you good, and to multiply you; so YHWH will rejoice over you to destroy you, and to bring you to nothing; and you shall be (a) plucked from off the land where you go to possess it. And YHWH shall (b) scatter you among all people, from the one end of the earth even to the other; and (c) there you shall serve other gods, which neither you nor your fathers have known, even wood and stone.

Lev 26:33–35: And I will (b) scatter you among the heathen, and will (d) **draw out a sword after you**: and your land shall be desolate, and your cities waste. Then shall the land (e) enjoy her sabbaths, as long as it lies desolate, and you be in your enemies' land; even then shall the land rest, and enjoy her sabbaths. As long as it lies desolate it shall rest; because it did not rest in your sabbaths, when you dwelled on it.

The previous (4th) epoch foretold Babylon's subjugation of the Levant and Jerusalem's final siege. The Prophetic Law was consistent in foretelling each national (a) deportation. Judah's third deportation occurred when Nebuchadnezzar

> carried away all Jerusalem, and all the princes, and all the mighty men of valor, even ten thousand captives, and all the craftsmen and smiths: none remained, save the poorest sort of the people of the land. And he carried away Jehoiachin to Babylon, and the king's mother, and the king's wives, and his officers, and the mighty of the land. (2 Kgs 24:14–15)

Judah's fourth and final deportation took place, in 583 BCE, when "in the three and twentieth year of Nebuchadnezzar Nebuzar-adan the captain of the guard carried away captive of the Jews seven hundred forty and five persons" (Jer 52:30; see Appendix A: Table 9.50/8, pp. 892–93). Nebuchadnezzar's siege and deportation of Judah's citizens specifically fulfilled the Testimony's curse, which prophesied that the entire nation would be (a) plucked up from the Promised Land, thus completely fulfilling the judgment of Numbers 33.

And YHWH shall (b) scatter you among all people, from the one end of the earth even to the other. (Deut 28:64)

And I will (b) scatter you among the heathen. (Lev 26:33)

> Moreover it shall come to pass, that I shall do to you, as I thought to do to them (the Canaanites). (Num 33:56)

The Law not only recognized Judah's deportation; it noted that she would be sifted through the nations, just like Ephraim. YHWH (b) would "scatter" Judah among all nations. Hence, the Law depicted an epoch longer than the reign of just one or two world powers, such as Babylon or Persia. The Testimony depicted a Diaspora that would last for many generations. When Cyrus freed Israel, many of Judah's citizens immigrated to Egypt or were satisfied to remain in exile.

> And YHWH shall scatter you among all people, from the one end of the earth even to the other; and (c) there you shall serve other gods, which neither you nor your fathers have known, even wood and stone. (Deut 28:64)

The curse of false gods occurs twice in Deuteronomy's Testimonial Law. The first time (Deut 28:36) was Samaria's fall, when Sargon banished Hoshea and deported the Northern Kingdom. With the final sack of Judah (Deut 28:64), Israel again began to serve gods of wood and stone that she and her "fathers had *not* known." As pointed out in the previous section, the deities worshiped by the kings of Akkad (Assyria) had not been known to Israel in the Promised Land. During her Diaspora, she would settle in Mesopotamian provinces, which were rich in physical manifestations of the gods (images of wood and stone). These were new gods to Israel: deities with different rites, rituals, and beliefs. Although the general doctrines held by Mesopotamia's deities were similar to the deities the Israelites had lusted after while they lived in YHWH's land, Mesopotamia's deities were new to Israel. YHWH would cause both Judah and Ephraim to serve the "whole host of heaven" (Deut 4:19) during their long Diaspora.

> And I will scatter you among the heathen, and will (d) **draw out a sword after you.** (Lev 26:33; see also the promise of Ezek 6:8)

Most of Israel's citizens did *not* return to the Promised Land with Zerubbabel when Cyrus ordered the First Temple restored. For this reason Leviticus's Testimony outlined the (d) events that would occur to Judah's and Ephraim's children during their Diaspora, prophesying that YHWH would "draw out a sword after them" (Lev 26:33). After Judah's deportation, YHWH pulled the sword out of its sheath. Leviticus's Prophetic Law alludes to the events that would occur during the subsequent epoch's hidden Judgment Day.

YHWH is consistent with this methodology of a "Hidden Judgment Day." The cultic judgment against YHWH's sanctuary is mentioned at the end of the plagues of 7 Times. When Leviticus's 350 years expired after the First Temple Era, the Prophetic Law foretold an era of judgment, which the prophets referred to as The Day of YHWH (or, "The Day of the Lord" in the KJV). Leviticus's Testimony (26:36–39) *overlaps* with the Second Temple phase when the 7-Times plagues are reinstated once more. When the five 7 Times or 70-year epochs expire without Israel's fully returning to the constitutional Law at the end of the 350-year Second Temple Era, the Day of YHWH would begin. YHWH would take the Jews living on the Promised Land in the very delusions they had lusted after for so long. These fallacies would provoke other nations' hatred and their enemies' desire to control Jerusalem as the city became a "stone of trembling" to all nations that fought over her (see Table 16.2).

Table 16.2. Cultic Judgment
Judgment Against Israel's Sanctuary

Second Temple (in disrepair)		
165 BCE	5th 7th Times ends/ Epiphanes has vandalized Temple, rips veil/ Temple Falls into ruin symbolizing Israel's future—Isa 2:5–9/**Day of Judgement begins**	
163-63 BCE	YHWH renews the Covenant/ Century of Blessing—Zechariah 12; Dan 9:27 **Judgment of Delusions—wine poured out, holocaust prepared**	**Israel—Day of YHWH** Lev 26:36–39, 43; Deut 28:58–68, 29:20–21; Deuteronomy 32; Amos 5:16–20; Zech 12:3–4; Psalms 79; Isa 2:10–3:12; 8:13–9:5; 10:15–19; ch. 13; 27:1–12; 66:1–4; Jer 4–6; ch. 46; Zephaniah 1; Ezekiel 13; Joel 1–3:15
63 BCE	Judea falls to Rome/Jerusalem becomes a cup of trembling to all nations of the earth—Zech 12:2, ch. 13–14:2	**Nations possess the Temple mount** Ps 83; 75:8; Isaiah 24; Zech 12:2-4—nations possess Jerusalem and drink her wine. Gog/Magog
Herod's Temple		
20–19 BCE	**Israel's Temple becomes Esau's Temple— Herod repairs Second Temple** symbolizing Esau's blessing of stregnth during Israel's Judgment Day	
Desolations —No Temple (Christian Shrine nearby)		
70 CE	Herod's Temple destroyed/ The seed of Israel banned from Jerusalem/ Temple: desolations— Ps 74:3/ Israel and all nations become drunk	
Dome of the Rock		
961-Present	**Dome of the Rock:** Esau's latter blessing—Gen 27:38–41; Book of Obadiah	
?	Israel reclaims all of Jerusalem, defeats Esau/Day of Salvation begins, curses fall on all Israel's enemies—Deut 30:7; Ezekiel 35	

The original Promised-Land Covenant postponed judgment of the Amorites for 430 years, waiting for their sins to "come to the full."[51] YHWH *hides* Israel's Day of Judgment in the Prophetic Law by alluding to the holocaust well in advance and waiting for Israel's sins also to become complete. This is the formula followed by Israel's prophets after the sun set on the prophet's words. In the next few chapters, we will examine the exact era when YHWH's judgment occurred during the great and terrible *Day of YHWH.*

> Then shall the land (e) enjoy her sabbaths, as long as it lies desolate, and you be in your enemies' land; even then shall the land rest, and enjoy her sabbaths. As long as it lies desolate it shall rest; because it did not rest in your sabbaths, when you dwelled on it. (Lev 26:34–35)

Scripture upholds the idea that land can bear a nation's iniquities.[52] When Cain shed Abel's innocent blood, YHWH said Abel's "blood cried to me from the ground" (Gen 4:10). YHWH saw all Israel's wickedness while she lived in the land.[53] If he drove her from the land he beheld, then his land would not see her wickedness any longer: the land would enjoy her Sabbath for one epoch (Jer 29:10) and (e) "rest" from its oppression. It may be remembered that Leviticus's Testimony inclined to the Northern Kingdom. This is why Leviticus states that the Promised Land would rest for "sabbaths," recognizing that the Northern Kingdom and many Judahites would be removed from the land in an era with a much greater duration than one 7 Time epoch.

YHWH considered the Promised Land to be vitally important in his relationship with Israel. He looked on the land and beheld all of Israel's actions while she lived on it. His glory filled the Temple. The Law states that YHWH always watched over Canaan. "A land which YHWH your God cares for: the *eyes of YHWH your God are always on it,* from the beginning of the year even to the end of the year" (Deut 11:12). When YHWH sent Israel into Diaspora, the people were literally taken out of YHWH's sight. Israel was divorced (Jer 3:8; Isa 50:1). The Law stipulated that once a wife had been given a bill of divorce she was to be sent out of her husband's house and away from her husband's tribal inheritance (Deut 24:1). YHWH's prophets provide a "written bill" for the Creator's divorce of his idolatrous wives—Judah and Samaria. Once his bills of divorce were written to the nation, she was sent away from her husband's (YHWH's) heritage, in the same way that Adam and Eve were sent out of the Garden for their sins (Gen 3:24). The significance of Israel's and Judah's deportations off the Promised Land was that YHWH would no longer look on the nation or be entreated for mercy toward *that generation.*[54] He would no longer act as a husband-protector. Freedom, which had been established in his covenant (Exod 20:2), would no longer belong to her. Once off the Land, divorced Israel would be fair game and a prey for all who desired her proud-hearted people (Lev 26:33–36).

IX. JUDAH UTTERLY DEPORTED (598–583 BCE)

Nebuchadnezzar's annihilation of Judah could be seen as a bloody Day of vengeance when Solomon's Temple was destroyed. While it is true that the Creator judged Israel and Judah, the merciful sentence rendered Israel-Samaria divorced and banished; it was not a death sentence.[55] YHWH's banishment fulfilled Israel's Effacement Judgment, which stated that Israel would be "driven off" her land (Num 33:56). Death or extermination through holocaust was not associated with Numbers' judgment. Thus, the verdict YHWH imposed at the razing of Solomon's Temple was quite mild when contrasted to the vividly horrid descriptions of the prophets' *Day of YHWH.*[56]

Assyria's and Babylon's deportations fulfilled YHWH's national divorce as Israel was cast out of her Creator's heritage. (Sennacherib deported 200,150 people from Judah—ANET, 288). In the interregnum between Assyria and Babylon's conquests, many Palestinian nations plundered and deported Judah from her land. Thus, only a few Judahites were left in the Temple's final days, because many local tribal nations had already raided and deported Judah before Nebuchadnezzar's final sieges.[57] As the Effacement Judgment neared fruition, Solomon's Temple was obliterated, and only a very small handful of people remained. This is what Scripture testifies of Judah's prior deportations:

> At that time did king Ahaz send to the kings of Assyria to help him. **For again the Edomites had come and smitten Judah, and carried away captives.** The **Philistines** also had invaded the cities of the low country, and of the south of Judah, and had taken Beth-Shemesh, and Ajalon, and Gederoth, and Shocho with the villages of it, and Timnah with the villages of it, Gimzo also and the villages of it: and they dwelled there. For YHWH brought Judah low because of Ahaz king of Israel; for he made Judah naked, and transgressed sore against YHWH. And Tiglath-pileser king of Assyria came to him, and distressed him, but strengthened him not. (2 Chr 28:16–20).

> In his (Jehoiakim's) days Nebuchadnezzar king of Babylon came up, and Jehoiakim became his servant three years: then he turned and rebelled against him. And YHWH sent against him bands of the **Chaldees, and bands of the Syrians, and bands of the Moabites, and bands of the children of Ammon,** and sent them against *Judah to destroy it,* according to the word of YHWH, which he spoke by his servants the prophets. Surely at the commandment of YHWH came this on Judah, *to remove them out of his sight,* for the sins of Manasseh, according to all that he did; And also for the innocent blood that he shed: for he filled Jerusalem with innocent blood; *which YHWH would not pardon.* (2 Kgs 24:1–4, parenthesis added).

Assyria, the Chaldees, Syrians, Moabites, Ammonites, Egyptians, and Philistines had already deported Judah before Nebuchadnezzar's siege of Jerusalem. *All* but a few poor people of Judah were deported from the land—out of YHWH's sight. Jeremiah also verifies Judah's captivity:

> To whom the word of YHWH came. . . . *to the carrying away of Jerusalem captive* in the fifth month. (Jer 1:2–3)

> For through the anger of YHWH it came to pass in Jerusalem and Judah, until he had *cast them out from his presence,* that Zedekiah rebelled against the king of Babylon. (2 Kgs 24:20)

He carried away all Jerusalem, and all the princes, and all the mighty men of valor, even *ten thousand captives*, and all the craftsmen and smiths: none remained, save the poorest sort of the people of the land. (2 Kgs 24:14)

Therefore YHWH was very angry with Israel, and *removed them* out of his sight: there was none left but the tribe of Judah only. Also *Judah kept not the commandments of YHWH their God*, but walked in the statutes of Israel which they made. And YHWH rejected all the seed of Israel, and afflicted them, and delivered them into the hand of spoilers, *until he had cast them out of his sight*. (2 Kgs 17:18–20)

He burnt the house of YHWH, and the king's house, and all the houses of Jerusalem, and every great man's house with fire. And all the army of the Chaldees, that were with the captain of the guard, brake down the walls of Jerusalem round about. . . . The rest of the people that were left in the city, and the fugitives that fell away to the king of Babylon, with *the remnant of the multitude, did Nebuzar-adan the captain of the guard carry away*. (2 Kgs 25:9–11)

Notice, these texts show that Israel was deported, *not* that she was put to death. Scripture reports that *only* the king's sons (Jer 52:8–11) and highest-ranking officials received the death sentence.

And the captain of the guard took Seraiah the chief priest, and Zephaniah the second priest, and the three keepers of the door: And out of the city he took an officer that was set over the men of war, and five men of them that were in the king's presence, which were found in the city, and the principal scribe of the host, which mustered the people of the land, and threescore men of the people of the land that were found in the city: And Nebuzar-adan captain of the guard took these, and brought them to the king of Babylon to Riblah: And the king of Babylon smote them, and slew them at Riblah in the land of Hamath. So Judah was carried away out of their land. (2 Kgs 25:18–21; see also Jer 34:18–21; 52:24–27)

In Nebuchadnezzar's 7th and 18th years, he deported 10,000 of Jerusalem's citizens. At the First Temple's destruction, Nebuchadnezzar deported 832 people who lived in Jerusalem (2 Kgs 24:15–16; see also Jer 52:28–29). During his last deportation (23rd year), Babylon carried away 745 people (Jer 52:30). These three deportations totaled 11,577 citizens and left only a few of the poorest citizens to care for Nebuchadnezzar's fields and vineyards (Jer 52:15–16; 2 Kgs 25:12). The above account (2 Kgs 25:18–21) indicates that 72 men were put to death out of the 4,600 who were carried away to Babylon.[58] Undoubtedly, there were others who perished, while clinging to their idols for salvation, when Jerusalem fell, however, they were a small number compared with the number of people taken into captivity or deported by other nations. Even at the destruction of Solomon's Temple, most Judahites were carried away into captivity and deported off the and—they were not put to death. The destruction of Solomon's Temple was *not* the *Day of Judgment*, the *Day of Atonement*, or the *Day of YHWH* referred to by Israel's prophets.

Jeremiah exhorted Judah's exiles, encouraging them that they would enjoy peace and would prosper in Babylon:

> Thus said YHWH of hosts, the God of Israel, to *all that are carried away captives*, whom I have caused to be carried away from Jerusalem to Babylon; Build you houses, and dwell in them; and plant gardens, and eat the fruit of them; Take you wives, and beget sons and daughters; and take wives for your sons, and give your daughters to husbands, that they may bear sons and daughters; that you may be increased there, and not diminished. And seek the peace of the city where I have caused you to be carried away captives, and pray to YHWH for it: *for in the peace of it shall you have peace*. (Jer 29:4–7).

YHWH promised these humiliated exiles peace as long as they humbled themselves and submitted to the foreign authority under which he had placed them. Jeremiah encouraged Israel's banned citizens to pray for Babylon's peace so that they could enjoy peace on Babylon's land as well. Babylon's deportation from the Promised Land began an era or day of national judgment for Israel and many Near Eastern nations (Jeremiah 45–51), but the destruction of the First Temple was not the specific event that Israel's prophets foretold when they were referring to the "Day of YHWH." The Creator hid his Judgment Day in prophecies regarding Israel's Diaspora.

17

Atonement through Sacrifices as Holocausts

In chap. 3, we saw that the initial covenants YHWH made with Noah and Abraham were sealed with sacrifices, a custom that prevailed in most ancient societies. We had seen that one eighth-century treaty reads, "As this calf is cut to pieces so may Mati'el be cut to pieces."[1] The tenor of the text was that, if Mati'el failed to uphold his end of the covenant, he would be cut into pieces, even as the sacrificial calf had been slaughtered; the sacrifice depicted Mati'el's fate should he fail to uphold his end of the bargain. Let us reexamine the precedent that Abraham's offering set for Israel's sacrifices.

> And he said to him, I am YHWH that brought you out of Ur of the Chaldees, to give you this land to inherit it. And he said, Lord YHWH, whereby shall I know that I shall inherit it? And he said to him, Take me an heifer of three years old, and a she goat of three years old, and a ram of three years old, and a turtledove, and a young pigeon. And he took to him all these, and divided them in the middle, and laid each piece one against another: but the birds divided he not. And when the fowls came down on the carcasses, Abram drove them away. (Gen 15:7–11)

Abraham's sacrifice depicted "the self-destruction of the one making the contract in an analogous way: that the fate of the animal should befall him in the event that he does not keep the *bᵉrît* (covenant)."[2] This explanation is supported by YHWH's interpretation of sacrifices and covenants in Jer 34:18. When Israel again used a divided sacrifice to seal her covenant with YHWH, the Creator plainly states that the sacrifice symbolized the people's fate should they fail to uphold their end of the covenant.

> I will give the men that have transgressed my covenant, which have not **per-formed the words of the covenant which they had made before me, *when they cut the calf in two, and passed between the parts of it,*** The princes of Judah, and the princes of Jerusalem, the eunuchs, and the priests, and all the people of the land, **which passed between the parts of the calf.** (Jer 34:18–19)

Jeremiah's prophecy demonstrates that this ceremony depicted the fate of those who covenanted by passing between the divided sacrifice pieces but failed to uphold their covenant with YHWH—the covenant breakers would be sacrificially slaughtered.

When YHWH made the Promised-Land Covenant, he passed between the pieces of the burnt offering as a devouring lamp (Gen 15:17–18). YHWH implicated himself and his own fate *should he sin* and fail to deliver the Promised Land birthright to Abraham and his offspring.[3] Later on, when YHWH covenanted with Israel, the entire nation entered into a self-imprecating sacrifice through the Passover ceremony (Exod 12:43–51). This ceremony recognized each person as a citizen of YHWH's covenantal nation and bound them to the self-imprecating penalties listed in the Testimonies (Leviticus 26 and Deuteronomy 27–30) should they repudiate YHWH's Law.

I. YHWH'S DAY OF JUDGMENT FORETOLD (515 BCE-??)

A. *No Assurance of Life*

Deut 28:65–67	Curses on the heart; uncertainty of life; the evening sacrifice:
Lev 26:36–39	world judgment for breaking the Noahic Covenant (Gen 9:5)

> Deut 28:65–67: And (a) **among these nations** shall you find no ease, neither shall the sole of your foot have rest: but YHWH shall give you there a (b) trembling heart, and (c) failing of eyes, and sorrow of mind. And (d) your life shall hang in doubt before you; and you shall fear day and night, **and shall have none assurance of your life**. In the morning you shall say, Would God it were even! and at even you shall say, Would God it were morning! for the fear of your heart with which you shall fear, and for (c) the sight of your eyes which you shall see.
>
>   Lev 26:36–39: And on them (a) **that are left alive of you** I will send a (b) faintness into their hearts in the lands of their enemies; and (d) the sound of a shaking leaf shall chase them; and they shall flee, as fleeing from a sword; and they shall fall when none pursues. (e) *And they shall fall one on another,* as it were before a sword, when none pursues: and you shall have (f) no power to stand before your enemies. And you shall perish among the heathen, and the land of your enemies shall eat you up. And they that are left of you shall pine away in their iniquity in your enemies' lands; and also (g) in the iniquities of their fathers shall they pine away with them.

This portion of the Testimonial Law begins with (a) the majority of Israel's former citizens living in Diaspora. The prophecy outlines the Judgment Day events that would occur during the nation's captivity. The most outstanding characteristic of this long epoch is (d) the uncertainty and dismal quality of life. Dispersed (b) Israel will tremble and be fainthearted from the lack of hope and courage to withstand her enemies.[4] Israel's (c) eyes will still fail to see truth (Lam 5:17, 15). The philosophy that the Israelites embrace during this era brings sadness, not joy. Her doctrine continues to cause her to (g) pine away in her forefathers' iniquities (See Exod 34:6–7). During the Diaspora, Israel's descendants have no assurance (d) of YHWH's protection and easily (f) fall before their enemies. Their affliction is so great that they tremble in fear of the next day, not knowing whether their next master will be kind or oppressive.

B. The Noahic Covenant's Judgment Day

When YHWH gave his Law to Israel, he incorporated all previous patriarchal covenants and prophecies in it. He validated the Noahic Covenant by upholding its penalty in Israel's covenantal Law (Lev 17:14). The penalty of Noah's Covenant stated:

> But flesh with the life thereof, which is the blood of it, shall you not eat. And surely your blood of your lives will I require; at the hand of every beast will I require it, and at the hand of man; *at the hand of every man's brother will I require the life of man.* (Gen 9:4–5)

Notice, Lev 26:37 (above) states that the Israelites would "fall one on one another."

It may be remembered that, when YHWH entered into the Promised-Land Covenant with Abraham, he hid in it a day when he would judge Egypt and set Israel free.[5] The Testimonial Law continues this precedent. Notice that YHWH effectively hides his Judgment Day in prophecies about the Diaspora.

When Lev 26:37 refers (d) to "falling one on another," YHWH is applying the Noahic Covenant's penalty for eating flesh "with the blood" to all humanity, not just Israel (see pp. 73–77). YHWH would pass this judgment on Israel and *all nations* that had violated this command. This was the reason that the prophets spoke against many Near East nations: the prophets looked to the Law, and YHWH's spirit showed them the Day YHWH would render judgment for eating animal flesh with the blood, thus causing "every man's brother" to "fall one on another" (see Illustration 17.1). When Haggai and Zechariah returned to the Promised Land, they knew that the *Judgment Day* for breaching the Noahic Covenant was not far from occurring.

Zechariah foretold the *Day of YHWH* when the Creator would require justice for breaching the Noahic Covenant.

> For I will no more pity the inhabitants of the land, said YHWH: but, lo, I will deliver the *men every one into his neighbor's hand*, and into the hand of his king: and they shall smite the land, and out of their hand *I will not deliver them*. (Zech 11:6)

Illustration 17.1. Depiction of a battle during the American Civil War when fellow countrymen shed each other's blood.

In accord with YHWH's Testimony, Zechariah continues to reveal that *Judgment Day* events would occur during the Second Temple Era, referring to many false and foolish shepherds who would tend "the sheep of the slaughter" (Zech 11:4–7; 13:7–9).[6] These foolish shepherds would lead the blind out of "the way" during this long rebellious epoch (Zech 11:15–17; 13:7; and Isa 42:16).

Zechariah's testimony—a brief ray of light—was blessed with one chronological prophecy that follows the Testimonial Law. Zechariah recognized YHWH's strengthening of Judah under the Maccabees (Zech 12:5–10) when Jerusalem would again establish her independence and "dwell by herself" as YHWH renewed the covenant with the nation for one day (Dan 9:27). Zechariah describes the mourning that would arise due to the desecration and desolation of the Second Temple and the lack of "word" from YHWH (Zech 12:11–14;[7] fulfilled—1 Mac 4:46; 9:27). Although this rebellious Remnant sought for YHWH's word, not a single prophet could be found (1 Mac 9:27). The final judgment commenced when the Syrians and Romans began to carve Canaan into pieces as a permanent inheritance for the heathen.

Zechariah continues by revealing another Diaspora, when the rebellious Second Temple Remnant would be given over to sacrificial slaughter, banished from the land, and exiled into captivity once more (Zech 14:1–2; see also Lev 26:43).

> Behold, *the day of YHWH comes*, and your spoil shall be divided in the middle of you. For I will gather all nations against Jerusalem to battle; and the city shall

be taken, and the houses rifled, and the women ravished; and *half of the city shall go forth into captivity*, and the residue of the people shall not be cut off from the city. (Zech 14:1–2)

Zechariah wrote his prophecy both during Judah's Diaspora in Babylon *and continued to write shortly after the Remnant's return*. His prophecy could not be applied to Nebuchadnezzar's siege, which had already occurred, but must refer to a future siege of Jerusalem and subsequent captivity.

The rest of Zachariah 14 describes YHWH's (modern) latter-day return to Israel, when he is for the nation once more. At his return, YHWH will execute a second judgment on the heathen for breaching the Noahic Covenant; He will save the righteous and judge the wicked once more.

And it shall come to pass in that day, that a great tumult from YHWH shall be among them; and they shall lay hold every one on the hand of his neighbor, and his hand shall rise up against the hand of his neighbor. (Zech 14:13)

After YHWH reestablishes Israel, he will take all her curses and place them on her enemies (Deut 30:7), once again issuing a world judgment for breaching the Noahic Covenant, as strife and civil war again prevail for those peoples who eat meat with the blood. Nations will be divided against nations, and YHWH will judge the nations who have spoiled Israel and desecrated the Temple mount (Zech 14:3, 12–13). The curses will fall on these nations until they too learn to walk in the freedom established by the way of YHWH (Zech 14:16–19). When this occurs, all nations will observe the Feast of Tabernacles in Jerusalem (Isa 2:3–4; Zech 14:16). YHWH will restore worldwide peace (Lev 26:6; Isa 32:4) and health,[8] saving all nations who walk in his Law of Life.

Haggai prophesied at the same time as Zechariah. He was one of the last prophets to receive word from YHWH. In Darius's 2nd year, Haggai prophesied to the newly returned Remnant, foretelling the *soon-coming* day, when YHWH would exact the penalty of the Noahic Covenant on all kingdoms.

And I will overthrow the throne of kingdoms, and I will destroy the strength of the kingdoms of the heathen; and I will overthrow the chariots, and those that ride in them; and the horses and their riders shall come down, *every one by the sword of his brother*. (Hag 2:22)

Haggai foretold the first world judgment, where YHWH would judge the nations that violated the Noahic Covenant by consuming an animal's blood with its meat. During the *Day of YHWH*, the Creator would overthrow the kingdoms of the earth, provoking fellow countrymen to arise to shed blood.[9] The Tabernacle of Testimony foretold this event through Israel's many sacrifices. YHWH would wear the high priest's robes and arise to slaughter, requiring atonement for the injustices wrought in the earth as he held humanity accountable for their deeds (compare Isa 63:3 with Exod 29:21 and Lev 8:30).

II. HOLOCAUSTS AS ATONEMENTS

A. *Justice and Atonement*

The Law's many ceremonies incorporated sacrifices as atonements for the nation's iniquities (Lev 4:20–25; 5:6–18). The Hebrew word for "atonement" is *kaphar*. The primitive root means 'to cover, or expiate, or condone; to placate or cancel.'[10] Perhaps the clearest translation of atonement is the English word 'expiate,' which Webster defines as: '*to put an end to; to extinguish the guilt incurred by; or, to make amends for.*' When a person commits an iniquity, he or she causes or produces a condition that is in disharmony with the laws of nature. The Law allowed animal sacrifices to "cover over" the guilt incurred by humanity's sins. In order to see how these sacrifices actually "covered" or "expiated" Israel's sins, it is important that we are well grounded in the precepts that govern the ceremonial sacrifice and atonement.

B. *Bloodguilt*

Justice has always been the focal point of Israel's Law—justice is the Law's founding precept. One of Israel's foremost responsibilities was to establish justice and righteousness on Israel's soil by putting evil off the land.[11] A pivotal point in her entire justice system was that Israel's land must not bear the weight of innocent blood. When Israel followed the Law's judgment concerning the atonement for a murderer's bloodguilt, YHWH would forgive this trespass.

> If you shall keep all these commandments to do them, which I command you this day, to love YHWH your God, and to walk ever in his ways; then shall you add three cities more for you, beside these three: *That innocent blood be not shed in your (a) land, which YHWH your God gives you for an inheritance, and so blood be on you.* But if any man hate his neighbor, and lie in wait for him, and rise up against him, and smite him mortally that he die, and flees into one of these cities: Then the elders of his city shall send and fetch him there, and deliver him into the hand of the avenger of blood, that he may die. *Your eye shall not (b) pity him, but you shall put away the guilt of innocent blood (c) from Israel, that it may go well with you.* (Deut 19:9–13; see also Josh 2:19).

The concept underlying this verse is the expiation of bloodguilt. Merriam Webster defines "bloodguilt" as the '*guilt resulting from the shedding of blood.*' Moses (c) indicates that the entire land can bear the guilt of the innocent victim. This is why YHWH commanded Israel's judges (b) not to pity the murderer. If the nation failed to find and convict the murderer, she would not have expiated the guilt incurred by the shedding of innocent blood, (a) so the nation would be culpable for failing to atone for the murderer's actions. David further clarified the Creator's concept of bloodguilt.

After Saul's death, Abner, Saul's general, sought to transfer the kingdom into David's hand. An alliance was struck, plans were forged, and Abner departed to make the necessary arrangements. A short time later, David's general Joab called Abner back to David's camp and murdered him.

> Afterward when David heard it, he said, *I and my kingdom are guiltless before YHWH forever from the blood of Abner* the son of Ner. (2 Sam 3:28)

David wanted to make it clear that he had not betrayed his friendship with Abner or shed innocent blood. David showed that he was not responsible for bringing bloodguilt on his people.

There is a distinction between blood shed during war and blood shed during peace (2 Sam 2:19–31). During the civil war between David and Saul, Abner had tried to dissuade Joab's brother Asahel from following him, but Asahel refused, so Abner killed him in self-defense. Joab and his brother sought to avenge Asahel's death themselves when the war had ended (2 Sam 3:30). The Law ordained that people should not take vengeance into their own hands. Rather, YHWH (similar to America's court system) only licensed judges to try and to mete out justice.

> You shall not avenge, nor bear any grudge against the children of your people, but you shall love your neighbor as yourself: I am YHWH. (Lev 19:18)

Joab broke this command by slaying Abner, so David issued a curse against Joab and his House, prophesying that Abner's blood should

> rest on the head of Joab, and on all his father's house; and let there not fail from the House of Joab one that has an issue, or that is a leper, or that leans on a staff, or that falls on the sword, or that lacks bread. (2 Sam 3:29)

On David's deathbed, he instructed Solomon to mete out justice to two unrighteous men. The first was Shemai, the cursing Benjamite, and the other was General Joab. Solomon obeyed, sending the priest Benaiah to render justice and expiate Joab's sin from David's kingdom (1 Kgs 2:4–6, 28–30). When Joab sought refuge and pleaded for mercy in YHWH's Temple, Priest Benaiah asked Solomon if he should still execute Joab. Solomon wisely commanded,

> Do as he has said, and fall on him, and bury him; that you *may take away the innocent blood*, which Joab shed, *from me, and from the house of my father*. (1 Kgs 2:31)

Atoning for Abner's death removed any possibility that David or his kingdom would bear bloodguilt from Abner's innocent death. Rightfully, the atonement would come from Joab's own life (Num 35:33).

C. By Him Who Commits the Crime

David's charge to Solomon had followed the precepts of Israel's Covenantal Law. When YHWH gave the Law to the nation, he strengthened the stipulation in the Noahic Covenant that forbade the eating of animal blood. Those who ingest blood from animals without properly draining the meat bear the "bloodguilt" for the animal's death.

> And whatsoever man there be of the House of Israel, or of the strangers that sojourn among you, that (a) **eats any manner of blood**; I will even set my face against (b) that soul that eats blood, and will cut him off from among his people. For the life of the flesh is in the blood: and **I have given it to you on the altar to make an (c) atonement for your souls: for it is the blood that makes an atonement for the soul.** Therefore I said to the Children of Israel, No soul of you shall eat blood, neither shall any stranger that sojournes among you eat blood. (Lev 17:10–12)

Leviticus is referring to those that (a) bear bloodguilt for breaching the Noahic Covenant. Consuming animal blood is of such importance that YHWH considers people who eat it guilty of the animal's death. Notice that YHWH does not hold (b) all humanity guilty of this crime, nor does he even hold the entire nation guilty if people have not actually injested an animal's blood. YHWH only attributes guilt to those who violate this command.

YHWH states that the (c) blood that the Levites were commanded to sprinkle on the altar is what atones for the life of man.[12] In chap. 13, we saw that the earthen altar represented the 12 tribes of Israel (pp. 648–50). When YHWH tells us that he had stipulated blood to "make atonement on the altar," the Law prophesied of an atonement that YHWH would make for Israel's sins.

The Book of Numbers provides further clarification regarding the above statute.

> Moreover you shall take no satisfaction[13] for the life of a murderer, which is guilty of death: but he shall surely be put to death. And you shall take no satisfaction for him that is fled to the city of his refuge, that he should come again to dwell in the land, until the death of the priest. So you shall not pollute the land where you are: for blood it defiles the land: and the land cannot be cleansed of the blood that is shed therein, **but by the blood of him that shed it**. (Num 35:31–33)

The Law states that atonement can only occur through the death of the person who actually commits murder. Israel's constitutional covenant does *not* allow for any sin offering for murder.

Israel's constitutional covenant outlaws vicarious atonement when murder is concerned: only the murderer's death can satisfy the penalty for the killing of an innocent person.[14]

Leviticus specifies that animal blood, placed on Israel's altar, atones for the soul, while Numbers states that this atonement or cleansing occurs only through the death of the person who commits offense. Thus the Law consistently condemns vicarious punishment altogether (Deut 24:16),[15] consistently maintaining its founding precept of eye for an eye, tooth for a tooth by establishing opposite and equal reactions. This was the law that David obeyed when he ordered Solomon to seek justice with regard to Joab. Solomon's execution of Joab released his House and his kingdom from any possibility of bearing the consequences of Joab's blood-guilt. David bore the responsibility as king to judge and render righteous judgments.[16] If his government failed to provide justice, then he and his House would bear bloodguilt for perverting justice. Solomon removed bloodguilt from his House and the land by atoning for Abner's death by shedding the blood of "him who shed Abner's blood." Thus Solomon cleansed the land from Joab's bloodguilt.

D. When a House Bears Its Forefather's Bloodguilt

YHWH held each individual personally responsible for his or her actions.[17] The nation's leaders and judges were also held responsible for establishing and maintaining justice in the Promised Land (Lev 19:15; Deut 1:15–17; 16:18–20). It was their God-given role as leaders. When Israel failed to follow YHWH, her pursuit of justice failed. During these times of injustice, atonement for a victim's death often went unexpiated. In these cases, where the murderer's life was not given to atone for bloodguilt, the murderer's children inherited the "bloodguilt" of their father's actions.

At Mt. Sinai YHWH told Moses, "I will make all my goodness pass before you, and I will proclaim the name of YHWH before you; and will be gracious to whom I will be gracious, and will show mercy on whom I will show mercy" (Exod 33:19). When Moses ascended the mount, YHWH fulfilled his promise by defining both justice and mercy as his most important character trait.

> "And YHWH passed by before him, and proclaimed, YHWH, YHWH God, merciful and gracious, longsuffering, and abundant in goodness and truth, keeping mercy for thousands, *forgiving iniquity and transgression and sin*, and *that will by no means clear the guilty; visiting the iniquity of the fathers on the children, and on the children's children, to the third and to the fourth generation*" (Exod 34:6–7). The Second Commandment contains further information, which helps to clarify this definition. "For I YHWH your God am a jealous God, visiting the iniquity of the fathers on the children unto the third and fourth generation (a) *of them that hate me*; and showing mercy to thousands (b) *of them that love me*, and keep my commandments." (Exod 20:5–6)

If a person (b) loves YHWH and keeps his commandments, then humanity's Judge will be "merciful, gracious, and longsuffering" with him. If, however, a man's children (a) hate

YHWH, and they are the third or fourth generation from the person who shed innocent blood, *these rebellious children will bear their forefather's unexpiated judgment.* This can be seen in the many times that YHWH gave the kings of Israel three generations to repent from "walking in the ways of Jeroboam who caused Israel to sin." When the third, or in the case of Jehu the fourth generation (2 Kgs 10:30–31), continued to walk in his father's wicked ways, YHWH annihilated or "sacrificed" their houses.

This precept is probably no more evident than in David's House. David's children continually rebelled against YHWH. Before the third or fourth generation had expired, a righteous and faithful prince was usually born in David's ruling House. YHWH had willingly forgiven David's wicked generations for overstepping their authority, oppressing the people, and trampling his constitutional covenant—at least until Manasseh's heinous reign. "YHWH was not willing to pardon" Manasseh's sins (2 Kgs 24:4). YHWH extended mercy to Manasseh's first generation, Amon; his brother Josiah; and his second generation, Jehoahaz. Jehoiakim and Zedekiah were the third generation from Manasseh (i.e., great-grandsons), while Jehoiachin was the fourth generation. When Manasseh's line continued to rebel against the constitutional covenant for four generations, YHWH removed his mercy and punished David's House, not willing to pardon their grotesque sins any longer.

> Manasseh
> 1. Amon, Josiah
> 2. Jehoahaz
> 3. Jehoiakim, Zedekiah
> 4. Jechoniah

Whether we discuss Jehu's wicked children or Manasseh's, each child was sacrificed or killed for his own sins. YHWH's mercy, as defined in his law, had exceeded its limits when these houses continued to denigrate his Law for three and four consecutive generations. Thus, holocausts or atonements were made for sin by the deaths of the very persons who hated YHWH and rebelled against his constitutional covenant.

This precept of personal accountability is evident in the Law again. When a man had turned from following YHWH and shed the blood of his own children by sacrificing to Molech, YHWH commanded,

> Again, you shall say to the Children of Israel, Whosoever (a) *he be* of the Children of Israel, or of the strangers that sojourn in Israel, that gives any of his seed to Molech; *he* shall surely be put to death: the people of the land shall stone him with stones. And I will set my face *against that man*, and will cut him off from among his people; because he has given of his seed to Molech, to defile my sanctuary, and to profane my holy name. And if the *people of the land* do any ways (b) hide their eyes from the man, when he gives of his seed to Molech, and kill him not: Then I will set my face (c) *against that man, and (d) against his family, and will cut him off*, and (e) all that go a whoring after him, to commit whoredom with Molech, from among their people. (Lev 20:2–5)

When Israel's (b) citizens were indifferent to a case of murder and unconcerned with expiating the bloodguilt of the victim's death, then YHWH did the judging. In cases where the bloodguilt was left unexpiated by the murderer's death, the murderer's children inherited his bloodguilt.

Notice again that YHWH does not hold (a) all humanity guilty for one man's crime. He holds (c) the person committing the crime personally responsible. If the individual's children do not repent from their father's sins (d) but continue in their (e) father's lawlessness, then the children will bear the father's bloodguilt, and atonement will be made in their households by their deaths (in the third and fourth generations or at a later, national epoch).

Perhaps no story provides as much detail about bloodguilt as the account of David's sin concerning Uriah. King David both murdered and committed adultery. The prophet Nathan, speaking on YHWH's behalf explained the consequences of David's sins.

> Why have you despised the commandment of YHWH, to do evil in his sight? you have killed Uriah the Hittite with the sword, and have taken his wife to be your wife, and have slain him with the sword of the children of Ammon. **Now therefore the (a) sword shall never depart from your house; because you have despised me**, and have taken the wife of Uriah the Hittite to be your wife. Thus said YHWH, Behold, I will raise up evil against you out of your own house, and I will take your wives before your eyes, and give them to your neighbor, and he shall lie with your wives in the sight of this sun. **For you did it secretly: but I will do this thing before all Israel**, and before the sun. And David said to Nathan, I have sinned against YHWH. And Nathan said to David, **YHWH also has put away your sin; you shall not die.** Howbeit, because by this deed you have given (b) great occasion to the enemies of YHWH to blaspheme, the child also that is born to you shall surely die. (2 Sam 12:9–14)

David had loved YHWH his whole life and wholeheartedly sought to obey his Creator and to walk in his ways. However, his actions betrayed the fact that he had in this instance despised his Creator. When Nathan exposed his sin, David repented. As a righteous judge, YHWH extended mercy to David and did not kill him as *justice demanded*. Instead, YHWH passed over David's sins in this matter (both crimes that carried the death penalty),[18] leaving the "bloodguilt" for his children to inherit. David's bloodguilt procured the untimely deaths of his own children *when they rebelled against YHWH*. As (a) a consequence of his bloodguilt, the "sword would never depart from his house."

This judgment played out in many ways for David's House in his lifetime. His first child with Bathsheba died (see below). Another one of David's sons sought an incestuous relationship with his sister, while Absolom tried to overthrow David's throne. In the 37th year of his reign, Adonijah, another son tried once again to usurp his father's authority—a move that YHWH's priesthood did not sanction (1 Kings 11). For the crime that David had committed against Bathsheba, David promised that her next son would be his heir (1 Kgs 1:13).

There was another factor affecting YHWH's merciful judgment of David so that YHWH did not demand the death penalty. David lived during the blessing phase of Israel's Prophetic Law. YHWH had given David his covenant of peace. Had YHWH taken David's life, the people would have seen YHWH as an unmercifully harsh and unforgiving judge who had no recollection of all the good David had done to establish Israel in the nation's constitutional covenant. Any judgment by YHWH of David, as king, or of his House would be "felt" by the people. As we have seen throughout Israel's history, few of David's descendants upheld the covenant as he had. If YHWH were to have ended David's life, the people of Israel would have suffered for David's sin through his oppressive heirs. This would not have been merciful for Israel, and it would not have been in line with the teaching of the Law, since the sin was David's alone. Had YHWH simply punished David with economic hardship or oppression (as he consistently did with Israel when the nation rebelled), this judgment would still have "trickled down" to the people. Thus, YHWH's only recourse, the only penalty he could impose was on David's unlawfully conceived child.

YHWH's judgment of David's sin was also determined by another statute in the Law.

> If a man shall take his brother's wife, it is an unclean thing: he has uncovered his brother's nakedness; *they shall be childless.* (Lev 20:21)

YHWH's judgment prevented a life that resulted from an unlawful affair. If David's child had had lived, YHWH's enemies would have (b) just cause to charge that YHWH had showed bias and favoritism to David. His enemies could claim that YHWH had not demanded justice for Uriah. If YHWH had not judged David's adultery, fault could be found in the Creator, so he had no choice but to require atonement for Uriah's untimely death. Bathsheba had been Uriah's wife when the child was conceived, and David had no right to an heir that should have been Uriah's. Thus, David's actions caused his own child's death in much the same manner as sexually transmitted diseases often result in an innocent child's death. However, the righteousness of David's life and his love for his God had spared David the lawful death penalty, because YHWH consistently shows mercy to those who love him and uphold his covenant. David repented, returned to walk in YHWH's laws and obey his commands once more, and YHWH spared his life. "For I, YHWH your God . . . show mercy to thousands (b) *of them that love me,* and keep my commandments" (Exod 20:5–6).

E. When a Land Becomes Laden with Guilt

As a national constitution, Israel's Law applied equally to all citizens, foreigners, and illegal aliens who resided on Israel's soil.[19] Thus, the Law was not for "Israel only." YHWH held each nation responsible for establishing righteousness and justice in its land. He held other nations to the same standard as he did Israel. At Sinai, YHWH placed the responsibility for equity and justice in the hands of each tribe's elders and chiefs. These formed one branch of the nation's judicial court. If a person committed an offense, the community bore the responsiblity to search for the truth in the matter and make sure that justice was served for the victims or the falsely accused. Exonerating the innocent in matters of justice was of utmost importance in Israel's court.

YHWH commanded:

Keep you far from a false matter; and *the innocent and righteous slay you not*: for I will not justify the wicked (Exod 23:7). If there be a controversy between men, and they come to judgment, that the judges may judge them; then *they shall justify the righteous, and condemn the wicked.* (Deut 25:1)

The innocent and righteous slay you not: for I will not justify the wicked. (Exod 23:7)

In the nation's covenant, YHWH had stated that he would not "clear the guilty" (Exod 34:7). YHWH commanded Israel's judges to walk in his way and follow his example. By justifying the righteous and condemning the wicked, the judges would impart equity, justice, truth, and joy firmly on the nation's soil. But what happened when the nation's judges rebelled against issuing righteous judgments and pitied the criminal? YHWH stated, "that innocent blood be not shed in your land, which YHWH your God gives you for an inheritance, *and so blood be on you*" (Deut 19:10). When injustice mounts and innocent blood is shed in a nation's land, the land itself becomes defiled. The houses (family lineages) that have turned from YHWH are judged. It was the duty of Israel's court to render both justice for the victim's sake and judgment against the guilty.[20] When society failed to provide this atonement, the community was deemed an accomplice to the victim's unresolved crime.[21] This is why YHWH stipulated that when the judges failed to discover the murderer, they should swear that they had not committed the murder nor known who had.

If one be found slain in the land which YHWH your God gives you to possess it, lying in the field, and it be not known who has slain him: Then your elders and your judges shall come forth, and they shall measure to the cities which are round about him that is slain: And it shall be, that the city which is next to the slain man, even the elders of that city shall take an heifer, which has not been worked with, and which has not drawn in the yoke; And the elders of that city shall bring down the heifer to a rough valley, which is neither eared nor sown, and shall strike off the heifer's neck there in the valley: *And the priests the sons of Levi shall come near*; for them YHWH your God has chosen to minister to him, and to bless in the name of YHWH; and *by their word shall every controversy and every stroke be tried*: And all the elders of that city, that are next to the slain man, shall wash their hands over the heifer that is beheaded in the valley: And they shall answer and say, Our hands have not shed this blood, neither have our eyes seen it. (Deut 21:1–7)

This was not some mystical ritual. Rather, YHWH sought to hold each person accountable. As the Levites watched the elders perform the Expiating Heifer Ritual, they had the opportunity to detect the guilt of a person among them who knew more about the murder than he had disclosed. In this way, the murderer could be ferreted out.

After the judges performed this ritual (even if the murderer(s) had been discovered), the Levites were to bless the elders and judges, saying,

> Be merciful, O YHWH, to your people Israel, whom you have redeemed, and *lay not innocent blood to your people of Israel's charge.* And the blood shall be forgiven them. *So shall you put away the guilt of innocent blood from among you,* when you shall do that which is right in the sight of YHWH. (Deut 21:8–9)

After participating in this ceremony, YHWH accepted the covenant of the sacrificial heifer ritual and forgave this heinous crime. The unexpiated bloodguilt was *not* laid to the nation or the city's charge, and the people were reconciled to their God. YHWH freely forgave this sin. What he did *not* do, however, was forgive the individual who had actually committed the crime (Exod 34:7; Num 14:18). This anonymous person still assumed bloodguilt for himself and his offspring.

Notice again the concept of a nation's bearing the bloodguilt of the innocent in the above text. The nation (the *'edah*) bore the responsibility to issue judgment by executing the murderer on behalf of the innocent victim.[22] If the leaders failed in this regard, they too bore guilt for failing to provide atonement for the victim's murder and transferred "innocent blood" onto their own houses if they did not participate in the Expiating Heifer Ritual (Num 35:31–33).

If the iniquities of a land are vast and unexpiated, the Creator holds the nation's leadership and its citizens responsible for the lack of justice (Isa 9:16–21). This is why many judgments such as tribute, famine, pestilence, war, and deportation affected the nation as a whole. Should the land be defiled by sins, such as immorality, YHWH stated, "And the land is defiled: therefore I do visit the iniquity thereof on it, and *the land itself vomits out her inhabitants*" (Lev 18:25). National deportation was only one method that YHWH used to cleanse Israel's land from her depraved, and dysfunctional ways. The whole land had become defiled by the nation's iniquities. The only way to rectify the situation was to expel the entire nation out of his sight.[23] Thus YHWH banished Israel from his presence, adhering to the same method of punishment he had formerly used for Adam and Eve when exiling them from their garden home.

III. SACRIFICES

A. *The Passover Burnt Offering*

When we began to investigate whether or not the Hebrew Scriptures contained truth, we found that YHWH's word had been established through his covenants with the nation's patriarchs. Many of these covenants had been ratified with self-imprecating sacrifices that depicted the fate of the covenantee, if he violated the terms of the contract.²⁴ Later, when we had examined the structure of the Tabernacle in ch. 13, we touched on the purpose of Israel's ceremonial sacrifices.

These sacrifices represented specific holocausts or "atonements" that would occur to Israel's descendants. When the bloodguilt of a man's house had been great, eventually atonement for the innocent victim(s) "by the hand of him who shed it" would occur through a violent holocaust. The holocaust "victims" were the guilty houses that continued to rebel against their Creator and walk in their forefather's evil ways. When YHWH offered the Burnt-Offering Covenant to Abraham (chap. pp. 98–101), the sacrifice of his firstborn son (Isaac) provided the prophetic sign. Using Isaac as a burnt offering ordained the deaths of Abraham's children *when they rebelled* against his covenant.

The Law incorporated the Burnt-Offering Covenant into Israel's Sinai Covenant. YHWH used the priesthood and its rituals to remind the Israelites of their agreement with YHWH while daily sacrifices reminded the people of the consequences for breaching it. YHWH ordained very specific regulations for the continual burnt offering. The priests presented the continual burnt offering every evening and again every morning. But most importantly, the fire was to be kept burning day and night, *never to be quenched.*

> Now this is that which you shall offer on the altar; two lambs of the first year day by day continually. The one lamb you shall offer in the morning; and the other lamb you shall offer at even: And with the one lamb a tenth deal of flour mingled with the fourth part of an hin of beaten oil; and the fourth part of an hin of *wine for a drink offering.* And the other lamb you shall offer at even, and shall do thereto according to the meat offering of the morning, and according to the drink offering of it, for a sweet savor, an offering made by fire to YHWH. *This shall be a continual burnt offering* throughout your generations at the door of the tabernacle of the congregation before YHWH: where I will meet you, to speak there to you. And there I will meet with the Children of Israel, and the tabernacle shall be sanctified by my glory. (Exod 29:38–43)

Notice that wine was associated with the continual burnt offering. Scripture consistently uses wine to denote doctrinal drunkenness and Scriptural blindness (see pp. 650–56). The Law for the continual burnt offering foretold that Israel's adherence to falsehood, which led the nation to depart from her covenant would provoke YHWH to render a holocaust *that would not be fully quenched until she returned to righteousness.*

When YHWH offered to deliver Israel out of the house of Egyptian bondage and to establish his covenants with Abraham's descendants, Israel sealed her agreement to uphold YHWH's covenant by participating in the yearly Passover sacrifice (Exod 12:43–48; Num 9:1–14). Shortly before Israel entered Canaan, YHWH stipulated that the only place Israel could offer the seal of her covenantal sacrifice was at the city in which he placed his name.

> You may not sacrifice the passover within any of your gates, which YHWH your God gives you: But at the place which YHWH your God shall choose to place his name in, there you shall sacrifice the passover at even, at the going down of the sun, at the season that you came forth out of Egypt. (Deut 16:5–6)

YHWH permanently placed his name in Jerusalem at the dedication of the First Temple (1 Kgs 8:29, 43; 2 Chr 6:20). What this meant for Israel's covenantal Passover sacrifice was that the prophetic sacrifice could only take place in Jerusalem—no other city would qualify (Gen 22:2; 2 Chr 3:1).

Jeremiah built on the law of the continual burnt offering. He understood YHWH's covenants with Israel when he foretold the day when YHWH would make rebellious Israel the holocaust in Jerusalem.

> But if you will *not* listen to me to hallow the sabbath day, and not to bear a burden, even entering in at the gates *of Jerusalem* on the sabbath day; *then will I kindle a fire* in the gates of it, and it shall devour the palaces of Jerusalem, and *it shall not be quenched.* (Jer 17:27; see also Jer 5:14)

The Sabbath had been the sign of the Sinai Covenant that Israel had contracted with YHWH (Exod 31:13). If she hallowed the Sabbath and rested on that day, YHWH would bless her with health, wealth, and prosperity. But if she rebelled, YHWH would *temporarily* annul his covenant with her, just as her covenantal Passover sacrifice had foretold. Jeremiah borrows from the sacrifice's symbolism by specifically tying Jerusalem's holocaust to the continual burnt offering (Exod 29:38–42) and stating that Jerusalem's sacrificial fire would "not be quenched."

Isaiah also bases a prophecy of Jerusalem's ensuing holocaust (during the Day of YHWH) on the continual burnt offering.

> For it is *the day of YHWH's vengeance,* and the year of recompenses for the controversy of Zion. And the streams of it shall be turned to pitch, and the dust of it to brimstone, and the land of it shall become burning pitch. *It shall not be quenched night nor day*; the smoke of it shall go up forever: from generation to generation it shall lie waste; none shall pass through it forever and ever. (Isa 34:8–10; see also Isa 1:31 and Jer 7:20; 17:4)

The sacrifice that YHWH would make in Jerusalem would never die out. As long as Israel rebelled against the Creator's Law, her citizens would face the torment of war, persecution, and destruction for her dysfunctional sins. The validity and influence of this unquenchable curse can be seen in Jerusalem's long history.

Antiochus VI of Syria was one of the first beasts whom YHWH employed to judge Israel for breach of covenant. Antiochus Epiphanes rendered one of the first blows against the wayward Jews in Jerusalem when he tried to force idolatry on the Jews in 168 BCE. Many chose martyrdom rather than accepting Epiphanes' religion during Jerusalem's civil war.[25] When Rome conquered Jerusalem in 63 BCE, Pompey devastated Judea's citizens; few Israelites survived the bloody onslaught, and those who did were excommunicated from the city altogether. When Herod the Great claimed governorship over Jerusalem, he exterminated Levi's ruling Hasmonean House.

In 70 CE, civil war again ravaged Jerusalem as brother rose against brother, and blood continued to flow down Jerusalem's streets. Persecutions against Christians in Jerusalem continued under Septimius Severus (202 CE) and other Roman leaders. Four hundred years later, Jerusalem's fire burned under the Ottoman Empire's occupation. While the Franks (1099 CE) sought to liberate the Holy Land from the Muslims, this effort too ended in further bloodshed for Jerusalem's inhabitants.

> Behold, I have refined you, but not with silver; *I have chosen you in the furnace of affliction* (Isa 48:10). Awake, awake, stand up, O Jerusalem, which has drunk at the hand of YHWH the *cup of his fury*; you have drunken the dregs of the cup of trembling, and wrung them out. . . Therefore hear now this, you *afflicted*, and drunken, but not with wine. (Isa 51:17, 21)

Notice that when YHWH tossed Israel into his fiery furnace she was not drunk with literal wine but with a spiritual delusion that caused her to depart from her God's covenantal Law. The Testimony and Moses' Song had prophesied that during exile she would serve foreign gods, "new gods," which had recently been invented by man (Deut 32:17, 22; 28:36, 64). These gods and their doctrine would provoke YHWH's jealousy as Israel made covenants with false deities and forsook her covenant with YHWH (Deut 32:18, 22).

Today, the many wars, suicide bombers, air raids, missile attacks, and political instabilities in the modern State of Israel and with her neighboring Palestinian, Jordanian, and Lebanese enemies still bear the curse of an ever-burning fire that continues to simmer well into our modern era that has yet to be quenched by the waters of righteousness and truth (Isa 10:22–3; 28:17–18. See Illustration 17.2.)

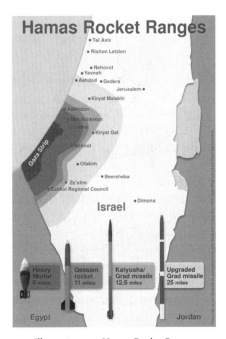

Illustration 17.2. Hamas Rocket Ranges

B. Penalty for Breaching the Noahic Covenant

When we looked at the prophecy established by Israel's national sanctuary, we saw that many sacrifices were associated with doctrinal drunkenness (see pp. 650–56). David and his prophets built on the statutes surrounding the Temple, incorporating them into songs that foretold Israel's many future holocausts. These massacres would occur when the people's sins became so grievous that the land could not bear their guilt any longer.

Isaiah continues to describe these holocausts further, clarifying the Levites' prophetic sacrifices.

> For the people turns not to him that smites them, neither do they seek YHWH of hosts. Therefore YHWH will cut off from Israel head and tail, branch and rush, (a) *in one day*. The (b) ancient and honorable, he is the head; and the prophet that teaches lies, he is the tail. *For the leaders of this people cause them to err; and they that are led of them are destroyed.* Therefore YHWH shall have no joy in their young men, neither shall have mercy on their fatherless and widows: for every one is an hypocrite and an evildoer, and every mouth speaks folly. For all this his anger is not turned away, but his hand is stretched out still. **For wickedness (c) burns as the fire: it shall devour the briers and thorns, and shall kindle in the thickets of the forest,** and they shall mount up like the lifting up of smoke. Through the wrath of YHWH of hosts is the land darkened, (d) **and the people shall be as the fuel of the fire: (e) no man shall spare his brother.** And he shall snatch on the right hand, and be hungry; and he shall eat on the left hand, and they shall not be satisfied: they shall eat every man the flesh of his own arm. (Isa 9:13–20; see also Isa 10:16–19; Jer 15:14)

Isaiah prophesies of a (a) specific prophetic "day" when YHWH would judge the rebellious nation. David established a prophetic day as 1,000 years (Ps 90:4). Thus, Israel's holocaust would last for 1,000 years, during which time YHWH would cleanse the land of her guilt.

YHWH had established Israel's ancient and honorable men as his executors of justice and judgment in the *'edah* congregation.[26] Because these leaders (b) had corrupted truth, perverted his judgments, oppressed, and caused the people to error, they would bear the brunt of the nation's future holocaust. Isaiah borrows the (d) symbolism found in animal sacrifice and applies it to Israel. Rather than an animal fueling YHWH's sacrifices, Israel's (c) wicked people would fuel the holocaust depicted by the nation's symbolic sacrifices (see also Ps 44:22). YHWH's sacrifice would burn up all the hypocrites, deceivers, and workers of iniquity as his holocaust burned in brotherly strife. Isaiah tied Israel's one-day holocaust to the Noahic Covenant's curse on consuming flesh with the blood, which depicted civil war.

When Isaiah states that "no man shall spare his brother" (e), he is quoting from the penalty for breaching Noah's Covenant, which stipulated "each man's hand being raised against his brother" (Gen 9:5). Israel's future Judgment Day, when fellow countrymen would rise against one another, would atone for or expiate the nation's bloodguilt for consuming blood with the meat. Not only would YHWH render justice for breaking Noah's Covenant, he would also judge for all the nation's sins. This is the same event that Haggai and Zechariah had prophesied after the Second Temple Remnant had been reestablished in the Promised Land.

The prophet Zephaniah continued to prophesy about YHWH's sacrifice, painting a vivid picture of the ensuing holocaust that would fall on the nation for her unexpiated bloodguilt:

> Fear you before YHWH God; for the Day of YHWH is near; for **YHWH has prepared his sacrifice,** and sanctified his guests. And it shall come to pass **in the Day of YHWH's sacrifice, that I will take vengeance on the princes, and on the king's house, and on all that wear strange apparel.** And I will openly take vengeance in the porches in that Day, on those that fill the house of YHWH their God with ungodliness and deceit. (Zeph 9:7–9, LXX)

The Temple's prophetic sacrifices were burned by fire. YHWH's future sacrifice of Israel, however, was not a literal burning by fire due to some apocalyptical catastrophe but a genocide that would be equally destructive. Israel's princes and her kings were the first part of YHWH's sacrifice. David's line bore the curse of Ahab's seed, and after Manasseh's heinous bloodguilt, YHWH stated that he would no longer pardon David's House for its wickedness (2 Kgs 21:10–16; 23:26; 24:2–4).

The second part of the sacrifice affected in the tribe that YHWH had sanctified to teach the nation YHWH's doctrine. The Levites had been given special garments to wear in their service in the Tabernacle, and it was the Levites who filled YHWH's house with unrighteousness, loathing the ordinance given to them as an inheritance. Although Israel's

Illustration 17.3. David Robert's depiction of the fall of Jerusalem to the Romans under Titus in 70 CE.

congregation had failed to establish and maintain justice in Israel's land, it was the leadership of the nation that YHWH held responsible. The first part of YHWH's sacrifice would be in David's and Phinehas's Houses. In later epochs, the bloodguilt of Israel's citizens would also be expiated.[27] Both bloodguilt and the burnt-offering sacrifice would be expiated in the city that carried YHWH's name. The expiation of all of Israel's sins would be witnessed in Jerusalem through holocausts and afflictions that would never be quenched until Israel's people finally forsook their own ways and returned to adhering to YHWH's covenant and seeking after righteousness (see Illustration 17.3)

IV. JERUSALEM'S HOLOCAUST (63 BCE–PRESENT DAY)

YHWH had tempted Abraham to sacrifice his firstborn son, Isaac (Gen 22:1). As a prophet (Gen 20:7), Abraham understood the prophetic implication of offering his firstborn son as a sacrifice, but he still obeyed. YHWH had commanded Abraham:

> Take now your son, your only son Isaac, whom you love, and get you to the land of Moriah; and offer him there for a burnt offering on one of the mountains which I will tell you of. (Gen 22:2)

Because Abraham was willing to sacrifice his only legitimate heir as a burnt offering, YHWH granted Abraham and his offspring the most incredible blessings imaginable. Years later, when YHWH called Israel out of Egypt, he placed the nation in Isaac's position as his firstborn heir. "You shall say to Pharaoh, Thus said YHWH, *Israel is my son, even my firstborn*" (Exod 4:22). The Burnt-Offering Covenant had prophesied the sacrifice that YHWH would render in Jerusalem on Mt. Zion, the mountain in the land of Moriah (Gen 22:2; 2 Chr 3:1). YHWH would there sacrifice Israel, his firstborn son, *for his people's own sins*. Though YHWH could have chosen another people, Abraham's willing obedience permitted YHWH to establish Abraham's descendants as the prophetic Burnt Offering, rewarding them with everlasting blessings when the family-nation finally chose to awake and to walk in his way of peace (Isa 59:8; see pp. 98–101).

 Isaiah continued the prophecy established in the Burnt-Offering Covenant, specifying Jerusalem as the place where YHWH's cup of fury and his flame of jealousy would smoke and consume his "only" son (Gen 22:2), Israel.

> And he shall pass over to his strong hold for fear, and his princes shall be afraid of the ensign, said YHWH, *whose fire is in Zion, and his furnace in Jerusalem.* (Isa 31:9)

YHWH's holocaust, the event prophesied through the nation's sin offerings would occur in Jerusalem. Jeremiah built on Isaiah's words, reiterating the prophetic day when YHWH would make a holocaust in Jerusalem for the Remnant's breach of the Sabbath's sign:

> But if you will not listen to me to hallow the Sabbath day, and not to bear a
> burden, even entering in at the gates of Jerusalem on the Sabbath day; *then will*
> *I kindle a fire in the gates of it, and it shall devour the palaces of Jerusalem,*
> *and it shall not be quenched.* (Jer 17:27; see also 5:14)

The only thing that would cause Israel to succumb to this holocaust was rebellion against
her covenant with YHWH. The Sabbath was the sign of that covenant and her perversion
and disregard of it would effect a violent judgment.

Isaiah again referred to the atonement that YHWH would render in Israel's wicked
houses for their bloodguilt, for Israel's government's failed court system, and for her citizens
who failed to uphold YHWH's Law and seek justice when murder and other sins had occurred in Israel's borders.

> Therefore shall YHWH, YHWH of hosts, send among his fat ones leanness;
> and under his glory he shall kindle a *burning like the burning of a fire. And the*
> *light of Israel shall be for a fire, and his Holy One*[28] *for a flame: and it shall*
> *burn and devour his thorns and his briers in one day*; And shall consume the
> glory of his forest, and of his fruitful field, both soul and body: and they shall
> be as when a standard bearer faints. And the rest of the trees of his forest shall
> be few, that a child may write them. (Isa 10:16–19; see also 34:8–10)

Israel's prophets based their prophecies on YHWH's Law. Isaiah, Jeremiah, Amos, Micah,
and others based their prophecies about the Day of YHWH on the many prophetic statutes
surrounding the Tabernacle's services. One stipulation that YHWH ordained was that one
sheep in every ten that passed under the rod would be holy or set apart for YHWH.

> And concerning the tithe of the herd, or of the flock, even of whatsoever passes
> under the rod, *the tenth shall be holy to YHWH*. He shall not search whether it
> be good or bad, neither shall he change it: and if he change it at all, then both it
> and the change thereof shall be holy; it shall not be redeemed. (Lev 27:32–33)

Isaiah continued this prophetic thread, building on the Law's statute, prophesying that
one-tenth of Israel would be given for prey after the Remnant returned at King Cyrus's
decree.

> Then said I, Lord, how long? And he answered, Until the cities be wasted with-
> out inhabitant, and the houses without man, and the land be utterly desolate,
> and YHWH have removed men far away, and there be a great forsaking in the
> midst of the land. But yet in it shall be *a tenth, and it shall return, and shall be*

> *eaten*: as a teil tree, and as an oak, whose substance is in them, when they cast their leaves: so the holy seed shall be the substance of it. (Isa 6:11–13)

Isaiah built on his former prophecy of the Second Temple Remnant's return as "soothsayers from the east" (Isa 2:6) like the Philistines. The Second Temple "soothsayers" would return from Babylon (the east), and one in ten would perish in Jerusalem's future holocaust. Though Judea and the surrounding countryside would experience most of the onset of the horrific Day of YHWH, Jerusalem's annihilating holocaust would be far more devastating as the city bore the brunt of YHWH's judgment for all the sins committed in her throughout the nation's history.

Ezekiel also referred to the Law's future one-tenth holocaust as the Day when YHWH would exact the penalties for breaching his covenant and purge the nation's transgressions. He referred to Leviticus's (27:32) statute, under which every tenth that passed under the rod was given for a sacrifice.

> And I will cause *you to pass under the rod*, and I will bring you into the bond of the covenant: And I will purge out from among you the rebels, and them that transgress against me: I will bring them forth out of the country where they sojourn, and they shall not enter into the land of Israel: and you shall know that I am YHWH. (Ezek 20:37–38)

YHWH's Law and his prophets prophesied of the Day of YHWH when one-tenth of the nation would be sacrificed. The Remnant had renewed the nation's covenant with YHWH under Ezra (Ezra 10:3; Neh 9:38), yet the same generation grossly rebelled against the very covenant that she contracted. Thus YHWH would once again bring her under the dreaded curse in his covenant and purge her rebellion. The Law's prophetic statute (Lev 27:32) was fulfilled when the Second Temple Remnant returned, and

> the rulers of the people dwelt at Jerusalem: the rest of the people also cast lots, *to bring one of ten to dwell in Jerusalem* the holy city, and nine parts to dwell in other cities. And the people blessed all the men, that willingly offered themselves to dwell at Jerusalem. (Neh 11:1–2)

One-tenth of the families who returned to Judea lived in Jerusalem. Their children would bear the brunt of YHWH's holocaust when Antiochus Epiphanes and Rome violently executed YHWH's judgment. Though the northern tribes that YHWH had scattered abroad would also bear his judgment during the Catholic Church's reign of terror with horrific inquisitions and persecutions, YHWH's long Judgment Day would begin in Judea. Israel, YHWH's only firstborn son, was the symbolic sacrifice ordained in the Burnt-Offering Covenant (see Illustration 17.5). YHWH fashioned Israel to be a servant to all nations. He

Illustration 17.4. Francesco Hayez depiction of the First Jewish-Roman War (*c.* 66 CE).

forsook his people, letting their own ways correct them, even though correction was very, very bitter (Jer 2:19). This is why dispersed Israel today will be the first righteous nation. It is the reason that Israel will inherit the blessings established as a double reward for her service as YHWH's firstborn son.

When the author of Lamentations prophesied, he looked backward as though he had come through all that had been spoken of Jerusalem. He depicted a scene as if he stood on the other side of Israel's holocausts, remembering all that had happened to her during the Day of YHWH. He accurately portrayed the fire that consumed YHWH's prophetic sacrifice, remembering:

> How has YHWH covered the *daughter of Zion* with a cloud in his anger, and cast down from heaven unto the earth the beauty of Israel, and remembered not his footstool in the day of his anger! YHWH has swallowed up all the habitations of Jacob, and has not pitied: he has thrown down in his wrath the strong holds of the daughter of Judah; he has brought them down to the ground: he has polluted the kingdom and the princes of it. He has cut off in his fierce anger all the horn of Israel: he has drawn back his right hand from before the enemy, and he *burned against Jacob like a flaming fire*, which devours round about. He has bent his bow like an enemy: he stood with his right hand as an adversary, and slew all that were pleasant to the eye in the tabernacle of the

daughter of Zion: he poured out his fury like fire. YHWH was as an enemy: he has swallowed up Israel, he has swallowed up all her palaces: he has destroyed his strong holds, and has increased in the daughter of Judah mourning and lamentation. And he has violently taken away his tabernacle, as if it were of a garden: he has destroyed his places of the assembly: YHWH has caused the solemn feasts and Sabbaths to be forgotten in Zion, and has despised in the indignation of his anger the king and the priest. YHWH cast off his altar, he has abhorred his sanctuary, *he has given up into the hand of the enemy* the walls of her palaces; they have made a noise in the house of YHWH, as in the day of a solemn feast. YHWH has purposed to destroy the wall of the daughter of Zion: *he has stretched out a line*, he has not withdrawn his hand from destroying: therefore he made the rampart and the wall to lament; they languished together. (Lam 2:1–8)

Indeed YHWH's servant Israel (Ps 136:22; Isa 41:8; 44:21; 49:3; Jer 30:10; 46:27) fulfilled the Burnt-Offering Covenant as YHWH began his sacrifice in Jerusalem under Antiochus Epiphanes and Rome, allowing it to continue through Jerusalem's Son of Man and his followers to all of Israel's scattered tribes (Ezek 14:10). YHWH put on the high priests garments (Isa 63:2–6) in order to sacrifice, purge, and refine his people into a new creation who are willing to humble themselves, call on his name, and obey his Law (Isa 13:12; 2 Chr 7:14). YHWH knew that it would be a very long time before Israel's people understood their own history or understood the reasons for their persecutions and afflictions. This is why he established many detailed prophecies in his Law and his prophets so that, in the Day when the veil cast over the nations is lifted (Isa 25:7–9), they may trace YHWH's words and his judgments (Isa 51:4–5) and see how his prophecies have been fulfilled in Abraham's only son and glorify YHWH their God. Israel is the servant who will finally sanctify YHWH alone. "You are my servant, O Israel, in whom I will be glorified" (Isa 49:3).

V. TRIED AND MADE TRUE: MERCIFUL SACRIFICE

In chap. 5, we saw that YHWH had tried his word in "the furnace of the earth" (Ps 12:6) to ensure it worked. The Creator consistently uses this "crucible" method to refine and purify his work. When YHWH judged Israel for her sins by sacrificing the wicked, he was refining the nation into a new creation that would listen and obey his word. Very early in Israel's history YHWH saw that, when his people were persecuted, they returned to him.

When he slew them, then they sought him: and they returned and inquired early after God. (Ps 78:34)

YHWH saw that war and persecution caused the Children of Israel to consider their ways and cry out to their God.

During the *day of YHWH*, he would sacrifice the wicked once more, giving them as an atonement for righteous (Prov 21:18) and making a new man: a man willing to obey his Creator's instructions.

> And I will punish the world for their evil, and the wicked for their iniquity; and I will cause the arrogancy of the proud to cease, and will lay low the haughtiness of the terrible. I will make a man more precious than fine gold; even a man than the golden wedge of Ophir. (Isa 13:11–12; see also Isa 48:10)
>
> And I will bring the third part *through the fire*, and will refine them as silver is refined, and will try them as gold is tried: they shall call on my name, and I will hear them: I will say, It is my people: and they shall say, YHWH is my God. (Zec 13:9; see also Ps 66:10–12)

The Burnt-Offering Covenant that YHWH contracted with Abraham will cause Abraham's descendants to become the firstborn (Exod 4:22–23) of all nations of the earth to seek righteousness. YHWH has used Israel's continual burnt offering to refine a latter-day generation into a people willing to obey his laws and abide by his covenants. It is YHWH's judgment used in the Day of YHWH that has re-created humanity into a creature finally willing to obey and follow his Creator-God.

18

The Daughter of Zion:
The Second Temple Remnant

I. ISRAEL RETURNS TO THE HOUSE OF BONDAGE—
DIASPORA (587-517 BCE)

Deut 28:68	**Curses**—Israel goes back to the "House of Bondage." (587–447 BCE) 6th 7 Times ends

Deut 28:68: And YHWH shall bring you into Egypt again with (a) ships, by the way whereof (b) I spoke to you, You shall see it no more again: and there you shall be sold to your enemies for slaves and bondwomen, and (c) no man shall buy you.

This point in the Testimonial Law refers to Israel seeking life outside YHWH's protective covenant; YHWH has divorced the entire nation. Israel's covenant at Sinai (b) promised: "I am YHWH your God, which have brought you out of the land of Egypt, *out of the house of bondage*" (Exod 20:2). Israel's symbolic return to Egypt was a literal return to the *house of bondage*. Oppression and heavy taxation define every government and religious system under which Israel and her descendants would live: comparable to Pharaoh's heavy yoke. Although YHWH sold Israel into slavery (Isa 50:1), her heavy toil would be (c) self-inflicted and no men would be sent to redeem her bondage (Deut 28:29).

When ships return to Egypt, YHWH is describing the nation's rulers whose disregard for the Law's precepts of liberty force the people into a controlled and compelled society. "Ships" symbolize (a) a nation's ruling body: ships ride over the sea, just as leaders rule over people. Because Israel breached her covenant with YHWH, Diaspora returned her to Egyptian bondage—a way that YHWH's covenant had guaranteed she should "see no more" *if* she obeyed.

Although the Testimony picks up again in Deuteronomy 29, the Prophetic Law left Israel in bondage throughout her Diaspora. She would serve foreign interests that prevented her from seeking her own welfare first; foreign interests would prevail above those of the exiled Israelite and Judahite offspring. Even at the end of the land's 70-year Sabbath, when the Second Temple Remnant returned to the Promised Land, she would continue to live in bondage.

Persia's monarchs were notorious for steep tribute. At her fall, Persia proved to have more gold and silver imaginable—most of it collected as tribute, then as war booty.[1] Zerubbabel's newly returned Remnant lived in oppression. As if this heavy tribute were not enough, the nobles charged usury—steep interest on personal debt that confiscated family land heritages (Neh 5:7; Lev 25:35-37)—from the common citizen. YHWH did not send a foreign nation to inflict this oppression; the Judean leaders chose to oppress their fellow citizens. The newly returned Second Temple Remnant reentered the house of bondage as her ships set a course away from Torah and toward Egypt's former oppressions.

II. COVENANT RENEWAL (516/15 BCE)

Deut 29:1-15	**Blessing—Renewal of Israel's Covenant.** The Remnant returns with Zerubbabel. The covenant is renewed with Ezra, Nehemiah, Yehoshua, and Zerubbabel. Jeremiah's 70 years are completed. The Temple's pillars are reestablished, and the golden fillet still exists.
Lev 26:40-42	7th 7 Times begins[2]—YHWH stretches Samaria's line over Jerusalem one last time (Zech 1:16; Dan 9:24).

Deut 29:1-15: You stand this day all of you before YHWH your God; your captains of your tribes, your elders, and your officers, with all the men of Israel, Your little ones, your wives, and your stranger that is in your camp, from the hewer of your wood to the drawer of your water: That *you should enter into covenant with YHWH your God, and into his oath*, which YHWH your God makes with you this day: That he may establish you today for a people to himself, and that he may be to you a God, as he has said to you, and as he has sworn to your fathers, to Abraham, to Isaac, and to Jacob. *Neither with you only do I make this covenant and this oath*; But with him that stands here with us this day before YHWH our God, and *also with him that is not here with us this day*.

Lev 26:40-42: If they shall confess their iniquity, and the iniquity of their fathers, with their trespass which they trespassed against me, and that also they have walked contrary to me; And that *I also have walked contrary to them, and have brought them into the land of their enemies*; if then their uncircumcised hearts be humbled, and they then accept of the punishment of their iniquity: Then will *I remember my covenant* with Jacob, and also my covenant with Isaac, and also my covenant with Abraham will I remember; and I will remember the land.

The last verse of Deuteronomy 28 left Israel in the house of bondage. Whether deported or returned to the Promised Land, her liberty fails. Taxation, slavery, and hard labor would define her life. This phase of Leviticus's and Deuteronomy's Prophetic Law coincided with the rebuilding of the First Temple, which reestablished the prophetic 35-cubit pillars. The Boaz and Jachin pillars prophesied that only 17 generations remained until YHWH rendered Numbers' Effacement Judgment once more by driving Israel off the land and rendering due judgment in *the Day of YHWH.*

When Ezra arrived in Jerusalem, he read the Law to Israel's congregation. The people pledged to renew and uphold the nation's constitutional covenant. This epoch of Israel's history parallels the Testimonial Law of Deut 29:1–15, indicating a time of covenant renewal.

Deut—29:14–15: Neither with you only do I make this covenant and this oath; But with him that stands here with us this day before YHWH our God, and also with him that is not here with us this day.

This renewal was fulfilled with the Remnant under Zerubbabel, Nehemiah, and the high priest Yehoshua:

> Behold, we are servants this day, and for the land that you gave to our fathers to eat the fruit of it and the good thereof, behold, we are servants in it: *And it yields much (a) increase to the kings whom you have set over us because of our sins*: also they have dominion over our bodies, and over our cattle, at their pleasure, and we are in great distress. And because of all this (b) *we make a sure covenant, and write it*; and our princes, Levites, and priests, seal to it. (Neh 9:36–38)

YHWH saw that sin and rebellion still existed among his people, so he left the Israelites under heavy mastery and confinement in order for (a) Persia's kings to test them, to see whether they would turn to him and obey his covenant or rebel further against it (Exod 20:20; Deut 8:2, 16). Ezra and Nehemiah witnessed the (b) congregation's covenant renewal to "walk in the way of Abraham, Isaac, and Jacob." If they obeyed the Law, YHWH would establish them as his people and set his kingdom among them.[3] If, on the other hand, they failed to uphold this covenant, they would bear the bitter curse of it.

A. *The First Remnant's Return (515–445 BCE)*

There are two generally accepted views regarding the Second Temple Remnant. The Christian view considers the Remnant to be cast off, awaiting the messiah.[4] In this view, the Remnant's righteousness or unrighteousness matters little: YHWH has already divorced Israel, so her actions have no bearing on future events. The messiah, whose death was predestined from the foundation of the world (Heb 9:26; 1 Pet 1:20; Rev 13:8), would save her *not* from her physical or national bondage but from her continual sins and sinful nature.[5] Israel's actions during the Second Temple Era were of little consequence.

Judaism views the Remnant's return quite differently. When the Remnant returned to the Promised Land, God no longer provided word through prophecy after Haggi and Zechariah—Israel's last two prophets.[6] It was up to her to figure out what God wanted, so her wise men (sages) began philosophical discussions (midrash) about the Law and how to apply it. The Jewish view is that the Second Temple Remnant was a righteous body of people who, despite their righteous efforts to understand God, were horribly persecuted and afflicted. This undue suffering and affliction somehow honored YHWH.

Jewish scholar Adin Steinsaltz sums up the Jewish position on the Second Temple Remnant thus:

> Though the people sometimes transgressed and were reproached by the prophets
> for their misdemeanors and sins, they continued to regard themselves as bound
> by insoluble ties to the body of law bestowed on them by divine revelation. This
> explains why Torah was studied and observed even in the most troubled and tragic
> eras. And almost from the first, the oral law . . . accompanied the written law.[7]

Contrary to both the Christian and Jewish views, Scripture shows that the Second Temple Remnant *did not return to righteousness* or obey YHWH's Law, which was *absolutely crucial* for those living on the Promised Land during the Second Temple Era. YHWH's Law, his covenant, and his commands were just as binding on Israel after she returned to the land as they had been during Isaiah's or Jeremiah's days. YHWH still desired Israel to turn to him and obey his constitutional covenant, which had been a thoroughly written document (see pp. 308–12) not an oral law or tradition (see below).

Throughout Israel's history, her rebellion had prevented her from fulfilling her fore-fathers' covenants. When Israel rebelled in the Wilderness of Sin, YHWH cast off or di-vorced that specific rebellious generation (Num 14:27–38), choosing its children to fulfill their forefathers' covenants (Num 32:13, 14) with their Creator. By casting off one rebellious generation and choosing its descendants to inherit the patriarchal covenants, YHWH re-mained true to the promises he had made to Israel's patriarchs. He did not reward good to an evil generation (Deut 1:35; Jer 18:10, 20). Instead, he let the wicked generation die out, yet still choose their children (Abraham's seed) to inherit the covenants in their forefathers' stead.

YHWH used this same method of national divorce at the end of the Monarchy. He divorced Ephraim and Judah, deporting them to Assyria and Babylon. After the 70-year desolation, YHWH proposed to choose Jerusalem yet again and grant his people the op-portunity to establish a righteous kingdom once more.

> For thus said YHWH of hosts, the God of Israel; Let not your prophets and
> your diviners, that be in the midst of you, deceive you, neither listen to your
> dreams which you cause to be dreamed. For they prophesy falsely to you in

my name: I have not sent them, said YHWH. For thus said YHWH, That after seventy years be accomplished at Babylon I will visit you, and *perform my good word toward you, in causing you to return to this place.* (Jer 29:8–10)

YHWH desired to bless Israel after disciplining her. He desired to choose Jerusalem as the seat of his government once more.

Thus said YHWH of hosts: My cities through prosperity shall yet be spread abroad; and YHWH shall yet comfort Zion, and shall yet choose Jerusalem . . . Sing and rejoice, O daughter of Zion: for, lo, I come, and I will dwell in the middle of you, said YHWH . . . And YHWH shall inherit Judah his portion in the holy land, and shall choose Jerusalem again. (Zech 1:17; 2:10, 12)

YHWH desired to choose Jerusalem, but he saw that she continually rebelled. Though he would deal mercifully with Jerusalem and cause his Temple to be rebuilt, he would once again set Samaria's measuring line over Jerusalem to see if she would sanctify his Law or turn from it.

Therefore thus said YHWH; I am returned to Jerusalem with mercies: my house shall be built in it, said YHWH of hosts, and *a line shall be stretched forth on Jerusalem.* (Zech 1:16)

After the Second Temple Remnant returned to the Promised Land, YHWH would allow one 7 Times epoch for the Remnant to turn from her sins and to sanctify YHWH. The prophet Daniel called Leviticus's 7-Time epoch "70 weeks," as the time allotted for Israel to sanctify YHWH:

Seventy weeks are determined on your people and on your holy city, *to finish the transgression, and to make an end of sins, and to make reconciliation for iniquity, and to bring in everlasting righteousness*, and to seal up the vision and prophecy (see Isa 8:16, 20), and to anoint the most Holy. (Dan 9:24)

Similar to other prophets, Daniel built his prophecy on Leviticus's 7 Times, but he termed the 70 years "70 weeks." If YHWH allowed 70 years for Jerusalem to end her sins, then the early Second Temple pioneers were responsible for steering the nation toward righteousness. They bore the responsibility of establishing YHWH's covenant, upholding it, and teaching their children to walk in it, just as the nation had at the Canaan Conquest. The righteousness of these early pioneers was crucial for averting the *Day of YHWH*. The critical question at this point is whether the Second Temple Remnant turned to righteousness when YHWH gave her the opportunity?

Before Nebuchadnezzar razed the First Temple, Judah's citizens covenanted with King Zedekiah to release their Hebrew slaves according the seventh-year Release Statute, but shortly thereafter, neglected their word, bringing their fellow citizens back into captivity (Jer 34:8–22). In return, YHWH gave Judah into the hands of her enemies, making her an oppressed captive, even as she had once been the oppressor. The Second Temple Remnant faced a similar situation.

Ezra and Nehemiah had been at the Second Temple's dedication, but official duties to the king had recalled them to Persia. When Nehemiah returned to Jerusalem, the people who had returned with Zerubbabel were as oppressive as their wicked forefathers by enslaving their countrymen.

> And there was a *great cry of the people and of their wives* against their brothers the Jews. . . . Yet now our flesh is as the flesh of our brothers, our children as their children: and, see, we *bring into bondage* our sons and our daughters to be servants, and some of our daughters are brought to bondage already: neither is it in our power to redeem them;[8] *for other men have our lands and vineyards*. And I was very angry when I heard their cry and these words. Then I consulted with myself, and I rebuked the nobles, and the rulers, and said to them, *You exact usury* (see Lev 25:37; Ezek 18:8, 13, 17), every one of his brother. And I set a great assembly against them. And I said to them, We after our ability have redeemed our brothers the Jews, which were *sold to the heathen* (see Exod 21:8; Lev 25:39–40, 45–46); and will you even sell your brothers? or shall they be sold to us? Then held they their peace, and found nothing to answer. Also I said, *It is not good that you do: ought you not to walk in the fear of our God* because of the reproach of the heathen our enemies? I likewise, and my brothers, and my servants, might exact of them money and corn: I pray you, *let us leave off this usury*.[9] *Restore, I pray you, to them, even this day, their lands, their vineyards, their oliveyards, and their houses*, also the hundredth part of the money, and of the corn, the wine, and the oil, **that you exact of them**. Then said they, We will restore them, and will require nothing of them; so will we do as you say. Then I called the priests, and took an oath of them, that they should do according to this promise. Also I shook my lap, and said, *So God shake out every man from his house, and from his labor, that performs not this promise, even thus be he shaken out, and emptied*. And all the congregation said, Amen, and praised YHWH. And the people did according to this promise. (Neh 5:1, 5–13)

These events occurred during the Remnant's first 70 years back on the Promised Land. Judea's newly returned Remnant followed all the corrupt ways of their rebellious forefathers! She exacted usury, compelled her citizens to be slaves, and sold them to foreign nations, even though the Law forbade it (Lev 25:42). At the Remnant's return, Judea was still a tribal-based community residing on ancestral lands (Jer 12:15). When usury accompanies landed heritages, lands are confiscated and Release Years ignored. The sabbatical years were the sign that Israel was "in covenant" with YHWH (Exod 31:13–17). The situation that Nehemiah describes demonstrates that the Remnant were once again trampling YHWH's constitutional covenant.

Notice Nehemiah's curse of "shaking" those of this Second Temple community who did not keep the oath to cease from oppression. When YHWH judged the nation, he would shake the houses that bore their forefather's bloodguilt or the people who had violated this oath with Nehemiah, destroying their lines during the ensuing *Day of YHWH*.

B. *Were the Second Temple Remnant Righteous?*

Nehemiah invested a great deal of energy in Israel's reorganization during the early Second Temple period (Neh 7:70). Artaxerxes appointed him Judah's governor (*tarshitha*).[10] As *tarshitha*, he forbade the priests to use the most holy utensils until a priest with the Urim and Thummim returned to Jerusalem.[11] Nehemiah was in Jerusalem when Priest Ezra arrived, and he stayed throughout the nation's recovenanting with YHWH. His duty as the king's cupbearer (1:11), however, soon recalled him to Persia. Nehemiah tried to return to Jerusalem whenever his duties to the king would permit. This may be why he feared asking the king to leave again in order to rebuild Jerusalem's walls. During his absence, Nehemiah yielded Judah's governorship to his brother Hanani and to Hananiah, the ruler of the palace (Neh 7:2). By Artaxerxes' 32nd year, when Nehemiah wrote his memoirs, he was a very old and wise man.

Upon his return from Persia in his later years (Artaxerxes 32nd year), Nehemiah had found Judea's citizens trespassing the Law even more than before—so much so that tithes had not been allocated for Levitical provisions, and the Second Temple was all but forsaken (Neh 13:7–14). Nehemiah discovered that even the sign of Israel's covenant with her Creator, the seventh-day Sabbath (see below), was being trampled and ignored by the rebellious Judean Remnant. Earlier in the nation's history, Jeremiah proclaimed the significance of the Sabbath sign, prophesying that Israel would become a powerfully righteous kingdom *if* she sanctified the Sabbath but would face continual persecution and affliction if she rebelled against the Sabbath (Jer 17:24–27).

YHWH desired to choose the Judean Remnant (the children of those whom he had divorced), seeking to reestablish his covenant of liberty with them. To this end, he faithfully ordained King Cyrus to release the captives and finance the Temple's reconstruction. Despite YHWH's blessing, the Remnant did not respond with humility or obedience. Rather, they rebelled against sanctifying the sign of Israel's covenant, just as their fathers had disobeyed only 70 years before.

> In those days saw I in Judah some treading wine presses *on the sabbath*, and bringing in sheaves, and lading asses; as also wine, grapes, and figs, and all manner of burdens, which they brought into Jerusalem on the sabbath day: and I testified against them in the day wherein *they sold victuals*. There dwelled men of Tyre also therein, which brought fish, and all manner of ware, and sold *on the sabbath* to the children of Judah, and in Jerusalem. Then I contended

with the *nobles of Judah*, and said to them, What evil thing is this that you do, and profane the sabbath day? *Did not your fathers thus, and did not our God bring all this evil on us, and on this city? yet you bring more wrath on Israel by profaning the Sabbath.* (Neh 13:15–18)

Judah's elders were the worst offenders. They disregarded the sign of their compliance with YHWH's freedom covenant, establishing city policies to trespass the Sabbath as well. The Second Temple Remnant was just as wicked after she returned to the Promised Land as before her exile. The Remnant had not repented. They committed another unlawful act by marrying individuals from the very nations that the Promised-Land Covenant stipulated Israel was to drive off the land (Gen 15:19–21; Num 33:50–56).

When YHWH your God shall bring you into the land where you go to possess it, and has cast out many nations before you, the Hittites, and the Girgashites, and the Amorites, and the Canaanites, and the Perizzites, and the Hivites, and the Jebusites, seven nations greater and mightier than you; And when YHWH your God shall deliver them before you; you shall smite them, and utterly destroy them; you shall make no covenant with them, nor show mercy to them: *Neither shall you make marriages with them; your daughter you shall not give to his son, nor his daughter shall you take to your son. For they will turn away your son from following me, that they may serve other gods:* **so will the anger of YHWH be kindled against you, and destroy you suddenly.** (Deut 7:1–4; see also Josh 23:12–13)

The Law forbade Israel's marriage to people from those nations that she was to have expelled. The Moabic-Shechem Testimony prophesied of the Day when YHWH would rage against her for disobeying. Regrettably, Israel never completely fulfilled Numbers' command during the Monarchy years, so the Effacement Judgment was still binding on Israel's children when they returned during the Second Temple Era. Instead of cleansing the land as YHWH commanded, the Remnant married into the very nations that YHWH forbade. In Artaxerxes 7th year, Ezra returned to Jerusalem. He and Nehemiah worked together to cleanse the people's violation of the Promise-Land Covenant (Neh 13:23–29). Twenty-five years later, when Nehemiah returned to the city in Artaxerxes' 32nd year, the people had once again intermarried with Canaan's descendants. Thus, the descendants of Jacob who lived on Israel's soil during the Second Temple Era became corrupted by marriages to the people who would "turn your sons and daughters from following YHWH" (see Tables 9.48 and 9.49 on pp. 426, 428).

In those days also saw I Jews that had (a) married wives of Ashdod, of Ammon, and of Moab: And their (b) children spoke half in the speech of Ashdod, and could not speak in the Jews' language, but according to the language of each people. And I contended with them, and cursed them, and smote certain of them, and plucked off their hair, and made them swear by God, saying, (c) *You shall not give your daughters to their sons, nor take their daughters to your sons, or for yourselves.*[12] Did not Solomon king of Israel sin by these things? yet among many nations was there no king like him, who was beloved of his God, and God made him king over all Israel: nevertheless even him did outlandish women cause to sin. Shall we then listen to you to do all this great evil, to transgress against our God in (d) marrying *strange* wives? And one of the sons of Joiada, the son of Eliashib *the high priest,* was son in law to Sanballat the Horonite: therefore I chased him from me. *Remember them,* O my God, because they have defiled the priesthood, and the covenant of the priesthood, and of the Levites. (Neh 13:23–29)

The Remnant's sin in the above account was (b) *not* that their children failed to speak Hebrew. Rather, it reveals the political and economic opportunity lost to the Remnant by not adhering to YHWH's constitutional Law.[13] The word (d) translated "strange," is the Hebrew *nokriy,* meaning 'foreigner.'[14] The Remnant sinned in marrying (a) foreign spouses who did not (c) love and adhere to YHWH's Law (Deut 7:1–4, above). Similar to America today, a multicultural nation loses its strong moral, judicial, fiscal, and constitutional foundation as the voice and short-sighted demand of the populace waters down sound precepts that had once constituted the national policy. Had Israel obeyed YHWH's Law, her economic and political strength would have naturally dictated that her people speak the language of the stronger, more influential nation.

Judea's newly returned Remnant reverted to the very sins for which YHWH had banished her forefathers only a century before! YHWH had established Levi as the tribe to lead and direct his people to obey his Law. Yet, during the Second Temple Era, Aaron's House was the worst offender (see Table 9.49. on p. 428). During the Maccabean era, when YHWH once again strengthened the Second Temple Remnant, giving them autonomy, Aaron's House did not drive the nations out of the land as YHWH commanded but tried to forcibly convert its people instead.[15] In the pages below, we will see that this was the reason YHWH had made a sure covenant with Phinehas, promising that he would always have offspring. In YHWH's future Judgment Day, much of the House of Aaron residing in Jerusalem would be exterminated during Herod's Hasmonean holocaust.

C. Zion's Daughter

Jerusalem's Temple mount became known as Zion, meaning 'a perfect defense,'[16] during David's administration. This citadel retained its name throughout the Monarchy years. Jeremiah built on David's and Asaph's many prophecies about Jerusalem and Mt. Zion. He addresses his words not to Zion but to *Zion's daughter.* He built on Amos's words (Amos 8), foretelling Israel's dark Passover and continuing Amos's prophecy aproximately 167 years after Amos had lived. This is what Jeremiah prophesies regarding the Noonday and the subsequent Judgment Day:

> Prepare you war against her; arise, and let us go up at noon. Woe to us! for the noonday goes away. For the shadows of the evening are stretched out. Arise, and *let us go by night, and let us destroy her palaces*. Thus said YHWH of hosts, They *shall thoroughly glean the remnant* of Israel as a vine: turn back your hand as a grape gathered into the baskets. (Jer 6:4–5, 9).

Jeremiah's chronology follows the Testimonial Law: the sun goes down at noon, yet destruction does not come until nightfall. A prophetic day is about 1,000 years (Ps 90:4; 84:10). If a "day" for the Children of Israel began at the institution of the Monarchy around 1000 BCE, then nightfall would begin at the close of the millennium, shortly before the Christian Era, when Rome began to afflict the Judean Remnant. This interpretation is consistent with the Prophetic Law, which prophesied that the sun would go down at Noonday, when YHWH rendered three days (millennia) of spiritual darkness (Deut 28:29).[17] If Noonday marks the mid part of a day (i.e., 400–500 years), then destruction occurs during the night of the first day of darkness.

The Noonday epoch began when Isaiah wrote his testimony during Pekah's first year and Uzziah's last year, in 745 BCE (Isa 6:1), and continued well into Hezekiah's reign, around 720 BCE.[18] The First Temple's destruction came a little over 100 years after Isaiah had fulfilled his commission to cause the sun to go down at Noonday. Sunset would occur about 400 years after the Second Temple Remnant had returned to the Promised Land, while "night" on Israel's first dark day would occur some 500 years after Solomon's Temple had been destroyed. A future generation springing from Zerubbabel's Remnant would endure the Judgment during the dark night when no word from YHWH and no true prophet could be found.

Notice, Jeremiah does not address this prophecy to Jerusalem or to Zion but to the "Daughter of Zion," the children of Nebechadnezzar's Diaspora—the Remnant that YHWH would glean. The rest of Jeremiah 6, continues to list chronological events: the destruction of Jerusalem by Babylon (v. 6), YHWH's departure from Jerusalem (v. 8), the day of YHWH's visitation (v. 15), and the stumbling-block prophecy of Ezek 3:20 (v. 21).

Jeremiah witnesses well in advance:

> Behold, a people come from the north country, and a great nation shall be raised from the sides of the earth. They shall lay hold on bow and spear; *they are cruel, and have no mercy*; their voice roars like the sea; and they ride on horses, set in array as men for war against you, *O daughter of Zion*. (Jer 6:22–23)

This cruel nation would show no mercy. Although the Babylonians had not regarded man, woman, or age when they carted away their captives, Jeremiah testified that in the short-term Judah and Israel would peacefully prosper on Babylonian soil (Jer 29:7). *The punishment dealt by Nebuchadnezzar was exile and banishment, not death.* YHWH would, however, deal with the "daughter of Zion" through fierce and merciless Syrian and Roman armies, who would affect his Judgment Day by devouring Zion's daughter in Jerusalem through a continually burning, unquenchable sacrifice.

III. THE CURSE (c. 165 BCE-PRESENT DAY)

A. *Leviticus's Diaspora Applied (Again) and the Day of YHWH*

Deut 29:16–28	The Day of Judgment or the Day of YHWH. Civil war; penalty of
Gen 9:5, ch. 22	Noah's Covenant is initiated. Moses' Judgment Song. Second Temple
Numbers 5	destroyed during Hellenistic and Roman eras. The Curse of Bitter
Deuteronomy 32	Waters. Israel is cast to the "molten sea" of 2,000 baths (Hos 6:2).
Lev 26:43	7th 7 Times is completed, and the 7 Times epochs end as YHWH hides his face from Israel's sins.

> Lev 26:43: The land also shall be left of them, and shall enjoy her sabbaths, while she lies desolate without them: and they shall accept of the punishment of their iniquity: because, even because they despised my judgments, and because their soul abhorred my statutes.

The previous stage of the Prophetic Law that we examined was Israel's return to the Promised Land and the Remnant's recovenanting with YHWH (Lev 26:40–42; Deut 29:10–15). Both Leviticus and Jeremiah had foretold the 70-year desolation during which the Promised Land would rest. When the Babylonian exile was exhausted, the Levitical Testimony ordained the restoration of YHWH's people to the land promised to Abraham.[19] They renewed their covenant with YHWH, acknowledging both the blessings for keeping his covenant and the curses should they again depart from his way of life.

B. *No Assurance of Life*

For many of the Remnant, the restoration on Israel's land was short-lived. This phase of Leviticus's Testimonial Law foresaw a renewed Diaspora sanctioned on the Promised Land. After the Second Temple Remnant renewed the covenant and promised to walk in the Creator's ways, they rebelled against YHWH's covenant to follow the traditions of the men (scribes, rabbis, elders, and sages) instead of the written word of God. In response, YHWH once again delivered a portion of this people to captivity, driving some of the Remnant off the Promised Land. This era of Diaspora began shortly after the world fell to Alexander the Great. Waves of forced deportation also compelled immigration. Political unrest, Hellenism, the many wars of succession fought by the Ptolemies in Egypt and the Seleucids in Syria for possession of the Promised Land, and taxes drove many Jews to immigrate to Egypt, Phoenicia, and other countries in hope of a peaceful, stable life.[20]

At no time during the Ptolemaic era did the Promised Land acquire the latter-day peace promised by Israel's prophets;[21] rather the Remnant reaped the opposite result as incessant battles, strife, and bloodshed continued to drive Abraham's descendants off the Promised

Land (yet again fulfilling Num 33:52, 56). Ptolemy I Soter—Alexander's successor in Egypt—deported a substantial portion of the Remnant in 311 BCE, enslaving most of those he deported. According to the *Letter of Aristeas*, Ptolemy Soter's son, Ptolemy II Philadelphus (285–247 BCE), sent a Hellenistic Jew named Aristeas as ambassador to Jerusalem.[22] Aristeas tells us (§§12–14) that Ptolemy I (367–283 BCE) forcibly transported 100,000 Jewish captives to Egypt, drafted 30,000 men into his army, and sold the rest (women, children, and elderly) into slavery. Though the Jewish captives were later redeemed by Ptolemy II Philadelphus (§§ 14–27, 37), many decided to make a new life among the Alexandrian Jews.[23] The deportations' net effect was the exile of a significant percentage of Abraham's children for their disobedience during the Second Temple Era, repeating the Diaspora and exile that had earlier occurred during Sennacherib's and Nebuchadnezzar's reigns during the First Temple Era.

Waves of migration continued to occur every time an enemy threatened Jerusalem. After six Syrian wars, Jerusalem fell prey to Antiochus Epiphanes' wicked designs. This conflict once again drove many Jews off the Promised Land, effecting massive migrations to Egypt.[24] Even the deposed and legitimate high priest Onias IV had been driven off the land promised to Abraham.[25] As in the Monarchic Era, YHWH continued to cause the "land to be left of his people to enjoy her Sabbaths," since the Remnant of his people (the Daughter of Zion) continued to follow the traditions of men (Isa 29:13)[26] over the word of their God during the long Day of YHWH.

Table 18.1 Second Temple Era 7 Times Cultic Judgment

BCE	Text	Event
520	Hag 2:10, 18	Temple begins to be rebuilt on Elul 24 in Darius's 2nd year.
516	Ezra 6:15	Temple is completed on Adar 3, in Darius' 6th year.
515		Since Adar 516 BCE was the last month of the year, the 7 Times Judgment begins in Nisan the following year at Sukkot in 515 BCE (cf. Solomon's dedication).
445		1st 7 Times ends
375		2nd 7 Times ends
305		3rd 7 Times ends
235		4th 7 Times ends
165		5th 7 Times ends/Antichus Epiphanes has vandalized the Temple, rips veil.
		Temple eventually falls into ruin and is forsaken.
		No legitimate Davidic or Aaronide heir rebuilds the Temple.
		An Edomite repairs the Temple.

515 -165 = 350 years for the 2nd Temple Era

Remember that the 7-Times judgment began again with the building of the Second Temple. There were 5 specific 7-Times judgments spanning 350 years. Similar to both the Tabernacle and First Temple, when the Sanctuary was destroyed or desecrated beyond salvation, the 350 years had expired. It is not coincidental then, that Antiochus Epiphanes desecrated the Second Temple in 168 BCE, right when the 350 years expired. History is repetitive. Antichus Epiphanes' act symbolically represented the many foreign nations that would oppress, desecrate, and make desolate the history of the very people that YHWH's Sanctuary symbolized (see Table 18.1).

C. Jeremiah's Test: Swearing by the Name of YHWH (515–165 BCE, cont.)

Jeremiah also recognized this era during which Israel's covenant was renewed. He reaffirmed the conditional nature of the promises in YHWH's Covenantal Law: as long as his people upheld his Law and loved to follow his way of life, YHWH would provide his blessings. One stipulation in YHWH's Law commanded that his people should swear by his name.

> You shall fear YHWH your God, and serve him, and **shall swear by his name**. (Deut 6:13)

Illustration 18.1. The name YHWH at the 5th Chapel of the Palace of Versailles, France.

The customary way that this oath done was by using the phrase "as YHWH lives" to state what one promised to do (See Illustration 18.1).[27] When David promised Bathsheba that Solomon would reign in his stead, he swore by YHWH's name:

> **As YHWH lives**, that has redeemed my soul out of all distress, even *as I swear to you by YHWH* God of Israel, saying, Assuredly Solomon your son shall reign after me, and he shall sit on my throne in my stead. (1 Kgs 1:29–30)

Jeremiah recognized that the people of his day had already departed from YHWH's Law to follow the scribes[28] (rather than YHWH's ordained Levites). He places a test before the Second Temple Remnant once they were restored to the Promised Land.

> And it shall come to pass, (a) *after that I have plucked them out I will return*, and have compassion on them, and will (b) bring them again, every man to his heritage, and every man to his land. And it shall come to pass, (c) *if they will diligently learn the ways of my people, to swear by my name, YHWH lives*; as they taught my people to swear by Baal; then shall they be built in the midst of my people. *But (d) if they will not obey, I will utterly pluck up and destroy that nation*, said YHWH. (Jer 12:15–17)[29]

Jeremiah promised that (a) after the 70 years allotted for the Promised Land to have enjoyed her Sabbaths, YHWH would (b) return to the nation and restore his people to their former heritage. The test during the Second Temple Era was whether his people would trust him enough (c) to obey his command to learn his ways, which culminated in vocalizing YHWH's name when swearing in his name. If the Remnant did not swear using the Creator's name, then YHWH (d) would once more drive Abraham's and Isaac's descendants from the Promised Land, divide them as their covenant sacrifice had foretold, and destroy them as a nation before him.

Sadly, the Remnant indeed failed this test after the postexilic restoration, because their teachers and sages disallowed the pronunciation of God's name.[30] They adopted a mystical approach to YHWH and his Scriptures,[31] by valuing the individual's state of cleanliness (*tahor*) when saying YHWH's name and emphasizing the way the Creator's name sounds when it is pronounced rather than heartfelt obedience to YHWH's actual command.[32]

Early rabbinic theology taught that

> from the mishnaic period onward, *the explicit name of God was never uttered except in the temple*. . . . The Talmud explains that only those few disciples who were outstanding for their spiritual qualities and profound moral standards were taught the name (i.e., YHWH) by their rabbis.[33]

> *Yud-Hay-Vov-Hay* (is) the ineffable Name of God. Known as the Tetragrammaton, the Name was permitted for everyday greetings until at least 586 B.C.E., when the First Temple was destroyed (*Mishnah Berakhot* 9:5). In time its pronunciation was permitted only to the priests (*Mishnah Sotah* 7:6), who would pronounce it in their public blessing of the people. After the death of the High Priest Shimon HaTzaddik around 300 B.C.E. (Babylonian Talmud, Tractate *Yoma* 39b) the name was pronounced only by the High Priest in the Holy of Holies on Yom Kippur (*Mishnah Sotah* 7:6; *Mishnah Tamid* 7:2). The sages then passed on the pronunciation of the Name to their disciples only once (some say twice) every seven years (Babylonian Talmud, Tractate *Kiddushin* 71a). Finally, on the destruction of the Second Temple in 70 C.E., the Name was no longer pronounced at all.[34]

Quite early in the postexilic restoration, common scribes taught the Remnant to refrain from pronouncing the name of Israel's God (a tradition that continues in most Jewish households today). The Jewish Remnant failed Jeremiah's test and received yet another penalty outlined in YHWH's covenantal Law. Judea's first deportation occurred when YHWH used Egypt once again to pluck her out of the land promised to Abraham during the closing years of the fourth century BCE. Less than 500 years after King Cyrus's decree for Jerusalem's restoration, YHWH would destroy the Judean remnant from being a nation before him because she followed the common scribes' and elders' teachings that prohibited mentioning YHWH's name instead of obeying YHWH's command to pronounce the name and swear by it, as upheld by the righteous priests of Zadok (Ezek 44:15).

Rome would finally quench any hopes that the Judean Remnant held for an autonomous government or religious existence when, in 70 CE, Titus razed the only remaining symbol of the Remnant's religious and political independence. For nearly 2,000 years, Rome would initiate many holocausts in the Promised Land; continual reminders that YHWH's people obeyed the traditions of men in lieu of God's Law (Isa 29:13). The continual oppressions that the Remnant faced throughout the long *Day of YHWH* demonstrate that YHWH's people had yet to return to him or his constitutional *way of life*.

D. Renewal of Diaspora in Deuteronomy's Prophetic Law

The Book of Deuteronomy does not explicitly acknowledge Diaspora and exile during the Second Temple Era as Leviticus 26 does. Deuteronomy does recognize that YHWH would bring on the Promised Land "all the curses that are written in this book" (Deut 29:27), which of course did include Diaspora and exile. Thus, in one very general statement in Deuteronomy, YHWH reissues the penalties that had previously been employed during the nation's kingdom years, fulfilling this curse once more during the long Day of YHWH. The next curse that the Moab-Shechem Covenant revealed was unlike any other.

E. The Dreaded Curse (c. 165 BCE-??)

1. The Man of Sin: The Dreaded Curse in the Testimonial Law

Although Deuteronomy's Testimonial Law does not establish 7 Times epochs in the way that Leviticus's Testimony does, Deuteronomy provides a very clear chronological picture for the Second Temple Remnant's future after the people return from the Babylonian Diaspora to the Promised Land. So far we have seen the fidelity with which the Prophetic Law foretold Israel's chronological history.

Deuteronomy's Testimony leaves the entire House of Israel (Northern and Southern Kingdoms) in bondage (Deut 28:68) and then picks up again with the covenant renewal made by the Judean Remnant (Deut 29:14–15). Deut 29:16 recognizes that Israel has passed through the nations, while v. 17 acknowledges that she has both seen and worshiped "new gods that her fathers have not known" (Deut 28:36, 64). When she returns to the Promised Land at Cyrus's decree, she does not leave the doctrines learned from Babylon's gods in Babylonia.

Rather, she returns to the Promised Land with a new set of delusions that she intends once again to blend with Israel's God's instructions (Isa 2:6).

> Deut 29:16–21: (For you know how we have dwelled in the land of Egypt; and how we came through the nations which you passed by; And you have seen their abominations, and their idols, wood and stone, silver and gold, which were among them:) Lest there should be among you man, or woman, or family, or tribe, whose heart turns away this day from YHWH our God, to go and serve the gods of these nations; lest there should be among you a root that bears gall and wormwood; And it come to pass, when he hears the words of this curse, that he bless himself in his heart, saying, I shall have peace, though I walk in the imagination of my heart, to add drunkenness to thirst: YHWH will *not* spare him, but then the anger of YHWH and his jealousy shall smoke against that man, and all the curses that are written in this book shall lie on him, and YHWH shall blot out his name from under heaven. And YHWH shall separate him to evil out of all the tribes of Israel, according to all the curses of the covenant that are written in this book of the law.

The Testimony of Deut 29:16 picks up where the curses of Deut 28:68 ended. The last curse of ch. 28 stated: "And YHWH *shall bring you to Egypt* again with ships, by the way whereof I spoke to you, You shall see it no more again: and there you shall be sold to your enemies for bondmen and bondwomen, and no man shall buy you" (Deut 28:68). This verse depicts self-inflicted oppression. Moses refers to this oppression by stating: "For you know how we have dwelled in the land of Egypt" (Deut 29:16). Hence, the prophecies contained in ch. 29 pick up where the curses of 28:68 end. Israel's sins and her departure from YHWH's covenant sold her into unredeemable bondage.

Verse 18 continues the Prophetic Law's chronology:

> Lest there should be (a) among you man, or woman, *or family, or tribe*, whose heart turns away this day from YHWH our God, to go and serve the gods of these nations; lest there should *be among you a (b) root that bears (c) gall and (d) wormwood*. (Deut 29:18)

Pen, the Hebrew word for "lest," is a conjunction that has the idea of averting or depreciating, "implying always that some precaution has been taken to avert the dreaded contingency."[35] The word "lest" signals this phase of the Testimony as the *dreaded contingency*. Should all the other curses fail to heal Israel of her sins, then this final dreaded curse surely would.

The dreaded curse has two parts. First, there will be (a) family in one of Israel's tribes who will turn from YHWH to serve other national deities and bear an evil (b) root. A root is the part of a seed from which a stem grows and blossoms; it forms the foundation of a future fruit. If this analogy is applied to Israel's history, the root of this curse would live during or after Israel's Babylonian Diaspora. He (or she) would be exposed to Babylon's deities (Deut 28:36, 64; 32:17) and theologies by embracing Babylon's doctrine and bringing these new and poisonous theologies back into Israel's land. The subsequent verses affirm this conclusion.

The Hebrew word for (c) "gall" is *ro'sh*; it means 'poison.'[36] *La'anah* is Hebrew for (d) the bitter herb "wormwood."[37] It also means poison, but more specifically it means 'to curse.'[38] A curse is a negative prophecy against a person and his offspring.[39] This can be seen in Noah's curse against Canaan (Gen 9:25), Jacob's curse against Levi and Simeon (Gen 49:5–7), or in the curse that Joshua spoke against the man who followed pagan child-sacrificing practices by placing his firstborn in Jericho's foundation and setting the city's gates on his youngest son (Josh 6:26; 1 Kgs 16:34). Israel's dreaded curse would grow out of a root or tribe in Israel that would issue "curses" and bring forth "poisonous doctrine." If this text prophesies of a man or woman who will become a poisonous "root," then what is the fruit that issues forth or blossoms out of this family's root?

The answer lies in the succeeding verse:

> And it come to pass, when he hears the *words of this (a) curse*, that he (b) *bless* himself in his heart, saying, I shall have peace, though I walk in the imagination of my heart, (b) *to add drunkenness to thirst*: YHWH will *not (c) spare him*, but then the (d) anger of YHWH and his (e) jealousy shall smoke against that man, and (f) all the curses that are written in this book shall lie on him, and the YHWH shall (g) *blot out his name from under heaven*. And YHWH shall separate *him* to evil out of all the tribes of Israel, according to (f) all the curses of the covenant that are written in this book of the law. (Deut 29:19–21).

The Septuagint may provide a better translation of this text:

> And it shall be if **one** shall hear the **words of this curse** and shall flatter himself in his heart, saying, **May holy things happen to me,** *for I will walk in the error of my heart,* (g) lest the sinner destroy the guiltless with him: God shall by no means be willing to pardon him, but then the wrath of YHWH and his jealousy shall flame out against *that man* and all the curses of this covenant shall attach themselves to him, which are written in this book, and YHWH shall blot out his name from under heaven. And YHWH shall separate *that man* for evil of all the Children of Israel, according to the curses of the covenant that are written in the book of this law. (Deut 29:19–21)

Verse 19 specifically states that the words in this part of the Law are (a) a "curse" against a particular family (root) in one of Israel's tribes. The poisonous root or tribe of v. 18 has budded and sprouted forth into "one" person who is a product of his forefathers' iniquities.[40] This deranged man will walk in (b) drunkenness (fermented doctrine) and error. He thinks he will have peace in his own life, even though his teachings imbibe the sins of his own imagination (see also Ps 62:4) by departing from YHWH's constitutional Law. Though the entire nation has rebelled against YHWH and corrupted the knowledge of truth, YHWH will separate this one drunk and evil man to make a public example out of him: YHWH will not show mercy or (c) spare him. The Septuagint states that YHWH will do this so that the (g) innocent will not perish with this drunken theologian.

The gall (poison) and bitter cursing (wormwood) that this family teach arise out of their love for false theology. This family's doctrine, and more specifically the teaching of one son, will provoke YHWH's (d) anger and (e) jealousy. *YHWH will place (f) all the curses of the law on this one evil man and his tribe* and righteously (g) blot out the remembrance of his name from under heaven. It may be remembered that YHWH previously employed the "blotting out" judgment when the wicked and unmerciful King Amalek attacked Israel as she journeyed out of Egypt (Deut 25:19).

Effacing a person's name and his memory is one of the Creator's tools for judgment (Num 33:52). YHWH continually seeks to expunge the memory and deface the honor of the wicked.

> The face of YHWH is against them that do evil, *to cut off the remembrance of them* from the earth (Ps 34:16).

Numbers' Effacement Judgment sought to erase the memory of unrighteous nations who lived in the Promised Land before Israel (Num 33:52–55). When YHWH turned the Effacement Judgment on Israel for her wickedness, Israel's archaeological memory was also "blotted out"—so much so that today very little evidence of her existence has survived and what did survive is buried under later occupations.[41] YHWH would use this same judgment and efface the memory of Israel's wicked teacher.

These verses (Deut 29:19–21) mark the advent of the *Day of YHWH* or the *Day of Vengeance,* where YHWH would judge those who partook of this *tribe's doctrines* and forsake the Law by placing man-made traditions above YHWH's written word. In vol. 2, I will demonstrate that one of Israel's high priests during the Babylonian Diaspora fulfilled Deuteronomy's prophecy of Israel's wicked "root." He was in a position to teach Israel and left his doctrine as a curse for his grandson, who would hear the words of Deut 29:18–19 and bless himself with peace. We will look at these and many other prophecies concerning Israel's Judgment Day in ch. 19. For now, we must finish the covenant's Testimonial Law before examining these particular events in the Testimony.

2. Bitter Waters: The Curse of Numbers 5

In order for YHWH to be righteous, he must abide by the same Law he has given to man. As discussed in chap. 1, he cannot act arbitrarily. YHWH knew this and placed many statutes in his religious constitution, allowing him to judge through various viable means if Israel proved obstinately rebellious. The curse of Numbers 5 is a case in point.

When Israel came out of Egypt, she encountered a much-needed water source that generated bitter-tasting water—so bitter that no one could drink it. YHWH used this bitter water at Marah to test Moses, Aaron, and the people of Israel. He incorporated this historical event into a statute later to be used as a test of an unfaithful people.

> And when they came to Marah, they could not drink of the waters of Marah, *for they were bitter*: therefore the name of it was called Marah. And the people murmured against Moses, saying, What shall we drink? And he cried to YHWH; and YHWH showed him a tree, which when he had cast into the

waters, the waters were made sweet: *there he made for them a statute and an ordinance, and there he proved them,* And said, If you will diligently listen to the voice of YHWH your God, and will do that which is right in his sight, and will give ear to his commandments, and keep all his statutes, I will put none of these diseases on you, which I have brought on the Egyptians: for I am YHWH that heals you. (Exod 15:23–26)

Notice that this verse ties YHWH's testing of Israel's obedience to disease. If she obeyed her Creator, she would be free from disease, but if she rebelled against his Law, she would inherit terminal diseases. *The Curse of Bitter Waters* in Numbers 5 was based on this precept and became the "statute of ordinance" to which Moses referred. If the nation turned from YHWH's Law to idolatry, she would contract a disease in her thigh that would terminate the life of her people. If, however, she did not rebel against the way of her God, then YHWH would heal her from all her diseases.

When Jacob wrestled with God's messenger, he touched Jacob's thigh, and it became disjointed (Gen 32:25). YHWH incorporated this prophetic sign into the curse he would later use against Israel, *if needed.* At Mt. Sinai Israel had sought the false god embedded in a graven image. Moses had followed the Bitter Water ordinance when he came down from the mount to discover a rebellious and short-sighted people. He melted the gold, beat it into powder, put it in water, causing the Children of Israel to drink the water of the idol they had sought (Exod 32:20). Jacob's disjointed thigh and the bitter water of Israel's idolatry were later incorporated into a prophetic curse in Numbers 5 that also dealt with drinking bitter water and a rotting thigh that would one day be used on Israel, *if* she should prove unfaithful to her Maker.

Deut 29:18–21 had recognized a particular family who would eat gall and drink wormwood. As we saw above (p. 804–6), both *La'anah,* Hebrew for "wormwood' and *Ro'sh,* Hebrew for "gall," connote bitterness. Gall symbolizes bitterly poisonous doctrine, while wormwood connotes bitter cursing.[42] YHWH bases Deuteronomy's dreaded curse in the Testimony on the former *Bitter Water Statute* ordained in Number's 5 for an unfaithful wife. Ezekiel further ties Numbers' curse of *Bitter Waters* in the Law to the method that YHWH would use to judge Jerusalem for all her sins: he would judge Israel as he would an adulterous woman:

And I will judge you, *as women that break wedlock* and shed blood are judged; and I will give you blood in fury and jealousy. (Ezek 16:38)

The Ten Commandments stipulated that adulterers and murderers should be judged with the death penalty.[43] After the Daughter of Zion had returned to the Promised Land, she professed to follow YHWH.[44] Yet, she had adopted so much pagan theology into her religion that it was difficult to find the original doctrine that YHWH had given to Abraham, David, and his prophets. The Second Temple Remnant claimed to follow Israel's God and guard his Torah, yet followed the precepts of men for doctrine (Isa 29:13). So YHWH put the Remnant to the test. He would test their fidelity to him to see if they would obey him or rebel.

When a wife's fidelity to her husband came into question, YHWH established a ritual to test the woman's faithfulness. He ordained very specific instructions when the wife was not actually caught in the act of adultery but was strongly suspected of it. This ritual solicited YHWH's divine justice in heart-wrenching cases, when it was uncertain whether the wife had broken covenant or not.

> Speak to the Children of Israel, and say to them, If any man's wife go aside, and commit a trespass against him, And a man lie with her carnally, and it be hid from the eyes of her husband, and be kept close, and she be defiled, and there be no witness against her, neither she be taken with the manner; And the spirit of jealousy come on him, and he be jealous of his wife, and she be defiled: or if the spirit of jealousy come on him, and he be jealous of his wife, and she be not defiled: Then shall the man bring his wife to the priest, and he shall bring her offering for her, the tenth part of an ephah of barley meal; he shall pour no oil on it, nor put frankincense thereon; for it is an *offering of jealousy, an offering of memorial, bringing iniquity to remembrance*. And the priest shall bring her near, and set her before YHWH: And the priest shall take holy water in an earthen vessel; and of the dust that is in the floor of the tabernacle the priest shall take, and put it into the water: And the priest shall set the woman before YHWH, and uncover the woman's head, and put the offering of memorial in her hands, which is the jealousy offering: and the priest shall have in his hand the (a) *bitter water that causes the curse*: And the priest shall charge her by an oath, and say to the woman, If no man have lain with you, and if you have not gone aside to uncleanness with another instead of your husband, be you free from this bitter water that causes the curse: But if you have gone aside to another instead of your husband, and if you be defiled, and some man have lain with you beside your husband: Then the priest shall *charge the woman with an (b) oath of cursing*, and the priest shall say to the woman, *YHWH make you a curse and an oath among your people*, when YHWH does make (c) *your thigh to rot*, and your belly to swell; And this water that causes the curse shall go into your bowels, to make your belly to swell, and your thigh to rot: And the woman shall say, Amen, amen. And the priest shall write these curses in a book, and (d) *he shall blot them out with the bitter water: And he shall cause the woman to drink the bitter water that causes the curse:* and the water that causes the curse shall enter into her, and become bitter. Then the priest shall take the jealousy offering out of the woman's hand, and shall wave the offering before YHWH, and offer it on the altar: And the priest shall take an handful of the offering, even the memorial of it, and burn it on the altar, and afterward shall cause the woman to drink the water. And when he has made her to drink the water, then it shall come to pass, that, if she be defiled, and have done trespass against her husband, that the water that causes the curse shall enter into her, and become bitter, and her belly shall swell, and her thigh shall rot: *and the woman shall be a curse among her people.* (Num 5:12–27)

If YHWH suspected that Israel had departed from him, he would be true to his own Law by applying the jealousy statute of Numbers 5, giving Israel (a) bitter water to drink. He would cause (b) the nation to take an oath of cursing (see below). *If the nation had indeed turned to YHWH and forsaken other gods, then she would be healed.* If, however, the people had given their hearts to former gods or to "gods which neither their fathers' had known" (Deut 28:64), then Israel's (c) thigh would rot and *this tribe* would become a curse to all nations where he scattered them. Notice also that, similar to Deuteronomy's dreaded curse, Numbers' (d) *Bitter Water* would naturally cleanse itself. In other words, after Numbers' horrible curse ran its course, it would naturally effect the healing of the very curses associated with it.

This curse was formally administered by Ezra when the Second Temple was dedicated.

> And the rest of the people, the priests, the Levites, the porters, the singers, the Nethinims, and all they that had separated themselves from the people of the lands to the law of God, their wives, their sons, and their daughters, *every one having knowledge, and having understanding;* They clave to their brethren, their nobles, and (b, see above) *entered into a curse, and into an oath*, to walk in God's law, which was given by Moses the servant of God, and to observe and do all the commandments of YHWH our Lord, and his judgments and his statutes. (Neh 10:28–29)

As a priest with *Urim* and *Thummim*, Ezra understood this phase of the Testimonial Law. He understood that YHWH would give this test by recovenanting with his people: if they obeyed, the oath of cursing would have no effect. If, however, the Remnant and their descendants set their hearts to accept foreign theologies, the curse would take hold and destroy them, making them an astonishment, byword, and curse among all nations where they emigrated.[45] This part of the curse is called *anti-Semitism* today. It was caused by the Remnant proudly accepting contradictory doctrines and traditions (many Jews still hold onto these doctrines of men today—Isa 29:13). We will discuss this curse more thoroughly in chap. 19 when we take a detailed look at the Day of YHWH. We will see further evidence that the Remnant, the Daughter of Zion, had indeed become unfaithful to YHWH. She had recovenanted with her God (Ezra 10:3; Neh 9:38), accepted the curses for breaching his covenant, then paid no heed to her God or to his Law.

IV. UNVEILING THE HOLY OF HOLIES (PRESENT DAY)

Deut 29:29	The third "Day of Darkness" is completed and the Noonday judgment is lifted. The veil cast over the nations is removed (Isa 25:7). Israel has hope of hastening redemption.

Deuteronomy's Prophetic Law leaves Israel under the dreaded curse until her latter-day restoration. In Deut 29:22, YHWH describes a future generation, born on the other side of the nation's plague of darkness. This generation will not be hardened or stiff-necked like its forefathers. Rather, YHWH's affliction has humbled this people to obedience (Ps 110:3; Isa 29:18–24; 51:7). This will allow their eyes to become fully open, so they can "see" that YHWH has indeed kept his word by performing and fulfilling the covenant's Testimony.

> Deut 29:22–29: So that (a) *the generation to come* of your children that shall rise up after you, and the stranger that shall come from a far land, shall say, when they see (b) the plagues of that land, and the sicknesses which YHWH has laid on it; And that the whole land of it is brimstone, and (c) salt, and burning, that it is not sown, (d) nor bears, nor any grass grows therein, like the overthrow of Sodom, and Gomorrah, Admah, and Zeboim,
>
> which YHWH overthrew in his anger, and in his wrath: Even (e) all nations shall say, Why has YHWH done thus to this land? what means the heat of this great anger? (f) Then men shall say, Because they have forsaken the covenant of YHWH God of their fathers, which he made with them when he brought them forth out of the land of Egypt: For they went and served other gods, and worshiped them, gods whom they knew not, and whom he had not given to them: And the anger of YHWH was kindled against this land, to bring upon it (g) *all the curses that are written in this book*: And YHWH rooted them out of their land in anger, and in wrath, and in great indignation, and cast them (h) *into another land, as it is this day.* The (i) secret things belong to YHWH our God: but those things which are revealed belong to us and to our children forever, that we may do all the words of this law.

Defacing an enemy's land was a commonly employed military tactic. Defacing caused famine and subdued obstinate vassals. Salt (c) burned the soil, rendering it useless for years to come.[46] YHWH even instructed Israel's military to deface their enemies' lands: "Smite every fenced city, and every choice city, and fell every good tree, and stop all wells of water, and mar every good piece of land with stones" (2 Kgs 3:19). Most ancient nations observed this practice. The ancient historian Megasthenes (330 BCE) mentions the practice of damaging farmlands as an andcient widespread war policy. He contrasts Indian war policies with other eastern nations.

> There are usages observed by the Indians which contribute to prevent the occurrence of famine among them; *for whereas among other nations it is usual, in the contests of war, to ravage the soil, and thus to reduce it to uncultivated waste,* among the Indians . . . even when battle is raging . . . allow those engaged in husbandry to remain quite unmolested. (Meg. Frag. I.36:14; corresponds to Diod. 2.35–42)

Indian policy prohibited burning enemy land or felling trees, as customary among other nations and Megasthenes observed that this prevented famine in India's conquered territories.

Assyria had installed war policies that reduced lands to "uncultivated wastes." When King Ashurbanipal wasted Susa, his men strode over Susa's sacred groves, defiled them, and set them on fire. His inscription records: "The people small and great I carried off to Assyria. Sixty double-hours of ground in Elam I laid waste, *scattering salt and tares thereon.*"[47] Ashurbanipal salted and wasted Elam the same way that he did Israel. Evidence

Illustration 18.2. Much of Israel is today a barren land and does not grow "any grass" (d, above in text).

of Ashurbanipal's ancient salting of Israel can be seen in the sparse agricultural resources found in the land of Israel today:

> Only about a fifth of the land is suitable for farming, and of that about half is irrigated. The rest of the country is too dry and has little or no potential for irrigation because of limited water supplies.[48]

This plague is still evident 2,500 years after YHWH enacted curses on the Promised Land! Only 1/5 or 20% of the land is arable (see Illustration 18.2) and only 10% is sustainable without irrigation. Compare this modern description of Israel with Scripture's *pre-Conquest* account of Canaan. Before Israel entered the Promised Land, Canaan needed no irrigation because frequent rains provided plenty of water for all the nation's needs.

> A land that flows with milk and honey. For the land, where you go in to possess it, is not as the land of Egypt, from where you came out, where you sowed your seed, *and watered it with your foot, as a garden of herbs*: But the land, were you go to possess it, is a land of hills and valleys, and *drinks water of the rain of heaven*. (Deut 11:9–11)

Archaeologist Rivka Gonen states that archaeology and history demonstrate that Canaan once had rich and fertile land:

> The fame of Canaan's "seven kinds" of produce is no exaggeration; the land was suitable for raising cereals, fruits, and vegetables, as well as for breeding livestock such as small and large cattle, donkeys, and horses.[49]

Today, Israel receives rain only during the winter months, and the land is heavily irrigated.[50] Israel's poor agricultural state does not compare with the many lush places of the earth. In the United Kingdom, for instance, 80% of the land is suitable for farming, while agricultural surpluses from the United States, Australia, and Canada help feed the rest of the world.[51] Even in Europe, 40% of the land is used for agricultural purposes.[52] If Israel was once a land flowing with milk and honey, she is now a land that must be irrigated by machine even more than a garden of herbs.

During the Diaspora, YHWH sent all of Egypt's plagues against Israel's health, offspring, and land. Since Israel's welfare hinged on following YHWH's constitutional Law, he knew that the Children of Israel would naturally succumb to these plagues when they rebelled against his way of life. YHWH hid and concealed himself (which included his Testimony) by a veil of darkness, from a people who did not desire his way of life so that in the latter days, Israel's circumcised descendants could seek and find that YHWH had wholly upheld his covenant.

YHWH applied Egypt's three days of darkness as a darkening of his word. The original Egyptian plague of darkness probably lasted for two and a half days. Since, counting in Israel was inclusive,[53] this remainder was rounded up to three, which may be the reason that the sun went down at noon on the first day, leaving only 2.5 days remaining. What this means for the prophecies of the Diaspora is that the veil can be lifted anytime after the 2.5 days or 2,500 years. Sunset prevailed against the knowledge of truth at noon on the first day of darkness, during Pekah's first year in office, in 745 BCE. Scripture defines a prophetic day as 1,000 years. This means that the first day would have begun with the Davidic monarchy *c.* 1023, or the building of the First Temple in 980 BCE, and the first day ended around the end of the millennium, at the beginning of the Christian Era. If we add the two days (2,000 years) of the Christian or Common Era, our generation today is roughly 2,800 years after the Noonday curse: at the dawn of the third day, when YHWH will lift the darkness curse.[54]

The Tabernacle of Testimony foretold the end of the Diaspora by means of the molten sea's 2,000 baths (1 Kgs 7:26). These baths represented 2,000 years of dispersion and exile outside Israel's Promised Land.[55] Hosea built on the Tabernacle's structure by prophesying that, after two prophetic days, YHWH would raise Israel up, heal her, and in the third day restore her to live in his sight in the Promised Land.

> Come, and let us return to YHWH: for he has torn, and he will heal us; he has smitten, and he will bind us up. *After two days will he revive us: in the third day he will raise us up*, and we shall live in his sight. Then shall we know, if we follow on to know YHWH: his going forth is prepared as the morning; and he shall come to us as the rain, as the latter and the former rain to the earth. (Hos 6:1–3)

Dispersed latter-day Israel has reached morning of the first day of light, when YHWH will lift the Noonday curse. We are the (a) future generation who will see and understand YHWH's word. Latter-day Israel will (b) see that plagues and enemy-inflicted sicknesses, such as salting, still cling to Israel's land in the latter days. This is the epoch Jeremiah refers to when he writes that:

> The fierce anger of YHWH shall not return, until he have done it, and until he have performed the intents of his heart: *in the latter days you shall consider it.* (Jer 30:24; see also Jer 23:20)

Latter-day Israel will both see the curses that YHWH has put on the Promised Land and understand that the land's plagues are consequences of her rebellion (f) against YHWH's covenant. She will see that YHWH has performed the entire Testimony embraced in the Prophetic Law. Not only will the seed of Israel acknowledge this truth, (e) all nations will see that Israel is today a cursed land—salted land, where nothing grows. Notice that, when the nations of the earth hear that modern Israel's poor condition results from her breach of YHWH's covenant, the land of Israel still manifests YHWH's plagues. The land of Israel will still bear the "plagues, sickness, and burning" when YHWH lifts the last day of darkness from the eyes of the world.

Deut 29:27 specifically states that the curses that remain in the Promised Land are curses (g) written in "this book." This is a reference to the Book of Deuteronomy, which records the Moab-Shechem Testimony. YHWH's Prophetic Law foretells that latter-day Israel will see and understand that YHWH has fulfilled all the curses of Deuteronomy in her land and in her descendants—many of whom may bear the curses of the Law at the time the veil is lifted. This is the case with the next phase of the Prophetic Law, which begins to remove the curses from Israel's children as they return to obey his Law.

Captivity (h) is one curse that will still be experienced by Israel's children when their eyes are opened to Deuteronomy's Testimony. When YHWH removes the stone of stumbling and the wine of false doctrine, Israel will still be "in another land"; she will not be in Israel when her eyes are opened. Rather, her salvation and restoration will come after she returns to her God and seeks his covenant.

Deuteronomy's Testimonial Law continues to acknowledge the latter-day lifting of the veil covering the Holy of Holies:

> Deut 29:29: The (i) secret things belong to YHWH our God: but those things which are revealed *belong to us and to our children forever, that we* **may do all the words of this law.**

This prophecy refers to the Day when YHWH will withdraw the veil cast over Israel and all nations, removing drunken doctrines that obscure who he is.

> He will destroy in this mountain the face of the covering cast over all people, and the veil that is spread over all nations. He will swallow up death in victory; and YHWH GOD will wipe away tears from off all faces; and the rebuke of his people shall he take away from off all the earth: for YHWH has spoken it. And it shall be said in that day, *See, this is our God; we have waited for him, and he will save us: this is YHWH; we have waited for him, we will be glad and rejoice in his salvation.* (Isa 25:7–9)

From the Day when his righteousness is revealed and onward in time, the Israelites and their descendants will return to obey the covenental Law, which will extend the length of their lives. Subsequently, Israel will be restored to the land promised, and the covenants (Diaspora, Circumcision, Prevailing, and Promised Land) with her forefathers will be fulfilled (Deut 30:1–6; Lev 26:45).

Notice that when YHWH reveals truth to Israel (i) he does not reveal absolutely everything: there are still "secret things" related to his covenants that are not yet revealed (Ps 25:14). This refers to the role that the New Testament has played in history that has yet to be revealed. The truth that he has revealed to Israel at the dawn of her first day of light, however, will never again be darkened! Israel and her children will walk in the light of YHWH. He will grant her the heart and the ability to obey all the words of the Law.

It is to this time that Isaiah refers when he writes:

> And I will rejoice in **Jerusalem**, and joy in my people: and the voice of weeping shall be no more heard in her, nor the voice of crying. There shall be no more

there an infant of days, nor an old man that has not filled his days: for the child shall die an hundred years old; but the sinner being an hundred years old shall be accursed. And *they shall build houses, and inhabit them*; and they shall plant vineyards, and eat the fruit of them. They shall not build, and another inhabit; they shall not plant, and another eat: for *as the days of a tree are the days of my people*, and my elect shall long enjoy the work of their hands. They shall not labor in vain, nor bring forth for trouble; for *they are **the seed** of the blessed* of YHWH, and *their offspring with them*. And it shall come to pass, that before they call, I will answer; and while they are yet speaking, I will hear. The wolf and the lamb shall feed together, and the lion shall eat straw like the bullock: and dust shall be the serpent's meat. They shall not hurt nor destroy in all my holy mountain, said YHWH. (Isa 65:19–25)

V. REDEMPTION: DIASPORA AND PROMISED-LAND COVENANTS FULFILLED (FUTURE)

Deut 30:1–6 **Lev 26:44–45**	Latter-Day Remnant returns to YHWH and obeys. Remnant is delivered (redeemed) to the Promised Land. The Diaspora, Circumcision, Prevailing, and Promised-Land Covenants are fulfilled. Israel finally obeys. Israel fulfills Numbers' Effacement Judgment against her enemies.

Deut 30:1–4: And it shall come to pass, when (a) all these things are come on you, *the blessing and the curse*, which I have set before you, and (b) **you shall call them to mind among all the nations, where YHWH your God has driven you,** And (c) shall return to YHWH your God, and *shall obey* his voice according to all that I command you this day, you and your children, with all your heart, and with all your soul; (d) That then YHWH your God will turn your captivity, and have compassion on you, and (e) will *return and gather you from all the nations, where YHWH your God has scattered you*. If (f) any of your be driven out to the outmost parts of heaven, from there will YHWH your God gather you, and from there will he fetch you.

Lev 26:44–45: And yet for all that, *when (b) they be in the land of their enemies, I will **not** cast them away,* neither will I abhor them, to destroy them utterly, *and (g) to break my covenant with them*: for I am YHWH their God. But I will for their sakes remember the covenant of their ancestors, whom I brought forth out of the land of Egypt in the sight of the heathen, *that I might be their God: I am YHWH.*

Israel remains under the curses of the Law until her latter-day redemption. When both the (a) blessing and the dreaded curse are fulfilled, (b) she will remember the covenant's blessing and its curse *while yet scattered among the nations*. This verse links to the previous text in Deut 29:16–29, where the final darkened day has been lifted and Israel understands the Testimonial Law while yet in Diaspora. After she remembers her forefathers' constitutional Law, (c) she will return to YHWH and obey all his commands with her whole heart and soul. It is Israel's (d) return to YHWH alone as her Creator and her obedience to his Law that enables him to "turn Israel's captivity." This is the same motif that YHWH had previously used in blessing Abraham. YHWH had commanded Abraham to walk in his way of life and to instruct his children in that way so "that YHWH may bring on Abraham that which he has spoken of him" (Gen 18:17–19). Likewise, it is Israel's return to YHWH alone as her God and her obedience to his constitutional Law that will enable him to bless the latter-day nation and heal her land (2 Chr 7:14).

Deut 30:3 (e) marks the end of the Diaspora! YHWH redeems Israel's descendants from (f) all the kingdoms where they have been scattered and returns them to the land promised to Abraham, Isaac, and Jacob. YHWH has returned to Israel to be her God, to walk with her (Ps 12:5; 44:23–26; Isa 51:15–23), and to heal "all of her diseases" (Ps 105:37; Jer 33:6–7).

Moses had previously prophesied of this day:

YHWH shall scatter you among the nations, and you shall be left few in number among the heathen, where YHWH shall lead you. And there you shall serve gods, the work of men's hands, wood and stone, which neither see, nor hear, nor eat, nor smell. But if from there you shall seek YHWH your God, you shall find him, if you seek him with all your heart and with all your soul. When you are in tribulation, and *all these things are come on you, even in the latter days*, if you turn to YHWH your God, and shall be obedient to his voice; (For YHWH your God is a merciful God;) he will not forsake you, neither destroy you, *nor forget the covenant of your fathers which he sware to them.*

For *ask now* of the days that are past, which were before you, since the day that God created man on the earth, and ask from the one side of heaven to the other, whether there has been any such thing as this great thing is, or has been heard like it? Did ever people hear the voice of God speaking out of the midst of the fire, as you have heard, and live? Or has God assayed to go and take him a nation from the middle of another nation, by temptations, by signs, and by wonders, and by war, and by a mighty hand, and by a stretched out arm, and by great terrors, according to all that YHWH your God did for you in Egypt before your eyes? To you it was showed, that *you might know that YHWH he is God; there is none else beside him.* (Deut 4:27–35)[56]

The Testimonial Law reveals that (g) YHWH will never forget the patriarchal covenants! *He will never rescind his promises to Abraham or to the nation of Israel.* YHWH will be faithful and remember the covenants and reestablish those covenant with the latter-day nation. This, remember, was our key criterion for determining whether or not Israel's God had been righteous. A God who waits well over 2,500 years for his people to return to him so that he can once again set about to fulfill his covenants is indeed a loyal and faithful God!

When she is redeemed to the Promised Land, Israel will finally fulfill Numbers' Effacement Judgment to destroy, drive out, dispossess, and divide the Promised Land.

And it shall come to pass in that day, that YHWH shall set his hand again the (a) *second time* to recover the remnant of his people, which shall be left, from Assyria, and from Egypt, and from Pathros, and from Cush, and from Elam, and from Shinar, and from Hamath, and from the islands of the sea. And **he shall set up an ensign for the nations,**[57] and shall assemble the outcasts of Israel, and gather together the dispersed of Judah from the (b) *four corners of the earth.* The (c) envy also of Ephraim shall depart, and the adversaries of Judah shall be cut off: Ephraim shall not envy Judah, and Judah shall not vex Ephraim.[58] But they shall (d) fly on the shoulders of the Philistines toward the west; they shall spoil them of the east together: they shall lay their hand on Edom and Moab; and the children of Ammon shall obey them. And YHWH shall utterly (e) destroy the tongue of the Egyptian sea; and with his mighty wind shall he shake his hand over the river, and shall smite it in the seven streams, and make (f) men go over dryshod. **And there shall be an (f) highway for the remnant of his people, which shall be left, from Assyria;** like *as it was to Israel* **in the day that he came up out of the land of Egypt**. (Isa 11:11–16; see also Isa 60:19–22)

YHWH will perform a (a) *second exodus* for Israel. While the first exodus under Moses only affected Abraham's children living in Egypt, the second exodus will deliver Israel from the (b) four corners of the earth. Restored Israel will no longer envy or resent the capitalistic wealth that Ephraim accumulates. Rather, she will see the (c) strength that Ephraim's commerce, innovation, entrepreneurial spirit, and wealth bring to a nation. Likewise, Ephraim will not be jealous of Judah's shepherding role but will willingly support Judah's Monarchy. YHWH's redeemed people will (d) have one heart and one spirit to fulfill Numbers' Efacement Judgment, despoiling and driving out the children of ancient nations. This signals that the people have circumcised their hearts and prevailed in the way of YHWH to fulfill those covenants. The tongue of the Egyptian sea refers to the main arteries of the Nile and the source of Egypt's strength. YHWH will dry up this strength and utterly weaken the nation so that Egypt cannot be a threat to the newly restored remnant. (This may be one ensign of Israel's restoration.) Throughout Egypt, Assyria, and the earth, YHWH will cause his name and his fame to be known with a *second exodus* as he had at the first exodus. YHWH will create highways out of lakes, oceans, and seas; and roads out of mountains.[59] The earth will reel and move as YHWH creates this miracle to deliver his people from their captivity, so they may freely return to his land to live without oppression.

VI. ETERNAL BLESSINGS (FUTURE)

A. Redemption and Circumcision of the Heart

Deut 30:5–6	YHWH pours his spirit on the House of Israel; she becomes a blessing to all other nations. The Circumcision Covenant, Prevailing Covenant, and Promised-Land Covenant are fulfilled. YHWH gives the nation a Covenant of Peace and a new name (Ezek 34:25; Isa 62:2), similar to the Circumcision Covenant.

Deut 30:5–6: And YHWH your God will bring you to the land which your fathers possessed, and you shall possess it; and he will do you good, and (a) multiply you above your fathers. And YHWH your God will (b) circumcise your heart, and the heart of your seed, to love YHWH your God with all your heart, and with all your soul, that you may live.

During this era of the Prophetic Law, YHWH has gathered Israel's children from all nations and reestablished them on the Promised Land. He has removed all their curses. Israel's (a) population and her blessings increase exponentially so that the Promised Land is not large enough to contain her multitude, and she asks for more land. The land that once swallowed her up cannot now contain her blessings.

> The land of your destruction shall even now be too narrow by reason of the inhabitants, and they that swallowed you up shall be far away. The children which you shall have, after you have lost the other, shall say again in your ears, The place is too strait for me: give place to me that I may dwell. (Isa 49:19–20)

As in the days of Joshua, Israel will be encouraged to colonize new territory (Josh 17:14–18) that will be "one portion above the rest" (Gen 48:22) of the nations of the earth, and YHWH will bless Israel with as much land as she needs.

YHWH will circumcise (b) Israel's heart and the heart of her future generations to love and serve YHWH only. During the previous epoch, when YHWH had lifted the veil of darkness, he began to pour his spirit out on those who believed and kept his covenant. This epoch, however, signals YHWH's pouring his spirit on the whole House of Israel, which will cause her to understand and obey his covenant and keep all his statutes, commandments, and laws. It is to this time that Ezekiel and Isaiah referred when they wrote:

> I will sanctify my great name, which was profaned among the heathen, which you have profaned in the middle of them; and the heathen shall know that I am YHWH, said YHWH GOD, when I shall be sanctified *in you* before their eyes. For I will take you from among the heathen, and gather you out of all countries, and will bring you into **your own land**. Then will I sprinkle clean

water on you, and you shall be clean: from all your filthiness, and from all your idols, will I cleanse you. **A new heart also will I give you, and a new spirit will I put within you: and I will take away the stony heart out of your flesh, and I will give you an heart of flesh.** And I will put my spirit within you, **and cause you to walk in my statutes, and you shall keep my judgments, and do them**. And you shall dwell in the land that I gave to your fathers; and you shall be my people, and I will be your God. I will also save you from all your uncleannesses: and I will call for the corn, and will increase it, and lay no famine on you. And I will multiply the fruit of the tree, and the increase of the field, that you shall receive no more reproach of famine among the heathen. Then shall you remember your own evil ways, and your doings that were not good, and shall lothe yourselves in your own sight for your iniquities and for your abominations. (Ezek 36:23–31)

Thus said YHWH GOD; Behold, O my people, I will open your graves, and cause you to come up out of your graves, and *bring you into the land of Israel*. And you shall know that I am YHWH, when I have opened your graves, O my people, and brought you up out of your graves, *And shall put my spirit in you*, and you shall live, and *I shall place you in your own land*: then shall you know that I YHWH have spoken it, and performed it, said YHWH. (Ezek 37:12–14)

Yet now hear, O Jacob my servant; and Israel, whom I have chosen: Thus said YHWH that made you, and formed you from the womb, which will help you; Fear not, O Jacob, my servant; and you, Jesurun, whom I have chosen. For I will pour water on him that is thirsty, and floods on the dry ground: *I will pour my spirit on your seed, and my blessing on your offspring*. (Isa 44:1–3)[60]

When Israel's heart is finally circumcised to YHWH alone, he will bless Israel in all she undertakes. She will walk with YHWH and be a light to all nations (Isa 60:1–5, 20–21). Once Israel sanctifies YHWH alone and wholeheartedly observes his Law, YHWH will establish a covenant with Israel so that his spirit will never depart from this generation or from any generation to come (Isa 59:21; Deut 29:29). She will finally fulfill the Deuteronomic promise to be a nation "who has God so near to them, as YHWH our God is in all things that his people call on him for" (Deut 4:6–7). When the entire land of Israel walks in YHWH's way of life, the obedience will naturally lead to life in which there is no death (Prov 12:28). YHWH, will restore them to life and cause the righteous to have complete dominion over the wicked (Ps 49:14).

B. All Israel's Curses Are Healed; Her Curses Fall on Her Enemies

Deut 30:7–15	Blessing: Day of Judgment against Israel's enemies. Curses fall on Israel's enemies. Temple is rebuilt. Judgment against the nations who have sought to destroy Israel and Jerusalem (Deut 32:39–43; 30:7; Zech 12:9). Israel becomes the "head," other nations the "tail" (Lev 26:45); Israel lends but does not borrow. Israel is blessed and becomes a blessing to all other nations by establishing righteousness and justice. Other nations then learn to walk in the way of YHWH and to enjoy constitutionally defined righteousness and justice in their own lands.

Once Israel is established in righteousness, YHWH will turn against any who seek to harm his people. He will take the curses that have reformed Israel and aim them at all the nations that have been the instruments of judgment during Israel's refining process.[61] Israel's Testimonial Law will prevail against other rebellious nations to refine them as well.

> Deut 30:7: And YHWH your God will put all these curses on your enemies, and on them that hate you, which persecuted you.

Israel's curses fall on all nations until they too become obedient. YHWH will then send national deliverers to lead other nations to strong national independence and freedom through obedience to the Torah's constitution. YHWH will give Egypt and many other nations saviors who will deliver them from oppression and sanctify YHWH.

> In that day shall there be an altar to YHWH in the middle of the land of Egypt, and a pillar at the border of it to YHWH. And it shall be for a sign and for a witness to YHWH of hosts in the land of Egypt: for they shall cry to YHWH *because of the oppressors*, and he shall send them a savior, and a great one, and he shall deliver them. And YHWH shall be known to Egypt, and the Egyptians shall know YHWH in that day, and shall do sacrifice and oblation; yes, they shall vow a vow to YHWH, and perform it. And YHWH shall smite Egypt: he shall smite and heal it: and they shall return even to YHWH, and he shall be entreated of them, and shall heal them. (Isa 19:19–22)

When YHWH redeems Israel out of all nations and restores her to the Promised Land, it will be a monumental event. Worldwide news coverage will show forth YHWH's praise to the world, causing many to believe and fear Yah. Many nations with rich heritages that are tied to Israel will fear YHWH very early on, so that when the curses fall on them, they are quick to repent while other nations may take longer. When YHWH removes the curses from all nations, he will then redeem and reestablish the nations on their forefathers' lands, just as he did Israel.

Woe be to you, O Moab! the people of Chemosh perishes: for your sons are taken captives, and your daughters captives. *Yet will I bring again the captivity of Moab in the latter days*, said YHWH. (Jer 48:46–47)

Concerning the Ammonites, thus said YHWH; Has Israel no sons? has he no heir? Why then does their king inherit Gad, and his people dwell in his cities? . . . And afterward I will *bring again the captivity of the children of Ammon*, said YHWH. (Jer 49:1, 6)

And I will set my throne in Elam, and will destroy from there the king and the princes, said YHWH. But it shall come to pass *in the latter days, that I will bring again the captivity of Elam*, said YHWH. (Jer 49:38–39)

Shuwh, the Hebrew for "bring again," means 'to return or to turn back.'[62] One of the first known deportations of Elam occurred during Assyria's campaigns, when Ashurbanipal deported Susa, Elam's capital city, relocating many Elamites to the Promised Land.[63] In the latter days, when YHWH restores the nations, he will return the Moabites, Ammonites, and the Elamites to their ancestral lands, providing them with the opportunity of the freedom from oppression to walk in his ways and become a righteous nation before him. He will judge all nations and restore them; Israel will simply be the first nation to complete the process and earn her place as the capital seat of YHWH's government. Hence, the Creator's method of judgment and restoration is impartial on this point, for YHWH will deal with other nations as he has dealt with Israel, the only difference being that Israel will be the *first nation* to sanctify him, walk in his ways, love him alone as God, and be redeemed to its land.[64]

World peace will not be effected by an ecumenical society that simply tolerates conflicting ideas of social justice and freedom (i.e., this is what religion has become). Rather, peace will be effected by every nation seeing the logic and the goodness of YHWH's constitutional Law for herself, taking hold of it, and basing her government, systems of justice, and economies on it. Only then will oppression cease, righteousness prevail, and a real freedom and world peace be realized.

C. National Humility and Obedience

The Moab-Shechem Testimony began in Deuteronomy 27 and ends in Deuteronomy 30:14. These texts, as we have seen, chronologically foretell Israel's future from the day she entered the Promised Land under the Canaan Conquest until our present day, YHWH has accurately prophesied Israel's future.

The final portion of Deuteronomy's Testimony is addressed to the nation of Israel. YHWH prophesies that the latter-day nation will return to him and obey his Law. This will enable YHWH to pour his everlasting blessings on the Children of Israel.

> Deut 30:8–14: And you shall return and obey the voice of YHWH, and do all his commandments which I command you this day. And YHWH your God will make you plenteous in every work of your hand, in the fruit of your body, and in the fruit of your cattle, and in the fruit of your land, for good: for YHWH will again rejoice over you for good, as he rejoiced over your fathers: If you shall listen to the voice of YHWH your God, to keep his commandments and his statutes which are written *in this book of the law*, and if you turn to YHWH your God with all your heart, and with all your soul. For this commandment which I command you this day, it is (a) **not** hidden from you, neither is it far off. It is not in heaven, that you should say, (b) Who shall go up for us to heaven, and bring it to us, that we may hear it, and do it? Neither is it beyond the sea, that you should say, Who shall go over the sea for us, and bring it to us, that we may hear it, and do it? But (c) the word is very near to you, in your mouth, and in your heart, that you may do it.

Because the above text appears in the Prophetic Law, one could argue that neither Israel nor the rest of humanity was capable of keeping the Law or understanding it until the latter days, when Israel is redeemed to the Promised Land. This interpretation, however, would completely take these verses out of context. We have seen how easy the Law is to observe. The above verses do not address the individual but the entire Israelite nation. While some curses were directed at the individual level, others were not. The curse of Diaspora, for instance, was a national penalty (Deut 28:41, 64). Likewise, the promise of national restoration once Israel has chosen to obey will also occur at the national level (Deut 30:3). The curses outlining diseases, however, target the individual, not the entire nation. When YHWH stipulated that Israel's seed would bear sickness of "sore and long continuance" (Deut 28:59–61), he did not intend for every Israelite descendant to endure this curse. If a person followed the Law, he or she could avert this penalty and so many other curses stemming from the consequences of breaching the covenant (which is why many European nations endured so many plagues during the Dark Ages, but many Jewish communities' averted plagues due to their adherence Torah's cleanliness protocols). Likewise, if an individual sought the Creator at anytime in Israel's history, he or she would find YHWH and understand and obey his covenantal Law.[65] This is why the prophet Abijah exhorted Judah *"to seek YHWH* God of their fathers, and *to do the law and the commandment"* (2 Chr 14:4). Abijah's words indicate that the nation could readily understand YHWH's Law and easily obey it.

Israel's history, both before and during Diaspora, has demonstrated that YHWH's people have discounted the truth in the above verses that proclaim *the Law's ease*. They continually looked to something else or someone else to add or to clarify his word rather than simply trusting that the constitution YHWH gave at Mt. Sinai is sufficient for them. Although many people throughout Israel's history have indeed heeded the above verses and taken to heart how easy the Law is to observe, wholehearted understanding and obedience to YHWH's Law has yet to occur on the *national level*; only among individuals and small groups in Israel's communities has Torah obedience thrived.[66]

When Israel does return to YHWH, and he redeems her to the Promised Land, the entire nation will finally realize how incredibly easy the Law is to obey. She will realize—on a national level—that the Law is not a (a) hidden formula but a practical guide for living: YHWH is her exceedingly great reward.

Israel will finally understand that (b) no one can obey the Law as a surrogate for her, and no one can save her from its penalties (curses). The entire nation will finally see that the Law is plain and simple to understand. The entire nation (having been restored to the Promised Land) will see that the Law is (c) so easy to do and to understand that she is able to figure it out for herself: she needs no oral law to explain it. Israel will become a kingdom of priests (Exod 19:6) that will bless all other nations[67] by teaching them to walk in the way of YHWH.

> And it shall come to pass, that every one that is left of all the nations which came against Jerusalem shall even go up from year to year to worship the King, YHWH of hosts, and to keep the feast of tabernacles. And it shall be, that whoever will not come up of all the families of the earth to Jerusalem to worship the King, YHWH of hosts, even on them shall be no rain. And if the family of Egypt go not up, and come not, that have no rain; there shall be the plague, wherewith YHWH will smite the heathen that come not up to keep the feast of tabernacles. This shall be the punishment of Egypt, and the punishment of all nations that come not up to keep the feast of tabernacles. In that day shall there be on the bells of the horses, HOLINESS UNTO YHWH; and the pots in YHWH's house shall be like the bowls before the altar. Yes, every pot in Jerusalem and in Judah shall be holiness to YHWH of hosts: and all they that sacrifice shall come and take of them, and seethe therein: and in that day there shall be no more the Canaanite in the house of YHWH of hosts. (Zech 14:16–21; see also Isa 66:23)

Many nations will join YHWH in the latter days. Nations will bring *a portion* of their tithes and offerings to Israel, which will provide the children of Jacob with incredible wealth. The nations will become Torah observant and send representatives to appear before YHWH in Jerusalem during the three annual feasts (Exod 23:14, 17; Deut 16:16). Nations will be at peace with neighboring nations, and war will no longer prevail (Isa 2:4; Mic 4:3). YHWH will restore peace to the whole the earth. This period will be the time when all nations finally obey the Noahic Covenant's prohibition against eating meat with the blood, disobedience to which had *formerly* caused "every man's hand to be raised against his brother." This final epoch marks an eternal era of blessing for all nations, as human beings finally conquer the evil imaginations of their hearts (Gen 6:5) and prevail in the *way of YHWH*.

Modern, dispersed Israel's joy will burst forth when she is healed and sees that the nation's Judgment Day, which her prophets termed the *Day of YHWH*, has already been fulfilled. She is free to inherit the blessings, redemption, and restoration ordained in YHWH's Testimonial Law.

> *When I shall bring again their captivity*; YHWH bless thee, O habitation of justice, and mountain of holiness. And there shall dwell in Judah itself, and

in all the cities of it together, husbandmen, and they that go forth with flocks. For I have satiated the weary soul, and I have replenished every sorrowful soul. *Upon this I awaked, and beheld; and my sleep was sweet to me.* Behold, the days come, says YHWH, that I will sow the house of Israel and the house of Judah with the seed of man, and with the seed of beast. And it shall come to pass, that like as I have watched over them, to pluck up, and to break down, and to throw down, and to destroy, and to afflict; so will I watch over them, to build, and to plant, says YHWH. (Jer 31:23–28)

When Israel "awakes" to see her latter-day restoration, the sweetness is in knowing that the bitter Judgment Day has passed. Understanding the events that transpired during the *Day of YHWH* helps us to better understand the poisonous wine that affected the deep slumber, which blinded Israel's descendants to see how important her history has been.

My quest has sought to reopened the case of *Israel v. YHWH*, to see if the Creator was righteous in his dealings with Israel. My study has demonstrated that YHWH has been constant, steadfast, and loyal to Israel. He has not rescinded any of his covenants. Even during times of duress, YHWH did not change his word; rather, his Testimony tells us that his promises will be fulfilled in the latter days, when Israel is finally willing to obey his Law. In vol. 2, we will see that YHWH's righteousness goes beyond the basic definitions of truth and faithfulness. He upheld his word *to his own injury* (Ps 15:4). He endeavored to refine a nation into a people capable of inheriting his blessings. Israel was a hard-headed nation. Though he tried to spare her, it had taken a long and bloody sacrifice to finally heal the breach of his covenant. Throughout her sacrifice, he has been afflicted as she was afflicted (Isa 63:9). Like a father pained to severely punish his obstinately wayward son, so YHWH has been pained to let Israel receive the consequences of her wickedness so that her children can be thoroughly healed today. At least this is my assessment thus far. It would be too premature for me to conclude that YHWH has been completely righteous when there is so much of Israel's history yet to consider. We still have to consider what has happened to Israel for the past 2,000 years.

19

The Day of YHWH

The Prophetic Law found in the covenant's Testimony was the formal Prophetic Code. It was not however, the only formula used to foretell Israel's future. Numbers' Effacement Judgment also warned of the day when YHWH would retribute all the crimes associated with Israel's breach of his covenant. In addition to the Testimony, YHWH specifically ordained a particular psalm to testify against the wayward nation. Moses' *Judgment Song* ordained judgment and retribution for all Israel's sins upon *a heinously wicked generation*. The Creator instructed Moses to write a Song of Judgment that would not be understood by the nation until his judgment had been fulfilled, and the veil that was cast over the eyes of her children was removed (in the latter days). As her redemption drew nigh and YHWH opened her eyes to see the righteousness of his Law, she would finally understand the prophecy fulfilled in Moses' Song (Deut 29:22–29; Isa 42:21).

During the Israelites' 40 years of wandering in the wilderness, YHWH was testing his people (Exod 20:20; Deut 8:2, 16). After enduring Israel's rebellion, hardheartedness and stubbornness, YHWH understood the heart and mind of his people. He instructed Moses to tell the Israelites that they would rebel against him and his Law so as to provoke his anger and his jealousy. This was YHWH's instruction to Moses:

> And YHWH said to Moses, Behold, you shall sleep with your fathers; and this people will rise up, and go a whoring after the gods of the strangers of the land, where they go to be among them, and will forsake me, and break my covenant which I have made with them. Then my anger shall be kindled against them in that DAY, and **I will forsake them, and I will hide my face from them**, **and they shall be devoured, and many evils and troubles shall befall them;** so that they will say in that DAY. Are not these evils come on us, *because our God is not among us*? And I will surely *hide my face in that DAY*[1] for all the evils which they shall have worked, in that they are turned to other gods. Now

therefore write you this song for you, and teach it the Children of Israel: put it in their mouths, that **this song may be a witness for me against the Children of Israel.** For when I shall have brought them into the land which I swore to their fathers, that flows with milk and honey; and they shall have eaten and filled themselves, and waxen fat; then will they turn to other gods, and serve them, and provoke me, and break my covenant. And it shall come to pass, *when many evils and troubles are befallen them, that this song shall testify against them as a witness;* for *it shall not be forgotten out of the mouths of their seed*: for I know their imagination which they go about, even now, *before I have brought them into the land which I swore.* (Deut 31:16–21)

Moses' Song follows the chronology set forth in the Testimonial Law. Moses wrote this testimony against a "perverse and crooked generation" (Deut 32:5). During the *Day of YHWH*, the Creator would hide his face from his divorced people, allowing many evils to overtake them. As a prophetic witness against them, YHWH ordained Moses to write this song as an early warning so that her descendants could, in the latter days, remember that the Testimony had formerly prophesied against their forefathers and see that YHWH's judgment had come to pass. The following text is Moses' Judgment Song in Deuteronomy 32. I will break this text into three short segments, similar to my investigation of the Testimonial Law.

I. MOSES' JUDGMENT SONG

Give ear, O you heavens, and I will speak; and hear, O earth, the words of my mouth. My doctrine shall drop as the rain, my speech shall distil as the dew, as the small rain on the tender herb, and as the showers on the grass: Because I will publish the name of YHWH: ascribe you greatness to our God. He is the Rock, his work is perfect: for *all his ways are judgment:* **a God of truth and without iniquity, just and right is he.** They have (a) corrupted themselves, their spot is not the spot of his children: *they are a perverse and crooked generation.* Do you thus requite YHWH, O foolish people and unwise? is not he your father that has bought you? has he not made you, and established you? *Remember the days of old,* consider the years of many generations: ask your father, and he will show you; your elders, and they will tell you. When the most High divided to the nations their inheritance, when he separated the sons of Adam, he set the bounds of the people according to the number of the Children of Israel. For YHWH's portion is his people; Jacob is the lot of his inheritance. He found him in a desert land, and in the waste howling wilderness; he led him about, he instructed him, he kept him as the apple of his eye. As an eagle stirs up her nest, flutters over her young, spreads abroad her wings, takes them, bears them on her wings: So YHWH *alone* did lead him, and (b) there was no strange god with him. He made him ride (c) on the high places of the earth, that he might eat the increase of the fields; and he made him to suck honey out of the rock, and oil out of the flinty rock; Butter of cows, and milk of sheep, with fat of lambs, and rams of the breed of Bashan, and goats, with the fat of kidneys of wheat; and you did drink the pure blood of the grape. (d) But Jeshurun waxed fat, and kicked: you are waxen fat, you are grown thick, you are covered with fatness; then he forsook God which made him, and lightly esteemed the Rock of his salvation. They provoked him to jealousy with strange gods, with abominations provoked they him to anger. They sacrificed to devils, not to God; to gods whom they knew not,(e) *to new gods that came newly up, whom your fathers feared not.* (Deut 32:1–17)

Moses wrote this song for (a) a people who had thoroughly corrupted themselves and rebelled against YHWH. He called the congregation to remember YHWH's benevolence: how he blessed Israel (c) with a land flowing with milk and honey, giving her one of the pristine places of the earth. He loved her and sought to give her all his benefits. YHWH not only bestowed physical blessings at Mt. Sinai, but he also gave the nation (b) pure doctrine and unfermented drink. Israel knew then that there was no god beside YHWH. It was he and only he who had delivered Israel from Egypt's oppression and established her freedom.

As the nation received the blessings from walking with her God, she grew fat, became a glutton, (d) and rebelled against her Maker. He disciplined her through exile, but she still sought the wine of other gods. This is why Moses refers to (e) "new gods." *Moses' Song parallels the Testimonial Law*, which showed that Israel would serve Babylonia's and Assyria's deities during the exile (Deut 28:36, 64). When Israel returned to the land with Zerubbabel, she brought her false beliefs with her, forgetting the way YHWH had taught her forefathers at Sinai's mount.

Of the Rock that begat you, you are unmindful, and have forgotten God that formed you. And when YHWH saw it, he abhorred them, because of the provoking of his sons, and of his daughters. And he said, (f) **I will hide my face from them**, **I will see what their end shall be: for they are a very fraudulent generation, children in whom is no faith.** They have moved me to jealousy *with that which is not God*; they have provoked me to anger with their vanities: and (g) I will move them to jealousy with those which are not a people; I will provoke them to anger with a foolish nation. For (h) *a fire* is kindled in my anger, and shall burn to the lowest hell, and shall consume the earth with her increase, and set on fire the foundations of the mountains. I will heap mischiefs on them; *I will spend my arrows on them. They shall* (i) *be burnt with hunger, and devoured with burning heat, and with bitter destruction: I will also send the teeth of beasts on them, with the poison of serpents of the dust. The sword without, and terror within, shall destroy both the young man and the virgin, the suckling also with the man of gray hairs.* (j) I said, **I would scatter them into corners, I would make the remembrance of them to cease from among men:** Were it not that I feared the wrath of the enemy, lest their adversaries should behave themselves strangely, and (k) **lest they should say, Our hand is high, and YHWH has not done all this.** For they are a nation void of counsel, neither is there any understanding in them. (Deut 32:18–28)

This portion of Moses' Song refers to Israel at a time when the nation is deported and given to serve gods alien to her forefathers (Deut 32:17). Whether in exile or on the Promised Land, YHWH would (f) forsake the succeeding generations, hiding his face from them until he could see the path that Israel would choose. Once the Creator saw that Israel had utterly corrupted herself, forsaken him, and fully embraced evil, he would send another nation against her;[2] this nation would not just destroy her through battle, *this nation would try to (g) supplant her as YHWH's people.* This judgment followed the precept of equity found in the Law. Israel had worshiped false gods both before and during the exile: gods that were gods only in man's superstitious imagination. YHWH would apply the opposite and equal reaction of the Law by provoking Israel with a people not chosen—a foolish people who did not walk in the freedom of his Law. YHWH's anger and his jealousy would then be unleashed against a particularly "perverse and crooked generation," causing the mountains (symbolic of nations) to burn to their very foundations during this judgment era.[3]

Moses compares YHWH's anger and jealousy to a (h) fire, clarifying that **YHWH's flame is not a literal fire but a symbol of afflictions that end in the bitter destruction of a future generation** (Isa 48:10). This is a reference to YHWH's sacrifice during the Day of YHWH. The Creator would sacrifice Israel using (i) four different methods to humble her:

> (1) hunger,
> (2) heat and destruction,
> (3) the teeth of beasts, and
> (4) the poison of serpents.

Both Jeremiah and Ezekiel based prophecies of "four sore judgments" on Deuteronomy's text (Jer 15:2–4; Ezek 14:21). These four sore judgments would devour and destroy Israel during the *Day of YHWH*, until her desire for wickedness was consumed (Amos 9:10).

When YHWH (j) scattered Israel among all nations, he purposed to efface the remembrance of his wicked people (Ps 34:16). Were it not for YHWH's covenants, he would leave his people wholly dispersed. If he did, however, other nations could boast that they had devoured Israel by their might and strength rather than recognizing the act of Israel's God. So YHWH will honor his covenants so that Israel's (k) devouring beasts can understand that the only reason they prevailed against her is because YHWH gave them Israel for a prey (see Illustration 19.1).

O that they were wise, that they understood this, that they would (l) consider their latter end! How should one chase a thousand, and two put ten thousand to flight, (m) except their Rock had sold them, and YHWH had shut them up? For their rock is not as our Rock, even our enemies themselves being judges. For their vine is of the vine of Sodom, and of the fields of Gomorrah: their grapes are (n) *grapes of gall*, their clusters are *bitter*: Their (o) wine is the poison of dragons, and the cruel venom of asps. Is not this laid up in store with me, and (p) *sealed up* among my treasures? **To me belongs vengeance, and recompense; their foot shall slide in due time:** (q) for the day of their calamity is at hand, and the things that shall come on them make haste.

Illustration 19.1. François-Joseph Heim's depiction of the destruction of Jerusalem by the Romans.

For YHWH shall judge his people, and (r) repent himself for his servants, when he sees that their power is gone, and there is none shut up, or left. And he shall say, Where are their gods, their rock in whom they trusted, Which did eat the fat of their sacrifices, and drank the wine of their drink offerings? let them rise up and help you, and be your protection. (s) *See now that I, even I, am he, and there is no god with me*: I kill, and I make alive; I wound, and I heal: neither is there any that can deliver out of my hand. For I lift up my hand to heaven, and say (i.e., swearing that), I live forever. If I whet my glittering sword, and my hand take hold on judgment; I will render vengeance to mine enemies, and will reward them that hate me. I will make my arrows drunk with blood, and my sword shall devour flesh; and that with the blood of the slain and of (t) the captives, from the beginning of revenges on the enemy.

Rejoice, O you nations, with his people: for (u) he will avenge the blood of his servants, and will render vengeance to his adversaries, and (v) *will be merciful to his land, and to his people*. And Moses came and spoke all the words of this song in the ears of the people, he, and Hoshea the son of Nun. (Deut 32:29–44, parenthesis added)

When Moses asks Israel to consider her latter end, he is (l) referring to Balaam's blessing as Israel came out of the Wilderness of Sin (Num 23:8–10). YHWH blessed Israel's latter end above all other nations well before she entered the Promised Land. This is the blessing that Micah indicated would absolve YHWH of Israel's charge of unrighteousness: though she had constantly rebelled against her God, in the day when her descendants chose to do right, YHWH would reestablished, strengthen, and eternally bless her latter end. The (m) only reason that Israel did not grow and prosper was because YHWH sold her into the bondage of foreign governments to pay for her iniquity (Deut 28:68; Isa 50:1).

The Prophetic Law foretold that a family would arise in Israel who would adhere to Babylon's idolatrous doctrines (Deut 29:18–21). Moses links this phase of his *Judgment Song* to the (n) bitterly poisonous doctrine that the Remnant would embrace at the ensuing Judgment Day (Deut 29:18). In ch. 13, we saw that the Tabernacle of the Testimony associates (o) wine with doctrinal error.[4] The Remnant would "return here" to Jerusalem, where "waters of a full cup would be wrung out to them" (Ps 73:10). The Second Temple Remnant would partake of Israel's dreaded curse. They would guzzle the idolaters' bitter waters (Numbers 5), reaping the idolaters' reward.

Once Israel's foot slid into doctrines of gall and wormwood, (q) YHWH's Day of Vengeance would quickly ensue: it would not delay. YHWH (p) sealed the understanding of this curse so that Israel's descendants (and the world) could not understand it until the latter days. In volume 2 of this book, we shall see this curse unsealed for the first time in history! This curse is key to the case questioning YHWH's righteousness. This particular curse is the judgment that rests as a light for (latter-day) Israel today (Isa 51:4; Zeph 3:5) and for us to see whether YHWH has been righteous.

Once the Creator's judgment has humbled Israel to obedience, YHWH (r) will sorrow for Israel's utterly helpless situation, similar to his sorrow for humanity's state of affairs shortly before the flood (Gen 6:6–7). As we saw in the Testimonial Law, YHWH will then strengthen his people, seeking to save, deliver, and redeem them out of all oppression once more. Moses draws the nation's (s) attention to the fact that YHWH has been Israel's *only* Savior: there are no other gods created with him or after him. There is YHWH alone and no other. He is the one who has wounded Israel (Isa 33:22). YHWH has judged his people, and no one can deliver any of them from his judgment: not now or in the future.[5] This statement in the chronology of *Moses' Song* indicates that Israel will finally realize this fact on a national level.

After Israel has drunk from the bitter wine of gall and wormwood to pervert Yah's truth, the Creator will begin an era of judgment during which the sword will fall on Israel during her (t) captivity and exile from the Promised Land.[6] Shortly thereafter, his sword will fall on all nations, rendering retribution for dismissing the Noahic Covenant. When Israel's darkened curse is lifted and YHWH chooses Israel again, all nations will rejoice with her. He will avenge the nations (u) that wounded Israel. This corresponds to the last phase of the Testimonial Law, when all Israel's curses will fall on her enemies (Deut 30:7; Zech 14:16–21). YHWH will be faithful and true to the covenants of Israel's forefathers and choose Abraham's descendants once more (Deut 30:1–14; Lev 26:44–45). When YHWH lifts the veil covering Israel's eyes in the latter days, the land of Israel will still evidence the Testimony's plagues and curses. Moses refers to the day when (v) YHWH will be merciful to the land and remove "all its diseases" (Exod 15:26; 2 Chr 7:14). *Moses' Song* very closely parallels the Testimonial Law, but it includes greater detail about Israel's Diaspora. Israel's prophets built on the statutes of the Tabernacle, the Testimony, and *Moses' Song* in their prophecies by depicting *a day of terrible tribulation,* when YHWH would hide his face from Israel, refusing to hear her cries for deliverance.

II. YHWH SHRUGS:
A PATIENT GOD HIDES HIS FACE

The second phase of Moses' Song depicts a day when YHWH shrugs. When Israel first apostacized after entering Canaan, YHWH subjected her to bondage. When she repented, YHWH sent saviors (Judg 3:9) to deliver her from oppression. Many saviors aided the nation during the Judges Era. Following the Monarchy, the king often acted as Israel's savior or deliverer. As the nation's idolatry continued, her savior-kings became fewer and fewer. Jehoash was one of the last kings empowered to save Samaria out of the hands of Syria (2 Kgs 13:25), and Judah's last deliverance came when Hezekiah subdued Philistine-occupied territories.

Up to this point, Israel's saviors had decreased, as the prophets or watchmen who warned against her wicked actions increased. In Hezekiah's day there were no less than five heralders prophesying the consequences of breaking covenant. As national idolatry persisted, these prophets—like her saviors—became fewer and fewer; in Jerusalem's final days, Jeremiah was the lone voice in the Promised Land. At the nation's twilight, YHWH told Jeremiah that he would no longer listen to prayers petitioning mercy for Jerusalem's citizens: "*pray not y*ou for this people, neither lift up cry *nor prayer for them, neither make intercession to me: for I will not hear you*" (Jer 7:16). YHWH refused to hear or show mercy to a mean-hearted and continuously rebellious nation. When YHWH reestablished the Remnant at Cyrus's decree, he once again began to send his word. Haggai and Zechariah were the last two prophets YHWH sent to the Second Temple Remnant. They were the only two prophets to receive "word" from YHWH when the Remnant returned with Zerubbabel and the high priest Yehoshua.[7] Both of these prophets exhorted the Remnant to turn from their evil ways, repent from serving other gods to return to obey the Law, but to no avail. After YHWH saw that the newly returned Remnant would not return to him, he hid his face and stopped sending word to the sons of Korah.[8]

YHWH forsook this Remnant until they, like the Amorites in former times (Gen 15:16) would "slide in due time" (Deut 32:35). Then, YHWH could righteously render judgment. YHWH would cause his Temple to be desolate and eventually be destroyed while his people were deported—during a second judgment era. The final time that YHWH sent word to his people was on the 4th day of the 9th month in Darius's 4th year (Zech 7:1). The final words of YHWH as recorded in Scripture are a plea for the Second Temple Remnant to do justly and to turn from evil.

> Thus said YHWH Almighty: Judge righteous judgment, and deal mercifully
> and compassionately every one with his brother: and oppress not the widow, or
> the fatherless, or the stranger, or the poor; and let not one of you remember in
> his heart the injury of his brother. But they refused to attend, and madly turned
> their back, and made their ears heavy, so that they should not hear. And they
> made their heart disobedient, so as not to listen to my law, and the words which
> YHWH Almighty sent forth by his spirit by the former prophets: so there *was*
> great wrath from YHWH Almighty. (Zech 7:9–12, LXX)

Zechariah is quoting Jer 22:2. He recites Israel's former history and uses it as the basis for
another prophecy. History would repeat itself. YHWH would judge Israel for her oppression
once more. When Zechariah wrote his prophecy in Darius's 4th year, he hid a prophecy
against the newly returned Remnant proclaiming the day when YHWH would hide his
face from the terrible tribulation that the Remnant had brought on themselves with their
rebellion.

> And it *shall* come to pass, as he spoke, and they listened not, so they *shall* cry,
> and *I will not listen*, said YHWH Almighty. And *I will* cast them out among
> all the nations, whom they know not; and the land behind them shall be made
> utterly destitute of any going through or returning: yes they have made the
> choice land a desolation. (Zech 7:13–14, LXX)

Zechariah's prophecy parallels Moses' Song. YHWH will hide his face from his people by
withholding warning.[9] He will not hear their cries for deliverance, and this future crooked
generation will experience the consequences. YHWH's trampled covenant could not grant
protection to those that rebelled against it. Jeremiah also indicates that the Creator will
forsake his idolatrous people:

> If you will not listen to me, to walk in my law, which I have set before you, listen
> to the words of my servants the prophets, whom I sent to you, both rising up
> early, and sending them, but you have not listened; *then* will I make this house
> [in Jerusalem] like Shiloh, and *will make this city a CURSE to all the nations
> of the earth* (Jer 26:4–6, brackets added; see through Jer 26:65)

What Jeremiah prophesied did *not* occur during the Monarchy when the First Temple was
destroyed. Rather, YHWH restored Jerusalem at Cyrus's decree, promising blessings for the
Remnant who returned, *if* they would follow him.[10] The Judean Remnant's rebellion against
YHWH's promises violated the natural laws that YHWH had ordained to protect them. After Antiochus Epiphanes desecrated the Second Temple, Jerusalem continued to sink down
into the dregs of tradition with countering religious and secular factions. YHWH did not

make Jerusalem like Shiloh until the country came under Roman control. In the subsequent era, Jerusalem became a curse to *all* nations when her conquerors also drank the bitter wine described in Jeremiah 25.

Zechariah also alludes to Jerusalem's curse after the Second Temple Remnant had rebelled:

> **Behold, I will make Jerusalem a cup of trembling to all the people round about**, when they shall be in the siege both against Judah and against Jerusalem. **And in that day will I make Jerusalem a burdensome stone for all people:** all that burden themselves with it shall be cut in pieces, though all the people of the earth be gathered together against it. In that day, said YHWH, **I will smite every horse with astonishment, and his rider with madness:** and I will open my eyes on the House of Judah, and will smite every horse of the people with blindness. (Zech 12:2–4)

Zechariah's testimony parallels Jeremiah 25–26. The nations that will drink Jerusalem's trembling cup and all who desire to conquer her shall themselves be made drunk and be judged by YHWH and destroyed (see Isa 29:8; Deut 32:43). Scripture uses horses, chariots, and their riders to symbolize a nation's military strength. Moses and Miriam's Victory Song is the first time that Scripture employs this terminology.

> I will sing to YHWH, for he has triumphed gloriously: **the horse and his rider has he thrown into the sea.** YHWH is my strength and song, and he is become my salvation: he is my God, and I will prepare him an habitation; my father's God, and I will exalt him. YHWH is a man of war: YHWH is his name. **Pharaoh's chariots and his host has he cast into the sea:** his chosen captains also are drowned in the Red sea. (Exod 15:1–3; see also Hag 2:22)

YHWH defeated Egypt's military strength at the Red Sea. Zechariah borrows this symbolism by stating that YHWH will strike *every* nation's horse and rider that comes against Jerusalem with "astonishment, madness, and blindness." This is the same curse that the Testimony issued against Israel: "YHWH shall smite you with madness, and blindness, and astonishment of heart" (Deut 28:28). When YHWH applied this curse on Israel during the Monarchy Era, he blinded her to knowledge of truth as she followed false doctrine. Zechariah indicates that YHWH will pour this same curse out on the nations that burdened themselves with Jerusalem during the subsequent Judgment era because they, too, will drink from Israel's talmudic doctrinal wine.

> And this shall be the plague with which YHWH will smite all the people that have fought against Jerusalem; Their (a) flesh shall consume away while your stand on their feet, and their eyes shall consume away in their holes, and their

> tongue shall consume away in their mouth. And it shall come to pass in that
> day, that a great tumult from YHWH shall be among them; and *they shall lay
> hold every one on the hand of his neighbor, and his hand shall (b) rise up
> against the hand of his neighbor.* (Zech 14:12–13)

The Law and the books of Psalms and Proverbs had established definitions for the prophets
to use for their words and symbolism. Zechariah follows this protocol by concealing the
meaning of his prophecy within a Scriptural definition.

In the Book of Proverbs, Solomon defines a sound heart as the life of the flesh:

> A sound heart is the life of the flesh: but envy the rottenness of the bones.
> (Prov 14:30)

A good, healthy, stable heart is what empowers the flesh with life. But if this proverb is reversed, it reads: "The flesh of life is a sound heart." When Zechariah states that YHWH will
cause the nation's (a) "flesh" to consume their bodies, he implies that the nations will lose
its sound heart. The loss of a sound heart will cause the hand of (b) "every man's brother" to
be raised in civil strife (Gen 9:5; Ezek 38:18–21; Isa 19:2; Jer 9:4). This is not some apocalyptic
event. It may be remembered that YHWH's initial promise in the Noahic Covenant promised to "never again smite every living thing" (Gen 8:21) as he had in the flood. Rather, this
was an era of war and incredible oppression.

Zechariah's testimony continued to coincide with the Noahic Covenant's judgment,
which forbade consuming bloody flesh (Gen 9:3–5). YHWH would judge all nations that
breached Noah's Covenant during the Day of YHWH. Zechariah did not stand alone in
warning Israel and the world of YHWH's soon-coming Judgment Day when the 7-Times
cultic epochs expired.

In Darius's 2nd year, Haggai also prophesied:

> And I will overthrow the throne of kingdoms, and I will destroy the strength
> of the kingdoms of the heathen; and I will overthrow the chariots, and those
> that ride in them; and the horses and their riders shall come down, *every one
> by the sword of his brother.* (Hag 2:22; Gen 9:4–5; see also Ps 76:6)

Haggai acknowledged that judgment for breaching the Noahic Covenant was not far from
his day. In the subsequent epoch, YHWH would smite the world with madness, causing
"the hand of every man to be raised against his brother" in the ensuing turbulent and violent era of world history, as the nations succumbed to the curse for breaching the Noahic
Covenant.

III. NON-ARBITRARY JUDGMENT

A. *Lawful Judgment*

Righteousness excludes individual discretion, even for God. For the Creator to be exonerated in the controversy *Israel vs. YHWH*, his actions must not be arbitrary. He must act in accord with the Law he gave to Israel. He cannot use "individual discretion" to override the Law nor can he use random chance in matters of justice and judgment. For the Creator to be free from guilt or sin, YHWH must obey his own Law and follow the truth he establishes for humanity. For these reasons, YHWH placed several injunctions in the Law that allowed him to render justice should the nation prove obstinate and rebellious.

One of these injunctions stated:

> If a man have a stubborn and rebellious son, which will not obey the voice of his father, or the voice of his mother, and that, when they have chastened him, will not listen to them: Then shall his father and his mother lay hold on him, and bring him out to the elders of his city, and to the gate of his place; and they shall say to the elders of his city, **This our son is stubborn and rebellious, he will not obey our voice; he is a glutton, and a drunkard. And all the men of his city shall stone him with stones that he shall die:** so shall you put evil away from among you; and all Israel shall hear, and fear. (Deut 21:18–21)

If no form of correction or rebuke effectively reformed a stubborn, rebellious son that was a threat to society, a parent could bring his wicked child to be judged and put to death.[11] This action would cause the community to fear and obey parental authority as well as their Creator, who ordained this authority. At the exodus YHWH stated that Israel was his first-born son. "Thus says YHWH, *Israel is my son, even my firstborn*" (Exod 4:22). If we apply the opposite and equal reaction of the Law to this command, then YHWH must obey his own Law and apply the same judgment to Israel. If Israel is a stubborn and rebellious son, Israel's death should be required so that people of all nations can hear, fear, and learn to obey. YHWH's actions on Judgment Day will show whether the Creator obeys his own Law and acts righteously (Isa 51:4; Zeph 3:5).

B. *YHWH Will Not Spare His Rebellious Son*

Throughout the ancient world, nations customary worshiped their enemies' gods in order to procure their gods' favor and deliverance.[12] After King Amaziah of Judah battled Edom, he worshiped and burned incense to Edom's gods, crediting them rather than YHWH with his victory over his foes (2 Chr 25:14). In times of crisis, people felt it best to pacify all the gods rather than rely on just one.[13] This appears to have been how Israel believed shortly before Jerusalem's demise under Nebuchadnezzar.

YHWH sent a vision to Ezekiel concerning Judah's small Remnant. At Israel's exile to Babylon, she was introduced to new deities that "her fathers had not known." The prophet

Ezekiel testifies that the most popular of these was a deity called Tammuz (Dumuzi), the shepherd-god and judge of the underworld (Ezekiel 8). He was the indigenous god of the kings of Akkad and the territory of Babylon.[14] In Ezekiel 8, Judah's elders came to listen to Ezekiel's prophecies (Ezek 8:1) when YHWH showed the prophet a vision of the abominations wrought in King Zedekiah's days.

> Behold, the glory of the God of Israel was there, according to the vision that I saw in the plain. Then said he to me, Son of man, lift up your eyes now the way toward the north. So I lifted up my eyes the way toward the north, and behold northward at the gate of the altar *this image of jealousy in the entry*. He said furthermore to me, Son of man, see you what they do? even the great abominations that the House of Israel commits here, *that I should go far off from my sanctuary*? but turn you yet again, and you shall see greater abominations. And he brought me to the door of the court; and when I looked, behold a hole in the wall. Then said he to me, Son of man, dig now in the wall: and when I had digged in the wall, behold a door. And he said to me, Go in, and behold the wicked abominations that they do here. So I went in and saw; and behold every form of creeping things, and abominable beasts, and all the idols of the House of Israel, **portrayed on the wall** round about. And there stood before them seventy men **of the ancients of the House of Israel**, and in the midst of them stood Jaazaniah the son of Shaphan, **with every man his censer in his hand**; and a thick cloud of incense went up. Then said he to me, Son of man, have you seen **what the ancients of the House of Israel** do in the dark, every man in the chambers of his imagery? for they say, YHWH sees us not; YHWH has forsaken the earth. (Ezek 8:4–12)

YHWH gives Ezekiel, whom he terms the Son of man, a vision of Judah's abominations. He tells Ezekiel that Judah's perversities will drive him from his earthly Sanctuary.[15] In the vision, Ezekiel, as the Son of man, goes unhindered through a wall to observe the wicked and detestable practices of the people in YHWH's holy Temple.[16] Israel's 70 elders participated in cultic rituals.[17] Judah's elders chose to believe that YHWH had become fed up with them and had deserted his people and forsaken the nation—without remedy. They believed that their only salvation must come from other nation's deities rather than turn to the God who rebuked and punished them only for their own sins (Ps 78:32–34).

Ezekiel may give us the first glimpse of the formal rise of the scribal Pharisee faction.[18] Shaphan, Jaazaniah's father, who read the Book of the Law to King Josiah (2 Kgs 22:10–14) was not a Levite but was one of the king's royal (Judahite) scribes. We find Jaazaniah among the 70 elders of Israel who led the nation away from YHWH to follow traditions of men. According to the Law, only Levites were allowed into the inner court (Lev 16:2; Ezek 44:7). YHWH shows Ezekiel that these elders had presumptuously entered the Temple's sanctified quarters to serve as priests of pagan traditions by portraying the traditional Egyptian scarab and other pagan religious symbols in the sacred precincts of YHWH's dwelling place.[19]

> Then he said to me, Turn you yet again, and you shall see greater abominations that they do. Then he brought me to the door of the gate of YHWH's house which was toward the north; and, behold, there sat women weeping for Tammuz. Then said he to me, Have you seen this, O son of man? Turn you yet again, and you shall see greater abominations than these. And he brought me into the inner court of YHWH's house, and, behold, at the door of the Temple of YHWH, between the porch and the altar, were about five and twenty men, with their backs toward the Temple of YHWH, and their faces toward the east; and they worshiped the sun toward the east. (Ezek 8:13–16)

Before the First Temple's final siege, Nebuchadnezzar had already deported the most valuable and productive people of Judah's population (2 Kgs 24:14). The people knew that Babylon's forces would soon face their lovely city. Jerusalem's dwindled Remnant did not return to the God whose prophets proclaimed his judgments; instead, these men looked to Babylon's gods to save them out of the hand of their forefathers' God.

Tammuz (Dumuzi) was Babylon's premier deity. People worshiped him as the judge of the underworld (judge of the dead).[20] In Sumerian hymns, Tammuz is immortalized as the "bridegroom." After his wife (Inanna) spent three days and nights in hell, she was released, and Tammuz was obliged to take her place.[21] Although he was an unwilling surrogate for his bride, he was resurrected from hell every spring. As a vegetation god, he returned to the underworld after six months at the end of the harvest season.[22] Every year women wept over Tammuz's unjust and untimely death.[23] In Babylon, women wept over his death in late June; thus, the later Jewish month called Tammuz, which usually falls in June/July.[24] The women who were weeping, in YHWH's Temple were weeping, not for the death of their men who had been slain at YHWH's hand, but for the imaginary death of their enemy's god. They were not weeping and showing grief over their own sins, but the death of a make-believe god. The Judeans sought another god to comfort YHWH's people.

> Have you seen this, O son of man? Is it a light thing to the House of Judah that they commit the abominations which they commit here? for they have filled the land with violence, and *have returned*[25] [to the Promised Land] to (1) provoke me to anger: and, lo, they put the branch to their nose. (2) Therefore will I also deal in fury: mine eye shall not spare, neither will I have pity:[26] and though they cry in mine ears with a loud voice, (3) *yet will I not hear them.* (Ezek 8:17–18, brackets and parenthesis added)

YHWH's words to Ezekiel follow the chronology of Moses' Song. First, YHWH will be angry at the Judean Remnant's violence, injustice, and idolatry. Second, he will forsake the Remnant (2 Kgs 21:14; Ezek 8:6). Third, he will allow trouble and affliction to devour the people (Deut 31:17–18). Ezekiel prophesies that, in YHWH's future day of fury, he will show no mercy; he will not spare the evil-doer.[27] This prophecy very accurately parallels the Testimony's dreaded curse (Deut 29:20) by depicting a generation that will follow the teachings of a wicked root (family) during the Second Temple Era and embrace poisonous doctrines that provoke YHWH's wrath and his jealousy. YHWH will not spare the cursed man who corrupted truth. Nor will YHWH spare his followers.

IV. THE LIGHT OF EZEKIEL

A. *The Divided Sacrifice*

The Book of Ezekiel is one of the most unique testimonies in the entire Tanakh (Old Testament).[28] While YHWH commissioned most prophets to simply relay his message to Israel, he gave Ezekiel many visions, charging him to perform numerous signs, wonders, and parables in front of the deported Israelites. Ezekiel (1:2–6:14) received YHWH's orders outlining his prophetic commission to Israel in the fifth year of his captivitiy.[29] This would have been about six years before Jerusalem fell to Nebuchadnezzar.

The first seven chapters of Ezekiel's work narrate YHWH's commission of his prophecy, while foretelling Jerusalem's impending destruction. Throughout Ezekiel's prophecies and signs, he consistently adheres to the Testimonial Law, shedding more light on Israel's dreaded curse than any other prophet in history (as we will see in vol. 2). Ezekiel's prophecies address the nation's continual rebellion and Jerusalem's coming destruction. However, they do not end there. Ezekiel continues to reveal the nation's future judgment, describing the holocausts that will follow Israel throughout the Diaspora.

One parable that YHWH told Ezekiel to act out prophesied Jerusalem's destruction at Nebuchadnezzar's hands while fully disclosing and blatantly foretelling the latter Day of YHWH, when the Creator would sacrifice his rebellious firstborn son. The statute of one in ten passing under the rod (Lev 27:32–33) was applied to the Judean Remnant who returned to the land of Israel (see p. 784–86), while Ezekiel's prophecy focused on the House of Israel (Ephraim's tribes that did not return to the land). Ezekiel foretells the judgment Israel's descendants will face during the ongoing Diaspora.

And you, son of man, take you a sharp knife, take you a barber's razor, and cause it to pass on your head and on your beard: then take you balances to weight, and **divide the hair.** You shall **burn with fire** a (a) **third part in the middle of the city,** when the days of the siege are fulfilled: and you shall take a (b) third part, and smite about it with a knife: and a (c) **third part you shall scatter in the wind; and I will draw out a sword after them.** You shall also take of it a few in number, and bind them in your skirts. (d) **Then take of them again, and cast them into the middle of the fire, and burn them in the fire; for of it shall a fire come forth into all the House of Israel.** (Ezek 5:1–4)

There are three parts to YHWH's sacrifice. The first third of the people are destroyed during (a) Jerusalem's destruction, when the city succumbed to Babylon's siege under

Nebuchadnezzar. This would have been six years after Ezekiel issued this warning. The (b) second third of the people who do not return to the land during the Second Temple Era are smitten with a devouring knife during the Diaspora through war and persecution. It is the remaining third of the people, however, who endure the long Day of YHWH. The Creator will take this final third of Israel's citizens who have been taken captive by Nebuchadnezzar and will scatter them through all nations.[30] While the people are in exile from the Promised Land, YHWH will send the sword to pursue and overtake the wicked among the Children of Israel. (d) Those who live through these wars will finally be cast into the fire to be smelted and refined into a new creation that is finally humble and willing to walk in the way of YHWH (Isa 13:12). Notice that the final (d, again) third whose offspring live through the Diapsora's sword is further subdivided into three parts: those who die by the sword, those who die by the fire; and the descendants of the final remnant that survive through all the holocausts and become willing to obey YHWH and enjoy his latter-day redemption. It is this final third that is refined to righteousness.

The prophet Zechariah builds on Ezekiel's prophecy, addressing this final third and reissuing Ezekiel's prophecy long *after* Nebuchadnezzar had destroyed Jerusalem and the Judean Remnant had returned to the Promised Land after Cyrus's decree.

> And it shall come to pass, that in all the land, said YHWH, **two parts** therein shall be cut off and die; but **the third shall be left therein**. And I will bring the **third part through the fire**, and will refine them as silver is refined, and will try them as gold is tried: *they shall call on my name*, and I will hear them: I will say, It is my people: and they shall say, YHWH is my God. (Zech 13:8–9; see also Isa 13:12)

Ezekiel's and Zechariah's testimonies parallel each other by foretelling that YHWH will sacrifice two-thirds of the Israelites during Babylon's siege and forthcoming Diaspora for their gross iniquities. The final third who survive this holocaust will live to endure other holocausts. YHWH will refine them as silver when he "punishes the world for their evil, and the wicked for their iniquity;" he causes "the arrogancy of the proud to cease, and lays low the haughtiness of the terrible. YHWH will make a man more precious than fine gold; even a man than the golden wedge of Ophir" (Isa 13:11–12). The final third's descendants will be refined into a pure and wholehearted creation, circumcised to YHWH alone.

Ezekiel and Zechariah both adhere to the Testimonial Law, which foretold the retribution, judgment, and sacrifice (holocaust) that would occur for Israel's many sins during the long Day of YHWH.

> **I will scatter you among the heathen, and (see c, above) will draw out a sword after you:** (Lev 26:33. Compare to Ezek 5:2). And they shall fall one on another (see Gen 9:5), as it were before a sword, when none pursues: and you shall have no power to stand before your enemies. And you shall perish among the heathen, and the land of your enemies

shall eat you up. And they that are left of you shall pine away in their iniquity in your enemies' lands; and also in the iniquities of their fathers shall they pine away with them. (Lev 26:37–39, parenthesis added)

And YHWH shall (see c, above) scatter you among all people, from the one end of the earth even to the other; and there you shall serve other gods, which neither you nor your fathers have known, even wood and stone. And among these nations shall you find no ease, neither shall the sole of your foot have rest: but YHWH shall give you there a trembling heart, and failing of eyes, and sorrow of mind. And your life shall hang in doubt before you; and you shall fear day and night, and shall have none assurance of your life. (Deut 28:64–66)

Notice that Ezekiel (5:2) actually quotes from Leviticus's Testimonial Law, which outlined the consequences for Israel's breach of pact. Both the Testimony and the prophets show that the day when Israel falls to the sword, when her life daily teeters in the balance, will be after the nation's exile, after she has been scattered among all peoples and nations. It is this epoch in time that Moses' Song had foretold: Israel would drink from the bitter wormwood waters of YHWH's curse during an era when the nation's sins had compounded as a run-away deficit that called out for justice and atonement of a people without self-control, when their hard-hearted and rebellious tendencies thwarted their ability to live productively.

B. Stubborn Scum

Ezekiel's parables provide the meaning of Israel's sacrifices and regulations. On the very day when Nebuchadnezzar sieged Jerusalem, YHWH commanded Ezekiel to act out a parable for Israel. He was to take a pot (the pot of Jer 1:13 and the cauldron of Mic 3:3) representing Jacob's rebellious House and put all the choice sacrificial pieces into it along with water and scum (Ezek 24:3–6).

Notice what Ezekiel prophesies in Babylon on the very day that Nebuchadnezzar begins to besiege Jerusalem:

For her blood is in the middle of her (i.e., bloodguilt); she set it on the top of a rock; she poured it not on the ground, to cover it with dust;[31] That it might cause fury to come up to take vengeance; I have set her blood on the top of a rock, that it should not be covered. Therefore thus said YHWH God; Woe to the bloody city! I will even make the pile for fire great. Heap on wood, kindle the fire, consume the flesh, and spice it well, and let the bones be burned. Then set it empty on the coals of it, that the brass of it may be hot, and may burn, and that the filthiness of it may be molten in it, that the scum of it may be consumed. She has wearied herself with lies, and her great scum went not forth out of her: her scum shall be in the fire. In your filthiness is lewdness: because I have purged you, and you were not purged, you shall not be purged from your filthiness any more, till I have caused my fury to rest on you. I YHWH have spoken it: it shall come to pass, and I will do it; I will not go back, neither will I spare, neither will

I repent; according to your ways, and according to your doings, shall they judge you, said YHWH God. (Ezek 24:7–14, parenthesis added)

YHWH had repeatedly purged and corrected Jerusalem through famines, wars, pestilence, tribute, deportations—all the curses in his covenantal Testimony. Still the city did not return to her Maker. Now, he had no choice but to use the final Bitter Curse found in Moab-Shechem's Testimonial Law. Notice that the chronology found in these verses above correlates directly with both the Testimoinal Law and Ezekiel's suffering while he bore Israel's sins (Ezek 4:1–6). YHWH would use a fire to consume Jerusalem, but this fire would not purge Israel's lewdness. Later, YHWH will refrain from correcting or purging Israel's sins until her sins mount to such a degree that YHWH's fury will rest on Jerusalem and its backsliding people (Zech 12:3; Jer 17:27). Then YHWH will use another nation to judge his wayward people and execute his judgments. Ezek 24:13 holds a key to Moses' Song. Ezekiel that states the city "shall not be purged from their filthiness any more, **till YHWH has caused his fury to rest on it**" (Ezek 24:13; see also Jer 26:6). This coincides with the time when YHWH hides his face and withholds warning to his people. At the end of this withholding, YHWH will pour his fury on the earth, specifically on Jerusalem.

Jeremiah had previously prophesied about this day:

And you shall say to them, Thus said YHWH; If you will not listen to me, to walk in my law, which I have set before you, To listen to the words of my servants the prophets, whom I sent to you, both rising up early, and sending them, but you have not listened; Then will I make this house like Shiloh, and **will make this city a curse to all the nations of the earth.** (Jer 26:4–6)

But if you will not listen to me to hallow the sabbath day, and not to bear a burden, even entering in at the gates of Jerusalem on the sabbath day; then will **I kindle a fire** in the gates of it, and it shall devour the palaces of Jerusalem, and **it shall not be quenched.** (Jer 17:27)

Hosea also builds his prophecy on the Testimonial Law, which long ago had prophesied of Israel's holocaust from Mt. Sinai. Hosea refers to the day when YHWH would withhold judgment and wait to discipline his rebellious people until their sins overcame them.

Prostitution and wine and new wine take away the heart. My people ask counsel at their stocks, and their staff declares to them: for the spirit of prostitutions has caused them to err, and they have gone a whoring from under their God. They sacrifice on the tops of the mountains, and burn incense on the hills, under oaks and poplars and elms, *because the shadow of it is good: therefore your daughters shall commit prostitution, and your spouses shall commit adultery.* **I will not punish** your daughters when they commit prostitution, nor your spouses when they commit adultery: for themselves are separated with whores, and they sacrifice with harlots: therefore **the people that does not understand shall fall**. Though you, Israel, play the harlot, yet let not Judah offend; and come not you to Gilgal, neither go you up to Bethaven, nor swear, YHWH lives. For Israel slides back as a backsliding heifer: now YHWH will feed them as a lamb in a large place. (Hos 4:11–16; see also 9:2)

Haggai and Zechariah were the last two prophets YHWH sent to warn the Children of Israel of their sins. After their testimony, YHWH hid his face from the Second Temple Remnant for their rebellion against his covenant, refusing to warn of the consequences of their way any longer. He would not punish the stubborn nation for her wickedness. Rather, he would let her sins build up until they violently unleashed their own retribution as the nation "pined away for her iniquities" (Ezek 24:23; Lev 26:39).

At the end of Ezekiel's 430 years (Ezek 4:6, see below), the Second Temple Remnant's foot would slide to such depths that their sins would again "come to the full," at which time YHWH would gather all the choice parts of the sacrifice—the final third part—and purge the scum out of them during his coming Judgment Day. Israel's bloodguilt would be atoned during the time of a future wicked generation. The Second Temple Remnant would continue to play the part of a rebellious son, walking in the light of his own oral traditions and the teachings of his sages. The gall and wormwood of his false doctrines would allow YHWH to judge his firstborn son, spue him out of the land once more, deliver him to sacrificial death for the son's own sins.

C. Ezekiel's Silent Parable

Ezekiel is without a doubt the most important prophet for understanding YHWH's hidden Judgment Day. Remember that the Noahic Covenant had set a precedent of blessings for obedience and curses or consequences for disobedience. The Promised-Land Covenant followed this same formula, however, the judgment against Egypt was a minor point of the entire prophecy (see pp. 65–72, 650–56). *YHWH's Judgment Day was simply obscured in the Book of Ezekiel by prophecies that received more attention.* YHWH continued to employ this formula in the Testimonial Law, referring to it only slightly in the Sinai (Leviticus 26's) Testimony, while Deuteronomy focused on the Judgment Day in greater detail. Ezekiel adheres to the Testimonial Law, filling in and reporting the details of YHWH's horrific *Judgment Day*.

Ezekiel's testimony, unlike any other prophet's, sets the stage for YHWH's dreaded curse to be poured out like wine on Israel during this judgment era and later to be removed when the nation returns to YHWH alone. In the fifth year of Ezekiel's captivity, YHWH outlines the duties for a nation's watchman, commissioning Ezekiel with the watchman's post (Ezekiel 3; 33:7). At the outset of this commission, YHWH tells Ezekiel that he will make Ezekiel mute—unable to speak—for a period of time and he will fail to be a reprover. Later when YHWH speaks with him, he will open Ezekiel's mouth so that he can speak YHWH's words of warning to a rebellious people.

But you, O son of man, behold, they shall put bands on you, and shall bind you with them, and you shall not go out among them: And *I will make your tongue cleave to the roof of your mouth, that you shall be dumb,* **and** *shall not be to them a reprover*: for they are a rebellious house. *But when I speak with you, I will open your mouth,* and you shall say to them, Thus said the Lord YHWH; He that hears, let him hear; and he that declines, let him forbear: *for they are a rebellious house.* (Ezek 3:25–27)

YHWH clarifies Ezekiel's mission as an act of judgment against Israel, YHWH's rebellious son. Ezekiel's parable is a sign to *test* the House of Israel to see whether the people will listen to Ezekiel's warning or will turn their ears from obeying. Although YHWH sent Ezekiel to reprove Israel's sins (Ezek 3:4–11), YHWH knew that his rebellious people would not heed the prophet's counsel (a point confirmed when Ezekiel prophesies against Israel's Babylonian captives—Ezek 14:1–7; 33:32). Although YHWH outlines the requirements for performing this parable, he does not state "when" Ezekiel will begin his mute or dumb parable and bear the nation's sins.

Understanding the chronological timeline in which Ezekiel's prophecies occur becomes increasingly important for understanding the Son of man's prophetic mission. Ezekiel was commissioned during the fifth year of his captivity (Ezek 3:25–27, above), and Ezekiel obeyed his commission to warn, reprove, and rebuke Israel's sins for another four years (chaps. 3; 8–9; 20–24). Ezekiel continued to relate YHWH's warnings, reproving the sins of the people in Diaspora and the sins of the people in the land of Israel until the day when Nebuchadnezzar began to besiege Jerusalem (Ezek 24:1).

The last time Ezekiel obeys YHWH's command to speak against Israel's sins is in December of Zedekiah's 9th year, the 10th month, on the 10th day of the month (2 Kgs 25:1; Ezek 24:1, 25–27). This is exactly the same day that Nebuchadnezzar builds forts and mounds and begins to besiege Jerusalem. At this point the prophet becomes mute and no longer issues YHWH's warning to Jerusalem. Two days later (12th day), the Son of Man's mouth is opened. The last prophecy he speaks to Israel as he bears the nation's sins does not reprove the nation for her sins but is concerned with foreign nations, such as Egypt (Ezek 29:1).

Nebuchadnezzar placed Jerusalem in utter peril. The Son of Man's last word of warning to the people in the Babylon Diaspora before Jerusalem fell, however, was not concerned with Israel's sins but with the sins of another nation. Thus, *during the time that was most perilous for Judah's homeland,* Ezekiel did not warn or rebuke the nation just as YHWH had predicted. During the rest of Zedekiah's reign, Ezekiel was mute and paralyzed for 430 days—14 1/2 months (Ezek 4:3–6). At the beginning of the new year (Nisan), the Son of Man continues to prophesy against every nation (Ezek 26:1; 28:2, 22; 30:20; 31:1), *but when he talks about Israel, he promises salvation* (Ezek 28:25) *although destruction and judgment are eminent.* After he completes his dumb parable, YHWH heales Ezekiel, so he can once again warn, rebuke, and prophecy of Israel's future (see Table 19.1).

Table 19.1. Chronology of Ezekiel's Prophecies*

Date	Year	Month	Day	Text	Month	Modern Equivalent	Prophecy
593	5	1?	5	Ezek 1:2	Nisan??	March/April	Sends Ezekiel to the rebellious House of Israel
592	6	6	5	Ezek 8:1, 11	Elul	August/September	Jaazaniah, the son of Shapha
591	7	5	10	Ezek 20:1	Ab	July/August	20:24—Despised Sabbaths; prophecy of future judgment of Israel
589	9	10	10	Ezek 24:1; 2 Kgs 25:1; Ezek 24:25–27	Tebeth	December/January	LAST TIME TO PROPHECY AGAINST JUDAH/Jerusalem beseiged
				Ezek 29:1	Tebeth	December/January	Prophecies against Egypt
588	10	10	12	Ezek 4:1-6			**430 Days** — Ezekiel is mute and unable to speak from the 10/12/10th yr. to 10/5/12th yr. (shaded below)
							Ezekiel speaks as the Son of Man to the House of Israel
	11	1	1	Ezek 3:26; Ezek 4:7	Nisan	March/April	*Ezekiel is not a reprover*
				Ezek 26:1			Prophecy against Tyre
		1	7	Ezek 28:2; Ezek 28:22; Ezek 28:25; Ezek 30:20	Nisan	March/April	Prophecy against Tyre / Prophecy against Zidon / Prophesies salvation for Israel / Prophecy Against Egypt
		3	1	Ezek 31:1	Sivan	May/June	Foretells Egypt's demise
587		4	9	2 Kgs 25:2	Tammuz	June/July	**Jerusalem falls**
		5	10	Jer 52:12	Ab	July/August	**Temple destroyed**
	12	10	5	Ezek 3:26; Ezek 24:25–27	Ab	July/August	Captive brings tidings to open Ezekiel's mouth, no longer mute / Mouth opened
				Ezek 33:21			
				Ezek 33:17–20			Prophesies against Israel and her watchman
		12	1	Ezek 32:1	Adar	February/March	Egypt
			15	Ezek 32:17			Egypt, Tyre, Edom, and other nations
568	25	1	10	Ezek 40:1	Nisan	March/April	Vision of New Temple—Reestablishes covenant
566	27	1	1	Ezek 29:17	Nisan	March/April	Egypt/Tyre given to Babylon
563	30	4	5	Ezek 1:1	Tammuz	June/July	4m/5day/30yr.—Near River Chebar and saw visions of God

*All calendric reckoning is Tishri for the new year.

D. *Ezekiel's 430 Years*

1. Ezekiel Bears Israel's Sins

Ezekiel's testimony is essential for understanding YHWH's Judgment Day as foretold in Moses' Song. The Creator veiled his prophecies to Ezekiel behind the prophet's symbolic actions. YHWH told Ezekiel that he would be dumb (unable to speak) for 430 days (Ezek 4:3–6). Both his speech and his mobility would be impaired during Jerusalem's siege until the day an escapee brought tidings of the destruction heaped on Jerusalem and Solomon's Temple (Ezek 4:1–6; 3:26).[32] Ezekiel's mouth would be "closed" for 430 days before he heard the tidings of the First Temple's demise, but an escapee's tidings would "open" Ezekiel's mouth to speak words of warning about a future wicked generation (Ezek 24:27; 33:22) *after* Jerusalem's destruction.[33] In this way, YHWH could hide an important judgment prophecy that seemed to be aimed at Judah, while in reality this prophecy and the sign of his dumbness were directed at the nation *after* the destruction of the First Temple. Ezekiel would sound an early warning for a later time when YHWH would hide his face (Deut 31:17–18; 32:20) and refuse to provide word or to prophesy to a wicked generation during the *Day of YHWH*, as had been openly foretold in both the Testimonial Law and Moses' Song for so long.

Ezekiel's testimony begins with visions and instructions that outline the prophet's service to Israel. Although YHWH commands Ezekiel to perform many signs and parables, the most significant calls for Ezekiel to reenact a parable about Nebuchadnezzar's battle-siege of Jerusalem. Ezekiel is to reconstruct Judah's battle scene using clay models. In his effort to topple Judah's capital city (2 Kgs 25:1–2; Jer 32:24–25), Nebuchadnezzar had built forts and mounts. Ezekiel is supposed to use small bricks to portray this scene by playing the part of the besieging Babylonian army while bearing Israel's sins for 430 days during this mock siege.

This was YHWH's commission to Ezekiel:

> You also, son of man, take you a tile, and lay it before you, and portray on it the city, even Jerusalem: and (a) lay siege against it, and build a fort against it, and cast a mount against it; set the camp also against it, and set battering rams against it round about. Moreover take to you an iron pan, and set it for a wall of iron between you and the city: and set your face against it, and it shall be besieged, and you shall lay siege against it. This shall be a sign to the House of Israel.
>
> *Lie you also on your left side*, and *lay the iniquity* of the House of Israel on it: according to the number of the days that you shall lie on it *you shall bear their iniquity*. For I have laid on you the years of their iniquity, according to the number of the days, three hundred and ninety days: so shall you bear the iniquity of the House of Israel. And when you have accomplished them, *lie again on your right side*, and you shall bear the iniquity of the House of Judah forty days: **I have appointed you each day for a year**[34] (430 years). **Therefore you shall set your face (b) toward the siege of Jerusalem, and your arm shall be uncovered, and you shall prophesy against it. And, behold, I will lay bands**

on you, and (c) **you shall not turn you from one side to another, till you have ended the days of your siege.** (Ezek 4:1–8, parentheses added)

Ezekiel's 430-day parable prophesies of Jerusalem's future test. His prophecy begins with the onset of Babylon's (a) siege of Jerusalem during the reign of Zedekiah, when forts, mounds, battering rams, and other war appliances were employed to conquer Jerusalem. Ezekiel bears the nation's sins for 430 days until (b) his arm is uncovered to prophecy against Jerusalem and her siege. During the 430 days that Ezekiel reenacts Nebuchadnezzar's siege, the prophet is paralyzed so that he cannot turn from one side to another or speak while he bears the nation's sins.[35] He simply lies on his left side for 390 days, then on his right side for 40 days. Thus the prophet was incapacitated for about 14 1/2 months. In the final days of the city's siege the (b) *Son of Man's arm is uncovered to specifically prophesy against Jerusalem.* The first 390 days of Ezekiel's reenactment are a sign to the House of Israel, which has already been deported off the land. The last 40 days of Ezekiel's paralysis are a sign to the House of Judah, many of whose citizens had been deported with Ezekiel and Jechoniah to Babylon. This parable is not a sign to Jerusalem's people who are under siege over 300 miles away but is a sign to those who have already been sent into Babylonian captivity and have come to Ezekiel for counsel.

YHWH continues his instructions for the reenactment parable by telling the prophet to procure food supplies for the time when he would be unable to move.

Take you also to you (a) wheat, and barley, and beans, and lentils, and millet, and fitches, and put them in one vessel, and make you bread of it, according to the number of the days that you shall (b) **lie on your side**, three hundred and ninety days shall you eat of it. And your (c) meat which you shall eat shall be by weight, twenty shekels a day:[36] from time to time shall you eat it. You shall drink also water by measure, the sixth part of an hin:[37] from time to time shall you drink. And you shall eat it as barley cakes, and you shall bake it with (d) dung that comes out of man, in their sight. And YHWH said, Even thus shall the children (e) of Israel eat their defiled bread among the Gentiles, where I will drive them. (Ezek 4:9–13)

Interestingly, Ezekiel's main staple is a (a) bread that is nutritionally complete[38] except for the fact that it is (d) mixed with human dung (replaced by cow dung at Ezekiel's request—4:14–15). Remember that YHWH had established his *show bread* to represent an unfermented food that is doctrinally pure and true (pp. 647–48). Ezekiel's actions prophesy that during the Diaspora Israel will forsake YHWH's pure *un*leavened bread for a different bread that, though healthy, will be mixed with defiled, human doctrine that she will (e) eat during the Diaspora (a point we will examine in vol. 2).

Ezekiel will ration his (c) meat, defiled bread, and water to last during (b) his paralysis (Ezek 4:9–12, 15) while he bears the nation's sins. At the end of Ezekiel's 430-day paralysis, his mouth will be opened, and he will speak according to the defiled bread he has eaten. He will face besieged Jerusalem (Ezek 4:7) but will not reprove the nation's sins, as YHWH commanded (Ezek 3:4, 26–27). Instead, he will be concerned with the welfare of the nations surrounding Israel while prophesying of salvation on the very day that YHWH's Temple, his holy dwelling place in Israel's midst, is about to be destroyed. Later, YHWH will open Ezekiel's mouth to speak for himself, and Ezekiel will reprove Israel. *All of Ezekiel's actions represent beliefs, behavior, and situations that the Israelites will experience in the future (Ezek 24:24).*

At first glance Ezekiel's parable of judgment appears to be aimed wholly at Nebuchadnezzar's siege.[39] Examining the timing of Ezekiel's parable reveals quite a different understanding. On the very day that Nebuchadnezzar began his siege of Jerusalem (Zedekiah's 9th year, Jer 52:4–9; Ezek 24:1–2), YHWH tells the Babylonian Diaspora that they—not Jerusalem's besieged citizens—will fulfill the signs and parables that Ezekiel has just performed:

> Thus Ezekiel is to you a sign: according to all that he has done *shall you do*: and when this comes, you shall know that I am the Lord YHWH. (Ezek 24:24)

This statement implies a twofold prophecy. The first was fulfilled at Jerusalem's demise when the people were vanquished by Nebuchadnezzar, and the second will be fulfilled by the Children of Israel during the long Diaspora. When Israel's latter-day generation sees and understands this parable, they will finally understand that there is singularly YHWH and no other.

When YHWH initially commissioned Ezekiel to bear Israel's sins, he did not provide a specific time for his parable to begin; he simply outlined instructions about how the "muted parable" should be performed. Understanding *when* Ezekiel actually performed this parable sheds incredible light on this prophetic parable and its purpose. Later in Ezekiel's work, we find the exact date when Ezekiel would perform his confining parable, when YHWH issues instructions for Ezekiel's commission.

> *Speak to the House of Israel*, Thus said the Lord YHWH; Behold, (a) *I will profane my sanctuary*, the excellency of your strength, the desire of your eyes, and that which your soul pities; and your sons and your daughters whom you have left shall fall by the sword. And you shall do as I (referring to Ezekiel) have done: (b) you shall not cover your lips, nor eat the bread of men. And your tires shall be on your heads, and your shoes on your feet: you shall not mourn nor weep; but you (c) shall pine away for your iniquities, and mourn one toward another. (d) Thus Ezekiel is to you a sign: according to (e) all that he has done shall you do: and when this comes you shall know that I am the Lord YHWH. (Ezek 24:21–25, parenthesis added.)

After being paralyzed for 430 days, Ezekiel would speak the word God gave him to the House of Israel. He would speak during a time when YHWH had (a) profaned his sanctuary.

YHWH created his holy Temple in Jerusalem to symbolize Israel's strength and power and the glory of her political independence (see chap. 13.IV). Zion was the city out of all the places in the earth where YHWH had placed his name and granted his blessing. Although YHWH's glory had once filled the First Temple (1 Kgs 8:11; 2 Chr 5:14; 7:1–3), the Creator would (a) destroy the Temple, which he had defined as the "excellency of Israel's strength."

In the ancient Near East, through time, and until the very recent Victorian era, people customarily demonstrated grief when death or national tragedy occurred. When Job faced horrific afflictions, he rent his clothes, then sat in sackcloth and ashes. Jacob mourned for Joseph's death in this same manner (Gen 37:34). When Joab murdered Abner, David commanded all Israel to demonstrate proper respect and grief over the loss of Abner's life and for his role in reuniting the kingdom. It was important to mourn the loss of life as well as grieving over the jealous iniquity and wickedness that had led to Abner's death (2 Sam 3:31–39). Showing grief meant humbling one's heart and mind (Prov 15:13). When King Ahab heard YHWH's judgment against him, he humbled himself by tearing his clothes, putting on sackcloth and ashes, and becoming very gentle. YHWH saw the change in Ahab's spirit and demeanor and extended his mercy to Ahab by forbearing to bring judgment against his children in Ahab's lifetime (1 Kgs 21:24–29). Unlike the hard-hearted Ahab, who could humble himself in the face of YHWH's judgment, the rebellious among the (b) Diaspora would not show any signs of grief to mourn the Temple's destruction or sorrow for their sins that had led to YHWH's judgment.

Similar to Ezekiel, the Diaspora would (b) not cover their mouths with shame or grief. They would not show any outward or inward humility or grief over YHWH's judgment. Rather, they would continue to wear their ordinary attire and hold to their usual beliefs, as though a mighty blow had not been dealt the nation. Their insensitivity and wandering hearts would continue to search for another way of life outside YHWH's covenant as they turned to another god, thus consuming (b) a new religious bread of doctrine that, though destructive, gave them great comfort and immediate hope. Their bread would mirror the substance of Ezekiel's bread—wholly complete except for the fact it was mixed with human dung.

The hard-hearted nation would not leave the comfortable theology found in the wine of their new Babylonian gods (Deut 28:64; 32:17) to return to the God who wanted to correct their ways so they could prosper (Isa 48:17–19). Rather, the sins of the Children of Israel would (c) consume them as they followed a comfortable, but destructive, theology. They would not humble themselves to seek and cry out to their Maker (Job 35:9–10; Isa 22:10–14; 51:12–14) for comfort. Instead, Israel would complain, as did her fathers in the wilderness, while God waited for her to return to him.

During this time, Ezekiel becomes a (d) sign to Israel as he obeys his commission to re-enact Jerusalem's siege. He is paralysed by bearing the nation's iniquities, leaving him unable to speak (Ezek 3:26; 4:4–6, 8) as YHWH withholds his judgment for 430 days, while the (c) iniquities of the people continue to mount. At the end of the Ezekiel's mock siege, Jerusalem falls into enemy hands. When Israel's people see Ezekiel's model siege (the prophet lying partially paralyzed and unable to speak, eating his daily rations with the hand from the side unaffected by the paralysis) they know that their nation will follow Ezekiel's example. Israel will become paralyzed under the weight of her own iniquities as she consumes her defiled spiritual bread, which never quite satisfies her hunger and thirst during the long Diaspora.[40]

YHWH completes his commission for Ezekiel, telling the prophet that he will fulfill this sign "in the day" the Temple—the joy of Israel's strength and glory—is destroyed.

> Also, you son of man, shall it not be in the day when I (a) take from them their strength, the joy of their glory, the desire of their eyes, and that whereon they set their minds, their sons and their daughters, that (b) **he that escapes in that day shall come to you**, to cause you to hear it with your ears? (c) **In that day shall your mouth be opened to him which is escaped, and you shall speak, and be no more dumb**: and (d) you shall be a sign to them; and (e) they shall know that I am YHWH. (Ezek 24:25–27)

YHWH tells Ezekiel that after (a) the Temple's destruction, (b) a prisoner will bring tidings of Jerusalem's fall. *On the (c) day that Ezekiel will hear of Jerusalem's destruction from one of the city's deported citizens, YHWH will open his mouth, so he can speak once again.* Both Ezekiel's (d) inability to speak and the opening of his mouth are signs to Israel, warning the nation of future judgment. Understanding Ezekiel's parables (e) will finally cause latter-day Israel to know YHWH exists.

Scripture does not tell us the exact date when Ezekiel began his "muted" parable except that it was near the time of the Temple's destruction. To discover this date, we must work backwards from the date that one of Jerusalem's captives brought the news that ended Ezekiel's suffering.

> And it came to pass in the **twelfth year of our captivity, in the tenth month, in the fifth day of the month**, that one that had escaped out of Jerusalem came to me, saying, The city is smitten. Now the hand of YHWH was on me **in the evening, before he that was escaped came**; and **had opened my mouth**, until he came to me in the morning; **and my mouth was opened, and I was no more dumb.** (Ezek 33:21–22)

Although YHWH opened Ezekiel's mouth on the evening before the escapee came, it was the same "day" when the refugee had arrived. At creation, a physical day began at evening (Gen 1:5–31); so when YHWH opened Ezekiel's mouth on the evening before, it was still on the day when the prisoner came to him. In this way YHWH obscured judgment prophecies against Zion's Daughter by opening Ezekiel's mouth on the evening before the prisoner came to him so the people would think that he was prophesying about Jerusalem's fall to Nebuchadnezzar rather than about the fate that awaited their rebellious descendants during the future Day of YHWH.

Jerusalem had fallen into Nebuchadnezzar's hands in the 4th month of the 11th year of Zedekiah's reign (2 Kgs 25:2; Jer 52:5–6). This was also the 4th month and 11th year of

Table 19.2 Ezekiel's Month-by-Month Chronology from the Closing of his Mouth until His Mouth is Opened*

Date	Year	Month	Postexilic	Modern Equivalent	Text	Prophecy	
589		8	Marcheshvan	October/November	2 Kgs 25:1; Ezek 24:1, 25–7	Jerusalem is under seige	
		9	Kislev	November/December			
		10	Tebeth	December/January	Ezek 29:1	Prophecy against Egypt	
					Ezekiel is mute and paralyzed for 430 days		
	10	10	Tebeth	December/January	Ezekiel 4:1–6		0.6 (17 days)
		11	Shebat	January/February			2
		12	Adar	February/March			3
		1	Nisan	March/April			4
		2	Iyyar	April/May			5
		3	Sivan	May/June		430 Days	6
		4	Tammuz	June/July			7
588		5	Ab	July/August			8
		6	Elul	August/September			9
		7	Tishri	September/October			10
		8	Marcheshvan	October/November			11
		9	Kislev	November/December			12
		10	Tebeth	December/January			13
		11	Shebat	January/February			14
		12	Adar	February/March			14.6 months
					The Son of Man speaks to the House of Israel		
	11	1	Nisan	March/April	Ezek 26:1	Prophecy against Tyre	
					Ezek 28:21	Prophecy against Zidon	
					Ezek 28:25	Prophecies salvation for Israel	
					Ezek 30:20	Prophecy against Egypt	
		2	Iyyar	April/May			
		3	Sivan	May/June	Ezek 31:1	Foretells of Egypt's demise	
		4	Tammuz	June/July	2 Kgs 25:2	Jerusalem Falls	Jerusalem beseiged/Ezekiel is not a reprover
587		5	Ab	July/August	Jer 52:12	Temple Destroyed	
		6	Elul	August/September		Ezekiel does not warn the people that Jerusalem has fallen even though he warns them when Jerusalem comes (Ezek 24:1–2) under seige.	
		7	Tishri	September/October			
		8	Marcheshvan	October/November			
		9	Kislev	November/December			
	12	10	Tebeth	December/January	Ezek 3:26	Captive brings tidings of Jerusalem's fall to open Ezekiel's mouth.	Ezekiel obeys YHWH's commands and prophesies against the House of Israel
					Ezek 24:26–27		
					Ezek 33:21	Ezekiel's mouth is opened	
					Ezek 33:17–20	Prophecies against Israel and her watchman	

*All calendric reckoning is according to Tishri: the months begin in Nisan (March–May), but the year begins in Tishri (September–November).

Ezekiel's captivity, since Zedekiah's reign and Ezekiel's captivity began at the same time. Six months later, in the *12th year and 10th month* of Ezekiel's captivity, he heard of the Temple's destruction from an escapee and his mouth was opened (see Table 19.2). So why is Ezekiel's parable so important?

> Ezekiel issues his warning against Jerusalem and her watchmen after Jerusalem had already fallen.

Once YHWH opened Ezekiel's mouth, the prophet continued to reprove Israel of her sins and warn of YHWH's ensuing Judgment Day. *This was 5 months after Jerusalem's utter destruction at Nebuchadnezzar's hand.* Ezekiel prophesied against the Babylonian Diaspora, foretelling that Israel's land would, in the future, lie desolate once again. The following prophecy was spoken during Adar, 6 months *after* Jerusalem had fallen to Nebuchadnezzar.

> Say you thus to them, Thus said the Lord YHWH; As I live, surely they that are in the wastes shall fall by the sword, and him that is in the open field will I give to the beasts to be devoured, and they that be in the forts and in the caves shall die of the pestilence. For *I will lay the land most desolate*, and the pomp of her strength shall cease; and the mountains of Israel shall be desolate, that none shall pass through. Then shall they know that I am YHWH, when I have laid the land most desolate because of all their abominations which they have committed. (Ezek 33:27–29)

YHWH's judgment had already fallen on the land when Babylon destroyed Jerusalem and burned the Temple five months earlier. Nebuchadnezzar's final campaign simply "tied up loose ends" when he commandeered 745 prisoners of war four years later (Jer 52:30). No doubt the people looked at the prophet as though he had a "screw loose" when he prophesied of an event that had already happened. They did not realize that Ezekiel's prophecy stood as a testimony, warning the Second Temple Remnant (Daughter of Zion) of YHWH's future Judgment Day, when the 430 days that Ezekiel had borne Israel's sins were fulfilled as 430 years (Ezek 4:6).

Not only did Ezekiel warn and reprove those who would live on Israel's soil; Ezekiel also addressed his prophecies to the sins of those who lived in Diaspora, regarding their sins.

> Also, you son of man, the children of your people still are talking against you by the walls and in the doors of the houses, and speak one to another, everyone to his brother, saying, Come, I pray you, and hear what is the word that comes forth from YHWH. And they come to you as the people come, and they sit before you as my people, and they hear your words, *but they will not do them*: for with their mouth they show much love, *but their heart goes after their covetousness*. And, lo, you are to them as a very lovely song of one that has a pleasant

voice, and can play well on an instrument: *for they hear your words, but they do them not*. And when this comes to pass, (lo, it will come,) then shall they know that a prophet has been among them. (Ezek 33:30–33)

YHWH points out that his dispersed people are no different from the proud Judahites back in their native homeland. Similar to the Jews who sought word from YHWH through Jeremiah about whether they should immigrate to Egypt (Jeremiah 42–43), Babylon's exiles will seek to know YHWH's will, to know his judgments, yet will have no desire to turn from their covetous ways to follow him. Ezekiel will become like a song that is sung without any tangible action behind it. His words would "feel good," and Israel would sing about them, but they would not take action to obey.

Exile and deportation have not yet healed the nation's hypocrisy or humbled her to love and obey her Maker. This is why YHWH ordained Ezekiel's parables to rebuke the Israelites' sins and warn of YHWH's future Judgment Day: they would know that there had been a prophet who had served as the nation's watchman, warning them of the consequences. After YHWH had opened Ezekiel's mouth, he continued to prophesy against (a, below) the selfish leaders and teachers, who would bear the brunt of YHWH's upcoming holocaust. At a much later time, YHWH would once again judge the nation, deliver the remnant of his flock to the Promised Land, never to be removed again.[41]

After Ezekiel's mouth was opened when a captive had told dispersed Israel that the Temple had been destroyed five months before, the Son of man prophesied:

And as for my flock, they eat that which you have trodden with your feet; and they drink that which you have fouled with your feet. Therefore thus said the Lord YHWH to them; Behold, I, even I, (a) will judge between the fat cattle and between the lean cattle. Because you have thrust with side and with shoulder, and pushed all the diseased with your horns, till you have scattered them abroad; Therefore will I save my flock, and they shall no more be a prey; and I will judge between cattle and cattle. And I will set up (b) one shepherd over them, and he shall feed them, even my servant David; he shall feed them, and he shall be their shepherd. And I YHWH will be their God, and my servant David a prince among them; I YHWH have spoken it. And I will make with them a (c) covenant of peace, and will cause the evil beasts to cease out of the land: and they shall dwell safely in the wilderness, and sleep in the woods. And I will make them and the *places* round about my hill a (d) blessing; and I will cause the shower to come down in his season; there shall be showers of blessing. (Ezek 34:19–26)

The events ordained in the Testimonial Law—the blessings, the curses—and the dreaded curse that coincides with the Day of YHWH all serve one purpose: to teach, refine, and heal the stubborn nation. YHWH intended for the judgments in his Testimony to correct, guide, and direct the Israelites through their wayward years until they finally learned to humble themselves, to listen and obey his words. When Israel is ready to obey, YHWH will redeem the nation from all lands where she has been scattered, and the Diaspora Covenant will be fulfilled. The Creator will either (b) resurrect King David[42] or establish David's descendant to be his governor on earth, as YHWH offers the entire nation of Israel a (c) covenant of peace, as he had formerly done with David and Phinehas (pp. 153–58). Once Israel is restored, YHWH will fill Israel's people and land with his (d) blessings, which will overflow from the righteousness that comes from following his way of life.

2. The 430-Year Precedent

When YHWH made the Promised-Land Covenant with Abraham (Genesis 15), he established 430 years as the time allotted for a society to reach utter degradation. The first time we find this formula employed is in the vision that YHWH gave to Abraham.

> Know of a surety that your seed shall be a stranger in a land that is not theirs, and shall serve them; and they shall afflict them four hundred years; And also that nation, whom they shall serve, will I judge. . . . But in the fourth generation they shall come here again: *for the iniquity of the Amorites is not yet full.* (Gen 15:13–16)

YHWH sent Jacob and his family to Egypt because the sins and idolatry of the Amorites' had not yet reached saturation. The foot of the Amorites had not yet fully slid (Deut 32:35). Melchizedek, the Amorite king of Jerusalem who was a priest of Elyon (the most high God), is evidence of a people who at least partially worshiped the Creator (Gen 14:18). Righteousness still existed in Canaan during Abraham's days.

YHWH sent Israel to Egypt until the Amorites' iniquities became wholly degenerate, and righteousness had entirely evaporated from the land (see pp 88–89). YHWH could then judge them, using Israel to cast them out and cleanse the land of their wickedness, according to Numbers' Effacement Judgment. During the time that Israel was waiting for the Amorites' sins to mature, Israel was brought into bondage in Egypt.

Throughout Scripture YHWH consistently uses 430 years as the benchmark for judgment, allotting this period for nations to establish righteousness on their land or fail to establish it. We see this precedent referred to repeatedly in Scripture. After Israel entered Canaan, she lived there for about 430 years before she rebelled against YHWH by asking for a king (See chap. 9.III.B.6., p. 356). When YHWH had established the Davidic Monarchy, the kingdom lasted another 430 years until Nebuchadnezzar finally vanquished the people whose wickedness, like the Amorites before had "come to the full." YHWH is consistent when he once again established this 430 years as the period for the Second Temple Remnant to become a righteous nation or degenerate into wanton wickedness during the Second Temple Period.

3. The Day of YHWH Begins

YHWH had told Ezekiel that, each day that he bore Israel's sins represented one year.

> Lie you also on your left side, and lay the iniquity of the House of Israel on it: according to the number of the days that you shall lie on it you shall bear their iniquity. For I have laid on you the years of their iniquity, according to the number of the days, three hundred and ninety days: so shall you bear the iniquity of the House of Israel. And when you have accomplished them, lie again on your right side, and you shall bear the iniquity of the House of Judah forty days: *I have appointed you each day for a year.* (Ezek 4:4–6)

If YHWH's judgment method is applied to Israel with *constancy*, the 430 years represented by Ezekiel bearing Israel's sins was the time when YHWH withheld total judgment, allowing the First Remnant's iniquity to "come to the full." When the Second Temple Remnant's sins did reach total reprobation, YHWH could righteously provoke a nation who would judge Israel and cast her out of the Promised Land—again. This activated Numbers Effacement Judgment with all the Testimony's curses a second time.

After this prophetic 430 years, YHWH would open the mouth of another prophet, who would not warn of Israel's sins but prophesy of salvation to her congregation. This Son of Man would not reprove the nation's sins but seek to establish YHWH's kingdom during an era of rebellion, wickedness, and worldwide judgment.

Four-hundred thirty years after Nebuchadnezzar destroyed the city, Jerusalem was besieged again, when Ezekiel's prophecies were uncovered and put into effect, as YHWH offered a great sacrifice in Jerusalem. Remember that YHWH had openly told Ezekiel that, after Jerusalem's final siege, he would divide Israel into a three-part sacrifice:

> Divide the hair. You shall burn with fire a third part **in the middle of the city, (a) when the days of the siege are fulfilled**: and you shall take a (b) third part, and smite about it with a knife: and a (c) **third part you shall scatter in the wind; and I will draw out a sword after them.** You (d) shall also take of it a few in number, and bind them in your skirts. **Then (e) take of them again, and cast them into the middle of the fire, and burn them in the fire; for of it shall a fire come forth (f) into all the House of Israel.** (Ezek 5:1–4)

We looked at this prophecy in depth above (pp. 838–40), but now we can gain understanding gleaned from Ezekiel's muted parable. From the inception of YHWH's covenant with Israel, the Creator used fire to consume his sacrifices or holocausts.[43] Israel's prophets had based their prophecies on the symbolism built into the sacrificial system to foretell the day when YHWH's fire would consume the sacrifice of his wicked firstborn son. YHWH's word to Ezekiel continues to use the symbolism found in the sacrificial system to describe the nation's future judgments.

YHWH tells Ezekiel to perform this parable (a) after the prophet has completed his 430-day enactment of Jerusalem.[44] The first third of Jerusalem's citizens were killed in a sacrificial holocaust when Nebuchadnezzar destroyed Judah in 587 BCE. The (b) second third of the people were killed by the sword during battle throughout the Diaspora. And the final (c) third were deported to Babylon, only to have their descendants die by war and persecution. Of this (d) final third, a few have humbled themselves enough for YHWH to safely hide them during the upcoming holocaust. YHWH will take the rest (e) of this final third to fuel his sacrifice that will begin in Jerusalem but quickly (f) spread to all the Diaspora. Although Jacob's descendants are living in other lands, YHWH's sacrificial fire will find the wicked among them.

We have seen that the final third of the House of Israel would fuel YHWH's sacrifice. But what does this mean in real terms? How does Ezekiel's 430 years reveal the beginning of the Day of YHWH? And why did Ezekiel need to bear Israel's sins for 430 days/years?

Nebuchadnezzar began to besiege Jerusalem in 589 BCE.[45] If Ezekiel bore Israel's sins for 430 years, the beginning of the Day of YHWH would be c. 159 BCE. Remember YHWH's 7-Times Judgment against his Sanctuary? These 7 Times symbolized the fact that, after 350 years of the Second Temple's being reestablished on YHWH's holy mount, the Temple would once again be made desolate (see pp. 799–801). Ezekiel's 430 years covered this same era, ending about 6 year later. The judgment at the end of the Second Temple Era, however, did not completely remove Israel from the land; rather, YHWH poured out the sacrificial wine of the Judgment of Delusions to the wicked generation that adhered to the teachings of men, which corrupted his constitutional Law. The Day of YHWH would begin during a time when Jerusalem would again be besieged and Second Temple left desolate.[46] This is how the prophecy works:

1st siege—Nebuchadnezzar begins to siege Jerusalem (Ezek 4:1–3)	589 BCE
Ezekiel bears the sins of Judah and Israel (Ezek 4:3–6)	−430 years
2nd siege begins the Day of YHWH (Ezek 4:7)	159 BCE
Judgment of Delusion begins	

The Day of YHWH began with Antiochus Epiphanes' siege of Jerusalem. Ever since Alexander the Great's death in 323 BCE, Syria and Egypt had vied for supremacy over the Promised Land. *Five wars* had been fought in this contest.[47] In 170 BCE, Antichus Epiphanes was invited into Jerusalem by Hellenizing Jews.[48] Syria's Jewish supporters opened the city gates to him and he killed the traditionalists who opposed his authority. Two years later, in desperate need of cash (168 BCE), Antiochus Epiphanes again slaughtered Jerusalem's citizenry—even his Hellenistic followers—in his quest for the riches that lay within the Temple's sacred precincts (*Ant.* 12.53–55) to finance his cash-strapped campaigns. This time, Antiochus violated the Second Temple's sacred precincts and emptied its treasure of its reserves, while ripping the veil that separated the most Holy Place. His generals fulfilled Ezekiel's prophecy of a three-part holocaust by burning Jerusalem with fire (1 Macc 1:31), massacring her citizens, and taking 10,000 captives (*Ant.* 12.5.4). Antiochus's second conquest was a reign of terror, an era of wholesale religious persecution, destined to be imitated by the Roman Empire, as both nations fulfilled YHWH's judgments against Jerusalem. During the long Day of YHWH, the Creator's fury rested on Jerusalem (Jer 30:7). Syria, and, later, Rome fiercely targeted religious thoughts, beliefs, ideals, and allegiances. Eventually, the whole House of Israel succumbed to the persecutions wrought by Rome's inquisitions.

V. THE DAY OF YHWH BEGINS TO BE FULFILLED

A. *In Judea: 1 Maccabees*

For over a century, Egypt and Syria fought wars for possession of Israel. Egypt maintained control until about 200 BCE, when Antiochus III won, and Judea was caught in the middle of the two strong nations.[49] This polarized the Judeans because some citizens favored Egyptian control while others favored Syrian.[50] Evidently, many Judeans had backed the Ptolemies during the sixth war, so when Antiochus won, he was furious with the people for partially siding with Egypt.[51]

Many modern scholars consider polarization to have been the Hellenizers' intent—wanting to change Israel's "outdated" theology.[52] While this view certainly has merit, we cannot overlook the religious divisions that already existed in Judea before any formal Hellenistic movement may have occurred. When Antiochus III secured Judea, he granted privileges for Judea's assistance in driving out Ptolemaic garrisons.[53] One of these privileges was the Judeans' right to live "according to their ancestral laws" (*Ant.* 12.138ff).[54] This presented a dilemma for the Remnant.

During the Monarchy years, the Pentateuch (first five books of Scripture) had been the basis for Israel's governmental laws and her religion. But during her exile and her early reestablishment in the land, her teachers *added an Oral Law* that many considered to be equal to the written Law.[55] Adherents of the Oral Law believed it was given to Israel at Mt. Sinai and handed down from Moses to succeeding generations.[56] This produced sects in the Jewish religion. The scribes, who later became known as rabbis (Pharisees) defended the Oral Law, believing that the written Law could not be understood without it, while the Sadducees condemned the Oral Law (*Ant.* 13.10.6).[57]

When Antiochus Epiphanes sought to secure Judea, the rift between religious factions (including the secular Hellenizers) had drifted far apart.[58] Opposing sides sought Epiphanes' sanction for their personal religious policies, and when he saw that his rule was not backed by the entire nation, he turned against Jerusalem's citizens. The Book of 1 Maccabees is the only historical narrative to date that has survived the late Second Temple Era. It describes the fulfillment of Moses' Judgment Song and Ezekiel's parables.

According to 1 Maccabees 1, Antiochus campaigned against Egypt during the 6th year of his reign, but he was defeated and humiliated by a simple Roman envoy.[59] On his return to Syria, he violated Jerusalem's Temple, removed the veil between the holy and Most Holy Place, confiscated gold and the Temple implements, then massacred Judea's citizens. His invasion began a horrible holocaust.[60] Two years later, he

> fell suddenly on the city, and smote it very sore, and destroyed much people of Israel. And when he had taken the spoils of the city, he set it on fire, and pulled down the houses and walls of it on every side. But the women and children took they *captive*, and possessed the cattle. (1 Mac 1:30–32; see Jeremiah 6)[61]

Antiochus Epiphanes may have seen Israel's "ancestral laws" as the source of his misery in Judea, since "ancestral laws" had divided its citizens allegiance between Syria and Egypt.[62] So he sought to ban the laws that had caused him so many headaches.[63] He outlawed Torah observance (1 Macc 1:41–49) and sought to change YHWH's ordinances (1 Mac 1:49). Most important to his control over the province, Epiphanes sought to install a new cult in Jerusalem, which many Judahites actually embraced (1 Macc 1:11, 43).[64] When Antiochus fell on Jerusalem, many soldiers in his legions were Judeans who shed their fellow countrymen's blood.[65] He put to death any that embraced the Torah or the rabbis. Later in the year, Epiphanes "set up the abomination of desolation on the altar" and built idol altars throughout the Judean countryside (1 Macc 1:54; *Ant.* 13.5.4). This was the first time in history that a conqueror had sought to divide and destroy a people's religious ideals.

Numbers 33 had commanded, "And you shall divide the land by lot for an inheritance" (Num 33:54). If Israel failed to follow Numbers' command, its judgment would be turned against those charged with carrying it out (Num 33:56). The author of 1 Maccabees witnesses the fulfillment of this collective judgment against Israel once again, reciting Antiochus Epiphanes' orders to Lysias, the governor of the land (1 Macc 3:32), to

> place *strangers in all their quarters, and divide their land by lot.* (1 Macc 3:36)

As we saw above (pp. 687–90, 797–99), the Judeans of this era were still failing to follow Numbers 33. At the end of 430 years, the exact same judgment that Israel was to have fulfilled against the natives living in the Promised Land was turned against the Judeans once more as they continued to corrupt the truth that YHWH had given to the nation at Mt. Sinai. Her fermented teachings prevented her from obeying Numbers 33 Judgment and, so YHWH did to the Judean Remnant what he had thought of doing to the Amorites before (Num 33:56). History records the fidelity of YHWH's judgments. The Creator adhered to his own Law by placing strangers (Num 33:55) in Israel's land and dividing it among them once again. Antiochus Epiphanes both divided Israel's land and drove her from it (1 Macc 1:32, 53).

During Epiphanes' 10th year, an Aaronic Levite, Judas Maccabee played the role of savior and defeated Lysias with 5,000 of his men. This temporarily deterred Israel's adversaries, granting Judas's company the opportunity to investigate the Temple's violation. They found the Temple dilapidated.

> Upon this all the host assembled themselves together, and went up into mount Sion (Zion). And when they saw the sanctuary desolate, and the altar profaned, and the gates burned up, and shrubs growing in the courts as in a forest, or in one of the mountains, yes, and the priests' chambers pulled down; they rent their clothes, and made great lamentation, and cast ashes on their heads, and fell down flat to the ground on their faces and blew an alarm with the trumpets, and *cried toward heaven.* (1 Macc 4:37–40, parenthesis and emphasis added)

The Remnant sought to cleanse the Temple. The priests removed the altar's defiled stones, "until there should come a prophet to show what should be done with them" (1 Macc 4:46). Five years later, the daughter of Zion was still awaiting her elusive prophet but to no avail.

YHWH had utterly forsaken this generation: he shrugged. He refused to hear her cry toward heaven, send word to her, or to act on her behalf. The author of 1 Maccabbess attests: "So was there a great affliction in Israel, the like whereof was not since the time that *a prophet was not seen among them*" (1 Macc 9:27). YHWH had "hid his face from a wicked and perverse generation" as he had prophesied in the Law and the prophets:

> Then my anger shall be kindled against them in that day, and I will *forsake them*, and I will *hide my face from them*, and they shall be devoured, and many evils and troubles shall befall them; so that they will say in that day. Are not these evils come on us, because our God is not among us? And I will surely hide my face in that day for all the evils which they shall have worked, in that they are turned to other gods. (Deut 31:17–18; see also 32:20–25 and Jer 4–6:9)
>
> They are corrupt, and speak wickedly concerning oppression: they speak loftily. They set their mouth against the heavens, and their tongue walks through the earth. Therefore *his people return here*: and waters of a full cup are wrung out to them. And they say, How does God know? and is there knowledge in the most High? Behold, these are the ungodly, who prosper in the world; they increase in riches. Truly I have cleansed my heart in vain, and washed my hands in innocency. For all the day long have I been plagued, and chastened every morning. If I say, I will speak thus; behold, I should offend against the generation of your children. When I thought to know this, it was too painful for me; Until I went into the sanctuary of God; then understood I their end. Surely you did set them in slippery places: you cast them down into destruction. *How are they brought into desolation, as in a moment! They are utterly consumed with terrors.* (Ps 73:8–19)

YHWH did not complete his judgment of the Amorites' iniquities in a single epoch; rather, his judgment spanned several centuries. Similarly, Israel's Judgment Day was not completed at the end of the 430 years when Ezekiel bore Israel's sins. A Scriptural day lasts for a 1,000 years (Ps 90:4; 84:10), so the Day of YHWH would last for a 1,000 years. Israel's judgment began when the prophet ceased to bear the nation's sins and would continue well into the Middle Ages.

B. Jeremiah's Migration Curse

Shortly after Nebuchadnezzar's final deportation of Judah, many Judahite refugees sought Egypt's safe harbors and the protection of Pharoah's vast army (i.e., horses). Johanan and the captains of Judah's remaining forces asked Jeremiah if migrating to Egypt was right in YHWH's sight. The refugees promised to follow YHWH's instructions through Jeremiah (Jer 42:3–6). The prophet replied emphatically, "No, do not return to Egypt." Yet the Remnant, after receiving YHWH's answer, disobeyed YHWH's instruction. This was their reply:

> Saying, No; but we will go to the land of Egypt, where we shall see no war, nor hear the sound of the trumpet, nor have hunger of bread; and there will we dwell. (Jer 42:14).

Jeremiah (42–44) outlined the future judgment these Jews would face for rebelling against YHWH's specific prohibition. This judgment would occur in Egypt during the Day of YHWH.

> Then it shall come to pass, that the (a) sword, which you feared, shall overtake you *there in the land of Egypt*, and the (b) *famine*, whereof you were afraid, *shall follow close after you there into Egypt*; and there you shall die. So shall it be with all the men that set their faces to go into Egypt to sojourn there; they shall die by the sword, by the famine, and by the (c) pestilence: and none of them shall remain or escape from the evil that I will bring on them. For thus said YHWH of hosts, the God of Israel; As **my anger and my fury has been poured forth on the inhabitants of Jerusalem; so shall my fury be poured forth on you, when you shall enter into Egypt:** and (d) you shall be an execration, and an astonishment, and (d) *a curse*, and a reproach; and you shall see this place no more. YHWH has said concerning you, O you remnant of Judah; Go you not into Egypt: know certainly that I have admonished you this day. For you dissembled in your hearts, when you sent me to YHWH your God, saying, Pray for us to YHWH our God; and according to all that YHWH our God shall say, so declare to us, and we will do it. And now I have this day declared it to you; but you have not obeyed the voice of the YHWH your God, nor any thing for the which he has sent me to you. Now therefore know certainly that *you shall die by the sword, by the famine, and by the pestilence, in the place where you desire to go and to sojourn.* (Jer 42:16–22)

Jeremiah prophesied four specific things that would happen to the rebellious Judahite Remnant: sword, famine, hatred (anti-Semitism), and pestilence. Furthermore, these curses were left as a legacy or "curse" for their children living on Egypt's soil. Jeremiah continued this prophecy (44:30), foretelling the unrest and civil war that would occur under Pharoah Hophra (Greek—Apries, 589–570 BCE).

Apries' Palestinian policy weakened his throne.[66] After a devastating defeat, he returned home to face civil war.[67] This was an ethnic battle, as native Egyptians rebelled against Apries and fought his foreign supporters.[68] Jeremiah's prophecy of (a) war came to pass no more than 15 years after the rebellious Jews migrated to Egypt. The final blow came in the 37th year of Nebuchadnezzar's reign (570 BCE), when he invaded Egypt, and the "sword, which they feared, overtook them there in the land of Egypt" during Egypt's ongoing civil war.[69]

Jeremiah also used his prophecy as a (d) curse on the descendants of the Judahites who had migrated to Egypt (see Deut 28:37; Ezek 5:15). It is this curse that germinated anti-Semitism throughout the Diaspora, as Jewish talmudic tendencies caused Abraham's offspring, once destined to be a blessing to all nations, to become a curse to all nations where they migrated.

The Jews who migrated to Egypt continued to face unrest and persecution. As early as 250 BCE, we see the first strong waves of anti-Semitism against Alexandrian Jews.[70] Among them, the Egyptian priest-historian Manetho was one of the most ardent and outspoken.[71] Noted Jewish historian Aryeh Kasher observes:

> The reign of Ptolemy IV Philopater (221–205 B.C.E.) was marked by religious fanaticism and the persecution of Egyptian Jews in general and Alexandrian Jews in particular.[72]

These persecutions culminated in forced participation in the cult of Dionysis (Greek for Tammuz).[73] It was the female aspect of this cult (Isis/Astarte) that Judah's women refused to let go of when they sought Jeremiah's council (Jer 44:17–25). Now the gods they had willingly apostacized to would be a source of oppression, as they were forced to worship the very gods for which they had lusted.[74] During the Ptolemaic era, the (d) Jews of Egypt increasingly became a "reproach and an astonishment" and a curse among the other cities in the Hellenistic world due to their new wine that commingled their doctrine once more.

After Philopater compelled the Jews to be registered by ethnic origin (3 Macc 2:27–32; 4:14), he tried to annihilate them.[75] According to 3 Macabees 7, the Alexandrian Jews escaped Philopater's persecution. The king then ordered those who had transgressed the law to be slain, and each man turned against his brother (3 Macc 7:10–16).[76] By the end of Philopater's reign, Egypt's Delta region was enveloped in a civil war,[77] as Jeremiah's sword continued to follow the Egyptian Jews throughout the Ptolemaic era.

Alexandria's large Jewish community played a key role in supporting Egyptian monarchs.[78] The consequences could be brutal if the community supported a pharaoh who did not retain the throne. Such was the case when they supported Cleopatra II—only to end up on the wrong side of the monarchy. This episode resulted in persecution by Ptolemy VIII Physcon (Euergetes II) in 145 BCE.[79] The Jewish involvement in Egypt's politics resulted in several civil wars in 124, 108, and again in 88 BCE.[80] Egypt's conflict soon spread to the Egyptian vassals of Antioch and Cyrene, where Jews were specifically targeted for their support of the competing monarch.[81]

Later, the Alexandrian Jews and their Egyptian garrisons would support Roman generals to their own detriment.[82] In 38 CE, under the Egyptian prefect (governor) Aulus Avilius Flaccus, the "severest persecutions ever encountered by the Jews of Alexandria began (Philo: *In Flaccum* and *Legatio ad Gaium*)."[83] Jewish solidarity broke down as Alexandria's allegiance to Roman rulers became divided.[84] Anti-Semitism culminated in Rome's "Jewish tax," part of the Roman campaign against Jews, even if they were Roman citizens. All these events culminated in the loss of political influence, as Jews both in Egypt and around the world became the outcasts of society throughout the remaining long Diaspora.[85] Remember, both this curse in the Law (Deut 28:37) and in Jeremiah 42 occurred only because the Jews followed their teachers in adding regulations and contradicting (Deut 4:2; 12:32) YHWH's Law. Had they returned to obey the written Law, without adding their own regulations, this curse could have been averted.

Famine (b) was another aspect of Jeremiah's curse. Interestingly, many of the famines during the Ptolemaic era were not caused by the lack of rainfall but by taxes and by the government's overproduction that rendered the land unfertile (anachoresis).[86] These harsh policies resulted in famines during Philopator's reign (217 BCE) and again during Philometor's reign (165 BCE). Josephus tells us that at some point during Cleopatra's reign (*c.* 45 BCE) there was a drought and famine in Egypt significant enough to merit food distribution. Cleopatra (*Against Apion* 2.60) intentionally discriminated against the Alexandrian Jews. Regarding the pre-Christian era, noted Egyptologist Günther Hölbl observes:

> The 40s were characterized by famines in Egypt because of the low levels of the flooding of the Nile river. Already in 48 the flooding was extremely poor (Plin. Nat. V 58: only 5 cubits) and apparently none took place at all in 43 and 42 (Sen Nat. IV2.16). We know that during the Roman civil war following Ceasar's death there was widespread famines and (b, c, p. 859) plagues in Egypt. . . ."[87]

Hölbl further states that, when the famine was especially difficult, Cleopatra had to open the Crown warehouses to distribute grain to Alexandria's citizens. "Since the Jews of Alexandria had not been granted citizenship they were passed over."[88] Thus, Jeremiah's curse continued to be fulfilled in Egypt as YHWH's holocausts in Jerusalem began.

VI. ORAL WINE

A. *Moses Wrote all the Words of YHWH*

When YHWH met with Israel at Mt. Sinai, he gave his constitutional Law to Moses on two stone tablets. The information was so great that YHWH inscribed these stones on both sides (Exod 32:15). YHWH wrote every law he gave to Moses as well as the penalties for breaking those laws on these two tablets: no law was overlooked. This is why the Pentateuch calls these tablets "the Tables of Testimony" (Exod 31:18; 32:15; 34:29). Moses took the written Law YHWH had given him and wrote it in a book, which Scripture refers to as the *Law of Moses* (Josh 8:31–32; 23:6; 1 Kgs 2:3; Ezra 3:2).

> And Moses *wrote all the words of YHWH*, and rose up early in the morning, and built an altar under the hill, and twelve pillars, according to the twelve tribes of Israel. (Exod 24:4)[89]

> And *Moses wrote this law*, and delivered it to the priests the sons of Levi, which bare the ark of the covenant of YHWH, and to all the elders of Israel. (Deut 31:9)

> And it shall be on the day when you shall pass over Jordan to the land which
> YHWH your God gives you, that you shall set you up great stones, and plaster
> them with plaster: And you shall write on them *all the words of this law*, when
> you are passed over, that you may go in to the land which YHWH your God
> gives you, a land that flows with milk and honey; as YHWH God of your fathers
> has promised you. Therefore it shall be when you be gone over Jordan, that you
> shall set up these stones, which I command you this day, in mount Ebal, and
> you shall plaster them with plaster. . . . *And you shall write on the stones all
> the words of this law very plainly.* (Deut 27:2–4, 8)

Moses wrote "all the words" YHWH had given to him in the books we today recognize as
the Pentateuch. Joshua transcribed Moses' work in the Book of Deuteronomy once Israel had
passed over Jordan (Josh 8:30–32), so the entire "Law of YHWH" had been written by the time
Israel entered Canaan. The Pentateuch followed the covenant formula, consisting of ten formal
parts, most importantly: the stipulations, penalties, and sign. The Book of Leviticus (Leviticus
26) preserved the penalties for Israel's breach of the Sinai Covenant, and Deuteronomy 27–30
contained the penalties for breaching the Moab-Shechem Covenant: nothing was forgotten
or overlooked. This is why David proclaims, "The Law of YHWH is perfect" (Ps 19:7).

Many Jews living in the Second Temple Era believed that YHWH had given an Oral or
spoken law along with the written Pentateuch. They believed the Oral Law helped to explain
the written Sinai Compact and had been faithfully handed down generation after generation.
Many Jews today still uphold this belief, considering the Oral Law (or Oral Torah) to uphold
traditions in the written Law when the people, government, and Levites had failed.[90] They
see the Oral Law as eliminating ambiguity in the written text. This position, however, fails
to merit validity.

The Book of Exodus is very clear that the only words YHWH spoke to Israel were
the Ten Commandments (Exod 19:18–20:21). YHWH intended to speak his whole Law
to Israel, but her elders were afraid and requested YHWH **not** to speak to them any more
(Exod 20:19). YHWH honored this request and gave the details of his Law *only* to Moses
(Exod 20:20–22).

> And all the people saw the thunderings, and the lightnings, and the noise of
> the trumpet, and the mountain smoking: and when the people saw it, they
> removed, and stood afar off. And they said to Moses, *Speak you with us, and
> we will hear: but let not God speak with us, lest we die.* (Exod 20:18–19)
>
> These words YHWH spoke to all your assembly in the mount out of the middle
> of the fire, of the cloud, and of the thick darkness, with a great voice: and *he
> added no more.* And *he wrote them in two tables of stone, and delivered them
> to me.* (Deut 5:22)

The words that YHWH spoke to Israel's congregation were the Ten Commandments (Exod 20:1–17). During the two times when YHWH called Israel's 70 elders before him (Exod 24:1–2, 14; Num 11:16–25), he did not speak his laws, statutes, or judgments to them. The first time, the elders stood afar off to worship YHWH (Exod 24:1, 14) while he gave Moses all his Law. The second time when the nation's elders appeared before YHWH, he placed his spirit on them so that they prophesied—they did not receive the Law because YHWH had already given it through Moses (Num 11:16–25).

Exod 20:22 begins the words that YHWH spoke *only to Moses* after the prophet had ascended the mountain (Exod 20:21). If YHWH spoke his Law *only to Moses*, then the only Law that Israel's elders received comprised "all the words" (Exod 24:4) that Moses had written down from his conversation with God. Scripture is clear that YHWH did not give the nation's elders any oral law, because YHWH did not speak to them (other than the Ten Commandments written in Exodus 20), and any words that YHWH did speak to the nation, Moses wrote down. Deut 5:22 plainly states that YHWH added "no more" words to what he had spoke at Mt. Sinai. So the elders did not have any information outside of what Moses had written down and given to them.

Many accounts demonstrate that ancient Israel preserved no tradition of an Oral Law, and if anything, her Oral Law developed centuries *after the Assyrian and Babylonia Diaspora.* For instance, when Joshua—who would have known every detail of the Oral Law (if it actually existed)—reconvened a new generation, which was unadulterated by the sin in worshiping the Golden Calf, what information did Joshua tell the people regarding YHWH's Law?

> *There was not a word of all that Moses commanded*, which **Joshua read not** before all the congregation of Israel, with the women, and the little ones, and the strangers that were conversant among them. (Josh 8:35)

Any word that Moses instructed Joshua was conveyed to the Israelites through Joshua's reading it to them. In other words, Joshua read a Law that was written: there was nothing of YHWH's Law that he did not *read.* The rabbis' support of an *Oral Torah* would also infer that Joshua then destroyed the Oral Law after writing and reading it to the people, so that it simply remained an "oral tradition" (for future generations to write down after YHWH destroyed his Temple and removed the priesthood and his people to pagan lands). Yet this blatantly contradicts Deuteronomy's command to "read" (something written, not an oral tradition) the Law to Israel during the sabbatical Release Years' holy days when the covenant was renewed every seven years (Deut 31:11).

Scripture indicates that, during Israel's and Judah's many eras of apostasy, public knowledge of the Deuteronomic Law had been lost—not only had the common citizens and elders lost knowledge of the Law (and any Oral Law that allegedly existed beside it), but the king and priest whose duty it was to preserve the Law had forgotten much of what YHWH's Law said:

> It came to pass in the eighteenth year of king Josiah . . . Hilkiah the high priest said to Shaphan the scribe, *I have found the book of the law* in the house of YHWH. And Hilkiah gave the book to Shaphan, and *he read it.* . . . And Shaphan the scribe showed the king, saying, Hilkiah the priest has delivered me a book. And *Shaphan read it* before the king. And it came to pass, when the king had heard the words of the book of the law, that he rent his clothes. And the king commanded Hilkiah the priest, and Ahikam the son of Shaphan, and Achbor the son of Michaiah, and Shaphan the scribe, and Asahiah a servant of the king's, saying, Go you, inquire of YHWH for me, and for the people, and for all Judah, concerning the words of this book that is found: for great is the wrath of YHWH that is kindled against us, because *our fathers have not listened to the words of this book,* to do according to *all that which is written* concerning us. (2 Kgs 22:3, 8–13; see also Isa 29:13–18)

Had King Josiah observed an Oral Law—supposedly handed down generation after generation since Mt. Sinai—there would have been no need to rend his clothing when the Torah was rediscovered in the Temple's dilapidated facilities. Moreover, Josiah could not say that "our fathers have not listened to the word of this book" if he knew an Oral Law (unless Josiah had practiced an Oral Law that contradicted the written Law and rent his clothes after hearing how his adherence to the Oral Law departed from the Book of the law found in the Temple).

A few years later, we find that Israel's 70 elders, who were the leaders of YHWH's people, had again failed to preserve truth in their traditions. Shortly before Jerusalem succumbed to Nebuchadnezzar' armies, scribes such as Yaazaniah, the son of Shaphan, led the way in supplanting YHWH's ordained Levitical priests with non-Levitical scribes by serving and teaching in YHWH's holy Temple (Ezek 8:11). Israel's 70 elders were with the scribe Yaazaniah, performing Egyptian abominations in YHWH's Temple, so any traditions these elders preserved were not found in the instructions that YHWH had given at Mt. Sinai. What this history does show, however, is that the scribal class rose as a faction that politically opposed the Levites' authority by seeking to interpret "God's word" by the precepts of men[91] rather than humbling themselves to follow his written instructions in the Pentateuch's constitutional Law.

It is interesting that the manifestation of YHWH's spirit on Israel's elders was their ability to prophesy. This is exactly the opposite of what we find in the Great Assembly that repopulated the Promised Land at the Second Temple Remnant's return. Jewish historians acknowledge that "prophecy died out in the era of the Great Assembly."[92] If Israel's elders had been following YHWH's Law as they did at Mt. Sinai, YHWH's spirit should have remained among them. Since prophecy indeed died out during the Second Temple period, it further evidences the departure of the nation's elders from YHWH's way of life found within his written Law. YHWH's Law had promised that if people seek YHWH, they will find him (Deut 4:29). If Judah's people did not find salvation during this period it is because they were seeking to follow the traditions of men (Isa 29:13) instead of the written word of God.

B. Mishnah, Talmud, and Gemara Wine

Scholars believe the Pharisees, predecessors of the modern rabbis, rose as a political sect out of Judah's scribal class. The Pharisees gained power during the Second Temple Era, as they almost replaced the Aaronic priesthood entirely.[93] One example of the Egyptian traditions to which these scribes and elders subscribed is the Jewish belief regarding YHWH's name.

When the rebellious Jews sought to migrate to Egypt, against YHWH's command, Jeremiah issued a special curse against them.

> Moreover Jeremiah said to all the people, and to all the women, Hear the word of YHWH, all Judah that are in the land of Egypt: Thus said YHWH of hosts, the God of Israel, saying; You and your wives have both spoken with your mouths, **and fulfilled with your hand**, saying, We will surely perform our vows that we have vowed, **to burn incense to the queen of heaven**, and to pour out drink offerings to her: you will surely accomplish your vows, and surely perform your vows. Therefore hear you the word of YHWH, all Judah that dwell in the land of Egypt; Behold, I have sworn by my great name, said YHWH, **that my name shall no more be named in the mouth of any man of Judah in all the land of Egypt**, saying, The Lord YHWH lives. (Jer 44:24–26)

It is not by accident that one of the primary prohibitions of Judaism is the use of YHWH's name (see rabbinic teachings in the Talmud: *Mishnah Sotah* 7:6; *Mishnah Tamid* 7:2; *Babylonian Talmud Sanhedrin 90a*; and in the *Tosefta*).

As the women of Judah made clear, they had no intention of refraining from their idolatrous worship of Isis, the Queen of Heaven (Jer 44:15–26).

> As for the word that you have spoken to us in the name of YHWH, we will not listen to you. But we will certainly do whatsoever thing goes forth out of our own mouth, to burn incense to the queen of heaven, and to pour out drink offerings to her, as we have done, we, and our fathers, our kings, and our princes, in the cities of Judah, and in the streets of Jerusalem: for then had we plenty of victuals, and were well, and saw no evil. But since we left off to burn incense to the queen of heaven, and to pour out drink offerings to her, we have wanted all things, and have been consumed by the sword and by the famine. And when we burned incense to the queen of heaven, and poured out drink offerings to her, did we make her cakes to worship her, and pour out drink offerings to her, without our men?
>
> Then Jeremiah said to all the people, to the men, and to the women, and to all the people which had given him that answer, saying, The incense that you burned in the cities of Judah, and in the streets of Jerusalem, you, and your fathers, your kings, and your princes, and the people of the land, did not YHWH remember them, and came it not into his mind? *So that YHWH could no longer bear, because of the evil of your doings,* and because of the abominations which you have committed; therefore is your land a desolation, and an astonishment,

and a curse, without an inhabitant, as at this day. Because you have burned incense, and because you have sinned against YHWH, and have not obeyed the voice of YHWH, nor walked in his law, nor in his statutes, nor in his testimonies; therefore this evil is happened to you, as at this day. (Jer 44:16–23)

The superstitious Jewish Remnant believed that the source of all their misery was their lack of support for the Queen of Heaven (whether Ashtarte, Isis, or Ishtar).[94] They had failed to procure her favor—all the while ignoring the fact that their people had covenanted with their forefathers' God, YHWH. Their Creator had simply applied the penalties for breaching his covenant for their idolatrous disobedience, as Jeremiah points out.

In response to the Remnant's idolatry and rebellion against YHWH, Jeremiah tells them that YHWH will take away his name, which they despised through their idolatry (Jer 23:27). If they did not wish to sanctify him, to call on him, or to swear by his name, then YHWH would take his name from them so they could not profane (Isa 48:10–11, 52:5; Jer 34:16) it any longer by co-mingling it with idols or corrupt doctrinal traditions of men (Isa 29:13; see "On God's Name" at the beginning of this book).

Therefore hear you the word of YHWH, all Judah that dwell in the land of Egypt; Behold, **I have sworn by my great name, said YHWH,** *that my name shall no more be named in the mouth of any man of Judah* **in all the land of Egypt, saying, The Lord YHWH lives.** Behold, *I will watch over them for evil*, and not for good: and all the men of Judah that are in the land of Egypt shall be consumed by the sword and by the famine, until there be an end of them. (Jer 44:26–27)

How did this curse naturally affect itself? Egypt's counterpart to Canaan's Queen of heaven (Ashteroth) was known as Isis, whom the Jews were worshiping when they responded to Jeremiah in Egypt.[95] Her cult was part of the Egyptian Mysteries.[96] Yet, Isis was only one part of Egypt's great Mysteries. Her husband/son, Osiris, was equally venerated. One aspect of these cults involved the god's known and unknown names, some of which were hidden.[97] From an early date, Osiris had the epithet "he of many names."[98] The same is attested in the Amun period: "he of many names, the number of which is not known."[99] During the Greco-Roman period, Isis was still simply the "one of many names."[100]

However, not all names were of equal value or status because the Egyptians believed in a hierarchy of names.[101] In the story of *Isis and Re*, during the New Kingdom Era, we find the following mythology regarding god's divine name.

The story describes the aged sun god in graphic terms and, as his opponent, the great magician goddess Isis, who knows everything 'in the sky and on earth' except the sun god's (true) name. But even *this most secret knowledge of all* will not remain hidden from her any longer. By means of her magic arts she creates a poisonous snake whose 'fire' makes the god suffer acute agony. Only Isis the magician can release Re from his agony through her knowledge of a powerful spell against the snake bite, but she demands to know his name before she will use it, for 'a man lives if he is addressed by his name.' The sun god then enumerates a long list of epithets that are his due as creator and guarantor of the world, ending with his three chief manifestations.... But the poison remains in his body, because his true name is not any of these appellations. In his agony he finally whispers this last, *most secret name* into Isis' ear, and then the poison leaves the 'burning god,' releasing him from his pain. Isis, the cunning magician, has achieved her purpose and *learned the most secret thing of all*.[102]

There is some indication that there was a ritual prohibition in Egypt against pronouncing some divine names. In his stele from Abydos, Ramesses IV claimed, "I have not pronounced the name of Tatenen."[103] The early Pyramid Texts also support the concept of a "hidden" name of god that was too holy to be pronounced. According to the Pyramid Texts, when a deceased king appeared among the gods as the highest god, even "his mother did not know his name."[104]

During the New Kingdom and later Greco-Roman period, the fascination with a god's hidden divine name reached an apogee, as Isis and other deities were given many new, and exotic appellations.[105] This, however, does not show how this Egyptian doctrine found its way into Judaism.

The Jewish immigrants in Egypt, worshiping in the Egyptian Mysteries, caught hold of these doctrines and appropriated them for their own idolatrous, rote human commands and customs (Isa 29:13). Throughout Israel's history, she had commingled her theology with local pantheons, as is so well attested by archaeology and her prophets.[106] She did this once again, adopting Egyptian mythology regarding a god's name and applying it to Israel's God. Notice what traditional Judaism teaches regarding YHWH's name.

By the time of the Talmud, it was the custom to use substitute Names for God. Some asserted that a person who pronounces YHVH according to its letters (instead of using a substitute) has no place in the World to Come, and should be put to death (Babylonian Talmud *Sanhedrin* 90a). Instead of pronouncing the four-letter Name, we usually substitute the Name "Adonai," or simply say "Ha-Shem" (lit., The Name).[107]

Although the prohibition on pronunciation applies only to the four-letter Name, Jews customarily do not pronounce any of God's many Names except in prayer or study. The usual practice is to substitute letters or syllables, so that Adonai becomes Adoshem or Ha-Shem, Elohaynu and Elohim become Elokaynu and Elokim, etc. The word "Jehovah" comes from the fact that ancient Jewish texts used to put the vowels of the Name "Adonai" (the usual substitute for YHVH) under the consonants of YHVH to remind people not to pronounce YHVH as written.[108]

From the mishnaic period onward, the explicit name of God was never uttered except in the Temple.... But even the name uttered in the Temple during prayer was not what is known as the "explicit Name," which was known only to a select few. A certain sage who had served as a Temple priest in his youth reported that the name was uttered during the priestly blessing, but was intentionally drowned out by singing of the Levites so that even the young priests never heard it. There is therefore no known tradition (except in the Kabbalah) on ways of uttering the Divine Name. . . . Furthermore, we know that the four-letter name, despite its sanctity, was not the explicit name and that there was a twelve-letter name, a forty-two-letter name, and even one with seventy-two letters.[109]

Does this sound a little like the ideals embraced in the god Re's many hidden names? Egyptian gods, such as Osiris or Isis were known as a god of "many names," with one name being the most sacred and most hidden—so hidden that Re would endure excruciating pain before divulging his most secret name to Isis. Jewish scholar Adin Steinsaltz continues:

The Talmud explains that only those few disciples who were outstanding for their spiritual qualities and profound moral standards were taught the name by their rabbis. The mystic and esoteric world was kept hidden for several reasons, One basic reason was that it was considered that matters pertaining to the greatness of God *should be left to those worthy of studying them.* But it was also feared that unworthy use might be made of the powers a man acquired from knowing the names and the secrets according to which the world was constituted.[110]

These concepts cannot be found anywhere in the Tanakh (Old Testament). However, they are readily found in Egyptian, Babylonian, and Hellenistic theologies. In direct contrast to Judaism's theology, YHWH taught his people to use his name in daily life. As we saw in chap. 2 (p. 47), Israel often used part of YHWH's name in their children's names. The Law commanded Israel to swear by his name (Deut 6:13), which was usually carried out in the phrase "as YHWH lives" to state what one promised to do.[111] During the Second Temple Period, YHWH did not rescind or change his covenantal Law.

Jeremiah, recognizing that the people of his day had already departed from YHWH's Law to follow the scribal class[112] (over the Levites or Torah), established a test for the Second Temple Remnant once they were restored to the Promised Land:

And it shall come to pass, *after that I have plucked them out I will return,* and have compassion on them, and will bring them again, every man to his heritage, and every man to his land. And it shall come to pass, **if they will diligently learn the ways of my people, to swear by my name, YHWH lives;** as they taught my people to swear by Baal; then shall they be built in the midst of my people. But if they will not obey, **I will utterly pluck up and destroy that nation,** said YHWH. (Jer 12:15–17)[113]

The test during the Second Temple Era was whether or not YHWH's people trusted him enough to obey his command to learn his ways, which culminated in swearing in YHWH's name. If the Remnant did not swear by using the Creator's name, then YHWH would once more drive Abraham and Isaac's descendants from the Promised Land, dividing them, as their covenant sacrifice symbolized, destroying them as a nation before him. Jeremiah's second prophecy (Jeremiah 44) prophesied that the Egyptian Jews would never fulfill this command because they would rebel against YHWH once more and would eventually forsake using YHWH's name altogether.

C. "You Shall Not Add to My Law"

Another text that demonstrates that the Jews did not have an Oral Law is Nehemiah's statement that Ezra and the Levites *read* the Law of Moses to the people, causing them "to understand the Law" (Neh 8:7–9). Nehemiah continues by saying that Ezra and the priests gave them the "sense" by explaining what had been read to them. If the Jews had accurately preserved an Oral Law from Mt. Sinai, they would have already understood the reading and had no need for Ezra and the priests to explain the Law to them. Furthermore, Nehemiah states that the people were ignorant of the fact that the day on which the Law had been read to them was a holy day (Neh 8:8–18).

The context implies that the people's gross idolatries had caused them to forget the holy days prescribed in YHWH's Law (Jer 23:27) to such an extent that they were not aware that the day on which Ezra read the Law was not only a holy day, but was also in a Release Year (Deut 31:10–13; see Appendix A: Table 9.50/9, pp. 894–95). If oral tradition failed to retain the sense and understanding of the Law of Moses and the holy days—the heart of YHWH's way of life—what did the Talmud and Mishna preserve other than the traditions of men (Isa 29:13)?

One of the commands that YHWH gave Moses forbade anyone to add to the Law that he had commanded Moses to write.

> You shall not add to the word which I command you, neither shall you diminish anything from it, that you may keep the commandments of the YHWH your God which I command you. (Deut 4:2; see also 12:32)

This command prohibited anyone or any assembly of elders from adding to YHWH's holy, perfect constitutional Law. Moses had written all of YHWH's commands, which Joshua had read to the entire congregation of Israel. If any later generation would claim to have received YHWH's word outside his written Law, they would—instead of teaching Torah—be teaching the oppressive philosophies and doctrines of men (Isa 29:13–16).

Despite Deuteronomy's injunction against adding to the Law, the Second Temple Remnant developed errant doctrines and precepts. The only part of the Law that Israel's forefathers' heard YHWH speak, was the Ten Commandments. Moses wrote "all" the remaining words that YHWH had spoken to him in the Law of Moses, and YHWH forbade anyone to add to this Law. However, the Second Temple Remnant desired to follow the unlawful oral traditions over YHWH's command, which forbade additions to his Law. So YHWH shrugged.

He forsook the Second Temple Remnant and delivered her over to delusion and desolation. She had recovenanted with her Maker during Ezra's administration but then breached her contract. So YHWH "shook her out" (Neh 5:13), emptying all her sins on a wicked generation during his judgment era. She would eagerly drink the gall and wormwood found in Deuteronomy's dreaded curse, as Jerusalem became a source of wine and spiritual drunkenness from which all nations would drink and corrupt themselves as Jerusalem's curse fell on nations that desired to acquire her land.

VII. THE LONG DAY OF YHWH

Although the Day of YHWH began when the cultic 7 Times (350 years ended) ended, the Creator's judgment would extend far beyond Antiochus Epiphanes reign of terror. Scripture defines a prophetic day as a thousand years, "For a thousand years in your sight are but as yesterday when it is past, and as a watch in the night" (Ps 90:4). Moses, who authored this psalm, describes the time from the Creator's infinite perspective. One thousand years are simply like yesterday: one day for YHWH compares to 1,000 years for humanity.[114] If one of YHWH's days equals 1,000 years on earth, this text implies that YHWH's long Judgment Day would extend for at least one millennium.

The prophets provide further understanding by indicating that YHWH would repay double for all of Israel's sins with a millennial judgment that would not last for one prophetic day, but for two:

> For my eyes are on all their ways: they are not hid from my face, neither is their iniquity hid from mine eyes. And first **I will recompense their iniquity and their sin double**; because they have defiled my land, they have filled my inheritance with the carcasses of their detestable and abominable things. (Jer 16:17–18)

> neither have I desired the woeful day; you know: that which came out of my lips was right before you. Be not a terror to me: you are my hope in the day of evil. Let them be confounded that persecute me, but let not me be confounded: let them be dismayed, but let not me be dismayed: **bring on them the day of evil, and destroy them with double destruction**. (Jer 17:16–19)

Jeremiah indicates that the woeful day of YHWH would continue not for one, but for two days, as YHWH tried humanity to make him into a new creation.[115] Jeremiah's prophecy parallels the molten sea's 2,000 baths, which ordained 2,000 years for Israel's Diaspora, to cleanse her from her desire to do wickedly.[116] If the Day of YHWH began in 165 BCE, then his persecution against Israel's rebellion would have continued until about 1835 CE. This means that the dispersed Children of Israel have only very recently emerged from the evil and dreaded Day of Judgment. (This is probably one reason that many Protestant back-to-Torah movements began in the early to mid 1800s).

Zechariah paints the most accurate description of the events that occured during the long Day of YHWH. He prophesies that the Creator would strengthen and employ the nations arising out of Greece to render his judgment on Israel's descendants during his long Judgment Day, until the final latter days, when the Day of YHWH has been fulfilled and the Creator will finally arise for Israel's salvation:

> As for you also, by the blood of your covenant I have sent forth your prisoners out of the pit wherein is no water. Turn you to the strong hold, you prisoners of hope: even today do I declare that *I will render **double** to you*; When I have bent Judah for me, filled the bow with Ephraim, *and raised up your sons, O Zion, against your sons, O Greece, and made you as the sword of a mighty man*. And YHWH shall be seen over them, and his arrow shall go forth as the lightning: and YHWH GOD shall blow the trumpet, and shall go with whirl-winds of the south. YHWH of hosts shall defend them; and they shall devour, and subdue with sling stones; and they shall drink, and make a noise as through wine; and they shall be filled like bowls, and as the corners of the altar. And YHWH their God shall save them in that day as the flock of his people: for they shall be as the stones of a crown, lifted up as an ensign on his land. For how great is his goodness, and how great is his beauty! corn shall make the young men cheerful, and new wine the maids. (Zech 9:11–17)

Zechariah's prophecy parallels that of Isaiah, who not only foretold Israel's double judgment but also Israel's double latter-day blessing:

> Speak you comfortably to Jerusalem, and cry to her, that her warfare is accomplished, that her iniquity is pardoned: *for she has received of YHWH's hand double for all her sins*. (Isa 40:2)

> For your shame you shall have double; and for confusion they shall rejoice in their portion: therefore in their land *they shall possess the double*: everlasting joy shall be to them. (Isa 61:7)

Isaiah's prophecy parallels Balaam's prophetic blessing, which he ordained for Israel shortly before she entered the Promised Land (Numbers 23–24). YHWH would make an example of Israel's rebellion, doubly avenging all her sins before the eyes of the nations of the earth. Her public example would, in the latter days, cause other nations to fear YHWH and to believe the unchanging words of his covenant. When Israel had finally become righteous and obedient to his covenant, YHWH would bestow his double blessing, granting her never-ending joy and a sure covenant of peace, which naturally resulted from observing "all the words of the covenant to do them" (Deut 29:9).

There was a blessing in YHWH's judgment. Not only would YHWH repay his righteous nation with a double latter-day blessing, but she would not even remember YHWH's former judgment. Her intoxicated state would effect a deep sleep, as though in a sweet dream. She would not see YHWH's judgments or understand her rebellion until he led her captivity

captive, calling her from all nations of the earth, to restore his constitutional covenants with
Abraham's seed.

The fierce anger of YHWH shall not return, until he has done it, and until he
has performed the intents of his heart: *in the latter days you shall consider it.
At the same time*, says YHWH, will I be the God of all the families of Israel,
and they shall be my people. (Jer 30:24–31:1; see also Isa 51:9, 17 and Jer 31:26)

YHWH has told us that we would not acknowledge that his fierce anger had been quenched
(fulfilled) until long after it had been executed. Israel's punishment is past! When Israel sees
that the Day of YHWH has been fulfilled—at the "same time"—he will return to be Israel's
God and to restore his covenants with Ephraim and Judah.

At the same time, says YHWH, will I be the God of all the families of Israel, and
they shall be my people. Thus says YHWH, The people who survived the sword
found grace in the wilderness; even Israel, when I went to give him rest. . . . Yes,
I have loved you with an everlasting love: therefore with lovingkindness have I
drawn you. Again I will build you, and you shall be built, O virgin of Israel: you
shall again be adorned with your timbrels, and shall go forth in the dances of
them that make merry. You shall yet plant vines on the *mountains of Samaria*:
the planters shall plant, and shall eat them as common things. For there shall
be a day, that the watchmen on *mount Ephraim* shall cry, Arise, and let us go
up to Zion to YHWH our God. (Jer 31:3–6)

This specific prophecy foretells Israel's salvation! When Israel sees that her judgment is past,
YHWH will again quickly become Israel's only God. He will pour out his lovingkindness on
the nation and restore the Promised-Land Covenant with them. This alludes to the latter-
day exodus, in which YHWH will soon restore—not just Judah, but also Ephraim to the
Promised Land—a people who will literally rise up in peace to go to worship at Mt. Zion.

Set up (a) signposts, make yourself landmarks: set your heart toward the highway, even the way which you went: turn again, O virgin of Israel, turn again
to these your cities. How long will you go about, O you backsliding daughter?
for YHWH has created a new thing in the earth, (b) A woman shall protect
a man. Thus says YHWH of hosts, the God of Israel; Yet again they shall use
this speech in the land of Judah and in its cities, when I shall bring again their
(c) captivity; YHWH bless you, O home of justice, and mountain of holiness.
And there shall dwell in Judah itself, and in all its cities together, farmers, and
they that go forth with flocks. For I have fully satisfied the weary soul, and I
have replenished every sorrowful soul. *Upon this I awaked, and beheld; and
my sleep was sweet to me.* Behold, the days come, says YHWH, that I will sow
the House of Israel and the House of Judah with the seed of man, and with the

seed of beast. And it shall come to pass, that as I have watched over them, to pluck up, and to break down, and to throw down, and to destroy, and to afflict; *so will I watch over them, to build, and to plant*, says YHWH. In those days they shall say no more, The fathers have eaten a sour grape, and the children's teeth are set on edge. But everyone shall die for his own iniquity: every man that eats the sour grape, his teeth shall be set on edge. (Jer 31:21–30)

The setting of this prophecy is at the dawn of salvation, as Israel's righteous shepherds issue the call to return to YHWH alone. Although she has rebelled, YHWH still desires to be her God. Jeremiah shows that the curse against the woman in Eden (Gen 3:16) has been fulfilled. Israel has prevailed; she has led her captivity captive (Judg 5:12). YHWH will create a highway to restore his people and renew the Promised-Land Covenant with them. Their hearts will be fulfilled with every joy. Then YHWH will awake from hiding his face (as though from slumber) to restore peace and unity among Israel and all nations. In these latter days, people will finally realize that they were punished for their own sins and no other: YHWH's controversy will be resolved!

Notice, however, that YHWH's slumber was sweet, as though he did not remember the former times of trouble Israel had brought to him. YHWH was not the only one to have slept. The "after effects" of the wine Israel imbibed led to a fitful sleep. She would not remember YHWH or see his judgments until all the curses in the Testimonial Law had been fulfilled.

Come, and let us return to YHWH: for he has torn, and he will heal us; he has smitten, and he will bind us up. *After two days will he revive us: in the third day he will raise us up*, and we shall live in his sight. . . . For I desired mercy, and not sacrifice; and the knowledge of God more than burnt offerings. (Hos 6:1–2, 6)

According to the chronology established by the Testimonial Law, we are on the dawn of the third day, when YHWH's salvation will be seen by all nations of the earth. Israel was cast off the land of Israel over 2,500 years ago. The long 2,000-Day of YHWH has passed. We are the generation that will finally see the complete extent to which YHWH desires obedience and mercy more than *any* sacrifice. If we do finally comprehend these ideas, if we are finally willing to do what is right in his sight, then the question remains: why does his salvation delay?

Throughout this trial, I have tried to give YHWH the benefit of the doubt whenever there was a question. We have seen so many promises of victory, almost touched the archaeological artifacts, and heard scientific evidence that confirms that YHWH's word is real; it seems almost certain that this case has been won. This judgment would be too hasty. There are still many obstacles for us to face before YHWH can be exonerated as a righteous God. The dreaded *Day of YHWH* ended a little over one and a half centuries ago (see p. 870). The Testimonial Law prophesied, that once Deuteronomy's curses had been fulfilled, YHWH would remember his covenants and restore Israel to the Promised Land, never to be removed again. Why has he waited so long? Has YHWH been righteous to cast off Abraham's descendants for 2,000 years?

Ephraim's history, as we will see, is intricately entwined with the doctrine of the New Testament. How does this Testimony fit into YHWH's redemption? What about Christianity's vastly differing interpretations of Scripture? Is YHWH righteous to allow religion to divide families and nations in our modern era? Can YHWH be exonerated in the case of *Israel vs. YHWH*? Or, will we yet find iniquity in him? We will find that some of the most challenging obstacles to YHWH's exoneration as a righteous God lie within the pages of the New Testament. It is here we will find that evidence exists for many prophecies' being fulfilled in unexpected ways and the questions regarding such a long Diaspora answered. The New Testament is where YHWH's righteousness will finally be revealed!

Acknowledgements

Many thanks to those who have encouraged this project over the years. My family has been incredibly supportive and understanding. It is not easy for children when Mom always has her nose in a book or says, "wait a minute, I need to write this down," when they have something important to share with her (nor is it any less difficult for a spouse). I would like to offer a special tribute to the incredible generous support my family has offered that has made it possible for this book come to life.

To Jack, for the support and encouragement you provided over the last fourteen years of research. For supporting this project in every way and for the many criticisms you offered along the way. To Ariyl, who has been a well-spring of joy and patient, but realistic encouragement: thank you for patiently stepping in so I could spend time researching and writing. I am honored to have you as my daughter. To Elisha, who knew exactly when I needed a glass of water, salad, chocolate, or other treat during those long days: thank you for stepping in so I could spend time researching and writing. I love you and appreciate your quest for truth. To Luke, who has learned to be extremely capable and self-reliant: thank you for your sense of humor and work-ethic that helped to ensure that I had the time to complete this project. To Brit, for whom this project was especially difficult: may the years spent on this project be returned to you in blessing that surpasses the years spent in writing and researching it. I appreciate your kindness and thoughtfulness and I love you. To Ethan, who has been understanding when Mom only had "a few more pages to go:" thank you for the good example you set for your brother, for being patiently kind, for your joy, love of learning, and for all those cuddles. I love your laughter and truthfulness. To Zack, who has generously shared "his mommy time" with this project: thank you for happy dances, funny faces, the love you have of learning and for a sweet desire to do right. I love spending time with you. I am so very proud of who each of you has become over the last fourteen years.

I would also like to thank Dr. Leviton, Jack, Steve, and Paul for the sharp editing "eye" they so graciously contributed to this project. Thanks to Chelle and Briann for putting so many of my ideas into tangible illustrations. Thanks to Phil and Martha for their support. Thanks to Yair for photographs. And, a special thanks to Steve M. for his excellent cartographic expertise and to Jennifer H. for the long late-night hours of bringing those ideas to life, even at the last minute. Thanks to countless others who have encouraged this project along the way.

Appendices

Appendix A: Table 9.50 Macro Synchronized Chronology of Israel and the Near East (p. 1)

BCE	Text	United Kingdom of Israel		Tyre	Egypt	Assyria	Babylon
		David	Ishbosheth				
1025	Continues Priestly/postdating reckoning						1033–1025: Nabu-shum-libur
1024						c.1028–987: Ashur-rabi II	Aramean invasion (should be dated later)
1023n	2 Sam 2:10–11, 5:4–5	1	1 (6 m)		1039–993: Psusennes I		1025–1008: Simbar-shipak (assasinated)
1022	2 Sam 5:5	2	2				
1021		3					
1020	2 Sam 2–3:10	4	civil war				
1019	Joab kills Abner?	5					
1018		6					
1017	2 Sam 5:1–5	7t	United Kingdom				
1016t	David installed over United Israel	8					
1015	2 Sam 5:9?	9					
1014		10					
1013	Ps 60:1 (superscription)?	11					
1013		12		Hiram			
1011	2 Sam 5:11; 1 Chr 14:1, 15:1?—David builds palaces	13		1			
1010		14		2			
1009	1 Chr 13; 2 Sam 6:1–11	15		3			1008: Ea-mukin-zeri (Usurper)
1008	$10^{th}/1^{st}$ Jubilee—Ark moved to Jerusalem	16		4			1008–1004: Kashshu-nadin-ahi
1007	2 Samuel 6:12–7; 1 Chr 15–17	17		5			
1006		18		6			
1005		19		7			
1004		20		8			1004–987: Eulma-shakin-shumi
1003		21		9			
1002		22		10			
1001		23		11			
1000	Bathsheba?	24		12			
999	Solomon born?	25		13			
998		26		14			
997		27		15			
996		28		16			
995		29		17			
994		30		18			
993		31		19	993–984: Amenemope		

Year	Scripture / Event	Reign	Solomon		Egypt	Assyria	Babylon
992		32		20			
991		33		21			
990		34		22			
989		35		23			
988		36		24			
987		37		25		c. 987–982: Ashur-resh-ishi II	987–985: Ninurta-kudurri-usur I
986		38		26			
985		39		27			985–979: Mar-biti-apla-usur
984		40		28	984–978: Osorkon the Elder		
983	Shift to Monarchy/antedating reckoning		Solomon 1t	29			
982			2	30		c. 982–950: Tiglath-pileser II	
981			3	31			
980	Temple construction begun		_4_	32			
979			5	33			979–943: Nabu-mukin-apli
978			6	34			
977			7	35			
976			8	36			
975			9	37			
974	1 Kgs 6:38		10	38			
973	1 Kgs 8:2—Temple construction completed, Sukkot observed		_11_	39			
972			12	40			
971	1 Kgs 7:1—Finished palace		13	41			
970			14	42			
969			15	43			
968			16	44			
967			17	45			
966			18	46			
965			19	47			
964			20	48			
963			21	49			
962			22				

LEGEND

	= Release year		= Jubilee	Year Underlined = Year specifically mentioned in Scripture	Ital. = accession year	H.P. = High Priest

Appendix A: Table 9.50 Macro Synchronized Chronology of Israel and the Near East (p. 2)

BCE	Year	Text	Judah	Israel	Edom/Damascus	Egypt	Assyria	Babylon	7 Times
961			Solomon		Hadad				
960			24						
959			25			959–945: Psusennes II			
958		11th/2nd Jubilee—Similar to the Judges Era,	26						
957		Solomon is considered to have	27						
956		forsaken YHWH after Jubilee missed	28						
955			29						
954		1 Kgs 11:14 –25?	30						
953			31						
952			32						
951			33						
950		1 Kgs 11:28–31—Ahijah the Shilonite's prophecy?	34				950–935: Ashur-Dan II		
949			35						
948			36						
947		1 Kgs 11:40—Jeroboam flees to Shoshenq	37						
946			38			946–924: Shoshenq I			
945			39			1			
944	1	1st 7 Times begins— Kgs 11:29–40; 2 Chr 10:15	Rehoboam 1t	Jeroboam I 1n		2		1st 7 Times begins—Lev 26:16-17	0
943	2	Gen 49:10—fulfilled, Tribes split	2	2		3		943: Ninurta-kudurri-usur II	70
942	3		3	3		4		943–920: Mar-biti-ahhe-iddina	69
941	4		4	4		5			68
940	5	1 Kgs 14:25; 2 Chr 12:2	5	5		6			67
939	6		6	6		7—Shoshenq (Biblical: Shishak) invades Judah			66
938	7		7	7		8			65
937	8		8	8	?Hezion	9			64
936	9		9	9		10			63
935	10		10	10		11			62
934	11		11	11		12			61
933	12		12	12		13			60
932	13		13	13		14			59
931	14		14	14		15			58
930	15		15	15		16			57
929	16		16	16		17			56
						18			

Year	#	Scripture	Judah (Abijam / Asa)	Israel (Jeroboam / Zimri·Tibni·Omri)	Israel (Nadab / Baasha / Elah)	Aram	Egypt	Assyria	Babylon	#
928	17		Abijam 1	17				19		55
927	18	1 Kgs 15:1–2	2	18				20 — 927–906: Adad-nirari II		54
926	19		3	19				21 — Builds Temple commemorating victory over Judah		53
925	20	1 Kgs 15:9–10	Asa 1t	20				22		52
924	21	1 Kgs 15:25	2t	21	Nadab 1n		924–889: Osorkon I			51
923	22	1 Kgs 15:28, 33	3t	22n	Nadab 2					50
922	23		4		Baasha 1n					49
921	24	1 Kgs 15:18	5		2	?Tabrimon				48
920	25		6		3				920–900: Shamash-mudammiq	47
919	26		7		4					46
918	27		8		5					45
917	28		9		6					44
916	29		10		7	Ben-Hadad I				43
915	30	1 Kgs 15:16–20	11		8					42
914	31		12		9					41
913	32		13		10					40
912	33	2 Chr 14:8:15	14		11		"Zerah the Nubian"			39
911	34	2 Chr 15:10 — Celebrated Shavout in 3rd month	15		12					38
910	35		16		13					37
909	36	Recovenanted—2 Chr 15:12–15; 1 Kgs 15:11–14	17		14					36
908	37	12th/2nd Jubilee	18		15					35
907	38		19		16					34
906	39		20		17			906–899: Tukulti-Ninurta II		33
905	40		21		18					32
904	41		22		19					31
903	42		23		20					30
902	43		24	Zimri /	21					29
901	44		25	Tibri /	22					28
900	45	1 Kgs 16:8	26	Omri 1	23				900–888: Nabu-shuma-ukin I	27
899	46	1 Kgs 16:10, 15, 16–23	27	2	24			899–874: Ashure-nasir-pal II — 1		26
898	47		28	3	Elah 1			2		25
897	48		29		2			3		24

LEGEND   [shaded] = Release year   [shaded box] = Jubilee   Year Underlined = Year specifically mentioned in Scripture   *Ital.* = accession year   H.P. = High Priest

Appendix A: Table 9.50   Macro Synchronized Chronology of Israel and the Near East (p. 3)

BCE	Year	Text	Judah	Israel	Assyria	Egypt	Babylon	7 Times
896	49		30		4			23
895	50		31t		5			22
894	51	1 Kgs 16:23	32		6n			21
893	52		33		7			20
892	53		34		8			19
891	54		35	Ahab	9			18
890	55	(Omri/Ahab co-regency)	36	1	10			17
889	56		37	2	11			16
888	57	1 Kgs 16:29	38 (uncounted)	3n (1)	12	889–874: Takelot I	888–855: Nabu-apla-iddini	15
887	58		co-regency	4 (2)	13			14
886	59		Jehoshephat	5 (3)	14			13
885	60	2 Chr 20:31; 1 Kgs 22:41—This was Ahab's 4th official	41	6 (4)	15			12
884	61	year after his father's death	1t	7	16			11
883	62		2	8	17			10
882	63		3	9	18			9
881	64		4	10	19			8
880	65		5	11	20			7
879	66		6	12	21			6
878	67	1 Kgs 20—Ahab wars with Ben-Hadad	7	13	22			5
877	68	1 Kgs 20:32–34—Ahab allies with Ben-Hadad (Damascus)	8	14	23			4
876	69		9	15	24			3
875	70	1 Kgs 21—Ahab steals Naboth's vineyard?	10	16	Shalmaneser III	874–850: Osorkon II		2
874	71	1st 7 Times ends	11	17	1		1st 7 Times ends	1
873	72		12	18	2			70
872	73		13	19	3			69
871	74		14	20	4			68
870	75		15	21	5			67
869	76	1 Kgs 22:51	16	22 / Ahaziah 1n	6—Shalmaneser confronts Ahab in battle (ANET, 279)/Battle of Qarqar			66
868	77	2 Kgs 3:1; 1 Kgs 22:47—No king in Edom, only a deputy	17	Ahaziah 2 / Joram 1n	7			65
867	78	2 Kgs 3:4–5—Mesha rebels	18	2	8			64
866	79		19	3	9			63
865	80	2 Kgs 8:13–15—Hazael (Damascus)	Jehoram	4	10			62
864	81	2 Kgs 8:16–17; 2 Chr 21:5	1t	5	11			61

Year	#	Scripture	Judah	Israel (Joram)	Jehu	Assyria	Egypt	Babylon	H.P.
863	82	2 Kgs 1:17—error	23 · 2	6		12			60
862	83		24 · 3	7		13			59
861	84	2 Chr 21:4—Jehoram kills royal brothers	25 · 4	8		14			58
860	85	13th/14th Jubilee—2 Kgs 9:29	5	9		15			57
859	86		6	10		16			56
858	87		7	11n		17			55
857	88	2 Kgs 8:25–26, 10:36; 2 Chr 22:2–12	8 · Ahaziah 1t	12	Jehu 1n	18—Shalmaneser receives tribute from Jehu (ANET, 281)			54
856	89	2 Chr 22:12, 23:1	Athaliah 1		2	19			53
855	90		2		3	20		855–819: Marduk-zakir-shum I	52
854	91		3		4	21			51
853	92		4		5	22			50
852	93		5		6	23			49
851	94	2 Kgs 11:3–4, 21; 12:1; 2 Chr 24:1	6 · Joash 1t		7	24			48
850	95		7 · Joash 2		8	25	850–825: Takelot II		47
849	96		Joash 3		9	26			46
848	97		4		10	27			45
847	98		5		11	28			44
846	99		6		12	29			43
845	100		7		13	30			42
844	101		8		14	31			41
843	102		9		15	32			40
842	103		10		16	33			39
841	104		11		17	34			38
840	105		12		18	Shamshi-Adad V · 1			37
839	106		13		19	2			36
838	107		14		20	3			35
837	108		15		21	4			34
836	109		16		22	5			33
835	110		17		23	6			32
834	111		18		24	7			31
833	112		19		25	8			32
832	113		20		26	9			33

LEGEND

	= Release year	Year Underlined = Year specifically mentioned in Scripture	Ital. = accession year	H.P. = High Priest
	= Jubilee			

Appendix A: Table 9.50 Macro Synchronized Chronology of Israel and the Near East (p. 4)

BCE	Year	Text	Judah	Israel	Assyria	Egypt	Babylon	7 Times
831	114		21	27	10			28
830	115		22	28 (co-regency)	11			27
829	116	2 Kgs 13:1	23t	Jehoahaz / 2n	12			26
828	117		24	3	Adad-nirari III / 1			25
827	118		25	4	2			24
826	119		26	5	3			23
825	120		27	6	4	825–773: Shoshonq III		22
824	121		28	7	5			21
823	122		29	8	6			20
822	123		30	9	7			19
821	124		31	10	8			18
820	125		32	11	9			17
819	126		33	12	10		819–813: Marduk-balassu-iqbi	16
818	127		34	13	11			15
817	128		35	14	12			14
816	129		36	15	13			13
815	130	2 Kgs 13:10	37	Jehoash / 1n	14			12
814	131	2 Kgs 14:1–2, 20; 2 Chr 25:1	38; Amaziah 1t	2	15			11
813	132	(Judah co-regency or coup)	39; 2	3	16		813–811: Baba-aha-iddina	10
812	133	2 Kgs 13:13, 22—Hazeal (King of Edom)	40; 3	4	17			9
811	134		4	5	18			8
810	135		5	6	19			7
809	136		6	7	20			6
808	137	14th/5th Jubilee	7	8	21			5
807	138		8	9	22			4
806	139		9	10	23			3
805	140		10	11	24			2
804	141	2nd 7 Times ends	11	12	25		2nd 7 Times ends	1
803	142		12	13	26			70
802	143		13	14	27			69
801	144		14	15				68
800	145	2 Kgs 14:17; 14:23; 2 Chr 25:15–27—War with Joash	15t; (1)	16	Shalmaneser IV / 1		800–790: Ninurta-apla-X	67
799	146		16; (2)	Jeroboam II / 1n				66

BC	No.	Scripture / Notes	(col)	(col)	(col)	Azariah (Uzziah)	Assyria	Egypt & Babylon	No.
798	147	2 Kgs 14:21–22; 2 Chr 15:27 —coup	17	(3)	2		2		65
797	148	Azariah crowned in Elah (not Jerusalem)	18	(4)	3	Azariah (Uzziah)	3		64
796	149	2 Kgs 15:2; 2 Chr 26:1–3	19	(5)	4	1a	4		63
795	150		20	(6)	5	2	5		62
794	151		21	(7)	6	3	6		61
793	152		22	(8)	7	4	7		60
792	153		23	(9)	8	5	8		59
791	154		24	(10)	9	6	9		58
790	155		25	(11)	10	7	Ashur-Dan III	790–780: Marduk-bel-zeri	57
789	156		26	(12)	11	8	1		56
788	157		27	(13)	12	9	2		55
787	158		28	(14)	13	10	3	787–757: Osorkon III/Takelot III	54
786	159	2 Kgs 14:17–15yrs; 2 Chr 25:1	29	(15)	14	11	4		53
785	160				15	12	5		52
784	161				16	13	6		51
783	162				17	14	7		50
782	163				18	15	8		49
781	164				19	16	9		48
780	165				20	17	10	780–769: Marduk-apla-usur	47
779	166				21	18	11		46
778	167				22	19	12		45
777	168				23	20	13		44
776	169				24	21	14		43
775	170				25	22	15		42
774	171				26	23	16		41
773	172	2 Kgs 15:1 —error			27	24	17	773–767: Pami	40
772	173	If Jeroboam reigned 41 yrs. and Uzziah			28	25	Ashur-niari V		39
771	174	reigned 52 yrs., this would make Jeroboam's			29	26	1		38
770	175	son Zechariah ascending Samaria's throne			30	27	2		37
769	176	in Uzziah's 14th yr., not his 38th			31	28	3		36
768	177				32	29	4		35
767	178				33	30	5	767–730: Shoshenq V	34

LEGEND   ▓ = Jubilee   Year Underlined = Year specifically mentioned in Scripture   *Ital.* = accession year   ▒ = Release year   H.P. = High Priest

Appendix A: Table 9.50 Macro Synchronized Chronology of Israel and the Near East (p. 5)

BCE	Year	Text	Judah	Israel	Assyria	Egypt	Babylon	7 Times
766	179		31	34	6			33
765	180		32	35	7			32
764	181		33	36	8			31
763	182		34	37	9			30
762	183		35	38	10 Tiglath-Pileser II			29
761	184		36	39	1		761–748: Nabu-shuma-ishkun	28
760	185	(shift to postdating reckoning)	37	40	2			27
759	186	2 Kgs 15:8	38t	Zechariah	3—Tribute from Azariah, king of Judah (L 1:274)			26
758	187	15th/6th Jubilee; 2 Kgs 15:13, 17	39t	6m	4			25
757	188		40	Shallum/Menahem In	5—Tiglath-Pileser receives tribute from Menahem, installs him as King of Israel (ANET, 283)	757–754: Rudamon		24
756	189		41	2	6—Pul invades Israel (2Kgs 15:19, 20)			23
755	190	2 Kgs 15:5—Jotham co-ruled because Uzziah	42 (unreckoned	3	7			22
754	191	contracted leprosy	43 co-regency)	4	8	754–715: Iuput		21
753	192	2 Kgs 15:19—Tiglath Pileser	44	5	9—Rezin mentioned (L 2:777)			20
752	193		45	6	10			19
751	194		46	7	11			18
750	195		47	8	12			17
749	196		48	9	13			16
748	197		49	Pekahiah	14		748–734: Nabu-nasir (Assyria conquers Babylon under Tiglath-Pilesser III)	15
747	198	2 Kgs 15:23	50	1	15	747–716: Piankhi (Piyi)		14
746	199		51	2	16			13
745	200	2 Kgs 15:27 Isaiah 6—Noonday Judgment	52 Jothom	Pekah 1	17—Tiglath-Pilesser deports Naphtali (2 Kgs 15:29)		Isaiah 6—Noonday Judgment	12
744	201	2 Kgs 15:32–33; 2 Ch 27:1 (Switch to Priestly reckoning)	1t	2	18—Naphtali deported (L 1:292)			11
743	202		2	3	19 (1)—Conquers Babylon			10
742	203		3	4	20 (2)			9
741	204		4	5	21 (3)			8
740	205		5	6	22 (4)			7
739	206		6	7	23 (5)			6
738	207		7	8	24 (6)			5
737	208		Ahaz 8	9	25 (7)			4
736	209		9	10	26 (8)			3
735	210		10	11	27 (9)—Rezin mentioned (L 2:777)			2
734	211	3rd 7 Times ends	11	12	28 (10)		3rd 7 Times ends	1

BC	No.	Scripture / Notes			Israel (Hoshea)		Judah (Hezekiah)	Assyria — regnal years & events	Egypt	Babylonia / Assyria	No.
733	212		12	13				29 (11)—Tribute to Tiglath-Pileser		734–732: Nabu-nadin-zeri	70
732	213		13	14				30 (12)			69
731	214		14	15				31 (13)			68
730	215		15	16				32 (14)	730–715: Osorkon IV		67
729	216	2 Kgs 16:1–2; 2 Chr 27:1; 28:1	16	17n		4		33 (15)		Merodach-baladan before Tiglath's yr. 17 (L:285)	66
728	217	Isa 7:1–12–65 yrs. until Ephraim is not a people	17	18		5		34 (16)			65
727	218	Isa 7:1–7—Syria cannot prevail	18	19		6		35 (17)	727–720: Tefnakht		64
726	219	Syria incorporated into Assyrian Empire	19	20	Hoshea	7		36 (18)			63
725	220	2 Kgs 17:1; 2 Kgs 15:30—scribal error	20		1	8		37 (19)—Installs Hoshea (L:293)			62
724	221				2	9t		38 (20)			61
723	222	2 Kgs 16—conspiracy against Ahaz?			3n	10	Hezekiah	Shalmaneser V — 1			60
722	223	2 Kgs 18:1			4	11	1t	2			59
721	224				5	12	2	3	720–715: Bakenrenef (Bochoris)	721–710: Marduk-apla-iddini II	58
720	225				6	13	3	4 — Sargon II			57
719	226	2 Kgs 18:9—Samaria seiged			7	14	4	5			56
718	227				8	15	5	1—Deports Samaria			55
717	228	2 Kgs 18:9—Samaria taken			9	16	6	2—Deports Syrian rebels (L 2:3)			54
716	229	Merodachbaladan of Babylon ruled for 12 yrs.			No more kings	17	7	3	716–702: Shabaka		53
715	230	Before Sargon's 15th yr. (Luckenbill 2:2, 33)					8	4			52
714	231						9	5			51
713	232						10	6			50
712	233						11	7			49
711	234						12	8—War against Babylon-Merodach baladan	Shebitku (Tang I Var)	Merodach-baladan of Babylon (L 2.2, 33)	48
710	235						13	9—Ashdod captured (L 2:31; ANET 286) Sennacherib			47
709	236	49th Release; 2 Kgs 18:13, 2 Chr 32:1–23—Sennacherib invades Judah					14	10			46
708	237	16th/17th, 50th Jubilee—2 Kgs 19:29; Isa 37:30; 2 Kgs 20:6					15	11—Tartan installed; Isaiah 20-Ashdod (2 Kgs 18:21, 24) Based on Taylor Prism—(2)	Battle of Eltekeh?		45
707	238	2 Kgs 20:12—Merodach-baladan sends letters to Hezekiah					16	12 (3)			44
706	239						17	13 (4)			43
705	240						18	14—Before yr. 15, Sibe, turtan of Egypt (L 2:26) 1/(5)			42
704	241						19	15—Against Egypt (Tang-i-Var) 2/(6)			41
703	242						20	16 3/(7)			40
702	243						21	17 4/(8)	702–690: Shebitku	702–700: Bel-ibni	39

Sennacherib count (continued): 5, 6

Appendix A: Table 9.50 Macro Synchronized Chronology of Israel and the Near East (p. 6)

BCE	Year	Text	Judah	Manasseh	Assyria & Babylon (based on Haran Inscription & Ptolemy's Canon)	Assyria	Haran Inscrip.	Egypt	Babylon	7 Times
701	244		22							38
700	245		23		7				699–694: Ashur-nadin-shumi	37
699	246		24		8					36
698	247		25		9					35
697	248		26		10					34
696	249		27		11					33
695	250	Manasseh	28		12					32
694	251	2 Kgs 21:1: Switch to Monarchy/antedating	29	1t	13					31
693	252			2	14				693: Nergal-ushezib	30
692	253			3	15				692–689: Mushezib-Marduk	29
691	254			4	16					28
690	255			5	17			690–644: Taharqa		27
689	256			6	18					26
688	257			7	19					25
687	258			8	20					24
686	259			9	21					23
685	260			10	22					22
684	261			11	23	Esarhaddon				21
683	262			12	24	1				20
682	263			13		2				19
681	264			14		3				18
680	265			15		4				17
679	266			16		5				16
678	267			17		6				15
677	268			18		7				14
676	269			19		8				13
675	270			20		9				12
674	271			21		10				11
673	272			22		11				10
672	273			23	Ashurbanipal based upon Haran	12				9
671	274			24	1					8
670	275			25	2					7

BC	No.	Left events	Manasseh / Amon / Josiah	Center (year / Scripture note)	Judah yr	Assyria / Egypt events	Right no.
669	276		26	3			6
668	277		27	4			5
667	278		28	5		667–648: Shamash-shum-ukin	4
666	279		29	6			3
665	280		30	7			2
664	281	4th 7 Times ends	31 — Manasseh deported	8		664–656: Tanutamun 4th 7 Times ends	1
663	282	2 Chr 33:11—Manasseh deported	32 (1)	9— Foriegners imported (Ezra 4:10)			1
662	283		33 (2)	10			2
661	284	Manasseh exiled in Assyria	34 (3)	11			3
660	285	2 Chr 33:12	35 (4)	12			4
659	286		36 (5)	13			5
658	287	17th/8th Jubilee	37 (6)	14			6
657	288	2 Chr 33:13	38 (7)	2 Kgs 21:13—Measuring line of Samaria stretched over Jerusalem			7
656	289		39	16			70
655	290		40	17			69
654	291		41	18			68
653	292		42	19			67
652	293		43	20			66
651	294		44	21	1		65
650	295		45	22	2		64
649	296		46	23	3		63
648	297		47	24	4		62
647	298		48	25	5		61
646	299		49	26	6		60
645	300		50	27	7		59
644	301		51	28	8		58
643	302		52	29	9		57
642	303		53	30	10		56
641	304		54	31	11		55
640	305	2 Kgs 19:21; 2 Chr 33:21	55 Amon	32	12		54
639	306	2 Kgs 21:19	1t	33	13		53
638	307	2 Kgs 22:1	2 Josiah 1t 2	34	14		52

LEGEND   = Release year   = Jubilee   Year <u>Underlined</u> = Year specifically mentioned in Scripture   Ital. = accession year   H.P. = High Priest   L = Luckenbill

Appendix A: Table 9.50 Macro Synchronized Chronology of Israel and the Near East (p. 7)

BCE	Year	Text	Judah	70 Yrs. of Desolation in Judah	Assyria & Babylon (based on Haran Inscription & Ptolemy's Canon)	Haran Inscrip.	Jeremiah's 23 Years	Jechoniah's Captivity	Egypt	7 Times
637	308		3		35	15				51
636	309		4		36	16				50
635	310		5		37	17				49
634	311		6		38	18				48
633	312		7		39	19				47
632	313		8		40	20				46
631	314		9		41	21				45
630	315		10		42 Ashure-etil-ilani	22				44
629	316		11		1	23				43
628	317		12		2	24				42
627	318		13		Babylon: Nabopolassar	25	1			41
626	319		14		1	26	2			40
625	320		15		2	27	3			39
624	321		16		3	28	4			38
623	322	Book of the Law found	17		4	29	5			37
622	323	2 Kgs 22:3	18		5	30	6			36
621	324		19		6	31	7			35
620	325		20		7	32	8			34
619	326		21		8	33	9			33
618	327		22		9	34	10			32
617	328		23		10	35	11			31
616	329		24		11	36	12			30
615	330		25		12	37	13			29
614	331		26		13	38	14			28
613	332		27		14	39	15			27
612	333		28		15	40	16			26
611	334		29		16	41	17			25
610	335		30 Jehoahaz/		17	42	18		610–595: Nekau (Necho)	24
609	336	2 Kgs 23:29, 31	31 Jehoiakim		Pharaoh-Necho went up against "King of Assyria" (2 Kgs 23:29)	43	19			23
608	337	18th/9th Jubilee; 2 Kgs 23:34–36, Jer 52:1	1		19	44	20			22
607	338	During Jubilee shift to Priestly/postdating	2		20	45	21			21
606	339	Jer 25:1, 46:2—Nebuchadnezzare destoys	3		Nebuchadnezzar	46	22			20

BC	No.	Scripture / Event (left)	Reign yr.	No.	Nebuchadnezzar's reign / Event (middle)	No.		Egypt / Event (right)	Captivity yr.	No.
605	340	Pharaoh-Necho Jehoiakim's 4th yr.;	4	1		47				19
604	341	Jer 25:1; chs. 36, 45	5	2		48	23			18
603	342		6	3		49				17
602	343		7	4	4— Nebuchadnezzar marches against Egypt (ANET, 562)	50				16
601	344		8	5		51				15
600	345		9	6		52				14
599	346	Jer 52:28	10	7	7— Baylonian Chronicle 5-Nebuchadnezzar encamps against Judah	53				13
598	347	2 Kgs 24:8, 12 (2nd Deportation)	11	8	8— Nebuchadnezzar sieges Jerusalem in Adar and "appoints a king of his choice."	54		1— Beginning of Jeconiah's	1	12
597	348	2 Kgs 24:18	1 (Jehoiachin/ Zedekiah)	9		55		2 captivity until his 37th yr.	2	11
596	349		2	10		56		3	3	10
595	350		3	11		57		4 595–589: Psamtik II	4	9
594	351	Jeremiah 34:8-10	4	12		58		5	5	8
593	352	Ezekiel 1–4, based on the 5th yr. of his captivity	5	13		59		6	6	7
592	353		6	14		60		7	7	6
591	354		7	15		61		8	8	5
590	355		8	16		62		9	9	4
589	356	Jer 52:4—Jerusalem seiged	9	17		63		10 589–570: Wahibre (Apries)	10	3
588	357	Jer 52:29—Deported 832 people; 2 Kgs 25:1	10	18	18— Jerusalem falls on the 11th yr. 4th mo, 9th day (Jer 52:5–8)	64		11	11	2
587	358	Jer 52:12-27; 2 Kgs 25:2/ 5th 7 Times ends	11	19	19— Temple burned with fire in the 19th yr. of the 5th mo., 10th day (Jer 52:12-27; 2 Kgs 25:8—7th day)	65		12 5th 7 Times ends	12	1
586		Jer 25:11, 29:10— / 70 yrs of desolation begins		20		66		13	13	1
585				21		67		14	14	2
584				22		68		15	15	3
583		Jer 52:30—Deportation		23		69		16	16	4
582				24		70		17	17	5
581				25		71		18	18	6
580				26		72		19	19	7
579				27		73		20	20	8
578				28		74		21	21	9
577				29		75		22	22	10
576				30		76		23	23	11
575				31		77		24	24	12

LEGEND   = Release year   = Jubilee   Year Underlined = Year specifically mentioned in Scripture   Ital. = accession year   H.P. = High Priest   L = Luckenbill

Appendix A: Table 9.50 Macro Synchronized Chronology of Israel and the Near East (p. 8)

BCE	70 Years of Desolation in Judah	Assyria & Babylon (based on Haran Inscription & Ptolemy's Canon)	Haran Inscrip.	Jechoniah's Captivity	Egypt	Persia	7 Times
574	Ezek 40:1—25ᵗʰ yr. of Ezekiel's captivity	32	78	25			13
573	Siege of Tyre?	33	79	26			14
572		34	80	27			15
571		35	81	28			16
570	Ezek 29:17—Tyre has fallen to Nebuchadnezzar by the 27ᵗʰ yr. of Jehoachin's captivity	36	82	29	570–526: Amose II		17
569	37ᵗʰ yr. Nebuchadnezzar marches against Egypt (ANET, 308)	37	83	30	(Amasis)		18
568	Ezek 1:1—Ezekiel begins to see visions of God	38	84	31			19
567		39	85	32			20
566		40	86	33			21
565		41	87	34			22
564		42	88	35			23
563		43 Evil Merodach	89	36			24
562	1ˢᵗ yr. of Amel-Merduk (Nebuchadnezzar's son) was the 37ᵗʰ yr. of Jehoachin's captivity	1	90	37			25
561		2	91				26
560	2 Kgs 25:27–30; Jer 52:31–34	(Neriglissar) 1	92				27
559		2	93				28
50th	19ᵗʰ/10ᵗʰ Jubilee; Jer 27:7—nations will serve Babylon until Nebuchadnezzar's grandson (3 generations)	3	94				29
557		4 Labasi-Maruk (a few mo.) 1	95				30
556		Nabonidus/Belshazzar					31
555		1					32
554		2					33
553	Dan 5:22—Belshazzar knew the story of "7 times" that had passed over his father	3					34
552		4					35
551		5					36
550		6					37
549		7					38
548		8					39
547		9					40
546		10					41
545		11					42
544		12					43
543		13					44
542		14					45
541		15					46
540		16					47
539		17					48

BCE	Event / Scripture	Cyrus, King of Persia	Cambyses	Darius I	
538	(70 yrs. of desolation continues)				49
537	Ezra 1:1, 2:2, 63—Cyrus frees captives; Ezra 3:1—Sukkot kept in 7th month/Remnant recovenant—Neh 7:65, 10:1	<u>1</u>			50
536	Ezra 3:6—2nd yr., The Temple's foundation has NOT been laid; Levites set in courses, Zerrubabal, Yeshua lead the deportees home	2			51
535	Yehosuah, H.P.	3			52
534		4			53
533		5			54
532		6			55
531		7			56
530	Neh 10:38—Recovenanting in either 537 or 530 BCE	8	Cambyses		57
529	Ezra 3:10—Foundation suspended all Cyrus' days until Darius' 2nd yr.; Dan 9:1; Ezek 29:13—Egypt in Diaspora for 40 yrs.	9	1		58
528	Ezra 4:6—Ezra calls Cambyses, "Ahasuerus"		2		59
527	(70 yrs. from Judah's, Jechoniah's, and Ezekiel's deportation)		3		60
526			4		61
525			5		62
524			6		63
523			7		64
522			8	Darius I	65
521	Hag 1:2—70 yrs. of desolation not yet complete in Darius' 2nd yr.; Hag 1:5–11—Drought for several years			1	66
520	Hag 2:10, 18—Foundation of Temple laid on the 20th day, 9th month, 2nd yr. of Darius			2	67
519				3	68
518				4	69
517	Jer 25:11, 29:10—70 yrs. of desolation complete			5	70
516	Ezra 6:15—Temple completed on Adar 3; Temple dedicated during Sukkot — 1st 7 Times begins			6	<u>1</u>
515				7	2
514				8	3
513	Jehoiakim, H.P.			9	4
512				10	5
511				11	6
510				12	7
509				13	8
508	20th/11th Jubilee			14	9
507				15	10
506				16	11

LEGEND   □ = Release year   ▩ = Jubilee   Year <u>Underlined</u> = Year specifically mentioned in Scripture   *Ital.* = accession year   H.P. = High Priest   L = Luckenbill

Appendix A: Table 9.50 Macro Synchronized Chronology of Israel and the Near East (p. 9)

BCE	Desolation & Return	Persia	7 Times
505	17		12
504	18		13
503	19		14
502	20		15
501	21		16
500	22		17
499	23		18
498	24		19
497	25		20
496	26		21
495	27		22
494	28		23
493	29		24
492	30		25
491	31		26
490	32		27
489	33		28
488	34		29
487	35		30
486	36	Xerxes I	31
485		1	32
484		2	33
483		3	34
482		4	35
481		5	36
480		6	37
479		7	38
478		8	39
477		9	40
476		10	41
475		11	42
474		12	43
473		13	44

Year	Events	Artaxerxes	Count
472	Eliashib, H.P.	14	45
471		15	46
470		16	47
469		17	48
468		18	49
467	Neh 1:3—Jerusalem's wall had been broken down/burned with fire; Heb 3:20—Eliashib was H.P. when wall was rebuilt	19	50
466	Neh 1:1—Artaxerxes 20th yr, Nehemiah receives word of Jerusalem in Shushan	20	51
465	Neh 5—Oppression by the Jews, usury	21	52
464		Artaxerxes I 1	53
463		2	54
462	Joiada, H.P.	3	55
461		4	56
460	(Jonathan)	5	57
459	Ezra 7:25—King gave Ezra power to establish judges and magistrates; Ezra 7:7—Takes Ezra 5 months to migrate from Babylon to Jerusalem	6	58
458	Ezra 9—Levites sin; Ezra 9:10—9th mo., 20th day of Artaxerxes 7th yr; "Great rain" Ezra 10:1—Evidences Temple is rebuilt	7	59
457		8	60
456	Ezra 10:14—flooding	9	61
455	Ezra 9—People had broken their covenant with YHWH by failing to release their Hebrew slaves, employing usury, and violating the Sabbath, just as during King Zedekiah's reign	10	62
454		11	63
453		12	64
452		13	65
451		14	66
450		15	67
449		16	68
448		17	69
447	Daniel 9:27 1st 7 Times ends	18	70
446		19	1
445	Neh 1:1; 5:14—Nehemiah returns to Jerusalem and is appointed governor	20	2
444		21	3
443	Neh 5:14—appointed governor for 12 yrs.	22	4
442		23	5
441		24	6
440		25	7
439		26	8
438		27	9
437		28	10
436		29	11
435		30	12
434		31	13
433	Nehemia writes his testimony	32	14
432		33	15
431	Jaddua, H.P.?	34	16
430		35	17

LEGEND   [shaded] = Release year   [shaded] = Jubilee   Year Underlined = Year specifically mentioned in Scripture   Ital. = accession year   H.P. = High Priest   L = Luckenbill

Appendix B: Table 9.51. Time: Flood to Abraham

BCE Dates	Post-Flood Date (P.F.)	Person	Age at Birth of Child	Years Lived after Child's Birth	Age at Death	Died in (Post-Flood Date/ BCE Dates):	Events (P.F./BCE Dates)	Genesis Text
		Noah			950		Lived 350 yrs. after the flood	9:28
2658		Shem	100	500	600			11:10–11
2560			Flood					7:6
2558	2	Arphaxad[1]	35	403	438			11:12–13
2523	37	Salah	30	403	433			11:14–15
2493	67	Eber	34	430	464			11:16–17
2459	101	Peleg	30	209	239			11:18–19
2429	131	Reu	32	207	239			11:20–21
2397	163	Serug	30	200	230			11:22–23
2367	193	Nahor	29	119	148			11:24–25
2338	222	Terah	70	135	205			11:26–32
2268	292	Abraham	100	75	175	Noah d. 350/2210 Peleg d. 340/2220 Nahor d. 341/2219 Reu d. 370/2190 Serug d. 393/2167	BABEL DESTROYED and EARTH DIVIDED 340/341 (2220/2219) 367/2193—Abram leaves Haran 391/2169—Abram receives Circumcision Covenant	Babel—10:25, 32; 11:8–9; 1 Chr 1:19/ Abram leaves Haran— 12:4/ Circumcision Cov.—17:1
2168	392	Isaac	60	120	180	Tarah d. 427/2133 Arphaxad d. 440/2120		
2108	452	Jacob[2]	130	17	147	Abraham d. 467/2093 Salah d. 470/2090 Shem d. 502/2058 Eber d. 531/2029 Isaac d. 572/1988	582/1978—Jacob was 130 yrs. when family migrated to Egypt—Gen 47:9	Abraham's death—25:7 Isaac's death—35:28

Appendix C:
The Habiru Hebrews

I. 1 SAMUEL

Before the twentieth century, scholars had never questioned the Hebrews' being Israelites. It was understood that anyone who was an Israelite was ethnically Hebrew. After ancient texts were discovered to refer to "Habiru" (Hebrews)[1] in Mesopotamia, Mari, Ugarit, and Egypt, long before Israel's Exodus, scholars began to question Scripture's use of the term *Hebrew* (עִבְרִי or עִבְרִית). Two of the most influential works on this issue are Henri Cazelles's "The Hebrews" and Mary Gray's *The Habiru-Hebrew Problem*.[2] Gray's work is more thorough, while Cazelles focuses on Scripture's use of the term *Hebrew* (*'ibri* or *ibriyim*). Many scholars consider this term to be distinct from other terms such as the *Children of Israel* or the *people of Israel*.[3] This distinction is based on three texts in 1 Samuel: 13:3; 13:6–7; 14:21, in which the story of Saul's campaign against the Philistines "can only be fully understood if a distinction is made between Israelites and Hebrews."[4] As Cazelles opines:

> 1 Sam 14:21 concerns the Hebrews "who had been with the Philistines before that time" and the Israelites who were fighting with Saul and Jonathan; the Hebrews change sides and join the Israelites. In the previous chapter (13:6 and 7) Hebrews and Israelites had taken different attitudes towards the Philistine army; the Israelites stayed where they were, even though they had to hide themselves in caves and among bushes and rocks, while the Hebrews crossed the Jordan to the land of Gad and Gilead. Finally there is 1 Sam 13:3, where the distinction is less clear. The text as we have it has perhaps been edited under the influence of the identification between Israelites and Hebrews. . . . Saul wishes to let all the "Hebrews" know of the victory of Jonathan over the Philistines; he also tries to attract to the side of the Israelites who had become odious to the Philistines, a more numerous following.[5]

Does Scripture support Cazelles's claim? Does Scripture distinguish between Hebrews and Israelites? It is important for us to establish the Scriptural context and usage of the term *Hebrew* (*'ibri*), especially as it relates to King Saul's early campaigns before we examine the historical evidence.

The first time the Book of Samuel mentions the Hebrews is during the Judges' Era, when Israel brought the Ark of the Covenant to the battlefield.

> And when the *ark of the covenant of YHWH came into the camp*, **all Israel** shouted with a great shout, so that the earth rang again. And when the Philistines heard the noise of the shout, they said, What means the noise of this

great shout in the **camp of the Hebrews**? And they understood that the ark of
YHWH was come into the camp. (1 Sam 4:5–6)

In this text, we see that the Ark of the Covenant came into the Israelite camp. We are also
told that these Israelites were identified as Hebrews (*'ibri*) by the Philistines. One obstacle
to viewing the Hebrews and Israelites as two distinct groups of people is that there was no
other nation or group of people that had control over the Ark of the Covenant other than
the Hebrew-Israelites (before the Philistines captured it). This is a point that Cazelles fails
to consider.

And the Philistines were afraid, for they said, God is come into the camp. . . .
Be strong, and quit yourselves like men, O you Philistines, that you be not
servants to the **Hebrews**, as they have been to you: quit yourselves like men,
and fight. (1 Sam 4:7, 9)

According to the author of this text, the Philistines continued to view the Israelites, who
brought the Ark of the Covenant into Israel's camp, as Hebrews. The Philistines rallied to
fight so as to avoid becoming servants to the Israelites, who are identified as Hebrews (perhaps similar to early American history, where an American could be identified as English,
Polish, or French in addition to being an American). In other ancient texts, such as those
discovered at Amarna, individuals who joined with the Habirus' campaigns in Canaan are
often said to have "become Habiru."[6] From a Torah context, this would imply that a person
had joined himself to Israel and her God and had integrated into the confederacy of Israel
(Exod 12:48–49; Lev 19:33–34).

After the Ark had been captured by the Philistines, Israel asked Samuel for a king. Saul
was appointed and began to campaign against the Philistines. In his second regnal year, Saul
formed a militia of 4,000 men. Two thousand men camped with Saul at Bethel, while his
son Jonathan took 1,000 forces to attack a Philistine garrison at Geba. Saul sent the rest of
the recruits home until he could see the outcome of his initial campaigns.

Saul chose him three thousand men of Israel; whereof two thousand were with
Saul in Michmash and in Mount Bethel, and a thousand were with Jonathan
in Gibeah of Benjamin: and the rest of the people he sent every man to his
tent. And Jonathan smote the garrison of the Philistines that was in Geba, and
the Philistines heard of it. And *Saul blew the trumpet throughout all the land*,
saying, **Let the Hebrews hear**. (4) **And all Israel heard** that Saul had smitten
a garrison of the Philistines, and that **Israel** also was held in abomination with
the Philistines. And the people were called together after Saul to Gilgal. (1 Sam
13:2–4)

In this text, we see that after Saul's initial success he blew the trumpet to call all the Hebrews that he had sent home back to the battlefront (compare to Gideon's battle, Map 11.6). Verse 4 clarifies that the Hebrews he called were "all Israel." Saul was following an instruction in the Law of Moses for calling the people of Israel to battle. Moses had commanded Israel to sound the trumpet *throughout the land* when the Children of Israel fought oppression (Num 10:8–9). Since the Law forbade Israel to make treaties with other nations or peoples within the Promised Land, which it appears Saul observed (Exod 23:32; Deut 7:2; 20:12), the only people Saul's trumpet was calling to battle were the Hebrew-Israelites. Nothing in these texts indicates that any non-Israelite Hebrews existed in Israel during Saul's campaigns.

As the story of Saul's campaign continues, we discover that a key battle did not bode well for Israel.

> When the **men of Israel** saw that they were in a strait (for the people were distressed), then the people did hide themselves in caves, and in thickets, and in rocks, and in high places, and in pits. (7) And *some of the Hebrews went over Jordan to the land of Gad and Gilead.* As for Saul, he was yet in Gilgal, and all the people followed him trembling. And he tarried seven days, according to the set time that Samuel had appointed: but Samuel came not to Gilgal; and **the people were scattered from him.** (1 Sam 13:6–8)

Once the battle soured, Israel hid in rocks and caves, fleeing the enemy's blow. Some soldiers followed Saul to Gilgal while others fled across the Jordan into Reuben and Gad's tribal inheritances, which Scripture appropriately recognizes as "the land of Gad" (v. 7). Cazelles and Gray posit a distinction between the Israelites and the Hebrews in these verses, viewing those that crossed the Jordan as Hebrews and those that followed Saul as Israelites.[7] Does the context of these verses support this distinction? Verse 7 states that the Hebrews fled from the battle while v. 8 tells us the "people" (of Israel) were "scattered" from Saul. There is nothing in this text that distinguishes the Hebrews from Israel. In fact, the text supports that the Hebrews were Israelites that "scattered" from Saul and fled into the land of Gad because they were being chased by the Philistines. This is in line with 1 Sam 14:22, which states that the "men of Israel" had fled to Mt. Ephraim. The fact that Israel retreated into two different territories does not make them a different people. Many armies, facing a tough battle will retreat by whatever means possible, even if they are well-trained, for which there is no evidence that Saul's men were.

Another fact that stands in opposition to Gray's and Cazelles's thesis is the Hebrews' route of retreat. Had the Hebrews fled to the coastal region or to the north, it could be argued that they were retreating to their homeland. Yet, the Hebrews who fled into the "land of Gad" were retreating to an Israelite territory that had already been conquered and settled by the Israelite tribes at least 300 years prior (Judg 11:26; see chap. 9.III.B.2., p. 350). The books of Deuteronomy, Joshua, and Judges tell us that the Amorites' old territory (Num 32:33; Deuteronomy 3; Josh 2:10), which lay just east of the Jordan between the Dead Sea and the Sea of Chinnereth (Galilee) had been allotted to the half-tribe of Manasseh, Gad, and Reuben (Num 32:32–33). In context, these Hebrews were fleeing to their tribal Israelite homes for refuge and perhaps to resupply. Once news of Saul's success spread across the land, the recruits rejoined Saul's campaign.

In another battle, Jonathan (Saul's son) and his armor-bearer attack another Philistine garrison (1 Samuel 14). According to 1 Sam 14:11, the Philistines referred to Jonathan and his bearer as Hebrews when the duo challenged them.

> Both of them discovered themselves unto the garrison of the Philistines: and the Philistines said, Behold, **the Hebrews** come forth out of the holes where they had hid themselves. (1 Sam 14:11)

Although Jonathan was a Benjaminite who may have been dressed as an Israelite prince, the Philistines thought him to be a Hebrew or *Habiru*. Remember, *Habiru* was the term that Egypt, Assyria, Ugarit, and Canaan used to identify the Israelites during the Amarna Period, as we saw in chap. 11. This appellation continued to be used by Egypt well into Seti's and Ramesses' reigns (*c.* 1275 BCE). It would therefore be natural for the Philistines to recognize the Israelites by their ethnic-linguistic distinction of Hebrews rather than Israelites since the Kingdom of Israel had only been formed two years prior and had not yet asserted itself as a distinct entity within the land of Canaan, despite Menerptah's inscription (1 Sam 13:1–2).

Now, this text is where Cazelles and Gray see the greatest distinction between the Hebrews and the Israelites.

> (v. 21) Moreover, *the Hebrews* **that were with the Philistines before that time,** which went up with them into the camp from the country round about, even they also turned to be with the Israelites that were with Saul and Jonathan. (22) Likewise **all the men of Israel which had hid themselves in Mount Ephraim,** when they heard that the Philistines fled, even they also followed hard after them in the battle. (1 Sam 14:21–22)

Cazelles and Gray consider the Hebrews who allied with the Philistines to be a separate entity from the Israelites who warred against the Philistines, since it is stated that the Hebrews (not the Israelites) had allied with the Philistines. This view is short-sighted, since this scenario is the same situation that the Book of Judges tells us occurrred, where the *Israelites* had allied with the Canaanites. It may be remembered that the angel that came to Shiloh had rebuked Israel for making a "league with the inhabitants of this land" (Judg 2:2; see also Exod 23:32; Deut 7:2; 20:12; Judg 1:21, 27–35; see pp. 363–64, 552–55, 562, 687). This is consonant with the statement in 1 Sam 14:21 regarding the Hebrews.

As we saw in chap. 11, Israel constantly allied with the very nations YHWH had commanded the Hebrews to expel. Once Samuel installed the Monarchy, many of these alliances were probably revoked as the tribal nation finally began to work together to assert its independence from the Philistine hold. In fact, 1 Sam 14:22 tells us that, when the Israelites scattered from Saul, not only did some flee to their homes in the land of Gad, others fled to Mount Ephraim (1 Sam 14:22). With Jonathan's success, all Israelites who had previously fled rallied and returned to aid the war effort. There is nothing in these texts that makes even a subtle distinction between the Hebrews and the Israelites. If Jonathan is an Israelite, he is ethnically a Hebrew, which the text supports. Nothing in these texts indicate that the Hebrews in 1 Sam 14:21 had a different attitude toward the Philistines[8] from the Hebrews in ch. 13. Rather, the context parallels that of Judges 1–3, where Israel is said to have settled alongside and allied with the very nations that God had commanded Israel to drive off the land and that had eventually oppressed Israel (Judg 21:27–2:3). Under Saul's and Samuel's leadership, the nation finally began to break free of these alliances and establish her own independence.

1 Samuel does not support Cazelles's assertion that the Hebrews and Israelites had two different attitudes toward the Philistines.[9] Originally, Saul had only gathered 3,000 men to battle (1 Sam 13:2). He chose these men to attack a small garrison in Geba (1 Sam 13:3), a city near Saul's hometown that had been allotted to Benjamin by Joshua (Josh 21:17). 1 Sam 13:6, 8 parallels Judg 6:2, where Israel had previously hid in caves when the Amalekites and Moabites had oppressed the tribal federation but in no way had they lost their ethnic tribal affiliation. 1 Sam 4:9 tells us that the Philistines did not want the Hebrews to rule over them, and so they rose against Israel to battle. Yet, v. 5 identifies these Hebrews as "all Israel" (1 Sam 4:5), as we saw above. The situation during Saul's campaign was aggravated by Samuel's delay, which further scattered the tribal federation (1 Sam 13:8). However, once these frightened soldiers saw that Saul and Jonathan had the upper hand, they reunited with their host (14:21–22) to rout the Philistines. Saul's incredible victory over this small garrison provoked the Philistines' declaration of war (1 Sam 13:4). Saul's attack provoked the Philistines' negative attitude toward the Hebrews, which caused the Hebrews to be an affront (odious or an abomination) to them. This hostility did not stem from their identity as a separate group, as Cazelles supposes;[10] rather, much like the modern 9/11 attack, it was Saul's assault on the Philistine garrison that provoked the Philistine sentiment—just as Americans now view many terrorist groups with contempt.

II. GREATER CONTEXT:
THE TERM 'IBRI IN SCRIPTURE

Scriptures' use of the term 'ibri ("Hebrew") to denote an Israelite is consistent throughout Scripture where Israel is considered to be a different ethnic group from the Egyptians (Exod 1:16–19; 2:7, 11–13; 5:3). When YHWH gave the Law at Mt. Sinai, he defined how to maintain justice and equity between fellow countrymen. The only term that is used to define Israel's "fellow countrymen" is "Hebrew" (Exod 21:2; Deut 15:12; Jer 34:14), which appears about 34 times, mostly in the Pentateuch and 1 Samuel. The term "Israelite" appears 18 times, with only 4 occurrences in the Pentateuch. While the more common designation "people of Israel" occurs over 400 times, and "children of Israel" occurs 630 times. The only term, however, that consistently conveys the concept of a fellow citizen or countryman is the term "Hebrew." The term *Hebrew* fell out of written use once the Monarchy was established.

Cazelles correctly points out that a distinction should be made between Israel and all Hebrews in general.[11] The term *Israel* usually designates the descendants of Jacob, while the term *Hebrew* is used to identify descendants of Eber, a much broader group (contra Cazelles and Gray, who distinguish between Hebrew Israelites and dismiss a language or ethnic affiliation; see below).

The Philistines responded to Saul's provocation with an immense army (1 Sam 13:5), the same way that America responded to 9/11 with a "War on Terror." When the Hebrews-Israelites saw this, they fled their tribal heritages to safer/peaceable territories (1 Sam 13:7). Cazelles's assertion that the Hebrews fled while the Israelites stayed[12] is a supposition, not supported by Scripture's use of the term *Hebrew* in these texts.

Saul chose Gilgal, near Jericho's borders (Josh 4:19) which had traditionally headquartered military campaigns during the Conquest (Josh 4:19–20; 5:9–10; ch. 10; 14:6). The *'ibiru* who fled[13] retreated to territories allotted to the Hebrew Israelites, not some other vaguely defined "Hebrew" peoples. The Book of Judges reports Israel's propensity to make alliances with local populations shortly after Joshua's death (Deut 7:2; Judg 1:21, 27–35; 2:2). YHWH had warned Israel that if she did not drive the native Canaanites out of the land, she would be assimilated into their culture and their communities (Exod 23:32–33). 1 Sam 14:21 shows that this was indeed the result. Many Israelites (Hebrews) had indeed lived peaceably among the Philistines "before that time" of war (1 Sam 14:21). Many had allied with the Philistines either out of economic and social convenience or due to the proximity of their tribal inheritance, which facilitated their mutual tolerance. 1 Samuel 13–14 continually alternates between the two terms, demonstrating that the Hebrew-Israelites were a singular group as is supported by a 16th-century Exodus date (see chaps. 9–10).

Another text Cazelles uses to support a non-Israelite affiliation of the term *Hebrew* (*'ibri*) is Balaam's blessing of the people of Israel shortly after the Exodus.[14]

> And ships shall come from the coast of Kittim, and shall afflict Asshur, and shall afflict Eber, and he also shall perish for ever. (Num 24:24)

Eber, in this text is not the term *'ibri* (*Hebrew*) but the family patriarch Eber (Gen 10:25) from whom the eponym *Hebrew* is derived.[15] Cazelles takes the verse out of context when he considers Eber to be "related to the Kittim."[16] The context does not imply that Eber and the Kittim were ethnically related. (According to Genesis 10, the Kittim were Greeks, sons of Javan, Gen 10:4, while Eber descended from Shem, Gen 10:22–24.) In context, Scripture implies that the Kittim will afflict the descendants of Assur (Assyria) and Eber (Hebrews). As is well known from history, Alexander the Great, perhaps a descendant of Kittim, did indeed subjugate the land of the Hebrews (Israel) and the land of Assyria and Babylon. Eber lived when the languages were divided among the families of the earth at Babel, and his descendants were scattered throughout Mesopotamia and Canaan.

Unto Eber were born two sons: the name of one was Peleg; for in his days was the earth divided. (Gen 10:25; see Appendix B: Table 9.51)

Since Scripture states that these languages were divided based on families (Gen 10:5), it would be only natural that all future descendants be known as Eber or *'iberus*, after the name of the family patriarch who was part of the first generation of divided languages.[17]

Cazelles accurately points out that Abraham's other children through Keturah, his grandson Esau,[18] or his nephews through Lot (Moabites) would also be considered Hebrews and may have been included in the broad Habiru group of people recognized by the Egyptians. Scripture, however, distinguishes these tribes (Midian, Edom, Moab) from the Israelites, never referring to any of their people as Hebrews.[19] *In fact, there is not one place in the entire Tanakh where any other group of people is called Hebrew other than the Israelites.* Thus the Israelites, at least from the Scriptural perspective, were the only group of people in Canaan who were "Hebrews."

Another argument levied against an ethnic affiliation of Israelite-Hebrews is that the ethnically mixed multitude (Exod 12:38) that departed from Egypt with Israel was considered Hebrew based on its social class rather than its ethnicity.[20] The fact that Israel left Egypt with a mixed multitude of Asiatic slaves does not change the fact that the core group that left Egypt was Hebrew-Israelite, descendants of Eber through Jacob. After other Asiatic groups intermarried with the Israelites for a few generations they, too, would have become ethnically Hebrews, just as most people today who marry into another nation, tribe, or family are absorbed into that culture or community after a few generations. (For example, many Germans who migrated to the U.S. in the early 1900s are simply known as Americans today. Yet, when a group continues to live as an ethnic community within the U.S., the people retain their ethnicity—i.e. the Serbian communities around Chicago, German communities in Texas, or many Jewish communities throughout the U.S.).

Cazelles also assumes that the word *Hebrew* disappeared from the spoken language after Saul's reign.[21] Since we do not know how people referred to themselves during this era, his statement is an argument from silence.[22] From the administrative perspective, Cazelles is correct that, after Saul's early victories, the word *Hebrew* virtually disappeared from the Hebrew Scriptures, with the exception of the Philistines' reference to David (1 Sam 29:3), the prophet Jonah's statement (*c.* 850 BCE) that he was a Hebrew (1:9), and Jeremiah's quote of the Law regarding releasing fellow Hebrew countrymen during the Release Year (Jer 34:9, 14). However, Cazelles fails to point out that the word *Hebrew* in Scripture is not replaced with any substitute; no term for either the Hebrews or the Israelites maintains the idea of ethnic affinity. Instead, Israel continues to be called "people of Israel" and "Children of Israel," two terms that had been instituted when Israel immigrated to Egypt. After the Israelite Kingdom split in two, the sister nations were termed the "House of Israel" and the "House of Judah."[23] Neither the word *Hebrew* nor the word *Israelite* was abandoned for another term (administratively) until the term *Jew* was coined for people in the Southern Kingdom after Samaria's fall (*c.* 717 BCE).[24] This evidence fits the theory that the Hebrews were an ethnic group who formed a nation, and the terms associated with nationhood replaced earlier ethnic affiliations when they were no longer needed.

III. ANACHRONISTIC IDEAS

The discussion about the Habirus has been colored by modern ideas of race and ethnicity. There is an increasing tendency to discount racial heritage and cultural values even when a person's ethnicity is relevant to a particular situation or discussion. The ancient world did not share this idea of universal humanity. Ancient texts demonstrate that race and country of origin were of primary importance. Legal contracts in Mesopotamia dealing with the Habirus (who were not Israelites) demonstrate that their country of origin is almost always specified.[25] A legal contract will state that a person is a Habiru from Akkad or a Habiru from Babylon in the same way we today may say that a person is a Hispanic from Honduras or Mexico. The same type of ethnic and geographic identifier can be seen in well-known Egyptian contracts where Nubians are often identified.

Most scholars take the term *Habiru* out of its context of ethnicity to denote a slave that has fled his master to become a rebellious "Habiru/servant."[26] For most scholars the statement by the Philistines that they do not want to become slaves to the Hebrews (1 Sam 4:9) implies that the Philistines did not want to become slaves to the rebellious slaves (i.e., Habiru). While this interpretation is certainly possible, it is out of context. Every time Scripture cites oppression, it is always by one ethnic group toward another ethnic group. Israel is oppressed by Moab, Amalek, Midian, and the Philistines— all racial/ethnic groups of people. In this context, it is not that the Philistines do not want to become slaves to another class of slaves. Rather, the Philistines do not wish to become slaves to the Hebrews, who are another ethnic group residing in Canaan. The term *Hebrew* has nothing to do with a social class of foreigners.

IV. NO ETHNIC HEBREWS?

The word *Habiru* is often linked to the root *'br*, meaning, 'to cross a boundary.' Of this etymology, Gray observes,

> Such a participle form could be used as an appellative noun describing a class of people as "those who cross or have crossed boundaries," "immigrants." The etymology from *'br* fits the historical evidence. As we have noticed, the place of origin of the Ḥâbirū is frequently noted in the texts, and it is usual to find that the Ḥâbirū has migrated, has come from some other place. As a group, they are classified as outsiders, away from their homeland; this classification accounts for the diversity of occupation, the stigma attached to the minority group, their frequent appearance in low economic circumstances, their apparent preference for living together in a group, and their coherence. The term cannot mean "those who continually cross boundaries, i.e., nomads" since the group is frequently described as living in a defined locality and is listed separately from the Bedouin.[27]

Mary Gray dismisses the possibility that ethnic origin could have united the Hebrews because they came from various national origins.[28] But, does the historical evidence disallow an ethnic affiliation?

The Habiru/Sa.Gaz are first attested as living in Ur,[29] the place where Abraham's family originated. Terah emigrated from Ur (Gen 11:31) before YHWH called Abraham "unto a land that he would show him" (Gen 12:1). The Habiru/Sa.Gaz are recognized as an entity around 2200 BCE.[30] This is the exact date supported by the Torah's account of Abram's migration out of Ur (see Table 9.22 on pg. 384). As we saw on pp. 519–21, Abraham was part of a larger migration out of Ur, as tribal-based families were displaced by temple-corporations that confiscated tribal lands. Temples began to amass more and more land in order to support their priesthoods and labor forces,[31] which in turn displaced more families. Clans were forced either to seek work inside a city or to become migratory (due to Mesopotamia's desert conditions). Without land, families often wandered around in search of food and home (Isocrates, *Panegyrikos,* 167–170).[32]

Hebrews may have been one of the primary groups affected by this shift in land ownership. This may be the reason Hebrews are often shown to have emigrated from another country.[33] As mentioned previously, it is quite possible that these displaced Hebrews gave rise to the concept 'to ḥabāru' or 'to migrate,'[34] because the trait of an ethnic tribe seemed to characterize the entire clan. A similar phenomenon occurred with the ethnic Medjay tribe, which aided Ahmose as "regular policemen" against the Hyksos, *c.* 1550 BCE.[35] The tribe performed the office so well that the term "'Medjay' virtually became synonymous with 'policeman.'"[36] Although the Medjay were law enforcers, their occupation did not discount their ethnic tribal association.[37] This same type of scenario occurred again in the modern early 19th century, when the term "Nigger," which had been a neutral term that referred to black men, broadened into a pejorative ethnic slur that often implied laziness or some other moral deficiency (so much so, that I hesitate to use it as an example). In the same way, the migration of ethnic Hebrews gave rise to the concept of "migration" and often provoked pejoratives as the immigrant Hebrews vied for resources (both natural and political) with a land's native inhabitants. This does not discount the possibility that the Hebrews in general could also have developed into a social class. I would be cautious with this association, since the pre-Israelite Hebrews such as Abraham and Lot gained vast amounts of wealth, had the ability to sustain a small militias, and some become kings.[38] Perhaps a similar situation can be seen with modern Hispanics who, back in the 1970s and 1980s were associated with cheap labor, but have now established themselves in America so that they can be found in many educated fields and among high-ranking politicians.

The Hebrews also became active in northern Syria (18–13th centuries) several centuries after Abraham migrated to Canaan (*c.* 2190).[39] While other groups of Hebrews were probably absorbed into other Near Eastern communities, the Hebrews in Canaan retained their own ethnic identity. This identity held particular significance for Abraham's descendants due to the patriarchal covenants, which based Abraham's claim to the land of Canaan on Noah's prophecy (Gen 9:24–27), which ceded Canaan's inheritance to Shem's descendants (see pp. 78–82). While one could theorize that Shem's progeny were known as "Shemites" before the languages were divided, once the division of families and languages occurred, not all Shemites spoke Hebrew, so Eber became an eponym for the entire Hebrew-speaking clan. As Hebrew families were displaced and migrated through various countries, their descendants were often given personal names (in Akkadian, Hurrian, etc.) relative to the nations through which they had migrated, perhaps in an attempt to fit into the local population. A similar phenomenon is seen not only in ancient Egypt during the Hyksos period, when foreigners adopted Egyptian names,[40] but also in America today as immigrants often choose English names that are easier for Americans to articulate. Similar to the Israelites, the Hebrews in general are "presented as part of a larger group having some coherence and unity," as Gray observes,[41] similar to many modern Jewish communities that emigrate from all over Europe and Asia but retain an ethnic-cultural heritage.

Gray points out that Abraham's life is consistent with what we know of the Habiru in general. He is a wanderer, an immigrant, he settles in a new land, he amasses great flocks and herds, and he is able to influence local politics.[42] While Gray accepts Abraham's designation as a Hebrew, she challenges that of Joseph, who came from the "Land of the Hebrews" (Gen 40:15) as an ethnic designation. She posits that the term *Hebrew* simply referred to a foreign class of immigrants that had a social status little higher than slaves.[43] Yet, as we have seen, no Hebrews exist outside of the Israelites in the Hebrew Scriptures. Ever since the Promised-Land Covenant that God contracted with Abraham, there was only one "land of the Hebrews" for Abram's descendants, which was Canaan. Scripture did not uphold Canaan as a land given to a social class but to the children of Abraham (Gen 15:18–21), just as Joseph's statement implies.

One of the strongest arguments against the Hebrews' simply being a social class is the definition of a "bondservant" (Heb. *'ebed*). Unlike free servants, who could make contracts, bondservants were sold into a plantation type of slavery.[44] We know that Joseph fell into this class because he was sold into slavery by his brothers (Gen 37:28), taken to Egypt by the Ishmaelites, and sold to Potiphar (Gen 37:36). When Potiphar's wife accused Joseph, she called him a "Hebrew servant." If the term *Habiru/Hebrew* denoted a social class right above bondslaves, as most scholars believe, then this statement is contradictory. Joseph would no longer fall into the social class of Habiru/Hebrew but into the lower social class of slave.[45] This does not make sense. If, however, the term *Hebrew* denotes ethnicity, it makes perfect sense because Potiphar's wife accuses a person of Hebrew origin who was a bondslave. Notice that the text still allows for a racial pejorative to be associated with the term *Hebrew*. In fact, the text almost implies this type of nuance since Potiphar's wife drives home the point that Potiphar's slave was a Hebrew.

Another text that implies ethnicity is Exod 1:19, where Shiphrah and Puah tell Pharaoh that the Hebrew women are not like the Egyptians when giving birth. Their statement implies a difference of one race in delivering babies more quickly than the other race. This context is nonsensical if it means that the Hebrew social class had the ability to deliver a child more quickly than the Egyptian social class.

Gray also dismisses ethnicity in Exod 2:11, where Scripture states that an Egyptian was beating a "Hebrew man, of his (Moses's) people."[46] Gray questions the reason that the text clarifies that the Hebrew was "of his people." She concludes that the text is differentiating the abused Hebrew as an Israelite versus other socially classed Hebrews in Egypt who had no relation to the Israelites, since stating that this Hebrew was an ethnic "brother" would be redundant.[47] This view is both myopic and unsupported by other texts in the Hebrew Scriptures. Deut 15:12 uses both words together in a text that clearly drives home the point of kindred (ethnicity):

> And if **your brother, a Hebrew man, or a Hebrew woman,** be sold to you, and serve you six years; then in the seventh year you shall let him go free from you. (Deut 15:12)

If one was a Hebrew, then he was a "brother" (*'ibri*) to all other Israelites.[48] This distinction is made with the stipulation that Israel could only take bondservants from the local, Canaanite population (Lev 25:44). If, according to Gray's theory, Habiru/Hebrew classes existed in these populations, her thesis would contradict Lev 25:44, and Israel could not make bondslaves of the native Canaanites (since many of them would be Hebrews according to Gray's theory). These texts do not imply social class but clearly refer to ethnicity. About a 1,000 years later, when Jeremiah (34:14) quoted from the Law, he maintained this context, which *equated Hebrews with Jews based on ethnicity* (i.e., "a brother") at the closing of the kingdom years.

Lewy and Gray point out that the limit of service for a Hebrew slave (Exod 21:2) was similar to the limits of service found in Nuzi contracts for the Hapiru.[49] Both scholars conclude that this demonstrates that *Habiru* was a social distinction, since the Torah upholds the commonly accepted rights of the Habiru. As we have seen, the Torah upholds many commonly accepted ancient laws and did not change them unless they were unjust. Gray's observation works equally as well if the Hebrews were an ethnic group of people whose rights to limited terms of service had been established and recognized *prior* to the Sinai Covenant. Remember that many of Israel's holy days are attested in Ugarit and Mesopotamia before the 14th century. Since we do not know how much of YHWH's Law Noah had knowledge of after the flood, we cannot discount the possibility that some of these laws and customs had been established early in Mesopotamia and passed down through the generations, then became lost or corrupted, but were reestablished by YHWH with the Hebrews at Mt. Sinai.

V. IMPLICATIONS FROM CHAPTER 9'S CHRONOLOGY

One last consideration that alters any discussion of the Habiru is the date of the exodus. A 13th-century exodus does indeed face many obstacles for the Habiru/Hebrew equation: for example, what are Hebrews doing attacking Canaanite cities when the Hebrew populace is in Egypt? A 16th-century exodus reflects the archaeological record, for which I have presented incontrovertible evidence in chaps. 9–11. The Amarna Tablets further evidence Habiru activity in the very places such as Shechem and Jerusalem where the Hebrew-Israelites had settled during the early Conquest and Judges Eras. This again reinforces an ethnic association of the Habiru with the Hebrew-Israelites.

Chronology continues to remain a factor when considering the identity of the Hebrews in Mesopotamia. Chushan-rishathaim/Kadashman-harbe I of Kassite Babylon (Judg 3:8)[50] probably deported the Hebrews in Canaan to Akkad and Babylon *c.* 1460 BCE. While this theory may seem speculative, if we accept the Hebrew text as an accurate account of Israel's past, it certainly cannot be dismissed as a possibility. In Egypt, the Habiru do not appear in any written texts until the campaigns of Tutmoses III and Amenhotep II into Canaan, where both pharaohs deported Habiru from the very territories where the Hebrew Scriptures tell us Israel had settled and was continuing to subdue the Canaanites (see chap. 11). This use of the term *Habiru* completely fits Scripture's ethnic-linguistic affiliation. Notice that Scripture also allows for other ethnic Hebrews to have existed outside the land of Canaan. Thus, we see that an ethnic-racial affiliation for the Hebrews does indeed accommodate the historical and Scriptural evidence.

VI. HABIRU AND SHASU

Another term that may have been applied to Israel is the Egyptian term *Shasu.* The controversy over this term is that it is never clearly defined by either Egyptian hieroglyphics or the images that often accompany the term *Shasu.*[51] Gray observes that the Shasu were often distinguished from the Hapiru, and Merneptah certainly distinguished them from Israel.[52] That being said, there does appear to be some overlap prior to Merneptah's and Gideon's days.

The most distinguishing feature of Shasus appears to have been that they (1) lived in the desert regions of southern Canaan or (2) across the Jordan and (3) used whatever means available to remain self-sufficient and free.[53] The Shasu were usually listed separately from Asiatics or Habiru since Asiatics were associated with the west-central parts of Canaan and the Habiru with the area north of the Dead Sea.[54] The people of Edom and Mt. Seir are identified as Shasu in Egyptian texts;[55] however, this term probably included the Moabites, Kenites, Amalekites, and Ammonites. While most Shasu are understood to have been seminomadic, some Shasu, such as those in Edom, built cities.[56] The question that arises is: When would this term apply to Israel?

Similar to the etymology of *Habiru,* which means "to wander," *shasu* as an Egyptian term also means "to wander about," although this etymology is not clear-cut.[57] Habiru and Shasu are often listed together in the same texts, although they do not appear to be identical. This is how one possible theory can be constructed. The Habiru may have been a more settled people, while some of the Habiru/Hebrews, who were still living a Bedouin lifestyle, were known as *shasu.* The only reference (in all known Egyptian texts to date) that would identify the *Shasu* with Israel or the Hebrews is the inscription attributed to Amenhotep III, which identifies a particular Shasu group as the "Shasu of Yhw."[58] The Egyptian word Yhw is phonetically the same as the Hebrew word *Yahweh.*[59] This may be evidence that much of Israel's society was at least seminomadic during the 18th Dynasty (see pp. 538–39). By the

Amarna Period, a little less than a century later, it appears that the Egyptians came to regard the Habiru and the Shasu as different entities.

Whether we approach the Israelites as being part of a group of Shasu or the Habiru, the historical evidence accommodates an ethnic and/or linguistic affiliation of the Habiru/ Hebrew with the Israelites. Both the terms *Hebrew* and *Israelite* had designated the children of Abraham during the early Conquest and up through Saul's reign. Neither the word *Hebrew* nor the word *Israelite* had been abandoned for another term until the term *Jew* was coined for the Southern Kingdom after Samaria's fall (*c.* 717 BCE). These facts support that the information that Israel's scribes were recording did not require referring to Hebrews or Israelites except as the collective *Israel*, with only a few exceptions (2 Kgs 3:24; 7:13; 1 Chr 9:2). Jonah's reference to himself and Jeremiah's quotation of the Law indicate that these two names continued to identify the children of Jacob well into the later Monarchy. If we accept that a definite event (i.e., the confusion at Babel) or politics had forced the Hebrews from their homelands and caused them to immigrate to other lands rather than face the oppression of the temple corporations, then it is reasonable to associate the Hebrews with the historical evidence of a migratory ethnic group. While the Habirus/Hebrews in other lands were eventually absorbed into local populations, the Hebrews in Canaan retained their ethnic Hebrew (Heber) identity. This overall evidence continues to support the historicity of the Hebrew Scriptures.

Companion Resource

When I completed this study a few years ago, life was quite lonely. Churches that embraced the foundational truths of Scripture did not exist. Thankfully, over the past couple years, many people have returned to the Hebrew Scriptures to discover the same ideas I have presented here. The following links offer community and resources for those that would like to research further.

The first resource is Roots of Faith. This group of believers offers a textual-based Scripture study on Saturdays at 10:30 a.m. (CST). Click on the "Service/Classes" tab at www.rootsoffaith.org.

You can find other resources at these sites:

www.yhwhexists.com
www.closertotruth.com/participant/James-Tabor/104
www.jcpa.org/dje/articles2/deut-const.htm
www.unitedisrael.org/home.html
www.britam.org

ON FACEBOOK:

www.facebook.com/YHWHExistsbooks
www.facebook.com/JewishJesusDaily

COMING IN 2015-2016:

www.TorahObservantIsrael.org
www.TorahObservantIsrael.com

BOOKS:

Restoring Abrahamic Faith by James Tabor
Shattering the Conspiracy of Silence by Nehemia Gordon
Scripture in Context, Eds. Carl Evans, William Hallo, and John White
Temples, Tithes, and Taxes by Marty Stevens
Essential Papers on Israel and the Ancient Near East by Frederick Greenspahn, ed.
Faith, Tradition, and History, Eds. A.R. Millard, J.K. Hoffmeier, and D.W. Baker
The Nine Commandments by David Noel Freedman
Egypt, Canaan, and Israel in Ancient Times by Donald Redford
None of These Diseases by S. I. McMillen and David Stern

Endnotes

SEEK AND YOU SHALL FIND

1. James Dobson, *Bringing Up Boys* (Wheaton, IL: Tyndale House, 2001) 199; emphasis is Dr. Dobson's.
2. See also Matt 6:33; John 8:32; and 1 Cor 5:8.
3. Ps 146:8; Isa 42:18; 29:18; 35:5; and Matt 15:14.
4. 2 Cor 13:5; 2 Pet 2:1; and 1 John 4:1.
5. Israel Finkelstein and Neil Asher Silberman, *The Bible Unearthed* (New York: Free Press, 2001) 275–95; Richard Elliott Friedman, *Who Wrote the Bible?* (San Francisco: Harper San Francisco, 2001) 108–16; J. D. Levenson, "Who Inserted the Book of the Torah," *HTR* 68 (1977) 203–33; R. D. Nelson, *The Double Redaction of the Deuteronomistic History*, JSOTSup 18; Sheffield: JSOT Press, 1981); S. L. McKenzie, *The Chronicler's Use of the Deuteronomistic History* (HSM 33; Atlanta: Scholars Press, 1983); and John Van Seters, *In Search of History:Historiography in the Ancient World and Origins of Biblical History* (New Haven, CT: Yale University Press, 1983).
6. Ps 71:22; Eph 4:14; John 4:23; 8:23; 17:17; 2 Tim 2:15; 2 Cor 13:5; 2 Pet 2:1; 1 Jn 4:1; Josh 24:14; 1 Sam 12:24; Ps 51:6; 25:10; 33:4; 40:11; 60:4; 85:10–13; 89:14; 96:13; 98:3; 100:5; 145:18; Isa 26:2; 65:16; and Jer 5:1; 33:6.

ON GOD'S NAME

1. Deut 4:7–8; 2 Sam 7:23–24; Ps 119:142, 151; 73:1; 147:19–20; Isa 26:2; and Zech 8:3.
2. Exod 20:3; 10:7; 23:33; Deut 7:16; 8:19; 11:16; 30:17; Judgs 2:3; 8:27; 1 Kgs 9:6; 2 Chr 7:9; Ps 97:7; 106:36; Jer 13:10; 25:6; Deut 6:4; 32:39; Isa 43:10, 15; 44:24; 46:5.
3. The word "nation" is a modern term. In Hebrew, this idea is termed *goy* or *gôyim*. These Hebrew terms, however, have modern connotations that are alien to the Scriptural text. The most important being that modern Judaism terms any non-Jew a *goy*; when in fact the Scriptural text applies the term to any group of people, even Israelites (Gen 12:2; 18:18; 21:18; 35:11; 46:3; Exod 19:6; 32:10; 33:13; Lev 18:26; Deut 4:6, 34; 9:14; 26:5; 32:28; 1 Chr 17:21; Ps 33:12; 83:4; Isa 26:2, 15; 51:4; Jer 31:36; 48:2; Ezek 37:22). In order to avoid confusion for the reader, I will use the word 'nation' to express the ancient concept of *goy* or *gôyim*.
4. Exod 23:13; Zech 13:2; and *JFB*, 768.

911

5. *UBD*, 413, plural—*Baalim* (*SEC* 1168; BDB, 127).

6. *GDSAM*, 128; and Kurt G. Jung, "Baal," *ISBE* (vol. 1) 377–78.

7. Ze'ev Meshel, *Kuntillet 'Ajrud (Horvat Teman): An Iron Age II Religious Site on the Judah-Sinai Border* (Jerusalem: Israel Exploration Society, 2012) 109; see also Hershel Shanks, "The Persisting Uncertainties of Kuntillet 'Ajrud," *BAR* 38/6 (2013) 29–37, 76.

8. John Day, *Yahweh and the Gods and Goddesses of Canaan* (London: Sheffield Academic Press, 2002) 68; emphasis added.

9. See also Exod 23:13; Zech 13:2; and Isa 52:5–6.

10. *SEC* 376; BDB 35; and *TWOT* (vol. 1) 38–39. *Baalim* is the plural form of the word *Baal* or *Bali*.

11. See also Ezek 39:25.

12. *SEC* 3068–69; BDB, 217–18; *TWOT* (vol. 1) 210–12.

13. *SEC* 1961; BDB, 226; Day, *Gods and Goddesses of Canaan*, 14, 20. For other discussions on the name, see William F. Albright, *Yahweh and the Gods of Canaan* (Winona Lake, IN: Eisenbrauns, 1994) 168–72.

14. Robert J. Wyatt, "Names of God," *ISBE* (vol. 2) 507.

15. Stephen Hawking, *A Brief History of Time* (New York: Bantam Books, 1988) 141. See also Day, *Gods and Goddesses of Canaan*, 14, 20.

CHAPTER ONE

1. Mic 6:3; Ezek 18:25, 29; 33:17–20.

2. Acts 13:39; Rom 3:19–20; 4:15; 7:1, 6; Gal 2:16, 21; 3:10–11; Heb 7:19; and Jas 2:10.

3. The present study differentiates between scientific "proof" and legal "evidence."

4. We will look at Balaam's prophecy in Part 2 of this volume.

5. Louis P. Pojman, *Philosophy: The Quest for Truth* (Belmont, CA: Wadsworth Publishing, 1989) 152; A. N. Prior, *The Encyclopedia of Philosophy* (vol. 2; ed. Paul Edwards; New York: Macmillan and The Free Press, 1962) 223–232; Robert Nola and Howard Sankey, *Theories of Scientific Method* (Montreal: McGill-Queen's University Press, 2007).

6. Ayn Rand, *Philosophy: Who Needs It?* (New York: Signet, 1982) 70–71.

7. Ibid., 71.

8. Kim Ryholt, *The Political Situation in Egypt during the Second Intermediate Period* (Copenhagen: Museum Tusculanum Press, 1997) 311–12.

9. To the best of my ability, I have ordered this investigative case based on the principles set forth in Robert Nola and Howard Sankey's, *Theories of Scientific Method*. Reflective equilibrium can be seen to deal with the chasm between (moral) law and those value judgments society actually follows. It does not call for justification but seeks to find the equilibrium between the two (Ibid., 91–98). I will not seek to justify the chasm. Rather I will employ a principle-based approach to a scientific set of "concept controls" that will allow us to test the Hebrew Scriptures (YHWH) to see if they support (i.e., meet our criteria) or if they fail. I have tried to avoid establishing controls that "maximize expected utility," opting instead for well-defined, empirical, logical set of ideals, which underlie a "concept of truth theorem." To achieve the aim of this research, we will appeal to value-based principles of confirmation. While these concepts, or principles, may not be conclusive, they should at least establish a foundation for a conceptual and ideological hypothesis to test the "concepts of truth" to see if ideological contradictions exist in Scripture.

10. Mary Joan Leith, "The Bible Divide," *BAR* 38/2 (March/April, 2012) 24, 66.

11. George Mendenhall, "Biblical History in Transition," in *The Bible and the Ancient Near East: Essays in Honor of William Foxwell Albright* (ed. George Earnest Wright; Garden City, NY: Anchor Books, 1965) 42.

12. If the Hebrew Scriptures appeal to mysticism in lieu of the principles of scholarship, then this study would be pointless.

13. Joachim Rehork, postscript in *The Bible as History,* by Werner Keller (New York: William Morrow and Company, 1981) 387. See also, Edwin Yamauchi, "The Current State of Old Testament Historiography," *FTH,* 5–7.

14. Rehork, postscript in *The Bible as History,* 387–88.

15. See definition of *truth* in the previous section.

16. Gordon Wenham, *Word Biblical Commentary: Genesis 16–50* (vol. 2; Dallas, TX: Word Books, 1994) 29.

17. Ibid.

18. Exod 9:27; Deut 4:8; Judg 5:11; 1 Sam 12:7; 2 Chr 12:6; Ezra 9:15; Neh 9:8; Ps 7:9; 7:17; 9:8; 11:7; 19:9; 22:31; 35:24, 28; 36:6, 10; 40:10; 50:6; 51:14; 71:2, 15–16, 19, 24; 72:2; 88:12; 89:16; 97:6; 98:2, 9; 99:4; 103:6; 111:3; 116:5; 119:7, 40, 62, 106, 123, 137–38, 142–4, 160, 164, 172; 129:4; 143:1, 11; 145:7, 17; Isa 5:16; 11:4–5; 41:10; 42:21; 45:19, 23; 46:13; 51:5–6, 8; 56:1; 59:16–17; Jer 12:1; Lam 1:18; Dan 9:7, 14, 16; Mic 6:5; and Zech 8:8.

19. *SEC* 6662; BDB, 843; and *TWOT* (vol. 2) 754–55.

20. *SEC* 6663; BDB, 842.

21. Victor Hamilton, *The Book of Genesis: 1–17* (Grand Rapids: Eerdmans, 1990) 273.

22. James Hoffmeier, *Israel in Egypt* (New York: Oxford University Press, 1996) 10–11; and Baruch Halpern, *The First Historians* (University Park: Penn State University Press, 1988) xix–xxiii.

23. Hoffmeier, *Israel in Egypt,* 10.

24. Ibid. See also Halpern, *The First Historians,* 5.

25. Hoffmeier, *Israel in Egypt,* 13.

26. Israel Finkelstein and Neil Asher-Silberman, *The Bible Unearthed* (New York: Freedom Press, 2001) 129.

27. Halpern, *First Historians,* 13.

28. The information that I am presenting in this trial is based on 12 years of research. Although I have already drawn my conclusions, I am presenting the evidence for the reader to see if ancient Israel's allegations have merit or if they fail. If you find I am being too lenient on Israel's God, please reserve judgment until volume II of this trial.

29. Geza Vermez, *The Complete Dead Sea Scrolls in English* (New York: Penguin, 1962) 23; Joel Hoffman, *In the Beginning: A Short History of the Hebrew Language* (New York: New York University Press, 2004) 142; James VanderKam and Peter Flint, *The Meaning of the Dead Sea Scrolls* (San Francisco: Harper, 2002) 103–152.

30. W. F. Bolton, *A Living Language* (New York: McGraw-Hill, 1982) 23–30, 77–94, 204–16; and Hoffman, *In the Beginning,* 142–62.

31. Sidney Jellicoe, *The Septuagint and Modern Study* (Winona Lake, IN: Eisenbrauns, 1993) 319; and VanderKam and Flint, *Meaning of the Dead Sea Scrolls,* 88–90.

32. Jellicoe, *Septuagint and Modern Study,* 319. See also VanderKam and Flint, *Meaning of the Dead Sea Scrolls,* 142–43.

33. Jellicoe, *Septuagint and Modern Study,* 29–35; *JHRE,* 4–6; and Sven K. Soderlund, "Septuagint," *ISBE* (vol. 4) 400–408.

34. Jellicoe, *Septuagint and Modern Study,* 318–19; Hoffman, *In the Beginning,* 146; and VanderKam and Flint, *Meaning of the Dead Sea Scrolls,* 142–43.

35. Jellicoe, *Septuagint and Modern Study,* 277; Vermez, *Dead Sea Scrolls,* 16; and Hoffman, *In the Beginning,* 146.

36. Vermes, *Dead Sea Scrolls,* 23–24; and VanderKam and Flint, *Meaning of the Dead Sea Scrolls,* 142–43.

37. The basis for my choice are threefold. First, to use a text that most people are familiar with or that they can easily access. Second, we will be examining many texts and do not want to be restricted in use of the textual evidence due to copyright or other legal limitations. Third, most research tools are based on the traditional KJV. My goal is to make the information readily accessible for others to check and verify or research further. I have chosen the American KJV version, which is easier to read since most of the outdated language has been updated to modern English.

38. Gary King, Robert Keohane, and Sidney Verba, *Designing Social Inquiry: Scientific Inference in Qualitative Research* (Princeton, NJ: Princeton University Press, 1994).

39. Thomas Kuhn, *The Structure of Scientific Revolutions* (Chicago: University of Chicago Press, 1970).

40. The word *Torah* designates the Pentateuch, the first five books of the Bible: Genesis, Exodus, Leviticus, Numbers, and Deuteronomy. I will use *Torah* and *Pentateuch* interchangeably when referring to the books of the Law.

41. *SEC* 7810; BDB, 1005; and *TWOT* (vol. 2) 914.

42. Throughout the ancient Near East, arable lands such as Ephron's field were customarily inherited by the owner's children or near kin. The only way to gain permanent ownership of properties in the rural countryside and to avoid the heirs' claim was by paying full market value (Raymond Westbrook and Bruce Wells, *Everyday Law* [Louisville, KY: John Knox, 2009] 109–10). Had Abram or David (2 Sam 24:22–24) paid a lesser amount for their properties the transfer would have been a temporary possession, which would revert to the estate's heirs upon the seller's death (see the 13th century contract no. 15.119 in Nougayrol 199, op cite: ibid.). Israel's Law forbid actual sale of the countryside by her citizenry even when full market price had been realized. Instead, YHWH opted for lease-only contracts (Lev 25:23). Other nations such as the Hittites did not follow this inalienable statute regarding land and therefore transferred permanent ownership to Abraham and his heirs if the full price of the field was met. Abraham's transaction not only obtained a permanent possession, but he also refused a less-permanent altruistic gift. See also, Raymond Westbrook, *Property and the Family in Biblical Law* (JSOTSup 113; Sheffield: JSOT Press, 1991) 24–35.

43. Wenham, *Genesis 16–50*, 127–29.

44. Wenham (ibid.) also points out that the political realities in accepting a gift naturally obligates the receiver to the donor.

45. *SEC* 1870; BDB, 202; *TWOT* (vol. 1) 196–97; and Victor Hamilton, *Genesis:18–50* (Grand Rapids: Eerdmans, 1995) 194.

46. Moshe Weinfeld, "Covenant of Grant," in *Essential Papers on Israel and the Ancient Near East* (ed. Frederick Greenspahn, New York: New York University Press, 1991) 70; and Hamilton, *Genesis:18–50*, 194.

47. YHWH's nonarbitrary selection is seen again in his covenant with David, where the Creator states that he chose David "because he kept my commandments and my statutes" (1 Kgs 11:34).

48. Wenham, *Genesis 16–50*, 29.

49. YHWH promised King David that Israel's monarchy (under a United Kingdom) would always descend through David's line. Likewise, YHWH promised Phinehas that the priesthood would always descend through his sons (Numbers 25). Jeremiah refers to these covenants in Jer 33:20–26.

50. Deut 28:15–68; and Roland K. Harrison, "Curse," *ISBE* (vol.1) 837–38.

51. See also Robert Wilson, *Genealogy and History in the Biblical World* (New Haven, CT: Yale University Press, 1977) 161.

52. Edward Young, *An Introduction to the Old Testament* (Grand Rapids: Eerdmans, 1958) 125. See also, A. R. Millard, J. K. Hoffmeier, and D. W. Baker, *Faith Tradition and History* (Winona Lake, IN: Eisenbrauns, 1994).

CHAPTER TWO

1. King, Keohane, and Verba, *Designing Social Inquiry*; John Stuart Mill, *Philosophy of Scientific Method* (New York: Dover, 2005); Nola and Sankey, *Theories of Scientific Method*. For an easily accessed overview, see: http://www.indiana.edu/~educy520/sec5982/week_1/inquiry_sci_method02.pdf (accessed December 2014).

2. Anthony Phillips, *Ancient Israel's Criminal Law* (Oxford: Basil Blackwell, 1970) 11; and Westbrook, *Property, Family in Biblical Law*, 38.

3. See also Deut 10:13; 26:11; Josh 1:8; 23:14; 1 Sam 12:23; 1 Kgs 8:36; 2 Chr 30:22; Ezra 3:11; Neh 9:13; Ps 25:8; 34:10; 119:39, 68; and Prov 4:2.

4. Phillips, *Israel's Criminal Law*, 11; and Westbrook, *Property, Family in Biblical Law*, 38.

5. *SEC* 1891, 1892; BDB 210–11; and *TWOT* (vol. 1) 204–5.

6. *CGAE*, 117, 229; Joseph Campbell, *The Mythic Image* (Princeton, NJ: Princeton University Press, 1974); and John Currid, *Ancient Egypt and the Old Testament* (Grand Rapids: Baker, 1997) 42.

7. David Noel Freedman, *The Nine Commandments* (New York: Doubleday, 2000) 34; James Hastings and John Selbie, *Encyclopedia of Religion and Ethics* (vol. 10; Whitefish, MT: Kessinger, 1908) 483–84; K. van der Toorn, *Sin and Sanction in Israel and Mesopotamia* (Maastricht, Netherlands: Van Gorcum, 1985) 23; and Campbell, *Mythic Image*, 15–44.

8. George Mendenhall, *Ancient Israel's Faith and History* (Louisville, KY: John Knox, 2001) 34.

9. *JM*, 5, 34–37; and van der Toorn, *Sin and Sanction*, 24, 94–97; Jan Assmann, *Death and Salvation in Ancient Egypt* (trans. David Lorton; Ithaca, NY: Cornell University Press) 115, 125; Currid, *Egypt and Old Testament*, 96–102; It should be pointed out that not all ancient religions had a concept of sin. Some cults, such as Egypt's Maat viewed right and wrong as a set of ethics (Maulana Karenga, *Maat, the Moral Ideal in Ancient Egypt: A Study in Classical African Ethics* [New York: Routledge, 2004] 233–35, 3–11). However, Bleeker has demonstrated ten Egyptian words associated with sin and six other words associated with guilt (C. J. Bleeker, "Guilt and Purification in Egypt," in *Proceedings of the Xth International Congress of the International Association of Religions* [vol. 2; Leiden: Brill, 1968] 81–87).

10. Assmann, *Death and Salvation*, 115–16. See also Donald Redford, *Oxford Encyclopedia of Ancient Egypt* (vol. 3; Oxford: Oxford University Press, 2001) 346; Ibid., (vol. 2) 211–14; Bleeker, "Guilt and Purification in Egypt," 81–87.

11. John Pedley, *Sanctuaries and the Sacred in the Ancient Greek World* (New York: Cambridge University Press, 2006) 1, 16, 116; *CGAE*, 135, 117, 136; Cambell, *Mythic Image*; Paul L. Garber and Roland K. Harrison, "Idol," *ISBE* (vol. 2) 794–97; and Othmar Keel and Christopher Uehlinger, *Gods, Goddesses, and Images of God* (trans. Thomas Trapp; Minneapolis, MN: Fortress Press, 1998) 7–9.

12. R. J. Hoffmann, trans., *Celsus on the True Doctrine* (Oxford: Oxford University Press, 1987) 71; and *JM*, 80–81.

13. *JM*, 16, 21–22, 25.

14. *JM*, 35. See also: Hastings and Selbie, *Encyclopedia Religion and Ethics: part 10*, 282–84; Assmann, *Death and Salvation*, 78; and Bleeker, *Guilt and Purification*, 87.

15. Assmann, *Death and Salvation*, 78–86. According to currently accepted Egyptian chronology, Moses lived during the New Kingdom Era of Egyptian history. This theory is challenged in chap. 10 of this volume.

16. Richard Wilkinson, *The Complete Gods and Goddesses of Ancient Egypt* (London: Thames and Hudson, 2003) 170–72; Ian Shaw and Paul Nicholson, *The British Museum Dictionary of Ancient Egypt* (London: British Museum Press, 2008) 38–39; and Patricia Turner and Charles Coulter, *Dictionary of Ancient Deities* (New York: Oxford University Press, 2000) 61–62. When Osiris reincarnated, he took a bull or apis form. The Hebrew word, *'egel*, usually translated "calf" actually means a bullock, almost full-grown thus embracing the idea of an apis (*SEC* 5695; BDB, 7222).

17. Camden M. Cobern and Carl E. Armerding, "Golden Calf," *ISBE* (vol. 1) 579–80; Molefi Asante and Ama Mazama, ed., *Encyclopedia of African Religion* (vol. 1; Thousand Oaks, CA: Sage Publication, 2009) 141. Hathor and Ihy are other Egyptian deities that could have been represented by the golden calf. One of the best treatments of the subject can be found by Walter Mattfeld, "The Egyptian Origins of Israel's Golden Calf Worship in the Sinai," Bible Origins, last updated November 21, 2009, http://www.bibleorigins.net/EgyptianOriginsGoldenCalf.html (accessed December 2014).

18. Robert Morkot, *The Egyptians* (New York: Routledge, 2005) 210; Assmann, *Death and Salvation*, 115–16, 125, 134–37; and George Hart, *The Routledge Dictionary of Egyptian Gods and Goddesses* (New York: Routledge, 2005) 70–72, 114–24.

19. Wilkinson, *Complete Gods and Goddesses,* 170–72; Shaw and Nicholson, *Dictionary of Ancient Egypt,* 38–39; and Turner and Coulter, *Dictionary of Ancient Deities,* 61–62.

20. In ancient Egypt, a golden calf always represented Pharaoh as a god. It was a dualistic synronization of the image of god and the monarch. Jeroboam, who had spent a significant time in Egypt (1 Kgs 11:40) no doubt turned to these gods to legitimize his reign (see also: http://www.bibleorigins.net/EgyptianOriginsGoldenCalf.html).

21. Hart, *Dictionary of Egyptian Gods and Goddesses,* 29–30.

22. Albright, *Yahweh and the Gods of Canaan*; Day, *Gods and Goddesses of Canaan*; and Keel and Uehlinger, *Gods, Goddesses, and Images,* 205, 236–81.

23. Sarah Johnston, ed., *Religions of the Ancient World* (Cambridge: Harvard University Press, 2004) 20, 81, 96, 110, 340, 368, 496–513, 507, 643–44, 648; Campbell, *Mythic Image,* 49, 167–69; Idem, *Oriental Mythology: The Masks of God* (New York: Penguin, 1962) 395; *JM,* 33, 57–58, 93, 178; Alexander Hislop, *The Two Babylons* (Neptune, NJ: Loizeaux Brothers, 1959) 20, 56; and James Frazer, *The Golden Bough* (New York: Macmillan, 1922). Although Hislop's book is outdated, his basic premise is quite justified. This present study draws from the portions of his book that remain valid.

24. Johnston, *Religions of the Ancient World,* 20, 81, 96, 110, 340, 368, 496–513, 507, 643–44, 648; Jean Bottéro, *Religion in Ancient Mesopotamia* (trans. Teresa Fagan; Chicago: University of Chicago Press, 2004); David Ulansey, *The Origins of the Mithraic Mysteries: Cosmology and Salvation in the Ancient World* (Oxford: Oxford University Press, 1991) 125; Frazer, *Golden Bough,* 445; Hislop, *The Two Babylons*; Joseph McCabe, *The Myth of the Resurrection* (Buffalo, NY: Prometheus Books, 1993); J. M. Robertson, *Pagan Christs* (New Hyde Park, NY: University Books, 1967); Kersey Graves, *The World's Sixteen Crucified Saviors* (Boston, MA: Colby and Rich, 1881). Graves' book is also outdated. He misidentifies many "crucified saviors" while other saviors arose during the New Testament era (after CE 200). Much of his polemic, however, remains valid and is easily accessible on the Internet.

25. Ralph Woodrow, *Babylon Mystery Religion* (Riverside, CA: Ralph Woodrow Evangelistic Association, 1966) 84.

26. Ibid., 47–54; T. W. Doane, *Bible Myths and Their Parallels in Other Religions* (New York: University Books, 1971) 339–58; Hislop, *Two Babylons,* 48–49; and *JM,* 50, 80, 166, 199.

27. Introductory works include: Wodrow, *Babylon Mystery Religion*; Hislop, *The Two Babylons*; McCabe, *The Myth of the Resurrection*; Robertson, *Pagan Christs*; Graves, *The World's Sixteen Crucified Saviors*; Freke and Gandy, *The Jesus Mysteries*; Campbell, *Hero with a Thousand Faces*; Idem, *Mythic Image*; and Emma J. Edelstein and Ludwig Edelstein, "T. 700," *Asclepius: Collection and Interpretation of the Testimonies* (2 vols.; Baltimore: Johns Hopkins University, 1998) 365.

28. One good translation of these mythological texts is: Stephanie Dally, trans., *Myths from Mesopotamia* (Oxford: Oxford University Press, 1989); see also N. Wyatt, *Religious Texts from Ugarit* (Sheffield; Sheffield Academic Press, 1998). Another very good discussion is Currid, *Egypt and Old Testament.* See also Campbell, *Mythic Image.*

29. Compare Exodus 29–30.

30. *SEC* 8552; BDB, 1070–71; and *TWOT* (vol. 2) 973–74.

31. *SEC* 1870; BDB, 202; and *TWOT* (vol. 1) 196–97.

32. *SEC* 6965; BDB, 877; *TWOT* (vol. 2) 793; and Hamilton, *Genesis: 1–17,* 316.

33. For example, see the following KJV verses. **Rise up**–Num 22:20, 23:18; Deut 2:24, 18:15, 19:15, 29:22; Judg 2:16, 5:7; 1 Sam 18:27. **Confirm**—Num 30:14; Deut 27:26; Esth 9:29, 32; Ezek 13:6. **Establish**—Gen 9:9, 11, 17; 17:7, 19, 21; Num 30:14; Deut 8:18, 28:9; 2 Chr 7:18; Esth 9:21. **Arise/arose**—Gen 31:17, 21, 35, 32:22, 46:5; Exod 21:19, 24:13; Lev 19:32, 26:1; Num 22:13, 24:17; 2 Chr 13:6. **Stand**—Num 30:5; Job 19:25; and Ps 1:5.

34. Weinfeld, "Covenant of Grant," 70.

35. Jer 33:20–21; and Gen 8:21–22. For further discussion, see chap. 1.VII.E.1.

36. Hamilton, *The Book of Genesis: 1–17,* 321.

37. This law did not condone personal retribution (Lev 19:18). Rather, the Israelite Law established social justice firmly administered through a community-based court system (Deut 1:13–18; 17:9–13).

38. *SEC* 1101; BDB, 117; *TWOT* (vol. 1) 111–12; *UBD*: 114–15; and Gordon Wenham, *Word Biblical Commentary: Genesis 1–15* (vol. 1; Waco, TX: Word Books, 1987) 241.

39. *TWOT* (vol. 1) 89; A. W. Fortune, "Babylon," *ISBE* (vol. 1) 385. For a contrary viewpoint, see David F. Payne, "Babel," *ISBE* (vol. 1) 382.

40. The regulations within the Pentateuch (Israel's Law) are another "control" in this case.

41. *SEC* 6389; BDB, 811; and UBD, 841.

42. Carl Rasmussen, "Peleg," *ISBE* (vol. 3) 736.

43. See Appendix B, 9.51. Flood to Abraham on pg. 896.

44. The KJV erroneously translates "flood" in lieu of "river" (*SEC* 5104; BDB, 625–26). Terah lived on the "other side" of the Euphrates River. Canaan would have been on "this" side of the river.

45. Victor Hamilton, *Genesis: 18–50* (Grand Rapids, MI: Eerdmans, 1995) 205.

46. Muata Ashby, *Egypt and India: Ancient Egyptian Religion and the Origins of Hinduism, Vedanta, Yoga, Buddhism and Dharma of India* (Miami: Curzian Mystic Books, 2002); R. Drew Griffith, *Mummy Wheat* (New York: University Press of America, 2008); Frazer, *Golden Bough,* 59. Also a good reference: Campbell, *Mythic Image,* 16; Idem, *Oriental Mythology,* 47–48, 70, 196, 255, 395; Sushama Londhe, *A Tribute to Hinduism* (New Delhi: Pragun Publications, 2008); and http://www.hinduwisdom.info/India_and_Egypt.htm (accessed December 2014).

47. Campbell, *Oriental Mythology,* 47–48, 70, 196, 255, 395; Idem, *Occidental Mythology:The Masks of God* (New York: Pinguin,1994) 6, 15, 23, 44, 54–55, 64, 73, 104–5, 107–9, 147–48, 173, 342–47; Ashby, *African Origins* (vol. 3) 174–382; and Frazer, *Golden Bough,* 378.

48. Peter Koslowski, ed., *Progress, Apocalypse, and Completion of History and Life after Death of the Human Person in the World Religions* (Dordrecht, Netherlands: Kluwer Academic Publishers, 2002) 75–80; and Prem Bhalla, *Hindu Rites, Rituals, Customs and Traditions* (Delhi: Pustak Mahal, 2006) 308.

49. *CGAE,* 29–32; J. H. Breasted, *The Development of Religion and Thought in Ancient Egypt* (New York: Scribner, 1912), http://www.sacred-texts.com/egy/rtae/rtae05.htm (accessed December 2014); Earnest Budge, *The Gods of the Egyptians Or, Studies in Egyptian Mythology* (2 vols.; London: Methuen, 1904); and Currid, *Egypt and Old Testament,* 47.

50. *CGAE,* 53, 58–59, 62–63, 132; Abeer El-Shahawy, *The Funerary Art of Ancient Egypt: A Bridge to the Realm of the Hereafter* (Cairo: Farid Atiya Press, 2005) 75–79; Assmann, *Death and Salvation,* 155–57; Redford, *Oxford Encyclopedia of Ancient Egypt* (vol. 3) 71; Morris Jastrow, *Religion of Babylonia and Assyria* (Boston: Athanaeum Press, 1898) 599, 605, 682–83; Walter Burkert, *Greek Religion* (trans. John Raffan; and Cambridge: Harvard University Press, 2008) 192–94.

51. Redford, ed., *Oxford Encyclopedia of Ancient Egypt* (vol. 1) 313, 330–31. Rosalie David points out that writing letters to the dead was also a customary practice as late as the Old Kingdom (Rosalie David, *Religion and Magic in Ancient Egypt* [New York: Penguin, 2003] 282, 422).

52. *CGAE,* 107, 140–42; and *KG,* 110, 132–39.

53. *CGAE,* 36–38.

54. Ibid., 36, 40.

55. Redford, *Oxford Encyclopedia of Ancient Egypt* (vol. 1) 330.

56. *CGAE,* 62.

57. Ibid., 217–23.

58. Assmann, *Death and Salvation,* 155.

59. Redford, *Oxford Encyclopedia of Ancient Egypt* (vol. 1) 330.

60. Assmann, *Death and Salvation,* 158, 337–38.

61. Augustine Pagolu, *The Religion of the Patriarchs* (Sheffield: Sheffield Academic Press, 1998) 37. See also *ANET,* 325; and Raymond Faulkner, *The Ancient Egyptian Pyramid Texts* (Oxford: Clarendon, 1969) 7, 20–21.

62. For examples of sacrifice for the dead in Ugarit, see Pagolu, *Religion of Patriarchs,* 42.

63. Van der Toorn, *Sin and Sanction,* 153. See also pp. 44, 70, 134; and *IHCANE,* 133, 138.

64. *GDSAM,* 27–28.

65. Ibid., 28.

66. Ibid.; Van der Toorn, *Sin and Sanction,* 153. See also: 44, 70, 134; and *IHCANE,* 133, 138.

67. *ESSP,* 472. See also Redford, *Oxford Encyclopedia of Ancient Egypt* (vol. 1) 330.

68. *GDSAM,* 28. See also Redford, *Oxford Encyclopedia of Ancient Egypt* (vol. 1) 330. Walter Burkert sees later Greek beliefs regarding death strongly tied to the Egyptian *Book of the Dead* (Burkert, *Greek Religion,* 294).

69. Allen C. Myers, "Death," *ISBE* (vol. 1) 899.

70. Campbell, *Mythic Image,* 32–51, 58–66, 196–97, 232, 243; Idem, *Oriental Mythology,* 40, 98, 100, 330, 384–85, 394–95; *JM,* 5–6, 18, 29–31, 57, 60, 76, 196; Doanne, *Bible Myths,* 326–38; Harold Willoughby, *Pagan Regeneration* (Chicago: Chicago University Press, 1929) 30–32; Hislop, *The Two Babylons,* 18–21, 74–90; Joycelyn Rhys, *Shaken Creeds: The Virgin Birth Doctrine and the Study of Its Origins* (Whitefish, MT: Kessenger Publishing, 1922); Simo Parpola, "Sons of God: The Ideology of Assyrian Kingship," *Archaeology Odyssey* 2/5 (1999) 16–27; *KK,* 266–67; and Thomas James Thorburn, *A Critical Examination of the Evidences for the Doctrine of the Virgin Birth* (New York: E. S. Gorham, 1908) 156–58. Thorburn, an unabashed apologetic, had to admit this myth was "abundantly common for generations before, and subsequent to, the time of Christ (that) there is no doubt whatever" (ibid., 157, parenthesis added). Buddhism also recognized a virgin holy mother well before the Christian era (see *Majjhima Nikaya* 123:10—*The Middle Length Discourses of the Buddha*).

71. Campbell, *Oriental Mythology,* 395; *JM,* 33, 57–58, 93, 178; *GDSAM,* 72–73; Willoughby, *Pagan Regeneration,* 30–32; Hislop, *The Two Babylons,* 20, 56; and Frazer, *Golden Bough,* 378.

72. Burkert, *Greek Religion,* 177–78.

73. *GDSAM,* 108, 72–73. There are well over 800 languages and dialects spoken in India; thus, the name Devaki and Krsna appear in many different spellings and transliterations.

74. A. C. Bhaktivedanta Swami Prabhupada, *KRSNA* (Juhu, India: Bhaktivedanta Book Trust, 1970) 28; Campbell, *Mythic Image,* 46; *JM,* 5–6, 29–31, 60, 76, 141. For other examples of immaculate conception in Egypt, see Barry J. Kemp, *Ancient Egypt: Anatomy of a Civilization* (New York: Routledge, 1989) 198–200; Jill Kamil, *The Ancient Egyptians: Life in the Old Kingdom* (Cairo: American University Press in Cairo, 1984) 183; and John Marshall, *Mohenjo Daro and the Indus Civilization* (vol. 1; New Delhi: Asian Educational Services, 1931) 58.

75. Prabhupada, *KRSNA,* 29–30; Campbell, *Mythic Image,* 49; Paul W. Gaebelein, Jr., "Tammuz," *ISBE* (vol. 4) 726. For a more detailed account of Krishna's conception and danger at birth, see T. R. Iyengar, *Dictionary of Hindu Gods and Goddesses,* (New Delhi: DK Printworld, 2003) 111–16.

76. Prabhupada, *KRSNA,* 30.

77. See also *JM,* 4, 9, 22–23, 29, 32–34; Campbell, *Mythic Image;* Idem, *Occidental Mythology;* Idem, *The Masks of God;* Burkert, *The The Orientalizing Revolution: Near Eastern Influence on Greek Culture in the Early Archaic Age* (trans. Margaret Pinder, Cambridge: Harvard University Press, 1995); Charles Penglase, *Greek Myths and Mesopotamian: Parallels and Influence in the Homeric Hymns and Hesiod* (New York: Routledge, 1994); Griffith, *Mummy Wheat;* and Willoughby, *Pagan Regeneration,* 30–32, 169–195.

78. For Oriental influence on Greek mythology, see Burkert, *The Orientalizing Revolution;* Griffith, *Mummy Wheat;* Penglase, *Greek Myths and Mesopotamia;* Freke and Gandy, *The Jesus Mysteries;* and Willoughby, *Pagan Regeneration,* 30–32, 111–12, 169–95.

79. Gae Callender, "The Middle Kingdom Renaissance," in *OHAE,* 166–67.

80. *CGAE,* 80; *KG,* 118, 210; J. E. Hartley, "Star," *ISBE* (vol. 4) 611; and *GDSAM,* 169–70.

81. Amar Annus, *The God Ninurta* (Helsinki: University of Helsinki Press, 2002) 138.

82. *CGAE,* 80 (emphasis added). See also, *KG,* 118, 210; Hartley, "Star," *ISBE* (vol. 4) 611; and *GDSAM,* 169–70.

83. Roland K. Harrison, "Queen of Heaven," *ISBE* (vol. 4) 8. In Babylon, Ishtar (Inana) was associated with Venus (*GDSAM,* 109; and Jastrow, *Babylonia and Assyria,* 81, 370, 458–59, 571).

84. *GDSAM,* 108; *KG,* 297 (Inanna was the Mesopotamian counterpart to Isis); and Harrison, "Queen of Heaven," 8.

85. Turner and Coulter, *Ancient Deities,* 367, 396.

86. *KG,* 281–83, 285, 291–94; *CGAE,* 155, 160–62; *JM,* 54–57, 59, 61, 121–23, 130; Currid, *Ancient Egypt,* 242. On Tammuz, Osiris's Babylonian counterpart, see *ANET,* 84; Burkert, *Greek Religion,* 176–78; Susan Ackerman, *Under Every Green Tree* (HSM 46; Eisenbrauns, 2001) 33; Assmann, *Death and Salvation,* 113–27; and Samuel Kramer, "Sumerian Literature," in *The Bible and the Ancient Near East* (Garden City, NY: Anchor, 1965) 338.

87. Assmann, *Death and Salvation,* 115; Jastrow, *Babylonia and Assyria,* 484; Willoughby, *Pagan Regeneration,* 117–18; and Thorkild Jacobsen, *The Treasures of Darkness: A History of Mesopotamian Religion* (New Haven, CT: Yale University Press, 1976) 47–62, 63–73.

88. *CGAE,* 152; *KG,* Violent death—30–31, 137–38, 146, 197, 201, 281–86 and Resurrection—128, 136, 186–87; Alberto Green, *The Storm-God in the Ancient Near East* (Biblical and Judaic Studies 8; Winona Lake, IN: Eisenbrauns, 2003) 5, 209, 212; Hislop, *The Two Babylons,* 55–74; Ezek 8:14–15; *GDSAM,* 72–73; Doanne, *Bible Myths,* 181–246; *JM,* 54–57, 59, 61, 119–21, 130; Willoughby, *Pagan Regeneration,* 31; Gerald Massey, *Ancient Egypt: The Light of the World* (vol. 2; Baltimore: Black Classic Press, 1907) 727–889; and Edelstein and Edelstein, *Asclepius* (vol. 2) 365. Concepts of a unified son who was sacrificed and descended into the "navel of the earth" then arose into the sky are also found in pre-Columbian Aztec images (Campbell, *Mythic Image,* 167–69).

89. *CGAE,* 160 (brackets added).

90. Redford, *Oxford Encyclopedia of Ancient Egypt* (vol. 3) 54–55; *JM,* 56 and n.251.

91. Redford, *Oxford Encyclopedia of Ancient Egypt* (vol. 3) 56. See also *GDSAM,* 57–58, 72–73; Willoughby, *Pagan Regeneration,* 65–67, 80, 127–28, 138–39, 159, 167; and Gaebelein, "Tammuz," 725–26.

92. *GDSAM,* 72–73; *CGAE,* 172, 181; *KG,* 39, 209 n.15; *JM,* 25; Assmann, *Death and Salvation,* 74, 77–78; Herbert Lockyer, ed., *Nelson's Illustrated Bible Dictionary* (Nashville: Thomas Nelson, 1986) 433.

93. For a better description of these plays, see Willoughby, *Pagan Regeneration,* 60–65.

94. Some of these rites have been preserved in the mystery plays recorded in the Egyptian Pyramid Texts. See *KG,* 128 and 136 for some common ritual elements to which Herodotus may be referring regarding Osiris's death and resurrection.

95. Willoughby, *Pagan Regeneration,* 30–32, 75, 76, 280.

96. For more information on these rites in Greece, see previous note.

97. Additional evidence of the Greeks' adopting Egyptian/Mesopotamian mythologies can be seen in Greek mythologies of the stars/constellations. Amar Annus cites K. van der Toorn, who proposes that Grecian mythologies of Osiris/Damuzi/Tammuz had become a "conflation of traditions," resulting in the idea that for the Greeks "the constellation of Orion instead of Sirius was the heavenly counterpart of the hunter Orion," since in Syriac, Orion is called *gabbar,* 'hero' (Amar Annus, *The God Ninurta,* 138). The early father Justin Matyr (*c.* 150 CE) in his apologetic defending Christianity argued that a crucified god was a readily accepted doctrine among pagan cults:

> "And when we say also that the Word, who is the first-birth of God, was produced without sexual union, and that He, Jesus Christ, our Teacher, was crucified and died, and rose again, and ascended into heaven, we propound nothing different from what you believe regarding those whom you esteem sons of Jupiter. For you know how many sons your esteemed writers ascribed to Jupiter: Mercury, the interpreting word and teacher of all; Asclepius, who, though he was a great physician, was struck by a thunderbolt, and so ascended to heaven; and Bacchus too, after he had been torn limb from limb; and Hercules, when he had committed himself to the flames to escape his toils; and the sons of Leda, and Dioscuri; and Perseus, son of Danae; and Bellerophon, who, though sprung from mortals, rose to heaven on the horse Pegasus. . . . This only shall be

said, that they are written for the advantage and encouragement of youthful scholars; for all reckon it an honorable thing to imitate the gods." (Alexander Roberts and James Donaldson, eds., The Ante-Nicene Fathers: The Apostolic Fathers, Justin Martyr, Irenaeus (vol. 1). Online at: http://www.ccel.org/ccel/schaff/anf01.viii.ii.xxi.html, accessed January 2015.)

Justin unwittingly confirms Herodutus' account that Greeks and Romans were schooled in the mysterious Passion cults that encouraged its adherants to follow the god's self-imulating example.

98. Assmann, *Death and Salvation,* 48–52.

99. Ibid., 51.

100. Ibid.

101. Ibid., 404.

102. Edwin Oliver James, *The Tree of Life: An Archaeological Study* (Leiden: Brill, 1966) 6, 24, 39, 98; Hislop, *Two Babylons,* 19–21, 70, 77; Campbell, *Mythic Image,* 32–51, 58–66, 167–69, 196–97, 232, 243, 248–253, 415–26, 484–97; Idem, *Oriental Mythology,* 188; Idem, *Masks of God,* 324; Parpola, "Sons of God," 16–27; *KK,* 266–67; Marshall, *Mohenjo Daro and the Indus Civilization* (vol. 1) 53, 57; Willoughby, *Pagan Regeneration,* 115–142, 148–49.

103. Hislop, *Two Babylons,* 20, 77, 199–200, 301–2; *JM,* 51–52, 56; and Gaebelein, "Tammuz," 725–26.

104. See also Frazer, *Golden Bough*; Doane, *Bible Myths,* 111–359; *JM,* 22–26; and Robertson, *Pagan Christs.*

105. Hislop, *Two Babylons,* 20–21. See also Burkert, *Greek Religion,* 177. Campell also observes strong parallels in Oriental myths. "When to the symbolic (unconsummated) self-offering of T'ang in the mulberry grove there is added the virgin birth of Yi Yin from a *k'ung sang,* all the elements of a myth of death and resurrection by a holy tree (compare Christ on Holy Rood) stand before us" (Campbell, *Oriental Mythology,* 394–95).

106. Green, *The Storm-God in the Ancient Near East,* 154.

107. Hos 2:16–18; Jer 23:27; 1 Kgs 16:33; 2 Kgs 13:6; 21:7; and Ezek 14:7. See also Keel and Uehlinger, *Gods, Goddesses, and Images,* 2–8, 177–248; Day, *Gods and Goddesses of Canaan,* 42–67; and Albright, *Yahweh and the Gods of Canaan.*

108. *JM,* 23. See also Campbell, *Mythic Image,* 168.

109. *KG,* 286–94.

110. Ibid., 287.

111. Ibid., 340–44.

112. Javier Teixidor, *The Pantheon of Palmyra* (Leiden: Brill, 1979) 9–11, 30–31; *CGAE,* 218–19, 56; Redford, *Oxford Encyclopedia of Ancient Egypt* (vol. 1) 372–73; Campbell, *Oriental Mythology,* 188, 395; Idem, *Masks of God,* 240, 265; Hislop, *Two Babylons,* 12–18; Doane, *Bible Myths,* 368–83; Edelstein, *Asclepius* (vol. 1; T 48) 31–32; David Patrick, ed., *Chambers's Encyclopaedia: A Dictionary of Universal Knowledge* (vol. 1; London: W. R. Chambers, 1901) 230, 336, 518, 535; Parpola, "Sons of God," 16–27; Marshall, *Mohenjo Daro and the Indus Civilization* (vol. 1) 53, 57–58; Jastrow, *Babylonia and Assyria,* 107–110, 145–50, 432; E. M. Yamauchi, "Religions: Persia, Artaxerxes II," *ISBE* (vol. 4) 126. Morkot, *The Egyptians,* 202. Morkot dates the development of Egyptian Trinitarian ideas to the New Kingdom.

113. *CGAE,* 88.

114. Ibid., 93.

115. Ibid., 56; and Hislop, *Two Babylons,* 12–18.

116. The word *godhead* may seem monotheistic; however, in ancient Egyptian or Mesopotamian times, it was not. There were many "godheads" within the Egyptian pantheon. My use of the term designates the synchronistic manifestation of the gods; they worked together for a common purpose (i.e., rebirth of the sun), which often occurred by their unification with the supreme sun-god.

117. *CGAE,* 91–99, 126, 235–36; and Redford, *Oxford Encyclopedia of Ancient Egypt* (vol. 1) 372–73.

118. *CGAE,* 97; and Redford, ibid., 372–73.

119. Ibid.

120. Hislop, *Two Babylons*, 19–21. For a similar evolution in the Asclepius cult, see Edelstein, *Asclepius* (vol. 2) 102.

121. *CGAE*, 60, 69–74; and Morkot, *The Egyptians*, 156–57.

122. J. B. Bury, ed., *The Cambridge Ancient History* (vol. 7; London: Cambridge University Press, 1969) 5.

123. Annus, *The God Ninurta*, 13–17, 22–23, 39–42.

124. *KK*, 266–67 (parenthesis added).

125. Parpola, "Sons of God," 16–27.

126. Ibid.

127. Ibid.

128. *KG*, 299–302.

129. *KK*, 282, 297.

130. *CGAE*, 137–42; *KG*, 299–302; and Parpola, "Sons of God," 16–27.

131. *KK*, 271.

132. For a more detailed view of this religious belief, see: Roderick Meredith, "Satan's Counterfeit Christianity," Tomorrow's World, http://www.tomorrowsworld.org/booklets/satans-counterfeit-christianity; Margaret Minnicks, "Satan's Counterfeits," April 28, 2011, http://www.examiner.com/article/satan-s-counterfeits; and Joe Crews, "Satan's Confusing Counterfeits," Amazing Facts, http://www.amazing-facts.org/media-library/book/e/47/t/satans-confusing-counterfeits.aspx (all sites accessed January 2015); and Raymond Capt, *Counterfeit Christianity—How Ancient Paganism Mixed with Christianity* (Muskogee, OK: Arisan Publishers, 2006).

133. Day, *Gods and Goddesses of Canaan*, 14–15.

134. See I.III.D. We we began this study into Israel's Scriptures to see if Israel's God could be vindicated as righteous in the trial *Israel vs. YHWH*. For YHWH to be cleared as a righteous God, he cannot act arbitrarily or be "above" his own Law or requirements for humanity.

135. *SEC* 8549; BDB, 1071.

136. "Have you not sinned if you have brought it rightly, but not rightly divided it?" (Gen 4:7, LXX). See also Jeff A. Benner, *A Mechanical Translation of the Book of Genesis: The Hebrew Text Literally Translated Word for Word* (College Station, TX: Virtual Bookworm, 2007), 30–31, http://www.ancient-hebrew.org/bookstore/e-books/mtg.pdf (accessed online January 2015), which indicates Abel would rule over ("regulate") Cain because Cain had erred in his donation (offering).

137. "Enos: he had faith to call on the name of the Lord God" (Gen 4:26, LXX). The Hebrew states this name is YHWH. See also Jeff Benner, *Mechanical Translation*, 34.

138. For a similar approach, see Keel and Uehlinger, *Gods, Goddesses, and Images of God*, 204–7.

139. David Diringer, "J," *Encyclopedia Britannica*: vol. 15 (Danbury, CT: Grolier, 2001) 636; Leon L. Bram and Norma H. Dickey, ed., "J," *Funk and Wagnalls Encyclopedia*: vol. 14 (New York: Funk and Wagnalls, 1975) 94; John P. Whalen, ed., "J," *New Catholic Encyclopedia*: vol. 14 (San Francisco, CA: McGraw-Hill, 1967) 1065; Allen P. Ross, *Introducing Biblical Hebrew* (Grand Rapids, MI: Baker Academic, 2001) 20–21; Hoffman, *In the Beginning*, 44 n.4.

140. *UBD*, 413.

141. *SEC* 5019; BDB, 613.

142. *SEC* 3106; BDB, 385. See also Albright, *Yahweh and Gods of Canaan*, 98, n119.

143. Based upon *yaval*, יָבַל, a verb meaning 'to lead.'

144. *SEC* 8423; BDB, 1063.

145. Wilson, *Genealogy and History*, 141–43.

146. Ibid., 143.

147. *SEC* 5279; BDB, 653.

148. Hamilton, *The Book of Genesis: 1–17*, 264–68, 271.

149. For a concise discussion of the various interpretations of Gen 6:2, see Hamilton, *The Book of Genesis: 1–17*, 261–66.

150. Another viable theory on the "sons of god," interprets Seth's Godly children as intermarrying with Cain's ungodly children (*Matthew Henry's Commentary on the Whole Bible Complete and Unabridged* [Peabody, MA: Hendrickson, 1991] 22; and *JFB,* 22).

151. *SEC* 7945, 1571; BDB, 979, 168–69.

152. Hamilton, *The Book of Genesis: 1–17,* 267–68.

153. Walter Kaiser, *Toward Old Testament Ethics* (Grand Rapids, MI: Academic Books, 1983) 182–83.

154. In fact, Moore's law states that technologies (in computing hardware) will double every two years. This law has held true for the past 50 years.

155. For more information, surf the Web by topics: "cloning history" or "genetic engineering history."

156. *SEC* 5303; BDB, 658; *TWOT* (vol. 2) 587; and James K. Hoffmeier, "Moses," *ISBE* (vol. 3) 518–19.

157. *SEC* 1368; BDB, 150; and *TWOT* (vol. 1) 148–49.

158. *Matthew Henry's Commentary,* 22; and *JFB,* 22.

159. *SEC* 8549; BDB, 1071; *TWOT* (vol. 2) 973–74; and Gary Pratico, "Noah," *ISBE* (vol. 3) 543.

160. Jastrow, *Babylonia and Assyria,* 178.

161. Green, *Storm-God in the Ancient Near East,* 209, 212.

162. *GDSAM,* 72–73; and Turner and Coulter, *Dictionary of Ancient Deities,* 158, 367.

163. *GDSAM,* 72–73.

164. Wilson, *Genealogy and History,* 79.

165. William Millar, "Oral Poetry and *Dumuzi's Dream,*" in *Scripture in Context: Essays on the Comparative Method* (vol. 1; PTMS 34; ed. Carl D. Evans, Pittsburgh: Pickwick Publications, 1980) 29.

166. Ibid.

167. Ibid., 29.

168. Robert Wilson, *Genealogy and History,* 79.

169. Ibid., 140.

170. Stephanie Dally, "Gilgamesh and the Arabian Nights," in *Gilgamesh: A Reader* (ed. John Maier, Wauconda, IL: Bolchazy-Carducci, 1997) 229–30; and Claus Westermann, *Genesis 1–11: A Continental Commentary* (Minneapolis: Fortress, 1994) 37, 58, 154–55, 163, 270.

171. Regarding the historicity of a Goliath in Gath, see "The Tell es-Safi/Gath Official (and unnofficial) Weblog," http://gath.wordpress.com/2006/02/16/comment-on-the-news-item-in-bar-on-the-goliath-inscription/ (accessed January 2015); see also p. 606.

172. Roland K. Harrison, "Giants," *ISBE* (vol. 2) 460.

173. 2 Sam 21:22; and 1 Chr 20:4–8. See also James Hastings, ed., *A Dictionary of the Bible* (vol. 2; New York: Scribner, 1898) 166.

174. *SEC* 7497; BDB, 952; *TWOT* (vol. 2) 858–59; and Roland K. Harrison and Nola J. Opperwall, "Lightning," *ISBE* (vol. 3) 136–37. For other theories about the *Rephaim,* see: Mark Shipp, *Of Dead Kings and Dirges: Myth and Meaning in Isaiah 14:4b–21* (Leiden: Brill, 2002) 120; Day, *Gods and Goddesses of Canaan,* 217–25; Dennis Baly, "The Pitfalls of Biblical Geography in Relation to Jordan," in *Studies in the History and Archaeology of Jordan* (vol. 3; Adnan Hadidi, ed., New York: Routledge and Kegan Paul, 1987) 128–29; and Hastings, ed., *Dictionary of the Bible,* 166–68.

175. *TWOT* (vol. 2) 858–59.

176. If this theory merits validity, it applies to other parallel accounts, such as Mesopotamian creation myths or flood motifs—i.e., the general history underlying the stories are indeed true, but the embellished mythology of warring gods and goddesses is not.

177. See also Deut 3:10–13.

178. This name does present some difficulties, not only attesting to an ancient text, but also to its corruption in later transcribing processes (J. Author Thompson, *1, 2 Chronicles* [vol. 9: New American Commentary 9; ed. E. Ray Clendenen, Nashville: Broadman and Holman, 1994] 157–58).

179. The account in 2 Samuel regarding the enormous size and weight of the Ammonite king's crown, identifies this particular king as a Rephaite/Anak descendant (Thompson, *1, 2 Chronicles,* 156).

180. Thompson, *1, 2 Chronicles,* 157–58.

181. Adrianus van Selms, "Valley of Rephaim," *ISBE* (vol. 4) 137–38.

182. *SEC* 1368; BDB, 150; and *TWOT* (vol. 1) 148–49. See also Hastings, *Dictionary of the Bible,* 166.

183. For an argument against this conclusion, see J. A. Soggin, "Sons of God(s), Heroes, and *Nephilim*: Remarks on Genesis 6:1–4," in *Texts, Temples, and Traditions* (ed. Michael V. Fox et al. Winona Lake, IN: Eisenbrauns, 1996) 135–36. It is quite probable that after the Giboriym/Rephaim became extinct, the Hebrew root *gbr* evolved to mean 'strength or might' in later times.

184. Patrick Miller, *Religion of Ancient Israel* (Louisville: Westminster John Knox, 2000) 63, 162; John Walton et al., *The IVP Bible Background Commentary of the Old Testament* (Downers Grove, IL: Inter-Varsity Press, 2000) 93, 272; Lamberg-Karlovsky, "Housholds, Land Tenure, and Communication, Systems in the 6th-4th Millennia of Greater Mesopotamia," in *ULO*, 189, 197.

185. The Hebrew word for Egypt is *Mitsrayim*. It is a derivative of *Mizraim*, the name of Ham's son (*SEC* 4714; BDB, 595; Donald Redford, *Egypt, Canaan, and Israel in Ancient Times* [Princeton, NJ: Princeton University Press, 1992] 228).

186. Day, *Gods and Goddesses of Canaan,* 217–19.

187. Ibid., 220–21.

188. Ibid., 221.

189. Ibid., 224.

190. Ibid.

191. Ibid., 223. While Day touches on the amelioration of the term *Rephaim*, he does not adequately address it. Scripture demonstrates that the meaning of the word *rp'um*, the root which appears in many Hebrew words, came to have more neutral connotations over time. Whereas in the nation's early history the term designated the deified ethnic *Rephaim*, after the race's extinction, it came to designate underworld deities in general. Day adeptly points out the evil god Molech's association with the Ashteroth Rephaim.

192. *SEC* 8034; BDB, 1027–28; and *TWOT* (vol. 2) 934.

193. *God's Word Translation* (Grand Rapids: Baker, 1995).

194. Hoffman, *In the Beginning,* 41.

195. Ibid.; and *GKC*, 396–401/§124.

196. *TWOT* (vol. 1) 44; *UBD*, "Gods," 411; and *GKC*, 428/§132.

197. *GKC*, 428, 463/§§132, 145.

198. *SEC* 410, 430; BDB, 42, 43; *TWOT* (vol. 1) 41–42, 44–45.

199. *SEC* 6440; BDB, 815–16; *TWOT* (vol. 2) 727.

200. See also 1 Sam 28:13–14, where Samuel's spirit is called *elohiym* ('god') and is termed 'he' (singular).

201. Geoffrey W. Bromiley, "God: God in the OT," *ISBE* (vol. 2) 497; Robert J. Wyatt, "Names of God: OT Name," *ISBE* (vol. 2) 505–8; *GKC*, 396–401, 428, 463/§124, §132, §145; and Nehemia Gordon, "Elohim: Plural or Singular?" http://www.karaite-korner.org/sources/6.pdf (accessed February 2015) and http://www.obcitydesigns.com/wayofthenazarene/uploads/pdf/God%20-%20Elohim%20Plural%20Or%20 Singular.pdf (accessed February 2015).

202. Hoffman, *In the Beginning,* 42.

203. Patrick Toner, "Etymology of the Word "God," in *The Catholic Encyclopedia* (vol. 6; New York: Robert Appleton, 1909) 10, http://www.newadvent.org/cathen/06608x.htm (accessed January 2015); and Hoffman, *In the Beginning,* 43.

204. Ibid.

205. See also Exod 23:24; 32:23; 34:15; Deut 7:4; 12:30–31; 29:26; 31:18, 20; 32:17, 37, where plural verbs are used to indicate the multiplicity of a godhead.

206. If the Apis depicted Moses as the intermediary god as suggested above (chap. 2.I), he was no doubt "synchronized" within a triad manifested by the Apis, thus granting him the same type of divinity to which Israel had been accustomed with Egypt's pharaohs; thus, Moses' anger at this blasphemy.

207. *SEC* 433; BDB, 43, 1080.

208. Ezek 20:6–8; Jer 10:3; and Isa 19:14.

209. See also Isa 28:15; 59:3–4; Ezek 13:8–9, 19, 22; 24:12; Hos 10:13; and Amos 2:4.

CHAPTER THREE

1. George Mendenhall, *Law and Covenant in Israel and the Ancient Near East* (Pittsburgh: Biblical Colloquium, 1955). See also idem, *Ancient Israel's Faith and History*.

2. Kenneth Kitchen, *Ancient Orient and the Old Testament* (Downers Grove, IL: InterVarsity Press, 1996) 99; J. A. Thompson, *Ancient Near Eastern Treaties and the Old Testament* (London: Tyndale, 1964) 14; Meredith Kline, *Treaty of the Great King* (Grand Rapids: Eerdmans, 1963) 42–43; J. A. Thompson, "Covenant," *ISBE* (vol. 1) 790–92; and Freedman, *The Nine Commandments,*17.

3. Mendenhall, *Law and Covenant* (part 2.15), http://home.earthlink.net/~cadman777/Law_Cov_Mendenhall_TITLE.htm#pt2 (accessed January 2015); Kline, *Treaty of the Great King,* 14–15; Albright, *Yahweh and the Gods of Canaan,* 167.

4. Dennis McCarthy, "Treaty and Covenant," in *Institution and Narrative* (Rome: Pontifical Biblical Institute, 1985) 43–44; Moshe Weinfeld, " Covenant of Grant," 69–102; Wenham, *Word Biblical Commentary: Genesis 1–15,* 333; and Westbrook and Wells, *Everyday Law,* 92.

5. Weinfeld, "Covenant of Grant," 69–87 (parenthesis added). While Mendenhall is correct regarding the composition of biblical covenants, his polemic on suzerainty vs. parity is more applicable to the Sinai and Moab Compacts and less convincing with regard to the patriarchal covenants. Weinfeld's Royal Grant thesis is much closer to the type of covenant that Scripture demonstrates YHWH made with the patriarchs.

6. Mendenhall, *Law and Covenant* (part 2.15), http://home.earthlink.net/~cadman777/Law_Cov_Mendenhall_TITLE.htm#pt2. For examples of different types of treaties recorded in the Hebrew Scriptures, see Thompson, *Treaties and the Old Testament,* 18–19. http://www.biblicalstudies.org.uk/pdf/tp/treaties_thompson.pdf (accessed January 2015); see also Weinfeld, "Covenant of Grant," 69–87. For various covenant theories, see Steven McKenzie, "The Typology of the Davidic Covenant," in *The Land That I Will Show You* (ed. Andrew Dearman and Patrick Graham; Sheffield: Sheffield Academic Press, 2001) 153–78.

7. Mendenhall, *Law and Covenant*; idem, *Ancient Israel's Faith.* 55–69; Kitchen, *Ancient Orient,* 90–101; McCarthy, *Institution and Narrative,* 67–73; J. M. Roberts, *The Bible and the Ancient Near East: Collected Essays* (Winona Lake, IN: Eisenbrans, 2001) 44–47; Thompson, *Treaties and Old Testament*; and Augustine Pagolu, *The Religion of the Patriarchs,* 64–65; Hoffmeier, *Anceint Israel in Sinai* (New York: Oxford University Press, 2005) 183–92.

8. Mendenhall, *Israel's Faith,* 57–58; Kitchen, *Ancient Orient,* 92–93; idem, *On the Reliability of the Old Testament* (Grand Rapids: Eerdmans, 2003) 283–94; Thompson, *Treaties and Old Testament,* 18–23; Kline, *Treaty of the Great King,* 28, 48, 50–51; and Deut 1:1–5. See also http://home.earthlink.net/~cadman777/Law_Cov_Mendenhall_TITLE.htm

9. Mendenhall, *Israel's Faith,* 57–58; Kitchen, *Ancient Orient,* 92–93; Thompson, *Treaties and Old Testament,* 18–23; Kline, *Treaty of the Great King,* 28; Exod 20:1–2; Deut 1:6–5; 5:1–6; and Westbrook and Wells, *Everyday Law,* 46. See also http://home.earthlink.net/~cadman777/Law_Cov_Mendenhall_TITLE.htm.

10. Mendenhall, *Israel's Faith,* 58–67; Kitchen, *Ancient Orient,* 93; and http://home.earthlink.net/~cadman777/Law_Cov_Mendenhall_TITLE.htm.

11. Deut 31:9–13; 1 Kgs 8:9; Mendenhall, *Law and Covenant* (part 2); Kitchen, *Ancient Orient,* 93; Thompson, *Treaty and Old Testament,* 23, 25; Kline, *Treaty of the Great King,* 28; McCarthy, *Institution and Narrative,* 38; Albright, *Yahweh and Gods of Canaan,* 167; and Phillips, *Israel's Criminal Law,* 4.

12. Ibid.

13. Ibid.

14. Mendenhall, *Israel's Faith,* 69; Kitchen, *Ancient Orient,* 94; http://home.earthlink.net/~cadman777/Law_Cov_Mendenhall_TITLE.htm.

15. Phillips, *Israel's Criminal Law,* 4.

16. Mendenhall, *Israel's Faith,* 57–58; Kitchen, *Ancient Orient,* 92–93; idem, *On the Reliability of the Old Testament,* 283–94; Thompson, *Treaties and Old Testament,* 18–23; Kline, *Treaty of the Great King,* 28, 48, 50–51; and Deut 1:1–5. See also http://home.earthlink.net/~cadman777/Law_Cov_Mendenhall_TITLE.htm.

17. Mendenhall, *Israel's Faith,* 57–58; Kitchen, *Ancient Orient,* 92–93; Thompson, *Treaties and Old Testament,* 18–23; Kline, *Treaty of the Great King,* 28; Deut 1:6–4:49; and Westbrook and Wells, *Everyday Law,* 46. See also http://home.earthlink.net/~cadman777/Law_Cov_Mendenhall_TITLE.htm.

18. Mendenhall, *Law and Covenant* (part 2); Kitchen, *Ancient Orient,* 93; Thompson, *Treaty and Old Testament,* 23, 25; Kline, *Treaty of the Great King,* 28; McCarthy, *Institution and Narrative,* 38; Albright, *Yahweh and Gods of Canaan,* 167; and Phillips, *Israel's Criminal Law,* 4.

19. *ANET,* 526.

20. Deut 31:9–13; 1 Kgs 8:9; Mendenhall, *Law and Covenant* (part 2); Kitchen, *Ancient Orient,* 93; Thompson, *Treaty and Old Testament,* 23, 25; Kline, *Treaty of the Great King,* 28; McCarthy, *Institution and Narrative,* 38; Albright, *Yahweh and Gods of Canaan,* 167; and Phillips, *Israel's Criminal Law,* 4.

21. Ibid.; Hudson, "From Sacred Enclave to Temple to City," in *ULO,* 119–27, 131–32; C. C. Lamberg-Karlovsky, "Households, Land Tenure, and Communication Systems," in *ULO,* 178–79, 185.

22. Mendenhall, *Law and Covenant* (part 2); Kitchen, *Ancient Orient,* 93; Thompson, *Treaty and Old Testament,* 23, 25; Kline, *Treaty of the Great King,* 28; McCarthy, *Institution and Narrative,* 38; Albright, *Yahweh and Gods of Canaan,* 167; and Phillips, *Israel's Criminal Law,* 4.

23. http://home.earthlink.net/~cadman777/Law_Cov_Mendenhall_PART2.htm.

24. Mendenhall, *Israel's Faith,* 69; Kitchen, *Ancient Orient,* 94; http://home.earthlink.net/~cadman777/Law_Cov_Mendenhall_TITLE.htm; Weinfeld, "Covenant of Grant," 80–82; Kline, *By Oath Consigned,* 16–17; Hamilton, *Genesis: 1–17,* 433, 436–37; Tremper Longman III, *How to Read Genesis,* 96; and Phillips, *Israel's Criminal Law,* 11.

25. McCarthy, *Institution and Narrative,* 60. Most scholars (Mendenhall, Kitchen, Kline, and Thompson) overlook the importance that the sign or seal played in the role of Israel's covenants. Although McCarthy touches on signs (*Institution and Narrative,* 11, 56–57, 60, 412), he does not demonstrate the role that a covenant's sign played in Israel's covenants or history.

26. As we chart Israel's foundational covenants, we will notice that prophecy is a fundamental element of Israelite covenants. We will also see the importance played by both prophecy and the "sign" of the covenant itself.

27. See Mendenhall, *Law and Covenant* (part 2), 25; and Weinfeld, "Covenant of Grant," 69–82.

28. The first penalty stated: "But of the tree of the knowledge of good and evil, you shall not eat of it: for in the day that you eat thereof you shall surely die" (Gen 2:17).

29. The consequence for eating blood is upheld and reiterated in the words of Israel's Law (Lev 17:10; 3:17; 7:26, 27; 19:26; Deut 12:16, 23). Israel's prophets uphold the stipulations for the Noahic Covenant as well. See Mic 7:2; Isa 9:19, 19:2; Jer 9:4; Ezek 38:21; Hag 2:22; and Deut 28:26, 54.

30. Hamilton, *The Book of Genesis, 1–17,* 316.

31. Deut 22:6–7 also upheld the rights of birds and their offspring.

32. *TWOT* (vol. 1) 457.

33. Weinfeld, *Covenant of Grant,* 80.

34. Ibid., 81.

35. McCarthy, *Institution and Narrative,* 210; Pagolu, *The Religion of the Patriarchs,* 64–65; *TWOT* (vol. 1) 457; Thompson, *Treaties and the Old Testament,* 25; Weinfeld, "Covenant of Grant," 80–82. We will explore the biblical concept of sacrifice in greater detail in Part 2 of this volume.

36. *TWOT* (vol. 1) 457; Victor Hamilton, *Genesis 1–17,* 430; and McCarthy, *Institution and Narrative,* 210. Weinfeld successfully argues that many of the patriarchal covenants were royal grant treaties in which the king bound himself to a loyal servant ("Covenant of Grant," 69–87).

37. Thompson, *Treaties and the Old Testament*, 25 (emphasis added). See also McCarthy, *Institution and Narrative*, 53–57; Weinfeld, "Covenant of Grant," 79–80; Kline, *Treaty of the Great King*, 23; and Victor Hamilton, *Genesis: 18–50*, 90.

38. Exod 21:24, 26; Lev 24:20; and Deut 19:21. The Hammurabi Code is available online: http://avalon.law. yale.edu/subject_menus/hammenu.asp (accessed January 2015).

39. For possible theories regarding this offense, see Hamilton, *Genesis: 1–17*, 322–23.

40. Wenham, *Word Biblical Commentary: Genesis 1–15*, 202.

41. Ibid., 203, 308.

42. The powerful Egyptians traditionally dominated the Canaanite region when Assyrian, Hebrew, Babylonian, Persian, or Roman interests failed.

43. Gen 10:22, 11; *SEC* 804; *BDB*, 78; and *UBD*, 100.

44. *ANET*, 274–75. For a possible Scriptural attestation of this event, see the title of Psalms 60, which states, "Mesopotamia strove with A'-ram-na-ha-ra'-im and with A'-ram-zo'-bah and Jo'-ab smote E'-dom" (Ps 60:1—title).

45. *ANET*, 275–76.

46. Redford, *Ancient Times*, 364; Alan B. Lloyd, "The Late Period," in *OHAE*, 365; and Peter Clayton, *The Chronicles of the Pharaohs* (London: Thames and Hudson) 192–23.

47. William Moran, "The Hebrew Language," in *The Bible and the Ancient Near East* (ed. Earnest Wrist; Garden City, NY: Doubleday, 1965) 63; Bill Arnold, "What Has Nebuchadnezzar to Do with David?" in *MB*, 331, 335; J. A. Brinkman, *A Political History of Post-Kassite Babylonia, 1158–722 BC* (AnOr 43; Rome: Pontifical Biblical Institute, 1968) 267–85; the Chaldean Berossos in Josephus, *Against Apion* 1.128–31; Gerald Verbrugghe and John Wickersham, *Berossos and Manetho* (Ann Arbor: University of Michigan Press, 2000) 3; see Gen 11:28, where Ur is listed as a Chaldean province. See also Lipiński, who classifies Chaldea as East Semitic (Edward Lipiński, *Semitic Languages: Outline of a Comparative Grammar* [Leuven: Peeters, 2001]).

48. Based upon Aramean (Deut 26:5) and Chaldean association. Arnold, "Nebuchadnezzar and David?" in *MB*, 333–35.

49. Egypt was also oppressed by foreigners during the *First Intermediate Period* (2181–2055 BCE) as well.

50. Ryholt, *Political Situation*, 69–203.

51. Ibid., 5 n.8, 118–50.

52. For evidence of Assyrian personal names in Egypt during this era, see ibid., n.102, 338, 130, 128. The name of Khayan (*c.* 1621 BCE), one "Asiatic" king of this era, is generally regarded the same as the Amorite name Ḥayanu. An Assyrian king's list registers this name as a remote ancestor of Shamshi-Adad I (*c.* 1800) thus evidencing an Assyrian connection (ibid., 128).

53. A Scriptural "heritage" refers to family tribal lands, see Exod 6:8.

54. For a most recent thorough discussion of Darius's lineage, see Pierre Briant, *From Cyrus to Alexander* (trans. Peter Daniels; Winona Lake, IN: Eisenbrauns, 2002) 15–17, 24–27, 110–13.

55. Briant, *Cyrus to Alexander*, 15. In his Behistun inscription, Darius also claims to be Hystaspes (Astyages) royal Persian heir. Two other inscriptions shorten this genealogy to include only Darius' great-grandfather and grandfather. While Herodotus' genealogy (7.11) differs from the Behistun inscription it does not undermine Cyrus I's genealogical ties to the Achaemenid Dynasty.

56. *SEC* 3120; *BDB*, 402; and *UBD*, 556.

57. John H. Marks, *Visions of One World* (Guilford, CT: Four Quarters, 1985) 21–22; and Herod. 2.167. See also, "Origin of the Macedonians," http://www.macedonia.com/english/origin.html (accessed January 2015).

58. *HPE*, 14.

59. *HCJ*, 14 (parenthesis added).

60. Weinfeld, "The Covenant of Grant," 69–83; Kline, *By Oath Consigned*, 21, 27; Thompson, *Treaties and the Old Testament*, 12–15, 21–23; Tim Hegg, "The Covenant of Grant and the Abrahamic Covenant"

(paper read at the Regional Evangelical Theological Society, 1989), http://www.torahresource.com/EnglishArticles/Grant%20Treaty.pdf (accessed February 2015).

61. Most scholars (e.g., Mendenhall, Thompson, Kline, Weinfeld) overlook the importance of the sign or seal in Scriptural covenants between God and man. Since the sign that sealed Israel's covenants was usually both theological (i.e., circumcision or the Sabbath) and prophetic in nature, we should not expect to find common parallels to this religious feature of the Hebrew covenants within the political treaties of the Near East (exception being given to the self-imprecating sacrifice discussed further within this chapter).

62. I have omitted the covenant YHWH's messengers made with Abraham in Genesis 18, which promised that Abraham's and Sarah's son would be born the following year (Gen 17:21, 18:10, 14).

63. Weinfeld, "Covenant of Grant," 69–82.

64. See Apendix, 9.51 Time: Flood to Abraham.

65. Kline, *Treaty of the Great King,* 67.

66. Weinfeld, "Covenant of Grant," 69–87.

67. Gerhard Hasel, "Heir," *ISBE* (vol. 2) 674.

68. Ibid.; and Westbrook, *Property, Family in Biblical Law,* 14.

69. Ibid.

70. *SEC* 4578; *BDB*, 589; and *TWOT* (vol. 1) 518–19.

71. If this covenant were not mutually binding on both YHWH and Abram, then YHWH could have allowed Eliezer, Lot, or an entirely new entity to inherit his covenants. In order for Abraham's children to inherit their father's covenants, YHWH had bound himself to his covenant without being able to act or proscribe measures arbitrary to this treaty with Abram.

72. A quick Web search for population statistics for Russia or France demonstrates this truth.

73. "World Fertility Report 2007" (New York: United Nations: Economic and Social Affairs, 2010) xi, http://www.un.org/esa/population/publications/worldfertilityreport2007/wfr2007-text.pdf (accessed January 2015).

74. U.S. census: see the "individual and aggregate" data, showing that almost every nation is projected to have declining birth rates over the next 20 years: http://www.census.gov/population/international/data/idb/region.php (accessed October 2013); David A. Hartman, "Remarks to The World Congress of Families III," Mexico City, March 29, 2004, http://www.worldcongress.org/wcf3_spkrs/wcf3_hartman.htm(accessed February 2013). Probably the best justification for large families, based on government statistics can be found at: http://www.youtube.com/watch?v=_kKkY5EpVpY (accessed February 2015); Anatoly Karlin, "Rite of Spring: Russia's Fertility Trends," *The Russia Blog,* April 29, 2009, http://darussophile.com/2009/04/rite-of-spring/ (accessed February 2015); and Craig Pirrong, "DR (or is it S-O?) on Russian Demographics," Streetwise Professor, April 28, 2009, http://streetwiseprofessor.com/?p=1832 (accessed January 2015).

75. Nicholas Eberstadt, "The Demographic Future: What Growth—and Decline—Means for the Global Economy," in *The Foreign Affairs Journal* (November 1, 2010), http://www.foreignaffairs.com/articles/66805/nicholas-eberstadt/the-demographic-future (accessed January 2015). See also Jeni Klugman, ed. *Poverty in Russia: Public Policy and Private Responses* (Washington, DC: World Bank, 1997) 92; and Nicholas Eberstadt and Apoova Shah, "No Amount of 'Reset' Can Avert the Looming Russian Disaster," Public Policy Blog of the American Enterprise Institute, July 8, 2009, http://www.aei-ideas.org/2009/07/no-amount-of-reset-can-avert-the-looming-russian-disaster/ (accessed January 2015).

76. Eberstadt, "The Demographic Future: World Fertility Report 2007" (New York: United Nations Economic and Social Affairs, 2010) xi. Online at http://www.un.org/esa/population/publications/worldfertilityreport2007/wfr2007-text.pdf; U.S. Census: See the "individual and aggregate" data option where almost every nation is projected to have declining birth rates over the next 20 years: http://www.census.gov/population/international/data/idb/region.php.

77. Robert Greenall, "Russia Turns Spotlight on Abortion," *BBC News,* September 2003, http://news.bbc.co.uk/2/hi/europe/3093152.stm (accessed January 2015); Fred Weir, "A Second Baby? Russia's

Mothers Aren't Persuaded," in the *Christian Science Monitor* (May 2006), http://www.csmonitor. com/2006/0519/p01s04-woeu.html (accessed January 2015); David A. Hartman, "Remarks to The World Congress of Families III."

78. Peeter Värnik, "Suicide Rates per 100,000 by Country, Year, and Sex (Table)," World Health Organization 2011 http://www.who.int/mental_health/prevention/suicide_rates/en/index.html (accessed November 2013); idem, Suicide in the World, *International Journal of Environmental Research and Public Health* 9/3 (2012) 760–771, http://www.ncbi.nlm.nih.gov/pmc/articles/PMC3367275/ (accessed February 2015); and Eberstadt, "The Demographic Future."

79. Klugman, *Poverty in Russia*.

80. Nicholas Eberstadt, "The Demographic future."

81. Marx had written, "Abolition of the family! Even the most radical flare up at this infamous proposal of the Communists." In other words, the Communists proposed that the family unit should be abolished. In the *Manifesto*, Marx also taught: "But, you will say, we destroy the most hallowed of relations (i.e., family), when we replace home education by social" (parenthesis added). Marx was advancing the idea of state education that taught children what to believe and disallowed family input, thus crippling family relations (Karl Marx and Friedrich Engels, *The Communist Manifesto* (1888), trans. Allen Lutins; The Gutenberg Ebook of the Communist Manifest, January 25, 2005, http://www.gutenberg. org/files/61/61.txt (accessed January 2015).

82. Henry Bowls, "Russia's Exploding Muslim Population," *Foreign Policy* (January 2007), http://blog. foreignpolicy.com/posts/2007/01/16/russias_exploding_muslim_population (accessed January 2015).

83. Thomas Jefferson, "Chapter 1809: To Doctor William Eustis," in *The Works of Thomas Jefferson* (vol. 11; federal edition; New York: Putnam, 1904–5), http://oll.libertyfund.org/titles/807#lf0054-11_head_042 (accessed February 2015). Jefferson also wrote: "The multitude possesses force, and wisdom must yield to that force" (Jefferson, "Chapter: *To P. S. Dupont De*," in *The Works of Thomas Jefferson*, http://oll. libertyfund.org/titles/807#Jefferson_0054-11_472 (accessed February 2015).

84. *TWOT* (vol. 1) 457, parenthesis added. See Thompson, "Covenant: OT," *ISBE* (vol. 1) 790–93; Weinfeld, "Covenant of Grant," 79–80; James Hastings et al., *Encyclopaedia of Religion and Ethics* (vol. 9) 430–34. *Contra* Pagolu, *The Religion of the Patriarchs*, 64.

85. McCarthy, *Institution and Narrative*, 53–57; and Weinfeld, "Covenant of Grant," 79. This judgment only ceded Mizriam's wealth to Abram, not his land.

86. Kline, *By Oath Consigned*, 16–17; Weinfeld, "Covenant of Grant," 79–82; and Hastings, *Encyclopaedia of Religion and Ethics* (vol. 9) 430–33.

87. Kline, *Treaty of the Great King*, 67.

88. Robert Morkot, *The Egyptians*, 189–92; Ogden Goelet, "'Town' and 'Country' in Ancient Egypt," *ULO*, 95; Gen 47:20–22.

89. Goelet, ibid., 94–96; Redford, *Ancient Times*, 266, 372; William Moran, *The Amarna Letters*, EA 365 (Baltimore: Johns Hopkins University Press, 1987) 363; and Steven Shubert and Kathryn Bard, eds., "Social Organization," *Encyclopedia of the Archaeology of Ancient Egypt* (New York: Routledge—Taylor and Francis, 1999) 745.

90. D. Henige, *The Chronology of Oral Tradition: Quest for a Chimera* (Oxford; Oxford University Press, 1974); M. L. Bierbrier, "Generation-Counting and Late New Kingdom Chronology," *JEA* 67 (1981) 182; idem, *The Late New Kingdom in Egypt (c. 1300–664 BC) A Genealogical and Chronological Investigation* (Warminster: Aris and Philips, 1975) xvi, 112f; and Chris Bennet, "Temporal Fugues," *JAMS* 13 (1996) 4–32.

91. Hamilton, *Genesis: 1–17*, 436.

92. That YHWH waits to render judgment until a society is wholly degenerate is also supported by Gen 18:23–33.

93. Weinfeld, "Covenant of Grant," 80–82; Kline, *By Oath Consigned*, 16–17; and Hamilton, *Genesis: 1–17*, 436–37, 433; Tremper Longman, III, *How to Read Genesis* (Downer's Grove, IL: InterVarsity Press, 2005) 96; Phillips, *Israel's Criminal Law*, 11. Contra Gerhard Hasel, "The Meaning of the Animal Rite in

Genesis 15," *JSOT* 19 (1981) 61–78. Hasel's thesis lacks credibility. He rejects YHWH's self-imprecation simply because it "demands almost too much from the Israelite picture of God" (p. 64). Yet he never presents evidence to support this thesis. While he rightly admits that animal sacrifice served to ratify the treaty (pp. 68–70), unlike McCarthy, Hasel does not examine the underlying symbolic meaning of the sacrificial ratification ritual.

94. Hamilton, *Genesis: 1–17,* 436–37.

95. It should be pointed out that YHWH also benefited from this covenant. We saw that YHWH had given the patriarchs and, later, the nation of Israel his "truth" in an effort to preserve it (see pp. 18, 23–28). Thus, YHWH would use Abram and his descendants to preserve his name and his knowledge through time.

96. Henige, *The Chronology of Oral Tradition*; Bierbrier, "Generation-Counting and Late New Kingdom Chronology," 182; idem, *The Late New Kingdom in Egypt (c 1300–664 BC),* xvi, 112f; and Bennet, "Temporal Fugues," 4–32.

97. See pp. 6–10 for discussion.

98. Kline, *Treaty of the Great King,* 23.

99. *SEC* 8549; *BDB,* 1071.

100. *SEC* 1980; *BDB,* 229–37; *TWOT* (vol. 1) 216; and Gary L. Knapp, "Walk," *ISBE* (vol. 4) 1003–5.

101. McCarthy points out that a treaty's reiteration of previous promises "appeals to a legal record, not to history." Thus YHWH upholds all of his legal contracts with Abram (*Treaty and Covenant,* 45).

102. A score is 20; thus, threescore is 60.

103. This is one of the controls or tests for this investigation, see pp. 6–11.

104. Remember that YHWH had pledged his loyalty to Abram and his descendants through sacrifice. When YHWH's flame passed between the divided sacrifice, it meant that if YHWH sinned by failing to uphold his covenant with Abram, he would perish in a similar holocaust.

105. *SEC* 226; *BDB,* 16–17; *TWOT* (vol. 1) 18; and *UBD,* 1105.

106. *SEC* 87, 85; *BDB,* 4; and *TWOT* (vol. 1) 5–6.

107. Wenham, *Genesis 16–50,* 31.

108. R. Martin-Achard, "Isaac," in *ABD* (vol. 3) 463; and Hamilton, *Genesis: 1–17,* 478.

109. Idem, *Genesis: 18–50,* 80–81.

110. Wenham, *Genesis 16–50,* 27.

111. J. M. Wilson and Roland K. Harrison, "Birthright," *ISBE* (vol. 1) 515.

112. Many ancient Near Eastern societies considered the wife's duty to secure her husband's offspring. The Nuzi texts specified that an upper-class wife who was childless should provide her husband with a slave girl by which to obtain offspring (*ANET,* 220; Hasel, "Heir," 674; and Wenham, *Genesis 16–50,* 7).

113. Hamilton, *Genesis: 1–17,* 444–45.

114. Hamiltion rightly points out that YHWH's blessing of Ishmael when Hagar (Gen 16:10–15) ran away from Sarah's judicial hand was in many ways quite restrained (*Genesis: 1–17,* 454). The only blessing Hagar/Ishmael receive is the promise that Ishmael will become a populous nation.

115. Hamilton, *Genesis: 18–50,* 103–4.

116. *SEC* 5254; *BDB,* 650; and *TWOT* (vol. 2) 581.

117. Ibid.

118. Wenham, *Genesis 16–50,* 116.

119. Hamilton, *Genesis: 18–50,* 103–4, 112; and Wenham, *Genesis 16–50,* 113.

120. Weinfeld, "Covenant of Grant," 80–82; Kline, *By Oath Consigned,* 16–17; and Hamilton, *Genesis:1–17,* 436–37, 433.

121. Lev 18:21; Deut 18:10; *Jer* 32:35; and Ezek 20:31.

122. Hamilton, *Genesis: 18–50,* 112.

123. For other Scriptural examples of covenants being ratified or sealed with sacrifices, see: Gen 31:48–54; Exod 24:5, 7–8; 34:15; Ps 50:5; Jer 34:18–19; Jonah 1:16; and Zech 9:11. See also: Mendenhall, *Law and Covenant,* 55–69; Kitchen, *Ancient Orient and the Old Testament,* 90–101; McCarthy, *Institution and*

Narrative, 67–73; Roberts, *The Bible and the Ancient Near East*, 44–47; Thompson, *Treaties and the Old Testament*; Pagolu, *The Religion of the Patriarchs*, 64–65; *TWOT* (vol. 1) 457; Weinfeld, "Covenant of Grant," 80–82; Kline, *By Oath Consigned*, 16–17; and Hamilton, *Genesis: 1–17*, 436–67, 433.

124. Thompson, *Treaties and the Old Testament*, 14; McCarthy, *Institution and Narrative*, 53–57; Phillips, *Israel's Criminal Law*, 11–12. See also Pagolu, *Religion of the Patriarchs*, 64–65; and *TWOT* (vol. 1) 457.

125. Hamilton adeptly points out that the ram substituted for sacrifice in this ritual carried strong prophetic connections with Israel's later priesthood (*Genesis: 18–50*, 113). We will examine this theory in greater detail in the second part of this book, chaps. 14–19.

126. Zeph 1:7–8; Jer 17:27; 5:4; 12:3; Ps 44:22; Isa 53:7; and Zech 11:4, 7. We will examine this in greater detail in chap. 18.

127. Hamilton, *Genesis: 18–50*, 194.

128. Remember that faithfulness is a control for the test of YHWH's truthfulness.

129. Wenham, *Genesis 16–50*, 191.

130. Hamilton, *Genesis: 18–50*, 200–202.

131. Merriam Webster, "Birthright." See also, *SEC* 1062; *BDB*, 114; and *TWOT* (vol. 1) 108–10.

132. Westbrook, *Property, Family in Biblical Law*, 18; Hasel, "Heir," (vol. 2) 674; Wilson and Harrison, "Birthright," (vol. 1) 515–16; *ANET*, 173, 220; Eryl Davies, "The Inheritance of the Firstborn in Israel and the Ancient Near East," *JSS* 38/2 (1993) 175–91; Abraham Malamat, *History of Biblical Israel* (Leiden: Brill, 2001) 36, 39; C. C. Lamberg-Karlovsky, "Households, Land Tenure, and Communication Systems in the 6th–4th Millennia of Greater Mesopotamia," in *ULO*, 189, 197; and Westbrook and Wells, *Everday Law*, 93–97.

133. Hamilton, *Genesis: 18–50*, 182–86.

134. Westbrook and Wells, *Everyday Law*, 97.

135. *Strong's Concordance* (*SEC* 1062) and Brown, Driver, Briggs are among the reference works that erroneously support this claim.

136. *SEC* 1288, 1293; *TWOT* (vol. 1) 285; Allen C. Myers, "Bless," *ISBE* (vol. 1) 523–24; K. H. Richards, "Bless/ Blessing," *ABD* (vol. 1) 754, 756; and Wenham, *Genesis 1–15*, 275.

137. *SEC* 1293, 1288; *BDB*,139, 138, respectively; *TWOT* (vol. 1) 285; and G. Johannes Botterweck and Helmer Ringgren, eds., *Theological Dictionary of the Old Testament* (vol. 2; Grand Rapids: Eerdmans, 1975) 279–297–300, see especially, p. 297. Patriarchal blessings were tied directly to land ownership (Josh 15:19; Malamat, *Biblical Israel*, 36, 39). Jacob denied independent tribal heritages to Simeon and Levi because of their unjust slaughter of Shechem (Gen 49:5–7; see also Josh 19:9 and Num 18:23). Simeon's inheritance fell within Judah's tribal lands while Jacob disallowed Levi from receiving any tribal inheritance.

138. Scripture usually recognizes the firstborn within each tribe as a *nasi'* or 'prince' (Num 1:16, 44, 7:2–84).

139. The reason that Isaac asked Esau to prepare a meal was to signify that this was a formal covenant, which was usually entered into with a sacrificial meal. Isaac partook of the meal and blessed Jacob. In the same vein, YHWH partakes of Israel's sacrifices, enters into covenants, and promises to bless the nation.

140. Raymond de Hoop, *Genesis 49 in Its Literary and Historical Context* (Society of Biblical Literature; Leiden: Brill, 1999) 52.

141. Harrison, "Curse," *ISBE* (vol. 2) 837–38; D. Stuart, "Curse," *ABD* (vol. 1) 1218; de Hoop, *Genesis 49*, 33, 45, 48, 52, 73; Esau's blessing (Gen 27:36–41) is in many ways a curse. Esau's children will live in continual warfare and serve Jacob's children; hence, we can appreciate Esau's anger.

142. *SEC* 3327; *BDB*, 50; and *TWOT* (vol. 2) 763.

143. *SEC* 7121; BDB 294–95; and *TWOT* (vol. 2) 810–11.

144. *SEC* 3290; BDB, 784; Leonid Kogan, "The Etymology of Israel" in *Babel und Bibel 3*: Annual of Ancient Near Eastern, Old Testament, and Semitic Studies (Winona Lake, IN: Eisenbrauns, 2006) 237–42; and Hamilton, *Genesis: 18–50*, 178–79.

145. *SEC* 3478, BDB, 975; Gary A. Lee, "Israel," *ISBE* (vol. 2) 907; Kogan, "Etymology," 237–55; Wenham, *Genesis 16–50*, 296–97. Wenham accurately points out that "the Bible generally takes the form of a

play on a name rather than a precise . . . etymology" (ibid., 296). *Ya'aqob* is Hebrew for 'Jacob' and *Yitschaq* is Hebrew for 'Isaac.' The name *Yisra' el* incorporated part of *Yitschaq*'s name, thus fulfilling YHWH's promise to Abraham that his nation of children would be called by Isaac's name (Gen 21:12).

146. See *Table 9.51. Time: Flood to Abram* in the Appendix B.

147. Wenham, *Genesis 16–50,* 211.

148. Ibid., 298–99.

149. Deut 30:2–6; Prov 1:23; Isa 44:3; Joel 2:28–29; and Ezek 11:17–19; 36:24–28; 39:27–29.

150. *JHRE,* 1–11, 289–92.

151. Karen Armstrong, *Jerusalem: One City Three Faiths* (New York: Knopf, 1996) 154; and William Sanford LaSor, "Jerusalem," *ISBE* (vol. 2) 1029–30.

152. Michael Avi-Yonah, *The Holy Land: A Historical Geography from the Persian to the Arab Conquest 536 BC to AD 640* (Jerusalem: Carta, 2002) 91, 114, 215; 1 Macc 3:36; and *JHRE,* 28.

153. This prophecy has yet to be fulfilled. There are many nations that have historically afflicted Israel that do not yet serve her. Neither has YHWH yet gathered his people out of all nations. The modern-day state has yet to meet the requirements of these many prophecies: she still has many enemies that afflict her, and violence still pours out of the land over issues of settlement. The modern population on the land of Israel has yet to embrace YHWH's covenants or his Law to walk in them but in fact disregards both.

154. Notice also the correlation of the elements within this prophecy: when YHWH shines on Israel, when Abraham's children learn to become righteous, and they are a joy and a praise to the earth. Notice that the wicked still exist, and if they do not submit to this strong nation, they will perish.

155. Exod 19:5; Deut 4:30; 11:27–28; 30:2, 8, 20; Job 36:11–12; Isa 1:18–20; 30:18; 56:1–2; Jer 26:13; 30:20–22; Hos 12:6; Zeph 3:8–13; and Zech 6:15.

156. Hamilton, *Genesis: 18–50,* 226–28.

157. Wenham*, Genesis 16–50,* 297.

158. Hamilton, *Genesis: 18–50,* 335.

159. Ibid., 334–35.

160. Deut 7:9; 1 Chr 16:15; and Ps 105:8.

CHAPTER FOUR

1. Matthew Henry's Commentary, §5–7, 91; and Thompson, *1, 2 Chronicles,* 90–91.

2. Notably, Isaiah chs. 44–45.

3. See LXX, 3 Kgdms 11:30–32; and 2 Chr 11:12.

4. The Law established tithes and offerings as the Levites' source of income. These taxes compensated their public service. In times when Israel gave their tithes and offerings to other gods, the Levite's ability to provide for their families became severely compromised because the tithes and offerings were given to rival temple organizations.

5. *SEC* 3064; BDB, 1095; *TWOT* (vol. 1) 368–69.

6. W. Ward Gasque, "Jew," *ISBE* (vol. 2) 1056.

7. Henri Cazelles, "The Hebrews," in *Essential Papers on Israel and the Ancient Near East* (ed. Frederick Greenspahn; New York: New York University Press, 1991) 269.

8. Joseph Jacobs, ed., "Jew," in *The Jewish Encyclopedia* (New York: Funk and Wagnalls, 1906) 174–75.

9. *ANET,* 283.

10. Assyria called the Northern Kingdom "Omri land," after the house of Omri (King Ahab's father).

11. *ANET,* 282, 287–88.

12. David Graubart, "Jews," in *New Standard Encyclopedia*: vol. 9 (ed. Douglas W. Downey; Chicago: Standard Educational Corporation, 1995) 65; ibid., "Judaism," 105; and *UBD,* 588. See also "Origins of the Word 'Jew,'" http://www.jewfaq.org/whoisjew.htm (accessed January 2015).

13. Remember that Benjamin was one of the four tribes in the Southern Kingdom.

14. Gasque, "Jew," *ISBE* (vol. 2) 1056; and Jacobs, "Jew," *The Jewish Encyclopedia*, 174–75.

15. *SEC* 319; BDB, 31; and *TWOT* (vol. 1) 34.

16. Deut 4:30; 29:22–29; 31:29; Jer 23:20; 30:24; 48:47; 49:39; Ezek 38:16; Hos 3:5; and de Hoop, *Genesis 49*, 86–87. In chaps. 15–16 we shall see evidence demonstrating that Israel's Testimonial Law provided the paradigm by which Israel's prophets established prophetic eras (i.e., "days") for their prophecies. By looking to the Testimony, we can judge if a particular prophet's "latter-day" prophecy falls within ancient Israel's history or at "the end time" when the patriarchal blessings are fulfilled.

17. See chap. V.C., pp. 92–95. Modern Jews may represent one small nation within Abrahamic lineage, however, their genealogical reckoning by the mother (contrary to Scripture) makes many lineage claims quite untenable. Although their communities may have fostered marriage with other descendants from the Southern Kingdom, given the vastness of time and the many migrations they were forced to make over the last 2,500 years, it does not allow for the modern *exclusive* claim for Jews being the only descendants of Jacob. The majority of biblical prophecies are about the redemption of both the descendants of the Southern Kingdom of Judah and the so-called "lost Ten Tribes" of the Northern Kingdom of Israel (see pp. 110–115, 124). *One house is not preferred or excluded for the other.*

18. *Matthew Henry's Commentary*, 91; and *JFB*, 52.

19. *SEC* 226; BDB, 16–17; *TWOT* (vol. 1) 18–19; Hastings, ed., *A Dictionary of the Bible* (vol. 1) 237–38.

20. *JFB*, 109–10; James Hastings et al., "Banners" in *Encyclopaedia of Religion and Ethics* (vol. 3; New York: Scribner, 1917) 348–50; Timothy Ashley, *The Book of Numbers* (Grand Rapids: Eerdmans, 1993) 73. See also, "ensign," Dicionary.com Unabridged (Random House, Inc., 2013), http://dictionary.reference.com/browse/ensign.

21. In the early Fourth Egyptian Dynasty (2575–2465 BCE), we see a similar legally binding "last will and testament" in the *Imet-per* (Jmjt-pr), "what-is-in-the-house" (-document) where the Pharaoh bequeaths his empire (de Hoop, *Genesis 49*, 72–73).

22. Hamilton, *Genesis: 18–50*, 647. *See also* de Hoop, *Genesis 49*, 225.

23. De Hoop, *Genesis 49*, 53–54; and Wenham, *Genesis 16–50*, 468.

24. De Hoop, *Genesis 49*, 33, 43, 52–53.

25. Rachel's and Leah's marriages present a legal conundrum. According the Israelite Law Code, once a woman was betrothed (engaged), she was legally viewed as though she was married (Exod 21:9; Deut 22:23–27). Rachel was betrothed to Jacob years before her sister Leah. Technically, however, Leah became Jacob's wife before Rachel. It appears that Rachel and Leah shared the legal status of *first wife* that normally granted their children the right to inherit the birthright and the blessing.

26. Exod 21:10. Deut 21:15 assumes the rights of the legal wife and in no way elevates a handmaid or her children to the same inheritance rights as the legal wife (Exod 21:10). Deuteronomy disallows a younger heir of a second or third wife to have preference over an older heir to the first wife simply because his mother is better loved. Hence, neither Joseph nor Benjamin receive the entire birthright and blessing, even though their mother was better loved.

27. De Hoop, *Genesis 49*, 225.

28. De Hoop translates this as "deceptive" or "as untrustworthy as water" (de Hoop, *Genesis 49*, 89). See also Job 6:15; and Jer 15:18.

29. For the problems facing translators of Genesis 49's blessings, see de Hoop, *Genesis 49*, 85–96. Unless duly warranted, I have opted to adhere to a translation of the traditional MT (rather than a translation of the LXX). Where the translation presents formidable obstacles, I will comment in either text or footnote.

30. De Hoop, *Genesis 49*, 87.

31. Ibid., 89–90.

32. Hamilton, *Genesis, 18–50*, 645–48.

33. We will discuss concepts associated with natural law in chapters 5–7.

34. LXX. This text is a play on words for circumcision. The root "to cut" כרת is used also in Exod 4:2, 5, referring to the cutting of circumcision (de Hoop, *Genesis 49*, 108–9).

35. For the greater reliability of the Septuagint on this text, see de Hoop, *Genesis 49*, 102–109.

36. De Hoop, *Genesis 49*, 101.

37. Hamilton, *Genesis: 18–50*, 371.

38. De Hoop, *Genesis 49*, 101.

39. Josh 13:14, 33, ch. 21; and Deut 18:1.

40. See also Ps 60:7; 108:8; and Prov 8:15.

41. Strong's *Concordance* (*SEC* 1062) and the Brown, Driver, Briggs *Lexicon* imply that the birthright and blessing are synonymous. This is not the case. Both the birthright and blessing were the firstborn's "right or privilege," but they were not the same institution. If they were the same, Isaac would not have planned to bestow the family blessing on Esau after his son had already sold the birthright to his brother Jacob.

42. Raymond Westbrook, "The Female Slave," in *Gender and Law in the Hebrew Bible and the Ancient Near East* (Ed. Victor Matthews et al.; Sheffield Academic, 1998) 214–38.

43. For further portrayal of military strength as a lion, see Nah 2:11, 12 and Hos 13:8.

44. *GDSAM*, 118. See also de Hoop, *Genesis 49*, 133–34.

45. Compare to Deut 29:22–29.

46. See also de Hoop, *Genesis 49*, 143 for the similarities in Jacob's blessing of Judah and Balaam's blessing of Israel.

47. Ps 14:7; 53:6; 85:1–2; Isa 10:20–21; 14:1; 46:3–4; Jer 46:27–28; and Ezek 28:24–26; 39:25.

48. Jacob blesses only his biological descendants. While many Jews today may or may not be descendants of Judah (or one of the Southern tribes), many individuals who have converted to Judaism are not Jacob's biological offspring. Another fact bearing on this prophecy is that many Judahites did not return to Judah at King Cyrus's proclamation, leaving their offspring in the Diaspora (see pp. 759–64 and chap. 18). Thus, Judah's latter-day leadership of Israel may not be found within modern Judaism, although leadership will be established with a descendant of Judah through David (see pp. 129–33).

49. *SEC* 7626; BDB, 986; John Collins, *The Septer and the Star* (Anchor Bible Reference Library; New York: Bantam Doubleday, 1995) 62.

50. Collins, *Scepter and Star*, 62.

51. *SEC* 7886; A. R. Fausset, *Faucet's Bible Dictionary* (Grand Rapids, MI: Zondervan, 1966) 646.

52. *SEC* 7951; BDB, 1017.

53. De Hoop, *Genesis 49*, 151–62.

54. *SEC* 6721; BDB, 850.

55. Wenham, *Genesis 16–50*, 463–64.

56. For variously proposed translations and problems facing this ancient text, see de Hoop, *Genesis 49*, 180–223.

57. De Hoop, *Genesis 49*, 224–28.

58. For a similar usage of military terms see Nah 2:12.

59. De Hoop, *Genesis 49*, 163–68.

60. See de Hoop, *Genesis 49*, 173–79.

61. Ibid., 170–72.

62. Westbrook and Wells, *Everyday Law*, 35.

63. For other examples, see Genesis 18–19; 22:15; 24:7; 24:40; 31:11; 48:16.

64. *SEC* 226; BDB, 16–17.

65. Freedman, *Nine Commandments*, 8.

66. James Tabor, *Restoring Abrahamic Faith* (Charlotte, NC: Genesis 2000, 2008) 18–21; On the pronunciation of the name, see article with discussion by Yaaqov ben Yisrael, "Is the Pronounciation of the Name of YHWH Lost?" Peshat—The Plain and Simple Meaning, http://peshat.com/index.php?itemid=32, July 20, 2009 (accessed March 2015); and Nehemiah Gordon, "The Pronounciation of the Name," Karite-Korner, http://karaite-korner.org/yhwh_2.pdf (accessed December 2013); Good Reads, http://www.goodreads.com/book/show/16170213-the-pronounciation-of-the-name (accessed January 2015).

67. See also Hosea 12:1–5. For further information on the pronunciation of the name of *YHWH* see http://www.goodreads.com/book/show/16170213-the-pronunciation-of-the-name; Ross, *Introducing Biblical Hebrew,* 20–22; and Joel Hoffman, *In the Beginning,* 44 n.4.

68. *ANET,* 21. Archaeology of the Holy Land reveals that during the Middle Bronze Age, Canaan received greater precipitation and enjoyed a wide variety and diversity of vegetaion that per square kilometer is unmatched by an nation today. [Avinoam Danin, "Man and the Natural Environment," in *The Archaeology of Society in the Holy Land* (New Approaches in Anthropological Archaeology; ed. Thomas E. Levy; London: Leicester University Pres, 1998) 24–37].

69. Notice that if Moses had not requested a spokesman, then he, "as God," would have spoken directly to the people without a prophet or intermediary.

70. Exod 21:24; Lev 24:20; and Deut 19:17–21.

71. If Pharaoh was already in need of judgment for his genocide, why would YHWH harden pharaoh's heart to perform another injustice? Given the human tendency to disclaim God, the Creator intended to leave no doubt that this judgment against Pharaoh came from Israel's God. YHWH wanted credit and did not want his people to see this judgment simply as a natural disaster. Additionally, as an idolator who did not walk in the way of YHWH, Pharaoh's son could *not* be classified as righteous or innocent in this situation.

72. W. L. Walker, "Hardened, Harden," *ISBE* (vol. 2) 615.

73. Genesis 18–19; 22:15; 24:7; 24:40; 31:11; and 48:16.

74. *SEC* 6963; BDB, 876–77; and *TWOT,* 1995.

75. Kline, *Treaty of the Great King,* 18.

76. Exod 13:3, 14; 20:2; Deut 5:6; 6:12; 8:14; 13:5, 10; Josh 24:17; and Judg 6:8.

77. See pp. 65–73 for further discussion. The reason the parity is still valid in this discussion is that YHWH still bound himself to the same stipulations as he had Israel. See also Weinfeld, "Covenant of Grant," 69–83; Kline, *By Oath Consigned,* 21, 27; Thompson, *Treaties and the Old Testament,* 12–15, 21–23; Hegg, *The Covenant of Grant and the Abrahamic Covenant.*

78. Exod 15:24; 16:2; 17:3; Num 14:2–29; 16:41; Numbers 21, 25; and Deut 1:26–27; 9:23–24.

79. Num 32:13–14; Deut 29:1.

80. Deut 1:1–2, 5; 2:18; 29:1.

81. Deut 1:3; 34:8; and Josh 1:11; 4:19; 5:6, 7, 10.

82. For some excellent photos of this site, check out: http://www.bibleplaces.com/shechem.htm. To see how all Israel could have heard these instructions from two points that are a mile apart, see: http://blog.bibleplaces.com/2008/12/acoustics-of-mounts-gerizim-and-ebal.html (both sites accessed January 2015).

83. Exod 12:25; 13:5–16; Lev 14:34; 19:23–25; 23:10–11; 25:2–18; Num 15:2–41; 33:51–56; 34:2–15; 35:10–15; Deut 7:1–11; 11:29–32; 12:10–18; 17:14–20; chaps. 26–27.

84. We will look at how this worked in chapter 8.

85. Phillips, *Israel's Criminal Law,* 11; and Westbrook, *Property, Family in Biblical Law,* 38.

86. *SEC* 1481; BDB, 157–58; and *TWOT* (vol. 1) 155–56.

CHAPTER FIVE

1. Phillips, *Israel's Criminal Law,* 11.

2. Corey S. Powell, *God in the Equation* (New York: Free Press, 2002) 20; and J. J. M. Roberts, *History of the World* (New York: Oxford University Press, 1993) 701.

3. Powell, *God in the Equation,* 20.

4. Ibid., 30. For more detailed information regarding the Church's medieval views, search the Web with the key words, "solar system," "church," and history."

5. *Encyclopædia Britannica Online*, s. v. "law of action and reaction,": http://www.britannica.com/EB-checked/topic/4447/law-of-action-and-reaction (accessed January 2015).

6. Exod 21:24; Lev 24:20; and Deut 19:21.

7. *TWOT* (vol. 1) 647–48; *SEC* 2451; and BDB, 315.

8. *SEC* 8394; BDB, 108; and *TWOT* (vol. 1) 104.

9. William Wilson, *Wilson's Old Testament Word Studies* (McLean, VA: MacDonald, 1990) 461.

10. *M'zuqqaq* is a *pual* active participle. *SEC* 2212; BDB, 279; *TWOT* (vol. 1) 250.

11. *Tsaruf* is a *qal* passive participle. See use of *Zaqaq* in: 1 Chr 28:18, 29:4; Job 28:1; and Mal 3:3.

12. *SEC* 6884; BDB, 864; and *TWOT* (vol. 2) 777.

13. Ps 119:140; 18:30; and 2 Sam 22:31.

14. *SEC* 5948; BDB, 760; and *TWOT* (vol. 1) 671.

15. *SEC* 8435; BDB, 410; and *TWOT* (vol. 1) 380.

16. Hawking, *History of Time*, 84 (emphasis added).

17. A. Douglas Stone, "What Is a Boson? Einstein Was the First to Know," *The Huffington Post: Science* (September 5, 2012), http://www.huffingtonpost.com/a-douglas-ston/higgs-boson-einstein_b_1849374.html (accessed January 2015).

18. Chris Quigg, "Particle physics: What exactly is the Higgs boson? Why are physicists so sure that it really exists?" Fermi National Accelerator Laboratory (January 13, 2012), http://lutece.fnal.gov/Drafts/Higgs.html (accessed January 2015).

19. The Collider Detector at Fermilab, "Search for the Standard Model Higgs Boson at CDF," December 14, 2005, http://www-cdf.fnal.gov/PES/higgs_pes/higgs_plain_english.html (accessed January 2015); R. Nave "The Higgs Boson." Georgia State University, January 13, 2012, http://hyperphysics.phy-astr.gsu.edu/hbase/forces/higgs.html (accessed January 2015); Laura Gardner, "Physicists Say They Are Near Epic Higgs Boson Discovery," Brandeis University, December 13, 2011, updated: Jan. 13, 2012, http://www.brandeis.edu/now/2011/december/particle.html (accessed January 2015).

20. Hawking, *History of Time*, 122–25; and Gerald L. Schroeder, *Genesis and the Big Bang* (New York: Bantam, 1990) 86. For a rebuttal of Schroeder's thesis, see Jay Wile: http://blog.drwile.com/?p=419 ("Genesis and the Big Bang: Part 1." Proslogian. December 28, 2009, accessed January 2015).

21. *SEC* 5948; BDB, 760.

22. Schroeder, *Genesis and the Big Bang*, 50. See also, Gerhard Hasel, "Day," *ISBE* (vol. 1) 877–78.

23. *SEC* 3117; BDB, 398–401; and *TWOT* (vol. 1) 370–71. See also Jay Wile's post http://blog.drwile.com/?p=31 (accessed January 2015).

24. *SEC* 4150; BDB, 417–18. The word translated "season" (*mo'ed* in Hebrew) means 'appointed times.'

25. See pp. 19, 73–77 for further discussion.

26. See Hawking, *History of Time*, 37–54 for further discussion.

27. Scripture often uses the word *water* to denote any liquid that resembles water in consistency. Such is the case in Gen 1:6 where the hot liquid after the Big Bang is termed "water." In the English language today, one of the concepts comprised by the word *water* is any liquid-type substance (MerriamWebster's 3rd Collegiate edition). Thus, the Genesis account does not necessarily denote H_2O but, rather, an extremely hot liquid configuration.

28. Schroeder, *Genesis' Big Bang*, 93–94.

29. Powell, *God in the Equation*, 226. Lambda was the Greek letter Albert Einstein employed in his equations as a cosmological constant. Lambda was the constant that made Einstein's Theory of General Relativity work.

30. *Tipach* is a piel verb. *SEC* 2946; BDB, 381.

31. *Noteh* is in the qal active participle. *SEC* 5186; BDB, 639.

32. *SEC* 7554; BDB, 955. See also Ps 136:6. Much of the terminology used throughout Scripture parallels that of other Semitic culture's creation accounts (see Babylonian Tiamat vs. Hebrew Tehom). I propose that similar to Mesopotamian laws that followed the earlier Noahic Covenant paradigm (i.e.,

Hammurabi Code—See pp. 32, 77, 103–4 for discussion), Genesis reflects a primary creation account that later cultures mythologized, adding stories to the various elements and facets of creation.

33. For a better understanding of the bent universe, see Stephen Hawking, *The Universe in a Nutshell* (New York: Bantam, 2001) 18–21; Kip S. Thorne, *Black Holes and Time Warps: Einstein's Outrageous Legacy* (New York: WW Norton, 1994) 87–120. The Prophet Isaiah's reference to stretching the earth also refers to gravitational forces that developed with every new mass or body that YHWH's creation brought into existence.

34. Mishneh Torah 4:10 (Moses Maimonides, *The Guide for the Perplexed* [trans. M. Friedlander; London: Routledge, 1928] and part 3, chap. 51).

35. With regard to the "creation" of the sun and light, Genesis does *not* actually say that YHWH created anything. More than likely, he had already established the laws of mass/energy conservation and simply fashioned the matter and energy from previous creative periods into the bundle of energy we call the sun.

36. Schroeder, *Genesis' Big Bang*, 86; and Hawking, *History of Time*, 120–25.

37. Schroeder, *Genesis' Big Bang*, 88–89 (emphasis added).

38. For further study on the dilation of time see Schroeder, *Genesis' Big Bang*, 42–48; Hawking, *History of Time*, 15; Ps 90:4; and Andrew Zimmerman Jones and Daniel Robbins, "Slowing Time to a Stanstill with Relativity," For Dummies, http://www.dummies.com/how-to/content/slowing-time-to-a-standstill-with-relativity.html (accessed March 2015).

39. *SEC* 2889; *tahowr* is derived from *taher* (*SEC* 2891), which means 'unadulterated, pure, or uncontaminated.'

40. See also Deut 7:6; 14:2, 21; and Isa 62:12.

41. *SEC* 5459; BDB, 688; and *TWOT* (vol. 2) 617.

42. One popular Christian Web site summarizes this belief: "This seems pretty clear to me: that I should not look like the world. . . . I should not dress like the world. . . . I should not talk like the world. . . . I should not want to be like the world. . . . *I should not want the things the world wants. . . . period*" (Trip Singer, "Church Come out and Separate Yourself from the World," All God.com: Jesus Saves, http://www.all-god.com/come-out-separate-yourself-from-the-world.html, [accessed January 2015]). Other scholarly works do not come right out and acknowledge this assumption, yet it underscores their basic polemic against authenticity. Some of the most popular books today that subscribe to this idea of what a peculiar people "should be" are *The Bible Unearthed* (Finkelstein and Silberman) and *Who Wrote the Bible?* (Friedman).

43. Bill Arnold, professor at Asbury Theological Seminary, observes, "Nearly every genre of the Old Testament has found its parallel in Mesopotamian literature; law, poetry, wisdom, and historical texts. (Arnold, "What has Nebuchadnezzar to do with David?" in *MB*, 330); and Currid, *Ancient Egypt and the Old Testament*.

44. Westbrook and Wells, *Everyday Law*, 23, 46; Nicholas H. Ridderbos and Peter Craigie, "Psalms," *ISBE* (vol. 3) 1039–40; and G. T. Sheppard, "Wisdom," *ISBE* (vol. 4) 1074–76.

45. *ANET*, 412–38, 589–601.

46. F. Brent Knutson, "Canticles," *ISBE* (vol. 1) 606–8.

47. *ANET*, 467–71; and Ridderbos and Craigie, "Psalms,"(vol. 3) 1039–40.

48. In subsequent chapters, I shall demonstrate that Israel's psalms served a specific purpose.

49. 1 Sam 28:6; 23:9–13; and Num 27:21.

50. Richard E. Averbeck, "Sumer, the Bible, and Comparative Method: Historiography and Temple Building," *Mesopotamia and the Bible*, (ed. Mark W. Chavalas and K. Lawson Younger, Jr.; Grand Rapids: Baker Academic, 2002) 88–125; and Ziony Zevit, "The Earthen Altar Laws of Exodus 20:24–26 and Related Sacrificial Restrictions in their Cultural Context," in *Texts, Temples, and Traditions:A Tribute to Menehem Haran* (ed. Michael V. Fox et al.; Winona Lake, IN: Eisenbrauns, 1996) 53–62.

51. A.T. Sandison and Edmund Tapp, "Disease in Ancient Egypt," in *MDAC,* 54.

52. *AEM*, 31, 169–171.

53. Stephen H. Langdon, *Babylonian Menologies and the Semitic Calendars* (London: Oxford University Press, 1935) 89, 10–11; and Hutton Webster, *Rest Days* (New York: MacMillan, 1916) 178–79, 255. It should be noted that this is the era where Daniel would have been active in Babylon.

54. See pp. 73–77 for further discussion.

55. Helmer Ringgren, *Theological Dictionary of the Old Testament* (vol. 15; Grand Rapids: Eerdman's, 2006) 564; Wayne R. Dynes and Stephen Donaldson, *Homosexuality in the Ancient World* (Routledge, 1992) vii–viii, 466.

56. Gerhard Hasel, "Cuttings in the Flesh," *ISBE* (vol. 1) 841; and *ANET*, 139.

57. Other laws unique to Israel were provisions for Refuge Cities in cases of involuntary manslaughter (Numbers 35, Joshua 21) and the recognition of the slaves' right to social justice (Exod 21:6–7, 20–21; Westbrook and Wells, *Everyday Law,* 75, 86–87). Another stipulation on polygyny greatly impeded a man's ability to add another wife to his family by commanding that any previous wife's standard of living could not diminish (Exod 21:10) by the addition of another wife. Desecration of the Sabbath and apostasy are other concepts and laws unique to Israel (Westrook and Wells, *Everyday Law,* 70).

58. Manfred Barthel, *What the Bible Really Says* (trans. Mark Howson; New York: Wings Books) 126–27; Stephen Westerholm, *Israel's Law and the Church's Faith: Paul and His Recent Interpreters* (Grand Rapids: Eerdmans, 1998) 16; Rolf P. Knierim, *The Task of Old Testament Theology: Substance, Method, and Cases: Essays* (Grand Rapids: Eerdmans, 1998) 107–8.

59. *Truth* means that the body of real things, real events, and real facts are in accord with fact or reality, while *omniscient* means composed of universal or complete knowledge. Many Hebrew Scriptures evidence that God is not omniscient. YHWH heard a report of Sodom and Gomorrah's wickedness and sent representatives to see if the report was true (Gen 18:20–21). God did not know if the report was true or not, but sent representatives to find out. During this same event, Abraham is able to argue with God and convince him to modify the qualifications of his judgment (Gen 18:23–33). When YHWH wanted to judge Ahab, he asked for advice from his heavenly counsel (1 Kgs 22:19–23). In another instance, Moses reasoned with God, so that God reserved his judgment (Num 14:11–21). Although YHWH may choose man's delusions (Isa 66:4), Scripture does not indicate that YHWH knows what man will do in every instance. Rather, YHWH uses conditional and limiting judgments to determine the future: "If you do this, then my response will be that." In no way do these judgment laws indicate that YHWH knows what every individual action will be but rather that he will choose his response to it when it does occur.

60. *IHCANE*, 308; James Strong, *The Tabernacle of Israel* (Grand Rapids, MI: Kregel, 1987).

61. Frank E. Hirsch and Kenneth J. Grider, "Crime," *ISBE* (vol. 1) 815–17; and Moshe Greenberg, "Some Postulates of Biblical Criminal Law," in *Essential Papers,* 336–52.

62. Wayne O. McCready, "Priests and Levites," *ISBE* (vol. 3) 965–68.

63. Westbrook and Wells, *Everyday Law,* 35, 39.

64. Donald A. Hagner, "Scribes," *ISBE* (vol. 4) 360.

65. Marty Stevens, *Temples, Tithes, and Taxes* (Grand Rapids: Baker Academic, 2006) 25.

66. Jastrow, "Did the Babylonian Temples Have Libraries?" *JAOS* 27/1 (1906) 147–150, 182.

67. Hudson, "From Sacred Enclave to Temple to City," in *ULO,* 119–27, 131–32; C. C. Lamberg-Karlovsky, "Households, Land Tenure, and Communication Systems," in *ULO,* 178–79, 185.

68. *IHCANE*, 228; Jer 32:11; 7–12; Deut 25:5–10; Ruth 4:2–5; and Van de Mieroop, "Thoughts on Urban Real Estate in Ancient Mesopotamia," in *ULO,* 278.

69. Hudson, "Sacred Enclave to Temple to City," in *ULO,* 119; and Num 7:13, 19, 25, 31, 37, 43, 49, 55, 61, 67, 73, 79; Hazel W. Perkin, "Money," *ISBE* (vol. 3) 403–4; and Stevens, *Temples, Tithes, and Taxes,* 24. Stevens observes: "The Temple was the central socioeconomic-religious institution in ancient Israel, combining the modern-day IRS, Supreme Court, National Cathedral, Congress, and CitiBank" (ibid.).

70. Hudson, "Sacred Enclave to Temple to City," in *ULO,* 129, 142, 146; and Roland K. Harrison, "Interest," *ISBE,* (vol. 2) 860–61.

71. Exod 22:25; Lev 25:35–37; Deut 23:19; Ps 15:5; and Ezek 18:13.

72. Deut 11:8; 15:6; 28:12; and Gen 22:17.

73. *IHCANE*, 256.

74. Erik Øtsby, "Twenty-five Years of Research on Greek Sanctuaries: a Bibliography," in *Greek Sanctuaries: New Approaches* (ed. Nanno Marinatos, Robin Hagg; New York: Routledge, 1993) 179–82; Pedley, *Sanctuaries and The Sacred in the Ancient Greek World*, 122, 150; and Michael Gagarin and Elaine Fantham (eds.), *The Oxford Encyclopedia of Ancient Greece and Rome*, (vol. 1; Oxford: Oxford University Press, 2010) 139, 153, 263, 330–33.

75. 2 Sam 12:28; and 1 Kgs 8:16–21; 9:3.

76. Hutton Webster, *Rest Days*, 223–31; S. Langdon, *Babylonian Menologies*, 10–11, 89; Eviatar Zerubavel, *The Seven Day Circle* (New York: Free Press, 1985); and Mark E. Cohen, *The Cultic Calendars of the Ancient Near East* (Bethesda, MD: CDL, 1993). Most ancient nations observed a Sabbath in one form or another; however, other nations had no penalty for working on the Sabbath as Israel did.

77. *SEC* 4150; BDB, 417–18; *TWOT* (vol. 1) 388–89.

78. Lev 23:3, 7–8, 21, 24, 27, 35–36, 38.

79. Harrison, "Interest," (vol. 4) 861.

80. Ibid., 861–62.

81. Hudson, "Sacred Enclave to Temple to City," in *ULO*, 129–31.

82. Ibid.

83. *SEC* 1293; BDB, 139.

84. Westbrook, *Property and the Family in Biblical Law*, 37.

85. Carlo Zaccagnini, "Economic Aspects of Land Ownership and Land Use in Northern Mesopotamia and Syria from the Late Third Millennium to the New-Assyrian Period," in *ULO*, 342; and Westbrook, *Property, Family in Biblical Law*, 11.

86. Lev 25:21; Deut 11:27. A land's blessing can still be witnessed in the United States, a country that possesses enough natural resources (blessings) to sell their blessings abroad and to hire their labor sector from nations such as India and Indonesia. America's blessings not only profit her own citizenry; her wealth is also shared with other nations via trade and employment exchange.

87. Phillips, *Israel's Criminal Law*, 12.

88. Today, the United States sets penalties for misdemeanor crimes such as traffic tickets at large, predetermined amounts. Instead of discouraging the offense, these penalties often contribute to poverty quite quickly. For instance, a person with an annual income of $20,000 receives a $200 speeding ticket, which he cannot pay. He needs to drive in order to work but receives another ticket and his license is revoked for not having the money to pay the first ticket. At this point, the offender either drives without a license and risks time in jail or loses his job. This system does not take into account the offender's personal income or allow graduated payments. Had the penalty been closer to $20 or $40, the offender could have paid for his offense without its snowballing into other penalties. The real discouragement for reckless driving or speeding in Israel's Law code is based on of the driver's actions. If the driver injured another person, he would be personally liable to pay for the victim's complete recovery. If an accident resulted in death, the driver would escape to a refuge city until the death of the high priest, unless it was determined the victim caused the accident (in which case the accused would go free). If the court found the death to be caused by gross or intentional negligence or a continual disregard for traffic laws was demonstrated, then the death penalty would apply. This strong system of accountability in itself would discourage reckless or negligent driving habits.

89. Lev 25:35–37; Deut 15:1–2, 7–10; 23:19–20.

90. Deut 4:6; 11:8–15; 22–32; 15:11.

91. North, *Tools of Dominion*, 137.

92. Wenham, *Genesis 16–50*, 449.

93. Israel's Law was unique in that it established equity and compensation for any injury that an owner had inflicted on his own slave. This was a progressive concept not recognized in other ancient Near Eastern law codes (Westbrook and Wells, *Everyday Law*, 85).

94. Westbrook and Wells, *Everyday Law,* 86–87.

95. Under the standard *antichretic pledge,* a contract between a creditor and the debtor originated at the onset of a loan: "The creditor enjoyed the income from the debtor's land and/or the debtors labor in lieu of interest payments. . . . neither the land nor the person so pledged became the property of the creditor, unless the debtor defaulted when the debt fell due" (ibid., 114–52). Israel's Law allowed for this type of pledge while providing permanent income-producing lands by which a person could avoid total bankruptcy that led to slavery.

96. *IHCANE,* 24.

97. Ibid., 419.

98. *AEM,* 110–12, 132; and *ESSP,* 17.

99. *AEM,* 160–61; *IHCANE,* 160–63, 202–16, 413; and Van der Toorn, *Sin and Sanction,* 123–24.

100. *IHCANE,* 311–15; *AEM,* 74–75; and Roland K. Harrison, "Leper; Leprosy," *ISBE* (vol. 3) 103–6. For further study see: E. V. Hulse, "The Nature of Biblical 'Leprosy' and the Use of Alternative Medical Terms in Modern Translations of the Bible," *Palestine Exploration Quarterly* 107 (1975) 87–105; J. Wilkinson, "Leprosy and Leviticus: The Problem of Description and Identification," *Scottish Journal of Theology* 30 (1977) 153–59; Idem, "Leprosy and Leviticus: A problem of Semantics and Translation," *Scottish Journal of Theology* 31 (1978) 153–66; and J. Lowe, "Comments on the History of Leprosy," *Leprosy Review* 9 (1955) 9, 25.

101. *SEC* 6883; BDB, 863.

102. *IHCANE,* 311–15.

103. Ibid., 315.

104. See Leviticus 5, 7, 11, 13–15; and *IHCANE,* 408–12.

105. Roland K. Harrison, "Disease," *ISBE* (vol. 1) 955; Van der Toorn, *Sin and Sanction,* 67–70; and *IHCANE,* 243.

106. *IHCANE,* 73.

107. Ibid.,74; and Daniel Snell, *Religions of the Ancient Near East* (Cambridge, UK: Cambridge University Press, 2010) 125.

108. *IHCANE,* 73–74, 78.

109. Van der Toorn, *Sin and Sanction,* 72–80; Harrison, "Disease" (vol. 1) 955; and *IHCANE,* 128, 133.

110. This would be in contrast to Israel's Law that stipulated that each man should bear the consequences of his own sin (Deut 24:16; Lev 20:20; 22:9; 24:15; and Num 27:3).

111. *IHCANE,* 140.

112. Ibid.,140, 186.

113. Lev 5:1, 17; Deut 24:16; Num 35:31–33; and Ezek 33:8–16.

114. *IHCANE,* 372.

115. Lev 16:2; and Num 3:30–31; 4:4–5.

116. *IHCANE,* 243; and Ezek 18:26–28; 33:8–16.

117. Prov 3:18, 22; 6:23; 9:11; 12:28; 13:14; 14:27; 15:30–31 (see also Prov 6:23); and Ezek 33:15.

118. *IHCANE,* 32.

119. Ibid., 32, 89.

120. Ibid., 390.

121. Ibid., 225.

122. Ibid., 409.

123. Deut 12:6–7; 14:23; Num 19:20; and Lev 14:36. Notice that a woman was not allowed to come to the sanctuary until after she had been cleansed of her issue and become clean—Lev 15:28–29, 31. See also Lev 13:46.

124. Gula or Ninisina was a visible constellation (*IHCANE,* 191; and *GDSAM,* 67–68, 101) and she was represented as a dog. Archaeologists have uncovered many sacred burial sites for "healing dogs" near temple precincts throughout Greece, Mesopotamia, and Egypt. In some cities, the goddess was also known as Ninkarrak, Bau, or Nintinugga (*GDSAM,* 101).

125. *IHCANE*, 189, 223, 227.

126. *ESSP*, 472.

127. *IHCANE*, 276.

128. Roland K. Harrison, "Physician," *ISBE* (vol. 3) 865; and Edelstein, *Asclepius* (vol. 2), 101.

129. *IHCANE*, 28.

130. *IHCANE*, 66–70; *AEM*, 110; and *GDSAM*, 81–82.

131. *AEM*, 110–11.

132. *IHCANE*, 160–61.

133. Ibid., 162.

134. Ibid., 189, 223.

135. *ESSP*, 482.

136. *AEM*, 149. Nunn observes that Egyptian medical books, like the Edwin Smith Surgical papyrus, which were written during the Old Kingdom period (*c*. 2686–2181 BCE) approached trauma, disease, and medicine from a scientific standpoint. After the instability of the First Intermediate Period (*c*. 2181–2040 BCE), medicine took on a significantly more "magical" approach to therapy, rituals, and healing incantations, whose unproven methods have survived until modern times (*AEM*, 11).

137. Harrison, "Physician," 865; and *IHCANE*, 244–80, 333, 371, 378–89, 394, 396, 295–98.

138. *IHCANE*, ibid.

139. Deut 32:39; 2 Kgs 20:5; 2 Chr 7:14; Ps 41:4; Jer 17:10–14; 30:14–17; and *IHCIANE*, 269.

140. *IHCANE*, 333; and 1 Sam 1:2–19.

141. Edelstein, *Asclepius*, (vol. 2) 102.

142. Exod 2:24; 3:7; 6:5; 16:9; and *IHCANE*, 254–62.

143. *IHCANE*, 275.

144. Westbrook and Wells, *Everyday Law*, 85; and Exod 21:18–19; 22:4–5.

145. Ibid., 85.

146. Deut 24:16; Lev 20:20; 22:9; 24:15; and Num 27:3.

147. See also 1 Kgs 8:10; and 2 Chr 5:13. For a great discussion on this topic, see Dr. James Tabor (chair, University of N. Carolina at Charlotte) blog: http://unitedisrael.org/the-firm-foundation-of-our-faith/ (accessed January 2015); and Freedman, *Nine Commandments*, 68–69, 76–77.

148. 1 Kgs 8:30–32; 2 Chr 7:14; Psalms 102; 51:17.

149. *IHCANE*, 357, 354.

150. Ps 99:8; 1 Kgs 8:39; Jer 17:10; 32:19; and Ezek 18:30.

151. *IHCANE*, 371.

152. Ibid.

153. Ibid., 396.

154. *AEM*, 136–38.

155. Edelstein, *Asclepius* (vol. 2), 73, 75, 81, 85.

156. *IHCANE*, 55.

157. Edelstein, *Asclepius* (vol. 1; T. 700), 365.

158. *IHCANE*, 89, parenthesis added.

159. Edelstein, *Asclepius*, (vol. 2) 180; and *IHCANE*, 55, 89.

CHAPTER SIX

1. *CGAE*, 282; and Turner and Coulter, *Dictionary of Ancient Deities*, 421.

2. *CGAE*, 276, 277–78; and Turner and Coulter, *Dictionary of Ancient Deities*, 98, 242–43.

3. Ps 18:25–26; 2 Sam 22:25; Exod 21:24; Lev 24:20; and Deut 19:21.

4. Deut 4:6, 40; 8:18; 16:20; 26:19; 30:16–20; Josh 1:7; 1 Kgs 2:3; Psalms 112; Isa 45:3; and Jer 23:22.

5. 1 Kgs 8:23; 2 Chr 6:23; Jer 2:19; 4:14; and Ezek 9:10; 16:43.

6. Scripture often refers to the "diseases of Egypt." See Deut 7:14–15; 28:60–61; 1 Kgs 8:37; 2 Chr 6:28; Ps 103:3; and Lev 18:24–27, 30.

7. *MDAC*, 49–50; and *AEM*, 85–87.

8. Ibid.

9. *MDAC*, 44–48; and *AEM*, 64–95.

10. *MDAC*, 38–44; *AEM*, 73; and *IHCIANE*, 122.

11. Khonsu was known as the moon god and keeper of time. In the course of history, his theology changed from a warring, vengeful god in the Old Kingdom to that of a loving child in the New Kingdom.

12. *AEM*, 75.

13. Ibid.

14. Cameron Walker, "Bubonic Plague Traced to Ancient Egypt," *National Geographic* (March 10, 2004).

15. *AEM*, 69; and *MDAC*, 39–44. During the 19th century, Napoleon Bonaparte's troops reported that Egypt was "the land of menstruating men." Today, this has been attributed to the troop's contact with schistosomiasis. In 1963, the Egyptian Ministry of Public Health estimated that 50% of Egypt's population harbored parasites such as Schistosoma (*MDAC*, 40).

16. *MDAC*, 50–51; and *AEM*, 81–82.

17. *ESSP*, 403–6; and *Ebers*, 813.

18. *AEM*, 81; and *MDAC*, 50–51.

19. *AEM*, 71.

20. Ibid., 16.

21. http://www.ers.usda.gov/topics/in-the-news/hogpork-sector-background-information-and-data.aspx (accessed January 2015); and http://www.ers.usda.gov/topics/animal-products/hogs-pork.aspx (accessed January 2015).

22. Personal communication from the National Marine Fisheries Service, Fisheries Statistics and Economics Division (Silver Spring, MD), http://usda.mannlib.cornell.edu/usda/nass/CatfProc/2000s/2002/CatfProc-07-22-2002.pdf (accessed January 2015) and http://www.st.nmfs.noaa.gov/st1/fus/current/index.html (accessed January 2015).

23. Ibid.; and http://citac.info/shrimp/new_releases/GrocerySalesJune2004.pdf (accessed November 2013).

24. Ibid.

25. R. L. Miller, et al., "Palaeoepidemiology of Schistosoma Infection in Mummies," *BMJ* 304/6826 (February 29, 1992) 555–56.

26. M. H. Criqui et al., "Mortality over a Period of 10 Years in Patients with Peripheral Arterial Disease," *NEJM* 326/6 (1992) 381–386; Michael J. Pentecost et al., "Guidelines for Peripheral Percutaneous Transluminal Angioplasty of the Abdominal Aorta and Lower Extremity Vessels: A Statement for Health Professionals From a Special Writing Group of the Counsels on Cardiovascular Radiology, Arteriosclerosis, Cardio-Thoracic and Vascular Surgery, Clinical Cardiology, and Epidemiology and Prevention, the American Heart Association," *Journal of Vascular and Interventional Radiology* 89/1 (1994) 511–31; Sheryl Benjamin, Executive Director for the Vascular Disease Foundation, personal communication to author, January 27, 2004.

27. A. M. Minino and B. L. Smith, "Preliminary Data for 2000," *National Vital Statistics Report* 49/12 (Hyatsville, MD; October 9, 2001), http://www.cdc.gov/nchs/data/nvsr/nvsr49/nvsr49_12.pdf (accessed January 2015).

28. Ibid.

29. Statistics from the American Academy of Orthopaedic Surgeons, "The Burden of Musculoskeletal Diseases in the United States: 2nd ed.," Bone and Joint Initiative USA (2011), http://www.boneandjointburden.org/ (accessed January 2015); and Statistics from the National Institute of Arthritis and Musculoskeletal and Skin Diseases (NIAMS) Bethesda: MD, 2012, http://www.niams.nih.gov/health_info/Arthritis/arthritis_rheumatic_qa.asp (accessed January 2015).

30. Staff, "Unlocking Mummies' Secrets to Study Today's Diseases," *Cancer Weekly Plus* (June 30, 1997) 24.

31. Palmer A. Orlandi, Dan-My T. Chu, "Parasites and the Food Supply," *Food Technology* 56/4 (April 2002) 72–80; Derek Wakelin, *Immunity to Parasites* (New York; Cambridge University, 1996) 122–45.

32. P. A. Orlandi and D. T. Chu, "Parasites and Food Supply," *Food Technology,* 77.

33. Over the last decade, several studies have demonstrated that returning to a plant-based diet not only reverses disease but eliminates disease all together. The problem credible researchers face in this field is that university or institutional funding (i.g., Johns Hopkins) usually comes from a source (government or industry) that stands to lose if a studies' results are published (i.e., the pork industry). One excellent study that reveals the benefits of a plant-based diet is by T. Colin Campbell and Thomas Campbell, *The China Study* (Dallas, TX: Benbella Books, 2006).

34. S. I. McMillen, *None of These Diseases*, (New York: Pyramid Books, 1963) 19. See also online see: Salynn Boyles, "Male Circumcision Cuts Women's Cervical Cancer Risk: Study Shows Circumcision May Help Reduce Spread of HPV," *WebMD Health News* (ed. Laura Martin, January 2011), http:// www.webmd.com/cancer/cervical-cancer/news/20110106/male-circumcision-cuts-womens-cervical-cancer-risk (accessed January 2015); Christine Rivet, MD, "Circumcision and Cervical Cancer Is There a Link?" *Canadian Family Physician* 49 (September 2003) 1096–97, http://www.ncbi.nlm.nih.gov/ pmc/articles/PMC2214289/pdf/14526861.pdf (accessed January 2015).

35. Xavier Castellsague, et al., "Male Circumcision, Penile Human Papillomavirus Infection, and Cervical Cancer in Female Partners," *NEJM* 346/15 (April 11, 2002) 1105–12.

36. Reynolds, Steven J., Mary E. Shepherd, Arun R. Risbud, et al. "Male Circumcision and Risk of HIV-1 and Other Sexually Transmitted Infections in India." *Lancet* 363 (2004) 1039–40. doi:10.1016/ S0140-6736(04)15840-6.PMID 15051285 (accessed December 2013); See also Rivet, "Circumcision and Cervical Cancer," 1096–97.

37. Reynolds, "Male Circumcision and Risk," 1039–40; Peggy Peck, "Circumcision Associated with 'Profound' Reduction in HIV-1 Risk," *Medscape* (October 11, 2003), http://www.medscape.com/view-article/462816 (accessed January 2015).

38. The researchers note that the participant's interaction with prostitutes was virtually the same in both groups.

39. Hiram N. Wineberg, "The Rare Occurrence of Cancer of the Womb Among Jewish Women," *Bulletin of Mt. Sinai* (1919); and William B. Ober, and Leopold Reiner, "Cancer of Cervix in Jewish Women," *NEJM* 251/14 (November 30, 1954) 555–59.

40. I. Kaplan and R. Rosh, "Carcinoma of the Cervix; Bellevue Hospital Method of Treatment over a Period of Twenty-One Years," *American Journal of Roentgenology* 57 (ed. Lawrence Reynolds, Springfield, IL: Charles Thomas, 1947) 659–64.

41. McMillen, *None of These Diseases,* 18; and William Ober and Leopold Reiner, "Cancer of Cervix in Jewish Women," *NEJM* 251/14 (1954) 556.

42. McMillen, *None of These Diseases*, 18.

43. Rex Russell, *What the Bible Says About Healthy Living* (Ventura, CA: Regal Books, 1996) 22.

44. For a very general understanding of prothrombin, see: *Encyclopædia Britannica Online*, s. v. "prothrombin," http://www.britannica.com/EBchecked/topic/480073/prothrombin (accessed January 2015).

45. McMillen, *None of These Diseases*, 21.

46. Ibid.

47. Aaron Tobian, Seema Kacker, Kevin Frick, Charlotte Gaydos et al., "Declining Rates of U.S. Infant Male Circumcision Could Add Billions to Health Care Costs, Experts Warn," *John Hopkins Medicine* (August 20, 2012), http://www.hopkinsmedicine.org/news/media/releases/declining_rates_of_us_in-fant_male_circumcision_could_add_billions_to_health_care_costs_experts_warn (accessed January 2015). See also Seema Kacker, et al., "Costs and Effectiveness of Neonatal Male Circumcision," *Archives of Pediatrics and Adolescent Medicine* 166/10 (2012) 910–18, http://archpedi.jamanetwork.com/article. aspx?articleid=1352167 (accessed January 2015).

48. Ibid.

49. Russell, *Healthy Living*, 146–47, 154.

50. Food and Drug Administration, "Foodborne Pathogenic Microorganisms and Natural Toxins Handbook" (1st ed., January 2001) 108, emphasis added.

51. Ibid., 34–36; Lewis Goldfrank and Neal Flomenbaum (eds.), *Goldfrank's Toxicologic Emergencies* (8th ed., New York: McGraw-Hill; 2006) 703–5; Thomas C. Arnold, Asim Tarabar, et al., "Shellfish Toxicity,"*Medscape* (Last modified May 6, 2011), http://emedicine.medscape.com/article/818505 (accessed January 2015); "Neurotoxic Shellfish Poisoning: Human Illness Associated with Harmful Algae," Woods Hole Oceanographic Institute http://www.whoi.edu/science/B/redtide/illness/illness. html#Neurotoxic%20Shellfish%20Poisoning (accessed January 2015).

52. "Epidemiologic Notes and Reports Paralytic Shellfish Poisoning—Massachusetts and Alaska, 1990." *Morbidity and Mortality Weekly Report* 40/10 (March 15, 1990) 157–161, http://www.cdc.gov/mmwr/ preview/mmwrhtml/00001927.htm (accessed January 2015); "Centers for Disease Control and Prevention. Update: Neurologic Illness Associated with Eating Florida Pufferfish." *Morbidity and Mortality Weekly Report* 51/19 (May 17 2002) 414–16; A. C. Bronstein, D. A. Spyker, et al., "2009 Annual Report of the American Association of Poison Control Centers' National Poison Data System, (NPDS): 27th Annual Report," *Clinical Toxicology (Philadelphia)* 48/10 (December 2010) 979–1178; B. D. Gessner BD, J. P. Middaugh, et al., "Paralytic Shellfish Poisoning in Kodiak, Alaska," *West Journal of Medicine* 167/5 (November 1997) 351–53; B. Jeffery, T. Barlow, et al., "Amnesic Shellfish Poison," *Food and Chemical Toxicology* 42/4 (April 2004) 545–57; V. Economou, C. Papadopoulou, et al. "Diarrheic Shellfish Poisoning Due to Toxic Mussel Consumption: The First Recorded Outbreak in Greece," *Food Additives and Contaminants* 24/3 (Mar 2007) 297–305; and Thomas C. Arnold, Asim Tarabar, et al., "Shellfish Toxicity," *Medscape* (Last modified May 6, 2011), http://emedicine.medscape.com/article/818505 (accessed January 2015).

53. "Foodborne Handbook," 37; T. M. Petrillo, "Enteritis Necroticans (Pigbel) in a Diabetic Child," *NEJM* 342/17 (April 27, 2000) 1250–53; K. J. Goh, "Clinical Features of Nipah Virus Encephalitis among Pig Farmers in Malaysia," *NEJM* 342/17 (April 27 , 2000) 1229–35.

54. "Foodborne Handbook," 37.

55. One excellent, albeit older treatment on this subject is by the famous *corn flake* inventor who revolutionized the American Breakfast industry: J. H. Kellogg, "The Dangers of Pork-Eating Exposed" (Battle Creek, MI: Good Health Publishing, 1897).

56. "Foodborne Handbook," 21–23.

57. Wakelin, *Immunity to Parasites,* xvi, 173–190; David N. Fredricks et al., "Rhinosporidium seeberi: A Human Pathogen From a Novel Group of Aquatic Protistan Parasites," *Emerging Infectious Diseases* 6/3 (2000) 273–82; David Moore et al., "Gnathostomiasis: An Emerging Imported Disease," *Emerging Infectious Diseases* 9/6 (2003) 647–50; Jerome Goddard, "Kissing Bugs and Chagas' Disease," *Infections in Medicine* 16/3 (1999) 172–80; and Matty de Wit et al., "Gastroenteritis in Sentinel General Practices, the Netherlands," *Emerging Infectious Diseases* 7/1 (2001) 82–91.

58. Jonathan Hardy et al., "Extracellular Replication of Listeria Monocytogenes in the Murine Gall Bladder," *Science* (Feb 6, 2004) 851–53.

59. Russell, *Healthy Living,* 154; see also, Jordan Rubin, *The Maker's Diet* (Lake Mary, FL: Siloam, 2004) 31–49.

60. Stacey Knobler and Alison Mack et al., eds., "The Story of Influenza," in *The Threat of Pandemic Influenza: Are We Ready? Workshop Summary,*" 1 (Washington, D.C; The National Academies Press, 2005) 75. http://books.nap.edu/openbook.php?isbn=0309095042&page=75; Some researchers believe humans contracted the 1918 epidemic from swine, see R. E. Shope, "Swine influenza. III: Filtration Experiments and Aetiology," in *Journal of Experimental Medicine* 54 (1931) 373–80; and Paul Heinen, "Swine Influenza: A Zoonosis," in *Veterinary Sciences Tomorrow* (September 15, 2003) 1–11.

61. World Health Organization, "Swine Influenza Frequently Asked Questions," (April 26, 2009) http://www.paho.org/english/ad/who_swineinfluenza_faq_eng.pdf (accessed February 2015). See also,http://www.cdc.gov/mmwr/preview/mmwrhtml/mm58d0430a2.htm (accessed February 2015).

62. Keith Bradsher, "The Naming of Swine Flu, a Curious Matter," *New York Times* (April 4, 2009).

63. Eileen Thacker and Bruce Janke, "Swine Influenza Virus: Zoonotic Potential and Vaccination Strategies for the Control of Avian and Swine Influenzas," *Journal of Infectious Diseases* 197 (Suppl 1; February, 2008) S19–24, http://www.journals.uchicago.edu/doi/abs/10.1086/524988 (accessed January 2015).

64. Ibid., "Swine Influenza Virus," 19–24.

65. Heinen, "Swine Influenza: A Zoonosis," 1–11.

66. Associated Press, "Pig-brain Mist Suspected in Worker's Disease," *MSNBC* (December 7, 2007), http://www.msnbc.msn.com/id/22150940/ (accessed January 2015).

67. Brandon Keim, 'Pig Brain Mist' Disease Concludes," ABC News (March 5, 2009). http://abcnews.go.com/Health/MindMoodNews/story?id=7015430&page=1&page=1 (accessed January 2015).

68. WHO: Western Pacific Region, "Fact Sheet: *Streptococcus suis*" (August 1, 2005), http://www.wpro.who.int/mediacentre/factsheets/fs_20050802/en/index.html (accessed January 2015).

69. Hongjie Yu, et al, "Human *Streptococcus suis* Outbreak, Sichuan, China" in *Emerging Infectious Diseases* 12/6 (June 2006) 914–20, http://www.cdc.gov/ncidod/eid/vol12no06/pdfs/05-1194.pdf (accessed January 2015).

70. Smith, T. C., et al., "Occupational Exposure to *Streptococcus suis* among US Swine Workers," *Emerging Infectious Diseases* 14/12 (December 2008) 1925–27, http://www.cdc.gov/eid/content/14/12/pdfs/08-0162.pdf (accessed January 2015); Marcelo Gottschalk, "Porcine *Streptococcus suis* Strains as Potential Sources of Infection in Humans: An Underdiagnosed Problem in North America?" *Journal of Swine Health and Production* 12 (2004) 197–99, PubMed DOI: 10.1017/S1466252307001247; idem, "Streptococcus suis Infections in Humans: The Chinese Experience and the Situation in North America," *Animal Health Research Reviews* 8 (2007) 29–45; K. Donsakul et al., "*Streptococcus suis* Infection: Clinical Features and Diagnostic Pitfalls," *Southeast Asian J Trop* 34/1 (2003) 154–58; M. C. Heidt et al., "Human Infective Endocarditis Caused by *Streptococcus suis* Serotype 2," *Journal of Clinical Microbiology* 43 (2005) 4898–4901. PubMed DOI: 10.1128/JCM.43.9.4898-4901.2005.

71. Gottschalk, "*Streptococcus suis* Infections in Humans," 29–45.

72. Donsakul, "*Streptococcus suis* Infection," *Southeast Asian J Trop Med Public Health* 34 (2003) 154; Heidt, "Human Infective Endocarditis," 898–901; Gottschalk, "*Streptococcus suis* Infections in Humans," 29–45; E. E. Mazokopakis et al., "First Case Report of *Streptococcus suis* Septicaemia and Meningitis from Greece," *European Journal of Neurology* 12 (2005) 487–89, PubMed DOI: 10.1111/j.1468-1331.2005.00998.x

73. Mazokopakis, " First case report of *Streptococcus suis*," 487–89.

74. J. P. Arends and H. C. Zanen, "Meningitis Caused by *Streptococcus suis* in Humans," *Review of Infectious Diseases* 10 (1988) 131–37.

75. I. D. Robertson and D. K. Blackmore, "Occupational Exposure to *Streptococcus suis* Type 2," *Epidemiology Infection* 103 (1989) 157–64.

76. WHO, "Fact Sheet: *Streptococcus suis*."

77. Hongjie, "Human *Streptococcus suis* Outbreak, Sichuan, China," 914–20.

78. Ibid.

79. Y. Guan, et al., "Isolation and Characterization of Viruses Related to the SARS Coronavirus from Animals in Southern China," *Science* 302 (2003) 276–78; Maggie Fox, "Chinese Researchers Confirm SARS Came from Animals," *Reuters* (September 4, 2003); Joe McDonald, "WHO Finds Evidence Animals Play SARS Role," *Associated Press* (January 16, 2004); Also see the official WHO Web site: http://www.who.int/csr/sars/conference/june_2003/materials/presentations/en/roleofAnimals180603.pdf (accessed April 2011. The article has since been abbreviated).

80. Angus Nicoll, chair, "Consensus Document on the Epidemiology of Severe Acute Respiratory Syndrome (SARS)," Department of Communicable Disease and Surveillance Response, *WHO* (Geneva, Switzerland; May 2003) 29.

81. Lev 11:8, 24–27; and Deut 14:8.

82. Eric M. Leroy et al., "Multiple Ebola Virus Transmission Events and Rapid Decline of Central African Wildlife," *Science* 303 (2004) 387–90.

83. Ibid.

84. Nathan Wolfe, interview on March 18, 2004 at Johns Hopkins. "Primate Viruses Transmitted to People through Bushmeat." Reproduced with permission of the Johns Hopkins Bloomberg School of Public Health, Baltimore, MD. Online at http://www.jhsph.edu/publichealthnews/press_releases/PR_2004/ape_viruses.html (accessed January 2015); Nathan Wolfe et al., "Naturally Acquired Simian Retrovirus Infections in Central African Hunters," *The Lancet* 363 (March 20, 2004) 932–37.

85. Patricia Reaney, "Bushmeat Sparks Fears of New AIDS-Type Virus," *Reuters* (March 19, 2004).

86. David Macht, "An Experimental Pharmacological Appreciation of Leviticus XI and Deuteronomy XIV," *Bulletin of Historical Medicine* 47/1 (Johns Hopkins University, April 1953) 444–50.

87. Ibid.

88. Russell, *Healthy Living,* 28, 47; and F. Gunby, "Battles Continue over DES Use in Fattening Cattle," *Journal of American Medical Association* 244/3 (July 1980) 228.

89. Russell, *Healthy Living,* 31–32.

90. Soewarta Kosen et al., "Communicable Diseases: Qualitative Study on Avian Influenza in Indonesia;" *Regional Health Forum* 13/1 (WHO Regional Office for South-East Asia, 2009) 35, http://whoindonesia.healthrepository.org/handle/123456789/610 (accessed January 2015).

91. Ibid.

92. Communicable Disease Surveillance and Response (CSR), "Bovine Spongiform Encephalopathy (BSE)," *WHO,* 2013, http://www.who.int/csr/disease/bse/en/ (accessed January 2015, emphasis added).

93. Greg Lardy, "Bovine Spongiform Encephalopathy, (BSE; Mad Cow Disease)," *North Carolina State University Department of Agriculture* (March 2004), http://www.ag.ndsu.edu/pubs/ansci/beef/as1206w.htm (accessed January 2015).

94. Suzette Priola, et al., "How Animal Prions Cause Disease in Humans," in *Microbe Magazine* 3/12 (December 2008), American Society for Microbiology 2009, http://www.microbemagazine.org/index.php?option=com_content&view=article&id=407:how-animal-prions-cause-disease-in-humans&catid=160:featured&Itemid=212 (accessed January 2015).

95. Num 12:14. See also *JFB,* 121.

96. Leviticus 15.

97. Lev 15:19–28.

98. Lev 15:16–18.

99. Lev 11:24, 25, 28, 31, 32, 39–40; 15:10; 16–23, 27.

100. George Rosen, *History of Public Health* (New York: MD Publications, 1958) 62–63.

101. Roberts, *History of the World,* 413.

102. J. Aberth, *The Black Death: The Great Mortality of 1348–1350: A Brief History with Documents* (New York: Palgrave Macmillan, 2005); "The Black Death and Early Public Health Measures: Science Museum," http://www.sciencemuseum.org.uk/broughttolife/themes/publichealth/blackdeath.aspx (accessed January 2015); and Peter Tyson, "A Short History of Quarantine," *NOVA* (October 12, 2004), http://www.pbs.org/wgbh/nova/body/short-history-of-quarantine.html (accessed November 2013).

103. Th. M. Vogelsang, *Leprosy in Norway,* http://www.ncbi.nlm.nih.gov/pmc/articles/PMC1033440/pdf/medhisto0156–0037.pdf (accessed January 2015).

104. Edgar B. Johnwick, "Hansen's Disease," *New Standard Encyclopedia* (ed. Douglas Downey; Chicago: Standard Educational Corporation, 1995) 45.

105. Tyson, "A Short History of Quarantine," *NOVA* (2004).

106. E. L. Tan et al., "Inhibition of SARS Coronavirus Infection in Vitro with Clinically Approved Antiviral Drugs," *Emerging Infectious Diseases* (April 10, 2004) 581–86; Mary Hansen et. al., "SARS Response Plan Version 1.2," IOWA Department of Public Health (July 2004) 2.

107. Ibid.

108. Nicoll, "Consensus Document on the Epidemiology of Severe Acute Respiratory Syndrome (SARS)," Department of Communicable Disease and Surveillance Response, *WHO* (Geneva, Switzerland; May 2003) 16.

109. Since then, SARS has reappeared in separated cases. In each case, SARS was associated with human consumption or handling of an infected animal.

110. Nicoll, "Consensus Document," 16.

111. Victor A. McKusick, *Mendelian Inheritance in Man: A Catalog of Human Genes and Genetic Disorders:* 12th ed, (Baltimore, MD: Johns Hopkins University Press, 1998). Also see the government-sponsored site based on McKusick's work, http://www.ncbi.nlm.nih.gov/omim/.

112. David Greenberg, *The Construction of Homosexuality* (Chicago: University of Chicago Press, 1990) 126; Vern Bullough, *Sexual Variance in Society and History* (John Wiley, 1976) 53; and Westbrook and Wells, *Everyday Law*, 71–73.

113. Norman Sussman et al., "Sex and Sexuality in History," in *The Sexual Experience* (ed. B. J. Sadock, et al.; Baltimore: Williams and Wilkins, 1976) 9.

114. Bruce L. Gerig, "Homosexuality in the Ancient Near East, Beyond Egypt," *Homosexuality and the Bible Supplement* (2005), http://epistle.us/hbarticles/neareast.html (accessed January 2015).

115. "*The Almanac of Incantations* contained prayers favoring on an equal basis the love of a man for a woman, of a woman for a man, and of a man for man. . . . *The Summa alu,* a manual used to predict the future, sought to do this in some cases on the basis of sexual acts, five of which are homosexual" (Gerig, "Homosexuality in the Ancient Near East," http://epistle.us/hbarticles/neareast.html). Scholars theorize that the lack of records detailing female homosexuality arises from women's low status, where laws and records dealing with female activity was not deemed valuable to a male-dominated society (ibid.) See also Dennis Prager's excellent article on homosexuality: "Judaism's Sexual Revolution: Why Judaism (and Christianity) Rejected Homosexuality," *Crisis* 11/8 (September 1993), http://www.orthodoxytoday.org/articles2/PragerHomosexuality.php (accessed January 2015).

116. Another factor that stands at odds with this logic is Scripture's use of the term *whoredom,* which did not depict prostitution but sexual promiscuity, a point that we will address in the next section.

117. Lesbianism can also spread disease. Whatever apparatus is used between the two partners shares both fluid and disease between female partners as well as any other diseases that may be contracted from other heterosexual or homosexual partners.

118. Koray Tanfer and Sevgi Aral, "Sexual Intercourse During Menstruation and Self-Reported Sexually Transmitted Disease History Among Women," *Sexually Transmitted Diseases* 23/5 (September/October 1996) 395–401, http://www.ncbi.nlm.nih.gov/pubmed/8885071 (accessed January 2015).

119. Ibid.

120. Ibid.

121. Ibid.

122. For a quick overview see: http://www.wisegeek.com/what-is-the-endometrium.htm (accessed January 2015).

123. James B. Maas, *Power Sleep* (New York: Villard Books, 1998) xvii, 22, 28–29, 50, 97, 113.

124. A mother's separation from marital relations was determined by the sex of her child (Lev 12:2–5). A daughter's birth always resulted in a longer separation period. It is possible that a woman needed more time to shed hormones and other chemicals required to form her daughter's life. The body may simply take longer to identify these compounds and separate them from the woman's natural hormone levels. It is hoped that scientific research in the future can allot resources to fund studies that may reveal the factors involved in the postpartum process.

125. Exod 20:14; Lev 20:10; and Deut 5:18.

126. We will discuss Israel's Congregation in chapter 10.

127. Exod 13:3, 14; 20:2; and Deut 5:6; 6:12; 8:14; 13:5, 10.

128. *SEC* 2181, 2183, 2184, and 8457; BDB, 275–76; and *TWOT* (vol. 1) 246. For an excellent treatise on ancient ideas on promiscuity, see Victor Matthews, Bernard Levinson, and Tikva Frymer-Kensky (eds.), *Gender and Law in the Hebrew Bible and the Ancient Near East* (London: Sheffield Academic, 1998) 79–112.

129. *TWOT* (vol. 1) 295.

130. Westbrook and Wells, *Everyday Law,* 86.

131. Ibid.

132. Ibid., 62–63.

133. Ibid., 63.

134. Ibid., 61.

135. Federal Interagency Forum on Child and Family Statistics, "America's Children: Key National Indicators of Wellbeing," (2002) 7, http://childstats.gov/americaschildren/index.asp (accessed January 2015).

136. Juliette Engel, Robert Aronson, et al., "Addressing the Needs of Children in Crisis: Single, Teen-age Motherism the Russian Federation" *for CHILDHOOD World Childhood Foundation* (Part I, Moscow, Russia: March 2002), http://www.miramed.org/pdf/ResearchReportonTeenPregnancies.pdf (accessed January 2015).

137. Peter Ford, "In Europe, Unmarried Parents on Rise" *Christian Science Monitor* (April 17, 2006), http://www.csmonitor.com/2006/0417/p01s03-woeu.html (accessed January 2015).

138. Ibid.

139. See pp. 85–87; *Elizabeth Lopatto,* "Births to Unwed Mothers Increase to Record Proportion in U.S.," *Bloomberg* (July 13, 2007), http://www.bloomberg.com/apps/news?pid=20601103&sid=aAexAvTGa7zk&refer=us (accessed January 2015); Hartman, "Diagnosing the Impending European Population Implosion," *Remarks to The World Congress of Families III* (Mexico City, Mexico: March 29, 2004), http://www.worldcongress.org/wcf3_spkrs/wcf3_hartman.htm (accessed January 2015).

140. Joe McIhaney, *Sexuality and Sexually Transmitted Diseases* (Grand Rapids, MI: Baker, 1990); and David Hager and Donald Joy, *Women at Risk: The Real Truth About Sexually Transmitted Disease* (Anderson, IN: Bristol, 1993).

141. Federal Interagency Forum on Child and Family Statistics, "America's Children," 8.

142. Ibid., 7.

143. Ibid.

144. Kyle D. Pruett, *Fatherneed: Why Father Care Is As Essential As Mother Care for Your Child* (New York: Broadway Books, 2000).

145. Ibid.; and Hartman: http://www.worldcongress.org/wcf3_spkrs/wcf3_hartman.htm.

146. See statistics in the next section, "STDs: All of These Diseases."

147. Linda L Anderson, ed., et al., "Sexually Transmitted Disease in America: How Many Cases and at What Cost?" *American Social Health Foundation* (December 1998) 10, http://www.kff.org/womenshealth/1445-std_rep.cfm (accessed January 2015).

148. Ibid., 13–20.

149. Centers for Disease Control and Prevention, "*Sexually Transmitted Disease Surveillance, 1997,*" U.S. Department of Health and Human Services, Public Health Service: Division of STD Prevention: Atlanta (September 1998) 5, http://www.cdc.gov/nchstp/dstd/Stats_Trends/1997_Surveillance_Report.pdf (accessed January 2015).

150. Ibid.

151. CDC, "*Sexually Transmitted Diseases in the United States, 2008: National Surveillance Data for Chlamydia, Gonorrhea, and Syphilis,*" National Prevention Prevention Network, (Last Updated April 16, 2013), http://www.cdcnpin.org/scripts/std/std.asp; and http://www.cdc.gov/std/stats08/2008survFactSheet.PDF (accessed January 2015).

152. CDC, "*Sexually Transmitted Disease Surveillance, 1997,*" 13.

153. Ibid., 5.

154. "Just the Facts: STDs," Richmond, Virginia, Metro Pregnancy Resource Center, http://prcrichmond.org/STDs.htm (accessed January 2015).

155. Ibid.

156. M. Watson, et al., "Burden of Cervical Cancer in the United States, 1998–2003," *Cancer* 113/10 (2008) 2855–2864; Centers for Disease Control and Prevention (CDC), "HPV-Associated Cervical Cancer Rates by Race and Ethnicity," Division of Cancer Prevention and Control, National Center for

Chronic Disease Prevention and Health Promotion (Last Updated August 13, 2013), http://www.cdc.gov/cancer/hpv/statistics/cervical.htm (accessed January 2015); and Xiaocheng Wu, et al., "Human Papillomavirus–Associated Cancers—United States, 2004–2008," *Morbidity and Mortality Weekly Report* 61/15 (2012) 258–261.

157. http://prcrichmond.org/STDs.htm; "How Serious of a Problem are Sexually Transmitted Infections (STIs) in the United States?" Medical Institute for Sexual Health (last modified June 29, 2012), https://www.medinstitute.org/faqs/how-serious-of-a-problem-are-sexually-transmitted-infections-stis-in-the-united-states/ (accessed January 2015); and "CDC/HRSA Advisory Committee on HIV and STD Prevention and Treatment: Draft Record of the Preceedings, November 2–3, 2009," Bethesda, Maryland, http://www.cdc.gov/maso/FACM/pdfs/CHACHSPT/2009110203_CHACHSPT.pdf (accessed January 2015).

158. http://prcrichmond.org/STDs.htm; Brochert, Adam, "STD—Sexually Transmitted Disease," Medicine Online (Last modified July 2001), http://www.medicineonline.com/articles/S/2/STD/Sexually-Transmitted-Disease.html (accessed January 2015).

159. CDC, "*Sexually Transmitted Disease Surveillance, 1997,*" 13–14.

160. CDC, "HIV in the United States," http://www.cdc.gov/hiv/topics/surveillance/resources/factsheets/us_overview.htm.

161. UNAIDS 2009, "2009 *AIDS Epidemic Update,*" Geneva: World Health Organization (WHO, 2009) 33, http://www.unaids.org/en/media/unaids/contentassets/dataimport/pub/report/2009/jc1700_epi_update_2009_en.pdf (accessed January 2015).

162. George Chang and Mark Welton, "Human Papillomavirus, Condylomata Acuminata, and Anal Neoplasia," *Clinics in Colon Rectal Surgery* 174 (November 2004) 221–30.

163. World Health Organization – Regional Office for the Eastern Mediterranean, "Aids and Sexually Transmitted Diseases," Fact Sheet for World AIDS Campaign 2003, http://www.emro.who.int/asd/wac2003-FactSheet-Statistics.htm (accessed January 2015).

164. UNAIDS 2009, "Global Summary of the AIDS Epidemic, 2009," WHO, http://www.who.int/hiv/data/2009_global_summary.png (accessed January 2015).

165. Purnima Mane and Ann P. McCauley, "Impact of Sexually Transmitted Infections Including AIDS on Adolescents: a Global Perspective," in *Towards Adulthood: Exploring the Sexual and Reproductive Health of Adolescents in South Asia* (WHO) 133–36.

166. Elise F. Jones and Jacqueline Darroch Forrest, "Contraceptive Failure in the United States: Revised Estimates from the 1982 National Survey of Family Growth," *Family Planning Perspectives* 21 (May 1989) 103–5; Lode Wigersma and Ron Oud, "Safety and Acceptability of Condoms for Use by homosexual Men as a Prophylactic Against Transmission of HIV during Anogenital Sexual Intercourse," *BMJ* 295/6590 (July 11, 1987) 94; Margaret A. Fischl, et al., "Heterosexual Transmission of Human Immunodeficiency Virus (HIV) Relationship of Sexual Practices to Seroconversion," III International Conference on AIDS (Abstracts Volume: June 1–5, 1987) 178; Marcia F. Goldsmith, "Sex in the Age of AIDS Calls for common Sense and Condom Sense," *JAMA* (257; May, 1987) 2262; Susan G. Arnold, et al., "Latex Gloves Not Enough to Exclude Viruses," *Nautre* 335 (September, 1988) 19; Nancy E. Dirubbo, "The Condom Barrier," *American Journal of Nursing,* (October, 1987)1306; "Condom Roulette," *In Focus* 25 (Washington: Family Research Counsel, February 1992) 2.

167. It may be remembered that both Black Death and leprosy were virtually extinguished by implementing Torah based protocols.

168. CDC, "*Sexually Transmitted Disease Surveillance, 1997,*" 4 (emphasis added).

169. Mane and McCauley, "Impact of Sexually Transmitted Infections," in *Towards Adulthood* (WHO) 133–36.

170. Desmond Cohen, "Economic Impact of the HIV Epidemic," HIV and Development Programme, United Nations Development Programme 2 (UNDP), http://www.undp.org/hiv/publications/issues/english/issue02e.htm (accessed November 2013). The article has since been moved to: http://www.heart-intl.net/HEART/HIV/Comp/TheEconomicImpactofhmic.htm (accessed January 2015).

171. Cohen, "Economic Impact of the HIV Epidemic."

172. Anderson, "Sexually Transmitted Disease in America: What Cost," 23.

173. Ibid.; see also David A. Hartman, " Impending European Population Implosion," *World Congress of Families III* 18/9 (Mexico City, March 31, 2004), http://www.profam.org/pub/fia/fia_1809.htm (accessed January 2015).

174. Carol Ezzell, "Care for a Dying Continent," *Scientific American* 282/5 (May 2000) 96–105.

175. Cohen, "Economic Impact of HIV Epidemic."

176. J. D. Unwin, *Sexual Regulations and Human Behaviour* (London: Williams and Northgate, 1933).

177. "Just the Facts: STDs," Richmond, Virginia, Metro Pregnancy Resource Center, http://prcrichmond.org/STDs.htm

178. CDC, "Sexually Transmitted Disease Surveillance, 1997," 24, 29.

179. UNAIDS "Report on the Global HIV/AIDSEpidemic," XIV International AIDS Conference (July 2002), http://data.unaids.org/pub/Report/2002/brglobal_aids_report_en_pdf_red_en.pdf (accessed February 2015).

180. McKusick, *Mendelian Inheritance in Man*; http://www.ncbi.nlm.nih.gov/Omim/mimstats.html. See also "heart disease" or "coronary heart disease" at John Hopkin's site based on McKusick's work at: http://www.ncbi.nlm.nih.gov/omim/ (accessed January 2015).

181. Barry M. Popkin and J. Richard Udry, "Adolescent Obesity Increases Significantly in Second and Third Generation U.S. Immigrants: The National Longitudinal Study of Adolescent Health," *Journal of Nutrition* 128/4 (April 1, 1998) 701–706; Heidi Enwald and Maija-Leena Huotari, "Preventing the Obesity Epidemic by Second Generation Tailored Health Communication: An Interdisciplinary Review," *Journal of Medical Internet Research* 12/2 (April–June, 2010) e24, PMCID: PMC2956235. See also the Mayo Clinic on childhood type 2 Diabetes, which lists both genetics and life-style as primary causes: http://www.mayoclinic.com/health/type-2-diabetes-in-children/DS00946/DSECTION=risk-factors (accessed January 2015).

CHAPTER SEVEN

1. See also Num 15:16, 29.

2. Richard Elliott Friedman, *Commentary on the Torah* (New York: Harper Collins, 2001) 212.

3. Westbrook and Wells, *Everyday Law,* 83; and *ANET,* 164–80.

4. Ibid.

5. Ibid.

6. The only way for indemnity to work according to Torah standards would be for the court to hold criminals culpable for their crimes and citizens culpable for their life-style choices. Similarly, for healthcare (another type of indemnity) to operate according to Torah standards, participation would be purely voluntary and individual life-style would remain a primary factor in cost. However, this requires a court system that uphold's a victim's rights and honestly pursues justice, even in small matters.

7. Westbrook and Wells, *Everyday Law,* 85.

8. Catherine Crier, *The Case Against Lawyers* (New York: Broadway Books, 2002) 19.

9. Exod 21:29, 13; and Num 35:20–23. See also Westbrook and Wells, *Everyday Law,* 75.

10. Throughout the Near East, nations practiced the custom of *satisfaction* or *ransom* (Heb. *Kopher—SEC* 3724). When convicted of murder, the criminal could buy his ransom with no further restraints (Leon Morris, "Ransom," *ISBE,* vol. 4, 44–45). Except for a few cases in which injury was not a person's fault (Exod 21:30–36), Israel's Law forbade this practice (Num 35:31–34). Satisfaction could *never* be used in a case involving premeditated murder or crime. See also, Westbrook and Wells, *Everyday Law,* 73–74, 78. In other words, there were no legal loopholes.

11. Hudson, "From Sacred Enclave to Temple to City," in *ULO*, 136–37; and Baruch Levin, "The Biblical 'Town' as Reality and Typology: Evaluating Biblical References to Towns and Their Functions," in *ULO*, 429–38.

12. Refuge Cities, which protected the man-slayer, were a unique characteristic of Israel's Law system. There is no evidence for this system in any other ancient Near Eastern Society (Westbrook and Wells, *Everyday Law*, 75).

13. Nor could a case be dismissed based on the defendant's state of mind. Hence, "insanity" was not a valid defense in Israel's courts.

14. Mendenhall, *Ancient Israel's Faith and History*, 62–63.

15. Dobson, *Bringing up Boy*, 53–54; emphasis added.

16. Hartman, "Diagnosing the Impending European Population Implosion," *Remarks to The World Congress of Families III* (Mexico City, March 29, 2004).

17. Modern society differs little in this respect from ancient Mesopotamia. The Code of Hammurabi (laws 127–193) dealt extensively with individual rights in divorce cases. If there was a need to address almost one-fourth of these laws to divorce issues or other elements dissolving the family unit, then it appears that family breakup was quite commonplace in ancient Mesopotamia during Hammurabi's reign.

18. Num 34:14–18; 33:54; 26:52–55.

19. The tribe's firstborn heir was the tribal "prince" (Num 17:6; 34:18–29).

20. Daughters were sometimes given heritages as well. Caleb gave his daughter land with natural springs (Josh 15:19).

21. Westbrook and Wells, *Everyday Law*, 91–104.

22. See Abraham Malamat, *History of Biblical Israel*, 36–40 for a good discussion on this practice.

23. Deut 13:5; 17:7, 12; 19:19; 21:21; 22:22–24; 24:7.

24. See Phinehas's actions on the Moab plains as well as the Altar of Ed incident (Num 25:7–13; and Josh 22:10–34).

25. Marc Van De Mieroop, "Thoughts on Urban Real Estate in Ancient Mesopotamia," in *ULO*, 259. See also Maria de Ellis, *Agriculture and the State in Ancient Mesopotamia: An Introduction to Problems of Land Tenure* (Occasional Publications of the Babylonian Fund 1. Philadelphia: Babylonian Fund, University Museum, 1976).

26. Ibid.

27. Van der Toorn, *Sin and Sanction*, 3.

28. Westbrook and Wells, *Everyday Law*, 120.

29. Michael Hudson, "Introduction: The New Economic Archaeology of Urbanization," in *ULO*, 14; Van de Mieroop, "Thoughts on Urban Real Estate," in *ULO*, 259.

30. Hudson, "New Economic Archaeology of Urbanization," in *ULO*, 15.

31. Ibid.

32. Idem, "Sacred Enclave to Temple to City," in *ULO*, 121, 125, 130–131; and Van der Toorn, *Sin and Sanction*, 3.

33. Hudson, "Sacred Enclave to Temple to City," in *ULO*, 120.

34. Ibid.

35. Ibid., 122.

36. Ibid., 130; and *KG*, 222–23.

37. Hudson, "Sacred Enclave to Temple to City ," in *ULO*, 130–31; Goelet, "'Town' and 'Country' in Ancient Egypt," in *ULO*, 90–96.

38. Alexander Fuks, *Social Conflict in Ancient Greece* (Leiden: Brill, 1984) 19–20; Isocrates, *Panegyricus*, 4:167 (Isocrates, *Isocrates with an English Translation*: 3 vols. [ed. George Norlin, Cambridge, MA: Harvard University Press: London, 1980]). http://www.perseus.tufts.edu/hopper/text?doc=Perseus:abo:tlg,0010,011:167. (accessed January 2015).

39. Ibid., 90.

40. Van de Mieroop, "Urban Real Estate in Ancient Mesopotamia," in *ULO*, 258.

41. Num 18:20–24; 26:62; 18:2; 35:2–8; Josh 14:3–4; and Lev 25:33.
42. Num 3:12; 8:17–19; 18:6.
43. Hudson, "Sacred Enclave to Temple to City," in *ULO*, 118, 129–30.
44. Ibid., 129; Harry E Barnes, *An Economic History of the Western World* (New York: Harcourt, Brace and Company, 1942) 507.
45. Westbrook and Wells, *Everyday Law*, 120.
46. E. M. Cook, "Weights and Measures," *ISBE* (vol. 4) 1051–54. If the Levites purchased grain at 50 shekels per homer and sold them for a half shekel per seah (2 Kgs 7:1), there would have been a loss of 2.33 shekels per seah (the break-even price would have been 3.33 shekels per seah). Since this is not sustainable, the constitutionally-defined purchase price had been abandoned or substantially lowered during Israel's rebellious eras. Another possibility is that a seah was a much smaller measurement.
47. Ibid., 1051.
48. Célestin Charles Alfred Bouglé, *Essays on the Caste System* (trans. D. F. Pocock; London: Cambridge University Press, 1971) 8, 44, 107.
49. Bouglé, *Caste System*, 97.
50. J. T. Wheeler, *Wheeler's History of India* (vol. 3; Coronet Books, 1969) 192.
51. *AEM*, 127, 129–131.
52. Num 4:3, 23, 30, 35, 39, 43, 47. Num 8:24–26 appears to have a scribal error of 5 years by establishing service age at age 25 rather than age 30.
53. Daniel B. Pecota and John W. Simpson, "Young(er) (Man)," *ISBE* (vol. 4) 1166.
54. Exod 12:49; Lev 7:7; Num 15:16, 29; and Ps 37:5.
55. If a stranger ate meat that had died of its own accord, the Law provided means for cleansing (Lev 17:15–16).
56. Kaiser, *Toward Old Testament Ethics*, 212–17.
57. The work week could not exceed six days (Exod 20:8–11).
58. Andrew Steinmann, *From Abraham to Paul: A Biblical Chronology* (St. Louis, MO: Concordia Publishing, 2011) 27.
59. Exod 23:8–11; and Lev 25:1–12.
60. Steinmann, *Abraham to Paul*, 25–30.
61. A. de Hingh, "The Archaeology of the Agricultural Landscape: Land-Use and Access to Land in Later Prehistoric Society in North-west Europe," in *Landless and Hungry?* (Leiden, Netherlands: CNWS Publications, 1998) 10–11; and Jan Wagenaar, *Origin and Transformation of the Ancient Israelite Festival Calendar* (Wiesbaden: Harrassowitz Verlag, 2005) 47–48.
62. Exod 23:11; and Lev 19:9–10.
63. The Release Years also helped to stabilize the national economy as any oversupply of agricultural products were consumed during the Release or Jubilee period. During normally productive years (years without drought, pests, or blight), this system helped to limit supply so the market demand for Israel's agriculture remained high. In reality, the Levites probably served as commodity brokers, who sold Israel's produce to other nations. The constant pressure on supply kept the value of produce very high.
64. Steinmann (*Abraham to Paul*, 33) points out that Lev 25:22 only allowed for one fallow year and argues that the 50th Jubilee was also counted as the first year of the new Jubilee cycle. This situation then provided a surplus for the 3rd year (Lev 25:21).
65. The Law did not ordain its citizens to sustain the foolish who burned their money on frivolity. Proverbs adeptly points out that these citizens received little aid (Prov 6:6–11; 10:4; 13:4, 25; 19:24; 20:4; 21:5, 25; 25:30–34). Rather, these citizens (KJV-"Sluggard/Slothful") were sold into slavery, the nation's welfare system.
66. S. Scott Bartchy, "Slavery," *ISBE* (vol. 4) 539–43; Westbrook and Wells, *Everyday Law*, 55, 132–33, 114; Westbrook, *Property, Family in Biblical Law*, 36–37.
67. Lev 25:24, 25, 26, 29, 48–52.

68. Another valid theory is that the debtor's land was "sold" to repay his debts. The first right of refusal was given to the nearest kinsmen. Thus the redemption right was "exercised for the redeemer's own benefit" (*Everyday Law,* 122) because the "sale" of the land was given to the nearest kin, and the land was kept in the family (ibid.). It appears that this land would revert to the debtor at the Jubilee.

69. Bartchy, "Slavery," (vol 4) 539–41. The limit established in the Code of Hammurabi (§117) was only three years of servitude (*ANET,* 107), which probably did little to discourage unnecessary indebtedness or unsustained frivolity.

70. Bartchy, ibid.; and Westbrook and Wells, *Everyday Law,* 55, 132–33.

71. Ibid.

72. Gary North, *Tools of Dominion: The Case Laws of Exodus* (Tyler, TX: Institute for Christian Economics, 1990) 134–35.

73. Lev 25:54 addresses citizens that are sold to foreigners living within Israel. The Law does not compel foreigners to forgive Hebrew debt, just as the Israelite is not commanded to forgive the debt of a foreigner (Deut 23:19–20). Citizens were to forgive fellow-countrymen's debt after six years (Exod 21:2; Deut 15:1–2, 12), but it appears that foreigners residing in the Promised Land were entitled to the full term of service paid for the Hebrew slave, limiting a full term to the time remaining until the 49th Jubilee, at which time all slaves in Israel were released.

74. Westbrook and Wells, *Everyday Law,* 64–65.

75. Ibid., 55, 132–33, 114; and Matthews, Levinson, and Kensky, *Gender and Law,* 147–84.

76. Westbrook and Wells, *Everyday Law,* 64–65.

77. Ibid., 64; and Exod 21:8.

78. Westbrook and Wells, *Everyday Law,* 55, 132–33, 114.

79. Ibid., 58–60, 63, 93, 99–100.

80. Ibid. 61–63.

81. Ibid. 64.

82. Deut 1:20–46; and Num 14:22.

83. Exod 12:49; Lev 7:7; and Num 15:16, 29. If we were to argue that these were two separate laws or standards, we would undermine the very meaning of God being one (*echad,* Deut 6:4).

84. Exod 22:25; Lev 25:36–37; and Deut 15:1–2; 23:20.

85. Exod 12:49; Lev 24:22; and Num 15:16.

86. The only type of slavery that would have survived would have been in cases of crime or wanton irresponsibility, when a person was slothful or lacked self-control. In these cases, slavery would offset and tame the undisciplined within Israel's society.

87. Exod 21:8; and Lev 25:42–46.

88. See also, Yehezkel Kaufmann, *The Biblical Account of the Conquest of Canaan* (Jerusalem: Magnes Press, 1985) 30–36, 51–56.

89. *ANET,* 287–88.

90. Lev 25:13–17; and Prov 31:16.

91. *ANET,* 288.

92. Thompson, *1, 2 Chronicles,* 64.

93. Ibid.

94. See also Ezra 2:61–62. Notice, also that the daughter's son could be heir to both the maternal grandfather's estate and the paternal grandfather's estate. As we will see, at the 50th Jubilee these two estates could be joined together because there would be no other heir to supersede the grandson's claim to both maternal and paternal heritages.

95. This was recognized as a common problem throughout the ancient world. Each nation had varying regulations regarding the daughter's privilege of inheritance. It was customary that, in lieu of a land inheritance, she received a dowry that was a large sum of her family's wealth to sustain her in the event of widowhood (Westbrook and Wells, *Everyday Law,* 97–101).

96. This statute only addresses the rights of the legal wife. If there were other wives (or concubines) involved, it is assumed that they would *not* have been entitled to the Levirate marriage. The story of Abraham and literature from the ancient Near East in general demonstrate that only the legal wife and her heirs could lay claim to her husband's estate. All other offspring had no legal claim to their father's assets, although, as with Abraham, it was customary to give those children gifts whenever possible.

97. Deut 25:6; and Robert K. Bower and Gary L. Knapp, "Marriage," *ISBE* (vol. 3) 263. See also Ruth 4:3–10 and Gen 38:9.

98. Westbrook and Wells, *Everyday Law,* 44. "Copies of private legal documents were kept in archives administered by the temples. These were repositories for all kinds of records: wills, deeds, cadastral records, birth registration, contracts etc." (André Dollinger, "Contracts and Other Legal Documents," An Introduction to the History and Culture of Pharaohic Egypt, last updated April 2004, http://www. reshafim.org.il/ad/egypt/law_and_order/contracts.htm [accessed January 2015]). Westbrook (*Property, Family in Biblical Israel*) dismisses the reference to the Jubilee in Num 36:4 as a mistaken gloss (p. 38). In doing so, Westbrook misses the implication this system had for the Levites' administrative and archival functions associated with the Jubilee.

99. Mendenhall *Law and Covenant* (part 2); Kitchen, *Ancient Orient,* 93; and Thompson, *Treaty and Old Testament,* 23, 25; and Albright, *Yahweh and Gods of Canaan,* 167.

100. *SEC* 249; BDB, 251–52; Exod 12:19, 48–49; Lev 16:29; 17:15; 18:26; 19:34; 23:42; 24:16, 22; Num 9:14; 15:13, 29–30; Josh 8:33; and Ezek 47:22.

101. *SEC* 5236, 5237; BDB, 648; Daniel I. Block, "Sojourner," *ISBE* (vol. 4) 561–63; Gen 17:27; Exod 12:43; Lev 22:25; Deut 31:16; 2 Sam 22:45–46; Neh 9:2; 13:30; Ps 18:44–45; and Isa 56:6; 60:10; 61:5; 62:8.

102. Gen 8:21–9:17; 15:8–11; and Jer 34:18–20.

103. Block, "Sojourner," *ISBE* (vol. 4) 562 (emphasis added).

104. *SEC* 2114; BDB, 266; and Block, "Sojourner," (vol. 4) 561–63.

105. Ibid., 463; and BDB, 266.

106. *TWOT* (vol. 1) 536; *SEC* 2114; and BDB, 266.

107. BDB, 266; *TWOT* (vol. 1) 238; and Craig L. Blomberg, "Stranger," *ISBE* (vol. 4) 635.

108. Phillips, *Israel's Criminal Law,* 11.

109. This social status was not inherited by the crimal's children—Deut 24:16.

110. *SEC* 8453; BDB, 444; Block, "Sojourner," (vol. 4) 562; and *TWOT* (vol. 1) 411–12.

111. Exod 12:45; Lev 22:10; 25:6, 40; *ger*—Gen 23:4; Lev 25:23, 35, 45, 47; Num 35:15; 1 Chr 29:15; and Ps 39:12.

112. *SEC* 1616; BDB, 158; Block, "Sojourner," (vol. 4) 561–63; and *TWOT* (vol. 1) 155–56.

113. Westbrook and Wells, *Everyday Law,* 53.

114. Friedman, *Commentary on Torah*, 212.

115. Westbrook and Wells, *Everyday Law,* 91.

116. Ezekiel ordains a similar situation at the nation's latter-day redemption, when the land is again divided among Israel and her converts (Ezek 47:21–23).

117. Freedman, *Nine Commandments*, 54.

118. Ezekiel's distribution of tribal lands will be a *one-time* apportioning of the Promised Land when Israel is again reestablished on YHWH's covenanted ground, when many have joined themselves to YHWH and his covenant (Isa 56:1–8).

119. Exod 22:21; 23:9; Deut 24:17; Jer 7:6; 22:3; and Ezek 22:7, 29.

120. If the disabled were also covered by the welfare system, their prohibition from the Temple meant they would forfeit any voting rights because they could not attend the Temple's congressional assemblies.

121. Neh 7:5–64; Ezra 2:1–62; and Westbrook and Wells, *Everyday Law,* 44.

122. See pp. 238–41.

123. The exception to this rule was the Levites, who were not given tribal heritages but smaller parcels of land. Their genealogy and "right" to serve in a government post was based on actual genealogical records (Ezra 2:62; Neh 7:63–64). Many of the differences in Scripture's genealogical lists may arise from generalized lists used by government administrators versus more-detailed lists, which were kept

by individual clans (Thompson, *1, 2 Chronicles*, 99). We also have records from Neo-Babylonian archives that similarly list holders of agricultural lands (Michael Jursa, "Accounting in Neo-Babylonian Institutional Archives: Structure, Usage, Implications" in Creating Economic Order [Bethesda, MD: CDL, 2004] 170–73). In very ancient times, the ownership of these lands was also determined by tribal systems (Hudson, "Sacred Enclave to Temple to City," in *ULO*, 130–31; and Elizabeth Stone, "The Constraints on State and Urban Form in Ancient Mesopotamia," in *ULO*, 207). Ancient Mesopotamia kept very detailed records of land ownership for quite some time (Van de Mieroop, "Thoughts on Urban Real Estate in Ancient Mesopotamia," in *ULO*, 258–59, 278; and Piotr Steinkeller, "Land-Tenure Conditions in Third-Millennium Babylonia: The Problem of Regional Variation," in *ULO*, 294).

124. This would contrast with the policies of the United States, which bases citizenship on birth within the borders of the country.

125. Although the Pentateuch does not spell out land ownership in this detail, given the stipulations regarding the land (i.e., all arable/tribal land had been divided among the 12 tribes so that only cities had available free market real estate), it is the only possible way to reconstruct a *ger*'s or *nechar*'s ability to gain arable land within Israel's borders.

126. Thompson, *1, 2 Chronicles*, 64. A text from ancient Egypt demonstrates how this worked. A soldier purchased a slave who had been captured in war. The slave became loved by the soldier who captured him and was given to marry the soldier's niece. The soldier then gave his niece part of his land inheritance. He did not give the land inheritance to the slave, but his niece, who shared the inheritance equally with her uncle's (the soldier's) wife since apparently the soldier had no male offspring (Donald Redford, *Akhenaten: The Heretic King* [Princeton, NJ: Princeton University Press, 1984] 23).

127. For example, see 1 Chr 2:31, 34–41.

128. Matthews, *Gender and Law*, 97–112, 172.

129. Ibid., 147–72, 214–38.

130. Ibid., 82–85, 147–72, 214–38.

131. Ibid., 147–72, 214–38. Ezekiel 18 and 33 indicate that many of these ancient customs will *not* be reestablished when YHWH restores Israel after the Diaspora.

132. Kaiser, *Toward Old Testament Ethics*, 154–55.

133. Matthews, *Gender and Law*, 172. I defined the term *citizenship* in its relationship to retaining tribal land heritages. I use the term *citizenship* in regard to women as it relates to their retention of Israel's land through inheritance.

134. Ibid., 172.

135. Levirate marriage was practiced in a few societies, such as the Hittites, Assyrians, Hurrians, and in parts of ancient Greece (Peter C. Craigie, "Idea of War," *ISBE* [vol. 4] 1091).

136. *Levir* comes from the Latin word for 'brother-in-law,' which can be misleading because the deceased's brother may not be the next eligible kin (Westbrook and Wells, *Everyday Law*, 96). See also Bower and Knapp, "Marriage," (vol. 3) 263.

137. Many of Jane Austen's novels depict the stress and financial hardship that women faced during the Georgian and Victorian eras in England without this protection under the law.

138. Donn F. Morgan, "Horse," *ISBE* (vol. 2) 759–60; and Deborah Cantrell, *The Horsemen of Israel* (Winona Lake, IN: Eisenbrauns, 2011) 11–136.

139. *KK*, 282, 297.

140. Westbrook, Property, *Family in Biblical Law*, 47.

141. Ibid.

142. In America, the Vice Presidency has become a powerless office. Although Israel's high priest could be viewed in modern terms as a hereditary vice presidency, his power and authority were much greater. He was imbued with the power to hold both the king and the congregation accountable to the national covenant and functioned as the nation's supreme court.

143. Nili Fox, *In the Service of the King: Officialdom in Ancient Israel and Judah* (Cincinnati, OH: Hebrew Union College Press, 2000) 103; and Num 27:18–23.

144. For good observations regarding Israel's government in the nation's early history, see Daniel Elazar, *The Book of Judges: The Israelite Tribal Federation and Its Discontents.* Jerusalem Center for Public Affairs. http://www.jcpa.org/dje/articles/judges.htm (accessed January 2015).

145. Westbrook and Wells, *Everyday Law,* 40.

146. *SEC* 5712; BDB, 416–17; and *TWOT* (vol. 1) 387–88.

147. *SEC* 3259; BDB, 416–17; and James T. Dennison, Jr., "Congregation," *ISBE* (vol. 1) 760–61.

148. Exod 23:14–17; Leviticus 23; and Deut 16:16.

149. *TWOT* (vol. 1) 338.

150. See Ps 1:5, where *'edah* denotes the "congregation of the righteous" and Ps 22:16 where *'edah* denotes "a congregation of the wicked."

151. Legal historian David Daube also recognizes a legal process involved in Abner's death (2 Sam 30:21–39). In this case the entire congregation of Israel finds or discerns David's innocence in Abner's death (David Daube, *Studies in Biblical Law* [Cambridge University Press, 1947] 6). It is assumed that the *'edah* had judged in this case.

152. The Torah prohibited women from serving in the military. "The woman shall not wear that which pertains to a *man,* neither shall a man put on a woman's garment: for all that do so are abomination to YHWH your God" (Deut 22:5). Although the general precept underlying this verse is gender-neutral by prohibiting cross-dressing, there is a direct prohibition on a woman's military service. The word for 'man' in this text is specifically *gibbor,* an ancient term that eventually designated men who were 'valiant warriors' (Josh 1:14; Judg 5:23; 10:7; 2 Sam 23:22; 1 Chr 23:3; 24:4).

153. David's mighty men broke through Philistine lines to bring him water from Bethlehem (1 Chr 11:15–19). 2 Samuel 1 is a lament for the fallen heroes, Saul and Jonathan, extolling their valiant deeds. Similarly, 2 Samuel 23 records the glories of various mighty men. 1 and 2 Chronicles contain many references to the mighty men of Israel, commonly employing the phrase *gibbôr hayil* "mighty man of valor" to describe them. Chronicles generally uses the term to express a 'warrior' or 'soldier.' (*TWOT* [vol. 1] 310). In a modern context, this text would not prohibit a woman from wearing pants or shirts, but it would prohibit a woman from wearing military attire because only men served in Israel's armies. When Deborah (Judg 4:9–24) led Israel's armies, the prophetess probably wore her normal attire without the traditional coat of mail or other traditional army implements.

154. See also Thompson, *1, 2 Chronicles,* 126.

155. Ancient armies had a variety of expenses: soldier's garments, provisions, bows, arrows, chariots, horses, production of siege engines, and even salaries (1 Sam 8:12 and K. N. Schoville, "War," *ISBE* [vol. 4] 1015–17). The Law provided no distribution of the tithe for military expenditures, nor did it ordain a standing army, so the *'Edah* had to determine how military threats would be funded.

156. It may be remembered that the birthright had been divided between Judah and Ephraim (see chap. 4. IV). Joshua was from the tribe of Ephraim (Num 13:8, 16), a tribe that had authority within the nation.

157. See also Deut 31:2; Judg 20:28; 1 Sam 28:1; 2 *Sam 11:1*; 1 Kgs 3:7; 15:17; 1 Chr 14:15; 1:10; and Jer 17:19.

158. While we have evidence of the priesthood working with the *'edah* when judgment was needed or treaties were reached (Exod 16:22; Lev 8:4–5; 24:14–16; Num 1:18; 14:10; 15:32–36; 35:12, 24–25; Josh 9:15–19; 20:6, 9; 22:12–16, 30; Judg 20:1–2; 21:10–16; 1 Kgs 12:20; Ps 111:1; and Jer 30:20), the later monarchy was virtually autonomous, the greatest exception being the *'edah'*s revolt against Rehoboam and subsequent installation of Jeroboam I.

159. Phillips, *Israel's Criminal Law,* 17–22. Baruch Halpern demonstrates the legitimacy of this type of reconstruction in relation to Ehud (*First Historians,* 39–63). Although Halpern's argument was aimed at historicity, he demonstrates the value of reconstructing Israel's history from the information provided within the historical narrative. "If the narrative conforms to the data in the sources, if it digests and represents them chiefly within a view to conveying the central historical data they provide, then we may claim that the account is historical" (*First Historians,* 61).

160. Westbrook and Wells, *Everyday Law,* 35, 39. Throughout the ancient Near East, kings such as David, Solomon, or even usurpers such as Absalom were the supreme judges of the land.

161. Josh 18:6, 8, 10; 1 Sam 14:42; 1 Chr 24:31; 25:8; 26:13–14; and Neh 10:34; 11:1.

162. See, Daniel Elezar, "The Book of Judges: The Israelite Tribal Federation and Its Discontents," http://www.jcpa.org/dje/articles/judges.htm for similar views on this topic.

163. Samuel was a priest of the sons of Korah (2 Chr 6:38–33—Samuel's genealogy is listed in descending order). He was also an Ephraimite (1 Sam 1:1) since Joshua had divided the territory of Ephraim (Josh 21:20–22) among the Koath descendants (See also, Thompson, *1, 2 Chronicles*, 85–87). This was the reason that Elkanah, Samuel's father, was compelled to go to the Tabernacle on a yearly basis to offer sacrifices and to serve at the Tabernacle in an annual service rotation similar to the system later instituted for the priests under Samuel and David (1 Chr 28:13, 21).

164. Phillips, *Israel's Criminal Law*, 19–20.

165. Deut 12:5, 11, 21; 14:23–4; 16:2, 6, 11; 16:11; 26:2; North, *Tools of Dominion*, 828. It should also be noted that the limited time allotted for these assemblies meant that only the most pressing matters could be addressed.

166. Deut 13:5; 17:7, 12; 19:19; 21:21–24; 24:7; and Judg 20:13.

167. Westbrook and Wells, *Everyday Law*, 36. See also Gen 18:19; Num 35:4; Ps 58:1; and Prov 21:3, 15.

168. *TWOT* (vol. 1) 388; and Dennison, "Congregation," (vol. 1) 761.

169. *SEC* 6951; BDB, 874; and *TWOT* (vol. 2) 789–90.

170. *SEC* 5387; BDB, 672.

171. See Numbers 2, where the KJV translates *nasi'* "captain." See also Num 3:24, 30, 32, 35; and Numbers 7; 27:1–2.

172. Exod 16:22; 34:21; Lev 4:15; Num 1:2, 16; 16:2; 31:13, 26; 32:2; and Josh 9:15, 18–21; 22:30.

173. Judg 20:2 appears to be the exception in references to the army that gathered in Mizpeh, calling it the "assembly (*qahal*) of God." The previous verse, however, Judg 20:1, had already established that the congress that convened at Mizpeh was the *'Edah*.

174. Exod 23:14–17; 34:23–24; Leviticus 23; and Deut 16:16–17; 31:10–13.

175. Num 10:9; Judg 3:26–30; 1 Sam 13:3; and 2 Sam 2:28.

176. Phillips, *Israel's Criminal Law*, 17.

177. North, *Tools of Dominion*, 828.

178. *SEC* 3772; BDB 503–4; and *TWOT* (vol. 1) 456–57.

179. Exod 30:33, 38; Lev 7:20–21, 25–27; 18:29; 19:8; and Num 19:13.

180. Exod 31:14; Lev 20:3–6, 17–18; 23:29–30.

181. Ancient Israel's lack of standardized scribal practices probably contributes to the confusion over the *qahal* and the *'edah* (We will discuss scribal practices in chaps. 8 and 11).

182. William Sanford LaSor, "Ezekiel," *ISBE* (vol. 2) 260–61.

183. Ibid.

184. Exod 13:3, 14; 20:2; Deut 5:6, 12; 8:14; 13:5, 10; Josh 24:17; and Judg 6:8.

185. Bartchy, "Slavery," (vol 4) 540; Goelet, "'Town' and 'Country in Ancient Egypt," in *ULO*, 95–96; Callender, "Middle Kingdom Renaissance," in *OHAE*, 161–64; and *Diad*, Book 1.80.

186. It was this corvée labor to which YHWH protested through Samuel, saying that a monarchy would return Israel's citizens back to the bondage from which they had been delivered (1 Sam 8:12–18; and 1 Kgs 5:13–17; 9:17–23).

187. Dobson, *Bringing up Boys*; Kyle Pruett, *FatherNeed*; William Pollock, *Real Boys: Rescuing Our Sons from the Myths of Boyhood* (New York: Henry Holt, 1998); Angela Phillips, *The Trouble with Boys* (New York: Basic Books, 1994); John Attarian, "Let Boys be Boys—Exploding Feminist Dogma, This Provocative Book Reveals How Educators are Trying to Feminize Boys while Neglecting their Academic and Moral Instruction," *The World and I* (October 1, 2000).

188. Lev 13:46; 15:31; and *IHCANE*, 390–91.

189. F. Charles Fensham, "Judicial Courts," *ISBE* (vol. 1) 788–89. When King David sinned by committing adultery then tried to cover it up with murder, he claimed that his sin was against YHWH (Ps 51:4).

190. Phillips, *Israel's Criminal Law*, 21–23.

191. Ibid., 18.

192. Ibid., 21–23.

193. Num 14:18; Deut 7:9; Ps 25:10; 86:5; 106:1; Prov 14:22; 20:28; Dan 4:27; 9:4; *Hos 6:6; 12:6*; and Mic 6:8.

194. It is unclear whether Israel used a formal (Levitical) prosecutor or not. In the Book of Job, satan accuses Job of wrongdoing. The word *satan* literally means an adversary or opponent (*SEC* 7853; BDB, 967). The role that Job's adversary played in this account would very closely parallel the role that modern prosecutors play today.

195. Westbrook and Wells, *Everyday Law,* 42. Likewise, the tainted virgin is also to bring forth evidence of her last menstrual cycle as a "witness" to her virginity (Deut 22:15).

196. Fensham, "Judicial Courts," (vol. 1) 789; and Westbrook and Wells, *Everyday Law,* 35.

197. Phillips, *Israel's Criminal Law,* 21.

198. Scripture is silent on how the high priest and king functioned in their respective roles. From all evidence, it appears that once the monarchy was established, the high priest's role as supreme judge was transferred to the king. The high priest became one of the king's chief advisers, or the prime minister. (For instance, see David's interaction with the high priests Abiathar and Zadok; 2 Samuel 15, 19:11; 1 Kgs 1:34–45; 2 Kgs 2:35.) Whatever the case may be, the priesthood often thwarted the Monarchy when its office was abused.

199. Phillip's, *Israel's Criminal Law,* 19.

200. Ibid., 20.

201. Ibid., 21.

202. Exod 13:3, 14; 20:2; Deut 5:6; 6:12; 8:14; 13:5, 10; Josh 24:17; and Judg 6:8.

203. The U.S. Constitution states: Article 1: Section 8: "Congress shall have Power to lay and collect Taxes, Duties, Imposts and Excises, to pay the Debts and provide for the common Defense and general Welfare of the United States. . . . to borrow Money on the credit of the United States. (The Heritage Foundation, http://www.heritage.org/constitution#!/articles/1/essays/34/spending-clause [accessed January 2015]). This broad stipulation did not place any limits on the taxes Congress could levy or the amount of debt the nation could secure in peaceful times.

204. Unfortunately for America, this undermining is quietly happening. Her various branches of government simply ignore the constitution and enact their own policies. And her people, like Jeshurun, have been lulled and distracted into complacency, unaware of the "progressive" threats to their constitutional liberties.

205. C. F. Keil and Franz Delitzsch, *Commentary on the Old Testament* (vol. 5; Peabody, MA: Hendrickson, 2006). *Elohiym* as used in Ps 82:1 probably also refers to local rulers (see also chap. 2.VII).

206. John Gill, *Gill's Exposition of the Entire Bible,* http://www.biblestudytools.com/commentaries/gills-exposition-of-the-bible/exodus-22/ (accessed February 2015).

207. Gen 18:25; 1 Sam 2:10; Ps 10:18; 50:4; 67:4; 82:8; 94:2; 96:13; Isa 11:4; Exod 23:7; and Ps 11:5–7; 7:9–11; 34:15–16; 119:155; 145:20.

208. Exod 15:24; 16:2; 17:3; 32:4–35; Num 14:2, 29; 16:41; 20:24; 25:1; 27:14; and Deut 1:26–27, 43.

209. Westbrook and Wells, *Everyday Law,* 12, 130–33.

210. Deut 1:3 records that Moses outlined the stipulations of the Moab-Shechem Covenant in the 11th month of the 40th year after Israel came out of Egypt. "This day" is a specific term that refers to that date.

211. See Westbrook and Wells, *Everyday Law,* 91–104; and Victor Matthews, *Gender and Law,* 97–112.

212. *SEC* 802; BDB, 61; Kaiser, *Toward Old Testament Ethics,* 153–54. See chapter 2.VI.A.

213. *SEC* 376; BDB, 35.

214. R. K. Bower and G. L. Knapp, "Marriage," *ISBE* (vol. 3) 262–63; and R. K. Harrison, "Polygamy," *ISBE* (vol. 3) 901.

215. Ibid.

216. See, for instance, Mark C. Roser, *The Cleansing of the Heavens* (Shippensburg, PA: Treasure House, 1998) 24–25.

217. M. R. De Haan, *Studies in Galatians* (Grand Rapids: Kregel Publications, 1995) 101; Erwin Lutzer, *Doctrines That Divide: A Fresh Look at the Historic Doctrines That Separate Christians* (Grand Rapids: Kregel, 1989) 169; Darwin Chandler, *The Royal Law of Liberty: Living in Freedom under Christ's Law of Love* (Victoria, BC: Trafford, 2003) 264.

218. See for instance, Fred McKinnon's blog, "The Sabbath—Do We Keep It?" (November 2, 2009), http://www.fredmckinnon.com/myblog/2009/11/02/the-sabbath-do-we-keep-it/ (accessed January 2015).

219. For a greater context of these beliefs, see the following sites and search for the key word "incapable." See Bruce Mills, "The Purpose of God's Law," Inverted Planet (June 29, 2009), http://invertedplanet. blogspot.com/2009/06/purpose-of-god-law.html (accessed January 2015); Matt Slick, "How Do You Present the Gospel Properly," Christian Apologetics and Research Ministry, http://www.carm.org/how-to-present-gospel-properly (accessed January 2015); K. T., "The God of the New Testament is the Very Same God as the One in the Old," The Whyman, http://www.thewhyman.jesusanswers. com/contact.html (accessed January 2015); M. R. De Haan, *Studies in Galatians,* 101; Erwin Lutzer, *Doctrines that Divide,* 169; and Darwin Chandler, *The Royal Law of Liberty,* 264.

220. See the following religious organizations' Web sites that support this belief: Thomas Watson, "Body of Divinity Contained in Sermons upon the Assembly's Catechism: The Law and Sin," Westminster Shorter Catechism Project, Last modified July 26, 2008, http://www.shortercatechism.com/resources/watson/wsc_wa_082.html (accessed March 2015); C. W. Wood, "God's Perfect Law Verses Man's Inability to Keep It," *Dewitt Tabernacle Teaching Series,* May 2011, http://www.dewitttabernacle.org/God%27s%20Perfect%20Law%20Mans%20Inability%20to%20Keep.htm (accessed January 2015).

221. Although Abraham lied to these kings, he did not defraud them. According to Torah, lying in itself is not wrong. It is wrong if lying defrauds another person. See pp. 300–1.

222. K. C. Hanson, "Teman," *ISBE* (vol. 4) 758; and William Sanford LaSor, "Teman, City," *ISBE* (vol. 4) 759.

223. Wenham, *Genesis 16–50,* 337.

224. Prov 3:2, 8; Exod 15:26; Prov 3:18, 22; 6:23; 9:11; *12:28*; 13:14; 14:27; 15:30–31 (relates to Prov 6:23); Ezek 33:15; and Ps 133:3.

225. Essential laborers, similar to the Levites, probably worked on a yearly rotating cycle.

226. *SEC* 1870; BDB, 202; *TWOT* (vol. 1) 196–97; and Hamilton, *Genesis: 18–50,* 194.

227. Gen 47:9; Lev 26:6; Ps 29:11; 119:165; 125:5; and Prov 3:1–2; 17:14.

228. It should be noted that under the Old Testament Law, Israel had access to YHWH's gift of eternal life—Deut 4:40; 5:29; Ps 133:3; Isa 26:15–19; Ezekiel 37, 33, 18; 34:22–31; Isa 1:25–28; 51:11–12; 25:8–9.

229. Ps 119:105; Prov 6:23; and Isa 8:20; 51:4.

230. *SEC* 2889; BDB, 372–73; and *TWOT* (vol. 1) 792–95.

231. 1 Sam 16:13; 2 Sam 23:2; and Ps 51:11–12.

232. There is a law that governs all prophecy. We will examine this law or, more accurately, the Testimony within Israel's covenantal Law in Part 2 of this volume.

233. Deut 4:7; 5:4; Gen 17:3, 22; 35:13–14; and Exod 20:22; 33:9–11.

234. *SEC* 4284; BDB, 364; and *TWOT* (vol. 1) 329–30.

235. *SEC* 2403; BDB, 308–10; and *TWOT* (vol. 1) 277–79.

236. Ibid.

237. Freedman, *Nine Commandments,* 20.

238. Joseph used this method to try his brothers to see if their hearts had changed (Genesis 43–45). King Solomon used this formula to judge which woman was a child's true mother (1 Kgs 3:25–26).

239. For examples, see the following Web sites or search for "what is sin" in your web browser to see the varied and conflicting theological opinions. See "What is Sin—Definition," All about God, http://www.allaboutgod.com/what-is-sin.htm (accessed January 2015); "What is Sin," The Restored Church of God, http://www.thercg.org/articles/wis.html (accessed January 2015); Jack Kelly, "What is Sin?" Gracethrufaith, (last updated December 13, 2008), http://gracethrufaith.com/selah/what-is-sin/

(accessed January 2015); Matt Slick, "What Is Sin?" Christian Apologetics and Research Center, http://www.carm.org/What%20is%20sin%3F (accessed January 2015).

240. *SEC* 2398, 2401, 2403; BDB, 306–8; and *TWOT* (vol. 1) 277–79. *Chata,* usually connotes judgment/punishment or guilt because Hebrew does not actually have a distinctive word for 'guilt.' A similar term is used in the ancient Ugaritic language (ibid.).

241. See Lev 4:26–28. See also Leviticus 5, 7, 11, 13, 15, and 20. For use of *chata'*, see Lev 6:4; Exod 32:31; 2 Kgs 13:34; 17:21.

242. *SEC* 5771; BDB, 730–31; and *TWOT* (vol. 2) 650–51 .

243. *TWOT* (vol. 2) 650–51. See also 1 Sam 25:24; 2 Sam 22:23–25. Job 13:23 and Jer 18:23 strongly imply that *chata'* and *'avon* had two different yet similar ideas.

244. *TWOT* (vol. 2) 650.

245. *SEC* 6588, 4604; BDB, 833, 591; *TWOT* (vol. 2) 741–42 and 519–20, respectively.

246. See Gen 50:17; Exod 34:7; Num 5:12; 14:18; Josh 22:22; 24:19–20; 1 Chr 9:1; 10:13; 2 Chr 28:19; 29:19; 33:19; 36:14; Ezek 14:13; 18:24, 28–32; 33:10–16; 37:23.

247. The Hebrew for "iniquity" is *'avon* (*SEC* 2304), transgression is *pesha'* (*SEC* 6588) and sin is *chata'ah* (*SEC* 5771).

248. See *'ashmah* (*SEC* 819) in Lev 4:3; 6:5–7; 22:16; BDB, 80; and *TWOT* (vol. 1) 79.

249. Lev 4:27–35 and 5:1–13. For expiation of guilt for intentional sins, see Lev 6:4–7. Forgiveness did not eliminate the consequences for one's actions (Exod 34:7).

250. For some theological views on this, see, Donald and Nina Young, "Receiving God's Holy Spirit," http://donimon.org/holyspirit.html (accessed January 2015); Robert Barnes, "Reformed Answers: Problem of Evil," Third Millennium Ministries, http://reformedanswers.org/answer.asp/file/99770.qna/category/ot/page/questions/site/; (accessed January 2015); Michael Patton, "Did the Holy Spirit Indwell Old Testament Believers?" Parchment and Pen Blog. Credo House Ministries (Last updated February 7, 2007), http://www.reclaimingthemind.org/blog/2007/02/did-the-holy-spirit-indwell-old-testament-believers/ (accessed January 2015).

251. The question is whether any of these texts support the belief that God gave his Law just to demonstrate humanity incapable of obeying it.

CHAPTER EIGHT

1. Finkelstein and Silberman, *The Bible Unearthed*; Richard Elliot Friedman, *Who Wrote the Bible?* (1997); Erik Eynikel, *The Reform of King Josiah and the Composition of the Deuteronomistic History* (Leiden: Brill, 1996); Thomas Dozeman and Konrad Schmid, eds., *A farewell to the Yahwist?: The Composition of the Pentateuch in Recent European Interpretation* 34 (Atlanta: Society of Biblical Literature, 2006); Joel Baden, *J, E, and the Redaction of the Pentateuch* 68 (Forschungen zum Alten Testament; Tubingen, Ger: Mohr Siebeck, 2009); Umberto Moshe David Cassuto, *The Documentary Hypothesis and the Composition of the Pentateuch*: Eight Lectures (trans. Israel Abrahams; Jerusalem: Central Press, 1941). Most scholarly works now maintain this view.

2. For further detail regarding this theory see the following sites: Michael Coogan, interviewed by Gary Glassman, Writers of the Bible, NOVA/PBS, November 8, 2008,http://www.pbs.org/wgbh/nova/ancient/writers-bible.html (accessed February 2015); Diana E. E. Kleiner, "Wellhausen's Documentary Hypothesis and Characteristics of Biblical Sources," (lecture, Yale University; *Open Yale Courses)*, http://oyc.yale.edu/religious-studies/rlst-145/lecture-5#ch0 (accessed February 2015); and Rolf Rendtorff, "What Happened to the 'Yahwist'?: Reflections after Thirty Years," SBL Forum Archive: *SBL*. http://www.sbl-site.org/publications/article.aspx?articleId=553 (accessed February 2015). One of the best books on the Documentary Hypothesis is Richard Elliot Friedman, *The Bible with Sources Revealed* (San Fransisco: HarperOne, 2005).

3. Ibid.

4. Matti Friedman, "Bible's Different Authors Revealed by New Language Software," *Huffington Post*, June 29, 2011, http://www.huffingtonpost.com/2011/06/29/an-israeli-algorithm-shed_n_886996.html (accessed January 2015); Friedman, *The Bible with Sources Revealed*, 1–31.

5. Yamauchi, "The Current Stat of Old Testament Historiography" in *FTH*, 5–7; Hoffmeier, *Israel in Egypt*, 3–24; and Idem, *Israel in Sinai*, 5–33.

6. Baden, *J, E, and the Redaction*, 66. See Hoffmeier, *Israel in Egypt*, 1–44; Idem, *Israel in Sinai*, 1–33; Willaim Hallo, "Biblical History in its Near Eastern Setting: The Contextual Approach," *Scripture in Context* (Pittsburgh: Pickwick, 1980) 1–26.

7. Extinguishing Amalek's "remembrance" did not necessarily mean that the memory of his name was forgotten. In the ancient Near Eastern context where families testified to their righteous ancestors, this statement often referred to a wicked man's lack of *any* offspring (see similar prophecies against Ahab; see pp. 155–54, 602–3).

8. *WWB*, 18–20.

9. David McKee, "Isaac De la Peyrère: A Precursor of Eighteenth-Century Critical Deists," in *Publications of the Modern Language Association* 59/2 (1944) 456–85; and *WWB*, 20.

10. *WWB*, 19–21; and Halpern, *First Historians*, 16–18.

11. Thomas Paine, *The Age of Reason* (New York: Prometheus Books, 1984) 80–84; and *WWB*, 20.

12. Kline, *Treaty of the Great King*, 47–48.

13. Josh 8:31–32; 23:6; 1 Kgs 2:3; 2 Kgs 14:6; 23:25; and Ezra 3:2.

14. *SEC* 5715; BDB, 730; and *TWOT* (vol. 2) 1576–77.

15. *SEC* 5707; BDB, 729; and *TWOT* (vol. 2) 649–50.

16. Kline, *Treaty of the Great King*, 16–17; and Phillips, *Israel's Criminal Law*, 4.

17. Exod 25:21; 31:18; 32:15; 34:29; 40:20; and *TWOT* (vol. 2) 1576–77; Kline, *Treaty of the Great King*, 16–17; See also chap. 4.VI.A.

18. Depositing legal treaties in a temple's sacred precincts was a common legal practice to which most nations (such as Hittite, Mari) adhered. See 1 Kgs 8:9; Mendenhall, *Law and Covenant* (part 2); Kitchen, *Ancient Orient*, 93; Thompson, *Treaty and Old Testament*, 23, 25; and Albright, *Yahweh and Gods of Canaan*, 167.

19. Kline, *Treaty of the Great King*, 16–18.

20. Exod 30:26; 31:7; 39:35; 40:3, 5, 20–21; Num 4:5; 7:89; and Josh 4:16.

21. Num 10:33; 14:44; Deut 10:8; 31:9, 25–26; Josh 3:3–14; 4:7, 9, 18; 6:6, 8; 8:33; Judg 20:27; 1 Sam 4:3–5; 2 Sam 15:24; 1 Kgs 3:15; 6:19; 8:1, 6, 9, 21; 1 Chr 15:25–29; 16:16, 37; 17:1; 22:9; 28:2, 18; 2 Chr 5:2, 7, 10; 6:11; and Jer 3:16.

22. McCarthy, *Institution and Narrative*, 44.

23. Similarly, the U.S. Constitution is housed in the National Archives and carefully guarded.

24. Phillips, *Israel's Criminal Law*, 4, 8.

25. Ryholt, *Political Situation*, 32.

26. Ibid., 28.

27. Kline, *Treaty of the Great King*, 18.

28. For further discussion on covenants, see chaps. 3–4. For discussion regarding the Sabbath as the sign of Israel's covenant, see chap. 4.VI.A.

29. David W. Baker, "Scribes as Transmitters of Tradition," in *FTH*, 72–73.

30. Ibid.; and Martha T. Roth, "The Series An-ta-gál = šaqû," in *MSL XVII* (ed. Antoine Cavigneaux; Pontificum Institutum Biblicum; Rome: Gregorian University Press, 1985) 134–35.

31. Ibid.; Alfonso Archi, "Archival Record-Keeping at Ebla 2400–2350 BC," in *Ancient Archives and Archival Traditions: Concepts of Record-Keeping in the Ancient World* (ed. Maria Brosius, Oxford University Press, 2003) 19–20.

32. Thomas Edward Payne, *Exploring Language Structure: A Student's Guide* (New York: Cambridge University Press, 2006).

33. Gilbert Dahan, "Genres, Forms and Various Methods in Christian Exegesis and the Middle Ages," in *Hebrew Bible/Old Testament: From the beginnings to the Middle Ages (until 1300) 1/2: The Middle Ages* (ed. Magne Saebo; Munich: Magne Sæbø; Vandenhoeck and Ruprecht, 2000) 216–220; Nicholas de Lange, "An Early Hebrew-Greek Bible Glossary from the Cairo Genizah and its Significance for the Study of Jewish Bible Translations into Greek," in *Studies in Hebrew Language and Jewish Culture* (Amsterdam Studies in Jewish Thought; ed. M. F. Martin, et al.; Dorddrecht, Netherlands: Springer, 2007) 34–39.

34. While it is almost certain that Moses was the person who actually recorded the original Law and Testimony, it would not be impossible for other documents to have been written by other scribes yet attributed to Moses, since they were ordained and approved under his administration.

35. See the dig's official site: http://qeiyafa.huji.ac.il/ (accessed January 2015).

36. See Gershon Galil's (Haifa University) direct translation and commentary on this text: http://newmedia-eng.haifa.ac.il/?p=2043 (accessed January 2015).

37. Ibid.

38. Clara Moskowitz, "Bible Possibly Written Centuries Earlier, Text Suggests," *Live Science* (January 15, 2010), http://www.livescience.com/8008-bible-possibly-written-centuries-earlier-text-suggests.html (accessed January 2015). See also, Hershel Shanks, "Prize Find: Oldest Hebrew Inscription Discovered in Israelite Fort on Philistine Border," *BAR* 36/2 (March/April, 2010) 51–54.

39. See Gershon Galil's translation and commentary on this text: http://newmedia-eng.haifa.ac.il/?p=2043.

40. Although chapter divisions are a modern invention, the location of this information (i.e., beginning, middle, end) in the book is still relevant.

41. For a great overview of this material, see Kitchen, *On the Reliability of the Old Testament,* 160–63.

42. We will examine this chronology in the next chapter.

43. K. Lawson Younger, *Ancient Conquest Accounts: A Study in Ancient Near Eastern and Biblical History Writing* (Sheffield: Sheffield Academic, 1990) 197–265; and James Hoffmeier, "The Structure of Joshua 1–11 and the Annals of Thutmose III," in *FTH,* 165–79.

44. Hoffmeier, "Joshua 1–11 and Thutmose III," in *FTH,* 170–79.

45. Ibid., 172–25.

46. Ibid., 172–29.

47. Baker, "Scribes as Transmitters of Tradition," in *FTH,* 75.

48. Scholars even critical of the biblical text pretty much agree that the Song of Deborah is one of the most anciently preserved accounts in Scripture (Raymond de Hoop, *Genesis 49,* 28–30, 36–37, 41–42; Edwin Yamauchi, "The Current State of Old Testament Historiography," in *FTH,* 7, 13, 199 n.21; and John E. Hartley, "Song of Deborah," *ISBE* [vol. 1] 904–6).

49. Frank Yurco, "Merenptah's Canaanite Campaign and Israel's Origins," in *Exodus: The Egyptian Evidence* (ed. Ernest Frerichs and Leonard Lesko; Winona Lake, IN: Eisenbrauns, 1997) 43, 45.

50. Thompson, *1, 2 Chronicles,* 87, 107.

51. 1 Chr 25:1–6; 15:15–19; 16:4; 6:32–36; and 2 Chr 5:12–14.

52. Samuel's life fulfills the prophecy laid out in Deut 18:15–19. See 1 Samuel 8 and 12. Samuel inherited Moses' role of speaking on YHWH's behalf, and YHWH indeed held the people accountable for listening to Samuel (2 Samuel 12).

53. A seer was a prophet, 1 Sam 9:9.

54. The Septuagint appears to be most credible with regard to title preservation.

55. The Septuagint contains several important, valid songs, such as Palms 5, 9, and 10, that are quite different from the MT's. However, the LXX also contains spurious, *in*valid songs, such as Psalms 151.

56. For instance, the Song of Deborah (Judges 5); Merriam's Song of the Sea (Exodus 15); or the Song of Moses (Deuteronomy 32).

57. Thompson, *1, 2 Chronicles,* 23.

58. 2 Chr 16:11; 25:26; 27:7; 28:26; 32:32; 35:27; 36:8; and Fox, *Service of the King,* 104.

59. The Kingdom Era began with Saul and David.

60. Philip Davies, *Scribes and Schools: The Canonization of the Hebrew Scriptures* (Louisville: KY; Westminster John Knox, 1998) 78–79; and Baker, "Scribes as Transmitters of Tradition," in *FTH*,73.

61. The Book of the Chronicles of the Kings of Judah—1 Kgs 8:23; 12:19; 14:29; 15:7, 23; 22:45; 2 Kgs 14:18; 15:6, 36; 16:19; 20:20; 21:17; 21:25; 23:28; 24:5. The Book of the Chronicles of the Kings of Israel—1 Kgs 14:19; 15:31; 16:5; 16:14, 20, 27; 22:39; 2 Kgs 1:18; 10:34; 13:8, 12; 14:15, 28; 15:11, 15, 21, 26, 31. For the latter, while it references particular deeds of Israel's kings, no chronicles are found within the texts that we have inherited.

62. Yamauchi, "The Current State of Old Testament Historiography," in *FTH,* 3.

63. Ibid., 5.

64. Hallo, "Biblical History in Its Near Eastern Setting: The Contextual Approach," in *Scripture in Context,* 8.

65. *SEC* 2142; BDB, 269; and Fox, *Service of the King,* 110–21.

66. *SEC* 5608; BDB, 708; and Fox, *Service of the King,* 96.

67. Fox, *Service of the King,* 99–100, 102; and Baker, "Scribes as Transmitters of Tradition," in *FTH*. Fox also cites various obstacles to determining the precise role that this position held.

68. Fox also points out that both Joash's unidentified scribe and Josiah's scribe Shaphan "fit the primary definition of the verb סָפַר 'count.' The two enterprises with which these men were involved pertain to counting and disbursement of Temple funds for repairs" (*Service of the King,* 102).

69. Fox, *Service of the King,* 116–17; and David O'Connor, "The Hyksos Period in Egypt," in *HP,* 60. See also Exod 17:14, where YHWH tells Moses to record the prophecy of Amalek's doomed progeny.

70. Fox, *Service of the King,* 112–21.

71. Ibid., 105; and Davies, *Scribes and Schools,* 78–79. Although Fox misses the Levitical establishment's connection to this office, she does recognize the hereditary nature of the office. Davies, however, also acknowledges the Levitical branch of the scribal class. Scripture (notably Jeremiah) also points to a royal scribal (Judahite or other tribes) class within the Monarchy administration (Jer 36:10–12, 20, 26; 36:2; 37:15, 20; 52:25).

72. See also 2 Sam 20:24–25; and 1 Chr 18:15–16.

73. For a thorough discussion about how the scribe's pen should be considered history, see Halpern, *The First Historians,* chaps. 5–6.

74. Ibid., 116–17. "Sigla stand for whole strands of minor revisions. *The revisions amplify, clarify, or defend claims in a received text.* This activity differs from writing history in the first instance: if the reviser wished to subvert the text, he would either have subverted it systematically or written a different text. That the reviser transmitted the text largely intact suggests that he or his community regarded it with reverence. It is a logical corollary that *the scribe's insertion must have been consonant with his reading of the text: they reconcile difficulties in the text or difficulties arising from the application of the text to changed realities*" (ibid., emphasis added). Halpern also points out that not even the most critical minimalist questions the editor's use of primary manuscripts. Noth, Smend, Wellhausen, Cross, and every scholar who has written on the Documentary Hypothesis do not deny the editor's use of original source material (ibid., 114–15, 121, 124).

75. "The editors' antiquarianism goes far to explain their inconsistent interventions in the narrative; *the interventions come where, and only where, they are called for, both by politics and by the logic of reconstruction*" (ibid., 118, emphasis added).

76. Another scribe's colophon clarifies that Hebron had been called Hezron by the former Canaanites.

77. This evidence indeed supports Halperns' criteria for reconstruction: the scribe only amended or inserted information when he needed to clarify textual difficulties arising from changed realities.

78. We will examine Israel's chronology in chap. 9.

79. Hoffemeier, *Israel in Egypt,* 122–23.

80. There are almost as many ancient sites in Egypt that have been proposed for the biblical Pithom as there are archaeologists giving opinions on the matter. See Hoffmeier, *Israel in Egypt,* 119–21; and Thomas V. Brisco, "Pithom," *ISBE* (vol. 3) 875–76.

81. Volume 2 (forthcoming) of the *YHWH Exists* series will conclusively demonstrate that the Deuter-onomist could not have written the Book of Deuteronomy late in the nation's history since there was a very important event that he could not have anticipated.

82. This colophon was appended just after the record of David's life. It had little to do with the actual text except to mention the authors of the annals that the scribe had just transcribed.

83. The use of the title "1st and 2nd Samuel" by the King James Version implies that Samuel actually wrote these books in their entirety. The Septuagint more accurately labels these books "1 and 2 Kings." The Septuagint acknowledges four books of the Kings of Judah and Israel.

84. Although Scripture refers to Manasseh's prayer (2 Chr 33:18), both the Catholic and Protestant can-ons lack this text. Manasseh's written prayer, however, is probably found in the Apocrypha of the Septuagint.

85. It appears Elijah was "taken into heaven" sometime during the reign of Jehoram, king of Judah—2 Chr 21:12.

86. See 1 Chronicles 1. After Rehoboam's reign, later scribes added the genealogies to the manuscript. As we shall see, Scripture usually records the author-scribe who registered these entries.

87. Thompson, *1, 2 Chronicles*, 23.

88. Callender, "The Middle Kingdom Renaissance," *OHAE*, 160.

89. I theorize that a later scribe inadvertently omitted Jehu's name.

90. Thompson, *1, 2 Chronicles*, 23.

91. Wilson, *Genealogy and History in the Biblical World*, 189–90.

92. Thompson, *1, 2 Chronicles*, 91.

93. Recorded in Judah's chronicles, no chronicle exists for the Northern Kingdom.

94. Recorded within Jehoshaphat's Chronicles of Judah. No Chronicle exists for the Northern Kingdom.

95. Thompson, 1, 2 Chronicles, 23.

96. A. T. Olmstead, *History of the Persian Empire* (Chicago: University of Chicago Press, 1948) ix.

97. Idem., "Tattenai, Governor of 'Across the River,'" *JNES* 3 (1944) 46; *PB*, 156; and Ronald F. Sweet and George A. Gay, "Tax; Tribute," *ISBE* (vol. 4) 739.

98. Carl Schultz, "The Political Tensions Reflected in Ezra-Nehemiah," in *Scripture in Context,* 232.

99. A.R. Millard, "A Decree of a Persian Governor," in *Buried History* (June 1974) 88. See also *PB*, 91–92.

100. See Halpern, *First Historians*, 30–31.

101. 1 Chr 8:38 and 9:44 exemplify some of the final genealogical entries.

102. The veracity of this conclusion will be demonstrated in Part 2 of this present volume.

103. James Hoffmeier, *Israel in Egypt*, 8–9.

104. Ezra need not have personally copied and edited all of Israel's ancient manuscripts. Similar to Samuel, he probably oversaw the Levitical scribes' work, gave advice along the way, and approved the final editions.

105. J. Llewellyn Thomas, *The Assyrian Invasions and Deportations of Israel* (Leicestershire, UK: Covenant Publishing, 1937) 7.

106. Compare 1 Chr 21:5 to 2 Sam 24:9 and 2 Sam 8:4 to 1 Chr 18:4, for example. See also, 2 Sam 8:4 vs. 1 Chr 18:4; 2 Sam 10:18 vs. 1 Chr 19:18; and 1 Chr 21:5 vs. 2 Sam 24:9.

107. Many scholars have pointed to the fallacy of those who minimize the Hebrew Scriptures. The arbi-trariness of their polemics is revealed by the fact that they see no obstacles to historicity in Assyrian or Babylonian records, even when those archives contain conflicting reports, such as the number of war captives or battle casualties or invoke the intervention of a deity. Yet when the same type of record is found in Israel's Scriptures it is suspect (Edwin Yamauchi, "Current Historiography," in *FTH*, 27–36; and James Hoffmeier, *Israel in Egypt*, 11).

108. *ANET*, 284–85; and *MB*, 295.

109. John M. Russell, *The Writing on the Wall* (Winona Lake, IN: Eisenbrauns, 1999) 141–42.

110. Ibid.

111. Ibid.

112. A.R. Millard, "Variable Spelling in Hebrew and Other Ancient Texts," *JTS* 42 (1991) 106–15; David Tsumura, "Scribal Errors or Phonetic Spellings? Samuel as an Aural Text," *Vestus Testamentum* 49 (July 1999) 390–411; and Donald Redford, "Textual Sources for the Hyksos Period," *in The Hyksos: New Historical and Archaeological Perspectives* (ed. Eliezer Oren; Ephrata, PA: University of Pennsylvania Museum, 1997) 21.

113. Ibid.

114. Davies, *Scribes and Schools*, 83–84.

115. Millard, "Variable Spelling in Hebrew and Other Ancient Texts," 106–15; Tsumura, "Scribal Errors or Phonetic Spellings? Samuel as an Aural Text," 390–411; and Redford, "Textual Sources for the Hyksos Period," in *HP*, 21.

116. Edward Kutscher, *The Language and Linguistic Background of the Isaiah Scroll: I Q Isaiah* (Netherlands: Brill, 1974) 46–71. Although Kutscher's thesis primarily applies to a later period, the same issues can be discerned in problems arising from dialects within ancient Israel as in the example of the Ephraimites (Judg 12:5–6).

117. Halpern, *The First Historians*, xxiv–xxxiii.

118. Jehoiachin—2 Kgs 24:6–15; 25:27; 2 Chr 36:8–9; Jer 52:31. Jeconiah—1 Chr 3:16–17; Esth 2:6; Jer 24:1; 27:20; 28:4; 29:2. Coniah—Jer 22:24–28; 37:1.

119. Jehoiachin–*SEC* 3078; BDB, 220. Jeconiah—*SEC* 3204; BDB, 220. And Coniah—*SEC* 3659: BDB, 220.

120. Rivkah Harris, "Notes on the Nomenclature of Old Babylonian Sippar," *Journal of Cuneiform Studies* 24 (ASOR, 1972) 104; and Nili Fox, *Service of the King*, 39, 40–42.

121. *WWB*, 29. For more information on this theory, search for "First Isaiah" or "Second Isaiah" in your Web browser.

122. Gen 28:10–16; see also chap. 3.VIII.B.

123. Prophecies against rebellious Israel—Isa 42:13–17; 22–25; 43:22–28; 44:9–20; 45:9–10, 16. Prophecies of Israel's righteous latter day generation—Isa 40:1–11; 42:1–12, 18–21; 43:1–21; 44:1–8, 21; 45:8, 11–25.

124. Michael D. Guinan, "Lachish Letters," *ISBE* (vol. 3) 58–60. Read the Lachish letters online at the British Museum: http://www.britishmuseum.org/explore/highlights/highlight_objects/me/l/lachish_letter_i.aspx (accessed January 2015).

125. Guinan, "Lachish Letters," *ISBE* (vol. 3) 60.

126. Ibid.

127. *WWB*, 148, brackets added.

CHAPTER NINE

1. For chronology in general, see: Paul Åstrom, ed., *High, Middle or Low: Acts of an International Colloquium on Absolute Chronology Held at the University of Gothenburg* 20th–22nd *August 1987, part 1 and 2* (Gothenburg: Paul Åstroms Forlage, 1987); Manfred Bietak, ed., *The Middle Bronze Age in the Levant: Proceedings of an International Conference on MB IIA Ceramic Material, Vienna*, 24th–26th *of January 2001* (Vienna: Verlag, 2002).

2. E. G. Richards, *Mapping Time* (Oxford University Press, 1999) 106, 217; and Jack Finegan, *Handbook of Biblical Chronology* (Peabody, MA: Hendrickson, 1998) 114.

3. Richards, *Mapping Time*, 106, 217.

4. Olmstead, *Persian Empire*, 57.

5. Rodger Young, "When Did Jerusalem Fall," in *JETS* 47/1 (March 2004) 21; Finegan, *Handbook*, 262–64; and Steinmann, *Abraham to Paul*, 164–67.

6. D. J. Wiseman, *Chronicles of Chaldean Kings in the British Museum* (London: Trustees of the British Museum, 1956) 73.

7. Ibid.

8. Finegan, *Handbook*, 262.

9. Young, "When Did Jerusalem Fall," 21; and Finegan, *Handbook,* 262–63.

10. Steinmann, *Abraham to Paul,* 164–69.

11. Ibid., 37.

12. Kitchen, *Reliability,* 23, 32–33; Steinmann, *Abraham to Paul,* 40–41; Karl Jansen-Winkeln, "Relative Chronology of Dyn. 21," in *Ancient Egyptian Chronology* 83/1 (Handbook of Oriental Studies; ed. Erik Hornung, et al.; Leiden: Brill, 2006) 232–33.

13. From Solomon's 4th year to his 40th year is 36 years. Under Solomon's administration, the monarchy began to use the Egyptian style of chronology by reckoning Solomon's last year as Rehoboam's 1st year, eclipsing either the last year of Solomon's reign or the 1st year of Rehoboam's reign. Thus one year must be subtracted from the transition from Solomon to Rehoboam (see Steinmann, *Abraham to Paul,* 38–40; and Thiele, *Mysterious Numbers,* 43–65).

14. Erik Hornung, "Introduction," *Ancient Egyptian Chronology* 83/1(Handbook of Oriental Studies; ed. Erik Hornung, et al.; Lieden: Brill, 2006) 8–12.

15. Ibid.

16. Redford, *Ancient Times,* 258. For discussion of the various problems with this era, see Elizabeth Bloch-Smith, "Bible, Archaeology, and the Social Sciences," in *The Hebrew Bible* (ed. Frederick Greenspahn; New York University Press, 2008) 27–37.

17. Finkelstein and Silberman, *Unearthed,* 129.

18. Bimson, *Redating,* 76, 89.

19. Kitchen, *Reliability*, 82–83; and Steinmann, *Abraham to Paul,* 37–44.

20. Malamat, *History of Biblical Israel,* 200.

21. Kitchen, *Reliability,* 23, 32–33; Steinmann, *Abraham to Paul,* 40–41. See also Jansen-Winkeln, "Relative Chronology of Dyn. 21," 232–33.

22. Kitchen, *Reliability,* 23, 32–33; Jansen-Winkeln, "Relative Chronology of Dyn. 21," 232–33.

23. Jansen-Winkeln, "Relative Chronology of Dyn. 21," 232–33; and Steinmann, *Abraham to Paul,* 41.

24. Jansen-Winkeln, ibid., 233 n.83.

25. Steinmann, *Abraham to Paul,* 7.

26. Jörg Klinger, "Chronological Links Between the Cuneiform World of the Ancient Near East and Ancient Egypt," in *Ancient Egyptian Chronology* 83/1 (Handbook of Oriental Studies; Ed. Erik Hornung, et al.; Lieden: Brill, 2006) 305.

27. Ibid., and Hornung, "Introduction," in *Ancient Egyptian Chronology,* 1, 8. The vote to accept the Low Chronology at the Gothenburg conference passed with only three votes against and three abstentions.

28. Hornung, "Introduction," *Ancient Egyptian Chronology,* 10 .

29. Jörg Klinger, "Chronological Links," in *Ancient Egyptian Chronology,* 232; Kitchen, *Reliability,* 16–45; James Hoffmeier, "What is the Biblical Date for the Exodus: A Response to Bryant Wood," *JETS* 50/2 (2007) 226–30; Bryant Wood, "Biblical Date of the Exodus is 1446 BC: A Response to James Hoffmeier," *JETS* 50/2 (June 2007) 249–58.

30. Rodger Young, "Evidence for Inerrancy from an Unexpected Source: Old Testament Chronology," *Bible and Spade* (Spring, 2008) 55.

31. Steinmann, *Abraham to Paul,* 50–65; William Shea, "Date of the Exodus," in *Giving the Sense* (ed. David Howard and Michael Grisanti; Grand Rapids: Kregel Academic, 2003) 245–48; ; Wood, "Biblical Date of the Exodus is 1446 BC," 249–58.

32. Steinmann, *Abraham to Paul,* 51.

33. Redford, *Ancient Times,* 155–213; Nicolas Grimal, *Ancient Egypt* (trans. Ian Shaw; Oxford, UK: Blackwell, 1994) 209–21; Shea, "The Date of the Exodus," *ISBE* (vol. 2) 233–38; Idem, "Date of the Exodus," in *Giving the Sense,* 236–55.

34. Redford, *Ancient Times,* 272–73; Meredith Kline, "The Ha-Bi-Ru," in *Westminster Theological Journal* 19 (1956) 5; Megan Bishop Moore and Brad Kelle, *Biblical History and Israel's Past* (Grand Rapids: Eerdmans, 2011) 109–10, 124–25; Alberto Greene, "Social Stratification and Cultural Continuity at Alalakh," in *The Quest for the Kingdom of God: Studies in Honor of George E. Mendenhall* (ed. H. B.

Huffmon, et. al., Winona Lake, IN: Eisenbrauns, 1985) 198–204; and Bryant Wood, "From Ramesses to Shiloh," in *Giving Sense* (ed. David Howard and Michael Grisanti; Grand Rapids: Kregel Academic, 2003) 269–71. See pp. 550–53, 556–62 and Appendix C for discussion on the *habiru*.

35. Redford, *Ancient Times*, 209, 207.

36. Ibid., 208.

37. Aram-Naharim, which the KJV translates "Mesopotamia," probably refers to a place near Haran. Abraham's servant Eliezer had traveled there in search of a wife among Abraham's kinsmen, specifically mentioning Abraham's brother, Nahor (Gen 24:10). Scripture gives Haran as the last city in which Nahor lived (Gen 11:26–31) although Aram-Naharim said to be Nahor's city in Gen 24:10.

38. Steinmann, *Abraham to Paul*, 59.

39. Ibid.

40. Dever, *Early Israelites*, 8, 26–30, 37–90; and Kitchen, *Reliability*, 137–216.

41. Dever, *Early Israelites*, 30–32.

42. Jansen-Winkeln, "Relative Chronology of Dyn. 21," in *Ancient Egyptian Chronology*, 232–33; and Steinmann, *Abraham to Paul*, 41.

43. Manfred Bietak and Felix Höflmayer, "Introduction: High and Low Chronology," in *The Synchronisation of Civilisations in the Eastern Mediterranean in the Second Millennium* BC III: *Proceedings of the SCIEM 2000 – 2nd EuroConference, Vienna 28th of May – 1st of June 2003* (ed. Manfred Bietak and E. Czerny; Verlag der Österreichischen Akademie der Wissenschaften, 2007).

44. Steinmann, *Abraham to Paul*, 37.

45. Ibid., 41.

46. Ibid., 37–44. See Rodger Young's work at: http://www.rcyoung.org/papers.html (accessed January 2015).

47. Rodger Young, "Three Verifications of Thiele's Date for the Beginning of the Divided Kingdom," *AUSS* 45/2 (2007) 163–89; and Steinmann, *Abraham to Paul*, 42–44.

48. Young, "Three Verifications of Thiele's Date for the Beginning of the Divided Kingdom," 163–89; Idem, "Evidence for Inerrancy from an Unexpected Source: OT Chronology," *Bible and Spade* 21 (2008) 56.

49. John Sietze Bergsma, *The Jubilee from Leviticus to Qumran: A History of Interpretation* (Lieden: Brill, 2007) 155–56; Israel Knohl, *The Sanctuary of Silence: The Priestly Torah and the Holiness School* (Winona Lake, IN: Eisenbrauns, 2007); and Floyd Jones, *Chronology of the Old Testament* (Green Forrest, AR: Master Books) 165–66.

50. This does not undermine the Talmud's value in dealing with issues contemporary with its authors. Using the Talmud (Babylonian or Jerusalem) to aid in understanding ancient Israel's history or theology at most adds confusion.

51. Rodger Young, "Tables of Reign Lengths from the Hebrew Court Recorders," *JETS* 48/2 (June 2005) 225–48; Idem, "The Parian Marble and Other Surprises from Chronologist V. Coucke," *AUSS* 50/2 (Fall 2010) 225–49; and Steinmann, *Abraham to Paul*, 20.

52. Steinmann, *Abraham to Paul*, 67–80.

53. For a scholarly discussion regarding these dates, see John Bimson, *Redating the Exodus and Conquest* (Sheffield: Almond Press, 1981) 74–84; and Jeremy Hughes, *Secrets of the Times: Myth and History in Biblical Chronology* (New York: Continuum, 1990) 55–77.

54. Some scholars (Kitchen, *Reliability*, 203) question 30–40 years for a generation during this era. However, if lifetime spanned 110 years, as it did for Joshua (Josh 24:29), or 120 years, as it did for Moses (Deut 34:7), or 123 for Aaron (Num 33:39), it would *not* be unreasonable for a generation to span 30 to 40 years during this era. For the validity of a 120-year life-span, see p. 377 n.1335.

55. Thompson, *1, 2 Chronicles*, 85. See also Bimson, *Redating*, 75–78.

56. Hoffmeier, "What is the Biblical Date for the Exodus: A Response to Bryant Wood," 236.

57. Steinmann, *Abraham to Paul*, 55–56.

58. Bimson, *Redating the Exodus,* 88; and Wood, "The Rise and Fall of the 13th-Century Exodus-Conquest Theory," *JETS* 48/3 (September 2005) 485–86.

59. Wood, "The Rise and Fall," 484, 486–87; and Steinmann, *Abraham to Paul,* 56.

60. Wood, "The Rise and Fall," 484, 486–87; idem, "Biblical Date of the Exodus is 1446 BC," 253; Steinmann, *Abraham to Paul,* 54–64.

61. Bimson, *Redating,* 84–86. See also, Hughes, *Secrets of the Times,* 53–58.

62. This is calculated as: 340 years of Judges (see next paragraph) + 5 years for the second conquest era (see Table 9.5, below) + 30 years for Joshua's administration.

63. For the validity of this, see Halpern, *First Historians,* 122–32.

64. Ibid., 122–40. See also, Kitchen, *Reliability,* 202–3; and idem, "The Exodus," *ABD* (vol. 2) 702.

65. Judg 3:8, 11, 14, 30, 31; 4:3; 5:31; 6:1; 8:28; 9:22; 10:2, 3, 8, (15:2); which are records of the length of the judges' reigns with the coinciding oppression time added to them.

66. Judg 12:7, 9, 11, 14; 13:1; 15:20. This formula only holds true for only the Book of Judges. The Book of Samuel makes no claim to this formula. In fact, as we will see (section IV–V below and chap. 11. XVIII) that Eli and Samuel were contemporary with other judges whose administrations are listed in the Book of Judges.

67. Steinmann, *Abraham to Paul,* 89–91; and Bimson, *Redating,* 80. See pp. 88–89 for further discussion on the 430-year hidden judgment precedent.

68. Steinmann, *Abraham to Paul,* 94.

69. 1 Kgs 6:1 = 480 yrs. minus the period of the judges, 410 = 70 minus David's 40 yrs. = 30 minus Solomon's 4 yrs. = 26 years that were possible for Saul to have reigned over Israel. Bimson supported 22 years for Saul's reign; see Bimson, *Redating,* 90. See also Hughes, *Secrets,* 59–60, 66–68; and Steinmann, *Abraham to Paul,* 114–15.

70. This is based on Saul being enthroned at the very point when Judge's linear chronology ends, which equals 410 years. David is enthroned 26 years later.

71. Hughes, *Secrets of the Times,* 59.

72. Ibid., 58. For evidence of Samuel's Levitical ancestry through Korah, see p. 942 n. 163 or p. 661.

73. Steinmann, *Abraham to Paul,* 62–64.

74. Scholars often posit three different names for Moses' father-in-law: Jethro, Reuel (Regual), and Hobab. Part of the reason for this confusion is a lack of understanding chronology as well as geneaology. The text gives Moses' father-in-law's name as Reuel (variant: Regual—Exod 2:18; Num 10:29). The term Jethro (Heb. *Yithrow*), meaning 'excellency or preeminence,' was more of a title associated with Reuel's role as priest of Midian (Exodus 18) than a name. Exod 2:18 demonstrates that Moses' father-in-law was indeed named Reuel, while passages that deal with Reuel's knowledge of priestly matters call him Jethro (Exod 18:10, 12). The last name, Hobab, is aided by chronology. Hobab I was Moses' brother-in-law (Num 10:29), who helped scout out the Midian territory during Israel's exile. The Midianite territory as well as Mt. Sinai (Horeb) lay on the east side of the Gulf of Aqaba. It was this sparsely populated area that Israel wandered in for 40 years. Hobab II was a descendant of Reuel (Judg 4:11). Judg 1:16 identifies Reuel (Moses' father-in-law) as a Kenite who lived in Midian's territory. There is some ambiguity here as to whether Reuel was a descendant of a Midianite or a Kenite. It appears that he was a Kenite who lived in the land of Midian. This connection with Midian (a descendant of Abraham, Gen 25:2) may explain Reuel's inherent understanding of the Law and his wisdom in advising Moses on political matters (Exodus 18). See the map of ancient Midian at: http://bibleatlas.org/midian.htm (accessed January 2015).

75. See Halpern, *First Historians,* 118; Finkelstein an Silberman, *Unearthed,* 76–81; and E. D. Isaacs, "Jabin," *ISBE* (vol. 2) 946.

76. Kitchen, *Reliability,* 213.

77. Finkelstein and Silberman, *Bible Unearthed,* 81.

78. Bimson, *Redating,* 84–86.

79. Kitchen, *Reliability,* 209.

80. Ibid., 203–9.

81. Ibid., 203; Steinmann, *Abraham to Paul*, 54–65; David Freedman, "Chronology of Israel," in *Bible and the Ancient Near East:* 270–71; and J. De Vries, "Chronology of the Old Testament, "*The Interpreter's Dictionary of the Bible* (vol. 1; ed. G.A. Buttrick; Nashville: Abingdon Press, 1962) 584.

82. Redford, *Ancient Times,* 259–60.

83. Hughes, *Secrets of the Times,* 59.

84. Judg 3:31; 10:3; 12:8, 11, 13.

85. Kitchen (*Reliability,* 203) and Freedman ("Chronology," in *Bible and ANE,* 271) posit that the 1 Kgs 6:1 colophon does not account for the time that Samuel (or Eli) "judged" Israel. Within the Book of Judges, the chronology is set up to recognize a judge who leads military campaigns and relieves Israel from her oppression at the hands of Canaanite overlords. There are no accounts in Scripture that indicate that Eli ever led military campaigns. While Samuel indeed aided the military effort, his priestly administration coincided with the formally elected judges. His childhood converged with the Philistines' capture of the Ark of the Testimony and subjugation of Israel. It is quite probable that the 40 years (Judg 13:1) when the Philistines oppressed Israel are included in Samuel's administration, which coincided with both Philistine oppression and the early years of Saul's reign over Israel (1 Sam 25:1), a topic we will return to in chap. 11.

86. Ibid., 203; Freedman, "Chronology of Israel," in *Bible Ancient Near East,* 270–71; and De Vries, "Chronology of the Old Testament," in *Interpreter's Dictionary,* 584.

87. Halpern, *First Historians,* 134–37.

88. See pp. 88–89 for further discussion of the 430-year hidden judgment precedent. We examine the 430-year precedent further in chap. 19.

89. See also Redford, *Ancient Times,* 258. For a similar observation, see Hughes, *Secrets of the Times,* 37 n.24, 61–62.

90. Kitchen, "The Exodus," in *ABD* (vol. 2) 702; Idem, *Reliability,* 202–3; and J. De Vries, "Chronology of the Old Testament," in *The Interpreter's Dictionary,* 584.

91. Halpern, *First Historians,* 121–40; and Steinmann, *Abraham to Paul,* 87–89.

92. Steinmann, *Abraham to Paul,* 86–87.

93. Steinmann, *Abraham to Paul,* 88.

94. Bimson, *Redating,* 80.

95. Calculated: 480 + 40 = 520 years. See Kitchen, "The Exodus," in *ABD,* 702; and J. De Vries, "Chronology of the Old Testament," in *The Interpreter's Dictionary,* 584. James Hoffmeier allows up to 633 years for this period (Hoffmeier, "What is the Biblical Date for the Exodus?" *JETS,* 226–230).

96. Calculated: 40 years in the desert + 30 years for Joshua to govern Israel inside Canaan + 30 years for the elders who outlived Joshua to rightly govern = 100 years at the upper limit.

97. See Steinmann, *Abraham to Paul,* 89–109; Eugene Merrill, *An Historical Survey of the Old Testament* (Nutley, NJ: Craig, 1966).

98. Kitchen, "The Exodus," in *ABD,* 702; and idem, *Reliability,* 203. It should be noted, however, that Kitchen does not accept this added 74 years or the 480 years found in the 1st Kings colophon. Rather, he telescopes the entire Conquest, Judges, and early Monarchy into a couple hundred years in order to support a thirteenth-century Exodus.

99. Bimson, *Redating,* 80.

100. Hoffmeier, *Israel in Egypt,* 125.

101. While scholars such as Kitchen, Redford, Finkelstein, and even Hoffmeier find 500–600 years for this era unreasonable, they never state why this chronology is untenable. Although the history of Egypt, Mari, Assyria, as well as Babylon and Elam are confirmed by many inscriptions, it is not outside the range of possibilities that Israel, during the Early Conquest, possessed the knowledge as well as the capability of accurately recording their own history as rescent archaeological discoveries have confirmed. More will be discussed on this topic in the next two chapters (10–11), below.

102. See also, Steinmann, *Abraham to Paul,* 89.

103. Josh 14:11–15; 15:13–16; and Judg 1:9–20.

104. See Exod 33:11 and Num 11:28, where Joshua is called a youth. For other examples of this term used to denote youth see: 1 Sam 1:24; 17:33, 42; 25:5. If Joshua were younger than 80 years of age when entering the Promised Land, then the Early Conquest Era would be lengthened by that amount of time: a maximum of 20–40 years, given the fact that YHWH's age stipulations regarding military service indicate that Caleb and Joshua were at least more than 20 years of age. Josh 6:23 indicates a military policy of using younger recruits (privates?) to scout out military objectives. This again indicates that Joshua may have been younger than 40 years of age.

105. There is no reason to doubt the ability of Joshua to live to 110 years or Moses and Aaron to 120 and 123 years, respectively. An AP article in 2011 cites over 47,000 people in Japan over 100 years of age (see below). *The China Study*, attributes Japan's long lifespan to the Japanese's predominantly vegetable-based diet. If Joshua and the elders had also eaten a vegan diet of manna, there is no reason to find fault with Scripture's account of their long lifespans. (Associated Press, "The Number of Centurions in Japan Tops 47,000," http://www.foxnews.com/health/2011/09/13/number-centenarians-in-japan-tops-47000/?test=latestnews [accessed January 2015]; and Colin and Thomas Campbell, *The China Study*.)

106. Besides Caleb and Joshua, no one could have been over 60 years of age when Israel arrived in Canaan (Num 14:29).

107. Bimson, *Redating*, 84–85.

108. Joshua is listed as a young man and may have been younger than 40 yrs. at the exile (Exod 33:11; Num 11:28).

109. Exod 33:11. For other examples of this term used to denote youth, see 1 Sam 1:24; 17:33, 42.

110. For a similar discussion, see Steinmann, *Abraham to Paul*, 70.

111. Kitchen, *Reliability*, 202–3.

112. Steinmann, *Abraham to Paul*, 48–53; and Rodger Young, "The Talmud's Two Jubilees and Their Relevance to the Date of the Exodus," *Westminster Theological Journal* 68 (2006) 71–83.

113. Westbrook, *Property, Family in Biblical Law*, 41.

114. Ibid., 26, 52, 149–51.

115. Compare to Lev 25:5.

116. Steinmann, *Abraham to Paul*, 148–50.

117. Westbrook, *Property, Family in Biblical Law*, 37.

118. Bergsma, *The Jubilee from Leviticus to Qumran*, 155.

119. Nadav Na'aman, "Sennacherib's 'Letter to God' on His Campaign to Judah," *BASOR* 214 (1974) 25–39.

120. Ibid., 28.

121. William Shea, "Sargon's Azekah Inscription: The Earliest Extrabiblical Reference to the Sabbath?" *AUSS* 32/3 (1994) 247–51.

122. Ibid., 251.

123. Bergsma, *The Jubilee From Leviticus to Qumran*, 29–30. In his book, *From Abraham to Paul*, 29–30, Steinmann presents a chart that is supposed to demonstrate the two-year fallowing of the land. The chart does not demonstrate two years, but one year. The harvest at the end of the 6th year and beginning of the 7th year sustained Israel for one agricultural year, not two. If Steinmann were to shorten his chart by one agricultural year to account for the 7th Release Year (not the Jubilee), the fallowing of the land according to his chart would last for only 6 months. Steinmann recognizes that Lev 25:20–22 addresses objections to the Jubilee year, not the 7th Release Year in which the bounty of the 6th year would last for 3 years (Steinmann, p. 28 n.57). Yet, if we were to apply the two fallow years that Scripture ordains for the Jubilee, Steinmann's method of reckoning would give 4 years for the Jubilee era instead of the 3 actual years that a 2-year fallowing of the land would logically allow. This error appears to stem from confusing the agricultural/civil calendar and the cultic calendar (see below). Steinmann's method places greater emphasis on extrabiblical talmudic sources (*b. Meg.* 14b and *b. 'Arak.* 12a) for reconstructing Israel's Jubilee chronology and less emphasis on the evidence of

Scripture regarding the Jubilee in Hezekiah's 14/15 year (Steinmann, pp. 48–53). Additionally, Steinmann's reconstruction is anachronistic. He readily acknowledges that the Tishri calendric reckoning (which he employs) did not develop until the Monarchy (Steinmann, pp. 17–21). Yet he imposes a civil Tishri form of reckoning the religious regulations of the *cultic calendar of the covenant*, which are tied to the cultic new year in Aviv/Nisan (Exod 12:2). Nothing in the Pentateuch indicates that Israel's cultic calendar would begin its new year in a month other than Aviv/Nisan. Thus his objection to Hezekiah's Jubilee year is unsubstantiated.

124. Finegan, *Handbook*, 127.

125. Steinmann, *Abraham to Paul*, 48–53, 148–51; Young, "The Talmud's Two Jubilees," *Westminster Theological Journal* 68/1 (2006) 71–83; and Finegan, *Handbook*, 127.

126. Ibid.

127. Saul's actual reign was probably closer to 18 years and 6 months, since David had already begun to rule over Judah six months prior, upon Saul's death. Civil war prevented David from reigning over the United Kingdom until Saul's general, Abner, sought to transfer the kingdom to David (2 Sam 3:10) but was killed by David's jealous general, Joab.

128. Phillips, *Israel's Criminal Law*, 4.

129. Samaria's measuring line is discussed on pp. 376–79, 680, 695, 701–2, 739–40.

130. Wilson, *Genealogy and History*, 9; and Steinmann, *Abraham to Paul*, 71–80.

131. See also Steinmann's similar reconstruction of this era, *Abraham to Paul*, 67–74.

132. Ibid., 72–73.

133. Ibid., 74–80.

134. For discussion on this 430 years, see pp. 88–89.

135. See also Steinmann's similar reconstruction of this era, *Abraham to Paul*, 37–64, 81–109.

136. This figure is supported by both Judges' linear chronology and 1 Kgs 6:1, respectively: 290 + 430 + 40 + 48 + 410 + (26) + 40 + 4 = 1,288 or 290 + 430 + 40 + 48 + 480 = 1,288.

137. Donald V. Etz, "The Genealogical Relationships of Jehoram and Ahaziah, and of Ahaz and Hezekiah, Kings of Judah," *JSOT* 21/71 (1996) 39–53; William H. Barnes, *Studies in the Chronology of the Divided Monarchy of Israel* 48 (Cambridge, MA: Harvard Semitic Monographs, 1991); Gershon Galil, *The Chronology of the Kings of Israel and Judah* (Amsterdam: Brill Academic (1996); and Freedman, "The Chronology of Israel," 272–94.

138. Edwin Thiele, "Synchronisms of the Hebrew Kings," *AUSS* 1 (1963) 124–25; and Rodger Young, "Tables of Reign Lengths from the Hebrew Court Recorders," 233–34.

139. Young, *Three Verifications*, 166–67; and Thiele, *Mysterious Numbers*, 55.

140. Thiele, *Mysterious Numbers*, 37–38, 48, 79–138. See also, Robb Andrew Young, *Hezekiah in History and Tradition* (Leiden: Brill, 2012) 11.

141. *SEC* 4150; BDB, 417–18; and *TWOT* (vol. 1) 388–89.

142. Wagenaar, *Israelite Festival Calendar*, 9–12; David Miano, *Shadow on the Steps, Time Measurement in Ancient Israel* (Atlanta: Society of Biblical Literature, 2010) 30, 35, 41, 203; Cohen, *Cultic Calendars*, 6–7; Finegan, *Handbook*, 16–17; Steinmann, *Abraham to Paul*, 12–17; and Richards, *Mapping Time*, 28–29.

143. Wagenaar, *Israelite Festival Calendar*, 30–44, 62–78; Steinmann, *Abraham to Paul*, 15–30; Miano, *Shadow Steps*, 31–32; Steinmann, *Abraham to Paul*, 12–30; Finegan, *Handbook*, 16–17, 25–31; Leo Depuydt, *Civil Calendar and Lunar Calendar in Ancient Egypt* (Belgium: Peeters, 1997) 15–20, 23, 43, 50–56, 61–63.

144. Finegan, *Handbook*, 29–33.

145. Aviv—Exod 13:4, 23:15; 34:18; Deut 16:1; Ziv—1 Kgs 6:1, 37; Ethanim—Judg 8:2; and Bul—1 Kgs 6:38. See also Steinmann, *Abraham to Paul*, 12–16.

146. Finegan, *Handbook*, 30–33 and Steinmann, *Abraham to Paul*, 13–16.

147. Steinmann, *Abraham to Paul*, 15. Nisan—Neh 2:1; Esth 3:7. Sivan—Esth 8:9. Kislev— Neh 1:1. Tebeth—Esth 2:16. Shebat—Zech 1:7. Adar—Ezra 6:15; Esth 3:7, 13; 8:12; 9:1, 15, 17, 19.

148. Finegan, *Handbook*, 21–22, 21, 33; Steinmann, *Abraham to Paul*, 17–21; Thiele, *Mysterious Numbers*, 44–50; and Wagenaar, *Origin and Transformation*, 13–24.

149. Finegan, *Handbook*, 21, 33–35; Steinmann, *Abraham to Paul*, 17–21; and Thiele, *Mysterious Numbers*, 44–50.

150. We will discuss Israel's calendar in greater detail when we look at the Exodus' plagues.

151. Finegan, *Handbook*, 21–22, 21, 33; Steinmann, *Abraham to Paul*, 17–21; Thiele, *Mysterious Numbers*, 44–50; and Wagenaar, *Origin and Transformation*, 13–24.

152. Wagenaar, *Origin and Transformation*, 13–14; and Finegan, *Handbook*, 29–31.

153. Finegan, *Handbook*, 21.

154. Wagenaar, *Origin and Transformation*, 14–17.

155. Ibid., 13–14; and Finegan, *Handbook*, 13–14, 19, 29–31.

156. The 50th Jubilee released slaves who had yoked themselves to longer service. This emancipation took place on the Day of Atonement during the 50th Jubilee—Lev 25:8–11. The sabbatical Release Years worked similarly; fields were left fallow and indebted slaves released. Although the 7th sabbatical Release Year does not specifically mention the Jubilee, when reconstructed it appears to have worked in the same manner, with fallowing of the land beginning in the spring of the 7th year, and the emancipation of indebted slaves occurring on the Day of Atonement in the fall. For more detail, see the discussion on Israel's Release and Jubilee years (see pp. 152, 178–80, 226–41, 248–285, 363, 367, 369–88).

157. Thiele, *Mysterious Numbers*, 51–53; and Steinmann, *Abraham to Paul*, 18–21.

158. Thiele, *Mysterious Numbers*, 51–53.

159. Many thanks to Rodger Young, who patiently and tirelessly explained Thiele's methods to me.

160. Thiele came to this same conclusion (*Mysterious Numbers*, 92).

161. 2 Kings 14:17—Amaziah lives 15 years after the death of Jehoash of Israel

162. 2 Kgs 14:2; 2 Chr 25:1—Amaziah reigns for 29 years.

163. 2 Kgs 14:23—Jeroboam begins to reign in Amaziah's 15th year.

164. Thiele, *Mysterious Numbers*, 43–48; Freedman, "Chronology of Israel," 272–73; Kim Ryholt, *Political Situation*, 16; and Steinmann, *Abraham to Paul*, 38–39.

165. Freedman, "Chronology of Israel," 273; and Thiele, *Mysterious Numbers*, 42–45.

166. Steinmann, *Abraham to Paul*, 38–39; and Thiele, *Mysterious Numbers*, 42–45.

167. Freedman, "Chronology of Israel," 273.

168. Steinmann, *Abraham to Paul*, 38–39.

169. Freedman, "Chronology of Israel," 273, emphasis added.

170. Steinmann, *Abraham to Paul*, 39. I differ here with Steinmann on his method of simply subtracting a year from each monarch's overlapping accession year. His method conflicts with the synchronisms Scripture provides for Judah's and Israel's monarchies.

171. Abijam's reign is the only exception to this format. It may be that the nation was still in transition, and older Levites used the priestly system to record Abijam's reign.

172. Bob Becking, *The Fall of Samaria: An Historical and Archaeological Study* (Leiden: Brill, 1992) 13–40.

173. Clayton, *Chronicle*, 79; and Rodger Young, "Evidence for Inerrancy," 55.

174. William Murnane, *Ancient Egyptian Co-regencies* 40 (Studies in Ancient Oriental Civilization; Chicago: The Oriental Institute, 1970) 59.

175. *KK*, 170, 260, 261; Hornung, "Introduction," *Ancient Egyptian Chronology*, 13; Kenneth Kitchen, *Third Intermediate Period* (Warminster, UK; Aris and Phillips, 1986) 155; Barnes, *Chronology of the Divided Monarchy*, 102–3; Murnane, *Ancient Egyptian Co-regencies*; See also Frederick Giles and M. D. Birrell, *The Amarna Age: Egypt* (Warminster, UK: Aris and Phillips, 2002) where the authors argue for the co-regency of Amenhotep and his son Akhenaten, and of Akhenaten and Smenkhkare.

176. *KK*, 170.

177. *KK*, 260–61.

178. K. Lawson Younger, Jr., "Recent Study on Sargon II, King of Assyria: Implications for Biblical Studies," in *MB*, 314.

179. *ANET*, 287.

180. "Now it came to pass in the fourteenth year of King Hezekiah that Sennacherib king of Assyria came up against all the defenced cities of Judah and took them. And the king of Assyria sent Rabshakeh . . . said to them . . . See, you trust in the staff of this broken reed, on Egypt; where on if a man lean, it will go into his hand, and pierce it: so is Pharaoh king of Egypt to all that trust in him . . . How then will you turn away the face of one captain of the least of my master's servants, and put your trust on Egypt for chariots and for horsemen?" (Isa 36:1–2, 4, 6, 9).

181. *ANET,* 287. See also Becking's treatment of the Samarian evidence, which paralells my supposition (Becking, *Fall of Samaria,* 24–40).

182. *MB,* 318, emphasis added. See also, Hornung, *Ancient Egyptian Chronology,* 13.

183. *ANET,* 287; and *MB,* 314.

184. Ryholt, *Political Situation,* 13–18.

185. Ibid., 16.

186. Dan Bruce, *Sacred Chronology of the Hebrew Kings* (Atlanta: The Prophecy Society, 2012) 23, 67–69.

187. *ANET,* 280; and Steinmann, *Abraham to Paul,* 38.

188. Steinmann, *Abraham to Paul,* 38.

189. Stuart W. Manning, "Radiocarbon Dating and Egyptian Chronology," in *Ancient Egyptian Chronology: Handbook of Oriental Studies* 83/1 (Leiden: Brill, 2006) 351.

190. Thiele, *Mysterious Numbers,* 118–23.

191. Azariah was Uzziah's throne name (Thompson, *1, 2 Chronicles,* 69).

192. Ryholt, *Political Situation,* 28.

193. Thiele had opted for the opposite method: accept 2 Kgs 15:1 and reject the consistent antedating system that the Northern Kingdom had employed. I find this option less realistic because it allows for Jehoash to reign independently for only 5 years and for Amaziah to have reigned independently for only 3 years after his father's death. Since Scripture cites a righteous era for Amaziah's initial regency (2 Kgs 14:1–7), it seems that he would have enjoyed many successful years on the throne before he campaigned against Edom and sought to confront his northern brothers. Thiele's dating would also contradict our current understanding of Assyrian chronology, by placing Menaehm's reign 12 years too early. Tiglath-pileser's inscriptions tell us that he received tribute from Menahem somewhere between his 3rd and 9th years (*ANET,* 283). Seeking Tiglath's sanction was the political move that secured Menahem's throne his 1st year. The synchronism presented here is in line with Assyrian chronology, which has Menahem paying tribute after Tiglath-pileser's third year. See Table 9.50 Macro Synchronized Chronology of Israel and the Near East in Appendix A.

194. Bruce, *Sacred Chronology,* 25.

195. For the difficulties involved in reconstructing this era, see Thiele, *Mysterious Numbers,* 106–38; and Rodger Young, "Tables of Reign Lengths from the Hebrew Court Recorders," 229–30.

196. Fox, *Service of the King,* 49, 81, 84–85.

197. *ANET,* 284.

198. Pekah's 17th to 20th years equals 4 actual years. Add to this another 12 years to allow for the full 16 years of Ahaz's reign, and one ends up with Hezekiah's ascension to the throne beginning at least 6 years after the Samarian (Israel's) monarchy had been abolished.

199. According to one scribe, Hoshea reigned on Samaria's throne in Jotham's 20th year (2 Kgs 15:30). This was a scribal error. According to 2 Kgs 15:33, Jotham died after ruling for 16 years. It appears that the scribe who registered or edited this entry became confused on the length of Jotham's reign.

200. Isaiah stated that Ahaz's protection in this prophecy was conditional: "*If* you will not believe, surely you shall not be established" (Isa 7:9). Ahaz did not "believe" that YHWH was the Deity who would establish his kingdom and he did not believe Isaiah's prophecy. He subsequently vandalized YHWH's Temple, trusting in other deities to deliver and establish his throne (2 Chr 28:1–5; 2 Kings 16). Indeed, YHWH did allow Resin and Pekah to assault Jerusalem (although the prophet Oded convinced the Northern Kingdom to restore its booty—2 Chr 28:9–15). YHWH still fulfilled Isaiah's prophecy by

sending Assyria a few years later to deport both Samaria and Rezin, vanquishing both their kings. We have a record of Isaiah's fulfilled prophecy in Assyria's archives, which we will examine in chap. 12.

201. Luckenbill, *Ancient Records of Assyria and Babylonia* (vol. 1; London: Histories and Mysteries of Man, 1989) 269.

202. Verbrugghe and Wickersham, *Berossos and Manetho,* 76.

203. Steven Holloway, "The Quest for Sargon, Pul and Tiglath-pileser," in *MB,* 73; and Jones, *Chronology of the Old Testament,* 170–73.

204. Ibid., 73 n.19. To see Ptolemy's King List see: http://www.livius.org/cg-cm/chronology/canon.html (accessed February 2015).

205. Holloway, "The Quest for Sargon, Pul and Tiglath-pileser," in *MB,* 73–78. Another explanation for Pul may be in the heir apparent, who died before his father or whose throne was compromised by another a rival before his father's death.

206. Hayim Tadmor and S. Yamada, *The Royal Inscriptions of Tiglath-pileser III and Shalmaneser V, Kings of Assyria* (Jerusalem: Israel Academy of Sciences and Humanities, 1994) 29.

207. Luckenbill, *Ancient Records of Assyria and Babylonia,* (vol. 1) 272–74.

208. *ANET,* 282–83.

209. Luckenbill, *Ancient Records of Assyria and Babylonia,* (vol. 1) 293.

210. Ibid.

211. See Becking, *Fall of Samaria,* 24–33. Tiglath-pileser's long reign could explain why his aged son Shalmaneser only lived long enough to reign for 5 years. His long reign could also be the reason that his other son, an aged Sargon, appointed a younger and more energetic Sennacherib as heir apparent.

212. Clayton, *Chronicles,* 188–196; John Taylor, "The Third Intermediate Period in Egypt," in *OHAE,* 332–54; Karl Jansen-Winkeln, "The Chronology of the Third Intermediate Period: Dynasty 22–24," in *Handbook of Ancient Egyptian Chronology* (ed. Erik Hornung; Leiden, Brill, 2006) 234–64; and Redford, *Ancient Times,* 350–64.

213. *KK,* 170, 260–61; Hornung, "Introduction," *Ancient Egyptian Chronology,* 13; Kitchen, *Third Intermediate Period,* 155; Barnes, *Chronology of the Divided Monarchy,* 102–3.

214. William Gallagher, *Sennacherib's Campaign to Judah* (Leiden: Brill, 1999) 18–19, 122–28, 149, 222.

215. Luckenbill, *Ancient Records of Assyria and Babylonia* (vol. 1) 430–39; and Thiele, *Mysterious Numbers,* 67–78, 221–26.

216. Ibid.

217. Luckenbill, *Ancient Records of Assyria and Babylonia* (vol. 1) 115, 438; Thiele, *Mysterious Numbers,* 67–78.

218. *ANET,* 287. See pp. 396–97 for discussion.

219. Kitchen, *Third Intermediate Period,* 550–59.

220. Young, "Tables of Reign Lengths from the Hebrew Court Recorders," 229.

221. Ibid., 229–30.

222. *MB,* 300.

223. Ibid., 301.

224. See also Appendix A, Table 9.50. Macro Synchronized Chronology of Israel and the Near East, p. 878.

225. *ANET,* 311–12, 560–61.

226. Leibel Reznick, *The Holy Temple Revisited* (Northvale, NJ: Jason Aronson, 1990) 2.

227. Steinmann, *Abraham to Paul,* 169; Young, "When Did Jerusalem Fall," 21; Daniel L. Smith-Christopher, "Exile," in *Eerdmans Dictionary of the Bible* (ed. David Noel Freedman, et al.; Grand Rapids: Eerdmans, 2000) 439.

228. Reznick, *Holy Temple Revisited,* xii.

229. Kyung-Jin Min, *The Levitical Authorship of Ezra-Nehemiah* (*JSOT*; London: T and T Clark, 2004) 82.

230. Calculated: 587 BCE – 538 BCE = 49 years.

231. Edwin Yamauchi, "The Eastern Jewish Diaspora Under the Babylonians," in *MB,* 366.

CHAPTER TEN

1. For a very pertinent overview of the various theories on the historical and archaeological data, see: James Hoffmeier, *Israel in Egypt*, 3–44; and Dever, *Early Israelites*.
2. Hoffmeier, *Israel in Egypt*, 3–17.
3. This theory was first advanced by C. R. Lepsius in 1849. It was later taken up by the famed archaeologist William F. Albright, although the dates were modified based on his interpretation of the archaeological data at Jericho, Lachish, and Bethel among other excavated sites. See also Kitchen, *Reliability*, 202–9.
4. Shea, "The Date of the Exodus," *ISBE* (vol. 2) 233. Donald Redford dates the Exodus to 1496 based on 1 Kgs 6:1, while he ignores both the Wilderness Exile and early Conquest years under Joshua's administration (*Ancient Times*, 258). Finkelstein and Silberman date the Exodus to 1440 (*Unearthed*, 56). Abraham Malamat considers dating the Exodus to be "futile" allowing a range from the 15th to 12th centuries BCE (*History of Biblical Israel*, 58).
5. Carl E. DeVries, "Hyksos," *ISBE* (vol. 2) 787; Manetho, *Aegyptiaca.*, frag. 42, 1.75–79.2; and Josephus, *Against Apion* 1.73, 93, 227. For various dates proposed for the reign of Amoses I, the pharaoh who expelled the Hyksos, see http://lists.ibiblio.org/pipermail/b-hebrew/2000-January/006340.html (accessed January 2015). The date 1570 BCE is suggested by Finkelstein and Silberman, *Bible Unearthed*, 56; 1530 BCE by William Dever, "Is There Any Archaeological Evidence for the Exodus?" in *Exodus: Egyptian Evidence* (ed. Ernest Frerichs and Leonard Lesko; Winona Lake, IN: Eisenbrauns, 1997) 71; and 1532 by Currid, *Egypt and Old Testament*, 125–36.
6. Shea, "Date of the Exodus," *ISBE* (vol. 2) 230–38; Freedman, "The Chronology of Israel," *ABD*, 270–71; Brimson, *Redating*, 17; and Hoffmeier, *Israel in Egypt*; Kitchen, "The Exodus" *ABD* (vol. 2) 702; Amihai Mazar, "The Patriarchs, Exodus, and Conquest Narratives in Light of Archaeology" in *The Quest for the Historical Israel* 17 (ed. Andrew Vaughn; Atlanta, GA: Society of Biblical Literature, 2007) 57–58, 61–62; Israel Finkelstein, "Patriarchs, Exodus, Conquest: Fact or Fiction?" in *The Quest for Historical Israel*: 44–46, 53; and Dever, *Early Israelites*, 8.
7. Clayton, *Chronicle*, 9–13.
8. Ibid., 11.
9. Janine Bourriau, "The Second Intermediate Period (c. 1650–1550)," in *The Oxford History of Ancient Egypt* (New York: Oxford Press, 204) 173.
10. Clayton, *Chronicle*, 11–12.
11. Bourriau, "Second Intermediate Period," *OHAE*, 179.
12. Clayton, *Chronicle of the Pharaohs*, 12.
13. Ibid., 9–13.
14. Shea, "The Date of The Exodus," 230–31; Kitchen, *Reliability*, 255; Dever, *Early Israelites*, 21, 23; and Hoffmeier, *Israel in Egypt*, 34.
15. Shea, "Date of The Exodus," 230–31; and Kitchen, *Reliability*, 255–56.
16. *ANET*, 199–203; and Shea, "Date of The Exodus," 232.
17. Shea, "Date of The Exodus," 232.
18. Finkelstein and Silberman, *Unearthed*, 57; Dever, *Early Israelites*, 135; Kitchen, *Reliability*, 206–207; and Yurco, "Merenptah's Campaign," in *Exodus: Egyptian Evidence*, 27–51.
19. P. Kyle McCarter, "Inscriptions," *ISBE* (vol. 2) 834; Finkelstein and Silberman, *Unearthed*, 57–60; Finkelstein and Mazar, *Quest for Israel*, 30, 39, 69, 74; Dever, *Early Israelites*, 135, 210–18; and Kitchen, *Reliability*, 206–7, 220.
20. Aharon Kempinski, "The Middle Bronze Age," *AOAI*, 179; and Bourriau, "SIP," *OHAE*, 172–75.
21. Kitchen, *Reliability*, 348; Mazar, "The Patriarchs, Exodus, and Conquest," in *The Quest*, 58. Egyptologist Robert Brier (who frequents the Discovery Channel) has also presented this position.
22. Shea, "Date of the Exodus," (vol. 2) 231–32; Kitchen, *Reliability*, 256–69; Currid, *Egypt and Old Testament*, 125–36; Dever, *Early Israelites*, 13–14; and Mazar, "Patriarchs, Exodus, and Conquest," in *The Quest*, 59.

23. Shea, "Date of the Exodus," (vol. 2) 232; and Mazar, "Patriarchs, Exodus, and Conquest," in *The Quest,* 59. The 19th Dynasty began during the reign of Ramesses I in 1295 BCE.

24. Shea, "Date of the Exodus," (vol. 2) 232; and Cazells, "The Hebrews," in *Essential Papers,* 272.

25. Clayton, *Chronicle,* 98.

26. Wood, "Rise and Fall," *JETS,* 484–47.

27. Ibid., 487; Bimson, *Redating,* 86–88; and Kitchen, *Reliability,* 204–8.

28. Wood, "Rise and Fall," *JETS,* 487–49; and Bimson, *Redating,* 86.

29. Bimson, *Redating,* 88; and Kitchen, *Reliability,* 204–8.

30. Shea, "Date of the Exodus," *ISBE* (vol. 2) 232–33.

31. Karel Van der Toorn, *Scribal Culture* (Cambridge: Harvard University Press, 2007) 148. Van der Toorn actually gives the figure closer to 40 years (p. 149). However, he also cites the scroll that sat in the Ark of the Covenant for quite a lengthy time without being transcribed for several generations; it was so long that the priests forgot about it (2 Chronicles 34). Therefore, many manuscripts may have lasted for several generations or until they showed signs of wear.

32. Ibid., 149. See also pp. 312, 314–16.

33. Shea, "Date of the Exodus," (vol. 2) 232–33.

34. Hoffmeier, *Israel in Egypt,* 3–44.

35. Shea, "Date of the Exodus," 232.

36. For the many problems with a 1200–1300 BCE Exodus date, see Finkelstein and Silberman, *The Bible Unearthed,* 48–96; Dever, *Early Israelites,* 7–35; and Finkelstein and Mazar, *The Quest for the Historical Israel,* 38–65.

37. Kenneth A. Kitchen, "Joseph," *ISBE* (vol. 2) 1129.

38. Mendenhall, *Ancient Israel,* 29 n.7; and Nicholas Reeves, *Akhenaten: Egypt's False Prophet* (New York: Thames and Hudson, 2001) 16, 48–51, 73, 89–90, 95, 97–98, 100–3, 108, 117–18, 140–47, 154.

39. Ezek 20:6–8; Jer 10:2–12, 14–16; and Joshua 24; see chap. 2 for further discussion.

40. Ibid.

41. Shea, "Date of the Exodus," 234.

42. Ibid., 235.

43. Ibid.

44. Ibid., 237.

45. Ibid.

46. Dever, *Early Israelites,* 8.

47. Ibid.; and Steinmann, *Abraham to Paul,* 45–53.

48. Finkelstein and Silberman, *Unearthed,* 77–79.

49. Ibid.; and Hoffmeier, *Israel in Egypt,* 25–44; and Shea, "Date of the Exodus," 236–38.

50. Shea, "Date of the Exodus," 236.

51. Walter Reinhold, "Exodus Problems: Scholarly Pitfalls Encountered in Setting a Date for the Exodus and Establishing Its Route on Maps," last updated October 17, 2010, http://www.bibleorigins.net/ ExodusProblems.html (accessed January 2015); and Idem, Exodus Memories of Southern Sinai (Linking the Archaeological Data to the Biblical Narratives," last updated November 21, 2009, http://www. bibleorigins.net/ExodusTimnaSerabitelKhadim.html (accessed January 2015).

52. James Weinstein, "Exodus and Archaeological Reality," in *Exodus: The Egyptian Evidence* (ed. Ernest S. Friedichs and Leonard H. Lesko; Winona Lake, IN: Eisenbrauns, 1997) 93.

53. Finkelstein, "Patriarchs, Exodus, Conquest: Fact or Fiction?" in *Quest,* 51–52.

54. Ryholt, *Political Situation,* 172; Redford, "Textual Sources for the Hyksos Period," in *HP,* 1–44.

55. Exception noted for First Intermediate Period (*c.* 2180–2040 BCE).

56. Clayton, *Chronicle,* 90–97; and Bourriau, "SIP," 172.

57. Bourriau, "SIP," in *OHAE,* 175; Nicolas Grimal, *Ancient Egypt,* 182; and Hoffmeier, *Israel in Egypt,* 53–60, 62, 68.

58. Bourriau, "SIP," in *OHAE,* 175; and Hoffmeier, *Israel in Egypt,* 61.

59. For a quick resource, see: J. Hill, "Hyksos," 2010, http://www.ancientegyptonline.co.uk/hyksos.html (accessed January 2015); Grimal, *Ancient Egypt,* 139, 144–45.

60. Bourriau, "SIP" in *OHAE,* 174; and Ryholt, *Political Situation,* 94–150.

61. Bourriau, "SIP," in *OHAE,* 174; John Van Seters, *The Hyksos: A New Investigation* (Eugene, OR: Wipf and Stock Publishers, 1966) 3; and Redford, *Ancient Times,* 100.

62. Dever, *Early Israelites,* 10; Van Seters, *The Hyksos,* 20–21, 29.

63. Ryholt, *Political Situation,* 102 n.338, 128, 130.

64. Van Seters, *Hyksos,* 75; and Clayton, *Chronicle,* 84–85.

65. Clayton, *Chronicle,* 84–85; and Van Seters, *Hyksos,* 93–94.

66. Van Seters, *Hyksos,* 93–94.

67. Ibid., 94; and Callender, "Middle Kingdom Renaissance," in *OHAE,* 146–47.

68. Grimal, *Ancient Egypt,* 186; and James Hoffmeier, *Israel in Egypt,* 53–68.

69. Grimal, *Ancient Egypt,* 186.

70. Bourriau, "SIP" in *OHAE,* 174–82; and Van Seters, *Hyksos,* 116.

71. Redford, *Ancient Times,* 113; John Van Seters, *Hyksos,* 54–55, 60–61, 83–84; and Ryholt, *Political Situation,* 111–12, 116, 131, 139, 142, 296, 299, 303.

72. Ryholt, *Political Situation,* 280, 318, 100 n.322, 101 n.327, 102 n.339, 128, 220, 293–94, 402; Bourriau, "SIP," in *OHAE,* 175; Van Seters, *Hyksos,* 20–21, 29; and Dever, *Early Israelites,* 10.

73. Callender, "Middle Kingdom," in *OHAE,* 162.

74. Bourriau, "SIP," in *OHAE,* 180; and O'Connor, "The Hyksos Period," in *HP,* 48, 52.

75. Grimal, *Ancient Egypt,* 184; and Bourriau, "SIP," in *OHAE,* 177.

76. As per Manetho (Against Apion I. 78). Donald Redford rejects this view (Redford, "Textual Sources," in *HP,* 25–26).

77. Ibid.

78. Robert Schiestl, "The Cemeteries of F/I in the Strata d/2 (H) and d/1 (G/4), Late 12th Dynasty and Early 13th Dynasty," (Tell el-Dabᶜa, 2008), http://www.auaris.at/html/stratum_f1_d1_en.html (accessed January 2015); Ernst Czerny, "The Orthogonal Planned Settlement of the Early Middle Kingdom (F/I, stratum e)," Tell el-Dabᶜa, 2008, http://www.auaris.at/html/stratum_e_en.html (accessed January 2015); Irmgard Hein, "Area A/IV," Tell el-Dabᶜa, 2008, http://www.auaris.at/html/areal_a4_en.html (accessed January 2015); Bourriau, "SIP," in *OHAE,*175; and Hoffmeier, *Israel in Egypt,* 63.

79. Bourriau, "SIP," in *OHAE,* 180.

80. Manfred Bietak, "The Center of Hyksos Rule: Avaris (Tell el-Daba)," in *HP,* 97–109; and Ryholt, *Political Situation,* 79, 103.

81. Grimal, *Ancient Egypt,* 183; Ryholt, *Political Situation,* 79; and Bourriau, "SIP," in *OHAE,* 177.

82. Bourriau, "SIP," in *OHAE,* 178; and Callender, "Middle Kingdom," in *OHAE,* 161–63.

83. Bourriau, "SIP," in *OHAE,* 183.

84. Van Seters, *Hyksos,* 192–93.

85. Bourriau, "SIP," in *OHAE,* 183, 198.

86. Ibid., 179, 209.

87. O'Connor, "Hyksos Period," in *HP,* 52.

88. Ibid.

89. Van Seters, *Hyksos,* 12, 17; and Ryholt, *Political Situation,* 142.

90. Grimal, *Ancient Egypt,* 186; and Van Seters, *Hyksos,* 90.

91. Hoffmeier, *Israel in Egypt,* 61; and Van Seters, *Hyksos,* 90.

92. Bourriau, "SIP," in *OHAE,* 198.

93. Ryholt, *Political Situation,* 139, 176–77, 182.

94. Ibid.; Grimal, *Ancient Egypt,* 190–95; and Clayton, *Chronicle,* 93–97.

95. Clayton, *Chronicle,* 90–97. Ryholt, however, dates Seqenenre's 4-year reign as beginning in 1558 (*Political Situation,* 204).

96. *ANET,* 232–33; and Grimal, *Ancient Egypt,* 190–95.

97. *ANET,* 232–33; and Redford, "Textual Sources," in *HP,* 13–14.

98. Redford, "Kamose II," in *HP,* 14–16.

99. Grimal, *Ancient Egypt,* 192–95; Redford, "Textual Sources," in *HP,* 13–16; *ANET,* 232–34; Clayton, *Chronicle,* 93–97. There is some question about who sacked Avaris: Kamose or Ahmose. The problem lies in the fact that Kamose II's stele states that Kamose returned to Thebes, apparently before the city was sacked (Grimal, 193). However, the same stele indicates that he indeed sacked Avaris but did not live long enough to chase the Hyksos out of Egypt. Another viewpoint considers Ahmose the pharaoh to have sacked Avaris due to the fact that the highest attested year for his brother Kamose is his 3rd year. Most scholars (Redford, Ryholt, Grimal) consider the brothers co-regents. Thus, the Kamose II Stele probably does not refer to Ahmose's assault on Avaris since the inscription does not indicate the pharaoh mentioned in the stele pursued the Hyksos to Sharuhen, but returned to Thebes. The two events can be seen as separate events with Ahmose having served coregent at Thebes during Kamose's sack of Avaris, but resuming the campaign upon his brother's untimely death and chasing Hyksos out of Egypt without the stele distinguishing between the brothers.

100. *ANET,* 232–33.

101. Dever, *Early Israelites,* 39–40.

102. Ibid., 40.

103. Bourriau, "SIP," in *OHAE,* 183, parentheses added for clarity.

104. The names associated with these cities can be confusing. While the Hyksos city was Avaris, the more-modern area is known as Tell el-Dab'a. A few thousand feet to the west of these ruins is the modern district of Qantir. Ramesses II built on top of Avaris. His 12th-century (BCE) city was known as Pi-Ramses.

105. Verbrugghe and Wickersham, trans., *Berossos and Manetho,* 156–67.

106. Redford, *Ancient Times,* 101.

107. Redford also acknowledges: the merits of Manetho's accounts, the reason for conflicting chronologies, and the legitimate reason for Salitis/Sheshy's requiring tribute from the southern kings (Redford, *Ancient Times,* 110–15). See also Thompson's approach to Manetho in Thomas Schneider, "The Relative Chronology of the Middle Kingdom and the Hyksos Period (Dyns. 12–17)" in *Ancient Egyptian Chronology: Handbook of Oriental Studies* (ed. Erik Hornung, et al.; Leiden, Brill: 2006) 193.

108. Redford, "Textual Sources," in *HP,* 2.

109. Ibid.

110. Bourriau, "SIP," in *OHAE,* 208.

111. Grimal, *Ancient Egypt,* 186.

112. William Matthew Flinders Petrie and John Garrow Duncan, *Hyksos and Israelite Cities* (London: British School of Archaeology, 1906) 4.z

113. Petrie and Duncan, *Hyksos and Israelite Cities;* Bourriau, "SIP," in *OHAE,* 175; Grimal, *Ancient Egypt,* 186; and Hoffmeier, *Israel in Egypt,* 67.

114. Verbrugghe and Wickersham, *Berossos and Manetho,* 160, parenthesis added.

115. Halpern, *First Historians,* xxxi–xxxiii. See also a similar comparison of Assyrian perspective in Hoffmeier, *Israel in Egypt,* 13. See also O'Connor's use of an "Egyptian perspective" or "Theban perspective" in "Hyksos Period," *HP,* 45, 62.

116. Van Seters, *Hyksos,* 3–4. The Hyksos's roots to Syria-Palestine seem to be confirmed by the archaeological evidence within Palestine based on ceramics and fortification systems (Van Seters, 20–21, 29). Redford defines the "Asiatics" based on their common West Semitic language (Redford, *Ancient Times,* 100).

117. For the validity of differing historical perspectives, see Halpern, *First Historians,* xxxi–xxxiii; and Hoffmeier, *Israel in Egypt,* 13.

118. Hoffmeier, *Israel in Egypt,* 122.

119. Ryholt, *Political Situation,* 75, 79

120. Ibid., 79.

121. Egypt has a long tradition of preserving its history. Not only do the Royal Canon of Turin, Royal List of Karnak, Royal List of Abydos, the Abydos King List, and the Rosetta Stone all attest the importance of written records of the kings, the mortuary temples, inscriptions, and written stories aim to preserve this history as well. Many viziers and other high officials indeed had mortuary complexes, and we know the names of quite a few viziers from both the Middle and the New Kingdoms (Wolfram Grajetzki, *Court Officials of the Egyptian Middle Kingdom* [London: Gerald Duckworth, 2009]).

122. Toby A. H. Wilkinson, *The Rise and Fall of Ancient Egypt* (New York: Random, 2010) 192–93; Bourriau, "SIP," in *OHAE,* 210; and Van Seters, *Hyksos,* 156, 168.

123. Erik Hornung, *History of Ancient Egypt: An Introduction* (trans. David Lorton, Cornell University, 1999) 113, 132; and *ANET,* 231.

124. Albert Barnes, *Barnes' Notes on the Bible,* http://www.sacred-texts.com/bib/cmt/barnes/exo001.htm (accessed January 2015); parenthesis added.

125. Ryholt, *Political Situation,* 34–65; and Redford, "Textual Sources for the Hyksos Period," in *HP,* 21.

126. Ibid., 40–52, 62; and Redford, *Ancient Times,* 106.

127. Spiros Zodhiates, *The Hebrew Greek Keyword Bible* (Chattanooga, TN: AMG Publishers, 1991) 78.

128. Ryholt, *Political Situation,* 117.

129. Ibid., 137, 165, 167.

130. Bietek, "A Palace of the Hyksos King Khayan at Avaris," 102, parenthesis added.

131. Zahi Hawass, "Press Release—New Discovery at Tel El-Daba," http://www.drhawass.com/blog/press-release-new-discovery-tel-el-daba (accessed November 2013).

132. Ryholt, *Political Situation,* 128; and Van Seters, *Hyksos,* 181.

133. Ryholt, *Political Situation,* 295.

134. Burials during this period affirm this view since male graves yield weapons, "which indicate that warriors played an important part in the society. . . . This observation suggests that the secession did not come about peacefully" (Ryholt, *Political Situation,* 295).

135. Ryholt, *Political Situation,* 200.

136. Bietak, "Center of Hyksos Rule," in *HP,* 113; Grimal, *Ancient Egypt,* 183; and Van Seters, *Hyksos,* 95.

137. Ryholt, *Political Situation,* 122–23, 126, 131.

138. Ibid., 296.

139. Ibid., 141.

140. Ibid., 189, 79, 120, 135.

141. O'Connor, "Hyksos Period," in *HP,* 53.

142. Ryholt, *Political Situation,* 408.

143. Ibid.

144. Ryholt, *Political Situation,* 124.

145. Ibid., 51.

146. Ibid., 43, 120, 189, 304, 307.

147. Ryholt, *Political Situation,* 201, 410. Ryholt dates Khayan's rise to power to *c.* 1621 BCE.

148. Hoffmeier, *Israel in Egypt,* 138.

149. Ibid.

150. Ian Bolling, "Adoption Trends in 2003: Infant Abandonment and Safe Haven Legislation," in *Report on Trends in the State Courts* (2003), http://www.uvm.edu/~vlrs/Safety/babysafehavens.pdf (accessed January 2015).

151. Redford, *Ancient Times,* 56–70.

152. Redford, *Akhenaten,* 22.

153. Ryholt, *Political Situation,* 93. See also Hoffmeier, *Israel in Egypt,* 94, 159.

154. Ronald Hendel, "The Exodus in Biblical Memory," *JBL* 12/4 (winter 2001) 615.

155. Hoffmeier, *Israel in Egypt,* 140.

156. Ryholt, *Political Situation,* 278.

157. Van Seters, *Hyksos,* 168. Tany is listed as a "daughter of Apophis," and a vase bearing her name was recovered from Ahmose's tomb. Van Seters interprets both Tany's Egyptian name and the presence of the vase in a Theban tomb as indicative of a family relationship. Thus the term "pharaoh's daughter" may have been used similarly to term "son of pharaoh" to indicate a friendly standing with the king.

158. Redford, *"Textual Sources,"* in *HP,* 10.

159. Ryholt, *Political Situation,* 121, 256, 288, 304, 307. Contra Bietak, "Avaris," in *HP,* 114.

160. Ibid.

161. *ANET,* 231.

162. Ryholt, *Political Situation,* 149–50; Redford, *Ancient Times,* 116–17; O'Connor, "Hyksos Period," in *HP,* 56; and Bourriau, "SIP," in *OHAE,* 177.

163. William Simpson, *The Literature of Ancient Egypt* (London: Yale University Press, 2003) 69. See also, *ANET,* 231.

164. *ANET,* 231.

165. *ANET,* 231 n.10.

166. Redford, "Textual Sources," in *HP,* 13.

167. Ibid., 14.

168. Ibid.

169. Redford, *Ancient Times,* 108.

170. Exod 13:3, 14; 20:2; Deut 5:6; 6:12; 8:14; 13:5, 10; 26:6; Josh 24:17; and Judg 6:8.

171. *SEC* 5656; BDB, 715; and *TWOT* (vol. 2) 1553.

172. Bartchy, "Slavery," (vol. 4) 542.

173. No person in Egypt, other than pharaoh, owned land in Egypt. Land-holding Egyptian citizens could only hold or "own" land for as long as pharaoh granted the privilege. There never was any concept of "private land ownership" in Egypt where land was a redistributive tool to reward loyalty or military service. See Goelet, "'Town' and 'Country' in Ancient Egypt," in *ULO,* 91, see also pp. 65–96.

174. Callender, "Middle Kingdom," in *OHAE,* 163–64; John Holladay, Jr., "The Eastern Nile Delta During the Hyksos and Pre-Hyksos Periods: Toward a Systemic/Socioeconomic Understanding," in *HP,* 202–3.

175. Diodorus Siculus (I.74, 81); and *AEM,* 127, 129–131. See pp. 214–15 for discussion.

176. Callender, "The Middle Kingdom Renaissance," in *OHAE,* 161–62, 171.

177. Ibid., 161–64.

178. See http://dictionary.reference.com/browse/corvee (accessed January 2015).

179. Bartchy, "Slavery," (vol. 4) 540.

180. Ibid., parenthesis added for clarity.

181. *SEC* 4522; BDB, 586–87; and *TWOT* (vol. 1) 516.

182. Bartchy, "Slavery," (vol. 4) 540. See also BDB, 586–87; and *TWOT* (vol. 1) 516.

183. The Law did not forbid voluntary service or cooperation, but it did view compulsory labor as a curse. Thus, noncompulsory insurance, healthcare, investments, or ventures that do not abrogate personal responsibility (i.e., diet or life-style) would not violate the precepts within the Torah. *Voluntary* co-operation is often beneficial to communities.

184. Jer 23:4; 30:20; and Ezek 34:10; 45:8; 46:17–18.

185. *SEC* 6635; BDB, 838–39; and *TWOT* (vol. 2) 749–51. See also Gen 21:22; Num 1:20, 22, where the Hebrew term *tseba'* also designates a standing army.

186. SEC 2571; BDB, 332; TWOT (vol 2) 299. Many thanks to David Levitan for drawing my attention to this text.

187. Ryholt, *Political Situation,* 185–89; Bourriau, "SIP," in *OHAE,* 191–204. The pharaoh to whom the reverse side of the *Rhind Mathematical Papyrus* refers is in dispute since it does not mention a name. Three kings are generally proposed: Kamose, Ahmose, and the last Hyksos pharaoh Khamudi (*OHAE,* 200).

188. O'Connor, "Hyksos Period," in *HP,* 60–61; and Ryholt, *Political Situation,* 295.

189. Ryholt, *Political Situation,* 172.

190. *SEC* 4543; BDB 698; *TWOT* (vol. 2) 625; and Hoffmeier, *Israel in Egypt,* 116, 119–20.

191. Bietak, "Center of Hyksos Rule," in *HP,* 116; and Bourriau, "SIP," in *OHAE,* 175–82, 185.

192. Holladay, "The Eastern Nile Delta During the Hyksos," in *HP,* 183–86.

193. Bourriau, "SIP," in *OHAE, 185.*

194. Verbrugghe and Wickersham, trans., *Berossos and Manetho,* 156–57, parenthesis added.

195. Redford, "Kamose II: Textual Sources," in *HP,* 14–15

196. Ibid.

197. Goelet, "'Town' and 'Country' in Ancient Egypt," in *ULO,* 78.

198. Hoffmeier, *Israel in Egypt,* 119.

199. Ibid.

200. David Silverman, ed., *Ancient Egypt* (Oxford: Oxford University Press, 1997) 27; http://www.philae. nu/akhet/LowerSepatMap.html (accessed December 2012. The site has since partially moved to "The Ancient Egyptian Calendar: The Egyptian World," Last updated October 26, 2007, http://www. ancientworlds.net/aw/Article/998323 [accessed January 2015]); "The Nomes of Egypt and Astronomy– E–Lower Egypt Nomes Explained—ANE BC P8," Ancient Egypt Web Blog, May 26, 2004, http:// ancientegyptweblog.blogspot.com/2004_05_01_archive.html (accessed January 2015); and Jenny Hill, "Map of Ancient Egypt: Lower Egypt," Ancient Egypt Online, http://www.ancientegyptonline.co.uk/ nomeslower.html (December 2013).

201. Hoffmeier, *Israel in Egypt,* 121.

202. Ibid.; and Kitchen, *Reliability,* 256.

203. Hoffmeier, *Israel in Egypt,* 120; Kitchen, *Reliability,* 257; and Bimson, *Redating,* 31, 40–43.

204. Holladay, "Eastern Nile Delta During the Hyksos," in *HP,* 194.

205. During the Old Kingdom, this would have been the 13th nome. See note 1665 on nomes above.

206. Geoffry Graham, "Tanis," *Oxford Encyclopedia of Ancient Egypt:* vol. 3 (ed. Robert Redford, New York: Oxford University Press, 2001) 348.

207. Staff, "Lost in Time, Found by Satellites," *Science Magazine* (June 2011) 1134; Francis Cronin, Egypian Pyramids Found by Infra-red Satellite Images," BBC News, May 24, 2011, http://www.bbc.co.uk/news/ world-13522957 (accessed January 2015); Ki Mae Heussner, "Lost Pyramids: Peering Beneath Egypt's Surface With Satellite Images," *ABC News* (May 27, 2011), http://abcnews.go.com/Technology/lost-pyramids-egypt-discovered-satellite-images/story?id=13693894 (accessed January 2015).

208. Ibid.

209. Goelet, "'Town' and 'Country' in Ancient Egypt," in *ULO,* 77.

210. Holladay "Eastern Nile Delta," in *HP,* 201.

211. Dever, *Early Israelites,* 41–74; and Finkelstein, *Quest,* 53. On Egyptologists' history of dating the Exodus, see Bimson, *Redating,* 10–41.

212. Bimson, *Redating,* 13–26; and Hoffmeier, *Israel in Egypt,* 3–44.

213. Kathleen Kenyon, *Digging Up Jericho* (London: Ernest Benn, 1957) 167–232.

214. For a good treatment on the subject, see Hoffmeier, *Israel in Egypt,* x, 14, 33, 38, 43; and Yamauchi, "Current State of Old Testament Historiography," in *FTH,* 1–36.

215. Redford, *Ancient Times,* 412.

216. Ibid., 258.

217. Finkelstein, *Quest,* 59.

218. Ryholt, *Political Situation,* 88 n.280, 100 n.318, n.322, 101 n.327, 102 n.339, 128, 220, 293–94, 402; Bourriau, "SIP," in *OHAE,* 175; Redford, *Ancient Times,* 108–11; and Hoffmeier, *Israel in Egypt,* 61.

219. Scriptural chronology deviates from the historical dating of these seals by 200 years. While there is a very slight possibility that the name Yakbim could indeed refer to the patriarch (as Israel's tribal king), the seal would have to have been passed down through the generations. The overall Egyptian evidence would not currently support this hypothesis.

220. Callender, "Middle Kingdom," in *OHAE,* 150–51; and Erik Hornung, *Ancient Egypt,* 41.

221. Ryholt, *Political Situation,* 293–94.

222. Bourriau, "SIP," in *OHAE*, 175; and Van Seters, *Hyksos*, 47.

223. Bourriau, "SIP," in *OHAE*, 175; and Hoffmeier, *Israel in Egypt*, 61.

224. A similar practice is also related in the story of Daniel and his three friends (Dan 1:6–7). Even today when people from Japan, China, or Russia move to the United States, they often adopt names that are easily pronounced in English.

225. Bourriau, "SIP," in *OHAE*, 175.

226. Dever, *Early Israelites*, 27, 77, 80, 103; and Finkelstein, *Quest*, 77.

227. Bourriau, "SIP," in *OHAE*, 176, 204.

228. Ryholt, *Political Situation*, 110; and Van Seters, *Hyksos*, 11.

229. Callender, "The Middle Kingdom," in *OHAE*, 161–62, 171; and Redford, *Ancient Times*, 101.

230. Callender, "The Middle Kingdom," in *OHAE*, 161. See also Van Seters, *Hyksos*, 110.

231. Van Seters, *Hyksos*, 91–92.

232. Callender, "Middle Kingdom," in *OHAE*, 161.

233. Bourriau, "SIP," in *OHAE*, 175.

234. Petrie and Duncan, *Hyksos and Israelite Cities*, 5.

235. Ibid.

236. Bietak, "The Center of Hyksos Rule," in *HP*, 91–97; Ryholt, *Political Situation*, 112–13, 123, 138–42; Callender, "Middle Kingdom," in *OHAE*, 165; Grimal, *Ancient Egypt*, 185–86; Redford, *Ancient Times*, 100; and Van Seters, *Hyksos*, 21–22, 26, 46, 49–52.

237. Callender, "Middle Kingdom Renaissance," in *OHAE*, 161.

238. Bourriau, "SIP," in *OHAE*, 182; and Bietak, "Center of Hyksos Rule," in *HP*, 91–97.

239. Manfred Bietak, "The Palatial Precinct at the Nile Branch (Area H)," http://www.auaris.at/html/ez_helmi_en.html#1, parenthesis added (accessed January 2015). See also: "Tall al-Yahudiyyah," GIS Center: Supreme Council of Antiquities, Egypt http://www.giscenter.gov.eg/uploads/of/ff/offffa2bb67d62d6ade49de69663c034/featured-site-layout.pdf (accessed January 2015).

240. O'Connor, "The Hyksos Period," in *HP*, 57.

241. William Waddell, trans., *Manetho* (Loeb Classical Library 350; Cambridge: Harvard university Press, 1940) 79, emphasis added.

242. Bietek, "A Palace of the Hyksos King Khayan at Avaris," 102.

243. Holladay "Eastern Nile Delta During the Hyksos," in *HP*, 208.

244. Grimal, *Ancient Egypt*, 186.

245. Bourriau, "SIP," in *OHAE*, 183; and *ANET*, 232–33. This peaceful alliance is attested by the reluctance of Kamose's counselors to engage the Hyksos pharaohs.

246. Bourriau, "SIP," in *OHAE*, 99, 175.

247. Ryholt, *Political Situation*, 141 n.506; and Redford, *Ancient Times*, 101.

248. Ryholt, *Political Situation*, 76, 303, 177.

249. Ibid., 177, 303.

250. Grimal, *Ancient Egypt*, 187–89; Bourriau "SIP," in *OHAE*, 182; Ryholt, *Political Situation*, 76, 111–12, 116, 138–43, 253, 296, 299–300, 307.

251. Ryholt, *Political Situation*, 295.

252. Ibid., 145–46.

253. Redford, "Kamose II: Textual Sources," in *HP*, 14–15.

254. Ryholt, *Political Situation*, 172–224, 182–83; O'Connor, "Hyksos Period," in *HP*, 45; Janine Bourriau, "SIP," in *OHAE*, 197–203; and Grimal, *Ancient Egypt*, 191–95.

255. Bourriau, "SIP," in *OHAE*, 200.

256. Ryholt, *Political Situation*, 183, 273.

257. Ibid., 172–74, 182–83; and Bietak, "Center of Hyksos Rule," in *HP*, 114.

258. O'Connor, "Hyksos Period," in *HP*, 63 n.1.

259. Ryholt, *Political Situation*, 137, 165.

260. Redford, "Kamose II: Textual Sources," in *HP*, 14–15.

261. For similar usage of "spoil" or plunder see Gen 31:9, 16; Exod 12:36, 33:6; 1 Sam 30:8, 18; 2 Chr 20:25; and Amos 3:12.

262. Bourriau "SIP" in *OHAE*, 177; and O'Connor, "Hyksos Period," in *HP,* 55

263. Bourriau "SIP," in *OHAE,* 177.

264. Erik Hornung, *The Ancient Egyptian Books of the Afterlife* (trans. David Lorton, London: Cornell University Press, 1997) and Jan Assmann, *Death and Salvation in Ancient Egypt*, 323–29.

265. Ryholt, *Political Situation*, 300.

266. Ibid., 301.

267. Bourriau "SIP," in *OHAE*, 176–77. See also, O'Connor, "Hyksos Period," in *HP,* 53; and Bietak, "Center of Hyksos Rule," in *HP,* 125–28.

268. Bietak, "Center of Hyksos Rule," in *HP,* 91; and O'Connor, "Hyksos Period," in *HP,* 45–56.

269. Bietak, "Center of Hyksos Rule," in *HP,* 91.

270. Bietak, "Center of Hyksos Rule," in *HP,* 105.

271. W. Kutschera, M. Bietak, E.M. Wild, C. Bronk Ramsey, M. Dee, R. Golser, K. Kopetzky, P. Stadler, P. Steirer, U. Thanheiser, F. Weninger, "The Chronology of Tell el-Daba: A Crucial Meeting Point of 14C Dating, Archaeology, and Egyptology in the 2nd Millennium BC", E. Boaretto & N.R. Rebollo Franco (eds.), *Proceedings of the 6th International Radiocarbon and Archaeology Symposium, Radiocarbon* (vol. 54, No. 3-4, 2012) 407–422. Fig. 3.

272. Bietak, "Center of Hyksos Rule," in *HP,* 105. For a general treatment of Exodus and the plagues in Egyptian memory, see Ronald Hendel, "The Exodus in Biblical Memory," 612–14.

273. Ibid.

274. Bietak, "Center of Hyksos Rule," in *HP,* 116.

275. Ibid.

276. Ryholt, *Political Situation*, 172–74, 182–83; O'Connor, "Hyksos Period," in *HP,* 45; Bourriau, "SIP," in *OHAE*, 197–203; and Grimal, *Ancient Egypt*, 191–95 .

277. Bourriau, "SIP," in *OHAE*, 200.

278. Grimal, *Ancient Egypt*, 192–93.

279. Ibid., 192.

280. Edward Wente, "Thutmose III's Accession and the Beginning of the New Kingdom," *JNES* 57/1 (1975) 271. If the reverse side of the Rhind Mathematical Papyrus is assigned to Kamose, it may indicate that his co-rengency with Ahmose lasted a number of years, perhaps in an effort to maintain stability both on the front and at home. Even in this case, however, it would be difficult to reconcile what appears to be a seven-year difference. Again, it is hoped that future studies can address these details.

281. Grimal, *Ancient Egypt*, 193.

282. Christopher Bronk Ramsey, et al., "Radiocarbon-Based Chronology for Dynastic Egypt," *Science* 325/5985 (June 2010) 1554–57.

283. Bourriau, "SIP," in *OHAE,* 177.

284. Holladay, "The Eastern Nile Delta," in *HP,* 185.

285. Redford, *Ancient Times*, 129, emphasis added.

286. Kitchen, *Reliability*, 247–49.

287. Grimal considers 1570, 1560, or 1551 BCE as possibilities for Kamose's death (*Ancient Egypt*, 193, 202); Ryholt holds to 1549 as the date of Kamose's death (*Political Situation*, 410); and O'Connor places his death at 1551 ("Hyksos Period," in *HP,* 56).

288. Hoffmeier, *Israel in Egypt*, 121; and Kitchen, *Reliability*, 256.

289. Holladay, "Eastern Nile Delta," in *HP,* 188. Holladay expects to find adult burials near this site; however, contemporary adult burials currently elude discovery.

290. Ibid.

291. Ibid., 194.

292. Ibid., 195.

293. Ibid., 196.

294. Ibid., 197.

295. Ibid.

296. Ibid., 208.

297. Ibid., 204.

298. Ryholt, *Political Situation,* 144.

299. Ibid., 144–48, 309; and Janine Bourriau "SIP," in *OHAE,* 204–5.

300. Malcolm Wiener and James Allen, "Separate Lives: The Ahmose Tempest Stela and the Theran Eruption," *JNES* 57/1 (January 1998) 21.

301. *KG,* 50–56; and O'Connor, "The Hyksos," in *HP,* 57.

302. Ryholt, *Political Situation,* 144.

303. Redford, "Kamose I and Kamose II: Textual Sources," in *HP,* 13.

304. Ibid.

305. James Allen, "Separate Lives: The Ahmose Tempest Stela," 3, 7, 17.

306. Ibid., 7.

307. Ibid. 7, 19.

308. Redford, "Textual Sources," in *HP,* 16, emphasis added.

309. Allen, "Separate Lives: The Ahmose Tempest Stele," 18.

310. Redford, "Textual Sources," in *HP,* 31 n.178.

311. Wiener and Allen render "corpses" ("Ahmose Tempest Stele," 11).

312. Both times this text has been revisited (Wiener and Allen, "Ahmose Tempest Stele," 11–12; and Karen Foster, Robert Ritner and Benjamin R. Foster, "Texts, Storms, and the Thera Eruption," *JNES* 55/1 [January 1996] 10–12), Egyptologists could find no other explanation than that a massive, "howling" storm flooded an area large enough to contain temples, tombs, and houses, and possibly left bodies in its wake.

313. Redford, "Textual Sources," in *HP,* 3.

314. Janine Bourriau, "Beyond Avaris: The Second Intermediate Period in Egypt Outside the Eastern Delta," in *HP,* 161–63.

315. Ibid.

316. Betsy Bryan, "The 18th Dynasty Before the Amarna Period," in *OHAE,* 210.

317. Ibid.

318. Allen, "Separate Lives: The Ahmose Tempest Stele," 11, 13, 18.

319. *CGAE,* 61–62; Allen, "Separate Lives: The Ahmose Tempest Stele," 18.

320. Allen renders "providing cover" (Ahmose Tempest Stele, 13) in lieu of "hidden faces, having no clothing on them"; however, this text could imply that during the storm his army had to cover their faces in order to breathe. I have not quoted this section of the text.

321. Redford, "Textual Sources," in *HP,* 16.

322. *KG,* 134; and Redford, *Ancient Times,* 242.

323. Redford, "Textual Sources," in *HP,* 16.

324. Allen, "Separate Lives: The Ahmose Tempest Stele," 15.

325. *KG,* 50–56.

326. Allen, "Separate Lives: The Ahmose Tempest Stele," 16.

327. *JFB,* 62; and Kitchen, *Reliability,* 249–53.

328. Allen, "Separate Lives: The Ahmose Tempest Stele," 13.

329. Bourriau "SIP," in *OHAE,* 205; Foster, et al., "Texts, Storms, and the Thera Eruption," 1–14; Dever, *Early Israelites,* 21. See also Ian Wilson, *Exodus Enigma* (London: Weidenfeld and Nicolson, 1985) 86–114.

330. Bietak, "Center of Hyksos Rule," in *HP,* 124.

331. The New Kingdom begins with Ahmose's ascension upon Kamose's death. Again the question is debated among scholars. Grimal considers 1570, 1560, or 1551 BCE as possibilities for Ahmose's enthronement (*Ancient Egypt,* 193, 202); Ryholt holds to 1549 (*Political Situation,* 410); and O'Connor dates Ahmose's reign to begin in 1551 ("Hyksos Period," in *HP,* 56).

332. Holladay, "Eastern Nile Delta," in *HP,* 212 n.28.

333. Bietak, "Center of Hyksos Rule," in *HP,* 124–25.

334. Ibid. Analysis was provided by Prof. Anton Preisinger and Dr. Max Bichler, Institute for Mineralogy of the Technical University and the Reactor Sibersdorf, Austria. For use of pumice and ash deposits in relation to chronological dating, see Caitlin Buck and Andrew Millard, *Tools for Constructing Chronologies: Crossing Disciplinary Boundaries* (Lecture Notes on Statistics: 177; London: Springer-Verlag, 2004) 84–93.

335. Bietak, "Center of Hyksos Rule," in *HP,* 125.

336. See also Wilson, *Exodus Enigma,* 97–114. I theorize that the significant gas emissions and large ash plumes that preceeded Thera's cataclysmic eruption contributed to Egypt's violent rainstorm. This rainstorm then contributed to the dome collapse that caused Thera to explode a short time later [see James Randerson, "Rainstorms Could Trigger Killer Eruptions," *NewScientist* (August 2002), http://www.newscientist.com/article/dn2755-rainstorms-could-trigger-killer-eruptions.html#.UcTcGPm-siqc (accessed January 2015); Staff, "Rainstorms Might Trigger Volcanic Blowouts," *Current Science* 88/8 (December 2002) 14]. For a general understanding of volcanos and weather, see Scott Rowland, et al., "How Do Volcanoes Affect the Atmosphere and Climate?" Volcano World (Department of Geosciences at Oregon State University), http://volcano.oregonstate.edu/how-do-volcanoes-affect-atmosphere-and-climate (accessed January 2015); "Volcanic Activity," Global Climate Change http://www.global-climate-change.org.uk/2-6-3.php (accessed January 2015); "Climate Effects of Volcanic Eruptions," How Volcanos Work (Geoloical Sciences at San Diego State University), http://www.geology.sdsu.edu/how_volcanoes_work/climate_effects.html (accessed January 2015).

337. Wilson, *Exodus Enigma,* 97–114. Wilson's associating Thera to Israel's pillar of cloud by day and pillar of fire by night (Exod 31:21–22; 14:19, 24; and Num 14:14) is sorely misplaced since Scripture demonstrates the movability of this phenomenon. For this present study, Thera is proposed simply as *a probable cause* for Egypt's three days of darkness and the violent rainstorm (via gases, heat release into the atmosphere, etc.), which pelted Egypt a month before.

338. Wiener, "Separate Lives: The Ahmose Tempest Stele," 27 n.53. Dever (*Early Israelites,* 21) had originally supported the high/early date of 1675 BCE for Thera's eruption. More recent archaeological discoveries (ash at Palestinian sites) and scientific data have virtually eliminated the high date. See Buck and Millard, *Tools for Constructing Chronologies: Crossing Disciplinary Boundaries,* 84–93; and Bietak, "The Center of Hyksos Rule," in *HP,* 115–17, 125–28. See also Tiziano Fantuzzi, "The Absolute Chronology of the Egyptian S.I.P. New Kingdom Transition and Implications for Late Minoan Crete," *Creta Antica* 10/2 (2009) 477–500.

339. Bourriau, "SIP," in *OHAE,* 204; Ryholt, *Political Situation,* 142–43; Grimal, *Ancient Egypt,* 200; and Fantuzzi, "Absolute Chronology of the Egyptian S.I.P. New Kingdom Transition and Implications for Late Minoan Crete," 477–500.

340. Bietak, "The Center of Hyksos Rule," in *HP,* 117. Unlike the archaeological evidence found at Pompeii, archaeologists have discovered very few corpses under lava flows that covered Thera's cities (Wilson, *Exodus Enigma,* 86–127). Volcanoes usually give warning signs such as earthquakes and ruptured steam vents before eruption (as Mt. St. Helen's did in 1980). This would have allowed the majority of Thera's population to evacuate months or years prior to the final blast. As Bietak concludes (*HP,* p. 124) the reason that a Minoan presence is so strong in Egypt's Delta versus Canaan—where Minoan artifacts also suddenly appear—is that Egypt probably needed their navy's sea power and thus formed an alliance.

341. Bietak, "The Center of Hyksos Rule," in *HP,* 125. After the epidemic (see above), Avaris began to expand again, perhaps as a result of pre-eruption Aegean migration into the Delta. This could account for both the increase in population and the evidence of Minoan wares for the first time. It should be noted that if Therans had not evacuated until the actual eruption, very few would have survived, given the massive destruction attested on the island. Therefore, a substantial migration should have

preceded Thera's eruption, with a continual flow of immigrants after the final explosion, as displaced communities regrouped in new cities of Diaspora.

342. Ryholt, *Political Situation,* 145.

343. Ibid.

344. Allen, "Separate Lives: The Ahmose Tempest Stele," 18, parentheses added.

345. Redford, "Textual Sources," in *HP,* 16–17.

346. Wiener, "Separate Lives: The Ahmose Tempest Stele," 24.

347. *ANET,* 252.

348. Ibid.

349. Ibid.

350. I have used Miriam Lichtheim's translations as they give the feel for the tone and the situation in Egypt. As an accurate translation, however, they are lacking. For a more accurate translation, see P. Montet, *Byblos et l'Egypte; quatre campagnes de fouilles a Gebeil* (2 vols.; Paris: P. Geutehr, 1928–29).

351. A.R. Millard, "Story, History, and Theology," in *FTH,* 53.

352. Halpern, *The First Historians,* 3–32; and Millard, "Story, History, and Theology," in *FTH,* 37–64.

353. Vincent Tobin, "The Admonitions of an Egyptian Sage," in *The Literature of Ancient Egypt* (ed. William Simpson, New Haven: Yale University Press, 2003) 188–210.

354. Tobin, "Admonitions," in *Literature of Ancient Egypt,* 188. Quite recently, Janine Bourriau has argued that in reality the Middle Kingdom extended to the end of the SIP (Bourriau, "Beyond Avaris: The Second Intermediate Period in Egypt Outside the Eastern Delta," in *HP,* 168).

355. Redford, *Ancient Times,* 66.

356. Ryholt, *Political Situation,* 2–3; and Tobin, "Admonitions" in *Literature of Ancient Egypt,* 188.

357. Miriam Lichtheim, *Ancient Egyptian Literature: The Old and Middle Kingdoms* (Berkeley: University of California Press, 2006) 149–62.

358. Redford, "Textual Sources," in *HP,* 16–17.

359. Ryholt, *Political Situation,* 137–38.

360. Ibid.,138.

361. Holladay, "Eastern Nile Delta," in *HP,* 196.

362. Lichtheim, *Ancient Egyptian Literature: The Old and Middle Kingdoms,* 149–62.

363. Clayton, *Chronicles,* 101.

364. Callender, "Middle Kingdom," in *OHAE,* 168.

365. Ibid.

366. Ibid.

367. Ibid., 169.

368. O'Connor, "Hyksos Period," in *HP,* 48, 52; and Ryholt, *Political Situation,* 34–65.

369. Ryholt, *Political Situation,* 94–117, 251–56.

370. Lichtheim, *Ancient Egyptian Literature, Old and Middle Kingdom,* 149. Attempts to see one of the plagues from the Exodus in this account are quite unjustified and take Ipuwer out of context.

371. Lichtheim, *Ancient Egyptian Literature, Old and Middle Kingdom,* 151–57.

372. Egypt did not recognize "private" land: all land belonged to Pharaoh. However, pharaohs would give land grants that would last until another pharaoh recalled the land and gave it to another (Goelet, "'Town' and 'Country' in Ancient Egypt," in *ULO,* 90–91).

373. Miriam Lichtheim, *Ancient Egyptian Literature: Old and Middle Kingdom,* 153.

374. Tobin, "The Admonitions of an Egyptian Sage," in *Literature of Ancient Egypt,* 193; and Van Seters, *Hyksos,* 108–9. See also, Lichtheim, *Ancient Egyptian Literature: Old and Middle Kingdom,* 152.

375. Perhaps meaning that the storekeeper is stretched out dead on the ground.

376. Lichtheim, *Ancient Egyptian Literature: Old and Middle Kingdom,* 153–56.

377. Tobin, "Admonitions," 208.

378. Ryholt, *Political Situation,* 300–1 n.1053. Attempts to associate these famines with Joseph are quite misplaced. These texts demonstrate that famine arose from a lack of civil order and the depletion of

food supplies, which was perhaps aided by low inundation levels. If Joseph had stored grain for seven years (Gen 41:34–36), it would have been emptied by the rebels during this era.

379. Redford, *Textual Sources*, 2–3.

380. Van Seters, *Hyksos*, 108; and John Wilson, *The Culture of Ancient Egypt* (Chicago: University of Chicago Press, 1951) 108. See also Lichtheim, *Ancient Egyptian Literature: Old and Middle Kingdom*, 152.

381. Van Seters, *Hyksos*, 109–10; and Ryholt, *Political Situation*, 177. Van Seters is basing his interpretation on *Admonitions* 3:6–10.

382. Redford, "Kamose I: Textual Sources," in *HP*, 13–14.

383. Lichtheim, *Ancient Egyptian Literature: Old and Middle Kingdom*, 154.

384. Ibid., 151, 154; and Tobin, "The Admonitions of an Egyptian Sage," in *Literature of Ancient Egypt*, 194, 196, 197.

385. Lichtheim, "Ipuwer," in *Ancient Egyptian Literature: Middle Kingdom*, 198.

386. *ANET*, 10.

387. Lichtheim, "Ipuwer," *in Ancient Egyptian Literature: Middle Kingdom*, 197–98.

388. Ibid., 198.

389. O'Connor, "Hyksos Period," in *HP*, 57.

390. Geraldine Pinch, *Egyptian Mythology* (Oxford: Oxford University Press, 2002) 74–75.

391. Ibid.; E. W. Budge, *Legends of the Gods* (London: Kegan Paul, Trench, Trubner, 1912) 26; *ANET*, 11; and Lichtheim, "Destruction of Mankind," in *Egyptian Literature: New Kingdom* (vol. 2; Berkeley: University of California Press, 2006) 198.

392. *ANET*, 11 n.11.

393. Lichtheim, "Destruction of Mankind," in *Egyptian Literature: New Kingdom*, 199; Edward Wente, "The Book of the Heavenly Cow," in *The Literature of Ancient Egypt* (New Heaven: Yale University, 2003) 291; and Pinch, *Egyptian Mythology*, 138, 187–89.

394. *ANET*, 11; and Budge, *Legends*, 27.

395. Budge, *Legends*, 25; and *ANET*, 11.

396. Ibid.

397. Budge, *Legends*, 26; and *ANET*, 11.

398. Lichtheim, *Egyptian Literature: New Kingdom*, 199; and Wente, "Book of the Heavenly Cow," in *Literature of Ancient Egypt*, 291.

399. Budge, *Legends*, 27.

400. Ibid., 28.

401. Grimal, *Ancient Egypt*, 224–25; Claude Traunecker, *The Gods of Egypt* (trans. David Lorton; Ithaca: Cornell University, 2001) 68–69; and *CGAE*, 63.

402. Allen, "Separate Lives: The Ahmose Tempest Stele," 19.

403. Redford, Textual Sources," in *HP*, 9; and Idem. *Ancient Times*, 112.

404. Bourriau, "Beyond Avaris," in *HP*, 160, 163, 168.

405. *CGAE*, 53, 185; and Lichtheim, *Egyptian Literature: New Kingdom*, 199.

406. *CGAE*, 63.

407. Ryholt, *Political Situation*, 149–50; Redford, *Ancient Times*, 116–17; O'Connor, "Hyksos Period," in *HP*, 56; and *OHAE*, 177.

408. Albright, *Yahweh and the Gods of Canaan*, 127.

409. Ibid.

410. Grimal, *Ancient Egypt*, 42.

411. Pinch, *Egyptian Mythology*, 106–8; and Hart, *Dictionary of Egyptian Gods and Goddesses*, 31–33.

412. Ibid.

413. *ANET*, 231 n.10.

414. *CGAE*, 158–59, 164, 169, 179; and Wilkinson, *The Complete Gods and Goddesses of Ancient Egypt*, 221–23.

415. Ibid.; Traunecker, *The Gods of Egypt*, 85–86; and Ian Shaw and Paul Nicholson, *British Museum Dictionary of Ancient Egypt*, 37–39, 295–97.

416. Wilkinson, *Gods and Goddesses of Ancient Egypt*, 223.

417. Traunecker, *The Gods of Egypt*, 82; and Wilkinson, *Gods and Goddesses of Ancient Egypt*, 221.

418. *CGAE*, 158–59, 208–9.

419. Wilkinson, *Complete Gods and Goddesses*, 221–23.

420. Ibid., 223.

421. For further discussion of the Exodus plagues, see Wilson, *Exodus Enigma*, 115–50; Hoffmeier, *Israel in Egypt*, 145–53; and Kitchen, *Reliability*, 149–51.

422. Wilson, *Exodus Enigma*, 149–50.

423. Richard Parker, *The Calendars of Ancient Egypt* 26 (Chicago: University of Chicago Press, 1950) 7; and Depuydt, *Civil Calendar and Lunar Calendar in Ancient Egypt*, 49. For questions regarding the various calendars employed in ancient Egypt, see Depuydt, 14–20.

424. Parker, *Calendars*, 11–13, 32; and Leo Depuydt, *Civil and Lunar Calendar*, 14, 49.

425. Leo Depuydt, *Civil and Lunar Calendar*, 18.

426. Ibid., 99.

427. Richards, *Mapping Time*, 46. See also Parker, *Calendars*, 31–34; and Depuydt, *Civil and Lunar Calendar*, 14–15.

428. Parker, *Calendars*, 31–32.

429. Hoffmeier, *Israel in Egypt*, 146. Kitchen also associates the plague cycle with the Egyptian civil calendar. The only difference between Kitchen's model and the one presented here is the occurrence of the 5th and 6th plagues, both of which Kitchen places in January (Kitchen, *Reliability*, 251).

430. Kitchen, *Reliability*, 249–51.

431. Miano, *Shadow on the Steps*, 31–35; Wagenaar, *Israelite Festival Calendar*, 16–17; Redford, *Ancient Times*, 211; and *ANET*, 238 n.1.

432. Paul Nicholson and Ian Shaw, ed., *Ancient Egyptian Materials and Technology* (New York: Cambridge University Press, 2000) 522, 524, 616.

433. Kitchen, *Reliability*, 250–51; and Miano, *Shadow on the Steps*, 33. Egypt's civil calendar varied over the centuries due to the fact that it was off by a quarter-day from the solar year. Thus, eventually the first month would fall in winter. Every 1,460 years, the calendar "reset" itself and was accurate again. Though the calendar "wandered," Depuydt posits that the overall concept of the "ideal" or "correct" Sothic calendar persisted so that Egyptians continually thought of the first month of the inundation as Akhet, even when the calendar had "slipped out of alignment" (*Civil and Lunar Calendar*, 15–20, 49–52). It is unknown if the priests used other means to keep the Egyptian calendar in line with a solar year. Note: A forensics approach uses a broad spectrum of sciences and technologies for use in court in order to reconstruct an event.

434. Grimal, *Ancient Egypt*, 114.

435. Ibid. See also Kitchen, *Reliability*, 247–48.

436. Hart, *Dictionary of Egyptian Gods and Goddesses*, 214–18; Pinch, *Egyptian Mythology*, 209–11; Parker, *Calendars*, 8; and Depuydt, *Civil and Lunar Calendar*, 110–121, 126–36.

437. Wilkinson, *The Complete Gods and Goddesses of Ancient Egypt*, 216.

438. Hart, *Egyptian Gods and Goddesses*, 75–76; Pinch, *Egyptian Mythology*, 136–37; and Wilkinson, *The Complete Gods and Goddesses of Ancient Egypt*, 106. See also, Mirjam Nebet, "The Ancient Egyptian Calendar," The Egyptian World (Last updated October 26, 2007) http://www.ancientworlds.net/aw/Article/998323 (accessed January 2015).

439. Scott Noegel, "Moses and Magic: Notes on the Book of Exodus," *JANES* 24 (1996) 46.

440. Hart, *Egyptian Gods and Goddesses*, 172–77; Pinch, *Egyptian Mythology*, 181–82; Parker, *Calendars*, 8; and Depuydt, *Civil and Lunar Calendar*, 110–121, 126–36. See also http://www.ancientworlds.net/aw/Article/998323.

441. Wilkinson, *Complete Gods and Goddesses*, 124–26.

442. Ibid., 106.

443. *CGAE*, 277.

444. Turner and Coulter, *Dictionary of Ancient Deities*, 206; and Pat Remier, *Egyptian Mythology A–Z* (New York: Chelsea, 2010) 75–77, 171–72.

445. *CGAE*, 277.

446. Pinch, *Egyptian Mythology*, 137–39.

447. Carl Friedrich Keil and Franz Delitzsh, *Biblical Commentary on the Old Testament* (http://www.sacred-texts.com/bib/cmt/kad/ex0008.htm (accessed January 2015).

448. Kitchen, *Reliability*, 250–51.

449. Corey J. Chimko, "Foreign Pharaohs: Self-Legitimization and Indigenous Reaction in Art and Literature," *JSSEA* 30 (2003) 20–22.

450. For further discussion see in this pp 479–82 in this chapter. See also Pinch, *Egyptian Mythology*, 187–89; and Hart, *Dictionary of Egyptian Gods and Goddesses*, 187–89.

451. *CGAE*, 53, 185; and Lichtheim, *Egyptian Literature: New Kingdom*, 199.

452. Budge, *Gods of the Egyptians* (vol. 1), 388, 392.

453. Parker, *Calendars*, 8; and Depuydt, *Civil and Lunar Calendar*, 110–121, 126–36.

454. Wilkinson, *Complete Gods and Goddesses*, 115–17, 153–56; Shaw and Nicholson, *Dictionary of Ancient Egypt*, 209, 215; Hart, Dictionary of Egyptian Gods and Goddesses, 128–29; Pinch, *Egyptian Mythology*, 168–69; and http://www.ancientworlds.net/aw/Article/998323.

455. Wilkinson, *Complete Gods and Goddesses*, 115–17; Pinch, *Egyptian Mythology*, 168–69; and Hart, *Dictionary of Gods and Goddesses*, 121–26.

456. Wilkinson, *Complete Gods and Goddesses*, 153–54; and Shaw and Nicholson, *Dictionary of Ancient Egypt*, 215

457. Wilkinson, *Complete Gods and Goddesses*, 153–54.

458. See in this chapter pp. 479–82 and Chimko, "Foreign Pharaohs," *JSSEA* 30 (2003) 20–22.

459. Wilkinson, *Complete Gods and Goddesses*, 155.

460. Gudrun Dahl and Anders Hjort, *Having Herds: Pastoral Hert Growth and Household Economy* (University of Stockholm, 1976) 89–91; and Wagenaar, *Israelite Festival Calendar*, 46.

461. Ancient Worlds, "The Ancient Egyptian Calendar," http://www.ancientworlds.net/aw/Article/998323; and Wilkinson, *Complete Gods and Goddesses*, 146–49.

462. *CGAE*, 88.

463. Parker, *Calendars*, 8; and Depuydt, *Civil and Lunar Calendar*, 110–121, 126–36.

464. *CGAE*, 86–88, 90, 274–75; Shaw and Nicholson, *Dictionary of Ancient Egypt*, 92–97; and Wilkinson, *Complete Gods and Goddesses*, 33; Hart, *Dictionary of Egyptian Gods and Goddesses*, 4–17; and Pinch, *Egyptian Mythology*, 100–102.

465. Ibid.

466. http://www.philae.nu/akhet/NetjeruA.html#Amun (accessed June 2012).

467. Ibid.

468. Parker, *Calendars*, 8; and Depuydt, *Civil and Lunar Calendar*, 110–121, 126–36.

469. Wilson, *The Exodus Enigma*, 115–127.

470. When Mt. St. Helen's erupted in 1980, I was living in Washington state and saw the unusual rain patterns that preceded the initial blast. Ian Wilson cites similar weather patterns with other volcanic eruptions in his book *The Exodus Enigma* (chaps. 6–8).

471. Ryholt, *Political Situation*, 309; and *ANET*, 231.

472. Nicholson and Shaw, *Ancient Egyptian Materials and Technology*, 270; and A. Lucas, *Ancient Egyptian Materials and Industries* (London: Edward Arnold, 1948) 166–68.

473. Ibid., 268–78.

474. Ibid., 166–68.

475. Alex J. Warden, *The Linen and Trade Ancient and Modern* (London: Longman, Green, Roberts, 1867) 4–7; and "Growing Flax," Flax Council of Canada, http://www.flaxcouncil.ca/english/index.jsp?p=growing5&mp=growing (accessed January 2015).

476. Ibid.; and Nicholson and Shaw, *Ancient Egyptian Materials and Technology*, 270.

477. Ibid.

478. Carl Friedrich Keil and Franz Delitzsh, "Exodus 9," in *Biblical Commentary on the Old Testament,* http://www.sacred-texts.com/bib/cmt/kad/exo009.htm (accessed January 2015).

479. Pliny, *Natural History,* Book XIX (ed. John Bostock and H.T. Riley; London: Henry Bohn, 1856) 131–32. In Egypt the months of summer began in mid-March to mid-April (see p. 500–2 below).

480. Nicholson and Shaw, *Ancient Egyptian Materials and Technology,* 270–71.

481. Ibid., 270.

482. Ibid., 569.

483. Ibid., 519, 270.

484. Ibid., 519.

485. Recent studies have shown that sowing diverse crops, such as cereal grains and legumes increases both the availability of nitrogen and the amount of protein within the plant while allowing more efficient use of the land (Elena N Pasynkova and Aleksander Pasynkov, "Efficiency of the Mixed Crops of Spring Cereals and Legumes Cultivated on Sod-podzolic Soil" *Agricultural and Forest Engineering* 57 (Kirov, Russia, 2011) 15–19; and K. Fujita, K. G. Ofosu-Budu and S. Ogata, "Biological Nitrogen Fixation in Mixed Legume-cereal Cropping Systems," *Plant and Soil* 141/1–2 [October, 2007] 155–175).

486. The *sha'atnez* garment prohibited in Lev 19:19 is a specific type of Egyptian priestly garment (*Sha'atnez* is an Egyptian loanword). Lev 13:47–59 cites other types of mixed linen and wool fabrics that are not prohibited. Thus the ban did not prohibit the mixing of fibers but the wearing of a garment typical of Egyptian priests (T. O. Lambdin, "Egyptian Loan Words in the Old Testament," *JAOS* 73/3 [1953] 155; and Ludwig Köhler and Walter Baumgartner, *The Hebrew and Aramaic Lexicon of the Old Testament* [vol. 2; trans. M. E. Richardson; Leiden: Brill, 2001] 1016–17).

487. Nicholson and Shaw, *Ancient Egyptian Materials and Technology,* 514, 270.

488. Carl Friedrich Keil and Franz Delitzsh, *Biblical Commentary on the Old Testament* (1857–78), http://www.sacred-texts.com/bib/cmt/kad/exo009.htm; and James Hoffmeier and Alfred H. Joy, "Hail," *ISBE* (vol. 2) 596.

489. James Hoffmeier and Alfred H. Joy, "Hail," *ISBE* (vol. 2) 596.

490. Wiener, "Separate Lives," 3, 7; Lichtheim, *Egyptian Literature: New Kingdom,* 199; and Wente "The Book of the Heavenly Cow," in *The Literature of Ancient Egypt,* 291.

491. Hart, *Dictionary of Egyptian Gods and Goddesses,* 182–85; Pinch, *Egyptian Mythology,* 185–86; Parker, *Calendars,* 8; and Depuydt, *Civil and Lunar Calendar,* 110–21, 126–36.

492. http://www.philae.nu/akhet/NetjeruR.html (accessed June 2012).

493. Hart, *Dictionary of Egyptian Gods and Goddesses,* 184.

494. Wagenaar, *Israelite Festival Calendar,* 16–17; and Miano, *Shadow on the Steps,* 25–48. In Egypt, flax ripened at the end of February, whereas in central Israel it ripened at the end of March.

495. Hazel W. Perkin and Gary A. Lee, "Gezer Calendar," *ISBE* (vol. 2) 460.

496. Wagenaar, *Israelite Festival Calendar,* 16.

497. Martin Enserink, "Can the War on Locusts Be Won," *Science Magazine* 306/5703 (December 10, 2004) 1880–82.

498. Kitchen, *Reliability,* 250–51; Ian Wilson, *Enigma,* 122–25; and Staff, "Locust Swarms Advance into Egypt," *BBC News* (November 18, 2004), http://news.bbc.co.uk/2/hi/middle_east/4022871.stm (accessed January 2015).

499. Staff, "Locust swarms advance into Egypt," *BBC News* (November 18, 2004); and Associated Press, "Egypt Swarms with Locusts," *USA Today* (November 17, 2004). Enserink, "Can the War on Locusts Be Won," *Science Magazine,* 1880–82. See also Raymond Kondos, "Swarms of Locusts Invade Egypt," December 1, 2004 (Issue 9), http://www.youregypt.com/issue9/news.htm (accessed January 2015).

500. Kitchen, *Reliability,* 250–51; and Staff, "Locust Swarms Advance into Egypt," *BBC News* (November 18, 2004), http://news.bbc.co.uk/2/hi/middle_east/4022871.stm. Enserink, "Can the War on Locusts Be Won?" 1882.

501. Enserink, "Can the War on Locusts Be Won," 1882.

502. Pinch, *Egyptian Mythology,* 155–56; *CGAE,* 155 n.36; Wilkinson, *Complete Gods and Goddesses,* 83, 113–14; Shaw and Nicholson, *Dictionary of Ancient Egypt,* 169–70; Hart, *Dictionary of Egyptian Gods and Goddesses,* 112–15; and http://www.ancientworlds.net/aw/Article/998323.

503. Parker, *Calendars,* 31; and Depuydt, *Civil and Lunar Calendar,* 16–17, 139, 187–215.

504. Depuydt *Civil and Lunar Calendar,* 40–41, 43, 49–63. See also Parker, *Calendars,* 27, 30–31.

505. Depuydt *Civil and Lunar Calendar,* 21–45, 49–63; and Parker, *Calendars,* 30–31.

506. Shaw and Nicholson, *Dictionary of Ancient Egypt,* 169–70; Wilkinson, *Complete Gods and Goddesses,* 83, 113–14. Pinch, *Egyptian Mythology,* 155.

507. Pinch, *Egyptian Mythology,* 143–45; Hart, *Dictionary of Egyptian Gods and Goddesses,* 87–97; Parker, *Calendars,* 8; and Depuydt, *Civil and Lunar Calendar,* 110–121, 126–36. See also http://www.ancientworlds.net/aw/Article/998323.

508. Wilkinson, *Complete Gods and Goddesses,* 200–3; Shaw and Nicholson, *Dictionary of Ancient Egypt,* 150–51.

509. Wilkinson, *Complete Gods and Goddesses,* 201.

510. *CGAE,* 277.

511. Parker, *Calendars,* 7, 30; Depuydt, *Civil and Lunar Calendar,* 14–18, 35; Richards, *Mapping Time,* 152; and Clayton, *Chronicles,* 12–13.

512. Wagenaar, *Israelite Festival Calendar,* 9–12; Miano, *Shadow Steps,* 30, 35, 41, 203; Cohen, *Cultic Calendars,* 6–7, 400; Finegan, *Handbook,* 16–17; and Steinmann, *Abraham to Paul,* 12–17.

513. Ibid. Other reasonable articles dealing with Israel's New Year and the equinoxes are on the Web. Search by the key words "Leviticus," "New Year," "Turn of the year" or see the following links: "Biblical Calendation: Reckoning the New Year," World's Last Chance.com, http://www.worldslastchance.com/yahuwahs-calendar/biblical-calendation-reckoning-the-new-year.html (accessed February 2015); "When Does the Biblical New Year Start?" YahSaves.org (January 29, 2013) http://yahsaves.org/bbs/viewtopic.php?t=610 (accessed February 2015); ; Don Esposito, "Aviv/Nissan 1 Cannot Start in the Winter" Iahushua.com, http://www.iahushua.com/ST-RP/PDF/Aviv-Nissan-1-Cannot-Start-in-Winter.pdf (accessed February 2015).

514. Cohen, *Cultic Calendars,* 7–8, 400–1; and Wagenaar, *Israelite Festival Calendar,* 10–11.

515. Wagenaar, *Israelite Festival Calendar,* 9–12; Miano, *Shadow Steps,* 30, 35, 41, 203; Cohen, *Cultic Calendars,* 6–7; Finegan, *Handbook,* 16–17; and Steinmann, *Abraham to Paul,* 12–17.

516. Wagenaar, *Israelite Festival Calendar,* 10.

517. Ibid., 9–12; and Cohen, *Cultic Calendars,* 377–86.

518. Wagenaar, *Israelite Festival Calendar,* 10–11, 144–46; and Cohen, *Cultic Calendars,* 400–1.

519. Wagenaar, *Israelite Festival Calendar,* 23, 60.

520. Cohen, *Cultic Calendars,* 400–1.

521. Wagenaar, *Israelite Festival Calendar,* 11, 24; and Cohen, *Cultic Calendars,* 33.

522. *SEC* 4150; BDB, 417–18; and *TWOT* (vol. 1) 388–89.

523. Wagenaar, *Israelite Festival Calendar,* 27–31, 33–44.

524. Ibid., 30–44, 62–78; and Steinmann, *Abraham to Paul,* 15–30. Miano also observes that the planting season lasted until mid-April, with the first barley harvest occurring in April or May (*Shadow Steps,* 31–32).

525. Depuydt makes up for this deficiency, touching on all the major concepts affecting an astronomically based calendar as well as its interplay with agricultural seasons. Any studies attempting to reconstruct Israel's ancient calendar should consider the calendrical concepts that Depuydt presents.

526. Steinmann, *Abraham to Paul,* 12–30; Depuydt, *Civil and Lunar Calendar,* 15–20, 23, 43, 50–56, 61–63.

527. Ibid.; Parker, *Calendars,* 30–31 (based on Sothis sighting, not the equinox). In the past, there has been a trend to associate Israel's new year with the sighting of "green ears," based on the studies of Ginsberg, Milgrom, Levine (Wagenaar, 30–31), coupled with a long-standing Karaite tradition. The idea expressed by the term *Abib* is better rendered 'fresh ears' than 'green ears' (Wagenaar, 31). If the above synchronism between Egyptian and Israelite calendars is correct, it further supports the idea of fresh rather than green ears as the state of barley development intended in Scripture. There is no indication

that Israel or any other ancient nation used the sighting of an agricultural crop to begin its new year. Instead, all calendars were based on some astronomically tied event, which for Israel is in accord with Gen 1:14 for a solar-based year and a lunar-based month.

528. *Shachath* (SEC 7843), translated "destroyer" is also used in Isa 54:16; Jer 12:10; 22:7; 48:18; 49:9; Dan 9:26. Each time the term refers to 'one who destroys' it is in the context of an invading king or Israel's monarchs that have abused Israel's citizens.

529. Schneider points out that since the inferior term, "King of the South" can only refer to a Theban king, the reverse of the Rhind must be based on the regnal years of an Asiatic ruler (Schneider, "The Relative Chronology of the Middle Kingdom and the Hyksos Period (Dyns. 12–17)," 194–95).

530. Van Seters, *Hyksos,* 93.

531. Ryholt, *Political Situation,* 188, emphasis added.

532. Ibid., 187.

533. Redford, "Kamose II Textual Sources," in *HP,* 14–15.

534. Van Seters, *Hyksos,* 93.

535. Finkelstein and Silberman, *Bible Unearthed,* 76–78, 160; and Willaim Dever, *Early Israelites,* 41–50.

536. Finkelstein and Silberman, *Bible Unearthed,* 60. For similar criticisms see Dever, *Early Israelites,* 26–30.

537. Hoffmeier, *Israel in Egypt,* 59–61.

538. Ibid. One of the best treatments regarding all the theories of the exodus route is on the Web site of a lay scholar, Walter Mattfeld at: http://www.bibleorigins.net/ExodusRouteMapsVarious.html, last updated June 14, 2009 (accessed January 2015).

539. One website which presents the Scriptural evidence the this case is: Steve Rudd, "The Exodus Route: Goshen to the Red Sea" Bible.ca., http://www.bible.ca/archeology/bible-archeology-exodus-route-goshen-red-sea.htm (accessed February 2015); idem, "Migdol 'Watchtower,'" http://www.bible.ca/archeology/bible-archeology-exodus-route-migdol.htm (accessed January 2015); Penny Caldwell, "The Split Rock," Split Rock Research, http://splitrockresearch.org/content/100/Field_Reports/The_Split_Rock (accessed January 2015). Gordan Franz ("Is Mount Sinai in Saudi Arabia?") presents a good counter-argument to Jabel el-Lawz at http://www.ldolphin.org/franz-sinai.html, last updated October 18, 2000 (accessed January 2015). Franz makes an excellent point that the many artifacts strewn throughout the region are of Nabatean origin (200BCE–100 CE). These later artifacts do not disqualify many of the other geological features and artifacts that are consonant with the Exodus account. In particular, according to Gen 24:62 Abraham and Isaac were living south of Mamre. Before his death, Abraham sent Midian to the "east country" (Gen 25:4–5). This would preclude the land of Midian from being in the Sinai Peninsula; however, it would not preclude the "Land of Midian" being east of Mt. Horeb or in a nearby location, thus Franz's argument against Jabel el-Lawz geographic location is weak. Given a 1548 Exodus date, there would be no political obstacle to this location.

540. For popular Exodus models, see Dever, *Early Israelites,* 16–26; Hoffmeier, *Israel in Egypt,* 164–215; Kitchen, *Reliability,* 254–74 and http://www.bibleorigins.net/ExodusRouteMapsVarious.html.

541. Bryant Wood's website has many excellent articles on the Exodus route at http://www.biblearchaeology.org. See: "Is Mount Sinai in Saudi Arabia?" and "New Evidence from Egypt on the Location of the Exodus Sea Crossing: Part I" and "Part II." Although Wood is adamant against associating Mt. Sinai with Jabel el Lawz in Saudi Arabia, this location has not yet had the privilege of an unbiased investigation, due mostly by the many constraints placed on the field by the Saudi Arabian government.

CHAPTER ELEVEN

1. Kuhn, *Structure of Scientific Revolutions,* 24–25.

2. Redford, *Ancient Times,* 258–60; and Hoffmeier, "What is the Biblical Date for the Exodus?" *JETS,* 226–39.

3. Amon Ben-Tor, "Introduction," in *AOAI*, 2. See Bimson's counter to the idea that all theories of the Conquest have been "exhausted" (*Redating*, 27).

4. Remember that Egyptian chronology differs by about 30–40 years, depending on where the Sothis sighting occurred at the beginning of the 18th Dynasty (See Grimal, *Ancient Egypt*, 202–3).

5. Redford, *Ancient Times*, 94. See also Dever, *Early Israelites*, 68.

6. Charles Krahmalkov, "Exodus Itinerary Confirmed by Egyptian Evidence," *BAR* 20/5 (Sept/Oct, 1994) 54–62; and Dever, *Early Israelites*, 67–68.

7. Dever, *Early Israelites*, 68.

8. Ibid., 45; Kenyon, *Digging Up Jericho*, 167–265; and Miriam Davis, *Dame Kathleen Kenyon: Digging Up the Holy Land* (Walnut Creek, CA: Left Coast Press, 2008) 101–127.

9. The noted exception is Bryant Wood, relying on John Garstang's former fieldwork at Jericho. For Wood's rebuttal to the lack of data supporting a fourteenth century Conquest, see http://www.biblearchaeology.org/post/2012/03/28/Dating-Jerichos-Destruction-Bienkowski-is-Wrong-on-All-Counts.aspx (accessed January 2015). See also, Hoffmeier, *Israel in Egypt*, 7.

10. Dever, *Early Israelites*, 46; and Finkelstein and Silberman, *Unearthed*, 81–82.

11. Hendrick Bruins and Johannes van der Plicht, "Tell Es-Sultan (Jericho) Radiocarbon Results of Short-Lived Cereal and Multiyear Charcoal Samples from the End of the Middle Bronze Age," *Radiocarbon* 37/2 (1995) 213–20.

12. Dever, *Early Israelites*, 31.

13. Bimson, *Redating*, 65. Based on the Egyptian chronology that is used, this date could vary by about 30 years.

14. Ibid., 59, 65.

15. Finkelstein and Silberman, *Bible Unearthed*, 72.

16. Redford, *Ancient Times*, 264.

17. *JPS Tanach* (Philadelphia, PA: Jewish Publication Society, 1988) 345.

18. Kenyon, *Digging Up Jericho*, 44–46, 210–65; and Dever, *Early Israelites*, 37–50, 56–68.

19. Kenyon, *Digging Up Jericho*, 45, 256–65; and Finkelstein and Silberman, *Unearthed*, 57–68, 81–94.

20. Finkelstein and Silberman, *Unearthed*, 82, see also 76–77.

21. Ibid., 105.

22. Ibid., 109–10.

23. Finkelstein and Silberman, *Bible Unearthed*, 72–94.

24. Kenyon, *Digging Up Jericho*, 44–46, 22, 228–29; and William Dever, "Settlement Patterns and Chronology of the Palestine in the Middle Bronze Age," in *HP*, 286–95.

25. Redford, *Ancient Times*, 121; and Aharon Kempinski, "The Middle Bronze Age," in *AOAI*, 184–93.

26. Kempinski, "The Middle Bronze Age," in *AOAI*, 166–73, 175–99.

27. Ibid., 182–99; and Dever, "Settlement Patterns and Chronology," in *HP*, 289–92.

28. Dever, "Settlement Patterns and Chronology," in *HP*, 291.

29. Rivka Gonen, "The Late Bronze Age," in *AOAI*, 217–18.

30. It may be remembered that there are numerous scholarly debates over chronology of this era. Manfred Bietak is working with other scholars, blending the world of archaeology with other scientific disciplines to create a comprehensive model. At this point in time, standard deviations for this era run 30–100 years (see Otto Cichocki, et al, "The Synchronization of Civilizations in the Eastern Mediterranean in the Second Millennium BC: Natural Science Dating Attempts" *in Tools for Constructing Chronologies: Crossing Disciplinary Boundaries* (Caitlin Buck, ed; London, Springer, 2004) 83–105.

31. Rivka Gonen, "The Late Bronze Age," in *AOAI*, 217–18.

32. Dever, "Settlement Patterns and Chronology," in *HP*, 288; and Kenyon, *Digging up Jericho*, 44–46, 170, 177, 180–81, 188–89, 214, 229–30, 261–62.

33. Ibid.

34. Kenyon, *Digging Up Jericho*, 186–232; Finkelstein and Silberman, *Unearthed*, 75–96; and Dever, *Early Israelites*, 23–100.

35. William Dever, "Settlement Patterns," in *HP*, 293–94. The parenthesis "(MB III)" is added, subsequent parenthesis are Dever's; bolding is mine. See also Redford, *Ancient Times*, 138; and Aharon Kempinski, "The Middle Bronze Age," in *AOAI*, 184–94.
36. Ibid.
37. Redford, *Ancient Times*, 138–39 (parenthesis added). See also Rivka Gonen, "The Late Bronze Age," in *AOAI*, 246.
38. Redford, *Ancient Times*, 137.
39. Dever, "Settlement Patterns and Chronology," in *HP*, 293; Manfred Bietak and Ernst Czerny, eds., "The Synchronisation of the Civilisations in the Eastern Mediterranean in the Second Millennium B.C. III,"*Proceedings of the SCIEM 2000–2nd EuroConverenceVienna, 28th of May—1st of June 2003* (Verlag der Osterreichishen Akademie der Wissenschaften, 2007); and Manfred Bietak and Felix Hoflmayer, "Introduction: High and Low Chronology, http://dendro.cornell.edu/articles/manning2007a. pdf (accessed January 2015).
40. Kitchen, *Reliability*, 204–8.
41. Kitchen, "The Exodus," in *ABD*, 702; and idem, *Reliability*, 203. Factors affecting this chronology would be Joshua's being younger than 80 when crossing the Jordan into Canaan; Othniel's living longer than the 108 years estimated in chap. 9; whether or not Samuel judged Israel separately from the "time of the Philistines" within the Judges chronology before King Saul; the length of King Saul's reign; whether Sampson was Shamgar. Each of these factors could push Israel's chronology further back in time. As noted previously, James Hoffmeier allows up to 633 years from the Exodus to Solomon's 4th year (Hoffmeier, "What is the Biblical Date for the Exodus?" *JETS*, 226–28).
42. Redford, *Ancient Times*, 93; and Georges Roux, *Ancient Iraq* (London: Penguin Books, 1966) 273–74.
43. Redford, *Ancient Times*, 100.
44. Ibid., 167–68.
45. Dever, "Settlements and Chronologies," in *HP*, 287.
46. Ibid.
47. Ibid.; Redford, *Ancient Times*, 63; and Kempinski, "The Middle Bronze Age," in *AOAI*, 167.
48. Dever, "Settlements and Chronologies," in *HP*, 287; and Redford, *Ancient Times*, 63.
49. Redford, *Ancient Times*, 64.
50. Ibid.
51. Ibid., 287; and 290.
52. Redford, *Ancient Times*, 93.
53. Dever, "Settlements and Chronologies," in *HP*, 292.
54. Ibid., 289; and Redford, *Ancient Times*, 95.
55. Dever, "Settlements and Chronologies," in *HP*, 286, 290.
56. Ibid.; Redford, *Ancient Times*, 96; Aharon Kempinski, "The Middle Bronze Age," in *AOAI*, 166–67.
57. Redford, *Ancient Times*, 79.
58. Dever, "Settlements and Chronologies," in *HP*, 290.
59. Stephan Seidlmayer, "The First Intermediate Period," in *OHAE*, 110–135.
60. Redford, *Ancient Times*, 80.
61. Dever, "Settlements and Chronologies," in *HP*, 292; and Kempinski, "The Middle Bronze Age," in *AOAI*, 166–72.
62. Dever, "Settlements and Chronologies," in *HP*, 291.
63. Redford, *Ancient Times*, 96.
64. Ibid.
65. Dever, "Settlements and Chronologies," in *HP*, 291.
66. Ibid., 292.
67. Aharon Kempinski, "The Hyksos: A View from Northern Canaan and Syria," in *HP*, 329. See also the official site: "Alakh Report," http://alalakh.org/report_main.asp (accessed January 2015). A similar site is Tel Kabri (Stuart Thornton, "Tel Kabri Project," September 19, 2013, National Geographic,

http://education.nationalgeographic.com/education/news/tel-kabri-project/?ar_a=1 (accessed January 2015).

68. "Tall el-Hammam Excavation Project," College of Archaeology, Trinity Southwest University and the Department of Antiquities of the Hashemite Kingdom of Jordan, 2015, http://www.tallelhammam.com/(accessed January 2015).

69. Eliezer Oren, "The 'Kingdom of Sharuhen' and the Hyksos Kingdom," in *HP,* 253–80.

70. Ibid., 255–59.

71. Ibid.

72. Redford, *Ancient Times,* 121.

73. Ibid., 253.

74. Ibid., 253; and Redford, *Ancient Times,* 129.

75. Redford, *Ancient Times,* 121.

76. Rivka Gonen, "The Late Bronze Age," in *AOAI,* 213; and Redford, *Ancient Times,* 206.

77. Oren, "Kingdom of Sharuhen," in *HP,* 271–72.

78. Dever, *Early Israelites,* 21.

79. Ibid.

80. Ibid., 359.

81. Bietak, "The Center of Kysos Rule: Avaris (Tell el-Daba)," in *HP,* 103–4.

82. Paula Wapnish, "Middle Bronze Equid Burials at Tell Jemmeh and a Reexamination of a Purportedly 'Hyksos' Practice," in *HP,* 353–55, 60.

83. Ibid., 361–62.

84. Ibid., 349–53.

85. Ibid.

86. Ibid., 337–43.

87. Ibid., 360.

88. Although many animals are categorized as unclean and would be disqualified for cultic offerings, the donkey/ass is the only unclean animal specifically prohibited.

89. This phrase is usually used poetically to describe the first shot fired in Lexington at the outset of the American Revolution. It can also refer to the killing of Austria's Archduke Ferdinand that thrust Europe into the first World War. Both were regional events that sent ripples throughout the world.

90. Bimson, *Redating,* 54.

91. Redford, *Ancient Times,* 268.

92. Davis, *Kathleen Kenyon,* 151; and Bimson, *Redating,* 56.

93. For other examples of YHWH's considering the armies of other nations to be acting as his force, see Jer 25:9; 27:6; Isa 7:18.

94. Redford, *Ancient Times,* 132; and Grimal, *Ancient Egypt,* 193.

95. Redford, *Ancient Times,* 132.

96. Ibid., 134.

97. Roux, *Ancient Iraq,* 254.

98. Redford, *Ancient Times,* 135–40; and Grimal, *Ancient Egypt,* 213.

99. Redford, *Ancient Times,* 216.

100. Finkelstein and Silberman, *Bible Unearthed,* 90.

101. Roux, *Ancient Iraq,* 254, 256.

102. Shaw and Nicholson, *Dictionary of Ancient Egypt,* 327–28; Redford, *Ancient Times,* 153–54; and Breasted, *Ancient Records of Egypt* (vol. 2; Champaign, IL: University of Illinois Press, 2001) 24–46.

103. *ANET,* 235.

104. Clayton, *Chronicle,* 101–2; Redford, *Ancient Times,* 146–56; and Breasted, *Ancient Records of Egypt* (vol. 2) 24–162.

105. Redford, *Ancient Times,* 149–52.

106. Clayton, *Chronicle,* 104–6; and Redford, *Ancient Times,* 153.

107. Albert Grayson, *Assyrian and Babylonian Chronicles* (Winona Lake, IN: Eisenbrauns, 2000) 59; Leonhard Sassmannshausen, "Babylonian Chronology of the 2nd half of the 2nd Millennium BC," in *Contributions to the Chronology of the Eastern Mediterranean Mesopotamian Dark Age Revisited* (ed. Regine Pruzsinszky and Herman Hunger; Vienna: Austrian Academy of Sciences, 2004) 61–69; and EA 195 and 318 in Moran, *The Amarna Letters,* 273, 317, respectively.

108. Clayton, *Chronicles,* 110.

109. Bimson, *Redating,* 71.

110. For date, see Redford, *Ancient Times,* 247.

111. A point *not* lost on Bimson, either (*Redating,* 69).

112. *ANET,* 279.

113. Grimal, *Ancient Egypt,* 213–17; and Redford, *Ancient Times,* 156–61.

114. Ibid., 159–60; and Grimal, *Ancient Egypt,* 215–16.

115. *ANET,* 235; and Redford, *Ancient Times,* 154–55.

116. Grimal, *Ancient Egypt,* 213; and George Steindorff and Keith Seele, *When Egypt Ruled the East* (Chicago: University of Chicago Press, 1942) 35–36.

117. *ANET,* 235.

118. *ANET,* 237.

119. Ibid., 237, 239.

120. See *ANET,* 237 n.38.

121. Ibid., 237.

122. Ibid., 237; and Grimal, *Ancient Egypt,* 213.

123. *ANET,* 237.

124. Ibid., 238.

125. Ibid.

126. Ibid., 240; and Grimal, *Ancient Egypt,* 213–16.

127. *ANET,* 241, 239; and Grimal *Ancient Egypt,* 215.

128. *ANET,* 240; and Grimal, *Ancient Egypt,* 218.

129. Gonen, "Late Bronze Age," in *AOAI,* 213; and *ANET,* 219.

130. *ANET,* 241; and Breasted, *Ancient Records of Egypt* (vol. 2) 227–34.

131. Redford, *Ancient Times,* 216–17.

132. Ibid., 218–19; and Gonen, "Late Bronze Age," in *AOAI,* 213.

133. Redford, *Ancient Times,* 160, 169; and Grimal, *Ancient Egypt,* 222.

134. Redford, *Ancient Times,* 163–66, 169; and Gonen, "Late Bronze Age," in *AOAI,* 213.

135. Breasted, *Ancient Records of Egypt* (vol. 2), 165–69.

136. *ANET,* 246, 240.

137. Ibid.

138. Redford, *Ancient Times,* 208; and *ANET,* 237–41.

139. Redford, *Ancient Times,* 168; and *ANET,* 247. Since Thutmoses and Amenhotep shared an unspecified number of years of co-regency, scholars are unsure the date this campaign actually occurred.

140. *ANET,* 251.

141. Redford, *Egypt, Ancient Times,* 168–69.

142. *ANET,* 247.

143. Ibid., 240.

144. Ibid., 246–47.

145. Ibid., 247.

146. Ibid., 242.

147. Ibid., 245.

148. Turner and Coulter, *Dictionary of Ancient Deities,* 423.

149. *ANET,* 242–43.

150. When Abraham defeated Chedorlaomer, he donated the spoils of war to Melchizedek, king of Salem. It is quite possible that Melchizedek was a priest to El before the Canaanite priesthood had thoroughly corrupted God's theology (Gen 15:16). Later Amorite kings in Jerusalem retained the common "zedek" affiliation with their ancestor, Melchizedek (Josh 10:1, 5) when Joshua fought against them at the initial Conquest.

151. *ANET*, 246–47.

152. Redford, *Ancient Times*, 272–73; and Kline, "The Ha-Bi-Ru," 5.

153. *ANET*, 247 n.47.

154. See pp. 312–14, 321–22, 334–35, 578–90 (below); Younger, *Ancient Conquest Accounts*, 197–265; and James Hoffmeier, "The Structure of Joshua 1–11 and the Annals of Thutmose III," in *FTH*, 165–79.

155. Exod 23:32; Deut 7:2; Josh 17:13; and Judg 1:21, 28, 32.

156. *ANET*, 242–43.

157. Ibid.

158. K. L. Noll, *Canaan and Israel in Antiquity: An Introduction* (London: Sheffield Academic, 2001) 121–23; Gary Rendsburg, "Israel without the Bible," in *The Hebrew Bible: New Insights and Scholarship* (ed. Frederick E. Greenspahn; New York University Press, 2008) 9–12; Moore and Kelle, *Biblical History and Israel's Past*, 124–25; and Redford, *Ancient Times*, 272–73.

159. Ibid.

160. Frank Yurco, "Merenptah's Canaanite Campaign," in *Journal of the American Research Center in Egypt* 23 (1986) 189–215; and Michael Hasel, "Merenptah's Inscription and Reliefs and the Origin of Israel," in *The Near East in the Southwest: Essays in Honor of William G. Dever* (ed. Beth Alpert Nakhai, Boston: ASOR, 2003) 19–44.

161. Rendsburg, "Israel Without the Bible," 11–12, 16–17; and Moore and Kelle, *Biblical History and Israel's Past*, 109–10, 124–25.

162. Mendenhall, *Faith and History*, 15–16.

163. Dever, *Early Israelites*, 11; and Finkelstein and Silberman, *Unearthed*, 60–61.

164. Peter van der Veen, Christoffer Theis, and Manfred Görg, "Israel in Canaan (Long) Before Pharaoh Merenptah?": A Fresh Look at Berlin Statue Pedestal Relief 21687," in *The Journal of Ancient Eagyptian Interconnections* 2/4 (2010) 15–25; Hoffmeier, "What is the Biblical Date for the Exodus?" 225–27; Wood, "Rise and Fall," 475–89; and Hershel Shanks, "When Did Ancient Israel Begin?" *BAR* 38/1 (January 2012) 60–62, 67.

165. Finkelstien and Silberman, *Bible Unearthed*, 60; Dever, *Early Israelites*, 218; Hoffmeier, *Israel in Egypt*, 27, 42; and Redford, *Ancient Times*, 275.

166. Van der Veen, Theis, and Görg, "Israel in Canaan," 16–18.

167. Ibid.

168. Manfred Görg, Christoffer Theis, Peter van der Veen, Bryant Wood, Raphael Giveon, and John Bimson.

169. Redford, *Ancient Times*, 292; Shanks, "When Did Ancient Israel Begin?" *BAR*, 61–62. Many revisions were made to "Classical Egyptian" during the Amarna Period that took hold during the reign of Ramesses II (*OHAE*, 292). The Berlin Canaan relief uses the earlier linguistic forms, which indicates that it was written before these revisions went into effect.

170. Ibid.; and Van der Veen, Theis, and Görg, "Israel in Canaan," 16–18.

171. Ibid.

172. Van der Veen, Theis, and Görg, "Israel in Canaan," 16, 20. Redford, *Ancient Times*, 292; and Jacobus van Dijk, "The Amarna Period and Later New Kingdom," in *OHEA*, 292.

173. Veen, Theis, and Görg, "Israel in Canaan," 16.

174. See also Manfred Görg, "Response to Prof. Hoffmeier's Objections," *JETS* 50/2 (June 2007) 255.

175. Ibid., 16–18.

176. Seti I lived about 20–30 years before the traditionally accepted 13th-century exodus. If Seti's inscription does refer to a Levitical town, it means that the Exodus must have occurred at least a century earlier.

177. Ibid.

178. Ibid., 16.

179. Ibid., 18–20. See also, Redford, *Ancient Egypt,* 236.

180. Hornung, "The New Kingdom," in *Ancient Egyptian Chronology,* 201–203.

181. Redford, *Ancient Times,* 156.

182. The dates provided in this table reflect a scenario that fits well with Israel's chronology; however, I adhere to the widely accepted dates in all other chronologies and synchronisms.

183. Ramesses had become co-regent while still "a child in his embrace" (*OHAE,* 288). Amenhotep could also have been a small child during co-regency and simply attributed his father's campaigns to himself.

184. Grimal, *Ancient Egypt,* 204–212.

185. Clayton, *Chronicle,* 119.

186. Ibid., 118.

187. Alan Gardiner, *Egypt of the Pharaohs* (Oxford University Press, 1964) 202.

188. Grimal, *Ancient Egypt,* 222.

189. Clayton, *Chronicle,* 117.

190. Ibid.; and Grimal, *Ancient Egypt,* 223.

191. Grimal, *Ancient Egypt,* 224–25.

192. Ibid., 223.

193. Ibid., 218–21, 223–37; and Redford, *Ancient Times,* 172–76.

194. Redford, *Ancient Times,* 173–77.

195. Ibid., 174–75.

196. Ibid., 175–77.

197. Kitchen has studied over 100 treaty texts and law codes in forming this conclusion (Kenneth A. Kitchen and P. J. N. Lawrence, *Treaty, Law and Covenant in the Ancient Near East,* 3 vols. [Wiesbaden: Harrassowitz, 2012]).

198. Kitchen, *Ancient Orient and Old Testament,* 93. See also Kitchen, *Reliability,* 289. For discussion and references on ancient covenants, see chap. 3.I–II. Also see Hoffmeier, "Biblical Date for the Exodus?" *JETS,* 246.

199. Ibid.

200. Kitchen, *Orient and Old Testament,* 90–102.

201. Redford, *Ancient Times,* 196–97.

202. Ibid., 298; and Malamat, *Biblical Israel,* 60.

203. Roux, *Ancient Iraq,* 273–76. See also Deut 26:5.

204. Hamilton, *Genesis: 1–17,* 344, 405; and Mendenhall, *Ancient Israel,* 16–17.

205. Malamat, *History of Biblical Israel,* 45.

206. Ibid., 47.

207. See Westbrook and Wells, *Everyday Law*; and Richard Hess, "The Bible and Alalakh," in *MB,* 213.

208. Abraham Malamat, *History of Biblical Israel,* 31.

209. Ibid., 43–53.

210. Richard Hess, "The Bible and Alalakh," in *MB,* 211–12.

211. Although I am not aware of any early Hebrew epigraphs in Canaan, this absence of evidence does not necessarily indicate that Hebrew was not at one time spoken in Mesopotamia. Today, there are many Chinese and Vietnamese dialects that are almost unintelligible from region to region for which we have no epigraphic evidence to support their existence, even in this modern age.

212. Malamat, *Biblical Israel,* 60.

213. Johannes Botterweck, Helmer Ringgren, Heinz-Josef Fabry, eds., *Theological Dictionary of the Old Testament: vol. 10* (Grand Rapids, Eerdmans, 1999) 430–37; and Barry Beitzel, "Habiru," *ISBE* (vol. 2) 586–89.

214. Moore and Kelle, *Biblical History and Israel's Past,* 13, 109–10, 124–25; Shea, "The Date of the Exodus," in *Giving the Sense,* 244–45, 247; Bryant Wood, "From Ramesses to Shiloh," in *Giving the Sense,*

269–71. See also "Habiru," TutorGig Encyclopedia, http://www.tutorgig.info/ed/Habiru (accessed February 2015).

215. Na'aman, "Habiru and Hebrews: the Transfer of a Social Term to the Literary Sphere," *JNES* 45/4 (1986) 272; Kline, "The Ha-Bi-Ru," in *Westminster Theological Journal*, 12; Mendenhall, *Ancient Israel*, 31–32; Cazelles, "The Hebrews," 269–90; and Beitzel, "Habiru," 586–89.

216. Na'aman, "Habiru and Hebrews," *JNES*, 272.

217. Kline, "The Ha-Bi-Ru," 17; and Beitzel, "Habiru," 587.

218. Beitzel, ibid.

219. Finkelstein and Silberman, *Bible Unearthed*, 103; David Wright, David Freedman, Avi Hurvitz, *Pomegranates and Golden Bells: Studies in Biblical, Jewish, and Near Eastern Ritual, Law and Literature in Honor of Jacob Milgrom* (Winona Lake, IN: Eisenbrauns , 1995) 481–90; and Samuel Mercer, *El-Amarna* (vol. 2) 843–44.

220. Beitzel, "Habiru," 589; Abraham Malamat, *Biblical Israel*, 60; Grimal, *Ancient Egypt*, 219; Mendenhall, *Ancient Israel*, 31; Finkelstein and Silberman, *Bible Unearthed*, 102–3; and Mirjo Salvini, "The Habiru Prism of King Tunip-Teššup of Tikunani," in *Documenta Asiana* (vol. 3; Rome. Istituti Editoriali e Poligrafici Internazionali, 1996).

221. Botterweck, *Theological Dictionary* (vol. 10), 430–37; and Beitzel, "Habiru," 586–89; Moore and Kelle, *Biblical History and Israel's Past*, 13, 109–10, 124–25; Shea, "The Date of the Exodus," in *Giving the Sense*, 244–45, 247; Wood, "Ramesses to Shiloh," in *Giving the Sense*, 269–71. For a quick reference see: http://www.tutorgig.info/ed/Habiru (accessed January 2015).

222. Botterweck, *Theological Dictionary of the Old Testament*: vol. 10, 430–37; and Beitzel, "Habiru," 586–89.

223. Mendenhall, *Ancient Israel*, 31–32; Henri Cazelles, "The Hebrews," in *Essential Papers*, 269–90; Moshe Greenberg, "Hab/piru and Hebrews," in *Patriarchs: World History of the Jewish People* (vol. 2; ed. Benjamin Mazar, New Brunswick, NJ: Rutger's University Press, 1970) 188–200, 279–81; Nadav Na'aman, "Habiru and Hebrews," 271–88; Kline, "The Ha-Bi-Ru," 1–24; and Beitzel, "Habiru," 586–60.

224. Redford, *Ancient Times*, 272–73.

225. Beitzel, "Habiru," 586–60; Mary Gray, *The Ḫâbirū-Hebrew Problem in the Light of the Source Material Available at Present* (Hebrew Union College Annual vol. 21; Jewish Institute of Religion: Cincinnati, 1958) 141–43, 154; and Cazelles, "Hebrews," in *Essential Papers*, 274–87.

226. Beitzel, "Habiru," 587.

227. Ibid., 587–88; and Gray, *Ḫâbirū-Hebrew Problem*, 138–168.

228. Kline, "The Ha-Bi-Ru," 21.

229. Ibid., 17.

230. Na'aman, "Habiru and Hebrews," 272; Kline, "The Ha-Bi-Ru," 8; Malamat, *Biblical Israel*, 25; and Gray, *Ḫâbirū-Hebrew Problem*, 141–154.

231. Steinkeller, "Land-Tenure Conditions in Third-Millennium Babylonia," in *ULO*, 294; Hudson, "Sacred Enclave to Temple to City," in *ULO*, 118,121, 130–31; Lamberg–Karlovsky, "Households, Land Tenure," in *ULO*, 167–91.

232. Hudson, "Sacred Enclave to Temple to City," in *ULO*, 117–46; and Marc Van De Mieroop, "Thoughts on Urban Real Estate in Ancient Mesopotamia," in *ULO*, 258–59.

233. Na'aman, "Habiru and Hebrews," 272.

234. Kline, "The Ha-Bi-Ru," 20–21, the reference to Rachel and Laban is added.

235. Ibid.; and Na'aman, "Habiru and Hebrews," 274.

236. Redford, *Ancient Times*, 207.

237. Ibid.

238. Ibid.

239. It is quite interesting that the Habiru do not appear in Egyptian sources prior to Israel's Exodus.

240. *ANET*, 247.

241. Malamat, *Biblical Israel*, 60.

242. Redford, *Ancient Times*, 208.

243. Redford, *Ancient Times,* 209, 207, emphasis added.

244. Ibid., 193, 245, 201–3.

245. Ibid., 197–98.

246. Gonen, "The Late Bronze Age," in *AOAI,* 213; and Donald Redford, *Akhenaten, The Heretic King* (Princeton, NJ: Princeton University Press, 1984) 21–22, 25–26.

247. Redford, *Ancient Times,* 199.

248. Grimal, *Ancient Egypt,* 242–43; and van Dijk, "The Amarna Period and Later New Kingdom," in *OHAE,* 279–94; and Redford, *Akhenaten,* 52–54, 157–68, 193–203.

249. For discussion of historicity of Ehud slaying Eglon, see Baruch Halpern, *The First Historians,* 39–75.

250. Finkelstein and Silberman, *Bible Unearthed,* 83.

251. Moran, *Amarna Letters,* 169.

252. Ibid., 218–19, 179–80.

253. Ibid., 298, 316.

254. Mendenhall, *Ancient Israel,* 19.

255. Hoffmeier, "What is the Date of the Exodus," 245.

256. Moran, *Amarna Letters,* xxxiv.

257. Mercer, *El Amarna Tablets,* (vol. 2) 703.

258. Na'aman, "Habiru and Hebrews," 276.

259. For a excellent discussion on Israel's similar guerilla warfare tactics during the initial Canaan Conquest, see Abraham Malamat, *History of Biblical Israel,* 74–94.

260. Grimal, *Ancient Egypt,* 214–25, 250–61.

261. Redford, *Ancient Times,* 170.

262. Redford, *Ancient Egypt,* 171–72, parenthesis added.

263. The brackets in the tablets quoted below are the translators. Translators use brackets to indicate damage to an inscription. The words or letters inside brackets indicate the most likely restoration.

264. Mercer, *Amarna Letters,* 485. Mercer's translations are often problematic. They are used here for their ease of highlighting the usage of *Habiru/Sa.Gaz* without the modern popular gloss (Moran), which simply obscures the relevance of both terms.

265. Moran, *The Amarna Letters,* 230.

266. Mercer, *El-Amarna Tablets* (vol. 2), 559–63.

267. Ibid., 687.

268. Ibid., 639.

269. Ibid., 715–17.

270. Ibid., 721–23.

271. Moore and Keele, *Biblical History and Israel's Past,* 13, 109–10, 124–25; and Rasmussen, "Conquest, Infiltration, Revolt, or Resettlement?" in *Giving the Sense,* 145–49.

272. See also, Yehuda Elitzur and Yehuda Keel, *The Daat Mikra Bible Atlas* (trans. Lenn J. Schramm; Jerusalem: 2011) 124–26; and Ernest Moyer, "The Mysterious Habiru," http://www.world-destiny.org/a29hab.htm (accessed January 2015).

273. Mercer, *El-Amarna* (vol. 2) 722 n.16; and Redford, *Ancient Times,* 269.

274. Hoffmeier, "What is the Date of the Exodus," *JETS,* 245.

275. Redford, *Ancient Times,* 179; emphasis added. Compare with Josh 13:6, 29–30, where Bashan and the Palestinian highlands are given to the Manasseh tribe as an inheritance.

276. Redford, *Ancient Times,* 179; and Wenham, *Genesis 1–15,* 314.

277. Finkelstein and Silberman, *Bible Unearthed,* 105–10.

278. Timothy Harrison, "The Battleground: Who Destroyed Megiddo," *BAR* 29/6 (November, 2003) 34.

279. Redford, *Ancient Times,* 208; and Yurco, "Merenptah and Israel's Origins," in *Exodus: Egyptian Evidence,* 31.

280. Redford, *Ancient Times,* 270.

281. Ibid., 271.

282. *ANET,* 255.

283. Redford, *Ancient Times,* 195.

284. Grimal, *Ancient Egypt,* 219.

285. Redford, *Ancient Times,* 268; emphasis added.

286. Hugo Winckler, *The Tell-el-Amarna Letters* (Berlin: Reuther and Reichard, 1896) 151.

287. *ANET,* 250; and Donald Redford, *Ancient Times,* 185.

288. Grimal, *Ancient Egypt,* 242–43; and Clayton, *Chronicle,* 138–39.

289. Grimal, *Ancient Egypt,* 243; and Gonen, "The Late Bronze Age," in *AOAI,* 215.

290. *ANET,* 252.

291. *ANET,* 251.

292. James Breasted, *Ancient Records of Egypt* (vol. 3; Chicago: University of Chicago Press, 1906) 7.

293. Clayton, *Chronicle,* 136–39.

294. Grimal, *Ancient Egypt,* 247.

295. Clayton, *Chronicle,* 137–39; and Grimal, *Ancient Egypt,* 242–44.

296. Breasted, *Ancient Records* (vol. 3) 23–24.

297. Clayton, *Chronicle,* 142.

298. Grimal, *Ancient Egypt,* 247.

299. Ibid.

300. Redford, *Ancient Times,* 117, 183.

301. Hornung, "The New Kingdom," in *Ancient Egyptian Chronology,* 210–212.

302. Gonen, "The Late Bronze Age," in *AOAI,* 216.

303. Redford, *Ancient Times,* 196, 199, 201.

304. Breasted, *Ancient Records of Egypt* (vol. 3) 40; and Redford, *Ancient Times,* 181.

305. Grimal, *Ancient Egypt,* 247.

306. Breasted, *Ancient Records of Egypt* (vol. 3) 55–56.

307. *ANET,* 255; and Grimal, *Ancient Egypt,* 247. Notice also this indicates Israel did not have control over Beth-shan during this time.

308. *ANET,* 255.

309. *ANET,* 254; Yurco, "Merenptah and Israel's Origins," in *Exodus: Egyptian Evidence,* 42–43; and Wright, *Pomegranates and Golden Bells,* 490.

310. Ibid.

311. Breasted, *Ancient Records of Egypt* (vol. 3) 38, 40, 50, 52.

312. *ANET,* 255.

313. Redford, *Ancient Times,* 93; and Roux, *Ancient Iraq,* 273–74.

314. Kitchen, *Reliability,* 466–67.

315. Breasted, *Ancient Records of Egypt* (vol. 3) 41–73; and Grimal, *Ancient Egypt,* 247.

316. Ibid.

317. Gonen, "The Late Bronze Age," in *AOAI,* 216, 218, 221; and Redford, *Ancient Times,* 203–7.

318. Gonen, "The Late Bronze Age," in *AOAI,* 216–17.

319. Ibid., 218.

320. Grimal, *Ancient Egypt,* 250; and Hornung, *Ancient Egyptian Chronology,* 210–12.

321. Clayton, *Chronicle,* 147–48.

322. Breasted, *Ancient Records of Egypt* (vol. 3) 158; and Redford, *Ancient Times,* 185–86.

323. Breasted, *Ancient Records of Egypt* (vol. 3) 123–29.

324. Kitchen, *Reliability,* 283–89. See pp. 65–73 for discussion.

325. Grimal, *Ancient Egypt,* 256.

326. Ibid., 257.

327. *ANET,* 255; Grimal, *Ancient Egypt,* 256.

328. *ANET,* 242.

329. Ibid., 243.

330. Grimal, *Ancient Egypt,* 256.

331. Redford, *Ancient Times,*189; Clayton, *Chronicle,* 150–55; and Grimal, *Ancient Egypt,* 250–59.

332. Redford, *Ancient Times,* 190–91; and Clayton, *Chronicle,* 150–55.

333. Redford, *Ancient Times,* 189, 191; and John Bimson, "Merneptah's Israel and Recent Theories of Israelite Origins," *JSOT* (49, 1991) 3–30.

334. Moran, *Amarna Tablets,* 235, 288–89.

335. Redford, *Ancient Times,* 193; Gonen, "The Late Bronze Age," in *AOAI,* 216; and Kempinski, "The Middle Bronze Age," in *AOAI,* 166.

336. Ibid.

337. Redford, *Ancient Times,* 202.

338. Yorco, "Merenptah and Israel's Origins," in *Exodus Evidence,* 29–30; and Redford, *Ancient Times,* 192.

339. Redford, *Ancient Times,* 202, 206.

340. Ibid., 195.

341. *ANET,* 237; and Gonen, "The Late Bronze Age," in *AOAI,* 213.

342. Gonen, "The Late Bronze Age," in *AOAI,* 216; and Redford, *Ancient Times,* 196.

343. Redford, *Ancient Times,* 199, 201.

344. Ibid.,189. See also "Tell Hazor," Biblewalks.com, last updated May 31, 2010, http://www.biblewalks.com/Sites/Hazor.html (accessed February 2015).

345. Ibid., 191.

346. Ibid., 264.

347. Wood, "The Rise and Fall," *JETS,* 487–88.

348. Dever, "Settlement Patterns," in *HP,* 286, 290–94; Gonen, "The Late Bronze Age," in *AOAI,* 217–20; and Amnon Ben-Tor, "Who Destroyed Canaanite Hazor?" *BAR* 39/4 (July 2013) 27–36.

349. Ibid.

350. Gonen, "The Late Bronze Age," in *AOAI,* 217–18.

351. Dever, *Early Israelites,* 66–67, parenthsis added.

352. Finkelstein and Silberman, *Bible Unearthed,* 89, 81.

353. Hoffmeier, "What is the Biblical Date for the Exodus?" *JETS,* 245.

354. Exod 34:12–16; Num 33:52; and Judg 2:3.

355. Ben-Tor, "Who Destroyed Canaanite Hazor?" *BAR,* 31.

356. Wood, "Biblical Date: Response to James Hoffmeier," *JETS,* 256.

357. Finkelstein and Silberman, *Bible Unearthed,* 90. See also Wood, "The Rise and Fall of the 13th Century Exodus," *JETS,* 487–88; and Amihai Mazar, "The Iron Age I," in *AOAI,* 260–62.

358. Gonen, "The Late Bronze Age," in *AOAI,* 231.

359. Finkelstein and Silberman, *Bible Unearthed,* 90.

360. Ibid.; Dever, *Early Israelites,* 50; Gonen, "The Late Bronze Age," in *AOAI,* 230; and Bimson, *Redatng,* 50.

361. Bimson, *Redating,* 48–49.

362. Finkelstein and Silberman, *Bible Unearthed,* 90; Dever, *Early Israelites,* 50; Gonen, "The Late Bronze Age," in *AOAI,* 230; and Bimson, *Redatng,* 50.

363. Dever, *Early Israelites,* 8. See also Gonen, "The Late Bronze Age," in *AOAI,* 216; and Bimson, *Redating,* 47.

364. Finkelstein and Silberman, *Bible Unearthed,* 109. See also Gonen, "The Late Bronze Age," in *AOAI,* 241–44.

365. Finkelstein and Silberman, *Bible Unearthed,* 119.

366. Ibid.

367. Gonen, "The Late Bronze Age," in *AOAI,* 217.

368. Ibid.

369. 1 Sam 7:14 is written reflectively. Samuel states that Israel had formerly lived in these territories but lost them during the Philistine assault, probably about the time the Ark was captured.

370. Bimson, *Redating,* 89.

371. Gonen, "The Late Bronze Age," in *AOAI*, 220.

372. Ibid.

373. Ibid.

374. Ibid.

375. Gonen, "The Late Bronze Age," *in AOAI*, 232.

376. Bimson, *Redating*, 51–53; and Gonen, "The Late Bronze Age," in *AOAI*, 218.

377. Bimson, *Redating*, 53–55; and Dever, *Early Israelites*, 121.

378. Gonen, "The Late Bronze Age," in *AOAI*, 218; and Redford, *Ancient Egypt*, 211.

379. Ibid., 218 .

380. Dever, *Early Israelites*, 121–25.

381. Gonen, "The Late Bronze Age," in *AOAI*, 217–18.

382. Ibid., 248.

383. Avraham Faust, "Early Israel: An Egalitarian Society," *BAR* 30/4 (July 2013) 46.

384. *SEC* 2710; BDB, 349; *TWOT* (vol. 1) 316–17; and Holladay, *Concise Hebrew and Aramaic Lexicon*, 114.

385. Redford, *Ancient Times*, 225.

386. Gonen, "The Late Bronze Age," in *AOAI*, 249.

387. Redford, *Ancient Times*, 202.

388. Ibid., 217.

389. Ibid.

390. Ibid.

391. Ibid.

392. See Gen 12:8; 13:3, 18; 14:14; 23:19; 37:14; Num 13:22; 14:45; Deut 1:44; 34:1; Josh 10:3, 5, 23, 36, 39; 11:21; 12:10; 14:13; 21:13; and Judg 1:20.

393. Bimson, *Redating*, 43; and Steinmann, *Abraham to Paul*, 56–58, 62–64.

394. Hoffmeier, "What is the Biblical Date for the Exodus?" *JETS*, 234.

395. Remember that evidence demonstrates that the books of Joshua and Judges were originally authored by many different scribes in different scrolls that were edited together into one book at a much later date (See chap. 8). See also Redford, *Ancient Times*, 235–36 for the influence of and interaction with literature from other nations in Egypt and the influence of Egypt's literature on other nations.

396. Kitchen, *Reliability*, 16; and Hoffmeier, *Israel in Egypt*, 87.

397. Hoffmeier, *Israel in Egypt*, 87.

398. Ibid., 86–88.

399. Ibid., 88.

400. A reference to the Philistine-like headdress.

401. Vincent Tobin, "Pyramid Texts," in *Literature of Ancient Egypt* (ed. William Simpson, New Haven, CT: Yale University Press, 2003) 357.

402. Breasted, *Ancient Records* (vol. 3) 264–68; and Tobin, "Pyramid Texts," in *Literature of Ancient Egypt*, 357–58.

403. Gonen, "The Late Bronze Age," in *AOAI*, 249–50.

404. Hoffmeier, *Israel in Egypt*, 143–44, 159 n.83.

405. Redford, *Ancient Egypt*, 209.

406. Ibid.

407. Gonen, "The Late Bronze Age," in *AOAI*, 217, 221.

408. Clayton, *Chronicle*, 156–57.

409. Ibid.

410. Ibid., 157; Nancy K. Sandars, *The Sea Peoples* (New York: Thames and Hudson, 1985) 29–47; and Grimal, *Ancient Egypt*, 269.

411. Clayton, *Chronicle*, 157.

412. Yurco, "Merenptah and Israel's Origins," in *Exodus: Egyptian Evidence*, 27.

413. Clayton, *Chronicle*, 157; Redford, *Ancient Times*, 262; and Grimal, *Ancient Egypt*, 258.

414. Sandars, *Sea Peoples*, 11, 21–24; Grimal, *Ancient Egypt*, 268; and Redford, *Ancient Times*, 244.

415. Edward Wente, "The Israel Stela," in *The Literature of Ancient Egypt* (ed. William Simpson; New Haven, CT: Yale University Press, 2003) 358.

416. Redford, *Ancient Times*, 203, 269–73, 275.

417. Yurco, "Merenptah and Israel's Origins," in *Exodus: Egyptian Evidence*, 30. Yurco considered the Israelites' meddling with Gezer and Ashkelon to be the cause of Merneptah's assault, based on the thirteenth-century Conquest theory. Joshua 6, however, indicates that Merneptah's campaign confronted Midian and Egyptian Shasu aggression, not Israelite.

418. Ibid., 39.

419. Wente, "The Israel Stela," in *Literature of Ancient Egypt*, 360, parenthesis added.

420. Ibid., 359.

421. Egypt may still have considered Israel's tent-dwelling tribes *shasu*. It is theorized that Israel began transitioning to more permanent homes after Deborah's administration. It is unknown how Israel's tribal affiliation distinguished her people from the Midianites or the Amalekites; however, Merneptah did seem to recognize that distinction.

422. Ibid.; parentheses added for clarity.

423. Winfield L. Thompson, Jr., "Succoth," *ISBE* (vol. 4) 648.

424. Redford, *Ancient Times*, 211.

425. Yurco, "Merenptah and Israel's Origins," in *Exodus: Egyptian Evidence*, 30. Israel could not have gained chariots any earlier than Deborah since the prophetess states the nation lacked armaments (Judg 5:8).

426. Ibid., 29.

427. Van Dijk, "The Amarna Period and Later New Kingdom," in *OHAE*, 295.

428. Yurco, "Merenptah and Israel's Origins," in *Exodus: Egyptian Evidence*, 29; Lawrence Stager, "Forging an Identity: The Emergence of Ancient Israel," in *The Oxford History of the Biblical World* (ed. Michael Coogan, Oxford University Press, 2001) 92.

429. Stager, "Forging an Identity," in *Oxford Biblical World*, 92.

430. Yurco, "Merenptah and Israel's Origins," in *Exodus: Egyptian Evidence*, 28.

431. For example see, Judges 5:3, 7, 8; 6:14; 12:11.

432. Grimal, *Ancient Egypt*, 269.

433. Ibid., 268.

434. Ibid.

435. Gonen, "The Late Bronze Age," in *AOAI*, 215

436. Clayton, *Chronicle*, 160.

437. Sandars, *Sea Peoples*, 11, 19, 24, 35, 105–137; and Redford, *Ancient Times*, 245–56.

438. Redford, *Ancient Times*, 250–51; Finkelstein and Silberman, *Bible Unearthed*, 87–89; and Clayton, *Chronicle*, 161–62.

439. Redford, *Ancient Times*, 250, 225–26.

440. Grimal, *Ancient Egypt*, 274–75; Clayton, *Chronicle*, 163; and Redford, *Ancient Times*, 250, 225–26.

441. Grimal, *Ancient Egypt*, 274–75.

442. Ibid., 275–92; and Redford, *Ancient Times*, 283–85.

443. Redford, *Ancient Times*, 255.

444. Ibid., 255.

445. Gonen, "The Late Bronze Age," in *AOAI*, 222–23.

446. Ibid., 223.

447. Lawrence Stager, "The Shechem Temple Where Abimelech Massacred a Thousand," *BAR* 29/4 (July, 2003) 26–35, 66, 68–69; and Gonen, "The Late Bronze Age," in *AOAI*, 223.

448. Wood, "Ramesses to Shiloh," in *Giving the Sense*, 277–79; and Gonen, "The Late Bronze Age," in *AOAI*, 223. See also http://www.biblearchaeology.org/post/2006/02/abimelech-at-shechem.aspx#Article (accessed February 2015).

449. William Sanford LaSor, "Philistines, Philistia," *ISBE* (vol. 3) 842–46.

450. Kempinski, "The Middle Bronze Age," in *AOAI*, 179, 182; Oren, "Kingdom of Sharuhen," in *HP*, 255, 271–73; Holladay, "Eastern Nile Delta," in *HP*, 184, 187, 198; Dever, "Settlement Patterns," in *HP*, 292; Kempinski, "Northern Canaan and Syria," in *HP*, 328–29; and Bourriau, "SIP," in *OHAE*, 204–5; See pp. 522–23.

451. LaSor, "Philistines; Philistia," 842, 844.

452. Redford, *Ancient Times*, 250; Finkelstein and Silberman, *Unearthed*, 37–38; Dever, *Early Israelites*, 23; and Malamat, *Biblical Israel*, 94.

453. Eliezer Oren, ed., *The Sea Peoples and Their World: A Reassessment* (Philadelphia: University of Pennsylvania Museum of Archaeology and Anthropology, 2000).

454. Gonen, "The Late Bronze Age," in *AOAI*, 215.

455. Ibid.

456. Redford, *Ancient Times*, 290–91.

457. Bimson, *Redating*, 93.

458. Dever, *Early Israelites*, 59–60; Gonen, "The Late Bronze Age," in *AOAI*, 216–17; Mazar, "Iron Age I," in *AOAI*, 260–61, 301; Bimson, *Redating*, 98–99; and Silberman and Finkelstein, *Bible Unearthed*, 90.

459. Christopher A. Rollston, What's the Oldest Hebrew Inscription?" *BAR* 38/3 (May 2012) 32–40, 66.

460. Gerard Leval, "Ancient Inscription Refers to Birth of Israelite Monarchy," *BAR* 38/3 (May, 2012) 41–43, 70.

461. Ibid.; Martin Sicker, *The Pre-Islamic Middle East* (Westport, CT: Praeger, 2000) 47–48; Roux, *Ancient Iraq*, 279; Grayson, *Assyrian and Babylonian Chronicles*, 67; and Luckenbill, *Ancient Records of Assyria and Babylon* (vol. 1) 83–85.

462. "Cultic Shrines from Time of King David," *Israel Ministry of Foreign Affairs* (May 8, 2012), http://www.mfa.gov.il/MFA/History/Early+History+-+Archaeology/Cultic_shrines_time_King_David_8-May-2012.htm (accessed February 2015). See also, "Breaking News—Evidence of Cultic Activity in Judah Discovered at Khirbet Qeiyafa," Bible History Daily, Biblical Archaeology Society (May 8, 2012) http://www.biblicalarchaeology.org/daily/biblical-artifacts/artifacts-and-the-bible/breaking-news%E2%80%94evidence-of-cultic-activity-in-judah-discovered-at-khirbet-qeiyafa/ (accessed February 2015).

463. Ibid.

464. Throughout Israel's early history, it appears that children were born when fathers were older. Isaac was 60 when the twins were born (Gen 25:26), and Moses' genealogy demonstrates similarly long generational cycles for the period of the nation's sojourn in Egypt (Exod 6:16–25). Therefore, my construction also allows for David's patriarchs to be 50–70 years of age when sons are born.

CHAPTER TWELVE

1. *ANET*, 267–68.

2. Luckenbill, *Ancient Records of Assyria and Babylonia* (vol. 2), 158.

3. Hornung, "Introduction," *Ancient Egyptian Chronology*, 1–2.

4. *ANET*, 328, parenthesis added.

5. Luckenbill, *Ancient Records* (vol. 2), 152.

6. *SEC* 4229; BDB, 562; and *TWOT* (vol. 1), 498–99.

7. Luckenbill, *Ancient Records* (vol. 2) 152; emphasis added

8. Avraham Biran and Joseph Naveh, "An Aramaic Stele Fragment from Tel Dan," *Israel Exploration Journal* 43/2–3 (1993).

9. Andre Lemaire "'House of David' Restored in Moabite Inscription," *BAR* 20/3 (1994) 30–37. See also Finkelstein and Silberman, *Bible Unearthed*, 129.

10. Avraham Biran and Joseph Naveh, "The Tel Dan Inscription: A New Fragment," in *Israel Exploration Journal* 45 (1995) 1–15.

11. Ibid., 9–11.

12. Hoffmeier, *Israel in Egypt,* 13.

13. Finkelstien and Silberman, *Bible Unearthed,* 129; Lemaire, "House of David," *BAR,* 33; and Anson Rainey, "The 'House of David,' and the House of the Deconstructionists," *BAR* 20/6 (November/December, 1994) 47.

14. See the excavation home page at: "The Tell es-Safi/Gath Excavations Official (and Unofficial) Weblog," February 16, 2006, http://gath.wordpress.com/2006/02/16/comment-on-the-news-item-in-bar-on-the-goliath-inscription/ (accessed January 2015).

15. Ibid.

16. Ibid.

17. See the dig's official site: http://qeiyafa.huji.ac.il/ (accessed January 2015); Yosef Garfinkel and Saar Ganor, "Khirbet Qeiyafa: Sha'arayim," *The Journal of Hebrew Scriptures* 8/22 (2008), http://www.jhsonline.org/Articles/article_99.pdf (accessed January 2015).

18. Shanks, "Prize Find," *BAR* 36/2 (2010) 51–54.

19. See the dig's official site: http://qeiyafa.huji.ac.il/; Garfinkel and Ganor, "Khirbet Qeiyafa: Sha'arayim," *The Journal of Hebrew Scriptures,* 1–10.

20. Ibid.

21. Ibid.

22. Hershel Shanks, "Prize Find," *BAR,* 52.

23. For the a few of the latest archaeological discoveries see: "King Solomon's Wall Excavated," Youtube, https://www.youtube.com/watch?feature=player_embedded&v=VH9ZDHUyu7A (accessed January 2015); "One of King David's Palaces Discovered Near Jerusalem," The Bridge Blog, Last updated July 18, 2013, http://blog.ifcj.org/post/one-king-davids-palaces-discovered-near-jerusalem?sm=Blog&s_src=FB&s_subsrc=NEX1307XXEXXX (accessed January 2015); "Archaeologists Claim to Have Found King David's Palace in Israel," *CBS News* (July 21, 2013), http://www.cbsnews.com/news/archaeologists-claim-to-have-found-king-davids-palace-in-israel/ (accessed January 2015); Helen Collis, "Archaeologists Baffled after Ancient Egyptian Sphinx Discovered in Northern Israel," *DailyMail Online*(July 10, 2013), http://www.dailymail.co.uk/news/article-2359396/Archaeologists-baffled-ancient-Egyptian-sphinx-discovered-northern-Israel.html (accessed January 2015); Eli Ashkenazi, "Fragment of Ancient Egyptian Sphinx Discovered in Northern Israel," *HAARETZ* (July 10, 2013), http://www.haaretz.com/news/national/.premium-1.534841 (accessed January 2015).

24. *UBD,* 17.

25. *PB,* 158–59.

26. Josh 13:3; Isa 23:3; and Jer 2:18. Although I understand Israel's borders to include the Sinai Peninsula to the Pelusiac Nile branch, the following Web site provides a great treatment of this location, see: http://www.bible.ca/archeology/bible-archeology-exodus-kadesh-barnea-southern-border-judah-territory-river-of-egypt-wadi-el-arish-tharu-rhinocolu.htm (accessed January 2015).

27. Kathleen Corley, "Tiphsah," *ISBE* (vol. 4) 858–59.

28. *UBD,* 1102.

29. Howard F. Vos, "Hamath," *ISBE* (vol. 2) 603.

30. Rendered from the BDB, 562. We will discuss this further when we examine Israel's Testimonial Law in chaps. 14–16.

31. *SEC* 4229; BDB, 562; and *TWOT* (vol. 1) 498–99.

32. Hoffmeier, *Israel in Egypt,* 22 n.85. See also Alan Millard, "Texts and Archaeology: Weighing the Evidence, The Case for King Solmon," *Palestine Exploration Quarterly* 123 (1991) 25.

33. Finkelstein and Silberman, *BibleUnearthed,* 257; and Ernest W. G. Masterman and J. Barton Payne, "Siloam," *ISBE* (vol 4) 510–11.

34. A quick reference source (in progress) regarding the veracity of persons and events mentioned in the Hebrew Scriptures can be found at: http://en.wikipedia.org/wiki/User:Lindert/BiblicalFigures_List (accessed January 2015). While the list is incomplete, it is nevertheless a good starting point.

35. *ANET*, 278–79.

36. Ibid.

37. *ANET*, 281.

38. For a lively discussion on the identification of Pul, see Holloway, "The Quest for Sargon, Pul, and Tiglath-pileser in the Nineteenth Century," in *MB*, 68–79.

39. *ANET*, 283–84.

40. Luckenbill, *Ancient Records* (vol. 1), 274.

41. Ibid., 275.

42. *ANET*, 282–84. Jahoahaz, may have been Ahaz's throne name.

43. Ibid., 283.

44. Ibid.

45. Ibid.

46. Ibid.

47. Young, *Hezekiah in History and Tradition*, 13–15; Younger, "Recent Study on Sargon II," in *MB*, 290; and Becking, *Fall of Samaria*, 24–40.

48. Ibid., 290–91. See also, *UBD*, 970–71.

49. Younger, "Recent Study on Sargon II," in *MB*, 293. Becking arrives at a similar conclusion (*Fall of Samaria*, 25–27).

50. Ibid., 292–93.

51. Holloway, "The Quest for Sargon, Pul and Tiglath-pileser," in *MB*, 68–69.

52. Younger, "Recent Study on Sargon II," in *MB*, 313–14.

53. A.R. Millard, *The Eponyms of the Assyrian Empire 910–612 BC* (SAAS, vol. 2; Helsinki: The Neo-Assyrian Text Corpus Project, 1994) 47, 60.

54. *ANET*, 284–85.

55. See Num 33:52–56.

56. *ANET*, 287–88, emphasis added.

57. Halpern adeptly points out that history written from different perspectives does not invalidate real historical events (Halpern, *First Historians*, xxxiii).

58. For a discussion on the two rebel brothers, see the article by Assyrianologist Parpola on Sennacherib's death: Simo Parpola, "The Murderer of Sennacherib," in *Death in Mesopotamia, XXVIeme Rencontre Assyriologique Internationale* (ed. Bendt Alster; Akademisk Forlag, 1980), http://www.gatewaysto-babylon.com/introduction/murderersennacherib.htm (accessed January 2015).

59. *ANET*, 302.

60. Luckenbill, *Ancient Records* (vol. 2) 200–1.

61. Ibid., 290.

62. Ibid., 288.

63. *ANET*, 290.

64. *PB*, 292, parenthesis added.

65. *ANET*, 291.

66. Carl Evans, "Judah's Foreign Policy from Hezekiah to Josiah," in *Scripture in Context*, vol. 1: *Essays on the Comparative Method*. (ed. Carl Evans, et al.; PTMS 34; Pitsburgh: Pickwick, 1980) 167.

67. Ibid., 298.

68. Austen H. Layard, *Nineveh and Its Remains* (vol. 2; New York: George Putnam, 1849) 247

69. Khorsabad cylinder inscription, lines 44–49. See also the evidence of satellite photographs to show Nineveh's extensive use of canal systems: Alvin Powell, "Ancient Canal Network is Recasting Archae-ologists' Understanding of the Assyrian Capital," Harvard News Office, http://news.harvard.edu/gazette/2006/03.16/11-canal.html (accessed January 2015).

70. H. A. Layard, "Nineveh" in *The Encyclopaedia Britannica, or Dictionary of Arts, Sciences, and General Literature* (vol. 16; Edinburgh: Encyclopaedia Britannica, 1858) 273.

71. *ANET*, 304.

72. Ibid., 304–5.

73. Ibid., 305.

74. Fox, *Service of the King*, 55.

75. Grayson, *Assyrian and Babylonian Chronicles*, 102; and *ANET*, 564.

76. Ibid., 307.

77. Leonard Greenspoon, "Strata," *BAR* 33/6 (November/December, 2007) 18; See online also: British Museum, "Tablet Recording Gold Delivery by the Chief Eunuch of Nebuchadnezzar II," http://www.britishmuseum.org/explore/highlights/highlight_objects/me/t/tablet_recording_gold_delivery.aspx (accessed January 2015); "Nabu-sharrussu-ukin, You Say?" *British Heritage* 28/6 (January 2008) 8, http://connection.ebscohost.com/c/articles/27191936/nabu-sharrussu-ukin-you-say (accessed January 2015).

78. Raymond Dougherty, *Nabonidus and Belshazzar* (London: Yale University Press, 1929) 2–10; and *ANET*, 561, 566.

79. *ANET*, 311.

80. Ibid., 315; and Briant, *From Cyrus to Alexander*, 43.

81. Edwin M. Yamauchi, "Nabonidus," *ISBE* (vol. 3) 468–70. Ancient peoples considered epigraphic material that attested to a former king's existence or to his deeds as a type of intellectual property to be conquered as booty and destroyed, thus supplanting the former king's memorabilia with their own.

82. Ibid., 469.

83. Ibid.; and Dougherty, *Nabonidus and Belshazzar*, 39.

84. Exod 20:5; 34:7; Num 14:18; and Deut 5:9.

85. *ANET*, 467; and Ridderbos and Craigie, "Psalms," *ISBE* (vol. 3) 1039–40.

86. Jer 46:19; 48:7, 46; 49:3; 49:31, 32; 51:50. See also Nah 2:7.

87. J. B. Bury, ed., *The Cambridge Ancient History* (vol. 4; London: Cambridge University, 1969) 1.

88. 1 Kgs 8:1; Ps 135:21; 147:12.

89. Nehemiah 9–10 probably refers to an earlier recovenanting, when the Remnant returned to the land shortly after Cyrus's decree in 539 BCE. Jeremiah is listed as having signed the constitutional covenant declaration, and it is highly doubtful he would still have been living at the 50th Jubilee in 458 BCE, Artaxerxes' 7th year.

90. Compare this prophecy against Babylon with Moses' prophecy against Israel (Deut 32:15). Both prophecies hold citizens and their leaders responsible for complacency with regard to righteousness and justice on the land, which all too often accompany prosperity.

91. *SEC* 319; BDB, 31.

92. *Bachuwr*, the Hebrew for "chosen" indicates youth in Jer 50:44 (*SEC* 970; BDB, 104).

93. Yamauchi, "Eastern Jewish Diaspora," in *MB*, 356, 368.

94. Ezra 4:9, 10; and *PB*, 292.

95. Olmstead, *Persian Empire*, 33.

96. *PB*, 296.

97. Ibid., 295.

98. Ibid.

99. *SEC* 7694; BDB, 993.

CHAPTER THIRTEEN

1. Deut 31:9–13; 1 Kgs 8:9; Mendenhall, *Law and Covenant* (part 2); Kitchen, *Ancient Orient*, 93; Thompson, *Treaty and Old Testament*, 23, 25; Kline, *Treaty of the Great King*, 28; McCarthy, *Institution and Narrative*, 38; and Albright, *Yahweh and Gods of Canaan*, 167.

2. Ibid.

3. When we had studied Israel's Law, we also saw that depositing the Testimony in the Tabernacle served to protect the document from emendation, allowing the priest to consult it should discrepancies arise, in much the same way as the actual U.S. Constitution is kept under lock and key. While these were the practical reasons for YHWH's stipulation, our discussion will now investigate the prophetic implications of these actions, which we will again compare to history.

4. Prov 25:2; Josh 24:14; Isa 6:10–13; 49:4–6; 42:1–10, 21; 43:1–11; 61:8; Jer 33:6–26; and Ezek 37:15–28.

5. YHWH contracted the Deuteronomy covenant with the children of those who entered into the earlier, Sinai compact. Though Deuteronomy's covenant (Testimony) also contained stipulations for breach of pact, these stipulations had not been given at the time of the Sinai compact and were not part of the original Testimony housed within the Ark of Testimony. It is assumed that the Moabic Covenant's stipulations were added to the original covenant and also housed within the Ark of the Covenant. Therefore, the final Testimony would encompass both the Sinai (Leviticus 26) and Deuteronomy (28–30) consequences for breach of the terms of YHWH's covenants. As we shall see, the Moabic (Deuteronomic) Covenant incorporated all aspects of the former Sinai Covenant.

6. We will discuss this further in chaps. 15–19.

7. See pp. 75, 88–89, 92.

8. See also Deut 17:6; and Num 35:30.

9. *SEC* 3940; BDB, 542; William L. Holladay, ed., *A Concise Hebrew and Aramaic Lexicon of the Old Testament* (Leiden: Brill, 1988) 246.

10. *SEC* 5216; BDB, 632.

11. Scripture maintains that history often repeats itself. In modern times, George Santayana drew attention to this natural phenomenon in his famous statement that "those who fail to learn from history are doomed to repeat it." (National Churchill Museum, "Category Archives: WC Quotes," National Churchill Museum Blog [January 31, 2014], http://www.nationalchurchillmuseum.org/blog/category/winston-churchill-quotes/ [accessed January 2015].

12. SEC 3899/6440; BDB, 536–37/815–19; Holladay, *Concise Hebrew and Aramaic Lexicon*, 175; J. H. Hertz, *The Pentateuch and Haftorahs* (2nd ed.; London: Soncino Press, 1997) 329.

13. G. L. Car and N. J. O., "Bread of the Presence," ISBE (vol 3) 955–56; and "Showbread," Jewish Encyclopedia (1906), http://www.jewishencyclopedia.com/articles/13611-showbread (accessed January 2015).

14. See also Zech 9:16.

15. *SEC* 68; BDB, 6–7, 1078.

16. *SEC* 6697; BDB, 849.

17. See also 2 Chr 18:10; and Ps 75:10.

18. Isa 6:10–13; 49:4–6; 42:1–10, 21; 43:1–11; 61:8; Jer 33:6–26; and Ezek 37:15–28.

19. *AEM*, 13.

20. Num 28:7; Isa 51:17–23.

21. Exod 29:40; Num 15:5–11; and Numbers 29. The Septuagint translates the word more accurately as "holocaust" in lieu of "sacrifice," to describe the complete slaughter prophesied through the Tabernacle's burnt sacrifices.

22. In the movie *The Matrix,* the *blue pill* represented mediocrity and the status quo, which was simply a facade, much like burying one's head in the sand in the face of opposition and pretending it will disappear. The *red pill* revealed an unpleasant truth that could affect change. It was the ostrich pulling its head out of the sand before the drunk driver came barreling down the road, saving itself from becoming roadkill.

23. See Ezekiel 18, 33; and Mic 6:2–5.

24. See Nehemiah, chap. 5.

25. See Ezek 33:24–25 for evidence of Judah's prideful expectations during the Babylonia Diaspora.

26. Ps 12:5–8; Isa 13:12; and Zech 13:9.

27. See also Jer 17:24–27.

28. Jeremiah 25; 48:26; 49:12; 51:7, 39–40; 56–57.

29. See also Isa 51:17–23; Zech 9:15–16; Isa 51:4–11, 16; 56:1; and Zeph 3:5.

30. A cubit equals about 18 inches or half a meter. The ark would have been about 45 inches or a meter and a quarter long.

31. *Aliyah* (SEC 5949; BDB, 760) which the KJV renders "inventions" means 'actions or doings' (see 1 Chr 16:8; Ps 9:11; 14:1; 66:5; 77:12; 78:11; 103:7; Ezek 14:22–23; 20:43–44; 21:24; 24:14; 36:17, 19). See also, Holladay, *Concise Hebrew and Aramaic Lexicon*, 245, 274.

32. See the Davidic and Phinehas covenants in chap. 4.VII.

33. W. H. Bennet, *Symbols of Our Celto-Saxon Heritage*, 201.

34. J. A. Thompson, *1, 2 Chronicles*, 85–87.

35. See chap. 8.V.A for discussion.

36. Remember Samuel requested that YHWH send a fierce thunderstorm to rebellious Israel—1 Sam 12:16–25. Both Moses and Samuel served as the two cherubim during the Tabernacle era. Elijah and Elisha served as the cherubim during the First Temple era.

37. Exod 14:21; 16:14, 31; 17:1–6; Num 11:7–9; 20:2–13; and Genesis 19.

38. Biographies were not unheard of during this era. The "Story of Sinuhe," one of the great works in Egyptian literature, dates to *c.* 1800 BCE and tells the very personal story of Sinuhe.

39. 1 Kgs 14:7–11; 15:27–30; and 1 Kgs 16:3–13.

40. *SEC* 4949; BDB, 1054; Holladay, *Concise Hebrew and Aramaic Lexicon*, 222.

41. The "line of Samaria" will be discussed in chap. 16.

42. It should be noted that even if the Second Temple had not corresponded with the First Temple, the prophecies laid in its structure of the First Temple still held true even though Nebuchadnezzar had demolished it. In other words, the destruction of Solomon's Temple could not alter *or rescind* the intended prophetic application. King David had established this prophetic structure through his understanding of the Law and the leading of YHWH's spirit (1 Chr 28:11–13, 18–19).

43. For further discussion see pp. 89–91.

44. 2 Mac 4:13–38; and Vermes, *Complete Dead Sea Scrolls*, 51–52.

CHAPTER FOURTEEN

1. When Israel had first entered the Promised Land, she entered during a time of blessing, and YHWH placed his name on Shiloh. After the Ark of the Testimony had been captured, YHWH removed his name from Shiloh until a more permanent sanctuary could be built, and a new era of blessings introduced. While the curse of 7 Times had been fulfilled during the Judges/Tabernacle era, it was reissued when the new Temple was erected after the people rebelled and the nation fractured in two.

2. 2 Chr 6:14–42; 7:1, 12–22; and 1 Kgs 8:22–61; 9:1–9.

3. We will return to look at these blessings when we examine the parallel Testimonial Law in Deuteronomy.

4. See LXX, 3 Kgdms 11:29–36.

5. Exod 23:14,17; Deut 16:16; 1 Kgs 9:25; and 2 Chr 8:13.

6. 1 Kgs 16:26; 22:52; 2 Kgs 3:3; 10:29, 31.

7. We will examine the historical evidence to support the chronological Testimony portion of Israel's Covenant when we delve into the Testimonial Law within Deuteronomy in the next few chapters.

8. Lev 25:1–7; see also pp. 370–79.

9. *SEC* 3254; BDB, 414–15.

10. See chapter pp. 628–31.

11. Gen 28:13–15; see also pp. 107–15.

12. For discussion of Jacob's Covenants see chap. 3.VIII.

13. See also: Jer 23:5; 31:23–40; 33:14–16; Isa 9:7; Zech 14:16–21; Ezek 34:22–31; 37:15–28; Hosea 3; Ps 14:7; ch. 48; 102:13–22; Isa 2:1–5; 18:7, 35; 40:1–11; 43:1–21; 49:1–26, 51; 52:1–12; 59:19–21; 61:1–11; 62:10–12.

14. James Scott, *Restoration: Old Testament, Jewish, and Christian Perspectives* (Leiden: Brill, 2000) 44–81. One popular Web site comments: "No time framework is here indicated into which we could place the words. What we know from subsequent history, however, is that the failure of the restored Judahite kingdom to live righteously before God and to rise up to be everything that God had desired His people to be must have been an undermining of its fulfilment. In 586 BC, with the exile of Judah into Babylon, the fulfilment of the promise received a terminal setback." (Lee Smith, "Amos 9:13–15: Quicker and larger Return from Exile," Old Doctrines, New Light, http://www.arlev.co.uk/amos23. htm [accessed January 2015]. See also: "The Kingdom Restored: When Did the Restoration of Israel Happen," Abide in Christ, last updated August 19, 2013, http://www.abideinchrist.com/messages/ amos9v11.html [accessed January 2015]).

15. Notice that this concept upholds the precept of an eye for an eye and a tooth for a tooth—opposite and equal reactions.

16. We will examine this specific curse in the next few chapters.

17. 1 Sam 30:8; 2 Sam 3:18; 5:20–21; 7:11; 22:38; 1 Chr 17:8; 22:9; and Ps 44:2, 5–6.

18. Exod 23:33; Num 33:55; and Judg 2:3.

19. Victor Tcherikover, *Hellenistic Civilization and the Jews* (Philadelphia: Jewish Publication Society, 1959) 1–39; Avi-Yonah, *Holy Land,* 32–41; Ephraim Stern, "Between Persia and Greece: Trade, Administration and Warfare in the Persian and Hellenistic Periods (539–63 BCE)," in *The Archaeology of Society in the Holy Land* (ed. Thomas E. Levy; London: Leicester University Press) 432–44; and William Sanford LaSor, "Territory of Judah," (vol. 2) 1150.

20. See also Charles Taylor, ed., *Calmet's Dictionary of the Holy Bible* (Boston: Crocker and Brewser, 1832) 38.

21. Joseph L. Gardner, ed., *Atlas of the Bible* (Pleasantville, NY: Reader's Digest, 1971) 154.

22. Avi-Yonah, *Holy Land,* 72.

23. Ibid., 74.

24. John Barton and John Muddiman, eds., *The Oxford Bible Commentary* (Oxford University Press, 2001) 622.

25. Ibid.

26. Isa 43:4–14; 11:12; Jer 31:7–12; Hosea 3; 9:17; Deut 4:27–31; 30:2–6; Ps 106:45–48; Amos 9:9–15; Ezek 34:11–16; 36:22–24; and Jer 23:3–8.

27. See descriptions of the Day of YHWH in: Joel 1:1–2:14; Mic 3:1–4; 6:1–7:6; Zephaniah 1–2; Isa 10:21–23; Jeremiah 6; 15:9; 44; Ezek 5:9–15; and 2 Kgs 21:14.

28. YHWH did not "choose" for humanity, neither did he predestine humanity's future. YHWH's Testimony always had an "open door" loophole that ordained blessings the moment the people returned to establish his covenant.

29. It should also be noted that YHWH's choice of Israel was not by election. He chose Abraham for his obedience (Gen 22:18; 26:5) and because YHWH discovered that Abraham's heart was faithful to him (Neh 9:8) in addition to the fact that Abraham was Shem's rightful heir to his birthright and blessing. YHWH chose Israel for the sake of his covenants (promises) with Abraham, Isaac, and Jacob (Deut 9:5), thus fulfilling his own words within his contracted covenants with Israel's patriarchs.

30. See pp. 663–72.

31. MW, "honor"; *SEC* 3513; *TWOT* (vol. 1) 426–27.

32. James Dobson, *The New Dare To Discipline* (Wheaton, IL: Tyndale, 1992) 18.

33. "Secretary General Zahi Hawass of Egypt's Supreme Counsel of Antiquities teamed up with paleogeneticist Carsten Pusch from the University of Tübingen in Germany, to examine Tutankhamen and 10 royal mummies. . . . The study revealed that King Tut's parents were siblings, a trend which might have continued in Tut's marriage. 'There are rumors that Tut's wife was his sister or half sister. If this is true we have at least two successive generations that had interfamilial marriages, and this is not a good thing,' Pusch says. 'We see it quite often in royal families that they marry each other. They thought: 'Better to stay close'. . . Pusch explains that Tutankhamen's family was plagued by malformations and

infections from family intermarriage" (Katie Moisse, "Tutankhamen's Familial DNA Tells Tale of Boy Pharaoh's Disease and Incest," *Scientific American* [February 16, 2010], http://www.scientificamerican. com/article.cfm?id=king-tut-dna [accessed January 2015]. See also: "Study Examines Family Lineage of King Tut, His Possible Cause of Death," *JAMA* [February 11, 2010], http://www.newswise.com/ articles/view/561303/ [accessed January 2015]).

34. Pharoh Hatshepsut is a case in point along with the many Ptolemaic brother-sister unions that provoked feuds.

35. See pp. 225, 669–70 for further discussion.

36. MW, "Truth."

CHAPTER FIFTEEN

1. Michael Mann, *The Sources of Social Power:* vol. 1 (Cambridge: Cambridge University Press, 1986) 83, 111, 164.

2. See use of "going out" and "coming in" to designate military campaigns—Josh 14:11; 1 Kgs 15:17; Isa 24:10; and Jer 17:19.

3. The account of 1 Sam 27:8–10 supports David invading many of the nations designated in the Promised-Land Covenant of Gen 15:18–21 and driving the wicked off the Promised Land (see also Josh 13:2–3; 10–13; and Num 14:25).

4. See pp. 132–33.

5. 2 Chr 12:1–12; and 1 Kgs 14:25–30.

6. Num 33:51–56; Judges 2:3; and Deut 7:1–9; 12:1–3.

7. *SEC* 7711; BDB, 995; *TWOT* (vol. 2) 907–8; Holladay, *Concise Hebrew and Aramaic Lexicon*, 361.

8. UBD, 148; and 730.

9. *SEC* 3420; BDB, 439; and Gerald L. Borchert, "Mildew," *ISBE* (vol. 3) 354.

10. UBD, 730; and Borchert, "Mildew," *ISBE* (vol. 3) 354.

11. Johannes Botterweck and Helmer Ringgren, ed., *Theological Dictionary of the Old Testament* (vol. 6; Grand Rapids: Eerdmans, 1990) 365–66.

12. *SEC* 6920; BDB, 869; and *TWOT* (vol. 2) 785; Holladay, *Concise Hebrew and Aramaic Lexicon*, 116.

13. Roland K. Harrison, "Fever," *ISBE* (vol. 2) 300.

14. *SEC* 2746; BDB, 359; *TWOT* (vol. 1) 326–27.

15. *ANET*, 279 (Assyria); and 320–21 (Moab).

16. See also Deut 11:16–17.

17. Allen C. Myers and James A. Patch, "Blasting," *ISBE* (vol. 1) 522 (emphasis added).

18. Deut 28:22.

19. *ANET*, 320–21 (brackets added).

20. Ibid., 278–79.

21. See Isa 21:8–9; and Jer 4:7; 5:6.

22. *ANET*, 283–84. See also 2 Kgs 15:20.

23. *IHCANE*, 311–15; *AEM*, 74–75; and Harrison, "Leper; Leprosy," 103–6.

24. See pp. 180–82, 192, 203–4.

25. ''*Olam*, the Hebrew word translated "forever" has a slightly different meaning in Hebrew. In biblical times, this word meant 'as long as the condition or circumstance continues' [*SEC* 5769; BDB, 761–63, 1106; *TWOT* (vol. 2), 672–73; Holladay, ed. *A Concise Hebrew and Aramaic Lexicon*, 267–68]. As long as Israel continued to obey the Law, the lives of her children would continue to increase (Isa 65:20, 22). Many texts in the Law refer to Israel's ability to live forever, as long as the Law is observed by society (Deut 4:40; 5:29; 12:28; 29:29).

26. *SEC* 1870; BDB, 202; *TWOT* (vol. 1) 196–97; and Hamilton, *Genesis: 18–50* (vol. 2) 194. See pp. 16–17.

27. See also the KJV translation of these verses.

28. Paraphrased; see also Ps 81:12; 78:18, 29; and Num 11:18–35.
29. See Isa 28:13.
30. We will return to this point below. Remember that YHWH does not stand in the way of humanity's lusts but gives people their heart's desires (for their own correction). The quail in the wilderness are a case in point (Num 11:18–35; Ps 78:18, 29; 81:12). See pp. 650–56, 723, 736–37..
31. See Table 8.1 on page 324–25 that shows when the prophets lived.
32. 2 Sam 23:2; 1 Chr 28:11–12; and Ps 119:23, 54.
33. Psalms 42, 44–49 are David's instructions to the sons of Korah. Asaph's instructions to Korah's sons are found in Psalms 84–85, 87– 88.
34. Thompson, *1, 2 Chronicles*, 87; and Davies, *Scribes and Schools*, 78. Based on 1 Chronicles 23, Davies estimates about 38,000 Levites served in managerial offices while 24,000 were in charge of the Temple, 6,000 Levites were officers and judges, and 4,000 were trained mucisians who served in the temple.
35. It may be remembered that Samuel was a priest of the sons of Korah (2 Chr 6:33–38, which is listed in ascending order).
36. See pp. 628–38 for discussion on Haddasseh and Jeremiah.
37. The Septuagint gives the title for Psalms 138 as: "A Psalm of David for Haggai and Zechariah."
38. "Those that rejoice" is a reference to the Temple's prophet-singers.
39. Amos's statement that he was not the son of a prophet (Amos 7:14) does not mean he was not a Korahite. His words indicate that his fathers, probably for a couple of generations, had not served the role of prophet. During times of Israel's apostasy, tithes declined and Levites often sought other lines of work. Very likely, this is the situation in which Amos's family had found itself.
40. For the importance of securing a legitimate succession with regard to YHWH's covenants, see Kline, *Treaty of the Great King*, 35–38. Although Kline focuses on Israel's ancient covenants, the same principle holds true for Israel's prophets. Through the Scriptures, YHWH designates successors who are authorized to interpret his word to Israel (i.e., his prophets).
41. Note that Isaiah, chaps. 6–12 do follow the chronological timeline defined in the Testimonial Law. The chapters after ch. 12, however, ease back and forth between various national epochs.
42. See pp. 650–56.
43. 1 Sam 8:5; 2 Sam 8:15; 15:2; 1 Kgs 3:9.

CHAPTER SIXTEEN

1. *ANET,* 283.
2. Paul Kern, *Siege Warfare* (Bloomington, IN: Indiana University Press: 1999) 116–17.
3. 2 Kgs 3:19, 25; Jer 6:6; and *Megasthenes* 1.14.
4. Kern, *Siege Warfare,* 116–17.
5. *ANET,* 284.
6. Ibid., 287–88.
7. *SEC* 2505; BDB, 323; Holladay, *Concise Hebrew and Aramaic Lexicon*, 106–7. "The word has legal connotations similar to *nahala*, 'give as a possession' but with the more specific implication of what is granted. It differs radically from the many Hebrew roots for 'divide' used in the sense of 'to break into parts.' The verb, used only in Qal and Piel (62 times). . . . The verb is commonly used of parceling out shares (RSV "allotments") of land (Num 26:53), inheritance (Prov 17:2), or other forms of division, whether of food at a feast (2 Sam 17:2), or other forms of division (Prov 22:19)." (*TWOT* [vol. 1] 292–93).
8. See pp. 34–46 for discussion.
9. Rolland K. Harrison, "Queen of Heaven," *ISBE,* (vol. 4) 8; and Alberto Green, *Storm God,* 202.
10. *CGAE,* 80; and *GDSAM,* 108–9; see chap. 2.V.
11. See also 1 Kgs 9:6–9; 2 Chr 7:20–22; Jer 24:9; 29:18; and Ps 44:13–14.

12. Exod 20:5; 34:14; Deut 4:24; Josh 24:19–20; 1 Kgs 14:22; Ps 78:58; Isa 42:13–14; Ezek 8:3–4; 16:38–43; Nah 1:2–3; and Zeph 3:8.

13. *SEC* 8148; BDB, 1042; and *TWOT* (vol. 2) 936–37.

14. *ANET,* 288.

15. Isa 7:8; Ezra 4:2; Hos 1:6; 2 Chr 33:11–13. See pp. 416–17.

16. See 2 Kgs 21:13–14; and p. 417.

17. Deut 28:1–13; Exod 15:26; and Lev 26:1–13.

18. Ackerman, *Under Every Green Tree,* 50, 177.

19. See Lev 26:32 (charts the same phase of the Prophetical Law).

20. See also Jer 52:6–7; 38:9.

21. "Enteroviral Infections." Health Protection Surveillance Centre. Doublin, Ireland, December 8, 2006. http://www.hpsc.ie/hpsc/A-Z/Gastroenteric/EnteroviralInfections/Factsheet/ (accessed December 2013). "Enteroviruses are small viruses that are made of ribonucleic acid (RNA) and protein. Enteroviruses belong to the Picornaviridae family of viruses and are divided into 5 groups with many types within each group, including polioviruses (3 types), coxsackieviruses A (23 types), coxsackieviruses B (6 types), echoviruses (33 types), and other enteroviruses (4 types)" (Ibid). This data does not reflect the many less severe fevers children and adults experience every year which do not end in mortality.

22. Ibid.

23. *SEC* 7829; BDB, 1006.

24. "How Common is Inflamitory Bowel Disease [IBD]?" Crohn's and Colitis Foundation of America, http://www.ccfa.org/info/about/crohns (accessed February 2015).

25. Ibid.

26. Jordan Rubin, *Patient Heal Thyself* (Topanga, CA: Freedom Press, 2003); and idem, *The Maker's Diet* (Lake mary, FL: Siloam, 2004).

27. See for instance: Colin Campbell, interview by Forks over Knives. "Colin Campbell on How the China Study Demonstrates Cause and Effect, (Nov 15, 2012)http://www.youtube.com/watch?v=xsoDOVfASsI (accessed February 2015); Brian Wendel, "Forks over Knives," http://www.forksoverknives.com/ (accessed February 2015); Kathy Freston, "Why Do Vegetarians Live Longer?" *Huffington Post*, October 28, 2012 (updated December 26, 2012), http://www.huffingtonpost.com/kathy-freston/ plant-based-diet_b_1981838.html (accessed February 2015); Paul Nison, "The Raw Life with Paul Nison," http://healthwatchman.com/about-paul/torah-life-ministries/ (accessed February 2015); idem, "Health According to the Scriptures by Paul Nison," (April 11, 2009), https://www.youtube.com/ watch?v=7btqjnlB1BI, (accessed February 2015); John Westerdahl and Colin Campbell, "The China Study Lecture, Indroduced by Dr. John Westerdahl," (September 28, 2011) https://www.youtube.com/ watch?v=LOEeTJY5zCM (accessed February 2015).

28. *SEC* 7711; BDB, 995; Holladay, *Concise Hebrew and Aramaic Lexicon,* 391. See also Deut 28:22 and pp. 185, 713–15.

29. *TWOT* (vol. 2) 907–8; and Allen and Patch, "Blasting," 522.

30. Johannes Botterweck and Helmer Ringgren (eds.), *Theological Dictionary of the Old Testament* (vol. 6; Grand Rapids: Eerdmans, 1990) 365–66.

31. "*Pesticide Use Trends in the United States,*" Economic Research Service: United States Department of Agriculture, http://www.ers.usda.gov/Briefing/Agchemicals/pestmangement.htm (accessed May, 2011). See also, Jorge Fernandez-Cornejo, Richard Nhering, et al., "Pesticide Use in U.S. Agriculture: 21 Selected Crops, 1960–2008," USDA (May 2014) http://www.ers.usda.gov/media/1424195/eib124_summary.pdf (accessed February 2015).

32. Arthur Grube, David Donaldson, et al. "Pesticides Industry Sales and Usage: 2006 and 2007 Market Estimates," United States Environmental Protection Agency; Washington, DC: 2011, http://www.epa.gov/pesticides/pestsales/07pestsales/market_estimates2007.pdf (accessed February 2015).

33. "Trends in Home and Garden Usage by Homeowners," US and International Pest Management Databases: Center for Pest Management (Raleigh, NC: North Carolina State University), http://www.pestmanagement.info/pesticide_history/SIX.pdf (accessed February 2015).

34. John Kent, "Pesticides in Agriculture," School of Agriculture, Charles Sturt University. Wagga Wagga, NSW, http://www.regional.org.au/au/roc/1992/roc1992031.htm (accessed February 2015); "Cancer Trends Progress Report-2011/2012 Update," Pesticides: National Cancer Institute, http://progressreport.cancer.gov/doc_detail.asp?pid=1&did=2007&chid=71&coid=713&mid (accessed February 2015); Georgetown University Medical Center, "Common Household Pesticides Linked to Childhood Cancer Cases In Washington Area," *ScienceDaily* (August 4, 2009), http://www.sciencedaily.com/releases/2009/07/090728102306.htm (accessed February 2015); Gordon Shetler, "Farm Pesticides Linked to Skin Cancer," *Scientific American* (March 31, 2010) http://www.scientificamerican.com/article.cfm?id=farm-pesticides-linked-to-skin-cancer (accessed February 2015); Jonathan Benson, "Research—Roundup Toxicity Much Worse Than What Monsanto, Government Claims," *Natural News* (July 11, 2013), http://www.naturalnews.com/041150_Monsanto_Roundup_glyphosate.html (accessed February 2015).

35. Everette L. Herndon, Jr. and Chin S. Yang, "Mold and Mildew: a Creeping Catastrophe," *Claims Magazine* (August 2000).

36. Ibid.

37. Ibid.

38. Robert Anderson, "Deaths: Leading Causes for 1999," *National Vital Statistics Report* 49/11 (October 12, 2001), www.cdc.gov/nchs/data/nvsr/nvsr49/nvsr49_11.pdf (accessed February 2015).

39. Arialdo Minino, et al., "Deaths: Preliminary Data for 2004," *National Vital Statistics Report* 54/11 (June 28, 2006), www.cdc.gov/nchs/data/nvsr/nvsr54/nvsr54_19.pdf (accessed February 2015).

40. MJW van de Laar, et al., "Lymphogranuloma Venereum among Men Who Have Sex with Men—Netherlands, 2003–2004," in *Morbidity and Mortality Weekly Report* 53/42 (CDC: October 29, 2004) 985–988, http://www.cdc.gov/mmwr/preview/mmwrhtml/mm5342a2.htm (accessed February 2015).

41. Ibid.

42. Statistics are based upon an estimated population under 1 year of age and are presented as rates per 100,000 of this age group. See Donna Hoyert, et al., "Deaths: Final Data for 1999," *National Vital Statistics Reports* 49/8 (September 21, 2001) 105, www.cdc.gov/nchs/data/nvsr/nvsr49/nvsr49_08.pdf (accessed February 2015).

43. Ibid., 11–12.

44. Ibid., 15.

45. Joyce Martin, et al., "Births: Final Data for 2000," *National Vital Statistics Reports* 50/5 (February 12, 2002) 16, http://www.cdc.gov/nchs/data/nvsr/nvsr50/nvsr50_05.pdf (accessed February 2015).

46. Kimberly Roots, "Ugandan President, Wife Key to AIDS Decline" *Science and Theology News* (September 2004) 1–2. It should be noted that these rates have risen the last couple of years as Uganda's citizens have returned to promiscuous sexual behavior.

47. For further study see: Yair Davidi, *Ephraim: The Gentile Children of Israel* (Jerusalem, Israel: Russell-Davis, 2001); Ziva Shavitsky, The Mystery of the Ten Lost Tribes (Newcastle, UK: Cambridge Scholars Publishing, 2015); J. H. Allen, *Judah's Sceptre and Joseph's Birthright* (Merrimac, MA: Destiny, 1917); J. Wilson, *Our Israelitish Origin* (Philadelphia, PA: Daniels and Smith, 1850); E. Raymond Capt, *Missing Links Discovered in Assyrian Tablets* (Muskogee, OK: Artisan Sales, 1985); William Goard, *The Post-Captivity Names of Israel* (UK: Covenant Publishing, 1934); W. H. Bennett, *Symobs of our Celto-Saxon Heritage* (Windsor, Ontario: Herald Press, 1976); Colonel H. W. J. Senior, *The British Israelites* (London: Samuel Bagster and sons); and www.britam.org. Unfortunately, an academic treatment tracing the Israelite people through the Diaspora has yet to be pursued by scholars. The main obstacle in conducting such a study would be identifying human remains that could be determined to be "Israelite" at the time of the Diaspora.

48. B. A. Robinson, "Grouping Christian Denominations into Families," Ontario Consultants on Religious Tolerance (last updated November 6, 2006) http://www.religioustolerance.org/chr_deno.htm (accessed February 2015) and "List of Christian Denominations," Wikipedia, http://en.wikipedia.org/wiki/List_of_Christian_denominations for a quick overview.

49. In chap. 9 we learned that Israel's method of counting always rounded up (see pp. 357, 388–89). Hence, any part of a day that exceeded two days would be rounded up to three days. This leaves open the possibility that the 3 days of darkness that YHWH placed on Egypt could have lasted for more than two days, but less than three days.

50. See pp. 108–15, 610–23, 743 for discussion.

51. Gen 15:16; see pp. 88–89.

52. Lev 18:25; Jer 16:18; 25:12–13; Ezek 9:9; and Zech 3:9.

53. Deut 11:12; Prov 15:3; Isa 1:16; and Jer 7:30.

54. See the example in Num 14:22–23, 27–31.

55. Jer 3:8; Hos 9:15; Isa 50:1; and Deut 24:3–5.

56. Amos 5:18–20; Mic 5:15; Isa 2:11–22; 13:6, 9; 34:8–10; Zeph 1:7–18; Jer 46:8–12; Ezek 24:3–14; 30:3; Zech 14:1; Joel 1:15; 2:1–31; 3:14; and Obad 1:15.

57. See Isa 39:6–7; and 2 Kgs 24:12–16.

58. Jer 52:24–27 provides a parallel account of this and may indicate that Jeremiah wrote the "prophet's entry" into 2 Kings 25. The 11,577 captives did not include many Israelites who fled or immigrated to other lands.

CHAPTER SEVENTEEN

1. *TWOT* (vol. 1) 457; see p. 76.

2. Ibid., parenthesis added.

3. Kline, *By Oath Consigned,* 16–17; Weinfeld, "Covenant of Grant," in *Essential Papers,* 79–82; and Hastings, et al., *Encyclopaedia of Religion and Ethics,* 430–33; Thompson, *Treaties and the Old Testament,* 14; and Dennis McCarthy, *Institution and Narrative,* 53–57. See also Augustine Pagolu, *The Religion of the Patriarchs,* 64–65.

4. See Isa 1:5; 13:7; Lam 1:1; Ezek 21:7. Though each of these verses uses a different Hebrew word for "faintness," these texts still convey the idea that Israel will lack hope to withstand her enemies. See also Amos 8:8–9; Zech 12:2; and Joel 2:1.

5. See pp. 88–89.

6. See also Jer 25:30–38; 50:6; and Ezek 34:2; 7–10.

7. See also Amos 8:12; and Deut 32:20.

8. Exod 15:26; Ps 103:3; 107:20; Jer 33:6; 2 Chr 7:14; Ezek 47:6–12; Hos 6:1–3; 14:4–9

9. Perhaps similar to what continues to occur among Sunnis and Shiites in the Middle-East.

10. *SEC* 3722; BDB, 497–98; *TWOT* (vol. 1) 452–53.

11. Deut 13:5; 17:7, 12; 19:19; 21:21; 22:22–24; 24:7.

12. Lev 5:9; 7:2; 16:14–19.

13. *Kopher* (*SEC* 3724; BDB, 497; Holladay, *Concise Hebrew and Aramaic Lexicon,* 163; Morris, "Ransom," *ISBE* [vol. 4] 44) means 'ransom.' It was customary in the ancient world (*Diya* in Sharia Law today) that when a guilty verdict had been rendered, the defendant could pay the ransom price and avoid the court's sentence. Although Israel's Law did allow ransom in a few limited cases (Exod 21:30), the Book of Numbers stipulates that ransom could *never* be a viable option where murder was concerned.

14. It is important to point out that YHWH does not view the shedding of innocent blood in the same way he views shedding the blood of the guilty. As the above verses demonstrate, shedding the blood of the *guilty* is what atones for the sins incurred (see Exod 21:24; 34:7; Num 14:18; Deut 19:13, 21; 21:8–9; and Lev 24:20).

15. Westbrook and Wells, *Everyday Law,* 74.

16. Deut 25:1; 1 Kgs 3:9; 7:7.

17. 1 Kgs 8:39; 2 Chr 6:30; Job 34:11; Jer 17:10; 32:19; Ezek 7:3; 8–9; 18:30; 24:14; Hos 12:2; Zech 1:6; and Num 5:6–8.

18. Lev 20:10, 21; Gen 9:6; and Num 35:16–21.

19. Exod 12:49; Num 15:16; 15:29.

20. See pp. 274–77.

21. Freedman, *Nine Commandments,* 56–57.

22. Deut 25:1–2; Ps 149:7–9; and Jer 7:3–7; 21:12.

23. Although the entire nation was part of the national judgment, those who were innocent among the nation lived and prospered during their exile, eventually being assimilated into new communities. Daniel, Ezra, and Mordecai, for instance, are examples of only a few righteous Israelites who prospered during captivity. Though they also were deported, YHWH blessed them so that exile was as comfortable as possible (Jer 29:5–7). See also, the private collection of tablets from Babylon, which demonstrate Jews enjoyed peace and prosperity in the Babylonian Empire. Ilan ben Zion "'By the Rivers of Babylon' Exhibit Breaths Live into Judean Exile," The Times of Israel, February 1, 2015, http://www.timesofisrael.com/by-the-rivers-of-babylon-exhibit-breathes-life-into-judean-exile/#ixzz3QtcvjbRQ (accessed February 2015) and Kathleen Abraham, "The Reconstruction of Jewish Communities in the Persian Empire: The Āl-Yahūdu Clay Tablets," in *Light and Shadows-The Catalog-The Story of Iran and the Jews,* ed. Hagai Segev and Asaf Schor (Beit Hatfutsot: Tel Aviv, 2011) 261–64, http://www.academia.edu/1383485/The_Reconstruction_of_Jewish_Communities_in_the_Persian_Empire_The_%C4%80l-Yah%C5%ABdu_Clay_Tablets (accessed February 2015).

24. Kline, *By Oath Consigned,* 16–17; Weinfeld, "Covenant of Grant," in *Essential Papers,* 79–82; Hastings, et al., *Encyclopaedia of Religion and Ethics,* 430–3; Thompson, *Treaties and the Old Testament,* 14; McCarthy, *Institution and Narrative,* 53–57; and Phillips, *Israel's Criminal Law,* 11–12. See also Augustine Pagolu, *The Religion of the Patriarchs,* 64–65.

25. 1 Maccabees 1–2; and Tcherikover, *Hellenistic Civilization and the Jews,* 77–89, 117–203.

26. Num 35:24–5; Josh 20:4–6; Deut 1:13–18; and Deut 17:9–13; see pp. 258–71.

27. Jer 21:12; Ezek 24:6–11; Mic 3:9–12; and referring to the bloodguilt of Edom—Joel 3:19–21 and Ezek 35:2–8.

28. The "Holy One" usually refers to the high priest (Deut 33:8).

CHAPTER EIGHTEEN

1. *PB,* 273–78; and Olmstead, *Persian Empire,* 298.

2. The Testimonial Law in Leviticus 26 only allotted five 7 Times epochs. Jeremiah continued these 7 Times epochs with 70 years of desolation for the land to enjoy its Sabbaths. The seventh 7 Times overlaps the rebuilding of the Second Temple. Hence, the seventh 7 Times for the First Temple is also the first 7 Times epoch for the Second Temple. Because these 7 Times are cultic judgments, it is more accurate to call this the 1st 7 Times of the Second Temple Era. I have chosen a continuous numbering system to avoid confusion. Whether we reckon this 7 Times period to the First or Second Temple era is irrelevant since the Second Temple was the First Temple rebuilt. What is important are the prophecies that the prophets tied to the Remnant's commitment to adhere to the constitutional covenant after the Second Temple was built. As we will see, the cultic judgments tied to the First Temple continue into the Second Temple Era through the Diaspora until the latter-day restoration of the descendants of Israel.

3. Jer 17:21–27; Isaiah 35; and Zech 8:1–17.

4. Randall Price offers a particularly lucid discussion on this topic. Ezekiel's Prophecy on the Temple can be found at: http://www.worldofthebible.com/Bible%20Studies/Ezekiel's%20Prophecy%20of%20the%20Temple.pdf (accessed February 2015).

5. Matt 1:21; 25:34; Luke 9:56; John 1:29; 12:47; 1 Titus 1:15; and Jas 5:15.

6. Adin Steinsaltz, *The Esssentail Talmud* (trans. Chaya Galai; New York: Basic Books, 1976) 16.

7. Ibid., 10.

8. Notice that Deut 28:68 is still being fulfilled because the Remnant did not have power to redeem their brethren.

9. Exod 22:25; Lev 25:36, 37; and Deut 23:19–20.

10. Neh 12:26; 5:14; 8:9; 10:1

11. Ezra 2:63; Neh 7:65; 8:9; 10:1.

12. See Deut 7:1–6.

13. The Testimonial Law refers to "stranger that is within you shall get up above you very high; and you shall come down very low" (Deut 28:43). This natural process occurs when a nation (1) does not adhere to tribal land ownership that protected against massive waves of immigration and (2) accepts a debt-based economy.

14. *SEC* 5237; BDB (vol. 2) 579–80. See 1 Kgs 8:41; 11:8; Deut 14:21; 15:3; 17:5.

15. See pp. 688–89 for discussion.

16. *BDB*, 764–65; and Anson F. Rainey, "Zion," *ISBE* (vol. 4) 1198.

17. See pp. 700–2, 721–30.

18. See pp. 726–29; and Appendix A, Table 9.50. Macro Synchronized Chronology of Israel and the Near East, p. 3.

19. It should also be noted that Antiochus III repatriated 2,000 Jewish families from Mesopotamia and Babylon to Judea in an effort to stave Greek uprisings in the region (Josephus, *Ant.* 12.149–53).

20. *JHRE*, 2–3.

21. Isa 32:15–18, 35, 51; 65:16–25; 66:22–24; Jer 24:6–7; and Zechariah 14.

22. Peter Kirby, "Letter of Aristeas," *Early Jewish Writings,* http://www.earlyjewishwritings.com/letter-aristeas.html (accessed February 2015); Wendland, ed., "Aristeas, Letter of," *Jewish Encyclopedia* (1916), http://www.jewishencyclopedia.com/articles/1765-aristeas-letter-of (accessed February 2015).

23. *JHRE*, 2–4; Olmstead, *Persian Empire,* 189–90; *HCJ*, 55–56; and Josephus (*Ant.* 13, 3–60).

24. *JHRE*, 2–13.

25. Olmstead, *Persian Empire*, 189–90.

26. Louis Finkelstein, ed., *Pharisaism in the Making* (Jersey City, NJ: KTAV Publishing, 1972) 456–57 n.6.

27. Judg 8:19; Ruth 3:13; 1 Sam 14:39, 45; 19:6; 20:3; 20:21; 25:26; 26:10, 16; 28:10; 2 Sam 12:5; 1 Kgs 1:29; 2 Kgs 2:4; and Jer 38:16.

28. John Kampen, *The Hasideans and the Origin of Pharisaism* (Atlanta, GA: Scholars Press, 1988) 1–43.

29. This verse uses the word *goy* to designate the Judean remnant as a nation. Modern Judaism (as a religious movement) sees this term as applying only to Gentiles and non-converts. This was not the Scriptural definition of the term, which often applied it to the nation of Israel—Gen 12:2; 17:4–6; 17:20; 18:18. Scripture also uses *goy* to refer directly to Jacob's children—Gen 25:23; 35:11; 46:3; Exod 19:6; 33:13; Deut 4:6–8; Ps 83:4; 106:5; Isa 1:3–4; 18:2, 7; and Jer 7:28.

30. Finkelstein, ed., *Pharisaism in the Making,* 175–76. Finkelstein sees the Pharisees's sect as arising in the early fourth century BCE.

31. Steinsaltz, *Essential Talmud,* 211–18.

32. Ibid., 213–14.

33. Steinsaltz, *Essential Talmud,* 213–14, parenthesis added.

34. Mark Sameth, "God's Hidden Name Revealed," *Reform Judaism* (Spring 2009), http://rjmag.org/Articles/index.cfm?id=1433(accessed February, 2015). According to Jewish tradition and beliefs, the Oral Law (today, the Mishnah) was given simultaneously with Moses' writing down the Pentateuch (*Ethics of the Fathers* 1:1). Hence, there is a contradiction. YHWH tells Moses and Israel to swear by his name. This is the same Israel that had already rebelled against him in the Sinai Wilderness several times. The group who exited Egypt could hardly have been considered pure or holy. However, YHWH commanded them to swear in his name (see Freedman, *Nine Commandments,* 1–50). The Pharisees' Mishnah teaches that God's name is too pure or holy to be pronounced, despite the fact that his name

was not too holy or pure to be pronounced by wicked, idolatrous Israel during the Monarchic Period when YHWH sent prophets such as Jeremiah to instruct his people to swear in his name. Thus, the Oral Law changes the written (Exod 24:4, 12; 34:27–28; Deut 28:58, 61; 29:20, 21, 27; *31:9*; Deut 27:3–8; and Josh 8:34–35) *Law of Moses*: an act that YHWH's Law had forbade (Deut 4:2; 12:32). Additionally, *according to Jewish tradition*, there were many names of God, so the Jews of the Second Temple era who followed the rabbis would not necessarily have known in which of God's names to swear, being more apt to consult a sage than a Torah scroll.

35. *SEC* 6435; *BDB*, 814. See also Gen 3:3.

36. *SEC* 7219; *BDB*, 912; Holladay, *Concise Hebrew and Aramaic Lexicon*, 329; George L. Kelm, "Wormwood," *I SBE* (vol. 4) 1117; and Roland K. Harrison, "Gall," *ISBE* (vol. 2) 392–93.

37. *SEC* 3939; *BDB*, 542; Holladay, *Concise Hebrew and Aramaic Lexicon*, 178.

38. *SEC* 3939; *BDB*, 542; *IBSE*, (vol. 2) 392; and Alexander Harkavy, *The Hebrew and Chaldee Dictionary* (New York: Hebrew Publishing, 1914) 60.

39. See pp. 66, 71–72, 103–04.

40. Exod 20:5; 34:7; Num 14:18; and Deut 5:9.

41. See chap. 12.

42. *SEC* 3939/7219; *BDB*, 542/912; Holladay, *Concise Hebrew and Aramaic Lexicon*, 16; and Kelm, "Wormwood," *ISBE* (vol. 4) 1117.

43. Exod 20:13–14; Lev 20:10; and Num 35:16–21, 29–34.

44. Steinsaltz, *Essential Talmud*, 10–23; and Abraham Cohen, *Everyman's Talmud* (New York: Schocken Books, 1949) x–xi.

45. Deut 28:37; Jer 42:18; 44:12; and Ezek 4:16; 12:19; 23:33.

46. Ridley, R.T. "To Be Taken with a Pinch of Salt: The Destruction of Carthage," *Classical Philology* 81/2 (April 1986) 140–46; Stanley Gevirtz, "Jericho and Shechem: A Religio–Literary Aspect of City Destruction," *Vetus Testamentum* 13/1 (January 1963) 52–62; and Susan Stevens, "A Legend of the Destruction of Carthage," *Classical Philology* 83/1 (January 1988) 39–41.

47. *PB*, 292; and R. Campbell Thompson, *The Prisms of Esar haddon and of Ashurbanipal* (London: British Museum, 1931) 34.

48. Graubart, David, "Israel," *NSE* (vol. 9) I–232. Also, compare to Deut 11:17.

49. Gonen, "The Late Bronze Age," *AOAI*, 246. See also Danin, "Man and the Natural Environment," in *The Archaeology of Society in the Holy Land*, 24–39.

50. Graubart, David, "State of Israel," *NSE* (vol. 9) I-230.

51. Douglas W. Downey, ed., "Great Britain," *NSE* (vol. 7) G-232; and Rufus F. Cox, Jonathan Garst, and Richard M. Highsmith, "Agriculture," *NSE* (vol. 1) 145, 150.

52. Ibid., 150.

53. Thiele, *Mysterious Numbers*, 51–53.

54. The actual estimate for the third day when the darkness is lifted is closer to 3,035 years, counting from the beginning of the Davidic Monarchy (1023 BCE), and thus well into the third day.

55. Remember that the false prophet Hananiah also saw the prophecy within the molten sea. Without looking to the Testimonial Law, he stated that the time of Israel's exile would last only two years (Jer 28:11). YHWH warned this prophet through Jeremiah that at least 70 years had been allotted for exile (Jer 25:11–14; 29:8–14). If she repented and returned to YHWH at the end of the 70 years, YHWH would walk with the nation again (Jer 29:8–14). If not, she would be cast off for 2,000 years (Jer 29:15–23; Hos 6:2).

56. See also Ps 106:45–48; Isa 43:14, 4–13; 49:14–26; Jer 31:7–13; 23:3–8; Amos 9:9–15; Ezek 34:11–31; 36:22–24; 37:21–28.

57. Compare with Isa 18:3–7.

58. See Ezek 37:16–19.

59. See also Isa 49:8–12; 54:10; 64:1–5; 19:23–25; 35:8–10.

60. See also Ps 104:30; Isa 32:15–20; Prov 1:23; Joel 2:28–29; and Ezek 11:17–20.

61. Isa 51:22–23; Mic 5:8–9; and Zech 12:9.

62. *SEC* 7725; BDB, 996–1000; and *TWOT* (vol. 2) 909–10.

63. *PB*, 292; and Ezra 4:9–10.

64. When Israel fulfills Numbers' Effacement judgment to expel the Promised-Land's native peoples, the refugees will be absorbed into other countries and other lands. They will find peace and salvation in their new homelands and learn to live righteously.

65. Deut 4:29; Prov 8:17; 1 Chr 28:9; and 2 Chr 15:2.

66. During the long Diaspora, Torah observance has not thrived in most Jewish communities due to their reliance on rabbinic theology, which perverts and distorts YHWH's written word. Although I have given some evidence for these perversions, we will examine this further in chap. 19.

67. Gen 18:18; 22:18; 27:29; Num 22:12; 23:20; 24:9; Jer 31:34; and Isa 44:1–3; 19:24.

CHAPTER NINETEEN

1. See Ezek 39:23–24; and Amos 8:11–13.

2. YHWH had previously adhered to this policy with the Amorites, waiting 430 years for their sins to come to the full. He redeemed Israel and at the same time judged the Amorites, sentencing them to be expelled from their homeland (Gen 15:13–16).

3. See also Micah 1:4; 3:12; 4:1, 2; Isa 22:5; 34:1–5; 42:14–17.

4. See pp. 651–56.

5. See also Deut 4:35; Isa 41:4; 43:10–11; 44:6; 45:5, 18, 22; 48:12.

6. Compare with Leviticus's and Deuteronomy's Testimonies—see p. 702 and chap. 17.

7. Finkelstien, *Pharisaism in the Making*, 13.

8. See pp. 317–18, 661, 726–28 for discussion regarding the function of the Sons of Korah.

9. For further discussion, see chapter 15.IV.B. on pp. 721–24.

10. Jer 29:10–12; Hag 1:8; Neh 2:18; 6:15–16.

11. See also Freedman's excellent observations in *Nine Commandments*, 76–79.

12. Ibid., 26.

13. See pp. 181–90.

14. Campbell, *Oriental Mythology*, 395; *JM*, 33, 57–58, 93, 178; *GDSAM*, 72–73; Willoughby, *Pagan Regeneration*, 30–32; Hislop, *The Two Babylons*, 20, 56; Frazer, *Golden Bough*, 378; *CGAE*, 172, 181; *KG*, 39, 209; *JM*, 25; Assmann, *Death and Salvation*, 74, 77–78; Lockyer, *Nelson's Illustrated Bible Dictionary*, 433.

15. Ackerman, *Under Every Green Tree*, 36.

16. For further study into this text see Ackerman, *Under Every Green Tree*, 37–99.

17. For lucid discussion on these cultic practices see: Ackerman, *Every Green Tree*, 67–79; Malamat, *History of Biblical Israel*, 316–18; and Walther Zimmerli, *Ezekiel I and II: A Commentary on the Book of the Prophet Ezekiel Chapters 25–48* (Minneapolis, MN: Fortress Press, 1983).

18. Finkelstein, *Pharisaism in the Making*, vii–viii, 13–15; and Kampen, *The Hasideans and the Origin of Pharisaism*, 17–22.

19. *JFB*, 678; and Malamat, *History of Biblical Israel*, 315–19. Contra Ackerman, *Under Every Green Tree*, 67–79.

20. *GDSAM*, 72–73; *CGAE*, 172, 181; *KG*, 39, 209; *JM*, 25; Assmann, *Death and Salvation*, 74, 77–78; Lockyer, *Nelson's Illustrated Bible Dictionary*, 433.

21. Albright, *Yahweh and the Gods of Canaan*, 126–27; Green, *Storm-God*, 209–10, 74–75; and Ackerman, *Every Green Tree*, 78–92.

22. Ibid.; Albright, *Yahweh and the Gods of Canaan*, 126–27; Green, *Storm-God*, 209–10, 74–75; Gaebelein, "Tammuz," (vol. 4) 725–26. See also, Walter Mattfeld, "Tammuz, Dumuzi, Ningishzida, and Jesus Christ," last updated April 27, 2004, http://www.bibleorigins.net/TammuzDumuziDamuSeal.html (accessed February 2015).

23. Albright, *Yahweh and Gods*, 126–27; Green, *Storm-God*, 74–75, 209–10; Ackerman, *Every Green Tree*, 78–92; and Millar, "Oral Poetry and *Dumuzi's Dream*," in *Scripture In Context*, 38.

24. Cohen, *Cultic Calendars*, 315–19.

25. See Ps 73:8–10; 75:8; Isa 2:6; 1:22; Jer 8:14; 9:15—referring to the returned remnant. The word for "return," *Shubh*, has a wide variety and many shades of meaning. It is often used to denote apostasy as rebelling against the covenant (William Holladay, *The Root SUBH in the Old Testament* [Leiden: Brill, 1958] 3, 9–12, 53–59, 112, 116–57).

26. Deut 7:16; 13:8; 19:13, 21.

27. Amos 9:10. See also Deut 7:16; 13:8; 19:13, 21.

28. Zimmerli, *Ezekiel 1: Commentary on Ezekiel, Chapters 1–24*, 19, 24, 30.

29. For a discussion on of the chronology in Ezekiel, see Zimmerli, *Ezekiel 1*, 9–10.

30. Isa 43:14, 4–13; Jer 31:7–12; Lev 26:33, 44–45; Deut 30:2–6; Ps 106:45–48; Amos 9:9–15; Ezek 11:17–19; 36:24–28; 39:27–29; 34:12–16; 36:22–24; Jer 23:3–8; Isa 11:12; and Deut 4:27–31.

31. See Gen 9:4–5; Lev 17:10–14; and Deut 12:23–24.

32. Zimmerli, *Ezekiel 1*, 8, 17, 20, 28.

33. Ibid., 8.

34. Compare this method with that of Num 14:34, where YHWH causes Israel to bear her iniquity for 40 years. God sentenced her to wander in the wilderness for 40 years for her rebellion until every man 20 years old and older died for his sins (Num 14:29). The 40 years represented the 40 days that the spies spent in Canaan (Num 14:34).

35. Zimmerli, *Ezekiel 1*, 8, 17, 20, 28.

36. About eight very meager ounces (John F. Walvoord and Roy B. Zuck, ed., *The Bible Knowledge Commentary* [Victor Books, 1985] 1236).

37. About 2/3 of a quart of water (ibid.).

38. Since Ezekiel's bread contains all the essential amino acids, it is a complete protein.

39. I am grateful to Rodger Young, who fleshed out the chronological method of reckoning for the Book of Ezekiel. See Rodger Young, "Inductive and Deductive Methods as Applied to OT Chronology," *TMSJ* 18/1 (Spring, 2007) 99–116.

40. Deut 28:48; Hos 2:3; Amos 8:11; Isa 32:6; 65:11–13; and Ezek 4:17.

41. Amos 9:9–15; Ezek 11:17–19; 34:22–24; 36:24–28; 39:21–29; Jer 23:3–8; and Isa 11:12.

42. Hos 3:5; Ezek 37:23–25; and Jer 30:9.

43. See pp. 644, 653–54, 689, and chap. 17.

44. Ezekiel did not know when Jerusalem fell until a deportee brought him the news (Ezek 33:21).

45. See chap. 9 for further discussion.

46. Some scholars begin this prophecy with Jehoiachin's exile in 597 BCE and end the prophecy in 168/67 (Walvoord and Zuck, *Bible Knowledge Commentary*, 1236.)

47. Olmstead, *Persian Empire*, 143–48.

48. *HCJ*, 179–203.

49. *HCJ*, 81.

50. Ibid., 81, 175–203.

51. Ibid., 75–89.

52. Ibid., 78–79.

53. Ibid., 80–81.

54. For discussion of historical validity, see *HCJ*, 49, 81–84.

55. Steinsaltz, *Essential Talmud*, 146.

56. Westbrook and Wells, *Everyday Law*, 15–16. The authors observe that the Oral Law was in reality "the jurisprudence of the Rabbis (Tannaim and later Amora'im) starting in the Hellenistic period" (p. 16).

57. Steinsaltz, *Essential Talmud*, 146.

58. Steinsaltz, *Essential Talmud*, xxxix, 146; and *HCJ*, 152–74.

59. *HPE*, 143–48; *HCJ*, 175–203; *Polybius xxxix, 27.10* http://penelope.uchicago.edu/Thayer/E/Roman/Texts/Polybius/28*.html (accessed February 2015).

60. The Book of 1 Maccabees and Josephus's *Antiquities* differ concerning the year that Epiphanes desecrated and plundered the Second Temple. 1 Maccabees holds that Epiphanes plundered the Temple in the 143rd year of the Seleucid Empire (170 BCE), while Josephus dates the event two years later, in the Empire's 145th year (168 BCE). According to Josephus, Epiphanes' primary intent in the second invasion (168 BCE) was the Temple's treasury, whose funding he desperately needed to secure foreign mercenaries and for campaigns. No other source exists to help settle the two-year discrepancy. See *HCJ* for Tcherikover's chronology, which accepts Maccabees' account, pp. 186–96.

61. This was not the only deportation of Israel to occur during the Second Temple era. Egypt, under Ptolemy II Philadelphus deported 100,000 Judean citizens—at least, that is the number given in *The Letter of Aristeas* (*JHRE*, 3–6; and *HCJ*, 56 n.45).

62. Olmstead, *Persian Empire*, 190–92; and *HCJ*, 81.

63. *HCJ*, 198–200.

64. Ibid., 200–203.

65. Ibid., 187.

66. Clayton, *Chronicle*, 196–97.

67. Ibid.

68. Ibid.

69. *JFB*, 646; John W. McCrindle, *Ancient India As Described by Megasthenês and Arrian* (trans. J. W. McCrindle; Munshiram Manoharlal Publishers, 2000) 113–14 (Frag XLIX, p.114); and *ANET*, 308.

70. *JHRE*, 6.

71. Aryeh Kasher, *Studies in the History of the Jewish People and the Land of Israel:* vol. 3 (Tübingen: Mohr Siebeck, 1978) 69–84.

72. *JHRE*, 7; *HPE*, 191. For a discussion on the credibility of 3 Macabees, see also *JHRE*, 211–20.

73. *JHRE*, 214–232.

74. Compare YHWH's judgment here to that in the wilderness. When Israel lusted for flesh, he gave it to them for a whole month until they became sick of it (Num 11:18–35).

75. *JHRE*, 7. On the reliability of 3 Maccabees see *JHRE*, 211–232.

76. Ibid., 230.

77. *HPE*, 154.

78. *JHRE*, 11–13, 58–62.

79. Ibid., 9.

80. Ibid., 9–12.

81. Ibid., 12.

82. Ibid., 13.

83. Ibid., 20–22.

84. Ibid., 23–28.

85. *JHRE*, 26–28.

86. *HPE*, 154, 157, 182. Anachoresis (flight) occurred when farmers faced excessive taxes and constant requisitions for corvée service. This was compounded with ruthless masters, miserable wages, and appalling living conditions. In despair, the farmer would lay down his tools, forsake family, home, and field to flee to another land (Sergio Donadoni, *The Egyptians* [Chicago: University of Chicago Press: 1997] 22).

87. *HPE*, 239.

88. Ibid.

89. See also Exod 24:12; Num 33:2; Deut 31:22; and Josh 8:32.

90. Steinsaltz, *Essential Talmud*, 5–17.

91. Kampen, *Hasideans and the Origin of Pharisaism*, 17–22, 27; Finkelstein, *Pharisaism in the Making*, viii–ix, 13–15; Steinsaltz, *Essential Talmud*, 14–16; Cohen, *Everyman's Talmud*, xxxvii–xl.

92. Adin Steinsaltz, *Essential Talmud*, 16.

93. Kampen, *The Hasideans and the Origin of Pharisaism,* 17–22, 27; and Finkelstein, *Pharisaism in the Making,* viii–ix, 13–15.

94. Harrison, "Queen of Heaven," *ISBE* (vol. 4) 8. In Babylon, Ishtar (Inana) was associated with Venus (*GDSAM,* 109; and Jastrow, *Babylonia and Assyria,* 81, 370, 458–59, 571).

95. See pp. 36–39.

96. *CGAE,* 117; and *JM* 3–6, 16–26.

97. *CGAE,* 86–90, 117.

98. *CGAE,* 86.

99. Ibid.

100. Ibid.

101. Ibid.

102. Ibid., 88.

103. Ibid.

104. Ibid.

105. Ibid., 89.

106. See Day, *YHWH and the Gods and Goddesses of Canaan* and Albright, *Yahweh and the Gods of Canaan.*

107. See, Tracy R. Rich, "The Name of G-d," Judaism 101, http://www.jewfaq.org/name.htm (accessed February 2015); Jewish Virtual Library, "The Name of God," American-Israel Cooperative Enterprise, http://www.jewishvirtuallibrary.org/jsource/Judaism/name.html (accessed February 2015); Freedman, *Nine Commandments,* 50–51.

108. Ibid.

109. Steinsaltz, *Essential Talmud,* 213–14.

110. Ibid., 214 (emphasis added).

111. Judg 8:19; Ruth 3:13; 1 Sam 14:39, 45; 19:6; 20:3; 20:21; 25:26; 26:10, 16; 28:10; 2 Sam 12:5; 1 Kgs 1:29; 2 Kgs 2:4; and Jer 38:16.

112. Kampen, *The Hasideans and the Origin of Pharisaism,* 1–43.

113. This verse uses the word *goy* to designate the Judean remnant as a nation. Modern Judaism (as a religious movement) sees this term applying only to Gentiles and non-converts. This was not the Scriptural definition of the term, which often applied to the nation of Israel—Gen 12:2; 17:4–6; 17:20; 18:18. Scripture also uses *goy* to refer directly to Jacob's children—Gen 25:23; 35:11; 46:3; Exod 19:6; 33:13; Deut 4:6–8; Ps 83:4; 106:5; Isa 1:3–4; 18:2, 7; and Jer 7:28.

114. For further study on the dilation of time see Hawking, *History of Time,* 15; Schroeder, *Genesis' Big Bang,* 42–48; and Ps 90:4; and http://www.dummies.com/how-to/content/slowing-time-to-a-standstill-with-relativity.html (accessed February 2015).

115. Isa 13:11–12; 48:10; Zech 13:9; Ps 66:10–12. For further discussion see pp. 299, 654, 786, 839.

116. See chap. 13.V.A. on pp. 659–60; and Hos 6:1–3.

APPENDIX B

1. In both Gen 10:24 and 11:13 the Septuagint adds Cainan. "And after he [Arphaxad] became the father of Cainan, Arphaxad lived 430 years and had other sons and daughters, and then he died. When Cainan had lived 130 years, he became the father of Shelah. And after he became the father of Shelah, Cainan lived 330 years and had other sons and daughters" (11:13). If the LXX is correct, we would need to add another 130 yrs. to the Post-Flood Chronology.

2. Jacob was born in 452 P.F. or 2108 BCE. Shem died 50 years later in 502 P.F or 2058 BCE and would have been alive to see Abraham leave Mesopotamia to claim his birthright. He would also have known that Isaac, Jacob, and their children would inherit both his blessing and his birthright. See pp. 382–83.

APPENDIX C

1. Gray, "The Ḥâbirū-Hebrew Problem," 173–76; George Mendenhall, *The Tenth Generation: The Origins of the Biblical Tradition* (Baltimore: Johns Hopkins University Press, 1973) 35–138.

2. Henri, "The Hebrews," in *Essential Papers*; Gray, "The Ḥâbirū-Hebrew Problem," 135–202. See also: Julius Lewy, "Ḥâbirū and Hebrews," *Hebrew Union College Annual* 14 (1930) 587–623; Niels Peter Lemche, *Early Israel: Anthropological and Historical Studies on the Israelite Society before the Monarchy* (Vetus Testamentum Supplement 37; Leiden: Brill, 1985); and Nadav Na'aman, "Habiru and Hebrews: The Transfer of a Social Term to the Literary Sphere," *JNES* 45 (1986) 271–88.

3. Cazelles, *Hebrews*, 271.

4. Ibid.

5. Ibid.

6. Wilson, *Exodus Enigma*, 176; Gray, "The Ḥâbirū-Hebrew Problem," 155–60; Norman Gottwald, *Tribes of Yahweh: A Sociology of the Religion of Liberated Israel: 1250–1050 BCE* (Biblical Seminar 66; New York: Continuum, 1999) 491–92; Na'aman, "Habiru and Hebrews, 271.

7. Cazelles, *Hebrews*, 271.

8. Ibid.

9. Cazelles, *Hebrews*, 271.

10. Ibid., 274–75, 77; and Gray, "The Ḥâbirū-Hebrew Problem," 168, 171.

11. Cazelles, *Hebrews*, 269–71.

12. Ibid., 271.

13. Ibid.

14. Ibid., 270.

15. Hamilton, *Genesis: 1–17,* 344, 405; Mendenhall, *Ancient Israel*, 16–17; Malamat, *Biblical Israel*, 31, 43–53.

16. Cazelles, *Hebrews*, 270.

17. Malamat, *Biblical Israel,* 25.

18. Cazelles, *Hebrews*, 270.

19. Egypt appears to have maintained this distinction as well since Edom and the tribes east of the Jordan River are not referred to as Habiru, but as Shasu (Ward, "Shasu," 51, 53); see below.

20. Cazelles, *Hebrews*, 269.

21. Ibid., 271.

22. Hoffmeier, *Israel in Egypt,* 34. See also, David Merling, "The Relationship between Archaeology and the Bible," in *The Future of Biblical Archaeology: Reassessing Methodologies and Assumptions* (Proceedings of a Symposium at Trinity International University, Aug. 21–14, 2001; ed. James Hoffmeier and Alan Millard; Grand Rapids, MI: Eerdmans, 2004) 33–34.

23. 2 Sam 12:8; 1 Kgs 12:21; 2 Kgs 19:30; Jer 3:18; 5:11; 11:10, 17; 13:11; 31:31; 33:14; Ezek 4:4–6; 9:9; 37:16–17.

24. See chap. 4.II, pp. 124–25.

25. Lewy, "The Hebrew Hebrews," 609–14.

26. Wilson, *Exodus Enigma,* 176; Gray, "The Ḥâbirū-Hebrew Problem," 155–60; Gottwald, *Tribes of Yahweh,* 491–92; Na'aman, "Habiru and Hebrews," 271.

27. Na'aman, "Habiru and Hebrews," 171–72.

28. Ibid., 169.

29. Gray, "The Ḥâbirū-Hebrew Problem," 137.

30. Ibid.; Beitzel, "Habiru," *ISBE* (vol. 2) 587.

31. Hudson, "Enclave," in *ULO,* 130–31; Goelet, "'Town' and 'Country,'" in *ULO,* 90–96.

32. Alexander Fuks, *Social Conflict in Ancient Greece* (Leiden: Brill, 1984) 19–20; Isocrates. *Isocrates with an English Translation* (3 vols.; ed. George Norlin, 167), http://www.perseus.tufts.edu/hopper/text?doc= Perseus:abo:tlg,0010,011:167 (accessed December). The other factor affecting migration during this era was the very recent destruction of Babel (according to the chronology set forth in Genesis). With the

failed project and confused languages, people migrated to establish their own communities (see Table 9.51 in Appendix B).

33. Naʾaman, "Habiru and Hebrews," 272; Kline, "The Ha-Bi-Ru," 8; Malamat, *Biblical Israel,* 25; and Gray, "The Ḫâbirū-Hebrew Problem," 141–54.

34. Ibid.; and Naʾaman, "Habiru and Hebrews," 274.

35. Redford, *Ancient Times,* 207.

36. Ibid.

37. Ibid.

38. Beitzel, "Habiru," 587–88; and Gray, "The Ḫâbirū-Hebrew Problem," 138–68.

39. This leaves open the possibility of kindred relationship to Abram, Lot, and their servants.

40. Grimal, *Ancient Egypt,* 186; and Van Seters, *Hyksos,* 90.

41. Gray, "The Ḫâbirū-Hebrew Problem," 168.

42. Ibid., 138–39, 176.

43. Ibid., 177–78.

44. *SEC 5650;* BDB, 713–14; TWOT (vol. 2) 639–40.

45. Gray, "The Ḫâbirū-Hebrew Problem," 177–78.

46. Ibid., 179.

47. Ibid.

48. See also the similar use of *Shabbath Shabatown,* which is also redundant but drives home the idea of resting on the Sabbath (Exod 16:23; 15:31; 35:2).

49. Gray, "The Ḫâbirū-Hebrew Problem," 183–85; and Lewy, *The Habiru Hebrews,* 619–23.

50. Grayson, *Assyrian and Babylonian Chronicles,* 59; Sassmannshausen, "Babylonian Chronology of the 2nd half of the 2nd Millennium B.C.," 61–69; and EA 195 and 318 in Moran, *The Amarna Letters,* 273, 317, respectively.

51. Ward, "Shasu," 47–48.

52. McCarter, "Inscriptions," *ISBE* (vol. 2) 834; Finkelstein and Silberman, *Unearthed,* 57–60; Finkelstein and Mazar, *Quest for Israel,* 30, 39, 69, 74; Dever, *Early Israelites,* 135, 210–18; and Kitchen, *Reliability,* 206–7, 220.

53. Ward, "Shasu," 50–51, 54.

54. Ibid., 53.

55. Ibid., 51; and *ANET,* 259.

56. Ward, "Shasu," 54.

57. Ibid., 58.

58. Noll, *Canaan and Israel in Antiquity,* 121–23; Rendsburg, "Israel without the Bible," 9–12; Moore and Kelle, *Biblical History,* 124–25; and Redford, *Ancient Times,* 272–73.

59. Ibid.

Bibliography

HISTORICAL AND THEOLOGICAL SOURCES

Abraham, Kathleen. "The Reconstruction of Jewish Communities in the Persian Empire: The Āl-Yahūdu Clay Tablets." *Light and Shadows-The Catalog-The Story of Iran and the Jews.* Ed. Hagai Segev and Asaf Schor. Beit Hatfutsot: Tel Aviv, 2011: 261–64. http://www.academia.edu/1383485/The_Reconstruction_of_Jewish_Communities_in_the_Persian_Empire_The_%C4%80l-Yah%C5%ABdu_Clay_Tablets (accessed February 2015).

Ackerman, Susan. *Under Every Green Tree.* HSM 46. Winona Lake, IN: Eisenbrauns, 2001.

Albright, William Foxwell. *Yahweh and the Gods of Canaan.* Winona Lake, IN: Eisenbrauns, 1994.

Allen, J. H. *Judah's Sceptre and Joseph's Birthright.* Merrimac, MA: Destiny, 1917.

Anderson, James D. "The Impact of Rome on the Periphery: The Case of Palestina—Roman Period (63 BCD-324 CE)." *The Archaeology of Society in the Holy Land.* Ed. Thomas E. Levy. London: Leicester University Press, 1995: 446–68.

Annus, Amar. *The God Ninurta.* Helsinki: University of Helsinki, 2002.

Archi, Alfonso. "Archival Record-Keeping at Ebla 2400–2350 BC." *Ancient Archives and Archival Traditions: Concepts of Record-Keeping in the Ancient World.* Ed. Maria Brosius. Oxford: Oxford University Press, 2003.

Armstrong, Karen. *Jerusalem: One City, Three Faiths.* New York: Knopf, 1996.

Arnold, Bill T. "The Weidner Chronicle and the Idea of History in Israel. *Faith, Tradition, and History.* Ed. A. K. Millard, J. K. Hoffmeier, and D. W. Baker. Winona Lake, IN: Eisenbrauns, 1994: 129–48.

———. "What has Nebuchadnezzar to Do with David? On the Neo-Babylonian Period and Early Israel." *Mesopotamia and the Bible.* Ed. Mark W. Chavalas and K. Lawson Younger, Jr. Grand Rapids: Baker Academic, 2002: 330–55.

Asante, Moleifi, and Ama Mazama, Ed. *Encyclopedia of African Religion*: vol. 1. Thousand Oaks, CA: Sage, 2009.

Ashby, Muata. *Egypt and India: Ancient Egyptian Religion and the Origins of Hinduism, Vedanta, Yoga, Buddhism and Dharma of India.* Miami: Curzian Mystic Books, 2002.

Ashley, Timothy. *The Book of Numbers.* Grand Rapids, MI: Eerdmans, 1993.

Assmann, Jan. *Death and Salvation in Ancient Egypt.* Trans. David Lorton. Ithaca, NY: Cornell University Press, 2005.

_____. *The Mind of Egypt.* Trans. Andrew Jenkins. New York: Metropolitan Books, 1996.

Åstrom, Paul, Ed. *High, Middle or Low: Acts of an International Colloquium on Absolute Chronology Held at the University of Gothenburg 20th–22nd August 1987, part 1 and 2* (Gothenburg: Paul Åstroms Forlage, 1987).

Avalos, Hector. *Illness and Health Care in the Ancient Near East.* HSM 54. Atlanta: Scholars Press, 1995.

Averbeck, Richard E. "Ancient Near Eastern Mythography as It Relates to Historiography in the Hebrew Bible: Genesis 3 and the Cosmic Battle." *The Future of Biblical Archaeology: Reassessing Methodologies and Assumptions.* Proceeding of a Symposium at Trinity International University, Aug. 12–14, 2001. Ed. James Hoffmeier and Alan Millard. Grand Rapids, MI: Eerdmans, 2004: 328–356.

_____. "Sumer, the Bible, and Comparative Method: Historiography and Temple Building." *Mesopotamia and the Bible.* Ed. Mark W. Chavalas and K. Lawson Younger, Jr. Grand Rapids: Baker Academic, 2002: 88–125.

_____. "The Sumerian Historiographic Tradition and Its Implications for Genesis 1–11." *Faith, Tradition, and History.* Ed. A. K. Millard, J. K. Hoffmeier, and D. W. Baker. Winona Lake, IN: Eisenbrauns, 1994: 79–102.

Avi-Yonah, Michael. *The Holy Land: A Historical Geography from the Persian to the Arab Conquest (536 B.C. to A.D. 640).* Jerusalem: Carta, 2002.

Baden, Joel. *J, E, and the Redaction of the Pentateuch.* Forschungen zum Alten Testament 68. Tubingen, Germany: Mohr Siebeck, 2009.

Baker, David W. "Scribes as Transmitters of Tradition." *Faith, Tradition, and History.* Ed. A. K. Millard, J. K. Hoffmeier, and D. W. Baker. Winona Lake, IN: Eisenbrauns, 1994: 65–78.

Baly, Dennis. "The Pitfalls of Biblical Geography in Relation to Jordan." *Studies in the History and Archaeology of Jordan*: vol. 3. Ed. Adnan Hadidi. New York: Routledge and Kegan Paul, 1987: 128–29.

Bard, Katheryn A. "The Emergence of the Egyptian State (*c.* 2686–2160 BC)." *The Oxford History of Ancient Egypt.* Ed. Ian Shaw. New York: Oxford University Press, 2004: 57–82.

Barnes, Albert. *Barnes' Notes on the Old and New Testaments*: 14 vols. Grand Rapids: Baker Books, 1996. http://www.sacred-texts.com/bib/cmt/barnes/exo001.htm (accessed February 2015).

Barnes, Harry E. *An Economic History of the Western World.* New York: Harcourt, Brace and Company, 1942.

Barnes, Robert. "Reformed Answers: Problem of Evil." Third Millennium Ministries. http://reformedanswers.org/answer.asp/file/99770.qna/category/ot/page/questions/site/ (accessed February 2015).

Barnes, William H. *Studies in the Chronology of the Divided Monarchy of Israel.* HSM 48. Atlanta: Scholars Press, 1991.

Bartchy, S. Scott. "Slavery." *International Standard Bible Encyclopedia*: vol. 4. Grand Rapids, MI: Eerdmans, 1979: 539–43.

Barthel, Manfred, Ed. *What the Bible Really Says.* Trans. Mark Howson. Oxford: Morrow, 1982.

Barton, John, and John Muddiman, Ed. *The Oxford Bible Commentary*. Oxford: Oxford University Press, 2001.

Bar-Yosef, "Prehistoric Chronological Framework." *The Archaeology of Society in the Holy Land*. Ed. Thomas E. Levy. London: Leicester University Press, 1995: xiv–xvi.

Beale, G. K. *We Become What We Worship: A Biblical Theology of Idolatry*. Downers Grove, IL: IVP Academic, 2008.

Becking, Bob. *The Fall of Samaria: An Historical and Archaeological Study*. Leiden: Brill, 1992: 13–40.

Beitzel, Barry. "Habiru." *International Standard Bible Encyclopedia*: vol. 2. Grand Rapids, MI: Eerdmans, 1979: 586–89.

Benner, Jeff A. *A Mechanical Translation of the Book of Genesis: The Hebrew Text Literally Translated Word for Word* (College Station, TX: Virtual Bookworm, 2007). http://www.ancient-hebrew.org/bookstore/e-books/mtg.pdf (accessed February 2015).

Bennet, Chris. "Temporal Fugues." *JAMS* 13 (1996).

Bennet, W. H. *Symobols of our Celto-Saxon Heritage*. Windsor, Ontario: Herald Press, 1976.

Ben-Tor, Amnon, Ed. *The Archaeology of Ancient Israel*. Trans. R. Greenberg. New Haven, CT: Yale University Press, 1992.

Ben-Zion, Ilan. "'By the Rivers of Babylon' Exhibit Breaths Live into Judean Exile." The Times of Israel (February 1, 2015). http://www.timesofisrael.com/by-the-rivers-of-babylon-exhibit-breathes-life-into-judean-exile/#ixzz3QtcvjbRQ (accessed February 2015)

Ben-Zvi, Ehud. "Shifting the Gaze: Historiographic Constraints in Chronicles and Their Implications." *The Land That I Will Show You*. Sheffield: Sheffield Academic Press, 2001: 38–60.

_____. "Who Destroyed Canaanite Hazor?" *BAR* 39/4 (2013) 27–36.

Bergsma, John Sietze. *The Jubilee from Leviticus to Qumran: A History of Interpretation*. Leiden: Brill, 2007.

Bhalla, Prem. *Hindu Rites, Rituals, Customs and Traditions*. Delhi: Pustak Mahal, 2006.

Bienkowski, Piotr. "New Evidence on Edom in the Neo-Babylonian and Persian Periods." *The Land That I Will Show You*. Sheffield: Sheffield Academic Press, 2001: 198–213.

Bierbrier, M. L. "Generation-Counting and Late New Kingdom Chronology." *JEA* 67 (1981) 182–84.

_____. *The Late New Kingdom in Egypt (c1300–664 BC): A Genealogical and Chronological Investigation*. Warminster: Aris and Phillips, 1975.

Bietak, Manfred, Ed. "The Center of Hyksos Rule: Avaris (Tell el-Daba)." *The Hyksos: New Historical and Archaeological Perspectives*. Ed. Eliezer Oren. University Museum Monograph 96/8. Philadelphia: University of Pennsylvania Museum, 1997.

_____. "A Palace of the Hyksos King Khayan at Avaris." *Proceedings of the 6th International Congress of the Archaeology of the Ancient Near East*: vol. 2. Ed. Paolo Matthiae, et al. Wiesbaden: Harrassowitz Verlag, 2010.

_____, et al. "The Chronology of Tell el-Daba: A Crucial Meeting Point of 14C Dating, Archaeology, and Egyptology in the 2nd Millennium BC." *Proceedings of the 6th International Radiocarbon and Archaeology Symposium*. Ed. E. Boaretto and N.R. Rebollo Franco. *Radiocarbon* 54(2012)3–4.

_____, Ed. *The Middle Bronze Age in the Levant: Proceedings of an International Conference on MB IIA Ceramic Material, Vienna, 24th–26th of January 2001* (Vienna: Verlag, 2002).

_____. "The Palatial Precinct at the Nile Branch (Area H)." http://www.auaris.at/html/ez_helmi_en.html(accessed February 2015).

Bietak, Manfred, Felix Höflmayer, et al. "Introduction: High and Low Chronology." *The Synchronisation of Civilisations in the Eastern Mediterranean in the Second Millennium B.C. III: Proceedings of the SCIEM 2000 — 2nd EuroConference, Vienna 28th of May – 1st of June 2003*. Ed. Manfred Bietak and E. Czerny. Vienna: Verlag der Österreichischen Akademie der Wissenschaften, 2007.

Beitzel, Barry. "Habiru." *International Standard Bible Encyclopedia*: vol. 2. Grand Rapids, MI: Eerdmans, 1979: 586–89.

Bimson, John. *Redating the Exodus and Conquest*. Sheffield: Almond Press, 1981.

_____. "Merneptah's Israel and Recent Theories of Israelite Origins." *JSOT* 49 (1991) 3–29.

Biran, Avraham. "The Tel Dan Inscription: A New Fragment." *Israel Exploration Journal* 45 (1995) 1–15.

_____. "A Palace of the Hyksos King Khayan at Avaris." *Proceedings of the 6th International Congress of the Archaeology*: vol. 2. Ed. Paolo Matthiae, et al. Harrassowitz Verlag, 2008: 102.

_____. "The Tel Dan Inscription: A New Fragment." *Israel Exploration Journal* 45 (1995) 1–18.

Biran, Avraham, and Joseph Naveh. "An Aramaic Stele Fragment from Tel Dan." *Israel Exploration Journal* 43/2–3 (1993) 81–99.

Black, Jeremy, and Anthony Green. *Gods, Demons and Symbols of Ancient Mesopotamia*. Austin: University of Texas, 1992.

Bleeker, C. J. "Guilt and Purification in Egypt." *Proceedings of the Xth International Congress of the International Association of Religions*: vol. 2. Leiden: Brill, 1968.

Blenkinsopp, Joseph. *Sage, Priest, Prophet: Religious and Intellectual Leadership in Ancient Israel*. Ed. Douglas Knight. Louisville: John Knox, 1995.

Bloch-Smith, Elizabeth. "Bible, Archaeology, and the Social Sciences." *The Hebrew Bible*. Ed. Frederick Greenspahn. New York: New York University Press, 2008.

Block, Daniel I. "Deborah among the Judges: The Perspective of the Hebrew Historian." *Faith, Tradition, and History*. Ed. A. R. Millard, J. K. Hoffmeier, and D. W. Baker. Winona Lake, IN: Eisenbrauns, 1994: 229–253.

_____. "Sojourner." *International Standard Bible Encyclopedia*: vol. 4. Grand Rapids, MI: Eerdmans, 1979: 561–63.

Blomberg, Craig L. "Stranger." *International Standard Bible Encyclopedia*: vol. 4. Grand Rapids, MI: Eerdmans, 1979: 635.

Bolling, Ian. "Adoption Trends in 2003: Infant Abandonment and Safe Haven Legislation." *Report on Trends in the State Courts* (2003). http://www.uvm.edu/~vlrs/Safety/babysafehavens.pdf (accessed December 2013).

Bolton, W. F. *A Living Language*. New York: McGraw-Hill, 1982.

Borchert, Gerald L. "Mildew," *International Standard Bible Encyclopedia*: vol. 3. Grand Rapids, MI: Eerdmans, 1979: 354.

Bottéro, Jean. *Religion in Ancient Mesopotamia*. Trans. Teresa Fagan. Chicago: University of Chicago Press, 2004.

Botterweck, Johannes, Helmer Ringgren, and Heinz-Josef Fabry, Ed. *Theological Dictionary of the Old Testament*: 15 vols. Grand Rapids, MI: Eerdman's, 2006.

Bouglé, Célestin C. A. *Essays on the Caste System*. Trans. D. F. Pocock, London: Cambridge University Press, 1971.

Bourriau, Janine. "Beyond Avaris: "The Second Intermediate Period in Egypt Outside the Eastern Delta." *The Hyksos: New Historical and Archaeological Perspectives*. Ed. Eliezer Oren. University Museum Monograph 96/8. University of Pennsylvania Museum, 1997.

_____. "The Second Intermediate Period (c. 1650–1550)." *The Oxford History of Ancient Egypt*. New York: Oxford University Press, 2004.

Bower, Robert K., and Gary L. Knapp. "Marriage." *International Standard Bible Encyclopedia*: vol. 3. Grand Rapids, MI: Eerdmans, 1979: 263.

Bowls, Henry. "Russia's Exploding Muslim Population." *Foreign Policy* (January 2007). http://blog.foreignpolicy.com/posts/2007/01/16/russias_exploding_muslim_population (accessed December 2013).

Bram, Leon L. and Norma H. Dickey, Ed. *Funk and Wagnalls Encyclopedia*: vol. 14. "J." New York, 1975: 94.

"Breaking News—Evidence of Cultic Activity in Judah Discovered at Khirbet Qeiyafa." *Bible History Daily*. Biblical Archaeology Society. May 8, 2012. http://www.biblicalarchaeology.org/daily/biblical-artifacts/artifacts-and-the-bible/breaking-news%E2%80%94evidence-of-cultic-activity-in-judah-discovered-at-khirbet-qeiyafa/ (accessed February 2015).

Breasted, James Henry. *Ancient Records of Egypt*: 5 vols. Champaign, IL: University of Illinois Press, 2001.

_____. *The Development of Religion and Thought in Ancient Egypt*. New York: Scribner, 1912.

_____, Ed. *The Edwin Smith Surgical Papyrus*. Chicago: University of Chicago, 1930.

_____. *The Papyrus Ebers*. Trans. Cyril P. Bryan. Letchworth, Herts: Garden City Press, 1930.

Brenton, C. L., Trans. *The Septuagint with Apocrypha: Greek and English*. London: Bagster, 1851. Repr. Peabody, MA: Hendrickson, 1986.

Briant, Pierre. *From Cyrus to Alexander*. Trans. Peter Daniels. Winona Lake, IN: Eisenbrauns, 2002.

Brinkman, J. A. *A Political History of Post-Kassite Babylonia, 1158–722 B.C.* AnOr 43. Rome: Pontifical Biblical Institute, 1968.

Brisco, Thomas V. "Pithom." *International Standard Bible Encyclopedia*: vol. 3. Grand Rapids, MI: Eerdmans, 1979: 875–76.

British Museum, "Tablet Recording Gold Delivery by the Chief Eunuch of Nebuchadnezzar II," http://www.britishmuseum.org/explore/highlights/highlight_objects/me/t/tablet_recording_gold_delivery.aspx (accessed December 2013).

Brody, Aaron. *"Each Man Cried Out to His God": The Specialized Religion of the Canaanite and Phoenician Seafarers*. Ed. Peter Machinist. HSM 58. Atlanta: Scholars Press, 1998.

Bromiley, Geoffrey W., Ed. *International Standard Bible Encyclopedia*: 4 vols. Grand Rapids, MI: Eerdmans, 1979.

_____. "God: God in the OT." *International Standard Bible Encyclopedia*: vol. 2. Grand Rapids, MI: Eerdmans, 1979: 497.

Brown, Francis, S. R. Driver, and C. Briggs. *The Brown-Driver-Briggs Hebrew and English Lexicon*. Peabody, MA: Hendrickson, 2003.

Bruce, Dan. *Sacred Chronology of the Hebrew Kings*. Atlanta: The Prophecy Society, 2012.

_____. *Lifting the Veil on the Book of Daniel*. Atlanta: The Prophecy Society, 2012.

Bruins, Hendrick, and Johannes van der Plicht. "Tell Es-Sultan (Jericho) Radiocarbon Results of Short-Lived Cereal and Multiyear Charcoal Samples from the End of the Middle Bronze Age." *Radiocarbon* 37/2 (1995) 213–20.

Bryan, Betsy. "The 18th Dynasty before the Amarna Period." *The Oxford History of Ancient Egypt*. Ed. Ian Shaw. New York: Oxford University Press, 2004: 207–264.

Buccellati, Giorgio. "Urkesh and the Question of Early Hurrian Urbanism." *Urbanization and Land Ownership in the Ancient Near East*: vol.2. Ed. Michael Hudson and Baruch Levine.

Cambridge: Peabody Museum of Archaeology and Ethnology of Harvard University, 1999: 229–52.

Bunimovitz, Shlomo. "On the Edge of Empires—Late Bronze Age (1500–1200 BCE)." *The Archaeology of Society in the Holy Land.* Ed. Thomas E. Levy. London: Leicester University Press, 1995: 320–30.

Buck, Caitlin, and Andrew Millard, Ed. *Tools for Constructing Chronologies: Crossing Disciplinary Boundaries.* Lecture Notes on Statistics 177. London: Springer-Verlag, 2004.

Budge, Ernest. *The Gods of the Egyptians: Or, Studies in Egyptian Mythology:* 2 vols. London: Methuen, 1904.

———. *Legends of the Gods.* London: Kegan Paul, Trench, Trubner, 1912.

Burkert, Walter. *Greek Religion.* Trans. John Raffan. Cambridge: Harvard University Press, 1985.

———. *The Orientalizing Revolution: Near Eastern Influence on Greek Culture in the Early Archaic Age.* Trans. Margaret Pinder. Cambridge: Harvard University Press, 1995.

Bury, J. B., Ed. *The Cambridge Ancient History:* 12 vols. Cambridge: Cambridge University, 1969.

Buss, Martin J. "A Projection for Israelite Historiography: With a Comparison between Qohelet and Nagarjuna." *The Land That I Will Show You.* Ed. Andrew Dearman and Patrick Graham. Sheffield: Sheffield Academic Press, 2001: 61–68.

Caldwell, Penny. "The Split Rock." Split Rock Research. http://splitrockresearch.org/content/100/Field_Reports/The_Split_Rock (accessed February 2015).

Callender, Gae. "Middle Kingdom Renaissance." *The Oxford History of Ancient Egypt.* Ed. Ian Shaw. New York: Oxford University Press, 2004.

Campbell, Joseph. *The Mythic Image.* Princeton: Princeton University Press, 1974.

———. *Occidental Mythology: The Masks of God.* New York: Penguin, 1991.

———. *Oriental Mythology: The Masks of God.* New York: Penguin, 1962.

———. *The Hero with a Thousand Faces.* Princeton: Princeton University Press, 1968.

Cantrell, Deborah. *The Horsemen of Israel: Horses and Chariotry in Monarchic Israel (Ninth–Eighth Centuries B.C.E.).* History, Archaeology, and Culture of the Levant. Winona Lake, IN: Eisenbrauns, 2011.

Capt, E. Raymond. *Counterfeit Christianity—How Ancient Paganism Mixed with Christianity.* Muskogee, OK: Artisan Publishers, 2006.

———. *Missing Links Discovered in Assyrian Tablets.* Muskogee, OK: Artisan Publishers, 1985.

Car, G. L., and N. J. O. "Bread of the Presence," *International Standard Bible Encyclopedia:* vol. 3. Grand Rapids, MI: Eerdmans, 1979: 955–56.

Cassuto, Umberto Moshe David. *The Documentary Hypothesis.* Trans. Israel Abraham. Skokie, IL: Varda Books, 2005.

Cazells, Henri. "The Hebrews." *Essential Papers on Israel and the Ancient Near East.* Ed. Frederick Greenspahn. New York: New York University Press, 1991.

Celsus on the True Doctrine. Trans. R. J. Hoffmann. Oxford: Oxford University Press, 1987.

Chandler, Darwin. *The Royal Law of Liberty: Living in Freedom under Christ's Law of Love.* Victoria, BC: Trafford, 2003.

Chavalas, Mark, W. "Genealogical History as 'Charter': A Study of Old Babylonian Period Historiography and the Old Testament." *Faith, Tradition, and History.* Ed. A. K. Millard, J. K. Hoffmeier, and D. W. Baker. Winona Lake, IN: Eisenbrauns, 1994: 103–128.

Chavalas, Mark, W., and K. Lawson Younger, Jr., Ed. *Mesopotamia and the Bible.* Grand Rapids, MI: Baker, 2002.

Chimko, Corey J. "Foreign Pharaohs: Self-Legitimization and Indigenous Reaction in Art and Literature." *JSSEA* 30 (2003) 15–57.

Cichocki, Otto, et al. "The Synchronization of Civilizations in the Eastern Mediterranean in the Second Millennium BC: Natural Science Dating Attempts." *Tools for Constructing Chronologies: Crossing Disciplinary Boundaries.* Ed. Caitlin Buck. London: Springer, 2004.

Clayton, Peter. *The Chronicles of the Pharaohs.* London: Thames and Hudson, 1994.

Cobern, Camden M., and Carl E. Armerding. "Golden Calf." *International Standard Bible Encyclopedia*: vol. 1. Grand Rapids, MI: Eerdmans, 1979: 579–80.

Cockburn, Aidan. Eve Cockburn, and Theodore Reyman, Ed. *Mummies, Disease, and Ancient Cultures.* Cambridge: Cambridge University Press, 1998.

Cohen, Abraham. *Everyman's Talmud.* New York: Schocken Books, 1949.

Cohen, Mark E. *The Cultic Calendars of the Ancient Near East.* Bethesda, MD: CDL Press, 1993.

Collins, John. *The Septer and the Star.* Anchor Bible Reference Library. New York: Bantam Doubleday, 1995.

Cook, E. M. "Weights and Measures." *International Standard Bible Encyclopedia*: vol. 4. Grand Rapids, MI: Eerdmans, 1979: 1051–54.

Corley, Kathleen. "Tiphsah." *International Standard Bible Encyclopedia*: vol. 4. Grand Rapids, MI: Eerdmans, 1979, 858–59.

Coward, Harold. *Sin and Salvation in the World Religions: A Short Introduction.* Oxford: Oneworld, 2003.

Cox, Rufus F., Jonathan Garst, and Richard M. Highsmith. "Agriculture." *New Standard Encyclopedia*: vol. 1. Chicago: Standard Educational, 1995: 145–150.

Craigie, Peter C. "Idea of War." *International Standard Bible Encyclopedia*: vol. 4. Grand Rapids, MI: Eerdmans, 1979: 1091.

Crier, Catherine. *The Case against Lawyers.* New York: Broadway Books, 2002.

Cronin, Frances. "Egyptian Pyramids Found by Infra-Red Satellite Images. *BBC News.* Last updated May 24, 2011. http://www.bbc.co.uk/news/world-13522957 (accessed February 2015).

Currid, John. *Ancient Egypt and the Old Testament.* Grand Rapids, MI: Baker Books, 1997.

Czerny, Ernst. "The Orthogonal Planned Settlement of the Early Middle Kingdom (F/I, stratum e)." Tell el-Dabᶜa, 2008, 2013. http://www.auaris.at/html/stratum_e_en.html (accessed February 2015).

Dahan, Gilbert. "Genres, Forms and Various Methods in Christian Exegesis and the Middle Ages." *Hebrew Bible/Old Testament: From the beginnings to the Middle Ages (until 1300), vol. 1/2: The Middle Ages.* Ed. Magne Saebo. Munich: Vandenhoeck and Ruprecht, 2000: 216–220.

Dahl, Gudrun, and Anders Hjort. *Having Herds: Pastoral Herd Growth and Household Economy.* Stockholm: University of Stockholm, 1976.

Dally, Stephanie, Trans. *Myths from Mesopotamia.* Oxford: Oxford University Press, 1989.

———. "Gilgamesh and the Arabian Nights." *Gilgamesh: A Reader.* Ed. John Maier. Wauconda, IL: Bolchazy-Carducci, 1997.

Dandamayev, Muhammed A. "Land Use in the Sippar Region During the Neo-Babylonian and Achaemenid Periods." *Urbanization and Land Ownership in the Ancient Near East*: vol. 2. Ed. Michael Hudson and Baruch Levine. Cambridge: Peabody Museum of Archaeology and Ethnology of Harvard University, 1999: 363–89.

Danin, Avinoam. "Man and the Natural Environment." *The Archaeology of Society in the Holy Land.* New Approaches in Anthropological Archaeology. Ed. Thomas E. Levy. London: Leicester University Press, 1998; 24–37.

Daube, David. *Studies in Biblical Law.* New York: Cambridge University Press, 1947.

Daviau, P. M. Michéle. "Assyrian Influence and Changing Technologies at Tall Jawa, Jordan." *The Land That I Will Show You.* Sheffield: Sheffield Academic Press, 2001: 214–38.

David, Rosalie. *Religion and Magic in Ancient Egypt.* New York: Penguin, 2003.

Davidi, Yair. *Ephraim: The Gentile Children of Israel.* Jerusalem, Israel: Russell-Davis, 2001.

Davies, Eryl. "The Inheritance of the First-born in Israel and the Ancient Near East." *JSS* 38 (1993) 175–91.

Davies, Philip. "The Intellectual, the Archaeologist and the Bible." *The Land That I Will Show You.* Ed. Andrew Dearman and Patrick Graham. Sheffield: Sheffield Academic Press, 2001: 239–254.

————. *Scribes and Schools: The Canonization of the Hebrew Scriptures.* Louisville: Westminster John Knox, 1998.

Davis, Miriam. *Dame Kathleen Kenyon: Digging Up the Holy Land.* Walnut Creek, CA: Left Coast Press, 2008.

Davis, Thomas W. "Theory and Method in Biblical Archaeology." *The Future of Biblical Archaeology: Reassessing Methodologies and Assumptions.* Proceedings of a Symposium at Trinity International University, Aug. 21–14, 2001. Ed. James Hoffmeier and Alan Millard. Grand Rapids, MI: Eerdmans, 2004: 20–28.

Day, John. *Yahweh and the Gods and Goddesses of Canaan.* JSOTSup. London: Sheffield Academic Press, 2002.

Dearman, Andrew, and Patrick Graham, Ed. *The Land That I Will Show You.* Ed. Andrew Dearman and Patrick Graham. Sheffield: Sheffield Academic Press, 2001.

DeHaan, M. R. *Studies in Galations.* Grand Rapids, MI: Kregel Publications, 1995.

Denniston, James T., Jr. "Congregation." *International Standard Bible Encyclopedia*: vol. 1. Grand Rapids, MI: Eerdmans, 1979: 760–61.

Depuydt, Leo. *Civil Calendar and Lunar Calendar in Ancient Egypt.* Leuven: Peeters, 1997.

Dever, William. "Is There Any Archaeological Evidence for the Exodus?" *Exodus: Egyptian Evidence.* Ed. Ernest Frerichs and Leonard Lesko. Winona Lake, IN: Eisenbrauns, 1997.

————. "Settlement Patterns and Chronology of Palestine in the Middle Bronze Age." *The Hyksos: New Historical and Archaeological Perspectives.* Ed. Eliezer Oren. University Museum Monograph 96/8. Philadelphia: University of Pennsylvania Museum, 1997.

————. "Social Structure in the Early Bronze IV Period in Palestine." *The Archaeology of Society in the Holy Land.* Ed. Thomas E. Levy. London: Leicester University Press, 1995: 282–95.

————. "Social Structure in Palestine in the Iron II Period on the Eve of Destruction." *The Archaeology of Society in the Holy Land.* Ed. Thomas E. Levy. London: Leicester University Press, 1995: 416–30.

————. *Who Were the Early Israelites and Where Did They Come From?* Grand Rapids, MI: Eerdmans, 2003.

De Vries, Carl E. "Hyksos." *International Standard Bible Encyclopedia*: vol. 2. Grand Rapids, MI: Eerdmans, 1979: 787.

De Vries, S. J. "Chronology of the Old Testament." *The Interpreter's Dictionary of the Bible*: 4 vols. Ed. G. A. Buttrick. Nashville: Abingdon Press, 1962.

Diodorus Siculus. Trans. Edwin Murphy. New Brunswick, NJ: Transaction Publishers, 1989.

Dijk, Jacobus van. "The Amarna Period and Later New Kingdom." *The Oxford History of Ancient Egypt*. Ed. Ian Shaw. New York: Oxford University Press, 2004.

Diringer, David. "J." *The Encyclopedia Britannica*: vol. 15. Danbury, CT: Grolier, 2001: 636.

Doane, T. W. *Bible Myths and Their Parallels in Other Religions*. New York: University Books, 1971.

Dollinger, André. "Contracts and Other Legal Documents." An Introduction to the History and Culture of Pharaohic Egypt. Last updated April 2004. http://www.reshafim.org.il/ad/egypt/law_and_order/contracts.htm (accessed February 2015).

Donadoni, Sergio. *The Egyptians*. Chicago: University of Chicago Press, 1997.

Dougherty, Raymond. *Nabonidus and Belshazzar*. New Haven, CT: Yale University Press, 1929.

Downey, Douglas W. Ed. *New Standard Encyclopedia*. Chicago: Standard Educational, 1995.

Dozeman, Thomas, and Konrad Schmid, Ed. *A Farewell to the Yahwist?: The Composition of the Pentateuch in Recent European Interpretation*. SBL Symposium Series 34. Atlanta: Society of Biblical Literature, 2006.

Dynes, Wayne R., and Stephen Donaldson. *Homosexuality in the Ancient World*. New York: Garland, 1992.

Eberstadt, Nicholas. "The Demographic Future: What Growth—and Decline—Means for the Global Economy." *The Foreign Affairs Journal*. November 1, 2010. http://www.foreignaffairs.com/articles/66805/nicholas-eberstadt/the-demographic-future (accessed February 2015).

Eberstadt, Nicholas, and Apoova Shah, "No Amount of 'Reset' Can Avert the Looming Russian Disaster," *Public Policy Blog of the American Enterprise Institute*. July 8, 2009. http://www.aei-ideas.org/2009/07/no-amount-of-reset-can-avert-the-looming-russian-disaster/ (accessed February 2015).

Edelstein, Emma J., and Ludwig Edelstein. *Asclepius: Collection and Interpretation of the Testimonies*: 2 vols. Baltimore, MD: Johns Hopkins University Press, 1998.

Edwards, Paul, Ed. *The Encyclopedia of Philosophy*: 8 vols. New York: Macmillan, 1967.

Eisenman, Robert. *James the Brother of Jesus and the Dead Sea Scrolls*: vol. 1. Nashville: Grave Distractions Publications, 2012.

Elazar, Daniel. "The Book of Judges: The Israelite Tribal Federation and Its Discontents." Jerusalem Center for Public Affairs. http://www.jcpa.org/dje/articles/judges.htm (accessed February 2015).

Elitzur, Yehuda, and Yehuda Keel. *The Daat Mikra Bible Atlas*. Trans. Lenn J. Schramm. Mosad Harav Kook: Jerusalem, 2011.

Ellis, Maria de. *Agriculture and the State in Ancient Mesopotamia: An Introduction to Problems of Land Tenure*. Occasional Publications of the Babylonian Fund 1. Philadelphia: Babylonian Fund, University Museum, 1976.

El-Shahawy, Abeer. *The Funerary Art of Ancient Egypt: A Bridge to the Realm of the Hereafter*. Cairo: Farid Atiya Press, 2005.

Enserink, Martin. "Can the War on Locusts Be Won?" *Science Magazine* 306/5703. AAAS (December 10, 2004) 1880–82.

Etz, Donald V. "The Genealogical Relationships of Jehoram and Ahaziah, and of Ahaz and Hezekiah, Kings of Judah." *JSOT* 21 (1996) 39–53.

Evans, Carl. "Judah's Foreign Policy from Hezekiah to Josiah." *Scripture in Context*: vol. 1: *Essays on the Comparative Method*. Ed. Carl Evans, et al. PTMS 34. Pitsburgh: Pickwick, 1980.

Evans, Paul. *The Invasion of Sennacherib in the Book of Kings: A Source-Critical and Rhetorical Study of 2 Kings 18–19*. Leiden: Brill, 2009.

Eynikel, Erik. *The Reform of King Josiah and the Composition of the Deuteronomistic History*. Leiden: Brill, 1996.

Fantuzzi, Tiziano. "The Absolute Chronology of the Egyptian S.I.P. New Kingdom Transition and Implications for Late Minoan Crete." *Creta Antica* 10/2 (2009) 477–500.

Faulkner, Raymond. *The Ancient Egyptian Pyramid Texts*. Oxford: Clarendon Press, 1969.

Fausset, A. R. *Faucet's Bible Dictionary*. Grand Rapids, MI: Zondervan Publishing, 1966.

Faust, Avraham. "Early Israel: An Egalitarian Society." *BAR* 30/4 (2013) 46.

Feldman, Rachel, Ed. "Most Ancient Hebrew Biblical Inscription Deciphered." University of Haifa. Last updated January 10, 2010. http://newmedia-eng.haifa.ac.il/?p=2043 (accessed February 2015).

Fensham, F. Charles. "Judicial Courts." *International Standard Bible Encyclopedia*: vol. 1. Grand Rapids, MI: Eerdmans, 1979: 788–89.

_____. "Widow, Orphan, and the Poor in Ancient Near Eastern Legal and Wisdom Literature." *Essential Papers on Israel and the Ancient Near East*. Ed. Greenspahn, Frederick. New York: New York University Press, 1991: 176–92.

Filer, Joyce. *Egyptian Bookshelf: Disease*. Austin, TX: University of Texas Press, 1995.

Finegan, Jack. *Handbook of Biblical Chronology*. Peabody, MA: Hendrickson, 1998.

Finkelstein, Israel. "The Great Transformation: The 'Conquest' of the Highlands Frontiers and the Rise of the Territorial States." *The Archaeology of Society in the Holy Land*. Ed. Thomas E. Levy. London: Leicester University Press, 1995: 349–66.

Finkelstein, Israel, and Amihai Mazar. *The Quest for Historical Israel*. Ed. Brian Schmidt. Atlanta: Society of Biblical Literature, 2007.

Finkelstein, Israel, and Neil Asher-Silberman. *The Bible Unearthed*. New York: Free Press, 2001.

Finkelstein, Jacob J. "Bible and Babel: A Comparative Study of the Hebrew and Babylonian Religious Spirit." *Essential Papers on Israel and the Ancient Near East*. Ed. Greenspahn, Frederick. New York: New York University Press, 1991: 355–80.

Finkelstein, Louis, Ed. *Pharisaism in the Making*. Jersey City, NJ: KTAV Publishing, 1972.

Fleming, Daniel. "Emar: On the Road from Harron to Hebron." *Mesopotamia and the Bible*. Ed. Mark W. Chavalas and K. Lawson Younger, Jr. Grand Rapids, MI: Baker, 2002: 222–50.

_____. "Genesis in History and Tradition: The Syrian Background of Israel's Ancestors, Reprise." *The Future of Biblical Archaeology: Reassessing Methodologies and Assumptions*. Proceeding of a Symposium at Trinity International University, Aug. 12–14, 2001. Ed. James Hoffmeier and Alan Millard. Grand Rapids, MI: Eerdmans, 2004: 193–232.

Fortner, Don. "The Law of the Lord is Perfect." Sovereign Grace of God. Last updated May 23, 2007. http://www.sovereigngraceofgod.com/sermons/fd-00811.htm (accessed November 2013).

Foster, Karen, Robert Ritner, and Benjamin R. Foster. "Texts, Storms, and the Thera Eruption." *JNES* 55 (1996) 1–14.

Fortune, A. W. "Babylon." *International Standard Bible Encyclopedia*: vol. 1. Grand Rapids, MI: Eerdmans, 1979, 385.

Fox, Michael V., et al., Ed. *Texts, Temples, and Traditions*. Winona Lake, IN: Eisenbrauns, 1996.

Fox, Nili. *Service of the King*. Cincinnati, OH: Hebrew Union College Press, 2000.

Frankfort, Henri. *Kingship and the Gods*. Chicago: University of Chicago Press, 1948.

Franz, Gordan. "Is Mount Sinai in Saudi Arabia?" Lambert Dolphin. http://www.ldolphin.org/franz-sinai.html (accessed February 2015).

Frazer, James G. *The Golden Bough: A Study in Magic and Religion.* New York: Macmillan Publishing, 1922.

Freedman, David Noel, Ed. *The Anchor Bible Dictionary*: 6 vols. New York: Doubleday, 1992.

_____. "The Chronology of Israel and the Ancient Near East." *The Bible and the Ancient Near East.* Ed. Earnest Wright. Garden City, NY: Doubleday, 1965.

_____. *The Nine Commandments.* New York: Doubleday, 2000.

Freke, Timothy, and Peter Gandy. *The Jesus Mysteries.* New York: Three Rivers Press, 1999.

Friedman, Matti. "Bible's Different Authors Revealed by New Language Software." *The Huffington Post* (June 29, 2011).

Friedman, Richard Elliot. *The Bible with Sources Revealed.* San Fransisco: HarperOne, 2005.

_____. *Commentary on the Torah.* San Francisco: Harper San Francisco, 2001.

_____. *Who Wrote the Bible?* San Francisco: Harper San Francisco, 2001.

Fritz, Vokmar. "Temple Architecture: What Can Archaeology Tell Us about Solomon's Temple?" *Essential Papers on Israel and the Ancient Near East.* Ed. Greenspahn, Frederick. New York: New York University Press, 1991: 116–28.

Frye, Richard. *The Heritage of Persia.* Bibliotheca Iranica, Reprint 1. Costa Mesa, CA: Mazda, 1993.

Fujita, K., G. Ofosu-Budu, and S. Ogata. "Biological Nitrogen Fixation in Mixed Legume-Cereal Cropping Systems." *Plant and Soil* 141/1–2 (October, 2007) 155–175.

Fuks, Alexander. *Social Conflict in Ancient Greece.* Leiden: Brill, 1984.

Gaebelein, Paul W., Jr. "Tammuz." *International Standard Bible Encyclopedia*: vol. 4. Grand Rapids, MI: Eerdmans, 1979: 726.

Gagarin, Michael, and Elaine Fantham. Ed. *The Oxford Encyclopedia of Ancient Greece and Rome*: 7 vols. New York: Oxford University Press, 2010.

Galil, Gershon. *The Chronology of the Kings of Israel and Judah.* Amsterdam: Brill Academic, 1996.

Gallagher, William. *Sennacherib's Campaign to Judah.* Leiden: Brill, 1999.

Garber, Paul L., and Rolland K. Harrison. "Idol." *International Standard Bible Encyclopedia*: vol. 2. Grand Rapids, MI: Eerdmans, 1979: 794–97.

Gardiner, Alan. *Egypt of the Pharaohs.* Oxford: Oxford University Press, 1964.

Gardner, Joseph L., Ed. *Atlas of the Bible.* Pleasantville, NY: Reader's Digest, 1971.

Garfinkel, Yosef, director. "Khirbet Qeiyafa Archaeological Project." Last updated August 12, 2013. http://qeiyafa.huji.ac.il/ (accessed February 2015).

Garfinkel, Yosef, and Saar Ganor. "Khirbet Qeiyafa: Sha'arayim." *The Journal of Hebrew Scriptures* 8/22 (2008) 1–10.

Gasque, W. Ward. "Jew." *International Standard Bible Encyclopedia*: vol 2. Grand Rapids, MI: Eerdmans, 1979, 1056.

Gerig, Bruce L. "Homosexuality in the Ancient Near East, Beyond Egypt." *Homosexuality and the Bible Supplement* (2005). http://epistle.us/hbarticles/neareast.html (accessed December, 2013).

Gesenius, Wilhelm. *Gesenius' Hebrew Grammar.* Trans. A. E. Cowley. Ed. E. Kautzsch. Mineola, NY: Dover Publications, 2006.

Gevirtz, Stanley. "Jericho and Shechem: A Religio-Literary Aspect of City Destruction." *Vetus Testamentum* 13 (1963) 52–62.

Giles, Federick, and M. D. Birrell. *The Amarna Age: Egypt.* Warminster, UK: Aris and Phillips, 2002.

Gill, John. *Gill's Exposition of the Entire Bible.* http://www.biblestudytools.com/commentaries/gills-exposition-of-the-bible/exodus-22/ (accessed February 2015).

Goard, William. *The Post-Captivity Names of Israel*. London: Covenant Publishing, 1934.

Goelet, Ogden. "'Town' and 'Country' in Ancient Egypt." *Urbanization and Land Ownership in the Ancient Near East*: vol.2. Ed. Michael Hudson and Baruch Levine. Cambridge: Peabody Museum of Archaeology and Ethnology of Harvard University, 1999: 65–115.

Goldberg, Paul. "The Changing Landscape." *The Archaeology of Society in the Holy Land*. Ed. Thomas E. Levy. London: Leicester University Press, 1995: 40–57.

Gonen, Rivka. "The Late Bronze Age." *The Archaeology of Ancient Israel*. Trans. R. Greenberg. Ed. Amnon Ben- Tor. New Haven, CT: Yale University Press, 1992.

Gophna, Ram. "Early Bronze Age Canaan: Some Spatial and Demographic Observations." *The Archaeology of Society in the Holy Land*. Ed. Thomas E. Levy. London: Leicester University Press, 1995: 269–80.

Gordon, Nehemia. "Elohim: Plural or Singular?" http://www.karaite-korner.org/sources/6.pdf (accessed February 2015) and http://www.obcitydesigns.com/wayofthenazarene/uploads/pdf/God%20-%20Elohim%20Plural%20Or%20Singular.pdf (accessed February 2015).

Gordon, Robert P. "In Search of David: The David Tradition in Recent Study." *Faith, Tradition, and History*. Ed. A. R. Millard, J. K. Hoffmeier, and D. W. Baker. Winona Lake, IN: Eisenbrauns, 1994: 285–97.

_____. "Who Made the Kingmaker? Reflections on Samuel and the Institution of Monarchy." *Faith, Tradition, and History*. Ed. A. R. Millard, J. K. Hoffmeier, and D. W. Baker. Winona Lake, IN: Eisenbrauns, 1994: 255–69.

Goren-Inbar, Naama, "The Lower Paleolithic of Israel." *The Archaeology of Society in the Holy Land*. Ed. Thomas E. Levy. London: Leicester University Press, 1995: 93–108.

Görg, Manfred. "Israel in Canaan (Long) Before Pharaoh Merenptah?": A Fresh Look at Berlin Statue Pedestal Relief 21687." *The Journal of Ancient Eagyptian Interconnections* 2/4 (2010) 15–25.

_____. "Response to Prof. Hoffmeier's Objections." *JETS* 50/2 (June 2007) 255.

Gottwald, Norman. *Tribes of Yahweh: A Sociology of the Religion of Liberated Israel, 1250–1050 BCE*. Issue 66 of Biblical Seminar. New York: Continuum, 1999.

Graham, Geoffry. "Tanis." *Oxford Encyclopedia of Ancient Egypt*: vol. 3. Ed. Robert Redford, New York: Oxford University Press, 2001: 348.

Graham, Matt Patrick. *The Utilization of 1 and 2 Chronicles in the Reconstruction of Israelite History in the Nineteenth Century*. Ed. J. M. Roberts. SBL Dissertation Series 116. Atlanta: Scholars Press, 1990.

Grajetzki, Wolfram. *Court Officials of the Egyptian Middle Kingdom*. London: Gerald Duckworth, 2009.

Graubart, David. "Jews." *New Standard Encyclopedia*: vol 9. Ed. Douglas W. Downey. Chicago: Standard Educational Corporation, 1995: 65.

_____. "Judaism." *New Standard Encyclopedia*: vol 9. Ed. Douglas W. Downey. Chicago: Standard Educational Corporation, 1995: 105.

_____. "State of Israel." *New Standard Encyclopedia*: vol 9. Ed. Douglas W. Downey. Chicago: Standard Educational Corporation, 1995: 230.

Gray, Mary P. *The Ḥâbirū-Hebrew Problem in the Light of the Source Material Available at Present*. Hebrew Union College Annual: vol. 21 (Cincinnati: Jewish Institute of Religion, 1958) 135–202.

Grayson, Albert. *Assyrian and Babylonian Chronicles*. Winona Lake: Eisenbrauns, 2000.

Green, Alberto. *The Storm-God in the Ancient Near East*. Biblical and Judaic Studies 8. Winona Lake, IN: Eisenbrauns, 2003.

_____."Social Stratification and Cultural Continuity at Alalakh." *In The Quest for the Kingdom of God: Studies in Honor of George E. Mendenhall*. Ed. H. B. Huffmon, et al. Winona Lake, IN: Eisenbrauns, 1985: 198–204.

Greenberg, Moshe. "Hab/piru and Hebrews." *World History of the Jewish People*: vol. 2. Patriarchs. Ed. Benjamin Mazar. New Brunswick, NJ: Rutger's University Press, 1970.

_____. "Some Postulates of Biblical Criminal Law." *Essential Papers on Israel and the Ancient Near East*. Ed. Greenspahn, Frederick. New York: New York University Press, 1991: 333–52.

_____. "Some Postulates of Biblical Criminal Law." *Essential Papers on Israel and the Ancient Near East*. Ed. Frederick Greenspahn. New York: New York University Press, 1991: 336–52.

Greenspahn, Frederick, Ed. *Essential Papers on Israel and the Ancient Near East*. New York: New York University Press, 1991.

_____ Ed. *The Hebrew Bible: New Insights and Scholarship*. New York: New York University Press, 2008.

Greenspoon, Leonard. "Strata," *BAR* 33/6 (2007) 18.

Griffith, R. Drew. *Mummy Wheat*. Lanham, MD: University Press of America, 2008.

Grigson, Caroline. "Plough and Pasture in the Early Economy of the Southern Levant." *The Archaeology of Society in the Holy Land*. Ed. Thomas E. Levy. London: Leicester University Press, 1995: 245–67.

Grimal, Nicolas. *Ancient Egypt*. Trans. Ian Shaw. Oxford, UK: Blackwell, 1994.

Grosby, Steven. *Biblical Ideas of Nationality Ancient and Modern*. Winona Lake, IN: Eisenbrauns, 2002.

"Growing Flax." Flax Council of Canada. http://www.flaxcouncil.ca/english/index.jsp?p=growing5&mp=growing (accessed February 2015).

Guinan, Michael D. "Lachish Letters." *International Standard Bible Encyclopedia*: vol. 3. Grand Rapids, MI: Eerdmans, 1979: 58–60.

Gwaltney, W. C., Jr. "The Biblical Book of Lamentations in the Context of Near Eastern Lament Literature." *Essential Papers on Israel and the Ancient Near East*. Ed. Greenspahn, Frederick. New York: New York University Press, 1991: 242–265.

Hadidi, Adnan, Ed. *Studies in the History and Archaeology of Jordan*. Amman: Department of Antiquities, 1987.

Hagner, Donald A. "Scribes." *International Standard Bible Encyclopedia*: vol. 4. Grand Rapids, MI: Eerdmans, 1979: 360.

Hall, Augustin F. C., and Thomas E. Levy. "Social Change and the Archaeology of the Holy Land: Prehistoric Lithic Production through Time. *The Archaeology of Society in the Holy Land*. Ed. Thomas E. Levy. London: Leicester University Press, 1995: 76–91.

Hallo, William. "Biblical History in Its Near Eastern Setting: The Contextual Approach." *Scripture in Context*, vol.1: *Essays on the Comparative Method*. Ed. Carl D. Evans, et al. PTMS 34. Pittsburgh: Pickwick, 1980.

_____. "New Moons and Sabbaths: A Case-Study in the Contrastive Approach." *Essential Papers on Israel and the Ancient Near East*. Ed. Greenspahn, Frederick. New York: New York University Press, 1991: 313–32.

_____. "Sumer and the Bible: A Matter of Proportion." *The Future of Biblical Archaeology: Reassessing Methodologies and Assumptions*. Proceeding of a Symposium at Trinity International

University, Aug. 12–14, 2001. Ed. James Hoffmeier and Alan Millard. Grand Rapids, MI: Eerdmans, 2004: 163–175.

Halpern, Baruch. *The First Historians*. University Park: Penn State University Press, 1988.

Hamilton, Victor. *The Book of Genesis: 1–17.* Grand Rapids, MI: Eerdmans, 1990.

_____. *The Book of Genesis: 18–50.* Grand Rapids, MI: Eerdmans, 1995.

Hanson, K. C. "Teman." *International Standard Bible Encyclopedia*: vol. 4. Grand Rapids, MI: Eerdmans, 1979: 758.

Harkavy, Alexander. *The Hebrew and Chaldee Dictionary*. New York: Hebrew Publishing, 1914.

Harris, R. Laird, Gleason Archer, Jr., and Bruce Waltke, Ed. *Theological Wordbook of the Old Testament*: 2 vols. Chicago, IL: Moody Bible Institute, 1980.

Harris, Rivkah. "Notes on the Nomenclature of Old Babylonian Sippar." *JCS* 24 (1972) 102–4.

Harrison, Roland K. "Curse." *International Standard Bible Encyclopedia*: vol.1. Grand Rapids, MI: Eerdmans, 1979: 837–38.

_____. "Disease." *International Standard Bible Encyclopedia*: vol. 1. Grand Rapids, MI: Eerdmans, 1979: 955.

_____. "Fever." *International Standard Bible Encyclopedia*: vol. 2. Grand Rapids, MI: Eerdmans, 1979: 300.

_____. "Gall." *International Standard Bible Encyclopedia*: vol. 2. Grand Rapids, MI: Eerdmans, 1979: 392–93.

_____. "Giants." *International Standard Bible Encyclopedia*: vol. 2. Grand Rapids, MI: Eerdmans, 1979: 460.

_____. "Interest." *International Standard Bible Encyclopedia*: vol. 2. Grand Rapids, MI: Eerdmans, 1979: 860–61.

_____. "Leper; Leprosy." *International Standard Bible Encyclopedia*: vol. 3. Grand Rapids, MI: Eerdmans, 1979: 103–6.

_____. "Physician." *International Standard Bible Encyclopedia*: vol. 3. Grand Rapids, MI: Eerdmans, 1979: 865.

_____. "Polygamy." *International Standard Bible Encyclopedia*: vol. 3. Grand Rapids, MI: Eerdmans, 1979: 901.

_____. "Queen of Heaven." *International Standard Bible Encyclopedia*: vol. 4. Grand Rapids, MI: Eerdmans, 1979: 8.

Harrison, Roland K., and Nola J. Opperwall. "Lightning." *International Standard Bible Encyclopedia*: vol. 3. Grand Rapids, MI: Eerdmans, 1979: 136–37.

Harrison, Timothy. "The Battleground: Who Destroyed Megiddo." *BAR* 29/6 (2003) 28–35, 60–64.

Hart, George. *A Dictionary of Egyptian Gods and Goddesses*. London: Routledge, 1986.

_____. *The Routledge Dictionary of Egyptian Gods and Goddesses*. New York: Routledge, 2005.

Hartley, John E. "Song of Deborah." *International Standard Bible Encyclopedia:* vol. 1. Grand Rapids, MI: Eerdmans, 1979: 904–6.

Hartman, David A. "Remarks to the World Congress of Families III." Mexico City. March 29, 2004. http://www.worldcongress.org/wcf3_spkrs/wcf3_hartman.htm (accessed February 2015).

_____."Star." *International Standard Bible Encyclopedia*: vol. 4. Grand Rapids, MI: Eerdmans, 1979: 611.

Hasel, Gerhard. "Day." *International Standard Bible Encyclopedia*: vol. 1. Grand Rapids, MI: Eerdmans, 1979: 877–78.

_____. "Cuttings in the Flesh." *International Standard Bible Encyclopedia*: vol. 1. Grand Rapids, MI: Eerdmans, 1979: 841.

_____. "Heir." *International Standard Bible Encyclopedia*: vol. 2. Grand Rapids, MI: Eerdmans, 1979: 674.

_____. "The Meaning of the Animal Rite in Genesis 15." *JSOT* 19 (1981) 61–78.

Hasel, Michael. "Merneptah's Inscription and Reliefs and the Origin of Israel." *The Near East in the Southwest: Essays in Honor of William G. Dever*. Ed. Beth Alpert Nakhai. Boston: ASOR, 2003.

Hastings, James, Ed. *A Dictionary of the Bible*: 5 vols. New York: Scribner, 1898–1904.

Hastings, James, and John Selbie, Ed. *Encyclopedia of Religion and Ethics*: 13 vols. New York: Scribner, 1908–26.

Hawass, Zahi, "Press Release-New Discovery at Tel El-Daba." http://www.drhawass.com/blog/press-release-new-discovery-tel-el-daba (accessed October 2013).

Hayes, John H. "The Beginning of the Regnal Year in Israel and Judah." *The Land That I Will Show You*. Ed. Andrew Dearman and Patrick Graham. Sheffield: Sheffield Academic Press, 2001: 92–95.

Hegg, Tim. "The Covenant of Grant and the Abrahamic Covenant." Paper read at the Regional Evangelical Theological Society, 1989. http://www.torahresource.com/EnglishArticles/Grant%20Treaty.pdf (accessed February 2015).

Hein, Irmgard. "Area A/IV." (Tell el-Dabᶜa, 2008, 2013). http://www.auaris.at/html/areal_a4_en.html (accessed February 2015).

Hendel, Ronald. "The Exodus in Biblical Memory." *JBL* 12/4 (2001) 601–22.

Henige, D. *The Chronology of Oral Tradition: Quest for a Chimera*. Oxford: Oxford University Press, 1974.

Henry, Matthew. *Matthew Henry's Commentary on the Whole Bible Complete and Unabridged*. Peabody, MA: Hendrickson, 1991.

Herodotus. *The Histories*. Trans. Aubrey de Sélincourt. London: Penguin, 1972.

Hertz, J. H. *The Pentateuch and Haftorahs*. 2nd Ed. London: Soncino Press, 1997: 329.

Hess, Richard. "Asking Historical Questions of Joshua 13–19: Recent Discussion Concerning the Date of the Boundry Lists." *Faith, Tradition, and History*. Ed. A. R. Millard, J. K. Hoffmeier, and D. W. Baker. Winona Lake, IN: Eisenbrauns, 1994: 191–206.

_____. "The Bible and Alalakh." *Mesopotamia and the Bible*. Ed. Mark W. Chavalas and K. Lawson Younger, Jr. Grand Rapids, MI: Baker, 2002.

_____. "Multiple-Month Ritual Calendars in the West Semitic World: Emar 446 and Leviticus 23." *The Future of Biblical Archaeology: Reassessing Methodologies and Assumptions*. Proceeding of a Symposium at Trinity International University, Aug. 12–14, 2001. Ed. James Hoffmeier and Alan Millard. Grand Rapids, MI: Eerdmans, 2004: 233–253.

Heussner, Ki Mae. "Lost Pyramids: Peering Beneath Egypt's Surface with Satellite Images." *ABC News* (May 27, 2011. http://abcnews.go.com/Technology/lost-pyramids-egypt-discovered-satellite-images/story?id=13693894 (accessed February 2015).

Hill, J. "Hyksos." Ancient Egypt Online. Last updated 2010. http://www.ancientegyptonline.co.uk/index.html (accessed February 2015).

Hingh, A. de. "The Archaeology of the Agricultural Landscape: Land-Use and Access to Land in Later Prehistoric Society in North-west Europe." *Landless and Hungry?* Ed. B. Haring and R. de Maaijer. Leiden: CNWS Publications, 1998.

Hirsch, Frank E., and Kenneth J. Grider. "Crime." *International Standard Bible Encyclopedia*: vol. 1. Grand Rapids, MI: Eerdmans, 1979: 815–17.

Hislop, Alexander. *The Two Babylons*. Neptune, NJ: Loizeaux Brothers, 1959.

Hoffman, Joel. *In the Beginning: A Short History of the Hebrew Language*. New York: New York University Press, 2004.

Hoffmann, R. J., Trans. *Celsus on the True Doctrine*. Oxford: Oxford University Press, 1987.

Hoffmeier, James. *Ancient Israel in Sinai*. New York: Oxford University Press, 2005.

_____. *Israel in Egypt*. New York: Oxford University Press, 1996.

_____. "Moses." *International Standard Bible Encyclopedia*: vol. 3. Grand Rapids, MI: Eerdmans, 1979: 518–19.

_____. "The Structure of Joshua 1–11 and the Annals of Thutmose III." *Faith, Tradition, and History*. Ed. A. R. Millard, et al. Winona Lake, IN: Eisenbrauns, 1994: 165–80.

_____. "What is the Biblical Date for the Exodus: A Response to Bryant Wood." *JETS* 50/2 (2007).

_____. "The North Sinai Archaeological Project's Excavations at Tell el-Borg (Sinai): An Example of the 'New' Biblical Archaeology?" *The Future of Biblical Archaeology: Reassessing Methodologies and Assumptions*. Proceeding of a Symposium at Trinity International University, Aug. 12–14, 2001. Ed. James Hoffmeier and Alan Millard. Grand Rapids, MI: Eerdmans, 2004: 53–68.

Hoffmeier, James, and Alfred H. Joy. "Hail." *International Standard Bible Encyclopedia*: vol. 2. Grand Rapids, MI: Eerdmans, 1979: 596.

Hoffner, Harr A., Jr. "Ancient Israel's Literary Heritage Compared with Hittite Textual Data." *The Future of Biblical Archaeology: Reassessing Methodologies and Assumptions*. Proceeding of a Symposium at Trinity International University, Aug. 12–14, 2001. Ed. James Hoffmeier and Alan Millard. Grand Rapids, MI: Eerdmans, 2004: 176–192.

Hölbl, Gunther. *A History of the Ptolemaic Empire*. Trans. Tina Saavedra. London: Routledge, 2001.

Holladay, John Jr. "The Eastern Nile Delta during the Hyksos and Pre-Hyksos Periods: Toward a Systemic/ Socioeconomic Understanding." *The Hyksos: New Historical and Archaeological Perspectives*. Ed. Eliezer Oren. University Museum Monograph 96/8. Philadelphia: University of Pennsylvania Museum, 1997.

_____. "The Kingdoms of Israel and Judah: Political and Economic Centralization in the Iron IIA-B (CA. 1000–750 BCE)." *The Archaeology of Society in the Holy Land*. Ed. Thomas E. Levy. London: Leicester University Press, 1995: 368–97.

Holladay, William, Ed. *A Concise Hebrew and Aramaic Lexicon of the Old Testament*. Leiden: Brill, 1988.

_____. *The Root SUBH in the Old Testament*. Leiden: Brill, 1958.

Holloway, Steven. "The Quest for Sargon, Pul, and Tiglath-pileser in the Nineteenth Century." *Mesopotamia and the Bible*. Ed. Mark W. Chavalas and K. Lawson Yonger, Jr. Grand Rapids, MI: Baker, 2002.

The Holy Bible, New Living Translation. Wheaton, IL: Tyndale House, 1996.

Hooker, Paul K. and John H. Hayes. "The Year of Josiah's Death: 609 or 610 BCE?" *The Land That I Will Show You*. Andrew Dearman and Patrick Graham, ed. Sheffield: Sheffield Academic Press, 2001: 96–103.

Hoop, Raymond de. *Genesis 49 in Its Literary and Historical Context*. Society of Biblical Literature 29. Leiden: Brill, 1999.

Hornung, Erik. *The Ancient Egyptian Books of the Afterlife*. Trans. David Lorton. Ithaca, NY: Cornell University Press, 1999.

_____. *Conceptions of God in Ancient Egypt*. Trans. John Baines. Ithaca: NY: Cornell University Press, 1982.

_____. *History of Ancient Egypt: An Introduction*. Trans. David Lorton. Ithaca, NY: Cornell University Press, 1999.

_____. Hornung, Erik. "Introduction," *Ancient Egyptian Chronology* 83/1. Handbook of Oriental Studies. Ed. Erik Hornung, et al. Leiden: Brill, 2006: 234–64.

Hornung, Erik. Rolf Krauss, and David Warburton, Ed. *Ancient Egyptian Chronology*. Handbuch der Orientalistik 83. Leiden: Brill, 2006.

Hudson, Michael. "From Sacred Enclave to Temple to City." *Urbanization and Land Ownership in the Ancient Near East*: vol. 2. Ed. Michael Hudson and Baruch Levine. Cambridge: Peabody Museum of Archaeology and Ethnology of Harvard University, 1999.

Hudson, Michael, and Marc Van de Mieroop, Ed. *Debt and Economic Renewal in the Ancient Near East*: vol. 3. Bethesda, MD: CDL Press, 2002.

Hulse, E. V. "The Nature of Biblical 'Leprosy' and the Use of Alternative Medical Terms in Modern Translations of the Bible." *Palestine Exploration Quarterly* 107 (1975) 87–105.

Hunger, Hermann, and Regine Pruzsinszky, Ed. *Mesopotamian Dark Age Revisited*. Proceedings of an International Conference of SCIEM 2000, Vienna 8–9th, November 2002. Vienna: Akademie der Wissenschaften, 2004.

Ilan, David. "The Dawn of Internationalism—The Middle Bronze Age." *The Archaeology of Society in the Holy Land*. Ed. Thomas E. Levy. London: Leicester University Press, 1995: 297–318.

Hughes, Jeremy. *Secrets of the Times: Myth and History in Biblical Chronology*. New York: Continuum, 1990.

Irvine, Stuart A. "The Rise of the House of Jehu." *The Land That I Will Show You*. Ed. Andrew Dearman and Patrick Graham. Sheffield: Sheffield Academic Press, 2001: 104–118.

Isaacs, E. D. "Jabin." *International Standard Bible Encyclopedia*: vol. 2. Grand Rapids, MI: Eerdmans, 1979: 946.

Isocrates. *Isocrates with an English Translation:* vol. 1. Ed. George Norlin. Cambridge: Harvard University Press, 1980) 167. http://www.perseus.tufts.edu/hopper/text?doc=Perseus:abo: tlg,0010,011 (accessed February 2015).

Israel Ministry of Foreign Affairs. "Cultic Shrines from Time of King David." May 8, 2012. http://www.mfa.gov.il/MFA/History/Early+History+-+Archaeology/Cultic_shrines_time_King_David_8-May-2012.htm (accessed February 2015).

Iyengar, T. R. *Dictionary of Hindu Gods and Goddesses*. New Delhi: DK Printworld, 2003.

Jacobs, Joseph, Ed. "Jew." *The Jewish Encyclopedia*. New York: Funk and Wagnalls, 1906: 174–75.

Jacobsen, Thorkild. *The Treasures of Darkness: A History of Mesopotamian Religion*. New Haven, CT: Yale University Press, 1976.

James, Edwin Oliver. *The Tree of Life: An Archaeological Study*. Leiden: Brill, 1966.

Jamieson, Robert. A. R. Fausset, and David Brown, *Jamieson, Fausset, and Brown's Commentary*. Grand Rapids, MI: Zondervan, 1961.

Jansen-Winkeln, Karl. "The Chronology of the Third Intermediate Period: Dynasty 22–24." *Handbook of Ancient Egyptian Chronology 83/1*. Handbook of Oriental Studies. Ed. Erik Hornung, et al. Leiden: Brill, 2006: 234–64.

_____. "Relative Chronology of Dynasty." *Ancient Egyptian Chronology* 83/1. Handbook of Oriental Studies, Ed. Erik Hornung, et al. Leiden: Brill, 2006: 232–33.

Janzen, Matthew. "The Biblical New Year." Ministers New Covenant. http://www.ministersnewcovenant.org/uploads/9/1/6/ 1/9161032/the_biblical_new_year_revised.pdf (accessed December 2013).

Jastrow, Morris. *Religion of Babylonia and Assyria*. Boston: Athenaeum Press, 1898.

_____. "Did the Babylonian Temples Have Libraries?" *JAOS* 27 (1906) 146–89.

Jefferson, Thomas. *The Works of Thomas Jefferson*: vol. 11. Federal Edition. New York: Putnam's, 1904–5. http://oll.libertyfund.org/titles/807#lf0054–11_head_042 (accessed February 2015).

Jellicoe, Sidney. *The Septuagint and Modern Study*. Winona Lake, IN: Eisenbrauns, 1993.

Johnston, Sarah, Ed. *Religions of the Ancient World*. Cambridge: Harvard University Press, 2004.

Jones, Floyd. *Chronology of the Old Testament*. Green Forest, AR: Master Books, 2004.

Josephus, *The Works of Josephus*. Trans. William Whiston. Peabody, MA: Hendrickson, 1987.

Joy, H. "Hail." *International Standard Bible Encyclopedia*: vol. 2. Grand Rapids, MI: Eerdmans, 1979: 596.

JPS Tanach. Philadelphia, PA: Jewish Publication Society, 1988.

Jung, Kurt G. "Baal." *International Standard Bible Encyclopedia*: vol. 1. Grand Rapids, MI: Eerdmans, 1979: 377–78.

Jursa, Michael. "Accounting in Neo-Babylonian Institutional Archives: Structure, Usage, Implications." *Creating Economic Order*. Bethesda, MD: CDL Press, 2004.

Kaiser, Walter. *Toward Old Testament Ethics*. Grand Rapids, MI: Academie Books, 1983.

Kamil, Jill. *The Ancient Egyptians: Life in the Old Kingdom*. Cairo: American University Press in Cairo, 1984.

Kampen, John. *The Hasideans and the Origin of Pharisaism*. SBL Septuagint and Cognate Studies 24. Atlanta: Scholars Press, 1988.

Karenga, Maulana. *Maat, the Moral Ideal in Ancient Egypt: a Study in Classical African Ethics*. New York: Routledge, 2004.

Karlin, Anatoly. "Rite of Spring: Russia's Fertility Trends." *The Russia Blog*. April 29, 2009. http://darussophile.com/2009/04/rite-of-spring/ (accessed February 2015).

Kasher, Aryeh. *The Jews in Hellenistic and Roman Egypt*: vol 3. Tübingen: Mohr Siebeck, 1978.

Kaufmann, Yehezkel. *The Biblical Account of the Conquest of Canaan*. Jerusalem: Magnes Press, 1985.

Keel, Othmar, and Christopher Uehlinger. *Gods, Goddesses, and Images of God*. Trans. Thomas Trapp. Minneapolis: Fortress Press, 1998.

Keil, C. F., and Franz Delitzsch. *Commentary on the Old Testament:* 10 vols. Peabody, MA: Hendrickson, 2006.

Kelly, Jack. "What Is Sin?" GracethruFaith. Last updated December 25, 2008. http://gracethrufaith.com/topical- studies/what-is-sin/ (accessed February 2015).

Kelm, George L. "Wormwood." *International Standard Bible Encyclopedia*: vol. 4. Grand Rapids, MI: Eerdmans, 1979: 1117.

Kemp, Barry J. *Ancient Egypt: Anatomy of a Civilization*. New York: Routledge, 1989.

Kempinski, Aharon. "The Hyksos: A View from Northern Canaan and Syria." *The Hyksos: New Historical and Archaeological Perspectives*. Ed. Eliezer Oren. University Museum Monograph 96/8. Philadelphia: University of Pennsylvania Museum, 1997.

_____. "The Middle Bronze Age." *The Archaeology of Ancient Israel*. Trans. R. Greenberg. Ed. Amnon Ben- Tor. New Haven, CT: Yale University Press, 1992.

Kenyon, Kathleen. *Digging Up Jericho*. London: Ernest Benn, 1957.

Kerényi, C. *The Gods of the Greeks*. London: Thames and Hudson, 1998.

Kern, Paul. *Ancient Siege Warfare*. Bloomington, IN: Indiana University Press, 1999.

King, Gary, Robert Keohane, and Sidney Verba. *Designing Social Inquiry: Scientific Inference in Qualitative Research*. Princeton, NJ: Princeton University Press, 1994.

"The Kingdom Restored: When Did the Restoration of Israel Happen." Abide in Christ. Last updated August 19, 2013. http://www.abideinchrist.com/messages/amos9v11.html (accessed February 2015).

Kitchen, Kenneth. *Ancient Orient and the Old Testament*. Downers Grove, IL: InterVarsity Press, 1996.

_____. "The Exodus." *The Anchor Bible Dictionary:* vol 2. Ed. David N. Freedman, et al. New York: Doubleday (1992) 700–708.

_____. "Joseph." *International Standard Bible Encyclopedia*: vol. 2. Grand Rapids, MI: Eerdmans, 1979: 1129.

_____. *On the Reliability of the Old Testament*. Grand Rapids, MI: Eerdmans, 2003.

_____. *The Third Intermediate Period in Egypt (1100–650 BC)*. Wiltshire, UK: Aris and Phillips, 1986.

Kitchen, Kenneth, and Gary L. Knapp. "Walk." *International Standard Bible Encyclopedia*: vol. 4. Grand Rapids, MI: Eerdmans, 1979: 1003–5.

Kitchen, Kenneth, and P. J. N. Lawrence. *Treaty, Law and Covenant in the Ancient Near East:* 3 vols. Wiesbaden: Harrassowitz, 2012.

Kirby, Peter. "Letter of Aristeas." *Early Jewish Writings*. http://www.earlyjewishwritings.com/letteraristeas.html (accessed February 2015).

Kline, Meredith. *By Oath Consigned*. Grand Rapids, Eerdmans, 1968.

_____. "The Ha-Bi-Ru: Kin or Foe of Israel?" *Westminster Theological Journal* 19 (1956) 1–24.

_____. *Treaty of the Great King*. Grand Rapids, MI: Eerdmans, 1963.

Klingbeil, Gerald A. *Bridging the Gap: Ritual and Ritual Texts in the Bible*. Bulletin for Biblical Research Supplement 1. Winona Lake, IN: Eisenbrauns, 2007.

Klinger, Jörg. "Chronological Links between the Cuneiform World of the Ancient Near East and Ancient Egypt." *Ancient Egyptian Chronology*. Handbook of Oriental Studies 83. Leiden: Brill, 2006.

Klugman, Jeni, Ed. *Poverty in Russia: Public Policy and Private Responses*. Washington, D.C.: World Bank, 1997.

Knauf, Ernst Axel. "Solomon at Megiddo?" *The Land That I Will Show You*. Ed. Andrew Dearman and Patrick Graham. Sheffield: Sheffield Academic Press, 2001: 119–134.

Knierim, Rolf P. *The Task of Old Testament Theology: Substance, Method, and Cases—Essays*. Grand Rapids, MI: Eerdmans, 1998.

Knohl, Israel. *The Sanctuary of Silence: The Priestly Torah and the Holiness School*. Winona Lake, IN: Eisenbrauns, 2007.

Knutson, Brent F. "Canticles." *International Standard Bible Encyclopedia*: vol. 1. Grand Rapids, MI: Eerdmans, 1979: 606–608.

Kochavi, Moshe. "Canaanite Aphek: Its Acropolis and Inscriptions." *Expedition* 20/4 (1978) 12–17.

Kogan, Leonid. "The Etymology of Israel." *Babel und Bibel 3*: Annual of Ancient Near Eastern, Old Testament, and Semitic Studies. Winona Lake, IN: Eisenbrauns, 2006.

Köhler, Ludwig, and Walter Baumgartner. *The Hebrew and Aramaic Lexicon of the Old Testament*: 5 vols. Trans. M. E. Richardson. Leiden: Brill, 1994.

Kolatch, Alfred J. *This is the Torah*. Middle Village, NY: Jonathan David Publishers, 1988.

Koslowski, Peter, Ed. *Progress, Apocalypse, and Completion of History and Life after Death of the Human Person in the World Religions*. Dordrecht, Netherlands: Kluwer Academic Publishers, 2002.

Kozyreva, Nelli V. "Sellers and Buyers of Urban Real Estate in South Mesopotamia at the Beginning of the 2nd Millennium BC." *Urbanization and Land Ownership in the Ancient Near East*: vol.2. Ed. Michael Hudson and Baruch Levine. Cambridge: Peabody Museum of Archaeology and Ethnology of Harvard University, 1999: 353–62.

Krahmalkov, Charles. "Exodus Itinerary Confirmed by Egyptian Evidence." *BAR* 20/5 (1994) 54–62, 79.

Kramer, Samuel. "Sumerian Lieterature." *The Bible and the Ancient Near East*. Garden City, NY: Anchor, 1965: 338.

Kreuzer, Siegfri, Ed. "Taanach." *Eerdmans Dictionary of the Bible* (Grand Rapids, MI: 2000) 1268–69. http://www.kreuzer-siegfriEd.de/texte-zum-at/taanach.pdf (accessed February 2015).

Kuan, Jeffrey K. "Šamši-ilu and the *Realpolitik* of Israel and Aram-Damascus." *The Land That I Will Show You*. Ed. Andrew Dearman and Patrick Graham. Sheffield: Sheffield Academic Press, 2001: 135–151.

Kuhn, Thomas. *The Structure of Scientific Revolutions*. Chicago: University of Chicago Press, 1970.

Kutscher, Edward. *The Language and Linguistic Background of the Isaiah Scroll: IQIsaiah*. Leiden: Brill, 1974.

LaBianca, Øystein S., and Randall W. Younker. "The Kingdoms of Ammon, Moab and Edom: The Archaeology of Society in Late Bronze/Iron Age Transjordan (CA. 1400–500 BCE)." *The Archaeology of Society in the Holy Land*. Ed. Thomas E. Levy. London: Leicester University Press, 1995: 399–414.

Lambdin, T. O. "Egyptian Loan Words in the Old Testament." *JAOS* 73 (1953) 1016–17.

Lamberg-Karlovsky, C. C. "Households, Land Tenure, and Communication Systems in the 6th–4th Millennia of Greater Mesopotamia." *Urbanization and Land Ownership in the Ancient Near East*: vol. 2. Ed. Michael Hudsonand Baruch A. Levine. Cambridge, MA: Peabody Museum of Archaeology and Ethnology of Harvard University, 1999.

Langdon, Stephen H. *Babylonian Menologies and the Semitic Calendars*. London: Oxford University Press, 1935.

Lange, Nicholas de. "An Early Hebrew-Greek Bible Glossary from the Cairo Genizah and its Significance for the Study of Jewish Bible Translations into Greek." *Studies in Hebrew Language and Jewish Culture*. Amsterdam Studies in Jewish Thought. Ed. M. F. Martin, et al. Dorddrecht, Netherlands: Springer, 2007: 34–39.

LaSor, William Sanford. "Ezekiel." *International Standard Bible Encyclopedia*: vol. 2. Grand Rapids, MI: Eerdmans, 1979: 260–61.

———. "Jerusalem." *International Standard Bible Encyclopedia*: vol. 2. Grand Rapids, MI: Eerdmans, 1979: 1029–30.

———. "Philistines; Philistia." *International Standard Bible Encyclopedia*: vol. 3. Grand Rapids, MI: Eerdmans, 1979: 842–46.

———. "Teman." *International Standard Bible Encyclopedia*: vol. 4. Grand Rapids, MI: Eerdmans, 1979: 759.

———. "Territory of Judah." *International Standard Bible Encyclopedia*: vol. 2. Grand Rapids, MI: Eerdmans, 1979: 1150.

Layard, Austen H. *Nineveh and Its Remains*: 2 vols. New York: Putnam, 1849.

———. "Nineveh." *The Encyclopaedia Britannica, or Dictionary of Arts, Sciences, and General Literature*: vol. 16. Edinburgh: Encyclopaedia Britannica, 1858: 273.

Lee, Gary A. "Israel." *International Standard Bible Encyclopedia*: vol. 2. Grand Rapids, MI: Eerdmans, 1979: 907.

Leith, Mary Joan. "The Bible Divide." *BAR* 38/2 (2012): 24, 66.

Lemaire, Andre. "House of David' Restored in Moabite Inscription." *BAR* 20/3 (1994) 30–37.

_____. "Lachish Letters." The British Museum. http://www.britishmuseum.org/explore/highlights/highlight_objects/me/l/lachish_letter_ii.aspx (accessed February 2015).

Lemche, Niels Peter. *Early Israel: Anthropological and Historical Studies on the Israelite Society Before the Monarchy*. Vetus Testamentum Supplement 37. Leiden: Brill, 1985.

Leval, Gerard. "Ancient Inscription Refers to Birth of Israelite Monarchy." *BAR* 38/3 (2012) 41–43, 70.

Levenson, J. D. "Who Inserted the Book of the Torah." *HTR* 68 (1977) 203–33.

Levin, Baruch. "The Biblical 'Town' as Reality and Typology: Evaluating Biblical References to Towns and Their Functions." *Urbanization and Land Ownership in the Ancient Near East*: vol.2. Ed. Michael Hudson and Baruch Levine. Cambridge: Peabody Museum of Archaeology and Ethnology of Harvard University, 1999: 429–38.

Levy, Thomas E., and Augustin F. C. Hall. "Social Change and the Archaeology of the Holy Land." *The Archaeology of Society in the Holy Land*. Ed. Thomas E. Levy. London: Leicester University Press, 1995: 2–8.

Levy, Thomas E. "Cult, Metallurgy and Rank Societies—Chalcolithic Period (CA. 4500–3500 BCE)." *The Archaeology of Society in the Holy Land*. Ed. Thomas E. Levy. London: Leicester University Press, 1995: 226–243.

Lewy, Julius. "Ḫâbirū and Hebrews." *Hebrew Union College Annual*: vol. 14 (1930) 587–623.

Lichtheim, Mariam. *Ancient Egyptian Literature: The Old and Middle Kingdoms*: vol 1. Berkeley: University of California Press, 2006.

_____. *Ancient Egyptian Literature: The New Kingdom*: vol. 2. Berkeley: University of California Press, 2006.

Lipiński, Edward. *Semitic Languages: Outline of a Comparative Grammar*. Leuven: Peeters, 2001.

Liverani, Mario. *Prestige and Interest: International Relations in the Near East c. 1600–1100 B.C.* Padova: Sargon, 1990.

Lloyd, Alan B. "The Late Period." *Oxford History of Ancient Egypt* (New York: Oxford University Press, 2000) 365.

Lockyer, Herbert, Ed. *Nelson's Illustrated Bible Dictionary*. Nashville: Thomas Nelson Publisher, 1986.

"Locust swarms advance into Egypt." *BBC News* (November 18, 2004). http://news.bbc.co.uk/2/hi/middle_east/4022871.stm (accessed February 2015).

Londhe, Sushama. *A Tribute to Hinduism*. New Delhi: Pragun Publications, 2008.

Long, V. Phillips. "How Did Saul Become King? Literary Reading and Historical Reconstruction." *Faith, Tradition, and History*. Ed. A. R. Millard, J. K. Hoffmeier, and D. W. Baker. Winona Lake, IN: Eisenbrauns, 1994: 271–84.

Longman, Tremper. *How to Read Genesis*. Downer's Grove, IL: InterVarsity Press, 2005.

"Lost in Time, Found by Satellites" *Science Magazine* (June 2011) 1134.

Lowe, J. "Comments on the History of Leprosy." *Leprosy Review* 9 (1955) 9, 25.

Lucas, A. *Ancient Egyptian Materials and Industries*. London: Edward Arnold, 1948.

Luckenbill, Daniel. *Ancient Records of Assyria and Babylon*: 2 vols. Chicago: University of Chicago Press, 1929.

Lutzer, Erwin. *Doctrines That Divide: A Fresh Look at the Historic Doctrines That Separate Christians*. Grand Rapids: Kregel, 1989.

Machinist, Peter. "The Question of Distinctiveness in Ancient Israel." *Essential Papers on Israel and the Ancient Near East.* Ed. Greenspahn, Frederick. New York: New York University Press, 1991: 420–442.

Majjhima Nikāya, The Middle Length Discourses of the Buddha: A New Translation of the Majjhima Nikāya. Translated from the Pali. Trans. Bhikkhu Ñānamoli. Ed. Bhikkhu Bodhi. Boston: Wisdom Publications (1995) 123:10.

Maimonides, Moses. *The Guide for the Perplexed.* Trans. M. Friedlander. London: Routledge, 1928.

Malamat, Abraham. "A Forerunner of Biblical Prophecy: The Mari Documents." *Essential Papers on Israel and the Ancient Near East.* Ed. Frederick Greenspahn. New York: New York University Press, 1991: 153–75.

_____. *History of Biblical Israel.* Leiden: Brill, 2001.

Malek, Jaromir. "The Old Kingdom (*c.* 2686–2160 BC)." *The Oxford History of Ancient Egypt.* Ed. Ian Shaw. New York: Oxford University Press, 2004: 83–107.

Mann, Michael. *The Sources of Social Power*: vol 1. Cambridge: Cambridge University Press, 1986.

Manning, Stuart W. "Radiocarbon Dating and Egyptian Chronology." *Ancient Egyptian Chronology.* Handbook of Oriental Studies 83. Leiden: Brill, 2006.

Marks, John H. *Visions of One World.* Guilford, CT: Four Quarters, 1985.

Marshack, Alexander. "Space and Time in Preagricultural Europe and the Near East: The Evidence for Early Structural Complexity." *Urbanization and Land Ownership in the Ancient Near East*: vol.2. Ed. Michael Hudson and Baruch Levine. Cambridge: Peabody Museum of Archaeology and Ethnology of Harvard University, 1999: 19–63.

Marshall, John. *Mohenjo Daro and the Indus Civilization*: 3 vols. New Delhi: Asian Educational Services, 1931.

Martens, Elmer A. "The Oscillating Fortunes of 'History' within Old Testament Theology." *Faith, Tradition, and History.* Ed. A. R. Millard, J. K. Hoffmeier, and D. W. Baker. Winona Lake, IN: Eisenbrauns, 1994: 313–39.

Martin-Achard, R. "Isaac." *Anchor Bible Dictionary*: vol. 6. Ed. David N. Freedman, et al. New York: Doubleday, 1992.

Martino, Stefano de. "A Tentative Chronology of the Kingdom of Mittani from Its Rise to the Reign of Tušratta." *Mesopotamian Dark Age Revisited.* Proceedings of an International Conference of SCIEM 2000. Ed. Hermann Hunger and Regine Pruzsinszky. Vienna: Verlag der Österreichischen Akademie der Wissenschaften, 2004: 35–42.

Massey, Gerald. *Ancient Egypt: The Light of the World*: 2 vols. Baltimore: Black Classic Press, 1907.

Masterman, Ernest W. G., and J. Barton Payne. "Siloam." *International Standard Bible Encyclopedia*: vol. 4. Grand Rapids, MI: Eerdmans, 1979: 510–11.

Mattfeld, Walter. "Exodus and the Hyksos." B-Hebrew Mailing List. Last updated January 17, 2000. http://lists.ibiblio.org/pipermail/b-hebrew/2000-January/006340.html (accessed December 2013).

_____. "Exodus Memories of Southern Sinai (Linking the Archaeological Data to the Biblical Narratives)." Bibleorigins. Last updated November 21, 2009. http://www.bibleorigins.net/ExodusTimnaSerabitelKhadim.html (accessed February 2015).

_____. "Exodus Problems: Scholarly Pitfalls encountered in Setting a Date for the Exodus and Establishing Its Route on Maps." Bibleorigins.net. Last updated October 17, 2010. http://www.bibleorigins.net/ExodusProblems.html (accessed February 2015).

_____. "Tammuz, Dumuzi, Ningishzida and Jesus Christ." Last updated April 27, 2004. http://www.bibleorigins.net/TammuzDumuziDamuSeal.html (accessed February 2015).

_____. "Various Map Proposals for the Route of the Exodus." Last updated June 14, 2009. http://www.bibleorigins.net/ExodusRouteMapsVarious.html (accessed February 2015).

Matthews, Victor. "Syria to the Early Second Millennium." *Mesopotamia and the Bible*. Ed. Mark W. Chavalas and K. Lawson Younger, Jr. Grand Rapids, MI: Baker, 2002: 168–90.

Matthews, Victor, Bernard Levinson, and Tikva Frymer-Kensky, Ed. *Gender and Law in the Hebrew Bible and in the Ancient Near East*. London: Sheffield Academic Press, 1998.

Marx, Karl, and Friedrich Engels. *The Communist Manifesto* (1888). Trans. Allen Lutins. The Gutenberg Ebook of the Communist Manifest, January 25, 2005. http://www.gutenberg.org/ebooks/61 (accessed February 2015).

Mazar, Amihai. "The Iron Age I." *The Archaeology of Ancient Israel*. Trans. R. Greenberg. Ed. Amnon Ben-Tor. New Haven, CT: Yale University Press, 1992.

_____. *Archaeology of the Land of the Bible—10,000–586 B.C.E.* Ed. David Noel Freedman. Anchor Bible Reference Library. New York: Doubleday, 1990.

_____. "Tel Beth Shean: History and Archaeology." *One God—One Cult—One Nation. Archaeological and Biblical Perspectives*. Ed. R. G. Kratz and H. Spieckermann. Berlin: Beihefte zur Zeitschrift für die alttestamentliche Wissenschaft 405, 2010: 239–72.

_____. "The Patriarchs, Exodus, and Conquest Narratives in Light of Archaeology." *The Quest for the Historical Israel*. Ed. Andrew Vaughn. SBL Archaeology and Biblical Studies 17. Atlanta: Society of Biblical Literature, 2007.

McCabe, Joseph. *The Myth of the Resurrection*. Buffalo, NY: Prometheus Books, 1993.

McCarter, P. Kyle. "Inscriptions." *International Standard Bible Encyclopedia*: vol. 2. Grand Rapids, MI: Eerdmans, 1979: 834.

McCarthy, Dennis. "Treaty and Covenant." *Institution and Narrative*. Rome: Pontifical Biblical Institute Press, 1985.

McCready, Wayne O. "Priests and Levites." *International Standard Bible Encyclopedia*: vol. 3. Grand Rapids, MI: Eerdmans, 1979: 965–68.

McKee, David. "Isaac de la Peyrère: A Precursor of the Eighteenth-Century Critical Deists." *Publications of the Modern Language Association* 59/2 (1944) 456–85.

McKenzie, Stephen L. *The Chronicler's Use of the Deuteronomistic History*. HSM 33. Atlanta: Scholars Press, 1983.

_____. "The Typology of the Davidic Covenant." *The Land That I Will Show You*. Ed. Andrew Dearman and Patrick Graham. Sheffield: Sheffield Academic Press, 2001) 153–78.

McKinnon, Fred, Ed. "The Sabbath—Do We Keep It?" Last updated November 2, 2009. http://www.fredmckinnon.com/myblog/2009/11/02/the-sabbath-do-we-keep-it/ (accessed February 2015).

McMahon, Gregory. "History and Legend in Early Hittite Hisoriography." *Faith, Tradition, and History*. Ed. A. K. Millard, J. K. Hoffmeier, and D. W. Baker. Winona Lake, IN: Eisenbrauns, 1994: 149–58.

McNeill, William, and Jean Sedlar, Ed. *The Ancient Near East*. Readings in World History: vol. 2. New York: Oxford University Press, 1968.

Mendenhall, George. *Ancient Israel's Faith and History*. Louisville: John Knox, 2001.

_____. "Biblical History in Transition." *The Bible and the Ancient Near East: Essays in Honor of William Foxwell Albright*. Ed. George Earnest Wright. Garden City, NY: Anchor Books, 1965: 42.

_____. *Law and Covenant in Israel and the Ancient Near East*. Pittsburgh: Biblical Colloquium, 1955.

_____. *The Tenth Generation, The Origins of the Biblical Tradition.* Baltimore: Johns Hopkins University Press. 1973.

Merling, David. "The Relationship between Archaeology and the Bible." *The Future of Biblical Archaeology: Reassessing Methodologies and Assumptions.* Proceedings of a Symposium at Trinity International University, Aug. 21–14, 2001. Ed. James Hoffmeier and Alan Millard. Grand Rapids, MI: Eerdmans, 2004: 29–42.

Merrill, Eugene. *An Historical Survey of the Old Testament.* Nutley, NJ: Craig, 1966.

_____. *Kingdom of Priests.* Grand Rapids, MI: Baker, 1987.

Meshel, Ze'ev. *Kuntillet 'Ajrud (Horvat Teman): An Iron Age II Religious Site on the Judah-Sinai Border.* Jerusalem: Israel Exploration Society, 2012.

Meyers, Eric M., Ed. *Galilee through the Centuries: Confluence of Cultures.* Winona Lake, IN: Eisenbrauns, 1999.

Miano, David. *Shadow on the Steps: Time Measurement in Ancient Israel.* Atlanta: Society of Biblical Literature, 2010.

Mill, John Stuart. *Philosophy of Scientific Method.* Mineola, NY: Dover, 2005.

Millar, William. "Oral Poetry and Dumuzi's Dream." *Scripture in Context,* vol.1: *Essays on the Comparative Method.* Ed. Carl D. Evans, et al. PTMS 34. Pittsburgh: Pickwick, 1980.

Millard, Alan R. "Amorites and Israelites: Invisible Invaders—Modern Expectation and Ancient Reality." *The Future of Biblical Archaeology: Reassessing Methodologies and Assumptions.* Proceeding of a Symposium at Trinity International University, Aug. 12–14, 2001. Ed. James Hoffmeier and Alan Millard. Grand Rapids, MI: Eerdmans, 2004: 148–162.

_____. A Decree of a Persian Governor." *Buried History* (1974) 88.

_____. *The Eponyms of the Assyrian Empire 910–612 BC.* SAAS 2. Helsinki: The Neo-Assyrian Text Corpus Project, 1994.

_____. "Story, History, and Theology." *Faith, Tradition, and History.* Ed. A. K. Millard, J. K. Hoffmeier, and D. W. Baker. Winona Lake, IN: Eisenbrauns, 1994: 37–64.

_____. "Texts and Archaeology: Weighing the Evidence—The Case for King Solmon." *Palestine Exploration Quarterly* 123 (1991) 25.

_____. "Variable Spelling in Hebrew and Other Ancient Texts." *Journal of Theological Studies* 42 (1991) 106–15.

Miller, Cynthia L. "Methodological Issues in Reconstructing Language Systems from Epigraphic Fragments." *The Future of Biblical Archaeology: Reassessing Methodologies and Assumptions.* Proceeding of a Symposium at Trinity International University, Aug. 12–14, 2001. Ed. James Hoffmeier and Alan Millard. Grand Rapids, MI: Eerdmans, 2004: 281–308.

Miller, Patrick. *Religion of Ancient Israel.* Louisville: Westminster John Knox, 2000.

Mills, Bruce. "The Purpose of God's Law." Inverted Planet (June 29, 2009). http://invertedplanet. blogspot.com/2009/06/purpose-of-god-law.html (accessed February 2015).

Min, Kyung-Jin. *The Levitical Authorship of Ezra-Nehemiah.* JSOTSup 409 (2004) 82.

Moisse, Katie. "Tutankhamen's Familial DNA Tells Tale of Boy Pharaoh's Disease and Incest." *Scientific American* (February 16, 2010). http://www.scientificamerican.com/article.cfm?id=king-tut-dna (accessed February 2015).

Monson, John M. "The Role of Context and the Promise of Archaeology in Biblical Interpretation from Early Judaism to Post Modernity." *The Future of Biblical Archaeology: Reassessing Methodologies and Assumptions.* Proceeding of a Symposium at Trinity International University, Aug. 12–14, 2001. Ed. James Hoffmeier and Alan Millard. Grand Rapids, MI: Eerdmans, 2004: 309–327.

Montet, P. *Byblos et l'Égypte: Quatre Campagnes de fouilles à Gebeil*: 2 vols. Paris: P. Geuthner, 1928–29.

Moore, Megan, and Brad Kelle. *Biblical History and Israel's Past: The Changing Study of the Bible and History*. Grand Rapids, MI: Eerdmans, 2011.

Moran, William. *The Amarna Letters*. Baltimore: Johns Hopkins University Press, 1987.

_____. "The Ancient Near Eastern Background of the Love of God in Deuteronomy." *Essential Papers on Israel and the Ancient Near East*. Ed. Greenspahn, Frederick. New York: New York University Press, 1991: 103–115.

_____. "The Hebrew Language." *The Bible and the Ancient Near East*. Ed. Earnest Wrist. Garden City, NY: Doubleday, 1965: 63.

Morgan, Donn F. "Horse." *International Standard Bible Encyclopedia*: vol. 2. Grand Rapids, MI: Eerdmans, 1979: 759–60.

Morkot, Robert. *The Egyptians*. New York: Routledge, 2005.

Morris, Leon. "Ransom." *International Standard Bible Encyclopedia*: vol.4. Grand Rapids, MI: Eerdmans, 1979: 44–45.

Moskowitz, Clara. "Bible Possibly Written Centuries Earlier, Text Suggests." *Live Science* (January 15, 2010). http://www.livescience.com/8008-bible-possibly-written-centuries-earlier-text-suggests.html (accessed February 2015).

Murnane, William. *Ancient Egyptian Coregencies*. Studies in Ancient Oriental Civilization 40. Chicago: The Oriental Institute, 1970.

Myers, Allen C. "*Bless*." *International Standard Bible Encyclopedia*: vol. 1. Grand Rapids, MI: Eerdmans, 1979: 523–24.

_____. "Death." *International Standard Bible Encyclopedia*: vol. 1. Grand Rapids, MI: Eerdmans, 1979: 899.

Myers, Allen C., and James A. Patch. "Blasting." *International Standard Bible Encyclopedia*: vol. 1. Grand Rapids, MI: Eerdmans, 1979: 522.

Na'aman, Nadav. "Habiru and Hebrews: The Transfer of a Social Term to the Literary Sphere." *JNES* 45/4 (1986) 271–88.

Nebet, Mirjam. "The Ancient Egyptian Calendar." The Egyptian World. Last updated October 26, 2007. http://www.ancientworlds.net/aw/Article/998323 (accessed February 2015).

_____. "Sennacherib's 'Letter to God' on His Campaign to Judah." *BASOR* 214 (1974) 25–39.

Nelson, Eric. *The Hebrew Republic: Jewish Sources and the Transformation of European Political Thought*. Cambridge: Harvard University Press, 2010.

Nelson, R. D. *The Double Redaction of the Deuteronomistic History*. JSOTSup 18. Sheffield: JSOT Press, 1981.

Nicholson, Paul, and Ian Shaw, Ed. *Ancient Egyptian Materials and Technology*. New York: Cambridge University Press, 2000.

Niehaus, Jeffrey J. "The Warrior and His God: The Covenant Foundation of History and Historiography." *Faith, Tradition, and History*. Ed. A. R. Millard, J. K. Hoffmeier, and D. W. Baker. Winona Lake, IN: Eisenbrauns, 1994: 299–311.

Noegel, Scott. "Moses and Magic: Notes on the Book of Exodus." *JANES* 24 (1996) 45–59.

Nola, Robert, and Howard Sankey. *Theories of Scientific Method*. Montreal: McGill-Queen's University Press, 2007.

Noll, K. L. *Canaan and Israel in Antiquity: An Introduction*. London: Sheffield Academic Press, 2001.

North, Gary. *Tools of Dominion: The Case Laws of Exodus*. Tyler, TX: Institute for Christian Economics, 1990.

"The Number of Centurions in Japan Tops 47,000." Associated Press. September 13, 2011. http://www.foxnews.com/health/2011/09/13/number-centenarians-in-japan-tops-47000/?test=latestnews (accessed February 2015).

Nunn, John F. *Ancient Egyptian Medicine*. Norman: University of Oklahoma, 1996.

O'Connor, David. "The Hyksos Period." *The Hyksos: New Historical and Archaeological Perspectives*. Ed. Eliezer Oren. University Museum Monograph 96/8. Philadelphia: University of Pennsylvania Museum, 1997.

Olmstead, A. T. *History of the Persian Empire*. Chicago: University of Chicago Press, 1948.

_____. "Tattenai, Governor of 'Across the River.'" *JNES* (1944) 46.

Oren, Eliezer, Ed. *The Sea Peoples and Their World: A Reassessment*. Philadelphia: University of Pennsylvania Museum of Archaeology and Anthropology, 2000.

_____. "The 'Kingdom of Sharuhen' and the Hyksos Kingdom." *The Hyksos: New Historical and Archaeological Perspectives*. Ed. Eliezer Oren. University Museum Monograph 96/8. Philadelphia: University of Pennsylvania Museum, 1997.

Ortiz, Steven M. "Deconstructing and Reconstructing the United Monarchy: House of David or Tent of David (Current Trends in Iron Age Chronology)." *The Future of Biblical Archaeology: Reassessing Methodologies and Assumptions*. Proceeding of a Symposium at Trinity International University, Aug. 12–14, 2001. Ed. James Hoffmeier and Alan Millard. Grand Rapids, MI: Eerdmans, 2004: 121–147.

Øtsby, Erik. "Twenty-five years of Research on Greek Sanctuaries: a Bibliography." *Greek Sanctuaries: New Approaches*. Eds. Nanno Marinatos and Robin Hagg. New York: Routledge, 1993: 179–82.

Pagolu, Augustine. *The Religion of the Patriarchs*. Sheffield: Sheffield Academic Press, 1998.

Paine, Thomas. *The Age of Reason*. New York: Prometheus Books, 1984.

Parker, Richard. *The Calendars of Ancient Egypt*. Studies in Ancient Oriental Civilization 26. Chicago: University of Chicago Press, 1950.

Parpola, Simo. "Sons of God: The Ideology of Assyrian Kingship." *Archaeology Odyssey* 2/5 (1999) 16–27.

_____. "The Murderer of Sennacherib." *Death in Mesopotamia: XXVIeme Rencontre Assyriologique Internationale*. Ed. Bendt Alster. Copenhagen: Akademisk Forlag, 1980: 171–82.

Patrick, David, Ed. *Chambers's Encyclopaedia: A Dictionary of Universal Knowledge*: 10 vols. London: W. B. R. Chambers, 1881–1901.

Patton, Michael. "Did the Holy Spirit Indwell Old Testament Believers?" *Parchment and Pen Blog*. Credo House Ministries. Last updated February 7, 2007. http://www.reclaimingthemind.org/blog/2007/02/did-the-holy-spirit-indwell-old-testament-believers/ (accessed February 2015).

Pasynkova, Elena N., and Aleksander V. Pasynkov. "Efficiency of the Mixed Crops of Spring Cereals and Legumes Cultivated on Sod-podzolic Soil." *Agricultural and Forest Engineering* 57. Kirov, Russia, 2011.

Payne, David F. "Babel." *International Standard Bible Encyclopedia*: vol. 1. Grand Rapids, MI: Eerdmans, 1979: 382.

Payne, Thomas Edward. *Exploring Language Structure: A Student's Guide*. New York: Cambridge University Press, 2006.

Pecota, Daniel B., and John W. Simpson. "Young(er) (Man)." *International Standard Bible Encyclopedia*: vol. 4. Grand Rapids, MI: Eerdmans, 1979: 1166.

Pedley, John Griffiths. *Sanctuaries and the Sacred in the Ancient Greek World*. Cambridge: Cambridge University Press, 2005.

Penglase, Charles. *Greek Myths and Mesopotamian: Parallels and Influence in the Homeric Hymns and Hesiod*. New York: Routledge, 1994.

Perkin, Hazel W., and Gary A. Lee. "Gezer Calendar." *International Standard Bible Encyclopedia*: vol. 2. Grand Rapids, MI: Eerdmans, 1979: 460.

_____. "Money." *International Standard Bible Encyclopedia*: vol. 3. Grand Rapids, MI: Eerdmans, 1979: 403–4.

Petrie, William Matthew Flinders, and John Garrow Duncan. *Hyksos and Israelite Cities*. London: British School of Archaeology, 1906.

Phillips, Anthony. *Ancient Israel's Criminal Law*. Oxford: Basil Blackwell, 1970.

Pinch, Geraldine. *Egyptian Mythology*. Oxford: Oxford University Press, 2002.

Pliny, *Natural History: Book XIX*. Ed. John Bostock and H. T. Riley. London: Henry Bohn, 1856.

Pojman, Louis. *Philosophy: The Quest for Truth*. Belmont, CA: Wadsworth Publishing, 1989.

Polybius, *The Histories of Polybius*. Loeb Classical Library 6. Trans. W. R. Paton. Cambridge: Harvard University Press, 1927.

Powell, Alvin. "Ancient Canal Network is Recasting Archaeologists' Understanding of the Assyrian Capital." Harvard News Office. http://news.harvard.edu/gazette/2006/ 03.16/ 11-canal.html (accessed February 2015).

Prabhupada, A. C. Bhaktivedanta Swami. *KRSNA*. Juhu, India: Bhaktivedanta Book Trust, 1970.

Prager, Dennis. "Judaism's Sexual Revolution: Why Judaism (and Christianity) Rejected Homosexuality." *Crisis* 11/8 (September 1993). http://www.orthodoxytoday.org/articles2/PragerHomosexuality.php (accessed March 2015).

Pratico, Gary. "Noah." *International Standard Bible Encyclopedia*: vol. 3. Grand Rapids, MI: Eerdmans, 1979: 543.

Price, Randall. "Ezekiel's Prophecy of the Temple." World of the Bible. http://www.worldofthebible.com/Bible%20Studies/Ezekiel's%20Prophecy%20of%20the%20Temple.pdf. (accessed December 2013).

Prior, A. N. *The Encyclopedia of Philosophy*: vol. 2. Ed. Paul Edwards. New York: Macmillan and The Free Press: 1962, 223–232.

Pritchard, James B., Ed. *Ancient Near Eastern Texts Relating to the Old Testament*. Princeton: Princeton University Press, 1969.

_____ . Ed. *The Ancient Near East: An Anthology of Texts and Pictures*. Princeton, NJ: Princeton University Press, 2011.

Pruzsinszky, Regine. "Evidence for the Short Chronology in Mesopotamia?" *Mesopotamian Dark Age Revisited*. Proceedings of an International Conference of SCIEM 2000. Ed. Hermann Hunger and Regine Pruzsinszky.Vienna: Verlag der Österreichischen Akademie der Wissenschaften, 2004: 43–50.

Rainey, Anson. "The 'House of David,' and the House of the Deconstructionists." *BAR* 20/6 (1994) 47.

_____. "Mesha' and Syntax." *The Land That I Will Show You*. Ed. Andrew Dearman and Patrick Graham. Sheffield: Sheffield Academic Press, 2001: 287–307.

_____."Zion." *International Standard Bible Encyclopedia*: vol. 4. Grand Rapids, MI: Eerdmans, 1979: 1198.

"Rainstorms Might Trigger Volcanic Blowouts." *Current Science* 88/8 (December 2002) 14.

Rand, Ayn. *Philosophy: Who Needs It?* New York: Signet, 1982.

Randerson, James. "Rainstorms Could Trigger Killer Eruptions." *NewScientist* (August 2002). http://www.newscientist.com/article/dn2755-rainstorms-could-trigger-killer-eruptions.html#.UsodvRDu8A (accessed February 2015).

Rasmussen, Carl. "Conquest, Infiltration, Revolt, or Resettlement?" *Giving the Sense.* Ed. David Howard and Michael Gristani. Grand Rapids, MI: Kregel Academic, 2003.

_____. "Peleg." *International Standard Bible Encyclopedia*: vol 3. Grand Rapids, MI: Eerdmans, 1979: 736.

Redford, Donald. *Akhenaten: The Heretic King.* Princeton, NJ: Princeton University Press, 1984.

_____. *Egypt, Canaan, and Israel in Ancient Times.* Princeton, NJ: Princeton University Press, 1992.

_____. "Textual Sources for the Hyksos Period." *The Hyksos: New Historical and Archaeological Perspectives.* Ed. Eliezer Oren. University Museum Monograph 96/8. Philadelphia: University of Pennsylvania Museum, 1997.

_____. Ed., *Oxford Encyclopedia of Ancient Egypt*: 3 vols. Oxford: Oxford University Press, 2001.

Reeves, Nicholas. *Akhenaten: Egypt's False Prophet.* New York: Thames and Hudson, 2001.

Rehork, Joachim. "Postscript in *The Bible as History*, by Werner Keller." New York: William Morrow, 1981.

Remier, Pat. *Egyptian Mythology A–Z.* New York: Chelsea House, 2010.

Rendsburg, Gary. "Israel without the Bible." *The Hebrew Bible: New Insights and Scholarship*. Ed. Frederick E. Greenspahn. New York: New York University Press, 2008.

Rendtorff, Rolf . "What Happened to the 'Yahwist'?: Reflections after Thirty Years." SBL Forum Archive. *Society of Biblical Literature.* http://www.sbl-site.org/publications/article.aspx?articleId=553 (accessed February 2015).

Reznick, Leibel. *The Holy Temple Revisited.* Northvale, NJ: Jason Aronson, 1990.

Rhys, Joycelyn. *Shaken Creeds: The Virgin Birth Doctrine and the Study of Its Origins.* Whitefish, MT: Kessenger, 1922.

Rich, Tracy R. "The Name of G-d." Judaism 101. http://www.jewfaq.org/name.htm (accessed February 2015).

Richards, E. G. *Mapping Time.* New York: Oxford University Press, 1999.

Richards, K. H. "Bless/Blessing." *The Anchor Bible Dictionary*: vol. 1. Ed. Richard Noel Freedman. New York: Doubleday, 1992: 754, 756.

Ridderbos, Nicholas H., and Peter Craigie. "Psalms." *International Standard Bible Encyclopedia*: vol. 3. Grand Rapids, MI: Eerdmans, 1979: 1039–40.

Ridley, R. T. "To Be Taken with a Pinch of Salt: The Destruction of Carthage." *Classical Philology* 81/2 (1986) 140–46.

Ringgren, Helmer. *Theological Dictionary of the Old Testament*: vol. 15. Grand Rapids: Eerdman's, 2006: 564.

Roberts, J. J. M. *The Bible and the Ancient Near East: Collected Essays.* Winona Lake, IN: Eisenbrans, 2001.

_____. *History of the World.* New York: Oxford University Press, 1993.

Robertson, J. M. *Pagan Christs.* New Hyde Park, NY: University Books, 1967.

Robinson, B. A. "Grouping Christian Denominations into Families." Ontario Consultants on Religious Tolerance Last updated November 6, 2006. http://www.religioustolerance.org/chr_deno.htm (accessed February 2015).

Rohl, David M. *Pharaohs and Kings: A Biblical Quest.* New York: Crown, 1995.

Rollston, Christopher A. "What's the Oldest Hebrew Inscription?" *BAR* 38/3 (2012) 32–40.

Roser, Mark C. *The Cleansing of the Heavens*. Shippensburg, PA: Treasure House, 1998.

Ross, Allen P. *Introducing Biblical Hebrew*. Grand Rapids, MI: Baker Academic, 2001.

Roth, Martha T. "The Series An-ta-gál = šaqû." *MSL XVII*. Ed. Antoine Cavigneaux. Pontificum Institutum Biblicum. Rome: Gregorian University Press (1985) 134–35.

Rouault, Oliver. "Chronological Problems Concerning the Middle Euphrates during the Bronze Age." *Mesopotamian Dark Age Revisited*. Proceedings of an International Conference of SCIEM 2000. Ed. Hermann Hunger and Regine Pruzsinszky.Vienna: Verlag der Österreichischen Akademie der Wissenschaften, 2004: 51–59.

Roux, Georges. *Ancient Iraq*. London: Penguin Books, 1966.

Rudd, Steve. "The Exodus Route: Goshen to the Red Sea." Bible.ca. http://www.bible.ca/archeology/bible- archeology-exodus-route-goshen-red-sea.htm (accessed February 2015).

_____. "Migdol 'Watchtower.'" http://www.bible.ca/archeology/bible-archeology-exodus-route-migdol.htm (accessed February 2015).

Russell, John Malcolm. *The Writing on the Wall*. Mesopotamian Civilizations 9. Winona Lake, IN: Eisenbrauns, 1999.

Ryholt, Kim. *The Political Situation in Egypt during the Second Intermediate Period*. Copenhagen: Museum Tusculanum Press, 1997.

Saggs, H. W. F. "The Divine History." *Essential Papers on Israel and the Ancient Near East*. Ed. Greenspahn, Frederick. New York: New York University Press, 1991: 17–48.

Salvini, Mirjo. *The Habiru Prism of King Tunip-Teššup of Tikunani*. Documenta Asiana 3. Rome: Istituti Editoriali e Poligrafici Internazionali, 1996.

Sameth, Mark. "God's Hidden Name RevealEd." *Reform Judaism Online* (Spring 2009) http://rjmag.org/Articles/index.cfm?id=1433 (accessed February, 2015).

Sandars, N. K. *The Sea Peoples: Warriors of the Ancient Mediterranean 1250–1150 BC*. New York: Thames and Hudson, 1985.

Sandison, A. T., and Edmund Tapp. "Disease in Ancient Egypt." *Mummies, Disease, and Ancient Cultures*. Ed. Aidan Cockburn et al. Cambridge: Cambridge University Press, 1998.

Sassmannshausen, Leonhard. "Babylonian Chronology of the 2nd half of the 2nd Millennium B.C." Contributions to the Chronology of the Eastern Mediterranean Mesopotamian Dark Age Revisited. Ed. Regine Pruzsinszky and Herman Hunger. Vienna: Austrian Academy of Sciences, 2004: 61–69.

Schiestl, Robert. "The Cemeteries of F/I in the Strata d/2 (H) and d/1 (G/4), Late 12th Dynasty and Early 13th Dynasty." Tell el-Dabca, 2008, 2013. http://www.auaris.at/html/stratum_f1_d1_en.html (accessed February 2015).

Schneider, Tammi. *An Introduction to Ancient Mesopotamian Religion*. Grand Rapids, MI: Eerdmans, 2011.

Schneider, Thomas. "The Relative Chronology of the Middle Kingdom and the Hyksos Period (Dyns. 12–17)." Ed. Erik Hornung, Rolf Krauss, and David Warburton. *Ancient Egyptian Chronology*. Handbuch der Orientalistik 83. Leiden: Brill, 2006.

Schniedewind, William. *How the Bible Became a Book*. New York: Cambridge University Press, 2004.

_____. "The Rise of the Aramean States." *Mesopotamia and the Bible*. Ed. Mark W. Chavalas and K. Lawson Younger, Jr. Grand Rapids, MI: Baker, 2002: 276–87.

Schoville, K. N. "War." *International Standard Bible Encyclopedia*: vol. 4. Grand Rapids, MI: Eerdmans, 1979: 1015–17.

Schultz, Carl. "The Political Tensions Reflected in Ezra-Nehemiah." *Scripture in Context*, vol. 1: *Essays on the Comparative Method*. Ed. Carl Evans, et al. PTMS 34. Pitsburgh: Pickwick, 1980.

Scolnic, Benjamin Edidin. "A New Working Hypothesis for the Identification of Migdol." *The Future of Biblical Archaeology: Reassessing Methodologies and Assumptions*. Proceeding of a Symposium at Trinity International University, Aug. 12–14, 2001. Ed. James Hoffmeier and Alan Millard. Grand Rapids, MI: Eerdmans, 2004: 91–120.

Scott, James. *Restoration: Old Testament, Jewish, and Christian Perspectives*. Leiden: Brill, 2000.

Seidlmayer, Stephan. "The First Intermediate Period." *The Oxford History of Ancient Egypt*. Ed. Ian Shaw. New York: Oxford University Press, 2004.

Shanks, Hershel. "The Persisting Uncertainties of Kuntillet 'Ajrud.'" *BAR* 38/6 (2013) 29–37, 76.

_____. "Prize Find: Oldest Hebrew Inscription Discovered in Israelite Fort on Philistine Border." *BAR* 36/2 (2010) 51–54.

_____. "When Did Ancient Israel Begin?" *BAR* 38/1 (2012) 59–62, 67.

Shaw, Ian. "Egypt and the Outside World." Ed. Ian Shaw. *The Oxford History of Ancient Egypt*. New York: Oxford University Press, 2000: 308–323.

Shaw, Ian, and Paul Nicholson. *The British Museum Dictionary of Ancient Egypt*. London: British Museum Press, 2008.

Shea, William. "The Date of the Exodus." *International Standard Bible Encyclopedia*: vol. 2. Grand Rapids, MI: Eerdmans, 1979: 233–38.

_____. "The Date of the Exodus." *Giving the Sense*. Ed. David Howard and Michael Grisanti. Grand Rapids: Kregel Academic, 2003.

_____. "Sargon's Azekah Inscription: The Earliest Extrabiblical Reference to the Sabbath?" *AUSS* 32/3 (1994) 247–51.

Shipp, Mark. *Of Dead Kings and Dirges: Myth and Meaning in Isaiah 14:4b–21*. Leiden: Brill, 2002.

Shubert, Steven, and Kathryn Bard, Ed. "Social Organization." *Encyclopedia of the Archaeology of Ancient Egypt*. New York: Routledge-Taylor and Francis, 1999.

Sicker, Martin. *The Pre-Islamic Middle East*. Westport, CT: Praeger, 2000.

Silberman, Neil Asher. "Power, Politics and the Past: The Social Construction of Antiquity in the Holy Land." *The Archaeology of Society in the Holy Land*. Ed. Thomas E. Levy. London: Leicester University Press, 1995: 9–23.

Silverman, David, Ed. *Ancient Egypt*. Oxford: Oxford University Press, 1997.

Simpson, William. *The Literature of Ancient Egypt*. New Haven, CT: Yale University Press, 2003.

Singer, Trip. "Jesus is the Only Way to God." AllGod.com: Jesus Saves. Baytown, TX. Last modified January 21, 2007. http://www.all-god.com/come-out-separate-yourself-from-the-world.html (accessed December 2013).

Slick, Matt. "How Do You Present the Gospel Properly." Christian Apologetics and Research Ministry. http://www.carm.org/how-to-present-gospel-properly (accessed February 2015).

_____. "What is sin?" Christian Apologetics and Research Ministry. http://www.carm.org/What%20is%20sin%3F (accessed December 2013).

Snell, Daniel. *Religions of the Ancient Near East*. Cambridge: Cambridge University Press, 2010.

Smith-Christopher, Daniel L. "Exile."*Eerdmans Dictionary of the Bible*. Ed. David Noel Freedman, et al. Grand Rapids: Eerdmans, 2000: 439.

Smith, Lee. "Amos 9:13–15: Quicker and larger Return from Exile." Old Doctrines, New Light. http://www.arlev.co.uk/amos23.htm (accessed February 2015).

Smith, Morton. "The Common Theology of the Ancient Near East." *Essential Papers on Israel and the Ancient Near East*. Ed. Greenspahn, Frederick. New York: New York University Press, 1991: 49–65.

Smith, Patricia. "People of the Holy Land from Prehistory to the Recent Past." *The Archaeology of Society in the Holy Land*. Ed. Thomas E. Levy. London: Leicester University Press, 1995: 58–74.

Soderlund, Sven K. "Septuagint." *International Standard Bible Encyclopedia*: vol 4. Grand Rapids, MI: Eerdmans, 1979: 400–408.

Soggin, J. A. "Sons of God(s), Heroes, and *Nephilim*: Remarks on Genesis 6:1–4." *Texts, Temples, and Traditions*. Ed. Michael V. Fox et al. Winona Lake, IN: Eisenbrauns, 1996: 135–36.

Soltau, Henry. *The Tabernacle, the Priesthood, and the Offerings*. Grand Rapids, MI: Kregel, 1972.

Spiegel, Shalom. "Noah, Danel, and Job, Touching on Canaanite Relics in the Legends of the Jews." *Essential Papers on Israel and the Ancient Near East*. Ed. Greenspahn, Frederick. New York: New York University Press, 1991: 193–241.

Stager, Lawrence. "Forging an Identity: The Emergence of Ancient Israel." *The Oxford History of the Biblical World*. Ed. Michael Coogan. Oxford: Oxford University Press, 2001.

———. "The Impact of the Sea Peoples (1185–1050 BCE)." *The Archaeology of Society in the Holy Land*. Ed. Thomas E. Levy. London: Leicester University Press, 1995: 332–47.

———. "The Shechem Temple Where Abimelech Massacred a Thousand." *BAR* 29/4 (2003) 26–35.

Steindorff, George, and Keith Seele. *When Egypt Ruled the East*. Chicago: University of Chicago Press, 1942.

Steinkeller, Piotr. "Land-Tenure Conditions in Third-Millennium Babylonia: The Problem of Regional Variation." *Urbanization and Land Ownership in the Ancient Near East*: vol. 2. Ed. Michael Hudson and Baruch Levine. Cambridge: Peabody Museum of Archaeology and Ethnology of Harvard University, 1999: 289–94.

Steinmann, Andrew. *From Abraham to Paul: A Biblical Chronology*. St. Louis, MO: Concordia Publishing, 2011.

Steinsaltz, Adin. *The Essential Talmud*. Trans. Chaya Galai. New York: Basic Books, 1976.

Stern, Ephraim. "Between Persia and Greece: Trade, Administration and Warfare in the Persian and Hellenisitic Periods (539–63 BCE)." *The Archaeology of Society in the Holy Land*. Ed. Thomas E. Levy. London: Leicester University Press, 1995: 432–44.

Stevens, Susan. "A Legend of the Destruction of Carthage." *Classical Philology* 83/1 (1988) 140–46.

Stone, Elizabeth. "The Constraints on State and Urban Form in Ancient Mesopotamia." *Urbanization and Land Ownership in the Ancient Near East*: vol. 2. Ed. Michael Hudson and Baruch Levine. Cambridge: Peabody Museum of Archaeology and Ethnology of Harvard University, 1999: 203–227.

Strong, James. *Strong's Exhaustive Concordance*. Grand Rapids, MI: Baker Books, 1997.

———. *The Tabernacle of Israel*. Grand Rapids, MI: Kregel, 1987.

Stuart, D. "Curse." *Anchor Bible Dictionary*: vol. 1. Ed. David N. Freedman. New York: Doubleday, 1992: 1218.

Sweet, Ronald F., and George A. Gay. "Tax; Tribute." *International Standard Bible Encyclopedia*: vol. 4. Grand Rapids, MI: Eerdmans, 1979: 739.

Tabor, James. *Restoring Abrahamic Faith*. Charlotte, NC: Genesis 2000 Press, 2008.

Tadmor, Hayim, and S. Yamada. *The Royal Inscriptions of Tiglath-pileser III and Shalmaneser V, Kings of Assyria*. Jerusalem: Israel Academy of Sciences and Humanities, 1994.

Tait, John, Ed. *'Never Had the Like Occurred': Egypt's View of Its Past*. London: UCL Press, 2003.

"Tall al-Yahudiyyah." GIS Center: Supreme Council of Antiquities, Egypt http://www.giscenter.gov.
eg/uploads/of/ff/offffa2bb67d62d6ade49de69663c034/featured-site-layout.pdf (accessed
January 2015).

Talmon, Shemaryahu. "The 'Comparative Method' in Biblical Interpretation—Principles and Problems." *Essential Papers on Israel and the Ancient Near East.* Ed. Greenspahn, Frederick. New
York: New York University Press, 1991: 381–419.

Taylor, Charles, Ed. *Calmet's Dictionary of the Holy Bible.* Boston: Crocker and Brewser, 1832.

Taylor, John. "The Third Intermediate Period in Egypt," Ed. Ian Shaw. *The Oxford History of Ancient
Egypt.* New York: Oxford University Press, 2000: 324–63.

Tcherikover, Victor. *Hellenistic Civilization and the Jews.* Philadelphia: Jewish Publication Society,
1959.

Teixidor, Javier. *The Pantheon of Palmyra.* Leiden: Brill, 1979.

"The Tell es-Safi/Gath Excavations Official (and Unofficial) Weblog." February 16, 2006. http://gath.
wordpress.com/2006/02/16/comment-on-the-news-item-in-bar-on-the-goliath-inscription/
(accessed February 2015).

Thiele, Edwin. *The Mysterious Numbers of the Hebrew Kings,* revised. Ed. Grand Rapids, MI: Kregel,
1983.

_____. "Synchronisms of the Hebrew Kings." *AUSS* 1 (1963) 124–25.

Thomas, J. Llewellyn. *The Assyrian Invasions and Deportations of Israel.* Leicestershire, UK: Covenant Publishing, 1937.

Thompson, J. Arthur. *Ancient Near Eastern Treaties and the Old Testament.* London: Tyndale Press,
1964.

_____. "Covenant." *International Standard Bible Encyclopedia*: vol 1. Grand Rapids, MI: Eerdmans,
1979: 790–92.

_____. *1, 2 Chronicles.* Ed. E. Ray Clendenen. The New American Commentary 9. Nashville: Broad-
man and Holman, 1994.

Thompson, R. Campbell. *The Prisms of Esarhaddon and of Ashurbanipal.* London: British Museum,
1931.

Thompson, Winfield L., Jr. "Succoth." *International Standard Bible Encyclopedia*: vol. 4. Grand Rapids, MI: Eerdmans, 1979: 648.

Thorburn, Thomas James. *A Critical Examination of the Evidences for the Doctrine of the Virgin Birth.*
New York: E. S. Gorham, 1908.

Thornton, Stuart, "Tel Kabri Project," September 19, 2013, National Geographic,http://education.
nationalgeographic.com/education/news/tel-kabri-project/?ar_a=1(accessed January 2015).

Tobin, Vincent. "The Admonitions of an Egyptian Sage." *The Literature of Ancient Egypt.* Ed. William
Simpson. New Haven, CT: Yale University Press, 2003.

_____. "Pyramid Texts." *The Literature of Ancient Egypt.* William Simpson, Ed. New Haven, CT:
Yale University Press, 2003.

Toner, Patrick. "Etymology of the Word 'God.'" *The Catholic Encyclopedia*: vol 6. New York: Robert
Appleton, 1909: 10.

Toorn, Karel van der. *Scribal Culture.* Cambridge: Harvard University Press, 2007.

_____. *Sin and Sanction in Israel and Mesopotamia.* Maastricht, Netherlands: Van Gorcum, 1985.

Török, László. *The Kingdom of Kush.* Leiden: Brill, 1997.

Traunecker, Claude. *The Gods of Egypt.* Trans. David Lorton. Ithaca, NY: Cornell University Press,
2001.

Tsumura, David. "Scribal Errors or Phonetic Spellings? Samuel as an Aural Text." *Vestus Testamentum* 49 (1999) 390–411.

Turner, Patricia, and Charles Coulter. *Dictionary of Ancient Deities.* New York: Oxford University Press, 2000.

Ulansey, David. *The Origins of the Mithraic Mysteries: Cosmology and Salvation in the Ancient World.* Oxford: Oxford University Press, 1991.

Unger, Merrill F. *Unger's Bible Dictionary.* Chicago, IL: Moody, 1957.

Van Dijk, Jacobus. "The Amarna Period and the Later New Kingdom." *The Oxford History of Ancient Egypt.* Ed. Ian Shaw. New York: Oxford University Press, 2004: 265–307.

Van de Mieroop, Mark. "Thoughts on Urban Real Estate in Ancient Mesopotamia." *Urbanization and Land Ownership in the Ancient Near East*: vol.2. Ed. Michael Hudson and Baruch Levine. Cambridge: Peabody Museum of Archaeology and Ethnology of Harvard University, 1999.

Van Selms, Adrianus. "Valley of Rephaim." *International Standard Bible Encyclopedia*: vol 4. Grand Rapids, MI: Eerdmans, 1979: 137–38.

Van Seters, John. "The Geography of the Exodus." *The Land That I Will Show You.* Ed. Andrew Dearman and Patrick Graham. Sheffield: Sheffield Academic Press, 2001: 255–77.

_____. *The Hyksos: A New Investigation.* New Haven, CT: Yale University Press, 1966.

_____. *In Search of History: Historiography in the Ancient World and Origins of Biblical History.* New Haven, CT: Yale University Press, 1983.

VanderKam, James, and Peter Flint. *The Meaning of the Dead Sea Scrolls.* San Francisco: Harper, 2002.

Vaughn, Andrew G. "Can We Write a History of Israel Today?" *The Future of Biblical Archaeology: Reassessing Methodologies and Assumptions.* Proceeding of a Symposium at Trinity International University, Aug. 12–14, 2001. Ed. James Hoffmeier and Alan Millard. Grand Rapids, MI: Eerdmans, 2004: 368–385.

Veen, Peter van der, Christoffer Theis, and Manfred Görg. "Israel in Canaan (Long) before Pharaoh Merenptah?: "A Fresh Look at Berlin Statue Pedestal Relief 21687." *Journal of Ancient Egyptian Interconnections* 2/4 (2010) 15–25.

Veenker, Ronald. "Syro-Mesopotamia: The Old Babylonian Period. *Mesopotamia and the Bible.* Ed. Mark W. Chavalas and K. Lawson Younger, Jr. Grand Rapids, MI: Baker, 2002: 149–67.

Verbrugghe, Gerald, and John Wickersham. *Berossos and Manetho.* Ann Arbor: University of Michigan Press, 2000.

Vermez, Geza. *The Complete Dead Sea Scrolls in English.* New York: Penguin Books, 1962.

Vos, Howard F. "Hamath." *International Standard Bible Encyclopedia*: vol. 2. Grand Rapids, MI: Eerdmans, 1979: 603.

Waddell, William, Ed. *Manetho.* Loeb Classical Library 350. Cambridge: Harvard University Press, 1940.

Wagenaar, Jan. *Origin and Transformation of the Ancient Israelite Festival Calendar.* Wiesbaden: Harrassowitz Verlag, 2005.

Walker, W. L. "Hardened, Harden." *International Standard Bible Encyclopedia*: vol 2. Grand Rapids, MI: Eerdmans, 1979: 615.

Walton, John. *Ancient Israelite Literature in Its Cultural Context.* Grand Rapids, MI: Zondervan, 1989.

_____. *Ancient Near Eastern Thought and the Old Testament.* Grand Rapids, MI: Baker Academic, 2006.

_____, et al. *The IVP Bible Background Commentary of the Old Testament.* Downers Grove, IL: InterVarsity Press, 2000.

_____. "Joshua 10:12–15 and Mesopotamian Celestial Omen Texts." *Faith, Tradition, and History.* Ed. A. R. Millard, J. K. Hoffmeier, and D. W. Baker. Winona Lake, IN: Eisenbrauns, 1994: 181–90.

Walvoord, John F., and Roy B. Zuck, Ed. *The Bible Knowledge Commentary.* Wheaton, IL: Victor Books, 1985.

Wapnish, Paula. "Middle Bronze Equid Murials at Tell Jemmeh and a Reexamination of a Purportedly 'Hyksos' Practice." *The Hyksos: New Historical and Archaeological Perspectives.* Ed. Eliezer Oren. University Museum Monograph 96/8. Philadelphia: University of Pennsylvania Museum, 1997.

Ward, William A. "The *Shasu 'Bedoin:'* Notes on A Recent Publication." *Journal of the Economic and Social History of the Orient* 15/1/2 (Brill) 35–60.

Warden, Alex J. *The Linen and Trade Ancient and Modern.* London: Longman, Green, Roberts, 1867.

Watson, Thomas. "Body of Divinity Contained in Sermons upon the Assembly's Catechism: The Law and Sin."

Westminster Shorter Catechism Project. Last modified July 26, 2008. http://www.shortercatechism. com/resources/watson/wsc_wa_082.html (accessed February 2015).

Webster, Hutton. *Rest Days.* New York: Macmillan, 1916.

Weinfeld, Moshe. "Covenant of Grant." *Essential Papers on Israel and the Ancient Near East.* Ed. Frederick Greenspahn. New York: New York University Press, 1991: 69–102.

Weinstein, James. "Exodus and Archaeological Reality." *Exodus: The Egyptian Evidence.* Ed. Ernest S. Friedrichs and Leonard H. Lesko. Winona Lake, IN: Eisenbrauns, 1997.

Weir, Fred. "A Second Baby? Russia's Mothers Aren't Persuaded." *Christian Science Monitor.* May 2006.

Weisberg, David B. "'Splendid Truths' or 'Prodigious Commotion'? Ancient Near Eastern Texts and the Study of the Bible." *The Future of Biblical Archaeology: Reassessing Methodologies and Assumptions.* Proceeding of a Symposium at Trinity International University, Aug. 12–14, 2001. Ed. James Hoffmeier and Alan Millard. Grand Rapids, MI: Eerdmans, 2004: 357–367.

Wendland, Paul, Ed., "Aristeas, Letter of." *Jewish Encyclopedia.* http://www.jewishencyclopedia.com/ articles/1765-aristeas-letter-of (accessed February 2015).

Wenham, Gordon. *Genesis 1–15.* Word Biblical Commentary 1. Waco, TX: Word Books, 1987.

_____. *Genesis 16–50.* Word Biblical Commentary 2. Dallas, TX: Word Books, 1994.

Wente, Edward. "The Book of the Heavenly Cow." *The Literature of Ancient Egypt.* Ed. William Simpson. New Haven, CT: Yale University Press, 2003.

_____. "The Israel Stela." *The Literature of Ancient Egypt.* Ed. William Simpson. New Haven, CT: Yale University Press, 2003.

_____. "Thutmose III's Accession and the Beginning of the New Kingdom." *JNES* 57/1 (1975) 271.

Westbrook, Raymond. "The Female Slave." *Gender and Law in the Hebrew Bible and the Ancient Near East.* Ed. Victor Matthews et al. Sheffield, UK: Sheffield Academic Press, 1998: 214–38.

_____. *Property and the Family in Biblical Law.* JSOTSup 113. Sheffield, UK: Sheffield Academic Press, 1991.

Westbrook, Raymond, and Bruce Wells. *Everyday Law in Biblical Israel.* Louisville: Westminster John Knox, 2009.

Westerholm, Stephen. *Israel's Law and the Church's Faith: Paul and His Recent Interpreters*. Grand Rapids, MI: Eerdmans, 1998.

Westermann, Claus. *Genesis 1–11: A Continental Commentary*. Minneapolis: Fortress Press, 1994.

Whalen, John P., Ed. "J." *New Catholic Encyclopedia*: vol. 14. San Francisco, CA: McGraw-Hill (1967) 1065.

"What is Sin?" The Restored Church of God. http://www.thercg.org/articles/wis.html (accessed February 2015).

"What is Sin—Definition." All about God. http://www.allaboutgod.com/what-is-sin.htm (accessed February 2015).

"When Does the Biblical New Year Start?" YahSaves.org. January 29, 2013. http://yahsaves.org/bbs/viewtopic.php?t=610 (accessed February 2015).

Wheeler, J. T. *History of India*: 3 vols. Delhi: Cosmo, 1973.

Wiener, Malcolm, and James Allen. "Separate Lives: The Ahmose Tempest Stela and the Theran Eruption." *JNES* 57/1 (1998) 1–28.

Wilhelm, Gernot. "Generation Count in Hittite Chronology." *Mesopotamian Dark Age Revisited*. Proceedings of an International Conference of SCIEM 2000. Ed. Hermann Hunger and Regine Pruzsinszky. Vienna: Verlag der Österreichischen Akademie der Wissenschaften, 2004: 71–79.

Wilkinson, J. "Leprosy and Leviticus: The Problem of Description and Identification." *Scottish Journal of Theology* 30 (1977) 153–59.

_____. "Leprosy and Leviticus: A Problem of Semantics and Translation." *Scottish Journal of Theology* 31 (1978) 153–66.

Wilkinson, Richard. *The Complete Gods and Goddesses of Ancient Egypt*. London: Thames and Hudson, 2003.

Wilkinson, Toby A. H. *The Rise and Fall of Ancient Egypt*. New York: Random House, 2010.

Willoughby, Harold. *Pagan Regeneration*. Chicago: University of Chicago Press, 1929.

Wilson, Ian. *Exodus Enigma*. London: Weidenfeld and Nicolson, 1985.

Wilson, J. Macartney, and Roland K. Harrison, "Birthright." *International Standard Bible Encyclopedia*: vol. 1. Grand Rapids, MI: Eerdmans, 1979: 515.

Wilson, John. *The Culture of Ancient Egypt*. Chicago: University of Chicago Press, 1951.

Wilson, Robert. *Genealogy and History in the Biblical World*. New Haven, CT: Yale University Press, 1977.

Wilson, William. *Wilson's Old Testament Word Studies*. McLean, VA: MacDonald, 1990.

Winckler, Hugo. *The Tell el-Amarna Letters*. Berlin: Reuther and Reichard, 1896.

Wiseman, D. J. *Chronicles of Chaldean Kings in the British Museum*. London: Trustees of the British Museum, 1956.

Wood, Bryant. "Biblical Date of the Exodus Is 1446 BC: A Response to James Hoffmeier." *JETS* 50/2 (2007) 249–58.

_____. "From Ramessess to Shiloh: Archaeological Discoveries Bearing on the Exodus–Judges Period." *Giving the Sense*. Ed. David Howard and Michael Gristani. Grand Rapids, MI: Kregel Academic, 2003.

_____. "The Rise and Fall of the 13th-Century Exodus-Conquest Theory." *JETS* 48/3 (2005) 475–90.

Woodrow, Ralph. *Babylon Mystery Religion*. Riverside, CA: Ralph Woodrow Evangelistic Association, 1966.

"World Fertility Report 2007." New York: United Nations: Economic and Social Affairs, 2010: xi. http://www.un.org/esa/population/publications/worldfertilityreport2007/wfr2007-text.pdf (accessed February 2015).

Wright, David, David N. Freedman, and Avi Hurvitz, Ed. *Pomegranates and Golden Bells: Studies in Biblical, Jewish, and Near Eastern Ritual, Law, and Literature in Honor of Jacob Milgrom.* Winona Lake, IN: Eisenbrauns , 1995.

Wright, George Ernest, Ed. *The Bible and the Ancient Near East: Essays in Honor of William Foxwell Albright.* Garden City, NY: Anchor Books, 1965.

Wunsch, Cornelia, "The Egibi Family's Real Estate in Babylon (6th Century BC)." *Urbanization and Land Ownership in the Ancient Near East*: vol.2. Ed. Michael Hudson and Baruch Levine. Cambridge: Peabody Museum of Archaeology and Ethnology of Harvard University, 1999: 391–419.

Würthwein, Ernst. "Egyptian Wisdom and the Old Testament." *Essential Papers on Israel and the Ancient Near East.* Ed. Greenspahn, Frederick. New York: New York University Press, 1991: 129–49.

Wyatt, N. *Religious Texts from Ugarit.* Sheffield, UK. Sheffield Academic Press, 1998.

Wyatt, Robert J. "Names of God, OT Name." *International Standard Bible Encyclopedia*: vol 2. Grand Rapids, MI: Eerdmans, 1979: 505–8.

Yadin, Yigael. "'And Dan, Why Did He Remain in Ships?'" *Essential Papers on Israel and the Ancient Near East.* Ed. Greenspahn, Frederick. New York: New York University Press, 1991: 294–310.

Yamauchi, Edwin. "The Current State of Old Testament Historiography." *Faith, Tradition, and History.* Ed. A. R. Millard, J. K. Hoffmeier, and D. W. Baker. Winona Lake, IN: Eisenbrauns, 1994: 1–36.

_____. "The Eastern Jewish Diaspora under the Babylonians." *Mesopotamia and the Bible.* Ed. Mark W. Chavalas and K. Lawson Younger, Jr. Grand Rapids, MI: Baker, 2002: 331–56.

_____. "Homer and Archaeology: Minimalists and Maximalists in Classical Context." *The Future of Biblical Archaeology: Reassessing Methodologies and Assumptions.* Proceeding of a Symposium at Trinity International University, Aug. 12–14, 2001. Ed. James Hoffmeier and Alan Millard. Grand Rapids, MI: Eerdmans, 2004: 69–90.

_____. "Nabonidus." *International Standard Bible Encyclopedia*: vol. 3. Grand Rapids, MI: Eerdmans, 1979: 468–70.

_____. *Persia and the Bible.* Grand Rapids, MI: Baker, 1990.

_____. "Religions: Persia, Artaxerxes II." *International Standard Bible Encyclopedia*: vol. 4. Grand Rapids, MI: Eerdmans, 1979: 126.

Young, Donald, and Nina Young. "Receiving God's Holy Spirit." http://donimon.org/holyspirit.html (accessed December 2013).

Young, Edward. *An Introduction to the Old Testament.* Grand Rapids, MI: Eerdmans, 1958.

Young, Robb Andrew. *Hezekiah in History and Tradition.* Leiden: Brill, 2012.

Young, Rodger. "Evidence for Inerrancy from an Unexpected Source: Old Testament Chronology." *Bible and Spade* (Spring, 2008) 55.

_____. "Inductive and Deductive Methods as Applied to OT Chronology." *TMSJ* 18/1 (2007) 99–116.

_____. "The Parian Marble and Other Surprises from Chronologist V. Coucke." *AUSS* 50/2 (2010) 225–49.

_____. "Rodger Young's Papers on Chronology." Last updated September 28, 2013. http://www. rcyoung.org/papers.html (accessed February 2015).

_____. "Tables of Reign Lengths from the Hebrew Court Recorders." *JETS* 48/2 (2005) 225–48.

_____."The Talmud's Two Jubilees and Their Relevance to the Date of the Exodus." *Westminster Theological Journal* 68/1 (2006) 71–83.

_____. "Three Verifications of Thiele's Date for the Beginning of the Divided Kingdom." *AUSS* 45/2 (2007) 163–89.

_____. "When Did Jerusalem Fall?" *JETS* 47/1 (2004) 21–38.

Younger, K. Lawson, Jr. *Ancient Conquest Accounts: A Study in Ancient Near Eastern and Biblical History Writing.* Sheffield: Sheffield Academic Press, 1990.

_____. "Recent Study on Sargon II, King of Assyria: Implications for Biblical Studies." *Mesopotamia and the Bible.* Ed. Mark W. Chavalas and K. Lawson Younger, Jr. Grand Rapids, MI: Baker, 2002: 207–28.

_____. "The Repopulation of Samaria (2 Kings 17:24, 27–31) in Light of Recent Study. *The Future of Biblical Archaeology: Reassessing Methodologies and Assumptions.* Proceeding of a Symposium at Trinity International University, Aug. 12–14, 2001. Ed. James Hoffmeier and Alan Millard. Grand Rapids, MI: Eerdmans, 2004: 254–280.

Younker, "Integrating Faith, the Bible, and Archaeology: A Review of the 'Andrews University Way' of Doing Archaeology." *The Future of Biblical Archaeology: Reassessing Methodologies and Assumptions.* Proceedings of a Symposium at Trinity International University, Aug. 21–14, 2001. Ed. James Hoffmeier and Alan Millard Grand Rapids, MI: Eerdmans, 2004: 43–52.

Yurco, Frank. "Merenptah's Canaanite Campaign." *Journal of the American Research Center in Egypt.* 23 (1986) 189–215.

_____. "Merenptah's Canaanite Campaign and Israel's Origins." *Exodus: The Egyptian Evidence.* Ed. Ernest Frerichs and Leonard Lesko. Winona Lake, IN: Eisenbrauns, 1997.

Zaccagnini, Carlo. "Economic Aspects of Land Ownership and Land Use in Northern Mesopotamia and Syria from the Late Third Millennium to the New-Assyrian Period." *Urbanization and Land Ownership in the Ancient Near East*: vol. 2. Ed. Michael Hudson and Baruch Levine. Cambridge: Peabody Museum of Archaeology and Ethnology of Harvard University, 1999: 242.

Zerubavel, Eviatar. *The Seven Day Circle.* New York: Free Press, 1985.

Zevit, Ziony. "The Biblical Archaeology versus Syro-Palestinian Archaeology Debate in Its American Institutional and Intellectual Contexts." *The Future of Biblical Archaeology: Reassessing Methodologies and Assumptions.* Proceedings of a Symposium at Trinity International University, Aug. 21–14, 2001. Ed. James Hoffmeier and Alan Millard. Grand Rapids, MI: Eerdmans, 2004: 3–19.

_____. "The Earthen Altar Laws of Exodus 20:24–26 and Related Sacrificial Restrictions in their Cultural Context." *Texts, Temples, and Traditions*: A Tribute to Menehem Haran. Ed. Michael V. Fox et al. Winona Lake, IN: Eisenbrauns, 1996: 53–62.

Zimmerli, Walther. *Ezekiel 1: Commentary on the Book of the Prophet Ezekiel: Chapters 1–24.* Philadelphia: Fortress Press, 1979.

_____. *Ezekiel II: A Commentary on the Book of the Prophet Ezekiel: Chapters 25–48.* Minneapolis, MN: Fortress Press, 1983.

Ziva Shavitsky. The Mystery of the Ten Lost Tribes. Newcastle, UK: Cambridge Scholars Publishing, 2015.

Zodhiates, Spiros, Ed. *The Hebrew-Greek Key Study Bible.* Chattanooga, TN: AMG Publishers, 1991.

MEDICAL AND SCIENTIFIC SOURCES

Aberth, J. *The Black Death: The Great Mortality of 1348–1350: A Brief History with Documents.* New York: Palgrave Macmillan, 2005.

American Academy of Orthopaedic Surgeons. "The Burden of Musculoskeletal Diseases in the United States: 2nd Ed." Bone and Joint Initiative USA (2011). http://www.boneandjointburden.org/ (accessed December 2013).

Anderson, Linda L. Ed., et al. "Sexually Transmitted Disease in America: How Many Cases and at What Cost?" *American Social Health Foundation* (December 1998) 10. http://www.kff.org/womenshealth/ 1445-std_rep.cfm (accessed February 2015).

Anderson, Robert. "Deaths: Leading Causes for 1999." *National Vital Statistics Report* 49/11. October 12, 2001. http://www.cdc.gov/nchs/data/nvsr49/nvsr49_11.pdf (accessed December 2013).

Arends, J. P., and H. C. Zanen. "Meningitis Caused by Streptococcus suis in Humans." *Review of Infectious Disease* 10 (1988) 131–37.

Arnold, Susan G., et al. "Latex Gloves Not Enough to Exclude Viruses." *Nautre* 335 (September 1988) 19.

Arnold, Thomas C., Asim Tarabar, et al. "Shellfish Toxicity." *Medscape.* Last modified May 6, 2011. http://emedicine.medscape.com/article/818505 (accessed March 2015).

Attarian, John. "Let Boys be Boys." *The World and I* 15/10 (2000) 238–43.

Benjamin , Sheryl. Executive Director for the Vascular Disease Foundation. Personal communication to author, January 27, 2004.

Benson, Jonathan. "Research—Roundup Toxicity Much Worse Than What Monsanto, Government Claims." *Natural News* (July 11, 2013). http://www.naturalnews.com/041150_Monsanto_Roundup_glyphosate.html (accessed March 2015).

Boyles, Salynn. "Male Circumcision Cuts Women's Cervical Cancer Risk: Study Shows Circumcision May Help Reduce Spread." *WebMD Health News.* http://www.webmd.com/cancer/cervical-cancer/news/20110106/male-circumcision-cuts-womens-cervical-cancer-risk (accessed March 2015).

Bradsher, Keith. "The Naming of Swine Flu: A Curious Matter." *New York Times* (April 4, 2009). http://www.nytimes.com/2009/04/29/world/asia/29swine.html?_r=0 (accessed March 2015).

Brochert, Adam. "STD - Sexually Transmitted Disease." Medicine Online. Last modified July 2001. http://www.medicineonline.com/articles/S/2/STD/Sexually-Transmitted-Disease.html (accessed March 2015).

Bronstein, A. C., D. A. Spyker, et al. "2009 Annual Report of the American Association of Poison Control Centers' National Poison Data System, (NPDS): 27th Annual Report." *Clinical Toxicology (Philadelphia)* 48/10 (December 2010) 979–1178.

Bullough, Vern. *Sexual Variance in Society and History.* New York: John Wiley, 1976.

Campbell, T. Colin, and Thomas Campell. *The China Study.* Dallas, TX: Benbella Books, 2006.

Cancer Weekly Plus. "Unlocking Mummies' Secrets to Study Today's Diseases." (June 30, 1997) 24.

Castellsague, Xavier, et al. "Male Circumcision, Penile Human Papillomavirus Infection, and Cervical Cancer in Female Partners." *NEJM* 346/15 (2002) 1105–12.

Centers for Disease Control and Prevention. "CDC/HRSA Advisory Committee on HIV and STD Prevention and Treatment: Draft Record of the Preceedings, November 2–3, 2009," Bethesda, Maryland. http://www.cdc.gov/maso/FACM/pdfs/CHACHSPT/2009110203_CHACHSPT.pdf (accessed February 2015).

_____. "HIV in the United States: An Overview." Division of Cancer Prevention and Control, National Center for Chronic Disease Prevention and Health Promotion. Last modified August 13, 2013. http://www.cdc.gov/hiv/topics/surveillance/resources/factsheets/pdf/HIV_overview_2012.pdf; http://www.cdc.gov/hiv/library/factsheets/index.html; http://www.cdc.gov/hiv/statistics/basics/ataglance.html (accessed February 2015).

_____. "HPV-Associated Cervical Cancer Rates by Race and Ethnicity (2009)." Division of Cancer Prevention and Control, National Center for Chronic Disease Prevention and Health Promotion. Last modified August 13, 2013. http://www.cdc.gov/cancer/hpv/statistics/cervical.htm (accessed February 2015).

_____. "Sexually Transmitted Disease Surveillance, 1997." U.S. Department of Health and Human Services, Public Health Service: Division of STD Prevention (September 1998) 5. http://www.cdc.gov/nchstp/dstd/Stats_Trends/1997_Surveillance_Report.pdf (accessed April 2013). Link has since moved to http://www.cdc.gov/std/stats97/default.htm (accessed February 2015).

_____. "Sexually Transmitted Diseases in the United States, 2008: National Surveillance Data for Chlamydia, Gonorrhea, and Syphilis." Prevention National Prevention Network. Last Updated April 16, 2013. http://www.cdcnpin.org/scripts/std/std.asp (accessed February 2015).

_____. "Update: Neurologic Illness Associated with Eating Florida Pufferfish." *Morbidity and Mortality Weekly Report* 51/19 (May 17 2002) 414–16.

Chang, George, and Mark Welton. "Human Papillomavirus, Condylomata Acuminata, and Anal Neoplasia." *Clinical of Colon Rectal Surgery* 17/4 (2004) 221–30.

Chohen, Desmond. "Economic Impact of the HIV Epidemic." *HIV and Development Programme, United Nations Development Programme* 2. http://www.heart-intl.net/HEART/HIV/Comp/TheEconomicImpactofthmic.htm (accessed February 2015).

The Collider Detector at Fermilab. "Search for the Standard Model Higgs Boson at CDF." December 14, 2005. http://www-cdf.fnal.gov/PES/higgs_pes/higgs_plain_english.html (accessed February 2015).

"Condom Roulette." *In Focus* 25. Washington: Family Research Council (February 1992) 2.

Criqui, M. H., et al. "Mortality over a Period of 10 Years in Patients with Peripheral Arterial Disease." *NEJM* 326/6 (1992) 381–86.

Dirubbo, Nancy E. "The Condom Barrier." *American Journal of Nursing* (October 1987) 1306.

Dobson, James. *Bringing Up Boys.* Wheaton, IL: Tyndale House, 2001.

_____. *The New Dare To Discipline.* Wheaton, IL: Tyndale House, 1992.

Donsakul, K., et al. "Streptococcus Suis Infection: Clinical Features and Diagnostic Pitfalls." *Southeast Asian Journal of Tropical Medicine and Public Health* 34 (2003) 154–58.

Economou, V., C. Papadopoulou, et al. "Diarrheic Shellfish Poisoning Due to Toxic Mussel Consumption: The First Recorded Outbreak in Greece." *Food Additives and Contaminants* 24/3 (Mar 2007) 297–305.

Encyclopædia Britannica Online. s. v. "prothrombin." http://www.britannica.com/EBchecked/topic/480073/prothrombin (accessed March 2015).

Engel, Juliette, Robert Aronson, et al. "Addressing the Needs of Children in Crisis: Single, Teen-Age Motherism the Russian Federation." *For CHILDHOOD World Childhood Foundation,* Part I. Moscow, Russia, March 2002. http://www.miramEd.org/pdf/ResearchReportonTeenPregnancies.pdf (accessed March 2015).

Enwald, Heidi, and Maija-Leena Huotari. "Preventing the Obesity Epidemic by Second Generation Tailored Health Communication: An Interdisciplinary Review." *Journal of Medical Internet Research* 12 (2010) e24.

"Enteroviral Infections." Health Protection Surveillance Centre. Doublin, Ireland. December 8, 2006. http://www.hpsc.ie/hpsc/A-Z/Gastroenteric/EnteroviralInfections/Factsheet/ (accessed March 2015).

"Epidemiologic Notes and Reports Paralytic Shellfish Poisoning—Massachusetts and Alaska, 1990." *Morbidity and Mortality Weekly Report* 40/10 (March 15, 1990) 157–161. http://www.cdc.gov/mmwr/preview/mmwrhtml/00001927.htm (accessed March 2015).

Ezzell, Carol. "Care for a Dying Continent." *Scientific American* 282/5 (May 2000) 96–105.

Federal Interagency Forum on Child and Family Statistics. "America's Children: Key National Indicators of Wellbeing." (2002) 7. http://childstats.gov/americaschildren/index.asp (accessed March 2015).

Fischl, Margaret A., et al. "Heterosexual Transmission of Human Immunodeficiency Virus (HIV) Relationship of Sexual Practices to Seroconversion." III International Conference on AIDS: Abstracts Volume (June 1–5, 1987) 178.

Food and Drug Administration. "Foodborne Pathogenic Microorganisms and Natural Toxins Handbook, 1st Ed." (January 2001).

Ford, Peter. "In Europe, Unmarried Parents on Rise." *Christian Science Monitor* (April 17, 2006). http://www.csmonitor.com/2006/0417/p01s03-woeu.html (accessed March 2015).

Fox, Maggie. "Chinese Researchers Confirm SARS Came from Animals." *Reuters* (September 4, 2003).

Fredricks, David N., et al. "Rhinosporidium Seeberi: A Human Pathogen from a Novel Group of Aquatic Protistan Parasites." *Emerging Infectious Diseases* 6/3 (2000) 273–82.

Fujita, K., K. G. Ofosu-Budu, and S. Ogata. "Biological Nitrogen Fixation in Mixed Legume-Cereal Cropping Systems." *Plant and Soil* 14/1–2 (2007) 155–75.

Gardner, Laura. "Physicists Say They Are Near Epic Higgs Boson Discovery." Brandeis University (Dec. 13, 2011, updated: Jan. 13, 2012). http://www.brandeis.edu/now/2011/december/particle.html (accessed March 2015).

Georgetown University Medical Center. "Common Household Pesticides Linked to Childhood Cancer Cases in Washington Area." *ScienceDaily* (August 4, 2009). http://www.sciencedaily.com/releases/2009/07/090728102306.htm (accessed March 2015).

Gessner B. D., J. P. Middaugh, et al. "Paralytic Shellfish Poisoning in Kodiak, Alaska." *West Journal of Medicine* 167/5 (November 1997) 351–53.

Goddard, Jerome. "Kissing Bugs and Chagas' Disease." *Infections in Medicine* 16/3 (1999) 172–180.

Goh, K. J. "Clinical features of Nipah Virus Encephalitis among Pig Farmers in Malaysia." *NEJM* 342 (2000) 1229–35.

Goldfrank, Lewis, and Neal Flomenbaum, Ed. *Goldfrank's Toxicologic Emergencies,* 8th Ed. New York McGraw-Hill, 2006.

Goldsmith, Marcia F. "Sex in the Age of AIDS Calls for Common Sense and Condom Sense." *JAMA* 257/17 (1987) 2262.

Gottschalk, Marcelo. "Porcine Streptococcus Suis Strains as Potential Sources of Infection in Humans: An Underdiagnosed Problem in North America?" *Journal of Swine Health and Production* 12 (2004) 197–99.

Gottschalk, Marcelo, Segura, and J. Xu. "Streptococcus suis Infections in Humans: The Chinese Experience and the Situation in North America." *Animal Health Research Reviews* 8 (2007) 29–45.

Greenall, Robert. "Russia Turns Spotlight on Abortion." *BBC News.* September, 2003. http://news.bbc.co.uk/2/hi/europe/3093152.stm (accessed February 2015).

Greenberg, David. *The Construction of Homosexuality*. Chicago: University of Chicago Press, 1990.

Grube, Arthur, David Donaldson, et al. "Pesticides Industry Sales and Usage: 2006 and 2007 Market Estimates." United States Environmental Protection Agency. http://www.epa.gov/pesticides/pestsales/07pestsales/market_estimates2007.pdf (accessed March 2015).

Guan, Y., et al. "Isolation and Characterization of Viruses Related to the SARS Coronavirus from Animals in Southern China." *Science* 302 (2003) 276–78.

Gunby, F. "Battles Continue over DES Use in Fattening Cattle." *JAMA* 244/3 (1980) 228.

Hager, David, and Donald Joy. *Women at Risk: The Real Truth about Sexually Transmitted Disease*. Anderson, IN: Bristol House, 1993.

Hansen, Mary, et al. "SARS Response Plan Version 1.2." *IOWA Department of Public Health.*July 2004. http://staging.ihaonline.globalreach.com/links/SARSResponseV1.2.pdf (accessed April 2013).

Hardy, Jonathan, et al. "Extracellular Replication of Listeria Monocytogenes in the Murine Gall Bladder." *Science* 303 (2004) 851–53.

Hartman, David A. "Impending European Population Implosion." *World Congress of Families III* 18/9. Mexico City, March 31, 2004. http://www.profam.org/pub/fia/fia_1809.htm (accessed March 2015).

Hawking, Stephen. *A Brief History of Time*. New York: Bantam Books, 1988.

_____. *The Universe in a Nutshell*. New York: Bantam, 2001.

Heidt, M. C., et al. "Human Infective Endocarditis Caused by Streptococcus Suis Serotype 2." *Journal of Clinical Microbiology* 43/9 (2005) 4898–4901.

Heinen, Paul. "Swine Iird nfluenza: A Zoonosis." *Veterinary Sciences Tomorrow* (September 15, 2003) 1–11.

Herndon, Everette L., and Chin S. Yang. "Mold and Mildew: a Creeping Catastrophe." *Claims Magazine* (August 2000).

Hongjie Yu, et al. "Human *Streptococcus suis* Outbreak, Sichuan, China." *Emerging Infectious Diseases* 12/6 (June 2006) 914–20.

"How Serious of a Problem are Sexually Transmitted Infections (STIs) in the United States?" Medical Institute for Sexual Health. Last modified June 29, 2012. https://www.medinstitute.org/faqs/how-serious-of-a-problem-are-sexually-transmitted-infections-stis-in-the-united-states/ (accessed December 2013).

Hoyert, Donna, et al. "Deaths: Final Data for 1999." *National Vital Statistics Reports* 49/8 (September 21, 2001) 105. www.cdc.gov/nchs/data/nvsr/nvsr49/nvsr49_08.pdf (accessed March 2015).

Israel, S. Leon. "Relative Infrequency of Cervical Carcinoma in Jewish Women is the Enigma Solved?" *Obstetrics and Gynecology* 5/3 (1955) 358–60.

Jeffery, B., T. Barlow, et al. "Amnesic Shellfish Poison." *Food and Chemical Toxicology* 42/4 (April 2004) 545–57.

Johnwick, Edgar B. "Hansen's Disease," *New Standard Encyclopedia*. Ed. Douglas Downey. Chicago: Standard Educational Corp., 1995: 45.

Jones, Andrew Zimmerman, and Daniel Robbins. "Slowing Time to a Standstill with Relativity." For Dummies. http://www.dummies.com/how-to/content/slowing-time-to-a-standstill-with-relativity.html (accessed March 2015).

Jones, Elise F., and Jacqueline Darroch Forrest. "Contraceptive Failure in the United States: Revised Estimates from the 1982 National Survey of Family Growth." *Family Planning Perspectives* 21 (May 1989) 103–5.

"Just the Facts: STDs," Richmond, Virginia, Metro Pregnancy Resource Center. http://prcrichmond. org/STDs.htm (accessed March 2015).

Kacker, Seema, et al. "Costs and Effectiveness of Neonatal Male Circumcision." *Archives of Pediatrics and Adolescent Medicine* 166/10 (2012) 910–18.

Kaplan, I., and R. Rosh. "Cancer of the Cervix; Bellevue Hospital Method of Treatment over a Period of Twenty- One Years." *American Journal of Roentgenology and Radium Therapy* 57. Ed. Lawrence Reynolds. Springfield, IL: Charles Thomas, 1947: 659–64.

Keim, Brandon. "'Pig Brain Mist' Disease Concludes." ABC News (March 5, 2009). http://abcnews. go.com/Health/MindMoodNews/story?id=7015430&page=1&page=1 (accessed March 2015).

Kellog, J. H. "The Dangers of Pork-Eating Exposed." Battle Creek, MI: Good Health Publishing, 1897.

Kent, John. "Pesticides in Agriculture." School of Agriculture: Charles Sturt University: Wagga Wagga, NSW. http://www.regional.org.au/au/roc/1992/roc1992031.htm (accessed March 2015).

Knobler, Stacey, and Alison Mack, et al., Ed. "The Story of Influenza." *The Threat of Pandemic Influenza: Are We Ready? Workshop Summary* 1. Washington, D.C.: The National Academies Press, 2005: 75.

Kosen, Soewarta, et al. "Communicable Diseases: Qualitative Study on Avian Influenza in Indonesia." *Regional Health Forum: Southeast Asia* 13/1. WHO Regional Office for South-East Asia, 2009: 35–47. http://whoindonesia.healthrepository.org/handle/123456789/610 (accessed March 2015).

Laar, MJW van de, et al. "Lymphogranuloma Venereum among Men Who Have Sex with Men— Netherlands, 2003-2004." *Morbidity and Mortality Weekly Report* 53/42 (October 29, 2004) 985–988. http://www.cdc.gov/mmwr/preview/mmwrhtml/mm5342a2.htm (accessed March 2015).

Lardy, Greg. "Bovine Spongiform Encephalopathy, (BSE; Mad Cow Disease)." *North Carolina State University Department of Agriculture.* March 2004. http://www.ag.ndsu.edu/pubs/ansci/beef/as1206w.htm (accessed March 2015).

Leroy, Eric M., et al. "Multiple Ebola Virus Transmission Events and Rapid Decline of Central African Wildlife." *Science* 303 (2004) 387–90.

Lopatto, Elizabeth. "Births to Unwed Mothers Increase to Record Proportion in U.S." *Bloomberg* (July 13, 2007). http://www.bloomberg.com/apps/news?pid=20601103&sid=aAexAvTGa7zk &refer=us. (accessed December 2013).

Maas, James B. *Power Sleep.* New York: Villard Books, 1998.

Macht, David. "An Experimental Pharmacological Appreciation of Leviticus XI and Deuteronomy XIV." *Bulletin of Historical Medicine* 47/1 (1953) 444–50.

Mane, Purnima, and Ann P. McCauley. "Impact of Sexually Transmitted Infections Including AIDS on Adolescents: A Global Perspective." *Towards Adulthood: Exploring the Sexual and Reproductive Health of Adolescents in South Asia.* Ed. Sarah Bott, et al. Geneva: Department of Reproductive Health and Research of the World Health Organization, 2003.

Martin, Joyce, et al. "Births: Final Data for 2000." *National Vital Statistics Reports* 50/5 (February 12, 2002) 16. http://www.cdc.gov/nchs/data/nvsr/nvsr50/nvsr50_05.pdf (accessed March 2015).

Mazokopakis, E. E., et al. "First Case Report of Streptococcus Suis Septicaemia and Meningitis from Greece." *European Journal of Neurology* 12 (2005) 487–89. PubMed DOI: 10.1111/j.1468-1331.2005.00998.x (accessed October 2013).

McDonald, Joe. "WHO Finds Evidence Animals Play SARS Role." *Associated Press* (January 16, 2004).

McIhaney, Joe. *Sexuality and Sexually Transmitted Diseases.* Grand Rapids, MI: Baker, 1990.

McKusick, Victor A. "Mendelian Inheritance in Man: A Catalog of Human Genes and Genetic Disorders, 12th Ed. Baltimore, MD: Johns Hopkins University Press, 1998. http://www.ncbi. nlm.nih.gov/Omim/mimstats.html. (accessed March 2015).

McMillen, S. I., and David Stern. *None of These Diseases.* Grand Rapids: Fleming H. Revell, 1984.

Miller, R. L., et al. "Palaeoepidemiology of Schistosoma Infection in Mummies." *British Medical Journal* 304 (1992) 555–56.

Minino, Arialdo, and B. L. Smith. "Preliminary Data for 2000." *National Vital Statistics Report* 49/12. Hyatsville, MD (October 9, 2001). http://www.cdc.gov/nchs/data/nvsr/nvsr49/nvsr49_12.pdf (accessed March 2015).

Minino, Arialdo, et al. "Deaths: Preliminary Data for 2004." *National Vital Statistics Report* 54/11. Hyatsville, MD, June 28, 2006. www.cdc.gov/nchs/data/nvsr/nvsr54/nvsr54_19.pdf (accessed December 2013).

Moore, David, et al. "Gnathostomiasis: An Emerging Imported Disease." *Emerging Infectious Diseases* 9/6 (2003) 647–650.

National Cancer Institute. "Cancer Trends Progress Report-2011/2012 Update." Pesticides. http://progressreport.cancer.gov/doc_detail.asp?pid=1&did=2007&chid=71&coid=713&mid (accessed March 2015).

National Institute of Arthritis and Musculoskeletal and Skin Diseases (NIAMS). "Statistics." Bethesda: MD, 2012. http://www.niams.nih.gov/health_info/Arthritis/arthritis_rheumatic_qa.asp (accessed March 2015).

Nave, R. "The Higgs Boson." Georgia State University. January 13, 2012. http://hyperphysics.phy-astr. gsu.edu/hbase/forces/higgs.html (accessed December 2013).

Nicoll, Angus. "Consensus Document on the Epidemiology of Severe Acute Respiratory Syndrome (SARS)." Department of Communicable Disease and Surveillance Response. *WHO:* Geneva, Switzerland, May 2003: 29.

Ober, William B. and Leopold Reiner. "Cancer of Cervix in Jewish Women." *NEJM* 251/14 (1954) 555–59.

"Open Letter to the Scientific Community." *New Scientist.* May 22, 2004. http://www.cosmologys-tatement.org/ (accessed December 2013).

Orlandi, Palmer A., and Dan-My T. Chu. "Parasites and the Food Supply." *FoodTechnology* 56/4 (April 2002) 72–80.

Peck, Peggy. "Circumcision Associated with 'Profound' Reduction in HIV-1 Risk." *Medscape* (October 11, 2003). http://www.medscape.com/viewarticle/462816 (accessed March 2015).

Pentecost, M. J., et al. "Guidelines for Peripheral Percutaneous Transluminal Angioplasty of the Abdominal Aorta and Lower Extremity Vessels: A Statement for Health Professionals from a Special Writing Group of the Councils on Cardiovascular Radiology, Arteriosclerosis, Cardio-Thoracic and Vascular Surgery, Clinical Cardiology, and Epidemiology and Prevention, the American Heart Association." *Journal of Vascular and Interventional Radiology* 89/1 (1994) 511–31.

"Pesticide Use Trends in the United States." Economic Research Service: United States Department of Agriculture. http://www.ers.usda.gov/Briefing/Agchemicals/pestmangement.htm (accessed May, 2011).

Petrillo, T. M. "Enteritis Necroticans (Pigbel) in a Diabetic Child." *NEJM* 342 (2000) 1250–53.

"Pig-brain Mist Suspected in Worker's Disease." *MSNBC* (December 7, 2007). http://www.msnbc. msn.com/id/22150940/ (accessed March 2015).

Pollock, William. *Real Boys: Rescuing Our Sons from the Myths of Boyhood.* New York: Henry Holt, 1998.

Phillips, Angela. *The Trouble with Boys.* New York: Basic Books, 1994.

Popkin, Barry M., and J. Richard Udry. "Adolescent Obesity Increases Significantly in Second and Third Generation U.S. Immigrants: The National Longitudinal Study of Adolescent Health." *Journal of Nutrition* 128/4 (1998) 701–6.

Powell, Corey S. *God in the Equation.* New York: Free Press, 2002.

Priola, Suzett, et al. "How Animal Prions Cause Disease in Humans." *Microbe Magazine* 3/12 (December 2008). http://forms.asm.org/microbe/index.asp?bid=62048 (accessed March 2015).

Pruett, Kyle D. *Fatherneed: Why Father Care Is as Essential as Mother Care for Your Child.* New York: Broadway Books, 2000.

Quigg, Chris. "Particle Physics: What Exactly is the Higgs Boson? Why Are Physicists So Sure That It Really Exists?" Fermi National Accelerator Laboratory. http://lutece.fnal.gov/Drafts/Higgs.html (accessed March 2015).

Reaney, Patricia. "Bushmeat Sparks Fears of New AIDS-Type Virus." *Reuters* (March 19, 2004).

Reynolds, D. L. et al. "Understanding, Compliance and Psychological Impact of the SARS Quarantine Experience." *Epidemiology and Infection* 136/7 (2008) 997–1007. *PMC.* Web. 1 Mar. 2015. http://www.ncbi.nlm.nih.gov/pmc/articles/PMC2870884/

Reynolds, Steven J., M. E. Shepherd, A. R. Risbud, et al. "Male Circumcision and Risk of HIV-1 and Other Sexually Transmitted Infections in India." *Lancet* 363 (2004) 1039–40. doi:10.1016/S0140-6736(04)15840-6.PMID 15051285.

Rivet, Christine. "Circumcision and Cervical Cancer: Is there a Link?" *Canadian Family Physician* 49 (September 2003) 1096–97. http://www.ncbi.nlm.nih.gov/pmc/articles/PMC2214289/pdf/14526861.pdf (accessed March 2015).

Robertson, I. D., and D. K. Blackmore. "Occupational Exposure to Streptococcus Suis Type 2." *Epidemiology Infection* 103 (1989) 157–64.

Rosen, George. *History of Public Health.* New York: MD Publications, 1958.

Rubin, Jordan. *The Maker's Diet.* Lake Mary, FL: Siloam, 2004.

———. *Patient Heal Thyself.* Topanga, CA: Freedom Press, 2003.

Russell, Rex. *What the Bible Says about Healthy Living.* Ventura, CA: Regal Books, 1996.

Schroeder, Gerald L. *Genesis and the Big Bang.* New York: Bantam, 1990.

———. *The Science of God.* New York: Free Press, 1997.

Shetler, Gordon. "Farm Pesticides Linked to Skin Cancer." *Scientific American* (March 31, 2010). http://www.scientificamerican.com/article.cfm?id=farm-pesticides-linked-to-skin-cancer (accessed December 2013).

Shope, R. E. "Swine Influenza. III: Filtration Experiments and Aetiology." *Journal of Experimental Medicine* 54 (1931) 373–380.

Sissam, Norman, et al. "Sex and Sexuality in History." *The Sexual Experience.* Baltimore: Williams and Wilkins, 1976.

Smith, T. C., et al. "Occupational Exposure to Streptococcus Suis among US Swine Workers." *Emerging Infectious Diseases* 14/12 (December 2008) 1925–27.

Stone, A. Douglas. "What Is a Boson? Einstein Was the First to Know." *Huffington Post: Science* (September 5, 2012). http://www.huffingtonpost.com/a-douglas-ston/higgs-boson-einstein_b_1849374.html (accessed March 2015).

"Suicide Rates per 100,000 by Country, Year, and Sex (Table)." *World Health Organization 2011.* http://www.who.int/mental_health/prevention/suicide_rates/en/index.html (accessed December 2013).

Sussman, Norman Sussman, et al. "Sex and Sexuality in History." *The Sexual Experience.* Ed. B. J. Sadock, et al. Baltimore: Williams and Wilkins, 1976: 9.

Tan, E. L., et al. "Inhibition of SARS Coronavirus Infection in Vitro with Clinically Approved Antiviral Drugs." *Emerging Infectious Diseases* 10 (2004) 581–86.

Tanfer, Koray, and Sevgi Aral. "Sexual Intercourse during Menstruation and Self-Reported Sexually Transmitted Disease History among Women." *Sexually Transmitted Diseases* 23/5 (1996) 395–401.

Thacker, Eileen, and Bruce Janke. "Swine Influenza Virus: Zoonotic Potential and Vaccination Strategies for the Control of Avian and Swine Influenzas." *Journal of Infectious Diseases* 197, Supplement 1 (February 2008) S19–24. http://www.journals.uchicago.edu/doi/abs/10.1086/524988 (accessed March 2015).

Thorne, Kip S. *Black Holes and Time Warps: Einstein's Outrageous Legacy.* New York: Norton, 1994.

Tobian, Aaron, Seema Kacker, Kevin Frick, Charlotte Gaydos et al. "Declining Rates of U.S. Infant Male Circumcision Could Add Billions to Health Care Costs, Experts Warn." *John Hopkins Medicine* (August 20, 2012). http://www.hopkinsmedicine.org/news/media/releases/declining_rates_of_us_infant_male_circumcision_could_add_billions _to_health_care_costs_experts_warn (accessed March 2015).

"Trends in Home and Garden Usage by Homeowners." US and International Pest Management Databases. Center for Pest Management. Raleigh, NC: North Carolina State University. http://www.pestmanagement.info/pesticide_history/SIX.pdf (accessed March 2015).

Tyson, Peter. "A Short History of Quarantine." *NOVA* (October 12, 2004). http://www.pbs.org/wgbh/nova/body/short-history-of-quarantine.html (accessed March 2015).

"Unlocking Mummies' Secrets to Study Today's Diseases." *Cancer Weekly Plus.* June 30, 1997: 24.

UNAIDS 2002. "Report on the Global HIV/AIDS Epidemic." XIV International Aids Conference. Geneva: UNAIDS (July 2002). http://data.unaids.org/pub/Report/2002/brglobal_aids_report_en_pdf_red_en.pdf (accessed March 2015).

UNAIDS 2009. "Global Summary of the AIDS Epidemic, 2009." Geneva: World Health Organization (WHO, 2009). http://www.who.int/hiv/data/2009_global_summary.png (accessed December 2013).

_____. "2009 AIDS Epidemic Update:" Geneva: World Health Organization (WHO, 2009) 33. http://data.unaids.org/pub/report/2009/jc1700_epi_update_2009_en.pdf (accessed March 2015).

Unwin, J. D. *Sexual Regulations and Human Behaviour.* London: Williams and Northgate, 1933.

Värnik, Peeter . "Suicide Rates per 100,000 by Country, Year, and Sex (Table)." World Health Organization 2011 http://www.who.int/mental_health/prevention/suicide_rates/en/index.html (accessed November 2013).

_____. Suicide in the World, *International Journal of Environmental Research and Public Health* 9/3 (2012) 760–771. http://www.ncbi.nlm.nih.gov/pmc/articles/PMC3367275/ (accessed February 2015)

Vogelsang, Th. M. *Leprosy in Norway.* http://www.ncbi.nlm.nih.gov/pmc/articles/PMC1033440/pdf/medhist00156–0037.pdf (accessed March 2015).

Wakelin, Derek. *Immunity to Parasites.* Cambridge: Cambridge University Press, 1996.

Bibliography

Walker, Cameron. "Bubonic Plague Traced to Ancient Egypt." *National Geographic* (March 10, 2004).

Watson, M., et al. "Burden of Cervical Cancer in the United States, 1998–2003." *Cancer* 113/10 (2008) 2855–64.

Wile, Jay. "Genesis and the Big Bang: Part 1." Proslogian. December 28, 2009. http://blog.drwile.com/?p=419 (accessed March 2015).

Wineberg, Hiram N. "The Rare Occurrence of Cancer of the Womb among Jewish Women." *Bulletin of Mt. Sinai Hospital*, 1919.

Wigersma, Lode, and Ron Oud. "Safety and Acceptability of Condoms for Use by Homosexual Men As a Prophylactic against Transmission of HIV during Anogenital Sexual Intercourse." *BMJ* 295/6590 (July 1987) 94.

Wit, Matty de, et al. "Gastroenteritis in Sentinel General Practices, the Netherlands." *Emerging Infectious Diseases* 7/1 (2001) 82–91. http://www.medscape.com/viewarticle/414365 (accessed March 2015).

Wolfe, Nathan, et al. *"Naturally Acquired Simian Retrovirus Infections in Central African Hunters." The Lancet 363 (March 2004) 932–37.*

Woods Hole Oceanographic Institute. "Neurotoxic Shellfish Poisoning: Human Illness Associated with Harmful Algae." http://www.whoi.edu/science/B/redtide/illness/illness.html#Neurotoxic%20Shellfish%20Poisoning (accessed March 2015).

World Health Organization. "Swine Influenza Frequently Asked Questions." Last updated April 26, 2009. http://www.paho.org/english/ad/who_swineinfluenza_faq_eng.pdf (accessed March 2015).

World Health Organization — Regional Office for the Eastern Mediterranean. "Aids and Sexually Transmitted Diseases." *Fact Sheet for World AIDS Campaign 2003*. http://www.emro.who.int/world-aids-campaigns/world-aids-campaigns-2003/advocacy-materials.html (accessed October 2013).

World Health Organization. "Role of Animals." International SARS Conference. Geneva: WHO (2003). http://www.who.int/csr/sars/conference/june_2003/materials/presentations/en/roleofAnimals180603.pdf (accessed April 2011, the article has since been greatly truncated).

World Health Organization—Western Pacific Region. "Fact Sheet: *Streptococcus suis*." (August 1, 2005). http://www.wpro.who.int/mediacentre/factsheets/fs_20050802/en/index.html (accessed March 2015).

World Health Organization—Communicable Disease Surveillance and Response (CSR). "Bovine Spongiform Encephalopathy (BSE)." http://www.who.int/zoonoses/diseases/bse/en/ (accessed December 2013).

Wu, Xiaocheng, et al. "Human Papillomavirus–Associated Cancers—United States, 2004–2008." *Morbidity and Mortality Weekly Report* 61/15 (2012) 258–261.

Indexes

Index of Biblical Citations

EXODUS

LEVITICUS

NUMBERS

DEUTERONOMY

JUDGES

2 KINGS

1 CHRONICLES

2 CHRONICLES

EZRA

NEHEMIAH

ESTHER

JOB

PSALMS

PROVERBS

ECCLESIASTES

ISAIAH

JEREMIAH

LAMENTATIONS

EZEKIEL

DANIEL

Index of Hebrew Terms

Index of Scholars

Index of Subjects

A

Aamu, 435, 439, 519, 549. *See also* Hyksos

Aaron, 385, 427, 469, 649
  birth of, 442,
  golden calf, 27, 59–60
  genealogies of, 350, 427, 648, 671,
  priesthood and rites of, 73, 333, 719
  as prophet, 59, 144–145, 485–487
  during Second Temple Period, 797, 800, 865

Abdi-Aširta, 555, 557

Abdi-Ḫiba, 556, 560–561

Abdi-Tishri, 561, 568

Abdon, 353

Abdon (Pirathonite), 571

Abel, 758

Abigail, 711

Abijah, 327, 714, 715, 822, 880

Abimelech, Abimelek, 102, 287, 353, 520, 570, 591–593

Abiram, 104, 264

Abner, 769–771, 848, 878

Abolition of slavery, 233–236

Abraham (Abram). *See also* ABRAHAMIC COVENANTS
  birth of, 381, 384
  birthright of, 95
  blessing of his leadership, 82, 121
  Burnt-Offering Covenant and, 98–101, 763
  childless, 92
  chronology of, 381, 384–385
  death of, 896
  father of many nations, 95, 121
  flood dating and, 896
  greatness of name, 82, 121
  Law of YHWH and, 284, 285, 287, 288
  Machpelah purchased by, 15

marriage to Keturah, 142
Migration Covenant and, 81–82
migration out of Ur, 905
migration to Canaan, 82
name changed by YHWH, 72, 94, 95, 121
neighborly love demonstrated by, 15
offspring blessed, 82, 92, 121
Promised-Land Covenant and, 84, 92
protection from enemies, 82, 121
reasoning with God, 1–2
righteousness of, 16–18, 31, 130, 169, 287–288
on having truth, 18, 24
walking in the way of YHWH, 16–17, 30–32, 71, 95, 99, 130
wealth of, 905

Abrahamic covenants, 81–101, 120
  Burnt-Offering Covenant, 98–101
  Circumcision Covenant, 92–96
  Migration Covenant, 81–82
  Promised-Land Covenant, 83–92
  prosperity under, 230
  Sarahic Covenant, 96–98

Absalom, 132, 183, 280, 284, 666

Abscesses, 181

Absolom, 773

Absolute chronology, 343–345

Abydos, 40, 430, 466–467, 475–476, 867

Accession-year system, 389, 391–392, 394–396, 398, 409

Accountability, 772

Achan, 321

Achzib, 518

Action-reaction law, 162

Acts of Solomon, 320, 323, 394, 661, 664

AD (Anno Domini), 342

Adad-apla-iddina, 571

Adad-nirari, 354, 881

Adad-nirari II, 881

Adad-nirari III, 884

Adam, 20, 30, 32, 75, 104, 109, 146, 285, 298, 758, 776

Admonitions of Ipuwer, 473–479, 482

Adonijah, 773

Adonis, 37

Adoni-zedek, 353

Adoption, 92

Adultery, 89, 209, 215, 223, 260, 295, 300–301, 773, 774, 807

Aegean pottery, 471

Aegyptiaca (Manetho), 438

Aelianus, 189

Africa, burden of disease in, 200, 214–215

Age
  day vs. age, 165–166
  elders vs. youth, 229–230
  human age after the fall, 49

Agricultural income, 225, 493–497

Ahab, 61, 70, 104, 158, 225, 284, 300, 324–325, 329, 378, 389–390, 398–401, 533, 605, 611–612, 628, 666–671,679, 694, 700, 707, 713, 715–717, 725, 740, 781, 848, 882

Ahaz, 257, 325, 329, 394, 408, 410–414, 416, 605, 614–615, 666–667, 701, 718, 739, 731, 739, 743, 759, 886–887

Ahaziah, 325, 329, 378, 393, 398–401, 605, 666–668, 679, 717, 882

Ahiah, 320, 388, 394, 882

Ahijah, 133, 323, 325, 667, 715, 880

Ahilud, 320
Ahmose I (Amosis), 438, 440,
 444, 460–462, 463–465, 466,
 466–473, 475, 479, 481–482,
 494, 499, 502–505, 517,
 522–523, 528, 530, 533, 548,
 552, 569, 905
Ahmose II, 892
Ahmose Tempest Stele (Storm
 Stele), 466–72, 473, 480, 493,
 497, 504, 509
Ai, 149, 321, 346, 514, 537
Aiab, 556
AIDS. *See* HIV INFECTIONS
Akhenaten. *See* AMENHOTEP IV
Akkad, 908
Akkadian documents, 312
Akkadians, 441, 501, 550, 551
Akko, 520
Akkub, 671
Alalakh, 521, 528, 550, 591
Aleppo, 528, 540
Alexander the Great, 80, 634,
 688, 799, 855, 902
Alexandria, 860
Allegorical lament, 581–82, 590
Altar of Ed, 258
Alzheimer's disease, 750
Amalek, 310, 312, 313, 357, 603,
 806, 904
Amalekites, 353, 554, 583, 584,
 598, 901, 908
Amarna,
 city, 192, 547, 563
 Period (1390–1332 BCE), 345,
  355, 542, 547–548, 555–563,
  590, 900, 909
 Tablets/Letters, 346, 468, 531,
  550–551, 555–558, 560–565,
  572, 908
Amaziah/Azariah, 256, 257,
 261, 325, 329, 395, 401–408,
 413–414, 613–614, 666–667,
 716, 718, 743, 835, 884–885
Amel-Merduk (Evil Mero-
 dach), 627, 892
Amenemape, 878
Amenemheb, 535
Amenemhet I, 382, 396
Amenemhet III, 457
Amenhotep I, 354, 475, 569
Amenhotep II, 345, 433, 534,
 536, 537, 542, 543, 545, 546,

552, 553, 555, 558, 569–571,
 599, 908
Amenhotep III, 537, 538, 546,
 547, 554, 555, 570, 908
Amenhotep IV (Akhenaten),
 345, 432–433, 547–548, 552,
 555–556, 563, 668, 570
Amish, 171
Ammon, 270, 350, 567, 594, 632,
 679, 759
Ammonites (and children of),
 53, 270–271, 351, 353, 541,
 554, 570, 575–576, 593–594,
 596, 613, 632, 682, 687, 701,
 741–742, 759, 773, 796, 817,
 821, 908
Amon (King of Judah), 94, 257,
 261, 325, 329, 379, 393, 419,
 666–667, 772, 889
Amon-Re, 447, 483
Amorites, 18, 33, 84, 89–92, 109,
 137, 142, 144, 206, 324, 350–51,
 357, 434, 520–530, 537, 555,
 608, 610, 696, 757, 831, 853,
 857–858, 899
Amos, 112, 206, 325, 716, 717,
 724– 726, 728–730, 783, 797
Amram, 89
Amun, 58, 493, 497
Amuru-Habiru alliance, 557
Anaharath, 540
Anakims, 52–54, 347
Anastasi I Papyrus, 568, 579
Anat, 41
Ancestor worship, 34–36
Anchor dates, 342, 365, 373
Ancient religions, 23–63
 Babylonian theology, 34–46
 commingled truth and error
  in, 32–34
 in Egypt, 23–28
 Egyptian theology, 34–46
 truth or myth in, 28–32
Angels (mal'ak), 59, 62, 67,
 105, 121
Animals to fear humans, 77
Anno Domini (AD), 342
Antedating system (non-acces-
 sion year), 391, 393–394, 399
Antediluvian period
 nephiyl in, 52–57
 perversion of truth in, 46–52
Antef decree, 446

Antioch, 860
Antiochus III, 856
Antiochus V Eupator, 671
Antiochus VI, 779
Antiochus IV (Epiphanes),
 380, 686, 757, 779, 784, 800,
 855–857, 870
Anti-Semitism, 809, 859, 860
Aphrodite, 37
Apiru. *See* HABIRU.
Apiru of Mount Yarmuta, 565
Apis, 27, 60
Apollo, 38, 41
Apophis, 445–447, 452, 460,
 463, 478, 481, 483–484, 487,
 490, 492, 494, 499, 503–504,
 552
Apprenticeship, 229
Aqiba (Rabbi), 13
Aram, 364
Aram-Naharim (Mesopota-
 mia), 346, 531, 553. *See also*
 MESOPOTAMIA
Araunah, 321
Arbitrary/Arbitrariness,
 xxxix, 8–9, 11–17, 19, 66, 158,
 182–184, 223, 806, 835–838
 as act of gods, 170–171, 191,
  285, 304
 arbitrary act, 89
 of Law, 158–159, 202, 216, 220,
  230, 231, 275, 285, 645, 651,
 nonarbitrary, 102, 170–171, 231
Aristeas, 800
Aristotle, 161
Ark of the Covenant (Ark of
 Testimony), 68, 176, 183,
 308–312, 348, 356, 370–372,
 374, 376, 469, 515, 570–571,
 593–594, 596, 599, 641–642,
 647, 651, 656–657, 661, 678
Aroer, 351
Arrian, 602
Artaxerxes, 426, 607, 633, 638,
 675, 795, 796, 895
Arteriosclerosis, 192
Arthritis, 192, 194
Asa, 256, 287, 319, 325, 327–329,
 374, 389–390, 392–394, 666,
 715, 881
Asahel, 769
Asaph, 318, 324–325, 453, 580,
 646, 653– 654, 726, 727, 797

D

I

M

O

T

X

Y